PrincetonReview.com

THE BEST VALUE COLLEGES

200 Schools

with Exceptional ROI

for Your Tuition Investment

2019 Edition

By Robert Franek,

David Soto, Stephen Koch, Danielle Correa, and

the Staff of The Princeton Review

Penguin
Random
House

The Princeton Review
110 East 42nd St, 7th Floor
New York, NY 10017
editorialsupport@review.com

ISBN: 978-0-525-56786-8
ISSN: 2163-6095

The Princeton Review is not affiliated with Princeton University.

Production: Best Content Solutions, LLC
Production Editor: Melissa Duclos

Printed in the United States of America.

9 8 7 6 5 4 3 2 1

2019 Edition

Editorial
Robert Franek, Editor-in-Chief
David Soto, Director of Content Development
Steven Koch, Student Survey Manager
Danielle Correa, Editor

Penguin Random House Publishing Team
Tom Russell, VP, Publisher
Alison Stoltzfus, Publishing Director
Ellen L. Reed, Production Manager
Amanda Yee, Associate Managing Editor
Suzanne Lee, Designer

CONTENTS

How Does College Pay You Back?

Introduction

The Princeton Review has long encouraged college applicants to seek out the schools that fit them best academically, culturally, and financially. As the cost of attending college continues to rise dramatically, applicants and their families are increasingly concerned about post-graduation job prospects. Tuition is an investment in the future, and like investors, students want to see a return on that investment. To continue our mission of helping students find the right college for them, we have combined alumni career outcome data with the institutional data and student surveys we collect to create a Return on Investment (ROI) rating for each of the 200 schools in this book. We know that students invest more than money in their educations, however—they invest their time, energy, and passion. The ROI on your education is much more than a high salary.

History

In 2008, we began publishing America's Best Value Colleges online (in partnership with USAToday), and in 2011, we turned that list into a book. The schools that we covered in *Best Value Colleges* were chosen based on more than thirty factors covering three areas: academics, cost of attendance, and financial aid, including student ratings of their financial aid packages. The aim of our Best Value Colleges franchise was to highlight schools that offer excellent academics as well as excellent need and non-need-based aid.

Career Outcomes

Career outcomes have become as important to students and parents as academic quality and campus life when choosing a school. Increasingly, colleges and universities are moving their offices of career services closer to their admissions offices, providing visiting prospective students with a glimpse of what they can offer. Career services advisors are engaging with students earlier in their time on campus, often in the first few weeks of their first year. These trends in career services aren't a result of colleges pressuring students to plan out their futures before they are ready—rather, colleges and universities are beginning to help students identify their interests, strengths, and passions, and use those to build the foundation of an effective long-term career strategy.

In order to provide meaningful career metrics for each school profiled in this book, we partnered with PayScale.com, which surveys alumni about salary and career. On each of the 200 school profiles in *The Best Value Colleges*, you'll find PayScale.com's median starting salary and mid-career salary for graduates of that school. To cover professions that have high social value but may offer lower salary numbers, such as teaching or non-profit management, we have also included the percentage of alumni who feel that their job makes the world a better place. All of these statistics are printed on each school's profile, and were incorporated into the overall ROI rating for each school. When available, salary data is broken out for alumni who pursued further study, and the percentage of alumni with science/technology/engineering/math (STEM) majors appears in some school profiles.

The Real Cost of College

When we set out to develop our ROI rating and determine which schools to include in this book, we started with the same cost analysis we used to create our Best Value Colleges criteria: We calculate the the sticker price of each college (often referred to as "cost of attendance," that figure includes tuition, required fees and room and board), and subtract the average gift aid (scholarships and grants) awarded to students. We don't subtract work-study or student loans, since those are costs that students ultimately have to bear. Out of the 657 schools we considered for this project, the 200 we chose as our "Colleges That Pay You Back" offer great academics, combined with affordable cost, and stellar career outcomes.

Going Beyond Cold Hard Cash

We defined "value" as inclusive of excellent academics, facilities, and on-campus resources in addition to generous financial aid packages, because we believe colleges pay you back in more than a high salary. The colleges and universities that appear in this book were chosen based on more than forty factors. These factors include PayScale.com's alumni career information, the cost of attendance, financial aid (based on both demonstrated need and merit), selectivity, academics, and student opinion surveys. This methodology goes beyond the bottom line to provide a complete picture of a school's value, and as a result the 200 colleges that pay you back are diverse in academic programs, size, region, and type.

26 Tips for Getting Financial Aid, Scholarships, and Grants and for Paying Less for College

When it comes to actually paying for college, there is a lot of information out there. A great resource is our book *Paying for College* by Kalman Chany. Here, we have some tips from Kal for applying for financial aid and trimming the costs of college.

Getting financial aid

1. Learn how financial aid works. The more and the sooner you know about how need-based aid eligibility is determined, the better you can take steps to maximize such eligibility.
2. Apply for financial aid no matter what your circumstances. Some merit-based aid can only be awarded if the applicant has submitted financial aid application forms.
3. Don't wait till the student is accepted to apply for financial aid. Do it when applying for admission.
4. Complete all the required aid applications. All students seeking aid must submit the FAFSA (Free Application for Federal Student Aid); other forms may also be required. Check with each college to see what's required and when.
5. Get the best scores you can on the SAT or ACT. They are used not only in decisions for admission but they can also impact financial aid. If your scores and other stats exceed the school's admission criteria, you are likely to get a better aid package than a marginal applicant.
6. Apply strategically to colleges. Your chances of getting aid will be better at schools that have generous financial aid budgets. (Check the "Colleges That Pay You Back" list and Financial Aid Ratings for schools in this book and on PrincetonReview.com.)
7. Don't rule out any school as too expensive. A generous aid award from a pricey private school can make it less costly than a public school with a lower sticker price.
8. Take advantage of education tax benefits. A dollar saved on taxes is worth the same as a dollar in scholarship aid. Look into Coverdells, 529 Plans, education tax credits, and loan deductions.

Scholarships and grants

9. Get your best possible score on the PSAT: It is the National Merit Scholarship Qualifying Test and also used in the selection of students for other scholarships and recognition programs.
10. Check your eligibility for grants and scholarships from your state. Some (but not all) states will allow you to use such funds out of state.
11. Look for scholarships locally. Find out if your employer offers scholarships or tuition assistance plans for employees or family members. Also look into scholarships from your community groups and high school, as well as your church, temple, or mosque.
12. Look for outside scholarships realistically: they account for less than five percent of aid awarded. Research them at PrincetonReview.com or other free sites. Steer clear of scholarship search firms that charge fees and "promise" scholarships.

Paying for college

13. Start saving early when the student is an infant. Too late? Start now. The more you save, the less you'll have to borrow.
14. Invest wisely. Considering a 529 plan? Compare your own state's plan which may have tax benefits with other states' programs. Get info at savingforcollege.com.
15. If you have to borrow, first pursue federal education loans (Direct or PLUS). Avoid private loans at all costs.
16. Never put tuition on a credit card. The debt is more expensive than ever given recent changes to interest rates and other fees some card issuers are now charging.
17. Try not to take money from a retirement account or 401(k) to pay for college. In addition to likely early distribution penalties and additional income taxes, the higher income will reduce your aid eligibility.

Paying less for college

18. Attend a community college for two years and transfer to a pricier school to complete the degree. Plan ahead: Be sure the college you plan to transfer to will accept the community college credits.
19. Look into "cooperative education" programs. Over 900 colleges allow students to combine college education with a job. It can take longer to complete a degree this way. But graduates generally owe less in student loans and have a better chance of getting hired.
20. Take as many AP courses as possible and get high scores on AP exams. Many colleges award course credits for high AP scores. Some students have cut a year off their college tuition this way.
21. Earn college credit via "dual enrollment" programs available at some high schools. These allow students to take college level courses during their senior year.
22. Earn college credits by taking CLEP (College-Level Examination Program) exams. Depending on the college, a qualifying score on any of the thirty-three CLEP exams can earn students three to twelve college credits. (See Princeton Review's *Cracking the CLEP*, 5th Edition.)
23. Stick to your college and your major. Changing colleges can result in lost credits. Aid may be limited/not available for transfer students at some schools. Changing majors can mean paying for extra courses to meet requirements.
24. Finish college in three years if possible. Take the maximum number of credits every semester, attend summer sessions, and earn credits via online courses. Some colleges offer three-year programs for high-achieving students.
25. Let Uncle Sam pay for your degree. ROTC (Reserve Officer Training Corps) programs available from U.S. Armed Forces branches (except the Coast Guard) offer merit-based scholarships up to full tuition via participating colleges in exchange for military service after you graduate.
26. Better yet: Attend a tuition-free college. Check out the nine institutions in this book on the "Tuition-Free Schools" list on p. 41.

Please visit PrincetonReview.com/college-advice online for the most up-to-date information on available financial aid programs.

Great Schools for the Highest Paying Majors

While choosing your major is not exactly choosing your fate, the major you choose can often impact your earning potential. There are certainly graduates who land in careers that are quite different from their college majors (we know a photojournalism major who became a statistical analyst, and a biology major who is now the chief technology officer at a start-up, just to name two examples). Your choice of major should not depend solely on your expected starting salary, but also on your academic interests, the subjects you are passionate about, and the type of career you're interested in. That said, in order to arm you with information you need to maximize the return on your education, below we have provided PayScale.com's median starting and mid-career salaries for forty-eight of the highest paying majors, and lists of schools that report awarding the most degrees and having the most students currently enrolled in those majors. You can find median starting and mid-career salary information for many more majors on PayScale.com.

BIOCHEMISTRY

Median starting salary: $44,500
Median mid-career salary: $87,600
% High job meaning: 59%

Agnes Scott College
Arizona State University at the Tempe campus
Barnard College
Bates College
Baylor University
Boston College
Bowdoin College
Brandeis University
Brigham Young University (UT)
Brown University
Bucknell University
Carleton College
Case Western Reserve University
Christopher Newport University
Claremont McKenna College
Clark University
Clemson University
Colgate University
The College of Wooster
Cornell University
Dartmouth College
Denison University
DePauw University
Dickinson College
Drew University
Franklin and Marshall College
Georgetown University
Georgia Institute of Technology
Gettysburg College
Grinnell College
Grove City College
Gustavus Adolphus College
Hamilton College
Harvard College
Hobart and William Smith Colleges

Illinois Institute of Technology
Kenyon College
Lafayette College
Lawrence University
Lehigh University
Miami University
Middlebury College
Mills College
Mount Holyoke College
Muhlenberg College
New College of Florida
North Carolina State University
Northeastern University
Oberlin College
Occidental College
The Ohio State University—Columbus
Oklahoma State University
Pennsylvania State University—University Park
Pitzer College
Purdue University—West Lafayette
Reed College
Rensselaer Polytechnic Institute
Rice University
Rose-Hulman Institute of Technology
Rutgers, The State University of New Jersey—New Brunswick
Santa Clara University
Scripps College
Smith College
Southwestern University
St. Anselm College
St. Lawrence University
St. Mary's College of Maryland
State University of New York at Binghamton (Binghamton University)
State University of New York—College of Environmental Science and Forestry
State University of New York—Stony Brook University

Stevens Institute of Technology
Swarthmore College
Texas A&M University—College Station
Trinity College (CT)
Trinity University
Tufts University
Tulane University
Union College (NY)
University of Arizona
University of California—Los Angeles
University of California—Riverside
University of California—San Diego
University of Colorado Boulder
University of Dallas
University of Dayton
University of Florida
University of Houston
University of Illinois at Urbana-
   Champaign
University of Maryland—College Park
University of Michigan—Ann Arbor
University of Minnesota—
   Twin Cities Campus
University of Notre Dame
University of Oklahoma
University of Pennsylvania
University of Richmond
University of Rochester
University of Southern California
The University of Texas at Austin
The University of Texas at Dallas
The University of Tulsa
University of Wisconsin—Madison
Vassar College
Villanova University
Virginia Tech
Wabash College
Washington University in St. Louis
Wellesley College
Wesleyan University
William Jewell College
Worcester Polytechnic Institute
Yale University

MOLECULAR BIOLOGY
Median starting salary: $47,600
Median mid-career salary: $91,000
% High job meaning: 68%

Arizona State University
   at the Tempe campus
Brigham Young University (UT)
Brown University
Bryn Mawr College
Bucknell University
California Institute of Technology

Centre College
Claremont McKenna College
Clark University
Coe College
Colby College
Colgate University
Colorado College
The College of Wooster
Gettysburg College
Harvard College
Harvey Mudd College
Illinois Institute of Technology
Johns Hopkins University
Kenyon College
Lawrence University
Lehigh University
Michigan Technological University
Middlebury College
Mills College
Ohio Wesleyan University
Princeton University
Purdue University—West Lafayette
Reed College
Rensselaer Polytechnic Institute
Rhodes College
Rutgers, The State University
   of New Jersey—New Brunswick
Scripps College
State University of New York at
   Binghamton (Binghamton University)
State University of New York—College of
   Environmental Science and Forestry
Texas A&M University—College Station
Trinity University
Tufts University
Tulane University
University of Arizona
University of California—Los Angeles
University of California—Berkeley
University of California—San Diego
University of California—Santa Barbara
University of California—Santa Cruz
University of Colorado Boulder
University of Denver
University of Florida
University of Georgia
University of Illinois at Urbana-
   Champaign
University of Massachusetts Amherst
University of Michigan—Ann Arbor
University of Pittsburgh—
   Pittsburgh Campus
University of Richmond
The University of Texas at Dallas
The University of Tulsa

University of Wisconsin—Madison
Vanderbilt University
Washington University in St. Louis
Wesleyan University
Whitman College
William Jewell College
Yale University

BIOTECHNOLOGY

Median starting salary: $46,100
Median mid-career salary: $82,500
% High job meaning: 49%

Brigham Young University (UT)
Carnegie Mellon University
City University of New York—
    City College
Rutgers, The State University
    of New Jersey—New Brunswick
State University of New York—College of
    Environmental Science and Forestry
Tufts University
University of California—Davis
University of Houston
University of Illinois at Urbana-
    Champaign
Washington State University
Worcester Polytechnic Institute

BUSINESS

ACTUARIAL SCIENCES

Median starting salary: $56,400
Median mid-career salary: $131,700
% High job meaning: 49%

Bentley University
Brigham Young University (UT)
Carnegie Mellon University
City University of New York—
    Baruch College
City University of New York—
    Queens College
Florida State University
Michigan Technological University
The Ohio State University—Columbus
Purdue University—West Lafayette
State University of New York at
    Binghamton
Texas Christian University
University of Illinois at Urbana-
    Champaign
University of Minnesota—Twin Cities
University of Nebraska—Lincoln

University of Pennsylvania
The University of Texas at Dallas
University of Wisconsin—Madison
Worcester Polytechnic Institute

CONSTRUCTION MANAGEMENT

Median starting salary: $56,800
Median mid-career salary: $97,600
% High job meaning: 56%

Arizona State University
Brigham Young University (UT)
Michigan Technological University
Purdue University—West Lafayette
State University of New York—College of
    Environmental Science and Forestry
University of Denver
University of Oklahoma
Virginia Polytechnic Institute and State
    University (Virginia Tech)
Washington State University

FINANCE

Median starting salary: $53,300
Median mid-career salary: $93,200
% High job meaning: 39%

Bentley University
Boston College
City University of New York—
    Baruch College
Fairfield University
Florida State University
Lehigh University
The Ohio State University—Columbus
St. Anselm College
Texas Christian University
The University of Alabama—Tuscaloosa
University of Denver
University of Georgia
University of Notre Dame
University of Pennsylvania
University of Pittsburgh—
    Pittsburgh Campus
University of Utah
Villanova University
Wofford College

INTERNATIONAL BUSINESS

Median starting salary: $48,500
Median mid-career salary: $93,200
% High job meaning: 40%

Bentley University
Bucknell University
Carnegie Mellon University

City University of New York—
Baruch College
College of the Ozarks
Dickinson College
Georgetown University
Gettysburg College
Grove City College
Northeastern University
The Ohio State University—Columbus
Oklahoma State University
Rhodes College
St. Anselm College
State University of New York
at Binghamton
Trinity University
University of Dayton
University of Denver
University of Maryland—College Park
University of Minnesota—Twin Cities
University of Pennsylvania
The University of Texas at Dallas
The University of Tulsa
University of Wisconsin—Madison
Villanova University
Washington University in St. Louis
William Jewell College

MANAGEMENT INFORMATION SYSTEMS

Median starting salary: $57,900
Median mid-career salary: $101,300
% High job meaning: 39%

Boston College
Brigham Young University (UT)
City University of New York—Baruch
College
Clarkson University
Fairfield University
Furman University
Georgetown University
Miami University
Michigan Technological University
Missouri University of Science
and Technology
Northeastern University
The Ohio State University—Columbus
Purdue University—West Lafayette
Saint Louis University
Santa Clara University
State University of New York
at Binghamton
Texas A&M University—College Station
The University of Alabama—Tuscaloosa
University of Colorado—Boulder

University of Dayton
University of Denver
University of Illinois at Urbana-
Champaign
University of Maryland—College Park
University of Minnesota—Twin Cities
University of Notre Dame
University of Oklahoma
University of Pennsylvania
The University of Texas at Dallas
The University of Tulsa
University of Utah
Villanova University
Washington State University
Worcester Polytechnic Institute

MARKETING

Median starting salary: $45,200
Median mid-career salary: $84,900
% High job meaning: 39%

Arizona State University at the Tempe
campus
Bentley University
Boston College
Bucknell University
Fairfield University
Florida State University
Georgetown University
Lehigh University
Loyola Marymount University
Miami University
Northeastern University
Oklahoma State University
Saint Louis University
San Diego State University
Santa Clara University
Stonehill College
Texas Christian University
Trinity University
Tulane University
University of Arizona
University of Connecticut
University of Dayton
University of Denver
University of Georgia
University of Houston
University of Nebraska—Lincoln
University of Notre Dame
University of Pennsylvania
The University of Texas at Dallas
The University of Tulsa
University of Utah
Washington State University

OPERATIONS & SUPPLY CHAIN MANAGEMENT

Median starting salary: $53,900
Median mid-career salary: $92,400
% High job meaning: 43%

Brigham Young University (UT)
Clarkson University
Lehigh University
The Ohio State University—Columbus
State University of New York
    at Binghamton
Texas A&M University—College Station
Texas Christian University
University of Houston
University of Illinois
    at Urbana-Champaign
University of Maryland—College Park
University of Nebraska—Lincoln
The University of Texas at Dallas

COMPUTER AND INFORMATION SCIENCES

COMPUTER INFORMATION SYSTEMS

Median starting salary: $53,500
Median mid-career salary: $93,000
% High job meaning: 45%

Boston College
Carnegie Mellon University
Clemson University
College of the Ozarks
Cornell University
Georgetown University
Gettysburg College
Lawrence University
Michigan Technological University
Missouri University of Science and
    Technology
Montana Tech of the University
    of Montana
North Carolina State University
Northwestern University
Oberlin College
Oklahoma State University
Pennsylvania State University—
    University Park
Purdue University—West Lafayette
Rensselaer Polytechnic Institute
Rutgers, The State University
    of New Jersey—New Brunswick
Scripps College

State University of New York
    at Binghamton
State University of New York—College of
    Environmental Science and Forestry
Stevens Institute of Technology
Texas A&M University—College Station
Trinity University
Tulane University
University of California—Berkeley
University of California—Davis
University of California—Santa Cruz
University of Dayton
University of Florida
University of Georgia
University of Houston
University of Illinois
    at Urbana-Champaign
University of Maryland—College Park
University of Massachusetts Amherst
University of Minnesota—Twin Cities
University of Notre Dame
University of Wisconsin—Madison
Virginia Polytechnic Institute and State
    University (Virginia Tech)
Washington University in St. Louis
Wellesley College
Worcester Polytechnic Institute

COMPUTER SCIENCE

Median starting salary: $65,900
Median mid-career salary: $110,100
% High job meaning: 40%

Arizona State University
Bowdoin College
Bradley College
Brandeis University
Brigham Young University (UT)
Bryn Mawr College
Carnegie Mellon University
Case Western Reserve University
Centre College
City University of New York—
    Hunter College
Colby College
Colgate University
College of the Ozarks
Cornell University
Emory University
Georgetown University
Gettysburg College
Grinnell College
Grove City College
Harvard College

Harvey Mudd College
Illinois Institute of Technology
Lake Forest College
Lawrence University
Lehigh University
Massachusetts Institute of Technology
Michigan Technological University
Middlebury College
Montana Tech of the University
  of Montana
Mount Holyoke College
North Carolina State University
Northwestern University
Pomona College
Purdue University—West Lafayette
Rhodes College
Rice University
Rochester Institute of Technology
Rose-Hulman Institute of Technology
Scripps College
St. Olaf College
Stanford University
State University of New York
  at Binghamton
State University of New York—
  Stony Brook University
Stevens Institute of Technology
Texas A&M University—College Station
Tufts University
University of California—Davis
University of California—Riverside
University of California—San Diego
University of California—Santa Barbara
University of California—Santa Cruz
The University of Chicago
University of Colorado—Boulder
University of Dayton
University of Denver
University of Georgia
University of Illinois
  at Urbana-Champaign
University of Massachusetts Amherst
University of Minnesota—Twin Cities
The University of North Carolina
  at Chapel Hill
University of Oklahoma
University of Pittsburgh—
  Pittsburgh Campus
University of Rochester
The University of Tulsa
University of Washington
Vanderbilt University
Washington University in St. Louis
Wellesley College
Wofford College

Wheaton College (IL)
Willamette University
Worcester Polytechnic Institute
Yale University

INFORMATION SYSTEMS
Median starting salary: $55,800
Median mid-career salary: $96,900
% High job meaning: 43%

Allegheny College
City University of New York—
  Baruch College
City University of New York—
  Brooklyn College
Missouri University of Science
  and Technology
New Jersey Institute of Technology
Northeastern University
Northwestern University
Ohio Wesleyan University
Pennsylvania State University—
  University Park
Purdue University—West Lafayette
Rutgers, The State University
  of New Jersey—New Brunswick
State University of New York—
  Stony Brook University
Stevens Institute of Technology
Tulane University
United States Military Academy
University of California—Santa Cruz
University of Houston
University of Maryland—College Park
University of Nebraska—Lincoln
The University of North Carolina
  at Chapel Hill
University of Oklahoma
University of Pittsburgh—
  Pittsburgh Campus
Washington State University
Washington University in St. Louis

INFORMATION TECHNOLOGY
Median starting salary: $52,300
Median mid-career salary: $86,300
% High job meaning: 45%

Brigham Young University (UT)
Clarkson University
College of the Ozarks
Cornell University
Furman University
Illinois Institute of Technology
Lehigh University
Missouri University of Science

and Technology
New Jersey Institute of Technology
Oklahoma State University
Purdue University—West Lafayette
Rensselaer Polytechnic Institute
Saint Louis University
San Diego State University
Texas Christian University
United States Military Academy
United States Naval Academy
University of Denver
The University of Tulsa

ENGINEERING

AEROSPACE ENGINEERING
Median starting salary: $66,300
Median mid-career salary: $113,300
% High job meaning: 52%

Arizona State University
California Institute of Technology
Case Western Reserve University
Clarkson University
Georgia Institute of Technology
Illinois Institute of Technology
Massachusetts Institute of Technology
Missouri University of Science and
   Technology
North Carolina State University
The Ohio State University—Columbus
Oklahoma State University
Pennsylvania State University—
   University Park
Purdue University—West Lafayette
Rensselaer Polytechnic Institute
Rochester Institute of Technology
Saint Louis University
San Diego State University
Stanford University
Texas A&M University—College Station
United States Air Force Academy
United States Naval Academy
The University of Alabama—Tuscaloosa
University of California—Davis
University of California—Los Angeles
University of California—San Diego
University of Colorado—Boulder
University of Florida
University of Houston
University of Illinois
   at Urbana-Champaign
University of Maryland—College Park
University of Michigan—Ann Arbor
University of Minnesota—Twin Cities
University of Notre Dame

University of Oklahoma
University of Southern California
The University of Texas at Austin
University of Virginia
University of Washington
Virginia Polytechnic Institute and State
   University (Virginia Tech)
Worcester Polytechnic Institute

ARCHITECTURAL ENGINEERING
Median starting salary: $61,200
Median mid-career salary: $95,100
% High job meaning: 53%

Allegheny College
Coe College
Georgia Institute of Technology
Illinois Institute of Technology
Missouri University of Science
   and Technology
New Jersey Institute of Technology
Ohio Wesleyan University
Oklahoma State University
Pennsylvania State University—
   University Park
Purdue University—West Lafayette
Saint Louis University
San Diego State University
Texas Christian University
Tufts University
The University of Alabama—Tuscaloosa
University of Colorado Boulder
University of Nebraska—Lincoln
University of Oklahoma
University of Pittsburgh—
   Pittsburgh Campus
The University of Texas at Austin
Washington State University
Washington University in St. Louis
Wheaton College (MA)
Worcester Polytechnic Institute

BIOMEDICAL ENGINEERING
Median starting salary: $62,900
Median mid-career salary: $103,500
% High job meaning: 72%

Arizona State University
Brown University
Bucknell University
Case Western Reserve University
City University of New York—
   City College
Clemson University
The College of New Jersey
Duke University
Fairfield University

Georgia Institute of Technology
Harvard College
Illinois Institute of Technology
Johns Hopkins University
Lehigh University
Massachusetts Institute of Technology
Miami University
Michigan Technological University
New Jersey Institute of Technology
North Carolina State University
Northwestern University
The Ohio State University—Columbus
Pennsylvania State University—
  University Park
Rensselaer Polytechnic Institute
Rice University
Rose-Hulman Institute of Technology
Rutgers, The State University
  of New Jersey—New Brunswick
Saint Louis University
Santa Clara University
Stanford University
State University of New York
  at Binghamton
State University of New York—
  Stony Brook University
Stevens Institute of Technology
Texas A&M University—College Station
Tufts University
Tulane University
Union College (NY)
University of California—Berkeley
University of California—Davis
University of California—Santa Cruz
University of Florida
University of Houston
University of Illinois
  at Urbana-Champaign
University of Michigan—Ann Arbor
University of Pennsylvania
University of Pittsburgh—
  Pittsburgh Campus
University of Rochester
University of Southern California
The University of Texas at Austin
The University of Texas at Dallas
University of Virginia
University of Washington
University of Wisconsin—Madison
Vanderbilt University
Washington State University
Washington University in St. Louis
Worcester Polytechnic Institute
Yale University

CHEMICAL ENGINEERING
Median starting salary: $70,300
Median mid-career salary: $124,500
% High job meaning: 57%

Arizona State University
Brigham Young University (UT)
Bucknell University
California Institute of Technology
Carnegie Mellon University
Case Western Reserve University
City University of New York—
  City College
Clarkson University
Clemson University
The Cooper Union for the Advancement
  of Science and Art
Cornell University
Georgia Institute of Technology
Harvard College
Illinois Institute of Technology
Johns Hopkins University
Lafayette College
Lehigh University
Massachusetts Institute of Technology
Miami University
Michigan Technological University
Missouri University of Science
  and Technology
New Jersey Institute of Technology
Northeastern University
North Carolina State University
Northwestern University
The Ohio State University—Columbus
Oklahoma State University
Pennsylvania State University—
  University Park
Princeton University
Purdue University—West Lafayette
Rensselaer Polytechnic Institute
Rice University
Rochester Institute of Technology
Rose-Hulman Institute of Technology
Rutgers, The State University
  of New Jersey—New Brunswick
Stanford University
State University of New York—College of
  Environmental Science and Forestry
State University of New York—
  Stony Brook University
Stevens Institute of Technology
Texas A&M University—College Station
Tufts University
Tulane University
United States Air Force Academy
United States Military Academy

The University of Alabama—Tuscaloosa
University of California—Berkeley
University of California—Davis
University of California—Los Angeles
University of California—Riverside
University of California—San Diego
University of California—Santa Barbara
University of Colorado—Boulder
University of Dayton
University of Florida
University of Houston
University of Illinois
  at Urbana-Champaign
University of Maryland—College Park
University of Massachusetts Amherst
University of Michigan—Ann Arbor
University of Minnesota—Twin Cities
University of Nebraska—Lincoln
University of Notre Dame
University of Oklahoma
University of Pennsylvania
University of Pittsburgh—
  Pittsburgh Campus
University of Rochester
University of Southern California
The University of Texas at Austin
The University of Tulsa
University of Virginia
University of Washington
University of Wisconsin—Madison
Vanderbilt University
Villanova University
Virginia Polytechnic Institute
  and State University (Virginia Tech)
Washington State University
Washington University in St. Louis
Worcester Polytechnic Institute
Yale University

CIVIL ENGINEERING
Median starting salary: $57,700
Median mid-career salary: $98,500
% High job meaning: 65%

Arizona State University
Brigham Young University (UT)
Bucknell University
Carnegie Mellon University
Case Western Reserve University
City University of New York—
  City College
Clarkson University
Clemson University
The College of New Jersey
The Cooper Union for the Advancement
  of Science and Art

Cornell University
Duke University
Georgia Institute of Technology
Harvard College
Illinois Institute of Technology
Johns Hopkins University
Lafayette College
Lehigh University
Massachusetts Institute of Technology
Michigan Technological University
Missouri University of Science
  and Technology
New Jersey Institute of Technology
Northeastern University
North Carolina State University
Northwestern University
The Ohio State University—Columbus
Oklahoma State University
Pennsylvania State University—
  University Park
Princeton University
Purdue University—West Lafayette
Rensselaer Polytechnic Institute
Rice University
Rose-Hulman Institute of Technology
Rutgers, The State University
  of New Jersey—New Brunswick
Saint Louis University
San Diego State University
Santa Clara University
Stanford University
State University of New York—College of
  Environmental Science and Forestry
State University of New York—
  Stony Brook University
Stevens Institute of Technology
Texas A&M University—College Station
Tufts University
United States Air Force Academy
United States Coast Guard Academy
United States Military Academy
The University of Alabama—Tuscaloosa
University of California—Berkeley
University of California—Davis
University of California—Los Angeles
University of California—San Diego
University of Colorado—Boulder
University of Dayton
University of Florida
University of Georgia
University of Houston
University of Illinois
  at Urbana-Champaign
University of Maryland—College Park
University of Massachusetts Amherst

University of Minnesota—Twin Cities
University of Nebraska—Lincoln
University of Oklahoma
University of Pennsylvania
University of Pittsburgh—
    Pittsburgh Campus
University of Southern California
The University of Texas at Austin
University of Utah
University of Virginia
University of Washington
University of Wisconsin—Madison
Vanderbilt University
Villanova University
Virginia Polytechnic Institute
    and State University (Virginia Tech)
Washington State University
Worcester Polytechnic Institute

COMPUTER ENGINEERING
Median starting salary: $70,300
Median mid-career salary: $116,000
% High job meaning: 45%

Allegheny College
Arizona State University
Brigham Young University (UT)
Bucknell University
California Institute of Technology
Carnegie Mellon University
Case Western Reserve University
Clarkson University
Clemson University
The College of New Jersey
Fairfield University
Georgia Institute of Technology
Harvard College
Illinois Institute of Technology
Johns Hopkins University
Lafayette College
Lehigh University
Miami University
Michigan Technological University
Missouri University of Science
    and Technology
Montana Tech of the University
    of Montana
New Jersey Institute of Technology
Northeastern University
North Carolina State University
Northwestern University
Oklahoma State University
Pennsylvania State University—
    University Park

Princeton University
Purdue University—West Lafayette
Rensselaer Polytechnic Institute
Rose-Hulman Institute of Technology
Saint Louis University
San Diego State University
Santa Clara University
State University of New York
    at Binghamton
State University of New York—
    Stony Brook University
Stevens Institute of Technology
Texas A&M University—College Station
Tufts University
Tulane University
United States Air Force Academy
United States Naval Academy
University of California—Berkeley
University of California—Davis
University of California—Los Angeles
University of California—Riverside
University of California—San Diego
University of California—Santa Barbara
University of California—Santa Cruz
University of Colorado—Boulder
University of Dayton
University of Denver
University of Florida
University of Georgia
University of Houston
University of Illinois
    at Urbana-Champaign
University of Maryland—College Park
University of Massachusetts Amherst
University of Michigan—Ann Arbor
University of Minnesota—Twin Cities
University of Nebraska—Lincoln
University of Notre Dame
University of Oklahoma
University of Pennsylvania
University of Pittsburgh—
    Pittsburgh Campus
University of Southern California
The University of Texas at Dallas
University of Virginia
University of Washington
University of Wisconsin—Madison
Vanderbilt University
Villanova University
Virginia Polytechnic Institute
    and State University (Virginia Tech)
Washington State University
Washington University in St. Louis
Worcester Polytechnic Institute

ELECTRICAL ENGINEERING

Median starting salary: $67,800
Median mid-career salary: $114,800
% High job meaning: 53%

Arizona State University
Brigham Young University (UT)
Bucknell University
California Institute of Technology
Carnegie Mellon University
Case Western Reserve University
City University of New York—
  City College
Clarkson University
Clemson University
The College of New Jersey
The Cooper Union for the Advancement
  of Science and Art
Cornell University
Duke University
Fairfield University
Franklin W. Olin College of Engineering
Georgia Institute of Technology
Grove City College
Harvard College
Illinois Institute of Technology
Johns Hopkins University
Lafayette College
Lehigh University
Massachusetts Institute of Technology
Miami University
Michigan Technological University
Missouri University of Science
  and Technology
Montana Tech of the University
  of Montana
New Jersey Institute of Technology
North Carolina State University
Northeastern University
Northwestern University
The Ohio State University—Columbus
Oklahoma State University
Pennsylvania State University—
  University Park
Princeton University
Purdue University—West Lafayette
Rensselaer Polytechnic Institute
Rice University
Rose-Hulman Institute of Technology
Rutgers, The State University
  of New Jersey—New Brunswick
Saint Louis University
San Diego State University
Santa Clara University
Stanford University
State University of New York
  at Binghamton
State University of New York—
  Stony Brook University
Stevens Institute of Technology
Texas A&M University—College Station
Tufts University
Union College (NY)
United States Air Force Academy
United States Coast Guard Academy
United States Military Academy
United States Naval Academy
The University of Alabama—Tuscaloosa
University of California—Berkeley
University of California—Davis
University of California—Irvine
University of California—Los Angeles
University of California—Riverside
University of California—San Diego
University of California—Santa Barbara
University of California—Santa Cruz
University of Colorado—Boulder
University of Dayton
University of Denver
University of Florida
University of Georgia
University of Houston
University of Illinois
  at Urbana-Champaign
University of Maryland—College Park
University of Massachusetts Amherst
University of Michigan—Ann Arbor
University of Minnesota—Twin Cities
University of Nebraska—Lincoln
University of Notre Dame
University of Oklahoma
University of Pennsylvania
University of Pittsburgh—
  Pittsburgh Campus
University of Rochester
University of Southern California
The University of Texas at Austin
The University of Texas at Dallas
The University of Tulsa
University of Virginia
University of Washington
University of Wisconsin—Madison
Vanderbilt University
Villanova University
Virginia Polytechnic Institute and State
  University (Virginia Tech)
Washington State University
Washington University in St. Louis
Worcester Polytechnic Institute
Yale University

INDUSTRIAL ENGINEERING
Median starting salary: $64,400
Median mid-career salary: $107,100
% High job meaning: 44%

Arizona State University
Clemson University
Georgia Institute of Technology
Lehigh University
Missouri University of Science
   and Technology
New Jersey Institute of Technology
North Carolina State University
Northeastern University
Northwestern University
The Ohio State University—Columbus
Oklahoma State University
Pennsylvania State University—
   University Park
Purdue University—West Lafayette
Rensselaer Polytechnic Institute
Rochester Institute of Technology
State University of New York
   at Binghamton
Texas A&M University—College Station
University of Florida
University of Houston
University of Illinois
   at Urbana-Champaign
University of Massachusetts Amherst
University of Michigan—Ann Arbor
University of Minnesota—Twin Cities
University of Oklahoma
University of Pittsburgh—
   Pittsburgh Campus
University of San Diego
University of Southern California
University of Washington
University of Wisconsin—Madison
Virginia Polytechnic Institute and State
   University (Virginia Tech)
Worcester Polytechnic Institute

MATERIALS SCIENCE AND
ENGINEERING
Median starting salary: $66,300
Median mid-career salary: $104,100
% High job meaning: 45%

Arizona State University
California Institute of Technology
Case Western Reserve University
Clarkson University
Clemson University
Cornell University

Georgia Institute of Technology
Harvard College
Illinois Institute of Technology
Johns Hopkins University
Lehigh University
Massachusetts Institute of Technology
Michigan Institute of Technology
Missouri University of Science
   and Technology
New Jersey Institute of Technology
North Carolina State University
Northwestern University
The Ohio State University—Columbus
Purdue University—West Lafayette
Rensselaer Polytechnic Institute
Rice University
Rochester Institute of Technology
Stanford University
University of California—Berkeley
University of California—Davis
University of California—Los Angeles
University of California—Riverside
University of Florida
University of Houston
University of Illinois
   at Urbana-Champaign
University of Maryland—College Park
University of Michigan—Ann Arbor
University of Minnesota—Twin Cities
University of Pennsylvania
University of Pittsburgh—
   Pittsburgh Campus
University of Rochester
University of Virginia
University of Wisconsin—Madison
Virginia Polytechnic Institute
   and State University (Virginia Tech)
Washington State University

MECHANICAL ENGINEERING
Median starting salary: $64,000
Median mid-career salary: $106,800
% High job meaning: 50%

California Institute of Technology
Clarkson University
The Cooper Union for the Advancement
   of Science and Art
Cornell University
Franklin W. Olin College of Engineering
Georgia Institute of Technology
Grove City College
Illinois Institute of Technology
Lafayette College

Lehigh University
Massachusetts Institute of Technology
Michigan Technological University
Missouri University of Science
  and Technology
New Jersey Institute of Technology
North Carolina State University
Princeton University
Purdue University—West Lafayette
Rochester Institute of Technology
Rose-Hulman Institute of Technology
Stevens Institute of Technology
The University of Alabama—Tuscaloosa
University of Florida
University of Idaho
The University of Tulsa
University of Utah
Worcester Polytechnic Institute

NUCLEAR ENGINEERING

Median starting salary: $69,000
Median mid-career salary: $127,500
% High job meaning: 72%

Georgia Institute of Technology
Massachusetts Institute of Technology
Missouri University of Science
  and Technology
North Carolina State University
The Ohio State University—Columbus
Pennsylvania State University—
  University Park
Purdue University—West Lafayette
Rensselaer Polytechnic Institute
Texas A&M University—College Station
United States Military Academy
United States Naval Academy
University of California—Berkeley
University of Florida
University of Illinois
  at Urbana-Champaign
University of Michigan—Ann Arbor
University of Wisconsin—Madison

PETROLEUM ENGINEERING

Median starting salary: $94,600
Median mid-career salary: $175,500
% High job meaning: 65%

Missouri University of Science
  and Technology
Montana Tech of the University
  of Montana
Pennsylvania State University—
  University Park
Texas A&M University—College Station

University of Houston
University of Oklahoma
University of Southern California
The University of Texas at Austin
The University of Tulsa
University of Utah

SOFTWARE ENGINEERING

Median starting salary: $66,300
Median mid-career salary: $104,300
% High job meaning: 38%

Arizona State University
Carnegie Mellon University
Harvard College
Michigan Technological University
Montana Tech of the University
  of Montana
New Jersey Institute of Technology
Purdue University—West Lafayette
Rose-Hulman Institute of Technology
University of Illinois
  at Urbana-Champaign
University of Nebraska—Lincoln
University of Southern California
The University of Texas at Dallas
Washington State University

INDUSTRIAL & SYSTEMS ENGINEERING

Median starting salary: $65,700
Median mid-career salary: $114,400
% High job meaning: 48%

Case Western Reserve University
Cornell University
Harvard College
Purdue University—West Lafayette
Stevens Institute of Technology
United States Military Academy
United States Naval Academy
University of California—Santa Cruz
University of Florida
University of Houston
University of Minnesota—Twin Cities
University of Pennsylvania
University of Virginia
Washington University in St. Louis

ENGINEERING TECHNOLOGIES

ELECTRICAL ENGINEERING TECHNOLOGY

Median starting salary: $60,400
Median mid-career salary: $93,400
% High job meaning: 45%

Arizona State University
Michigan Technological University
Oklahoma State University
Purdue University—West Lafayette
Texas A&M University—College Station
University of Dayton

ENVIRONMENTAL ENGINEERING

Median starting salary: $55,300
Median mid-career salary: $96,000
% High job meaning: 68%
North Carolina State University
Purdue University—West Lafayette
United States Military Academy

INDUSTRIAL TECHNOLOGY

Median starting salary: $54,600
Median mid-career salary: $86,600
% High job meaning: 50%

Arizona State University
Purdue University—West Lafayette
University of Dayton
Washington State University

MECHANICAL ENGINEERING TECHNOLOGY

Median starting salary: $58,000
Median mid-career salary: $90,000
% High job meaning: 49%

Arizona State University
City University of New York—
  City College
City University of New York—
  Hunter College
Miami University
Michigan Technological University
Oklahoma State University
Purdue University—West Lafayette
United States Military Academy
University of Dayton
University of Florida
University of Houston

FOOD SCIENCE

Median starting salary: $47,800
Median mid-career salary: $89,500
% High job meaning: 51%

Amherst College
Brigham Young University (UT)
Case Western Reserve University
City University of New York—
  City College
City University of New York—
  Hunter College
Clemson University
Colby College
The College of Wooster
Colorado College
Cornell University
Dartmouth College
Emory University
Hamilton College
Lafayette College
Lawrence University
Miami University
Middlebury College
North Carolina State University
Oberlin College
Oklahoma State University
Pennsylvania State University—
  University Park
Purdue University—West Lafayette
Rhodes College
San Diego State University
Scripps College
St. Olaf College
Texas A&M University—College Station
Trinity College (CT)
Tufts University
Tulane University
Union College (NY)
University of California—Los Angeles
University of California—Riverside
University of California—San Diego
The University of Chicago
University of Colorado—Boulder
University of Dayton
University of Florida
University of Georgia
University of Illinois
  at Urbana-Champaign
University of Maryland—College Park
University of Massachusetts Amherst
University of Michigan—Ann Arbor
University of Minnesota—Twin Cities
University of Nebraska—Lincoln

University of Richmond
University of Rochester
University of Southern California
The University of Texas at Austin
The University of Tulsa
University of Wisconsin—Madison
Washington State University
Wellesley College
Wheaton College (MA)
Yale University

PRODUCT DESIGN

Median starting salary: $50,600
Median mid-career salary: $86,400
% High job meaning: 39%

Arizona State University
Brigham Young University (UT)
Carnegie Mellon University
City University of New York—
   Brooklyn College
Georgia Institute of Technology
North Carolina State University
The Ohio State University—Columbus
Purdue University—West Lafayette
Stanford University
University of Houston
University of Michigan—Ann Arbor
University of Washington
Virginia Polytechnic Institute and State
   University (Virginia Tech)

MATHEMATICS AND STATISTICS

MATHEMATICS

Median starting salary: $54,200
Median mid-career salary: $99,000
% High job meaning: 43%

Bowdoin College
Bryn Mawr College
California Institute of Technology
Carleton College
Harvey Mudd College

APPLIED MATHEMATICS

Median starting salary: $57,600
Median mid-career salary: $113,200
% High job meaning: 40%

Arizona State University
Barnard College
Berea College
Boston College

Brown University
California Institute of Technology
Carnegie Mellon University
Case Western Reserve University
City University of New York—
   Baruch College
City University of New York—
   Brooklyn College
Clarkson University
Clark University
Colgate University
Emory University
Georgia Institute of Technology
Gettysburg College
Harvard College
Illinois Institute of Technology
Missouri University of Science
   and Technology
New College of Florida
New Jersey Institute of Technology
North Carolina State University
Northwestern University
Ohio Wesleyan University
Purdue University—West Lafayette
Rensselaer Polytechnic Institute
Rice University
San Diego State University
Southwestern University
Stanford University
State University of New York—
   Stony Brook University
Stevens Institute of Technology
Texas A&M University—College Station
Texas Christian University
Tufts University
Tulane University
University of California—Berkeley
University of California—Davis
University of California—Los Angeles
University of California—San Diego
University of California—Santa Barbara
University of California—Santa Cruz
University of Colorado—Boulder
University of Houston
University of Illinois
   at Urbana-Champaign
University of Minnesota—Twin Cities
University of Rochester
University of Southern California
The University of Texas at Dallas
The University of Tulsa
University of Wisconsin—Madison
Vanderbilt University

Washington State University
Washington University in St. Louis
Whitman College
Willamette University
Worcester Polytechnic Institute
Yale University

STATISTICS
Median starting salary: $60,000
Median mid-career salary: $104,600
% High job meaning: 34%

Arizona State University
Barnard College
Brigham Young University (UT)
Carnegie Mellon University
Case Western Reserve University
City University of New York—
  Baruch College
Colby College
Cornell University
Hampden-Sydney College
Harvard College
Lehigh University
Miami University
Michigan Technological University
Missouri University of Science
  and Technology
Montana Tech of the University of
  Montana
Mount Holyoke College
New Jersey Institute of Technology
North Carolina State University
Northwestern University
Oklahoma State University
Purdue University—West Lafayette
Rice University
Rutgers, The State University
  of New Jersey—New Brunswick
San Diego State University
Stanford University
Stevens Institute of Technology
United States Military Academy
University of California—Berkeley
University of California—Davis
University of California—Los Angeles
University of California—Riverside
University of California—San Diego
University of California—Santa Barbara
The University of Chicago
University of Denver
University of Florida
University of Illinois
  at Urbana-Champaign

University of Michigan—Ann Arbor
University of Minnesota—Twin Cities
University of Pennsylvania
University of Rochester
University of Virginia
University of Washington
University of Wisconsin—Madison
Virginia Polytechnic Institute and State
  University (Virginia Tech)
Wake Forest University
Washington University in St. Louis
Williams College

HEALTH PROFESSIONS

ENVIRONMENTAL HEALTH & SAFETY
Median starting salary: $51,900
Median mid-career salary: $91,800
% High job meaning: 34%

Purdue University—West Lafayette
State University of New York—College of
  Environmental Science and Forestry
Tulane University
University of Georgia
University of Minnesota—Twin Cities
University of North Carolina
  at Chapel Hill
University of Washington
Willamette University

NURSING
Median starting salary: $58,200
Median mid-career salary: $76,300
% High job meaning: 82%

Arizona State University
Baylor University
Boston College
Case Western Reserve University
Coe College
College of the Ozarks
Creighton University
Emory University
Fairfield University
Northeastern University
Saint Louis University
San Diego State University
St. Anselm College
St. Olaf College
State University of New York
  at Binghamton
State University of New York—
  Stony Brook University

Texas Christian University
Truman State University
The University of Alabama—Tuscaloosa
University of Arizona
University of California—Los Angeles
University of Central Florida
University of Massachusetts Amherst
University of Michigan—Ann Arbor
University of Pennsylvania
University of Pittsburgh—
    Pittsburgh Campus
The University of Tulsa
University of Utah
University of Wisconsin—Madison
Villanova University
Washington State University
William Jewell College

PHYSICAL THERAPY

Median starting salary: $42,800
Median mid-career salary: $89,700
% High job meaning: 90%

Clarkson University
Northeastern University
Purdue University—West Lafayette
University of Florida
University of Minnesota—Twin Cities
University of Utah

PHYSICIAN ASSISTANT STUDIES

Median starting salary: $87,800
Median mid-career salary: $107,600
% High job meaning: 82%

Purdue University—West Lafayette
University of Florida
University of Washington
Wake Forest University

PHYSICAL SCIENCES

GEOLOGY

Median starting salary: $45,400
Median mid-career salary: $83,800
% High job meaning: 54%

Amherst College
Arizona State University
    at the Tempe campus
Bates College
Boston College
Bowdoin College
Brigham Young University (UT)

Brooklyn College, City University
    of New York
Brown University
Bryn Mawr College
Bucknell University
California Institute of Technology
Carleton College
Case Western Reserve University
Clemson University
Colby College
Colgate University
College of William and Mary
The College of Wooster
Colorado College
Cornell University
Dartmouth College
Denison University
DePauw University
Dickinson College
Duke University
Furman University
Gustavus Adolphus College
Hamilton College
Haverford College
Johns Hopkins University
Lawrence University
Macalester College
Massachusetts Institute of Technology
Miami University
Michigan Technological University
Middlebury College
Missouri University of Science
    and Technology
Mount Holyoke College
North Carolina State University
Northeastern University
Northwestern University
Oberlin College
Occidental College
Oklahoma State University
Pennsylvania State University—
    University Park
Purdue University—West Lafayette
The Ohio State University—Columbus
Rensselaer Polytechnic Institute
Rice University
Rutgers, The State University
    of New Jersey—New Brunswick
Scripps College
Skidmore College
Smith College
St. Lawrence University
Stanford University

State University of New York at
Binghamton (Binghamton University)
State University of New York—
Stony Brook University
Texas A&M University—College Station
Trinity University
Tufts University
Tulane University
Union College (NY)
University of California—Davis
University of California—Los Angeles
University of California—Riverside
University of California—San Diego
University of California—Santa Barbara
University of California—Santa Cruz
University of Colorado Boulder
University of Dayton
University of Florida
University of Georgia
University of Houston
University of Illinois
at Urbana-Champaign
University of Maryland—College Park
University of Massachusetts Amherst
University of Michigan—Ann Arbor
University of Minnesota—
Twin Cities Campus
The University of North Carolina
at Chapel Hill
University of Oklahoma
University of Pennsylvania
University of Pittsburgh—
Pittsburgh Campus
University of Rochester
University of Southern California
The University of Texas at Austin
The University of Texas at Dallas
The University of Tulsa
University of Washington
University of Wisconsin—Madison
Vanderbilt University
Vassar College
Virginia Tech
Washington University in St. Louis
Wellesley College
Wesleyan University
Wheaton College (IL)
Whitman College
Yale University

METEOROLOGY

Median starting salary: $42,600
Median mid-career salary: $91,100
% High job meaning: 50%

Cornell University
North Carolina State University
Penn State University Park
Purdue University—West Lafayette
Rutgers, The State University
of New Jersey—New Brunswick
State University of New York—College of
Environmental Science and Forestry
State University of New York—
Stony Brook University
Texas A&M University—College Station
United States Air Force Academy
University of California—Davis
University of Houston
University of Illinois
at Urbana-Champaign
University of Maryland—College Park
University of Michigan—Ann Arbor
University of Oklahoma
University of Washington
University of Wisconsin—Madison
Virginia Tech

PHYSICS

Median starting salary: $58,000
Median mid-career salary: $108,000
% High job meaning: 45%

Bryn Mawr College
California Institute of Technology
Carleton College
The College of Wooster
Colorado College
Furman University
Gustavus Adolphus College
Harvey Mudd College
Haverford College
Kalamazoo College
Massachusetts Institute of Technology
Pitzer College
Princeton University
Rhodes College
St. Olaf College
United States Coast Guard Academy
United States Naval Academy
The University of Chicago
Wabash College
Whitman College
Willamette University
Williams College

SOCIAL SCIENCES

ECONOMICS

Median starting salary: $54,100
Median mid-career salary: $103,200
% High job meaning: 40%

Allegheny College
Amherst College
Beloit College
Boston College
Bowdoin College
Brandeis University
Brown University
Bucknell University
Centre College
Christopher Newport University
City University of New York—
    Queens College
Claremont McKenna College
Colby College
Colgate University
College of the Holy Cross
Colorado College
Cornell University
Dartmouth College
Denison University
DePauw University
Duke University
Emory University
Grinnell College
Hamilton College
Hampden-Sydney College
Harvard College
Hobart and William Smith Colleges
Hollins University
Kalamazoo College
Kenyon College
Lafayette College
Macalester College
Middlebury College
Mount Holyoke College
Northwestern University
Occidental College
Ohio Wesleyan University
Pitzer College
Princeton University
Rice University
Smith College
St. Lawrence University
St. Mary's College of Maryland
St. Olaf College
Swarthmore College
Trinity College (CT)

Tufts University
Union College (NY)
United States Military Academy
United States Naval Academy
University of California—Davis
University of California—San Diego
University of California—Santa Barbara
The University of Chicago
University of Maryland—College Park
University of Michigan—Ann Arbor
The University of North Carolina
    at Chapel Hill
University of Pennsylvania
University of Rochester
University of Wisconsin—Madison
Vassar College
Washington College
Wellesley College
Wesleyan University
Wheaton College (MA)
Willamette University
Williams College
Yale University

INTERNATIONAL RELATIONS

Median starting salary: $46,400
Median mid-career salary: $86,100
% High job meaning: 46%

Beloit College
Brigham Young University (UT)
Brown University
Bucknell University
Carleton College
Carnegie Mellon University
Case Western Reserve University
City University of New York—
    City College
Claremont McKenna College
Colgate University
The College of New Jersey
College of William and Mary
The College of Wooster
Denison University
Dickinson College
Georgetown University
Georgia Institute of Technology
Gettysburg College
Hamilton College
Hampden-Sydney College
Harvard College
Hobart and William Smith Colleges
Johns Hopkins University
Lafayette College

Lake Forest College
Lehigh University
Miami University
Middlebury College
Mount Holyoke College
Muhlenberg College
Northeastern University
Northwestern University
Occidental College
The Ohio State University—Columbus
Reed College
Rhodes College
Skidmore College
Southwestern University
Stanford University
State University of New York
   at Binghamton
Trinity University
Tufts University
United States Military Academy
University of California—Davis
The University of Chicago
University of Denver
University of Florida
University of Minnesota—Twin Cities
University of Pennsylvania
University of Southern California
The University of Tulsa
University of Virginia
Vassar College
Virginia Polytechnic Institute
   and State University (Virginia Tech)
Washington University in St. Louis
Wellesley College
Wheaton College (IL)
William Jewell College
Yale University

POLITICAL SCIENCE AND GOVERNMENT

POLITICAL SCIENCE

Median starting salary: $44,600
Median mid-career salary: $82,000
% High job meaning: 47%

Agnes Scott College
Amherst College
Arizona State University
Barnard College
Bates College
Beloit College
Berea College

Boston College
Bowdoin College
Brigham Young University (UT)
Brown University
Bryn Mawr College
Bucknell University
California Institute of Technology
Carleton College
Case Western Reserve University
Centre College
Christopher Newport University
City University of New York—
   Baruch College
City University of New York—
   Brooklyn College
City University of New York—
   City College
City University of New York—
   Hunter College
Claremont McKenna College
Clarkson University
Clark University
Clemson University
Colby College
Colgate University
College of the Holy Cross
The College of New Jersey
College of William and Mary
College of Wooster
Colorado College
Columbia University
Cornell University
Dartmouth College
Davidson College
Denison University
DePauw University
Dickinson College
Duke University
Emory University
Franklin & Marshall College
Furman University
Georgetown University
Gettysburg College
Grinnell College
Grove City College
Gustavus Adolphus College
Hamilton College
Hampden-Sydney College
Harvard College
Haverford College
Illinois Institute of Technology
Johns Hopkins University
Kalamazoo College
Kenyon College

Lafayette College
Lake Forest College
Lehigh University
Macalester College
Marlboro College
Massachusetts Institute of Technology
Miami University
Middlebury College
Mount Holyoke College
Muhlenberg College
New College of Florida
Northeastern University
North Carolina State University
Northwestern University
Oberlin College
Occidental College
Ohio State University—Columbus
Pennsylvania State University—
   University Park
Pitzer College
Princeton University
Purdue University—West Lafayette
Reed College
Rhodes College
Rice University
Rutgers, The State University
   of New Jersey—New Brunswick
Saint Anselm College
Santa Clara University
Scripps College
Skidmore College
Smith College
Southwestern University
Stanford University
State University of New York at
   Binghamton
State University of New York—Purchase
   College
State University of New York—
   Stony Brook University
St. Lawrence University
St. Olaf College
Swarthmore College
Texas A&M University—College Station
Trinity College (CT)
Trinity University
Truman State University
Tulane University
Union College (NY)
United States Coast Guard Academy
United States Military Academy
United States Naval Academy
University of California—Berkeley
University of California—Davis

University of California—Los Angeles
University of California—Riverside
University of California—San Diego
University of California—Santa Cruz
The University of Chicago
University of Colorado—Boulder
University of Dayton
University of Denver
University of Florida
University of Georgia
University of Houston
University of Maryland—College Park
University of Massachusetts Amherst
University of Michigan—Ann Arbor
University of Minnesota—Twin Cities
University of North Carolina
   at Chapel Hill
University of Notre Dame
University of Oklahoma
University of Pennsylvania
University of Pittsburgh—
   Pittsburgh Campus
University of Richmond
University of Rochester
University of Southern California
University of Texas at Austin
The University of Texas at Dallas
University of Tulsa
University of Utah
University of Virginia
University of Washington
University of Wisconsin—Madison
Vanderbilt University
Vassar College
Villanova University
Virginia Tech
Wabash College
Wake Forest University
Washington University in St. Louis
Wellesley College
Wesleyan University
Wheaton College (IL)
Willamette University
William Jewell College
Williams College
Wofford College
Yale University

GOVERNMENT
Median starting salary: $49,400
Median mid-career salary: $107,000
% High job meaning: 51%

Amherst College
Barnard College
Bates College
Bowdoin College
Claremont McKenna College
Clark University
College of the Holy Cross
Columbia University
Dartmouth College
Davidson College
Dickinson College
Franklin & Marshall College
Furman University
Georgetown University
Gettysburg College
Grinnell College
Hamilton College
Hampden-Sydney College
Harvard College
Hobart and William Smith Colleges
Lafayette College
Middlebury College
New College of Florida
Princeton University
Scripps College
Smith College
St. Lawrence University
Swarthmore College
Trinity College (CT)
United States Coast Guard Academy
United States Naval Academy
University of California—Berkeley
The University of Chicago
University of Illinois
    at Urbana-Champaign
University of Notre Dame
University of Wisconsin—Madison
Vassar College
Wake Forest University
Wellesley College
Yale University

About Our Student Survey

Surveying tens of thousands of students on hundreds of campuses is a mammoth undertaking. In 1992, our survey was a paper survey. We worked with school administrators to set up tables in centrally-trafficked locations on their campuses at which students filled out the surveys. To reach a range of students, freshmen to seniors, this process sometimes took place over several days and at various on-campus locations. That process yielded about 125 surveys per college.

However, the launch of our online survey several years ago made our survey process more efficient, secure, and representative. Our student survey is also now a continuous process. Students submit surveys online from all schools in the book and they can submit their surveys at any time at http:// survey.review.com. (However, our site will accept only one survey from a student per academic year per school (it's not possible to "stuff" the ballot box, as it were).) In addition to those surveys we receive from students on an ongoing basis, we also conduct "formal" surveys of students at each school in the book at least once every three years. (We conduct these more often once every three years if the colleges request that we do so (and we can accommodate that request) or we deem it necessary.)

How do we do conduct those "formal" surveys? First, we notify our administrative contacts at the schools we plan to survey. We depend upon these contacts for assistance in informing the student body of our survey (although we also get the word out to students about our survey via other channels independent of the schools). An increasing number of schools have chosen to send an e-mail to the entire student body about the availability of our online survey; in such cases this has yielded robust response rates. Our average number of student surveys (per college) is now 359 students per campus (and at some schools we hear from more than 3,000 students).

And of course, surveys we receive from students outside of their schools' normal survey cycles are always factored into the subsequent year's ranking calculations, so our pool of student survey data is continuously refreshed.

The survey has more than eighty questions divided into four sections: "About Yourself," "Your School's Academics/Administration," "Students," and "Life at Your School." We ask about all sorts of things, from "How many out-of-class hours do you spend studying each day?" to "How do you rate your campus food?" Most questions offer students a five-point grid on which to indicate their answer choices (headers may range from "Excellent" to "Awful"). Eight questions offer students the opportunity to expand on their answers with narrative comment. These essay-type responses are the sources of the student quotations that appear in the school profiles. Once the surveys have been completed and responses stored in our database, every college is given a score (similar to a grade point average) for its students' answers to each question. This score enables us to compare students' responses to a particular question from one college to the next. We use these scores as an underlying data point in our calculation of the ratings in the profile sidebars and the ranking lists in the section of the book titled "School Rankings and Lists."

Once we have the student survey information in hand, we write the college profiles. Student quotations in each profile are chosen because they represent the sentiments expressed by the majority of survey respondents from the college; or, they illustrate one side or another of a mixed bag of student opinion, in which case there will also appear a counterpoint within the text. In order to guard against producing a write-up that's off the mark for any particular college, we send our administrative contact at each school a copy of the profile we intend to publish prior to its publication date, with ample opportunity to respond with corrections, comments, and/or outright objections. In every case in which we receive requests for changes, we take careful measures to review the school's suggestions against the student survey data we collected and make appropriate changes when warranted.

How To Use This Book

It's pretty self-explanatory. We have done our best to include lots of helpful information about choosing colleges and gaining admission. The profiles we have written contain the same basic information for each school and follow the same basic format. The Princeton Review collects all of the data you see in the sidebars of each school. As is customary with college guides, our numbers usually reflect the figures for the academic year prior to publication. Since college offerings and demographics significantly vary from one institution to another and some colleges report data more thoroughly than others, some entries will not include all of the individual data described. Please know that we take our data-collection process seriously. We reach out to schools numerous times through the process to ensure we can present you with the most accurate and up-to-date facts, figures, and deadlines. Even so, a book is dated from the moment it hits the printing press. Be sure to double-check with any schools to which you plan to apply to make sure you are able to get them everything they need in order to meet their deadlines.

How This Book Is Organized

Each of the colleges and universities in this book has its own two-page profile. To make it easier to find and compare information about the schools, we've used the same profile format for every school. First, at the very top of the profile you will see the school's address, telephone, and fax numbers for the admissions office, the telephone number for the financial aid office, and the school's website and/or e-mail address. Second, there are two sidebars (the narrow columns on the outside of each page, which consist mainly of statistics) divided into the categories of Campus Life, Academics, Selectivity, and Financial Facts. Third, at the bottom of the page you will find a PayScale.com Career Information box with the each school's ROI rating and salary figures. Finally, there are seven headings in the narrative text: About the School, Bang for Your Buck, Student Life, Career, General Info, Financial Aid, and The Bottom Line.

Sidebars

The sidebars contain various statistics culled from our surveys of students attending the school and from questionnaires that school administrators complete at our request in the fall of each year. Keep in mind that not every category will appear for every school—in some cases the information is not reported or not applicable. We compile the eight ratings—Quality of Life, Fire Safety, Green Rating, Academic, Profs Interesting, Profs Accessible, Admissions Selectivity, and Financial Aid—listed in the sidebars based on the results from our student surveys and/or institutional data we collect from school administrators.

These ratings are on a scale of 60–99. If a 60* (60 with an asterisk) appears as any rating for any school, it means that the school reported so few of the rating's underlying data points by our deadline that we were unable to calculate an accurate rating for it. (These measures are outlined in the ratings explanation below.) Be advised that, because the Admissions Selectivity Rating is a factor in the computation that produces the Academic Rating, a school that has 60* (60 with an asterisk) as its Admissions Selectivity Rating will have an Academic Rating that is lower than it should be. Also bear in mind that each rating places each college on a continuum for purposes of comparing colleges within this edition only. Since our ratings computations may change from year to year, it is invalid to compare the ratings in this edition to those that appear in any prior or future edition.

PayScale.com Career Information Box

This box includes up to seven data points: our unique ROI rating; median starting salary reported by alumni and median mid-career salary reported by alumni, both those holding a bachelor's degree and those with at least a bachelor's degree which includes students who have gone on to a higher degree; the percentage of alumni that report having high job meaning (i.e., feeling that their job makes the world a better place); and the percentage of degrees the school awarded in STEM (science, technology, engineering, and math). Alumni survey information comes from PayScale.com's 2017–2018 College Salary Report. Some school profiles do not include all of these data points, as PayScale.com only reports survey results based on a statistically significant sample of responses. The data used for PayScale.com's annual College Salary Report is collected through their ongoing, online compensation survey. You can read more about their survey and methodology online at www.PayScale.com/college-salary-report/methodology.

ROI Rating
Our ROI rating is based on data we collected from fall 2017 through fall 2018 via our institutional and student surveys. It is calculated using more than forty data points covering academics, costs, financial aid, career outcomes, and student and alumni survey data.

We asked students to rate their schools career services office, the opportunities for internships and experiential learning, and the strength of their alumni network on campus. Starting and mid-career salary data was taken from PayScale.com's 2017–18 College Salary Report. In addition to salary data, PayScale.com provided data on alumni who reported high job meaning.

Also considered are the percentage of graduating seniors who borrowed from any loan program and the average debt those students had at graduation. The percentage of students graduating within four and six years was also taken into account.

Additional criteria included the following breakdown of Princeton Review's ratings:

Academic Rating
To tally this rating, we analyze a large amount of data the schools report to us about their academic selectivity and admissions, plus opinion data we collect from students reporting on the education they are receiving at their schools. The admissions statistics shed light on how difficult it is to gain acceptance: they include SAT/ACT scores and high school GPA of enrolled freshmen as well as other data factors. The student data reveals how students at the school rate their professors' teaching ability as well as how accessible the professors are outside of class.

Financial Aid Rating
This rating measures how much financial aid a school awards and how satisfied students are with that aid. This rating is based on school-reported data on the percentage of students who were determined to have need and received aid, the percentage of need met for those students, and the percentage of students whose need was fully met. Student survey data that measures students' satisfaction with the financial aid they receive is also considered.

Nota Bene: *The following ratings appear in each school profile, but were not included in the ROI methodology.*

Quality of Life Rating
On a scale of 60–99, this rating is a measure of how happy students are with their campus experiences outside the classroom. To compile this rating, we weighed several factors, all based on students' answers to questions on our survey. They included the students' assessments of: their overall happiness; the beauty, safety, and location of the campus; comfort of dorms; quality of food; ease of getting around campus and dealing with administrators; friendliness of fellow students; and the interaction of different student types on campus and within the greater community.

Fire Safety Rating

On a scale of 60–99, this rating measures how well prepared a school is to prevent or respond to campus fires, specifically in residence halls. We asked schools several questions about their efforts to ensure fire safety for campus residents. We developed the questions in consultation with the Center for Campus Fire Safety (www.campusfiresafety. org). Each school's responses to seven questions were considered when calculating its Fire Safety Rating. They cover:

1. The percentage of student housing sleeping rooms protected by an automatic fire sprinkler system with a fire sprinkler head located in the individual sleeping rooms.

2. The percentage of student housing sleeping rooms equipped with a smoke detector connected to a supervised fire alarm system.

3. The number of malicious fire alarms that occur in student housing per year.

4. The number of unwanted fire alarms that occur in student housing per year.

5. The banning of certain hazardous items and activities in residence halls, like candles, smoking, halogen lamps, etc.

6. The percentage of student housing fire alarm systems that, if activated, result in a signal being transmitted to a monitored location, where security investigates before notifying the fire department.

7. The percentage of student housing fire alarm systems that, if activated, result in a signal being transmitted immediately to a continuously monitored location.

Schools that did not report answers to a sufficient number of questions receive a Fire Safety Rating of 60* (60 with an asterisk). You can also find Fire Safety Ratings for our *Colleges That Pay You Back* (and several additional schools) in *The Complete Book of Colleges*, 2018 Edition and in *Best 382 Colleges* book.

Green Rating

We asked all the schools we collect data from annually to answer a number of questions that evaluate the comprehensive measure of their performance as an environmentally aware and responsible institution. The questions were first developed in consultation with ecoAmerica (www.ecoAmerica.org), a research and partnership-based environmental nonprofit that convened an expert committee to design this comprehensive rating system, and cover: 1) whether students have a campus quality of life that is both healthy and sustainable; 2) how well a school is preparing students not only for employment in the clean energy economy of the twenty-first century, but also for citizenship in a world now defined by environmental challenges; and 3) how environmentally responsible a school's policies are.

Additionally, The Princeton Review, the Association for the Advancement of Sustainability in Higher Education (AASHE) and Sierra magazine continue to collaborate on an effort to streamline the reporting process for institutions that choose to participate in various higher education sustainability assessments. The intent of this initiative is to reduce and streamline the amount of time campus staff spend tracking sustainability data and completing related surveys.

Please find more information here:

http://www.princetonreview.com/green-data-partnership

Each school's responses to ten questions were considered when calculating The Princeton Review's Green Rating.

They include:

1. The percentage of food expenditures that go toward local, organic, or otherwise environmentally preferable food.

2. Whether the school offers programs including mass transit programs, bike sharing, facilities for bicyclists, bicycle and pedestrian plan, car sharing, carpool discount, carpool/vanpool matching, cash-out of parking, prohibiting idling, local housing, telecommuting, and condensed work week.

3. Whether the school has a formal committee that is devoted to advancing sustainability on campus.

4. Whether school buildings that were constructed or underwent major renovations in the past three years are LEED certified.

5. The schools overall waste-diversion rate.

6. Whether the school offers at least one sustainability-focused undergraduate major, degree program, or equivalent.

7. Whether the school's students graduate from programs that include sustainability as a required learning outcome or include multiple sustainability learning outcomes.

8. Whether the school has a formal plan to mitigate its greenhouse gas emissions.

9. What percentage of the school's energy consumption is derived from renewable resources.

10. Whether the school employs a dedicated full-time (or full-time equivalent) sustainability officer.

Colleges that did not supply answers to a sufficient number of the green campus questions for us to fairly compare them to other colleges receive a Green Rating of 60*.

Check out our free resource area, The Princeton Review's Guide to 399 Green Colleges at www.princetonreview.com/green-guide.

In addition to these ratings, we have compiled the following information about each school. Keep in mind that not all schools responded to our requests for information, so not all of this information will appear in every profile.

Type of school: Whether the school is public or private.

Affiliation: Any religious order with which the school is affiliated.

Environment: Whether the campus is located in an urban, suburban, or rural setting.

Total undergrad enrollment: The total number of degree-seeking undergraduates who attend the school. The total number of undergraduates who attend the school.

"% male/female" through "# countries represented": Demographic information about the full-time undergraduate student body, including male to female ratio, ethnicity, and the number of countries represented by the student body. Also included are the percentages of the student body who are from out of state, attended a public high school, freshmen living on campus, and belong to Greek organizations.

Academic Rating: On a scale of 60–99, this rating is a measure of how hard students work at the school and how much they get back for their efforts. The rating is based on results from our surveys of students and data we collect from administrators. Factors weighed included how many hours students reported that they study each day outside of class, students' assessments of their professors' teaching abilities and of their accessibility outside the classroom and the quality of students the school attracts as measured by admissions statistics.

4-year graduation rate: The percentage of degree-seeking undergraduate students graduating in four years or less.

6-year graduation rate: The percentage of degree-seeking undergraduate students graduating within six years.

Calendar: The school's schedule of academic terms. A "semester" schedule has two long terms, usually starting in September and January. A "trimester" schedule has three terms, one usually beginning before Christmas and two after. A "quarterly" schedule has four terms, which go by very quickly: the entire term, including exams, usually lasts only nine or ten weeks. A "4-1-4" schedule is like a semester schedule, but with a month-long term in between the fall and spring semesters. (Similarly, a "4-4-1" has a short term following two longer semesters.) It is always best to call the admissions office for details.

Student/faculty ratio: The ratio of full-time undergraduate instructional faculty members to all undergraduates.

Profs interesting rating: On a scale of 60–99, this rating is based on levels of surveyed students' agreement or disagreement with the statement: "Your instructors are good teachers."

Profs accessible rating: On a scale of 60–99, this rating is based on levels of surveyed students' agreement or disagreement with the statement: "Your instructors are accessible outside the classroom."

Most common regular class size; Most common lab size: The most commonly occurring class size for regular courses and for labs/discussion sections.

Most popular majors: The majors with the highest enrollments at the school.

Admissions Selectivity Rating: On a scale of 60–99, this rating is a measure of how competitive admission is at the school. This rating is determined by several factors, including the class rank of entering freshmen, test scores, and percentage of applicants accepted.

% of applicants accepted: The percentage of applicants to whom the school offered admission.

% of acceptees attending: The percentage of accepted students who eventually enrolled at the school.

 # accepting a place on wait list: The number of students who decided to take a place on the wait list when offered this option.

% admitted from wait list: The percentage of applicants who opted to take a place on the wait list and were subsequently offered admission. These figures will vary tremendously from college to college, and should be a consideration when deciding whether to accept a place on a college's wait list.

# of early decision applicants: The number of students who applied under the college's early decision or early action plan.

% accepted early decision: The percentage of early decision or early action applicants who were admitted under this plan. By the nature of these plans, the vast majority who are admitted ultimately enroll.

Range SAT Critical Reading, Range SAT Math, Range SAT Writing, Range ACT Composite: The average and the middle fifty percent range of test scores for entering first-year students.

An Important Note About SAT Scores Published in *The Best Value Colleges, 2019 Edition*:

 The SAT underwent major changes in March 2016. The test now consists of 2 sections and is scored out of 1600 points. Prior to the redesign, the test consisted of 3 sections and was scored out of 2400 points.

The admission data reported in this book reflects the entering first-year class of fall 2017, a population that submitted applications in fall 2016 subsequent to the SAT redesign. Schools reported SAT score ranges for this class on the 1600 scale using concordance information published by the College Board. The College Board's SAT concordance methodology and tools are available at: https://collegereadiness.collegeboard.org/educators/higher-ed/scoring-changes/concordance.

We made the above information available to contacts at each school for review and approval. You may also cross-reference our print profiles with our online school profiles at PrincetonReview.com, which list the most up-to date data as reported by schools.

Don't be discouraged from applying to the school of your choice even if your combined SAT scores are 80 or even 120 points below the average, because you may still have a chance of getting in. Remember that many schools value other aspects of your application (e.g., your grades, how good a match you make with the school) more heavily than test scores.

Minimum TOEFL: The minimum test score necessary for entering freshmen who are required to take the TOEFL (Test of English as a Foreign Language). Most schools will require all international students or non-native English speakers to take the TOEFL in order to be considered for admission.

Average HS GPA: The average grade point average of entering freshman. We report this on a scale of 1.0–4.0 (occasionally colleges report averages on a 100 scale, in which case we report those figures). This is one of the key factors in college admissions.

% graduated top 10%, top 25%, top 50% of class: Of those students for whom class rank was reported, the percentage of entering freshmen who ranked in the top tenth, quarter, and half of their high school classes.

Early decision/action deadlines: The deadline for submission of application materials under the early decision or early action plan.

Early decision, early action, priority, and regular admission deadlines: The dates by which all materials must be postmarked (we suggest "received in the office") in order to be considered for admission under each particular admissions option/cycle for matriculation in the fall term.

Early decision, early action, priority, and regular admission notification: The dates by which you can expect a decision on your application under each admissions option/cycle.

Nonfall registration: Some schools will allow incoming students to register and begin attending classes at times other than the fall term, which is the traditional beginning of the academic calendar year. Other schools will allow you to register for classes only if you can begin in the fall term. A simple "yes" or "no" in this category indicates the school's policy on nonfall registration.

Financial Aid Rating: On a scale of 60–99, this rating is a measure of the financial aid the school awards and how satisfied students are with the aid they receive. It is based on school-reported data on financial aid and students' responses to the survey question, "If you receive financial aid, how satisfied are you with your financial aid package?"

Annual in-state tuition: The tuition at the school, or for public colleges, the cost of tuition for a resident of the school's state. Usually much lower than out-of-state tuition for state-supported public schools.

Annual out-of-state tuition: For public colleges, the tuition for a non-resident of the school's state. This entry appears only for public colleges, since tuition at private colleges is generally the same regardless of state of residence.

Room and board: Estimated annual room and board costs.

Required fees: Any additional costs students must pay beyond tuition in order to attend the school. These often include fitness center fees and the like. A few state schools may not officially charge in-state students tuition, but those students are still responsible for hefty fees.

Tuition and fees: In cases when schools do not report separate figures for tuition and required fees, we offer this total of the two.

Comprehensive fee: A few schools report one overall fee that reflects the total cost of tuition, room and board, and required fees. If you'd like to see how this figure breaks down, we recommend contacting the school.

Books and supplies: Estimated annual cost of necessary textbooks and/or supplies.

Average need-based scholarship: The average need-based scholarship and grant aid awarded to students with need.

% needy frosh receiving need-based scholarship or grant aid: The percentage of all degree-seeking freshmen who were determined to have need and received any need-based scholarship or grant.

% needy UG receiving need-based scholarship or grant aid: The percentage of all degree-seeking undergraduates who were determined to have need and received any need-based scholarship or grant.

% needy frosh receiving non-need-based scholarship or grant aid: The percentage of all degree-seeking freshmen, determined to have need, receiving any non-need based scholarship or grant aid.

% needy UG receiving non-need-based scholarship or grant aid: The percentage of all degree-seeking undergraduates, determined to have need, receiving any non-need based scholarship or grant aid.

% needy frosh receiving need-based self-help aid: The percentage of all degree-seeking freshmen, determined to have need, who received any need-based self-help aid.

% needy UG receiving need-based self-help aid: The percentage of all degree-seeking undergraduates, determined to have need, who received any need-based self-help aid.

% frosh receiving any financial aid: The percentage of all degree-seeking freshmen receiving any financial aid (need-based, merit-based, gift aid).

% UG receiving any financial aid: The percentage of all degree-seeking undergraduates receiving any financial aid (need-based, merit-based, gift aid).

% UG borrow to pay for school: The percentage who borrowed at any time through any loan programs (institutional, state, Federal Stafford Subsidized and Unsubsidized, private loans that were certified by your institution, etc., exclude parent loans). Includes both Federal Direct Student Loans and Federal Family Education Loans (prior to the FFEL program ending in June 2010).

Average Indebtedness: The average per-borrower cumulative undergraduate indebtedness of those who borrowed at any time through any loan programs (institutional, state, Federal Stafford Subsidized and Unsubsidized, private loans that were certified by your institution, etc.; excluding parent loans).

% frosh and ugrad need fully met: The percentage of needy degree-seeking students whose needs were fully met (excludes PLUS loans, unsubsidized loans and private alternative loans).

Average % of frosh and ugrad need met: On average, the percentage of need that was met of students who were awarded any need-based aid. Excludes any aid that was awarded in excess of need as well as any resources that were awarded to replace EFC (PLUS loans, unsubsidized loans and private alternative loans).

Nota Bene: *The statistical data reported in this book, unless otherwise noted, was collected from the profiled colleges from fall 2017 through the fall of 2018. In some cases, we were unable to publish the most recent data because schools did not report the necessary statistics to us in time, despite our repeated outreach efforts. Because the enrollment and financial statistics, as well as application and financial aid deadlines, fluctuate from one year to another, we recommend that you check with the schools to make sure you have the most current information before applying.*

The Narrative
These sections share the straight-from-the-campus feedback we get from the school's most important customers: The students attending them. They summarize the opinions of freshmen through seniors we've surveyed and they include direct quotes from scores of them. When appropriate, they also incorporate statistics provided by the schools. The sections based on student survey responses are divided into four subsections:

About the School
This section provides a general overview of the school including student descriptions of the school environment and often tells you which programs or academic departments students rated most favorably and how professors interact with students. Student opinion regarding administrative departments also works its way into this section.

Bang For Your Buck
Here you will find information about scholarship and fellowship programs, the school's commitment to meeting demonstrated need, and student opinion regarding financial aid. Details on particular offerings related to funding are also included.

Student Life
The student life section describes life outside the classroom and addresses questions ranging from "How comfortable are the dorms?" to "How popular are fraternities and sororities?" In this section, students describe what they do for entertainment both on-campus and off, providing a clear picture of the social environment at their particular school. This section will also give you the lowdown on the types of students the school attracts and how the students view the level of interaction among various groups, including those of different ethnic, socioeconomic, and religious backgrounds.

Career

In this section, you will find information about the career resources at each school including career services departments, job fairs, and internship programs. We spotlight specific experiential learning opportunities that could have real-world advantages in terms of your career and include student opinions about the career services offered to them.

The other three sections included in the profile are:

General Info

This section lists student activities, organizations, athletics, and other campus highlights that each school's admissions office would you to know about their institution.

Financial Aid

Here you'll find out what you need to know about the financial aid process at the school, namely what forms you need and what types of merit-based aid and loans are available. Information about need-based aid is contained in the financial aid sidebar. This section includes specific deadline dates for submission of materials as reported by the colleges. We strongly encourage students seeking financial aid to file all forms—federal, state, and institutional—carefully, fully, and on time.

The Bottom Line

Here we breakdown the cost of attendance for each school by tuition, fees, and housing, and give you the final totals for in-state and out-of-state students.

Ranking Lists

The Best Value Colleges contains seven ranking lists, all of which focus on different aspects of financial aid and career preparation. For lists that cover sixty-two topics on academics, facilities, and campus culture, check out our book *Best 384 Colleges*, or visit PrincetonReview.com.

Top 50 Best Value Colleges

The fifty schools that received the highest ROI rating (described on page 29), ranked in order. Each of these school's profiles also includes a banner with its rank.

1. California Institute of Technology
2. Stanford University
3. Princeton University
4. Massachusetts Institute of Technology
5. Williams College
6. Harvey Mudd College
7. Yale University
8. Harvard College
9. The Cooper Union for the Advancement of Science and Art
10. University of Virginia
11. University of California—Berkeley
12. Vanderbilt University
13. Rice University
14. Columbia University
15. Dartmouth College
16. University of North Carolina at Chapel Hill
17. Amherst College
18. Georgia Institute of Technology
19. Swarthmore College
20. Brown University
21. University of California—Santa Barbara
22. Bowdoin College
23. Cornell University
24. Pomona College
25. University of Pennsylvania
26. Duke University
27. University of Chicago
28. Colgate University
29. Wabash College
30. Worcester Polytechnic Institute
31. Brigham Young University (UT)
32. Haverford College
33. Claremont McKenna College
34. Carleton College
35. University of California—Los Angeles
36. Union College (NY)
37. Babson College
38. Emory University
39. College of William and Mary
40. Grinnell College
41. Vassar College
42. Carnegie Mellon University
43. University of Richmond
44. Lehigh University
45. University of California—San Diego
46. Washington University in St. Louis
47. University of Florida
48. City University of New York—Baruch College
49. Bates College
50. Johns Hopkins University

Top 25 Best Value Colleges for Students With No Demonstrated Need

To create this list, we used the same methodology for our ROI rating, but removed need-based aid information. If you don't qualify for financial aid, these are your twenty-five best value schools.

1. Georgia Institute of Technology
2. Harvey Mudd College
3. University of California—Berkeley
4. Stanford University
5. California Institute of Technology
6. University of Virginia
7. Massachusetts Institute of Technology
8. University of North Carolina at Chapel Hill
9. University of California—Santa Barbara
10. Brigham Young University (UT)
11. College of William and Mary
12. Princeton University
13. University of Florida
14. Rice University
15. Williams College
16. Dartmouth College
17. Yale University
18. Worcester Polytechnic Institute
19. State University of New York at Binghamton
20. University of California—Los Angeles
21. University of Wisconsin-Madison
22. Brown University
23. Vanderbilt University
24. State University of New York—Stony Brook University
25. Cornell University

Best Alumni Network

These twenty-five schools have the strongest and most active alumni networks, based on current students' ratings of alumni activity and visibility on campus.

1. Pennsylvania State University—University Park
2. Wabash College
3. St. Lawrence University
4. Hampden-Sydney College
5. Dartmouth College
6. Bucknell University
7. University of Virginia
8. Clemson University
9. Georgia Institute of Technology
10. Stanford University
11. Agnes Scott College
12. Lake Forest College
13. Texas Christian University
14. Fairfield University
15. Hobart and William Smith Colleges
16. Williams College
17. Hollins University
18. Bryn Mawr College
19. University of Wisconsin—Madison
20. Gettysburg College
21. Emory University
22. Wheaton College (IL)
23. Worcester Polytechnic Institute
24. University of Oklahoma
25. Wofford College

Best Schools for Internships

This top twenty-five list is based on students' ratings of accessibility of internships at their school.

1. Bentley University
2. Franklin W. Olin College of Engineering
3. Wabash College
4. University of Richmond
5. Northeastern University
6. College of William and Mary
7. Clemson University
8. Texas Christian University
9. Lake Forest College
10. The University of Alabama—Tuscaloosa
11. Grove City College
12. College of Wooster
13. Wake Forest University
14. Fairfield University
15. Coe College
16. Gettysburg College
17. Vanderbilt University
18. Southwestern University
19. Hampden-Sydney College
20. University of Dayton
21. Worcester Polytechnic Institute
22. Stevens Institute of Technology
23. Skidmore College
24. St. Lawrence University
25. Pennsylvania State University—University Park

Best Career Placement

This top twenty-five list is based on students' ratings of career services at their school, and on PayScale.com's median starting and mid-career salary information.

1. Harvey Mudd College
2. California Institute of Technology
3. Stanford University
4. Massachusetts Institute of Technology
5. Princeton University
6. Worcester Polytechnic Institute
7. Stevens Institute of Technology
8. Babson College
9. Carnegie Mellon University
10. Harvard College
11. Dartmouth College
12. University of Pennsylvania
13. Yale University
14. Rose-Hulman Institute of Technology
15. Georgia Institute of Technology
16. Rice University
17. Columbia University
18. Duke University
19. Lehigh University
20. Cornell University
21. Williams College
22. Santa Clara University
23. Brown University
24. Clarkson University
25. The Cooper Union for the Advancement of Science and Art

Best Financial Aid

The twenty-five schools in this book that receive the highest financial aid rating (described on page 29).

1. Bowdoin College
2. Vassar College
3. Princeton University
4. Yale University
5. Pomona College
6. Vanderbilt University
7. Williams College
8. Washington University in St. Louis
9. California Institute of Technology
10. Colgate University
11. Grinnell College
12. Cornell University
13. Stanford University
14. Lafayette College
15. Brown University
16. Haverford College
17. Middlebury College
18. Amherst College
19. Kenyon College
20. Carleton College
21. Mount Holyoke College
22. Rice University
23. Franklin W. Olin College of Engineering
24. University of Chicago
25. Dartmouth College

Best Schools for Making an Impact

These twenty-five schools were selected based on student ratings and responses to our survey questions covering community service opportunities at their school, student government, sustainability efforts, and on-campus student engagement. We also took into account PayScale.com's percentage of alumni from each school that reported that they had high job meaning.

1. Wesleyan University
2. Hobart and William Smith Colleges
3. Southwestern University
4. Lawrence University
5. Brown University
6. Saint Louis University
7. Dickinson College
8. Williams College
9. Furman University
10. Whitman College
11. Clark University
12. Brandeis University
13. Tulane University
14. Wheaton College (IL)
15. College of William and Mary
16. Colby College
17. Reed College
18. Tufts University
19. Bates College
20. St. Olaf College
21. Union College (NY)
22. Emory University
23. Washington University in St. Louis
24. Vanderbilt University
25. Creighton University

Tuition-Free Schools

Berea College
College of the Ozarks
Deep Springs College
United States Air Force Academy
United States Coast Guard Academy
United States Merchant Marine Academy
United States Military Academy (West Point)
United States Naval Academy
Webb Institute

Nota Bene: *For tuition-free schools, we have included neither Financial Aid or ROI ratings. Because our ratings are calculated on a continuum for each edition, giving tuition-free schools ratings of 99 would drastically skew the ratings for the other 200 schools in this book. Rest assured, each of these nine schools will provide an excellent return on each student's education.*

Berea College

CPO 2220, Berea, KY 40404 • Admissions: 859-985-3500 • Fax: 859-985-3512

CAMPUS LIFE

Quality of Life Rating	85
Fire Safety Rating	96
Green Rating	92
Type of school	Private
Environment	Village

STUDENTS

Total undergrad enrollment	1,610
% male/female	42/58
% from out of state	52
% frosh live on campus	99
% ugrads live on campus	89
% African American	15
% Asian	2
% Caucasian	56
% Hispanic	11
% Native American	<1
% Pacific Islander	<1
% Two or more races	7
% Race and/or ethnicity unknown	1
% international	8
# of countries represented	76

ACADEMICS

Academic Rating	89
% students returning for sophomore year	80
% students graduating within 4 years	49
% students graduating within 6 years	66
Calendar	Semester
Student/faculty ratio	10:1
Profs interesting rating	81
Profs accessible rating	82
Most classes have 10–19 students.	

MOST POPULAR MAJORS

Family and Consumer Sciences/Human Sciences; Biology/Biological Sciences; Business/Commerce

ABOUT THE SCHOOL

Perhaps best known for its tuition-free, four-year education, Berea has a whole lot more goin' on. At this predominantly Appalachian school in Kentucky, students can select from a curriculum that includes undergraduate research, service learning, and numerous study abroad opportunities, and expect to receive the full support of the school along the way. Since Berea's objective is to provide an education to students of limited economic resources, the school makes it clear that there is no slacking off; your spot here is an opportunity that could have gone to someone else. Academics are rigorous, classroom attendance is mandatory, and students are happy to be given an opportunity.

With such a distinct and regional mission, students here are not just faces in the crowd. All classes are taught by full professors, and everyone has access to the learning center, math and language labs, and tutors for assistance with papers, presentations, and homework. Service is also a way of life here, and Berea is one of the top schools in the nation for service learning. When students do need a rest from their studies, do-gooding, and work, there are more than seventy-five clubs and organizations available, as well as performing arts programs, theaters, and plenty of nature nearby.

Berea College is "about bringing underprivileged high school graduates from the Appalachian region and beyond together for a chance at a higher education, a career, and a better life." Thanks to a labor program that requires all students to work ten to fifteen hours each week (not to mention a ton of donated cash), tuition is entirely covered for each student, with a laptop thrown in for the duration of the school year to boot. In addition to a decent range of liberal arts and sciences majors, there are several career-oriented programs, all of which combines to make "a comfortable place for students to learn and grow."

BANG FOR YOUR BUCK

The school doesn't think your income should dictate your outcome, which is why it only admits students who have financial need. The school's endowment is what allows it to be so generous in awarding full scholarships to deserving students, and these scholarships work in conjunction with any other grants or scholarships students receive to completely cover the cost of tuition (as well as that laptop). In many cases, the school can even offer additional financial aid to assist with room, board, and other fees—not loans—according to each student's need. Simply put, students at Berea College pay what they can afford.

STUDENT LIFE

The student body at Berea is "so genuinely diverse" (though most are from Appalachia) that the only unifying ribbon is "the desire to learn and a craving for knowledge, and . . . a certain drive for self-improvement." That being said, "We also have an unusually high number of what you might call 'hipsters'," says a student. Though town life is admittedly slow, there is a regular shuttle to Richmond, and the campus is almost never quiet. Student organizations "are constantly holding events to keep Berea students occupied and having fun." "We still find ways to keep ourselves entertained," says one. For example, every semester a game called humans versus zombies is held, where people chase each other all over campus with Nerf guns and "sometimes even the professors join in." For those into hiking and being outdoors, "the Pinnacles (a popular hiking spot) are beautiful."

Berea College

FINANCIAL AID: 859-985-3310 • E-MAIL: ADMISSIONS@BEREA.EDU • WEBSITE: WWW.BEREA.EDU

CAREER

The job program at Berea inherently infuses students with a "rigorous, real world experience" that they might not receive elsewhere, and students are afforded "so much opportunity," such as internships, study/travel abroad, and the ability to attend conferences and workshops off-campus. The Office of Internships and Career Development centralizes all of the school's career development resources in one place, and offers peer consultations, workshops, alumni networking, and job search tools. The volunteer program at the Center for Excellence and Learning Through Service (CELTS) also offers students the chance to develop leadership and social justice backgrounds through academic service learning and student-led community service.

GENERAL INFO

Activities: Choral groups, dance, drama/theater, jazz band, literary magazine, music ensembles, pep band, student government, student newspaper, yearbook, campus ministries, international student organization. **Organizations:** 75 registered organizations, 14 honor societies, 5 religious organizations. **Athletics (Intercollegiate):** *Men:* Baseball, basketball, cross-country, golf, soccer, tennis, track/field (outdoor). *Women:* Basketball, cross-country, soccer, softball, tennis, track/field (outdoor), volleyball. **On-Campus Highlights:** Carillon (in Draper building tower), EcoVillage (married and single parent housing), Alumni Building (cafeteria, lounge, gameroom), Woods-Penn Complex (post office, cafe, etc.), Seabury Center (gym). **Environmental Initiatives:** 1. Sustainability and Environmental Studies academic program; 2. Ecological Renovations (including 1st LEED-certified building in Kentucky and the Ecovillage residential complex for student families); 3. Local Food Initiative.

FINANCIAL AID

Students should submit: FAFSA. Priority filing deadline is 10/1. The Princeton Review suggests that all financial aid forms be submitted as soon as possible after October 1. *Need-based scholarships/grants offered:* College/university scholarship or grant aid from institutional funds, Federal Pell, private scholarships, SEOG, state scholarships/grants. *Loan aid offered:* Direct PLUS Loans, Direct Subsidized Loans, Direct Unsubsidized Loans. Applicants will be notified of awards on a rolling basis beginning 11/1. Federal Work-Study Program available.

BOTTOM LINE

Tuition costs are quite simple: every admitted student is provided with a four-year tuition scholarship, knocking tuition down to zero. No tuition does not mean a full ride, however, and extra costs such as technology fees, insurance, food plans, etc., add up quickly (room, board, and fees run around $7,100 a year). However, about two-thirds of the students receive additional financial aid to help offset these costs. Each student is required to take an on-campus job for a certain number of hours per week as part of the school's work program, giving them valuable experience that translates into real-world skills, as well as a salary (about $1,200 in the first year) to assist with living expenses.

SELECTIVITY

Admissions Rating	**93**
# of applicants	1,744
% of applicants accepted	34
% of acceptees attending	72

FRESHMAN PROFILE

Range SAT EBRW	480–590
Range SAT Math	490–610
Range ACT Composite	22–27
Minimum paper TOEFL	520
Minimum internet-based TOEFL	68
Average HS GPA	3.5
% graduated top 10% of class	24
% graduated top 25% of class	64
% graduated top 50% of class	93

DEADLINES

Regular	
Deadline	4/30
Nonfall registration?	No

FINANCIAL FACTS

Financial Aid Rating	**60***
Annual tuition	$0
Room and board	$0
Required fees	
Books and supplies	$700
Average frosh need-based scholarship	$33,290
Average UG need-based scholarship	$32,288
% needy frosh rec. need-based scholarship or grant aid	100
% needy UG rec. need-based scholarship or grant aid	100
% needy frosh rec. non-need-based scholarship or grant aid	0
% needy UG rec. non-need-based scholarship or grant aid	0
% needy frosh rec. need-based self-help aid	100
% needy UG rec. need-based self-help aid	100
% frosh rec. any financial aid	100
% UG rec. any financial aid	100
% UG borrow to pay for school	25
Average cumulative indebtedness	$7,468
% frosh need fully met	0
% ugrads need fully met	0
Average % of frosh need met	98
Average % of ugrad need met	95

CAREER INFORMATION FROM PAYSCALE.COM

ROI Rating	NA
Bachelors and No Higher	
Median starting salary	$39,600
Median mid-career salary	$71,000
At Least Bachelors	
Median starting salary	$41,000
Median mid-career salary	$71,600
Alumni with high job meaning	52%
Degrees awarded in STEM subjects	27%

College of the Ozarks

Office of Admissions, P.O. Box 17, Point Lookout, MO 65726 • Admissions: 417-690-2636 • Fax: 417-335-2618

CAMPUS LIFE

Quality of Life Rating	89
Fire Safety Rating	83
Green Rating	70
Type of school	Private
Affiliation	Evangelical Christian
	Interdenominational
Environment	Rural

STUDENTS

Total undergrad enrollment	1,491
% male/female	45/55
% from out of state	24
% frosh from public high school	78
% frosh live on campus	93
% ugrads live on campus	90
# of fraternities (% ugrad men join)	0 (0)
# of sororities (% ugrad women join)	0 (0)
% African American	1
% Asian	1
% Caucasian	90
% Hispanic	2
% Native American	<1
% Pacific Islander	<1
% Two or more races	2
% Race and/or ethnicity unknown	2
% international	1
# of countries represented	17

ACADEMICS

Academic Rating	83
% students returning for sophomore year	73
% students graduating within 4 years	55
% students graduating within 6 years	72
Calendar	Semester
Student/faculty ratio	14:1
Profs interesting rating	83
Profs accessible rating	79

Most classes have 10–19 students. Most lab/discussion sessions have 10–19 students.

MOST POPULAR MAJORS
Agriculture, Agriculture Operations, and Related Sciences; Elementary Education and Teaching; Health Professions and Related Programs

ABOUT THE SCHOOL

College of the Ozarks, affectionately known as "Hard Work U," is a Christian liberal arts college in Missouri that provides its student body with the unique opportunity to graduate from college without any debt. To pay off their tuition, students work on campus each semester for fifteen hours a week, developing important transferable skills like reliability, teamwork, and communication. Work performance from students' participation at any of eighty work sites on campus, such as the Computer Center, Child Development Center, Ralph Foster Museum, or McDonald Clinic, are included on student transcripts alongside their academic GPA. Students know what to expect before they enroll, and are up to the task. One student says, "College of the Ozarks challenges us so that, when we graduate, we will be ready for life in the outside world." A small school where everyone works together there's also a strong sense of community, "the faculty and staff genuinely care about the students and exert extra effort to enhance student learning and development. The mission of the college promotes the development of foundational beliefs and values." You can also expect most of the student body to share the same values of "[seeking] to develop Christ-like, hard-working, and patriotic citizens" and being "[a] Christian influence to the world."

BANG FOR YOUR BUCK

In addition to their weekly gigs during the semester, students work on campus for two forty-hour work weeks per year. This offsets tuition for either in-state or out-of-state applicants, and College of the Ozarks additionally offers its own scholarships on top of state and federal aid. The college is committed to "providing students who have financial need with a faith-based college education to prepare them for future careers." Many students revealed that the "work-scholarship program for tuition as well as room and board for some select students" was a deciding factor in choosing College of the Ozarks. There's a strong sense of pride in "working for [their] education," among current students.

STUDENT LIFE

Students at College of the Ozarks stay very busy since they "manage a large schedule of going to class, working their on-campus job, studying, going to required chapel services and convocations, sleeping, sports, friends, and more." With an enrollment of about 1,500 students, C of O creates a strong community. As one student reports, "On campus life is great. When students aren't doing homework there are many things to do. My personal favorite thing to do is to go to swing dance classes. I've also been involved in the theater department. About three times a semester there is a 'coffee house' where students can perform, drink coffee, and spend time with other students. There are also many other fun events each semester." The location of the 1,000-acre campus, overlooking Lake Taneycomo, also influences student life. "During the nicer months the students like to hammock, play football, and go on hikes. Winter months require indoor activities like intramural sports." A current students sums up the campus atmosphere: "College of the Ozarks is a unique institution where true friendships are made and a sense of community is prevalent."

CAREER

College of the Ozarks has a Career Center on campus that is committed to each student's success by helping this hardworking bunch choose majors, evaluate career paths, find jobs in various fields of study, and conduct research on potential careers. This is in addition to the jobs that the students will have on campus, which is an opportunity for them to build their résumés and network with employers before they graduate. Additionally, students report that

College of the Ozarks

FINANCIAL AID: 417-690-3292 • E-MAIL: E-MAIL: ADMISS4@COFO.EDU • WEBSITE: WWW.COFO.EDU

"College of the Ozarks provides students with incredible leadership opportunities that other schools do not seek to offer," such as a the Patriotic Education Program that matches students with veterans, from World War II, the Cold War, the Korean War, and the Vietnam War, sending both veteran and student to historic battlegrounds. It's no wonder that with such a unique approach to education that the school boasts a 75 percent post-graduation employment rate, with 15 percent of students going on to graduate programs.

GENERAL INFO

Activities: Choral groups, concert band, drama/theater, jazz band, literary magazine, music ensembles, musical theater, pep band, radio station, student government, student newspaper, yearbook, campus ministries. **Organizations:** 45 registered organizations, 6 honor societies, 10 religious organizations. **Athletics (Intercollegiate):** *Men:* Baseball, basketball, cheerleading, cross country, golf, track. *Women:* Basketball, cheerleading, cross country, track, volleyball. **On-Campus Highlights:** Howell W. Keeter Athletic Complex, Ralph Foster Museum, Williams Memorial Chapel, The Keeter Center, Agriculture, Edwards Mill, Fruitcake and Jelly Kitchen. **Environmental Initiatives:** The College ensures proper management of hazardous, special and universal waste. There is campus-wide recycling: plastic bottles, corrugated cardboard, aluminum cans, tin cans, batteries, tires, light bulbs and electronic products. Light bulb reclamation (recycle of bulbs) and energy efficient lights. Agricultural Livestock Waste Containment program (protects area lakes). Lake water cools many buildings.

FINANCIAL AID

Students should submit: FAFSA. Priority filing deadline is 11/15. The Princeton Review suggests that all financial aid forms be submitted as soon as possible after October 1. *Need-based scholarships/grants offered:* College/university scholarship or grant aid from institutional funds, Federal Pell, private scholarships, SEOG, state scholarships/grants. Applicants will be notified of awards on or about 7/1. Federal Work-Study Program available. Institutional employment available.

BOTTOM LINE

A student can attend College of the Ozarks with absolutely no cash due for tuition and no student loans. Instead, student earnings from participation in the C of O work program, the C of O Cost of Education Scholarship, plus any federal and state awards cover the cost of education. The only other costs are $7,100 per semester for room and board, with $500 for books and $10 for parking permits. These additional costs can be also covered by state or federal aid or grants from the school itself or an outside entity.

CAREER INFORMATION FROM PAYSCALE.COM

ROI Rating	NA
Bachelors and No Higher	
Median starting salary	$38,600
Median mid-career salary	$68,300
At Least Bachelors	
Median starting salary	$40,100
Median mid-career salary	$72,000
Alumni with high job meaning	54%
Degrees awarded in STEM subjects	8%

SELECTIVITY

Admissions Rating	97
# of applicants	2,879
% of applicants accepted	16
% of acceptees attending	78
# offered a place on the wait list	586
% accepting a place on wait list	100
% admitted from wait list	4

FRESHMAN PROFILE

Range SAT EBRW	560–625
Range SAT Math	543–605
Range ACT Composite	21–26
Minimum paper TOEFL	550
Minimum internet-based TOEFL	79
Average HS GPA	3.7
% graduated top 10% of class	25
% graduated top 25% of class	62
% graduated top 50% of class	96

DEADLINES

Regular	
Priority	12/31
Notification	2/15
Nonfall registration?	Yes

FINANCIAL FACTS

Financial Aid Rating	60*
Annual tuition	$0
Room and board	$7,400
Required fees	$460
Books and supplies	$1,100
Average frosh need-based scholarship	$11,182
Average UG need-based scholarship	$11,182
% needy frosh rec. need-based scholarship or grant aid	100
% needy UG rec. need-based scholarship or grant aid	100
% needy frosh rec. non-need-based scholarship or grant aid	36
% needy UG rec. non-need-based scholarship or grant aid	94
% needy frosh rec. need-based self-help aid	64
% needy UG rec. need-based self-help aid	94
% frosh rec. any financial aid	100
% UG rec. any financial aid	100
% UG borrow to pay for school	0
% frosh need fully met	18
% ugrads need fully met	40
Average % of frosh need met	75
Average % of ugrad need met	81

Deep Springs College

APPLICATIONS COMMITTEE, HC 72 BOX 45001, DYER, NV 89010 • ADMISSIONS: 760-872-2000 • FAX: 760-872-4466

CAMPUS LIFE

Quality of Life Rating	**95**
Fire Safety Rating	**88**
Green Rating	**60***
Type of school	Private
Environment	Rural

STUDENTS

Total undergrad enrollment	28
% male/female	100/0
% from out of state	82
% frosh from public high school	67
% frosh live on campus	100
% ugrads live on campus	100
# of fraternities (% ugrad men join)	0 (0)
# of sororities (% ugrad women join)	0 (0)
% African American	0
% Asian	14
% Caucasian	64
% Hispanic	4
% Native American	0
% Pacific Islander	0
% Two or more races	4
% Race and/or ethnicity unknown	0
% international	14
# of countries represented	5

ACADEMICS

Academic Rating	**99**
% students returning for sophomore year	92
Calendar	Continuous
Student/faculty ratio	4:1
Profs interesting rating	99
Profs accessible rating	99
Most classes has fewer than 10 students.	

MOST POPULAR MAJORS

Liberal Arts and Sciences, General Studies and Humanities

ABOUT THE SCHOOL

You know the feeling you get when you look back at your second-grade class picture and you can remember every single person's name, no matter how long ago that was? That is the level of camaraderie that is achieved at Deep Springs College, a teeny-tiny, uber-selective, formerly all-male school located on a cattle ranch and alfalfa farm in California's High Desert. Deep Springs is now going co-ed with applications open to all young people beginning Fall 2018. Founded in 1917, the curriculum is based on the three pillars of academics, labor, and self-governance, offering "a unique liberal arts education that gives you very much freedom and requires a lot of responsibility for your classmates and environment." Every student must also work on the school's ranch and farm, which helps drive home the school's unique mission of service. After two years at Deep Springs (with full scholarship), students go on to complete a four-year degree at the world's most prestigious universities.

Whereas at some colleges, professors' doors are always open, at Deep Springs, professors' porch lights are always on. Classes are intense and bleed into activities around the clock, and they're sometimes also held in unconventional locations, like professors' homes or the irrigation ditch. Some students must wake up early to feed the cattle; some must stay up late to mend fences on the alfalfa farm. At every hour of the day, there are at least a few people awake and discussing Heidegger, playing chess, or strumming guitars. To say that the school's twenty-eight students (along with its staff and faculty) form a close community would be an understatement. Everyone is on a first-name basis and knows each other like the back of their own hand. There is no other school like it, and students receive an education that transcends simply learning from books, as well as an unprecedented education in citizenship.

BANG FOR YOUR BUCK

Deep Springs is one of the best educations a student can receive after high school, and though you may not have heard of the school before, the nation's top universities certainly have. Although percentages are somewhat moot for a school that has only twenty-eight students over two class years, in the past five years, nearly 45 percent of students have gone on to Harvard, Yale, Brown, and the University of Chicago, as well as winning numerous prestigious scholarships and fellowships.

Deep Springs College

E-MAIL: APCOM@DEEPSPRINGS.EDU • WEBSITE: WWW.DEEPSPRINGS.EDU

STUDENT LIFE

With only twenty-eight people, one student's life is every student's life here. Students play a significant part in running the college, which means that from day one, every student is involved in some meaningful and essential way in the everyday workings of the college. "When you are helping hire faculty, review applications, milk cows, cook meals for the community, and working in the organic garden, it's hard not to fit in or find a place where you belong," says a student. The typical student here is "driven and deeply committed to the 'common project'." This individual is also "permanently exhausted." Most people here "think about thinking, though of course there are students who exist more in feeling, but they aren't the majority." Hikes and horseback riding tend are popular ways to get away, physically and mentally.

CAREER

The academic rigor and work ethic required to get into Deep Springs is well-known, and mandatory public speaking and composition studies only further set the intellectual foundation. As students learning to be citizens of the world, many eventually go on to "a life of service" following the completion of a degree. Since Deep Springs is a two-year school, most everyone transfers to a more typical four-year institution, and Deep Springers are generally successful in their transfers. Of forty-seven students transferring from the entering years 2007–2011, over half transferred to either Yale, Brown, or the University of Chicago.

GENERAL INFO

Activities: Student government. **Organizations:** 1 registered organization. **On-Campus Highlights:** Boarding House, Dairy Barn, Horse Stables, The Upper Reservoir, The Druid.

FINANCIAL AID

Every single student accepted at Deep Springs receives a comprehensive scholarship that covers tuition and room and board in full, an estimated value of over $50,000.

BOTTOM LINE

As Deep Springs covers annual tuition and room and board in full, students are only expected to pay for books, incidentals, and travel, which the school estimates run less than $2,800 per year.

SELECTIVITY

Admissions Rating	99
# of applicants	200
% of applicants accepted	10
% of acceptees attending	84
# offered a place on the wait list	5
% accepting a place on wait list	100
% admitted from wait list	100

FRESHMAN PROFILE

% graduated top 10% of class	100
% graduated top 25% of class	100
% graduated top 50% of class	100

DEADLINES

Regular	
Deadline	11/7
Notification	4/15
Nonfall registration?	No

FINANCIAL FACTS

Financial Aid Rating	60*
Annual tuition	$0
Room and board	$0
Required fees	
Room and board	NR
Books and supplies	$1,200
% frosh rec. any financial aid	100
% UG rec. any financial aid	100
Average % of frosh need met	0
Average % of ugrad need met	0

United States Air Force Academy

HQ USAFA/RRS, 2304 Cadet Drive, Suite 2400, USAF Academy, CO 80840-5025 • Admissions: 719-333-2520

CAMPUS LIFE

Quality of Life Rating	90
Fire Safety Rating	99
Green Rating	74
Type of school	Public
Environment	Metropolis

STUDENTS

Total undergrad enrollment	4,276
% male/female	74/26
% from out of state	90
% frosh from public high school	76
% frosh live on campus	100
% ugrads live on campus	100
# of fraternities (% ugrad men join)	0 (0)
# of sororities (% ugrad women join)	0 (0)
% African American	6
% Asian	5
% Caucasian	63
% Hispanic	11
% Native American	<1
% Pacific Islander	1
% Two or more races	7
% Race and/or ethnicity unknown	5
% international	1
# of countries represented	22

ACADEMICS

Academic Rating	91
% students returning for sophomore year	94
% students graduating within 4 years	77
% students graduating within 6 years	79
Calendar	Semester
Student/faculty ratio	9:1
Profs interesting rating	84
Profs accessible rating	96

Most classes have 10–19 students. Most lab/discussion sessions have 10–19 students.

MOST POPULAR MAJORS

Aerospace, Aeronautical and Astronautical/Space Engineering; Systems Engineering; Business Administration and Management

ABOUT THE SCHOOL

The elite United States Air Force Academy is a selective institution, and for good reason: those who attend USAFA receive a world-class STEM education, supplemented with arts and humanities classes, intensive physical training, and a guaranteed job after graduation for no cost. While 1,200 cadets enter, only around one thousand will graduate this rigorous program, which offers twenty-seven majors and four minors, airmanship training, and numerous research opportunities. Between the third and fourth years, cadets undergo training in Air Force operations in a deployed environment and can specialize in various airmanship areas such as Space Operations, Cyber, Unmanned Air Vehicles, Powered Flight, Glider and Freefall Parachute. Professors "are always accessible outside of the classroom," and classes all have fewer than twenty cadets. As a current cadet explains, "All students take the same track of classes so the help and assistance is unending."

BANG FOR YOUR BUCK

When your annual tuition is $0, it's not hard to calculate the return on your investment. At USAFA, "you are a part of the best of the best and have ultimate job security," sums up a student. Each cadet is even given a monthly stipend of around $1,027 to covers the cost of uniforms, books, supplies, and personal spending. The academy is divided into around forty squadrons, and character and leadership are the driving forces behind everything: "Everyone understands what we are striving for, and having other cadets be motivated for their future really separates us from other schools," says one current cadet. Not all may make it to graduation, but those that do leave "competent and dedicated officers who will serve and protect the country."

STUDENT LIFE

The academy is "hard, [and] not always fun, but it is always rewarding," and people who are drawn to that kind of experience will find success here. Days are expectedly routine, with training, classes, athletics, formation, and meals comprising waking hours. For fun, "most people participate in winter sports or go camping when it is warm." All cadets live in one of two dormitories and are required to participate in an intercollegiate or intramural sport each semester. While there is not a lot of diversity gender-wise, each cadet comes from a unique background "which adds to our development into officers."

CAREER

Cadets are committed to serve in the military for a certain number of years following graduation, when nearly half enter flight training. This is a school of go-getters, and over four thousand people all dreaming of becoming officers in the United States Air Force "makes it very competitive." A few graduates receive scholarships to attend military or civilian graduate schools immediately after graduation, and many graduates receive funding for post-graduate programs. One way or another, the people that graduate from the academy "go on to do amazing things in the military and are great leaders who influence their airmen's lives." Of the Air Force Academy alumni visiting PayScale.com, 71 percent report that they derive a high level of meaning from their jobs.

United States Air Force Academy

Fax: 719-333-3012 • E-mail: rr_webmail@usafa.edu • Website: www.academyadmissions.com

GENERAL INFO

Activities: Choral groups, dance, drama/theater, marching band, musical theater, pep band, radio station, yearbook, campus ministries. **Organizations:** 93 registered organizations, 12 honor societies, 14 religious organizations. **Athletics (Intercollegiate):** *Men:* Baseball, basketball, boxing, cheerleading, cross-country, diving, fencing, football, golf, gymnastics, ice hockey, lacrosse, riflery, soccer, swimming, tennis, track/field (outdoor), track/field (indoor), water polo, wrestling. *Women:* Basketball, cheerleading, cross-country, diving, fencing, gymnastics, riflery, soccer, swimming, tennis, track/field (outdoor), track/field (indoor), volleyball. **On-Campus Highlights:** USAF Academy Chapel, Thunderbird Lookout and Air Field, Falcon Stadium, Cadet Sports Complex, Visitor Center. **Environmental Initiatives:** Solar Hydro Geo Thermal.

FINANCIAL AID

Aside from the free tuition, room and board, students receive a nominal monthly stipend. Each cadet will owe at least five years of service as an active duty officer upon graduation, though additional programs (such as attending higher education, or becoming a pilot) can add to the commitment.

BOTTOM LINE

Cost may not be a hurdle the Air Force Academy, but admission certainly is. All who apply here must receive a letter of recommendation from a United States. Congress member, and must be in peak academic, physical, and mental condition, which will need to be proven through an intense application and testing process.

CAREER INFORMATION FROM PAYSCALE.COM	
ROI Rating	NA
Bachelors and No Higher	
Median starting salary	$74,000
Median mid-career salary	$137,300
At Least Bachelors	
Median starting salary	$76,000
Median mid-career salary	$142,900
Alumni with high job meaning	69%
Degrees awarded in STEM subjects	43%

SELECTIVITY	
Admissions Rating	99
# of applicants	10,202
% of applicants accepted	12
% of acceptees attending	99

FRESHMAN PROFILE	
Range SAT EBRW	630–700
Range SAT Math	640–710
Range ACT Composite	29–33
Average HS GPA	3.9
% graduated top 10% of class	54
% graduated top 25% of class	83
% graduated top 50% of class	96

DEADLINES	
Early action	
Deadline	11/1
Notification	1/15
Regular	
Deadline	12/31
Nonfall registration?	No

FINANCIAL FACTS	
Financial Aid Rating	60*
Annual in-state tuition	$0
Annual out-of-state tuition	$0
Room and board	$0
Required fees	$0
% UG borrow to pay for school	0
Average % of frosh need met	0
Average % of ugrad need met	0

United States Coast Guard Academy

31 MOHEGAN AVENUE, NEW LONDON, CT 06320-8103 • ADMISSIONS: 860-444-8503 • FAX: 860-701-6700

CAMPUS LIFE

Quality of Life Rating	81
Fire Safety Rating	91
Green Rating	61
Type of school	Public
Environment	City

STUDENTS

Total undergrad enrollment	1045
% male/female	65/35
% from out of state	95
% frosh from public high school	76
% frosh live on campus	100
% ugrads live on campus	100
# of fraternities (% ugrad men join)	0 (0)
# of sororities (% ugrad women join)	0 (0)
% African American	6
% Asian	7
% Caucasian	65
% Hispanic	9
% Native American	<1
% Pacific Islander	<1
% Two or more races	9
% Race and/or ethnicity unknown	1
% international	3
# of countries represented	13

ACADEMICS

Academic Rating	87
% students returning for sophomore year	95
% students graduating within 4 years	78
% students graduating within 6 years	81
Calendar	Semester
Student/faculty ratio	7:1
Profs interesting rating	76
Profs accessible rating	96
Most classes have 10–15 students.	

MOST POPULAR MAJORS
Oceanography, Chemical and Physical;
Political Science and Government; Business
Administration and Management

ABOUT THE SCHOOL

There is a special sense of pride at the Coast Guard Academy—pride in America, service, each class, each company, and in one's accomplishments. With a student body of about 1,000, it's easy to see why graduates of the Coast Guard Academy form such a lifelong dedication to the school and each other. The USCGA graduates young men and women with "sound bodies, stout hearts, and alert minds, [and] with a liking for the sea and its lore," not to mention a four-year Bachelor of Science degree. The curriculum is heavily oriented toward math, science, and engineering, with a nationally recognized engineering program, as well as other programs in government, management, marine and environmental sciences, and more.

Given the intensity of academy life, most cadets are eager for the opportunity to participate in extracurricular activities, and social events and organized activities are an integral part of the cadet experience. There are a number of long-standing traditions that cement the Coast Guard bond, from organized dress-white formals. While the opportunities afforded by a degree from this highly selective institution are impressive enough, top performers spend their senior summer traveling on exciting internships around the nation and overseas, and all graduates serve on ships, airplanes or in other Coast Guard fields upon graduation—with 80 percent of applicants accepted to flight school in the ensuing years.

BANG FOR YOUR BUCK

All graduates go on to become commissioned officers in the U.S. Coast Guard, and every junior officer in the Coast Guard can apply for the opportunity to obtain advanced education at Coast Guard expense (and additional service obligation). While in graduate school, officers continue to receive full pay and benefits—their job is to study and earn a degree in an area of study directly related to Coast Guard missions. While acceptance into these programs is based on job performance and academic potential, there is such a broad range of opportunities (especially in engineering fields) that nearly 80 percent of all graduates are selected for one of the programs and go on to complete a master's degree. Also of interest: up to 10 percent (approximately twenty cadets) of the graduating class may attend flight training immediately upon completion of the four-year academy program.

STUDENT LIFE

Most of the people that choose to come here are of the same mindset: "determined to become good officers." It's a military academy, so "life is orderly and predictable from day to day, but very busy." Students schedules are full from 6:00 A.M. until 10:00 P.M. but include set time in the afternoons for sports or other activities, and after 10:30 PM the halls are generally quiet and empty. The dorms reflect this, and "cleanliness is great, and things get fixed (if anything breaks) rather quickly." "Getting off campus is a top priority to have fun," since the rules to be followed are very stringent. Every weekend, cadets leave campus whenever they can: the mall is a huge hot spot for freshman/sophomores, and the surrounding area up to Boston and down to New York is popular for juniors/seniors. When not in class or at military trainings, "students are either working on academic work or watching movies, playing video games, or working out to de-stress from cadet life." Over 60 percent of the Corps of Cadets are members of CGA's NCAA Division III varsity athletics teams, one of the highest percentages in the country."

United States Coast Guard Academy

WEBSITE: WWW.USCGA.EDU

CAREER

The Academy opens doors and equips cadets with the skills and resume they need to get upper echelon jobs. All students go on to become officers in the U.S. Coast Guard once they graduate and report for duty aboard cutters, at sector offices in ports around the country, to flight school, or into the Coast Guard's cybersecurity command, and serve out a five year commitment to the military. "I will have a guaranteed job once I graduate. And I am now a part of the military family that takes care of its own," says a student. Students are eager to begin their "very noble career" and many go on past their five years to become lifetime military officers.

GENERAL INFO

Activities: Choral groups, dance, drama/theater, jazz band, marching band, pep band, yearbook, campus ministries, cyber team, mock trial, Model UN, Cheerleading, and Dance. **Organizations:** 2 honor societies, 7 religious organizations. **Athletics (In-tercollegiate):** *Men:* Baseball, basketball, crew/rowing, cross-country, diving, football, pistol, riflery, sailing, soccer, swimming, tennis, track/field (outdoor), track/field (indoor), wrestling. *Women:* Basketball, crew/rowing, cross-country, diving, pistol, riflery, sailing, soccer, softball, swimming, track/ field (outdoor), track/field (indoor), volleyball. **On-Campus Highlights:** Otto Graham Hall of Athletic Excellence, Coast Guard Museum, Sailing Center and Waterfront, Souvenir Shop (Military Exchange), Coast Guard Academy Chapel and Crown Park. **Environmental Initiatives:** Federal Electronic Recycling Challenge Participant. RecycleMania.

FINANCIAL AID

Aside from the free tuition, room, and board, students receive a nominal monthly stipend, totaling approximately $12,000 per year. Each cadet will owe at least five years of service as a commissioned Coast Guard officer upon graduation.

BOTTOM LINE

Cadets don't pay a penny for tuition, room, or board at the Coast Guard Academy. All cadets receive pay totaling $11,530 per year. Students have a five-year service commitment after graduation, but that can be lengthened by the many available postgraduate degrees and training made available to USCGA alum. Approximately 90 percent of academy graduates go to sea after graduation, and the other 10 percent of academy graduates go to flight training, ashore operations, or cybersecurity positions.

CAREER INFORMATION FROM PAYSCALE.COM	
ROI Rating	NA
Bachelors and No Higher	
Median starting salary	$66,400
Median mid-career salary	$110,900
At Least Bachelors	
Median starting salary	$69,600
Median mid-career salary	$128,400
Alumni with high job meaning	71%
Degrees awarded in STEM subjects	69%

SELECTIVITY	
Admissions Rating	97
# of applicants	2,021
% of applicants accepted	18
% of acceptees attending	75
# offered a place on the wait list	148
% accepting a place on wait list	100
% admitted from wait list	24
# of early decision applicants	686
% accepted early decision	24

FRESHMAN PROFILE	
Range ACT Composite	26–31
Minimum paper TOEFL	560
Minimum internet-based TOEFL	90
Average HS GPA	3.8
% graduated top 10% of class	45
% graduated top 25% of class	79
% graduated top 50% of class	96

DEADLINES	
Early action	
Deadline	11/15
Notification	2/1
Regular	
Priority	11/15
Deadline	2/1
Notification	4/15
Nonfall registration?	No

FINANCIAL FACTS	
Financial Aid Rating	60*
Annual in-state tuition	$0
Annual out-of-state tuition	$0
Room and board	$0
Required fees	$978
Books and supplies	$2,199
% frosh rec. any financial aid	0
% UG rec. any financial aid	0

United States Merchant Marine Academy

OFFICE OF ADMISSIONS, KINGS POINT, NY 11024-1699 • ADMISSIONS: 516-773-5391 • FAX: 516-773-5390

CAMPUS LIFE

Quality of Life Rating	67
Fire Safety Rating	98
Green Rating	63
Type of school	Public
Environment	Town

STUDENTS

Total undergrad enrollment	952
% male/female	83/17
% from out of state	87
% frosh from public high school	75
% frosh live on campus	100
% ugrads live on campus	100
# of fraternities (% ugrad men join)	0 (0)
# of sororities (% ugrad women join)	0 (0)
% African American	3
% Asian	8
% Caucasian	75
% Hispanic	10
% Native American	1
% Pacific Islander	<1
% Two or more races	0
% Race and/or ethnicity unknown	3
% international	1
# of countries represented	4

ACADEMICS

Academic Rating	64
% students returning for sophomore year	89
% students graduating within 4 years	81
% students graduating within 6 years	87
Calendar	Trimester
Student/faculty ratio	8:1
Profs interesting rating	63
Profs accessible rating	61
Most classes have 20–29 students.	

MOST POPULAR MAJORS

Engineering; Naval Architecture and Marine
Engineering; Transportation and Materials
Moving

ABOUT THE SCHOOL

Known for having the hardest academics out of all the military academies, the United States Merchant Marine Academy offers students free tuition, rigorous academics, and the widest range of career options available to graduates of U.S. service academies following graduation (including officers in any branch of the armed forces, or a number of civilian occupations). Professors are undoubtedly more than qualified in their fields of study, ranging from former NASA scientists to highly decorated and accomplished officers in the military.

The notorious freshman year is spent inducting students into a completely new way of life, in which they learn new terms, the quality of endurance, how to perform under pressure, and the definition of a wakeup call at "0-dark-thirty." The "sea year" spent studying on merchant vessels gives students a hands-on perspective that not many other engineering schools offer, and students typically visit ten to fifteen countries in the course of the school year. When liberty time is allowed, students have access to New York City, as well as a multimillion-dollar waterfront packed with powerboats (not to mention the know-how to use them). At the end of it all, students graduate with a Bachelor of Science degree, as well as the specialized training for licensing as a merchant marine officer, the military knowledge for commissioning in a reserve component of the armed forces, and a strong network of alumni that know how capable a USMMA graduate really is.

The United States is a maritime nation, and every hour of every day, ships of all types ply the waters in and around it. It's a dangerous and lucrative business, and that's why the country relies on graduates of the United States Merchant Marine Academy in Kings Point, New York, to serve the economic and defense interests of the United States through the maritime industry and armed forces. This "prestigious academy, paid for by the federal government" offers "opportunities upon graduation [that] are endless."

BANG FOR YOUR BUCK

After graduation, students are automatically qualified to enter any branch of the armed forces as an officer, including Army, Navy, Air Force, Marines, Coast Guard, or NOAA. Virtually 100 percent of graduates obtain well-paying employment within six months of commencement, with the majority at work within three months, and most with offers of employment before graduation day. Most students that attend the USMMA have their sights set on a solid job that only requires them to work six months out of the year. The Academy's four-year program centers on a regimental system that turns its students—called midshipmen (a term used for both men and women)—into "top notch officers who are not only capable at sea, but have the ability to work under stress in any situation."

STUDENT LIFE

The student body can be classified into two groups: those who want to serve in the military and serve their country, and those who want to sail commercially for a living after graduation. The first year is designed to build unity in each graduating class, so camaraderie is apparent from the start. "Because of the regimental/military experience here everyone is smashed together and forced to work together to some extent so for the most part everyone gets along and or works together," says a student. The typical student "has tons on his plate," whether it be regimental duties or academic ones, and "people strongly focus on graduating and doing whatever it takes to reach that big goal." Students are restricted to the campus grounds during the week until senior year, so "most time is spent either in class, studying or working out."

United States Merchant Marine Academy

FINANCIAL AID: 516-773-5295 • E-MAIL: ADMISSIONS@USMMA.EDU • WEBSITE: WWW.USMMA.EDU

CAREER

Depending on whether one's focus was on transportation or engineering, a graduate can sit for different licenses and certifications that determine their career. Unlike the other military academies, USMMA graduates are required to fulfill their service obligation on their own in a wide variety of occupations, and must just provide proof of employment. Acceptable options include employment on any U.S. flagged merchant vessels, as civilians in the maritime industry, or as active duty officers in any branch of the U.S. armed forces. All graduates must maintain their merchant marine officer's license for six years.

GENERAL INFO

Activities: Choral groups, concert band, drama/theater, marching band, student government, student newspaper, yearbook, campus ministries. **Organizations:** 3 religious organizations. **Athletics (Intercollegiate):** *Men:* Baseball, basketball, crew/rowing, cross-country, diving, football, golf, lacrosse, riflery, sailing, soccer, swimming, tennis, track/field (outdoor), volleyball, water polo, wrestling. *Women:* Basketball, crew/rowing, cross-country, diving, golf, riflery, sailing, softball, swimming, tennis, track/field (outdoor), volleyball.

FINANCIAL AID

Students should submit: FAFSA; Institution's own financial aid form. The Princeton Review suggests that all financial aid forms be submitted as soon as possible after October 1. *Need-based scholarships/grants offered:* Federal Pell; Private scholarships; State scholarships/grants. *Loan aid offered:* Direct PLUS Loans, Direct Subsidized Loans, Direct Unsubsidized Loans. Applicants will be notified of awards on a rolling basis beginning 5/1.

BOTTOM LINE

The federal government pays for all of a student's education, room and board, uniforms, and books; however, midshipmen are responsible for the payment of fees for mandatory educational supplies not provided by the government, such as the prescribed personal computer, activity fees (athletic, cultural events, health services, student newspaper, yearbook, etc.), and personal fees. These fees along with books and supplies come to approximately $4,000, though totals may vary depending on class year (loans are available). The service commitment for each student is determined by their choice of career following graduation.

SELECTIVITY

Admissions Rating	**97**
# of applicants	1,855
% of applicants accepted	22
% of acceptees attending	68
# offered a place on the wait list	204
% accepting a place on wait list	100
% admitted from wait list	65

FRESHMAN PROFILE

Range SAT EBRW	570–660
Range SAT Math	630–660
Minimum paper TOEFL	540
Minimum internet-based TOEFL	83
% graduated top 10% of class	22
% graduated top 25% of class	64
% graduated top 50% of class	96

DEADLINES

Regular	
Deadline	3/1
Nonfall registration?	No

FINANCIAL FACTS

Financial Aid Rating	**60***
Annual in-state tuition	$0
Annual out-of-state tuition	$0
Room and board	$0
Required fees	$1,167
Books and supplies	$1,000
% frosh rec. any financial aid	33
% UG rec. any financial aid	30
% UG borrow to pay for school	15
Average cumulative indebtedness	$5,500

CAREER INFORMATION FROM PAYSCALE.COM	
ROI Rating	NA
Bachelors and No Higher	
Median starting salary	$80,800
Median mid-career salary	$136,600
At Least Bachelors	
Median starting salary	$81,400
Median mid-career salary	$141,300
Alumni with high job meaning	64%
Degrees awarded in STEM subjects	56%

United States Military Academy—West Point

646 Swift Road, West Point, NY 10996-1905 • Admissions: 845-938-4041 • Fax: 845-938-3021

CAMPUS LIFE

Quality of Life Rating	88
Fire Safety Rating	91
Green Rating	60*
Type of school	Public
Environment	Village

STUDENTS

Total undergrad enrollment	4,491
% male/female	78/22
% from out of state	94
% frosh from public high school	80
% frosh live on campus	100
% ugrads live on campus	100
# of fraternities (% ugrad men join)	0 (0)
# of sororities (% ugrad women join)	0 (0)
% African American	12
% Asian	8
% Caucasian	62
% Hispanic	10
% Native American	1
% Pacific Islander	<1
% Two or more races	3
% Race and/or ethnicity unknown	1
% international	1
# of countries represented	29

ACADEMICS

Academic Rating	99
% students returning for sophomore year	98
% students graduating within 4 years	82
% students graduating within 6 years	86
Calendar	Semester
Student/faculty ratio	7:1
Profs interesting rating	98
Profs accessible rating	99

Most classes have 10–19 students. Most lab/discussion sessions have 10–19 students.

MOST POPULAR MAJORS

Engineering/Industrial Management; Economics; Business Administration and Management

ABOUT THE SCHOOL

The United States Military Academy at West Point is one of the most storied institutions in America, turning out leaders trained to the highest levels of academic, military, and physical prowess. The curriculum offers more than forty majors (heavily STEM-oriented) and includes the West Point Writing Program designed to make cadets into clear and thoughtful communicators across all disciplines and aspects of military life. Students admit that academics "are hard but there is much help provided," and professors "are highly intelligent and completely dedicated to their students." The more than two dozen West Point research centers bring context to the classroom, and allow students to focus their studies and collaborate with scientists and scholars in areas such as robotics, combating terrorism, and cyber research. West Point has an impeccable reputation for sending "committed and competent leaders into the U.S. Army," and "cadets can do almost anything if they want it bad enough," academically speaking. If a cadet is interested in doing something unique, regardless of how outlandish it may sound at first, they "actually have the potential to make it come true, especially if you have a solid argument for how it can develop you or your peers in a desirable fashion (i.e. militarily, academically, physically)."

BANG FOR YOUR BUCK

What makes a West Point education such a good value? "It is completely free and everyone has a guaranteed job after graduation" should sum it up. Cadets all leave with a Bachelor's of Science, and instructors devote themselves to giving cadets a full experience because "[they] know in a matter of years they could be serving with us and are more invested in developing us and making us the best officers we can be." There are also excellent resources for cadets, such as the Center for Enhanced Performance, which "helps cadets learn skills to better manage their time, study more effectively, and prepare for tests."

STUDENT LIFE

All the time in a day is accounted for at West Point; whether it is going to class, working out, studying, or performing duties, "each minute holds a task to be done." In fact, cadets are required to participate in athletics at the intramural, club, or intercollegiate level for every season at the academy. Lunch is family style, with twelve cadets sharing a table: "All 4,400 of us are seated and served within fifteen minutes of the beginning of lunch." Though upperclassmen sometimes find a couple of hours to head into town before Taps, underclassmen mainly "play video games, go to clubs, play instruments, and go to New York City on the weekends" for fun.

CAREER

West Point's specialized courses and its wide range of majors are "good preparation for a both a military and civilian career in the future. "People just trust you more because they understand that the type of people West Point produces are top-notch," says one. Almost all West Point graduates become commissioned officers in the U.S. Army, starting off as a 2nd Lieutenant and possibly working their way up to a Colonel, though a small number can "cross-commission" and go to another branch of the military. During their second summer, all undergo cadet field training at a nearby camp, where they may serve as instructors the following summer. Of the United States Military Academy alumni visiting PayScale.com, 65 percent report that they derive a high level of meaning from their jobs.

United States Military Academy—West Point

E-MAIL: ADMISSIONS@USMA.EDU • WEBSITE: WWW.WESTPOINT.EDU

GENERAL INFO

Activities: Choral groups, drama/theater, jazz band, music ensembles, pep band, radio station, student government, student newspaper, television station, yearbook, campus ministries, international student organization. **Organizations:** 105 registered organizations, 7 honor societies, 13 religious organizations. **Athletics (Intercollegiate):** *Men:* Baseball, basketball, cross-country, football, golf, gymnastics, ice hockey, lacrosse, riflery, soccer, swimming, tennis, track/field (outdoor), track/field (indoor), wrestling. *Women:* Basketball, cross-country, riflery, soccer, softball, swimming, tennis, track/field (outdoor), track/field (indoor), volleyball. **On-Campus Highlights:** Cadet Chapel, West Point Museum, Eisenhower Hall, Michie Stadium, Trophy Point, Fort Putnam, West Point Cemetery.

FINANCIAL AID

Financial aid is not required. You must serve at least five years of active duty and three years in a Reserve Component for a total of eight years after graduation. The active duty obligation is the nation's return on a West Point graduate's fully funded, four-year college education.

BOTTOM LINE

Tuition, room and board, and expenses are fully covered, but that's the easy part. Getting in to West Point requires a congressional nomination from either an applicant's representative in Congress, their two U.S. senators, or the vice president of the United States.

CAREER INFORMATION FROM PAYSCALE.COM	
ROI Rating	NA
Bachelors and No Higher	
Median starting salary	$79,300
Median mid-career salary	$141,900
At Least Bachelors	
Median starting salary	$83,500
Median mid-career salary	$151,200
Alumni with high job meaning	63%
Degrees awarded in STEM subjects	39%

SELECTIVITY	
Admissions Rating	99
# of applicants	12,973
% of applicants accepted	10
% of acceptees attending	98

FRESHMAN PROFILE	
Range SAT EBRW	585–690
Range SAT Math	600–710
Range ACT Composite	23–28
Minimum paper TOEFL	500
Minimum internet-based TOEFL	75
% graduated top 10% of class	46
% graduated top 25% of class	74
% graduated top 50% of class	94

DEADLINES	
Regular	
Deadline	2/28
Nonfall registration?	No

FINANCIAL FACTS	
Financial Aid Rating	60*
Annual in-state tuition	$0
Annual out-of-state tuition	$0
Room and board	$0
Required fees	$0
% frosh rec. any financial aid	0
% UG rec. any financial aid	0

United States Naval Academy

117 Decatur Road, Annapolis, MD 21402 • Admissions: 410-293-1914 • Fax: 410-293-4348

CAMPUS LIFE

Quality of Life Rating	89
Fire Safety Rating	77
Green Rating	60*
Type of school	Public
Environment	Town

STUDENTS

Total undergrad enrollment	4,495
% male/female	73/27
% from out of state	94
% frosh from public high school	60
% frosh live on campus	100
% ugrads live on campus	100
# of fraternities (% ugrad men join)	0 (0)
# of sororities (% ugrad women join)	0 (0)
% African American	7
% Asian	7
% Caucasian	63
% Hispanic	12
% Native American	<1
% Pacific Islander	1
% Two or more races	9
% Race and/or ethnicity unknown	1
% international	1
# of countries represented	29

ACADEMICS

Academic Rating	94
% students returning for sophomore year	95
% students graduating within 4 years	90
% students graduating within 6 years	91
Calendar	Semester
Student/faculty ratio	8:1
Profs interesting rating	78
Profs accessible rating	96
Most classes have 10–19 students.	

MOST POPULAR MAJORS
Mechanical Engineering; Economics;
Political Science and Government

ABOUT THE SCHOOL

The deeply historic United States Naval Academy is one of the few colleges in the world that prepares students morally, mentally, and physically. There's an intense focus not only on regimentation, but also on the shaping of students' moral character, and students here thrive on the academic and militaristic discipline required to make it as a midshipman. Those that decide to apply here—and receive the necessary congressional recommendation to do so—are looking for more than a college degree, and so this self-selecting pool of the best and the brightest young men and women are ready to become the next military leaders of the world from the second they set foot in the Yard.

Through the school's well-worn system, students learn to take orders from practically everyone (Plebe Summer Training certainly provides an introduction to this) but before long acquire the responsibility for making decisions that can affect hundreds of other midshipmen. Small class sizes, protected study time, academic advising, and a sponsor program for newly arrived midshipmen all help ensure that students are given the tools to succeed at this tough school. After four years at the Naval Academy, the life and customs of the naval service become second nature, and most midshipmen go on to careers as officers in the Navy or Marines.

The scenic Naval Academy campus, known as the Yard, is located in historic Annapolis, Maryland, and has been the home to some of the country's foremost leaders, astronauts, scholars, and military heroes. With its combination of early-twentieth-century and modern buildings ("the facilities are unmatched"), the USNA is a blend of tradition and state-of-the-art technology, and the school's history is felt even in the most high tech of classrooms.

BANG FOR YOUR BUCK

All graduates go on to become an ensign in the Navy or a second lieutenant in the Marine Corps and serve five years as an officer, followed by reserve commissions. Many also go on for additional training, including nuclear power, aviation, submarine warfare, and special operations. Especially capable and highly motivated students are able to enroll in the school's challenging honors programs, which provide opportunities to start work on postgraduate degrees while still at the academy. Graduates of USNA tend to spread themselves beyond the military, and the school has produced one president and numerous astronauts, and more than 990 noted scholars in a variety of academic fields are academy graduates, including fifty Rhodes Scholars and twenty-eight Marshall Scholars.

STUDENT LIFE

Monday to Friday midshipmen "put every hour of their lives into their development" and weekdays are scheduled tightly with a "six-period class schedule, lunch together, sports period from 3:45 to 6:00, dinner together, then study period from 8:00 to 10:00." World conflicts are always being discussed "because in a few short years that is where we are possibly going to be." Fun activities involve Army Week, Halloween trick-or-treating, walking around downtown Annapolis ("a beautiful, quaint little town"), or going to the mall. While free time is extremely scarce, most students spend the afternoon working out or participating on varsity or intramural teams and head into DC or Baltimore on the weekends during one of their allotted weekends away. "Eating out and going to the movies" are also always popular activities on the weekends. Friendships are forged by fire during freshman year: "When you get the same haircut and wear the same outfit, 'fitting in' never seems to be a problem."

United States Naval Academy

FINANCIAL AID: 410-293-1858 • E-MAIL: INQUIRE@USNA.EDU • WEBSITE: WWW.USNA.EDU

CAREER

Midshipmen life is very difficult, but "the rewards are so great in four short years." "It [is] a fantastic opportunity to serve my country and to secure a fantastic education and job immediately after I finish my undergraduate degree," says one midshipman. Those who make it through all four years receive a Bachelor of Science degree and then are commissioned as Ensigns in the Navy or Second Lieutenants in the Marine Corps, and must fulfill a minimum military commitment of five years. Graduates of the academy who visited PayScale.com had an median starting salary of $80,600, and 64 percent reported feeling that their job had a meaningful impact on the world.

GENERAL INFO

Activities: Choral groups, concert band, drama/theater, jazz band, literary magazine, marching band, musical theater, pep band, radio station, student government, yearbook, campus ministries, international student organization. **Organizations:** 70 registered organizations, 10 honor societies, 8 religious organizations. **Athletics (Intercollegiate):** *Men:* Baseball, basketball, crew/rowing, cross-country, diving, football, golf, gymnastics, lacrosse, light weight football, riflery, sailing, soccer, squash, swimming, tennis, track/field (outdoor), track/field (indoor), water polo, wrestling. *Women:* Basketball, crew/ rowing, cross-country, diving, golf, lacrosse, riflery, sailing, soccer, swimming, tennis, track/field (outdoor), track/field (indoor), volleyball. **On-Campus Highlights:** Bancroft Hall, U.S. Naval Academy Museum, Armel-Leftwich Visitor Center, U.S. Naval Academy Chapel, Lejeune Hall.

FINANCIAL AID

Aside from the free tuition, room and board, medical and dental care costs, students receive a nominal monthly stipend. In return, Navy midshipmen owe at least five years of active duty service upon graduation. Midshipmen enjoy other benefits like access to military commissaries and exchanges and space-available seats on military aircrafts around the world.

BOTTOM LINE

The Navy pays for the tuition, room and board, and medical and dental care of Naval Academy midshipmen. Midshipmen also enjoy regular active-duty benefits, including access to military commissaries and exchanges, commercial transportation and lodging discounts, and the ability to fly space-available in military aircraft around the world. Midshipmen are also given a monthly salary of $1,062, from which laundry, barber, cobbler, activities fees, yearbook, and other service charges are deducted. Actual cash pay is less than $100 per month your first year, increasing each year to $400 per month in your fourth year.

SELECTIVITY

Admissions Rating	98
# of applicants	16,299
% of applicants accepted	8
% of acceptees attending	87
# offered a place on the wait list	193
% accepting a place on wait list	83
% admitted from wait list	3

FRESHMAN PROFILE

Range SAT EBRW	560–680
Range SAT Math	590–690
Average HS GPA	4.1
% graduated top 10% of class	57
% graduated top 25% of class	83
% graduated top 50% of class	97

DEADLINES

Regular	
Deadline	1/31
Nonfall registration?	No

FINANCIAL FACTS

Financial Aid Rating	60*
Annual in-state tuition	$0
Annual out-of-state tuition	$0
Room and board	$0
Required fees	$0
% frosh rec. any financial aid	0
% UG rec. any financial aid	0
% UG borrow to pay for school	0
Average % of frosh need met	0
Average % of ugrad need met	0

CAREER INFORMATION FROM PAYSCALE.COM	
ROI Rating	NA
Bachelors and No Higher	
Median starting salary	$78,600
Median mid-career salary	$149,800
At Least Bachelors	
Median starting salary	$83,500
Median mid-career salary	$154,100
Alumni with high job meaning	65%
Degrees awarded in STEM subjects	58%

Webb Institute

298 Crescent Beach Road, Glen Cove, NY 11542 • Admissions: 516-671-8355 • Fax: 516-674-9838

CAMPUS LIFE

Quality of Life Rating	**96**
Fire Safety Rating	**98**
Green Rating	**61**
Type of school	Private
Environment	Village

STUDENTS

Total undergrad enrollment	98
% male/female	80/20
% from out of state	78
% frosh from public high school	81
% frosh live on campus	100
% ugrads live on campus	100
# of fraternities (% ugrad men join)	0 (0)
# of sororities (% ugrad women join)	0 (0)
% African American	0
% Asian	11
% Caucasian	81
% Hispanic	1
% Native American	0
% Pacific Islander	0
% Two or more races	5
% Race and/or ethnicity unknown	2
% international	0
# of countries represented	2

ACADEMICS

Academic Rating	**96**
% students returning for sophomore year	93
% students graduating within 4 years	68
% students graduating within 6 years	77
Calendar	Semester
Student/faculty ratio	9:1
Profs interesting rating	96
Profs accessible rating	99

Most classes have 20–29 students. Most lab/discussion sessions have 20–29 students.

ABOUT THE SCHOOL

Ever wondered what goes into designing an America's Cup yacht, U.S. Navy destroyer, or a cruise liner? That's the exact sort of curiosity that brings students to Webb Institute, an engineering college that has produced the nation's leading ship designers for more than a century. Imagine a tiny student body living, eating, sleeping, and learning ship design in a mansion in a residential area overlooking the beautiful Long Island Sound. Then imagine that when that tiny student body leaves their manse, they find a 100 percent placement rate in careers and graduate schools. That's Webb Institute.

As the only school of its kind in the country, Webb enjoys an unrivaled reputation within the marine industry, which is also where students (happily) complete their mandatory two-month internships each January and February. Life—and that includes study, work, and play—on a twenty-six-acre beachfront estate with just 100 students and eleven full-time professors is a rare combination of challenge, focus, and adventure, so in a sense, every day at Webb is a beach day.

Webb Institute is a four-year, fully accredited engineering college that has specialized in naval architecture and marine engineering for the last 123 years. Founded in 1889 by prominent New York shipbuilder William H. Webb, the school's rigorous curriculum couples seamlessly with a total immersion in real-world experience. The school's curriculum goes beyond mechanical, electrical, and civil engineering, taking a systems-engineering approach to problem-solving, meaning Webb graduates are capable of working across engineering disciplines. "If you're passionate about architecture and engineering, you cannot hope for a better learning environment." Everyone majors in naval architecture and marine engineering, although nonengineering electives are available to juniors and seniors, and Webbies are exposed to a smattering of the liberal arts and a ton of advanced math and physics.

BANG FOR YOUR BUCK

Webb's full-tuition scholarship creates the lowest average student loan indebtedness of any four-year college in the nation besides the military academies. Job prospects are phenomenal; every Webb student goes to work in the marine industry for two months every year, creating a professional network and résumé content of eight months or more industry experience. In part due to this experience, as well as the school's specialized nature and excellent reputation, every graduate has a job at graduation or within two months after.

STUDENT LIFE

Classes are so small that "you learn to like everyone to an extent" (everyone being "obsessed about boats" also helps), and from the start "every student fits right into the freshman class through a week of dedicated trips and activities." "When you're going to spend four years with the same people in a room that's not very big, you learn to appreciate all types of people," says a student. This "very hardworking" group "knows how to have a good time when we put our minds to it," and students will often go sailing, fishing, or kayaking on the Long Island Sound with the school-funded boats. Webb students are given a lot of freedom outside of their classes (which "must be attended"), and "[New York City] is never too far away and offers anything you could want." Sports are also a great way to relax, and "anyone can join."

Webb Institute

FINANCIAL AID: 516-671-2213 • E-MAIL: ADMISSIONS@WEBB-INSTITUTE.EDU • WEBSITE: WWW.WEBB-INSTITUTE.EDU

CAREER

With only one academic major and a mandatory internship program, Webb has a pretty established reputation for the students it sends out into the world, and a one hundred percent job placement rate reflects this. "Webb Institute is THE college for Naval Architecture, and a job offer is basically guaranteed after graduating." The focus is on preparing the students for a marine engineering or naval architecture job by teaching them everything they might need to know, and students can expect one-on-one attention when lining up a post-graduation job. "Webb students are very prepared for a future career," says one.

GENERAL INFO

Activities: Choral groups, drama/theater, music ensembles, student government, yearbook. **Organizations:** 2 registered organizations. **Athletics (Intercollegiate):** *Men:* Basketball, cross-country, sailing, soccer, tennis, volleyball. *Women:* Basketball, cross-country, sailing, soccer, tennis, volleyball. **On-Campus Highlights:** Stevenson Taylor Hall, Brockett Pub, Waterfront Facility.

FINANCIAL AID

Students should submit: Business/Farm Supplement; FAFSA; Institution's own financial aid form. Priority filing deadline is 4/1. The Princeton Review suggests that all financial aid forms be submitted as soon as possible after October 1. *Need-based scholarships/grants offered:* College/university scholarship or grant aid from institutional funds; Federal Pell; Private scholarships; State scholarships/grants. *Loan aid offered:* Direct PLUS Loans, Direct Subsidized Loans, Direct Unsubsidized Loans. Applicants will be notified of awards on or about 6/1.

BOTTOM LINE

Every Webb student receives a full-tuition scholarship founded by Mr. Webb, and continued by the generous contributions of alumni/ae, friends of Webb, parents, corporations, and the U.S. government. All admitted students also get paid for two months of internships every year. The only costs are room, board, books, and supplies, which come to $15,500 each year. You can also expect to pay another $4,850 in personal expenses (including transportation and a laptop). There are some additional scholarships available to deserving students to help defray these costs, and if a student needs additional financial assistance, the school recommends pursuing federal grants and loans (and they'll help you do so).

CAREER INFORMATION FROM PAYSCALE.COM

ROI Rating	NA
Bachelors and No Higher	
Median starting salary	$79,100
Median mid-career salary	$134,700
At Least Bachelors	
Median starting salary	$79,700
Median mid-career salary	$141,900
Alumni with high job meaning	
Degrees awarded in STEM subjects	100%

SELECTIVITY

Admissions Rating	97
# of applicants	106
% of applicants accepted	35
% of acceptees attending	76
# offered a place on the wait list	8
% accepting a place on wait list	63
% admitted from wait list	80
# of early decision applicants	22
% accepted early decision	59

FRESHMAN PROFILE

Range SAT EBRW	680–750
Range SAT Math	760–790
Range ACT Composite	30–34
Average HS GPA	4.0
% graduated top 10% of class	44
% graduated top 25% of class	56
% graduated top 50% of class	0

DEADLINES

Early decision	
Deadline	10/15
Notification	12/15
Regular	
Priority	10/15
Deadline	2/1
Nonfall registration?	No

FINANCIAL FACTS

Financial Aid Rating	60*
Annual tuition	$49,750
Annual out-of-state tuition	$0
Room and board	$14,750
Required fees	$425
Books and supplies	$700
Average frosh need-based scholarship	$570
Average UG need-based scholarship	$1,950
% needy frosh rec. need-based scholarship or grant aid	100
% needy UG rec. need-based scholarship or grant aid	100
% needy frosh rec. non-need-based scholarship or grant aid	100
% needy UG rec. non-need-based scholarship or grant aid	100
% needy frosh rec. need-based self-help aid	100
% needy UG rec. need-based self-help aid	100
% frosh rec. any financial aid	25
% UG rec. any financial aid	32
% UG borrow to pay for school	43
Average cumulative indebtedness	$17,870
% frosh need fully met	0
% ugrads need fully met	0
Average % of frosh need met	95
Average % of ugrad need met	95

School Profiles

Agnes Scott College

141 EAST COLLEGE AVENUE, DECATUR, GA 30030-3770 • ADMISSIONS: 404-471-6285 • FAX: 404-471-6414

CAMPUS LIFE

Quality of Life Rating	94
Fire Safety Rating	96
Green Rating	60*
Type of school	Private
Affiliation	Presbyterian
Environment	Metropolis

STUDENTS

Total undergrad enrollment	890
% male/female	0/100
% from out of state	46
% frosh from public high school	75
% frosh live on campus	88
% ugrads live on campus	84
% African American	30
% Asian	7
% Caucasian	35
% Hispanic	12
% Native American	<1
% Pacific Islander	<1
% Two or more races	7
% Race and/or ethnicity unknown	2
% international	7
# of countries represented	34

ACADEMICS

Academic Rating	93
% students returning for sophomore year	87
% students graduating within 4 years	62
% students graduating within 6 years	67
Calendar	Semester
Student/faculty ratio	10:1
Profs interesting rating	92
Profs accessible rating	93
Most classes have 20–29 students.	

MOST POPULAR MAJORS
Psychology; Public Health; Business Management

ABOUT THE SCHOOL

With fewer than one thousand undergraduates, Agnes Scott College can devote its full attention and resources to the development of students as leaders, critical thinkers, and well-rounded students of the liberal arts. SUMMIT is Agnes Scott's unique college experience where every student, regardless of major, completes a core curriculum focused on global learning and leadership development. The Decatur-based school offers 34 undergraduate majors and 31 minors (spread out across courses with "thoughtful syllabi") and is affiliated with nearby institutions such as Georgia Tech and Emory University, giving undergraduates the chance to supplement their curriculum via cross-registration and partake in larger social events. Professors "are supportive, yet expect a lot," and resources such as the Science Center for Women and the Center for Writing and Speaking help students keep up. The 10:1 student-to-faculty ratio is a huge perk, and "there is nothing like having specialized time with expert professors in a classroom setting at an undergraduate level." Classes are "interactive and engaging" because professors are "open to different teaching styles and make sure all students can bring their own perspective into the discussion"; the faculty/student relationship is "academic but still extremely personable."

BANG FOR YOUR BUCK

The real benefit is in the people at Agnes Scott: Teachers have the chance to "really get to know you and care about you." "Professors write me letters of recommendation, let me know about global programs I'd be good for, and even send me job postings they saw that they know I'd be interested in," says one student. For those worried about the initial price, Agnes Scott offers both merit-based and need-based aid, but only students who apply early decision or early action are automatically considered for merit-based scholarships, such as the Elizabeth Kiss Trailblazer Scholarship for high academic achievement ($25,000 a year) and the Marvin B. Perry Presidential Scholarship, which awards full tuition and room and board to top applicants.

STUDENT LIFE

Agnes Scott is filled with "smart and thoughtful women who form a community that thrives together." These are "enthusiastic and welcoming" students who "are liberal and very aware of the important issues in our world today." Scotties are "very hard working and spend large amount of time studying," but the programming board at Agnes Scott does a great job of arranging events so "usually there is something to do," though the "campus is very chill" overall. Most Agnes Scott students are involved in at least one extracurricular ("many of us more than one") because "it's really easy to get involved here." Downtown Decatur is a two-minute walk away, and the train to Atlanta is only five minutes away. The local music scene is thriving, and "there are lots of festivals in the spring and lots of cool concert venues around the city."

CAREER

The Office of Internship & Career Development offers Major to Career roadmaps, a HireAScottie job board, and job, internship, and volunteer fairs. As part of a longstanding tradition, members of the senior class ring the campus bell and sign their names in the college's bell tower when they receive acceptance into graduate/professional school or a job offer. There are "fantastic internship opportunities" available due to the proximity to Atlanta, and professors are supportive of all student career goals and "push you to go after internships, clubs, leadership positions, and jobs." Agnes Scott College alumni who visited PayScale.com report an average

Agnes Scott College

FINANCIAL AID: 404-471-6395 • E-MAIL: ADMISSION@AGNESSCOTT.EDU • WEBSITE: WWW.AGNESSCOTT.EDU

starting salary of $42,900, and 55 percent say that they derive a high level of meaning from their jobs.

GENERAL INFO

Activities: Choral groups, dance, drama/theater, literary magazine, marching band, music ensembles, musical theater, pep band, student government, student newspaper, symphony orchestra, television station, yearbook, campus ministries, international student organization. **Organizations:** 80 registered organizations, 12 honor societies, 12 religious organizations. **Athletics (Intercollegiate):** *Women:* basketball, cross-country, soccer, softball, tennis, volleyball. **On-Campus Highlights:** LEED Gold Certified Campbell Hall Living and Learning community, recently renovated Elizabeth Kiss Welcome Center in Rebekah Scott Hall, Bradley Observatory and Planetarium, five solar arrays, McCain Library.

FINANCIAL AID

Students should submit: FAFSA. Priority filing deadline is 3/15. The Princeton Review suggests that all financial aid forms be submitted as soon as possible after October 1. *Need-based scholarships/grants offered:* College/university scholarship or grant aid from institutional funds, Federal Pell, private scholarships, SEOG, state scholarships/grants. *Loan aid offered:* Direct PLUS Loans, Direct Subsidized Loans, Direct Unsubsidized Loans. Applicants will be notified of awards on a rolling basis beginning 3/1. Federal Work-Study Program available. Institutional employment available.

BOTTOM LINE

It costs $40,920 in tuition to attend Agnes Scott, with another $12,330 going to room and board and $240 in Student Activity Fees. More than two-thirds of incoming students qualify for and receive need-based financial aid, with another quarter of the class receiving merit-based aid only.

CAREER INFORMATION FROM PAYSCALE.COM	
ROI Rating	88
Bachelors and No Higher	
Median starting salary	$44,700
Median mid-career salary	$82,700
At Least Bachelors	
Median starting salary	$46,000
Median mid-career salary	$82,700
Alumni with high job meaning	54%
Degrees awarded in STEM subjects	26%

SELECTIVITY	
Admissions Rating	86
# of applicants	1,534
% of applicants accepted	66
% of acceptees attending	25
# of early decision applicants	24
% accepted early decision	92

FRESHMAN PROFILE	
Range SAT EBRW	580–690
Range SAT Math	530–610
Range ACT Composite	24–30
Minimum internet-based TOEFL	80
Average HS GPA	3.8
% graduated top 10% of class	30
% graduated top 25% of class	65
% graduated top 50% of class	91

DEADLINES	
Early decision	
Deadline	11/1
Notification	12/1
Early action	
Deadline	11/15
Notification	12/15
Regular	
Priority	1/15
Deadline	5/1
Nonfall registration?	No

FINANCIAL FACTS	
Financial Aid Rating	87
Annual tuition	$40,920
Room and board	$12,330
Required fees	$240
Books and supplies	$1,000
Average frosh need-based scholarship	$31,186
Average UG need-based scholarship	$30,022
% needy frosh rec. need-based scholarship or grant aid	100
% needy UG rec. need-based scholarship or grant aid	100
% needy frosh rec. non-need-based scholarship or grant aid	18
% needy UG rec. non-need-based scholarship or grant aid	21
% needy frosh rec. need-based self-help aid	84
% needy UG rec. need-based self-help aid	84
% frosh rec. any financial aid	100
% UG rec. any financial aid	99
% UG borrow to pay for school	64
Average cumulative indebtedness	$32,276
% frosh need fully met	20
% ugrads need fully met	22
Average % of frosh need met	85
Average % of ugrad need met	85

Allegheny College

Allegheny College, Meadville, PA 16335 • Admissions: 814-332-4351 • Fax: 814-337-0431

CAMPUS LIFE	
Quality of Life Rating	**86**
Fire Safety Rating	**86**
Green Rating	**89**
Type of school	Private
Environment	Town

STUDENTS	
Total undergrad enrollment	1,764
% male/female	46/54
% from out of state	50
% frosh from public high school	86
% frosh live on campus	98
% ugrads live on campus	96
# of fraternities (% ugrad men join)	6 (26)
# of sororities (% ugrad women join)	5 (24)
% African American	9
% Asian	3
% Caucasian	70
% Hispanic	9
% Native American	<1
% Pacific Islander	<1
% Two or more races	4
% Race and/or ethnicity unknown	3
% international	3
# of countries represented	50

ACADEMICS	
Academic Rating	**88**
% students returning for sophomore year	81
% students graduating within 4 years	69
% students graduating within 6 years	75
Calendar	Semester
Student/faculty ratio	10:1
Profs interesting rating	88
Profs accessible rating	88

Most classes have 10–19 students. Most lab/discussion sessions have 10–19 students.

MOST POPULAR MAJORS
Biology/Biological Sciences; Psychology; Economics

ABOUT THE SCHOOL

At Allegheny College, a small liberal arts school in rural Meadville, Pennsylvania, the "general attitude of the student body and faculty are what define Allegheny as a great place." The Allegheny curriculum promotes collaboration and exploration across all subject areas. Students take classes across three "divisions of knowledge"—humanities, natural sciences and social sciences—and eventually combine their interests and skills in order to declare a major and a minor by the end of their sophomore year. The school encourages unusual academic combinations, and all seniors are required to complete and defend a comprehensive research project, known as "The Senior Comp," in order to graduate. Small class sizes allow for "as much one-on-one time as you need during office hours," and professors are supportive of the accepting environment and culture established on campus and "work these ideals into class discussion by promoting opposing ideas" rather than forcing students to confront them.

BANG FOR YOUR BUCK

Allegheny students thrive among a body of individuals that "don't necessarily fit the bill for a liberal arts student because of the comparatively awesome financial aid" versus at some other liberal arts colleges. In addition to federal and state grants, Allegheny doled out more than $45 million in institutional assistance. Trustee Scholarships are awarded based on achievement and academic excellence in high school rather than financial need. These scholarships automatically renew and can amount up to $28,000 per year. Additionally, individual scholarships are available based on specific academic departments and achievements, and even international students are eligible for some scholarships. Over half of all students are employed by graduation, while 30 percent move on to graduate or professional school (a sizable percentage also join the Peace Corps).

STUDENT LIFE

The college's academic reputation as a place where students create "unusual combinations" of interests is also "the perfect way to describe the Allegheny community." All first-year students live on Allegheny's small campus, which means that there are "certain unifying jokes and experiences that truly bind everyone together and they are rarely the ones the school has built into its tours." Several clubs and organizations offer activities for students such as "bingo nights, cactus planting, crocheting, movies, [and] bubble tea making" as well as weekend or day trips, and the school also "does a good job of offering school-wide activities, such as our annual Springfest, several performances, and other celebrations." Within the quiet town of Meadville there are "plenty of reasonably priced restaurants, cute cafés, bars and even a winery and critically-acclaimed brewery." The school is close to both Pittsburgh and Erie so it is common for students to take trips off campus.

CAREER

Allegheny is a place where students have full control over the education they want to have and "can put their talents and skills to their future careers." Students say the college wants them "to think about things in a completely different perspective which aims to make us unique and specifically individualized for potential careers." The tradition of Gator Days is an excellent example of the school's dedication to practical career prep. One day each semester is set aside for students to explore what they'll need to know beyond the classroom via alumni panels, department open houses, professional headshot sessions, with no classes, extracurricular activities, or practices scheduled. Allegheny's Office of Career Education is "very helpful and proactive with internships and job placement," and faculty members are excellent resources as well. "Most of my internships have come from [a] professor recommendation; as in they found the opportunity, made me aware that I would be a good candidate, and then helped me with the application process," says a student. The school hosts

Allegheny College

FINANCIAL AID: 800-835-7780 • E-MAIL: ADMISSIONS@ALLEGHENY.EDU • WEBSITE: WWW.ALLEGHENY.EDU

a summer job fair and a Work Local job fair designed to place students in jobs and internships in the area, and there is Experiential Learning Funding available to students offered exceptional hands-on opportunities not found nearby, such as international internships, volunteering, or independent research. Out of Allegheny alumni visiting PayScale.com, 44 percent report that they derive a high level of meaning from their jobs.

GENERAL INFO

Activities: Choral groups, concert band, dance, drama/theater, jazz band, literary magazine, music ensembles, musical theater, radio station, student government, student newspaper, symphony orchestra, television station, yearbook, campus ministries, Model UN. 110 registered organizations, 14 honor societies, 9 religious organizations. 6 fraternities, 5 sororities. **Athletics (Intercollegiate):** *Men:* baseball, basketball, cross-country, diving, football, golf, lacrosse, soccer, swimming, tennis, track/field (outdoor), track/field (indoor). *Women:* basketball, cross-country, diving, field hockey, golf, lacrosse, soccer, softball, swimming, tennis, track/field (outdoor), track/field (indoor), volleyball. **On-Campus Highlights:** Augmented Reality Sandbox, neuroscience and psychology research facility, Geographic Information Systems Learning Lab, Rustic Bridge, Wise Sport and Fitness Center, Henderson Campus Center, Pelletier Library, World's largest solid-volume glass sculpture group, State-of-the-art, nationally acclaimed science complex dedicated to biology and chemistry; Patricia Bush Tippie Alumni Center; seismographic network station; Center for Political Participation; Center for Business and Economics; radio and TV stations, Grounds For Change Coffeehouse, Vukovich Communication Arts Building and Environmental Roof Garden; Robertson athletic fields and recreation area.

FINANCIAL AID

Students should submit: FAFSA. Priority filing deadline is 2/15. The Princeton Review suggests that all financial aid forms be submitted as soon as possible after October 1. *Need-based scholarships/grants offered:* College/university scholarship or grant aid from institutional funds, Federal Pell, private scholarships, SEOG, state scholarships/grants. *Loan aid offered:* Direct PLUS Loans, Direct Subsidized Loans, Direct Unsubsidized Loans. Applicants will be notified of awards on a rolling basis beginning 12/1. Federal Work-Study Program available. Institutional employment available.

BOTTOM LINE

Allegheny College's tuition is $47,040 per year, with room and board, and activities fees running an additional $12,640.

CAREER INFORMATION FROM PAYSCALE.COM	
ROI Rating	88
Bachelors and No Higher	
Median starting salary	$48,700
Median mid-career salary	$96,100
At Least Bachelors	
Median starting salary	$51,100
Median mid-career salary	$99,900
Alumni with high job meaning	44%
Degrees awarded in STEM subjects	37%

SELECTIVITY	
Admissions Rating	85
# of applicants	5,114
% of applicants accepted	68
% of acceptees attending	14
# offered a place on the wait list	223
% accepting a place on wait list	100
% admitted from wait list	6
# of early decision applicants	163
% accepted early decision	50

FRESHMAN PROFILE	
Range SAT EBRW	580–670
Range SAT Math	560–650
Range ACT Composite	23–29
Minimum paper TOEFL	550
Minimum internet-based TOEFL	80
Average HS GPA	3.5
% graduated top 10% of class	33
% graduated top 25% of class	65
% graduated top 50% of class	88

DEADLINES	
Early decision	
Deadline	11/15
Notification	11/30
Other ED Deadline	2/1
Other ED Notification	2/15
Early action	
Deadline	12/1
Notification	1/1
Regular	
Deadline	2/15
Notification	3/15
Nonfall registration?	Yes

FINANCIAL FACTS	
Financial Aid Rating	88
Annual tuition	$47,040
Room and board	$12,140
Required fees	$500
Books and supplies	$1,000
Average frosh need-based scholarship	$36,480
Average UG need-based scholarship	$34,310
% needy frosh rec. need-based scholarship or grant aid	100
% needy UG rec. need-based scholarship or grant aid	100
% needy frosh rec. non-need-based scholarship or grant aid	18
% needy UG rec. non-need-based scholarship or grant aid	16
% needy frosh rec. need-based self-help aid	85
% needy UG rec. need-based self-help aid	86
% frosh rec. any financial aid	100
% UG rec. any financial aid	99

Amherst College

CAMPUS BOX 2231, AMHERST, MA 01002 • ADMISSIONS: 413-542-2328 • FAX: 413-542-2040

CAMPUS LIFE

Quality of Life Rating	84
Fire Safety Rating	60*
Green Rating	82
Type of school	Private
Environment	Town

STUDENTS

Total undergrad enrollment	1,836
% male/female	51/49
% from out of state	86
% frosh from public high school	54
% frosh live on campus	100
% ugrads live on campus	97
# of fraternities (% ugrad men join)	0 (0)
# of sororities (% ugrad women join)	0 (0)
% African American	11
% Asian	14
% Caucasian	44
% Hispanic	13
% Native American	1
% Pacific Islander	<1
% Two or more races	5
% Race and/or ethnicity unknown	3
% international	9
# of countries represented	58

ACADEMICS

Academic Rating	94
% students returning for sophomore year	96
% students graduating within 4 years	90
% students graduating within 6 years	95
Calendar	Semester
Student/faculty ratio	8:1
Profs interesting rating	88
Profs accessible rating	85
Most classes have 10–19 students.	

MOST POPULAR MAJORS

English Language And Literature;
Psychology; Economics

#17 BEST VALUE COLLEGE

ABOUT THE SCHOOL

Situated on a lush 1,015-acre campus in Amherst, Massachusetts, Amherst College offers students an intellectual atmosphere fostered by friendly and supportive faculty members. Amherst College has an exploratory vibe with a virtually requirement-free curriculum that gives students unprecedented academic freedom. There are no core or general requirements. Beyond the first-year seminar and major coursework, students can choose what they want to study. One student told us, "I love the open curriculum and that you can do whatever you want here." That doesn't mean you can slack off, though: students say you must be "willing to read a text forward and backward and firmly grasp it" and "skimming will do you no good." The most popular majors are economics, political science, and English, and alumni have a solid track record in gaining admission to postgraduate programs. In fact, some students view Amherst as "prep school for grad school." Students can also receive credit for courses at neighboring colleges Smith, Mount Holyoke, Hampshire, and the University of Massachusetts Amherst for a total selection of more than 6,000 courses. Students say that they love the "abundant academic and social opportunities" provided by the consortium. Almost half of Amherst students also pack their bags during junior year to study abroad. Students say that professors "are always available, and they want to spend time with us outside of the classroom."

BANG FOR YOUR BUCK

Amherst College is a no-loan institution, which means the college does not include loans in its financial aid packages but focuses on providing grant and scholarship aid instead. It is possible to graduate from Amherst with no debt. In addition to a need-blind admissions policy, Amherst meets 100 percent of students' demonstrated need, be they international or domestic. Every year, Amherst awards grants and scholarships to more than half the student body. All students who apply for financial aid are automatically considered for grant and scholarship funds. In 2014–15, the school provided just over $52 million in scholarship and grant aid to students, and the average award was just over $47,000.

STUDENT LIFE

While students at Amherst are "focused first and foremost on academics, nearly every student is active and enjoys life outside of the library." In their spare time, "students love to get involved in extracurriculars. It seems like everyone plays a sport, is a member of an a cappella group, and has joined an affinity group." "There's a club or organization for every interest" here, and students assure us that if there isn't one that you're interested in, "the school will find the money for it." Amherst's small size "means that no group is isolated, and everyone interacts and more or less gets along." And truly, "diversity—racial, ethnic, geographic, socioeconomic—is more than a buzzword here." The campus is also "a politically and environmentally conscious" place, and the town of Amherst and the surrounding areas are "incredibly intellectual." Still, the "awesome" dorms tend to serve as the school's social hubs, as Amherst did away with its Greek system in 1984.

Amherst College

FINANCIAL AID: 413-542-2296 • E-MAIL: ADMISSION@AMHERST.EDU • WEBSITE: WWW.AMHERST.EDU

CAREER

The Career Center at Amherst is focused on empowering students to think about their futures reflectively and strategically. The Amherst Select Internship Program allows students to get a taste of different fields over the summer and truly test out their options. Other resources like Quest, Career Beam, and the Liberal Arts Career Network list job and internship opportunities for gaining professional experience. Students can easily connect with alumni through Pathways, the alumni-student mentoring program that helps undergrads set goals and make informed career decisions. Those grads who visited PayScale.com report starting salaries of about $60,200, and 47 percent believe their work makes the world a better place.

GENERAL INFO

Activities: Choral groups, concert band, dance, drama/theater, jazz band, literary magazine, music ensembles, musical theater, opera, radio station, student government, student newspaper, student-run film society, symphony orchestra, yearbook, international student organization. **Organizations:** 100-plus registered organizations, 2 honor societies, 7 religious organizations. **Athletics (Intercollegiate):** *Men:* Baseball, basketball, cross-country, football, golf, ice hockey, lacrosse, soccer, squash, swimming and diving, tennis, track/field (outdoor), track/field (indoor). *Women:* Basketball, cross-country, field hockey, golf, ice hockey, lacrosse, soccer, softball, squash, swimming and diving, tennis, track/field (outdoor), track/field (indoor), volleyball. **On-Campus Highlights:** Mead Art Museum, Beneski Museum of Natural History, Center for Russian Culture, Japanese Yushien Garden, Wilder Observatory.

FINANCIAL AID

Students should submit: CSS Profile; FAFSA; Noncustodial PROFILE. Priority filing deadline is 3/1. The Princeton Review suggests that all financial aid forms be submitted as soon as possible after October 1. *Need-based scholarships/grants offered:* College/university scholarship or grant aid from institutional funds, Federal Pell, private scholarships, SEOG, state scholarships/grants. *Loan aid offered:* Direct PLUS Loans, Direct Subsidized Loans, Direct Unsubsidized Loans. Applicants will be notified of awards on or about 4/1. Federal Work-Study Program available. Institutional employment available.

BOTTOM LINE

Annual tuition, fees, and room and board cost roughly $63,000 at Amherst. Once you consider books, supplies, personal expenses, and transportation, you can expect to spend anywhere from $66,000 to $70,000 per year. In the end, you'll get much more than what you pay for. The school meets 100 percent of its student body's demonstrated need without loans, and those who choose to take them out graduate with little debt (relative to the indebtedness of graduates of many similar schools). Students feel it is "hard to find somewhere better" and believe Amherst is "the best of the small, elite New England colleges."

CAREER INFORMATION FROM PAYSCALE.COM

ROI Rating	94
Bachelors and No Higher	
Median starting salary	$62,300
Median mid-career salary	$123,700
At Least Bachelors	
Median starting salary	$65,200
Median mid-career salary	$133,300
Alumni with high job meaning	43%
Degrees awarded in STEM subjects	32%

SELECTIVITY

Admissions Rating	**98**
# of applicants	9,285
% of applicants accepted	13
% of acceptees attending	39
# offered a place on the wait list	1,144
% accepting a place on wait list	52
% admitted from wait list	10
# of early decision applicants	502
% accepted early decision	34

FRESHMAN PROFILE

Range SAT EBRW	720–770
Range SAT Math	710–790
Range ACT Composite	32–34
Minimum internet-based TOEFL	100
% graduated top 10% of class	83
% graduated top 25% of class	94
% graduated top 50% of class	100

DEADLINES

Early decision	
Deadline	11/1
Notification	12/15
Regular	
Deadline	1/1
Notification	4/1
Nonfall registration?	No

FINANCIAL FACTS

Financial Aid Rating	**97**
Annual tuition	$55,520
Room and board	$14,740
Required fees	$906
Books and supplies	$1,000
Average frosh need-based scholarship	$52,482
Average UG need-based scholarship	$51,841
% needy frosh rec. need-based scholarship or grant aid	100
% needy UG rec. need-based scholarship or grant aid	100
% needy frosh rec. non-need-based scholarship or grant aid	0
% needy UG rec. non-need-based scholarship or grant aid	0
% needy frosh rec. need-based self-help aid	84
% needy UG rec. need-based self-help aid	86
% frosh rec. any financial aid	54
% UG rec. any financial aid	58
% UG borrow to pay for school	29
Average cumulative indebtedness	$19,075
% frosh need fully met	100
% ugrads need fully met	100
Average % of frosh need met	100
Average % of ugrad need met	100

Arizona State University

PO Box 870112, Tempe, AZ 85287-0112 • Admissions: 480-965-7788 • Fax: 480-965-3610

CAMPUS LIFE

Quality of Life Rating	87
Fire Safety Rating	92
Green Rating	98
Type of school	Public
Environment	Metropolis

STUDENTS

Total undergrad enrollment	58,866
% male/female	53/47
% from out of state	24
% frosh live on campus	69
% ugrads live on campus	21
# of fraternities (% ugrad men join)	45 (8)
# of sororities (% ugrad women join)	28 (12)
% African American	4
% Asian	7
% Caucasian	50
% Hispanic	23
% Native American	1
% Pacific Islander	<1
% Two or more races	4
% Race and/or ethnicity unknown	1
% international	10
# of countries represented	121

ACADEMICS

Academic Rating	73
% students returning for sophomore year	86
% students graduating within 4 years	53
% students graduating within 6 years	63
Calendar	Semester
Student/faculty ratio	21:1
Profs interesting rating	72
Profs accessible rating	72

Most classes have 10–19 students. Most lab/discussion sessions have 10–19 students.

MOST POPULAR MAJORS

Business, Management, Marketing; Biology and Biological Sciences; Psychology

ABOUT THE SCHOOL

Arizona State University is a top-ranked public university with multiple campus locations in the Phoenix metropolitan area. ASU does a great job of extending ample resources and research opportunities to every branch: "Finding an expert in your field of interest on campus is simple," according to one student. Additionally, the university's many interdisciplinary research centers and institutes have helped to make it the fastest-growing research institution in the United States: Its annual research expenditures have more than quadrupled to $546 million according to https://research.asu.edu/about-us/facts-figures in the last fifteen years. ASU is similarly "very ambitious in its goals toward innovative efforts," such as fostering next generation service corps, sustainability goals, and "the commitment to promoting entrepreneurship." Classes are "engaging and interactive," and the size of ASU with its four distinct campuses across the Phoenix area is a huge strength: "Going to one of the largest universities in the world means being exposed to infinite opportunities, people, and ideas," says a student.

BANG FOR YOUR BUCK

ASU excels at "providing resources for all students regardless of their specific field," and sets students up "to network and create solid relationships that will be used for years to come." "They try to make it really accessible no matter what your background," says a student about the school's alumni network. Of the many need- and merit based grants available, the primary merit-based scholarships are the New American University Awards, which for out-of-state students range from approximately $7,000 to $15,000, and for Arizona residents range from $3,000 to $10,000 per year. Additionally, Arizona resident Pell eligible students are able to attend tuition free through the College Attainment Grant or the Obama Scholars Program. . For those unsure of where they stand in terms of scholarship qualifications, the school website's freshman merit scholarship estimator can let students know whether they are candidates.

STUDENT LIFE

You'll find it all at ASU—"students who focus strictly on academics and those who are more interested in the parties they have attended." ASU students love the "diversity" on campus, which makes for "an exciting and…vibrant feel to the student body." The Tempe campus is known as "the hub for athletes and Greek life," and the city itself "is a great place to hang out and there is a ton to do." Many students here work part-time jobs or internships, and there are "weekly music series, viewing parties for various sporting events, Friday night activities and other events." Most here (particularly in Barrett, The Honors College) are "very serious about their education and future goals, yet still know how to balance their studies and fun."

CAREER

ASU is a school that "prepares you greatly for your future while also giving you experience to feel confident moving into the workforce." The Career and Professional Development Services department has numerous resources available to students looking to map out their career plan, including career fairs, workshops, and the My ASU Career Milestones tool, which helps students to keep track of their professional goals. There are plenty of off-campus opportunities provided by the school through internships, study abroad, and a "crazy amount of research opportunities," so "it's hard to not fall in love with something." Of ASU's Tempe campus alumni visiting PayScale.com, 51 percent report that they derive a high level of meaning from their jobs.

Arizona State University

FINANCIAL AID: 855-278-5080 • E-MAIL: ADMISSIONS@ASU.EDU • WEBSITE: WWW.ASU.EDU

GENERAL INFO

Activities: Choral groups, concert band, dance, drama/theater, jazz band, marching band, music ensembles, musical theater, pep band, radio station, student government, student newspaper, student-run film society, symphony orchestra, television station, campus ministries, International Student Organization, Model UN. **Organizations:** 1,069 registered organizations, 30 honor societies, 66 religious organizations, 45 fraternities, 28 sororities. **Athletics (Intercollegiate):** *Men:* baseball, basketball, cross-country, diving, football, golf, ice hockey, swimming, tennis, track/field (outdoor), wrestling. *Women:* basketball, beach volleyball, cross-country, diving, golf, gymnastics, lacrosse, soccer, softball, swimming, tennis, track/field (outdoor), triathalon, volleyball, water polo.

FINANCIAL AID

Students should submit: FAFSA. Priority filing deadline is Jan. 1. The Princeton Review suggests that all financial aid forms be submitted as soon as possible after Oct. 1. *Need-based scholarships/grants offered:* College/university scholarship or grant aid from institutional funds; Federal Pell; Private scholarships; SEOG; State scholarships and grants; United Negro College Fund. *Loan aid offered:* Direct PLUS Loans, Direct Subsidized Loans, Direct Unsubsidized Loans. Applicants will be notified of awards on a rolling basis beginning Jan. 1. Federal Work-Study Program available. Institutional employment available.

BOTTOM LINE

Arizona residents must pay $10,822 in tuition and fees as well as $12,583 in room and board; out-of-state residents pay $28,336 in tuition and fees. More than 92 percent of freshmen received financial aid to ASU, and more than 85 percent of all ASU students receive some form of financial assistance every year.

CAREER INFORMATION FROM PAYSCALE.COM	
ROI Rating	87
Bachelors and No Higher	
Median starting salary	$53,200
Median mid-career salary	$98,900
At Least Bachelors	
Median starting salary	$54,400
Median mid-career salary	$102,600
Alumni with high job meaning	52%
Degrees awarded in STEM subjects	30%

SELECTIVITY

Admissions Rating	82
# of applicants	34,181
% of applicants accepted	82
% of acceptees attending	37

FRESHMAN PROFILE

Range SAT EBRW	560–660
Range SAT Math	550–670
Range ACT Composite	22–28
Minimum paper TOEFL	500
Minimum internet-based TOEFL	61
Average HS GPA	3.5
% graduated top 10% of class	33
% graduated top 25% of class	65
% graduated top 50% of class	91

DEADLINES

Regular	
Priority	11/1
Nonfall registration?	Yes

FINANCIAL FACTS

Financial Aid Rating	82
Annual in-state tuition	$10,104
Annual out-of-state tuition	$27,618
Room and board	$12,583
Required fees	$718
Books and supplies	$1,125
Average frosh need-based scholarship	$12,970
Average UG need-based scholarship	$10,297
% needy frosh rec. need-based scholarship or grant aid	99
% needy UG rec. need-based scholarship or grant aid	93
% needy frosh rec. non-need-based scholarship or grant aid	14
% needy UG rec. non-need-based scholarship or grant aid	8
% needy frosh rec. need-based self-help aid	51
% needy UG rec. need-based self-help aid	67
% frosh rec. any financial aid	92
% UG rec. any financial aid	85
% UG borrow to pay for school	51
Average cumulative indebtedness	$23,439
% frosh need fully met	22
% ugrads need fully met	19
Average % of frosh need met	70
Average % of ugrad need met	61

Babson College

231 Forest Street, Babson Park, MA 02457 • Admission: 781-239-5522 • Fax: 781-239-4006

CAMPUS LIFE

Quality of Life Rating	92
Fire Safety Rating	95
Green Rating	93
Type of school	Private
Environment	Village

STUDENTS

Total undergrad enrollment	2,342
% male/female	52/48
% from out of state	73
% frosh live on campus	100
% ugrads live on campus	79
# of fraternities (% ugrad men join)	4 (13)
# of sororities (% ugrad women join)	3 (26)
% African American	5
% Asian	12
% Caucasian	37
% Hispanic	11
% Native American	<1
% Pacific Islander	<1
% Two or more races	2
% Race and/or ethnicity unknown	5
% international	28
# of countries represented	77

ACADEMICS

Academic Rating	88
% students returning for sophomore year	96
% students graduating within 4 years	90
% students graduating within 6 years	92
Calendar	Semester
Student/faculty ratio	11:1
Profs interesting rating	90
Profs accessible rating	93
Most classes have 20–29 students.	

MOST POPULAR MAJORS
Business Administration and Management

#37 BEST VALUE COLLEGE

ABOUT THE SCHOOL

At its core, Babson College is a "prestigious, competitive business school that does an exceptional job at preparing you for a career in the business world." Undergrads here find that their courses are "difficult but extremely useful" with their core classes covering everything from "basic accounting, finance [and] marketing [to] statistics [and] operations." Students get a solid sense of how these subjects "build off each other" and ultimately gain a "well-rounded foundation." Many undergrads point out that Babson attracts many "international students," which helps everyone attending develop a "global outlook." And they adore that Babson encourages and nurtures "innovation and entrepreneurship." Professors here receive high marks as well. They really "push [students] to go beyond [their] limits and excel." They also "provide real life insight in to discussions and give constructive feedback regarding class or other matters." Best of all, they are "always accessible."

BANG FOR YOUR BUCK

Many undergrads here rave about Babson's awesome financial aid. As part of the Global Scholars Program a small, highly talented group of international students is awarded need-based scholarships each year. As one student boasts, "Babson met all of my demonstrated financial need, and I know many of my friends also have need or merit aid." More specifically, the college awards an impressive $45 million in aid annually. And $36 million of that funding is in the form of grants and scholarships. What's more, 50 percent of Babson's undergrads receive assistance. The school meets an astonishing 100 percent of students' demonstrated need. Merit awards include the Dean's Scholarship which provides up to $5,000 per year and the Honors Program Scholarship which provides up to $3,000. And then there's the Weissman Scholarship which covers full tuition and offers additional financial support.

SCHOOL LIFE

Most undergrads at Babson are "very involved," which can make life hectic at times. Of course, these curious and ambitious individuals wouldn't have it any other way. Students are fairly athletic and a large percentage "[hit] the gym or [participate in] intramural sports." Undergrads also join "various activities, clubs, and organizations such as Greek life, Business Greek life…[and] cultural [organizations as well as] business-related [ones.]" It's also quite normal for students to attend numerous "conferences or networking events." Additionally, a handful of people reveal that it's "pretty typical for students to go out to parties on Thursdays and Saturdays." We're told that "trips to Boston are common when students want to be off campus."

CAREER

Babson seems to attract students who are "very career and goal oriented." "Nearly all students have internships" at some point during their undergraduate tenure. Many individuals find these positions through their professors who frequently "open up their networks to students." Of course, the "Center for Career Development (CCD) has numerous connections that ease [the] search for internships and full-time opportunities" as well. Additionally, the CCD provides multiple resources to assist students on their professional journey. For

FINANCIAL AID: 781-239-4015 • E-MAIL: UGRADADMISSION@BABSON.EDU • WEBSITE: WWW.BABSON.EDU

example, Babson undergrads can learn how to sharpen their personal branding tools through classes on cover letter writing, interview techniques and social media practices. Babson is great at bringing employers and recruiters to campus, where students can attend a myriad of industry panels and career expos and meet representatives from companies such as Fidelity Investments, Digitas, Bank of America/Merrill Lynch, Goldman Sachs, and Hubspot.

GENERAL INFO

Activities: Dance, drama/theater, jazz band, literary magazine, musical theater, radio station, student government, student newspaper, television station. **Organizations:** 115 registered organizations, 8 religious organizations. 4 fraternities, 3 sororities. **Athletics (Intercollegiate):** *Men:* baseball, basketball, cross-country, diving, golf, ice hockey, lacrosse, skiing (downhill/alpine), soccer, swimming, tennis, track/field (outdoor), track/field (indoor). *Women:* basketball, cross-country, diving, field hockey, lacrosse, skiing (downhill/alpine), soccer, softball, swimming, tennis, track/field (outdoor), track/field (indoor), volleyball. **On-Campus Highlights:** Institute for Family Entrepreneurship, The Lewis Institute for Social Innovation, Sorenson Arts Center, Blank Center for Entrepeneurship, Glavin Family Chapel, Reynolds Student Center, Webster Athletic Center, Cutler Center for Investments and Finance, Center for Women's Entrepreneurial Leadership.

FINANCIAL AID

Students should submit: CSS Profile; FAFSA; Noncustodial PROFILE. Priority filing deadline is 2/1. The Princeton Review suggests that all financial aid forms be submitted as soon as possible after October 1. *Need-based scholarships/grants offered:* College/university scholarship or grant aid from institutional funds, Federal Pell, private scholarships, SEOG, state scholarships/grants. *Loan aid offered:* Direct PLUS Loans, Direct Subsidized Loans, Direct Unsubsidized Loans. Applicants will be notified of awards on or about 4/1. Federal Work-Study Program available. Institutional employment available.

THE BOTTOM LINE

Babson College currently charges $51,104 for its annual tuition. Undergrads (and their families) should also expect to pay $10,528 for room (the price of the average double) and an additional $5,784 for a meal plan. Books and classroom supplies will likely cost another $1,080. The college also estimates that personal expenses come to roughly $1,112. And there's a $50 federal direct loan fee. That makes the total (estimated) cost of attendance about $70,428.

CAREER INFORMATION FROM PAYSCALE.COM	
ROI Rating	92
Bachelors and No Higher	
Median starting salary	$69,300
Median mid-career salary	$139,200
At Least Bachelors	
Median starting salary	$70,000
Median mid-career salary	$145,500
Alumni with high job meaning	35%
Degrees awarded in STEM subjects	0%

SELECTIVITY	
Admissions Rating	95
# of applicants	7,122
% of applicants accepted	24
% of acceptees attending	32
# offered a place on the wait list	1,723
% accepting a place on wait list	40
% admitted from wait list	0
# of early decision applicants	432
% accepted early decision	38

FRESHMAN PROFILE	
Range SAT EBRW	610–680
Range SAT Math	620–730
Range ACT Composite	27–32
Minimum paper TOEFL	600
Minimum internet-based TOEFL	100

DEADLINES	
Early decision	
Deadline	11/1
Notification	12/15
Early action	
Deadline	11/1
Notification	1/1
Regular	
Priority	11/1
Deadline	1/2
Notification	4/1
Nonfall registration?	Yes

FINANCIAL FACTS	
Financial Aid Rating	92
Annual tuition	$51,104
Room and board	$16,312
Required fees	$0
Average frosh need-based scholarship	$40,546
Average UG need-based scholarship	$39,436
% needy frosh rec. need-based scholarship or grant aid	95
% needy UG rec. need-based scholarship or grant aid	96
% needy frosh rec. non-need-based scholarship or grant aid	9
% needy UG rec. non-need-based scholarship or grant aid	15
% needy frosh rec. need-based self-help aid	90
% needy UG rec. need-based self-help aid	82
% frosh rec. any financial aid	46
% UG rec. any financial aid	46
% UG borrow to pay for school	40
Average cumulative indebtedness	$35,013
% frosh need fully met	100
% ugrads need fully met	65
Average % of frosh need met	100
Average % of ugrad need met	98

Barnard College

3009 BROADWAY, NEW YORK, NY 10027 • ADMISSIONS: 212-854-2014 • FINANCIAL AID: 212-854-2154

CAMPUS LIFE

Quality of Life Rating	91
Fire Safety Rating	79
Green Rating	74
Type of school	Private
Environment	Metropolis

STUDENTS

Total undergrad enrollment	2,600
% male/female	0/100
% from out of state	73
% frosh from public high school	50
% frosh live on campus	99
% ugrads live on campus	91
# of sororities	10
% African American	6
% Asian	15
% Caucasian	52
% Hispanic	12
% Native American	<1
% Pacific Islander	<1
% Two or more races	6
% Race and/or ethnicity unknown	<1
% international	9
# of countries represented	66

ACADEMICS

Academic Rating	92
% students returning for sophomore year	95
% students graduating within 4 years	87
% students graduating within 6 years	93
Calendar	Semester
Student/faculty ratio	10:1
Profs interesting rating	88
Profs accessible rating	86
Most classes have 10–19 students.	

MOST POPULAR MAJORS
Economics; Psychology; Political Science;
English; Art History

ABOUT THE SCHOOL

Students of Barnard College say wonderful things about the school, such as "I loved the idea of a small liberal arts college in New York City." "Barnard is a school where students are challenged and given countless opportunities but are given support and guidance from professors, advisors, administrators, and other students to achieve their goals." When asked about her choice, another student tells us, "I wanted to attend a school that had very small classes (two-thirds have nineteen or fewer students), a community, and was still in the heart of New York City, specifically Manhattan, a wonderful island of activity." The academic environment is one where all students are able to find something of value. A sophomore mentions, "Barnard is all about educating young women in the most effective ways to help create the future leaders of the world." A student in her senior year adds, "At Barnard, you are not a face in the crowd. Professors want to get to know their students, even if the class is a larger lecture. The professors are extremely passionate about their specialties and go out of their way to make sure students benefit from their classes. Another added benefit is having access to all of Columbia University's classes."

BANG FOR YOUR BUCK

The value of the school is in the people, the location, and the satisfaction found throughout the years by successful Barnard graduates. One recent graduate tells us, "The school has a strong faculty, outstanding students, fabulous career-development services, a great alumnae network, and an important mission." Barnard College practices need-blind admissions for U.S. citizens and permanent residents, which means that admissions officers are unaware of a student's financial circumstances when evaluating an application or debating an application in committee. Financial need is not considered when considering the qualifications of potential Barnard students. Once accepted, undergraduates have access to many financial-assistance options; also included are study-abroad opportunities for qualified students.

STUDENT LIFE

"Barnard has so many resources for the students to live healthy, academically and socially strong lives," and students praise its "vibrant culture" and long-standing traditions, like Midnight Breakfast "a breakfast buffet served by administrators on the night before finals each semester" and Spirit Day, "a full day of programming each Spring which celebrates everything Barnard." Students also take advantage of Barnard's proximity to Columbia University and its shared resources: "I loved the way Barnard empowers women...and how it's a small school while still having the resources and accessibility of a big university across the street." The school's Manhattan location is also a big draw, with students noting that "in New York City the opportunities are really endless." An added perk is that as a "Barnard or Columbia student you get into almost all of the museums in New York City for free."

CAREER

Barnard's Beyond Barnard area strives to "support all students and alumnae of Barnard College as they define, pursue, and achieve success in their careers and communities." In addition to career fairs held every semester, Barnard also offers the Senior Initiative Program, which the school says "provides graduating seniors with the tools to navigate today's job market in order to prepare for life post-Barnard." Likewise, free Leadership Lab workshops, put on by the Athena Center for Leadership Studies, and the three-year Athena Scholars Program

Barnard College

E-MAIL: ADMISSIONS@BARNARD.EDU 2038 • FAX: 212-854-6220 • WEBSITE: WWW.BARNARD.EDU

engage students to develop their leadership potential. Students note that "internships in finance and publishing are popular" and praise the "strong alumnae network." According to PayScale.com, 57 percent of Barnard graduates report that their jobs are of high social value. The average starting salary for a Barnard graduate is $53,500, with popular jobs including director of a non-profit, research analyst, and marketing director. PayScale.com reports that the most popular majors at Barnard include Economics, Psychology, Political Science, English, and Art History.

GENERAL INFO

Activities: Choral groups, concert band, dance, drama/theater, jazz band, literary magazine, marching band, music ensembles, musical theater, opera, pep band, radio station, student government, student newspaper, student-run film society, symphony orchestra, television station, yearbook, campus ministries. **Organizations:** 100 registered organizations, 1 honor society. **Athletics (Intercollegiate):** Archery, basketball, crew/rowing, cross-country, diving, fencing, field hockey, golf, lacrosse, soccer, softball, swimming, tennis, track/field (outdoor), volleyball. **On-Campus Highlights:** Diana Center Art Gallery, Arthur Ross Greenhouse, Held Auditorium, Milstein Center for Teaching and Learning with a Digital Humanities Center, Design Center, Movement Lab, Computational Science Center and Empirical Reasoning Center, Liz's Place Cafe.

FINANCIAL AID

Students should submit: CSS Profile; FAFSA; Noncustodial PROFILE; State aid form. Regular filing deadline is 3/1. The Princeton Review suggests that all financial aid forms be submitted as soon as possible after October 1. *Need-based scholarships/grants offered:* College/university scholarship or grant aid from institutional funds, Federal Pell, private scholarships, SEOG, state scholarships/grants. *Loan aid offered:* Direct PLUS Loans, Direct Subsidized Loans, Direct Unsubsidized Loans. Applicants will be notified of awards on or about 3/31. Federal Work-Study Program available. Institutional employment available.

BOTTOM LINE

An education as valuable as one from Barnard College does not come without its costs; yearly tuition is $53,252. With fees and room and board totaling $19,005 (not to mention books, supplies, and other personal expenses), students are making a substantial investment. Forty-eight percent of all students benefit from some form of financial aid. Over 40 percent of recent graduates needed to pay for school, and, on average, graduate with a cumulative debt of federal loans of $17,233—extremely reasonable given the cost of attending the college.

CAREER INFORMATION FROM PAYSCALE.COM	
ROI Rating	90
Bachelors and No Higher	
Median starting salary	$56,800
Median mid-career salary	$108,300
At Least Bachelors	
Median starting salary	$58,800
Median mid-career salary	$113,800
Alumni with high job meaning	55%
Degrees awarded in STEM subjects	19%

SELECTIVITY	
Admissions Rating	98
# of applicants	7,716
% of applicants accepted	15
% of acceptees attending	51
# offered a place on the wait list	1,703
% accepting a place on wait list	72
% admitted from wait list	4
# of early decision applicants	934
% accepted early decision	31

FRESHMAN PROFILE	
Range SAT EBRW	660–760
Range SAT Math	650–740
Range ACT Composite	30–33
Minimum paper TOEFL	600
Minimum internet-based TOEFL	100
Average HS GPA	4.0
% graduated top 10% of class	84
% graduated top 25% of class	93
% graduated top 50% of class	100

DEADLINES	
Early decision	
Deadline	11/1
Notification	12/15
Regular	
Deadline	1/1
Notification	4/1
Nonfall registration?	No

FINANCIAL FACTS	
Financial Aid Rating	95
Annual tuition	$53,252
Room and board	$19,005
Required fees	$1,780
% frosh rec. any financial aid	44
% UG rec. any financial aid	41
Average % of frosh need met	100
Average % of ugrad need met	100

Bates College

23 Campus Avenue, Lindholm House, Lewiston, ME 04240 • Admissions: 207-786-6000 • Fax: 207-786-6025

#49 BEST VALUE COLLEGE

CAMPUS LIFE	
Quality of Life Rating	91
Fire Safety Rating	98
Green Rating	97
Type of school	Private
Environment	Town

STUDENTS

Total undergrad enrollment	1,787
% male/female	49/51
% frosh from public high school	53
% frosh live on campus	100
# of fraternities (% ugrad men join)	0 (0)
# of sororities (% ugrad women join)	0 (0)
% African American	5
% Asian	4
% Caucasian	70
% Hispanic	9
% Native American	<1
% Pacific Islander	<1
% Two or more races	5
% Race and/or ethnicity unknown	<1
% international	7
# of countries represented	71

ACADEMICS

Academic Rating	93
% students returning for sophomore year	95
% students graduating within 4 years	89
% students graduating within 6 years	92
Calendar	4/4/2
Student/faculty ratio	10:1
Profs interesting rating	93
Profs accessible rating	94
Most classes have fewer than 10 students.	

MOST POPULAR MAJORS

Psychology; Political Science and Government; History

ABOUT THE SCHOOL

Bates was founded in 1855, more than 150 years ago, by people who believed strongly in freedom, civil rights, and the importance of a higher education for all who could benefit from it. Bates is devoted to undergraduates in the arts and science, and commitment to teaching excellence is central to the college's mission. The college is recognized for its inclusive social character; there are no fraternities or sororities, and student organizations are open to all. Bates College has stood firmly for the ideals of academic rigor, intellectual curiosity, egalitarianism, social justice, and freedom since its founding just before the Civil War. "The willingness of everyone to hear differing viewpoints and opinions even if they disagree" is very attractive to one student. Another is impressed that "Bates is an institution that challenges me to critically think in a way I never have before." Students who can demonstrate the intellectual soundness and potential value of an initiative—whether it's for a senior thesis project, a performance, or an independent study—will receive every possible backing from the college. And one enrollee is very pleased to find that "you will not find it hard to gain access to resources." Bates has long understood that the privilege of education carries with it responsibility to others. Commitment to social action and the environment is something students here take seriously. Learning at Bates is connected to action and to others beyond the self. Bates faculty routinely incorporate service-learning into their courses, and about half of students take part in community-based projects in the Lewiston-Auburn region.

BANG FOR YOUR BUCK

With 200 instructors at the school, those students fortunate enough to actually enroll can expect to find an outstanding student-to-faculty ratio of 10:1. More than 90 percent of freshmen return as sophomores and just a few percent less graduate within four years. Diversity is paramount at Bates; 89 percent of students are from out-of-state, and fifty-five different countries are represented on campus—extremely impressive for such a small institution. Internships and experiential learning opportunities are heavily encouraged; through the Purposeful Work Internship program, for example, students explore the world of work throughout their four years. Ninety-eight percent of students complete a senior thesis and the other 2 percent complete a capstone project. More than two-thirds of alumni enroll in graduate study within ten years. Bates highly values its study-abroad programs, unique calendar (4-4-1), and the many opportunities available for one-on-one collaboration with faculty. "The size of the student body allows for a relationship beyond that of typical professor-student and creates a sense of academic equality that produces incredible levels of scholarship at the undergraduate level."

STUDENT LIFE

Bates undergrads promise you'll never have a dull moment on this campus. A lot of the fun can be attributed to the industrious "Student Activities Office, [which] puts on a tremendous [number] of exciting events/shows/trips for students to participate in." For example, they sponsored "the Snoop Dog concert last year, D.E.A.P. ('drop everything and play') concert in May, [the] weekly 'Village Club Series' concerts where up-and-coming artists perform café-style shows [and] the annual Winter Carnival in January." There are also nearly 100 student-run clubs to join, ranging "from Chess Club to Environmental Club to the DJ Society and, of course, the champion debating society." Additionally, you'll find "wild dances with all different themes, as well as crazy traditions like the puddle jump."

Bates College

FINANCIAL AID: 207-786-6096 • WEBSITE: WWW.BATES.EDU

And, of course, the minute that first snow fall hits, plenty of Batesies will head to the slopes to ski and/or snowboard.

CAREER

Bates' tremendous Career Development Center really helps undergrads plot their post-collegiate life. To begin with, the office provides the standard workshops in resume building, cover letter writing and interviewing techniques. Students can also participate in a new, short-term job shadowing program that offers both career insight and networking opportunities. Additionally, undergrads have access to JobCat, an exclusive Bates-only site that gives them the opportunity to browse a number of job postings/openings. Batesies looking to continue their education can attend the office's annual graduate and professional school fair. This event usually brings around 100 admissions representatives to campus. And, of course, the Career Development Center invites numerous employers (from various industries) to campus each year to conduct interviews and information sessions. Finally, recent graduates have managed to nab jobs with companies such as Sony Music Entertainment, Boston Consulting Group, GoldmanSachs, The Metropolitan Museum of Art, High Mountain Institute, and Trapeze School New York.

GENERAL INFO

Activities: Choral groups, dance, drama/theater, jazz band, literary magazine, music ensembles, pep band, radio station, student government, student newspaper, student-run film society, symphony orchestra, yearbook, campus ministries, international student organization. **Organizations:** 99 registered organizations, 3 honor societies, 9 religious organizations.

FINANCIAL AID

Students should submit: CSS Profile; FAFSA; Noncustodial PROFILE. Regular filing deadline is 2/1. The Princeton Review suggests that all financial aid forms be submitted as soon as possible after October 1. *Need-based scholarships/grants offered:* College/university scholarship or grant aid from institutional funds, Federal Pell, private scholarships, SEOG, state scholarships/grants. *Loan aid offered:* Direct PLUS Loans, Direct Subsidized Loans, Direct Unsubsidized Loans. Applicants will be notified of awards on or about 4/1. Federal Work-Study Program available. Institutional employment available.

BOTTOM LINE

The education that one receives at an institution like Bates College does not come without a price. The total cost of tuition, room, board, and fees comes to $64,500. But, have no fear, students and parents: on average Bates College also meets 100 percent of need. The average total need-based scholarship is a whopping $41,478. Forty-two percent of all undergrads receive financial aid. The average graduate can expect to leave school with about $22,845 of loan debt. Additionally, scholarships and grants are plentiful, for international as well as domestic students. One student was excited that Bates "provided me the greatest amount of financial aid. It was very generous."

CAREER INFORMATION FROM PAYSCALE.COM	
ROI Rating	92
Bachelors and No Higher	
Median starting salary	$57,500
Median mid-career salary	$120,300
At Least Bachelors	
Median starting salary	$59,500
Median mid-career salary	$123,200
Alumni with high job meaning	51%
Degrees awarded in STEM subjects	23%

SELECTIVITY	
Admissions Rating	96
# of applicants	5,316
% of applicants accepted	22
% of acceptees attending	42
# offered a place on the wait list	1,640
% accepting a place on wait list	47
% admitted from wait list	1
# of early decision applicants	721
% accepted early decision	48

FRESHMAN PROFILE	
Range SAT EBRW	640–730
Range SAT Math	630–720
Range ACT Composite	29–32
% graduated top 10% of class	63
% graduated top 25% of class	86
% graduated top 50% of class	97

DEADLINES	
Early decision	
Deadline	11/15
Notification	12/20
Other ED Deadline	1/1
Other ED Notification	2/15
Regular	
Deadline	1/1
Notification	4/1

FINANCIAL FACTS	
Financial Aid Rating	96
Annual tuition	$50,310
Room and board	$14,190
Required fees	
Average frosh need-based scholarship	$44,063
Average UG need-based scholarship	$42,804
% needy frosh rec. need-based scholarship or grant aid	100
% needy UG rec. need-based scholarship or grant aid	100
% needy frosh rec. non-need-based scholarship or grant aid	0
% needy UG rec. non-need-based scholarship or grant aid	0
% needy frosh rec. need-based self-help aid	97
% needy UG rec. need-based self-help aid	99
% frosh rec. any financial aid	42
% UG rec. any financial aid	42
% UG borrow to pay for school	42
Average cumulative indebtedness	$20,715
% frosh need fully met	100
% ugrads need fully met	100
Average % of frosh need met	100
Average % of ugrad need met	100

Baylor University

ONE BEAR PLACE #97056, WACO, TX 76798-7056 • ADMISSIONS: 254-710-3435 • FAX: 254-710-3436

CAMPUS LIFE

Quality of Life Rating	**88**
Fire Safety Rating	**91**
Green Rating	**83**
Type of school	Private
Affiliation	Baptist
Environment	City

STUDENTS

Total undergrad enrollment	14,284
% male/female	41/59
% from out of state	30
% frosh live on campus	99
% ugrads live on campus	35
# of fraternities (% ugrad men join)	17 (18)
# of sororities (% ugrad women join)	21 (33)
% African American	6
% Asian	6
% Caucasian	63
% Hispanic	15
% Native American	<1
% Pacific Islander	<1
% Two or more races	5 %
Race and/or ethnicity unknown	<1
% international	3
# of countries represented	73

ACADEMICS

Academic Rating	**88**
% students returning for sophomore year	90
% students graduating within 4 years	60
% students graduating within 6 years	77
Calendar	Semester
Student/faculty ratio	14:1
Profs interesting rating	85
Profs accessible rating	86

Most classes have 10–19 students. Most lab/discussion sessions have 10–19 students.

MOST POPULAR MAJORS

Biology/Biological Sciences; Registered Nursing; Accounting

ABOUT THE SCHOOL

Texas' Baylor University integrates academics and commitment to a Christian community through excellence in teaching, cutting edge research, and a mission of service, as exhibited in the more than 150,000 hours of local community service performed by Baylor faculty, staff, and students annually. Baylor drives its nearly 15,000 undergraduates "to be their very best through discipline and academic rigor," all while balancing the social and spiritual elements of the collegiate experience. Professors are similarly understanding of how loaded with work students can be, and "while they still hold us accountable, they're willing to give us a break every now and then." Baylor "strives to employ the best professors" and it shows: they are "amazing and extremely caring and will go above and beyond to assure your success." From the faculty and staff to each individual student, "it seems like everyone just wants everyone else to be the best possible version of themselves that they can be," according to a student.

BANG FOR YOUR BUCK

The focus here is "academics first, God/religion second, campus-affiliated organizations next, and sports fourth," and Baylor provides resources and opportunities for students to hit all four. The beautiful campus has "superior facilities to most campuses," and Baylor gives incoming students a lot of support though their Campus Living & Learning program, which helps first-years shape ideals, build relationship systems, and achieve personal growth through residential living. There are "plentiful resources," and "there are many academic resources available to struggling students." Students love the dedication to the "very pronounced Christian mission statement," and the fact that "it tries to stick to that as much as possible." "Some universities may have that in name, but don't act on it. Baylor is certainly not in this category," says a student.

STUDENT LIFE

Baylor University students "desire to learn and to make a positive impact in the world," and everyone is "generally very genuine and kind to all people." Sorority and fraternity life is "predominant" throughout the school, so most students have Greek obligations or on- or off-campus jobs to fill some of their non-academic time, but there are "a vast number of clubs for people to participate in" as well. The outdoors is big at Baylor, and the school provides free access to a marina on the Brazos River, where students can "kayak, paddleboard, [and] canoe," and there is also nearby Cameron Park, which is "great for hiking, running, biking, or hammocking." Baylor is "a social school" where everyone hangs out on campus—even the library is fun—and students "like to work hard between Sunday [and] Thursday and make sure they have fun Friday and Saturday." The student population is healthy and so the rec center is often packed in the afternoons and on weekdays.

CAREER

Baylor's Career Services department helps students to achieve "Success Beyond Baylor," and assists in résumés, job recruitment, career fairs, and networking, which is a solid reason why around eighty-six percent of students found a job or started graduate school within ninety days of graduation. The school's great reputation, combined with "a prestigious private school setting," gives students

Baylor University

FINANCIAL AID: 254-710-2611 • E-MAIL: ADMISSIONS@BAYLOR.EDU • WEBSITE: WWW.BAYLOR.EDU

a solid foundation for internships and the professors "all have an open-door policy and will help you find jobs." They "are connected not only to the academic world but also the workforce" and have "knowledge about future jobs and internships." Out of Baylor alumni visiting PayScale.com, 49 percent report that they derive a high level of meaning from their jobs.

GENERAL INFO

Activities: Campus Ministries; Choral groups; Concert band; Dance; Drama/theater; International Student Organization; Jazz band; Literary magazine; Marching band; Model UN; Music ensembles; Musical theater; Opera; Pep band; Radio station; Student government; Student newspaper; Symphony orchestra; Television station; Yearbook 222 registered organizations, 32 honor societies, 11 religious organizations. 22 fraternities, 20 sororities. **Athletics (Intercollegiate):** *Men:* baseball, basketball, cheerleading, cross-country, football, golf, tennis, track/field (outdoor), track/field (indoor). *Women:* basketball, cheerleading, cross-country, equestrian sports, golf, soccer, softball, tennis, track/field (outdoor), track/field (indoor), volleyball. **On-Campus Highlights:** Bear Habitat, Armstrong Browning Library, Baylor Sciences Building, Student Life Center, McLane Stadium.

FINANCIAL AID

Students should submit: FAFSA if seeking federal need-based aid. CSS Profile is required for all Early Decision applicants and those seeking institutional need-based aid. Priority filing deadline is 2/1. The Princeton Review suggests that all financial aid forms be submitted as soon as possible after October 1. *Need-based scholarships/grants offered:* College/university scholarship or grant aid from institutional funds, Federal Pell, private scholarships, SEOG, state scholarships/grants. *Loan aid offered:* Direct PLUS Loans, Direct Subsidized Loans, Direct Unsubsidized Loans. Applicants will be notified of awards on a rolling basis beginning 12/15. Federal Work-Study Program available. Institutional employment available.

CAREER INFORMATION FROM PAYSCALE.COM

ROI Rating	88
Bachelors and No Higher	
Median starting salary	$53,900
Median mid-career salary	$101,800
At Least Bachelors	
Median starting salary	$55,300
Median mid-career salary	$105,500
Alumni with high job meaning	50%
Degrees awarded in STEM subjects	16%

SELECTIVITY

Admissions Rating	91
# of applicants	37,083
% of applicants accepted	39
% of acceptees attending	23
# offered a place on the wait list	7,558
% accepting a place on wait list	19
% admitted from wait list	92

FRESHMAN PROFILE

Range SAT EBRW	600–680
Range SAT Math	590–680
Range ACT Composite	26–31
Minimum paper TOEFL	540
Minimum internet-based TOEFL	76
% graduated top 10% of class	44
% graduated top 25% of class	75
% graduated top 50% of class	96

DEADLINES

Early decision	
Notification	11/1
Other ED Notification	12/15
Early action	
Deadline	11/1
Notification	1/15
Regular	
Deadline	4/10
Nonfall registration?	Yes

FINANCIAL FACTS

Financial Aid Rating	82
Annual tuition	$41,194
Room and board	$7,800
Required fees	$4,348
Books and supplies	$1,230
Average frosh need-based scholarship	$27,714
Average UG need-based scholarship	$24,420
% needy frosh rec. need-based scholarship or grant aid	100
% needy UG rec. need-based scholarship or grant aid	97
% needy frosh rec. non-need-based scholarship or grant aid	98
% needy UG rec. non-need-based scholarship or grant aid	94
% needy frosh rec. need-based self-help aid	85
% needy UG rec. need-based self-help aid	83
% UG borrow to pay for school	52
Average cumulative indebtedness	$44,859
% frosh need fully met	15
% ugrads need fully met	15
Average % of frosh need met	72
Average % of ugrad need met	67

Beloit College

700 COLLEGE STREET, BELOIT, WI 53511 • ADMISSIONS: 608-363-2500 • FAX: 608-363-2075

CAMPUS LIFE

Quality of Life Rating	85
Fire Safety Rating	85
Green Rating	78
Type of school	Private
Environment	Town

STUDENTS

Total undergrad enrollment	1,324
% male/female	48/52
% from out of state	85
% frosh from public high school	75
% frosh live on campus	98
% ugrads live on campus	88
# of fraternities	3
# of sororities	3
% African American	7
% Asian	3
% Caucasian	56
% Hispanic	10
% Native American	<1
% Pacific Islander	<1
% Two or more races	4
% Race and/or ethnicity unknown	4
% international	15
# of countries represented	28

ACADEMICS

Academic Rating	89
% students returning for sophomore year	85
% students graduating within 4 years	75
% students graduating within 6 years	86
Calendar	Semester
Student/faculty ratio	11:1
Profs interesting rating	95
Profs accessible rating	90

Most classes have fewer than 10 students.
Most lab/discussion sessions have fewer than 10 students.

MOST POPULAR MAJORS

Health And Society; Psychology; Anthropology

ABOUT THE SCHOOL

Wisconsin's Beloit College is a small liberal arts school, offering its 1,300 undergraduates a true liberal arts curriculum via more than fifty majors and thirty minors; if none of these appeal to a student, they can create their own. All students complete a "Liberal Arts in Practice" requirement before they graduate, in which they apply their knowledge through hands-on experiences like internships, research-related fieldwork, or community engagement projects; understandably, faculty "strongly support study abroad and experiential learning programs." Professors "are accessible night and day" and are "excellent mentors" who "work hard to put together classes that are meaningful and interesting." They are "very creative with their lesson plans" and "will go out of their way for their students to have a better educational experience." Classes are usually discussion-oriented, and students have "a lot of freedom and openness to try what they want" in this welcoming community. To top it off, the courses offered at Beloit are "unique and interesting," and subjects such as "the history of rock and roll," "artificial intelligence in fact and fiction," "the human animal," and "the works of J.R.R. Tolkien" prompt in-depth discussions about society and culture and spark creativity and abstract thinking.

BANG FOR YOUR BUCK

The school has several distinctive offerings, including two museums ("wonderful resources for research"); renowned international programs; several residencies that bring luminaries and award winners to campus to teach for several weeks; as well as "so many" support programs, such as "free tutoring and free counseling for any and every subject." The small class sizes and the relationships made with professors are "incomparable," and the financial aid is beyond generous: "It seems as if they want you to come to this college with all the money that they throw at you." Many students find friendships with their professors and can speak frankly about their fears and challenges, which "allows professors the ability to provide the support students need to find success at Beloit."

STUDENT LIFE

"If you're bored at Beloit, there's something wrong with you." This is an "aggressively creative place," and the community "puts a lot of emphasis on making leisure time productive." The theatre programs are top notch, and student congress "devotes incredible time and effort to make sure there are fun and cultural events going on quite literally every day." There is a "really and truly" incredible community here, and the campus special interest housing is second to none. Students can live in "amazingly diverse sorts of learning communities, from [the] sexuality and gender alliance house, to [the] Beloit science fiction and fantasy club." There are "tons of clubs, ample Greek life, sports, and student government" as well as students who are always ready to join them, with "nerds, jocks, musicians, artists, rebels, and average joes…all there co-mingling."

Beloit College

FINANCIAL AID: 608-363-2663 • E-MAIL: ADMISS@BELOIT.EDU • WEBSITE: WWW.BELOIT.EDU

CAREER

Beloit allows students to explore all outlets of opportunity during their college career via the liberal arts curriculum structure, and the school itself "provides endless opportunities." The school has a three-story, storefront student business incubator located downtown, and there are a "vast amount of internship and community involvement opportunities" and funding to match, which is part of the reason why more than ninety-three percent of Beloit students are employed or in graduate school within six months of graduation. Beloit is about "taking the idea of a liberal arts education and transferring it into a fun and usable state for modern society." According to Beloit alumni visiting PayScale.com, sixty-one percent report that they derive a high level of meaning from their jobs.

GENERAL INFO

Activities: Campus Ministries; Choral groups; Dance; Drama/theater; International Student Organization; Jazz band; Literary magazine; Model UN; Music ensembles; Musical theater; Radio station; Student government; Student newspaper; Television station 50+ registered organizations, 6 honor societies, 3 religious organizations. 3 fraternities, 3 sororities. **Athletics (Intercollegiate):** *Men:* baseball, basketball, cross-country, football, golf, soccer, swimming, tennis, track/field (outdoor), track/field (indoor). *Women:* basketball, cross-country, soccer, softball, swimming, tennis, track/field (outdoor), track/field (indoor), volleyball. **On-Campus Highlights:** Logan Museum of Anthropology, Wright Museum of Art, Sanger Center for the Sciences, Hendricks Center for the Performing Arts, Laura H. Aldrich Neese Theatre Complex.

FINANCIAL AID

Students should submit: FAFSA. The Princeton Review suggests that all financial aid forms be submitted as soon as possible after October 1; students who submit their FAFSAs to Beloit by the time of their chosen admission plan deadline will receive a financial aid package one month after their admission decision. The preferred financial aid deadline is March 1. *Need-based scholarships/grants offered:* College/university scholarship or grant aid from institutional funds, Federal Pell, private scholarships, SEOG, state scholarships/grants. *Loan aid offered:* Direct PLUS Loans, Direct Subsidized Loans, Direct Unsubsidized Loans. Federal Work-Study Program available. Institutional employment available.

CAREER INFORMATION FROM PAYSCALE.COM

ROI Rating	88
Bachelors and No Higher	
Median starting salary	$46,500
Median mid-career salary	$85,100
At Least Bachelors	
Median starting salary	$48,900
Median mid-career salary	$89,200
Alumni with high job meaning	58%
Degrees awarded in STEM subjects	20%

SELECTIVITY

Admissions Rating	86
# of applicants	5,400
% of applicants accepted	54
% of acceptees attending	11
# offered a place on the wait list	25
% accepting a place on wait list	60
% admitted from wait list	20
# of early decision applicants	140
% accepted early decision	20

FRESHMAN PROFILE

Range SAT EBRW	510–650
Range SAT Math	530–660
Range ACT Composite	24–30
Minimum paper TOEFL	550
Minimum internet-based TOEFL	80
Average HS GPA	3.3
% graduated top 10% of class	30
% graduated top 25% of class	57
% graduated top 50% of class	92

DEADLINES

Early decision	
Deadline	11/1
Notification	12/1
Other ED Deadline	1/15
Other ED Notification	2/15
Early action	
Deadline	12/1
Notification	1/1
Regular	
Priority	1/15
Notification	4/1
Nonfall registration?	Yes

FINANCIAL FACTS

Financial Aid Rating	91
Annual tuition	$49,564
Room and board	$8,830
Required fees	$476
Books and supplies	$1,400
Average frosh need-based scholarship	$32,586
Average UG need-based scholarship	$30,133
% needy frosh rec. need-based scholarship or grant aid	97
% needy UG rec. need-based scholarship or grant aid	98
% needy frosh rec. non-need-based scholarship or grant aid	51
% needy UG rec. non-need-based scholarship or grant aid	52
% needy frosh rec. need-based self-help aid	83
% needy UG rec. need-based self-help aid	79
% frosh rec. any financial aid	99
% UG rec. any financial aid	99

Bentley University

175 Forest Street, Waltham, MA 02452 • Admissions: 781-891-2244 • Fax: 781-891-3414

CAMPUS LIFE

Quality of Life Rating	**90**
Fire Safety Rating	**99**
Green Rating	**97**
Type of school	Private
Environment	Town

STUDENTS

Total undergrad enrollment	4,272
% male/female	59/41
% from out of state	58
% frosh from public high school	67
% frosh live on campus	99
% ugrads live on campus	78
# of fraternities (% ugrad men join)	8 (16)
# of sororities (% ugrad women join)	3 (19)
% African American	3
% Asian	8
% Caucasian	61
% Hispanic	7
% Native American	0
% Pacific Islander	<1
% Two or more races	2
% Race and/or ethnicity unknown	4
% international	15
# of countries represented	71

ACADEMICS

Academic Rating	**84**
% students returning for sophomore year	92
% students graduating within 4 years	87
% students graduating within 6 years	91
Calendar	Semester
Student/faculty ratio	11:1
Profs interesting rating	87
Profs accessible rating	85

Most classes have 20–29 students. Most lab/discussion sessions have 20–29 students.

MOST POPULAR MAJORS

Accounting; Finance; Business, Management,Marketing, and Related Support Services

ABOUT THE SCHOOL

A small, private institution located in the greater Boston, Massachusetts area, Bentley University is, according to one student, all about "crafting young professionals into the future business leaders of the world." Armed with a curriculum that blends liberal arts with a business education, the 4,200 undergraduates on this gorgeous, classic college campus tend to be "well-dressed and ambitious people," who "have a clear vision of what they want to do in the future," reports one student. Class sizes are small and the faculty, for the most part, strive to be supportive. Not only do most have "extensive work experience in their field," but many are described as "not only accessible but willing to go out of their way to provide further assistance beyond the classroom." With a top-notch academic library and well-liked residential and recreation facilities, Bentley is a place where students are united in "their strong work ethic and desire to be successful no matter what."

BANG FOR YOUR BUCK

While Bentley is a private school that some call "pricey," there are, according to one student, "plenty of resources for students" trying to pay for it, including "incredible financial aid." More than 70 percent of students receive help covering costs through scholarships or grants. Students who enter with a demonstrated track record of success are automatically eligible for merit-based scholarships, and, to promote gender inclusivity, the Women's Leadership Program provides awards to incoming women who have "demonstrated leadership potential while in high school." Contrary to external perceptions about Bentley, as one student puts it, "Not all students here are wealthy… [and] there is still a huge amount of financial aid for those who need it."

STUDENT LIFE

While, for some, the singular, business focus at Bentley detracts from social life on campus, other students note "the student body…is very friendly and not as competitive as one would think…There is respect that we are all trying to reach a common goal." While studying takes up a great deal of time, students relax by taking part in "intramural sports like dodgeball or soccer" notes one undergrad, and "there are a lot of clubs on campus like Campus Activities Board, Bentley Consulting Group, or College Kindness" that create a thriving on-campus culture. With over 100 student-run clubs and organizations on campus, varsity sports, as well as several fraternities and sororities, there's no shortage of opportunities to meet people and network because "everyone lives on campus all four years so your friends are always nearby."

Bentley University

FINANCIAL AID: 781-891-3441 • E-MAIL: UGADMISSION@BENTLEY.EDU • WEBSITE: WWW.BENTLEY.EDU

CAREER

Through internships, student activities, and countless opportunities to network, Bentley does a lot to serve its "motivated students seeking high quality business education." On average, the starting salary of a graduate is an impressive $62,900 per year, according to PayScale.com, with 36 percent of them noting that their work has high meaning to them. Given that this is a business-oriented school, most students feel particularly supported by a Career Services Office that "does a great job in placing in internships as well as full-time jobs." Bentley is an institution that, as one student puts it, "is all about knowing what the business world wants" and "sets out to create the best for its students" as they step into the professional world.

GENERAL INFO

Activities: Academic Groups, debating club, international student groups, literary magazine, music ensembles, radio station, student government, student film society, student newspaper, television station, campus ministries, Model UN. **Organizations:** 110 registered organizations, 4 honor societies, 5 religious organizations. 8 fraternities, 3 sororities. **Athletics (Intercollegiate):** *Men:* baseball, basketball, cross-country, diving, football, golf, ice hockey, lacrosse, soccer, swimming, tennis, track/field (outdoor), track/field (indoor). *Women:* basketball, cross-country, diving, field hockey, lacrosse, soccer, softball, swimming, tennis, track/field (outdoor), track/field (indoor), volleyball. **On-Campus Highlights:** Student center, Dana Athletic Center, Library, green space, and currito burrito.

FINANCIAL AID

Students should submit: Business/Farm Supplement; CSS Profile; FAFSA; Noncustodial PROFILE. Students must also submit Federal Tax Returns, including all schedules for parents and student. Regular filing deadline is 1/7. The Princeton Review suggests that all financial aid forms be submitted as soon as possible after October 1. *Need-based scholarships/grants offered:* College/university scholarship or grant aid from institutional funds, Federal Pell, private scholarships, SEOG, state scholarships/grants. *Loan aid offered:* Direct PLUS Loans, Direct Subsidized Loans, Direct Unsubsidized Loans, State Loans. Applicants will be notified of awards on or about 3/31. Federal Work-Study Program available. Institutional employment available.

BOTTOM LINE

Tuition at Bentley University is $48,180 per year, with on-campus housing and dining services adding an additional $16,320. Don't forget to budget for additional costs, such as for books and supplies, which runs about $1,290 an academic year. The technology fee and student activities fee amounts to $1,700 when lumped together..

CAREER INFORMATION FROM PAYSCALE.COM	
ROI Rating	89
Bachelors and No Higher	
Median starting salary	$64,600
Median mid-career salary	$116,100
At Least Bachelors	
Median starting salary	$65,600
Median mid-career salary	$120,600
Alumni with high job meaning	36%
Degrees awarded in STEM subjects	7%

SELECTIVITY	
Admissions Rating	90
# of applicants	8,867
% of applicants accepted	44
% of acceptees attending	26
# offered a place on the wait list	2,082
% accepting a place on wait list	33
% admitted from wait list	0
# of early decision applicants	313
% accepted early decision	66

FRESHMAN PROFILE	
Range SAT EBRW	590–670
Range SAT Math	620–710
Range ACT Composite	27–31
Minimum paper TOEFL	577
Minimum internet-based TOEFL	90
% graduated top 10% of class	34
% graduated top 25% of class	74
% graduated top 50% of class	94

DEADLINES	
Early decision	
Deadline	11/15
Notification	Late Dec
Regular	
Deadline	1/7
Notification	Late March
Nonfall registration?	Yes

FINANCIAL FACTS	
Financial Aid Rating	89
Annual tuition	$48,180
Room and board	$16,320
Required fees	$1,700
Books and supplies	$1,290
Average frosh need-based scholarship	$31,621
Average UG need-based scholarship	$31,187
% needy frosh rec. need-based scholarship or grant aid	99
% needy UG rec. need-based scholarship or grant aid	99
% needy frosh rec. non-need-based scholarship or grant aid	20
% needy UG rec. non-need-based scholarship or grant aid	14
% needy frosh rec. need-based self-help aid	92
% needy UG rec. need-based self-help aid	95
% frosh rec. any financial aid	75
% UG rec. any financial aid	70
% UG borrow to pay for school	54
Average cumulative indebtedness	$31,889
% frosh need fully met	41
% ugrads need fully met	39
Average % of frosh need met	93
Average % of ugrad need met	93

Boston College

140 COMMONWEALTH AVENUE, DEVLIN HALL 208, CHESTNUT HILL, MA 02467-3809 • ADMISSIONS: 617-552-3100

CAMPUS LIFE

Quality of Life Rating	88
Fire Safety Rating	98
Green Rating	76
Type of school	Private
Affiliation	Roman Catholic
Environment	City

STUDENTS

Total undergrad enrollment	9,358
% male/female	47/53
% from out of state	74
% frosh from public high school	48
% frosh live on campus	100
% ugrads live on campus	84
# of fraternities (% ugrad men join)	0 (0)
# of sororities (% ugrad women join)	0 (0)
% African American	4
% Asian	10
% Caucasian	62
% Hispanic	11
% Native American	<1
% Pacific Islander	<1
% Two or more races	3
% Race and/or ethnicity unknown	4
% international	7
# of countries represented	68

ACADEMICS

Academic Rating	84
% students returning for sophomore year	95
% students graduating within 6 years	93
Calendar	Semester
Student/faculty ratio	12:1
Profs interesting rating	82
Profs accessible rating	80
Most classes have 10–19 students.	

MOST POPULAR MAJORS
Communication and Media Studies;
Economics; Finance

ABOUT THE SCHOOL

Boston, one of the finest college towns in the United States, is home to some of the most prestigious institutions of higher learning around. Boston College shoulders this pedigree effortlessly. Within a rich and challenging environment, while promoting "Jesuit ideals in the modern age," the school offers a rigorous and enlightening education. A student says, "Upon my first visit I knew this was the place for me." Students benefit greatly from Boston College's location just outside of downtown Boston, which affords them internship, service-learning, and career opportunities that give them world-class, real-world experiences before they graduate. In addition, Boston College has an excellent career-services office that works in concert with BC's renowned network of more than 175,000 alumni to assist students in career placement. Unique Jesuit-inspired service and academic reflection in core courses develop teamwork and analytical-thinking skills. Many students are amazed at their own development: "I have never been so challenged and motivated to learn in my life." "I leave virtually every class with useful knowledge and new opinions."

BANG FOR YOUR BUCK

Boston College is one of a very few elite private universities that is strongly committed to admitting students without regard to their family's finances and that also guarantees to meet a student's full demonstrated financial need through to graduation. (That means your aid won't dry up after the heady generosity of freshman year.) For the 2016–2017 school year, Boston College awarded over $147 million in student financial aid, including over $112 million in need-based undergraduate financial aid. In addition, BC offers a highly selective program of merit-based aid that supports selected students from among the top 1 or 2 percent of high school achievers in the country. While Boston College is committed to helping superior students attend with need-based financial aid, it is also highly selective. The college's Presidential Scholars Program, in existence since 1995, selects candidates who are academically exceptional and who exhibit through personal interviews the leadership potential for high achievement at a Jesuit university. In addition to offering four-year, full-tuition scholarships to students, the program offers built-in supports for a wide range of cocurricular opportunities, including summer placements for advanced internships and independent study. The Office of International Programs is extremely helpful in getting students interested in and ready for studying abroad and "encourages a 'citizen of the world' mindset."

STUDENT LIFE

Of Boston College, one student says "being just outside of Boston is a huge draw for BC students. As a student, I often go into the city to hang out, run errands, go to a sporting event, eat, or shop." As for staying on campus, "BC has an awesome sports program that semi-dominates the social scene in the Fall and Winter (football, hockey and basketball seasons) and the school also hosts a variety of weekend events like concerts, student dances and dance/theater shows that many people attend," while another adds, of the school's mission of "men and women for others," "BC doesn't force Catholicism on anyone. Rather, BC simply presents this simple mission of helping one another," and still another says, "Once you've settled in, you'll find that it's not at all difficult to find a group of friends" no matter who you are. Students feel that "Boston College seeks to educate the whole person with an emphasis on giving back to those who are unable to receive such a privileged education." In addition, Boston College's Division I ranking means there are plenty of athletes and sports fans.

Boston College

FAX: 617-552-0798 • FINANCIAL AID: 617-552-3300 • WEBSITE: WWW.BC.EDU

CAREER

The typical Boston College graduate has a median starting salary of $59,200, and 42 percent of graduates feel their jobs make the world a better place. Students feel that Boston College has "an excellent career center," both for current students and alumni, and a "great alumni network." In particular, the alumni network is "very supportive and strong...They really try to help students find internships and jobs." Some students feel that the career center is "really good for students in the business school, but it could be better in helping students in the humanities find internships."

GENERAL INFO

Activities: Choral groups, concert band, dance, drama/theater, jazz band, literary magazine, marching band, music ensembles, musical theater, pep band, radio station, student government, student newspaper, student-run film society, symphony orchestra, television station, yearbook, campus ministries, international student organization. **Organizations:** 225 registered organizations, 12 honor societies, 14 religious organizations. **Athletics (Intercollegiate):** *Men:* Baseball, basketball, cross-country, diving, fencing, football, golf, ice hockey, lacrosse, sailing, skiing (downhill/alpine), soccer, swimming, tennis, track/field (outdoor), track/field (indoor). *Women:* Basketball, crew/rowing, cross-country, diving, fencing, field hockey, golf, ice hockey, lacrosse, sailing, skiing (downhill/alpine), soccer, softball, swimming, tennis, track/field (outdoor), track/field (indoor), volleyball.

FINANCIAL AID

Students should submit: Business/Farm Supplement; CSS Profile; FAFSA; Noncustodial PROFILE. Priority filing deadline is 2/1. The Princeton Review suggests that all financial aid forms be submitted as soon as possible after October 1. Need-based scholarships/grants offered: College/university scholarship or grant aid from institutional funds, Federal Pell, private scholarships, SEOG, state scholarships/grants. Loan aid offered: Direct PLUS Loans, Direct Subsidized Loans, Direct Unsubsidized Loans. Applicants will be notified of awards on or about 4/1. Federal Work-Study Program available. Institutional employment available.

BOTTOM LINE

The sticker price for tuition, fees, room and board, and everything else at Boston College comes to about $69,942 per year. But you don't have to be an old-guard Bostonian to be able to afford to go here. The average need-based financial aid package is $37,894. "Their stellar academics and their generous financial aid were a combination that I couldn't find anywhere else," one grateful student exclaims.

CAREER INFORMATION FROM PAYSCALE.COM	
ROI Rating	88
Bachelors and No Higher	
Median starting salary	$61,600
Median mid-career salary	$117,700
At Least Bachelors	
Median starting salary	$63,300
Median mid-career salary	$121,600
Alumni with high job meaning	43%
Degrees awarded in STEM subjects	13%

SELECTIVITY	
Admissions Rating	95
# of applicants	28,454
% of applicants accepted	32
% of acceptees attending	26
# offered a place on the wait list	6,477
% accepting a place on wait list	59
% admitted from wait list	0

FRESHMAN PROFILE	
Range SAT EBRW	660–760
Range SAT Math	660–730
Range ACT Composite	31–33
Minimum paper TOEFL	600
Minimum internet-based TOEFL	100
% graduated top 10% of class	78
% graduated top 25% of class	95
% graduated top 50% of class	99

DEADLINES	
Early action	
Deadline	11/1
Notification	12/24
Regular	
Deadline	1/1
Notification	4/15
Nonfall registration?	Yes

FINANCIAL FACTS	
Financial Aid Rating	92
Annual tuition	$54,600
Room and board	$14,478
Required fees	$864
Books and supplies	$1,250
Average frosh need-based scholarship	$38,238
Average UG need-based scholarship	$37,716
% needy frosh rec. need-based scholarship or grant aid	91
% needy UG rec. need-based scholarship or grant aid	89
% needy frosh rec. non-need-based scholarship or grant aid	3
% needy UG rec. non-need-based scholarship or grant aid	2
% needy frosh rec. need-based self-help aid	92
% needy UG rec. need-based self-help aid	92
% frosh rec. any financial aid	63
% UG rec. any financial aid	67
% UG borrow to pay for school	50
Average cumulative indebtedness	$20,481
% frosh need fully met	100
% ugrads need fully met	100
Average % of frosh need met	100
Average % of ugrad need met	100

Bowdoin College

5000 COLLEGE STATION, BOWDOIN COLLEGE, BRUNSWICK, ME 04011-8441 • ADMISSIONS: 207-725-3100

#22 BEST VALUE COLLEGE

ABOUT THE SCHOOL

Located in Brunswick, Maine, Bowdoin College prides itself in offering a comprehensive liberal arts education on a picturesque, dynamic campus. With a student population of around 1,800, the school ensures that class sizes are small—the students-to-faculty ratio is an impressive 9:1—and it offers 44 majors in a range of humanities and science disciplines. Students describe themselves as "very academically focused…and genuinely interested in learning at the highest level." Students come to Bowdoin because they genuinely want to be there," notes one current student, and most feel supported by the "strong community" there. The professors are well-liked and have been described as "some of the brightest most understanding people," who are "eager to get to know their students." One student puts it succinctly: "Bowdoin is home to everyone."

BANG FOR YOUR BUCK

Bowdoin strives to make private higher education affordable for its students. The school's financial aid philosophy is summed up as "Meeting Full-Need," meaning that "we subtract your family share from the total cost to attend Bowdoin, and then provide financial aid to cover the difference." "The college provides every resource you could possibly imagine" including "generous financial aid," one student says. Between a well-endowed college grant budget and other sources of funding, an impressive 52 percent of the latest incoming class received need-based aid. In addition, Bowdoin helps students find a range of other scholarship and grant opportunities, and students can also participate in work-study programs. On average, the financial aid award (including school aid and state and federal grants) for incoming students is $47,275. Bowdoin does not require loans in its aid packages. Those who do borrow (about 25 percent of the class) graduate with around $23,000 of loan debt.

STUDENT LIFE

If there's a word that students most often use to describe life on campus, it's "community," and, as one student puts it, "Bowdoin definitely has a more diverse student body than a lot of other liberal arts schools." While most spend a great deal of time studying, "whether it's a sport, or swing dancing, students always are doing something with their time" another says. There are numerous clubs and activities on campus, and one student reports: "Many of the college houses offer programs, such as visiting authors, cheese tastings, or a cappella performances. Outing Club trips are fairly popular as well." In addition, the dining services at the school are very popular, and the campus, itself, allows easy access to Portland (Maine), Boston, as well as to excellent hiking areas. Even with rigorous academics, "there isn't a negative, competitive feeling between the students," one student reports.

Bowdoin College

Fax: 207-725-3101 • Financial Aid: 207-725-3273 • E-mail: admissions@bowdoin.edu • Website: www.bowdoin.edu

CAREER

Between its small class sizes, its rigorous academic environment, and careful attention given to every student, Bowdoin does as much as it can to ensure graduates succeed in the job market. The school's Career Planning Office hooks students up with a range of internships, volunteering opportunities, as well as one-on-one professional counseling sessions. At the core of Bowdoin's career prep commitment is fostering critical thinkers. "I believe my liberal arts education is so valuable because I learned how to learn," says one student, who adds, "I feel prepared for my career." The Bowdoin philosophy pays off—the average starting salary of graduates is $55,500 a year, according to PayScale.com, and 54 percent of alumni report finding high meaning in their work.

GENERAL INFO

Activities: Choral groups, concert band, dance, drama/theater, jazz band, literary magazine, music ensembles, musical theater, radio station, student government, student newspaper, student-run film society, symphony orchestra, television station, yearbook, international student organization. **Organizations:** 109 registered organizations, 1 honor society, 4 religious organizations. **Athletics (Intercollegiate):** *Men:* Baseball, basketball, cross-country, diving, football, golf, ice hockey, lacrosse, sailing, skiing (nordic/cross-country), soccer, squash, swimming, tennis, track/field (outdoor), track/field (indoo). *Women:* Basketball, cross-country, diving, field hockey, golf, ice hockey, lacrosse, rugby, sailing, skiing (nordic/cross-country), soccer, softball, squash, swimming, tennis, track/field (outdoor), track/field (indoor), volleyball.

FINANCIAL AID

Students should submit: Business/Farm Supplement; CSS Profile; FAFSA; Noncustodial PROFILE. Regular filing deadline is 3/15. The Princeton Review suggests that all financial aid forms be submitted as soon as possible after October 1. *Need-based scholarships/grants offered:* College/university scholarship or grant aid from institutional funds, Federal Pell, private scholarships, SEOG, state scholarships/grants. *Loan aid offered:* Direct Subsidized Loans; Direct Unsubsidized Loans. Applicants will be notified of awards on or about 3/25. Federal Work-Study Program available. Institutional employment available.

THE BOTTOM LINE

Tuition for new students at Bowdoin is $53,418 per year, with an additional $504 student activities fee. The on-campus housing and meal plans add another $14,698 to the total, but these amenities are recognized as being some of the best in the nation. After factoring in tuition, fees, and books the annual cost of attendance is roughly 69,460.

CAREER INFORMATION FROM PAYSCALE.COM	
ROI Rating	94
Bachelors and No Higher	
Median starting salary	$59,700
Median mid-career salary	$116,000
At Least Bachelors	
Median starting salary	$62,300
Median mid-career salary	$131,000
Alumni with high job meaning	56%
Degrees awarded in STEM subjects	37%

SELECTIVITY	
Admissions Rating	98
# of applicants	7,251
% of applicants accepted	14
% of acceptees attending	51
# of early decision applicants	870
% accepted early decision	28

FRESHMAN PROFILE	
Range SAT EBRW	650–750
Range SAT Math	640–760
Range ACT Composite	30–34
Minimum paper TOEFL	600
Minimum internet-based TOEFL	100
% graduated top 10% of class	86
% graduated top 25% of class	96
% graduated top 50% of class	100

DEADLINES	
Early decision	
Deadline	11/15
Notification	12/15
Other ED Deadline	1/1
Other ED Notification	2/15
Regular	
Deadline	1/1
Notification	early April
Nonfall registration?	No

FINANCIAL FACTS	
Financial Aid Rating	99
Annual tuition	$53,418
Room and board	$14,698
Required fees	$504
Books and supplies	$840
Average frosh need-based scholarship	$45,625
Average UG need-based scholarship	$44,824
% needy frosh rec. need-based scholarship or grant aid	100
% needy UG rec. need-based scholarship or grant aid	100
% needy frosh rec. non-need-based scholarship or grant aid	0
% needy UG rec. non-need-based scholarship or grant aid	0
% needy frosh rec. need-based self-help aid	91
% needy UG rec. need-based self-help aid	94
% frosh rec. any financial aid	54
% UG rec. any financial aid	48
% UG borrow to pay for school	25
Average cumulative indebtedness	$23,174
% frosh need fully met	100
% ugrads need fully met	100
Average % of frosh need met	100
Average % of ugrad need met	100

Brandeis University

415 South St, MS003, Waltham, MA 02454-9110 • Admissions: 781-736-3500 • Financial Aid: 781-736-3700

CAMPUS LIFE

Quality of Life Rating	87
Fire Safety Rating	98
Green Rating	81
Type of school	Private
Environment	Metropolis

STUDENTS

Total undergrad enrollment	3,635
% male/female	41/59
% from out of state	71
% frosh from public high school	61
% frosh live on campus	99
% ugrads live on campus	75
# of fraternities (% ugrad men join)	0 (0)
# of sororities (% ugrad women join)	0 (0)
% African American	5
% Asian	13
% Caucasian	47
% Hispanic	7
% Native American	<1
% Pacific Islander	<1
% Two or more races	3
% Race and/or ethnicity unknown	3
% international	21
# of countries represented	54

ACADEMICS

Academic Rating	92
% students returning for sophomore year	94
% students graduating within 4 years	83
% students graduating within 6 years	90
Calendar	Semester
Student/faculty ratio	10:1
Profs interesting rating	89
Profs accessible rating	88
Most classes have 10–19 students.	

MOST POPULAR MAJORS

Biology/Biological Sciences; Psychology; Economics

ABOUT THE SCHOOL

Located in the suburbs of Boston, Brandeis University "is both a place where students are directly involved in research and where [they] get a broad, liberal arts education." With an undergraduate enrollment of 3,635, this student-centered university is "small, but with many opportunities." Because Brandeis embraces a policy of academic "flexibility," students feel free "to study whatever they want" with the comfort that there will be an "abundance of undergraduate research opportunities in all majors." One student says "I chose [Brandeis] because of how easy it was to double major and customize my college experience to my interests. It was hard to find a school that would make it so easy to study two very different majors and more." Academics, here, are "well-rounded." "We don't just have one great program. We have incredibly brilliant professors and researchers in all departments at Brandeis who care about helping students learn and succeed." Intangible benefits abound, too. Brandeis attracts passionate students "who tackle some of the world's toughest issues related to social justice." As one student describes it, "Our involvement in creating an open and passionate community that will change the world."

BANG FOR YOUR BUCK

Brandeis offers more than $57 million in funded grants and scholarships to undergraduates. Each year, a select group of students is awarded a Dean, Presidential, or Justice Brandeis Scholarship, that recognizes a student's potential to contribute in the classroom. These scholarship awards range in value from $10,000 to $20,500 annually. There are also interest-based fellowships that give accepted students unique academic opportunities, in addition to a financial award, such as the Quantitative Biology Research Community fellowship for excellence within the sciences and the Humanities Fellowship for intellectually promising students with interest in the humanities. One student says "An amazing thing about this school is the amount of opportunities this school has in terms of grants, internships, work study, leadership roles, clubs, abroad trips, community services, you name it we have it!"

STUDENT LIFE

"Brandeis students have incredible pride and love for this community that we've built." Student say there is "an insane number of clubs and extracurriculars"—over 250 student-run organizations—"from music groups to improv to cultural organizations and academic-based clubs." "Our student body is very proactive and we stand up for what we believe in," says one student, and another notes that Waltham Group, "our community service organization, is the biggest group on campus." Overall, one student explains, "There is no normal Brandeis. I love that I can wear whatever I want because I know there's nowhere where it will be a problem that I don't fit in or feel judged. Everyone's attitude is kind of 'do whatever you want to/need to do.'"

CAREER

Hiatt Career Center at Brandeis is a full service career center for undergraduate students and alumni for life. They work with students and alumni to develop career skills and strategies that develop and harness adaptability, creativity, entrepreneurship, and resiliency to be successful in an ever-changing professional world. Hiatt partners with over 8,000 local, national and international, non-profit and for profit organizations in diverse industries to create opportunities for Brandeis students. They offer position postings, industry meetups, job treks, company information sessions, employer spotlights, on-campus interviews and career fairs. Brandeis is also generous with funding for internship experiences. For example, The World of Work fellowship program awards approximately forty stipends annually to

Brandeis University

E-MAIL: ADMISSIONS@BRANDEIS.EDU • FAX: 781-736-3536 • WEBSITE: WWW.BRANDEIS.EDU

undergraduates who pursue summer internships with organizations that are unable to provide a salary. Brandeis alumni who visited PayScale.com reported an average starting salary of $55,300 and an average mid-career salary of $114,200.

GENERAL INFO

Activities: Choral groups, concert band, dance, drama/theater, jazz band, literary magazine, music ensembles, musical theater, radio station, student government, student newspaper, student-run film society, symphony orchestra, television station, yearbook, campus ministries, international student organization. **Organizations:** 253 registered organizations, 17 intercultural organizations, 4 honor societies, 19 religious organizations. **Athletics (Intercollegiate):** *Men:* Baseball, basketball, cross-country, swimming & diving, fencing, soccer, tennis, track/field (outdoor), track/field (indoor). *Women:* Basketball, cheerleading, cross-country, swimming & diving, fencing, soccer, softball, tennis, track/field (outdoor), track/field (indoor), volleyball. **On-Campus Highlights:** Shapiro Science Center, Spingold Theater, Shapiro Campus Center, Rapaporte Treasure Hall. **Environmental Initiatives:** The Brandeis University Climate Action Plan has aggressive goals for future energy and climate impact reductions. Brandeis has invested significantly in energy reduction efforts.

FINANCIAL AID

Students should submit: CSS Profile; FAFSA; Noncustodial PROFILE. Regular filing deadline is 1/1. The Princeton Review suggests that all financial aid forms be submitted as soon as possible after October 1. *Need-based scholarships/grants offered:* College/university scholarship or grant aid from institutional funds, Federal Pell, private scholarships, SEOG, state scholarships/grants. *Loan aid offered:* Direct PLUS Loans, Direct Subsidized Loans, Direct Unsubsidized Loans. Applicants will be notified of awards on or about 4/1. Federal Work-Study Program available. Institutional employment available.

BOTTOM LINE

Tuition at Brandeis comes to $53,260 with an additional $1,780 for required fees. There are also cost of living expenses to budget for: $15,440 for on-campus room and board and an estimated $1,000 for books and supplies. Undergraduate students with need receive an average gift aid package of $39,606.

CAREER INFORMATION FROM PAYSCALE.COM	
ROI Rating	90
Bachelors and No Higher	
Median starting salary	$58,000
Median mid-career salary	$118,400
At Least Bachelors	
Median starting salary	$60,000
Median mid-career salary	$121,000
Alumni with high job meaning	47%
Degrees awarded in STEM subjects	29%

SELECTIVITY	
Admissions Rating	**96**
# of applicants	11,721
% of applicants accepted	34
% of acceptees attending	21
# offered a place on the wait list	1,826
% accepting a place on wait list	37
% admitted from wait list	1
# of early decision applicants	786
% accepted early decision	41

FRESHMAN PROFILE	
Range SAT EBRW	630–710
Range SAT Math	650–760
Range ACT Composite	29–33
Minimum paper TOEFL	600
Minimum internet-based TOEFL	100
Average HS GPA	3.9
% graduated top 10% of class	65
% graduated top 25% of class	90
% graduated top 50% of class	99

DEADLINES	
Early decision	
Deadline	11/1
Notification	12/15
Other ED Deadline	1/1
Other ED Notification	2/1
Regular	
Deadline	1/1
Notification	4/1
Nonfall registration?	Yes

FINANCIAL FACTS	
Financial Aid Rating	**92**
Annual tuition	$53,260
Room and board	$15,440
Required fees	$1,780
Average frosh need-based scholarship	$41,854
Average UG need-based scholarship	$39,606
% needy frosh rec. need-based scholarship or grant aid	98
% needy UG rec. need-based scholarship or grant aid	96
% needy frosh rec. non-need-based scholarship or grant aid	11
% needy UG rec. non-need-based scholarship or grant aid	9
% needy frosh rec. need-based self-help aid	87
% needy UG rec. need-based self-help aid	89
% frosh rec. any financial aid	63
% UG rec. any financial aid	58
% UG borrow to pay for school	54
Average cumulative indebtedness	$33,522
% frosh need fully met	94
% ugrads need fully met	71

Brigham Young Universit

A-153 ASB, Provo, UT 84602-1110 • Admissions: 801-422-2507 • Fax: 801-422-0005

#31 BEST VALUE COLLEGE

CAMPUS LIFE

Quality of Life Rating	89
Fire Safety Rating	76
Green Rating	60*
Type of school	Private
Affiliation	Church of Jesus Christ of Latter-day Saints
Environment	City

STUDENTS

Total undergrad enrollment	31,233
% male/female	51/49
% from out of state	64
% frosh live on campus	70
% ugrads live on campus	19
# of fraternities (% ugrad men join)	0 (0)
# of sororities (% ugrad women join)	0 (0)
% African American	1
% Asian	2
% Caucasian	82
% Hispanic	6
% Native American	<1
% Pacific Islander	1
% Two or more races	4
% Race and/or ethnicity unknown	1
% international	3
# of countries represented	121

ACADEMICS

Academic Rating	79
% students returning for sophomore year	90
% students graduating within 4 years	23
% students graduating within 6 years	83
Calendar	Semester
Student/faculty ratio	20:1
Profs interesting rating	80
Profs accessible rating	76
Most classes have 10–19 students.	

MOST POPULAR MAJORS

Elementary Education and Teaching;
Exercise Physiology; Business/Commerce

ABOUT THE SCHOOL

Owned by the Church of Jesus Christ of Latter-Day Saints, BYU is all about "high moral standards" and "educating the best LDS students efficiently." Students love the "religious atmosphere" that helps in "isolating its students from what they believe will wrongly influence their choices." Also, "the tuition cost is relatedly cheap." The "academically accomplished" professors are "smart and interesting people" and "very well trained in their field." The school offers a "large variety of majors" with almost 200 in total. Popular majors include exercise science, elementary education, psychology, management, and English. The roughly 30,000 students on campus—25,733 of whom are undergraduates—make it the largest religious university in the United States. "It offers everything I wanted," one student says, "good education, my major, people who would support me in my beliefs and morals, large campus, and it was all at a great price!"

BANG FOR YOUR BUCK

Tuition is affordable, especially if you are an LDS member. BYU cuts tuition in half for LDS members, claiming it is the equivalent of in-state tuition for state universities. In addition, BYU offers about one quarter of their incoming freshmen academic scholarships of varying amounts. These scholarships are mostly paid for by tithes on LDS church members. The scholarships do not renew, but instead are awarded on a yearly basis. Students must apply every year, which also means that you may receive a scholarship in later years even if you do not get one initially. Students may also apply for federal grants and loans.

STUDENT LIFE

BYU's student population "is pretty homogeneous due to the fact that 98 percent of us are LDS." "The average student is kind, conservative, dedicated to school, and very religious," one student explains. "Everyone pretty much fits in," "as long as a person doesn't wear clothes or have a hairstyle that stands out obnoxiously." Student life is shaped in large part by the school's religious rules, which enforce standards of appearance and ban alcohol, drugs, and premarital sex. Consequentially, many "people think about getting married...[and] for fun, people go on dates." "Good clean fun" is the rule, and students enjoy outdoor activities "like skiing, mountain biking, hiking, climbing, etc." "There are many social activities either through the church you attend or through the school" and students "like to watch movies, dance, cook, play games, sing, or make up their own ways to have fun."

Brigham Young University

FINANCIAL AID: 801-422-4104 • E-MAIL: ADMISSIONS@BYU.EDU • WEBSITE: WWW.BYU.EDU

CAREER

"Professors are very attuned to career opportunities" at BYU and help students get connected with jobs. "The alumni network is amazing" although "there needs to be more help for incoming freshman to figure out what they want to do." PayScale.com reports an average starting salary of $55,400 for BYU graduates. "BYU does emphasize book smarts but that is not the main emphasis," one student explains. "Hands-on experience, internships, and study abroad are highly encouraged," which helps students get a jump start on their post-college career.

GENERAL INFO

Activities: Choral groups, concert band, dance, drama/theater, jazz band, literary magazine, marching band, music ensembles, musical theater, opera, pep band, radio station, student government, student newspaper, student-run film society, symphony orchestra, television station. **Organizations:** 390 registered organizations, 22 honor societies, 25 religious organizations. **Athletics (Intercollegiate):** *Men:* baseball, basketball, cheerleading, cross-country, diving, football, golf, swimming, tennis, track/field (outdoor), track/field (indoor), volleyball. *Women:* basketball, cheerleading, cross-country, diving, golf, gymnastics, soccer, softball, swimming, tennis, track/field (outdoor), track/field (indoor), volleyball. **On-Campus Highlights:** Monte L. Bean Life Science Museum, The Museum of Art, Gordon B. Hinckley Alumni & Visitors Cen, Harold B. Lee Library, Wilkinson Student Center, Creamery on 9th, the Marriott Center.

FINANCIAL AID

Students should submit: FAFSA. Priority filing deadline is 4/15. The Princeton Review suggests that all financial aid forms be submitted as soon as possible after October 1. *Need-based scholarships/grants offered:* College/university scholarship or grant aid from institutional funds; Federal Pell; Private scholarships. *Loan aid offered:* Direct PLUS Loans, Direct Subsidized Loans, Direct Unsubsidized Loans.

BOTTOM LINE

The cost of BYU depends on your religious affiliation. LDS members pay $5,460 a year while non-LDS members pay roughly double that amount. Room and board will bring those totals to just about $13,000 for LDS members and about $18,450 for non-LDS students.

CAREER INFORMATION FROM PAYSCALE.COM	
ROI Rating	93
Bachelors and No Higher	
Median starting salary	$57,400
Median mid-career salary	$109,200
At Least Bachelors	
Median starting salary	$59,900
Median mid-career salary	$117,500
Alumni with high job meaning	59%
Degrees awarded in STEM subjects	25%

SELECTIVITY	
Admissions Rating	93
# of applicants	12,858
% of applicants accepted	52
% of acceptees attending	81

FRESHMAN PROFILE	
Range SAT EBRW	610–710
Range SAT Math	600–700
Range ACT Composite	27–32
Minimum paper TOEFL	500
Average HS GPA	3.8
% graduated top 10% of class	54
% graduated top 25% of class	85
% graduated top 50% of class	98

DEADLINES	
Regular	
Priority	N/A
Deadline	12/15
Notification	3/1
Nonfall registration?	Yes

FINANCIAL FACTS	
Financial Aid Rating	76
Annual tuition	$5,620
Room and board	$7,628
Required fees	$0
Average frosh need-based scholarship	$4,721
Average UG need-based scholarship	$5,017
% needy frosh rec. need-based scholarship or grant aid	49
% needy UG rec. need-based scholarship or grant aid	79
% needy frosh rec. non-need-based scholarship or grant aid	65
% needy UG rec. non-need-based scholarship or grant aid	50
% needy frosh rec. need-based self-help aid	26
% needy UG rec. need-based self-help aid	25
% frosh rec. any financial aid	53
% UG rec. any financial aid	64
% UG borrow to pay for school	26
Average cumulative indebtedness	$14,998
% frosh need fully met	2
% ugrads need fully met	2
Average % of frosh need met	28
Average % of ugrad need met	33

Brown University

Box 1876, 45 Prospect St, Providence, RI 02912 • Admissions: 401-863-2378 • Fax: 401-863-9300

CAMPUS LIFE

Quality of Life Rating	94
Fire Safety Rating	91
Green Rating	95
Type of school	Private
Environment	City

STUDENTS

Total undergrad enrollment	6,670
% male/female	47/53
% from out of state	94
% frosh from public high school	57
% frosh live on campus	100
% ugrads live on campus	74
# of fraternities (% ugrad men join)	10 (10)
# of sororities (% ugrad women join)	8 (9)
% African American	6
% Asian	15
% Caucasian	44
% Hispanic	12
% Native American	<1
% Pacific Islander	<1
% Two or more races	6
% Race and/or ethnicity unknown	6
% international	11
# of countries represented	105

ACADEMICS

Academic Rating	96
% students returning for sophomore year	98
% students graduating within 4 years	86
% students graduating within 6 years	95
Calendar	Semester
Student/faculty ratio	7:1
Profs interesting rating	96
Profs accessible rating	91

Most classes have 10–19 students. Most lab/discussion sessions have 10–19 students.

MOST POPULAR MAJORS
Computer And Information Sciences; Applied Mathematics; Econometrics and Quantitative Economics

#20 BEST VALUE COLLEGE

ABOUT THE SCHOOL
Ivy League Brown University's fervent dedication to free inquiry and undergraduate freedom means that rather than fulfilling distribution requirements, students are educated through the school's famous Open Curriculum and may dictate the course of their own liberal arts study. Under this plan, students can pick whether a course is taken for a letter grade, and have the option to pursue more than eighty majors, with a strong advising network and numerous centers and institutes (such as the public service-oriented Swearer Center) to aid in their research and action. Brown is "about constantly questioning what could make the world and our school a better place," and study abroad programs and international collaboration are stressed, as is social action. No matter what area of study a student may choose to focus on, Brown provides "an atmosphere of both strong support and intense debate."

BANG FOR YOUR BUCK
Brown allows students to "gain both practical knowledge and a traditional liberal arts education," and the Open Curriculum ensures that students can mesh very different studies into a unique blend and "gets the opportunity to map their own journey." With a "Shopping Period" to test out classes during the first two weeks of the semester and "the ability to design your own courses easily," students can easily get exactly what they pay for no matter what they're paying. Indeed, a lot of students are paying a reduced price; around 93 percent of needy students receive need-based scholarship or grant aid, with the average award totaling $45,644.

STUDENT LIFE
Everyone at Brown is "absolutely brilliant in one way or another" and "spends as much time developing skills outside of the classroom as within," yet still strives to have a thriving social life. There is a "strong activist culture" with demonstrations happening frequently, and there are "lectures, movie screenings, improv shows, dance performances, [and] a cappella showcases constantly" happening around campus. Generally, people "fill their weekdays with schoolwork and extracurricular activities and their weekends with friends and leisure." For fun, there are clubs in downtown Providence, parties or low-key room hangs, and people "dance, work out, paint, tutor, cook…and have fun in any way possible." "Really anyone can have fun in their own way at Brown, and that's lovely," says a student.

CAREER
These free-thinkers are more likely to carve their own paths than "just go to the normative career options," and Brown welcomes this approach with open arms. All post-graduate coordination is done through the CareerLAB, the Center for Careers and Life after Brown, which arranges for on-campus recruiting, job fairs, skills workshops, boot camps, and more. "Career and internship placement has become a top priority of the new university administration," and students enjoy the fruits of Brown's reputation when applying for jobs. Brown grads who visited PayScale.com report an average starting salary of $63,000 and 46 percent believe their work makes the world a better place.

Brown University

FINANCIAL AID: 401-863-2721 • E-MAIL: ADMISSION_UNDERGRADUATE@BROWN.EDU • WEBSITE: WWW.BROWN.EDU

GENERAL INFO
Activities: Choral groups, concert band, dance, drama/theater, jazz band, literary magazine, marching band, music ensembles, musical theater, opera, pep band, radio station, student government, student newspaper, student-run film society, symphony orchestra, television station, yearbook, campus ministries, international student organization.

FINANCIAL AID
Students should submit: CSS Profile; FAFSA; Noncustodial PROFILE. Regular filing deadline is February 1. The Princeton Review suggests that all financial aid forms be submitted as soon as possible after October 1. *Need-based scholarships/grants offered:* College/university scholarship or grant aid from institutional funds, Federal Pell, private scholarships, SEOG, state scholarships/grants. *Loan aid offered:* The Brown Promise Initiative eliminates loans in all financial aid packages, beginning fall 2018. Families may choose to pursue various loans, but Brown has eliminated all loans from its packages and replaced them with University scholarships that do not have to be repaid. Applicants will be notified of awards on or about 4/1. Federal Work-Study Program available. Institutional employment available.

BOTTOM LINE
Brown tuition is a steep $54,320 per year with another $14,670 for room and board and $1,236 in fees. But aid is everywhere; 100 percent of every student's demonstrated need is met with a financial aid award that includes scholarship and work only—no loans.

CAREER INFORMATION FROM PAYSCALE.COM	
ROI Rating	94
Bachelors and No Higher	
Median starting salary	$65,400
Median mid-career salary	$131,600
At Least Bachelors	
Median starting salary	$67,400
Median mid-career salary	$138,000
Alumni with high job meaning	46%
Degrees awarded in STEM subjects	42%

SELECTIVITY
Admissions Rating	99
# of applicants	32,723
% of applicants accepted	9
% of acceptees attending	59
# of early decision applicants	3183
% accepted early decision	22

FRESHMAN PROFILE
Range SAT EBRW	705–780
Range SAT Math	700–790
Range ACT Composite	31–35
% graduated top 10% of class	94
% graduated top 25% of class	99
% graduated top 50% of class	100

DEADLINES
Early decision Deadline	11/1
Notification	12/15
Regular	
Deadline	1/1
Nonfall registration?	No

FINANCIAL FACTS
Financial Aid Rating	98
Annual tuition	$54,320
Room and board	$14,670
Required fees	$1,236
Average frosh need-based scholarship	$44,435
Average UG need-based scholarship	$45,644
% needy frosh rec. need-based scholarship or grant aid	93
% needy UG rec. need-based scholarship or grant aid	93
% needy frosh rec. non-need-based scholarship or grant aid	0
% needy UG rec. non-need-based scholarship or grant aid	0
% needy frosh rec. need-based self-help aid	88
% needy UG rec. need-based self-help aid	88
% frosh rec. any financial aid	59
% UG rec. any financial aid	52
% UG borrow to pay for school	34
Average cumulative indebtedness	$25,471
% frosh need fully met	100
% ugrads need fully met	100
Average % of frosh need met	100
Average % of ugrad need met	100

Bryn Mawr College

101 NORTH MERION AVENUE, BRYN MAWR, PA 19010-2859 • ADMISSIONS: 610-526-5152 • FAX: 610-526-7471

CAMPUS LIFE

Quality of Life Rating	**96**
Fire Safety Rating	**86**
Green Rating	**86**
Type of school	Private
Environment	Metropolis

STUDENTS

Total undergrad enrollment	1,328
% male/female	0/100
% from out of state	82
% frosh from public high school	63
% frosh live on campus	100
% ugrads live on campus	91
# of fraternities (% ugrad men join)	0 (0)
# of sororities (% ugrad women join)	0 (0)
% African American	6
% Asian	12
% Caucasian	37
% Hispanic	9
% Native American	0
% Pacific Islander	<1
% Two or more races	6
% Race and/or ethnicity unknown	7
% international	23
# of countries represented	58

ACADEMICS

Academic Rating	**95**
% students returning for sophomore year	92
% students graduating within 4 years	76
% students graduating within 6 years	83
Calendar	Semester
Student/faculty ratio	8:1
Profs interesting rating	97
Profs accessible rating	94

Most classes have 10–19 students. Most lab/discussion sessions have 10–19 students.

MOST POPULAR MAJORS
Mathematics; Biology/Biological Sciences; Psychology

ABOUT THE SCHOOL

An intellectually engaging college like Bryn Mawr delivers an invaluable experience. This all-women's college delivers professors that "are not only passionate about their respective fields but are also incredibly accessible," and many are on a first-name basis with the students. Labs and facilities are state-of-the-art. Classes here are intense and small, and students emphasize that "the social science and hard science departments are very strong." Stress is a way of life, especially when midterms and finals roll around, but the "passionate" women here say they "manage to find time to form a tight community, despite mounds of schoolwork." The administration is well liked, not least because it gives students all manner of support in their academic endeavors. Bryn Mawr has a bi-college relationship with Haverford College, meaning that students from either school can live, study, and even major at both schools. Bryn Mawr and Haverford are also part of the Tri-College Consortium with Swarthmore College, which allows students from all three schools to use libraries and attend social functions, performances, and lectures on any campus. Cross-registration with Haverford, Swarthmore, and the University of Pennsylvania gives students access to more than 6,000 courses. Students praise the "vast resources offered through the Tri-Co," as well as the opportunities this system provides to "to grow culturally, academically, socially, and politically." Upon graduation, Mawrters can take advantage of a loyal network of successful alumnae who maintain a strong connection to the school.

BANG FOR YOUR BUCK

Bryn Mawr College is deeply committed to enrolling outstanding scholars. To eliminate financial barriers to attendance, the college meets 100 percent of the demonstrated financial need of enrolling students. In 2016–2017 alone, the college awarded $31.8 million dollars in grant assistance to 71 percent of undergraduate students. The average grant is approximately $33,000. If you are a veteran—or will soon be one—Bryn Mawr offers very generous benefits. In addition, graduates of Bryn Mawr are very competitive when the time comes to find a job.

STUDENT LIFE

Life at Bryn Mawr has somehow achieved the perfect balance of being both "relaxed" yet "busy." Certainly, these undergrads are quite focused on their studies. Yet they also manage to carve out time to kick back. And, fortunately, there are plenty of "musical, poetic and comedy events" as well as a movie series for those who "prefer a low-key night." Indeed, prospective students looking for a raucous scene be warned; "there are only a few big parties a year at Bryn Mawr, so if you want a party scene you have to go to one of the other schools in the area." However, a political science major counters that "you can find groups of people drinking with friends on any night of the week, and campus-wide parties for birthdays etc. are relatively common." Finally, since the college is in close proximity to Philadelphia, students love to "take advantage of everything going on in the city from concerts to restaurants."

Bryn Mawr College

FINANCIAL AID: 610-526-5245 • E-MAIL: ADMISSIONS@BRYNMAWR.EDU • WEBSITE: WWW.BRYNMAWR.EDU

CAREER

Bryn Mawr's Leadership Innovation and Liberal Arts Center integrates the Office of Civic Engagement and Career and Professional Development to prepare liberal arts and sciences students to become effective, self-aware leaders in their chosen life pursuits through experiential education. Undergrads here can schedule one-on-one appointments at any time and receive assistance in crafting their personal job strategy. Of course, they can get help both crafting and tweaking their résumés and cover letters. And they can learn the secrets to successful networking. Importantly, they may also participate in the college's recruiting program. Here, undergrads can meet with prospective employers interested in hiring Bryn Mawr students for internships, entry-level positions and gap-year fellowships. According to PayScale.com, the typical starting salary for alumnae after graduation is $50,200. Companies that have recently recruited undergrads include J.P. Morgan and Cornerstone Research.

GENERAL INFO

Environment: Metropolis. **Activities:** Choral groups, dance, drama/theater, jazz band, literary magazine, music ensembles, musical theater, radio station, student government, student newspaper, student-run film society, yearbook. **Organizations:** 158 registered organizations, 13 religious organizations. **Athletics (Intercollegiate):** Badminton, basketball, crew/rowing, cross-country, field hockey, lacrosse, soccer, swimming, tennis, track/field (outdoor), track/field (indoor), volleyball. **On-Campus Highlights:** College Hall (National Historic Landmark), Erdman Hall (designed by famed architect, Louis Kahn), The Cloisters, Taft Garden, Rhys Carpenter Library, Goodhart Theater.

FINANCIAL AID

Students should submit: CSS Profile; FAFSA; Noncustodial PROFILE. Regular filing deadline is 1/15. The Princeton Review suggests that all financial aid forms be submitted as soon as possible after October 1. *Need-based scholarships/grants offered:* College/university scholarship or grant aid from institutional funds, Federal Pell, private scholarships, SEOG, state scholarships/grants. *Loan aid offered:* Direct PLUS Loans, Direct Subsidized Loans, Direct Unsubsidized Loans. Federal Work-Study Program available. Institutional employment available.

BOTTOM LINE

Tuition, fees, room and board costs approximately $64,000 each year. While that may seem like a lot, the college's need-based financial aid programs are among the most generous in the country.

CAREER INFORMATION FROM PAYSCALE.COM	
ROI Rating	90
Bachelors and No Higher	
Median starting salary	$52,900
Median mid-career salary	$88,900
At Least Bachelors	
Median starting salary	$56,600
Median mid-career salary	$108,600
Alumni with high job meaning	49%
Degrees awarded in STEM subjects	18%

SELECTIVITY	
Admissions Rating	94
# of applicants	2,936
% of applicants accepted	38
% of acceptees attending	32
# offered a place on the wait list	734
% accepting a place on wait list	43
% admitted from wait list	7
# of early decision applicants	276
% accepted early decision	53

FRESHMAN PROFILE	
Range SAT EBRW	650–730
Range SAT Math	660–770
Range ACT Composite	29–33
Minimum paper TOEFL	600
Minimum internet-based TOEFL	100
% graduated top 10% of class	68
% graduated top 25% of class	91
% graduated top 50% of class	97

DEADLINES	
Early decision	
Deadline	11/15
Notification	12/15
Other ED Deadline	1/1
Other ED Notification	2/1
Regular	
Deadline	1/15
Notification	4/1
Nonfall registration?	No

FINANCIAL FACTS	
Financial Aid Rating	95
Annual tuition	$51,130
Room and board	$16,500
Required fees	$1,230
Average frosh need-based scholarship	$41,891
Average UG need-based scholarship	$42,244
% needy frosh rec. need-based scholarship or grant aid	100
% needy UG rec. need-based scholarship or grant aid	100
% needy frosh rec. non-need-based scholarship or grant aid	15
% needy UG rec. non-need-based scholarship or grant aid	12
% needy frosh rec. need-based self-help aid	85
% needy UG rec. need-based self-help aid	92
% frosh rec. any financial aid	67
% UG rec. any financial aid	72
% UG borrow to pay for school	55
Average cumulative indebtedness	$25,448
% frosh need fully met	100
% ugrads need fully met	100
Average % of frosh need met	100

Bucknell University

Freas Hall, Bucknell University, Lewisburg, PA 17837 • Admissions: 570-577-1101 • Financial Aid: 570-577-1331

CAMPUS LIFE

Quality of Life Rating	88
Fire Safety Rating	94
Green Rating	97
Type of school	Private
Environment	Village

STUDENTS

Total undergrad enrollment	3,588
% male/female	49/51
% from out of state	78
% frosh from public high school	60
% frosh live on campus	100
% ugrads live on campus	91
# of fraternities (% ugrad men join)	8 (32)
# of sororities (% ugrad women join)	9 (48)
% African American	4
% Asian	5
% Caucasian	74
% Hispanic	7
% Native American	0
% Pacific Islander	0
% Two or more races	4
% Race and/or ethnicity unknown	<1
% international	6
# of countries represented	42

ACADEMICS

Academic Rating	95
% students returning for sophomore year	94
% students graduating within 4 years	86
% students graduating within 6 years	90
Calendar	Semester
Student/faculty ratio	9:1
Profs interesting rating	93
Profs accessible rating	95

Most classes have 10–19 students. Most lab/discussion sessions have fewer than 20 students.

MOST POPULAR MAJORS

Psychology; Economics; Accounting and Finance

ABOUT THE SCHOOL

Bucknell University delivers the quintessential East Coast college experience, and one student says it offers a balanced combination of "great academics, a liberal arts education, sterling reputation, and a great social scene." Lewisburg is located in central Pennsylvania, and the campus is described as both beautiful and safe. Another student shares his experience, saying, "Bucknell was the perfect next step from my high school; it is small enough that your teachers know your name but big enough that you don't know every person on campus. I felt the most comfortable at Bucknell, and I felt that the school actually cared about me as a person, compared to some of the larger state schools to which I applied." Overall, Bucknell balances reputation with accessibility in a neat package. "It's extremely prestigious, beautiful, and the perfect size," shares one junior. A recent graduate sums up by saying, "Bucknell University is small enough to affect change, but big enough to attract national attention. It is a school where academics are amazing, school spirit is everywhere, and the people genuinely care." Another new student is excited that "campus pride is obvious, and as a large liberal arts college there are a myriad of opportunities, but I don't have to compete with a ton of people to take advantage of them."

BANG FOR YOUR BUCK

Bucknell pride extends into the community, and students become involved socially in many area projects and activities. One student relates, "Bucknell just felt like home. It is big enough where alumni and community connections are a huge benefit, but the campus is small enough that I'm not just a number. Professors take time to know me, and being included in class discussions is not a challenge." Another resident "wanted a small school where I could form close relationships with faculty and have the opportunity to do undergraduate research. So far it has exceeded my expectations, and the faculty and administration have made sure opportunities are within my reach." As another student notes appreciatively, "I also received a scholarship that allowed me to have an internship on campus, giving me work experience on top of my education."

STUDENT LIFE

At Bucknell "more than half of eligible students are members of a Greek Organization." "The typical student at Bucknell is upper/ middle class, friendly, driven, well educated and preppy." Still, "people tend to be very accepting of alternate cultures and lifestyles." "Generally, academics are the number one priority" and "Bucknellians work extremely hard all week." In addition to Greek life, Bucknell hosts "engaging guest speakers" and concerts at the Weis Center for the Performing Arts. "Lewisburg, a quaint town, feels like a true metropolis" with "an adorable old fashioned movie theater" and late night carnivals. In general, student sentiment echoes that at Bucknell, "there is a place for everyone." "Most people find one, two, or 100 extracurricular activities to join."

CAREER

"Bucknell University allows students, no matter what their academic or social preferences are, to find opportunities to really explore their interests. Students are encouraged to develop projects or clubs to enhance the campus community." Most are "impressed" with the career services and "networking opportunities" available, especially the alumni "dedication." Alumni are "valuable" assets to future Bucknellians and

Bucknell University

E-MAIL: ADMISSIONS@BUCKNELL.EDU • FAX: 570-577-3538 • WEBSITE: WWW.BUCKNELL.EDU

remain involved with the school and students long after graduation. Also, the career development center is "amazing" as are the study abroad programs, internships, and undergrad research opportunities. Bucknell "has a huge focus on service learning and community service which is phenomenal." Students receive guidance and opportunities through their professors and pre-professional advisors. According to the website PayScale.com, the average starting salary for graduates is $62,300 with a mid-career average at $124,700.

GENERAL INFO

Activities: Choral groups, concert band, dance, drama/theater, jazz band, literary magazine, music ensembles, musical theater, opera, pep band, radio station, student government, student newspaper, student-run film society, symphony orchestra, yearbook, campus ministries, international student organization. **Organizations:** 150 registered organizations, 23 honor societies, 12 religious organizations. 8 fraternities, 9 sororities. **Athletics (Intercollegiate):** *Men:* Baseball, basketball, cross-country, diving, football, golf, lacrosse, soccer, swimming, tennis, track/field, water polo, wrestling. *Women:* Basketball, crew/rowing, cross-country, diving, field hockey, golf, lacrosse, soccer, softball, swimming, tennis, track/field, volleyball, water polo.

FINANCIAL AID

Students should submit: CSS Profile; FAFSA. Regular filing deadline is 2/1. The Princeton Review suggests that all financial aid forms be submitted as soon as possible after October 1. *Need-based scholarships/grants offered:* College/university scholarship or grant aid from institutional funds, Federal Pell, private scholarships, SEOG, state scholarships/grants. *Loan aid offered:* Direct PLUS Loans, Direct Subsidized Loans, Direct Unsubsidized Loans. Applicants will be notified of awards on or about 4/1. Federal Work-Study Program available. Institutional employment available.

BOTTOM LINE

Bucknell University provides students with a fine educational experience. The yearly tuition does reflect that monetarily, at $55,788 a year. With room and board adding another $13,662, students are making a large but wise investment in their future. The school does provide a variety of options to offset the cost of attending here, with 69 percent of needy freshmen receiving need-based scholarships or grants. Forty-seven percent of students borrow to pay for school, and around 62 percent of students receive some form of financial aid. Upon graduating, for those who take out loans, the average total loan debt is $33,000. "The school has been generous and fair in financial assistance, and easy to work with," relates a satisfied undergraduate.

CAREER INFORMATION FROM PAYSCALE.COM	
ROI Rating	91
Bachelors and No Higher	
Median starting salary	$64,800
Median mid-career salary	$125,200
At Least Bachelors	
Median starting salary	$66,400
Median mid-career salary	$134,500
Alumni with high job meaning	40%
Degrees awarded in STEM subjects	40%

SELECTIVITY	
Admissions Rating	94
# of applicants	10,253
% of applicants accepted	31
% of acceptees attending	31
# offered a place on the wait list	2,883
% accepting a place on wait list	45
% admitted from wait list	4
# of early decision applicants	762
% accepted early decision	55

FRESHMAN PROFILE	
Range SAT EBRW	620–700
Range SAT Math	630–720
Range ACT Composite	28–31
Minimum paper TOEFL	600
Minimum internet-based TOEFL	100
Average HS GPA	3.6
% graduated top 10% of class	60
% graduated top 25% of class	89
% graduated top 50% of class	100

DEADLINES	
Early decision	
Deadline	11/15
Notification	12/15
Other ED Deadline	1/15
Other ED Notification	2/15
Regular	
Deadline	1/15
Notification	4/1
Nonfall registration?	No

FINANCIAL FACTS	
Financial Aid Rating	93
Annual tuition	$55,788
Room and board	$13,662
Required fees	$304
Books and supplies	$900
Average frosh need-based scholarship	$32,700
Average UG need-based scholarship	$29,000
% needy frosh rec. need-based scholarship or grant aid	69
% needy UG rec. need-based scholarship or grant aid	93
% needy frosh rec. non-need-based scholarship or grant aid	22
% needy UG rec. non-need-based scholarship or grant aid	24
% needy frosh rec. need-based self-help aid	100
% needy UG rec. need-based self-help aid	100
% frosh rec. any financial aid	54
% UG rec. any financial aid	62
% UG borrow to pay for school	47
Average cumulative indebtedness	$33,000
Average % of frosh need met	91

California Institute of Technology

1200 East California Boulevard, Pasadena, CA 91125 • Admissions: 626-395-6341

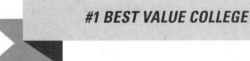

#1 BEST VALUE COLLEGE

ABOUT THE SCHOOL

Caltech's swagger is completely out of proportion with its small size of about 1,000 students. Thirty-seven Caltech alumni and faculty have won the Nobel Prize; fifty-eight have won the National Medal of Science; thirteen have won the National Medal of Technology and Innovation; and 125 have been elected to the National Academies combined. To say that this science and engineering powerhouse is world-class is an understatement. Located in the suburbs of Los Angeles ("Where else do you have beaches, mountains, and desert all within a two-hour drive?"), Caltech boasts a long history of excellence, with a list of major research achievements that reads like a textbook in the history of science. It goes without saying that academics are highly rigorous and competitive; if you are used to getting straight As, Caltech may be a shock to the system. "If you were the top student all your life, prepare to experience a big dose of humility, because you'll have to work hard just to stay in the middle of the pack," says a student. Techers say the learning experience here is "like trying to drink from a firehose," which is "as accurate a statement as can be made, given the breadth, intensity, and amount of coursework required."

BANG FOR YOUR BUCK

Caltech is extremely affordable, while the school's immense reputation and plethora of opportunities ensure a bright future in research or academia for Caltech graduates. Caltech operates need-blind admissions for all U.S. citizens and permanent residents. Every year, financial aid awards meet 100 percent of demonstrated student need. Of particular note, the school makes every effort to limit a student's debt, awarding aid packages with little work-study or loans. Across the board, the maximum loan expectation for Caltech students is just around $5,500 annually, and the average loan debt for Caltech students is just over $18,200 for all four years. The school also offers substantial need-based packages for international students, a rarity among private institutions. Caltech scholarships are awarded based on demonstrated financial need.

STUDENT LIFE

We're told that at Caltech, most "of the social interaction is centered around the eight student houses, which are somewhere between dorms and frats/sororities, but closest to the houses in Harry Potter." Indeed, undergrads here can participate in a myriad of activities through their respective houses. Events might include "scavenger hunts, inter-house dodgeball [and] frisbee, paint balling...pumpkin carving competition, Project Euler new problem solving session and New Yorker caption contest." Outside of the houses, "there are many music and theatre groups on campus, and countless clubs" in which students can participate. It's common for "most people [to be] involved with at least one non-academic thing." And while there is a small party scene, it's "much less traditional...than at other schools." A senior clarifies, "We're more likely to throw themed parties, with things to do other than dance, because we're kind of awkward."

California Institute of Technology

FINANCIAL AID: 626-395-6280 • E-MAIL: UGADMISSIONS@CALTECH.EDU • WEBSITE: ADMISSIONS.CALTECH.EDU

CAREER

We'll get right to the point—Caltech students do very well for themselves. In fact, according to PayScale.com, the median starting salary for recent graduates is $78,800. Certainly, the school's Career Development Center should take some of the credit for this success. After all, the office provides some stellar career counseling. It also hosts a number of workshops covering an array of topics such as connecting with recruiters, projecting confidence in interviews and social media networking. Undergrads also have access to the TecherLink which connects them with job, internship and work study opportunities as well as the career center's activities. Perhaps most importantly, the office hosts two big career fairs each year (one in the fall, one in the winter). Finally, companies that frequently hire Caltech grads include Google, Inc., National Institutes of Health (NIH) and Oracle Corp.

GENERAL INFO

Activities: Choral groups, concert band, dance, drama/theater, jazz band, literary magazine, music ensembles, musical theater, opera, pep band, student government, student newspaper, student-run film society, symphony orchestra, yearbook. **Organizations:** 113 registered organizations, 2 honor societies, 7 religious organizations. **Athletics (Intercollegiate):** *Men:* Baseball, basketball, cross-country, diving, fencing, soccer, swimming, tennis, track/field (outdoor), water polo. *Women:* Basketball, cross-country, diving, fencing, swimming, tennis, track/field (outdoor), volleyball, water polo.

FINANCIAL AID

Students should submit: Business/Farm Supplement; CSS Profile, FAFSA; Institution's own financial aid form, Noncustodial PROFILE; State aid form. Priority filing deadline is 3/15. The Princeton Review suggests that all financial aid forms be submitted as soon as possible after October 1. *Need-based scholarships/grants offered:* College/university scholarship or grant aid from institutional funds, Federal Pell, private scholarships, SEOG, state scholarships/grants. *Loan aid offered:* Direct PLUS Loans, Direct Subsidized Loans, Direct Unsubsidized Loans. Applicants will be notified of awards on or about 4/15. Federal Work-Study Program available. Institutional employment available.

THE BOTTOM LINE

In 2015 Caltech's endowment was just under $2.1 billion. It's no wonder generous financial aid and scholarship packages are commonplace here. Tuition at Caltech is $48,111 annually, plus another $1,700-plus in student fees. Once you factor in $14,796 for room and board and $1,300 more for books and supplies, the estimated annual cost is $66,004 per year. Few students pay the full cost, while everyone benefits from the world-class education, making this school a best buy. Financial aid packages for undergraduates include a $41,901 need-based grant on average.

CAREER INFORMATION FROM PAYSCALE.COM

ROI Rating	99
Bachelors and No Higher	
Median starting salary	$83,400
Median mid-career salary	$143,100
At Least Bachelors	
Median starting salary	$87,300
Median mid-career salary	$150,800
Alumni with high job meaning	54%
Degrees awarded in STEM subjects	96%

SELECTIVITY

Admissions Rating	99
# of applicants	7,339
% of applicants accepted	8
% of acceptees attending	41
# offered a place on the wait list	376
% accepting a place on wait list	80
% admitted from wait list	14

FRESHMAN PROFILE

Range SAT EBRW	750–790
Range SAT Math	780–800
Range ACT Composite	34–35
Minimum internet-based TOEFL	110
% graduated top 10% of class	93
% graduated top 25% of class	100
% graduated top 50% of class	100

DEADLINES

Early action	
Deadline	11/1
Notification	12/15
Regular	
Deadline	1/3
Notification	3/15
Nonfall registration?	No

FINANCIAL FACTS

Financial Aid Rating	99
Annual tuition	$48,111
Room and board	$14,796
Required fees	$1,797
Books and supplies	$1,323
Average frosh need-based scholarship	$43,675
Average UG need-based scholarship	$45,797
% needy frosh rec. need-based scholarship or grant aid	100
% needy UG rec. need-based scholarship or grant aid	100
% needy frosh rec. non-need-based scholarship or grant aid	0
% needy UG rec. non-need-based scholarship or grant aid	1
% needy frosh rec. need-based self-help aid	66
% needy UG rec. need-based self-help aid	67
% frosh rec. any financial aid	75
% UG rec. any financial aid	60
% UG borrow to pay for school	34
Average cumulative indebtedness	$16,777
% frosh need fully met	100
% ugrads need fully met	100
Average % of frosh need met	100
Average % of ugrad need met	100

Carleton College

100 South College Street, Northfield, MN 55057 • Admissions: 507-222-4190 • Fax: 507-222-4526

CAMPUS LIFE

Quality of Life Rating	94
Fire Safety Rating	97
Green Rating	90
Type of school	Private
Environment	Village

STUDENTS

Total undergrad enrollment	2,023
% male/female	49/51
% from out of state	85
% frosh from public high school	60
% frosh live on campus	100
% ugrads live on campus	96
# of fraternities (% ugrad men join)	0 (0)
# of sororities (% ugrad women join)	0 (0)
% African American	5
% Asian	8
% Caucasian	61
% Hispanic	8
% Native American	<1
% Pacific Islander	0
% Two or more races	6
% Race and/or ethnicity unknown	2
% international	10
# of countries represented	41

ACADEMICS

Academic Rating	98
% students returning for sophomore year	96
% students graduating within 4 years	89
% students graduating within 6 years	94
Calendar	Trimester
Student/faculty ratio	9:1
Profs interesting rating	98
Profs accessible rating	98

Most classes have 10–19 students. Most lab/discussion sessions have 10–19 students.

MOST POPULAR MAJORS
Computer And Information Sciences; Biology/Biological Sciences; Economics

ABOUT THE SCHOOL

Carleton College emphasizes rigor and intellectual growth without competition or hubris. Students attracted to Carleton's campus seek meaningful collaboration without the distraction of divisive academic one-upping. The opportunities to work with bright and engaged students and professors are plentiful. One student explains that "Carleton is not a research college, so while professors do some research, they are much more focused on students." Carleton operates on a trimester calendar, which many students enjoy, saying that "it's nice to be only taking three classes, though more intensely, rather than spreading yourself over four or five." An endless array of social and cocurricular activities is on offer at Carleton, as well as numerous programs for off-campus studies. These opportunities combine rural and urban experiences in a friendly Midwestern environment; students can master Chinese, Japanese, Arabic, and modern Hebrew; they can study in the shadow of a wind turbine generating electricity for the campus; they can choose to live in an environmentally conscious way from their dorm arrangements to the food they eat. Students love the "great study abroad office," which provides students here with "opportunities to travel to China, Thailand, Spain, and Africa." Experiential learning opportunities are immense here. Carleton Scholars is Carleton's highest-visibility experiential learning program and consists of taste-of-industry tours that introduce a variety of organizations in a particular field of interest, through site visits, panel discussions, receptions, and social activities. The 30 Minutes initiative provides students with access to one-on-one time, group discussion, and candid interviews with Carleton alumni luminaries in many fields. Carleton's Mentor Externships program connects students with alumni for one- to four-week short internships, most with a focus project, and generally including home-stays with their alumni hosts.

BANG FOR YOUR BUCK

Carleton's financial aid program is primarily need-based, and the college commits to meeting the need of admitted students fully. This means that a student's aid award will include grants and scholarships from Carleton, applicable government grants, on-campus work, and a reasonable amount of loan. Students graduate with about $21,000 in loan debt on average. Carleton's financial aid program helps support the unique culture and character of this college through its goal of enrolling diverse students regardless of their ability to pay for college. With nearly three-fifths of the student body receiving need-based grant aid, there is a broad socioeconomic representation across the student body, and students laud Carleton for its "generous financial aid."

STUDENT LIFE

The "creative, warm, compassionate, and helpful" undergrads of Carleton are "quirky," but "everyone is accepting of these little eccentricities." One physics major praises the inclusive nature of the school, noting that "the moment that I first stepped foot on campus I felt as if I belong here." The "average Carl is . . . very physically active and loves to spend time outdoors." Even the cold Minnesota weather can be a good thing: "Minnesota winters teach you how to appreciate sunny, forty degree Spring days!" Carleton is "everything I wanted in a school: small, Midwest, great campus community, professors who really care," notes an English major. Despite the academically rigorous atmosphere, on the weekends there are "movie screenings, plays, dance performances, lectures, [and] musicians [on] campus." "Carleton boasts a tight-knit community, strong

Carleton College

FINANCIAL AID: 507-222-4138 • E-MAIL: ADMISSIONS@CARLETON.EDU • WEBSITE: WWW.CARLETON.EDU

academics and fun campus life." One undergrad details weekend plans—"on Fridays I go to the Sci-Fi interest house . . . then go to an improv/sketch comedy group"—and highlights the general camaraderie of the school: "Conversations are often simultaneously totally goofy and deeply intellectual. I just love it here, and I'm convinced there's no better place for me."

CAREER

PayScale.com reports that 46 percent of Carleton graduates feel their careers help make the world a better place. The median starting salary for a Carleton grad is $56,100. Biology, economics, and computer science are three of the most popular majors at the school. A biology major notes that "there are great resources for academic and career help, and all kinds of interests are encouraged." Carleton's Career Center offers assistance to students at all levels of the job (and internship) hunting process. According to the school's website, two online resources, The Tunnel and Going Global, give students the opportunity to search for internships, participate in on-campus recruiting, and learn about international job and internship opportunities, respectively. Students note that Carleton professors "are very helpful in finding students summer...job opportunities."

GENERAL INFO

Activities: Choral groups, concert band, dance, drama/theater, jazz band, literary magazine, music ensembles, musical theater, radio station, student government, student newspaper, student-run film society, symphony orchestra, yearbook, campus ministries, international student organization.

FINANCIAL AID

Students should submit: CSS Profile; FAFSA; Noncustodial PROFILE. Priority filing deadline is 1/15. The Princeton Review suggests that all financial aid forms be submitted as soon as possible after October 1. *Need-based scholarships/grants offered:* College/university scholarship or grant aid from institutional funds, Federal Pell, private scholarships, SEOG, state scholarships/grants. *Loan aid offered:* Direct PLUS Loans, Direct Subsidized Loans, Direct Unsubsidized Loans. Applicants will be notified of awards on or about 3/31. Federal Work-Study Program available. Institutional employment available.

BOTTOM LINE

At Carleton College, the total cost for tuition and fees and room and board comes to about $68,000 annually. Fortunately, the folks writing the checks at Carleton believe that cost should not be an obstacle to achieving a Carleton education. The average financial aid package for frosh includes scholarships and grants totaling $41,917—that gets you halfway there. When you factor in Carleton's other financial aid offerings in the form of work-study and loans, the dollar amount will seem much more manageable.

CAREER INFORMATION FROM PAYSCALE.COM	
ROI Rating	92
Bachelors and No Higher	
Median starting salary	$56,100
Median mid-career salary	$115,300
At Least Bachelors	
Median starting salary	$58,200
Median mid-career salary	$119,400
Alumni with high job meaning	45%
Degrees awarded in STEM subjects	45%

SELECTIVITY	
Admissions Rating	**97**
# of applicants	6,499
% of applicants accepted	21
% of acceptees attending	38
# offered a place on the wait list	1,315
% accepting a place on wait list	40
% admitted from wait list	8
# of early decision applicants	725
% accepted early decision	30

FRESHMAN PROFILE	
Range SAT EBRW	680–760
Range SAT Math	680–770
Range ACT Composite	31–34
Minimum paper TOEFL	600
% graduated top 10% of class	86
% graduated top 25% of class	98
% graduated top 50% of class	100

DEADLINES	
Early decision	
Deadline	11/15
Notification	12/15
Other ED Deadline	1/15
Other ED Notification	2/15
Regular	
Deadline	1/15
Notification	3/31
Nonfall registration?	No

FINANCIAL FACTS	
Financial Aid Rating	**97**
Annual tuition	$54,438
Room and board	$14,085
Required fees	$321
Books and supplies	$823
Average frosh need-based scholarship	$41,917
Average UG need-based scholarship	$40,675
% needy frosh rec. need-based scholarship or grant aid	100
% needy UG rec. need-based scholarship or grant aid	100
% needy frosh rec. non-need-based scholarship or grant aid	10
% needy UG rec. non-need-based scholarship or grant aid	11
% needy frosh rec. need-based self-help aid	99
% needy UG rec. need-based self-help aid	98
% frosh rec. any financial aid	54
% UG rec. any financial aid	56
% UG borrow to pay for school	44
Average cumulative indebtedness	$21,035
% frosh need fully met	100
% ugrads need fully met	100
Average % of frosh need met	100

Carnegie Mellon University

5000 FORBES AVENUE, PITTSBURGH, PA 15213 • ADMISSIONS: 412-268-2082 • FAX: 412-268-7838

CAMPUS LIFE

Quality of Life Rating	89
Fire Safety Rating	89
Green Rating	98
Type of school	Private
Environment	Metropolis

STUDENTS

Total undergrad enrollment	6,804
% male/female	51/49
% from out of state	85
% frosh live on campus	100
% ugrads live on campus	60
# of fraternities (% ugrad men join)	13 (16)
# of sororities (% ugrad women join)	10 (11)
% African American	4
% Asian	29
% Caucasian	26
% Hispanic	9
% Native American	<1
% Pacific Islander	<1
% Two or more races	4
% Race and/or ethnicity unknown	5
% international	22
# of countries represented	56

ACADEMICS

Academic Rating	90
% students returning for sophomore year	96
% students graduating within 4 years	76
% students graduating within 6 years	89
Calendar	Semester
Student/faculty ratio	13:1
Profs interesting rating	82
Profs accessible rating	84

Most classes have 10–19 students. Most lab/discussion sessions have 20–29 students.

MOST POPULAR MAJORS
Computer Science; Electrical and Electronics Engineering; Systems Science and Theory.

#42 BEST VALUE COLLEGE

ABOUT THE SCHOOL
Primarily known for its incredibly strong STEM and drama programs, Carnegie Mellon University enjoys a worldwide reputation as a research university. Professors are experts in their respective fields, and the difficulty of the classes and high expectations from faculty push students to do their best work. In return, they are given "a lot of trust from the administration" in regards to self-governance and their courses of study. "I am not limited to take classes in any one particular college," says a student. "It is nice to know I will get a good degree, but that it is also unique to me." The school offers "more opportunities to excel than you could possibly use in one four-year period" and most here treat the university as an intellectual and creative playground. "Carnegie Mellon is the only place where you will see engineers working while an art installation goes in above their heads," says a student.

BANG FOR YOUR BUCK
Students who fill out and submit the requisite forms and materials for federal and state grants and the CSS financial aid profile will be considered for a Carnegie Mellon Undergraduate Grant. Thirty-nine percent of students receive some form of need-based financial aid, and 93.8 percent of all such need is met. Additionally, there are many student employment opportunities on campus, both need-based and non-need based.

STUDENT LIFE
Students report that "there are a million ways to find your niche on campus" beginning with orientation, and "eventually the labels 'artist' or 'scientist' fade and you become friends with people from all over campus." The challenging academics put everyone in the same time constrained boat, and so "the work-heavy culture becomes a social thing." The student body "isn't so small that you'll know everyone… [but] it's not so big that you'll disappear either." Everyone here fits in somewhere, and even people who were outcasts in high school "easily find large groups of people just like them on campus." Students at CMU are very dedicated to a variety of clubs and interests, and adhere to the logic "study or be trampled, but make sure you still have some fun."

CAREER
At CMU, the interdisciplinary approach to education means that students are taught to be versatile problem solvers with a key sense of community. The school is "great for engineering, math, science, or physics students (or drama or design)," who find that the world "practically throws opportunities (internships, guidance) at these majors." You would be hard-pressed to find a junior or senior who did not have an internship in the summer; "it almost seems expected of you because of the caliber of student you are." CMU's academic diversity and rigor "put its students in an excellent position to start their careers." "People will hire you because they know you can work since you have been doing nothing but working the past four years of your life," says a student. For those students who visited PayScale.com, 46 percent reported feeling that their job was making a meaningful impact on the world.

Carnegie Mellon University

FINANCIAL AID: 412-268-8186 • E-MAIL: ADMISSION@ANDREW.CMU.EDU • WEBSITE: WWW.CMU.EDU

GENERAL INFO

Activities: Choral groups, concert band, dance, drama/theater, literary magazine, marching band, music ensembles, musical theater, pep band, radio station, student government, student newspaper, student-run film society, symphony orchestra, television station, yearbook, campus ministries, International Student Organization. **Organizations:** 325 registered organizations, 34 religious organizations. 13 fraternities, 10 sororities. **Athletics (Intercollegiate):** *Men:* basketball, cross country, football, golf, soccer, swimming and diving, tennis, track and field (indoor and outdoor). *Women:* basketball, cross country, golf, soccer, softball, swimming and diving, tennis, track and field (indoor and outdoor), volleyball. **On-Campus Highlights:** Cohon Center, Hunt Library, The Cut, The Fence, The Underground, Pausch Bridge, Gates Café, Tepper Quad, Bagpiping.

FINANCIAL AID

Students should submit: CSS Profile; FAFSA; Noncustodial PROFILE, if applicable. Priority filing deadline is February 15. The Princeton Review suggests that all financial aid forms be submitted as soon as possible after October 1. *Need-based scholarships/grants offered:* College/university scholarship or grant aid from institutional funds, Federal Pell, SEOG, state scholarships/grants, private scholarships. *Loan aid offered:* Direct PLUS Loans, Direct Subsidized Loans, Direct Unsubsidized Loans. Applicants will be notified of awards on or about April 15. Federal Work-Study Program available. Institutional employment available.

BOTTOM LINE

As a private institution, the cost of tuition is set at $54,244 for all students regardless of state residence; add on another $14,418 for room and board (all incoming freshmen are required to live on campus). Once all fees and additional expenses (such as books and supplies) are factored in, incoming freshmen can expect to pay about $72,283. International students are not eligible to receive financial aid.

CAREER INFORMATION FROM PAYSCALE.COM	
ROI Rating	92
Bachelors and No Higher	
Median starting salary	$73,600
Median mid-career salary	$131,200
At Least Bachelors	
Median starting salary	$75,500
Median mid-career salary	$136,300
Alumni with high job meaning	46%
Degrees awarded in STEM subjects	66%

SELECTIVITY	
Admissions Rating	98
# of applicants	20,497
% of applicants accepted	22
% of acceptees attending	37
# offered a place on the wait list	5,609
% accepting a place on wait list	51
% admitted from wait list	0
# of early decision applicants	1384
% accepted early decision	25

FRESHMAN PROFILE	
Range SAT EBRW	700–760
Range SAT Math	730–800
Range ACT Composite	32–35
Minimum internet-based TOEFL	102
Average HS GPA	3.8
% graduated top 10% of class	74
% graduated top 25% of class	94
% graduated top 50% of class	99

DEADLINES	
Early decision	
Deadline	11/1
Notification	12/15
Regular	
Deadline	1/1
Notification	4/15
Nonfall registration?	No

FINANCIAL FACTS	
Financial Aid Rating	92
Annual tuition	$54,244
Room and board	$14,418
Required fees	$908
Books and supplies	$2,400
Average frosh need-based scholarship	$41,167
Average UG need-based scholarship	$37,531
% needy frosh rec. need-based scholarship or grant aid	97
% needy UG rec. need-based scholarship or grant aid	96
% needy frosh rec. non-need-based scholarship or grant aid	44
% needy UG rec. non-need-based scholarship or grant aid	44
% needy frosh rec. need-based self-help aid	90
% needy UG rec. need-based self-help aid	91
% UG borrow to pay for school	54
Average cumulative indebtedness	$31,077
% frosh need fully met	94
% ugrads need fully met	67
Average % of frosh need met	99
Average % of ugrad need met	94

Case Western Reserve University

WOLSTEIN HALL, CLEVELAND, OH 44106-7055 • ADMISSIONS: 216-368-4450 • FAX: 216-368-5111

CAMPUS LIFE

Quality of Life Rating	91
Fire Safety Rating	88
Green Rating	96
Type of school	Private
Environment	Metropolis

STUDENTS

Total undergrad enrollment	5,020
% male/female	56/44
% from out of state	72
% frosh from public high school	70
% frosh live on campus	97
% ugrads live on campus	80
# of fraternities (% ugrad men join)	18 (27)
# of sororities (% ugrad women join)	9 (26)
% African American	4
% Asian	21
% Caucasian	49
% Hispanic	7
% Native American	<1
% Pacific Islander	<1
% Two or more races	5
% Race and/or ethnicity unknown	2
% international	13
# of countries represented	46

ACADEMICS

Academic Rating	91
% students returning for sophomore year	93
% students graduating within 4 years	66
% students graduating within 6 years	83
Calendar	Semester
Student/faculty ratio	11:1
Profs interesting rating	81
Profs accessible rating	83
Most classes have 10–19 students.	

MOST POPULAR MAJORS

Bioengineering and Biomedical Engineering; Mechanical Engineering; Biology/Biological Sciences

ABOUT THE SCHOOL

More than seventy-five majors, small class sizes, and a 11:1 student-to-faculty ratio guarantee that students at Case Western Reserve University have access to a unique combination of all the opportunities of a big school with all of the individual attention of a small school. The research behemoth stresses a lot of interdisciplinary learning from a research, clinical, experiential, classroom, and social perspective, and the strong SAGES program (Seminar Approach to General Education and Scholarship) offers undergrads a series of small, interdisciplinary seminars throughout the entirety of their time at CWRU. Professors are "sociable and eminently approachable" and "truly believe that their job is to educate students, be it in the laboratory or in the classroom." CWRU relies heavily on student initiative, creating "a close knit community centered around the cultivation of the intellect."

BANG FOR YOUR BUCK

CWRU doesn't want sticker prices to deter any student from receiving an education, and is "very generous with aid, whether it is financial or merit-based," working with each student to develop a tailored assistance package. Case Western Reserve meets 100% of demonstrated need (beginning with the class that started in fall of 2017). In addition to need-based scholarships, students may receive general academic scholarships, including a variety of awards based on specific academic interests, such as the Bolton Scholarship, Michelson-Morley STEM Scholarship, and University Scholarship. Students are automatically considered for most available scholarships when they apply to CWRU.

STUDENT LIFE

Case Western Reserve's location in Cleveland offers a campus that still feels "collegiate" with the cultural benefits of a city; the school has a free access program to most museums, and the programming board "does a great job of planning events to restaurants, events, and concerts." In the summer, the beach is nearby, and skiing and snowboarding are equally a cinch in the winter. Students tend to be "Renaissance men and women," "jack[s]-of-all-trades" who get along "because there is something we end up working on together at some point." Most balance a full schedule, multiple campus organizations, and "still find time to go out and have fun on weekends." Leaders on campus often talk about how CWRU is "over-programmed"; there are "so many active organizations putting together events all the time that it`s impossible to go to everything."

CAREER

The academic atmosphere at CWRU is "competitive and full of opportunities for research or internship experience." Opportunities for co-ops, lab experience, shadowing, and volunteering with some of the world's top organizations help to overlay classroom theory with hands-on applications, and Case Western Reserve's science and tech programs act as a natural feeder to the booming healthcare and biotechnology industries in Cleveland. "A student need only simply look, or ask career services," says one. In addition to being academics, professors include "professionals in the work force who bring those experiences to the classroom for a much more enhanced education," and can become the foundation of a contact network for jobs after graduation. Many engineering students at Case Western Reserve also take part in a co-op, which is a full-time, two-semester-long, paid work experience that gives students a head start with potential employers. Students in the College of Arts & Sciences can take part in a similar (but shorter) experience called a practicum. The average starting salary for graduates who visited PayScale.com was $62,400, and 45 percent of these same graduates reported feeling that their job had a meaningful impact on the world.

Case Western Reserve University

FINANCIAL AID: 216-368-4530 • E-MAIL: ADMISSION@CASE.EDU • WEBSITE: WWW.CASE.EDU

GENERAL INFO

Activities: Choral groups, concert band, dance, drama/theater, jazz band, literary magazine, marching band, music ensembles, musical theater, pep band, radio station, student government, student newspaper, student-run film society, symphony orchestra, yearbook, campus ministries, International Student Organization, Model UN. **Organizations:** 200 registered organizations, 8 honor societies, 4 religious organizations. 18 fraternities, 9 sororities. **Athletics (Intercollegiate):** *Men:* baseball, basketball, cross-country, football, soccer, swimming, tennis, track/field (outdoor), track/field (indoor), wrestling. *Women:* basketball, cross-country, soccer, softball, swimming, tennis, track/field (outdoor), track/field (indoor), volleyball. **On-Campus Highlights:** North Residential Village, Peter B. Lewis Building, Kelvin Smith Library, Veale Convocation and Athletic Center, Tinkham Veale University Center , think[box] makerspace.

FINANCIAL AID

Students should submit: CSS Profile, FAFSA; Institution's own financial aid form, Noncustodial PROFILE. Priority filing deadline is two weeks after the application deadline. The Princeton Review suggests that all financial aid forms be submitted as soon as possible after October 1. *Need-based scholarships/grants offered:* College/university scholarship or grant aid from institutional funds, Federal Pell, private scholarships, SEOG, state scholarships/grants. *Loan aid offered:* Direct PLUS Loans, Direct Subsidized Loans, Direct Unsubsidized Loans. Applicants will be notified of awards upon admission. Federal Work-Study Program available. Institutional employment available.

BOTTOM LINE

Tuition runs at $47,074, with $14,784 being added on for room and board. With $426 in fees incorporated, the total cost for freshman year is $62,284. CWRU suggests that students all live on campus, but those returning students who choose to commute typically receive less need-based grant assistance (around $12,300 less) than those who live on campus.

CAREER INFORMATION FROM PAYSCALE.COM	
ROI Rating	91
Bachelors and No Higher	
Median starting salary	$65,100
Median mid-career salary	$113,800
At Least Bachelors	
Median starting salary	$66,700
Median mid-career salary	$120,200
Alumni with high job meaning	45%
Degrees awarded in STEM subjects	36%

SELECTIVITY

Admissions Rating	94
# of applicants	25,380
% of applicants accepted	33
% of acceptees attending	16
# offered a place on the wait list	7,178
% accepting a place on wait list	59
% admitted from wait list	14
# of early decision applicants	485
% accepted early decision	38

FRESHMAN PROFILE

Range SAT EBRW	650–740
Range SAT Math	690–780
Range ACT Composite	30–33
Minimum paper TOEFL	577
Minimum internet-based TOEFL	90
% graduated top 10% of class	70
% graduated top 25% of class	95
% graduated top 50% of class	100

DEADLINES

Early decision	
Deadline	11/1
Notification	12/15
Other ED Deadline	1/15
Other ED Notification	2/1
Early action	
Deadline	11/1
Notification	12/15
Regular	
Deadline	1/15
Notification	3/20
Nonfall registration?	Yes

FINANCIAL FACTS

Financial Aid Rating	93
Annual tuition	$48,604
Room and board	$15,190
Required fees	$438
Books and supplies	$1,200
Average frosh need-based scholarship	$36,474
Average UG need-based scholarship	$30,713
% needy frosh rec. need-based scholarship or grant aid	98
% needy UG rec. need-based scholarship or grant aid	97
% needy frosh rec. non-need-based scholarship or grant aid	35
% needy UG rec. non-need-based scholarship or grant aid	17
% needy frosh rec. need-based self-help aid	94
% needy UG rec. need-based self-help aid	96
% frosh rec. any financial aid	83
% UG rec. any financial aid	87
% UG borrow to pay for school	49

Centre College

600 WEST WALNUT STREET, DANVILLE, KY 40422 • ADMISSIONS: 800-423-6236 • FAX: 859-238-5373

CAMPUS LIFE	
Quality of Life Rating	87
Fire Safety Rating	84
Green Rating	78
Type of school	Private
Affiliation	Presbyterian
Environment	Small town

STUDENTS	
Total undergrad enrollment	1,441
% male/female	49/51
% from out of state	44
% frosh from public high school	66
% frosh live on campus	99
% ugrads live on campus	98
# of fraternities (% ugrad men join)	6 (36)
# of sororities (% ugrad women join)	5 (40)
% African American	5
% Asian	5
% Caucasian	73
% Hispanic	5
% Native American	<1
% Pacific Islander	<1
% Two or more races	3
% Race and/or ethnicity unknown	1
% international	7
# of countries represented	15

ACADEMICS	
Academic Rating	94
% students returning for sophomore year	91
% students graduating within 4 years	80
% students graduating within 6 years	82
Calendar	4/1/4
Student/faculty ratio	10:1
Profs interesting rating	96
Profs accessible rating	97

Most classes have 10–19 students. Most lab/discussion sessions have 10–19 students.

MOST POPULAR MAJORS
Biology/Biological Sciences; Economics

ABOUT THE SCHOOL

Centre College provides its students with a personal education that enables them to achieve extraordinary success in advanced study and their careers, "bringing a worldwide cultural intellect and perspective to a small town in Kentucky," according to a grateful undergraduate. Professors challenge their students and give them the individual attention and support they need. Courses are "pertinent to modern issues and thought," says a student. This results in graduates with a can-do attitude and the ability to accomplish their goals. "Preparing students to be actively engaged global citizens" is important here, one student tells us. Academics are of course paramount, but Centre also puts emphasis on community involvement and the social development of its students; there is "a big movement on getting out of the classroom with the community-based learning." "If a professor doesn't require that kind of learning," a student explains, "then they almost always will still make connections outside the classroom whether to real life or to other classes." While Centre is in a small town in rural Kentucky, "there is never a dull moment." Centre College has an active campus life. Fraternities and sororities have a big presence, but one student says, "There are a lot of students who are involved in Greek life, but there are a fair amount who are not involved in any way."

BANG FOR YOUR BUCK

Centre offers a multitude of advantages, such as a recognized academic reputation, a plethora of majors to choose from, and exposure to internationally known artists and scholars; benefits like these produce extraordinary success. For example, entrance to top graduate and professional schools; the most prestigious postgraduate scholarships (Rhodes, Fulbright, Goldwater); interesting, rewarding jobs (97 percent of graduates are either employed or engaged in advance study within ten months of graduation). Centre has an impressively strong study abroad program, and about eighty-five percent of their students take advantage; it "allows every student the chance to study abroad, regardless of major or financial situation," reports one student. Another undergrad states proudly that Centre "looks toward the future...of our world and the need for students to be prepared for it." Just about everyone gets a job or accepted into some sort of graduate school after graduation. "They took a chance by letting me attend. I had a below average ACT score than the college accepted. They offered me a great scholarship that made attending their school financially feasible. I honor their decision by doing my best, which has led me not only to good grades but also a life changing experience."

STUDENT LIFE

"When you go to Centre," says one behavioral neuroscience major, "you know that there is always someone to keep you accountable, to listen to you, and to help you when you need it." With eighty-one student organizations to choose from and 98 percent of students living on campus, this small Kentucky school—enrollment is roughly 1,440—provides many options for its students. Greek life plays a large role on campus, with five sororities and six fraternities available to pledge; nearly half the students (40 percent of women and 42 percent of men) join a sorority or fraternity. While weekends are often dominated by frat parties, "during the week, there are sporting events and tailgates sponsored by the Student Activities Council, religious group meetings, Midnight Movie events, convocations, and concerts at the Norton Center for the Arts." One English and Religion major noted that "we have this phrase at Centre called 'The Centre Bubble'—we get...wrapped up in life at Centre." While students agree that there aren't many social opportunities in the town of Danville, the "Student Activities Council always has something up [its sleeve] that is fun."

Centre College

FINANCIAL AID: 859-238-5365 • E-MAIL: ADMISSION@CENTRE.EDU • WEBSITE: WWW.CENTRE.EDU

CAREER

The Center for Career & Professional Development at Centre promises students that its staff "are here to help you apply for internships, jobs and graduate school, as well as explore your career options and interests." From the career center's website, students can watch tutorial videos from CareerSpots.com, which provides "a series of short videos on career related topics such as networking, interviewing, job fairs, etiquette, and more." One Computer Science major raved that Centre "guarantees an internship" or research experience, and other students praise the professors' helpfulness in tracking down and applying for internships. After graduating, a Biology major noted that the "alumni network is HUGE, and really helpful once you leave Centre." Popular majors for Centre students include economics and finance, philosophy, and history with popular post-Centre fields like financial services, education, and health/medicine.

GENERAL INFO

Activities: Choral groups, dance, drama/theater, jazz band, literary magazine, music ensembles, musical theater, opera, pep band, student government, student newspaper, symphony orchestra, television station, campus ministries, International Student Organization, 70 registered organizations, 12 honor societies, 6 religious organizations. 6 fraternities, 5 sororities. **Athletics (Intercollegiate):** *Men:* baseball, basketball, cross-country, diving, football, golf, lacrosse, soccer, swimming, tennis, track/field (outdoor). *Women:* basketball, cross-country, diving, field hockey, golf, lacrosse, soccer, softball, swimming, tennis, track/field (outdoor), volleyball.

FINANCIAL AID

Students should submit: FAFSA; Institution's own financial aid form. Regular filing deadline is 1/15. The Princeton Review suggests that all financial aid forms be submitted as soon as possible after October 1. *Need-based scholarships/grants offered:* College/university scholarship or grant aid from institutional funds, Federal Pell, private scholarships, SEOG, state scholarships/grants. *Loan aid offered:* Direct PLUS Loans, Direct Subsidized Loans, Direct Unsubsidized Loans. Applicants will be notified of awards on or about 1/10. Federal Work-Study Program available. Institutional employment available.

BOTTOM LINE

Centre's small but capable student body reflects solid academic preparation from high school. If you're ranked in the top quarter of your graduating class and have taken challenging courses throughout high school, you should have no difficulties with the admissions process. Tuition, room, board, books, and supplies will come to $47,800 at Centre College. However, 96 percent of undergraduates receive financial aid, so a Centre education is still within reach for most applicants. The average need-based scholarship package is substantial, at around $28,880. Centre College provided one undergraduate with a "good financial aid package and made it possible for a student with little financial means to study abroad." Upon graduation, student loan debt is a very reasonable $24,917.

CAREER INFORMATION FROM PAYSCALE.COM

ROI Rating	90
Bachelors and No Higher	
Median starting salary	$48,900
Median mid-career salary	$88,200
At Least Bachelors	
Median starting salary	$50,900
Median mid-career salary	$97,700
Alumni with high job meaning	52%
Degrees awarded in STEM subjects	17%

SELECTIVITY

Admissions Rating	89
# of applicants	2,454
% of applicants accepted	76
% of acceptees attending	21
# offered a place on the wait list	107
% accepting a place on wait list	18
% admitted from wait list	21
# of early decision applicants	88
% accepted early decision	76

FRESHMAN PROFILE

Range SAT EBRW	590–680
Range SAT Math	580–730
Range ACT Composite	26–31
Minimum paper TOEFL	580
Minimum internet-based TOEFL	90
Average HS GPA	3.6
% graduated top 10% of class	64
% graduated top 25% of class	86
% graduated top 50% of class	99

DEADLINES

Early decision	
Deadline	11/15
Notification	12/15
Early action	
Deadline	12/1
Notification	1/15
Regular	
Deadline	1/15
Notification	3/31
Nonfall registration?	No

FINANCIAL FACTS

Financial Aid Rating	87
Annual tuition	$41,700
Room and board	$10,480
Required fees	$0
Average frosh need-based scholarship	$31,901
Average UG need-based scholarship	$30,467
% needy frosh rec. need-based scholarship or grant aid	100
% needy UG rec. need-based scholarship or grant aid	100
% needy frosh rec. non-need-based scholarship or grant aid	0
% needy UG rec. non-need-based scholarship or grant aid	0
% needy frosh rec. need-based self-help aid	58
% needy UG rec. need-based self-help aid	65
% frosh rec. any financial aid	97
% UG rec. any financial aid	96
% UG borrow to pay for school	45
Average cumulative indebtedness	$24,917
% frosh need fully met	37

Christopher Newport University

1 Avenue of the Arts, Newport News, VA 23606-3072 • Admissions: 757-594-7015 • Fax: 757-594-7333

CAMPUS LIFE

Quality of Life Rating	94
Fire Safety Rating	95
Green Rating	60*
Type of school	Public
Environment	City

STUDENTS

Total undergrad enrollment	4,950
% male/female	44/56
% from out of state	8
% frosh from public high school	80
% frosh live on campus	98
% ugrads live on campus	78
# of fraternities (% ugrad men join)	10 (22)
# of sororities (% ugrad women join)	10 (34)
% African American	7
% Asian	3
% Caucasian	75
% Hispanic	5
% Native American	<1
% Pacific Islander	<1
% Two or more races	5
% Race and/or ethnicity unknown	4
% international	<1
# of countries represented	34

ACADEMICS

Academic Rating	86
% students returning for sophomore year	88
% students graduating within 4 years	63
% students graduating within 6 years	75
Calendar	Semester
Student/faculty ratio	15:1
Profs interesting rating	89
Profs accessible rating	91

Most classes have 10–19 students.

MOST POPULAR MAJORS
Speech Communication and Rhetoric;
Biology/Biological Sciences; Psychology

ABOUT THE SCHOOL

Virginia's Christopher Newport University is a relatively young public university that focuses on the study of leadership via the nationally-recognized President's Leadership Program, encourages civic engagement through community service, and develops students' intellectual capacities through a liberal learning-based core curriculum. Teaching undergraduates is a number one priority, and "classes are considered [students'] full time jobs." There is "a sense of expectation" in all things faculty and students pursue, "not because it's required, but because we know we are capable of achieving great things." To that end, faculty are "encouraging, engaging," and "truly helpful and brilliant professors in their fields," and work to connect classroom material to real life situations. Without decades of wear and tear, CNU has an incredible campus that "looks like a castle" but has up-to-date facilities, and "everything is new and has the best technology." It provides all of the spaces for rigorous academic study "and yet it is an oasis from the stressful life as a student."

BANG FOR YOUR BUCK

Christopher Newport is a small liberal arts and sciences university that "provides a private school atmosphere at a public school cost." The school creates an atmosphere "where students are urged to seek excellence and not settle," and meticulously sets its students up "to be a power in the real world and to invoke change." Students here strive for high achievement in their courses, but "are also motivated to be involved on campus." The Honors program especially promotes this type of involvement, and allows for the especially academically gifted to take seminar-style courses "that promote critical thinking and other skills necessary for graduate programs."

STUDENT LIFE

CNU is "small enough to know people of various majors and interests, but large enough to continue to meet new people every day." The student body has a large focus on service, and most people "do a lot of volunteering or are involved in service organizations." Greek life is big (and also "has a culture of kindness associated with it"), so "a lot of people are involved in their organization and help with fundraisers and host events." Dorms are "spacious and high quality" and the campus is "stunning," and many people play "Frisbee, soccer, or flag football on the Great Lawn at the heart of campus," or "set up hammocks in the trees around school and chill in them." Many people explore Newport News or visit family on the weekends, and many are athletic so "the gym is often crowded" and "intramural sports fill up quick."

CAREER

The Center for Career Planning offers workshops, career panels, campus interviews and career fairs, connecting students with alumni who can speak to how the CNU curriculum works in the real world. Christopher Newport is "located near some big companies who offer internships" as well as Jefferson Labs and NASA Langley Research Center, and there are "wide opportunities for students." Eager, caring professors "share their research interests with you," and as this is an "up-and-coming" school, there are "so many opportunities to become a founder of something," as well as lots of room for leadership roles. Out of CNU alumni visiting PayScale.com, 53 percent report that they derive a high level of meaning from their jobs.

Christopher Newport University

FINANCIAL AID: 757-594-7170 • E-MAIL: ADMIT@CNU.EDU • WEBSITE: WWW.CNU.EDU

GENERAL INFO

Activities: Campus Ministries; Choral groups; Concert band; Dance; Drama/theater; International Student Organization; Jazz ensembles; Literary magazine; Marching band; Model UN; Music ensembles; Musical theater; Opera; Pep band; Radio station; Student government; Student newspaper; Student-run film society; Symphony orchestra; Television station, 139 registered organizations, 23 honor societies, 12 religious organizations. 9 fraternities, 10 sororities. **Athletics (Intercollegiate):** *Men:* baseball, basketball, cheerleading, cross-country, football, golf, lacrosse, sailing, soccer, tennis, track/field (outdoor), track/field (indoor). *Women:* basketball, cheerleading, cross-country, dance team, field hockey, golf, lacrosse, sailing, soccer, softball, tennis, track/field (outdoor), track/field (indoor), volleyball. **On-Campus Highlights:** Trible Library, Ferguson Center for the Arts, David Student Union, Christopher Newport Hall, Freeman Center.

FINANCIAL AID

Students should submit: FAFSA. Priority filing deadline is 3/1. The Princeton Review suggests that all financial aid forms be submitted as soon as possible after October 1. *Need-based scholarships/grants offered:* College/university scholarship or grant aid from institutional funds, Federal Pell, private scholarships, SEOG, state scholarships/grants. *Loan aid offered:* Direct PLUS Loans, Direct Subsidized Loans, Direct Unsubsidized Loans. Applicants will be notified of awards on a rolling basis beginning 3/1. Federal Work-Study Program available. Institutional employment available.

CAREER INFORMATION FROM PAYSCALE.COM	
ROI Rating	87
Bachelors and No Higher	
Median starting salary	$49,600
Median mid-career salary	$84,000
At Least Bachelors	
Median starting salary	$50,300
Median mid-career salary	$90,100
Alumni with high job meaning	56%
Degrees awarded in STEM subjects	25%

SELECTIVITY	
Admissions Rating	83
# of applicants	6,948
% of applicants accepted	72
% of acceptees attending	26
# offered a place on the wait list	921
% accepting a place on wait list	30
% admitted from wait list	39
# of early decision applicants	400
% accepted early decision	81

FRESHMAN PROFILE	
Range SAT EBRW	570–650
Range SAT Math	540–620
Range ACT Composite	23–28
Minimum paper TOEFL	530
Minimum internet-based TOEFL	71
Average HS GPA	3.8
% graduated top 10% of class	18
% graduated top 25% of class	50
% graduated top 50% of class	84

DEADLINES	
Early decision	
Deadline	11/15
Notification	12/15
Early action	
Deadline	12/1
Notification	1/15
Regular	
Priority	2/1
Deadline	2/1
Notification	3/15
Nonfall registration?	Yes

FINANCIAL FACTS	
Financial Aid Rating	81
Annual in-state tuition	$9,032
Annual out-of-state tuition	$21,498
Room and board	$11,460
Required fees	$5,722
Average frosh need-based scholarship	$6,906
Average UG need-based scholarship	$6,982
% needy frosh rec. need-based scholarship or grant aid	69
% needy UG rec. need-based scholarship or grant aid	67
% needy frosh rec. non-need-based scholarship or grant aid	39
% needy UG rec. non-need-based scholarship or grant aid	29
% needy frosh rec. need-based self-help aid	72
% needy UG rec. need-based self-help aid	79
% frosh rec. any financial aid	74
% UG rec. any financial aid	69

City University of New York—Baruch College

Undergraduate Admissions, 151 East 25th Street, New York, NY 10010 • Admissions: 646-312-1400 • Fax: 646-312-1363

#48 BEST VALUE COLLEGE

CAMPUS LIFE

Quality of Life Rating	90
Fire Safety Rating	60*
Green Rating	61
Type of school	Public
Environment	Metropolis

STUDENTS

Total undergrad enrollment	14,903
% male/female	51/49
% from out of state	3
% frosh from public high school	87
% frosh live on campus	9
% ugrads live on campus	2
# of fraternities (% ugrad men join)	0 (0)
# of sororities (% ugrad women join)	0 (0)
% African American	9
% Asian	31
% Caucasian	20
% Hispanic	26
% Native American	<1
% Pacific Islander	<1
% Two or more races	1
% Race and/or ethnicity unknown	0
% international	11
# of countries represented	168

ACADEMICS

Academic Rating	80
% students returning for sophomore year	90
% students graduating within 4 years	41
% students graduating within 6 years	70
Calendar	Semester
Student/faculty ratio	19:1
Profs interesting rating	83
Profs accessible rating	75

Most classes have 20–29 students. Most lab/discussion sessions have 20–29 students.

MOST POPULAR MAJORS
Accounting; Finance

ABOUT THE SCHOOL

Situated in the heart of New York City, Baruch College and its three schools—Weissman School of Arts and Sciences, Marxe School of Public and International Affairs, and the Zicklin School of Business, which is the largest—maintains a strong "academic reputation" as one of the ten senior colleges within the City University of New York system. Here students can gain a "quality" education that won't break the proverbial bank. Many students rush to highlight the "great business school" and note that it's "one [of] the nation's finest." Others call out the School of Public and International Affairs as "extremely good" and say it does a great job of maintaining a "family-like feel" on a larger campus of about 15,000 undergrads. Should a student find themselves struggling, Baruch provides several "amazing resources such as peer counseling, the writing center and tutoring." Of course, they can also turn to their "excellent" professors who clearly have "a passion for what they teach." Many instructors have "first-hand experience," which they readily bring into the classroom. As one undergrad explains, "Some of my business professors came from leading huge corporations, and their anecdotes...help students internalize the material." Most importantly, Baruch professors "want the students to thrive and succeed."

BANG FOR YOUR BUCK

Many undergrads are drawn to Baruch in large part due to its "affordability." After all, "tuition is not expensive" and "the financial aid is generous." As one grateful student shares, "I am on a full tuition scholarship with free laptops and priority scheduling and even a study abroad stipend....[Baruch] really hook[s] you up." More specifically, the Baruch College Fund (BCF) distributes over $2 million in scholarship funds annually. Designed to encourage both academic excellence and leadership, many of these scholarships are awarded to students who maintain a high level of academic performance. For example, the Arthur Milton Memorial Scholarship is given to incoming freshmen who earned a strong SAT score and maintained a high GPA throughout high school. The Barbara and Arthur Gallagher Scholarship is awarded to students who demonstrate both financial need and a commitment to service.

SCHOOL LIFE

When asked about life at Baruch, many undergrads caution that Baruch is "a commuter school" and "most students go to classes and go home." Thankfully, they acknowledge that "there are great clubs and events always happening [on campus]." When they find a break in their day, students often head over to "the game room where there are foosball tables and a billiards table as well." Additionally, "Baruch's student affairs [office frequently sponsors] fun weekend trips" to places like "Boston," "Niagara Falls," or even "apple picking" at an orchard just outside the city. These students certainly capitalize on their prime Manhattan location. As one student points out, whether "you like art, music, galleries, museums, theater, [or] partying," there is "always something to do in New York City."

City University of New York—Baruch College

FINANCIAL AID: 646-312-1360 • E-MAIL: ADMISSIONS@BARUCH.CUNY.EDU • WEBSITE: WWW.BARUCH.CUNY.EDU

CAREER

Students at Baruch have access to some "impressive" career resources. To begin with, undergrads can easily tap into "a strong alumni network." Baruch's Star Career Services Center routinely invites "top companies [to campus] to network with students and talk about their jobs." The Center "provides services to help students prepare for these events," which can cover everything from LinkedIn 101—for students to learn how to leverage the site and make their profile stand out—to mastering a job interview. Additionally, the Career Services Center offers some unique programs like the dining etiquette workshop, which allows students to prep for networking events that involve food. Of course, most importantly, Baruch hosts some amazing career fairs that put students in direct contact with top firms like Bank of America, Citi, Target, and Goldman Sachs.

GENERAL INFO

Activities: Choral groups, dance, drama/theater, literary magazine, musical theater, radio station, student government, student newspaper, yearbook, campus ministries, Model UN 172 registered organizations, 9 honor societies, 7 religious organizations. **Athletics (Intercollegiate):** *Men:* baseball, basketball, cross-country, soccer, swimming, tennis, volleyball. *Women:* basketball, cheerleading, cross-country, softball, swimming, tennis, volleyball. **On-Campus Highlights:** Student Club Area—Vertical Campus, NewMan Library, Lobby—23 St. Building, Food Court—Vertical Campus Building, College Fitness Center—Vertical Campus.

FINANCIAL AID

Students should submit: FAFSA, state aid form. Priority filing deadline is 11/1. The Princeton Review suggests that all financial aid forms be submitted as soon as possible after October 1. *Need-based scholarships/grants offered:* College/university scholarship or grant aid from institutional funds, Federal Pell, private scholarships, SEOG, state scholarships/grants. *Loan aid offered:* Direct PLUS Loans, Direct Subsidized Loans, Direct Unsubsidized Loans. Applicants will be notified of awards on a rolling basis beginning 4/15. Federal Work-Study Program available. Institutional employment available.

THE BOTTOM LINE

New York residents who attend Baruch full-time face a relatively modest tuition bill of $6,730 per year. Undergraduates who hail from out-of-state should expect to pay $18,000. Students should budget about $1,364 for books and supplies and $1,054 for transportation. Undergrads living away from home will need a minimum of $17,926 for room and board. Additionally, the college estimates that personal expenses might amount to $4,342 for the academic year. Lastly, all full-time students must pay a $150 technology fee, $60–180 activity fee and a $15 consolidated service fee.

CAREER INFORMATION FROM PAYSCALE.COM

ROI Rating	92
Bachelors and No Higher	
Median starting salary	$57,100
Median mid-career salary	$107,600
At Least Bachelors	
Median starting salary	$57,600
Median mid-career salary	$110,100
Alumni with high job meaning	36%
Degrees awarded in STEM subjects	8%

SELECTIVITY

Admissions Rating	92
# of applicants	21,432
% of applicants accepted	29
% of acceptees attending	26

FRESHMAN PROFILE

Range SAT EBRW	580–660
Range SAT Math	610–690
Minimum paper TOEFL	550
Minimum internet-based TOEFL	80
Average HS GPA	3.3
% graduated top 10% of class	48
% graduated top 25% of class	75
% graduated top 50% of class	92

DEADLINES

Early decision	
Deadline	12/13
Notification	1/7
Regular	
Priority	12/1
Deadline	2/1
Notification	12/1
Nonfall registration?	Yes

FINANCIAL FACTS

Financial Aid Rating	80
Annual in-state tuition	$6,730
Annual out-of-state tuition	$18,000
Room and board	$17,926
Required fees	$531
Books and supplies	$1,364
Average frosh need-based scholarship	$7,504
Average UG need-based scholarship	$6,574
% needy frosh rec. need-based scholarship or grant aid	92
% needy UG rec. need-based scholarship or grant aid	91
% needy frosh rec. non-need-based scholarship or grant aid	8
% needy UG rec. non-need-based scholarship or grant aid	6
% needy frosh rec. need-based self-help aid	11
% needy UG rec. need-based self-help aid	25
% frosh rec. any financial aid	64
% UG rec. any financial aid	62
% UG borrow to pay for school	14
Average cumulative indebtedness	$12,117
% frosh need fully met	4
% ugrads need fully met	3
Average % of frosh need met	36
Average % of ugrad need met	37

City University of New York—Brooklyn College

2900 BEDFORD AVENUE, BROOKLYN, NY 11210 • ADMISSIONS: 718-951-5001 • FAX: 718-951-4506

CAMPUS LIFE

Quality of Life Rating	**82**
Fire Safety Rating	**60***
Green Rating	**60***
Type of school	Public
Environment	Metropolis

STUDENTS

Total undergrad enrollment	13,712
% male/female	43/57
% from out of state	2
% frosh from public high school	86
% frosh live on campus	0
% ugrads live on campus	0
# of fraternities (% ugrad men join)	7 (3)
# of sororities (% ugrad women join)	9 (3)
% African American	21
% Asian	20
% Caucasian	30
% Hispanic	23
% Native American	<1
% Pacific Islander	<1
% Two or more races	2
% Race and/or ethnicity unknown	0
% international	3
# of countries represented	138

ACADEMICS

Academic Rating	**69**
% students returning for sophomore year	82
% students graduating within 4 years	28
% students graduating within 6 years	58
Calendar	Semester
Student/faculty ratio	18:1
Profs interesting rating	67
Profs accessible rating	64

Most classes have 20–29 students. Most lab/discussion sessions have 20–29 students.

MOST POPULAR MAJORS

Computer Science; Psychology; Accounting

ABOUT THE SCHOOL

Respected nationally for its rigorous academic standards, the college takes pride in such innovative programs as its award-winning Freshman Year College; the Honors Academy, which houses six programs for high achievers; and its nationally recognized core curriculum. Its School of Education is ranked among the top twenty in the country, for graduates who go on to be considered among the best teachers in New York City. Brooklyn College's strong academic reputation has attracted an outstanding faculty of nationally renowned teachers and scholars. Among the awards they have won are Pulitzers, Guggenheims, Fulbrights, and many National Institutes of Health grants. The Brooklyn College campus, considered to be among the most beautiful in the nation, is in the midst of an ambitious program of expansion and renewal.

Education at the college is taken seriously, and the curriculum is challenging. Students mention that "the material is engaging and interesting while the professors are first-rate"; "I find myself learning beyond the course description." There is respect for the opinions of their students, and "each professor allows students to have free reign of their thoughts and ideas," one student says admiringly. Another satisfied undergrad tells us that "it is hard to estimate my academic gains, but they have been substantial." Additionally, each student is assigned a peer mentor and a counseling class that "helps us adapt to college life. I think that it helped me to be a more active student."

STUDENT LIFE

"The typical student at Brooklyn College is hardworking, from the New York metro area, and a commuter." Many "hold part-time jobs and pay at least part of their own tuition, so they are usually in a rush because they have a lot more responsibility on their shoulders than the average college student." Like Brooklyn itself, "the student body is very diversified," with everyone from "an aspiring opera singer to quirky film majors to single mothers looking for a better life for their children," and so "no student can be described as being typical. Everyone blends in as normal, and little segregation is noticed (if it exists)." Students here represent more than 100 nations and speak nearly as many languages. There are even students "that come from Long Island to North Carolina, from Connecticut to even Hong Kong." The college's accessibility by subway or bus allows students to further enrich their educational experience through New York City's many cultural events and institutions. It should be noted that there are now new dorms for students, and that this is very exciting.

CAREER

Brooklyn College alumni who visited PayScale.com reported a median starting salary of $48,200, and 43 percent of graduates feel their jobs have a lot of meaning in their lives. Students feel that Brooklyn College "is an outstanding school with a very good reputation of successful alumni," and that "there are a lot of volunteering programs and internships available." Students feel that "Brooklyn College is a school that attempts to provide an effective education for people in need of career advancement." The Magner Career Center partners with employers, faculty and staff, alumni and students to provide career programs, services and resources.

City University of New York—Brooklyn College

FINANCIAL AID: 718-951-5045 • WEBSITE: WWW.BROOKLYN.CUNY.EDU

GENERAL INFO

Activities: dance, drama/theater, literary magazine, music ensembles, musical theater, radio station, student government, student newspaper, television station, yearbook, international student organization. **Organizations:** 171 registered organizations, 7 honor societies, 8 fraternities, 9 sororities. **Athletics (Intercollegiate):** *Men:* Basketball, cross-country, soccer, tennis, track/field (outdoor), track/field (indoor), volleyball. *Women:* Basketball, cross-country, softball, tennis, track/field (outdoor), track/field (indoor), volleyball. **On-Campus Highlights:** Library, Student Center, Lily Pond, Library Cafe, Cafeteria, Dining Hall, Magner Center, James Hall. **Environmental Initiatives:** Reduce consumption; awareness.

FINANCIAL AID

Students should submit: FAFSA, state aid form. Priority filing deadline is 12/15. The Princeton Review suggests that all financial aid forms be submitted as soon as possible after October 1. *Need-based scholarships/grants offered:* College/university scholarship or grant aid from institutional funds, Federal Pell, private scholarships, SEOG, state scholarships/grants. *Loan aid offered:* Direct PLUS Loans, Direct Subsidized Loans, Direct Unsubsidized Loans. Applicants will be notified of awards on a rolling basis beginning 5/1. Federal Work-Study Program available. Institutional employment available.

BOTTOM LINE

Brooklyn College provides students with an excellent education for a cost that will not break any banks—piggy or otherwise. Fortunately, in-state tuition runs only $6,330 or so; out-of-state tuition comes to $20,160. Perhaps most importantly, the institution is able to meet 92 percent of all need. The average need-based scholarship is $3,400.

CAREER INFORMATION FROM PAYSCALE.COM	
ROI Rating	87
Bachelors and No Higher	
Median starting salary	$50,100
Median mid-career salary	$97,400
At Least Bachelors	
Median starting salary	$51,000
Median mid-career salary	$98,800
Alumni with high job meaning	42%
Degrees awarded in STEM subjects	8%

SELECTIVITY	
Admissions Rating	88
# of applicants	20,642
% of applicants accepted	40
% of acceptees attending	20

FRESHMAN PROFILE	
Range SAT EBRW	510–590
Range SAT Math	520–600
Minimum paper TOEFL	500
Average HS GPA	3.3

DEADLINES	
Regular	
Priority	2/1
Nonfall registration?	Yes

FINANCIAL FACTS	
Financial Aid Rating	88
Annual in-state tuition	$6,730
Annual out-of-state tuition	$18,000
Room and board	$14,824
Required fees	$510
Books and supplies	$1,364
Average frosh need-based scholarship	$10,070
Average UG need-based scholarship	$8,870
% needy frosh rec. need-based scholarship or grant aid	94.7
% needy UG rec. need-based scholarship or grant aid	94
% needy frosh rec. non-need-based scholarship or grant aid	73.8
% needy UG rec. non-need-based scholarship or grant aid	26.9
% needy frosh rec. need-based self-help aid	18.5
% UG borrow to pay for school	15
Average cumulative indebtedness	$11,550

City University of New York—City College

160 Convent Avenue, Wille Administration Building, New York, NY 10031 • Admissions: 212-650-6977 • Fax: 212-650-6417

CAMPUS LIFE

Quality of Life Rating	**84**
Fire Safety Rating	**97**
Green Rating	**95**
Type of school	Public
Environment	Metropolis

STUDENTS

Total undergrad enrollment	12,480
% male/female	49/51
% from out of state	1
% frosh from public high school	85
% ugrads live on campus	0
# of fraternities	6
# of sororities	5
% African American	16
% Asian	25
% Caucasian	16
% Hispanic	37
% Native American	<1
% Pacific Islander	<1
% Two or more races	2
% Race and/or ethnicity unknown	0
% international	6
# of countries represented	155

ACADEMICS

Academic Rating	**71**
% students returning for sophomore year	92
% students graduating within 4 years	12
% students graduating within 6 years	50
Calendar	Semester
Student/faculty ratio	15:1
Profs interesting rating	68
Profs accessible rating	64

Most classes have fewer than 10 students.
Most lab/discussion sessions have 10–19 students.

MOST POPULAR MAJORS

Communication and Media Studies;
Mechanical Engineering/Mechanical
Technology/Technician; Psychology

ABOUT THE SCHOOL

Founded in 1847, City College offers a prestigious education to a diverse student body. With its "astonishingly low cost," "great engineering program," "strong ties to research collaborators and institutions," and an art program that's "also one of the best" in the metro area, indeed, City College earns its claim of being one of "America's finest democratic achievements." When it comes to the school's main draws, students cite the three C's: "convenience, cost, and concentration." The school "is known for its rigorous academic programs," which "rival that of the nation's premier universities." Additionally, "it is affordable," which students are quick to note "is an important factor in these tough economic times." With total undergraduate enrollment at just under 13,000, City College is all about embracing diversity and harnessing personal dedication. Professors are "attentive" and classes are "challenging." Professors "exhibit great love for the materials they teach and generally go above and beyond to ensure that students are able to grasp and apply the material." What's better? All this learning takes place in New York City, with its wealth of professional opportunities.

BANG FOR YOUR BUCK

More than 80 percent of the entering class at City College receives some type of financial aid. In addition, in the last three years, City has increased the dollar amount going to student scholarships by 35 percent. It pays to be an exceptional student when your application comes through the admissions office, as many of the students receiving merit-based awards are members of the City College Honors program. In addition, the Macaulay Honors College at City College offers students a free laptop computer and a cultural passport to New York City. Many scholarships are awarded on the basis of the major or entrance to a specific school of the college.

STUDENT LIFE

As one student proudly contends, "We (the student body in the aggregate) speak over 100 languages and come from places most people have never heard of." The diversity at CCNY is not just limited to ethnicity—it also spans political leanings, economic background, academic interest, age, and professional experience, and—regardless of their origins—most CCNY students "identify first and foremost as New Yorkers." One student says, "CCNY is definitely a diamond in the rough. It should be considered by any student who wants to experience New York City college life at an affordable rate without sacrificing education quality," but warns that one should "expect to hunt for an apartment or a roommate on your own IN ADDITION TO, and not instead of, opting for on-campus housing." Most CCNY students are not looking for the "typical college experience," but rather are interested "in the intellectual and emotional growth that comes with higher education."

CAREER

City College graduates who visited PayScale.com reported a median starting salary of $51,400, and 55 percent of graduates feel their jobs have a lot of meaning in their lives. Students feel that City College "thoroughly prepares its students for their future careers, with emphasis placed on the effects of the current economic climate," and that there are veritable "tons of internship/research opportunities," which students receive frequent email updates about. City College's Career and Professional Development Institute offers a number of services to students and alumni including individual career counseling, internship and job opportunities, resume writing, career fairs, and workshops aimed at developing the professional identity of students and alumni.

City University of New York—City College

FINANCIAL AID: 212-650-5819 • E-MAIL: ADMISSIONS@CCNY.CUNY.EDU • WEBSITE: WWW.CCNY.CUNY.EDU

GENERAL INFO

Activities: Choral groups, concert band, dance, drama/theater, jazz band, literary magazine, radio station, student government, student newspaper, student-run film society, yearbook. **Organizations:** International Student Organization, Model UN. 145 registered organizations, 8 religious organizations. 2 fraternities, 1 sorority. **Athletics (Intercollegiate):** *Men:* baseball, basketball, cross-country, soccer, tennis, track/field (outdoor), track/field (indoor), volleyball. *Women:* basketball, fencing, soccer, tennis, track/field (outdoor), track/field (indoor), volleyball. **On-Campus Highlights:** NAC Rotunda and Plaza, Spitzer School of Archtiecture, Wingate Hall Athletic Center, North Campus Quad in warm weather, The Towers—Residence Hall. **Environmental Initiatives:** Signed on to ACUPCC and NYC Mayor's Campus 30in10 Challenge to reduce GHG emissions; task force to place sustainability at forefront in all operations, outreach and educational mission; undergraduate and graduate programs in sustainability, interdisciplinary with science, engineering, architecture, and economics.

FINANCIAL AID

Students should submit: FAFSA, state aid form. Priority filing deadline is 4/1. The Princeton Review suggests that all financial aid forms be submitted as soon as possible after October 1. *Need-based scholarships/grants offered:* College/university scholarship or grant aid from institutional funds; Federal Pell; SEOG; State scholarships/grants. *Loan aid offered:* Direct PLUS Loans, Direct Subsidized Loans, Direct Unsubsidized Loans. Applicants will be notified of awards on a rolling basis beginning 4/1. Federal Work-Study Program available. Institutional employment available.

BOTTOM LINE

With in-state tuition holding steady at $6,530 and out-of-state tuition at $17,400 (15 credits per semester), for many, CCNY offers a real opportunity to realize their future at a remarkably affordable cost. Due to its "close ties to the business community of New York City," CCNY "provides an extensive array of contacts and networking opportunities leading to internships and real-life work experiences." Located in historic West Harlem, "students are minutes away from leading organizations in the fields of business, theatre, music, art, law, education, finance, retail, engineering, architecture, science, and medicine." For those career-minded individuals looking to get a jumpstart in the workforce, CCNY provides "true work experience in day-to-day settings."

CAREER INFORMATION FROM PAYSCALE.COM

ROI Rating	87
Bachelors and No Higher	
Median starting salary	$53,000
Median mid-career salary	$93,500
At Least Bachelors	
Median starting salary	$53,800
Median mid-career salary	$98,500
Alumni with high job meaning	56%
Degrees awarded in STEM subjects	33%

SELECTIVITY

Admissions Rating	88
# of applicants	25,373
% of applicants accepted	41
% of acceptees attending	16

FRESHMAN PROFILE

Range SAT EBRW	480–570
Range SAT Math	500–620
Minimum paper TOEFL	500
Minimum internet-based TOEFL	61

DEADLINES

Regular	
Priority	2/1
Nonfall registration?	Yes

FINANCIAL FACTS

Financial Aid Rating	90
Annual in-state tuition	$6,530
Annual out-of-state tuition	$17,400
Room and board	$11,516
Required fees	$410
Books and supplies	$1,364
Average frosh need-based scholarship	$8,589
Average UG need-based scholarship	$8,552
% needy frosh rec. need-based scholarship or grant aid	86
% needy UG rec. need-based scholarship or grant aid	74
% needy frosh rec. non-need-based scholarship or grant aid	15
% needy UG rec. non-need-based scholarship or grant aid	38
% needy frosh rec. need-based self-help aid	21
% needy UG rec. need-based self-help aid	18
% frosh rec. any financial aid	80
% UG rec. any financial aid	79
% frosh need fully met	70
% ugrads need fully met	95
Average % of frosh need met	85
Average % of ugrad need met	84

City University of New York—Hunter College

695 Park Ave, Room N203, New York, NY 10065 • Admissions: 212-772-4490 • Fax: 212-650-3472

CAMPUS LIFE

Quality of Life Rating	83
Fire Safety Rating	97
Green Rating	87
Type of school	Public
Environment	Metropolis

STUDENTS

Total undergrad enrollment	15,820
% male/female	35/65
% from out of state	3
% frosh from public high school	75
# of fraternities (% ugrad men join)	2 (0)
# of sororities	2
% African American	12
% Asian	30
% Caucasian	30
% Hispanic	22
% Native American	<1
% international	6
# of countries represented	162

ACADEMICS

Academic Rating	74
% students returning for sophomore year	83
% students graduating within 4 years	24
% students graduating within 6 years	52
Calendar	Semester
Student/faculty ratio	14:1
Profs interesting rating	72
Profs accessible rating	68

Most classes have 10–19 students. Most lab/discussion sessions have 10–19 students.

MOST POPULAR MAJORS

English Language and Literature; Chemistry; Psychology

ABOUT THE SCHOOL

The City University of New York—Hunter College has a lot to offer beyond its miniscule tuition. For many New Yorkers seeking a top-notch college degree, Hunter offers the best, most affordable option available. Hunter's 15,000-plus students choose from more than seventy undergraduate programs. Regardless of their area of concentration, all Hunter students are encouraged to have broad exposure to the liberal arts: "Hunter is all about bringing people from all different parts of the world together in one place to learn from one another and to be exposed to almost every subject imaginable to help one find their true calling in life," says one sophomore. Though a Hunter College education doesn't come with a lot of frills, the school's faculty is a huge asset. Professors are very often experts in their fields, and they work hard to accommodate undergraduates. One student says, "Many of the professors teach at other, more expensive universities. Throughout my Hunter career, I have had professors who also teach at NYU, Hofstra, Cooper Union, and Yale! So it really is quite the bargain...I am not missing out on a challenging, intellectual educational process by attending a public school."

BANG FOR YOUR BUCK

Extraordinarily low tuition makes Hunter affordable, and more than 1,000 scholarships, awards, and special program opportunities offered throughout the CUNY campuses complement that affordability. The usual combination of work-study jobs, need-based grants, scholarships, and credit-bearing internships helps students fund their educations. Need-based grants from the state of New York are available. Hunter offers a variety of scholarship programs for entering freshman who have maintained a high level of academic achievement while in high school and who demonstrate potential for superior scholarship at the college level. Institutional scholarships at Hunter College are offered to more than 50 percent of the aid-eligible population. The Macaulay Honors College is definitely one of the highlights. Accepted students receive a full-ride scholarship (except for fees), a laptop computer, and additional funds to pursue research, internships, or service activities. One student boasts: "The Macaulay Honors College allows me access to the best Hunter and CUNY has to offer, and to the wide resources of New York City itself, while paying no tuition." Also, financial sessions are offered at Hunter to incoming students and cover topics such as loans, credit cards, and budgeting. All new students are considered for Hunter College sponsored scholarships automatically—no separate application is required.

STUDENT LIFE

Like many of the CUNY institutions, Hunter College is primarily a commuter school. Fortunately, there's still plenty of camaraderie among these undergrads. Indeed, "Hunter encourages student interaction through Student Government run parties and other student-run activities." And many undergrads are quick to take advantage of the numerous "great events, visiting authors and scientists, guest lectures" happening around campus. Of course, being located in the heart of New York City is also a boon for these students. As one political science major boasts, "It's nearly impossible not to find stuff to do, no matter what your tastes are. The city is our campus, and it's up to you to use it to the fullest."

City University of New York—Hunter College

FINANCIAL AID: 212-772-4820 • E-MAIL: ADMISSIONS@HUNTER.CUNY.EDU • WEBSITE: WWW.HUNTER.CUNY.EDU

CAREER

Hunter's Career Development Services truly does a tremendous job for its students. Undergrads have the opportunity to attend a variety of career panels throughout the year, featuring guest speakers and assorted alumni from a number of industries. Hunter also presents students with many chances to attend different career expos. There, undergrads are able to network, learn about specific corporations and career fields and discover potential job openings. Naturally, the college also works hard to capitalize on its New York City location. Each semester, Hunter invites companies to campus to meet with students regarding internships, part-time jobs and entry-level positions. Undergrads can attend recruiting events in a number of areas: social services, public affairs, film and media, financial services, scientific research, etc. All students, no matter their interests, are bound to find an opening that piques their curiosity.

GENERAL INFO

Activities: Choral groups, concert band, dance, drama/theater, jazz band, literary magazine, music ensembles, musical theater, radio station, student government, student newspaper, student-run film society, symphony orchestra, television station, yearbook. **Organizations:** 150 registered organizations, 20 honor societies, 2 fraternities, 2 sororities. **Athletics (Intercollegiate):** *Men:* Basketball, cross-country, fencing, soccer, tennis, track/field (outdoor), track/field (indoor), volleyball, wrestling. *Women:* Basketball, cross-country, diving, fencing, softball, swimming, tennis, track/field (outdoor), track/field (indoor), volleyball. **On-Campus Highlights:** More than 100 campus clubs, CARSI Geography Lab, Television Studio, Learning Center and Computer Lab, Sports Complex.

FINANCIAL AID

Students should submit: FAFSA, state aid form. Priority filing deadline is 12/15. The Princeton Review suggests that all financial aid forms be submitted as soon as possible after October 1. *Need-based scholarships/grants offered:* College/university scholarship or grant aid from institutional funds; Federal Pell; State scholarships/grants. *Loan aid offered:* Direct PLUS Loans, Direct Subsidized Loans, Direct Unsubsidized Loans. Applicants will be notified of awards on a rolling basis beginning 5/15. Federal Work-Study Program available. Institutional employment available.

BOTTOM LINE

Full-time tuition for New York residents comes to approximately $6,730. That's ridiculously cheap. If you can't claim state residency, you'll pay about three times that amount. Also, as you know if you are a New Yorker and probably have heard if you aren't, New York City can be a painfully expensive place to live. But that shouldn't dissuade prospective students, since about 94 percent of students receive aid.

CAREER INFORMATION FROM PAYSCALE.COM	
ROI Rating	89
Bachelors and No Higher	
Median starting salary	$50,900
Median mid-career salary	$91,300
At Least Bachelors	
Median starting salary	$51,900
Median mid-career salary	$92,200
Alumni with high job meaning	52%
Degrees awarded in STEM subjects	8%

SELECTIVITY	
Admissions Rating	89
# of applicants	29,326
% of applicants accepted	40
% of acceptees attending	20

FRESHMAN PROFILE	
Range SAT EBRW	520–610
Range SAT Math	550–650
Minimum paper TOEFL	500
Average HS GPA	3.4

DEADLINES	
Regular	
Deadline	2/1

FINANCIAL FACTS	
Financial Aid Rating	89
Annual in-state tuition	$6,730
Annual out-of-state tuition	$18,000
Room and board	$13,718
Required fees	$450
Books and supplies	$1,364
Average frosh need-based scholarship	$8,983
Average UG need-based scholarship	$7,789
% needy frosh rec. need-based scholarship or grant aid	88
% needy UG rec. need-based scholarship or grant aid	86
% needy frosh rec. non-need-based scholarship or grant aid	78
% needy UG rec. non-need-based scholarship or grant aid	45
% needy frosh rec. need-based self-help aid	9
% needy UG rec. need-based self-help aid	17
% frosh rec. any financial aid	91
% UG rec. any financial aid	94
% UG borrow to pay for school	15
Average cumulative indebtedness	$12,122
% frosh need fully met	32
% ugrads need fully met	53
Average % of frosh need met	94
Average % of ugrad need met	79

City University of New York—Queens College

65-30 Kissena Boulevard, Queens, NY 11367 • Admissions: 718-997-5600 • Fax: 718-997-5617

CAMPUS LIFE	
Quality of Life Rating	**84**
Fire Safety Rating	**97**
Green Rating	**91**
Type of school	Public
Environment	Metropolis

STUDENTS	
Total undergrad enrollment	15,762
% male/female	46/54
% from out of state	1
% frosh from public high school	75
% frosh live on campus	1
% ugrads live on campus	1
# of fraternities (% ugrad men join)	6 (1)
# of sororities (% ugrad women join)	5 (1)
% African American	9
% Asian	28
% Caucasian	26
% Hispanic	29
% Native American	<1
% Pacific Islander	<1
% Two or more races	1
% Race and/or ethnicity unknown	0
% international	5
# of countries represented	143

ACADEMICS	
Academic Rating	**74**
% students returning for sophomore year	84
% students graduating within 4 years	29
% students graduating within 6 years	54
Calendar	Semester
Student/faculty ratio	15:1
Profs interesting rating	72
Profs accessible rating	69
Most classes have 10–19 students.	

MOST POPULAR MAJORS
Computer Science; Psychology; Accounting

ABOUT THE SCHOOL

For more than eighty years, Queens College has offered a first-rate education to generations of students from all different backgrounds, maintaining an incredibly affordable price tag while constantly expanding its offerings, programs, centers and institutes, and even its physical campus. Now a lynchpin of the City University of New York (CUNY) system, the school's academic programs are divided into four divisions that offer both day and night courses, and the school is the only CUNY institution in the borough participating in the noted Macaulay Honors College. "Any course you can think of, they have," one undergrad attests. Students also call out the "endless ways to help a student pick the correct major for them," abundant "research opportunities," and supportive academic counseling staff as particular Queens College highlights. Professors, especially in the sciences, are "all experts in their fields" and "encourage students to go beyond what's expected": "Everybody is willing to help as much as possible without hesitation."

BANG FOR YOUR BUCK

Plain and simple, "there are not many other schools that will give you what Queens does for anywhere near the same price." With its rock solid reputation, plethora of resources, and an alumni network that resides almost exclusively (85 percent) in the New York metropolitan area, the reward is high for students. Queens College has numerous merit- and need-based scholarships available to students, including the $2,000 John S. and Yorka C. Linakis Scholarship for students helping to better their communities; multiple $5,000 issuances of the Donald I. Brownstein/John McDermott Scholarship in Humanities for students excelling in a related humanities major; and four-year merit awards through the Queens College Scholars program.

STUDENT LIFE

People generally commute to the Queens College campus only on class days, when it "is common to see peers on the trains or buses on your way to and from school, but before and after classes students can usually be found hanging out around the campus, studying in the library, or using the exercise and recreational facilities, which include "a gym, track, pool, tennis courts, and more." The college's lush 80-acre campus is a green oasis located in residential Flushing, and is a "lovely campus that is well-balanced in terms of facilities on site versus how spread out they are." The students at Queens College are "from a highly diverse population that comes from both New York and around the globe" (more than half of all students were born abroad), and "there are many different clubs and programs that offer you plenty to experience no matter what interests you."

CAREER

One of the biggest boons for Queens College students are the professors, who "support students beyond the classroom via letters of recommendation or trying to help them enter internships [and] various programs" if the student has proven themselves to be hardworking and capable. Thanks to the campus proximity to city many students already tend to have some sort of job, whether it's a part-time gig or a full-time career. Potential opportunities are posted daily on the school's Symplicity portal by the Office of Career Development & Internships, which also runs workshops such as Résumé Preparation, Job Interview Techniques, and Job Search Strategies. Additionally, the Jeannette K. Watson Summer Fellowship Program is a three-summer paid internship program that provides annual funding to promising students of New York City partner colleges so that they may participate in seminars, cultural events, fieldwork, and internships. Out of Queens College alumni visiting PayScale.com, 43 percent report that their jobs make the world a better place.

City University of New York—Queens College

FINANCIAL AID: 718-997-5123 • E-MAIL: VINCENT.ANGRISANI@QC.CUNY.EDU • WEBSITE: WWW.QC.CUNY.EDU

GENERAL INFO

Activities: Choral groups, concert band, dance, drama/theater, jazz band, literary magazine, music ensembles, musical theater, radio station, student government, student newspaper, student-run film society, symphony orchestra, television station, yearbook, Student Organization. 114 registered organizations, 5 honor societies, 12 religious organizations. 7 fraternities, 6 sororities. **Athletics (Intercollegiate):** *Men:* baseball, basketball, cross-country, diving, soccer, swimming, tennis, track/field (outdoor), water polo. *Women:* basketball, cross-country, diving, fencing, lacrosse, soccer, softball, swimming, tennis, track/field (outdoor), volleyball, water polo. **On-Campus Highlights:** Rosenthal Library, Student Union, Athletic Center, Dining Hall, Classrooms and Laboratory Facilities, Cafes around campus. **Environmental Initiatives:** Retrofit and completion of mechanical upgrade 27M for the new Science Building that will significally reduce energy consumption.

FINANCIAL AID

Students should submit: FAFSA; Institution's own financial aid form; State aid form. The Princeton Review suggests that all financial aid forms be submitted as soon as possible after October 1. *Need-based scholarships/grants offered:* College/university scholarship or grant aid from institutional funds, Federal Pell, private scholarships, SEOG, state scholarships/grants. *Loan aid offered:* Direct PLUS Loans, Direct Subsidized Loans, Direct Unsubsidized Loans. Federal Work-Study Program available. Institutional employment available.

BOTTOM LINE

Tuition runs at a bargain $6,330 for full-time students who are New York State residents, with another $608 needed to cover fees. Though most students live off-campus, there is limited residential college housing available in The Summit Apartments, which cost around $12,020 per academic year for a two-bedroom or $15,074 for a four-bedroom apartment. More than 50 percent of students receive financial aid in some form, including plenty of available work-study options.

CAREER INFORMATION FROM PAYSCALE.COM	
ROI Rating	88
Bachelors and No Higher	
Median starting salary	$50,900
Median mid-career salary	$96,600
At Least Bachelors	
Median starting salary	$51,800
Median mid-career salary	$98,000
Alumni with high job meaning	45%
Degrees awarded in STEM subjects	8%

SELECTIVITY	
Admissions Rating	88
# of applicants	18,180
% of applicants accepted	43
% of acceptees attending	22

FRESHMAN PROFILE	
Range SAT EBRW	520–600
Range SAT Math	540–620
Minimum paper TOEFL	500
Minimum internet-based TOEFL	62
Average HS GPA	3.5

DEADLINES	
Regular	
Priority	2/1
Nonfall registration?	Yes

FINANCIAL FACTS	
Financial Aid Rating	87
Annual in-state tuition	$6,530
Annual out-of-state tuition	$17,400
Room and board	$15,352
Required fees	$608
Books and supplies	$1,364
Average frosh need-based scholarship	$8,877
Average UG need-based scholarship	$7,486
% needy frosh rec. need-based scholarship or grant aid	91
% needy UG rec. need-based scholarship or grant aid	88
% needy frosh rec. non-need-based scholarship or grant aid	74
% needy UG rec. non-need-based scholarship or grant aid	26
% needy frosh rec. need-based self-help aid	11
% needy UG rec. need-based self-help aid	18
% frosh rec. any financial aid	85
% UG rec. any financial aid	53
% frosh need fully met	3
% ugrads need fully met	3
Average % of frosh need met	57
Average % of ugrad need met	49

Claremont McKenna College

888 COLUMBIA AVENUE, CLAREMONT, CA 91711 • ADMISSIONS: 909-621-8088 • FAX: 909-621-8516

#33 BEST VALUE COLLEGE

CAMPUS LIFE

Quality of Life Rating	97
Fire Safety Rating	88
Green Rating	60*
Type of school	Private
Environment	Town

STUDENTS

Total undergrad enrollment	1,334
% male/female	52/48
% from out of state	55
% frosh live on campus	100
% ugrads live on campus	97
# of fraternities (% ugrad men join)	0 (0)
# of sororities (% ugrad women join)	0 (0)
% African American	4
% Asian	11
% Caucasian	41
% Hispanic	15
% Native American	<1
% Pacific Islander	<1
% Two or more races	6
% Race and/or ethnicity unknown	6
% international	17
# of countries represented	43

ACADEMICS

Academic Rating	91
% students returning for sophomore year	97
% students graduating within 4 years	84
% students graduating within 6 years	90
Calendar	Semester
Student/faculty ratio	8:1
Profs interesting rating	96
Profs accessible rating	95
Most classes have 10–19 students.	

MOST POPULAR MAJORS
Economics; Government; International Relations; Psychology; Economics-Accounting

ABOUT THE SCHOOL

Part of a new generation of liberal arts colleges, Claremont McKenna was founded in 1946—more than a century later than many of its East Coast counterparts—but it has steadily built a reputation as one of the nation's best small schools. With a total enrollment of just 1,300 students, the average class size is under twenty, making it easy for students to work directly with the school's talented faculty. One literature and government major gushes that her "academic experience has been so rich—full of dinners with professors outside of class and conversations that make me a better scholar and person. I have been doing research on Robert Frost's letters that would usually be reserved for graduate students." Despite the comfortable environment, academics are surprisingly rigorous and varied. Offering a pragmatic approach to the liberal arts, the college is divided into twelve academic departments offering major programs in fields like biochemistry and history, as well as minor programs or "sequences" in areas such as Asian-American studies and leadership. The most popular majors are government, international relations, psychology, and economics-accounting. A psychology major relates that "the campus environment is extremely friendly, open, and career-focused. Students at CMC are motivated to make something of themselves in the world." As a part of the five Claremont colleges, Claremont McKenna offers students the intimacy of a small college with the variety of a larger system. Jointly, the colleges offer more than 2,500 courses, and cross-registration is encouraged (as is eating in neighboring colleges' dining halls).

BANG FOR YOUR BUCK

Not only is CMC need-blind in its admission policies, but the college is committed to meeting every student's financial need through a combination of merit-based scholarships and need-based awards. In addition to state and federal grants, the school offers a number of merit-based scholarship awards derived from gifts and endowments given to the college. Army ROTC Scholarships are also available. The school's website offers detailed information about the amount of aid granted to incoming students in recent years based on their family's income level. Furthermore, for students interested in an unpaid internship with a public or nonprofit organization, the Sponsored Internship & Experiences Program will provide funding for students to pursue internships anywhere in the world.

STUDENT LIFE

The incredibly content undergrads here happily declare that "life at CMC is unbeatable." For starters, students love to take advantage of the beautiful SoCal weather. And many an individual "can often be found throwing around a Frisbee, playing bocce ball, or setting up a slip-n-slide." Of course, these smart students also enjoy intellectual pursuits. Indeed, "there are numerous 'academic' things that people do for fun, such as Mock Trial or attending lectures." Students also rave about the welcoming and fun social scene. Unlike a lot of other schools, the "student government sends out emails weekly informing the students of the events taking place that weekend." This helps to "unify the whole school and creates a really fun community." Lastly,

Claremont McKenna College

FINANCIAL AID: 909-621-8356 • E-MAIL: ADMISSION@CMC.EDU • WEBSITE: WWW.CMC.EDU

when undergrads are itching to get away, they can head to "amazing places...such as Los Angeles, the beaches, the San Gabriel Mountains, and even as far as Las Vegas and Lake Tahoe."

CAREER

Undergrads at Claremont McKenna love to shower the "AMAZING career services center" with praise. And it's no secret why! The office is with students every step of the way, from initial career exploration to landing that first job offer. Through their alumni career contacts database, the office makes it fairly simple for current students to connect with alums working in industries of interest. Even better, their Experts-in-Residence program allows students to find an accomplished alum or parent and engage with him/her to provide valuable insights into his/her working world, offer professional (and educational) guidance and networking opportunities. Beyond alumni, CMC's extensive internship database allows undergrads to search through a myriad of interesting opportunities. With all of these outlets, it's no wonder CMC grads are so successful.

FINANCIAL AID

CMC is a need-blind institution that meets 100% of a student's demonstrated need. *Students should submit:* Business/Farm Supplement; CSS Profile; FAFSA; State aid form. Priority filing deadline is 1/5. The Princeton Review suggests that all financial aid forms be submitted as soon as possible after October 1. *Need-based scholarships/grants offered:* College/university scholarship or grant aid from institutional funds, Federal Pell, private scholarships, SEOG, state scholarships/grants. *Loan aid offered:* Direct PLUS Loans, Direct Subsidized Loans, Direct Unsubsidized Loans. Applicants will be notified of awards on or about 4/1. Federal Work-Study Program available. Institutional employment available.

BOTTOM LINE

Full-time tuition at Claremont McKenna College is $54,160 annually. Meal plans and housing range in price, but together room and board generally run about $16,705 per year. As at any private school, the annual cost to attend CMC can be a bit pricey; however, the school offers aid to students in a wide range of financial situations.

CAREER INFORMATION FROM PAYSCALE.COM	
ROI Rating	93
Bachelors and No Higher	
Median starting salary	$66,800
Median mid-career salary	$127,400
At Least Bachelors	
Median starting salary	$70,100
Median mid-career salary	$137,500
Alumni with high job meaning	45%
Degrees awarded in STEM subjects	16%

SELECTIVITY

Admissions Rating	98
# of applicants	6,349
% of applicants accepted	10
% of acceptees attending	53
# offered a place on the wait list	723
% accepting a place on wait list	56
% admitted from wait list	0
# of early decision applicants	667
% accepted early decision	31

FRESHMAN PROFILE

Range SAT EBRW	660–740
Range SAT Math	680–770
Range ACT Composite	30–34
Minimum paper TOEFL	600
Minimum internet-based TOEFL	100
% graduated top 10% of class	82
% graduated top 25% of class	96
% graduated top 50% of class	100

DEADLINES

Early decision	
Deadline	11/1
Notification	12/15
Other ED Deadline	1/5
Other ED Notification	2/15
Regular	
Deadline	1/5
Notification	4/1
Nonfall registration?	No

FINANCIAL FACTS

Financial Aid Rating	94
Annual tuition	$54,160
Room and board	$16,705
Required fees	$245
Average frosh need-based scholarship	$49,208
Average UG need-based scholarship	$46,324
% needy frosh rec. need-based scholarship or grant aid	97
% needy UG rec. need-based scholarship or grant aid	97
% needy frosh rec. non-need-based scholarship or grant aid	46
% needy UG rec. non-need-based scholarship or grant aid	52
% needy frosh rec. need-based self-help aid	91
% needy UG rec. need-based self-help aid	91
% frosh rec. any financial aid	53
% UG rec. any financial aid	46
% UG borrow to pay for school	31
Average cumulative indebtedness	$21,421
% frosh need fully met	97
% ugrads need fully met	98
Average % of frosh need met	100

Clark University

950 Main Street, Worcester, MA 01610-1477 • Admissions: 508-793-7431 • Fax: 508-793-8821

CAMPUS LIFE

Quality of Life Rating	89
Fire Safety Rating	98
Green Rating	91
Type of school	Private
Environment	City

STUDENTS

Total undergrad enrollment	2,192
% male/female	39/61
% from out of state	62
% frosh from public high school	69
% frosh live on campus	98
% ugrads live on campus	67
# of fraternities (% ugrad men join)	0 (0)
# of sororities (% ugrad women join)	0 (0)
% African American	4
% Asian	8
% Caucasian	58
% Hispanic	8
% Native American	<1
% Pacific Islander	0
% Two or more races	2
% Race and/or ethnicity unknown	6
% international	14
# of countries represented	65

ACADEMICS

Academic Rating	90
% students returning for sophomore year	86
% students graduating within 4 years	77
% students graduating within 6 years	83
Calendar	Semester
Student/faculty ratio	10:1
Profs interesting rating	90
Profs accessible rating	89
Most classes have 10–19 students.	

MOST POPULAR MAJORS
Biology/Biological Sciences; Psychology; Political Science and Government

ABOUT THE SCHOOL

Clark University, in Worcester, Massachusetts, attracts students who can think critically, and act decisively, thoughtfully, and compassionately to create change on a local, national, and global scale. The university uses an educational model called LEEP (Liberal Education and Effective Practice) that "combines a comprehensive liberal arts-based curriculum with experiential learning opportunities…" and culminates in a senior capstone project. The school also offers qualified students a tuition-free fifth year to complete a combined bachelor's and master's degree. Students say that Clark's faculty "[are its] strongest attribute. I have never taken a class at Clark where the professors haven't been enthusiastic and knowledgeable…. The one-on-one connection between professor and student allows for networking opportunities outside the campus and a far stronger understanding of the material than one would get through textbooks and large lectures."

BANG FOR YOUR BUCK

Clark's fifth year accelerated masters program is tuition-free—an "amazing" value and time-saving opportunity. Currently, 25 percent of seniors participate in Clark's accelerated master's degree program. Students report that the university charges a "significantly lower tuition" than comparable schools, and "…offers a tremendous amount of financial aid at a level that exceeds the expectations of what a typical private university would give." Students can also apply for significant funding for their senior LEEP project.

STUDENT LIFE

Clarkies, as students call themselves, are engaged with clubs and student organizations on campus. The absence of Greek life means that campus "party culture is less overwhelming," and students socialize in relaxed settings or through participation in one (or more) of the 130 clubs and student organizations. Students are also highly active in the various programming sponsored by the university, like "bringing down guest speakers like Janet Mock, Junot Díaz, [and] Arthur Klineman" to host dialogue and conversation series. Downtown Worcester offers a variety of dining options, and "a train from Union Station gets students…to Boston within an hour-and-a half."

CAREER

As part of the LEEP Program, the Clark's office of Career Development helps "connect students with opportunities to explore their co-curricular and professional interests, gain relevant experience, and achieve their personal and professional goals." ClarkCONNECT prepares students for employment after graduation by promoting internships "which may take place in a nonprofit organization, government office, or for-profit business." According to PayScale.com, 42 percent of Clark University alumni report that they derive a high level of meaning from their careers.

Clark University

FINANCIAL AID: 508-793-7478 • E-MAIL: ADMISSIONS@CLARKU.EDU • WEBSITE: WWW.CLARKU.EDU

GENERAL INFO

Activities: Choral groups, concert band, dance, drama/theater, jazz band, literary magazine, marching band, music ensembles, musical theater, pep band, radio station, student government, student newspaper, student-run film society, symphony orchestra, television station, yearbook, campus ministries, International Student Organization, Model UN. **Organizations:** 110 registered organizations, 10 honor societies, 7 religious organizations. **Athletics (Intercollegiate):** *Men:* baseball, basketball, cross-country, diving, lacrosse, soccer, swimming, tennis. *Women:* basketball, crew/rowing, cross-country, diving, field hockey, lacrosse, soccer, softball, swimming, tennis, volleyball. **On-Campus Highlights:** Larger than life statue of Freud, rare book room, Goddard Library, Traina Center for the Arts, Dolan Field House and updated fields, The Green on a warm spring day.

FINANCIAL AID

Students should submit: CSS Profile; FAFSA; Noncustodial PROFILE. Regular filing deadline is 1/15. The Princeton Review suggests that all financial aid forms be submitted as soon as possible after October 1. *Need-based scholarships/grants offered:* College/university scholarship or grant aid from institutional funds; Federal Pell; SEOG; State scholarships/grants. *Loan aid offered:* Direct PLUS Loans, Direct Subsidized Loans, Direct Unsubsidized Loans. Applicants are typically notified of awards within two weeks of receiving their admissions decision, if they submitted the FAFSA and PROFILE by the deadline. Federal Work-Study Program available. Institutional employment available.

BOTTOM LINE

Clark University's tuition is $45,380, with housing ranging from $6,000 to $11,120, and dining from a bare-bones $1,920 (one meal every weekday) to $4,460 according to https://clarkdining.sodexomyway.com/my-meal-plan. Merit scholarships are awarded to 65 percent of students and the accelerated degree program offers an affordable and time-saving way of gaining a graduate degree in five years.

CAREER INFORMATION FROM PAYSCALE.COM	
ROI Rating	88
Bachelors and No Higher	
Median starting salary	$50,200
Median mid-career salary	$105,900
At Least Bachelors	
Median starting salary	$52,600
Median mid-career salary	$112,100
Alumni with high job meaning	43%
Degrees awarded in STEM subjects	11%

SELECTIVITY	
Admissions Rating	89
# of applicants	8,355
% of applicants accepted	56
% of acceptees attending	13
# offered a place on the wait list	590
% accepting a place on wait list	46
% admitted from wait list	3
# of early decision applicants	75
% accepted early decision	53

FRESHMAN PROFILE	
Range SAT EBRW	600–700
Range SAT Math	580–680
Range ACT Composite	27–31
Minimum paper TOEFL	550
Minimum internet-based TOEFL	80
Average HS GPA	3.6
% graduated top 10% of class	37
% graduated top 25% of class	75
% graduated top 50% of class	96

DEADLINES	
Early decision	
Deadline	11/1
Notification	12/15
Early action	
Deadline	11/1
Notification	12/15
Regular	
Deadline	1/15
Notification	4/1
Nonfall registration?	Yes

FINANCIAL FACTS	
Financial Aid Rating	87
Annual tuition	$45,380
Room and board	$9,170
Required fees	$350
Books and supplies	$800
Average frosh need-based scholarship	$28,199
Average UG need-based scholarship	$26,780
% needy frosh rec. need-based scholarship or grant aid	78
% needy UG rec. need-based scholarship or grant aid	79
% needy frosh rec. non-need-based scholarship or grant aid	46
% needy UG rec. non-need-based scholarship or grant aid	48
% needy frosh rec. need-based self-help aid	74
% needy UG rec. need-based self-help aid	72
% frosh rec. any financial aid	91
% UG rec. any financial aid	89
% UG borrow to pay for school	64
Average cumulative indebtedness	$34,305

Clarkson University

Holcroft House, Potsdam, NY 13699 • Admissions: 315-268-6480 • Fax: 315-268-7647

CAMPUS LIFE

Quality of Life Rating	**84**
Fire Safety Rating	**96**
Green Rating	**91**
Type of school	Private
Environment	Village

STUDENTS

Total undergrad enrollment	2,991
% male/female	70/30
% from out of state	27
% frosh from public high school	90
% frosh live on campus	98
% ugrads live on campus	80
# of fraternities (% ugrad men join)	10 (14)
# of sororities (% ugrad women join)	4 (12)
% African American	2
% Asian	4
% Caucasian	81
% Hispanic	5
% Native American	<1
% Pacific Islander	0
% Two or more races	3
% Race and/or ethnicity unknown	2
% international	3
# of countries represented	22

ACADEMICS

Academic Rating	**74**
% students returning for sophomore year	87
% students graduating within 4 years	58
% students graduating within 6 years	74
Calendar	Semester
Student/faculty ratio	13:1
Profs interesting rating	72
Profs accessible rating	76
Most classes have 2–9 students.	

MOST POPULAR MAJORS
Civil Engineering; Mechanical Engineering; Engineering/Industrial Management

ABOUT THE SCHOOL

A private research university in a rural setting, Clarkson University boasts an impressive engineering program and a main campus situated in far northern New York (the "North Country") against the backdrop of the beautiful Adirondack Mountains. One student says, "If you want to be an engineer, this is the best school to come to in my opinion. [The] curriculum is rigorous and the work prepares you for the real world." Of course, there are nearly three dozen other academic programs from the digital arts to mathematics to choose from: "The specific programs are the greatest strength of the school." In the Clarkson community, a "small student body makes it easy to know your peers and your professors to know you." One student explains, "All of the professors I have had are genuinely interested in helping students learn. We are presented with real world problems and get good feedback on the ways we solve them. My experience here helped prepare me for my internships which definitely helped me get a job and feel confident that I will be able to learn and succeed in my field."

BANG FOR YOUR BUCK

Clarkson students feel confident about their post-college prospects. For example, the university appealed to one student for its "job placement assistance both for internships and actual jobs before and after graduation. Most students have jobs lined up before they graduate." The university works with students to make their college experience affordable through grants, scholarships, work study, loans, and other sources of financial aid. Notable scholarships include the Clarkson National CO-OP Scholarship Program, which offers up to $6,000 per year based on academic record. Incoming undergrads may also receive scholarships for robotics and engineering competitions at the high school level or location-based scholarships for academically excellent students from the five boroughs of New York City or from the North Country.

STUDENT LIFE

Clarkson University's main campus sits in Potsdam, New York, just a few hours from Lake Placid and the Adirondacks. Current students boast about the available outdoor adventures like the "trail system on campus, great outing club, hiking, biking, [and] skiing." There are also "over 200 student organizations to choose from." When not hiking in the mountains or enjoying hockey games, Clarkson students spend time working together on school projects: "The student body works well together to support each other, encourage each other, and help each other to learn and succeed. Rather than competing for grades and caring more about your personal grade, the school encourages an atmosphere of cooperation and group work. The library and other study areas are constantly full of student groups, whether classmates or friends, working on homework assignments, lab reports, or group projects." Many students cited the student body as one of the best facets of the school because members are "diverse in background and goal oriented. [They] have a wide range of plans for the future. You meet people who you may never have crossed paths with otherwise."

CAREER

Clarkson students praise the "availability of resources" for career prep on campus, "specifically the Career Center." Here they can browse for local and national internship listings using the online system Knightlink, or make career appointments to build a résumé, find and apply for jobs, and get feedback on mock interviews. Clarkson University also offers study abroad at 55 partner institutions, an unlimited number of co-op opportunities (many at Fortune 500

Clarkson University

FINANCIAL AID: 315-268-6480 • E-MAIL: ADMISSION@CLARKSON.EDU • WEBSITE: WWW.CLARKSON.EDU

companies), and internships to students while they're still in school, and hosts a corporate sponsor day, career fair, and interview day each semester. Clarkson boasts a 95 percent undergraduate placement rate for the Class of 2016. Seventy-five percent of students are employed and 16 percent continued to graduate school. With top employers like Amazon, General Electric, and Lockheed Martin for Clarkson grads, current students feel confident about their prospects: "The school genuinely cares about helping students succeed, and [has] reasonable financial aid to assist in making college education affordable."

GENERAL INFO

Activities: Choral groups, drama/theater, jazz band, musical theater, pep band, radio station, student government, student newspaper, symphony orchestra, television station, yearbook, international student organizations. **Organizations:** 292 registered organizations, 23 honor societies, 4 religious organizations. 10 fraternities, 4 sororities. **Athletics (Intercollegiate):** *Men:* baseball, basketball, cross-country, diving, golf, ice hockey, lacrosse, skiing (downhill/alpine), cross-country, soccer, swimming. *Women:* basketball, cross-country, diving, ice hockey, lacrosse, skiing (downhill/alpine), cross-country, soccer, softball, swimming, volleyball. **On-Campus Highlights:** Our most recent RDS submission listed: Student Center Forum & Java City, Wooded Recreational Trails, Cheel Campus Center & Arena, Adirondack Lodge, Residence Hall Rooms.

FINANCIAL AID

Students should submit: FAFSA, state aid form. Priority filing deadline is 12/1. The Princeton Review suggests that all financial aid forms be submitted as soon as possible after October 1. *Need-based scholarships/grants offered:* College/university scholarship or grant aid from institutional funds, Federal Pell, private scholarships, SEOG, state scholarships/grants. *Loan aid offered:* Direct PLUS Loans, Direct Subsidized Loans, Direct Unsubsidized Loans. Applicants will be notified of awards on a rolling basis beginning 2/17. Federal Work-Study Program available. Institutional employment available.

BOTTOM LINE

Tuition at Clarkson is $48,194 a year. With $15,222 for room and board, students can budget an annual $68,426 in expenses. When students submit the FAFSA, Clarkson will automatically check their eligibility for federal, state, and institutional, need-based programs as well as Clarkson Grants, which are awarded based on strong potential for success. The average amount of loan debt per graduate comes to $24,500.

CAREER INFORMATION FROM PAYSCALE.COM	
ROI Rating	89
Bachelors and No Higher	
Median starting salary	$65,100
Median mid-career salary	$128,200
At Least Bachelors	
Median starting salary	$66,700
Median mid-career salary	$134,300
Alumni with high job meaning	59%
Degrees awarded in STEM subjects	83.1%

SELECTIVITY	
Admissions Rating	86
# of applicants	7,000
% of applicants accepted	66
% of acceptees attending	15
# offered a place on the wait list	59
% accepting a place on wait list	63
% admitted from wait list	19
# of early decision applicants	199
% accepted early decision	55

FRESHMAN PROFILE	
Range SAT EBRW	563–650
Range SAT Math	580–680
Range ACT Composite	24–29
Minimum paper TOEFL	550
Minimum internet-based TOEFL	80
Average HS GPA	3.6
% graduated top 10% of class	37
% graduated top 25% of class	74
% graduated top 50% of class	96

DEADLINES	
Early decision	
Deadline	12/1
Notification	1/1
Regular	
Deadline	1/15
Nonfall registration?	Yes

FINANCIAL FACTS	
Financial Aid Rating	87
Annual tuition	$48,194
Room and board	$15,222
Required fees	$1,250
Books and supplies	$1,446
Average frosh need-based scholarship	$35,300
Average UG need-based scholarship	$32,061
% needy frosh rec. need-based scholarship or grant aid	99
% needy UG rec. need-based scholarship or grant aid	99
% needy frosh rec. non-need-based scholarship or grant aid	15
% needy UG rec. non-need-based scholarship or grant aid	14
% needy frosh rec. need-based self-help aid	79
% needy UG rec. need-based self-help aid	81
% frosh rec. any financial aid	97
% UG rec. any financial aid	97
% UG borrow to pay for school	82
Average cumulative indebtedness	$24,500
% frosh need fully met	21
% ugrads need fully met	21
Average % of frosh need met	90
Average % of ugrad need met	89

Clemson University

105 SIKES HALL, BOX 345124, CLEMSON, SC 29634-5124 • ADMISSIONS: 864-656-2287 • FINANCIAL AID: 864-656-2280

CAMPUS LIFE

Quality of Life Rating	**92**
Fire Safety Rating	**97**
Green Rating	**60***
Type of school	Public
Environment	Village

STUDENTS

Total undergrad enrollment	19,172
% male/female	51/49
% from out of state	35
% frosh from public high school	89
% frosh live on campus	98
% ugrads live on campus	41
# of fraternities (% ugrad men join)	26 (10)
# of sororities (% ugrad women join)	17 (15)
% African American	7
% Asian	2
% Caucasian	83
% Hispanic	4
% Native American	<1
% Pacific Islander	<1
% Two or more races	3
% Race and/or ethnicity unknown	<1
% international	1
# of countries represented	84

ACADEMICS

Academic Rating	**81**
% students returning for sophomore year	93
% students graduating within 6 years	82
Calendar	Semester
Student/faculty ratio	16:1
Profs interesting rating	78
Profs accessible rating	81

Most classes have 10–19 students. Most lab/discussion sessions have 20–29 students.

MOST POPULAR MAJORS

Engineering; Biology/Biological Sciences; Business/Commerce

ABOUT THE SCHOOL

Established in 1889, South Carolina's Clemson University is a world-class research university that is steeped in academic and school traditions. Offering more than 80 undergraduate majors, the university places an emphasis on "engaged learning" through both classroom and nontraditional opportunities such as Living-Learning communities, co-ops, and Creative Inquiry projects, which are faculty-supervised small group research projects that can span the course of several undergraduate years. Overall, the university has a 18:1 faculty/student ratio, and most Clemson classes have fewer than 20 students. "Endless opportunities" are everywhere (even the library is open 24 hours a day on weekdays). "Students love their Clemson experience." "It's an all-in-this-together mentality that keeps our family united," says one. Professors similarly "go out of their way to help" and "try to think of various ways to help the students." Beyond how involved and close the students, faculty, and staff are, "everything at Clemson is done with integrity and pride."

BANG FOR YOUR BUCK

The "co-op and internship program run through the career center is top notch," and is an excellent way for students to take advantage of Clemson's establishment and resources. The University Professional Internship/Co-op Program arranges paid positions for students that build their résumés with significant work toward a future career, and the International Internship Program helps students spend eight weeks of their summer working abroad at one of four locations. The university does an excellent job of "giving students opportunities to explore new ideas and take part in new experiences" and to that end, makes plenty of assistance available and easily applied for. There are several university academic recruiting scholarships such as the National Scholars Program, which offers a full ride and expenses, and Trustee Scholarships for South Carolina residents; additionally, there are varying levels of scholarships for diversity and need.

STUDENT LIFE

Fall social life at Clemson is easy, as football rules the schedule. Everyone "spends all Saturday tailgating before the game" and getting there before the team runs down the hill (a school tradition) is "important." Clemson, South Carolina is "the definition of a college town," and it "floods with people in orange on game days and is a quiet town on all the other days of the week." Football isn't the only binding agent though, and "there are a lot of different types of people" and "you can easily find a niche here." As for outdoor enthusiasts, "lots of students hang out on Bowman Field, kayak in Lake Hartwell, or hike the surrounding mountains." Most students enjoy "bowling, ping pong, and other arcade games" at the Underground Rec Center, attending "movie nights and game nights" and playing for "intramural teams." The school itself "does a great job of drumming up school spirit for everything from big football games to minor organization events."

CAREER

The Center for Career and Professional Development offers a full schedule of events and workshops throughout the year, including career fairs (for both specialized industries and general employment), mock interviews, career counseling, and meet-ups. Plenty more services are available through the Michelin Career Center. The Clemson Tiger pride extend long beyond graduation, and Clemson's alumni are "very involved with current operations of the University." Alumni are also a major contributor to the high job placement rate. It is common for many past alumni to contact department heads asking specifically for Clemson students to work for their business. "I knew that once I graduate from Clemson I would have no problem getting a job because so many people have heard how wonderful Clemson is," says a student. Of the Clemson University alumni visiting PayScale.com, 51 percent report that they derive a high level of meaning from their jobs.

Clemson University

E-MAIL: CUADMISSIONS@CLEMSON.EDU • FAX: 864-656-2464 • WEBSITE: WWW.CLEMSON.EDU

GENERAL INFO

Activities: Choral groups, concert band, dance, drama/theater, jazz band, literary magazine, marching band, music ensembles, pep band, radio station, student government, student newspaper, television station, yearbook. **Organizations:** 292 registered organizations, 23 honor societies, 24 religious organizations. 26 fraternities, 17 sororities. **Athletics (Intercollegiate):** *Men:* Baseball, basketball, cheerleading, cross-country, diving, football, golf, soccer, swimming, tennis, track/field (outdoor), track/field (indoor). *Women:* Basketball, cheerleading, crew/rowing, cross-country, diving, soccer, swimming, tennis, track/field (outdoor), track/field (indoor), volleyball. **On-Campus Highlights:** SC Botanical Garden/Discovery Center/Geology Muse, Hendrix Student Center–Clemson Ice Cream, Conference Center and Inn at Clemson/Walker Golf Course, Fort Hill–John C. Calhoun House, Lee Art Gallery.

FINANCIAL AID

Students should submit: FAFSA. Priority filing deadline is 4/1. The Princeton Review suggests that all financial aid forms be submitted as soon as possible after October 1. *Need-based scholarships/grants offered:* College/university scholarship or grant aid from institutional funds, Federal Nursing Scholarships, Federal Pell, Private scholarships, SEOG, State scholarships/grants. *Loan aid offered:* Direct PLUS Loans, Direct Subsidized Loans, Direct Unsubsidized Loans. Applicants will be notified of awards on a rolling basis beginning 4/1. Federal Work-Study Program available. Institutional employment available.

BOTTOM LINE

In-state tuition at Clemson runs $13,186 with an additional $9,144 going to room and board. Out-of-state residents pay a higher tuition of $32,738. Though the non-resident price is steep in comparison, the school works hard to make financial aid available, and over 70 percent of Clemson students do receive some type of financial assistance.

CAREER INFORMATION FROM PAYSCALE.COM	
ROI Rating	90
Bachelors and No Higher	
Median starting salary	$56,300
Median mid-career salary	$104,100
At Least Bachelors	
Median starting salary	$57,400
Median mid-career salary	$107,100
Alumni with high job meaning	51%
Degrees awarded in STEM subjects	39%

SELECTIVITY	
Admissions Rating	93
# of applicants	26,242
% of applicants accepted	47
% of acceptees attending	29
# offered a place on the wait list	2,649
% accepting a place on wait list	35
% admitted from wait list	95

FRESHMAN PROFILE	
Range SAT EBRW	620–690
Range SAT Math	600–700
Range ACT Composite	27–31
Minimum paper TOEFL	550
Average HS GPA	4.0
% graduated top 10% of class	62
% graduated top 25% of class	91
% graduated top 50% of class	99

DEADLINES	
Regular	
Priority	12/1
Deadline	5/1
Nonfall registration?	Yes

FINANCIAL FACTS	
Financial Aid Rating	80
Annual in-state tuition	$13,186
Annual out-of-state tuition	$32,738
Room and board	$9,144
Required fees	$1,132
Books and supplies	$1,308
Average frosh need-based scholarship	$10,918
Average UG need-based scholarship	$9,183
% needy frosh rec. need-based scholarship or grant aid	92
% needy UG rec. need-based scholarship or grant aid	83
% needy frosh rec. non-need-based scholarship or grant aid	92
% needy UG rec. non-need-based scholarship or grant aid	83
% needy frosh rec. need-based self-help aid	70
% needy UG rec. need-based self-help aid	75
% frosh rec. any financial aid	87
% UG rec. any financial aid	71
% UG borrow to pay for school	46
Average cumulative indebtedness	$30,201
% frosh need fully met	21
% ugrads need fully met	16
Average % of frosh need met	59
Average % of ugrad need met	54

Coe College

1220 First Avenue NE, Cedar Rapids, IA 52402 • Admissions: 319-399-8500 • Fax: 319-399-8816

CAMPUS LIFE

Quality of Life Rating	89
Fire Safety Rating	88
Green Rating	81
Type of school	Private
Affiliation	Presbyterian
Environment	City

STUDENTS

Total undergrad enrollment	1,323
% male/female	43/57
% from out of state	53
% frosh live on campus	90
% ugrads live on campus	86
# of fraternities (% ugrad men join)	5 (24)
# of sororities (% ugrad women join)	5 (26)
% African American	7
% Asian	2
% Caucasian	73
% Hispanic	9
% Native American	<1
% Pacific Islander	<1
% Two or more races	3
% Race and/or ethnicity unknown	3
% international	3
# of countries represented	12

ACADEMICS

Academic Rating	91
% students returning for sophomore year	75
Calendar	Semester
Student/faculty ratio	11:1
Profs interesting rating	90
Profs accessible rating	90

Most classes have 10–19 students. Most lab/discussion sessions have 10–19 students.

MOST POPULAR MAJORS

Biology/Biological Sciences; Psychology; Business Administration and Management.

ABOUT THE SCHOOL

Iowa's Coe College is a private, four-year residential liberal arts college, offering its 1,400+ students more than 60 areas of study, as well as a host of experiential learning opportunities that fall under the Coe Plan. One hundred percent of students are guaranteed to conduct research, complete an internship or study off campus which is designed to put Coe students in front of industry and academic professionals around the world. With an average class size of 16 and an 11:1 student to faculty ratio, small classes are the standard here, a perk that often results in "opportunities for undergraduate research and travel with your professors." Rigorous academics plus Coe's focus on residence life (students must live on campus for all four years) complete a holistic education for these students, who are typically "passionate for more than what they get out of the classroom" and "truly emanate a joy for learning, living, and giving."

BANG FOR YOUR BUCK

Coe College students find success after graduation—year after year, nearly 100 percent of reporting graduates have been employed or in graduate school within one year. Fifty percent of grads go on to medical school, law school or graduate school within three years of graduation. Students who apply for admission to Coe are automatically considered for a Trustee Scholarship valued up to $28,000 per year. In addition, there are several full- and partial-tuition scholarships such as Williston Jones Full-Tuition Scholarships, which are available to select students based on their academic accomplishments, commitment to sustainability, positive impact potential and diversity of background. Siblings of current Coe students or graduates are eligible to receive $500 annually. Legacy students are eligible to receive $1,000 annually.

STUDENT LIFE

Home to the fighting Kohawks, Coe College boasts "an amazingly diverse and loving student body" for an undergraduate enrollment of 1,400+ students, and students find that "everyone looks out for one another and holds each other accountable." There are 21 men's and women's NCAA Division III Athletic Teams and more than 80 clubs and organizations ranging "anywhere from Greek life to lacrosse to horror flicks." Campus improvements, most notably the new Athletics and Recreation Complex, bring state-of-the-art facilities to campus that rank among the best in the region. Coe's ambitious Student Activities Committee hosts activities including an annual ski trip, bowling, laser tag and free movie Fridays. Outside of campus, there are many great food options and activities in downtown Cedar Rapids, including "midnight farmer's markets, live music, 5Ks, BBQ festivals, museums," and more.

CAREER

Nestled in the heart of Cedar Rapids, one of America's most prosperous midwest cities, Coe students benefit from the lowest unemployment rate for college graduates in the nation. Coe's Center for Creativity & Careers — a catalyst for inclusion in The Princeton Review's Top 25 Best Schools for Internships — connects students to Coe's business partners and successful alumni located in the Cedar Rapids Corridor and beyond. Google, Corning Incorporated, Mayo Clinic and the Chicago Board of Trade are just some of the businesses routinely reserving internships for Coe students. The study abroad program at Coe College is similarly helpful. With domestic and international options in locales like Southeast Asia or Washington D.C., as well as opportunities for a semester or year-long study, Coe "offers a wide variety of locations to suit everyone's interests at a reasonable price."

Coe College

FINANCIAL AID: 319-399-8540 • E-MAIL: ADMISSION@COE.EDU • WEBSITE: WWW.COE.EDU

GENERAL INFO

Activities: Choral groups, concert band, dance, drama/theater, jazz band, literary magazine, music ensembles, musical theater, pep band, radio station, student government, student newspaper, symphony orchestra, yearbook and campus ministries. 60 registered organizations, 8 honor societies, 4 religious organizations. 5 fraternities, 5 sororities. **Athletics (Intercollegiate):** *Men:* baseball, basketball, cross-country, diving, football, golf, soccer, swimming, tennis, track/field (outdoor), track/field (indoor), wrestling. *Women:* basketball, cheerleading, cross-country, diving, golf, soccer, softball, swimming, tennis, track/field (outdoor), track/field (indoor), volleyball. **On-Campus Highlights:** Student Union/Coffee Shop, Dows Theatre, Library/Art Galleries, Racquet Center and the Athletics and Recreation Complex.

FINANCIAL AID

Students should submit: FAFSA. Priority filing deadline is March 1. The Princeton Review suggests that all financial aid forms be submitted as soon as possible after October 1. *Need-based scholarships/grants offered:* College/university scholarship or grant aid from institutional funds, Federal Pell, private scholarships, SEOG, state scholarships/grants. *Loan aid offered:* Direct PLUS Loans, Direct Subsidized Loans, Direct Unsubsidized Loans. Applicants will be notified of financial aid awards on a rolling basis beginning 12/15. Federal Work-Study Program available. Institutional employment available.

BOTTOM LINE

Tuition runs at the private school price of $43,700 per year, with room and board adding an additional $9,480 and student fees another $350. Coe College is committed to making education affordable to students of all means. The average financial aid award for incoming students in the fall of 2018 was $42,130 per year.

CAREER INFORMATION FROM PAYSCALE.COM	
ROI Rating	88
Bachelors and No Higher	
Median starting salary	$46,000
Median mid-career salary	$86,700
At Least Bachelors	
Median starting salary	$47,100
Median mid-career salary	$88,600
Alumni with high job meaning	41%
Degrees awarded in STEM subjects	24%

SELECTIVITY	
Admissions Rating	87
# of applicants	6,725
% of applicants accepted	50
% of acceptees attending	11

FRESHMAN PROFILE	
Range ACT Composite	22–28
Minimum paper TOEFL	520
Minimum internet-based TOEFL	68
Average HS GPA	3.6
% graduated top 10% of class	30
% graduated top 25% of class	65
% graduated top 50% of class	89

DEADLINES	
Early action	
Deadline	12/10
Notification	1/20
Regular	
Priority	12/10
Deadline	3/1
Nonfall registration?	Yes

FINANCIAL FACTS	
Financial Aid Rating	87
Annual tuition	$43,700
Room and board	$9,480
Required fees	$350
Books and supplies	$1,000
Average frosh need-based scholarship	$31,524
Average UG need-based scholarship	$28,610
% needy frosh rec. need-based scholarship or grant aid	100
% needy UG rec. need-based scholarship or grant aid	100
% needy frosh rec. non-need-based scholarship or grant aid	14
% needy UG rec. non-need-based scholarship or grant aid	14
% needy frosh rec. need-based self-help aid	85
% needy UG rec. need-based self-help aid	82
% frosh rec. any financial aid	99
% UG rec. any financial aid	99
% UG borrow to pay for school	82
Average cumulative indebtedness	$35,782
% frosh need fully met	20
% ugrads need fully met	21
Average % of frosh need met	85
Average % of ugrad need met	83

Colby College

4000 Mayflower Hill, Waterville, ME 04901-8848 • Admissions: 207-859-4800 • Fax: 207-859-4828

CAMPUS LIFE

Quality of Life Rating	**86**
Fire Safety Rating	**98**
Green Rating	**98**
Type of school	Private
Environment	Village

STUDENTS

Total undergrad enrollment	1917
% male/female	48/52
% from out of state	88
% frosh from public high school	52
% frosh live on campus	100
% ugrads live on campus	100
# of fraternities (% ugrad men join)	0 (0)
# of sororities (% ugrad women join)	0 (0)
% African American	4
% Asian	7
% Caucasian	64
% Hispanic	7
% Native American	<1
% Pacific Islander	<1
% Two or more races	5
% Race and/or ethnicity unknown	2
% international	10
# of countries represented	74

ACADEMICS

Academic Rating	**92**
% students returning for sophomore year	94
% students graduating within 4 years	89
% students graduating within 6 years	92
Calendar	4/1/4
Student/faculty ratio	10:1
Profs interesting rating	91
Profs accessible rating	94

Most classes have 10–19 students. Most lab/discussion sessions have 10–19 students.

MOST POPULAR MAJORS
Government; Biology/Biological Sciences; Economics

ABOUT THE SCHOOL

Challenging academics and professors who work closely with students are the backbone of Colby College's reputation as a small and desirable liberal arts college. The school's location in Waterville, Maine, may have some applicants asking, "Where?" But what that means is that students and professors who go to Colby do so because they want to be there. Academics are the focus here, so the work is challenging. Incoming students should be prepared to deal with a hefty workload, but those who are aiming high will find that Colby is "heaven for students who excel at everything." Studying abroad is also a major part of most Colby programs, and some two-thirds of students here spend time abroad. "Colby's greatest strengths lie in its people," one student notes. "From the administrators to the faculty, staff, students, and alumni, Colby's community is one that is genuinely caring, genuinely smart, and genuinely engaging." The dorms are mixed-class, and most activities at Colby center around the self-contained campus, so that sense of community is essential for student contentment. Nightlife here isn't necessarily thriving or hectic, with outdoor activities such as skiing and hiking the focus of much off-campus entertainment. Students who don't enjoy the outdoors or extra study time—a major pastime among Colby students—may find the campus "suffocating." Colby does not sponsor Greek life, so partying tends to be limited to small dorm parties or drinking at local pubs. Colby does offer a wide array of school-sponsored events, though, a natural extension of the community feeling fostered here. Most students find the intimacy of the campus to be a positive, not a negative.

BANG FOR YOUR BUCK

Colby College has a highly selective admissions process that sees fewer than a third of applicants accepted. However, Colby will meet the financial needs of students they accept, and it does so via grants rather than loans so as to alleviate the burden of loan debt. The school also sponsors National Merit Scholarships. Loan aid is available in the form of Direct Subsidized Stafford, Direct Unsubsidized Stafford, Direct PLUS, state loans, university loans from institutional funds. An array of campus jobs are available for those interested in student employment.

STUDENT LIFE

Due to its challenging academics and driven student body, "during the week, people think about finishing their homework, meeting deadlines, and attending lectures." Due to its small-town setting, "our campus has a great sense of community because most students spend all their time on campus." Colby provides no shortage of things for students to do, with "activities going on every day of the week such as lectures, dances, theatre productions, musical productions, and guest performers." Once the week is over, students cite Colby as having a "work hard, play hard" mentality and "have a blast on weekends." "There is a huge party culture," says a student "but also supportive friend groups and activities sponsored on the weekends for students to participate in." And though social life is largely centered on campus, "plenty of people take advantage of being in Maine. Without too much effort, you can spend a day on the coast or in the mountains regardless of the season." "Skiing is the big thing to do" and many students cite nearby Sugarloaf Mountain as an extremely enjoyable weekend excursion. No matter what their hobbies or how intense the workload, students agree that "life at Colby is a whole lot of fun!"

Colby College

FINANCIAL AID: 207-859-4832 • E-MAIL: ADMISSIONS@COLBY.EDU • WEBSITE: WWW.COLBY.EDU

CAREER

Colby's new DavisConnects program will provide every student with meaningful global, research, and internship experiences. The goal of the program is to integrate classroom learning with a set of universal experiences that will position students for career and graduate school success. Internship partners include Accenture, Citi, Goldman Sachs, the Institute for the International Education of Students, MarketAxess, Memorial SloanKettering Cancer Center, Ocean Spray, and the Smithsonian's Freer and Sackler galleries. Colby alumni visiting PayScale.com report a median starting salary of $55,200, and 42 percent say that their jobs make the world a better place.

GENERAL INFO

Activities: Choral groups, concert band, dance, drama/theater, jazz band, literary magazine, music ensembles, musical theater, radio station, student government, student newspaper, student-run film society, symphony orchestra, yearbook, international student organization. **Organizations:** 106 registered organizations, 4 honor societies, 5 religious organizations. **Athletics (Intercollegiate):** *Men:* Baseball, basketball, crew/rowing, cross-country, diving, football, golf, ice hockey, lacrosse, skiing (downhill/alpine), skiing (nordic/cross-country), soccer, squash, swimming, tennis, track/field (outdoor), track/field (indoor). *Women:* Basketball, crew/rowing, cross-country, diving, field hockey, golf, ice hockey, lacrosse, skiing (downhill/alpine), skiing (nordic/cross-country), soccer, softball, squash, swimming, tennis, track/field (outdoor), track/field (indoor), volleyball.

FINANCIAL AID

Students should submit: CSS Profile; FAFSA; Regular filing deadline is 1/15. The Princeton Review suggests that all financial aid forms be submitted as soon as possible after October 1. *Need-based scholarships/grants offered:* College/university scholarship or grant aid from institutional funds, Federal Pell, private scholarships, SEOG, state scholarships/grants. Applicants will be notified of awards on or about 4/1. Federal Work-Study Program available. Institutional employment available.

BOTTOM LINE

Yearly comprehensive fees at Colby College are $66,780, plus another $700 for books, though officials there say, "We don't want any student not to come to Colby because of concerns about paying off student loans." The college meets all calculated need with grants and scholarships. Limited off-campus job opportunities mean many students will look toward aid and on-campus jobs. Students graduate with an average debt of $23,343.

CAREER INFORMATION FROM PAYSCALE.COM	
ROI Rating	90
Bachelors and No Higher	
Median starting salary	$57,800
Median mid-career salary	$102,000
At Least Bachelors	
Median starting salary	$60,300
Median mid-career salary	$108,300
Alumni with high job meaning	47%
Degrees awarded in STEM subjects	24%

SELECTIVITY	
Admissions Rating	95
# of applicants	11,190
% of applicants accepted	16
% of acceptees attending	31
# offered a place on the wait list	2,242
% accepting a place on wait list	44
% admitted from wait list	3
# of early decision applicants	708
% accepted early decision	50

FRESHMAN PROFILE	
Range SAT EBRW	670–740
Range SAT Math	670–760
Range ACT Composite	31–33
Minimum internet-based TOEFL	100
% graduated top 10% of class	78
% graduated top 25% of class	94
% graduated top 50% of class	100

DEADLINES	
Early decision	
Deadline	11/15
Notification	12/15
Other ED Deadline	1/1
Other ED Notification	2/15
Regular	
Deadline	1/1
Notification	4/1
Nonfall registration?	Yes

FINANCIAL FACTS	
Financial Aid Rating	95
Annual tuition	$50,890
Room and board	$13,660
Required fees	$2,230
Books and supplies	$735
Average frosh need-based scholarship	$49,873
Average UG need-based scholarship	$46,775
% needy frosh rec. need-based scholarship or grant aid	100
% needy UG rec. need-based scholarship or grant aid	100
% needy frosh rec. non-need-based scholarship or grant aid	3
% needy UG rec. non-need-based scholarship or grant aid	1
% needy frosh rec. need-based self-help aid	81
% needy UG rec. need-based self-help aid	80
% frosh rec. any financial aid	47
% UG rec. any financial aid	42
% UG borrow to pay for school	28
Average cumulative indebtedness	$34,745
% frosh need fully met	100
% ugrads need fully met	100
Average % of frosh need met	100

Colgate University

13 OAK DRIVE, HAMILTON, NY 13346 • ADMISSIONS: 315-228-7401 • FAX: 315-228-7544

#28 BEST VALUE COLLEGE

ABOUT COLGATE UNIVERSITY

Since 1819, Hamilton, New York, has hosted Colgate University, a small liberal arts college that has a "very rigorous academic curriculum" and that will prove challenging to students—gratifyingly so, since those who choose Colgate tend to be looking for a focus on "high-intensity" academics. The science, medicine and health, music, and other programs at this "prestigious institution" win praise from those who attend. Students will be taught by professors who "love being at Colgate as much as the students do." Incoming students should expect small classrooms and hands-on teaching by professors, with class sizes that "allow for personal attention and a higher level of learning." Yet it's not all academics at Colgate. Those attending will also enjoy "strong Division I athletics, a wide variety of extracurricular activities, and a very special community." Football, softball, tennis, and other sports give students challenges to overcome outside the classroom. Students say Colgate offers "the perfect balance between academics and extracurricular activities." A strong sense of community helps. Success both in school and beyond is attributed to the "Colgate connection," a bond among the school's 2,900 students that lasts beyond their years here. The school's philosophical core, and by extension its student body, is career-minded. This is reflected in an extensive set of career-development programs and services. Among others, these include shadowing programs, internship recruiting and off-campus recruiting, and the innovative Colgate on the Cuyahoga program, which gives those accepted an unprecedented opportunity to network with executives, politicians, and business owners. According to the school administration, "These programs offer many dynamic opportunities for students to connect with alumni, staff, faculty, and others to learn about and discuss interests and goals."

BANG FOR YOUR BUCK

Financial aid packages can be sizable at Colgate, averaging just more than $52,075 for the class of 2021. The list of available grants and scholarships is extensive; graduating students call it "strong" and "generous." Over the next several years, school administration aims to lower the average debt for exiting students—and even that may be washed away easily for many students. One year after graduation, 80.5 percent of the class of 2015 is employed and nearly 15 percent are attending graduate school.

STUDENT LIFE

Colgate boasts a "happy and enthusiastic student body" that "follows the motto 'work hard, play hard.'" A sophomore says, "Imagine J. Crew models. Now give them brains, and that is who is walking around Colgate's campus." Fraternities and sororities are popular: "Greek life does have a huge presence in the social life at Colgate," but "it is not exclusive to just those who are members," a sentiment backed up by an art history major who states that "many students do not take part in the preppy, Greek, party-every-night lifestyle that dominates Colgate's reputation," and that "there IS diversity at Colgate, but you have to work quite hard to find it. It is nice to know that it DOES exist if you want to seek it out," while an English major adds that "with the addition of the Ho Science Building, the science department is getting more popular, but be warned because the chemistry major is one of the toughest in the country. No one tells you this before you apply but it falls just behind MIT and CalTech in difficulty."

Colgate University

FINANCIAL AID: : 315-228-7431 • E-MAIL: ADMISSION@COLGATE.EDU • WEBSITE: WWW.COLGATE.EDU

CAREER

The typical Colgate University graduate has a starting salary of around $61,400, and 37 percent of graduates feel their jobs have a lot of meaning in their lives. Students feel that Colgate University has "good financial aid and good career prep." One student feels that "the alumni system is amazing," and that said alumni would "jump over any hurdle for you." Students feel that "the Career Services is phenomenal," due to offering "an incredible selection of opportunities for students to prepare for life after graduation, starting with a major event for sophomores called Soph*MORE* Connections which gives students an opportunity to connect with the alumni network and learn more about career paths, job opportunities, and networking in general." Colgate also offers many grants to support summer career exploration, internships, and research. Benton Hall will be the new home of Career Services at Colgate—opening July 2018.

GENERAL INFO

Activities: Choral groups, concert band, dance, drama/theater, jazz band, literary magazine, music ensembles, musical theater, pep band, radio station, student government, student newspaper, student-run film society, symphony orchestra, television station, yearbook, campus ministries, international student organization. **Organizations:** 253 registered organizations, 3 honor societies, 12 religious organizations. 5 fraternities, 3 sororities. **Athletics (Intercollegiate):** *Men:* Baseball, basketball, cross-country, diving, football, golf, soccer, swimming, tennis, track/field (outdoor), water polo. *Women:* Basketball, cross-country, diving, golf, lacrosse, soccer, softball, swimming, tennis, track/field (outdoor), volleyball, water polo.

FINANCIAL AID

Students should submit: CSS Profile; FAFSA; Noncustodial PROFILE. Priority filing deadline is 1/15. The Princeton Review suggests that all financial aid forms be submitted as soon as possible after October 1. *Need-based scholarships/grants offered:* College/university scholarship or grant aid from institutional funds; Federal Pell; SEOG. *Loan aid offered:* Direct PLUS Loans, Direct Subsidized Loans, Direct Unsubsidized Loans. Applicants will be notified of awards on or about 3/20. Federal Work-Study Program available. Institutional employment available.

BOTTOM LINE

If the $53,650 in annual tuition seems daunting, your fears should be offset by the fact that the school's generous need-based financial aid programs help carry a large share of that burden. Colgate meets 100 percent of student need through need-based scholarships, grants, and self-help aid.

CAREER INFORMATION FROM PAYSCALE.COM	
ROI Rating	93
Bachelors and No Higher	
Median starting salary	$65,000
Median mid-career salary	$137,300
At Least Bachelors	
Median starting salary	$65,400
Median mid-career salary	$139,900
Alumni with high job meaning	38%
Degrees awarded in STEM subjects	26%

SELECTIVITY

Admissions Rating	97
# of applicants	8,542
% of applicants accepted	28
% of acceptees attending	32
# offered a place on the wait list	1,500
% accepting a place on wait list	50
% admitted from wait list	5
# of early decision applicants	851
% accepted early decision	44

FRESHMAN PROFILE

Range SAT EBRW	660–730
Range SAT Math	650–770
Range ACT Composite	31–33
Average HS GPA	3.7
% graduated top 10% of class	77
% graduated top 25% of class	94
% graduated top 50% of class	99

DEADLINES

Early decision	
Deadline	11/15
Notification	12/15
Other ED Deadline	1/15
Other ED Notification	Rolling
Regular	
Deadline	1/15
Notification	4/1
Nonfall registration?	No

FINANCIAL FACTS

Financial Aid Rating	98
Annual tuition	$53,650
Room and board	$13,520
Required fees	$330
Books and supplies	$2,360
Average frosh need-based scholarship	$49,397
Average UG need-based scholarship	$48,369
% needy frosh rec. need-based scholarship or grant aid	100
% needy UG rec. need-based scholarship or grant aid	100
% needy frosh rec. non-need-based scholarship or grant aid	0
% needy UG rec. non-need-based scholarship or grant aid	0
% needy frosh rec. need-based self-help aid	83
% frosh rec. any financial aid	31
% UG rec. any financial aid	36
% UG borrow to pay for school	35
Average cumulative indebtedness	$24,761

College of the Holy Cross

Admissions Office, 1 College Street, Worcester, MA 01610-2395 • Admissions: 508-793-2443 • Fax: 508-793-3888

CAMPUS LIFE

Quality of Life Rating	81
Fire Safety Rating	97
Green Rating	91
Type of school	Private
Affiliation	Roman Catholic
Environment	City

STUDENTS

Total undergrad enrollment	3,020
% male/female	48/52
% from out of state	59
% frosh from public high school	50
% frosh live on campus	99
% ugrads live on campus	91
# of fraternities (% ugrad men join)	0 (0)
# of sororities (% ugrad women join)	0 (0)
% African American	4
% Asian	5
% Caucasian	70
% Hispanic	10
% Native American	<1
% Pacific Islander	<1
% Two or more races	3
% Race and/or ethnicity unknown	3
% international	3
# of countries represented	24

ACADEMICS

Academic Rating	86
% students returning for sophomore year	95
% students graduating within 4 years	91
% students graduating within 6 years	92
Calendar	Semester
Student/faculty ratio	10:1
Profs interesting rating	88
Profs accessible rating	92

Most classes have 10–19 students. Most lab/discussion sessions have fewer than 20 students.

MOST POPULAR MAJORS
Psychology; Economics; Political Science and Government

ABOUT THE SCHOOL

The College of the Holy Cross is a small liberal arts college of fewer than 3,000 students offering rigorous academic preparation in more than thirty degree programs. Students are thrilled to discover the value of a Holy Cross education. "I realized with a degree from here, I can get a job almost anywhere," and the "large and strong" alumni network provides further professional connections. Students say that College of the Holy Cross "does an incredible job of giving its students a very broad education [and] preparing them with the tools for the real world."

But it's the professors that make students' four years at Holy Cross an extraordinary value. "The emphasis here is on teaching and learning, not research," enthused a freshman. All first-year students take part in full-year seminars that are heavy on intellectual development, and the college values effective communication skills. Faculty is accessible in and out of the classrooms. "At Holy Cross, the professors will keep you busy throughout the week." "Classes are hard," warns a biology major. Good grades are hard to come by. "You have to work your tail off to just get an A–." At the same time, students love their "caring" and "amazing" professors.

Holy Cross has a top-notch Career Planning Center and Summer Internship Program that connect students with alumni working in business, government, media, medicine, law, public policy, research, and many other fields. In fact, the alumni network at Holy Cross is legendary for its willingness to mentor and assist students and graduates throughout their careers. Opportunities such as academic internships, community-based learning courses, a prestigious Washington semester, and experiences through study abroad and immersion trips also provide students with invaluable "real-world" experience. Holy Cross has extensive summer internship and study abroad opportunities.

BANG FOR YOUR BUCK

No student or family should be dissuaded from applying to Holy Cross because of the price tag. Holy Cross is need-blind in its admissions policy, which means the decision to admit students to this highly selective liberal arts college is made without regard to a student's ability to pay. Additionally, Holy Cross meets 100 percent of a student's demonstrated financial need with a combination of scholarship grants, loans, and work-study.

STUDENT LIFE

The campus is exceptionally beautiful, and the sense of community within the first-year dorms is "outstanding." Students love going to sporting events (especially football and basketball), and Boston is a shuttle ride away. Though academics and extracurriculars dominate weekdays, "the weekends are the time to relax from the hectic pace of the week." "The library is full all week, but that nerdy chem major you see working hard all week can turn into the girl riding the mechanical bull at a local bar." For those who don't want to partake in the going out scene, SGA-sponsored events such as trivia nights, karaoke and dances are "a blast," and there are "plenty of comedians and musical performers to satisfy us on Friday nights." It is not unusual to find a group of friends hanging out watching movies and ordering in food on a lazy weekend night.

College of the Holy Cross

FINANCIAL AID: 508-793-2265 • E-MAIL: ADMISSIONS@HOLYCROSS.EDU • WEBSITE: WWW.HOLYCROSS.EDU

CAREER

"Holy Cross equips their students with an intangible set of skills that not only prepares them for a job, but for life," says a student. There are a ton of good connections to jobs after college, and students "have a lot of good programs to prepare us for those opportunities." Alumni networking, research and internship opportunities and career planning services all make going to Holy Cross "a fulfilling and active experience." The Career Planning Office's annual fall career fair and the "Crusader Connections" portal help students link up with employers, and the Career Advisor Network helps them to network with alumni. Of those Holy Cross graduates who visited PayScale.com, 45 percent said they felt their job had a meaningful impact on the world. The average starting salary for these same graduates is $56,000.

GENERAL INFO

Activities: Choral groups, concert band, dance, drama/theater, jazz band, literary magazine, marching band, music ensembles, musical theater, pep band, radio station, student government, student newspaper, yearbook, campus ministries, international student organization. **Organizations:** 97 registered organizations, 20 honor societies, 4 religious organizations. **Athletics (Intercollegiate):** *Men:* Baseball, basketball, crew/rowing, cross-country, diving, football, golf, ice hockey, lacrosse, soccer, swimming, tennis, track/field (outdoor), track/field (indoor). *Women:* Basketball, crew/rowing, cross-country, diving, field hockey, golf, ice hockey, lacrosse, soccer, softball, swimming, tennis, track/field (outdoor), track/field (indoor), volleyball. **On-Campus Highlights:** Library, Smith Hall, St. Joseph Chapel, Hart Recreation Center, Hogan Campus Center.

FINANCIAL AID

Students should submit: Business/Farm Supplement; CSS Profile; FAFSA; Noncustodial PROFILE. Regular filing deadline is 2/1. The Princeton Review suggests that all financial aid forms be submitted as soon as possible after October 1. *Need-based scholarships/grants offered:* College/university scholarship or grant aid from institutional funds, Federal Pell, private scholarships, SEOG, state scholarships/grants. *Loan aid offered:* Direct PLUS Loans, Direct Subsidized Loans, Direct Unsubsidized Loans. Federal Work-Study Program available. Institutional employment available.

BOTTOM LINE

At Holy Cross, the total cost for tuition and fees and room and board comes to about $64,300 annually. Don't fret; financial aid is generous here. The average need-based financial aid package for freshman includes gift aid totaling approximately $38,000. Additional aid is available in the form of work-study and loans.

CAREER INFORMATION FROM PAYSCALE.COM	
ROI Rating	89
Bachelors and No Higher	
Median starting salary	$58,800
Median mid-career salary	$121,000
At Least Bachelors	
Median starting salary	$60,800
Median mid-career salary	$124,700
Alumni with high job meaning	46%
Degrees awarded in STEM subjects	24%

SELECTIVITY	
Admissions Rating	92
# of applicants	6,622
% of applicants accepted	40
% of acceptees attending	31
# offered a place on the wait list	1,109
% accepting a place on wait list	40
% admitted from wait list	0
# of early decision applicants	445
% accepted early decision	78

FRESHMAN PROFILE	
Range SAT EBRW	630–700
Range SAT Math	640–710
Range ACT Composite	28–31
Minimum paper TOEFL	600
Minimum internet-based TOEFL	100
% graduated top 10% of class	57
% graduated top 25% of class	90
% graduated top 50% of class	100

DEADLINES	
Early decision	
Deadline	12/15
Regular	
Deadline	1/15
Nonfall registration?	No

FINANCIAL FACTS	
Financial Aid Rating	93
Annual tuition	$49,980
Room and board	$13,690
Required fees	$650
Books and supplies	$1,000
Average frosh need-based scholarship	$36,511
Average UG need-based scholarship	$36,836
% needy frosh rec. need-based scholarship or grant aid	85
% needy UG rec. need-based scholarship or grant aid	83
% needy frosh rec. non-need-based scholarship or grant aid	2
% needy UG rec. non-need-based scholarship or grant aid	2
% needy frosh rec. need-based self-help aid	91
% needy UG rec. need-based self-help aid	94
% frosh rec. any financial aid	65
% UG rec. any financial aid	61
% UG borrow to pay for school	52
Average cumulative indebtedness	$26,258
% frosh need fully met	100
% ugrads need fully met	100
Average % of frosh need met	100
Average % of ugrad need met	100

The College of New Jersey

PO Box 7718, Ewing, NJ 08628-0718 Admissions: 609-771-2131 • Financial Aid: 609-771-2211

CAMPUS LIFE

Quality of Life Rating	89
Fire Safety Rating	98
Green Rating	83
Type of school	Public
Environment	Town

STUDENTS

Total undergrad enrollment	6,850
% male/female	42/58
% from out of state	6
% frosh from public high school	70
% frosh live on campus	89
% ugrads live on campus	55
# of fraternities (% ugrad men join)	14 (15)
# of sororities (% ugrad women join)	14 (13)
% African American	6
% Asian	11
% Caucasian	66
% Hispanic	12
% Native American	<1
% Pacific Islander	<1
% Two or more races	<1
% Race and/or ethnicity unknown	3
% international	<1
# of countries represented	32

ACADEMICS

Academic Rating	82
% students returning for sophomore year	94
% students graduating within 4 years	73
% students graduating within 6 years	87
Calendar	Semester
Student/faculty ratio	13:1
Profs interesting rating	84
Profs accessible rating	81

Most classes have 20–29 students. Most lab/discussion sessions have 10–19 students.

MOST POPULAR MAJORS

Education; Psychology; Marketing

ABOUT THE SCHOOL

The College of New Jersey is situated on 289 acres in Ewing. The small, state-run public school starts incoming freshmen off on the right foot with a strong foundation of core requirements, which eventually leads to a final capstone course their senior year. Students start their TCNJ career with the First Year Experience, participating in the program for the duration of the year and receiving support related to their transition from high school to college. The group is required to sign up for a First Seminar course, where they will discuss issues that may arise while adjusting and be housed on the same floor in their dorm.

No courses are complete without outstanding professors, and students at TCNJ say theirs are the best. "I think the personal attention is the greatest strength," a student shares. "I loved that all of my professors knew my name. The classes are small and you really get to know both your professor and the other students in the class." The faculty goes above and beyond, even inviting their students in on the hiring process. "Whenever a position opens up in a department, the students are encouraged to attend lectures by prospective candidates and offer their input," one student writes. They also "find no cake-walk when it comes to classes."

BANG FOR YOUR BUCK

Over 60 percent of full-time undergraduates benefit from financial aid, which can come in the form of merit-based scholarships, work-study programs, loans, or government or institutional grants. Title IV students may compete for the college's merit scholarships, which are funded by the state government as well as private donors. These awards are offered to those applicants with top SAT scores and class rankings. Over the last six years, TCNJ has given scholarships totaling more than $12 million. Almost three-quarters of students graduate within four years, and more than a third pursue graduate studies. In addition to "top-notch faculty and the newest technology," students have the opportunity to develop their own special-interest learning communities on campus. Also, commitment to sustainability has been incorporated into the curriculum at TCNJ. The college's Municipal Land Use Center is authoring the state's sustainability and climate neutrality plans, and the school has committed to offsetting greenhouse gas produced by faculty and staff travel on an annual basis through the purchase of carbon offsets

STUDENT LIFE

At the College of New Jersey, it's "not uncommon [for] someone who you don't know [to] say hello and ask [how your] day is going—that's pretty much [the] norm around campus." With approximately 6,600 students—the majority of them New Jersey residents—there are roughly 223 registered student organizations on campus. A little more than half the students live on campus and the school does assist in finding off-campus housing for those who don't want to live in dorms. Greek life is a presence at the school, particularly sororities: there are thirteen sororities and eleven fraternities at the College of New Jersey, with 11 percent of women joining a sorority and 14 percent of men joining a fraternity. Despite these numbers, students note that while the Greek system is "definitely a presence on campus," they "don't feel obliged to join in order to have a social life" and the "College Union Board offers plenty of weekend entertainment for people who do not want to go out to parties." According to one Marketing major, "There is no way to define the typical student at TCNJ. With [so many] clubs and activities, there is something for everyone."

CAREER

According to PayScale.com, 45 percent of College of New Jersey graduates would describe their careers as helping to improve the

The College of New Jersey

E-MAIL: TCNJINFO@TCNJ.EDU • FAX: 609-637-5174 • WEBSITE: WWW.TCNJ.EDU

world. With a median starting salary of $54,400 for alumni, the most popular post-TCNJ jobs include software engineer, project engineer, and marketing coordinator. The most popular majors are Computer Science, Finance, and Psychology. Professors "often email students with internship...opportunities" and students praise the plethora of internships available and the study abroad options, which help connect them to the global job market. With its strong "academic focus," The College of New Jersey produces "successful and prepared graduates." The school's Career Center puts on events such as the Fall Engineering and Computer Science Networking event, the Fall Opportunities Fair, and Student Career Forums. According to one Political Science major, students "think about their futures here at TCNJ, and they're always wondering what the next step will be" when it comes to jobs or graduate school.

GENERAL INFO

Environment: Village. **Activities:** Choral groups, concert band, dance, drama/theater, jazz band, literary magazine, music ensembles, musical theater, opera, pep band, radio station, student government, student newspaper, symphony orchestra, television station, yearbook, campus ministries, international student organization, Model UN. **Organizations:** 205 registered organizations, 16 honor societies, 11 religious organizations. 11 fraternities, 13 sororities.

FINANCIAL AID

Students should submit: FAFSA. Priority filing deadline is 2/1. The Princeton Review suggests that all financial aid forms be submitted as soon as possible after October 1. *Need-based scholarships/grants offered:* College/university scholarship or grant aid from institutional funds, Federal Pell, private scholarships, SEOG, state scholarships/grants. *Loan aid offered:* Direct PLUS Loans, Direct Subsidized Loans, Direct Unsubsidized Loans. Applicants will be notified of awards on a rolling basis beginning 6/1. Federal Work-Study Program available. Institutional employment available.

BOTTOM LINE

"A smaller school that is a bargain for its quality of education," the College of New Jersey lives up to these words, according to one happy undergrad. With in-state tuition and fees amounting to just more than $15,000, and plenty of aid available, the school makes college a possibility for most every budget. Seventy percent of freshmen receive financial aid, with the average total need-based package being close to $13,200. Out-of-state students are looking at a bit more than $22,300 per year; room and board for all students is $12,880. The college meets on average 46 percent of all need, and the average need-based gift aid is more than $12,000. "Many of my friends... got into very prestigious schools...but chose TCNJ because of its unbeatable cost," reports one undergrad. There is also a respectable 13:1 student-to-faculty ratio, within such a large campus; there are 6,600 students in all.

CAREER INFORMATION FROM PAYSCALE.COM	
ROI Rating	89
Bachelors and No Higher	
Median starting salary	$57,200
Median mid-career salary	$101,000
At Least Bachelors	
Median starting salary	$59,000
Median mid-career salary	$106,700
Alumni with high job meaning	44%
Degrees awarded in STEM subjects	16%

SELECTIVITY	
Admissions Rating	89
# of applicants	12,898
% of applicants accepted	48
% of acceptees attending	25
# offered a place on the wait list	2,405
% accepting a place on wait list	25
% admitted from wait list	3
# of early decision applicants	710
% accepted early decision	62

FRESHMAN PROFILE	
Range SAT EBRW	590–660
Range SAT Math	580–670
Range ACT Composite	25–30
Minimum paper TOEFL	550
Minimum internet-based TOEFL	90
% graduated top 10% of class	36
% graduated top 25% of class	73
% graduated top 50% of class	98

DEADLINES	
Early decision	
Deadline	11/1
Notification	12/1
Other ED Deadline	1/1
Other ED Notification	2/1
Regular	
Priority	11/1
Deadline	2/1
Nonfall registration?	Yes

FINANCIAL FACTS	
Financial Aid Rating	78
Annual in-state tuition	$12,947
Annual out-of-state tuition	$24,662
Room and board	$13,617
Required fees	$3,604
Books and supplies	$1,200
Average frosh need-based scholarship	$13,272
Average UG need-based scholarship	$11,951
% needy frosh rec. need-based scholarship or grant aid	39
% needy UG rec. need-based scholarship or grant aid	39
% needy frosh rec. non-need-based scholarship or grant aid	35
% needy UG rec. non-need-based scholarship or grant aid	25
% needy frosh rec. need-based self-help aid	67
% needy UG rec. need-based self-help aid	77
% frosh rec. any financial aid	70
% UG rec. any financial aid	62
% UG borrow to pay for school	63
Average cumulative indebtedness	$35,798
% frosh need fully met	11

College of William and Mary

Office of Admissions, PO Box 8795, Williamsburg, VA 23187-8795 • Admissions: 757-221-4223 • Fax: 757-221-1242

CAMPUS LIFE

Quality of Life Rating	98
Fire Safety Rating	92
Green Rating	81
Type of school	Public
Environment	Town

STUDENTS

Total undergrad enrollment	6,243
% male/female	42/58
% from out of state	35
% frosh from public high school	77
% frosh live on campus	100
% ugrads live on campus	72
# of fraternities (% ugrad men join)	18 (27)
# of sororities (% ugrad women join)	14 (31)
% African American	7
% Asian	8
% Caucasian	59
% Hispanic	9
% Native American	<1
% Pacific Islander	<1
% Two or more races	5
% Race and/or ethnicity unknown	5
% international	6
# of countries represented	81

ACADEMICS

Academic Rating	89
% students returning for sophomore year	95
% students graduating within 4 years	85
% students graduating within 6 years	91
Calendar	Semester
Student/faculty ratio	12:1
Profs interesting rating	94
Profs accessible rating	97

Most classes have 20–29 students. Most lab/discussion sessions have 10–19 students.

MOST POPULAR MAJORS

Biology/Biological Sciences; Political Science and Government; Business Administration and Management

#39 BEST VALUE COLLEGE

ABOUT THE SCHOOL

The minute incoming students set foot on the campus of William & Mary in Williamsburg, Virginia, they join an "extremely close-knit and supportive" community. What's more, students here say the school's "incredible academic reputation" is well deserved noting the "rigor" of their coursework. William & Mary attracts students who love learning and maintain a desire to "satisfy…[their] curiosity." To that end, many individuals here relish the fact that "opportunit[ies] for undergraduate research" abound. They also value receiving a "liberal arts education" which helps to foster "well-rounded" individuals. "Small class sizes" allow for an intimate learning environment. Just as important, undergrads are greeted by professors who "challenge [students] to think for [themselves]" and encourage them "to come up with answers" on their own. They're also "extremely knowledgeable." As a satisfied student notes, "Professors seem like they really are here for us rather than their personal research which is nice."

BANG FOR YOUR BUCK

Affordability is synonymous with a William & Mary education. For starters, the college meets 100 percent of the demonstrated need for Virginia residents. Out-of-state students fear not; you won't be left in the dust. Indeed, qualified undergrads receive grant aid that covers 25 percent of the total cost of attendance. The college also provides numerous scholarships. For example, the James Monroe Scholars Program is offered to the top 10 to 15 percent of the applicant pool. Recipients receive a $3,000 research stipend, special housing and priority course registration. And the William & Mary Scholars Program is given to incoming students who come from underrepresented communities and/or have overcome adversity. The program awards the equivalent amount of in-state tuition. It's also renewable assuming the student remains in good academic standing.

SCHOOL LIFE

It's virtually impossible to be bored at William & Mary. After all, the college "is home to over 450 clubs and organizations." These groups "range from the Quidditch team to the Exotic Cheese club." Additionally, the school invites "many [prominent] speakers" to campus. Past lecturers have included "the Dali Lama [and] Condoleezza Rice." Many students also highlight "Alma Mater Productions (AMP) [which] plans and hosts free (or very low cost) events almost every day of the weekend." For example, there's "Screen on the Green, an inflatable movie screen that plays a double feature on the Sunken Gardens… [along with] more interactive activities like Zombie Apocalypse…[where] students have to fight zombies with nerf guns." Of course, when students want to get off campus, they often head to "neighboring Colonial Williamsburg" which always provides a nice respite from studying.

College of William and Mary

FINANCIAL AID: 757-221-2420 • E-MAIL: ADMISSION@WM.EDU • WEBSITE: WWW.WM.EDU

CAREER

William & Mary students have little trouble on the job market. Undergrads readily assert that this is because the "school has a powerful reputation that allows employers and graduate schools to feel comfortable with William & Mary student's ability to perform in a real job situation." "William & Mary does a great job networking their students with alumni," plus, undergrads can turn to the fantastic Cohen Career Center for insight and support. Students have access to top notch services including resume review and mock interviews. Undergrads can also participate in unique programs like "Ask an Executive," wherein executives from a range of industries meet with students to answer their career questions.

GENERAL INFO

Activities: Choral groups, concert band, dance, drama/theater, jazz band, literary magazine, music ensembles, musical theater, opera, pep band, radio station, student government, student newspaper, student-run film society, symphony orchestra, television station, yearbook, campus ministries, international student organization. **Organizations:** 450 registered organizations, 32 honor societies, 32 religious organizations. 17 fraternities, 13 sororities.

FINANCIAL AID

Students should submit: CSS Profile; FAFSA. Priority filing deadline is 3/1. The Princeton Review suggests that all financial aid forms be submitted as soon as possible after October 1. *Need-based scholarships/grants offered:* College/university scholarship or grant aid from institutional funds, Federal Pell, private scholarships, SEOG, state scholarships/grants. *Loan aid offered:* Direct PLUS Loans, Direct Subsidized Loans, Direct Unsubsidized Loans. Applicants will be notified of awards on or about 4/15. Federal Work-Study Program available. Institutional employment available.

THE BOTTOM LINE

As with all state schools, William & Mary's price tag varies depending on each student's residency. Undergrads who are from Virginia face a tuition bill of $13,127 and miscellaneous fees of $5,560. Students from out-of-state are charged $36,158 for tuition along with $6,245 for fees. Room and board for all students comes to $11,382. Books, travel and incidental expenses can range from $3,544 to $3,622 (depending on residency).

CAREER INFORMATION FROM PAYSCALE.COM	
ROI Rating	92
Bachelors and No Higher	
Median starting salary	$57,100
Median mid-career salary	$113,600
At Least Bachelors	
Median starting salary	$58,900
Median mid-career salary	$120,900
Alumni with high job meaning	44%
Degrees awarded in STEM subjects	21%

SELECTIVITY	
Admissions Rating	96
# of applicants	14,921
% of applicants accepted	36
% of acceptees attending	29
# offered a place on the wait list	4,392
% accepting a place on wait list	54
% admitted from wait list	3
# of early decision applicants	1021
% accepted early decision	52

FRESHMAN PROFILE	
Range SAT EBRW	660–740
Range SAT Math	640–740
Range ACT Composite	29–33
Minimum internet-based TOEFL	100
Average HS GPA	4.2
% graduated top 10% of class	81
% graduated top 25% of class	97
% graduated top 50% of class	100

DEADLINES	
Early decision	
Deadline	11/1
Notification	12/1
Regular	
Deadline	1/1
Notification	4/1
Nonfall registration?	No

FINANCIAL FACTS	
Financial Aid Rating	84
Annual in-state tuition	$15,864
Annual out-of-state tuition	$38,735
Room and board	$12,236
Required fees	$5,966
Average frosh need-based scholarship	$15,468
Average UG need-based scholarship	$15,892
% needy frosh rec. need-based scholarship or grant aid	82
% needy UG rec. need-based scholarship or grant aid	86
% needy frosh rec. non-need-based scholarship or grant aid	45
% needy UG rec. non-need-based scholarship or grant aid	37
% needy frosh rec. need-based self-help aid	50
% needy UG rec. need-based self-help aid	61
% frosh rec. any financial aid	54
% UG rec. any financial aid	53
% UG borrow to pay for school	35
Average cumulative indebtedness	$26,400
% frosh need fully met	24
% ugrads need fully met	23
Average % of frosh need met	79
Average % of ugrad need met	80

The College of Wooster

847 College Avenue, Wooster, OH 44691 • Admissions: 330-263-2322 • Fax: 330-263-2621

CAMPUS LIFE

Quality of Life Rating	93
Fire Safety Rating	86
Green Rating	79
Type of school	Private
Affiliation	Presbyterian
Environment	Town

STUDENTS

Total undergrad enrollment	1,970
% male/female	46/54
% from out of state	63
% frosh from public high school	62
% frosh live on campus	100
% ugrads live on campus	99
# of fraternities (% ugrad men join)	4 (14)
# of sororities (% ugrad women join)	7 (17)
% African American	9
% Asian	5
% Caucasian	66
% Hispanic	5
% Native American	1
% Pacific Islander	0
% Two or more races	0
% Race and/or ethnicity unknown	1
% international	13
# of countries represented	37

ACADEMICS

Academic Rating	96
% students returning for sophomore year	86
% students graduating within 4 years	70
% students graduating within 6 years	77
Calendar	Semester
Student/faculty ratio	11:1
Profs interesting rating	97
Profs accessible rating	99

Most classes have 20–29 students. Most lab/discussion sessions have 10–19 students.

MOST POPULAR MAJORS
Psychology; English; Political Science; History

ABOUT THE SCHOOL

Students who attend the College of Wooster in Ohio will find that they have access to mentored-research in a liberal arts setting. Wooster students praise their ability to "shape, direct and achieve [their academic] goals [all] while being supported by a community of peers, professors and mentors." What's more, they proclaim that a Wooster education truly allows individuals to uncover their "passions." One of Wooster's greatest strengths is the college's "emphasis on research": Students have many opportunities "to work one on one with a professor [to] co-author and publish papers [as well as] present at conferences." They are also required to complete a "senior thesis" during Independent Study, in the form of a major research paper, art exhibit, or performance, that demonstrates the analytical, creative, and communication skills they've honed at Wooster. Current students shower their "incredibly knowledgeable" and "engaging" professors with praise. These individuals "are entirely committed to giving each student the opportunity to succeed." And they excel at "tailor[ing] the learning experience to the particular needs of [their] students.

BANG FOR YOUR BUCK

Undergrads at Wooster love to highlight how "affordable" their school is and often remark on the "generous scholarships" they receive. In fact, the college provides some form of aid to over 85 percent of their student body. More specifically, it distributes over $50 million in the form of merit scholarships and need-based grants. Importantly, all applicants are automatically considered for any available merit scholarships. These can range from the Clarence Beecher Allen Scholarship, which provides up to $32,000 annually, to the Performing Arts Scholarship, which provides between $2,000 and $8,000 per year. Beyond scholarships, Wooster offers over $1 million in on-campus employment opportunities.

STUDENT LIFE

Academics certainly take priority at Wooster. Nevertheless, these undergrads manage to squeeze in some socializing. Ninety-nine percent of students live on campus, where they can participate in a wide variety of "clubs/organizations, sports, music [and] campus events." In fact, a third of Wooster students perform in at least one musical ensemble, a third compete on a varsity team, and one quarter participate in theatre or dance. And we'd be remiss if we didn't note that "many students do a lot of community service" as well. The Wooster Activities Crew continually organizes events like "crafts nights," "salsa classes and movie nights," and actively recruits "bands to play on campus."

CAREER

Wooster's "outstanding" career services truly helps students prepare for their post graduate life. From the moment undergrads set foot on campus, they can visit APEX, Wooster's center for Advising, Planning, and Experiential Learning, to begin exploring where certain majors might lead. As they ready themselves for their job and internship hunts, students can receive one-on-one advice on resume writing, interviews and more. APEX also hosts numerous events and workshops throughout the year. These frequently include information sessions with various companies (City Year and Urban Teachers to name a few) as well as local entrepreneurs. And students eyeing careers in medicine or law can take advantage of programs that help them plan and prep for their graduate school applications.

The College of Wooster

FINANCIAL AID: 800-877-3688 • E-MAIL: ADMISSIONS@WOOSTER.EDU • WEBSITE: WWW.WOOSTER.EDU

GENERAL INFO

Activities: Choral groups, concert band, dance, drama/theater, jazz band, literary magazine, marching band, music ensembles, musical theater, pep band, radio station, student government, student newspaper, Moot Court, symphony orchestra, yearbook, campus ministries, International Student Organization, Model UN. **Organizations:** 100 registered organizations, 6 honor societies, 9 religious organizations. 4 fraternities, 6 sororities. **Athletics (Intercollegiate):** *Men:* baseball, basketball, cross-country, diving, football, golf, lacrosse, soccer, swimming, tennis, track/field (outdoor), track/field (indoor). *Women:* basketball, cross-country, diving, field hockey, lacrosse, soccer, softball, swimming, tennis, track/field (outdoor), track/field (indoor), volleyball. **On-Campus Highlights:** Kauke Hall, Ruth W. Williams Hall of Life Science., Timken Science Library, Ebert Art Center, Burton D. Morgan Hall, Gault Manor (residence hall).

FINANCIAL AID

Students should submit: CSS Profile; FAFSA; Institution's own financial aid form. Priority filing deadline is 2/15. The Princeton Review suggests that all financial aid forms be submitted as soon as possible after October 1. *Need-based scholarships/grants offered:* College/university scholarship or grant aid from institutional funds, Federal Pell, private scholarships, SEOG, state scholarships/grants. *Loan aid offered:* Direct PLUS Loans, Direct Subsidized Loans, Direct Unsubsidized Loans. Applicants will be notified of awards on a rolling basis beginning 3/15. Federal Work-Study Program available. Institutional employment available.

THE BOTTOM LINE

For the 2017-2018 academic year, Wooster is charging $49,810 for combined tuition and fees. Students (and their families) will have to fork over another $11,850 for housing (estimated based on the cost of a double room) and a meal plan bringing the total with required fees to $62,100. Of course, undergrads will also require funds for books, supplies, personal expenses and travel.

CAREER INFORMATION FROM PAYSCALE.COM	
ROI Rating	89
Bachelors and No Higher	
Median starting salary	$47,800
Median mid-career salary	$90,700
At Least Bachelors	
Median starting salary	$50,500
Median mid-career salary	$92,300
Alumni with high job meaning	56%
Degrees awarded in STEM subjects	27%

SELECTIVITY	
Admissions Rating	89
# of applicants	5,615
% of applicants accepted	56
% of acceptees attending	18
# offered a place on the wait list	727
% accepting a place on wait list	18
% admitted from wait list	9
# of early decision applicants	151
% accepted early decision	77

FRESHMAN PROFILE	
Range SAT EBRW	570–680
Range SAT Math	580–700
Range ACT Composite	24–30
Minimum internet-based TOEFL	81
Average HS GPA	3.7
% graduated top 10% of class	45
% graduated top 25% of class	75
% graduated top 50% of class	92

DEADLINES	
Early decision	
Deadline	11/1
Notification	11/15
Other ED Deadline	1/15
Other ED Notification	2/1
Early action	
Deadline	11/15
Notification	12/31
Regular	
Priority	2/15
Deadline	2/15
Notification	4/1
Nonfall registration?	Yes

FINANCIAL FACTS	
Financial Aid Rating	91
Annual tuition	$49,810
Room and board	$11,850
Required fees	$440
Books and supplies	$1,000
Average frosh need-based scholarship	$34,309
Average UG need-based scholarship	$32,621
% needy frosh rec. need-based scholarship or grant aid	97
% needy UG rec. need-based scholarship or grant aid	98
% needy frosh rec. non-need-based scholarship or grant aid	18
% needy UG rec. non-need-based scholarship or grant aid	14
% needy frosh rec. need-based self-help aid	79
% needy UG rec. need-based self-help aid	82
% frosh rec. any financial aid	100
% UG rec. any financial aid	99

Colorado College

14 EAST CACHE LA POUDRE STREET, COLORADO SPRINGS, CO 80903 • PHONE: 719-389-6344 • FINANCIAL AID PHONE: 719-389-6651

CAMPUS LIFE

Quality of Life Rating	89
Fire Safety Rating	96
Green Rating	91
Type of school	Private
Environment	Metropolis

STUDENTS

Total undergrad enrollment	2,091
% male/female	46/54
% from out of state	83
% frosh live on campus	100
% ugrads live on campus	78
# of fraternities	3
# of sororities	3
% African American	3
% Asian	4
% Caucasian	66
% Hispanic	9
% Native American	1
% Pacific Islander	<1
% Two or more races	9
% Race and/or ethnicity unknown	1
% international	8
# of countries represented	53

ACADEMICS

Academic Rating	95
% students returning for sophomore year	94
% students graduating within 4 years	82
% students graduating within 6 years	88
Calendar	8 sessions each 3.5 weeks long, 1 class
Student/faculty ratio	10:1
Profs interesting rating	94
Profs accessible rating	94

Most classes have 20–29 students. Most lab/discussion sessions have 10–19 students.

MOST POPULAR MAJORS
Economics; Political Science and Government; Sociology

ABOUT THE SCHOOL

Colorado College provides an education without boundaries. With an average class size of sixteen students and a 10:1 student/faculty ratio, students have access to an intimate learning experience where the focus is on immersion and independence. Pair a liberal arts education with the college's signature feature, the "Block Plan" (students take, and professors teach, one course at a time in intensive three-and-a-half week segments), locate the school in Colorado Springs, and you create unparalleled opportunities for field studies and experiential learning, as well as total subject immersion. "Taking one class at a time allows you to devote all of your time to it. It is definitely nice when you are in a class that you love, because you don't have to sacrifice any time for another class that you may like less, or that you have a harder time with."

On average, there are 750 independent study blocks completed by students each year. Colorado College also offers $100,000 annually in Venture Grants, enabling students to pursue original research or an academic project of their choosing. "CC students care about the world. They are idealists and dreamers [who] want to change the world for the better. CC fosters an arena where dreams can grow and students can learn how to go about pursuing them." A Public Interest Fellowship Program awards students paid summer and year-long postgraduate fellowships annually, a number of which have evolved into permanent positions.

BANG FOR YOUR BUCK

Overall, Colorado College provides a nontraditional learning opportunity where young adults can develop their passions in a beautiful and supportive environment. Not only is the educational opportunity perfect for individual learners, it is attainable. Great financial aid is a major selling point. The school is committed to the philosophy that cost should not deter a student from considering Colorado College. "The staff is very nice. If you go into to any office to ask anything they are very helpful. Financial Aid has been exceptionally helpful." Once Colorado College determines a student's eligibility for CC grant and scholarship funds, the school will make a four-year commitment to the family (except in limited circumstances) and renew the CC funds automatically each year at the same level. Funds have been specially designated to assist families who have been adversely impacted by the downturn in the economy.

STUDENT LIFE

Due to the unusual "Block Plan" academic structure, "life at CC is filled with class from 9–12, then the rest of the day is open for activities or resting or doing homework." Beyond studying, campus life involves "a ridiculously large array of different student groups, and there's a lot of good programming put on by them (concerts, speeches, performers, etc.). Also, the Student Activities office on campus also does a lot of its own events and they're always pretty good." Off campus events are popular too: "Due to the glorious set up of the block plan, we get five day adventures every three and a half weeks. These include rafting trips in Utah, backpacking trips throughout Colorado, skiing in the mountains or doing just about anything you'd like to do for five days." Partying plays a role in on and off campus fun as well. "Drinking is a big part of the culture here. That being said people are really good about looking out for each other, and I feel really safe." But while there is definitely an active party scene "it's not overwhelming and a large portion of the student body doesn't participate." The bottom line is that students are involved and friendly: "Most people are extremely outgoing, social, and because it is such a small school there are few faces that aren't familiar."

Colorado College

E-MAIL: ADMISSION@COLORADOCOLLEGE.EDU • FAX: 719-389-6816 • WEBSITE: WWW.COLORADOCOLLEGE.EDU

CAREER

The Colorado College Career Center offers many services: advising and counseling to help students explore their interests; professional services such as resume, cover letter, and interview coaching; opportunities for networking; and internship and job search resources. Colorado College also offers funding for student internships both through the Career Center and through certain academic departments. Most students agree that Colorado College gives students "a unique academic experience that provides you with the tools and foundation for your future career." Fifty-three percent of Colorado College alumni who visited PayScale.com believe that their jobs make the world a better place.

GENERAL INFO

Activities: Choral groups, concert band, dance, drama/theater, jazz band, literary magazine, music ensembles, musical theater, radio station, student government, student newspaper, student-run film society, yearbook, campus ministries, international student organization. **Organizations:** 147 registered organizations, 13 honor societies, 20 religious organizations. 3 fraternities, 3 sororities. **Athletics (Intercollegiate):** *Men:* Basketball, cross-country, ice hockey, lacrosse, soccer, swimming, tennis, track/field (outdoor). *Women:* Basketball, cross-country, lacrosse, soccer, swimming, tennis, track/field (outdoor), track/field (indoor), volleyball. **On-Campus Highlights:** Worner Student Center, Palmer Hall, Shove Chapel, Cutler Hall–Admission, View of Pikes Peak. **Environmental Initiatives:** The newly opened Tutt Library is a large-scale library that is net-zero energy and net-zero carbon.

FINANCIAL AID

Students should submit: CSS Profile; FAFSA; Noncustodial PROFILE. Priority filing deadline is 1/15. The Princeton Review suggests that all financial aid forms be submitted as soon as possible after October 1. *Need-based scholarships/grants offered:* College/university scholarship or grant aid from institutional funds; Federal Pell; Private scholarships; SEOG; State scholarships/grants; United Negro College Fund. *Loan aid offered:* Direct PLUS Loans, Direct Subsidized Loans, Direct Unsubsidized Loans. Applicants will be notified of awards on or about 2/15. Federal Work-Study Program available. Institutional employment available.

BOTTOM LINE

Students are attracted to Colorado College for more than its stunning landscape. "Life at Colorado College is intense—everything from class to social life to long-weekend vacations—have yet to meet someone who doesn't meet every opportunity with enthusiastic energy." Tuition and fees at Colorado College may total close to $55,470, but the average undergraduate need-based scholarship is $45,251.

CAREER INFORMATION FROM PAYSCALE.COM	
ROI Rating	89
Bachelors and No Higher	
Median starting salary	$51,100
Median mid-career salary	$98,500
At Least Bachelors	
Median starting salary	$53,100
Median mid-career salary	$99,100
Alumni with high job meaning	50%
Degrees awarded in STEM subjects	19%

SELECTIVITY	
Admissions Rating	97
# of applicants	8,223
% of applicants accepted	15
% of acceptees attending	44
# offered a place on the wait list	763
% accepting a place on wait list	28
% admitted from wait list	8
# of early decision applicants	910
% accepted early decision	33

FRESHMAN PROFILE	
Range SAT EBRW	650–730
Range SAT Math	650–760
Range ACT Composite	29–33
% graduated top 10% of class	70
% graduated top 25% of class	94
% graduated top 50% of class	99

DEADLINES	
Early decision	
Deadline	11/10
Notification	12/15
Other ED Deadline	1/15
Other ED Notification	2/10
Early action	
Deadline	11/10
Notification	12/20
Regular	
Priority	1/15
Deadline	1/15
Notification	4/1
Nonfall registration?	Yes

FINANCIAL FACTS	
Financial Aid Rating	96
Annual tuition	$54,996
Room and board	$12,076
Required fees	$474
Books and supplies	$1,220
Average frosh need-based scholarship	$47,140
Average UG need-based scholarship	$45,251
% needy frosh rec. need-based scholarship or grant aid	97
% needy UG rec. need-based scholarship or grant aid	96
% needy frosh rec. non-need-based scholarship or grant aid	7
% needy UG rec. non-need-based scholarship or grant aid	6
% needy frosh rec. need-based self-help aid	82
% needy UG rec. need-based self-help aid	79
% frosh rec. any financial aid	51
% UG rec. any financial aid	51
% UG borrow to pay for school	34
Average cumulative indebtedness	$25,470

Columbia University

212 Hamilton Hall MC 2807, 1130 Amsterdam Ave., New York, NY 10027 • Phone: 212-854-2522

CAMPUS LIFE	
Quality of Life Rating	91
Fire Safety Rating	86
Green Rating	96
Type of school	Private
Environment	Metropolis

STUDENTS	
Total undergrad enrollment	6,231
% male/female	52/48
% from out of state	78
% frosh from public high school	56
% frosh live on campus	100
% ugrads live on campus	93
# of fraternities (% ugrad men join)	17 (24)
# of sororities (% ugrad women join)	11 (16)
% African American	12
% Asian	22
% Caucasian	34
% Hispanic	12
% Native American	2
% Race and/or ethnicity unknown	2
% international	16
# of countries represented	90

ACADEMICS	
Academic Rating	92
% students returning for sophomore year	99
% students graduating within 4 years	88
% students graduating within 6 years	96
Calendar	Semester
Student/faculty ratio	6:1
Profs interesting rating	79
Profs accessible rating	72
Most classes have 10–19 students.	

MOST POPULAR MAJORS
Engineering; English Language and Literature; Political Science and Government

#14 BEST VALUE COLLEGE

ABOUT THE SCHOOL
Columbia University provides prestigious academics and top-of-the-line resources for an Ivy League education with a liberal arts college feel. Located on the Upper West Side of New York City, Columbia attracts prospective students with its "high academic rigor, amazing diversity, unlimited resources, the city of New York, [and the] beautiful campus." The Core Curriculum is a large draw, providing students with a solid liberal arts education on which to base their future studies. Pair this with a location that provides unparalleled access to internships, community service, and research opportunities, and you have a recipe for a melting pot of possibility. Columbia undergraduates represent every socioeconomic, racial, and ethnic background and hail from all fifty states and all over the world. Students' distinct interests and talents are reflected by their diverse academic pursuits: undergraduates study in more than ninety different academic fields. Engagement within the global community is central at Columbia, where "the students are very aware of the world around them" and "activism is essential to the Columbia experience, in fact, it is encouraged by the school itself." Being in the heart of the city is like holding a passport to opportunity with a side of arts, culture, and entertainment.

BANG FOR YOUR BUCK
With nearly all undergraduate students living on campus, students are active participants in campus life through the "multitude of opportunities that extend from clubs to study abroad programs and its proximity to one of the greatest cities in the world," which offers "so much to do outside of class [to] learn about culture and meet other people." Students boast about the "range and quality of classes, academic resources, [and] many opportunities to satiate intellectual curiosity," including "Nobel Professors" and events like the "World Leaders Forum with speakers [who] historically have included presidents and prime ministers from countries far and wide." Columbia's Core Curriculum, a broad range of humanities and science classes required for all students, "teaches you to think critically and develop your opinion," which students say allows them to step outside their field: "Finally, I could escape the STEM bubble I was already part of and get myself to read books from Greek Literature, take a writing class, study philosophy, arts and music," one student explains.

STUDENT LIFE
It is no surprise that at an academically rigorous school, "the Monday to Thursday grind is usually pretty tough," "but since Columbia students generally don't have classes on Fridays, we still have enough time to enjoy the perks of living in New York City." Students enjoy going "into a city and watch plays or go to galleries," or stay on campus and "[party] at the most popular senior dorm or at one of the fraternities." While some students point out that taking advantage of the cultural experiences in NYC can be expensive, "Columbia also has a great Arts Initiative which is perfect for getting things cheaper." Student clubs and organizations are popular "and almost every student is part of at least one." "Even though studying at Columbia is pretty intense," students have plenty of opportunities to "get out of the Columbia bubble" and "devote...time to extracurriculars that [they] enjoy."

Columbia University

Fax: 212-894-1209 • Website: undergrad.admissions.columbia.edu

CAREER

The Columbia University brand goes far in this country, even though many students only need it to work downtown. Students are thankful for the wealth of resources (referring primarily to internships) available to a student at Columbia University, as well as the accessible professors and the "enormous investment in undergraduate research." Internships in New York are an excellent entry point for students trying to make themselves known to employers, and it doesn't hurt that the city is rife with Columbia alumni. The Center for Career Education offers a multitude of resources to get students on their way, including counseling sessions, practice interviews, dossier assessments, and old reliable career fairs. Graduates who visited PayScale.com reported median starting salary of $66,000; 46 percent of these students said they felt their job had a meaningful impact on the world.

GENERAL INFO

Activities: Choral groups, concert band, dance, drama/theater, jazz band, literary magazine, marching band, music ensembles, musical theater, opera, pep band, radio station, student government, student newspaper, student-run film society, symphony orchestra, television station, yearbook, campus ministries, international student organization.
Athletics (Intercollegiate): *Men:* Baseball, basketball, crew/rowing, cross-country, diving, fencing, football, golf, soccer, squash, swimming, tennis, track/field (outdoor), track/field (indoor), wrestling. *Women:* Archery, basketball, crew/rowing, cross-country, diving, fencing, field hockey, golf, lacrosse, soccer, softball, squash, swimming, tennis, track/field (outdoor), track/field (indoor), volleyball.

FINANCIAL AID

Students should submit: CSS Profile; FAFSA; Noncustodial PROFILE. Priority filing deadline is 2/15. The Princeton Review suggests that all financial aid forms be submitted as soon as possible after October 1. *Need-based scholarships/grants offered:* College/university scholarship or grant aid from institutional funds, Federal Pell, private scholarships, SEOG, state scholarships/grants. *Loan aid offered:* Direct PLUS Loans, Direct Subsidized Loans, Direct Unsubsidized Loans. Applicants will be notified of awards on or about 4/1. Federal Work-Study Program available. Institutional employment available.

BOTTOM LINE

Earning an acceptance letter from Columbia is no easy feat. Admissions officers are looking to build a diverse class that will greatly contribute to the university. It's the Ivy League, folks, and it's New York City, and there is a price tag that goes with both. A year's tuition is $56,608. Additionally, count on $14,016 in room and board. Columbia's New York City campus means that every manner of distraction is literally at your fingertips, so you'll want to factor in another nice chunk of change for things like transportation, personal expenses, outings, etc. These figures are nothing to sneeze at. Take heart: If you get over the first hurdle and manage to gain admittance to this prestigious university, you can be confident that the university will help you pay for it.

CAREER INFORMATION FROM PAYSCALE.COM

ROI Rating	95
Bachelors and No Higher	
Median starting salary	$69,200
Median mid-career salary	$127,500
At Least Bachelors	
Median starting salary	$71,000
Median mid-career salary	$134,600
Alumni with high job meaning	44%
Degrees awarded in STEM subjects	30%

SELECTIVITY

Admissions Rating	99
# of applicants	37,389
% of applicants accepted	6
% of acceptees attending	62
# of early decision applicants	4086
% accepted early decision	17

FRESHMAN PROFILE

Range SAT EBRW	720–780
Range SAT Math	730–800
Range ACT Composite	32–35
Minimum paper TOEFL	600
Minimum internet-based TOEFL	100

DEADLINES

Early decision	
Deadline	11/1
Notification	12/15
Regular	
Deadline	1/1
Notification	4/1
Nonfall registration?	No

FINANCIAL FACTS

Financial Aid Rating	95
Annual tuition	$56,608
Room and board	$14,016
Required fees	$2,822
Books and supplies	$1,270
Average frosh need-based scholarship	$56,504
Average UG need-based scholarship	$53,879
% needy frosh rec. need-based scholarship or grant aid	99
% needy UG rec. need-based scholarship or grant aid	99
% needy frosh rec. non-need-based scholarship or grant aid	7
% needy UG rec. non-need-based scholarship or grant aid	3
% needy frosh rec. need-based self-help aid	72
% needy UG rec. need-based self-help aid	78
% frosh rec. any financial aid	51
% UG rec. any financial aid	50
% UG borrow to pay for school	22
Average cumulative indebtedness	$25,402
% frosh need fully met	100
% ugrads need fully met	100
Average % of frosh need met	100
Average % of ugrad need met	100

The Cooper Union for the Advancement of Science and Art

30 COOPER SQUARE, NEW YORK, NY 10003 • ADMISSIONS: 212-353-4120 • FAX: 212-353-4342

CAMPUS LIFE

Quality of Life Rating	86
Fire Safety Rating	97
Green Rating	60*
Type of school	Private
Environment	Metropolis

STUDENTS

Total undergrad enrollment	853
% male/female	66/34
% from out of state	50
% frosh from public high school	65
% frosh live on campus	80
% ugrads live on campus	25
# of fraternities (% ugrad men join)	2 (2)
% African American	3
% Asian	20
% Caucasian	31
% Hispanic	10
% Native American	0
% Pacific Islander	0
% Two or more races	8
% Race and/or ethnicity unknown	10
% international	19

ACADEMICS

Academic Rating	89
% students returning for sophomore year	95
% students graduating within 4 years	62
% students graduating within 6 years	83
Calendar	Semester
Student/faculty ratio	8:1
Profs interesting rating	84
Profs accessible rating	81

MOST POPULAR MAJORS
Electrical and Electronics Engineering;
Mechanical Engineering;
Fine and Studio Arts

ABOUT THE SCHOOL

Believe it or not, the generous scholarship policy isn't the only reason gifted students clamor for a spot at The Cooper Union for the Advancement of Science and Art. The school's reputable, rigorous academics and location in the heart of New York's East Village are equally big draws. Classes are small (total enrollment is fewer than 900), and students must handle a highly demanding workload. The size of the school allows for very close relationships between the faculty and the students, and that partnership is the intellectual pulse of the institution. Practicing architects, artists, and engineers come to The Cooper Union while continuing their own personal research and work at various points in their careers, giving students frontline access to real-world experience and insight from professionals who want to teach. Group projects are a major part of the curriculum, regardless of academic discipline, furthering the school's problem-solving philosophy of education. A degree from The Cooper Union is enormously valuable in the job market, and many graduates become world-class leaders in the disciplines of architecture, fine arts, design, and engineering. As an all-honors private college, The Cooper Union offers talented students rigorous, humanistic learning enhanced by the process of design and augmented by the urban setting. In addition to outstanding academic programs in architecture, art, and engineering, it offers a Faculty of Humanities and Social Sciences. "An institution of the highest caliber," the school has a narrow academic focus, conferring degrees only in fine arts, architecture, and engineering, with "plenty of opportunities for independent study in your field." All students take a core curriculum of required courses in the humanities and social sciences in their first two years, and those that go on to the School of Art have easy "access to established and interesting artists."

BANG FOR YOUR BUCK

The school's founder, Peter Cooper, believed that an "education of the first rank" should be "as free as air and water," and while the current economic climate has recently changed the school's scholarship practices, The Cooper Union remains committed to providing financial support to its accomplished, ambitious student body. An example of this is every enrolled student receives a minimum half-tuition scholarship. The engineering program is considered one of the best in the nation, and a degree from The Cooper Union is a ticket into an excellent professional career. Forty percent of graduates go on to top-tier graduate programs, and the small school has produced thirty-four Fulbright scholars since 2001. The Cooper Union's location in the East Village adds value to students' experience as well. In the limited time they spend outside of the lab or the studio, students here have access to the nearly infinite range of cultural events, restaurants, museums, and other adventures available in New York City.

STUDENT LIFE

Artists, engineers, and architects abound on this East Village campus filled with "very unique, interesting people" eager to learn and cross-pollinate between departments. This goal is supported by the architecture of The Cooper Union's distinctive academic building which was designed by Thom Mayne to enhance interaction between enrollees of all three schools. Across the board, students in every major are serious about their studies, and most of The Cooper Union's selective admits are "super intelligent, super creative, and/or just super hardworking." Still, The Cooper Union's prime location allows the City That Never Sleeps to act as The Cooper Union's extended campus with plenty of "comedy

The Cooper Union for the Advancement of Science and Art

FINANCIAL AID: 212-353-4130 • E-MAIL: ADMISSIONS@COOPER.EDU • WEBSITE: WWW.COOPER.EDU

clubs, movies, bowling, lounges, and bars" to entice students to take a break from their studies. Students say their school will "push you to your limits, push you to succeed, and this common goal unites all the students as well," which makes for a "close-knit community," not to mention an exciting, motivating experience.

CAREER

The Center for Career Development encourages "self-accountability," "initiative," and "autonomy" in all Cooper students as they transition to a professional practice. With that in mind, the Center offers ample resources to help students find their way, like online timelines and career counseling tailored to each school as well as the Cooper Career Connection that informs students about all career-related events, programs, and forums. The Career Resource Library is another excellent way to keep abreast of trends and ideas in your relevant field. Alumni lead by example, and the CU @ Lunch program allows recent grads to "speak about the vital issues they face following graduation." Those graduates who visited PayScale.com report a median starting salary of $63,900, and 49 percent believe their work makes the world a better place.

GENERAL INFO

Activities: Choral groups, concert band, dance, drama/theater, jazz band, literary magazine, music ensembles, student government, student newspaper, student-run film society, symphony orchestra, yearbook. **Organizations:** 90 registered organizations, 18 honor societies, 8 religious organizations. 1 fraternity. **Athletics (Intercollegiate/Varsity):** *Men:* Basketball, soccer, tennis, volleyball. *Women:* Basketball, soccer, tennis, volleyball.

FINANCIAL AID

Students should submit: FAFSA. Priority filing deadline is March 1. The Princeton Review suggests that all financial aid forms be submitted as soon as possible after October 1. *Need-based scholarships/grants offered:* College/university scholarship or grant aid from institutional funds, Federal Pell, private scholarships, SEOG, state scholarships/grants. *Loan aid offered:* Direct PLUS Loans, Direct Subsidized Loans, Direct Unsubsidized Loans. Applicants will be notified of awards on a rolling basis beginning 12/20. Federal Work-Study Program available. Institutional employment available.

BOTTOM LINE

Students are accepted on the basis of student's academic achievement as well as their potential, creativity, talent and critical thinking skills. As of Fall 2015 every admitted student receives a half-tuition scholarship valued at $21,000 annually. For remaining expenses, including room and board, The Cooper Union provides additional aid based upon financial need. Health insurance adds an additional $1,200 for those that require it. Financial aid is available to assist with payment of all fees.

CAREER INFORMATION FROM PAYSCALE.COM

ROI Rating	95
Bachelors and No Higher	
Median starting salary	$65,900
Median mid-career salary	$128,300
At Least Bachelors	
Median starting salary	$68,900
Median mid-career salary	$135,000
Alumni with high job meaning	46%
Degrees awarded in STEM subjects	56%

SELECTIVITY

Admissions Rating	98
# of applicants	2,574
% of applicants accepted	13
% of acceptees attending	61
# offered a place on the wait list	136
% accepting a place on wait list	97
% admitted from wait list	14
# of early decision applicants	173
% accepted early decision	24

FRESHMAN PROFILE

Range SAT EBRW	650–740
Range SAT Math	660–790
Range ACT Composite	28–34
Minimum paper TOEFL	600
Minimum internet-based TOEFL	100
Average HS GPA	3.6
% graduated top 10% of class	51
% graduated top 25% of class	85
% graduated top 50% of class	99

DEADLINES

Early decision	
Deadline	12/1
Notification	12/23
Other ED Deadline	12/1
Other ED Notification	2/15
Regular	
Priority	12/1
Deadline	1/9
Notification	4/1
Nonfall registration?	No

FINANCIAL FACTS

Financial Aid Rating	96
Annual tuition	$44,550
Room and board	$16,638
Required fees	$2,150
Books and supplies	$1,650
Average frosh need-based scholarship	$24,749
Average UG need-based scholarship	$25,221
% needy frosh rec. need-based scholarship or grant aid	100
% needy UG rec. need-based scholarship or grant aid	100
% needy frosh rec. non-need-based scholarship or grant aid	100
% needy UG rec. non-need-based scholarship or grant aid	100
% needy frosh rec. need-based self-help aid	34
% needy UG rec. need-based self-help aid	29
% frosh rec. any financial aid	100
% UG rec. any financial aid	100
% UG borrow to pay for school	18
Average cumulative indebtedness	$17,037

SCHOOL PROFILES ■ 145

Cornell University

Undergraduate Admissions, 410 Thurston Ave, Ithaca, NY 14850 • Admissions: 607-255-5241 • Fax: 607-255-0659

CAMPUS LIFE

Quality of Life Rating	90
Fire Safety Rating	90
Green Rating	99
Type of school	Private
Environment	Town

STUDENTS

Total undergrad enrollment	14,815
% male/female	48/52
% from out of state	59
% frosh live on campus	100
% ugrads live on campus	54
# of fraternities (% ugrad men join)	43 (32)
# of sororities (% ugrad women join)	21 (31)
% African American	7
% Asian	19
% Caucasian	38
% Hispanic	13
% Native American	<1
% Pacific Islander	<1
% Two or more races	5
% Race and/or ethnicity unknown	8
% international	10
# of countries represented	88

ACADEMICS

Academic Rating	94
% students returning for sophomore year	97
% students graduating within 4 years	85
% students graduating within 6 years	93
Calendar	Semester
Student/faculty ratio	9:1
Profs interesting rating	83
Profs accessible rating	83

Most classes have 10–19 students. Most lab/discussion sessions have 10–19 students.

MOST POPULAR MAJORS

Biology/Biological Sciences; Hotel Administration; Labor and Industrial Relations; Computer Science/Info Science; Engineering

#23 BEST VALUE COLLEGE

ABOUT THE SCHOOL

"Any person, any study." Perhaps no motto does a better job of summing up the spirit of a school than Ithaca, New York's Cornell University, an Ivy League school in upstate New York consisting of seven undergraduate colleges and schools. Cornell University is not just Ivy League, it's the largest of the Ivy League schools—and it has a curriculum to match. The "unbelievably broad curriculum" at Cornell offers a "large variety of academic programs" and "a plethora of classes to chose from," giving credence to the school's famous motto. There are nearly forty different majors at the College of Arts and Sciences alone. Factor in six other colleges and schools, and it's clear that students have a wealth of options before them. Specializations in science, agriculture, and environmental studies are especially popular here, though engineering, premed, and other studies receive just as much attention by attendees. "The research opportunities have been incredible," one student says. Another notes that, thanks to the hard work it demands of students and the school's great reputation, Cornell is a "difficult school with great job placement after." With all the educational opportunities Cornell has to offer, it should come as no surprise that the campus features an "intellectually mature student body" who are intent on focusing on the school's "rigorous" academics. "The intellectual caliber of the student body here is really unmatched." When study time ends, students exploring the "bustling student life" will see that "diversity here is definitely apparent...I love the fact that you can be surrounded by dairy farmers and Wall Street wannabes all in the same quad." About the only thing tying Cornell's student population together is the fact that everyone is "very focused on performing well in the classroom." Outside the classroom, recreation is just as diverse as the classes. Being in Ithaca, New York, opportunities for outdoor adventure abound, and Greek life thrives. Sports are as popular here as partying—wrestling, track, and hockey are the school's top sports—and students note that "if I want to go study in a library at 3 A.M. on Saturday night, I will find a busy library full of other eager students, but if I want to go to a hockey game on a Saturday afternoon, I will find just as many screaming fans to share the fun."

BANG FOR YOUR BUCK

Need-based Federal Pell, SEOG, state scholarships/grants, private scholarships, school scholarship, or grant aid from institutional funds are all available to prospective students. Loan aid is also available in the form of Direct Subsidized Stafford loans, Direct Unsubsidized Stafford, Direct PLUS, and university loans from institutional funds.

STUDENT LIFE

Since Cornell is such a rigorous school, it's not surprising that "most of the time people are thinking about studying and getting their work done." "People are always thinking about the next prelim or paper they have to suffer through, but it's not always immediately at the forefront of their mind," says a student, so "people work hard here, and people certainly know how to play hard as well. "People here do anything and everything they can for fun: sports, parties, hanging out with friends or even getting involved with the clubs here on campus." With 30 to 40 percent of kids participating, "Greek life is big here. Not overwhelming, but definitely big." "Frat parties are really popular freshman and sophomore years, but then the crowd tends to migrate to the bars in Collegetown during junior and senior years." But while "it is not hard to find alcohol on campus,

Cornell University

FINANCIAL AID: 607-255-5147 • E-MAIL: ADMISSIONS@CORNELL.EDU • WEBSITE: WWW.CORNELL.EDU

there really is no pressure to drink, [and] there are also a lot of campus run events on the weekends and also throughout the week to encourage students to do other things." "The campus is so diverse and the range of activities is endless. You will find a club or organization here that interests you, and there's always the possibility of establishing something new if that's what you're interested in here." So even if "the size of the student body may be overwhelming at first," students will find that "it's easy to find a close group of people."

CAREER

Cornell students are definitely a career-focused bunch: "People are kind of paranoid of failure," says a student. "They go crazy looking for internships and career opportunities as early as second semester freshman year." Fortunately for those students, consensus seems to be that "Cornell offers great career assistance to help students write resumes, cover letters, and find jobs/internships." The center offers counseling for students looking to explore their interests and determine a career path, resources for finding jobs and internships, career fairs and on campus recruiting, and even resources for those seeking international work experience. In addition to a central office in Barnes Hall that serves all students, each of Cornell's seven undergraduate colleges has its own office with resources tailored to the students in that college.

GENERAL INFO

Environment: Town. **Activities:** Choral groups, concert band, dance, drama/theater, jazz band, literary magazine, marching band, music ensembles, musical theater, pep band, radio station, student government, student newspaper, student-run film society, symphony orchestra, television station, yearbook, campus ministries, international student organization.

FINANCIAL AID

Students should submit: CSS Profile; FAFSA; Noncustodial PROFILE. Regular filing deadline is 2/15. The Princeton Review suggests that all financial aid forms be submitted as soon as possible after October 1. *Need-based scholarships/grants offered:* College/university scholarship or grant aid from institutional funds, Federal Pell, private scholarships, SEOG, state scholarships/grants. *Loan aid offered:* Direct PLUS Loans, Direct Subsidized Loans, Direct Unsubsidized Loans. Applicants will be notified of awards on or about 4/1. Federal Work-Study Program available. Institutional employment available. International applicants should see the university website for deadlines and further details.

BOTTOM LINE

An Ivy League education at Cornell University will cost attendees just more than $55,188 per year in tuition and fees. Add to that $14,816 for room and board, and another $950 for books and supplies, and costs come to about $71,000 annually. Students are graduating from Cornell with an average accumulated debt of $25,542.

CAREER INFORMATION FROM PAYSCALE.COM	
ROI Rating	94
Bachelors and No Higher	
Median starting salary	$68,200
Median mid-career salary	$127,100
At Least Bachelors	
Median starting salary	$70,500
Median mid-career salary	$132,700
Alumni with high job meaning	45%
Degrees awarded in STEM subjects	43%

SELECTIVITY	
Admissions Rating	97
# of applicants	47,039
% of applicants accepted	12.67
% of acceptees attending	56
# offered a place on the wait list	5,714
% accepting a place on wait list	65
% admitted from wait list	1.3
# of early decision applicants	5401
% accepted early decision	26

FRESHMAN PROFILE	
Range SAT EBRW	690–760
Range SAT Math	700–790
Range ACT Composite	31–34
Minimum paper TOEFL	600
Minimum internet-based TOEFL	100
% graduated top 10% of class	86
% graduated top 25% of class	98
% graduated top 50% of class	100

DEADLINES	
Early decision	
Deadline	11/1
Notification	mid-Dec
Regular	
Deadline	1/2
Notification	Early Apr
Nonfall registration?	Yes

FINANCIAL FACTS	
Financial Aid Rating	98
Annual tuition	$54,584
Room and board	$14,816
Required fees	$604
Books and supplies	$950
Average frosh need-based scholarship	$42,053
Average UG need-based scholarship	$40,540
% needy frosh rec. need-based scholarship or grant aid	98
% needy UG rec. need-based scholarship or grant aid	96
% needy frosh rec. non-need-based scholarship or grant aid	0
% needy UG rec. non-need-based scholarship or grant aid	0
% needy frosh rec. need-based self-help aid	86
% needy UG rec. need-based self-help aid	91
% frosh rec. any financial aid	60
% UG rec. any financial aid	57
% UG borrow to pay for school	41
Average cumulative indebtedness	$25,542
% frosh need fully met	100
% ugrads need fully met	100
Average % of frosh need met	100
Average % of ugrad need met	100

Creighton University

2500 CALIFORNIA PLAZA, OMAHA, NE 68178 • ADMISSIONS: 402-280-2703 • FAX: 402-280-2685

CAMPUS LIFE

Quality of Life Rating	**86**
Fire Safety Rating	**93**
Green Rating	**86**
Type of school	Private
Affiliation	Roman Catholic Jesuit
Environment	Metropolis

STUDENTS

Total undergrad enrollment	4,212
% male/female	44/56
% from out of state	77
% frosh from public high school	51
% frosh live on campus	96
% ugrads live on campus	57
# of fraternities (% ugrad men join)	6 (32)
# of sororities (% ugrad women join)	8 (51)
% African American	3
% Asian	9
% Caucasian	71
% Hispanic	8
% Native American	<1
% Pacific Islander	<1
% Two or more races	5
% Race and/or ethnicity unknown	1
% international	3
# of countries represented	27

ACADEMICS

Academic Rating	**85**
% students returning for sophomore year	89
% students graduating within 4 years	73
% students graduating within 6 years	81
Calendar	Semester
Student/faculty ratio	11:1
Profs interesting rating	86
Profs accessible rating	83

Most classes have 10–19 students. Most lab/discussion sessions have 10–19 students.

MOST POPULAR MAJORS
Biology; Psychology; Nursing

ABOUT THE SCHOOL

Nebraska's Creighton University offers a top education in the Jesuit tradition, letting students take advantage of a flexible curriculum, an 11:1 student-to-faculty ratio, and more than 100 academic programs, degrees and majors. The school stresses a mission of caring for all people and striving for social justice, and "instills good values in its students to use their education to make a difference." Communications 101 is a class required for all first-years, and the school is "big enough to take care of the needs of the students, but small enough to know students personally and have small class sizes." Professors have a "diversity of views and encourage students to hold different views as well." They are "accessible, understanding, educated, and willing to work with every student to see everyone succeed," and the approaches they take in the classroom "are that beyond traditional lectures and seminars." They "find ways to get students involved in the lectures to assure that students are learning the course content" and are able to apply those principles to real life or topics outside the course.

BANG FOR YOUR BUCK

Academically, Creighton can be tough, but "there are so many resources on campus for students to obtain academic help," and it "is known for taking good care of their students." There is a "lot of intensive work, but you get an education that is really worth the cost." The university "excels at multiple majors" and doesn't just focus on a few flagship programs, and niche opportunities abound; for instance, Creighton offers Faculty Lead Programs Abroad (FLPA) where professors teach a class on a specific focus, normally overseas. Lectures hosted by the school featuring famous speakers and experts "make outside learning fun and engaging," and the school is "always updating the technology available in classes," such as cameras in the science labs that allow for a birds-eye view of the professor's lab table or computer labs designed for psychology majors to collect data from studies. Students agree that the academic experience at Creighton is "truly... second-to-none."

STUDENT LIFE

Creighton is "a faith-dominated community, where peers will "encourage everyone to lead and live lives influenced by Jesuit values," but without pressure. Most students are from middle- to upper-class families and from the suburbs of bigger cities, and the school is "full of high achievers." Nobody ever seems bored—"people are more overwhelmed than anything else"—which makes sense, given that "everyone gets involved in extracurricular activities such as intramural sports, clubs, and other organizations." The school is "a goldilocks size, not too big, but not too small," and most students tend to live on campus, but Omaha has lots of nearby restaurants so students "go off-campus on weekends to eat and go to parties." Basketball games are "super popular," and most students "arrive an hour and a half early to get a seat in the student section."

Creighton University

FINANCIAL AID: 402-280-2731 • E-MAIL: ADMISSIONS@CREIGHTON.EDU • WEBSITE: WWW.CREIGHTON.EDU

CAREER

The school's Center for Undergraduate Research and Scholarship serves as a resource for students looking to participate in research or creative projects, find funding and scholarships, and match up with professors/mentors that can help them develop hands-on skills; additionally, it helps two hundred —students present their findings at scholarly conferences each year. The job placement rate is stellar, as "you are receiving a world-class education here at Creighton University, and you can be sure when you graduate that you will have many opportunities for jobs." To wit, 99 percent of students are employed, volunteering, or attending a graduate or professional school within six months of graduation. No matter what, "there are endless opportunities for a Creighton grad." Out of Creighton alumni visiting PayScale.com, fifty-seven percent report that they derive a high level of meaning from their jobs.

GENERAL INFO

Activities: Campus Ministries; Choral groups; Dance; Drama/theater; International Student Organization; Model UN; Music ensembles; Musical theater; Pep band; Student government; Student newspaper; Symphony orchestra 182 registered organizations, 11 honor societies, 6 religious organizations. 5 fraternities, 8 sororities. **Athletics (Intercollegiate):** *Men:* baseball, basketball, cross-country, golf, soccer, tennis. *Women:* basketball, crew/rowing, cross-country, golf, soccer, softball, tennis, volleyball. **On-Campus Highlights:** Heider College of Business/Harper Center, Hixson-Lied Science Building, a 100,000 square foot science facility, Morrison Soccer Stadium, nationally acclaimed collegiate soccer stadium, Wayne and Eileen Ryan Athletic Center and D.J. Sokol Arena, St. John's Church, the "heart" of campus

FINANCIAL AID

Students should submit: FAFSA; Institution's own financial aid form. Priority filing deadline is 1/15. The Princeton Review suggests that all financial aid forms be submitted as soon as possible after October 1. *Need-based scholarships/grants offered:* College/university scholarship or grant aid from institutional funds, Federal Pell, private scholarships, SEOG, state scholarships/grants. *Loan aid offered:* Direct PLUS Loans, Direct Subsidized Loans, Direct Unsubsidized Loans. Applicants will be notified of awards on a rolling basis beginning 2/15. Federal Work-Study Program available. Institutional employment available.

CAREER INFORMATION FROM PAYSCALE.COM

ROI Rating	87
Bachelors and No Higher	
Median starting salary	$52,400
Median mid-career salary	$93,100
At Least Bachelors	
Median starting salary	$53,900
Median mid-career salary	$99,800
Alumni with high job meaning	56%
Degrees awarded in STEM subjects	9%

SELECTIVITY

Admissions Rating	86
# of applicants	9,727
% of applicants accepted	72
% of acceptees attending	16

FRESHMAN PROFILE

Range SAT EBRW	520–640
Range SAT Math	550–650
Range ACT Composite	25–30
Minimum paper TOEFL	570
Minimum internet-based TOEFL	88
Average HS GPA	3.8
% graduated top 10% of class	33
% graduated top 25% of class	69
% graduated top 50% of class	93

DEADLINES

Early action	
Deadline	11/1
Notification	Rolling
Regular	
Priority	12/1
Deadline	2/15
Nonfall registration?	Yes

FINANCIAL FACTS

Financial Aid Rating	85
Annual tuition	$38,200
Room and board	$11,036
Required fees	$1,716
Books and supplies	$1,200
Average frosh need-based scholarship	$21,759
Average UG need-based scholarship	$21,635
% needy frosh rec. need-based scholarship or grant aid	100
% needy UG rec. need-based scholarship or grant aid	97
% needy frosh rec. non-need-based scholarship or grant aid	26
% needy UG rec. non-need-based scholarship or grant aid	19
% needy frosh rec. need-based self-help aid	75
% needy UG rec. need-based self-help aid	79
% frosh rec. any financial aid	99
% UG rec. any financial aid	96
% UG borrow to pay for school	54
Average cumulative indebtedness	$34,766
% frosh need fully met	30
% ugrads need fully met	26
Average % of frosh need met	83
Average % of ugrad need met	79

Dartmouth College

6016 McNutt Hall, Hanover, NH 03755 • Admissions: 603-646-2875 • Fax: 603-646-1216

CAMPUS LIFE

Quality of Life Rating	**91**
Fire Safety Rating	**89**
Green Rating	**90**
Type of school	Private
Environment	Village

STUDENTS

Total undergrad enrollment	4,410
% male/female	51/49
% from out of state	97
% frosh from public high school	55
% frosh live on campus	100
% ugrads live on campus	85
# of fraternities (% ugrad men join)	17 (44)
# of sororities (% ugrad women join)	11 (46)
% African American	7
% Asian	15
% Caucasian	50
% Hispanic	10
% Native American	2
% Pacific Islander	<1
% Two or more races	5
% Race and/or ethnicity unknown	2
% international	9
# of countries represented	70

ACADEMICS

Academic Rating	**94**
% students returning for sophomore year	97
% students graduating within 4 years	88
% students graduating within 6 years	96
Calendar	Quarter
Student/faculty ratio	7:1
Profs interesting rating	88
Profs accessible rating	95

Most classes have 10–19 students. Most lab/discussion sessions have 10–19 students.

MOST POPULAR MAJORS

Psychology; Economics; Political Science and Government

#15 BEST VALUE COLLEGE

ABOUT THE SCHOOL

A member of the Ivy League, Dartmouth is a small, student-centered undergraduate and graduate college, with three leading professional schools—Geisel School of Medicine, Thayer School of Engineering, and the Tuck School of Business. It is known for its commitment to excellence in undergraduate education and has a reputation as a place where intellectual rigor and creativity collide. This comes from a flexible academic curriculum that emphasizes an interdisciplinary approach. The campus community is generally relaxed, accepting, a bit outdoorsy, and usually bundled up under eight layers of clothing to get through the New Hampshire winters. What students learn outside the classroom is often as meaningful as what they learn inside. All incoming freshmen live in residential housing clusters located throughout the campus, and more than 80 percent of upperclassmen choose to do so as well. Almost all of the student body comes from outside the college's New Hampshire base. Greek groups add to the social mix because everyone is welcome to attend fraternity and sorority parties and events. Intramural athletics are insanely popular on campus as well.

BANG FOR YOUR BUCK

Dartmouth's approximately 4,300 undergraduate students enjoy the college's strong reputation as a member of the Ivy League, as well as its high-quality academics through twenty-nine departments and ten multidisciplinary programs. Academics at New Hampshire's preeminent college, comparable with other Ivy League schools, are demanding, but Dartmouth students feel they are up to the challenge. Unlike many of the other Ivies, though, the student-faculty ratio of 7:1 favors the undergrads, who find graduate assistants in their classes to have the same open willingness to help them learn as the regular professors do.

STUDENT LIFE

Dartmouth students are continually on the go and they "wouldn't have it any other way." As one senior shares, "After attending classes in the morning, we run from meetings to debates to the library and finally to Frat Row. It is a relentless, fast-paced cycle, but it is so unbelievably fun and rewarding." More specifically, undergrads can enjoy "movies playing at our arts center . . . activities night (games, movies, etc. . . .), performance groups (dance troupes, a cappella groups, plays), outdoor activities (skiing, camping, hiking, sailing, etc.), and much more." We're told that "a very large percentage" of the student body chooses to go Greek. Fortunately, it's a "unique and VERY welcoming [scene] and much more low key than at other schools." And, of course, these undergrads love participating in Dartmouth traditions like "running around a giant three-story bonfire hundreds of times or streaking the green or singing karaoke with a milkshake close by."

CAREER

A Dartmouth degree and professional success typically go hand-in-hand. After all, according to PayScale.com, the average starting salary for Dartmouth grads is an impressive $66,300. Some of this success can indeed be attributed to the college's extensive alumni network. As one grateful psych major shares, "Alumni are...a HUGE resource; they love to stay involved with the college and are often willing to talk to current students about careers (and many have been known to give

Dartmouth College

FINANCIAL AID: 603-646-2451 • WEBSITE: WWW.DARTMOUTH.EDU

internships and jobs to Dartmouth students).” Certainly, students can also turn to the fantastic Center for Professional Development as well. Undergrads may use the office to find funding for unpaid internships, receive graduate and professional school advising and even get help finding housing for when they head out into the world. And, perhaps most important, the center hosts numerous recruiting sessions throughout the year.

GENERAL INFO

Activities: Choral groups, concert band, dance, drama/theater, jazz band, literary magazine, marching band, music ensembles, musical theater, opera, pep band, radio station, student government, student newspaper, student-run film society, symphony orchestra, television station, yearbook, campus ministries, international student organization. **Organizations:** 330 registered organizations, 26 religious organizations. 17 fraternities, 10 sororities. **Athletics (Intercollegiate):** *Men:* Baseball, basketball, crew/rowing, cross-country, diving, equestrian sports, fencing, football, golf, ice hockey, lacrosse, sailing, skiing (downhill/alpine), skiing (nordic/cross-country), soccer, squash, swimming, tennis, track/field (outdoor), track/field. *Women:* Basketball, crew/rowing, cross-country, diving, equestrian sports, fencing, field hockey, golf, ice hockey, lacrosse, sailing, skiing (downhill/alpine), skiing (nordic/cross-country), soccer, softball, squash, swimming, tennis, track/field (outdoor), track/ field, volleyball.

FINANCIAL AID

Students should submit: CSS Profile; FAFSA; Noncustodial PROFILE. Regular filing deadline is 2/1. The Princeton Review suggests that all financial aid forms be submitted as soon as possible after October 1. *Need-based scholarships/grants offered:* College/university scholarship or grant aid from institutional funds, Federal Pell, private scholarships, SEOG, state scholarships/grants. *Loan aid offered:* Federal Direct Subsidized Loans, Federal Direct Unsubsidized Loans. Parents may apply for Federal Direct PLUS Loans. Applicants will be notified of awards on or about 4/2. Federal Work-Study Program available. Institutional employment available.

BOTTOM LINE

To enjoy an Ivy League education with a nod to the New England collegiate experience, incoming freshmen at Dartmouth can expect to pay about $51,468 in tuition and roughly another $1,482 in required fees. On-campus room and board totals more than $15,159. Over half of Dartmouth students receive financial aid to help defray these costs, as the school maintains the philosophy that no one should hesitate to apply for fear they won’t be able to afford it. A recent graduate shares her experience: “The administration is great to work with. Opportunities for funding to travel and do research, internships, volunteer, etc. are AMAZING.”

CAREER INFORMATION FROM PAYSCALE.COM

ROI Rating	95
Bachelors and No Higher	
Median starting salary	$68,900
Median mid-career salary	$137,500
At Least Bachelors	
Median starting salary	$70,800
Median mid-career salary	$147,500
Alumni with high job meaning	44%
Degrees awarded in STEM subjects	35%

SELECTIVITY

Admissions Rating	98
# of applicants	20,035
% of applicants accepted	10
% of acceptees attending	58
# offered a place on the wait list	2,021
% accepting a place on wait list	67
% admitted from wait list	0
# of early decision applicants	1999
% accepted early decision	28

FRESHMAN PROFILE

Range SAT EBRW	710–770
Range SAT Math	720–790
Range ACT Composite	30–34
Minimum internet-based TOEFL	100
% graduated top 10% of class	93
% graduated top 25% of class	98
% graduated top 50% of class	99

DEADLINES

Early decision	
Deadline	11/1
Notification	12/15
Regular	
Deadline	1/1
Notification	4/1

FINANCIAL FACTS

Financial Aid Rating	96
Annual tuition	$51,468
Room and board	$15,159
Required fees	$1,900
Books and supplies	$1,260
Average frosh need-based scholarship	$51,461
Average UG need-based scholarship	$48,772
% needy frosh rec. need-based scholarship or grant aid	94
% needy UG rec. need-based scholarship or grant aid	96
% needy frosh rec. non-need-based scholarship or grant aid	0
% needy UG rec. non-need-based scholarship or grant aid	0
% needy frosh rec. need-based self-help aid	88
% needy UG rec. need-based self-help aid	92
% frosh rec. any financial aid	58
% UG rec. any financial aid	54
% UG borrow to pay for school	52
Average cumulative indebtedness	$19,571
% frosh need fully met	100
% ugrads need fully met	100
Average % of frosh need met	100

Davidson College

PO Box 7156, DAVIDSON, NC 28035-7156 • ADMISSIONS: 704-894-2230 • FAX: 704-894-2016

CAMPUS LIFE

Quality of Life Rating	**86**
Fire Safety Rating	**60***
Green Rating	**63**
Type of school	Private
Affiliation	Presbyterian
Environment	Village

STUDENTS

Total undergrad enrollment	1,800
% male/female	51/49
% from out of state	77
% frosh from public high school	47
% frosh live on campus	100
% ugrads live on campus	98
# of fraternities (% ugrad men join)	8 (39)
# of sororities (% ugrad women join)	6 (70)
% African American	7
% Asian	6
% Caucasian	67
% Hispanic	8
% Native American	<1
% Pacific Islander	<1
% Two or more races	5
% Race and/or ethnicity unknown	1
% international	7
# of countries represented	42

ACADEMICS

Academic Rating	**85**
% students returning for sophomore year	95
Calendar	Semester
Student/faculty ratio	9:1
Profs interesting rating	80
Profs accessible rating	82

Most classes have 10–19 students. Most lab/discussion sessions have 10–19 students.

MOST POPULAR MAJORS
Biology/Biological Sciences; Psychology; Political Science and Government

ABOUT THE SCHOOL

Davidson is a place where serious students can thrive and really throw themselves into the world of academia, all while surrounded by similarly energetic, curious, and quirky students. At this small, "really beautiful" school north of Charlotte, North Carolina, students come from nearly every state in the union and from dozens of foreign countries to immerse themselves in the "intellectually challenging, academically rigorous" cocoon that Davidson provides. The school offers a classic liberal arts education, encouraging students to take classes in all areas, and "all of these people come out smarter than they came in." Classes are small and intensive, with significant contact between students and faculty both in and out of the classroom, and faculty, while emphasizing teaching, involve students in significant research projects. There is a lot of work, but it "is accompanied by even more resources with which it can be successfully managed." "I have never witnessed people so eager to come do their job every day. [Professors] are almost too willing to help," says a student. The honor code also helps contribute "to having a safe and reliable environment."

BANG FOR YOUR BUCK

Davidson is consistently regarded as one of the top liberal arts colleges in the country, and its small size (and twenty-person class limits) give students access to a level of academic guidance and greatness that most college students can only dream of, at a price that students can afford. The school has just 1,791 undergraduates but offers $17 million a year in financial aid. On top of the holy triumvirate of financial aid, Davidson offers merit scholarships ranging from $1,000 to the full cost of education. The school is also need-blind to life experience: Need and merit aid can go with students on approved study-abroad programs, thereby eliminating a potential barrier to having an international experience.

STUDENT LIFE

Davidson is "an amalgamation of all types of people, religiously, ethnically, politically, economically, etc.," all "united under the umbrella of intellectual curiosity" and their devotion to the school as a community. The typical Davidson student is "probably white," but in the past few years, admissions has been making progress in racially diversifying the campus, which students agree is necessary. Though there are plenty of Southern, preppy, athletic types to fit the brochure examples, there are many niches for every type of "atypical" student. "There are enough people that one can find a similar group to connect with, and there are few enough people that one ends up connecting with dissimilar [people] anyway," says a student. Everyone here is smart and well-rounded; admissions "does a good job...so if you're in, you'll probably make the cut all the way through the four years." Most students have several extracurriculars to round out their free time, and they have a healthy desire to enjoy themselves when the books shut. "During the week we work hard. On the weekends we play hard. We don't do anything halfway," says a senior. Though the majority of students lean to the left, there's a strong conservative contingent, and there are no real problems between the two.

CAREER

Davidson's Center for Career Development keeps its student body on track with thorough career planning checklists for each class year (Step One: Sign up for career services announcements!). Students can drop-in to get advice on topics like career exploration and major selection or they can take part in a Job Shadowing Program over winter break when they will spend time with alumni at work. WildcatLink is the online gateway to Davidson-specific opportunities like fellowships,

Davidson College

E-MAIL: ADMISSION@DAVIDSON.EDU • WEBSITE: WWW.DAVIDSON.EDU

jobs, and internships. Recent graduates have also participated in the Davidson Impact Fellows program, working for a year with organizations focused on the environment, social entrepreneurship, and other issues. Alumni visiting PayScale.com reported a median starting salary of $53,100.

GENERAL INFO

Activities: Choral groups, concert band, dance, drama/theater, jazz band, literary magazine, music ensembles, musical theater, pep band, radio station, student government, student newspaper, symphony orchestra, yearbook, campus ministries, international student organization. **Organizations:** 151 registered organizations, 15 honor societies, 16 religious organizations. 8 fraternities, 6 sororities. **Athletics (Intercollegiate):** *Men:* Baseball, basketball, cross-country, diving, football, golf, soccer, swimming, tennis, track/field (outdoor), wrestling. *Women:* Basketball, cross-country, diving, field hockey, lacrosse, soccer, swimming, tennis, track/field (outdoor), volleyball. **On-Campus Highlights:** Belk Visual Arts Center, Baker-Watt Science Complex, Baker Sports Complex, Campus Center, Lake Campus.

FINANCIAL AID

Students should submit: Business/Farm Supplement; CSS Profile; FAFSA; Noncustodial PROFILE. Priority filing deadline is 2/15. The Princeton Review suggests that all financial aid forms be submitted as soon as possible after October 1. *Need-based scholarships/grants offered:* College/university scholarship or grant aid from institutional funds, Federal Pell, private scholarships, SEOG, state scholarships/grants. *Loan aid offered:* Direct PLUS Loans, Direct Subsidized Loans, Direct Unsubsidized Loans. Applicants will be notified of awards on or about 4/1. Federal Work-Study Program available. Institutional employment available.

BOTTOM LINE

Tuition runs about $49,454, with an additional $13,954 or so needed for room and board. However, the school hits three major financial aid points: it admits domestic students on a need-blind basis, meets 100 percent of all students' calculated need, and does so with grant and work funds only, not requiring students to utilize loans to have their need met. Aid is also guaranteed throughout the four years if a family's financial circumstances stay the same.

CAREER INFORMATION FROM PAYSCALE.COM	
ROI Rating	91
Bachelors and No Higher	
Median starting salary	$55,000
Median mid-career salary	$116,100
At Least Bachelors	
Median starting salary	$58,900
Median mid-career salary	$123,500
Alumni with high job meaning	50%
Degrees awarded in STEM subjects	28%

SELECTIVITY	
Admissions Rating	98
# of applicants	5,673
% of applicants accepted	20
% of acceptees attending	45

FRESHMAN PROFILE	
Range SAT EBRW	660–740
Range SAT Math	650–730
Range ACT Composite	30–33
Minimum paper TOEFL	600
Minimum internet-based TOEFL	100
Average HS GPA	3.9
% graduated top 10% of class	76
% graduated top 25% of class	95
% graduated top 50% of class	99

DEADLINES	
Early decision	
Deadline	11/15
Notification	12/15
Other ED Deadline	1/2
Other ED Notification	2/1
Regular	
Deadline	1/2
Notification	4/1
Nonfall registration?	Yes

FINANCIAL FACTS	
Financial Aid Rating	94
Annual tuition	$49,454
Room and board	$13,954
Required fees	$495
Books and supplies	$1,000
Average frosh need-based scholarship	$43,859
Average UG need-based scholarship	$44,434
% needy frosh rec. need-based scholarship or grant aid	100
% needy UG rec. need-based scholarship or grant aid	99
% needy frosh rec. non-need-based scholarship or grant aid	35
% needy UG rec. non-need-based scholarship or grant aid	26
% needy frosh rec. need-based self-help aid	59
% needy UG rec. need-based self-help aid	64
% frosh rec. any financial aid	52
% UG rec. any financial aid	52
% UG borrow to pay for school	26
Average cumulative indebtedness	$20,431
% frosh need fully met	100
% ugrads need fully met	100
Average % of frosh need met	100
Average % of ugrad need met	100

Denison University

100 W. College St., Granville, OH 43023 • Admissions: 740-587-6276 • Fax: 740-587-6306

CAMPUS LIFE

Quality of Life Rating	**90**
Fire Safety Rating	**96**
Green Rating	**89**
Type of school	Private
Environment	Village

STUDENTS

Total undergrad enrollment	2,321
% male/female	45/55
% from out of state	74
% frosh from public high school	67
% frosh live on campus	100
% ugrads live on campus	99
# of fraternities (% ugrad men join)	9 (30)
# of sororities (% ugrad women join)	9 (49)
% African American	7
% Asian	4
% Caucasian	65
% Hispanic	9
% Native American	0
% Pacific Islander	<1
% Two or more races	3
% Race and/or ethnicity unknown	2
% international	10
# of countries represented	37

ACADEMICS

Academic Rating	**93**
% students returning for sophomore year	91
Calendar	Semester
Student/faculty ratio	9:1
Profs interesting rating	92
Profs accessible rating	95

Most classes have 10–19 students. Most lab/discussion sessions have 10–19 students.

MOST POPULAR MAJORS

Biology; Psychology; Economics

ABOUT THE SCHOOL

Ohio's Denison University is a liberal arts college that prioritizes "connections...between students, faculty, alumni, and the community [at large.]" Many undergrads remark that the school "feel[s] like home." Academics here are "rigorous," but, thankfully, there's plenty of "support available." For example, students can take advantage of amazing "tutor[ing services," and they can turn to "the Writing Center and the library [for assistance with] researching and writing." "Small class size[s]" are a staple of a Denison education, which guarantees that students will encounter "engaged professors who love teaching undergraduates." Denison routinely hires instructors who are "expert[s] in their field" and who maintain "very high expectations for student performance and push students to produce their best work." These "very accessible" professors are "usually very excited to help when students have questions and...eager to meet... outside the classroom."

BANG FOR YOUR BUCK

Denison is steadfast in its commitment to remain affordable for students with financial need. And many undergrads here remark on their "generous" aid packages. Of course, that should be expected considering every year the university awards over $60 million in both need and merit-based aid. It's also important to mention that less than half of Denison's undergraduates incur any debt. (The average amount of loan debt per graduate is $28,833.) All accepted students are considered for merit scholarships with awards that generally range from $5,000 to full tuition coverage. Even better, they are all renewable. Students are selected based on superior academic achievement, leadership potential, and commitment to community.

SCHOOL LIFE

Rest assured, at Denison "there's never an absence of things to do outside of classes and work." In fact, some students suggest that "the school is actually over programmed, since so much goes on." You can always find a "concert, a speaker or a club/organization event" to attend. Additionally, "movie nights" and "student run comedy [shows]" always yield a big crowd. Intramural sports are also rather "popular." And many individuals enjoy participating in "arcade game night, galas [and] food truck festivals." We're also told that "if it's a Wednesday, Friday or Saturday, there are parties around campus in suites or senior apartments." These are typically "hosted by fraternities." When students need a little bit of breather, they often "explore downtown Granville" or head to "nearby Columbus," just thirty miles from campus.

CAREER

Undergrads at Denison receive a tremendous amount of "career support...[from] the college." And they are quick to sing the praises of the Knowlton Center, which "offers a variety of help with career decisions." Here, students "practice interviews, [get] career coaching, résumé building, and more." The center also runs some innovative programs such as First Looks, which helps students at the start of their professional journey to gain a better understanding of certain jobs and industries via information sessions, networking opportunities, and company tours. Through these events, undergrads connect with industry insiders to ask questions about company culture, daily responsibilities, and individual career paths. Ideally, this kind of information and early networking helps students clarify their own dreams and ambitions.

Denison University

FINANCIAL AID: 800-336-4766 • E-MAIL: ADMISSIONS@DENISON.EDU • WEBSITE: WWW.DENISON.EDU

FINANCIAL AID

Students should submit: CSS Profile; FAFSA; Noncustodial PROFILE. Priority filing deadline is 1/15. The Princeton Review suggests that all financial aid forms be submitted as soon as possible after October 1. *Need-based scholarships/grants offered:* College/university scholarship or grant aid from institutional funds; Federal Pell; Private scholarships; SEOG; State scholarships/grants; United Negro College Fund. *Loan aid offered:* Direct PLUS Loans, Direct Subsidized Loans, Direct Unsubsidized Loans. Applicants will be notified of awards on or about 3/15. Federal Work-Study Program available. Institutional employment available.

THE BOTTOM LINE

Tuition at Denison University currently costs $50,790. The school charges another $7,000 for room and $5,710 for board. There are also mandatory activity and health center fees. These are $490 and $680 respectively. Denison estimates that undergraduates will need another $2,320 for both books/classroom supplies and personal expenses. This brings the total annual figure to $66,990.

CAREER INFORMATION FROM PAYSCALE.COM	
ROI Rating	91
Bachelors and No Higher	
Median starting salary	$52,400
Median mid-career salary	$108,200
At Least Bachelors	
Median starting salary	$54,200
Median mid-career salary	$110,500
Alumni with high job meaning	44%
Degrees awarded in STEM subjects	22%

SELECTIVITY	
Admissions Rating	93
# of applicants	7,540
% of applicants accepted	37
% of acceptees attending	22
# offered a place on the wait list	1,502
% accepting a place on wait list	22
% admitted from wait list	17
# of early decision applicants	377
% accepted early decision	65

FRESHMAN PROFILE	
Range SAT EBRW	600–690
Range SAT Math	600–690
Range ACT Composite	28–31
Minimum paper TOEFL	550
Minimum internet-based TOEFL	80
% graduated top 10% of class	65
% graduated top 25% of class	87
% graduated top 50% of class	100

DEADLINES	
Early decision	
Deadline	11/15
Notification	12/15
Other ED Deadline	1/15
Other ED Notification	2/15
Regular	
Priority	1/15
Deadline	1/15
Notification	4/1
Nonfall registration?	No

FINANCIAL FACTS	
Annual tuition	$50,790
Room and board	$12,710
Required fees	$1,170
Average frosh need-based scholarship	$41,557
Average UG need-based scholarship	$38,832
% needy frosh rec. need-based scholarship or grant aid	100
% needy UG rec. need-based scholarship or grant aid	100
% needy frosh rec. non-need-based scholarship or grant aid	19
% needy UG rec. non-need-based scholarship or grant aid	11
% needy frosh rec. need-based self-help aid	100
% needy UG rec. need-based self-help aid	85
% frosh rec. any financial aid	93
% UG rec. any financial aid	95
% UG borrow to pay for school	53
Average cumulative indebtedness	$27,823
% frosh need fully met	100
% ugrads need fully met	91
Average % of frosh need met	100

DePauw University

204 E. Seminary, Greencastle, IN 46135 • Admissions: 765-658-4006 • Fax: 765-658-4067

CAMPUS LIFE

Quality of Life Rating	**84**
Fire Safety Rating	**73**
Green Rating	**60***
Type of school	Private
Affiliation	None
Environment	Village

STUDENTS

Total undergrad enrollment	2,137
% male/female	48/52
% from out of state	61
% frosh from public high school	83
% frosh live on campus	100
% ugrads live on campus	96
# of fraternities (% ugrad men join)	13 (74)
# of sororities (% ugrad women join)	11 (67)
% African American	5
% Asian	4
% Caucasian	66
% Hispanic	7
% Native American	<1
% Pacific Islander	0
% Two or more races	5
% Race and/or ethnicity unknown	2
% international	10
# of countries represented	34

ACADEMICS

Academic Rating	**88**
% students returning for sophomore year	89
% students graduating within 4 years	76
% students graduating within 6 years	81
Calendar	4/1/4
Student/faculty ratio	9:1
Profs interesting rating	88
Profs accessible rating	93

Most classes have 10–19 students. Most lab/discussion sessions have 10–19 students.

MOST POPULAR MAJORS
Speech Communication and Rhetoric; Economics

ABOUT THE SCHOOL

Serious-minded students are drawn to DePauw University for its "small classes," "encouraging" professors, and the "individual academic attention" they can expect to receive. Academically, DePauw is "demanding but rewarding" and "requires a lot of outside studying and discipline" in order to keep up. Professors lead small, discussion-based classes and hold their students firmly to high academic standards. Professors' "expectations are very high," which means "you can't slack off and get good grades." Be prepared to pull your "fair share of all-nighters."

Beyond stellar professors, DePauw's other academic draws include "extraordinary" study-abroad opportunities and a "wonderful" alumni network great for "connections and networking opportunities." Alums also "keep our endowment pretty high, making it easy for the school to give out merit scholarships," which undergraduates appreciate. DePauw emphasizes life outside the classroom, too. The school operates several fellowships to support independent projects by high-achieving students, and four out of five DePauw students will complete a professional internship during college. The DePauw curriculum includes an Extended Studies requirement. These can be completed during a Winter Term or May Term course, approved externship, travel experience or service learning program, semester-long off-campus study opportunity or internship, and/or independent study, research project or creative project. Arts and culture are at the forefront of campus life, and the school's annual ArtsFest allows students and invited artists to exhibit or perform for the campus and community.

BANG FOR YOUR BUCK

Small class sizes, close community, athletic opportunities, alumni network, great scholarships, and campus involvement make DePauw a good value. Need-based aid is available, and DePauw is also strong in the area of merit-based awards. All first-year applicants are automatically considered for scholarships, and awards are determined based on a student's GPA, course load, class rank, and standardized test scores. Almost 80 percent of the school's scholarship assistance comes from institutional funds rather than state or federal sources. Once a student is enrolled at DePauw, the only scholarships available come through individual academic departments. In addition to these general scholarships, the school operates several scholarship programs for students that meet specific criteria. To apply for need-based aid, students must submit the FAFSA. More than half of DePauw's student body receives some form of need-based financial aid through grants, loans, and work-study. The average financial aid package totals $28,000. Students who aren't eligible for work-study may still apply for campus jobs through the financial aid office.

STUDENT LIFE

Students at DePauw are a hardworking lot and many say that there's "a heavy emphasis on studying" around here. Of course, even intellectual types need to relax every once in awhile and there's certainly plenty of fun to be had on campus. Undergrads here report that the "majority of social life is centered around fraternity parties." However, they immediately explain that it's "mostly because fraternities provide a large gathering space for people." And they insist that Greek life "is a very open and non-exclusive environment." Aside from fraternities and sororities, lots of students can be found "work[ing] out...running outside or play[ing] football and frisbee in the park." And "every weekend there is some philanthropy event, music school concert, or speaker brought in by the school."

DePauw University

FINANCIAL AID: 765-658-4030 • E-MAIL: ADMISSION@DEPAUW.EDU • WEBSITE: WWW.DEPAUW.EDU

CAREER

DePauw students "are very focused on getting their degrees and [landing] really good jobs." Considering that Dension grads report at median starting salary of $52,300, (according to PayScale.com), we'd say they're achieving their goals. This is no doubt due to DePauw's "amazing" resources to help students find internships, jobs, etc. To begin with, undergrads love to highlight the "alumni database [which is teeming with] successful people." Additionally, students can scour TigerTracks, an internal site that allows undergrads to search for jobs and internships listed specifically for DePauw students. The Hubbard Center for Student Engagement also offers some really unique programs beyond the traditional resume workshops and mock interviews. For example, collaborating with Indiana University's Kelly School of Business, DePauw offers the Liberal Arts Management Program, which teaches how businesses are created and how they function. The insight gleaned from programs like this is enormous.

GENERAL INFO

Activities: Choral groups, concert band, dance, drama/theater, jazz band, literary magazine, music ensembles, musical theater, opera, pep band, radio station, student government, student newspaper, student-run film society, symphony orchestra, television station, campus ministries, international student organization. **Organizations:** 119 registered organizations, 13 honor societies, 10 religious organizations. 13 fraternities, 11 sororities. **Athletics (Intercollegiate):** *Men:* Baseball, basketball, cross-country, diving, football, golf, lacrosse, soccer, swimming, tennis, track/field (outdoor), track/field (indoor). *Women:* Basketball, cross-country, diving, field hockey, golf, lacrosse, soccer, softball, swimming, tennis, track/field (outdoor), track/field (indoor), volleyball.

FINANCIAL AID

Students should submit: FAFSA; Institution's own financial aid form. Priority filing deadline is 1/1. The Princeton Review suggests that all financial aid forms be submitted as soon as possible after October 1. *Need-based scholarships/grants offered:* College/university scholarship or grant aid from institutional funds, Federal Pell, private scholarships, SEOG, state scholarships/grants. *Loan aid offered:* Direct Subsidized Loans; Direct Unsubsidized Loans. Applicants will be notified of awards on a rolling basis beginning 2/1. Federal Work-Study Program available. Institutional employment available.

BOTTOM LINE

DePauw tuition and fees are about $48,860 with an additional $13,020 for room and board. Incoming students are also required to purchase a laptop. Families have the option of paying their college costs monthly (with no deferred payment charge) or each semester. Although DePauw does not guarantee meeting full demonstrated need for each student, the school's track record is good, with many students receiving all the funding they need.

CAREER INFORMATION FROM PAYSCALE.COM	
ROI Rating	89
Bachelors and No Higher	
Median starting salary	$54,900
Median mid-career salary	$102,900
At Least Bachelors	
Median starting salary	$57,100
Median mid-career salary	$110,600
Alumni with high job meaning	46%
Degrees awarded in STEM subjects	24%

SELECTIVITY	
Admissions Rating	87
# of applicants	5,173
% of applicants accepted	67
% of acceptees attending	17

FRESHMAN PROFILE	
Range SAT EBRW	560–650
Range SAT Math	550–680
Range ACT Composite	24–29
Minimum paper TOEFL	560
Average HS GPA	3.8
% graduated top 10% of class	40
% graduated top 25% of class	70
% graduated top 50% of class	95

DEADLINES	
Early decision	
Deadline	11/1
Notification	12/1
Early action	
Deadline	12/1
Notification	1/15
Regular	
Deadline	2/1
Nonfall registration?	Yes

FINANCIAL FACTS	
Financial Aid Rating	87
Annual tuition	$48,860
Room and board	$13,020
Required fees	$844
Books and supplies	$900
Average frosh need-based scholarship	$38,681
Average UG need-based scholarship	$37,234
% needy frosh rec. need-based scholarship or grant aid	100
% needy UG rec. need-based scholarship or grant aid	100
% needy frosh rec. non-need-based scholarship or grant aid	24
% needy UG rec. non-need-based scholarship or grant aid	19
% needy frosh rec. need-based self-help aid	73
% needy UG rec. need-based self-help aid	79
% UG borrow to pay for school	66
Average cumulative indebtedness	$23,635
% frosh need fully met	32
% ugrads need fully met	28
Average % of frosh need met	91
Average % of ugrad need met	91

Dickinson College

PO Box 1773, Carlisle, PA 17013-2896 • Admissions: 717-245-1231 • Fax: 717-245-1442

CAMPUS LIFE	
Quality of Life Rating	**88**
Fire Safety Rating	**91**
Green Rating	**99**
Type of school	Private
Environment	Town

STUDENTS	
Total undergrad enrollment	2,339
% male/female	42/58
% from out of state	79
% frosh from public high school	55
% frosh live on campus	100
% ugrads live on campus	95
# of fraternities (% ugrad men join)	5 (16)
# of sororities (% ugrad women join)	4 (27)
% African American	5
% Asian	4
% Caucasian	66
% Hispanic	8
% Native American	<1
% Pacific Islander	<1
% Two or more races	4
% Race and/or ethnicity unknown	1
% international	13
# of countries represented	44

ACADEMICS	
Academic Rating	**91**
% students returning for sophomore year	90
% students graduating within 4 years	80
% students graduating within 6 years	83
Calendar	Semester
Student/faculty ratio	9:1
Profs interesting rating	96
Profs accessible rating	95
Most classes have 10–19 students.	

MOST POPULAR MAJORS
Biology; Economics; International Business & Management

ABOUT THE SCHOOL
A small liberal arts college in Carlisle, Pennsylvania, Dickinson College is "a school that pushes [its students] forward with an encouraging, supportive hand." Undergrads love that the curriculum here emphasizes a "global" perspective and maintains a "pragmatic" bent. They note that students can really "explore various fields and pursue interdisciplinary study." And many express pride in the college's "commitment to sustainability," highlighting the school-run "organic farm." Quite a few individuals mention the popularity of "study abroad programs." With a student/faculty ratio of 9:1, Dickinson students benefit from their "small class sizes" and "discussion-based" courses. They also have access to "wonderful" professors who have "very impressive credentials and connections." These instructors are often "engaging" and "thought-provoking" and really work to "challenge [student] assumptions." Students feel their professors really "want their students to excel in and out of the classroom."

BANG FOR YOUR BUCK
Dickinson students agree that the college "give[s] out great financial aid." In fact, the college awarded $52.8 million in institutional grants and scholarships last year. All successful applicants are automatically considered for merit scholarships (provided they submit the optional writing supplement), and recipients are selected based on academic achievement, standardized test scores, and leadership abilities. Potential scholarships include the John Dickinson Scholarship, which is the highest recognition for academic achievement and leadership and provides $20,000 per year for up to four years; Benjamin Rush Scholarship, which provides $15,000 per year for up to four years; the John Montgomery Scholarship, which provides $10,000 per year for up to four years; and the Founders Scholarship, which provides $7,500 per year for up to four years. We should note that students who meet the criteria will only be given one of these scholarships.

STUDENT LIFE
Prospective students who end up attending Dickinson should expect to become "very busy." After all, most undergrads here "are involved in many different extracurricular organizations and [often] take leadership roles in at least one [club]." Students also maintain healthy lifestyles, meaning "the gym is always bustling [no matter the] time of the day." We're told that several individuals "participate in sports, [both] varsity [and] club" as well. Plenty of events happen on campus, too, each week, such as "a movie showing, lecture, interfaith event, National Coming Out Day, international potluck dinner, simulation on poverty, fun runs [and/or] improv shows." There's also "an organization called MOB," the student-run programming board at the college that is sponsored by the Student Senate, "which puts on free concerts, food events and arts and crafts sessions." And, for those interested individuals, we hear the "party scene is very inclusive and energetic." Lastly, students report that "the surrounding town has great restaurants and shops."

CAREER
Dickinson's Center for Advising, Internships & Lifelong Careers (CAILC) provides personalized support and development through academic advising, internships, externships and student and alumni career services. Before first-year students set foot on campus, CAILC begins the advising and career support process, with phone calls from faculty members helping students select their first semester classes. Workshops, networking opportunities, alumni guest speakers, one-on-one consultations and more are designed to equip students with the tools they need for success as students and as graduates. They take on internships, research experiences, volunteer opportunities and study abroad to build their portfolios.

Dickinson College

FINANCIAL AID: 717-245-1308 • E-MAIL: ADMISSIONS@DICKINSON.EDU • WEBSITE: WWW.DICKINSON.EDU

GENERAL INFO

Activities: Choral groups, concert band, dance, drama/theater, jazz band, literary magazine, music ensembles, musical theater, radio station, student government, student newspaper, student-run film society, symphony orchestra, yearbook, International Student Organization, Model UN. **Organizations:** 100+ registered organizations, 16 honor societies, 5 religious organizations. 5 fraternities, 5 sororities. **Athletics (Intercollegiate):** *Men:* baseball, basketball, cross-country, football, golf, lacrosse, soccer, squash, swimming, tennis, track/field (outdoor), track/field (indoor). *Women:* basketball, cross-country, field hockey, golf, lacrosse, soccer, softball, squash, swimming, tennis, track/field (outdoor), track/field (indoor), volleyball. **On-Campus Highlights:** Old West (designed by Benjamin Latrobe), Holland Union Building, Waidner-Spahr Library/Biblio Cafe, newly expanded Kline Athletic Center, Rector Science Complex, The Quarry (coffee shop; Mermaid Society Trellis and late night party/gathering space), Weiss Center for the Arts, Trout Gallery, Durden Athletic Training Center.

FINANCIAL AID

Students should submit: CSS Profile; FAFSA; Noncustodial PROFILE; State aid form. Priority filing deadline is 1/15. The Princeton Review suggests that all financial aid forms be submitted as soon as possible after October 1. *Need-based scholarships/grants offered:* College/university scholarship or grant aid from institutional funds, Federal Pell, private scholarships, SEOG, state scholarships/grants. *Loan aid offered:* Direct PLUS Loans, Direct Subsidized Loans, Direct Unsubsidized Loans. Applicants will be notified of awards on or about 3/23. Federal Work-Study Program available. Institutional employment available.

THE BOTTOM LINE

Dickinson currently charges $54,636 for combined tuition and student activity fees. Additionally, undergrads living on campus will be billed $13,698 for room and board. The college estimates that students spend roughly $1,210 on books and supplies. And they suggest undergrads will need another $1,770 for personal expenses. Keep in mind that Dickinson also charges $1,857 to individuals who opt to get health insurance through the school.

CAREER INFORMATION FROM PAYSCALE.COM	
ROI Rating	88
Bachelors and No Higher	
Median starting salary	$54,200
Median mid-career salary	$100,700
At Least Bachelors	
Median starting salary	$56,000
Median mid-career salary	$106,700
Alumni with high job meaning	48%
Degrees awarded in STEM subjects	22%

SELECTIVITY	
Admissions Rating	90
# of applicants	5,941
% of applicants accepted	49
% of acceptees attending	21
# offered a place on the wait list	628
% accepting a place on wait list	40
% admitted from wait list	14
# of early decision applicants	376
% accepted early decision	68

FRESHMAN PROFILE	
Range SAT EBRW	620–700
Range SAT Math	610–720
Range ACT Composite	27–32
Minimum internet-based TOEFL	90
% graduated top 10% of class	48
% graduated top 25% of class	77
% graduated top 50% of class	96

DEADLINES	
Early decision	
Deadline	11/15
Notification	12/15
Other ED Deadline	1/15
Other ED Notification	2/15
Early action	
Deadline	12/1
Notification	2/15
Regular	
Deadline	1/15
Notification	3/23
Nonfall registration?	No

FINANCIAL FACTS	
Financial Aid Rating	93
Annual tuition	$54,186
Room and board	$13,698
Required fees	$450
Books and supplies	$1,210
Average frosh need-based scholarship	$40,052
Average UG need-based scholarship	$39,595
% needy frosh rec. need-based scholarship or grant aid	97
% needy UG rec. need-based scholarship or grant aid	98
% needy frosh rec. non-need-based scholarship or grant aid	6
% needy UG rec. non-need-based scholarship or grant aid	5
% needy frosh rec. need-based self-help aid	91
% needy UG rec. need-based self-help aid	93
% frosh rec. any financial aid	78
% UG rec. any financial aid	76
% UG borrow to pay for school	54
Average cumulative indebtedness	$25,881

Drew University

OFFICE OF COLLEGE ADMISSIONS, MADISON, NJ 07940-1493 • ADMISSIONS: 973-408-3739 • FAX: 973-408-3068

CAMPUS LIFE

Quality of Life Rating	86
Fire Safety Rating	92
Green Rating	88
Type of school	Private
Affiliation	Methodist
Environment	Village

STUDENTS

Total undergrad enrollment	1,404
% male/female	41/59
% from out of state	35
% frosh from public high school	60
% frosh live on campus	87
% ugrads live on campus	79
# of fraternities (% ugrad men join)	0 (0)
# of sororities (% ugrad women join)	0 (0)
% African American	7
% Asian	5
% Caucasian	55
% Hispanic	13
% Native American	0
% Pacific Islander	0
% Two or more races	5
% Race and/or ethnicity unknown	5
% international	10
# of countries represented	49

SURVEY SAYS ...

Students love Madison, NJ
Theater is popular
Active student government

ACADEMICS

Academic Rating	82
% students returning for sophomore year	85
% students graduating within 4 years	59
% students graduating within 6 years	62
Calendar	Semester
Student/faculty ratio	10:1
Profs interesting rating	78
Profs accessible rating	77

Most classes have 20–29 students. Most lab/discussion sessions have 20–29 students.

MOST POPULAR MAJORS

Biology/Biological Sciences; Psychology; Business Administration and Management

ABOUT THE SCHOOL

Located in New Jersey, Drew University is an experiential learning-focused school that offers "real world opportunities" and proximity to the industries of New York City, which is just an hour away. The university has thirty majors, fifty-one minors, and ten pre-professional programs, and emphasizes its role in "creating and encouraging all students to be leaders." Professors are "amazing" and keep students interested, and if students are having trouble with concepts, they "are more than willing to talk...for a VERY long time outside of class." This focus on faculty mentorship stems from the school's mission to cultivate the student as a whole person, and a commitment to life beyond the campus; to that end, nearly three-quarters of the student body participates in a study abroad program. All in all, the school is all about "making sure everybody feels comfortable with what they are studying and...that everybody gets a support they need."

BANG FOR YOUR BUCK

One of Drew's greatest strengths is the resources they provide to help students succeed: "If we look for them, they are there," says one. Notable opportunities include the chance to perform research at the Charles A. Dana Research Institute for Scientists Emeriti (RISE) or the Drew Summer Science Institute (DSSI), or to study at the Center for Civic Engagement. Nearly 80 percent of the student body receives some form of financial aid, and the school recently lowered its tuition by 20 percent in a rollback effort to drive down the costs of attending college.

STUDENT LIFE

Drew's leafy home in Madison, New Jersey provides for a "lovely environment" in which students can take walks in the woods, go into town, or just "hang out with friends in lounges." Students also enjoy going to New York once in a while for shopping and sightseeing, and "the movie theater in Morristown is also popular." The student body is small—around just 1,500 undergraduates—but is a "diverse group of people from so many walks of life" that are all "passionate about different things." Students are "dynamic and exciting" and really take the opportunity to "learn so much from each other." The university community as a whole is very welcoming and "it's hard to find yourself lost" when "there are always people who you can go to when you need anything."

CAREER

The school's Center for Internships and Career Development provides services to students to assist in any and all career goals, and the comprehensive advising program is one of the main reasons that 94 percent of Drew alumni are employed or in graduate school one year after graduation. The school's location near New York City results in hundreds of internship opportunities for students, and students are able to attend immersive classes in New York City, which focus on topics such as Wall Street, the United Nations, or Communications and Media. Out of Drew alumni visiting PayScale.com, 41 percent report that they derive a high level of meaning from their jobs.

Drew University

FINANCIAL AID: 973-408-3112 • E-MAIL: CADM@DREW.EDU • WEBSITE: WWW.DREW.EDU

GENERAL INFO

Activities: Campus Ministries; Choral groups; Dance; Drama/theater; International Student Organization; Jazz band; Literary magazine; Model UN; Music ensembles; Musical theater; Pep band; Radio station; Student government; Student newspaper; Student-run film society; Symphony orchestra; Yearbook 80 registered organizations, 17 honor societies, 9 religious organizations. **Athletics (Intercollegiate):** *Men:* baseball, basketball, cross-country, fencing, lacrosse, soccer, swimming, tennis. *Women:* basketball, cross-country, fencing, field hockey, lacrosse, soccer, softball, swimming, tennis. **On-Campus Highlights:** The Commons, Ehinger Center, Dorothy Young Center for the Arts, Simon Forum, Rose Memorial Library.

FINANCIAL AID

Students should submit: FAFSA. The deadline for filing the FAFSA is the same as the deadline for the admissions application for your admissions plan (Early Decision, Early Action, Regular Decision). The Princeton Review suggests that all financial aid forms be submitted as soon as possible after October 1. *Need-based scholarships/grants offered:* College/university scholarship or grant aid from institutional funds, Federal Pell, private scholarships, SEOG, state scholarships/grants. *Loan aid offered:* Direct PLUS Loans, Direct Subsidized Loans, Direct Unsubsidized Loans. Applicants will be notified of their awards at the time of admission. Federal Work-Study Program available. Institutional employment available.

CAREER INFORMATION FROM PAYSCALE.COM

ROI Rating	88
Bachelors and No Higher	
Median starting salary	$51,000
Median mid-career salary	$92,600
At Least Bachelors	
Median starting salary	$52,200
Median mid-career salary	$97,900
Alumni with high job meaning	36%
Degrees awarded in STEM subjects	16%

SELECTIVITY

Admissions Rating	85
# of applicants	3,205
% of applicants accepted	63
% of acceptees attending	18
# offered a place on the wait list	106
% accepting a place on wait list	18
% admitted from wait list	37
# of early decision applicants	118
% accepted early decision	81

FRESHMAN PROFILE

Range SAT EBRW	560–660
Range SAT Math	540–640
Range ACT Composite	23–28
Minimum paper TOEFL	550
Minimum internet-based TOEFL	80
Average HS GPA	3.5
% graduated top 10% of class	24
% graduated top 25% of class	60
% graduated top 50% of class	84

DEADLINES

Early decision	
Deadline	11/15
Notification	12/15
Other ED Deadline	1/15
Other ED Notification	2/15
Early action	
Deadline	12/15
Notification	2/15
Regular	
Priority	11/15, 1/15
Deadline	2/1
Notification	3/18
Nonfall registration?	Yes

FINANCIAL FACTS

Financial Aid Rating	84
Annual tuition	$38,668
Room and board	$14,108
Required fees	$832
Books and supplies	$1,200
Average frosh need-based scholarship	$40,105
Average UG need-based scholarship	$38,899
% needy frosh rec. need-based scholarship or grant aid	100
% needy UG rec. need-based scholarship or grant aid	100
% needy frosh rec. non-need-based scholarship or grant aid	7
% needy UG rec. non-need-based scholarship or grant aid	6
% needy frosh rec. need-based self-help aid	84
% needy UG rec. need-based self-help aid	83
% frosh rec. any financial aid	98

Duke University

2138 CAMPUS DRIVE, BOX 90586, DURHAM, NC 27708-0586 • ADMISSIONS: 919-684-3214

CAMPUS LIFE

Quality of Life Rating	**73**
Fire Safety Rating	**60***
Green Rating	**91**
Type of school	Private
Affiliation	Methodist
Environment	City

STUDENTS

Total undergrad enrollment	6,692
% male/female	50/50
% from out of state	85
% frosh from public high school	65
% frosh live on campus	100
% ugrads live on campus	81
# of fraternities (% ugrad men join)	21 (29)
# of sororities (% ugrad women join)	14 (42)
% African American	10
% Asian	21
% Caucasian	44
% Hispanic	9
% Native American	1
% Pacific Islander	<1
% Two or more races	2
% Race and/or ethnicity unknown	3
% international	10
# of countries represented	89

ACADEMICS

Academic Rating	**91**
% students returning for sophomore year	97
% students graduating within 6 years	95
Calendar	Semester
Student/faculty ratio	6:1
Profs interesting rating	78
Profs accessible rating	77
Most classes have 10–19 students.	

MOST POPULAR MAJORS
Psychology; Public Policy Analysis;
Economics

#26 BEST VALUE COLLEGE

ABOUT THE SCHOOL

Duke University offers students a word-class education and freedom in choosing the academic path that best meets their needs. The school's research expenditures rank in the top ten nationally, the library system is extensive, and the school's Division I sports teams are legendary. Still, the undergraduate experience is the heart and soul of the school. Students are required to live on campus for three years. First-year students live together on East Campus, where about a quarter of them participate in FOCUS, a living/learning program organized around academic themes, which gives them access to faculty mentoring and a smaller community of students they get to know well. Maybe it's the mild North Carolina climate, but the students say their campus is way more laid-back than what you'd find at any of the Ivy League schools. It's also breathtakingly beautiful, featuring soaring Gothic buildings, modern teaching and research facilities, accessible athletic fields and recreational spaces, and a lush botanical garden. It's true that Duke students are focused on academics, but they are just as enthusiastic about attending campus events, participating in Greek functions, or cheering on the teams at Duke sporting events, especially when it's the school's top-ranked basketball team that's playing.

BANG FOR YOUR BUCK

Duke is dedicated to making its outstanding education affordable. More than half of undergraduates receive some sort of financial assistance, including need-based aid, and merit or athletic scholarships. Students are evaluated for admission without regard to their ability to pay. If admitted, Duke pledges to meet 100 percent of need. There are no loans or parental contributions required for families with incomes under $40,000. Families with incomes under $60,000 are not required to make a parental contribution, and the school offers capped loans for eligible families with incomes of more than $100,000. The biggest value is the academic experience. One student explains, "Every single one of my professors actually knows me very well. They know where I'm from; they know what I actually find funny in class; they know when I'm sick and are incredibly parental in making sure that I get all of my work done and stay healthy; they know ME. How many other students can say that in any university?" Another student adds, "I wanted a medium college that was not too large but had research opportunities. I liked the culture at Duke and the choice was easy because they also gave me the best financial package."

STUDENT LIFE

Life involves "getting a ton of work done first and then finding time to play and have fun," and the typical student here wears five or more hats: "He/she is studious but social, athletic but can never be seen in the gym, job hunting but not worrying, and so on and so forth." Of course, "Duke basketball games are a must" and sorority/fraternity life is popular but not necessary. The school has an on-campus movie theater and events happening all the time, and students also can just do their own thing, such as "exploring, going skiing or to the beach for a weekend, [or] making a bonfire in the forest." No matter what your weekend plan is, "people will be hitting the books on Sundays (all-nighters are common) in order to maintain their grades."

Duke University

FINANCIAL AID: 919-684-6225 • E-MAIL: UNDERGRAD-ADMISSIONS@DUKE.EDU • WEBSITE: WWW.DUKE.EDUWWW.DUKE.EDU

CAREER

Duke students "are focused on graduating and obtaining a lucrative and prosperous career." The "engaged Career Center" provides a range of services (such as seminars, workshops, and online databases) that help students fine-tune their skills. Career fairs are held throughout the year (including the "Just-in-Time" Career Fair in the spring, for employers who have immediate openings for graduating students. Drop-in advising is always available. Fifty-three percent of Duke graduates who visited PayScale.com reported feeling their jobs had a meaningful impact on the world. The median starting salary for Duke grads is $65,300.

GENERAL INFO

Activities: Choral groups, concert band, dance, drama/theater, jazz band, literary magazine, marching band, music ensembles, musical theater, opera, pep band, radio station, student government, student newspaper, student-run film society, symphony orchestra, television station, yearbook. **Organizations:** 200 registered organizations, 10 honor societies, 25 religious organizations. 21 fraternities, 14 sororities. **Athletics (Intercollegiate):** *Men:* Baseball, basketball, cross-country, diving, fencing, football, golf, lacrosse, soccer, swimming, tennis, track/field (outdoor), track/field (indoor), volleyball, wrestling. *Women:* Basketball, crew/rowing, cross-country, diving, fencing, field hockey, golf, lacrosse, soccer, swimming, tennis, track/field (outdoor), track/field (indoor), volleyball. **On-Campus Highlights:** Primate Center, Sarah P. Duke Gardens, Duke Forest, Levine Science Research Center.

FINANCIAL AID

Students should submit: Business/Farm Supplement; CSS Profile; FAFSA; Noncustodial PROFILE. Regular filing deadline is 1/1. The Princeton Review suggests that all financial aid forms be submitted as soon as possible after October 1. *Need-based scholarships/grants offered:* College/university scholarship or grant aid from institutional funds, Federal Pell, private scholarships, SEOG, state scholarships/grants. *Loan aid offered:* Direct PLUS Loans, Direct Subsidized Loans, Direct Unsubsidized Loans. Applicants will be notified of awards on or about 4/1. Federal Work-Study Program available. Institutional employment available.

BOTTOM LINE

With a moderately sized campus of almost 6,500 undergraduates, students have the opportunity to work closely with the school's accomplished faculty. Academics are challenging, especially in the quantitative majors like science and mathematics. However, there are plentiful student resources, including a writing center and a peer-tutoring program, not to mention the constant support from the school's teaching staff. Innovation and independence are encouraged; the school offers grants for undergraduate research projects, as well as travel grants and awards for artistic endeavors.

CAREER INFORMATION FROM PAYSCALE.COM	
ROI Rating	93
Bachelors and No Higher	
Median starting salary	$68,700
Median mid-career salary	$133,100
At Least Bachelors	
Median starting salary	$71,200
Median mid-career salary	$142,800
Alumni with high job meaning	50%
Degrees awarded in STEM subjects	26%

SELECTIVITY	
Admissions Rating	98
# of applicants	33,077
% of applicants accepted	10
% of acceptees attending	48
# of early decision applicants	3,451
% accepted early decision	25

FRESHMAN PROFILE	
Range SAT EBRW	680–780
Range SAT Math	710–800
Range ACT Composite	31–35
% graduated top 10% of class	90
% graduated top 25% of class	95
% graduated top 50% of class	99

DEADLINES	
Early decision	
Deadline	11/1
Notification	12/15
Priority	12/20
Deadline	1/3
Nonfall registration?	No

FINANCIAL FACTS	
Financial Aid Rating	93
Annual tuition	$53,760
Room and board	$15,178
Required fees	$1,935
Books and supplies	$1,260
Average frosh need-based scholarship	$49,174
Average UG need-based scholarship	$47,556
% needy frosh rec. need-based scholarship or grant aid	96
% needy UG rec. need-based scholarship or grant aid	95
% needy frosh rec. non-need-based scholarship or grant aid	6
% needy UG rec. non-need-based scholarship or grant aid	9
% needy frosh rec. need-based self-help aid	82
% needy UG rec. need-based self-help aid	85
% UG borrow to pay for school	33
Average cumulative indebtedness	$23,819
% frosh need fully met	100
% ugrads need fully met	100
Average % of frosh need met	100
Average % of ugrad need met	100

Earlham College

801 National Road West, Richmond, IN 47374-4095 • Admissions: 765-983-1600 • Fax: 765-983-1560

CAMPUS LIFE

Quality of Life Rating	84
Fire Safety Rating	93
Green Rating	91
Type of school	Private
Affiliation	Quaker
Environment	Town

STUDENTS

Total undergrad enrollment	1,027
% male/female	46/54
% from out of state	82
% frosh from public high school	73
% frosh live on campus	98
% ugrads live on campus	92
# of fraternities (% ugrad men join)	0 (0)
# of sororities (% ugrad women join)	0 (0)
% African American	11
% Asian	6
% Caucasian	52
% Hispanic	7
% Native American	1
% Pacific Islander	<1
% Two or more races	<1
% Race and/or ethnicity unknown	2
% international	22
# of countries represented	76

ACADEMICS

Academic Rating	94
% students returning for sophomore year	86
% students graduating within 4 years	58
% students graduating within 6 years	68
Calendar	Semester
Student/faculty ratio	10:1
Profs interesting rating	95
Profs accessible rating	95

Most classes have 10–19 students. Most lab/discussion sessions have 10–19 students.

MOST POPULAR MAJORS

Biology/Biological Sciences; Multi-/Interdisciplinary Studies; Psychology.

ABOUT THE SCHOOL

Earlham College, a small liberal arts school in Indiana founded in the Quaker tradition, makes its reputation on teaching excellence. The forty majors available to students all offer a "rich academic experience where students are given assignments that require thoughtful responses." In 2016 Earlham reorganized its curriculum and advising to integrate a student's academic major with transformative learning experiences: study abroad, research, internships, and leadership development. To support this initiative, they offer guaranteed funding for every student to have a paid internship or research opportunity. Earlham also provides resources for students to develop as autodidacts, including free peer tutoring through the Academic Enrichment Center, a Writing Center, and optional May Term intensives (which take place both on- and off-campus). Social justice is also a tenet of the Earlham education, and the school emphasizes volunteer work—to the tune of more than 23,000 reported hours each year.

BANG FOR YOUR BUCK

Earlham is an outcome-oriented school, and students leave prepared with hands-on experiences, résumés, and career plans. About half of all graduates will go on to graduate studies, and the school is in the top 2 percent nationally for students who go on to earn a PhD. There is "strong financial aid and availability of merit scholarships" available to students, including the Quaker Fellows Scholarship, a $2,500 annual four-year scholarship for students with an active interest in the Religious Society of Friends.

STUDENT LIFE

Students here are "incredibly passionate about diverse causes and activities" and the liberal arts atmosphere "allows us to take part in anything and everything that occurs on campus." This is a school of balance, and "there is always both a steady academic culture and a steady social culture" and students choose when and how much to participate in each. The school has plenty of fun traditions and events such as concerts, bingo, and dances, and students also run "events often such as open mics, parties, [and] game nights." The "incredibly beautiful" campus dorms have "tons of lounge-able areas around," and the campus climate is "one of respect and love." Earlham has "a large number of international students who contribute to a diversified living experience," and "students here are quirky, but there is a wide variety of quirkiness."

CAREER

At Earlham, students start thinking about their lifelong career and learning goals—not to mention how they will make a difference in the world—from the moment they matriculate. The Center for Career and Community Engagement (CCCE) is the school's hub for experiential education, and it helps to arrange scholarly research, internships, community service, and on-campus jobs for students, as well as providing a variety of career education services, including personality assessments, mock interviews, and presentations by alumni. Currently, the CCCE coordinates over fifty internships around the United States and the world, all funded by grants and donors.

Earlham College

FINANCIAL AID: 765-983-1217 • E-MAIL: ADMISSIONS@EARLHAM.EDU • WEBSITE: WWW.EARLHAM.EDU

GENERAL INFO

Activities: Choral groups, concert band, dance, drama/theater, jazz band, literary magazine, music ensembles, radio station, student government, student newspaper, student-run film society, symphony orchestra, yearbook, campus ministries, Student Organization, Model UN. 70 registered organizations, 1 honor society, 15 religious organizations. **Athletics (Intercollegiate):** *Men:* baseball, basketball, cross-country, football, golf, lacrosse, soccer, tennis, track/field (outdoor), track/field (indoor). *Women:* basketball, cross-country, field hockey, golf, lacrosse, soccer, tennis, track/field (outdoor), track/field (indoor), volleyball. **On-Campus Highlights:** Center for Science and Technology, Center for Visual and Performing Arts, Landrum Bolling Center—Interdisciplinary Studies, Athletics and Wellness Center, Runyan Center, Natural History Museum, Coffee Shop. **Environmental Initiatives:** Their sustainability plan, updated in 2016, has been embedded in daily operations and has helped the school achieve increasingly higher Sustainability Tracking and Rating System (STARS) recognition.

FINANCIAL AID

Students should submit: FAFSA. Priority filing deadline is 2/1. The Princeton Review suggests that all financial aid forms be submitted as soon as possible after October 1. *Need-based scholarships/grants offered:* College/university scholarship or grant aid from institutional funds, Federal Pell, private scholarships, SEOG, state scholarships/grants. *Loan aid offered:* Direct PLUS Loans, Direct Subsidized Loans, Direct Unsubsidized Loans. Applicants will be notified of awards on a rolling basis beginning 3/15. Federal Work-Study Program available. Institutional employment available.

BOTTOM LINE

It costs $45,500 annually for tuition at Earlham, with another $10,400 for room and board and an additional $930 in fees. Students should also expect to spend around $1,000 on books each year. Fortunately, nearly 96 percent of Earlham students receive some form of financial assistance, and the school's sizeable endowment and alumni network are used in service of making Earlham affordable to all who want to and are able to attend.

CAREER INFORMATION FROM PAYSCALE.COM

ROI Rating	90
Bachelors and No Higher	
Median starting salary	$48,400
Median mid-career salary	$85,600
At Least Bachelors	
Median starting salary	$48,900
Median mid-career salary	$94,600
Alumni with high job meaning	62%
Degrees awarded in STEM subjects	31%

SELECTIVITY

Admissions Rating	89
# of applicants	2,799
% of applicants accepted	52
% of acceptees attending	20
# offered a place on the wait list	364
% accepting a place on wait list	0
# of early decision applicants	56
% accepted early decision	80

FRESHMAN PROFILE

Range SAT EBRW	610–700
Range SAT Math	580–700
Range ACT Composite	25–31
Minimum paper TOEFL	550
Minimum internet-based TOEFL	80
Average HS GPA	3.7
% graduated top 10% of class	36
% graduated top 25% of class	67
% graduated top 50% of class	93

DEADLINES

Early decision	
Deadline	11/15
Notification	12/15
Early action	
Deadline	12/1
Notification	1/15
Regular	
Priority	12/1
Deadline	2/15
Notification	4/1
Nonfall registration?	Yes

FINANCIAL FACTS

Financial Aid Rating	91
Annual tuition	$45,500
Room and board	$10,400
Required fees	$950
Books and supplies	$1,200
Average frosh need-based scholarship	$38,564
Average UG need-based scholarship	$37,896
% needy frosh rec. need-based scholarship or grant aid	100
% needy UG rec. need-based scholarship or grant aid	100
% needy frosh rec. non-need-based scholarship or grant aid	19
% needy UG rec. non-need-based scholarship or grant aid	20
% needy frosh rec. need-based self-help aid	81
% needy UG rec. need-based self-help aid	81
% frosh rec. any financial aid	98
% UG rec. any financial aid	96
% UG borrow to pay for school	58
Average cumulative indebtedness	$27,830

Emory University

1390 Oxford Road NE, Atlanta, GA 30322 • Admissions: 404-727-6036 • Fax: 404-727-6039

#38 BEST VALUE COLLEGE

ABOUT THE SCHOOL
Emory University, just 15 minutes outside of Atlanta in Decatur, Georgia, is known for its excellent pre-professional programs, academic rigor, and strong focus on research. Students say the university's emphasis on community-building shapes a culture that prizes non-competitive achievement and a balance of challenging coursework with an engaged life on the "gorgeous" campus. The business and pre-med schools are top-rated, and students are given opportunities from freshman year onward to form close relationships with faculty, "renowned experts in their fields" who are generally "accessible and supportive" and include President Jimmy Carter, Salman Rushdie, and the Dalai Lama. Students appreciate that they are "encouraged to pursue their interests, both in the classroom and outside of it, and to pave their own paths." Emory has recently eliminated some of their liberal arts majors (journalism, visual arts, and education), to focus on core programs and growing areas.

BANG FOR YOUR BUCK
Emory offers generous financial aid packages and pledges a "commit[ment] to meeting 100 percent of demonstrated financial need for all accepted domestic students." In 2016–17, the average student received $42,277 in financial aid. Twenty percent of students receive federal Pell grants. All students who apply for need-based aid will automatically be considered for Emory Advantage funding, "available to students from families with annual total incomes of $100,000 or less." The Loan Replacement Grant "replaces loans for dependent undergraduate students whose families' annual total incomes are $50,000 or less," and the Loan Cap Program caps federal loans at 15,000 for any student whose family's income is between $50,000 and $100,000.

STUDENT LIFE
Students can get involved in wealth of campus activities, including Greek life (who throw most of the weekend's parties), intramural and varsity sports, and downtown Atlanta offers all the restaurants, shopping, arts and culture students could ask for. Downtown Decatur has a shopping district, as well. There's a farmer's market every Tuesday, and "Wonderful Wednesdays" are a "favorite Emory tradition," showcasing student clubs and providing free food, music, and the occasional quirky event (i.e. petting zoo). Students also "play nighttime soccer on McDonough Field," play video games at the Cox Computing Center, or write for The Emory Wheel, the college newspaper. "I love the fact that Emory's school spirit is not solely wrapped around athletics," one student says. "At Emory, all events are well attended and respected by all students. Community is something that Emory strives accomplished from day one, utilizing the orientation and residence life programs."

CAREER
As a leading research university, Emory gives students ample opportunity to get hands-on experience working with renowned scholars, as well as internships and training "…at the Emory University Hospital, the Center for Disease Control, the Carter Center, and other organizations that Emory partners with…including the Tibet Science program with our honorary faculty member, the Dalai Lama." Pre-med and pre-

Emory University

FINANCIAL AID: 404-727-6039 • E-MAIL: ADMISSION@EMORY.EDU • WEBSITE: WWW.EMORY.EDU

nursing students have valuable access to the lauded Woodruff Health Sciences Center, comprised of the School of Medicine, the Nell Hodgson Woodruff School of Nursing, the Rollins School of Public Health, the Winship Cancer Institute, and the Yerkes National Primate Research Center. According to PayScale.com, 44 percent of Emory University alumni report that their work makes the world a better place. The median yearly starting salary is $56,700.

GENERAL INFO

Activities: Choral groups, concert band, dance, drama/theater, jazz band, literary magazine, marching band, music ensembles, musical theater, opera, pep band, radio station, student government, student newspaper, student-run film society, symphony orchestra, television station, campus ministries, international student organization. **Organizations:** 400+ registered organizations. 17 fraternities, 12 sororities. **Athletics (Intercollegiate):** *Men:* Baseball, basketball, cross-country, diving, golf, soccer, swimming, tennis, track/field (outdoor). *Women:* Basketball, cross-country, diving, soccer, softball, swimming, tennis, track/field (outdoor), volleyball.

FINANCIAL AID

Students should submit: CSS Profile; FAFSA; Noncustodial PROFILE. Priority filing deadline is 2/15. The Princeton Review suggests that all financial aid forms be submitted as soon as possible after October 1. *Need-based scholarships/grants offered:* College/university scholarship or grant aid from institutional funds; Federal Pell; Private scholarships; SEOG. *Loan aid offered:* Direct PLUS Loans, Direct Subsidized Loans, Direct Unsubsidized Loans. Applicants will be notified of awards on or about 4/1. Federal Work-Study Program available. Institutional employment available.

BOTTOM LINE

Students studying business and the sciences will benefit from expert faculty and well-funded departments. Emory estimates the total costs of attendance in 2017-18 at $66,950, including $48,690 in tuition and $13,894 in room and board. Lower-income to middle-class students, however, are aided by the Emory Advantage funding, which leaves students in far less debt upon graduation.

CAREER INFORMATION FROM PAYSCALE.COM	
ROI Rating	92
Bachelors and No Higher	
Median starting salary	$59,900
Median mid-career salary	$111,800
At Least Bachelors	
Median starting salary	$62,300
Median mid-career salary	$121,400
Alumni with high job meaning	44%
Degrees awarded in STEM subjects	20%

SELECTIVITY	
Admissions Rating	98
# of applicants	23,747
% of applicants accepted	22
% of acceptees attending	27
# offered a place on the wait list	2,992
% accepting a place on wait list	70
% admitted from wait list	41
# of early decision applicants	2475
% accepted early decision	27

FRESHMAN PROFILE	
Range SAT EBRW	670–740
Range SAT Math	680–780
Range ACT Composite	30–33
Minimum internet-based TOEFL	100
Average HS GPA	3.8
% graduated top 10% of class	83
% graduated top 25% of class	97
% graduated top 50% of class	100

DEADLINES	
Early decision	
Deadline	11/1
Notification	12/15
Other ED Deadline	1/1
Other ED Notification	2/15
Regular	
Deadline	1/1
Notification	4/1
Nonfall registration?	No

FINANCIAL FACTS	
Financial Aid Rating	96
Annual tuition	$50,590
Room and board	$14,456
Required fees	$716
Books and supplies	$1,224
Average frosh need-based scholarship	$41,305
Average UG need-based scholarship	$39,571
% needy frosh rec. need-based scholarship or grant aid	95
% needy UG rec. need-based scholarship or grant aid	95
% needy frosh rec. non-need-based scholarship or grant aid	34
% needy UG rec. non-need-based scholarship or grant aid	23
% needy frosh rec. need-based self-help aid	91
% needy UG rec. need-based self-help aid	91
% frosh rec. any financial aid	57
% UG rec. any financial aid	56
% UG borrow to pay for school	36
Average cumulative indebtedness	$28,262
% frosh need fully met	100

Fairfield University

1073 North Benson Road, Fairfield, CT 06824-5195 • Admissions: 203-254-4100 • Fax: 203-254-4199

CAMPUS LIFE

Quality of Life Rating	97
Fire Safety Rating	98
Green Rating	80
Type of school	Private
Affiliation	Roman Catholic-Jesuit
Environment	Town

STUDENTS

Total undergrad enrollment	4,023
% male/female	40/60
% from out of state	71
% frosh from public high school	60
% frosh live on campus	94
% ugrads live on campus	71
# of fraternities (% ugrad men join)	0 (0)
# of sororities (% ugrad women join)	0 (0)
% African American	2
% Asian	2
% Caucasian	78
% Hispanic	8
% Native American	<1
% Pacific Islander	<1
% Two or more races	2
% Race and/or ethnicity unknown	5
% international	3
# of countries represented	47

ACADEMICS

Academic Rating	90
% students returning for sophomore year	90
% students graduating within 4 years	79
% students graduating within 6 years	81
Calendar	Semester
Student/faculty ratio	12:1
Profs interesting rating	94
Profs accessible rating	92

Most classes have 20–29 students.

MOST POPULAR MAJORS
Registered Nursing; Finance; Marketing/
Marketing Management, General.

ABOUT THE SCHOOL

A Jesuit school in Connecticut, Fairfield University offers forty-five majors and twenty interdisciplinary minors and puts a focus on providing students with experiential learning opportunities and imbuing them with a sense of social responsibility. Service learning is an essential part of Fairfield's mission, and students say service-learning programs are highlights of their time here. "There are so many different ways to do service whether it is at soup kitchens, mentoring kids, or going on mission trips." The "phenomenal" nursing school is a huge draw, and the school's location and reputation "draws a lot of renowned academics." These professors are all "extraordinarily dedicated and compassionate about teaching" and "take a vested interest in their students." Fairfield "truly is a school that embodies the Jesuit values of men and women for others and care of the whole person."

BANG FOR YOUR BUCK

Fairfield's stellar academic reputation extends both in-state and nationally. The nursing school, for instance, has a 100 percent post-graduation placement rate, and 98 percent of the Class of 2017 had secured full-time employment, enrolled in a graduate or professional school, or were participating in a volunteer service program within six months of graduating. Fairfield's proximity to New York City with its internship and job opportunities is a huge benefit, and students are well aware of how fortunate they are to get these types of experiences under their belts: "If you look at many colleges and university they don't have the opportunities to get involved in internships or community like we do," says one.

STUDENT LIFE

Fairfield students are extremely dedicated to their studies: "You are never alone in the library no matter what day of the week or time of day." Additionally, the university runs "a tremendous amount of programs of all sorts" from sporting events to intellectual lectures and arts programs; "there is really nothing that Fairfield does not offer to students." The coastline location means "going to the beach is a big thing." "Most seniors have houses on Lantern Point and on nice days the student body spends the day down there." The town of Fairfield itself is "a quick run/bike/stag bus away," and it has everything a student could need or want. "It's very fun to spend a day in a coffee shop or shopping down there," says one. For those who live on campus, housing provides "fun things to do on the nights of the week," and as it gets closer to the end of the semester there are "an astounding amount of opportunities to see the talent at Fairfield," at student concerts and expeditions.

CAREER

Students find that Fairfield "provides excellent resources for internships and alumni connections," and "there are tons of research opportunities, if you pursue them." Professors themselves are readily available; they "always have office hours" and leads for opportunities "whether it's a job or internship." The Academic & Career Development Center offers key services like career counseling, panels, an alumni shadowing program, career fairs, and on- and off-campus recruiting opportunities. Of Fairfield University alumni visiting PayScale.com, 43 percent report that they derive a high level of meaning from their jobs.

Fairfield University

FINANCIAL AID: 203-254-4125 • E-MAIL: ADMIS@FAIRFIELD.EDU • WEBSITE: WWW.FAIRFIELD.EDU

GENERAL INFO

Activities: Choral groups, dance, drama/theater, jazz band, literary magazine, music ensembles, pep band, radio station, student government, student newspaper, student-run film society, television station, yearbook, campus ministries, Student Organization, Model UN. 121 registered organizations, 24 honor societies, 22 religious organizations. **Athletics (Intercollegiate):** *Men:* baseball, basketball, crew/rowing, cross-country, diving, golf, lacrosse, soccer, swimming, tennis. *Women:* basketball, crew/rowing, cross-country, diving, field hockey, golf, lacrosse, soccer, softball, swimming, tennis, volleyball. **On-Campus Highlights:** Quick Center for the Arts (includes Walsh Art Gallery, Kelley Theatre and Wien Experimental Theater), Egan/Loyola Chapel, DiMenna-Nyselius Library, Leslie C. Quick, Jr. Recreation Complex, Barone Campus Center (Student Center).

FINANCIAL AID

Students should submit: Business/Farm Supplement; CSS Profile; FAFSA; Noncustodial PROFILE. Regular filing deadline is 1/15. The Princeton Review suggests that all financial aid forms be submitted as soon as possible after October 1. *Need-based scholarships/grants offered:* College/university scholarship or grant aid from institutional funds, Federal Nursing Scholarships, Federal Pell, Private scholarships, SEOG, State scholarships/grants. *Loan aid offered:* Direct PLUS Loans, Direct Subsidized Loans, Direct Unsubsidized Loans and Federal Nursing Loans, State Loans, private/alternative loans. Applicants will be notified of awards on or about 4/1. Federal Work-Study Program available. Institutional employment available.

BOTTOM LINE

Tuition runs a hefty $47,650 and room and board in the residence halls is another $14,710; the price may be steep, but there are plenty of institutional scholarships and aid available. Ninety-one percent of current students finance their education through a combination of scholarships, grants, work-study, graduate assistantships, and loans. All admitted students are automatically considered for a merit scholarship. Approximately 40 percent of the class of 2022 received aid that was exclusively merit-based, ranging from $9,000 to $25,000.

CAREER INFORMATION FROM PAYSCALE.COM

ROI Rating	89
Bachelors and No Higher	
Median starting salary	$59,600
Median mid-career salary	$118,700
At Least Bachelors	
Median starting salary	$61,400
Median mid-career salary	$123,300
Alumni with high job meaning	41%
Degrees awarded in STEM subjects	17%

SELECTIVITY

Admissions Rating	88
# of applicants	11,218
% of applicants accepted	61
% of acceptees attending	15
# offered a place on the wait list	3,757
% accepting a place on wait list	30
% admitted from wait list	5
# of early decision applicants	182
% accepted early decision	81

FRESHMAN PROFILE

Range SAT EBRW	590–660
Range SAT Math	590–660
Range ACT Composite	25–29
Minimum paper TOEFL	550
Minimum internet-based TOEFL	80
Average HS GPA	3.5
% graduated top 10% of class	41
% graduated top 25% of class	79
% graduated top 50% of class	98

DEADLINES

Early decision	
Deadline	11/15
Notification	12/15
Other ED Deadline	1/15
Other ED Notification	2/15
Early action	
Deadline	11/1
Notification	12/20
Regular	
Deadline	1/15
Notification	4/1
Nonfall registration?	Yes

FINANCIAL FACTS

Financial Aid Rating	88
Annual tuition	$47,650
Room and board	$14,710
Required fees	$700
Books and supplies	$1,150
Average frosh need-based scholarship	$28,236
Average UG need-based scholarship	$27,572
% needy frosh rec. need-based scholarship or grant aid	82
% needy UG rec. need-based scholarship or grant aid	86
% needy frosh rec. non-need-based scholarship or grant aid	92
% needy UG rec. non-need-based scholarship or grant aid	87
% needy frosh rec. need-based self-help aid	78
% needy UG rec. need-based self-help aid	81
% frosh rec. any financial aid	91
% UG rec. any financial aid	87

SCHOOL PROFILES ■ 169

Florida State University

PO Box 3062400, TALLAHASSEE, FL 32306-2400 • ADMISSIONS: 850-644-6200 • FAX: 850-644-0197

CAMPUS LIFE

Quality of Life Rating	91
Fire Safety Rating	90
Green Rating	60*
Type of school	Public
Environment	City

STUDENTS

Total undergrad enrollment	33,008
% male/female	44/56
% from out of state	11
% frosh from public high school	79
% frosh live on campus	81
% ugrads live on campus	20
# of fraternities (% ugrad men join)	27 (19)
# of sororities (% ugrad women join)	26 (24)
% African American	8
% Asian	2
% Caucasian	62
% Hispanic	20
% Native American	<1
% Pacific Islander	<1
% Two or more races	4
% Race and/or ethnicity unknown	2
% international	2
# of countries represented	109

ACADEMICS

Academic Rating	79
% students returning for sophomore year	94
% students graduating within 4 years	63
% students graduating within 6 years	80
Calendar	Semester
Student/faculty ratio	22:1
Profs interesting rating	81
Profs accessible rating	82

Most classes have 10–19 students. Most lab/discussion sessions have 20–29 students.

MOST POPULAR MAJORS
Psychology; Criminal Justice/Safety Studies; Finance

ABOUT THE SCHOOL
Founded in 1851, Florida State University is one of the largest and oldest of the state's colleges, seeking to create lifelong learners out of its 31,000 undergraduates. The school's student-centered curriculum encourages interdisciplinary study and pursuit of interests, and the Center for Undergraduate Research and Academic Engagement helps students take advantage of all of the opportunities the research university has to offer. The faculty are "very willing to help undergraduate students with classes, research, career prospects, and everything in between," and students are "both challenged and supported in...academics by the professors and administration." Classes are "discussion-based and experimental," and an excellent study abroad program lets students expand their horizons with ease. The school is "constantly growing," and "no matter how successful a college or program is at Florida State, it never stays stagnant." The professors, students and alumni "are actively putting their energy into you making for the state an incredible academic institution." The university also pays heed to its roots as well; it is "continuously upholding school traditions, which gives a greater meaning to our time here."

BANG FOR YOUR BUCK
FSU has an extreme devotion to changing and adapting; a few years ago, the school put together a council of low-income students to design a program that would help them succeed (CARE), and now it has the best four-year graduation rate of any public college in the state. There are "ample amounts of resources at your fingertips": "the research, service, scholarship, and extracurricular opportunities are endless." Florida State is "all about ensuring [its] students have the opportunity to make the most of their college experience." Tuition is already affordable, but Presidential Scholarships almost completely cover the cost, essentially allowing in-state students to "go to school for free while receiving a once-in-a-lifetime opportunity to pursue an opportunity to the fullest."

STUDENT LIFE
There is "a great sense of school pride" at FSU, and everyone is "very supportive of sports, rankings, and school organizations." The campus is gorgeous, the weather is always nice, and "a car is not required to get to any classes." There is a reservation where students can rent canoes and kayaks to use on the lake (which is "absolutely beautiful at sunset"), and during fall, football games are "the best." People are "very inquisitive," and most are involved in extracurriculars. This large student body is "a unique mixture of south Floridians, crunchy granolas, Northern snowbirds, sorority girls, and good ole boys, with a nice international population mixed in there," with one thing in common: "Everyone you see seems genuinely happy."

Florida State University

FINANCIAL AID: 850-644-5716 • E-MAIL: ADMISSIONS@ADMIN.FSU.EDU • WEBSITE: WWW.FSU.EDU

CAREER

One of the greatest boons of FSU is that the school "makes it really easy to get multiple, seemingly unrelated majors which benefits future careers." Students can hodge-podge together a course of study from the thousands of classes with their own individual job goals in mind, and upperclassmen are "not only willing but excited to serve as mentors to incoming students." The school's Career Center hosts a plethora of internship and career fairs ("incredible and attended by a large amount of employers") and workshops, and offers a series of skill-developing videos called CareerSpots. People are "happy and proud to be a part of FSU" and the Nole alumni network absolutely blankets the country. Out of FSU alumni visiting PayScale.com, 50 percent report that they derive a high level of meaning from their jobs.

GENERAL INFO

Activities: Campus Ministries; Choral groups; Concert band; Dance; Drama/theater; International Student Organization; Jazz band; Literary magazine; Marching band; Model UN; Music ensembles; Musical theater; Opera; Pep band; Radio station; Student government; Student newspaper; Student-run film society; Symphony orchestra; Television station; Yearbook 520 registered organizations, 23 honor societies, 30 religious organizations. 32 fraternities, 28 sororities. **Athletics (Intercollegiate):** *Men:* baseball, basketball, cheerleading, cross-country, diving, football, golf, swimming, tennis, track/field (outdoor), track/field (indoor). *Women:* basketball, cheerleading, cross-country, diving, golf, soccer, softball, swimming, tennis, track/field (outdoor), track/field (indoor), volleyball. **On-Campus Highlights:** Suwannee Dining Hall, Bobby E. Leach Student Recreation Center, Bobby Bowden Field at Doak Campbell Stadium, National High Magnetic Field Laboratory, FSU Reservation.

FINANCIAL AID

Students should submit: FAFSA, state aid form. The Princeton Review suggests that all financial aid forms be submitted as soon as possible after October 1. *Need-based scholarships/grants offered:* College/university scholarship or grant aid from institutional funds; Federal Pell; Private scholarships; SEOG; State scholarships/grants; United Negro College Fund. *Loan aid offered:* Direct PLUS Loans, Direct Subsidized Loans, Direct Unsubsidized Loans. Applicants will be notified of awards on a rolling basis beginning 4/5. Federal Work-Study Program available. Institutional employment available.

CAREER INFORMATION FROM PAYSCALE.COM

ROI Rating	90
Bachelors and No Higher	
Median starting salary	$49,000
Median mid-career salary	$93,500
At Least Bachelors	
Median starting salary	$50,400
Median mid-career salary	$97,000
Alumni with high job meaning	50%
Degrees awarded in STEM subjects	18%

SELECTIVITY

Admissions Rating	90
# of applicants	35,334
% of applicants accepted	49
% of acceptees attending	38

FRESHMAN PROFILE

Range SAT EBRW	600–670
Range SAT Math	590–660
Range ACT Composite	26–30
Minimum paper TOEFL	550
Minimum internet-based TOEFL	80
Average HS GPA	4.0
% graduated top 10% of class	41
% graduated top 25% of class	83
% graduated top 50% of class	99

DEADLINES

Regular	
Deadline	2/7
Nonfall registration?	Yes

FINANCIAL FACTS

Financial Aid Rating	82
Annual in-state tuition	$4,640
Annual out-of-state tuition	$19,806
Room and board	$10,666
Required fees	$1,877
Books and supplies	$1,000
Average frosh need-based scholarship	$13,458
Average UG need-based scholarship	$10,859
% needy frosh rec. need-based scholarship or grant aid	92
% needy UG rec. need-based scholarship or grant aid	88
% needy frosh rec. non-need-based scholarship or grant aid	70
% needy UG rec. non-need-based scholarship or grant aid	55
% needy frosh rec. need-based self-help aid	54
% needy UG rec. need-based self-help aid	64
% frosh rec. any financial aid	96
% UG rec. any financial aid	87
% UG borrow to pay for school	47
Average cumulative indebtedness	$23,777
% frosh need fully met	21
% ugrads need fully met	11
Average % of frosh need met	70
Average % of ugrad need met	65

Franklin & Marshall College

PO Box 3003, Lancaster, PA 17604-3003 • Admissions: 717-358-3953 • Fax: 717-358-4389

CAMPUS LIFE

Quality of Life Rating	87
Fire Safety Rating	97
Green Rating	95
Type of school	Private
Environment	Town

STUDENTS

Total undergrad enrollment	2,283
% male/female	46/54
% from out of state	77
% frosh from public high school	64
% frosh live on campus	99
% ugrads live on campus	99
# of fraternities (% ugrad men join)	7 (20)
# of sororities (% ugrad women join)	4 (26)
% African American	6
% Asian	5
% Caucasian	57
% Hispanic	10
% Native American	<1
% Pacific Islander	<1
% Two or more races	2
% Race and/or ethnicity unknown	4
% international	16
# of countries represented	52

ACADEMICS

Academic Rating	94
% students returning for sophomore year	92
% students graduating within 4 years	80
% students graduating within 6 years	85
Calendar	Semester
Student/faculty ratio	9:1
Profs interesting rating	90
Profs accessible rating	96

Most classes have 10–19 students. Most lab/discussion sessions have 10–19 students.

MOST POPULAR MAJORS
Psychology; Political Science and Government; Business Administration, Management and Operations

ABOUT THE SCHOOL

Located in Lancaster, Pennsylvania, Franklin & Marshall College is "a small, liberal arts school" that "offers a great education and a leg up in today's competitive job marketplace." The school's small class sizes and 9:1 student to faculty ratio means "professor accessibility." "I've been able to meet personally with all of my professors outside of class multiple times," an astrophysics major attests. The school has 2,400 undergraduates and a faculty of 250. Students like the "general atmosphere of academic excellence" and say professors "challenge students in order to provide the best future opportunities." "The professors at F&M are the best at what they do" and each one "brings his or her own spin to a class." "F&M is such a happy school," one student explains. "I immediately felt welcomed on campus because it has such a warm, friendly, and happy vibe."

BANG FOR YOUR BUCK

"We all know that we're paying $52,000 a year to be here, it's no secret," one student says. However, more than half of the student body receives need-based financial aid. F&M is committed to meeting 100 percent of students' financial needs. The school determines those needs "based on an institutional methodology that analyzes family income, assets, and other circumstances." The school eliminated merit-based scholarships—which one student calls "a huge mistake"— in order to commit to enrolling "highly qualified students who could not otherwise afford a Franklin & Marshall College education." The school does provide students with guidance about where to find other potential outside financial assistance for college.

STUDENT LIFE

At F&M, "the typical student is clean-cut, perhaps a little preppy, [and] dedicated to academics," while the student body as a whole is increasingly diverse. School is a priority, but when the weekend roles around students let loose. The social life of the school is heavily influenced by Greek life and "everyone goes to the frats every weekend." However, "it's not a huge deal if you decide not to be a part of it." Downtown Lancaster offers a lot of things to do, such as art galleries, restaurants, and live music, and F&M offers a shuttle service to and from downtown. There's plenty to do on campus, such as "orchestra concerts," "regular documentary screenings," and "guest lecturers." Students are very involved in campus life at F&M. Most undergrads are "either in a fraternity/sorority, sports team, the house system or a theme house, or a time-consuming club" such as "debate, ultimate Frisbee, and French Club."

CAREER

"F&M is all about good undergrad programs and tight-knit networking," one student says. Students praise the alumni network that helps F&M get a leg-up in their post-college careers. One says, "there are interesting opportunities for volunteer activities and internships everywhere I look." PayScale.com reports an average starting salary of $53,700 and a mid-career average of $112,400 for F&M graduates. Lancaster is the third most common post-college employment location after New York and Philadelphia. Popular companies for F&M grads include Morgan Stanley, Citi, Deloitte, and Merrill Lynch.

Franklin & Marshall College

FINANCIAL AID: 717-358-3991 • E-MAIL: ADMISSION@FANDM.EDU • WEBSITE: WWW.FANDM.EDU

GENERAL INFO

Activities: Choral groups, concert band, dance, drama/theater, jazz band, literary magazine, music ensembles, musical theater, radio station, student government, student newspaper, symphony orchestra, yearbook, campus ministries, International Student Organization, Model UN. **Organizations:** 90 registered organizations, 13 honor societies, 8 religious organizations. 8 fraternities, 4 sororities. **Athletics (Intercollegiate):** *Men:* baseball, basketball, crew/rowing, cross-country, football, golf, lacrosse, soccer, squash, swimming, tennis, track/field (outdoor), track/field (indoor), wrestling. *Women:* basketball, crew/rowing, cross-country, field hockey, golf, lacrosse, soccer, softball, squash, swimming, tennis, track/field (outdoor), track/field (indoor), volleyball. **On-Campus Highlights:** Alumni Sports and Fitness Center, Barshinger Center in Hensel Hall, Barnes and Noble Bookstore and Zime Cafe, Roschel Performing Arts Center, Writers House, International Center, Center for Jewish Life.

FINANCIAL AID

Students should submit: CSS Profile; FAFSA; Noncustodial PROFILE. Priority filing deadline is 3/15. The Princeton Review suggests that all financial aid forms be submitted as soon as possible after October 1. *Need-based scholarships/grants offered:* College/university scholarship or grant aid from institutional funds, Federal Pell, private scholarships, SEOG, state scholarships/grants. *Loan aid offered:* Direct PLUS Loans, Direct Subsidized Loans, Direct Unsubsidized Loans. Applicants will be notified of awards on or about 4/1. Federal Work-Study Program available.

BOTTOM LINE

The basic tuition at F&M currently stands at $56,450. Student housing costs range from $8,030 to $9,416 depending on the rooming situation. Meal plans and other fees bring up the room and board total to an average of $14,050. While F&M meets 100 percent of students' financial needs, they do not offer merit-based scholarships.

CAREER INFORMATION FROM PAYSCALE.COM	
ROI Rating	91
Bachelors and No Higher	
Median starting salary	$54,600
Median mid-career salary	$114,800
At Least Bachelors	
Median starting salary	$57,800
Median mid-career salary	$121,200
Alumni with high job meaning	43%
Degrees awarded in STEM subjects	23%

SELECTIVITY	
Admissions Rating	**94**
# of applicants	6,720
% of applicants accepted	34
% of acceptees attending	28
# offered a place on the wait list	2,335
% accepting a place on wait list	0
# of early decision applicants	559
% accepted early decision	62

FRESHMAN PROFILE	
Range SAT EBRW	620–700
Range SAT Math	640–720
Range ACT Composite	28–32
Minimum paper TOEFL	600
% graduated top 10% of class	68
% graduated top 25% of class	90
% graduated top 50% of class	100

DEADLINES	
Early decision	
Deadline	11/15
Notification	12/15
Other ED Deadline	1/15
Other ED Notification	2/15
Regular	
Deadline	1/15
Notification	4/1
Nonfall registration?	Yes

FINANCIAL FACTS	
Financial Aid Rating	**96**
Annual tuition	$56,450
Room and board	$14,050
Required fees	$100
Books and supplies	$1,200
Average frosh need-based scholarship	$48,311
Average UG need-based scholarship	$46,102
% needy frosh rec. need-based scholarship or grant aid	100
% needy UG rec. need-based scholarship or grant aid	99
% needy frosh rec. non-need-based scholarship or grant aid	29
% needy UG rec. non-need-based scholarship or grant aid	27
% needy frosh rec. need-based self-help aid	91
% needy UG rec. need-based self-help aid	93
% frosh rec. any financial aid	59
% UG rec. any financial aid	56
% UG borrow to pay for school	57
Average cumulative indebtedness	$27,011
% frosh need fully met	100
% ugrads need fully met	100
Average % of frosh need met	100
Average % of ugrad need met	100

Franklin W. Olin College of Engineering

Olin Way, Needham, MA 02492-1245 • Admissions: 781-292-2222 • Fax: 781-292-2210

CAMPUS LIFE

Quality of Life Rating	94
Fire Safety Rating	99
Green Rating	70
Type of school	Private
Environment	Town

STUDENTS

Total undergrad enrollment	345
% male/female	52/48
% from out of state	88
% frosh from public high school	71
% frosh live on campus	100
% ugrads live on campus	100
# of fraternities (% ugrad men join)	0 (0)
# of sororities (% ugrad women join)	0 (0)
% African American	3
% Asian	12
% Caucasian	53
% Hispanic	9
% Native American	0
% Pacific Islander	0
% Two or more races	8
% Race and/or ethnicity unknown	8
% international	8
# of countries represented	11

ACADEMICS

Academic Rating	99
% students returning for sophomore year	99
% students graduating within 4 years	79
% students graduating within 6 years	91
Calendar	Semester
Student/faculty ratio	8:1
Profs interesting rating	99
Profs accessible rating	96

Most classes have 10–19 students. Most lab/discussion sessions have fewer than 10 students.

MOST POPULAR MAJORS

Engineering; Electrical and Electronics Engineering; Mechanical Engineering

ABOUT THE SCHOOL

Located in Needham, Massachusetts, near Boston, the incredibly selective and tiny Olin College of Engineering is a young institution—just about 15 years old—"founded to radically change engineering education with the goal of fueling the technical innovation needed to solve the world's complex future challenges." Innovative project-based learning excites students and attracts talented faculty with "fascinating backgrounds" who are "heavily invested in experiential learning and refining…teaching methods [through] feedback" from students. The student body and professors make up a tight-knit community of "inquisitive, creative…, ambitious, and colorful" people, "diverse in their skillsets." Notably, the college has committed to maintaining gender diversity among the student body: half of its nearly 400 students are women, balancing the historically male-dominated STEM sector. Olin students get unparalleled attention from faculty, with an average 8:1 student/faculty ratio. Students say that Olin is providing an "academic revolution, essentially changing what it means to get an engineering education" and "preparing engineers to go forth and work on meaningful, global, interdisciplinary problems…and effectively communicate to both engineers [and other stakeholders]."

BANG FOR YOUR BUCK

Olin commits to providing every student "a four-year, half-tuition scholarship valued at more than $100,000 over four years." Furthermore, the college commits to "meeting full demonstrated financial need" for students and families eligible for further financial assistance.

STUDENT LIFE

"Life here is busy," Olin students say. Students are often working together on teams and preparing for international engineering competitions. Popular teams include Robotic Sailing, Electric Motorsports, Human Powered Vehicle Team, Olin Baja, and AERO. When not building, Oliners engage in a quirky variety of activities, which include riding unicycles, circus arts, improv theater, glass sculpting, ultimate Frisbee, and fencing. Educational partnerships with Babson, Wellesley, and Brandeis colleges invite students to take classes and participate in athletics like rugby and soccer. Students are generally collaborative and supportive, and comply with an honor code that leaves students at ease about the often expensive materials and equipment in their possession. Self-identified "nerds" and "geeks" get together at the Board Game Club to play games like the student-built 3-D Settlers of Catan, or join the Steampunk Society and Dr. Who fan club TARDIS.

CAREER

Olin College of Engineering offers career planning in its Office of Post-Graduate Planning, which helps students "identify meaningful research, internship, scholarship, professional and graduate school opportunities." Olin's forward-thinking initiatives, close student-faculty relationships, and emphasis on "real-world problems and solutions" prepare students to enter the job market not just as valuable employees, but as potential innovators and entrepreneurs. According to PayScale.com, the median starting salary for Olin graduates is $81,900.

Franklin W. Olin College of Engineering

FINANCIAL AID: 781-292-2343 • E-MAIL: INFO@OLIN.EDU • WEBSITE: WWW.OLIN.EDU

GENERAL INFO

Activities: Choral groups, dance, drama/theater, jazz band, music ensembles, musical theater, student government, student-run film society, symphony orchestra, yearbook. **Organizations:** 55 registered organizations. Large Project Building provides workspace for large-scale, hands-on student projects.

FINANCIAL AID

Students should submit: FAFSA. Regular filing deadline is 2/15. The Princeton Review suggests that all financial aid forms be submitted as soon as possible after October 1. *Need-based scholarships/grants offered:* College/university scholarship or grant aid from institutional funds; Federal Pell; SEOG. *Loan aid offered:* Direct PLUS Loans, Direct Subsidized Loans, Direct Unsubsidized Loans. Applicants will be notified of awards on or about 3/24. Institutional employment available.

BOTTOM LINE

Olin College's mission is to "prepare students to become exemplary engineering innovators who recognize needs, design solutions and engage in creative enterprises for the good of the world." The 2017-18 tuition is $50,400 while room and board runs $16,300. All students automatically receive a half-tuition merit scholarship, which helps offset the price, and financial aid packages help students meet all costs.

CAREER INFORMATION FROM PAYSCALE.COM

ROI Rating	91
Bachelors and No Higher	
Median starting salary	$81,900
Median mid-career salary	$134,200
At Least Bachelors	
Median starting salary	$84,800
Median mid-career salary	$141,500
Degrees awarded in STEM subjects	100%

SELECTIVITY

Admissions Rating	98
# of applicants	1,062
% of applicants accepted	13
% of acceptees attending	63
# offered a place on the wait list	58
% accepting a place on wait list	66
% admitted from wait list	5

FRESHMAN PROFILE

Range SAT EBRW	710–770
Range SAT Math	740–800
Range ACT Composite	33–35
Average HS GPA	3.8

DEADLINES

Regular	
Deadline	1/1
Nonfall registration?	No

FINANCIAL FACTS

Financial Aid Rating	97
Annual tuition	$50,400
Room and board	$16,300
Required fees	$680
Books and supplies	$200
Average frosh need-based scholarship	$49,471
Average UG need-based scholarship	$45,637
% needy frosh rec. need-based scholarship or grant aid	100
% needy UG rec. need-based scholarship or grant aid	100
% needy frosh rec. non-need-based scholarship or grant aid	100
% needy UG rec. non-need-based scholarship or grant aid	99
% needy frosh rec. need-based self-help aid	70
% needy UG rec. need-based self-help aid	73
% frosh rec. any financial aid	100
% UG rec. any financial aid	100
% UG borrow to pay for school	54
Average cumulative indebtedness	$23,098
% frosh need fully met	100
% ugrads need fully met	99
Average % of frosh need met	100
Average % of ugrad need met	100

Furman University

3300 POINSETT HIGHWAY, GREENVILLE, SC 29613 • ADMISSIONS: 864-294-2034 • FAX: 864-294-2018

CAMPUS LIFE

Quality of Life Rating	**94**
Fire Safety Rating	**90**
Green Rating	**92**
Type of school	Private
Environment	City

STUDENTS

Total undergrad enrollment	2,740
% male/female	41/59
% from out of state	69
% frosh live on campus	99
% ugrads live on campus	89
# of fraternities (% ugrad men join)	6 (30)
# of sororities (% ugrad women join)	7 (58)
% African American	6
% Asian	2
% Caucasian	76
% Hispanic	5
% Native American	<1
% Pacific Islander	0
% Two or more races	3
% Race and/or ethnicity unknown	3
% international	5
# of countries represented	49

ACADEMICS

Academic Rating	**93**
% students returning for sophomore year	93
% students graduating within 4 years	73
% students graduating within 6 years	81
Calendar	Semester
Student/faculty ratio	10:1
Profs interesting rating	95
Profs accessible rating	98

Most classes have fewer than 10 students.
Most lab/discussion sessions have fewer than 10 students.

MOST POPULAR MAJORS

Political Science and Government; Health
Professions and Related Clinical Sciences;
Business/Commerce

ABOUT THE SCHOOL

Furman University is a small, highly-acclaimed liberal arts and sciences university that offers its 2,780 students "an intense undergraduate experience" both in and out of the classroom and boasts a "great capacity for supporting students." Students are "constantly challenged to do better, learn more subjects, and get more involved in the community," and professors "encourage self-teaching" and are willing to meet with students and work around their schedules. "I've been to dinner with my professors before and they are always willing to help you in your journey," says one. The administration "knows what it's doing and is neither overbearing nor a non-existent presence." Not for the academically faint-of-heart, students work hard in the hopes of being rewarded with a well-reputed undergraduate education. "I wake up every day thrilled to be a part of this community," says a happy student. In fall 2016, the university launched The Furman Advantage, which promises every student an engaged learning experience that is tracked and integrated with academic and professional goals.

BANG FOR YOUR BUCK

The school also offers renewable merit-based scholarships such as the Herman W. Lay Scholarships for full tuition and partial other costs; James B. Duke Scholarships for full tuition; John D. Hollingsworth Scholarships for incoming students from South Carolina; and Charles H. Townes Scholarships for students coming from outside South Carolina.

STUDENT LIFE

The typical Furman student in this "close-knit, southern community" is "very studious but still very active in social life." "Pulling all-nighters is not uncommon but neither is staying out late." The school "has a lot of interesting things to do on campus, from music concerts to improv shows to sports games"; people visit "fun and safe" downtown Greenville on the weekends to shop or go to dinner. Football games are well-attended and most everyone is "overinvolved in many clubs." "Studying is a necessity," and students say Furman has done a good job at making studying convenient with "two coffee shops, four parlors, and fifteen to twenty study rooms in the library."

CAREER

This "bubble community" allows for "strong research/internships if you want them"; "graduate schools like the Furman name," and the professors associated with the school serve as great references and connections to a broader future. "Furman has given me a great opportunity to learn, challenge myself, and find incredible internships," says one student. The Malone Center for Career Engagement organizes job fairs and campus recruiting to help aid students in their search. For those Furman graduates who visited PayScale.com, 51 percent reported feeling that their career had a high social value. Ninety-seven percent of graduates gain admission to graduate school or find a job within six months of graduation.

Furman University

FINANCIAL AID: 864-294-2204 • E-MAIL: ADMISSIONS@FURMAN.EDU • WEBSITE: WWW.FURMAN.EDU

GENERAL INFO

Activities: Choral groups, concert band, dance, drama/theater, jazz band, literary magazine, marching band, music ensembles, musical theater, opera, pep band, student government, student newspaper, student-run film society, symphony orchestra, television station, yearbook, campus ministries, International Student Organization. **Organizations:** 150 registered organizations, 29 honor societies, 15 religious organizations, 7 diversity/inclusion organizations. 6 fraternities, 8 sororities. **Athletics (Intercollegiate):** *Men:* baseball, basketball, cheerleading, cross-country, football, golf, soccer, tennis, track/field (outdoor), track/field (indoor). *Women:* basketball, cheerleading, cross-country, golf, soccer, softball, tennis, track/field (outdoor), track/field (indoor), volleyball. **On-Campus Highlights:** Charles Townes Science Center, Timmons Arena, James B. Duke Library, 18-hole Golf Course, Physical Activities Center, Place of Peace, David Shi Center for Sustainability, Riley Institute, Institute for the Advancement of Community Health, Furman Lake, Bell Tower.

FINANCIAL AID

Students should submit: CSS Profile; FAFSA. Priority filing deadline is 10/15. The Princeton Review suggests that all financial aid forms be submitted as soon as possible after October 1. *Need-based scholarships/grants offered:* College/university scholarship or grant aid from institutional funds, Federal Pell, private scholarships, SEOG, state scholarships/grants. *Loan aid offered:* Direct PLUS Loans, Direct Subsidized Loans, Direct Unsubsidized Loans. Applicants will be notified of awards on or about 4/1. Federal Work-Study Program available. Institutional employment available.

BOTTOM LINE

Tuition costs $47,968 with $12,712 being added on for room and board. The vast majority of students receive need-based financial aid, with packages averaging $35,508, and merit-based scholarships are in no short supply for the eligible. Thirty-seven percent of students will graduate with loans, with the average debt coming in at $36,846.

CAREER INFORMATION FROM PAYSCALE.COM	
ROI Rating	89
Bachelors and No Higher	
Median starting salary	$49,600
Median mid-career salary	$103,000
At Least Bachelors	
Median starting salary	$52,000
Median mid-career salary	$106,900
Alumni with high job meaning	49%
Degrees awarded in STEM subjects	16%

SELECTIVITY	
Admissions Rating	87
# of applicants	5,002
% of applicants accepted	61
% of acceptees attending	23
# offered a place on the wait list	1,412
% accepting a place on wait list	0
# of early decision applicants	112
% accepted early decision	93

FRESHMAN PROFILE	
Range SAT EBRW	600–690
Range SAT Math	590–690
Range ACT Composite	26–31
% graduated top 10% of class	38
% graduated top 25% of class	71
% graduated top 50% of class	94

DEADLINES	
Early decision	
Deadline	11/1
Notification	11/15
Early action	
Deadline	11/1
Notification	12/20
Regular	
Deadline	1/15
Notification	3/1
Nonfall registration?	No

FINANCIAL FACTS	
Financial Aid Rating	89
Annual tuition	$47,968
Room and board	$12,712
Required fees	$380
Books and supplies	$1,230
Average frosh need-based scholarship	$36,996
Average UG need-based scholarship	$37,333
% needy frosh rec. need-based scholarship or grant aid	98
% needy UG rec. need-based scholarship or grant aid	98
% needy frosh rec. non-need-based scholarship or grant aid	30
% needy UG rec. non-need-based scholarship or grant aid	30
% needy frosh rec. need-based self-help aid	66
% needy UG rec. need-based self-help aid	67
% frosh rec. any financial aid	98
% UG rec. any financial aid	94
% UG borrow to pay for school	39
Average cumulative indebtedness	$32,919
% frosh need fully met	40
% ugrads need fully met	39
Average % of frosh need met	83
Average % of ugrad need met	81

Georgetown University

37TH AND O STREETS, NW, 103 WHITE-GRAVEN, WASHINGTON, D.C. 20057 • ADMISSIONS: 202-687-3600

CAMPUS LIFE

Quality of Life Rating	**64**
Fire Safety Rating	**88**
Green Rating	**60***
Type of school	Private
Affiliation	Roman Catholic
Environment	Metropolis

STUDENTS

Total undergrad enrollment	7,124
% male/female	44/56
% from out of state	98
% frosh from public high school	49
# of fraternities (% ugrad men join)	0 (0)
# of sororities (% ugrad women join)	0 (0)
% African American	6
% Asian	10
% Caucasian	54
% Hispanic	10
% Native American	0
% Pacific Islander	<1
% Two or more races	5
% Race and/or ethnicity unknown	2
% international	13
# of countries represented	138

ACADEMICS

Academic Rating	**81**
% students returning for sophomore year	96
% students graduating within 4 years	90
% students graduating within 6 years	95
Calendar	Semester
Student/faculty ratio	11:1
Profs interesting rating	65
Profs accessible rating	61

Most classes have 10–19 students. Most lab/discussion sessions have 10–19 students.

MOST POPULAR MAJORS

English Language and Literature; International Relations and Affairs; Political Science and Government

ABOUT THE SCHOOL

Georgetown was founded in 1789 by John Carroll, who concurred with his contemporaries Benjamin Franklin and Thomas Jefferson in believing that the success of the young democracy depended upon an educated and virtuous citizenry. Carroll founded the school with the dynamic Jesuit tradition of education, characterized by humanism and committed to the assumption of responsibility and action. Georgetown is a national and international university, enrolling students from all fifty states and more than 100 foreign countries. Undergraduate students are enrolled in one of four undergraduate schools: the College of Arts and Sciences, School of Foreign Service, Georgetown School of Business, and Georgetown School of Nursing and Health Studies. All students share a common liberal arts core and have access to the entire university curriculum.

This moderately sized elite academic establishment stays true to its Jesuit foundations by educating its students with the idea of "cura personalis," or "care for the whole person." The "well-informed" student body perpetuates upon itself, creating an atmosphere full of vibrant intellectual life that is "also balanced with extracurricular learning and development." "Georgetown is...a place where people work very, very hard without feeling like they are in direct competition," says an international politics major.

BANG FOR YOUR BUCK

Professors tend to be "fantastic scholars and teachers" and are "generally available to students," as well as often being "interested in getting to know you as a person (if you put forth the effort to talk to them and go to office hours)." Though Georgetown has a policy of grade deflation, meaning "As are hard to come by," there are "a ton of interesting courses available," and TAs are used only for optional discussion sessions and help with grading. The academics "can be challenging, or they can be not so much (not that they are ever really easy, just easier);" it all depends on the courses you choose and how much you actually do the work. Internship opportunities in the DC area are valuable and often take place "in the heart of the nation's capital." People know the importance of connections and spend time making sure they get to know the people here. One student is very enthusiastic about these opportunities. "The location in DC and the pragmatism of people who come here make for people that are fun to be around but are serious about their ambitions. There's a reason that Georgetown tends to draw political junkies. It's because there's no better place in the United States to get involved with politics on a national level."

STUDENT LIFE

There are "a lot of wealthy students on campus," and preppy-casual is the fashion de rigueur; this is "definitely not a 'granola' school," but students from diverse backgrounds are typically welcomed by people wanting to learn about different experiences. Indeed, everyone here is well-traveled and well-educated, and there are "a ton of international students." "You better have at least some interest in politics, or you will feel out-of-place," says a student. The school can also be "a bit cliquish, with athletes at the top," but there are "plenty of groups for everybody to fit into and find their niche," and "there is much crossover between groups."

Georgetown University

FINANCIAL AID: 202-687-4547 • FAX: 202-687-5084 • E-MAIL: GUADMISS@GEORGETOWN.EDU • WEBSITE: WWW.GEORGETOWN.EDU

CAREER

The Cawley Career Education Center can help students answer that perennial question: "What can I do with my major?" The Career Exploration resource on its website allows students to learn about the transferable skills that different majors at Georgetown will help them develop and see jobs and internships that alumni from those programs have held. The Hoya Career Connection and the iNet Internship network are the Career Education Center's online management systems that allow students to search and apply for jobs, internships, fellowships and volunteer gigs. Finally, the Center brings a number of potential employers to campus through the Career Fair, Government & Nonprofit Expo, and various Industry Weeks. Graduates who visited PayScale.com report a median starting salary of $61,400.

GENERAL INFO

Activities: Choral groups, concert band, dance, drama/theater, jazz band, literary magazine, music ensembles, musical theater, pep band, radio station, student government, student newspaper, student-run film society, symphony orchestra, television station, yearbook. **Organizations:** 139 registered organizations, 14 honor societies, 20 religious organizations. **Athletics (Intercollegiate):** *Men:* Baseball, basketball, crew/rowing, cross-country, diving, football, golf, lacrosse, sailing, soccer, swimming, tennis, track/field (outdoor), track/field (indoor). *Women:* Basketball, crew/rowing, cross-country, diving, field hockey, golf, lacrosse, sailing, soccer, softball, swimming, tennis, track/field (outdoor), track/field (indoor), volleyball. **On-Campus Highlights:** Yates Field House, Uncommon Grounds, The Observatory, The Quadrangle, Healy Hall.

FINANCIAL AID

Students should submit: The Princeton Review suggests that all financial aid forms be submitted as soon as possible after October 1. *Loan aid offered:* Federal Work-Study Program available. Institutional employment available.

BOTTOM LINE

Georgetown University has a well-deserved reputation for the outstanding quality of its curriculum and the fantastic overall educational experience it provides. Of course, the cost of tuition reflects that to a great extent, amounting to nearly $50,547 with fees. Room and board tacks on another $14,962. At the same time, Georgetown meets 100 percent of student need; with an average need-based scholarship of $40,104, it is easy to see that a Georgetown education is still accessible to a large segment of potential students. Students can envision a loan debt of about $23,067 once they graduate from the university.

SELECTIVITY	
Admissions Rating	98
# of applicants	21,462
% of applicants accepted	16
% of acceptees attending	47
# offered a place on the wait list	2,473
% accepting a place on wait list	64
% admitted from wait list	3

FRESHMAN PROFILE	
Range SAT EBRW	680–760
Range SAT Math	670–760
Range ACT Composite	30–34
% graduated top 10% of class	90
% graduated top 25% of class	97
% graduated top 50% of class	100

DEADLINES	
Early action	
Deadline	11/1
Notification	12/15
Regular	
Deadline	1/10
Notification	4/1
Nonfall registration?	No

FINANCIAL FACTS	
Financial Aid Rating	94
Annual tuition	$53,520
Room and board	$15,588
Required fees	$684

CAREER INFORMATION FROM PAYSCALE.COM	
ROI Rating	89
Bachelors and No Higher	
Median starting salary	$63,700
Median mid-career salary	$128,300
At Least Bachelors	
Median starting salary	$65,700
Median mid-career salary	$140,000
Alumni with high job meaning	43%
Degrees awarded in STEM subjects	14%

Georgia Institute of Technology

GEORGIA INSTITUTE OF TECHNOLOGY, ATLANTA, GA 30332-0320 • ADMISSIONS: 404-894-4154 • FAX: 404-894-9511

#18 BEST VALUE COLLEGE

CAMPUS LIFE

Quality of Life Rating	90
Fire Safety Rating	96
Green Rating	97
Type of school	Public
Environment	Metropolis

STUDENTS

Total undergrad enrollment	14,812
% male/female	62/38
% from out of state	33
% frosh live on campus	97
% ugrads live on campus	43
# of fraternities (% ugrad men join)	39 (55)
# of sororities (% ugrad women join)	16 (45)
% African American	7
% Asian	20
% Caucasian	49
% Hispanic	7
% Native American	<1
% Pacific Islander	<1
% Two or more races	4
% Race and/or ethnicity unknown	4
% international	9
# of countries represented	127

ACADEMICS

Academic Rating	88
% students returning for sophomore year	97
% students graduating within 4 years	39
% students graduating within 6 years	85
Calendar	Semester
Student/faculty ratio	22:1
Profs interesting rating	78
Profs accessible rating	76

Most classes have 20–29 students. Most lab/discussion sessions have 20–29 students.

MOST POPULAR MAJORS

Computer and Information Sciences; Mechanical Engineering; Industrial Engineering

ABOUT THE SCHOOL

One of the nation's top-ranked public research universities, Georgia Tech offers its 15,500 undergraduate students "a technologically focused education" that emphasizes critical inquiry and dynamic problem solving. Despite the rigor of its engineering, science, computing, business, and liberal arts programs, "there isn't a sense of cut-throat academic rivalry; everyone is...helpful and supportive of one another," notes one student. Described as "driven, passionate, and relentless," the students here are "constantly striving to pursue academic excellence, as well as technological advancement." Georgia Tech professors are leaders in their fields and are "truly passionate about what they're teaching," making themselves "highly approachable outside of classroom time." A shared sense of purpose unites this diverse student body, who feel that Georgia Tech is helping them become "better able to work together to solve the world's problems."

BANG FOR YOUR BUCK

Georgia Tech is a public institution that is committed not only to ensuring that education is as affordable as possible, but also, through its many co-op and internship programs, that students are exceedingly prepared for the job market. There are numerous scholarships and grants available, including those that are merit and need-based. In addition, the school's highly-rated study-abroad and international internship programs help make students "ideal for competitive positions in today's global economy." The university's Center for Career Discovery and Development is considered one of the nation's best in helping place students in competitive jobs and fostering recruitment opportunities. As one student puts it, "Georgia Tech has great job placement...it gives you the tools to get wherever you want to go."

STUDENT LIFE

Asked to describe their peers, many students point out that "people here are diverse, fun, friendly." While the academic environment at Georgia Tech is rigorous, "everybody has time to unwind," says one student. There are plenty of opportunities for extracurricular activities; the fitness-minded go to the school's state-of-the-art sports and recreation center, and there are over 500 clubs and societies to take part in. As one student puts it, "There is always something going on or an event I want to attend." Greek life here is vibrant, too, and a great deal of the student community rallies around the school's Division I football team; "if it's game day, the campus goes nuts" notes one fan. Located in Atlanta, many attending Georgia Tech love that they can experience the city while living in a "lush, green, bustling campus." The students here "make their best efforts to show goodwill toward [each] other...and generally strive to better their community."

Georgia Institute of Technology

FINANCIAL AID: 404-894-4160 • E-MAIL: ADMISSION@GATECH.EDU • WEBSITE: WWW.GATECH.EDU

CAREER

A Georgia Tech education is widely considered an excellent investment, with graduates earning $68,100 per year on average, and 47 percent of alumni noting their work has "high meaning" to them. Since it's located in Atlanta, students at the school have access to countless internships, co-ops, and other career-advancement opportunities with local companies. The university also emphasizes partnerships with business and engineering communities through its VentureLab and Advanced Technology Development Center, two of the country's most successful and dynamic innovation incubators. Not only that, Georgia Tech's Center for Career Discovery and Development offers a range of programs to help students become more competitive in the job market, including resume and cover letter coaching as well as career fairs. Through it all, as one student puts it, "Georgia Tech is about producing competitive students with valuable and unique research, job, and international experiences in order to lead them to successful careers."

GENERAL INFO

Activities: Choral groups, concert band, dance, drama/theater, jazz band, literary magazine, marching band, music ensembles, musical theater, pep band, radio station, student government, student newspaper, student-run film society, symphony orchestra, television station, yearbook, campus ministries, international student organization. **Organizations:** 548 registered organizations, 22 honor societies, 41 religious organizations. 41 fraternities, 16 sororities. **Athletics (Intercollegiate):** *Men:* Baseball, basketball, cheerleading, cross-country, diving, football, golf, swimming, tennis, track/field (outdoor), track/field (indoor). *Women:* Basketball, cheerleading, cross-country, diving, softball, swimming, tennis, track/field (outdoor), track/ field (indoor), volleyball.

FINANCIAL AID

Students should submit: CSS Profile; FAFSA; Institution's own financial aid form. Priority filing deadline is 1/15. The Princeton Review suggests that all financial aid forms be submitted as soon as possible after October 1. *Need-based scholarships/grants offered:* College/university scholarship or grant aid from institutional funds, Federal Pell, private scholarships, SEOG, state scholarships/grants. *Loan aid offered:* Direct PLUS Loans, Direct Subsidized Loans, Direct Unsubsidized Loans. Applicants will be notified of awards on or about 4/15. Federal Work-Study Program available. Institutional employment available.

BOTTOM LINE

Tuition for Georgia residents is $9,812 a year with out-of-state students paying $30,004. Annual room and board costs are $13,640, and books and other supplies run about $800. That said, the university offers several scholarships and grants, with the average undergraduate need-based scholarship totaling $11,070.

CAREER INFORMATION FROM PAYSCALE.COM	
ROI Rating	94
Bachelors and No Higher	
Median starting salary	$70,800
Median mid-career salary	$131,900
At Least Bachelors	
Median starting salary	$71,800
Median mid-career salary	$135,500
Alumni with high job meaning	48%
Degrees awarded in STEM subjects	80%

SELECTIVITY	
Admissions Rating	98
# of applicants	31,497
% of applicants accepted	23
% of acceptees attending	39
# offered a place on the wait list	4,241
% accepting a place on wait list	67
% admitted from wait list	1

FRESHMAN PROFILE	
Range SAT EBRW	370–730
Range SAT Math	720–790
Range ACT Composite	30–34
Average HS GPA	4.0
% graduated top 10% of class	88
% graduated top 25% of class	98
% graduated top 50% of class	99

DEADLINES	
Early action	
Deadline	10/15
Notification	1/13
Regular	
Priority	10/15
Deadline	1/1
Notification	3/15
Nonfall registration?	Yes

FINANCIAL FACTS	
Financial Aid Rating	83
Annual in-state tuition	$10,008
Annual out-of-state tuition	$30,604
Room and board	$14,126
Required fees	$2,410
Books and supplies	$800
Average frosh need-based scholarship	$7,831
Average UG need-based scholarship	$7,194
% needy frosh rec. need-based scholarship or grant aid	41
% needy UG rec. need-based scholarship or grant aid	52
% needy frosh rec. non-need-based scholarship or grant aid	69
% needy UG rec. non-need-based scholarship or grant aid	60
% needy frosh rec. need-based self-help aid	58
% needy UG rec. need-based self-help aid	65
% frosh rec. any financial aid	63
% UG rec. any financial aid	72
% UG borrow to pay for school	40
Average cumulative indebtedness	$32,398
% frosh need fully met	52
% ugrads need fully met	40
Average % of frosh need met	66
Average % of ugrad need met	54

Gettysburg College

Admissions Office, Eisenhower House, Gettysburg, PA 17325-1484 • Admissions: 717-337-6100 • Fax: 717-337-6145

CAMPUS LIFE

Quality of Life Rating	92
Fire Safety Rating	98
Green Rating	80
Type of school	Private
Affiliation	Lutheran
Environment	Village

STUDENTS

Total undergrad enrollment	2,405
% male/female	47/53
% from out of state	74
% frosh from public high school	70
% frosh live on campus	100
% ugrads live on campus	94
# of fraternities (% ugrad men join)	9 (32)
# of sororities (% ugrad women join)	7 (35)
% African American	4
% Asian	2
% Caucasian	75
% Hispanic	8
% Native American	<1
% Pacific Islander	0
% Two or more races	3
% Race and/or ethnicity unknown	2
% international	7
# of countries represented	38

ACADEMICS

Academic Rating	95
% students returning for sophomore year	90
% students graduating within 4 years	79
% students graduating within 6 years	84
Calendar	Semester
Student/faculty ratio	9:1
Profs interesting rating	92
Profs accessible rating	93

Most classes have 10–19 students. Most lab/discussion sessions have fewer than 10 students.

MOST POPULAR MAJORS
Psychology, Political Science, Business/ Commerce, Biology/Health Sciences

ABOUT THE SCHOOL

Gettysburg is a national college of liberal arts and sciences located in Gettysburg, Pennsylvania. Gettysburg's 2,500 students are actively involved in an academically rigorous and personally challenging educational experience offered through a wonderful "combination of small student-body and world-class faculty and administrative" members. "The small class sizes are a huge benefit for students, as they get individual attention, [something] so hard to find at most other institutions." With an average class size of seventeen and a student-to-faculty ratio of 9:1, there are no bystanders here—personal interactions and supports are part of the educational process. Don't be surprised if professors here know you by first name. One visiting, prospective undergraduate explains: "I met a biology professor in the college parking lot [who] took two hours out of his day to show us around the Science Center, the labs, and classrooms and even introduce me to the chair of the biology department." At Gettysburg, first-years participate in the First-Year Seminar, in which students analyze, investigate, research, discuss, and debate a diverse range of topics and themes. "The small environment provides the best conditions for participating in class, getting to know professors on a personal basis, and having a voice on campus," all while brazenly engaging whatever academic pursuits the student desires. "There is something for everyone," a sophomore expresses, "from trumpet performance to Latin studies to globalization to health sciences." Gettysburg's world-famous Sunderman Conservatory of Music attracts many artists to its campus and enables students to "seriously study music while allowing [them] to explore other areas of study as well." Research opportunities are copious, and students graduate from Gettysburg with hands-on learning experiences attractive to employers and graduate schools alike. "The Center for Career Engagement does a great job of helping students of all class years find internships, externships, and job-shadowing opportunities."

BANG FOR YOUR BUCK

Gettysburg College awarded about 60.2 million (2017-18) in merit scholarships and need-based grants benefiting 64 percent of the student body. Both need-based and merit-based awards are available. Merit-based scholarships range from $10,000 to $26,000 per year. A separate application is not required; decisions on merit scholarship recipients are made as part of the admissions process. Music talent scholarships are also available. The average first-year student grant and/or scholarship award was $36,718 (2017-18).

STUDENT LIFE

Students at Gettysburg love the place. A lot of students "spend a significant amount of time volunteering and are involved in on-campus groups during the week." There's always something going on at Gettysburg, meaning "it is never 'what is there to do tonight?' but instead 'what am I going to choose to do?'" The Campus Activities Board usually has something going on, whether they are hosting a concert, showing a movie, or having a dance in the Attic (an on-campus hangout spot), and the diverse Greek-oriented social life makes "a place for everyone regardless of who you are." Studying abroad is hugely popular, and most students "participate in sports on some level or take advantage of our amazing fitness facility."

Gettysburg College

FINANCIAL AID: 717-337-6611 • E-MAIL: ADMISS@GETTYSBURG.EDU • WEBSITE: WWW.GETTYSBURG.EDU

CAREER

There is excellent financial support for students who "want to do really cool things with their education" such as study abroad, internships, or academic conferences. The study abroad program is "impressively large," and the opportunities for gaining work experience both in the United States and abroad are "endless." The Center for Career Engagement "does a great job of helping students find internships, externships and job shadowing opportunities" and "the support from the alumni helps with having lots of options for internships and jobs," says a student. Aside from job fairs, resume reviews, and online resources, the center's Career Immersion Trips are three-day intensive career programs that offer students a chance to get firsthand insight into their possible career up close and in person. Of the Gettysburg graduates who visited PayScale.com 40 percent reported a feeling that their job had a meaningful impact on the world, and an average starting salary of $52,600.

GENERAL INFO

Athletics (Intercollegiate): *Men:* Baseball, basketball, cross-country, football, golf, lacrosse, soccer, swimming, tennis, track/field (outdoor), track/field (indoor), wrestling. *Women:* Basketball, cross-country, field hockey, golf, lacrosse, soccer, softball, swimming, tennis, track/field (outdoor), track/field (indoor), volleyball.

FINANCIAL AID

Students should submit: CSS Profile; FAFSA. Regular filing deadline is 1/15. The Princeton Review suggests that all financial aid forms be submitted as soon as possible after October 1. *Need-based scholarships/grants offered:* College/university scholarship or grant aid from institutional funds, Federal Pell, private scholarships, SEOG, state scholarships/grants. *Loan aid offered:* Direct PLUS Loans, Direct Subsidized Loans, Direct Unsubsidized Loans. Applicants will be notified of awards on or about 4/1. Federal Work-Study Program available. Institutional employment available.

BOTTOM LINE

At Gettysburg College, tuition and fees cost about $54,480 per year. Room and board on campus costs about $13,010. Prospective students should also factor in the annual cost of books, supplies, transportation, and personal expenses. Overall, about 64 percent of Gettysburg students receive some sort of funding from their "irresistible...and generous financial aid program."

CAREER INFORMATION FROM PAYSCALE.COM	
ROI Rating	91
Bachelors and No Higher	
Median starting salary	$55,900
Median mid-career salary	$113,600
At Least Bachelors	
Median starting salary	$57,600
Median mid-career salary	$114,900
Alumni with high job meaning	41%
Degrees awarded in STEM subjects	24%

SELECTIVITY	
Admissions Rating	92
# of applicants	6,384
% of applicants accepted	46
% of acceptees attending	25
# of early decision applicants	415
% accepted early decision	69

FRESHMAN PROFILE	
Range SAT EBRW	640–710
Range SAT Math	630–700
Range ACT Composite	26–30
% graduated top 10% of class	65
% graduated top 25% of class	84
% graduated top 50% of class	99

DEADLINES	
Early decision	
Deadline	11/15
Notification	12/15
Other ED Deadline	1/15
Other ED Notification	2/15
Regular	
Priority	1/15
Deadline	1/15
Notification	4/1

FINANCIAL FACTS	
Financial Aid Rating	94
Annual tuition	$54,480
Room and board	$13,010
Books and supplies	$500
Average frosh need-based scholarship	$36,718
Average UG need-based scholarship	$36,153
% needy frosh rec. need-based scholarship or grant aid	97
% needy UG rec. need-based scholarship or grant aid	97
% needy frosh rec. non-need-based scholarship or grant aid	54
% needy UG rec. non-need-based scholarship or grant aid	50
% needy frosh rec. need-based self-help aid	89
% needy UG rec. need-based self-help aid	84
% frosh rec. any financial aid	60
% UG rec. any financial aid	60
% UG borrow to pay for school	62
Average cumulative indebtedness	$31,323
% frosh need fully met	90
% ugrads need fully met	90
Average % of frosh need met	90
Average % of ugrad need met	90

Grinnell College

1103 PARK STREET, GRINNELL, IA 50112 • ADMISSIONS: 641-269-3600 • FAX: 641-269-4800

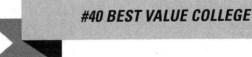

#40 BEST VALUE COLLEGE

ABOUT THE SCHOOL

Grinnell College is a smorgasbord of intellectual delights in a tiny, quintessential Iowa town that is surrounded by cornfields. The arts and sciences facilities here are world-class. The academic atmosphere is extremely challenging and stressful. Classes are hard and demanding. The ability to handle a lot of reading and writing is vital. Even though Grinnell boasts of an "open curriculum [and] low faculty-to-student ratio," the setting demands that students "work hard [and] play hard." Undergrads here often complete work that would be considered graduate-level at other institutions. At the same time, there isn't much in the way of competition; students bring the pressure on themselves. Classes are small and intimate. Professors are crazy accessible. The curriculum is completely open except for a freshman tutorial—a writing-intensive course that introduces academic thinking and research. Beyond that, there are no subject- matter requirements for obtaining a degree from Grinnell, as the school "encourages liberal arts academic exploration." Students are free to design their own paths to graduation. Mentored advanced projects provide a chance to work closely with a faculty member on scholarly research or the creation of a work of art. Fifty to 60 percent of every graduating class is accepted onto a wide range of off-campus study programs both domestic and abroad. On campus, Scholars' Convocation enriches the college's academic community by bringing notable speakers to campus.

BANG FOR YOUR BUCK

Grinnell was founded by a group of Iowa pioneers in 1843, and that pioneering spirit still informs the college's approach to education. Grinnell's endowment these days is in the range of a billion dollars. That's billion, with a B, so admission here is in no way contingent on your economic situation. If you can get admitted here (no small feat), Grinnell will meet 100 percent of your financial need. The college is even moving to meet the full demonstrated institutional need of select international students. In a typical year, Grinnell awards over ten times more in grants than in loans. As part of the culture of alumni support, the college also raises specific funds from alumni to reduce, at the time of graduation, the indebtedness of seniors who have demonstrated a solid work ethic both academically and cocurricularly. Eligible students may designate one summer devoted to either an approved Grinnell-sponsored internship or summer research at Grinnell. In return, the expected summer earnings contribution of $2,500 will be eliminated for that one summer only. One student notes that "on-campus employment is virtually guaranteed."

STUDENT LIFE

Undergrads here seem to live at fairly frenzied clip. Indeed, "Grinnellians pride themselves on working hard, but also playing hard." And, thankfully, there's plenty of fun to be had. To begin with, "every weekend there are movies, concerts, and parties planned and run by students all going on in addition to other events planned by the college." Additionally, "a lot of students volunteer for fun at the animal shelter or our Liberal Arts in Prison program, or they join an organization to learn something new or change the world." Moreover, Grinnell definitely has a party scene, one that is viewed as "thriving, quirky, welcoming, and casual." And "even [when it does get] raucous...you will [still] find people discussing 17th

Grinnell College

FINANCIAL AID: 641-269-3250 • E-MAIL: ASKGRIN@GRINNELL.EDU • WEBSITE: WWW.GRINNELL.EDU

century literature or debating hot political topics." Overall, Grinnell provides "an amazing mix of silly times and very smart people."

CAREER

Grinnell undergrads do pretty well for themselves. Indeed, according to PayScale.com, the average starting salary for these students is $48,800. Students are thankful that the "Grinnell College alumni...are very proactive in providing students with assistance in the form of... employment, or mentorship." And, even if undergrads are unable to hook up with an alum, they can always turn to the Center for Careers, Life and Service (CLS). Besides interview prep, job shadowing programs, and on-campus recruiting, the center also houses the Service Learning and Civic Engagement Program, which helps students find co-curricular service learning opportunities. Grinnellink internships are specific (and paid!) opportunities with college alumni and friends and are open exclusively to Grinnell students. Off-campus study experiences, whether abroad like Grinnell-in-London, or at a U.S. location like Grinnell-in Washington, offer more ways for experiential learning to complement coursework.

GENERAL INFO

Activities: Choral groups, concert band, dance, drama/theater, jazz band, literary magazine, music ensembles, musical theater, pep band, radio station, student government, student newspaper, student-run film society, symphony orchestra, yearbook, campus ministries, international student organization. **Organizations:** 240 registered organizations, 2 honor societies, 12 religious organizations. **Athletics (Intercollegiate):** *Men:* Baseball, basketball, cross-country, diving, football, golf, soccer, swimming, tennis, track/field (outdoor), track/field (indoor). *Women:* Basketball, cross-country, diving, golf, soccer, softball, swimming, tennis, track/field (outdoor), track/field (indoor), volleyball.

FINANCIAL AID

Students should submit: CSS Profile; FAFSA; Noncustodial PROFILE. Priority filing deadline is 1/15. The Princeton Review suggests that all financial aid forms be submitted as soon as possible after October 1. *Need-based scholarships/grants offered:* College/university scholarship or grant aid from institutional funds, Federal Pell, private scholarships, SEOG, state scholarships/grants. *Loan aid offered:* Direct PLUS Loans, Direct Subsidized Loans, Direct Unsubsidized Loans. Applicants will be notified of awards on or about 4/1. Federal Work-Study Program available. Institutional employment available.

BOTTOM LINE

The tab for tuition, fees, room and board, and everything else at Grinnell comes to about $62,864 per year. About 88 percent of Grinnell's first-year students receive some form of financial aid, though. On average, need-based financial aid packages for freshman includes a $39,444 scholarship.

CAREER INFORMATION FROM PAYSCALE.COM	
ROI Rating	92
Bachelors and No Higher	
Median starting salary	$51,200
Median mid-career salary	$96,700
At Least Bachelors	
Median starting salary	$53,800
Median mid-career salary	$103,500
Alumni with high job meaning	47%
Degrees awarded in STEM subjects	41%

SELECTIVITY	
Admissions Rating	95
# of applicants	5,850
% of applicants accepted	29
% of acceptees attending	26
# offered a place on the wait list	1,126
% accepting a place on wait list	47
% admitted from wait list	2
# of early decision applicants	322
% accepted early decision	61

FRESHMAN PROFILE	
Range SAT EBRW	640–740
Range SAT Math	670–770
Range ACT Composite	30–34
% graduated top 10% of class	69
% graduated top 25% of class	91
% graduated top 50% of class	99

DEADLINES	
Early decision	
Deadline	11/15
Notification	mid Dec
Other ED Deadline	1/1
Other ED Notification	late Jan
Regular	
Deadline	1/15
Nonfall registration?	No

FINANCIAL FACTS	
Financial Aid Rating	98
Annual tuition	$51,924
Room and board	$12,810
Required fees	$468
Books and supplies	$900
Average frosh need-based scholarship	$41,902
Average UG need-based scholarship	$41,344
% needy frosh rec. need-based scholarship or grant aid	100
% needy UG rec. need-based scholarship or grant aid	100
% needy frosh rec. non-need-based scholarship or grant aid	13
% needy UG rec. non-need-based scholarship or grant aid	12
% needy frosh rec. need-based self-help aid	87
% needy UG rec. need-based self-help aid	88
% frosh rec. any financial aid	86
% UG rec. any financial aid	87
% UG borrow to pay for school	55
Average cumulative indebtedness	$19,392
% frosh need fully met	100
% ugrads need fully met	100
Average % of frosh need met	100
Average % of ugrad need met	100

Grove City College

100 CAMPUS DRIVE, GROVE CITY, PA 16127-2104 • ADMISSIONS: 724-458-2100 • FAX: 724-458-3395

CAMPUS LIFE

Quality of Life Rating	**89**
Fire Safety Rating	**94**
Green Rating	**63**
Type of school	Private
Environment	Village

STUDENTS

Total undergrad enrollment	2,327
% male/female	51/49
% from out of state	44
% frosh from public high school	59
% frosh live on campus	98
% ugrads live on campus	95
# of fraternities (% ugrad men join)	10 (14)
# of sororities (% ugrad women join)	8 (20)
% African American	1
% Asian	2
% Caucasian	92
% Hispanic	1
% Native American	<1
% Pacific Islander	0
% Two or more races	3
% Race and/or ethnicity unknown	0
% international	1
# of countries represented	13

ACADEMICS

Academic Rating	**87**
% students returning for sophomore year	89
% students graduating within 4 years	78
% students graduating within 6 years	83
Calendar	Semester
Student/faculty ratio	13:1
Profs interesting rating	83
Profs accessible rating	93

Most classes have 10–19 students. Most lab/discussion sessions have 20-29 students.

MOST POPULAR MAJORS
Speech Communication and Rhetoric; Mechanical Engineering; Biology/Biological Sciences

ABOUT THE SCHOOL

Pennsylvania's Grove City College is a small, faith-based school with a strong liberal arts and sciences curriculum and a high job placement rate for graduates. One student says, "I wanted to attend a school that would not simply challenge me academically, but grow me as a whole individual. The opportunities to serve and grow spiritually, emotionally, and socially are tremendous at Grove City College." Students come here for a rigorous curriculum in sixty programs of study, and appreciate the perks of the small college enrollment: "My professors are extremely accessible and helpful. The student-to-teacher ratio is very low and professors know you on a very personal level." Grove City College provides a unique opportunity for a Christ-centered education because "the environment is friendly, the classes are insightful, the professors are accessible, and the campus is beautiful." It is a place for "pursuing Christ and pursuing your personal best."

BANG FOR YOUR BUCK

Students going to Grove City feel confident that their education will give them a head start once they graduate. One student says, "In my opinion, the greatest strength of my school is the job placement rate. The academics are known to be excellent, so employers look to hire Grove City grads. It was reassuring to know that after four years all the hard work would pay off because a large majority of students are employed. In addition, as an accounting major, hearing that almost 100 percent of accounting majors have jobs before the senior year made a large impact on my college decision." Be forewarned that "Grove City College doesn't accept federal financial aid or grants, but that doesn't mean students can't receive financial assistance from the states in which they live." The college website has information detailing specific grants available to students in each state, and also encourages students to apply for merit and need based aid from the school when they apply for admission. Additionally, Grove City College offers work programs for students up to 20 hours per week (or 10 hour maximum for frosh).

STUDENT LIFE

Grove City College attracts serious students with "a culture that focuses on religion and academics." As one student explains, "The college as a whole does not have many restricting or molding codes and protocols. Yes, we have chapel credit requirements, and yes, we have restrictive visitation hours, but the codes and rules are not what make Grove City campus the way it is. The students are what bring the Christian atmosphere." Dorm life is big here as 96 percent of Grove City College students choose to live in one of eleven on-campus residence halls and one on-campus apartment complex.

Choosing from approximately 200 on-campus organizations from Greek life to athletics, arts, business, and worship, Grove City students have a real voice on campus: "Students run the Bible studies and the outreach programs. Students are the ones to choose how to dress, or how to speak. As a whole, the student body is hardworking, and chooses to live up to, and create, the Christian atmosphere at Grove City."

CAREER

Boasting "very high job placement rates," Grove City prides itself on helping students succeed during and after their formal education. One student says, "The greatest strength of my school is how dedicated they are to helping students find a job and create a future.

Grove City College

FINANCIAL AID: 724-458-3300 • E-MAIL: ADMISSIONS@GCC.EDU • WEBSITE: WWW.GCC.EDU

The Career Services Office is dedicated to helping students in any way that they can and have special events to help students network." Last year alone, over 170 employers and graduate schools attended the fall Career Fair and the college hosted 247 on-campus recruiting events with employers like Amazon, IBM, PNC Financial Services Group, and Nestle. In 2016, 96 percent of Grove City graduates secured employment or admission to graduate school.

GENERAL INFO

Activities: Choral groups, concert band, dance, drama/theater, jazz band, literary magazine, marching band, music ensembles, musical theater, opera, pep band, radio station, student government, student newspaper, symphony orchestra, television station, yearbook, campus ministries, International Student Organization. **Organizations:** More than approximately 200 registered organizations, 26 honor societies, 19 religious organizations. 10 fraternities, 8 sororities. **Athletics (Intercollegiate):** *Men:* baseball, basketball, cross-country, diving, football, golf, lacrosse, soccer, swimming, tennis, track/field (indoor and outdoor). *Women:* basketball, cross-country, diving, golf, soccer, softball, swimming, tennis, track/field (indoor and outdoor), volleyball, water polo. **On-Campus Highlights:** Student Union, Chapel, Hall of Arts and Letters, Fitness Center, Ketler Recreation Room.

FINANCIAL AID

Students should submit: Institution's own financial aid form. Regular filing deadline is April 15. The Princeton Review suggests that all financial aid forms be submitted as soon as possible after October 1. *Need-based scholarships/grants offered:* College/university scholarship or grant aid from institutional funds; Private scholarships; State scholarships/grants. *Loan aid offered:* State and private alternative loans. Applicants will be notified of awards on a rolling basis beginning 3/1. Institutional employment available.

BOTTOM LINE

Tuition is $17,930, plus room and board, $9,770. Again, the college offers many scholarships and student employment. The college does not accept federal aid, as a means of safeguarding its institutional autonomy, but it does offer plenty of alternative funding options for any student who may need assistance in subsidizing their tuition.

CAREER INFORMATION FROM PAYSCALE.COM	
ROI Rating	89
Bachelors and No Higher	
Median starting salary	$52,600
Median mid-career salary	$98,300
At Least Bachelors	
Median starting salary	$53,500
Median mid-career salary	$103,300
Alumni with high job meaning	53%
Degrees awarded in STEM subjects	29%

SELECTIVITY	
Admissions Rating	86
# of applicants	1,783
% of applicants accepted	80
% of acceptees attending	45
# offered a place on the wait list	114
% accepting a place on wait list	21
% admitted from wait list	63
# of early decision applicants	349
% accepted early decision	85

FRESHMAN PROFILE	
Range SAT EBRW	537–587
Range SAT Math	534–662
Range ACT Composite	23–32
Minimum paper TOEFL	550
Minimum internet-based TOEFL	79
Average HS GPA	3.7
% graduated top 10% of class	35
% graduated top 25% of class	84
% graduated top 50% of class	90

DEADLINES	
Early decision	
Deadline	11/1
Notification	12/15
Other ED Deadline	12/1
Other ED Notification	1/15
Regular	
Deadline	1/20
Notification	2/20
Nonfall registration?	Yes

FINANCIAL FACTS	
Financial Aid Rating	79
Annual tuition	$17,930
Room and board	$9,770
Required fees	$0
Average frosh need-based scholarship	$7,989
Average UG need-based scholarship	$7,424
% needy frosh rec. need-based scholarship or grant aid	100
% needy UG rec. need-based scholarship or grant aid	99
% needy frosh rec. non-need-based scholarship or grant aid	12
% needy UG rec. non-need-based scholarship or grant aid	8
% needy frosh rec. need-based self-help aid	56
% needy UG rec. need-based self-help aid	65
% frosh rec. any financial aid	75
% UG rec. any financial aid	78
% UG borrow to pay for school	59
Average cumulative indebtedness	$40,747
% frosh need fully met	13
% ugrads need fully met	9

Gustavus Adolphus College

800 College Avenue, Saint Peter, MN 56082 • Admissions: 507-933-7676 • Fax: 507-933-7474

CAMPUS LIFE	
Quality of Life Rating	94
Fire Safety Rating	96
Green Rating	60*
Type of school	Private
Affiliation	Lutheran
Environment	Village

STUDENTS	
Total undergrad enrollment	2,190
% male/female	44/56
% from out of state	17
% frosh from public high school	94
% frosh live on campus	99
% ugrads live on campus	95
# of fraternities (% ugrad men join)	5 (13)
# of sororities	5
% African American	2%
% Asian	5%
% Caucasian	78%
% Hispanic	5%
% Native American	<1%
% Pacific Islander	<1%
% Two or more races	4%
% Race and/or ethnicity unknown	1%
% international	5%
# of countries represented	26

ACADEMICS	
Academic Rating	97
% students returning for sophomore year	88
students graduating within 4 years	79%
students graduating within 6 years	80%
Calendar	4/1/4
Student/faculty ratio	11:1
Profs interesting rating	96
Profs accessible rating	94
Most classes have 20-29 students.	
Most lab/discussion sessions have 10-19 students.	

MOST POPULAR MAJORS
Biology/Biological Sciences; Psychology; Business/Commerce

ABOUT THE SCHOOL

Students who attend Gustavus Adolphus, a private liberal arts college in Saint Peter, Minnesota, join a "very welcoming" and "close" community of academics and intellectuals. Not to mention they have access to a "nationally acclaimed dining hall!" Perhaps more importantly, Gustavus offers some phenomenal academic programs. Along with its renowned music department, the college is especially "strong in [the] natural sciences, psychology and economics." Moreover, it does a tremendous job of fostering "personal relationships...between faculty and students." As one impressed undergrad shares, "The professors and administrators truly care about each student, and are involved in our lives. I have watched hockey games on campus while sitting next to President Bergman." Professors are also "really passionate about they are teaching" and work diligently to make sure their lectures are "engaging." Further, they make it abundantly clear that "their research/other interests come second to their students." And they're often "in reach either through office hours or email practically 24/7."

BANG FOR YOUR BUCK

By and large, students find that Gustavus Adolphus provides "excellent" financial aid. As one amazed undergrad shares, "You can get all the help that you need simply by asking because [the administration] genuinely want[s] you to stay." These statements are certainly bolstered by the fact that 90 percent of students here receive some type of aid, be it scholarships, loans or work-study gigs. In fact, the college doles out over $14 million in scholarships and grants to incoming students. Even better, Gustavus Adolphus simplifies the process by automatically considering all applicants for renewable, merit-based scholarships. These include the Dean's Scholarship which provides select students with between $13,000 to $23,000 annually and the President's Scholarship which awards up to $26,000 per year. There's also the Gustavus Legacy Award which offers $2,500 (for four years) to students who are the children or siblings of alumni.

STUDENT LIFE

Be forewarned: "Life at Gustavus is very busy." Most students "keep their days as full...as possible" by getting involved with "athletics, clubs and the performing arts" as well as "community service." Plus, "there are always fun activities around campus." For example, there are "movies in [the] auditorium every weekend" and in the winter, you will often find students "sledding on trays down one of the hills on campus." Undergrads can also enjoy "bingo nights," "comedians," "Greek life," and "Harry Potter themed...trivia." Additionally, the college sponsors numerous "guest speakers, big concerts (with performers such as Timeflies and Gavin DeGraw) and [hosts the] annual President's Ball." And though the "surrounding community is quite small...there are many good sports bars and a bowling alley to visit."

CAREER

Undergrads at Gustavus can easily reap the benefits of a "wonderful career development [staff]." Thanks to the efforts of the Office of Career Development, "over 90 percent of [students] participat[e] in [an] internship, career exploration, clinical, student-teaching...[or] service-learning [project]" prior to graduation. Undergrads can also utilize Career Development for résumé reviews and to schedule mock interviews. The office also hosts numerous events like the health professions fair, nursing fair, education fair, and a non-profit job and internship fair. To motivate students, Career Development sponsors the Gustavus Network Challenge which encourages undergrads to network and then submit their stories and experiences. The office

Gustavus Adolphus College

FINANCIAL AID: 507-933-7527 • E-MAIL: ADMISSION@GUSTAVUS.EDU • WEBSITE: WWW.GUSTAVUS.EDU

chooses the top submissions and the selected students win gift cards. If you need any more proof, just consider the fact that the average starting salary for Gustavus grads is $48,200 and the average mid-career salary is $94,000, according to PayScale.com.

GENERAL INFO

Activities: Choral groups, concert band, dance, drama/theater, jazz band, literary magazine, music ensembles, musical theater, pep band, radio station, student government, student newspaper, symphony orchestra, television station, yearbook. 120 registered organizations, 11 honor societies, 8 religious organizations. 5 fraternities, 5 sororities. **Athletics (Intercollegiate):** *Men:* baseball, basketball, cross-country, diving, football, golf, ice hockey, skiingnordiccross-country, soccer, swimming, tennis, track/field (outdoor), track/field (indoor). *Women:* basketball, cross-country, diving, golf, gymnastics, ice hockey, skiing (nordic/cross-country), soccer, softball, swimming, tennis, track/field (outdoor), track/field (indoor), volleyball. **On-Campus Highlights:** Campus Center, Courtyard Cafe, Lund Athletic Center, Christ Chapel, Linnaeus Arboretum, With over 75% of students remaining on campus during a typical weekend (according to our Dining Service), our students actively use the entire campus. As there are no city streets intersecting our campus, Gusties enjoy their home on the hill.

FINANCIAL AID

Students should submit: FAFSA. Priority filing deadline is 4/1. The Princeton Review suggests that all financial aid forms be submitted as soon as possible after October 1. Need-based scholarships/grants offered: College/university scholarship or grant aid from institutional funds; Federal Pell; Private scholarships; SEOG; State scholarships/grants. Loan aid offered: Direct PLUS loans; Direct Subsidized Stafford Loans; Direct Unsubsidized Stafford Loans. Applicants will be notified of awards on a rolling basis beginning 12/15. Federal Work-Study Program available. Institutional employment available.

THE BOTTOM LINE

For the 2017-2018 academic year, Gustavus Adolphus College is charging $43,590 for tuition. Additionally, students living on campus can expect to pay to pay $6,160 for housing. Individuals on the meal plan will be charged another $3,510. All students can expect to pay $683 in miscellaneous fees and should budget for books as well as personal expenses.

CAREER INFORMATION FROM PAYSCALE.COM

ROI Rating	89
Bachelors and No Higher	
Median starting salary	$49,700
Median mid-career salary	$96,500
At Least Bachelors	
Median starting salary	$51,100
Median mid-career salary	$100,500
Alumni with high job meaning	47%
Degrees awarded in STEM subjects	22%

SELECTIVITY

Admissions Rating	84
# of applicants	4,834
% of applicants accepted	68
% of acceptees attending	18

FRESHMAN PROFILE

Range ACT Composite	24–30
Minimum paper TOEFL	550
Minimum internet-based TOEFL	80
Average HS GPA	3.6
% graduated top 10% of class	33
% graduated top 25% of class	65
% graduated top 50% of class	93

DEADLINES

Early action	
Deadline	11/1
Notification	11/15
Regular	
Deadline	4/1
Nonfall registration?	Yes

FINANCIAL FACTS

Financial Aid Rating	86
Annual tuition	$44,900
Room and board	$9,910
Required fees	$500
Books and supplies	$900
Average frosh need-based scholarship	$32,990
Average UG need-based scholarship	$32,482
% needy frosh rec. need-based scholarship or grant aid	100%
% needy UG rec. need-based scholarship or grant aid	100%
% needy frosh rec. non-need-based scholarship or grant aid	14%
% needy UG rec. non-need-based scholarship or grant aid	9%
% needy frosh rec. need-based self-help aid	100%
% needy UG rec. need-based self-help aid	100%

Hamilton College

Office of Admission, Clinton, NY 13323 • Admissions: 315-859-4421 • Fax: 315-859-4457

CAMPUS LIFE

Quality of Life Rating	**89**
Fire Safety Rating	**92**
Green Rating	**60***
Type of school	Private
Environment	Rural

STUDENTS

Total undergrad enrollment	1,885
% male/female	47/53
% from out of state	70
% frosh from public high school	58
% frosh live on campus	100
% ugrads live on campus	100
# of fraternities (% ugrad men join)	9 (26)
# of sororities (% ugrad women join)	7 (16)
% African American	4
% Asian	7
% Caucasian	64
% Hispanic	9
% Native American	<1
% Pacific Islander	0
% Two or more races	4
% Race and/or ethnicity unknown	6
% international	6
# of countries represented	45

ACADEMICS

Academic Rating	**94**
% students returning for sophomore year	96
% students graduating within 4 years	90
% students graduating within 6 years	94
Calendar	Semester
Student/faculty ratio	9:1
Profs interesting rating	96
Profs accessible rating	92
Most classes have 10–19 students.	

MOST POPULAR MAJORS

Mathematics; Economics; Political Science and Government

ABOUT THE SCHOOL

Hamilton provides about 140 research opportunities for students to work closely with science and nonscience faculty mentors each summer. Many students' choice of college depends on the strength of the school's academic department most relevant to their major: "I am amazed by the incredible resources—especially for the sciences—and couldn't believe all of the opportunities and grants they offer to students who are passionate about pursuing their studies outside of the classroom," says one sophomore. Oftentimes, the work leads to a paper published in a professional journal and gives the student a leg-up when competing for national postgraduate fellowships and grants. The college also provides about eighty stipends each summer so students can get career-related experience pursuing internships that are otherwise unpaid. A student contends that "the school has a lot of active alumni, so the networking opportunities are great. Many students find internships or jobs just through the alumni connections."

BANG FOR YOUR BUCK

Once you are accepted, the financial aid office will make your Hamilton education affordable through a comprehensive program of scholarships, loans, and campus jobs. The financial aid budget is approximately $40 million annually, enabling the school to make good on its commitment to meet 100 percent of students' demonstrated need. One student says, "The school offered me a generous amount of financial aid." The average financial aid package for students is $47,372. The average Hamilton College grant is $42,968 and does not have to be repaid.

STUDENT LIFE

There are two types of students at Hamilton: "Light-siders" are more preppy, and "dark-siders" are typically more artistic or hipster. No matter which group they fall into, students "are incredibly devoted to their school work, but they are also devoted to having a good time." People attend athletic events, student improv comedy shows, poetry readings, community service events, plays and concerts, and "very successfully compensate for our isolated location with themed parties, clubs, and other eclectic activities." In addition to all-campus parties, Hamilton has "Late Nights" every weekend, which are alcohol-free events "like a Glowstick party or a MarioKart Tournament where students can enjoy great local Indian takeout and a fun night." Hamilton has "a very intellectually stimulating academic environment," and it is not at all uncommon to find a whole dorm room debating about an economic theory. People who have cars can also go downtown or into New Hartford in their free time, but most students choose to spend their time on campus.

CAREER

At Hamilton, there is "a real investment in ensuring that every student is successful and happy both here and after graduation." The Career Center suggests that every student have two career-related experiences before they graduate, and the Handshake career development platform helps to link students up with internships or

Hamilton College

FINANCIAL AID: 800-859-4413 • E-MAIL: ADMISSION@HAMILTON.EDU • WEBSITE: WWW.HAMILTON.EDU

jobs, including many that come via Hamilton alumni. There are many workshops, industry-focused programs, and employer visits held throughout the year, including the half-day Sophomore Jumpstart! for second-year students beginning their career or internship search. Peer Advisors are students who are trained to critique cover letters and resumes, and offer advice on all aspects of finding jobs through events such as the popular How I Got My Internship lunch series. All incoming students are assigned a dedicated career advisor to work with during their four years at Hamilton. Of the Hamilton graduates who visited PayScale.com, the average starting salary was $60,400.

GENERAL INFO

Activities: Choral groups, dance, drama/theater, jazz band, literary magazine, music ensembles, musical theater, radio station, student government, student newspaper, student-run film society, symphony orchestra, yearbook, campus ministries, International Student Organization. **Organizations:** 189 registered organizations, 8 honor societies, 6 religious organizations. 9 fraternities, 6 sororities. **Athletics (Intercollegiate):** *Men:* baseball, basketball, crew/rowing, cross-country, diving, football, golf, ice hockey, lacrosse, soccer, squash, swimming, tennis, track/field (outdoor), track/field (indoor). *Women:* basketball, crew/rowing, cross-country, diving, field hockey, golf, ice hockey, lacrosse, soccer, softball, squash, swimming, tennis, track/field (outdoor), track/field (indoor), volleyball. **On-Campus Highlights:** Wellin Museum of Art, Root Glen, Outdoor Leadership Center, Café Opus and Café Opus 2, Arthur Levitt Public Affairs Center.

FINANCIAL AID

Students should submit: CSS Profile, FAFSA; Institution's own financial aid form, Noncustodial PROFILE. Regular filing deadline is 1/15. The Princeton Review suggests that all financial aid forms be submitted as soon as possible after October 1. *Need-based scholarships/grants offered:* College/university scholarship or grant aid from institutional funds, Federal Pell, private scholarships, SEOG, state scholarships/grants. *Loan aid offered:* Direct PLUS Loans, Direct Subsidized Loans, Direct Unsubsidized Loans. Applicants will be notified of awards on or about 4/1. Federal Work-Study Program available. Institutional employment available.

THE BOTTOM LINE

Hamilton College is one of the nation's top liberal arts colleges, and you certainly get what you pay for here. The total cost of tuition, room and board, and everything else adds up to about $66,170 per year. Hamilton is need-blind and pledges to meet 100 percent of students' demonstrated need.

CAREER INFORMATION FROM PAYSCALE.COM	
ROI Rating	91
Bachelors and No Higher	
Median starting salary	$61,000
Median mid-career salary	$96,100
At Least Bachelors	
Median starting salary	$62,100
Median mid-career salary	$105,400
Alumni with high job meaning	48%
Degrees awarded in STEM subjects	25%

SELECTIVITY	
Admissions Rating	97
# of applicants	5,678
% of applicants accepted	24
% of acceptees attending	35
# offered a place on the wait list	1,299
% accepting a place on wait list	48
% admitted from wait list	5
# of early decision applicants	620
% accepted early decision	41

FRESHMAN PROFILE	
Range SAT EBRW	680–750
Range SAT Math	680–760
Range ACT Composite	31–33
% graduated top 10% of class	77
% graduated top 25% of class	96
% graduated top 50% of class	100

DEADLINES	
Early decision	
Deadline	11/15
Notification	12/15
Other ED Deadline	1/1
Other ED Notification	2/15
Regular	
Deadline	1/1
Notification	4/1
Nonfall registration?	Yes

FINANCIAL FACTS	
Financial Aid Rating	95
Annual tuition	$52,250
Room and board	$13,400
Required fees	$520
Books and supplies	$1,000
Average frosh need-based scholarship	$42,570
Average UG need-based scholarship	$42,968
% needy frosh rec. need-based scholarship or grant aid	100
% needy UG rec. need-based scholarship or grant aid	100
% needy frosh rec. non-need-based scholarship or grant aid	0
% needy UG rec. non-need-based scholarship or grant aid	0
% needy frosh rec. need-based self-help aid	80
% needy UG rec. need-based self-help aid	81
% frosh rec. any financial aid	58
% UG rec. any financial aid	51
% UG borrow to pay for school	43
Average cumulative indebtedness	$19,281
% frosh need fully met	100
% ugrads need fully met	100
Average % of frosh need met	100
Average % of ugrad need met	100

Hampden-Sydney College

PO Box 667, Hampden-Sydney, VA 23943-0667 • Admissions: 434-223-6120 • Fax: 434-223-6346

CAMPUS LIFE

Quality of Life Rating	**89**
Fire Safety Rating	**88**
Green Rating	**65**
Type of school	Private
Affiliation	Presbyterian
Environment	Rural

STUDENTS

Total undergrad enrollment	1,046
% male/female	100/0
% from out of state	32
% frosh from public high school	66
% frosh live on campus	100
% ugrads live on campus	98
# of fraternities (% ugrad men join)	10 (30)
# of sororities (% ugrad women join)	0 (0)
% African American	4
% Asian	<1
% Caucasian	86
% Hispanic	4
% Native American	<1
% Pacific Islander	<1
% Two or more races	3
% Race and/or ethnicity unknown	2
% international	<1
# of countries represented	6

ACADEMICS

Academic Rating	**90**
% students returning for sophomore year	84
% students graduating within 4 years	61
% students graduating within 6 years	63
Calendar	Semester
Student/faculty ratio	10:1
Profs interesting rating	95
Profs accessible rating	96
Most classes have 10–19 students.	

MOST POPULAR MAJORS
Economics; Business/Managerial
Economics; History

ABOUT THE SCHOOL

Established in 1775, Hampden Sydney has the oldest private charter in the South, and its faculty and students are understandably proud of their school's traditions and history. Hampden-Sydney is also notable as one of the only all-male liberal arts schools in America. With twenty-seven majors and a twenty-four minors available to the 1,100 men who come here, the school provides "a small, intimate setting that fosters individualized learning." The college's required Rhetoric Program provides training in writing and speech and the interdisciplinary Core Cultures program ensures students learn about the past from both a Western and a global cultures perspective. Students like "the rural setting," "beautiful campus," and "the instant brotherhood" that an all-male education provides. "My school is a strong, intellectual community that seeks to transform boys into good men and good citizens," a Mathematics major says. The "great professors" are "incredibly helpful" and always accessible even outside of class. "Many even invite their students to have dinner at their homes," another student confirms. The school is also known for its strict "student-run honor code." "You will not get an education like this anywhere else," attests one Biology major.

BANG FOR YOUR BUCK

Although tuition alone is just over $42,400, Hampden-Sydney offers plenty of opportunities for scholarships and aid. The school offered over $31 million in financial assistance to the roughly 1,100 undergraduates last year. The school has several academic and "Citizen-Leader Scholarships." The academic scholarships are awarded based on GPA and SAT or ACT scores. The Citizen-Leadership Scholarships are the Eagle Scout Scholarship, the Boys State Participant Scholarship, and the Student Government President Scholarship. Hampden-Sydney has federal, state, and institutional work-study programs available. Virginia residents can also apply for the Virginia Tuition Assistance Grant.

STUDENT LIFE

The average Hampden-Sydney student is "a scholar," "an outdoorsman," "a leader," and "a gentleman." "The style of HSC is very southern prep," one student explains, adding that "the vast majority have Republican views and like to hunt, fish, and generally spend time outdoors." "Topsiders, khakis and button down Oxfords" are the required look. "Students here are very friendly because we like to promote an environment of gentlemanliness," and "brotherhood" rules the day here. "Farmville is a small town that is really about an hour away from anything that could be considered a major city," one student says. This means that students have to make their own fun. Luckily, the school provides a "plethora of extracurricular activities" and students enjoy going "to concerts that our activities committee provides" or "hang[ing] out with friends in their dorms" and, of course, "Greek life." "The Tiger Inn is a great hang-out place with couches, TVs, ping-pong tables, pool, arcade games, and computers."

Hampden-Sydney College

FINANCIAL AID: 434-223-6119 • E-MAIL: HSAPP@HSC.EDU • WEBSITE: WWW.HSC.EDU

CAREER

Hampden-Sydney's motto is "you can do anything with a degree from Hampden-Sydney College." The school works hard to help students get a leg up in an ever-competitive job market and the "reputation [of the] alumni network" at Hampden-Sydney is a major draw for applicants. One way that the school uses its impressive fifth nationally-ranked alumni network is through the use of "Handshake." The Internship Scholarship Program provides thousands of dollars to students who may not be able to afford an unpaid internship. PayScale.com reports an average starting salary of $54,800 for Hampden-Sydney grads.

GENERAL INFO

Activities: Choral groups, drama/theater, literary magazine, music ensembles, pep band, radio station, student government, student newspaper, yearbook, campus ministries, International Student Organization. **Organizations:** 45 registered organizations, 14 honor societies, 6 religious organizations. 11 fraternities. **Athletics (Intercollegiate):** *Men:* baseball, basketball, cross-country, football, golf, lacrosse, soccer, swimming, tennis, wrestling. **On-Campus Highlights:** Bortz Library, Brown Student Center, Viar-Christ Center for the Arts.

FINANCIAL AID

Students should submit: FAFSA, state aid form. Priority filing deadline is 3/1. The Princeton Review suggests that all financial aid forms be submitted as soon as possible after October 1. *Need-based scholarships/grants offered:* College/university scholarship or grant aid from institutional funds, Federal Pell, private scholarships, SEOG, state scholarships/grants. *Loan aid offered:* Direct PLUS Loans, Direct Subsidized Loans, Direct Unsubsidized Loans. Applicants will be notified of awards on a rolling basis beginning 12/15. Federal Work-Study Program available. Institutional employment available.

BOTTOM LINE

Annual tuition at Hampden-Sydney is $43,446. On-campus room and board averages about $13,558. Combined with other fees, students can expect to spend roughly $60,000 before any aid. The school's TigerWeb system lets students pay bills easily online.

CAREER INFORMATION FROM PAYSCALE.COM	
ROI Rating	89
Bachelors and No Higher	
Median starting salary	$55,800
Median mid-career salary	$114,000
At Least Bachelors	
Median starting salary	$57,200
Median mid-career salary	$117,700
Alumni with high job meaning	52%
Degrees awarded in STEM subjects	20%

SELECTIVITY	
Admissions Rating	86
# of applicants	3,573
% of applicants accepted	55
% of acceptees attending	16
# of early decision applicants	226
% accepted early decision	33

FRESHMAN PROFILE	
Range SAT EBRW	530–635
Range SAT Math	520–630
Range ACT Composite	21–27
Minimum paper TOEFL	600
Minimum internet-based TOEFL	100
Average HS GPA	3.4
% graduated top 10% of class	11
% graduated top 25% of class	30
% graduated top 50% of class	66

DEADLINES	
Early decision	
Deadline	11/1
Notification	12/1
Early action	
Deadline	1/15
Notification	2/15
Regular	
Priority	Fall prior
Deadline	3/1
Notification	4/15
Nonfall registration?	Yes

FINANCIAL FACTS	
Financial Aid Rating	87
Annual tuition	$43,446
Room and board	$13,558
Required fees	$1,950
Books and supplies	$1,000
Average frosh need-based scholarship	$29,916
Average UG need-based scholarship	$29,908
% needy frosh rec. need-based scholarship or grant aid	100
% needy UG rec. need-based scholarship or grant aid	76
% needy frosh rec. non-need-based scholarship or grant aid	19
% needy UG rec. non-need-based scholarship or grant aid	17
% needy frosh rec. need-based self-help aid	80
% needy UG rec. need-based self-help aid	17
% frosh rec. any financial aid	100
% UG rec. any financial aid	99
% UG borrow to pay for school	65
Average cumulative indebtedness	$35,921
% frosh need fully met	26
% ugrads need fully met	23

Harvard College

86 Brattle Street, Cambridge, MA 02138 • Admissions: 617-495-1551 • Fax: 617-495-8821

CAMPUS LIFE

Quality of Life Rating	**69**
Fire Safety Rating	**60***
Green Rating	**97**
Type of school	Private
Environment	City

STUDENTS

Total undergrad enrollment	6,701
% male/female	52/48
% from out of state	84
% frosh from public high school	58
% frosh live on campus	100
% ugrads live on campus	98
# of fraternities (% ugrad men join)	0 (0)
# of sororities (% ugrad women join)	0 (0)
% African American	8
% Asian	21
% Caucasian	40
% Hispanic	12
% Native American	<1
% Pacific Islander	<1
% Two or more races	7
% Race and/or ethnicity unknown	2
% international	11
# of countries represented	100

ACADEMICS

Academic Rating	**82**
% students returning for sophomore year	97
% students graduating within 4 years	84
% students graduating within 6 years	96
Calendar	Semester
Student/faculty ratio	6:1
Profs interesting rating	64
Profs accessible rating	61

Most classes have 20–29 students. Most lab/discussion sessions have 10–19 students.

MOST POPULAR MAJORS

Social Sciences; Economics; Political Science and Government

ABOUT THE SCHOOL

At Harvard College you will find a faculty of academic rock stars, intimate classes, a cosmically vast curriculum, world-class facilities (including what is arguably the best college library in the United States), a diverse student body from across the country and around the world ("The level of achievement is unbelievable"), and a large endowment that allows the college to support undergraduate and faculty research projects. When you graduate, you'll have unlimited bragging rights and the full force and prestige of the Harvard brand working for you for the rest of your life. All first-year students live on campus, and Harvard guarantees housing to its students for all four years. All freshmen also eat in the same place, Annenberg Hall, and there are adult residential advisers living in the halls to help students learn their way around the vast resources of this "beautiful, fun, historic, and academically alive place." Social and extracurricular activities at Harvard are pretty much unlimited: "Basically, if you want to do it, Harvard either has it or has the money to give to you so you can start it." With more than 400 student organizations on campus, whatever you are looking for, you can find it here. The off-campus scene is hopping, too. Believe it or not, Harvard kids do party, and "there is a vibrant social atmosphere on campus and between students and the local community," with Cambridge offering art and music, not to mention more than a couple of great bars. Downtown Boston and all of its attractions is just a short ride across the Charles River on the "T" (subway).

BANG FOR YOUR BUCK

Harvard is swimming in cash, and financial need simply isn't a barrier to admission. In fact, the admissions staff here often looks especially favorably upon applicants who have stellar academic and extracurricular records despite having to overcome considerable financial obstacles. About 90 percent of the students who request financial aid qualify for it. If you qualify, 100 percent of your financial need will be met. Just so we're clear: by aid, we mean free money—not loans. Harvard doesn't do loans. Instead, Harvard asks families that qualify for financial aid to contribute somewhere between zero and 10 percent of their annual income each year. If your family income is less than $65,000, the odds are very good that you and your family won't pay a dime for you to attend. It's also worth noting that Harvard extends its commitment to full financial aid for all four undergraduate years. Families with higher incomes facing unusual financial challenges may also qualify for need–based scholarship assistance. Home equity is no longer considered in Harvard's assessment of the expected parent contribution.

STUDENT LIFE

As you might expect, ambition and achievement are the ties that bind at Harvard. Most every student can be summed up in three bullet points: "Works really hard. Doesn't sleep. Involved in a million extracurriculars." Diversity is found in all aspects of life, from ethnicities to religion to ideology, and "there is a lot of tolerance and acceptance at Harvard for individuals of all races, religions, socioeconomic backgrounds, life styles, etc." Campus on the Charles River is a "beautiful, fun, historic, and academically alive place," with close to 400 student organizations to stoke your interests. "Arts First Week" annually showcases the talents of the arts and culture

Harvard College

FINANCIAL AID: 617-495-1581 • E-MAIL: COLLEGE@FAS.HARVARD.EDU • WEBSITE: WWW.COLLEGE.HARVARD.EDU

groups, and students gather each June (in Connecticut) for the Harvard-Yale Regatta. Nearby Cambridge and Boston are quintessential college towns, so students never lack for options. As one satisfied undergrad puts it, "Boredom does not exist here. There are endless opportunities and endless passionate people to do them with."

CAREER

As befits a school known for graduating presidents, CEOs, and literary legends, Harvard's Office of Career Service is tireless in working to educate, connect, and advise students about their options and opportunities. At its three locations, OCS offers specialized resources for finding internships, jobs, global opportunities, research and funding opportunities, or just getting your foot in the door of the field of your choice. Crimson Careers lists jobs and internships tailored for Harvard students only, including listings posted by alumni, and an impressive career fair and expo lineup ensures students always have access to hiring companies. Alumni who visited PayScale.com report an average starting salary of $69,200 and 56 percent believe their work makes the world a better place.

GENERAL INFO

Activities: Choral groups, concert band, dance, drama/theater, jazz band, literary magazine, marching band, music ensembles, musical theater, opera, pep band, radio station, student government, student newspaper, student-run film society, symphony orchestra, television station, yearbook, campus ministries, international student organization. **Organizations:** 393 registered organizations, 1 honor societies, 28 religious organizations.

FINANCIAL AID

Students should submit: Business/Farm Supplement; CSS Profile; FAFSA; Noncustodial PROFILE. Regular filing deadline is 1/1. The Princeton Review suggests that all financial aid forms be submitted as soon as possible after October 1. *Need-based scholarships/grants offered:* College/university scholarship or grant aid from institutional funds, Federal Pell, private scholarships, SEOG, state scholarships/grants. *Loan aid offered:* Direct PLUS Loans, Direct Subsidized Loans, Direct Unsubsidized Loans. Applicants will be notified of awards on or about 4/1. Federal Work-Study Program available. Institutional employment available.

THE BOTTOM LINE

The sticker price to attend Harvard is as exorbitant as its opportunities. Tuition, fees, room and board, and expenses cost about $63,025 a year. However, financial aid here is so unbelievably ample and generous that you just shouldn't worry about that. The hard part about going to Harvard is getting in. If you can accomplish that, Harvard will help you find a way to finance your education. Period.

CAREER INFORMATION FROM PAYSCALE.COM	
ROI Rating	96
Bachelors and No Higher	
Median starting salary	$72,600
Median mid-career salary	$142,600
At Least Bachelors	
Median starting salary	$75,300
Median mid-career salary	$151,600
Alumni with high job meaning	55%
Degrees awarded in STEM subjects	19%

SELECTIVITY	
Admissions Rating	99
# of applicants	39,506
% of applicants accepted	5
% of acceptees attending	83

FRESHMAN PROFILE	
Range SAT EBRW	730–790
Range SAT Math	730–800
Range ACT Composite	32–35
Average HS GPA	4.2
% graduated top 10% of class	95
% graduated top 25% of class	99
% graduated top 50% of class	100

DEADLINES	
Early action	
Deadline	11/1
Notification	12/15
Regular	
Deadline	1/1
Notification	4/1
Nonfall registration?	No

FINANCIAL FACTS	
Financial Aid Rating	94
Annual tuition	$46,340
Room and board	$17,160
Required fees	$4,080
Books and supplies	$1,000
Average frosh need-based scholarship	$53,120
Average UG need-based scholarship	$50,699
% needy frosh rec. need-based scholarship or grant aid	100
% needy UG rec. need-based scholarship or grant aid	100
% needy frosh rec. non-need-based scholarship or grant aid	0
% needy UG rec. non-need-based scholarship or grant aid	0
% needy frosh rec. need-based self-help aid	74
% needy UG rec. need-based self-help aid	84
% frosh rec. any financial aid	54
% UG rec. any financial aid	56
% UG borrow to pay for school	20
Average cumulative indebtedness	$15,114
% frosh need fully met	100
% ugrads need fully met	100
Average % of frosh need met	100
Average % of ugrad need met	100

Harvey Mudd College

301 Platt Boulevard, 301 Platt Blvd, Claremont, CA 91711-5990 • Admissions: 909-621-8011 • Fax: 909-621-8360

#6 BEST VALUE COLLEGE

CAMPUS LIFE

Quality of Life Rating	90
Fire Safety Rating	84
Green Rating	60*
Type of school	Private
Environment	Town

STUDENTS

Total undergrad enrollment	844
% male/female	52/48
% from out of state	57
% frosh from public high school	56
% frosh live on campus	100
% ugrads live on campus	92
# of fraternities (% ugrad men join)	0 (0)
# of sororities (% ugrad women join)	0 (0)
% African American	4
% Asian	17
% Caucasian	34
% Hispanic	18
% Native American	<1
% Pacific Islander	<1
% Two or more races	11
% Race and/or ethnicity unknown	5
% international	10
# of countries represented	26

ACADEMICS

Academic Rating	97
% students returning for sophomore year	98
% students graduating within 4 years	86
% students graduating within 6 years	96
Calendar	Semester
Student/faculty ratio	8:1
Profs interesting rating	98
Profs accessible rating	99
Most classes have 10–19 students.	

MOST POPULAR MAJORS
Computer and Information Sciences;
Engineering; Mathematics

ABOUT THE SCHOOL

A member of the Claremont Consortium, Harvey Mudd shares resources with Pitzer, Scripps, Claremont McKenna, and Pomona Colleges. It is the "techie" school of the bunch and focuses on educating future scientists, engineers, and mathematicians. "Mudd is a place where everyone is literate in every branch of science." The college offers four-year degrees in chemistry, mathematics, physics, computer science, biology, and engineering, as well as interdisciplinary degrees in mathematical and computational biology, and a few joint majors for students seeking extra challenges. Harvey Mudd is "small, friendly, and tough. Professors and other students are very accessible. The honor code is an integral part of the college." The honor code is so entrenched in campus culture that the college entrusts the students to twenty-four-hour-per-day access to many buildings, including some labs, and permits take-home exams, specified either as open-book or closed-book, timed or untimed. "Our honor code really means something," insists one student. "It isn't just a stray sentence or two that got put into the student handbook; it's something that the students are really passionate about." Academics at Harvey Mudd may seem "excessive [and] soul-crushing," but there are "great people and community," nonetheless. In order to ensure that all students receive a well-rounded education, students enrolled at Harvey Mudd are required to take a core component of humanities courses. Research opportunities are literally limitless. The Clinic program is open to students of all majors, who collaborate to satisfy the requests of an actual company. Best of all, these opportunities are available without the cutthroat competition of other similar schools.

BANG FOR YOUR BUCK

Harvey Mudd believes that college choice is more about fit than finances. That's why the college offers a robust program of need-based and merit-based awards to help insure that a Harvey Mudd education is accessible to all who qualify. Eighty-two percent of students receive financial aid, and 40 percent qualify for merit-based awards. In determining who will receive merit-based awards, the Office of Admission looks primarily at academic achievement—financial need is not considered. While these awards are granted independent of financial need, students who receive a merit-based award and are also eligible for need-based aid. Standout programs include the Harvey S. Mudd Merit Award, in which students receive a $40,000 scholarship distributed annually in the amount of $10,000 per year. The President's Scholars Program is a renewable, four-year, full-tuition scholarship that promotes excellence and diversity at Harvey Mudd by recognizing outstanding young men and women from populations that are traditionally underrepresented at HMC.

STUDENT LIFE

Mudders say they are united by "a brimming passion for science and a love of knowledge for its own sake." "All students are exceptionally intelligent and are able to perform their work in a professional manner." Beyond that, there's "a really diverse group of personalities" at Mudd, who are "not afraid to show their true colors" and who all have "a unique sense of humor." Students say they "are all friendly, smart, and talented, which brings us together. Upperclassmen look out for underclassmen, and students tend to bond together easily over difficult homework." In such a welcoming community, "students primarily fit

Harvey Mudd College

FINANCIAL AID: 909-621-8055 • E-MAIL: ADMISSION@HMC.EDU • WEBSITE: WWW.HMC.EDU

in by not fitting in—wearing pink pirate hats, or skateboarding while playing harmonica, or practicing unicycle jousting are all good ways to fit in perfectly," though it should be noted that several student have "never seen a dorm swordfight." The speed of the Wi-Fi network on campus has been deemed "great."

CAREER

Harvey Mudd College graduates who visit PayScale.com report a median starting salary of $81,000, and 55 perent of graduates feel their jobs have a lot of meaning in the world. Students feel that at Mudd, "the Office of Career Services finds more than enough summer internships," and one student in particular notes that one dedicated adviser "worked very hard to help me find a summer internship, calling many of his friends and passing around my resume." Students especially feel that their professors have been very helpful about finding them jobs and internships, and that Mudd provides "first-rate preparation for graduate study or (especially for the engineering major) success in the job market."

GENERAL INFO

Activities: Choral groups, concert band, dance, drama/theater, jazz band, literary magazine, music ensembles, musical theater, pep band, radio station, student government, student newspaper, student-run film society, symphony orchestra, yearbook, campus ministries, international student organization. **Organizations:** 109 registered organizations, 4 honor societies, 6 religious organizations. **Athletics (Intercollegiate):** *Men:* Baseball, basketball, cross-country, diving, football, golf, soccer, swimming, tennis, track/ field (outdoor), water polo. *Women:* Basketball, cross-country, diving, golf, lacrosse, soccer, softball, swimming, tennis, track/field (outdoor), volleyball, water polo.

FINANCIAL AID

Students should submit: Business/Farm Supplement; CSS Profile; FAFSA; Noncustodial PROFILE; State aid form. Regular filing deadline is 1/1. The Princeton Review suggests that all financial aid forms be submitted as soon as possible after October 1. *Need-based scholarships/grants offered:* College/university scholarship or grant aid from institutional funds, Federal Pell, private scholarships, SEOG, state scholarships/grants. *Loan aid offered:* Direct PLUS Loans, Direct Subsidized Loans, Direct Unsubsidized Loans. Applicants will be notified of awards on or about 4/1. Federal Work-Study Program available. Institutional employment available.

BOTTOM LINE

The retail price for tuition, room and board, and fees at Harvey Mudd ends up being a little more than $72,228 a year. Financial aid is plentiful here, though, so please don't let cost scare you away from applying. The average need-based scholarship is $39,799, and some students report receiving "excellent financial aid packages," including a "full-tuition scholarship."

CAREER INFORMATION FROM PAYSCALE.COM	
ROI Rating	98
Bachelors and No Higher	
Median starting salary	$85,600
Median mid-career salary	$157,400
At Least Bachelors	
Median starting salary	$88,000
Median mid-career salary	$154,700
Alumni with high job meaning	56%
Degrees awarded in STEM subjects	85%

SELECTIVITY	
Admissions Rating	**98**
# of applicants	4,078
% of applicants accepted	15
% of acceptees attending	36
# offered a place on the wait list	510
% accepting a place on wait list	71
% admitted from wait list	17
# of early decision applicants	504
% accepted early decision	16

FRESHMAN PROFILE	
Range SAT EBRW	720–770
Range SAT Math	750–800
Range ACT Composite	33–35
Minimum paper TOEFL	600
Minimum internet-based TOEFL	100
% graduated top 10% of class	90
% graduated top 25% of class	100
% graduated top 50% of class	100

DEADLINES	
Early decision	
Deadline	11/15
Notification	12/15
Other ED Deadline	1/5
Other ED Notification	2/15
Regular	
Deadline	1/5
Notification	4/1
Nonfall registration?	No

FINANCIAL FACTS	
Financial Aid Rating	**96**
Annual tuition	$54,347
Room and board	$17,592
Required fees	$289
Books and supplies	$800
Average frosh need-based scholarship	$41,649
Average UG need-based scholarship	$40,138
% needy frosh rec. need-based scholarship or grant aid	95
% needy UG rec. need-based scholarship or grant aid	97
% needy frosh rec. non-need-based scholarship or grant aid	37
% needy UG rec. non-need-based scholarship or grant aid	43
% needy frosh rec. need-based self-help aid	56
% needy UG rec. need-based self-help aid	68
% frosh rec. any financial aid	76
% UG rec. any financial aid	74
% UG borrow to pay for school	49
Average cumulative indebtedness	$25,041
% frosh need fully met	100
% ugrads need fully met	100

Haverford College

370 LANCASTER AVENUE, HAVERFORD, PA 19041 • ADMISSIONS: 610-896-1350 • FINANCIAL AID: 610-896-1350

#32 BEST VALUE COLLEGE

ABOUT THE SCHOOL

Haverford College prides itself on the type of student that it draws. Academically minded and socially conscious are two words that often describe the typical Haverford student. Many are drawn to the college due to the accessibility of the professors and attention each student receives in the classroom. They don't have to fight for attention in a large lecture hall, since the most common class size is around fourteen students, and most professors live on or around campus and regularly invite students over for a lively talk over dinner or tea. There is also a larger sense of community on campus that is proliferated by the much-lauded honor code, which, according to one surprised student, "really works, and we actually do have things like closed-book, timed, take-home tests." Many find that the honor code (which includes proctorless exams) brings a certain type of student looking for a mature academic experience that helps prepare students by treating them as intellectual equals. In fact, even comparing grades with other students is discouraged, which tends to limit competitiveness and creates a greater sense of community. This sense of togetherness is prevalent throughout campus. Students are actively involved in student government since they have Plenary twice a year, where at least two-thirds of students must be present to make any changes to documents such as the student constitution and the honor code.

BANG FOR YOUR BUCK

Students with family income below $60,000/year will not have loans included in their financial aid package; loan levels for incomes above this line range from $1,500–$3,000 each year. Though they don't offer any merit-based aid, the school does meet the demonstrated need of all students who were deemed eligible according to the college. Many students are able to find on-campus jobs to help support themselves. Haverford also encourages students to take internships through one of its three Academic Centers, which connect students with opportunities for paid research or internship experiences. The Center for Peace and Global Citizenship, for example, helps Haverfordians find fields that are simpatico with the college's ideals of trust and creating civically minded adults. The Center for Career and Professional Advising also has numerous programs that coordinate with alumni and help students expand their networking abilities and create job opportunities for when they graduate.

STUDENT LIFE

Many students describe themselves as a little "nerdy" or "quirky," but in the best possible way. "For the most part, Haverfordians are socially awkward, open to new friends, and looking for moral, political, [or] scholarly debate." As for the honor code in place at Haverford—"students who are not fully committed to abiding by Haverford's academic and social honor code will feel out of place. Students here are really in love with the atmosphere the honor code creates and feel uncomfortable with those who feel differently." Most are "liberal-minded" and "intellectual" and "want to save the world after they graduate." Some students found that "a lot of people were actually way more mainstream than I expected—not everyone is an awkward nerd with no social skills!" and in addition, "the party scene is open to everyone, and generally consists of music provided by student DJs, some dancing, the options to drink hard alcohol or beer (or soft drinks) and a generally fun environment."

Haverford College

E-MAIL: ADMISSIONS@HAVERFORD.EDU • FAX: 610-896-1338 • WEBSITE: WWW.HAVERFORD.EDU

CAREER

The typical Haverford College graduate has a starting salary of around $54,700. Students feel that Haverford offers a great deal of internship opportunities, especially ones with financial support. Koshland Integrated Natural Sciences Center and the Hurford Center for Arts and Humanities act as grant-making organizations to fund internships and research experiences on-campus, locally in the city of Philadelphia, across the U.S. and abroad. The Integrated Natural Science Center offers "plenty of internship opportunities." The Center for Career and Professional Advising, with a mission to "empower" past and enrolled students to "translate their Haverford liberal arts education into a rewarding life," offers several job boards like CareerConnect as well as other helpful resources.

GENERAL INFO

Activities: Choral groups, dance, drama/theater, literary magazine, music ensembles, musical theater, student government, student newspaper, yearbook, campus ministries, international student organization. **Organizations:** 144 registered organizations, 1 honor societies, 6 religious organizations. **Athletics (Intercollegiate):** *Co-ed:* Cricket. *Men:* Baseball, basketball, cross-country, fencing, lacrosse, soccer, squash, tennis, track/field (outdoor), track/field (indoor). *Women:* Basketball, cross-country, fencing, field hockey, lacrosse, soccer, softball, squash, tennis, track/field (outdoor), track/field (indoor), volleyball. **On-Campus Highlights:** Integrated Natural Sciences Center, John Whitehead Campus Center, Cantor Fitzgerald Gallery, Arboretum. **Environmental Initiatives:** Our athletic center is the first gold LEED-certified recreation center in the United States (opened in 2005). We have reached 75 to 85 percent for grounds recycling. We have completed a master plan to identify utility and powerhouse improvements, and will commence work on these improvements immediately.

FINANCIAL AID

Students should submit: Business/Farm Supplement; CSS Profile; FAFSA; Noncustodial PROFILE. Regular filing deadline is 1/1. The Princeton Review suggests that all financial aid forms be submitted as soon as possible after October 1. *Need-based scholarships/grants offered:* College/university scholarship or grant aid from institutional funds; Federal Pell; SEOG; State scholarships/grants. *Loan aid offered:* Direct PLUS Loans, Direct Subsidized Loans, Direct Unsubsidized Loans. Applicants will be notified of awards on or about 3/25. Federal Work-Study Program available. Institutional employment available.

BOTTOM LINE

Though the annual tuition is $52,278 per year, Haverford offers more than half of its students financial aid. The average cumulative indebtedness is around $18,932. The price may seem high on paper, but Haverford helps its students afford the education.

CAREER INFORMATION FROM PAYSCALE.COM	
ROI Rating	93
Bachelors and No Higher	
Median starting salary	$56,100
Median mid-career salary	$131,400
At Least Bachelors	
Median starting salary	$59,100
Median mid-career salary	$132,600
Alumni with high job meaning	44%
Degrees awarded in STEM subjects	36%

SELECTIVITY	
Admissions Rating	98
# of applicants	4,408
% of applicants accepted	20
% of acceptees attending	39
# offered a place on the wait list	1,152
% accepting a place on wait list	42
% admitted from wait list	8
# of early decision applicants	419
% accepted early decision	42

FRESHMAN PROFILE	
Range SAT EBRW	700–760
Range SAT Math	690–770
Range ACT Composite	31–34
Minimum internet-based TOEFL	100
% graduated top 10% of class	96
% graduated top 25% of class	99
% graduated top 50% of class	100

DEADLINES	
Early decision	
Deadline	11/15
Notification	12/15
Other ED Deadline	1/1
Other ED Notification	2/15
Regular	
Deadline	1/15
Notification	4/1
Nonfall registration?	No

FINANCIAL FACTS	
Financial Aid Rating	97
Annual tuition	$52,278
Room and board	$15,958
Required fees	$476
Average frosh need-based scholarship	$46,673
Average UG need-based scholarship	$48,895
% needy frosh rec. need-based scholarship or grant aid	100
% needy UG rec. need-based scholarship or grant aid	100
% needy frosh rec. non-need-based scholarship or grant aid	0
% needy UG rec. non-need-based scholarship or grant aid	0
% needy frosh rec. need-based self-help aid	94
% needy UG rec. need-based self-help aid	94
% frosh rec. any financial aid	51
% UG rec. any financial aid	51
% UG borrow to pay for school	29
Average cumulative indebtedness	$18,932
% frosh need fully met	100
% ugrads need fully met	100
Average % of frosh need met	100
Average % of ugrad need met	100

Hobart and William Smith Colleges

629 South Main Street, Geneva, NY 14456 • Admissions: 315-781-3622 • Fax: 315-781-3914

CAMPUS LIFE

Quality of Life Rating	**87**
Fire Safety Rating	**96**
Green Rating	**95**
Type of school	Private
Environment	Village

STUDENTS

Total undergrad enrollment	2,237
% male/female	49/51
% from out of state	60
% frosh from public high school	61
% frosh live on campus	100
% ugrads live on campus	90
# of fraternities (% ugrad men join)	8 (18)
# of sororities (% ugrad women join)	1 (2)
% African American	6
% Asian	3
% Caucasian	75
% Hispanic	5
% Native American	<1
% Pacific Islander	<1
% Two or more races	0
% Race and/or ethnicity unknown	5
% international	6
# of countries represented	45

ACADEMICS

Academic Rating	**90**
% students returning for sophomore year	86
% students graduating within 4 years	75
% students graduating within 6 years	81
Calendar	Semester
Student/faculty ratio	10:1
Profs interesting rating	93
Profs accessible rating	91

Most classes have 10–19 students. Most lab/discussion sessions have 10–19 students.

MOST POPULAR MAJORS
Economics; Mass Communication/Media Studies; Biology

ABOUT THE SCHOOL

Hobart and William Smith Colleges were founded separately in 1822 and 1908 respectively, but now operate together as a coordinate system. Men graduate from Hobart and women graduate from William Smith. The Colleges share the same campus and teachers, but have separate traditions and athletic departments. Students love their "beautiful campus"—located on about 320 acres in Geneva, New York—and "the GORGEOUS LAKE outside my window!" The Colleges have about 2,300 students between them, which means "the atmosphere is beyond friendly" within this "close-knit community." Students also recommend the "fantastic study abroad opportunities" and "personal relationships between the faculty and students." "Professors are always accessible, and a good number of them reach out to their students as opposed to simply expecting students to take initiative for help. They easily become friends with students and keep in touch with and mentor them after graduation." These professors show themselves to be "very respectful while simultaneously maintaining high standards of work," and one student comments, "I've never had a professor that did not inspire me while here."

BANG FOR YOUR BUCK

HWS's website states that they view financial aid as "a partnership": staff work "one-on-one with each accepted student and his or her family to create a total financial aid package that makes sense." In addition to federal and state need-based awards, there are numerous merit and scholarships available. Examples include the Elizabeth Blackwell Scholarships for students doing advanced science coursework and the Environmental Sustainability Trustee Scholarship for students dedicated to environmental leadership. On average, 79 percent of undergraduate financial need is fully met.

STUDENT LIFE

Students love the sense of inclusiveness at HWS. As one geoscience major explains about her decision to attend: "I did not want to be a number in a classroom; I wanted to be a person." "As soon as I got on campus it felt like 'my people' were here," a sociology major added. Students who are attracted to HWS include those who are interested in developing their own approach to their education, as the school's popular curriculum allows (they are a high-achieving bunch for sure: A top Fulbright producer, HWS boasts eighteen Fulbright U.S. Student Award recipients in the past three years). Plenty of students engage with the Colleges' offerings in "athletics, leadership and entrepreneurship, study abroad opportunities, alum network and connections," but they also enjoy weekend excursions off-campus. "Many people are involved in outing club trips" or drive to spots where they can "go hiking, kayaking, ice climbing," or just "go shopping at the Outlets fifteen minutes away."

Hobart and William Smith Colleges

FINANCIAL AID: 315-781-3315 • E-MAIL: ADMISSIONS@HWS.EDU • WEBSITE: WWW.HWS.EDU

CAREER

Students say HWS has "an extensive alumni network" that helps students find work after college. They also report excellent "access to great internships." In fact, in 2014 HWS started a "guaranteed internship program" where every student of "good academic and social standing" who completes their Pathways Program is assured an internship or research experience. HWS provides a stipend if the internship is unpaid. Students also say Career Services is very good at "helping students access...jobs during and after graduation." PayScale.com reports a median starting salary of $52,400 for HWS graduates and a mid-career average of $116,400.

GENERAL INFO

Activities: Choral groups, culture clubs, club and intramural sports, dance, drama/theater, international student organization, jazz band, literary magazine, music ensembles, radio station, student government, student newspaper, student-run film society, yearbook. **Organizations:** 101 registered organizations, 15 honor societies, 7 religious organizations. 7 fraternities. **Athletics (Intercollegiate):** *Men:* basketball, crew/rowing, cross-country, football, golf, ice hockey, lacrosse, sailing, soccer, squash, tennis. *Women:* basketball, crew/rowing, cross-country, field hockey, golf, ice hockey, lacrosse, sailing, soccer, squash, swimming and diving, tennis. **On-Campus Highlights:** Melly Academic Center, Centennial Center for Leadership, Entrepreneurship and Innovation and Bozzuto Center for Entrepreneurship, Scandling Campus Center, de Cordova Hall, Stern Hall, Caird Hall, Bristol Field House, Trinity Hall, Gearan Center for the Performing Arts, Perkin Observatory, Elliott Studio Arts Building and HWS Fribolin Farm.

FINANCIAL AID

Students should submit: CSS Profile; FAFSA; Noncustodial PROFILE; State aid form. Priority filing deadline is 2/1. The Princeton Review suggests that all financial aid forms be submitted as soon as possible after October 1. *Need-based scholarships/grants offered:* College/university scholarship or grant aid from institutional funds, Federal Pell, private scholarships, SEOG, state scholarships/grants. *Loan aid offered:* Direct PLUS Loans, Direct Subsidized Loans, Direct Unsubsidized Loans. Applicants will be notified of awards upon acceptance. Federal Work-Study Program available. Institutional employment available.

BOTTOM LINE

Tuition at HWS is $54,060. Room, board, and fees bring that total to $69,290. The school estimates an additional $1,300 for books and other supplies. Don't let that price tag detour you though, at HWS 92 percent of students receive some form of financial assistance.

CAREER INFORMATION FROM PAYSCALE.COM	
ROI Rating	89
Bachelors and No Higher	
Median starting salary	$53,600
Median mid-career salary	$120,400
At Least Bachelors	
Median starting salary	$54,600
Median mid-career salary	$118,200
Alumni with high job meaning	49%
Degrees awarded in STEM subjects	18%

SELECTIVITY	
Admissions Rating	**87**
# of applicants	4,409
% of applicants accepted	61
% of acceptees attending	24
# offered a place on the wait list	504
% accepting a place on wait list	35
% admitted from wait list	6
# of early decision applicants	360
% accepted early decision	89

FRESHMAN PROFILE	
Range SAT EBRW	610–680
Range SAT Math	600–680
Range ACT Composite	NR
Minimum paper TOEFL	550
Minimum internet-based TOEFL	80
Average HS GPA	3.4
% graduated top 10% of class	33
% graduated top 25% of class	59
% graduated top 50% of class	83

DEADLINES	
Early decision	
Deadline	11/15
Notification	12/15
Other ED Deadline	1/15
Other ED Notification	2/15
Regular	
Deadline	2/1
Nonfall registration?	Yes

FINANCIAL FACTS	
Financial Aid Rating	**91**
Annual tuition	$54,060
Room and board	$14,035
Required fees	$1,195
Books and supplies	NR
Average frosh need-based scholarship	$33,012
Average UG need-based scholarship	$32,527
% needy frosh rec. need-based scholarship or grant aid	99
% needy UG rec. need-based scholarship or grant aid	99
% needy frosh rec. non-need-based scholarship or grant aid	18
% needy UG rec. non-need-based scholarship or grant aid	16
% needy frosh rec. need-based self-help aid	79
% needy UG rec. need-based self-help aid	82
% frosh rec. any financial aid	96
% UG rec. any financial aid	94
% UG borrow to pay for school	65
Average cumulative indebtedness	$33,879

Hollins University

Box 9707, Roanoke, VA 24020-1707 • Admissions: 540-362-6401 • Fax: 540-362-6218

CAMPUS LIFE

Quality of Life Rating	86
Fire Safety Rating	84
Green Rating	79
Type of school	Private
Environment	City

STUDENTS

Total undergrad enrollment	628
% male/female	0/100
% from out of state	47
% frosh from public high school	80
% frosh live on campus	95
% ugrads live on campus	87
# of fraternities (% ugrad men join)	0 (0)
# of sororities (% ugrad women join)	0 (0)
% African American	12
% Asian	2
% Caucasian	66
% Hispanic	6
% Native American	1
% Pacific Islander	<1
% Two or more races	6
% Race and/or ethnicity unknown	3
% international	5
# of countries represented	20

ACADEMICS

Academic Rating	90
% students returning for sophomore year	78
% students graduating within 4 years	58
% students graduating within 6 years	62
Calendar	4/1/4
Student/faculty ratio	10:1
Profs interesting rating	90
Profs accessible rating	87

Most classes have 10–19 students. Most lab/discussion sessions have fewer than 10 students.

MOST POPULAR MAJORS

English Language and Literature; Biology; Business/Commerce

ABOUT THE SCHOOL

An all-female institution, Hollins University provides a "welcoming environment" where women feel "empower[ed]" and can easily "thrive." Students say they greatly benefit from "small class sizes," noting that most courses have "fewer than 20 people." And when it comes to specific academic disciplines, Hollins undergrads boast of the "incredible" English and psychology departments and quickly proclaim the theater program "excellent" as well. Many students are also drawn to the "fantastic study abroad" opportunities. However, no matter where or what they study, applicants should prepare for "rigorous" academics. Indeed, inside the classroom, students are taught to "challenge ideas" and encouraged to "formulate opinions." They are also greeted by "engaging and passionate" professors who "truly seem to care about [their] students." As one grateful undergrad explains, "they take the time to listen and offer feedback if you have questions." Best of all, professors here "generally go out of their way to make sure that you understand the concepts that they are trying to teach."

BANG FOR YOUR BUCK

A Hollins education is an affordable education. And students are thrilled to report that the Financial Aid Office is nothing short of "fantastic." Importantly, through a combination of need-based aid, scholarships, and cost-effective loans and grants, the university is able to distribute over $24 million annually in financial aid. More specifically, Hollins offers a handful of academic excellence scholarships including the Batten Scholar Award which provides full tuition coverage for four years. There's also the Hollins Scholar Award which provides at least $24,000 annually. And artistically inclined students will be happy to learn that the university offers scholarships to individuals exceptionally talented in dance, creative writing, theater, and music. These typically gift recipients up to $2,000/year.

STUDENT LIFE

Hollins offers plenty of excitement beyond the classroom. For starters, the school frequently "hosts famous speakers, poets, authors, and political figures." Hollins also maintains an active "Outdoors Program" which provides numerous opportunities for "kayaking, canoeing, hiking, and caving." And we've also been informed that "the student activities office is on top of their game...constantly bringing in theater companies, hosting intramural sports [and] screening movies." However, prospective applicants dreaming of raucous keg parties be forewarned— drinking culture is practically non-existent here. Students report that "there are apartment parties about once or twice a month but other than that there is no party scene here. Most people leave and go to other schools on the weekends."

Hollins University

Financial Aid: 540-362-6332 • E-mail: huadm@hollins.edu • Website: www.hollins.edu

CAREER

The career outlook for Hollins students is pretty rosy. That's partially thanks to the fact that undergrads are able to tap into a "highly active alumni base." They also have a wonderful Career Center at their disposal. Indeed, from the beginning of the first year, undergrads can swing by the office and start plotting their path to career success. Students have the opportunity to take assessment tests, sit for mock interviews and everything in between. Career Services also continually hosts workshops on topics such as workplace etiquette, crafting the perfect cover letter and how to find a good work/life balance. Aside from learning how to maximize their job and internship hunts, students can also receive top-notch guidance on applying to graduate programs.

GENERAL INFO

Activities: Campus Ministries; Choral groups; Dance; Drama/theater; International Student Organization; Literary magazine; Model UN; Music ensembles; Musical theater; Student government; Student-run film society 28 registered organizations, 15 honor societies, 5 religious organizations. **Athletics (Intercollegiate):** *Women:* basketball, equestrian sports, golf, lacrosse, soccer, swimming, tennis. **On-Campus Highlights:** Front Quadrangle, Wetherill Visual Arts Center and Wilson Museum, Wyndham Robertson Library, Moody Center, Gymnasium, Northern Swim Cntr, Tayloe Fitness Cntr Environmental Initiatives: Signing the President's Climate Agreement.

FINANCIAL AID

Students should submit: FAFSA, state aid form. Priority filing deadline is 2/15. The Princeton Review suggests that all financial aid forms be submitted as soon as possible after October 1. *Need-based scholarships/grants offered:* College/university scholarship or grant aid from institutional funds, Federal Pell, private scholarships, SEOG, state scholarships/grants. *Loan aid offered:* Direct PLUS Loans, Direct Subsidized Loans, Direct Unsubsidized Loans. Applicants will be notified of awards on a rolling basis beginning 3/1. Federal Work-Study Program available. Institutional employment available.

CAREER INFORMATION FROM PAYSCALE.COM

ROI Rating	88
Bachelors and No Higher	
Median starting salary	$40,900
Median mid-career salary	$81,900
At Least Bachelors	
Median starting salary	$43,800
Median mid-career salary	$88,500
Alumni with high job meaning	44%
Degrees awarded in STEM subjects	12%

SELECTIVITY

Admissions Rating	87
# of applicants	2,842
% of applicants accepted	48
% of acceptees attending	11
# of early decision applicants	5
% accepted early decision	100

FRESHMAN PROFILE

Range SAT EBRW	580–680
Range SAT Math	530–615
Range ACT Composite	23–28
Minimum paper TOEFL	550
Minimum internet-based TOEFL	80
Average HS GPA	3.8
% graduated top 10% of class	29
% graduated top 25% of class	66
% graduated top 50% of class	89

DEADLINES

Early decision	
Deadline	11/1
Notification	11/15
Early action	
Deadline	11/15
Notification	12/1
Regular	
Priority	2/1
Deadline	until full
Nonfall registration?	Yes

FINANCIAL FACTS

Financial Aid Rating	88
Annual tuition	$37,650
Room and board	$13,120
Required fees	$635
Books and supplies	$600
Average frosh need-based scholarship	$33,368
Average UG need-based scholarship	$32,377
% needy frosh rec. need-based scholarship or grant aid	100
% needy UG rec. need-based scholarship or grant aid	100
% needy frosh rec. non-need-based scholarship or grant aid	100
% needy UG rec. non-need-based scholarship or grant aid	100
% needy frosh rec. need-based self-help aid	73
% needy UG rec. need-based self-help aid	74
% frosh rec. any financial aid	99
% UG rec. any financial aid	96
% UG borrow to pay for school	74
Average cumulative indebtedness	$31,211
% frosh need fully met	25
% ugrads need fully met	24
Average % of frosh need met	85

Illinois Institute of Technology

10 West Thirty-third Street, Chicago, IL 60616 • Admissions: 312-567-3025 • Fax: 312-567-6939

CAMPUS LIFE

Quality of Life Rating	**83**
Fire Safety Rating	**83**
Green Rating	**61**
Type of school	Private
Environment	Metropolis

STUDENTS

Total undergrad enrollment	2,722
% male/female	69/31
% from out of state	26
% frosh from public high school	87
% frosh live on campus	77
% ugrads live on campus	39
# of fraternities (% ugrad men join)	7 (10)
# of sororities (% ugrad women join)	3 (13)
% African American	6
% Asian	14
% Caucasian	33
% Hispanic	16
% Native American	<1
% Pacific Islander	<1
% Two or more races	3
% Race and/or ethnicity unknown	7
% international	21
# of countries represented	94

ACADEMICS

Academic Rating	**74**
% students returning for sophomore year	93
% students graduating within 4 years	32
% students graduating within 6 years	72
Calendar	Semester
Student/faculty ratio	2:1
Profs interesting rating	71
Profs accessible rating	69

Most classes have 10–19 students. Most lab/discussion sessions have 10–19 students.

MOST POPULAR MAJORS

Architecture; Computer and Information Sciences; Mechanical Engineering

ABOUT THE SCHOOL

The Chicago-based Illinois Institute of Technology provides small class sizes, a "diverse and innovative" curriculum, and a fantastic learning environment to just under 3,000 undergrads, who study across six different academic divisions (including engineering, applied science, and architecture). Students are encouraged (and sometimes required) to take courses across the different colleges to complete their degrees, a practice which fortifies their interdisciplinary education. "Campus facilities are great": The school's Idea Shop—a giant "innovation hub" replete with computer visualization tools, a rapid-prototyping lab, and a 3-D printer—allows all students to flesh out concepts and then actualize them. Professors here are "erudite researchers and educators, accomplished in their fields," "really possess abundant knowledge," and "are well-updated about the current trends," as well.

BANG FOR YOUR BUCK

Job assurance is quite high for IIT grads in STEM fields, and the school makes sure there is "plenty of help with job search, homework tutoring, or advising" when needed. Practical knowledge is acquired through the assignments and projects typically found in IIT courses not to mention key resources like the "staff's professional network and connection to industry." Distinctive programs, like the Duchossois Leadership Scholars Program, which challenges students to think creatively across disciplines, offer further support for students to personalize their studies. IIT is committed to helping students secure necessary funding for college, and the Financial Aid office regularly updates its Scholarship Opportunities spreadsheet with available outside scholarships.

STUDENT LIFE

At this rigorous research university, "most of the time in the day is occupied by academic work," but "college sport teams and clubs provide for fun and development." IIT students "hang out, play games and sports, and just talk to each other" at The BOG, an on-campus facility that is home to all the current video game systems, Pinball and Pacman machines, darts, pool, ping pong, and even an 8-land bowling alley. And people can always hop on the El downtown to seek out entertainment. Current students note that there is "a lot of structure on campus" in terms of when students study and play. If you participate in student organizations you will have meetings during the weekdays with events "typically available every day of the week," while those who do research "will spend most of their free time in the labs." There is also "a huge international student base," and this makes the campus "a unique environment full of different people and cultures."

CAREER

Life at IIT is very organized, and "the institution is very focused on getting students placed in jobs after commencement." Career Services hosts several career fairs throughout the year (they even have accompanying prep nights), and offer a variety of services from day one, including career development/peer career coaching, workshops, and mock interviews. Academic departments also help students to apply for experiential learning opportunities such as internships, co-ops, and research opportunities in relevant fields. IIT's proximity to downtown Chicago is a huge plus for employment, and "almost every student either has a job concurrent with their classes or is working on a personal project of some sort." Of the Illinois Institute of Technology alumni visiting PayScale.com, 50 percent report that they derive a high level of meaning from their jobs.

Illinois Institute of Technology

FINANCIAL AID: 312-567-7219 • E-MAIL: ADMISSION@IIT.EDU • WEBSITE: WWW.IIT.EDU

GENERAL INFO

Activities: Choral groups, concert band, dance, drama/theater, literary magazine, music ensembles, musical theater, radio station, student government, student newspaper, student-run film society, television station, yearbook, campus ministries, International Student Organization. **Organizations:** 100 registered organizations, 4 honor societies, 10 religious organizations. 7 fraternities, 3 sororities. **Athletics (Intercollegiate):** *Men:* baseball, cross-country, diving, soccer, swimming. *Women:* cross-country, diving, soccer, swimming, volleyball. **On-Campus Highlights:** S.R. Crown Hall (Architecture Building), McCormick Tribune Center, Keating Athletic Center, Hermann Hall, State Street Village.

FINANCIAL AID

Students should submit: FAFSA. Priority filing deadline is 2/1. The Princeton Review suggests that all financial aid forms be submitted as soon as possible after October 1. *Need-based scholarships/grants offered:* College/university scholarship or grant aid from institutional funds, Federal Pell, private scholarships, SEOG, state scholarships/grants. *Loan aid offered:* Direct PLUS Loans, Direct Subsidized Loans, Direct Unsubsidized Loans. Applicants will be notified of awards on a rolling basis beginning 2/15. Federal Work-Study Program available. Institutional employment available.

BOTTOM LINE

Tuition costs $44,150, with an additional $1,384 in fees and another $13,007 for room and board. For those experiencing sticker shock, worry not: IIT strives to meet a family's entire need through grants, work (or work-study), and loans.

CAREER INFORMATION FROM PAYSCALE.COM

ROI Rating	88
Bachelors and No Higher	
Median starting salary	$62,800
Median mid-career salary	$115,900
At Least Bachelors	
Median starting salary	$64,900
Median mid-career salary	$121,800
Alumni with high job meaning	48%
Degrees awarded in STEM subjects	64%

SELECTIVITY

Admissions Rating	88
# of applicants	4,708
% of applicants accepted	54
% of acceptees attending	19

FRESHMAN PROFILE

Range SAT EBRW	580–680
Range SAT Math	650–730
Range ACT Composite	25–31
Minimum internet-based TOEFL	70

DEADLINES

Regular	
Priority	12/1
Deadline	8/1
Nonfall registration?	Yes

FINANCIAL FACTS

Financial Aid Rating	83
Annual tuition	$45,872
Room and board	$12,762
Required fees	$1,424
Books and supplies	$1,250
Average frosh need-based scholarship	$35,496
Average UG need-based scholarship	$33,045
% needy frosh rec. need-based scholarship or grant aid	99
% needy UG rec. need-based scholarship or grant aid	100
% needy frosh rec. non-need-based scholarship or grant aid	20
% needy UG rec. non-need-based scholarship or grant aid	12
% needy frosh rec. need-based self-help aid	65
% needy UG rec. need-based self-help aid	71
% frosh rec. any financial aid	100
% UG rec. any financial aid	99
% UG borrow to pay for school	54
Average cumulative indebtedness	$32,671
% frosh need fully met	22
% ugrads need fully met	13
Average % of frosh need met	85
Average % of ugrad need met	77

Johns Hopkins University

OFFICE OF UNDERGRADUATE ADMISSIONS, MASON HALL, 3400 N. CHARLES STREET, BALTIMORE, MD 21218 • ADMISSIONS: 410-516-8171

#50 BEST VALUE COLLEGE

CAMPUS LIFE	
Quality of Life Rating	90
Fire Safety Rating	98
Green Rating	92
Type of school	Private
Environment	Metropolis

STUDENTS	
Total undergrad enrollment	5,421
% male/female	49/51
% from out of state	89
% frosh from public high school	57
% frosh live on campus	99
% ugrads live on campus	64
# of fraternities (% ugrad men join)	10 (19)
# of sororities (% ugrad women join)	12 (30)
% African American	6
% Asian	26
% Caucasian	33
% Hispanic	14
% Native American	<1
% Pacific Islander	<1
% Two or more races	5
% Race and/or ethnicity unknown	5
% international	9
# of countries represented	65

ACADEMICS	
Academic Rating	92
% students returning for sophomore year	97
% students graduating within 4 years	88
% students graduating within 6 years	94
Calendar	4/1/4
Student/faculty ratio	8:1
Profs interesting rating	80
Profs accessible rating	81

Most classes have 20–29 students. Most lab/discussion sessions have 10–19 students.

MOST POPULAR MAJORS

Bioengineering And Biomedical Engineering; Neuroscience; Public Health; International Studies.

ABOUT THE SCHOOL

Without a doubt, Johns Hopkins University's reputation for academic rigor and its wide array of programs in the sciences and humanities make it a magnet for its top-notch students. In addition to its lauded biochemical engineering, international studies, and writing programs, this research university also offers opportunities for its students to study at its other divisions, including the Peabody Conservatory, the Nitze School of Advanced International Studies, the Carey Business School, and the Bloomberg School of Public Health. Students appreciate the school's flexible curriculum, small class size, and emphasis on academic exploration and hands-on learning. Around two-thirds of the students are involved in some kind of research opportunity, and an equal amount of students complete internships. Many of the distinguished professors at Johns Hopkins often serve as mentors and collaborators on these research projects. According to one student, "Johns Hopkins puts you shoulder-to-shoulder with some of the greatest minds in the world while promoting a work ethic that forces you to push yourself to your intellectual limits."

BANG FOR YOUR BUCK

To apply for financial aid, students must submit the FAFSA. Johns Hopkins distributes more than 90 percent of its financial aid awards on the basis of need and also provides need- and merit-based scholarships, including the Hodson Trust Scholarship, Bloomberg Scholarship, Clark Scholarship for engineers, and the Daniels-Rosen First Generation Scholarship. Along with financial aid, students receive a lot of support from the school's Career Center and Office of Pre-Professional Programs and Advising, as well as the extensive and loyal alumni network, to help them tackle their career-development and postgraduation goals.

STUDENT LIFE

For some reason, Hopkins developed a reputation as a school where "studies are more important than having fun." However, many undergrads here balk at that notion and insist that it couldn't be further from the truth. Indeed, while the academics are certainly rigorous there's also plenty of fun to be had. As one international studies major asserts, "There's never a dull moment at Johns Hopkins: you just have to step outside your room and look for five seconds." For starters, there are plenty of "free on-campus movies, plays, dance and a cappella performances" to catch. Additionally, the MSE symposium "always has interesting speakers (like Will Ferrell)." Moreover, about "one fourth of the school population is involved in Greek life." Of course, should students (temporarily) grow weary of campus life, Hodson Trust Scholarship, Bloomberg Scholarship, Clark Scholarship for engineers, and the Daniels-Rosen First Generation Scholarship. And, as an added bonus, D.C. and Philadelphia are both roughly an hour away.

CAREER

If you asked Hopkins undergrads to summarize their career services office in one word, it would likely be "awesome." And that's no surprise. After all, when the average starting salary for graduates is $63,200 (according to PayScale.com), you know the school is doing

Johns Hopkins University

Fax: 410-516-6025 • Financial Aid: 410-516-8028 • E-mail: gotojhu@jhu.edu • Website: www.jhu.edu

something right. The Career Center truly bends over backwards to help students prepare for the job market. With Career Academies in arts, media, and marketing; consulting; finance; health sciences; nonprofit and government; and STEM and innovation, the Career Center provides students with employer connections and industry-specific knowledge. Impressively, undergrads can request customized workshops on any career-related topic they deem important. They can also participate in programs and internships during intersession, the university's winter semester. Locally, some popular internships are at Baltimore-based Under Armour as well as T. Rowe Price and the Baltimore Sun newspaper. In addition, undergrads can receive more traditional guidance such as resume and cover letter writing, mock interviews, and networking opportunities.

GENERAL INFO

Activities: Choral groups, concert band, dance, drama/theater, jazz band, literary magazine, music ensembles, musical theater, pep band, radio station, student government, student newspaper, student-run film society, symphony orchestra, yearbook, campus ministries. **Organizations:** Over 400 student organizations, including 13 honor societies, 14 religious groups, 43 cultural groups, and 43 advocacy groups. 11 fraternities, 14 sororities. **Athletics (Intercollegiate):** *Men:* Baseball, basketball, cross-country, fencing, football, lacrosse, soccer, swimming, tennis, track/field (outdoor), track/field (indoor), water polo, wrestling. *Women:* Basketball, cross-country, fencing, field hockey, lacrosse, soccer, swimming, tennis, track/field (outdoor), track/field (indoor), volleyball. **On-Campus Highlights:** Mattin Student Arts Center, Homewood House Museum, Undergraduate Teaching Labs, Ralph S. O'Connor Recreation Center, Charles Commons, Brody Learning Commons, a state-of-the-art collaborative learning space, and "The Lab" student-designed social space. **Environmental Initiatives:** Commitment to reduce greenhouse gas emissions by 51 percent by 2025.

FINANCIAL AID

Students should submit: CSS Profile; FAFSA; Noncustodial PROFILE. Priority filing deadline is 1/5. Financial aid deadlines are 12/15 for Early Decision and 1/15 for Regular Decision applicants. The Princeton Review suggests that all financial aid forms be submitted as soon as possible after October 1. *Need-based scholarships/grants offered:* College/university scholarship or grant aid from institutional funds, Federal Pell, private scholarships, SEOG, state scholarships/grants. *Loan aid offered:* Direct PLUS Loans, Direct Subsidized Loans, Direct Unsubsidized Loans. Applicants will be notified of awards, along with their admissions decision, around 12/15 for Early Decision and 3/15 for Regular Decision. Federal Work-Study Program available. Institutional employment available.

CAREER INFORMATION FROM PAYSCALE.COM

ROI Rating	92
Bachelors and No Higher	
Median starting salary	$65,500
Median mid-career salary	$113,200
At Least Bachelors	
Median starting salary	$68,300
Median mid-career salary	$123,000
Alumni with high job meaning	57%
Degrees awarded in STEM subjects	31%

SELECTIVITY

Admissions Rating	99
# of applicants	26,576
% of applicants accepted	12
% of acceptees attending	43
# offered a place on the wait list	2,741
% accepting a place on wait list	59
% admitted from wait list	<1
# of early decision applicants	1934
% accepted early decision	30

FRESHMAN PROFILE

Range SAT EBRW	720–780
Range SAT Math	740–800
Range ACT Composite	33–35
Minimum paper TOEFL	600
Average HS GPA	3.9
% graduated top 10% of class	93
% graduated top 25% of class	99
% graduated top 50% of class	100

DEADLINES

Early decision	
Deadline	11/1
Notification	12/14
Regular	
Deadline	1/2
Notification	4/1
Nonfall registration?	No

FINANCIAL FACTS

Financial Aid Rating	94
Annual tuition	$53,740
Room and board	$15,836
Required fees	$500
Average frosh need-based scholarship	$44,318
Average UG need-based scholarship	$39,636
% needy frosh rec. need-based scholarship or grant aid	95
% needy UG rec. need-based scholarship or grant aid	94
% needy frosh rec. non-need-based scholarship or grant aid	14
% needy UG rec. non-need-based scholarship or grant aid	10
% needy frosh rec. need-based self-help aid	87
% needy UG rec. need-based self-help aid	90
% UG borrow to pay for school	45
Average cumulative indebtedness	$26,193
% frosh need fully met	100
% ugrads need fully met	100
Average % of frosh need met	100
Average % of ugrad need met	100

Kalamazoo College

1200 ACADEMY STREET, KALAMAZOO, MI 49006 • ADMISSIONS: 269-337-7166 • FAX: 269-552-5083

CAMPUS LIFE

Quality of Life Rating	86
Fire Safety Rating	83
Green Rating	60*
Type of school	Private
Environment	City

STUDENTS

Total undergrad enrollment	1,436
% male/female	43/57
% from out of state	32
% frosh from public high school	80
% frosh live on campus	100
% ugrads live on campus	60
# of fraternities (% ugrad men join)	0 (0)
# of sororities (% ugrad women join)	0 (0)
% African American	8
% Asian	8
% Caucasian	57
% Hispanic	13
% Native American	0
% Pacific Islander	<1
% Two or more races	4
% Race and/or ethnicity unknown	3
% international	4
# of countries represented	28

ACADEMICS

Academic Rating	90
% students returning for sophomore year	90
% students graduating within 4 years	82
% students graduating within 6 years	86
Calendar	Quarter
Student/faculty ratio	13:1
Profs interesting rating	87
Profs accessible rating	89

Most classes have 10–19 students. Most lab/discussion sessions have fewer than 10 students.

MOST POPULAR MAJORS

English Language and Literature;
Psychology; Economics

ABOUT THE SCHOOL

A private liberal arts college in Michigan with a "small, close-knit community," Kalamazoo College is a school "focuse[d] on helping people succeed." Undergraduates here benefit from "an emphasis on integrating academic experiences with service learning, study abroad, and senior independent research." Kalmazoo's Open Curriculum means that students do not have to take a fixed set of general education requirements. Instead, it "offers students [the opportunity] to explore exactly what they want to learn, rather than being required to take classes in which they have no interest." Other aspects of the colleges' K-Plan, each student's personalized four-year plan, include career development internships, study abroad, and a senior thesis. Kalamazoo students love to highlight the fact that both "small class sizes and commit[ed]...professors...make it easy to get one on one attention." And though professors have "very high expectations," they're also "very passionate about their material and are always willing to help students outside of class." Just as welcome, they "view their students as equals and peers and are open to listening to everyone's ideas in classes." Best of all, the clear majority "form strong bonds with students."

BANG FOR YOUR BUCK

Kalamazoo College is practically synonymous with affordability. After all, more than 98 percent of their student benefits from some type of aid, be it need-based or merit scholarships. More specifically, Kalamazoo awards over $44 million every year. And they make the process rather easy; all accepted students are considered for scholarships. Selected individuals are notified at the same time as their admissions decision. Kalamazoo College Scholarships typically range between $20,000 and $32,000. Additionally, music and theater students are considered for the Enlightened Leadership Award for the Performing Arts. Given to undergrads who demonstrate significant achievement in the arts, recipients are awarded $5,000 per year for up to $20,000. The K Tradition Scholarship is awarded to students who maintained a minimum 3.0 in high school and whose parents or grandparents are Kalamazoo alums. Those chosen receive $5,000 per year for up to four years.

SCHOOL LIFE

Students at Kalamazoo are often on the go. To begin with, "athletics are popular and easy to get into." As one student shares, "people [love] to workout in our new fitness center and join intramural sports." Beyond athletics, there are "lot[s] of student organizations... including symphonic band, philharmonic orchestra, a strong theater program, circus, swing dancing, and many others." Plus, "every Friday the school shows a different movie." Plenty of students head into downtown Kalamazoo since it's "close to campus and easily accessible."

CAREER

Current students say that Kalamazoo College is bursting with "career development opportunities." No matter where students are in their academic career or job search, they can easily turn to the fabulous Center for Career and Professional Development. The office smartly breaks the job hunt into digestible categories like exploration and goals, navigating the application process, and building connections. Students can receive help with everything from taking career assessments and conducting industry and salary research to dealing with rejection and finding mentors. Undergrads can put all that training and newfound confidence to good use at one of the numerous

Kalamazoo College

FINANCIAL AID: 269-337-7192 • E-MAIL: ADMISSION@KZOO.EDU • WEBSITE: WWW.KZOO.EDU

career expos Kalamazoo hosts. These events often attract companies such as Northwestern Mutual, the Peace Corps, Morgan Stanley Wealth Management, YWCA of Kalamazoo, Teach for America, Bell's Brewery, Inc., and the Kalamazoo Public Schools.

GENERAL INFO

Activities: Choral groups, concert band, dance, drama/theater, jazz band, literary magazine, music ensembles, musical theater, pep band, radio station, student government, student newspaper, symphony orchestra, yearbook, campus ministries, International Student Organization, Model UN. **Organizations:** 60 registered organizations, 3 honor societies, 5 religious organizations. **Athletics (Intercollegiate):** *Men:* baseball, basketball, cross-country, diving, football, golf, lacrosse, soccer, swimming, tennis. *Women:* basketball, cross-country, diving, golf, lacrosse, soccer, softball, swimming, tennis, volleyball. **On-Campus Highlights:** Upjohn Library Commons, The Quad, Water Street Coffee Joint, Hicks Student Center, Anderson Athletic Center, Arcus Center for Social Justice Leadership.

FINANCIAL AID

Students should submit: FAFSA. Priority filing deadline is 11/15. The Princeton Review suggests that all financial aid forms be submitted as soon as possible after October 1. *Need-based scholarships/grants offered:* College/university scholarship or grant aid from institutional funds, Federal Pell, private scholarships, SEOG, state scholarships/grants. *Loan aid offered:* Direct PLUS Loans, Direct Subsidized Loans, Direct Unsubsidized Loans. Applicants will be notified of awards on a rolling basis beginning 1/15. Federal Work-Study Program available. Institutional employment available.

THE BOTTOM LINE

Before financial aid, Kalamazoo students and their families face an annual tuition bill of $48,162. Additionally, the combined cost of room and board comes to $9,746, upon a double room and meal plan of 20 meals per week. There's also a $354 activity fee. The optional health insurance plan is $1,439

CAREER INFORMATION FROM PAYSCALE.COM	
ROI Rating	91
Bachelors and No Higher	
Median starting salary	$49,900
Median mid-career salary	$99,500
At Least Bachelors	
Median starting salary	$52,200
Median mid-career salary	$104,600
Alumni with high job meaning	52%
Degrees awarded in STEM subjects	31%

SELECTIVITY	
Admissions Rating	88
# of applicants	3,434
% of applicants accepted	73
% of acceptees attending	13
# offered a place on the wait list	214
% accepting a place on wait list	75
% admitted from wait list	3
# of early decision applicants	56
% accepted early decision	75

FRESHMAN PROFILE	
Range SAT EBRW	600–690
Range SAT Math	580–690
Range ACT Composite	26–30
Minimum paper TOEFL	550
Minimum internet-based TOEFL	84
Average HS GPA	3.8
% graduated top 10% of class	50
% graduated top 25% of class	87
% graduated top 50% of class	99

DEADLINES	
Early decision	
Deadline	11/1
Notification	12/1
Other ED Deadline	2/1
Other ED Notification	2/15
Early action	
Deadline	11/1
Notification	12/20
Regular	
Deadline	1/15
Notification	4/1
Nonfall registration?	No

FINANCIAL FACTS	
Financial Aid Rating	90
Annual tuition	$48,162
Room and board	$9,756
Required fees	$354
Books and supplies	$825
Average frosh need-based scholarship	$34,678
Average UG need-based scholarship	$32,723
% needy frosh rec. need-based scholarship or grant aid	98
% needy UG rec. need-based scholarship or grant aid	98
% needy frosh rec. non-need-based scholarship or grant aid	27
% needy UG rec. non-need-based scholarship or grant aid	19
% needy frosh rec. need-based self-help aid	76
% needy UG rec. need-based self-help aid	82
% frosh rec. any financial aid	98

Kenyon College

KENYON COLLEGE, ADMISSION OFFICE, GAMBIER, OH 43022-9623 • ADMISSIONS: 740-427-5776 • FAX: 740-427-5770

CAMPUS LIFE

Quality of Life Rating	**89**
Fire Safety Rating	**89**
Green Rating	**80**
Type of school	Private
Affiliation	Episcopal
Environment	Rural

STUDENTS

Total undergrad enrollment	1,661
% male/female	44/56
% from out of state	85
% frosh from public high school	50
% frosh live on campus	100
% ugrads live on campus	100
# of fraternities (% ugrad men join)	7 (27)
# of sororities (% ugrad women join)	4 (32)
% African American	3
% Asian	3
% Caucasian	72
% Hispanic	6
% Native American	0
% Pacific Islander	0
% Two or more races	7
% Race and/or ethnicity unknown	3
% international	6
# of countries represented	49

ACADEMICS

Academic Rating	**97**
% students returning for sophomore year	93
% students graduating within 4 years	86
% students graduating within 6 years	91
Calendar	Semester
Student/faculty ratio	9:1
Profs interesting rating	97
Profs accessible rating	98
Most classes have 10–19 students.	

MOST POPULAR MAJORS
English Language and Literature;
Psychology; Economics

ABOUT THE SCHOOL

Kenyon College, the oldest private college in Ohio, was founded in 1824 by Episcopalian Bishop Philander Chase. This small liberal arts college—about 1,600 students attend—sports an idyllic hilltop campus that is considered one of the most beautiful in the United States. The school's collegiate Gothic architecture is especially renowned. Kenyon College's strong academic reputation in the liberal arts and sciences rests on the back of its faculty. "The professors are what make Kenyon so great," as one student says. In addition to being "intelligent and stimulating," they "encourage discussion and constantly [ask] provoking questions." These are professors who "legitimately care about students." It is not uncommon for Kenyon professors to "invite [students] over for dinner, bring snacks to class, plan extracurricular departmental events, and...always [be] willing to help with schoolwork." Professors and students get to know each other here instead of being mere faces in giant, crowded lecture halls. In 2006, the college opened the Kenyon Athletic Center, a 263,000-square-foot building that is home to school athletics and a popular hangout spot for students. One of Kenyon College's strengths is its long and proud literary tradition, which includes the celebrated and still active *The Kenyon Review* magazine. Founded in 1937 by the poet John Crowe Ransom, *The Kenyon Review* has published such leading literary figures as Robert Lowell (also a Kenyon alum), Robert Penn Warren, Flannery O'Connor, and Dylan Thomas. The college believes its "small classes, dedicated teachers, and friendly give-and-take set the tone" of college life. Kenyon is a school that fosters a sense of community in which cooperation and shared intellectual growth is valued over competition. As one student sums up a common sentiment: "It just feels like a tight-knit, loving family, and it has made me feel at home here."

BANG FOR YOUR BUCK

The small classroom sizes and talented and personable faculty are real draws for Kenyon's students. With about 200 faculty members and only 1,600 students, the faculty-to-student ratio is simply outstanding. A full 92 percent of freshmen return for sophomore year, and 89 percent graduate within four years. The college boasts a diverse student body, "ethnically but also in terms of types of people and personality," that makes for a stimulating atmosphere. As the administration explains, "Life in this small college community is fueled by the talents and enthusiasm of our students, so the admission staff seeks students who have a range of talents and interests." Kenyon also has a commitment to student success beyond college. All seniors work with the career-development office to help plan their postcollege life and career, whatever path the student chooses to take.

STUDENT LIFE

At this rural Ohio liberal arts school, students "don't have much around [them] besides corn fields, so student life revolves around student groups, large [all-campus] parties, and lectures and performances." The parties are "welcoming and there is practically no exclusion in social life." With roughly, 1,600 students, Kenyon is an insular community and there are approximately 128 registered student organizations. Greek life plays a presence on campus—which has four sororities and seven fraternities—and roughly 20 percent of men and women pledge. Ninety-nine percent of the undergraduates live on campus, adding to the close-knit feeling. One International Studies major notes that students "mostly stay on campus, so [it's] a very social place. This gives most people a chance to get involved in

Kenyon College

FINANCIAL AID: 740-427-5240 • E-MAIL: ADMISSIONS@KENYON.EDU • WEBSITE: WWW.KENYON.EDU

some way," such as in "clubs [and] [intramural] sports." Aside from clubs to join and sports to play, "almost every week there is a cool concert...or a movie screening" on campus.

CAREER

Forty-seven percent of Kenyon graduates would classify their careers as jobs that help make the world a better place, according to PayScale. com. Popular degrees include Economics, Psychology, and English. One Kenyon Biochemistry major praises the school's professors, who provide "amazing resources both inside and outside the classroom" and "can provide insight not only [about] classroom topics, but on life and careers as well." Kenyon's Career Development office—whose mission is to "facilitate [students'] career success"—regularly brings in alumni for career-oriented presentations, such as the Kenyon Finance Panel led by Kenyon alumni working in the finance industry. According to the school's website, Kenyon offers lifetime services for alumni, which include networking opportunities and the ability to search, as an employer, for a Kenyon graduate to fill a position.

FINANCIAL AID

Students should submit: CSS Profile; FAFSA; Noncustodial PROFILE. Priority filing deadline is 1/15. The Princeton Review suggests that all financial aid forms be submitted as soon as possible after October 1. *Need-based scholarships/grants offered:* College/university scholarship or grant aid from institutional funds, Federal Pell, private scholarships, SEOG, state scholarships/grants. *Loan aid offered:* Direct PLUS Loans, Direct Subsidized Loans, Direct Unsubsidized Loans. Federal Work-Study Program available. Institutional employment available.

BOTTOM LINE

Kenyon College has an annual tuition of $49,220, and students can expect to spend an additional $12,130 on room and board. However, Kenyon has a strong commitment to bringing in talented students regardless of their financial situation. All students with financial aid needs can expect to find help at Kenyon. The school makes sure they meet students' financial needs for all their years attending the school, even if those needs change over the course of the student's college career. About forty-two percent of undergraduates receive some form of financial aid, with the average need-based scholarship totaling $39,897.

CAREER INFORMATION FROM PAYSCALE.COM	
ROI Rating	91
Bachelors and No Higher	
Median starting salary	$52,700
Median mid-career salary	$111,500
At Least Bachelors	
Median starting salary	$55,000
Median mid-career salary	$116,100
Alumni with high job meaning	49%
Degrees awarded in STEM subjects	17%

SELECTIVITY	
Admissions Rating	95
# of applicants	5,603
% of applicants accepted	34
% of acceptees attending	24
# offered a place on the wait list	1,656
% accepting a place on wait list	46
% admitted from wait list	5
# of early decision applicants	345
% accepted early decision	66

FRESHMAN PROFILE	
Range SAT EBRW	640–730
Range SAT Math	623–730
Range ACT Composite	29–33
Minimum internet-based TOEFL	100
Average HS GPA	3.9
% graduated top 10% of class	63
% graduated top 25% of class	86
% graduated top 50% of class	100

DEADLINES	
Early decision	
Deadline	11/15
Notification	12/15
Other ED Deadline	1/15
Other ED Notification	2/1
Regular	
Priority	1/15
Deadline	1/15
Notification	4/1
Nonfall registration?	No

FINANCIAL FACTS	
Financial Aid Rating	97
Annual tuition	$53,830
Room and board	$12,510
Required fees	$2,100
Average frosh need-based scholarship	$43,736
Average UG need-based scholarship	$42,258
% needy frosh rec. need-based scholarship or grant aid	100
% needy UG rec. need-based scholarship or grant aid	100
% needy frosh rec. non-need-based scholarship or grant aid	42
% needy UG rec. non-need-based scholarship or grant aid	34
% needy frosh rec. need-based self-help aid	76
% needy UG rec. need-based self-help aid	89
% frosh rec. any financial aid	42
% UG rec. any financial aid	42
% UG borrow to pay for school	40
Average cumulative indebtedness	$22,025
% frosh need fully met	100
% ugrads need fully met	100

Lafayette College

118 MARKLE HALL, EASTON, PA 18042 • ADMISSIONS: 610-330-5100 • FAX: 610-330-5355

CAMPUS LIFE

Quality of Life Rating	87
Fire Safety Rating	91
Green Rating	79
Type of school	Private
Environment	City

STUDENTS

Total undergrad enrollment	2,567
% male/female	48/52
% from out of state	81
% frosh from public high school	61
% frosh live on campus	100
% ugrads live on campus	93
# of fraternities (% ugrad men join)	3 (22)
# of sororities (% ugrad women join)	6 (34)
% African American	5
% Asian	4
% Caucasian	66
% Hispanic	7
% Native American	0
% Pacific Islander	<1
% Two or more races	2
% Race and/or ethnicity unknown	6
% international	10
# of countries represented	61

ACADEMICS

Academic Rating	95
% students returning for sophomore year	95
% students graduating within 4 years	86
% students graduating within 6 years	90
Calendar	Semester
Student/faculty ratio	10:1
Profs interesting rating	89
Profs accessible rating	94

Most classes have 10–19 students. Most lab/discussion sessions have 20–29 students.

MOST POPULAR MAJORS

Mechanical Engineering; Biology/Biological Sciences; Economics

ABOUT THE SCHOOL

Thinking across disciplines has defined the Lafayette College experience since its founding in 1826. With a total student body of 2,500, the focus is exclusively on undergraduates at this top liberal arts college. Lafayette graduates are well-trained in cross-disciplinary thinking and practical application. Here's what that looks like in real terms: computer science, art, biology, and neuroscience students might work together on brain research. A team of engineering, economics, psychology, and English students might take on a consulting project to redesign a new arts and cultural center in New Orleans. Lafayette sees the world through this interdisciplinary lens, and an ability to pursue those intersections in a practical way is a big reason Lafayette students land top research, academic, and employment opportunities. Students love that "even though the school is a small liberal arts college, its strengths in math, science, and engineering give it a very practical feel," and students also "think our greatest strength is our academic diversity." Undergrads are quite pleased to discover that "classes are mostly small and even our lecture classes don't get bigger than roughly seventy-five students." The small student-to-teacher ratio allows students to build a relationship with their professors and, according to a contented undergrad, "creates a spectacular class dynamic and sense of trust."

BANG FOR YOUR BUCK

Lafayette College is part of a very small group of colleges and universities throughout the United States, that provide reduced-loan or no-loan financial aid awards to lower- and middle-income students who gain admission and seek financial assistance. Scholarships are also offered to top applicants (no additional application needed). There are two major merit-based programs: The Marquis Fellowship, worth $40,000 per year and the Marquis Scholarship, worth $24,000 per year. The majority of Marquis winners are selected solely on the merits presented in their application. Both awards come with special mentoring activities with faculty and other campus scholars, and an additional $4,000 scholarship for an off-campus course during the interim period (in winter or summer). These awards are based on superior academic performance and evidence of leadership and major contribution to school or community activities. Said one thankful student, "I was lucky enough to be chosen as a Marquis Scholar, giving me ample opportunity to study abroad."

STUDENT LIFE

Life at Lafayette "is everything you make it. There are as many or as few social opportunities as any one person can handle." With 250 registered student organizations—at a school with only roughly 2,500 students—there really is something for everyone. Greek life plays a role in the social scene, with six sororities and four fraternities on campus. Roughly 34 percent of women join a sorority and 23 percent of men join a fraternity. According to one Mathematics major, "Greek life and [Division I] sports teams dominate the social scene after freshmen year." Lafayette students "work hard...but also know how to have a good time" and "tend to go to a lot of events on campus[,] whether it be musicians or comedians." There is "very little to do in Easton itself," so most students stick to campus activities sponsored by the school, various sports teams, or one of the Greek houses.

Lafayette College

FINANCIAL AID: 610-330-5055 • E-MAIL: ADMISSIONS@LAFAYETTE.EDU • WEBSITE: WWW.LAFAYETTE.EDU

CAREER

The average starting salary for a Lafayette graduate is roughly $61,500, according to PayScale.com, which also reports that 42 percent of Lafayette graduates consider their careers to be in keeping with making the world a better place. Popular jobs after graduation include project engineer, civil engineer, and marketing coordinator, with the most popular majors being Mechanical Engineering, Economics, and Civil Engineering. "Career counseling services start freshman year and are readily available to any student who wants to utilize them," says one Government/Law and Spanish double major. The Office of Career Services is "proud to be a national leader in career development," according to the school's website, and is ranked as one of the top twenty higher education career services offices. Students are encouraged to join Gateway, the school's four-year individualized career exploration program, and Lafayette's website reports that 85 percent of each undergraduate class signs up. A Psychology and Government double major praises the school's "strong career services program that provides excellent opportunities and...works closely with alumni to provide career exposure opportunities even to first year students."

GENERAL INFO

Activities: Choral groups, concert band, dance, drama/theater, jazz band, literary magazine, music ensembles, musical theater, pep band, radio station, student government, student newspaper, student-run film society, symphony orchestra, yearbook, campus ministries, international student organization.

FINANCIAL AID

Students should submit: CSS Profile; FAFSA; Noncustodial PROFILE. Priority filing deadline is 1/15. The Princeton Review suggests that all financial aid forms be submitted as soon as possible after October 1. *Need-based scholarships/grants offered:* College/university scholarship or grant aid from institutional funds, Federal Pell, private scholarships, SEOG, state scholarships/grants. *Loan aid offered:* Direct PLUS Loans, Direct Subsidized Loans, Direct Unsubsidized Loans. Applicants will be notified of awards on or about 4/1. Federal Work-Study Program available. Institutional employment available.

BOTTOM LINE

The tab for tuition, fees, and room and board at Lafayette College comes to about $63,355 per year. Fortunately, Lafayette's strong endowment enables the college to aggressively offset costs for students. Financial aid packages are generous and the average need-based scholarship is $40,285. Students thoroughly understand and appreciate the value of a Lafayette College education. "It's no secret that the education is expensive, but I feel like I'm really getting my money's worth from Lafayette."

CAREER INFORMATION FROM PAYSCALE.COM

ROI Rating	91
Bachelors and No Higher	
Median starting salary	$64,200
Median mid-career salary	$121,200
At Least Bachelors	
Median starting salary	$66,200
Median mid-career salary	$128,200
Alumni with high job meaning	41%
Degrees awarded in STEM subjects	47%

SELECTIVITY

Admissions Rating	95
# of applicants	8,469
% of applicants accepted	31
% of acceptees attending	25
# offered a place on the wait list	1,708
% accepting a place on wait list	24
% admitted from wait list	27
# of early decision applicants	726
% accepted early decision	46

FRESHMAN PROFILE

Range SAT EBRW	630–710
Range SAT Math	630–730
Range ACT Composite	28–31
Minimum paper TOEFL	550
Minimum internet-based TOEFL	80
Average HS GPA	3.5
% graduated top 10% of class	60
% graduated top 25% of class	91
% graduated top 50% of class	99

DEADLINES

Early decision	
Deadline	11/15
Notification	12/15
Other ED Deadline	2/1
Other ED Notification	2/15
Regular	
Deadline	1/15
Notification	4/1
Nonfall registration?	Yes

FINANCIAL FACTS

Financial Aid Rating	98
Annual tuition	$52,415
Room and board	$14,470
Required fees	$465
Books and supplies	$1,000
Average frosh need-based scholarship	$44,113
Average UG need-based scholarship	$43,399
% needy frosh rec. need-based scholarship or grant aid	98
% needy UG rec. need-based scholarship or grant aid	96
% needy frosh rec. non-need-based scholarship or grant aid	18
% needy UG rec. non-need-based scholarship or grant aid	17
% needy frosh rec. need-based self-help aid	91
% needy UG rec. need-based self-help aid	92
% frosh rec. any financial aid	61
% UG rec. any financial aid	58
% UG borrow to pay for school	48
Average cumulative indebtedness	$32,974
% frosh need fully met	100

Lake Forest College

555 North Sheridan Road, Lake Forest, IL 60045 • Admissions: 847-735-5000 • Fax: 847-735-6291

CAMPUS LIFE

Quality of Life Rating	92
Fire Safety Rating	89
Green Rating	60*
Type of school	Private
Environment	Village

STUDENTS

Total undergrad enrollment	1,483
% male/female	43/57
% from out of state	38
% frosh live on campus	87
% ugrads live on campus	75
# of fraternities (% ugrad men join)	3 (17)
# of sororities (% ugrad women join)	4 (19)
% African American	6
% Asian	6
% Caucasian	58
% Hispanic	15
% Native American	<1
% Pacific Islander	0
% Two or more races	4
% Race and/or ethnicity unknown	4
% international	8
# of countries represented	71

ACADEMICS

Academic Rating	92
% students returning for sophomore year	85
% students graduating within 4 years	66
% students graduating within 6 years	72
Calendar	Semester
Student/faculty ratio	12:1
Profs interesting rating	94
Profs accessible rating	95

Most classes have fewer than 10 students.
Most lab/discussion sessions have 10–19 students.

MOST POPULAR MAJORS
Psychology; Business/Commerce; Finance

ABOUT THE SCHOOL

When students enroll in Lake Forest College, they join a "close-knit [community] of intellectuals" who are truly passionate about their school. And it's easy to understand why. Indeed, undergrads quickly point out that they benefit from a "liberal arts education that is centered around student and professor relationships." This can partially be ascribed to "small class sizes" which virtually guarantee "individualized attention." Undergrads also highly value "the great opportunities available to [both]...study abroad and obtain hands on experience." And they rave about their professors who are "very passionate about what they are teaching" and "have very high expectations for student performance." Perhaps most importantly, professors here are "great at facilitating discussion and making students think deeply about issues." All in all, as one ecstatic senior concludes, "Lake Forest College is about expanding your horizons, your intellectual abilities, and opening your eyes to the world wider than imaginable."

BANG FOR YOUR BUCK

At first glance, Lake Forest might seem a tad pricey on paper. Thankfully, an active and caring financial aid office strives to help families mitigate costs. These efforts don't go unnoticed. After all, a handful of students report that their "financial aid [package] was a big factor" in deciding to attend Lake Forest. As a sociology major explains, "the financial aid office bends over backwards to help students and offers many grants. It was cheaper to attend LFC than the other private schools I was accepted to." In fact, 95 percent of undergraduates receive some form of need-based aid. Some of this money comes from the Lake Forest College Grant which awards gifts ranging from $5,000 to $30,000 each year. The Illinois Monetary Award Program also helps students meet their need with grants up to $4,720.

STUDENT LIFE

Academics usually take priority at Lake Forest. Therefore, it's not surprising that "during the week life revolves around studying and classes." But don't let these workhorses fool you! They find plenty of ways to kick back as well. On the weekends, students head to the Mohr Student Center for "Mohr at Midnight" events, such as Casino Night and Silent Dance Party as well as student-sponsored All Campus Parties (ACPs). School sponsored events such as "'Global Fest' [and] 'Casino Night' are also well attended. And undergrads love to take advantage of the fact that Lake Michigan, and a beautiful beach, are only half a mile from campus." Lastly, "Chicago is [merely] a train ride away so many weekends are spent exploring the city."

CAREER

Rest assured that when it comes time to cross the dais on graduation day, Lake Forest students are prepared to meet the future head on! In fact, 97% of these ... grad school within six months of graduation. More specifically, over 90 percent of Lake Forest students who applied to medical school were accepted. And nearly 100 percent of finance majors pursued at least one internship, many resulting in securing jobs before graduation. This success is certainly made possible through the guiding hand of a fantastic career services office. For example, undergrads here participate in the Career Pathways Program, joining specialized career communities that match their interests with career preparation opportunities and networks. This action plan really helps undergrads to focus their goals and professional aspirations. And, of course, the office hosts plenty of fun (and effective!) events from major and career exploration workshops, industry-focused events, to Speed Networking.

Lake Forest College

FINANCIAL AID: 847-735-5103 • E-MAIL: ADMISSIONS@LAKEFOREST.EDU • WEBSITE: WWW.LAKEFOREST.EDU

GENERAL INFO

Activities: Choral groups, concert band, dance, drama/theater, jazz band, literary magazine, music ensembles, musical theater, radio station, student government, student newspaper, symphony orchestra, campus ministries, International Student Organization, Model UN. **Organizations:** 80 registered organizations, 12 honor societies, 6 religious organizations. 3 fraternities, 4 sororities. **Athletics (Intercollegiate):** *Men:* basketball, cross-country, diving, football, handball, ice hockey, soccer, swimming, tennis. *Women:* basketball, cross-country, diving, handball, ice hockey, soccer, softball, swimming, tennis, volleyball. **On-Campus Highlights:** The Lillard Science Center, Donnelley and Lee Library, Mohr Student Center, Sports Center, Center for Chicago Programs, Career Advancement Center.

FINANCIAL AID

Students should submit: FAFSA. Priority filing deadline is 2/15. The Princeton Review suggests that all financial aid forms be submitted as soon as possible after October 1. *Need-based scholarships/grants offered:* College/university scholarship or grant aid from institutional funds, Federal Pell, private scholarships, SEOG, state scholarships/grants. *Loan aid offered:* Direct PLUS Loans, Direct Subsidized Loans, Direct Unsubsidized Loans. Applicants will be notified of awards on a rolling basis beginning 12/15. Federal Work-Study Program available. Institutional employment available.

BOTTOM LINE

Students choosing to enroll in Lake Forest College will receive a tuition bill of $46,320 Undergrads face an additional $744 in required fees. They can also expect to spend roughly $800 for books and various academic supplies. And, of course, room and board is estimated to cost $10,390. Fortunately, these figures become a little more palatable after learning that the average need-based scholarship is $35,723.

CAREER INFORMATION FROM PAYSCALE.COM	
ROI Rating	90
Bachelors and No Higher	
Median starting salary	$53,700
Median mid-career salary	$107,800
At Least Bachelors	
Median starting salary	$54,600
Median mid-career salary	$115,100
Alumni with high job meaning	47%
Degrees awarded in STEM subjects	21%

SELECTIVITY	
Admissions Rating	86
# of applicants	4,303
% of applicants accepted	53
% of acceptees attending	16
# of early decision applicants	41
% accepted early decision	68

FRESHMAN PROFILE	
Range SAT EBRW	550–650
Range SAT Math	560–660
Range ACT Composite	24–29
Minimum paper TOEFL	550
Minimum internet-based TOEFL	83
% graduated top 10% of class	38
% graduated top 25% of class	67
% graduated top 50% of class	93

DEADLINES	
Early decision	
Deadline	11/15
Notification	12/15
Other ED Deadline	1/15
Other ED Notification	1/30
Early action	
Deadline	11/15
Notification	12/15
Regular	
Deadline	2/15
Nonfall registration?	Yes

FINANCIAL FACTS	
Financial Aid Rating	88
Annual tuition	$46,320
Room and board	$10,390
Required fees	$744
Books and supplies	$1,000
Average frosh need-based scholarship	$35,723
Average UG need-based scholarship	$34,550
% needy frosh rec. need-based scholarship or grant aid	100
% needy UG rec. need-based scholarship or grant aid	100
% needy frosh rec. non-need-based scholarship or grant aid	0
% needy UG rec. non-need-based scholarship or grant aid	0
% needy frosh rec. need-based self-help aid	85
% needy UG rec. need-based self-help aid	88
% frosh rec. any financial aid	94
% UG rec. any financial aid	95
% UG borrow to pay for school	60
% frosh need fully met	30
% ugrads need fully met	32
Average % of frosh need met	85
Average % of ugrad need met	85

Lawrence University

711 EAST BOLDT WAY, APPLETON, WI 54911-5699 • ADMISSIONS: 920-832-6500 • FAX: 920-832-6782

CAMPUS LIFE

Quality of Life Rating	**88**
Fire Safety Rating	**86**
Green Rating	**89**
Type of school	Private
Environment	City

STUDENTS

Total undergrad enrollment	1,441
% male/female	46/54
% from out of state	71
% frosh live on campus	100
% ugrads live on campus	94
# of fraternities (% ugrad men join)	4 (10)
# of sororities (% ugrad women join)	4 (14)
% African American	5
% Asian	5
% Caucasian	65
% Hispanic	9
% Native American	<1
% Pacific Islander	<1
% Two or more races	4
% Race and/or ethnicity unknown	1
% international	12
# of countries represented	52

ACADEMICS

Academic Rating	**91**
% students returning for sophomore year	88
% students graduating within 4 years	65
% students graduating within 6 years	80
Calendar	Trimester
Student/faculty ratio	8:1
Profs interesting rating	91
Profs accessible rating	93

Most classes have 10–19 students. Most lab/discussion sessions have fewer than 10 students.

MOST POPULAR MAJORS
Biology/Biological Sciences; Psychology; Music Performance

ABOUT THE SCHOOL

Lawrence University is a liberal arts school and conservatory of music in Wisconsin that aims to "broaden students' minds" and "prepare [them] to be intellectual leaders in whatever field they enter." Centered around "Engaged Learning," or learning by doing, the curriculum begins with the Freshman Studies program, in which students are grouped into course sections of about fifteen students, and commence the reading and discussion of great works. "Small" class sizes and "individual attention" are hallmarks of the university as well, which together foster a "welcoming and friendly community." Lawrence also provides "many opportunities for experiential learning [such as] off-campus study, visits, field trips [and] grants." Academically, Lawrence has many "prestigious" programs, though its music conservatory, in particular, garners much renown. Thankfully, no matter the course of study, undergrads here tend to speak highly of their professors. These "dedicated" instructors are "very passionate and knowledgeable about what they teach." They also "really go out of their way to help individual students." As one undergrad elaborates, "I have gotten to know each one of my professors by name and continually interact with them even long after I have taken a course with them." And perhaps best of all, they push [their students] to learn and strengthen [their] opinions."

BANG FOR YOUR BUCK

Lawrence is a school that prides itself on "its ability to provide significant financial aid and scholarship opportunities." What's more, the "financial aid…department is [truly] willing to work with students individually" to ensure that their needs are met. All applicants are eligible to earn renewable academic scholarships that range up to half the tuition. Selected students will be notified shortly after receiving their letter of admission. Additionally, there are scholarships specifically set aside for music students that are renewable and can range up to half the tuition as well. All Lawrence undergraduates, as part of their Senior Experience Requirement, may apply for university grants of up to $3,000 to support particularly ambitious or distinctive projects.

STUDENT LIFE

Rest assured there's ample opportunity for fun at Lawrence. Students here love being active and you'll find that most of them are involved with "many different clubs or committees whether for the student government, towards our major, or just for fun like long boarding club or painting club." A good number also have an altruistic bent and "give lots of time to volunteer opportunities." Since so many people are involved with the music school you can guarantee that "there is ALWAYS [some] type of concert going on." Rumor has it that "Monday jazz sessions are [a] highlight." The school also sponsors plenty of weekly events like "bubble soccer at the gym," a "weekend… improv show," or "laser tag."

CAREER

The Career Services office at Lawrence really helps students approach the job hunt with confidence and purpose. To begin with, freshmen are encouraged to schedule an initial visit to introduce themselves, share their interests and learn how they can best use the office's resources in the years to come. Seniors (and upperclassmen in general) can participate in a 5-week program titled "Strategies for Career Success." This provides undergrads with the tools and skills they need to kick start their job search and successfully market themselves. Additionally, Career Services hosts numerous workshops on topics such as setting goals, resume writing, networking, branding and social media and exploring whether grad school is right for you. All undergrads can log into LU Works, a website through Lawrence, to find and manage job and internship opportunities.

Lawrence University

FINANCIAL AID: 920-832-6583 • E-MAIL: ADMISSIONS@LAWRENCE.EDU • WEBSITE: WWW.LAWRENCE.EDU

GENERAL INFO

Activities: Choral groups, concert band, dance, drama/theater, jazz band, literary magazine, music ensembles, musical theater, opera, pep band, radio station, student government, student newspaper, student-run film society, symphony orchestra, International Student Organization, Model UN. **Organizations:** 150+ registered organizations, 4 honor societies, 3 religious organizations. 4 fraternities, 4 sororities. **Athletics (Intercollegiate):** *Men:* baseball, basketball, cross-country, diving, fencing, football, ice hockey, soccer, swimming, tennis, track/field (outdoor), track/field (indoor). *Women:* basketball, cross-country, diving, fencing, soccer, softball, swimming, tennis, track/field (outdoor), track/field (indoor), volleyball. **On-Campus Highlights:** Wriston Art Gallery, Music Conservatory, Warch Campus Center, Bjorklunden(441-acre campus in Door County, WI), newly renovated Banta Bowl (football and soccer stadium).

FINANCIAL AID

Students should submit: CSS Profile; FAFSA; Noncustodial PROFILE. Priority filing deadline is 2/1. The Princeton Review suggests that all financial aid forms be submitted as soon as possible after October 1. *Need-based scholarships/grants offered:* College/university scholarship or grant aid from institutional funds, Federal Pell, private scholarships, SEOG, state scholarships/grants. *Loan aid offered:* Direct PLUS Loans, Direct Subsidized Loans, Direct Unsubsidized Loans. Applicants will be notified of awards on or about 1/15. Federal Work-Study Program available. Institutional employment available.

THE BOTTOM LINE

Lawrence University charges $47,175 in annual tuition. Students can expect to pay an additional $5,172 for on-campus housing (rate applies to a standard double room) as well as $5,169 for board for the year. Further, all undergrads are charged $285 for an activity fee and $15 for an environmental fee. These charges add up to $57,816. Of course, students should also set aside additional funds for books and personal expenses.

CAREER INFORMATION FROM PAYSCALE.COM	
ROI Rating	90
Bachelors and No Higher	
Median starting salary	$48,500
Median mid-career salary	$102,900
At Least Bachelors	
Median starting salary	$52,100
Median mid-career salary	$110,700
Alumni with high job meaning	63%
Degrees awarded in STEM subjects	25%

SELECTIVITY	
Admissions Rating	88
# of applicants	3,612
% of applicants accepted	61
% of acceptees attending	16
# offered a place on the wait list	176
% accepting a place on wait list	46
% admitted from wait list	1

FRESHMAN PROFILE	
Range SAT EBRW	620–730
Range SAT Math	600–730
Range ACT Composite	25–32
Minimum paper TOEFL	577
Minimum internet-based TOEFL	80
Average HS GPA	3.5
% graduated top 10% of class	38
% graduated top 25% of class	68
% graduated top 50% of class	94

DEADLINES	
Early decision	
Deadline	10/31
Notification	12/1
Other ED Deadline	11/1
Other ED Notification	12/15
Early action	
Deadline	12/1
Notification	1/25
Regular	
Deadline	1/15
Nonfall registration?	Yes

FINANCIAL FACTS	
Financial Aid Rating	91
Annual tuition	$47,175
Room and board	$10,341
Required fees	$300
Books and supplies	$900
Average frosh need-based scholarship	$36,619
Average UG need-based scholarship	$33,921
% needy frosh rec. need-based scholarship or grant aid	98
% needy UG rec. need-based scholarship or grant aid	98
% needy frosh rec. non-need-based scholarship or grant aid	0
% needy UG rec. non-need-based scholarship or grant aid	0
% needy frosh rec. need-based self-help aid	79
% needy UG rec. need-based self-help aid	82
% frosh rec. any financial aid	97
% UG rec. any financial aid	97
% UG borrow to pay for school	60
Average cumulative indebtedness	$32,488

Lehigh University

27 Memorial Drive West, Bethlehem, PA 18015 • Admissions: 610-758-3100 • Fax: 610-758-4361

#44 BEST VALUE COLLEGE

CAMPUS LIFE

Quality of Life Rating	85
Fire Safety Rating	97
Green Rating	93
Type of school	Private
Environment	City

STUDENTS

Total undergrad enrollment	5,057
% male/female	55/45
% from out of state	73
% frosh live on campus	99
% ugrads live on campus	65
# of fraternities (% ugrad men join)	17 (38)
# of sororities (% ugrad women join)	11 (45)
% African American	4
% Asian	8
% Caucasian	64
% Hispanic	9
% Native American	<1
% Pacific Islander	<1
% Two or more races	3
% Race and/or ethnicity unknown	4
% international	9
# of countries represented	62

ACADEMICS

Academic Rating	88
% students returning for sophomore year	96
% students graduating within 4 years	76
% students graduating within 6 years	86
Calendar	Semester
Student/faculty ratio	9:1
Profs interesting rating	77
Profs accessible rating	78

Most classes have 10–19 students. Most lab/discussion sessions have 10–19 students.

MOST POPULAR MAJORS
Mechanical Engineering; Accounting; Finance

ABOUT THE SCHOOL

Rigorous academics, a low student-to-faculty ratio, and a host of traditions are just a few of the many advantages at Lehigh University. A private research university in Bethlehem, Pennsylvania, the school's 100+ majors include more than twenty interdisciplinary programs spread across its colleges and departments. Around 87 percent of students graduate with at least one internship or co-op under their belts and nearly half study abroad. Lehigh's flexible curriculum lets students explore their interests and tailor a major, and the school encourages students to work side-by-side with faculty in research endeavors. The coursework is "difficult, keeping even the brightest students on their toes," but "the kinship formed through the struggle and triumph are irreplaceable," and students can even enroll in graduate classes while undergrads to get a head start. "Different colleges easily mix and can blend together," and professors are "always willing to help with any concerns or confusions about class matters or those outside of the classroom as well."

BANG FOR YOUR BUCK

According to students, "Lehigh is limitless." Though the school is known for engineering, "all programs and organizations are extremely dedicated to what they do" and "there are myriad opportunities available in all fields." "Make sure to get to know [professors] outside of the classroom since they often give out career advice," says a student. There are "so many research, internship, study abroad, and community service opportunities. Even though tuition is high, help is available. Students are considered for most merit-based scholarships just by applying to Lehigh, but some require an additional application. Dean's Scholarships are given for academic and leadership achievement to the tune of $12,000 per year; full tuition is given via Founder's and Trustees' Scholars to top students in the applicant pool.

STUDENT LIFE

Many students from Lehigh come from the states in proximity to Pennsylvania, though "there is a growing environment of diverse individuals from around the country (and other countries)." This group does it all. They are "hard working, smart, motivated, career-driven" who "spend countless hours in the library and still go out on average 3 to 4 times a week." "You are constantly doing school work and going out. It is nuts," says a student. Lehigh is big into Greek life, which "is a primary component to a lot of students"; the school's sixteen themed residential communities also help smaller subsets form. There is a "prevalence of the arts on campus," many students enjoy volunteering, and "most people hit the gym daily." The school throws Lehigh after Dark events, as well as "gym nights, music events, and cultural events where they always have food."

CAREER

Lehigh University's priority "is giving students the best chance for professional success." The Center for Career & Professional Development works with students on their individual plan at every step of the way, and 95 percent of students fulfill ones of the outcomes they had laid out, whether that be employment, graduate school,

Lehigh University

FINANCIAL AID: 610-758-3181 • E-MAIL: ADMISSIONS@LEHIGH.EDU • WEBSITE: WWW.LEHIGH.EDU

or other opportunities. Fall and spring career expos help students make connections, career coaches are embedded in each of the undergraduate colleges, and the alumni network "always reaches out to the school and are willing to help out current students." Currently, the school has over three thousand full-time positions and internships posted on the CCPD's job board. Of the Lehigh University alumni visiting PayScale.com, 46 percent report that they derive a high level of meaning from their jobs.

GENERAL INFO

Activities: Choral groups, concert band, dance, drama/theater, jazz band, literary magazine, marching band, music ensembles, musical theater, pep band, radio station, student government, student newspaper, student-run film society, symphony orchestra, yearbook, campus ministries, International Student Organization, Model UN. **Organizations:** 18 honor societies, 12 religious organizations. 18 fraternities, 12 sororities. **Athletics (Intercollegiate, Division I):** *Men:* baseball, basketball, cross-country, diving, football, golf, lacrosse, soccer, swimming, tennis, track/field (outdoor), track/field (indoor), wrestling. *Women:* basketball, crew/rowing, cross-country, diving, field hockey, golf, lacrosse, soccer, softball, swimming, tennis, track/field (outdoor), track/field (indoor), volleyball. **On-Campus Highlights:** Zoellner Arts Center LU Art Galleries, Campus Square, Taylor Gymnasium, Ulrich Student Center, Goodman Campus.

FINANCIAL AID

Students should submit: Business/Farm Supplement; CSS Profile; FAFSA; Noncustodial PROFILE. Regular filing deadline is 1/1. The Princeton Review suggests that all financial aid forms be submitted as soon as possible after October 1. *Need-based scholarships/grants offered:* College/university scholarship or grant aid from institutional funds, Federal Pell, private scholarships, SEOG, state scholarships/grants. *Loan aid offered:* Direct PLUS Loans, Direct Subsidized Loans, Direct Unsubsidized Loans. Applicants will be notified of awards on or about 3/30. Federal Work-Study Program available. Institutional employment available.

BOTTOM LINE

Tuition is a steep $50,320, with room and board costing another $13,120, but Lehigh is committed to meeting 100 percent of demonstrated need for all admitted students. The school caps loans at $5,000 per year to reduce student debt at graduation, and around half of all students receive some form of financial aid.

CAREER INFORMATION FROM PAYSCALE.COM	
ROI Rating	92
Bachelors and No Higher	
Median starting salary	$67,200
Median mid-career salary	$135,700
At Least Bachelors	
Median starting salary	$68,800
Median mid-career salary	$138,900
Alumni with high job meaning	45%
Degrees awarded in STEM subjects	52%

SELECTIVITY	
Admissions Rating	95
# of applicants	13,871
% of applicants accepted	25
% of acceptees attending	35
# offered a place on the wait list	6,516
% accepting a place on wait list	43
% admitted from wait list	2
# of early decision applicants	1116
% accepted early decision	60

FRESHMAN PROFILE	
Range SAT EBRW	620–700
Range SAT Math	650–730
Range ACT Composite	29–32
Minimum paper TOEFL	570
Minimum internet-based TOEFL	90
% graduated top 10% of class	63
% graduated top 25% of class	89
% graduated top 50% of class	99

DEADLINES	
Early decision	
Deadline	11/15
Notification	12/15
Other ED Deadline	1/1
Other ED Notification	2/15
Regular	
Deadline	1/1
Notification	4/1
Nonfall registration?	Yes

FINANCIAL FACTS	
Financial Aid Rating	93
Annual tuition	$50,320
Room and board	$13,120
Required fees	$420
Books and supplies	$1,000
Average frosh need-based scholarship	$41,234
Average UG need-based scholarship	$40,472
% needy frosh rec. need-based scholarship or grant aid	91
% needy UG rec. need-based scholarship or grant aid	93
% needy frosh rec. non-need-based scholarship or grant aid	15
% needy UG rec. non-need-based scholarship or grant aid	17
% needy frosh rec. need-based self-help aid	93
% needy UG rec. need-based self-help aid	94
% frosh rec. any financial aid	59
% UG rec. any financial aid	58
% UG borrow to pay for school	51
Average cumulative indebtedness	$35,440
% frosh need fully met	75
% ugrads need fully met	76

Macalester College

1600 GRAND AVENUE, ST. PAUL, MN 55105 • ADMISSIONS: 651-696-6357 • FAX: 651-696-6724

CAMPUS LIFE

Quality of Life Rating	91
Fire Safety Rating	98
Green Rating	95
Type of school	Private
Environment	Metropolis

STUDENTS

Total undergrad enrollment	2,116
% male/female	40/60
% from out of state	83
% frosh from public high school	65
% frosh live on campus	100
% ugrads live on campus	60
# of fraternities (% ugrad men join)	0 (0)
# of sororities (% ugrad women join)	0 (0)
% African American	3
% Asian	7
% Caucasian	61
% Hispanic	8
% Native American	<1
% Pacific Islander	<1
% Two or more races	6
% Race and/or ethnicity unknown	<1
% international	15
# of countries represented	90

ACADEMICS

Academic Rating	89
% students returning for sophomore year	93
% students graduating within 4 years	85
% students graduating within 6 years	87
Calendar	Semester
Student/faculty ratio	10:1
Profs interesting rating	94
Profs accessible rating	92

MOST POPULAR MAJORS
Mathematics; Economics; Political Science and Government

ABOUT THE SCHOOL

Macalester College has been preparing its students for world citizenship and providing a rigorous, integrated international education for over six decades. (Kofi Annan is an alumnus.) With a total campus size of just over 2,000 undergraduates, students benefit from a curriculum designed to include international perspectives, a multitude of semester-long study abroad programs, faculty with worldwide experience, and a community engaged in issues that matter. With more than 90 countries represented on campus, Macalester has one of the highest percentages of international-student enrollment of any U.S. college. Students affirm that the school's "commitment to internationalism is unmatched by any other institution." As a result, Macalester immerses students in a microcosm of the global world from the day each moves into a dorm room, walks into the first classroom, and begins to make friends over global cuisine in Café Mac. One student notes that the student body is "diverse and interesting; some of my best friends are from countries I had hardly heard of before I got here." Over a quarter of domestic students are people of color, further contributing to diverse perspectives in the classroom.

Macalester's location in a major metropolitan city offers students a wealth of research and internship opportunities in business, finance, medicine, science, government, law, the arts, and more. The internship program and career-development center help students gain experience and connections that frequently lead to employment opportunities in the United States and around the world. Students say that "one of Macalester's greatest strengths is its commitment to providing students with opportunities to apply their learning in real settings. Most students do an internship and/or participate in some kind of civic engagement during their time here, and the school is great about supporting that." In addition to teaching, Macalester's science and math faculty are very active in research. The college ranks among the top ten U.S. liberal arts colleges for active National Science Foundation (NSF) grants relative to faculty size. This results in incredible opportunities for students to work with their professors on cutting-edge, real-world research projects.

BANG FOR YOUR BUCK

Macalester meets the full demonstrated financial need of every admitted student in order to ensure that classes are filled with talented, high-achieving students from a broad variety of backgrounds. Support is provided by the college's endowment and gifts to the college, which remains fiscally strong. Every student benefits both academically and financially from this support.

STUDENT LIFE

Life at Macalester "is ruled by randomness," and these undergrads wouldn't have it any other way. As one delighted political science major shares, "Studying in the Campus Center can be broken up by an impromptu performance by one of our a cappella groups, or the water polo team running through to raise awareness about a match." The fun and whimsy doesn't end there. As another contented undergrad tells us, "I've gone sledding in full-body trash bag 'sleds', held election night viewing parties in the dorm lounges, and sat around talking until 3:30 in the morning about different religions with people who each brought a different experience to the table." Naturally, there are

Macalester College

FINANCIAL AID: 651-696-6214 • E-MAIL: ADMISSIONS@MACALESTER.EDU • WEBSITE: WWW.MACALESTER.EDU

plenty of more structured and school-sponsored activities. Indeed, "there's usually at least one dance a week as well as a healthy variety of other performances, sporting events, or discussions." Lastly, the surrounding Twin Cities offer plenty of entertainment should students decide to venture off-campus.

CAREER

Macalester provides its undergrads with "many opportunities and [lots of] encouragement [in finding] internships, research [opportunities], careers [paths], etc." And a lot of that is supplied by the awesome Career Development Center. To begin with, students unsure of what they might want to pursue can reap the benefits of career counseling. They can meet with counselors to discuss their passions and take career assessment tests. The office also helps undergrads to connect with alumni for both mentoring and networking purposes. Through the Macalester Career Connection, students can search through numerous job postings. And for those undergrads confident they want to attend grad school—fear not! The Career Development Center offers plenty of guidance in that department as well.

GENERAL INFO

Athletics (Intercollegiate): *Men:* Baseball, basketball, cross-country, diving, football, golf, soccer, swimming, tennis, track/field (outdoor), track/field (indoor). *Women:* Basketball, cross-country, diving, golf, soccer, softball, swimming, tennis, track/field (outdoor), track/field (indoor), volleyball, water polo.

FINANCIAL AID

Students should submit: CSS Profile; FAFSA; Noncustodial PROFILE. Regular filing deadline is 1/15. The Princeton Review suggests that all financial aid forms be submitted as soon as possible after October 1. *Need-based scholarships/grants offered:* College/university scholarship or grant aid from institutional funds, Federal Pell, private scholarships, SEOG, state scholarships/grants. *Loan aid offered:* Direct PLUS Loans, Direct Subsidized Loans, Direct Unsubsidized Loans. Federal Work-Study Program available. Institutional employment available.

BOTTOM LINE

The cost of tuition for a year at Macalester is about $54,114. Room and board is approximately $12,156. Daunting though that may seem, the college is committed to helping. The average undergraduate need-based scholarship is $39,177. Not to mention additional aid offered through scholarships and loans.

CAREER INFORMATION FROM PAYSCALE.COM	
ROI Rating	89
Bachelors and No Higher	
Median starting salary	$51,300
Median mid-career salary	$101,000
At Least Bachelors	
Median starting salary	$53,100
Median mid-career salary	$103,600
Alumni with high job meaning	50%
Degrees awarded in STEM subjects	31%

SELECTIVITY	
Admissions Rating	93
# of applicants	5,900
% of applicants accepted	41
% of acceptees attending	23
# offered a place on the wait list	356
% accepting a place on wait list	54
% admitted from wait list	54
# of early decision applicants	272
% accepted early decision	52

FRESHMAN PROFILE	
Range SAT EBRW	660–740
Range SAT Math	640–740
Range ACT Composite	29–32
% graduated top 10% of class	67
% graduated top 25% of class	91
% graduated top 50% of class	100

DEADLINES	
Early decision	
Deadline	11/15
Notification	12/15
Other ED Deadline	1/1
Other ED Notification	2/1
Regular	
Priority	None
Deadline	1/15
Notification	3/30
Nonfall registration?	No

FINANCIAL FACTS	
Financial Aid Rating	95
Annual tuition	$54,114
Room and board	$12,156
Required fees	$230
Books and supplies	$1,168
Average frosh need-based scholarship	$42,208
Average UG need-based scholarship	$39,177
% needy frosh rec. need-based scholarship or grant aid	99
% needy UG rec. need-based scholarship or grant aid	99
% needy frosh rec. non-need-based scholarship or grant aid	8
% needy UG rec. non-need-based scholarship or grant aid	6
% needy frosh rec. need-based self-help aid	89
% needy UG rec. need-based self-help aid	92
% frosh rec. any financial aid	83
% UG rec. any financial aid	82
% UG borrow to pay for school	61
Average cumulative indebtedness	$24,381
% frosh need fully met	100
% ugrads need fully met	100
Average % of frosh need met	100

Marlboro College

PO Box A, Marlboro, VT 05344-0300 • Admissions: 802-258-9236 • Fax: 802-451-7555

CAMPUS LIFE
Quality of Life Rating	85
Fire Safety Rating	82
Green Rating	60*
Type of school	Private
Environment	Rural

STUDENTS
Total undergrad enrollment	174
% male/female	47/53
% from out of state	89
% frosh from public high school	66
% frosh live on campus	100
% ugrads live on campus	66
# of fraternities (% ugrad men join)	0 (0)
# of sororities (% ugrad women join)	0 (0)
% African American	4
% Asian	1
% Caucasian	78
% Hispanic	3
% Native American	1
% Pacific Islander	0
% Two or more races	5
% Race and/or ethnicity unknown	7
% international	2
# of countries represented	4

ACADEMICS
Academic Rating	93
% students returning for sophomore year	85
Calendar	Semester
Student/faculty ratio	5:1
Profs interesting rating	99
Profs accessible rating	93
Most classes have 10–19 students.	

MOST POPULAR MAJORS
English Language and Literature; Social Sciences; Visual and Performing Arts

ABOUT THE SCHOOL

Tiny Vermont liberal arts gem Marlboro College is an intentionally small community of just 500 undergraduates and graduates, which stresses cross-disciplinary, student-designed study. A student-to-faculty ratio of 6:1 means professors act as "both a mentor and a friend," and upper level classes are often tutorials involving just one or two students. Students here are encouraged to address their professors by their first names in order to" implement a feeling of peerage rather than hierarchy," and students are elected to committees that have a say in admission decisions, punishments for broken rules, and which faculty receive tenure. In addition, a town meeting is held every week in which "new additions to the school or changes to the bylaws are presented in front of the entire Marlboro community, and everyone is given one vote."

Student autonomy is also present in the curriculum: Marlboro students must choose a Plan of Concentration in their junior year, which is more of an interdisciplinary academic theme than a single major; independent of the student's concentration, there is a strong emphasis on clear writing throughout all courses. Classes all pretty much take place "around tables," and faculty really "bring the coursework to life." Other options to interact with the material come in the form of guest speakers, interviews, and even hands-on experience such as working on the campus farm.

BANG FOR YOUR BUCK

The "academic freedom" at Marlboro is its greatest gift; it has just one professor for each field, which means those professors really 'know their stuff." Students "can study whatever [they] want in great depth" and this makes the academic work "deeply personal" and "that much more enriching." Each course is so highly-tailored to the individual student that "often changes to the syllabus are made as students find a related topic that interests them." All students can receive one-on-one support from the director of academic support services, who can arrange individual tutoring and coaching, access to the writing tutorial center, and academic skills and strategies workshops. Additionally, the school's unique World Studies Program integrates liberal arts with international study, and involves a six-to-eight month internship in a foreign culture.

STUDENT LIFE

As a small college, Marlboro's heart "runs in community values." Students, faculty, and staff all interact "without any boundaries" in the dining hall and "everyone blends in no matter who you are." Even though there are just a few hundred students at Marlboro, they still manage to come from all over: thirty-five states are represented within this surprisingly diverse student body. Every single student at Marlboro "is absolutely brilliant" and all are "studying vastly different and hugely interesting things." The gorgeous setting is removed from society and the school's Outdoor Program offers "gear, games, [and] tools to do what you need and want." The "great housing" often goes unnoticed: "the rooms are all fairly large…and every dorm has a unique personality. No brick buildings here!"

Marlboro College

FINANCIAL AID: 802-258-9312 • E-MAIL: ADMISSIONS@MARLBORO.EDU • WEBSITE: WWW.MARLBORO.EDU

CAREER

The career path for a Marlboro students is typically a long one: more than three-quarters of Marlboro undergraduates go on to graduate school, which is a relatively seamless transition given the nature of the courses. Students can easily supplement their studies with research and experience: "I've been able to practice paleography of early medieval manuscripts, analyze Marlboro College's food sustainability, work in the woodshop, and in one class visit an apiary and ferment our own foods," says one student. The Plan is rigorous and requires an oral defense, making it akin to a "master's-level thesis." The school's Clear Writing Requirement is "no joke" and requires submission of a portfolio of clear and concise writing samples for approval by the faculty, which is an excellent tool for a student to have in their belt; there are "ample opportunities to practice and improve on one's writing."

GENERAL INFO

Activities: Choral groups; Dance; Drama/theater; Jazz band; Literary magazine; Music ensembles; Radio station; Student government; Student newspaper; Student-run film society. 22 registered organizations. **On-Campus Highlights:** The Rice-Aron Library, Whittemore Theatre, Gander World Studies Center, Serkin Center for the Performing Arts, Persons Auditorium.

FINANCIAL AID

Students should submit: FAFSA. Priority filing deadline is 3/10. The Princeton Review suggests that all financial aid forms be submitted as soon as possible after October 1. *Need-based scholarships/grants offered:* College/university scholarship or grant aid from institutional funds, Federal Pell, private scholarships, SEOG, state scholarships/grants. *Loan aid offered:* Direct PLUS Loans, Direct Subsidized Loans, Direct Unsubsidized Loans. Applicants will be notified of awards on a rolling basis beginning 3/1. Federal Work-Study Program available. Institutional employment available.

CAREER INFORMATION FROM PAYSCALE.COM

ROI Rating	87
Bachelors and No Higher	
Median starting salary	$51,300
Median mid-career salary	$100,500
At Least Bachelors	
Median starting salary	$51,300
Median mid-career salary	$100,600
Degrees awarded in STEM subjects	13%

SELECTIVITY

Admissions Rating	75
# of applicants	120
% of applicants accepted	97
% of acceptees attending	24
# of early decision applicants	8
% accepted early decision	50

FRESHMAN PROFILE

Range SAT EBRW	600–710
Range SAT Math	550–630
Range ACT Composite	24–32
Minimum paper TOEFL	577
Minimum internet-based TOEFL	90
Average HS GPA	3.1
% graduated top 10% of class	0
% graduated top 25% of class	0
% graduated top 50% of class	0

DEADLINES

Early decision	
Deadline	11/15
Notification	12/1
Early action	
Deadline	1/15
Notification	2/1
Regular	
Priority	3/1
Nonfall registration?	Yes

FINANCIAL FACTS

Financial Aid Rating	88
Annual tuition	$39,870
Room and board	$12,385
Required fees	$970
Books and supplies	$1,200
Average frosh need-based scholarship	$40,587
Average UG need-based scholarship	$32,707
% needy frosh rec. need-based scholarship or grant aid	100
% needy UG rec. need-based scholarship or grant aid	100
% needy frosh rec. non-need-based scholarship or grant aid	29
% needy UG rec. non-need-based scholarship or grant aid	19
% needy frosh rec. need-based self-help aid	100
% needy UG rec. need-based self-help aid	94
% frosh rec. any financial aid	98
% UG rec. any financial aid	94
% frosh need fully met	33
% ugrads need fully met	34
Average % of frosh need met	72
Average % of ugrad need met	74

Massachusetts Institute of Technology

77 MASSACHUSETTS AVENUE, CAMBRIDGE, MA 02139 • ADMISSIONS: 617-253-3400 • FAX: 617-258-8304

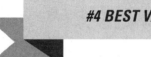

#4 BEST VALUE COLLEGE

ABOUT THE SCHOOL

The essence of Massachusetts Institute of Technology is its appetite for problems. Students here tend to be game-changers, capable of finding creative solutions to the world's big, intractable, complicated problems. A chemical engineering major says that "MIT is different from many schools in that its goal is not to teach you specific facts in each subject. MIT teaches you how to think, not about opinions but about problem-solving. Facts and memorization are useless unless you know how to approach a tough problem." While MIT is a research university committed to world-class inquiry in math, science, and engineering, MIT has equally distinguished programs in architecture, the humanities, management, and the social sciences. No matter what their field, almost all MIT students get involved in research during their undergraduate career, making contributions in fields as diverse as biochemistry, artificial intelligence, and urban planning. "Research opportunities for undergrads with some of the nation's leading professors" is a real highlight for students here. The school also operates an annual Independent Activities Period during the month of January, during which MIT faculty offer hundreds of noncredit activities and short for-credit classes, from lecture and film series to courses like Ballroom Dance or Introduction to Weather Forecasting (students may also use this period to work on research or independent projects). Students are frequently encouraged to unite MIT's science and engineering excellence with public service. Recent years have focused on projects using alternative forms of energy, and machines that could be used for sustainable agriculture. MIT's D-Lab, Poverty Action Lab, and Public Service Center all support students and professors in the research and implementation of culturally sensitive and environmentally responsible technologies and programs that alleviate poverty.

BANG FOR YOUR BUCK

Aid from all sources totals more than $115.6 million, and 72 percent of that total is provided by MIT Scholarships. Sixty-two percent of undergraduates qualify for need-based MIT Scholarships, and the average scholarship award exceeds $32,000. MIT is one of only a few number of institutions that have remained wholly committed to need-blind admissions and need-based aid. (There are no purely merit-based scholarships.) What truly sets MIT apart, however, is the percentage of students from lower-income households. Twenty-eight percent of MIT undergraduates are from families earning less than $75,000 a year, and 19 percent qualify for a federal Pell Grant. MIT also educates a high proportion of first-generation college students, including 16 percent of the current freshman class.

STUDENT LIFE

"As soon as you arrive on campus," students say, "you are bombarded with choices." Extracurricular options range from "building rides" (recent projects have included a motorized couch and a human-sized hamster wheel) "to partying at fraternities to enjoying the largest collection of science fiction novels in the United States at the MIT Science Fiction Library." Students occasionally find time to "pull a hack," which is an ethical prank, like changing digital construction signs on Mass Ave to read "Welcome to Bat Country," or building a "life-size Wright brothers' plane that appeared on top of the Great Dome for the 100th anniversary of flight." Luckily, "there actually isn't one typical student at MIT,"

Massachusetts Institute of Technology

FINANCIAL AID: 617-258-4917 • E-MAIL: ADMISSIONS@MIT.EDU • WEBSITE: WEB.MIT.EDU

students here assure us. "The one thing students all have in common is that they are insanely smart and love to learn. Pretty much anyone can find the perfect group of friends to hang out with at MIT."

CAREER

MIT's Global Education & Career Development "seeks to empower" students and alumni by taking a holistic approach to career services. A few offerings (among many) include career counseling and mock interviews, study abroad informational sessions, and graduate school advising. Frequent career fairs connect undergrads with potential employers (and the Career Fair Online Workshop will help you make the most of your time with them) or you can also peruse job and internship listings on CareerBridge. Students definitely get a hand-up from the rock-solid alumni network, and the surrounding areas of Cambridge and Boston abound with tech and research companies, offering students abundant opportunities for networking and internships. Alumni who visited PayScale.com reported starting salaries at about $81,500 and 53 percent felt that they do meaningful work.

GENERAL INFO

Activities: Choral groups, concert band, dance, drama/theater, jazz band, literary magazine, marching band, music ensembles, musical theater, radio station, student government, student newspaper.

FINANCIAL AID

Students should submit: CSS Profile; FAFSA; Noncustodial PROFILE. Priority filing deadline is 2/15. The Princeton Review suggests that all financial aid forms be submitted as soon as possible after October 1. *Need-based scholarships/grants offered:* College/university scholarship or grant aid from institutional funds; Federal Pell; Private scholarships; SEOG; State scholarships/grants; United Negro College Fund. *Loan aid offered:* Direct PLUS Loans, Direct Subsidized Loans, Direct Unsubsidized Loans. Applicants will be notified of awards on or about 3/15. Federal Work-Study Program available. Institutional employment available.

BOTTOM LINE

For the fall and spring terms, MIT tuition is about $49,580. Room and board averages about $14,720 per academic year, though those costs vary depending on a student's living situation. Books run about $1,000. MIT admits students without regard to their familys' circumstances and awards financial aid to students solely on the basis of need. The school is very clear that its sticker price not scare away applicants; approximately 76 percent of undergrads receive some form of aid. They also try to limit the amount of aid provided in loan form, aiming to meet the first $6,000 of need with loans or on-campus work, and covering the remainder of a student's demonstrated need with a scholarship.

CAREER INFORMATION FROM PAYSCALE.COM	
ROI Rating	99
Bachelors and No Higher	
Median starting salary	$83,600
Median mid-career salary	$150,400
At Least Bachelors	
Median starting salary	$86,800
Median mid-career salary	$156,500
Alumni with high job meaning	53%
Degrees awarded in STEM subjects	69%

SELECTIVITY	
Admissions Rating	99
# of applicants	20,247
% of applicants accepted	7
% of acceptees attending	76
# offered a place on the wait list	527
% accepting a place on wait list	74
% admitted from wait list	4

FRESHMAN PROFILE	
Range SAT EBRW	720–770
Range SAT Math	770–800
Range ACT Composite	33–35
Minimum internet-based TOEFL	90
% graduated top 10% of class	98
% graduated top 25% of class	100
% graduated top 50% of class	100

DEADLINES	
Early action	
Deadline	11/1
Notification	12/20
Regular	
Deadline	1/1
Notification	3/20
Nonfall registration?	No

FINANCIAL FACTS	
Financial Aid Rating	94
Annual tuition	$51,520
Room and board	$15,510
Required fees	$312
Books and supplies	$1,000
Average frosh need-based scholarship	$45,215
Average UG need-based scholarship	$45,570
% needy frosh rec. need-based scholarship or grant aid	98
% needy UG rec. need-based scholarship or grant aid	97
% needy frosh rec. non-need-based scholarship or grant aid	3
% needy UG rec. non-need-based scholarship or grant aid	2
% needy frosh rec. need-based self-help aid	73
% needy UG rec. need-based self-help aid	75
% frosh rec. any financial aid	82
% UG rec. any financial aid	71
% UG borrow to pay for school	29
Average cumulative indebtedness	$20,048
% frosh need fully met	100
% ugrads need fully met	100
Average % of frosh need met	100
Average % of ugrad need met	100

Miami University (OH)

301 SOUTH CAMPUS AVENUE, OXFORD, OH 45056 • ADMISSIONS: 513-529-2531 • FAX: 513-529-1550

CAMPUS LIFE

Quality of Life Rating	90
Fire Safety Rating	95
Green Rating	88
Type of school	Public
Environment	Village

STUDENTS

Total undergrad enrollment	16,816
% male/female	50/50
% from out of state	36
% frosh from public high school	68
% frosh live on campus	98
% ugrads live on campus	45
# of fraternities (% ugrad men join)	25 (19)
# of sororities (% ugrad women join)	20 (31)
% African American	3
% Asian	2
% Caucasian	72
% Hispanic	5
% Native American	<1
% Pacific Islander	<1
% Two or more races	3
% Race and/or ethnicity unknown	<1
% international	14
# of countries represented	89

ACADEMICS

Academic Rating	77
% students returning for sophomore year	91
% students graduating within 4 years	67
% students graduating within 6 years	79
Calendar	Semester
Student/faculty ratio	17:1
Profs interesting rating	87
Profs accessible rating	86

Most classes have 20–29 students. Most lab/discussion sessions have 10-19 students.

MOST POPULAR MAJORS

Biology/Biological Sciences; Finance; Marketing/Marketing Management

ABOUT THE SCHOOL

Oxford, Ohio's Miami University offers students a number of opportunities to gain practical, hands-on experience through "education, student activities, networking, and preparation for the future." The school maintains a strong core academic curriculum (called the Global Miami Plan for Liberal Education) and keeps the standards expected of students consistent. This education "insists students take classes to make them a well-rounded individual rather than focus only on their major," which pushes students to interact and learn in areas they wouldn't normally encounter outside of the major they select from more than the one hundred on offer. The "very accessible and teaching-focused" professors make learning meaningful and provide "many resources to help us to achieve our goals in their class as well as outside of their class." "Miami does a good job of providing a small college feel all the while encompassing over 15,000 students," says a student.

BANG FOR YOUR BUCK

Each year Miami gives out millions of dollars of scholarships based on academics, special achievements, and financial need; the application for admissions to Miami University doubles as an application for academic scholarships. Numerous scholarships, including up to full tuition, are available to high-achieving Ohio and non-resident students who have demonstrated academic merit. Miami's University Academic Scholars Program offers additional scholarship opportunities to exceptional students pursuing academic and professional interests in specific areas like Sustainability or the Humanities or Mathematic, and Statistics. Need-based grants and scholarships include full tuition for first-time, academically competitive freshmen from Ohio who have been admitted to the Oxford campus and who have a total family income of less than $35,000 (courtesy of the Miami Access Initiative). Several academic departments and athletic teams also offer financial awards.

STUDENT LIFE

Everyone is required to live on-campus for the first two years, and "the residence halls put a lot of effort into providing different activities for their students." Late night programming is also offered through Miami, as well as athletic events and other cultural events; people are often studying or "just hanging out on Miami's beautiful campus." On weekends, many choose to go uptown or take part in Greek life (more than 26 percent are involved); Oxford "may be a small town but it is the perfect college town to be in." Students can also travel to nearby Hueston Woods to engage in outdoor activities such as, hiking, boating, swimming, camping, and horseback riding.

CAREER

Miami University has a strong focus on preparing students for the workplace after graduation, "many of the students treat their education like a job—dress code and all." They applaud the commitment of the school in providing tools to help them to find jobs after college, including "career fairs, relationships with recruiters, supporting alumni, mock interview/resume workshops/career services, and teaching material that is applicable to future endeavors," as well as the Miami CAREERlink database. "Career Services will help anyone find an internship or job," says a student. Forty-six percent of Miami graduates who visited PayScale.com reported feeling their jobs highly impacted the world.

Miami University (OH)

FINANCIAL AID: 513-529-0001 • E-MAIL: ADMISSION@MIAMIOH.EDU • WEBSITE: WWW.MIAMIOH.EDU

GENERAL INFO

Activities: Choral groups, concert band, dance, drama/theater, Engineers Without Borders, Genetics Club, Greenhawks Media (sustainability publication), literary magazine, marching band, MU Dropouts Skydiving Club, music ensembles, radio station, student government, Quidditch, student newspaper, student-run film society, symphony orchestra, television station, varsity eSports, yearbook, campus ministries, international student organization, Model UN. **Organizations:** 636 registered organizations, 22 honor societies, 26 religious organizations. 26 fraternities, 20 sororities. **Athletics (Intercollegiate):** *Men:* baseball, basketball, cross-country, diving, football, golf, ice hockey, swimming, track/field (outdoor). *Women:* basketball, cross-country, diving, field hockey, soccer, softball, swimming, tennis, track/field (outdoor), volleyball. **On-Campus Highlights:** Armstrong Student Center, Institute for Entrepreneurship, Center for Student Engagement and Leadership, Howe Writing Center, Office of Research for Undergraduates, Human Immersive Virtual Environment, Center for the Performing Arts, Recreational Sports Center, Outdoor Pursuit Center.

FINANCIAL AID

Students should submit: FAFSA. Priority filing deadline is 2/15. The Princeton Review suggests that all financial aid forms be submitted as soon as possible after October 1. *Need-based scholarships/grants offered:* College/university scholarship or grant aid from institutional funds, Federal Pell, private scholarships, SEOG, state scholarships/grants. *Loan aid offered:* Direct PLUS Loans, Direct Subsidized Loans, Direct Unsubsidized Loans. Applicants will be notified of awards on a rolling basis beginning 3/20. Federal Work-Study Program available. Institutional employment available.

BOTTOM LINE

In-state students pay $13,722 for base tuition, while out-of-state students pay $31,962; room and board is an additional $12,725. With all associated fees and living costs added in, the total annual cost for in-state Ohio residents is $27,011, and out-of-state residents is $44,306. Around 51 percent of students borrow money to pay for school.

CAREER INFORMATION FROM PAYSCALE.COM	
ROI Rating	87
Bachelors and No Higher	
Median starting salary	$55,400
Median mid-career salary	$108,100
At Least Bachelors	
Median starting salary	$56,400
Median mid-career salary	$110,700
Alumni with high job meaning	46%
Degrees awarded in STEM subjects	22%

SELECTIVITY

Admissions Rating	87
# of applicants	33,255
% of applicants accepted	62
% of acceptees attending	19
# offered a place on the wait list	2,860
% accepting a place on wait list	21
% admitted from wait list	7
# of early decision applicants	915
% accepted early decision	77

FRESHMAN PROFILE

Range SAT EBRW	580–670
Range SAT Math	610–710
Range ACT Composite	26–31
Minimum paper TOEFL	550
Minimum internet-based TOEFL	80
Average HS GPA	3.8
% graduated top 10% of class	39
% graduated top 25% of class	66
% graduated top 50% of class	94

DEADLINES

Early decision	
Deadline	11/15
Notification	12/15
Early action	
Deadline	12/1
Notification	2/1
Regular	
Deadline	2/1
Notification	3/15
Nonfall registration?	Yes

FINANCIAL FACTS

Financial Aid Rating	81
Annual in-state tuition	$13,966
Annual out-of-state tuition	$32,718
Room and board	$13,031
Required fees	$859
Books and supplies	$1,216
Average frosh need-based scholarship	$11,417
Average UG need-based scholarship	$10,087
% needy frosh rec. need-based scholarship or grant aid	85
% needy UG rec. need-based scholarship or grant aid	84
% needy frosh rec. non-need-based scholarship or grant aid	20
% needy UG rec. non-need-based scholarship or grant aid	15
% needy frosh rec. need-based self-help aid	62
% needy UG rec. need-based self-help aid	69
% UG borrow to pay for school	51
Average cumulative indebtedness	$29,596
% frosh need fully met	27

Michigan Technological University

1400 TOWNSEND DRIVE, HOUGHTON, MI 49931 • ADMISSIONS: 906-487-2335 • FAX: 906-487-2125

CAMPUS LIFE

Quality of Life Rating	92
Fire Safety Rating	96
Green Rating	74
Type of school	Public
Environment	Village

STUDENTS

Total undergrad enrollment	5,917
% male/female	73/27
% from out of state	22
% frosh live on campus	93
% ugrads live on campus	45
# of fraternities (% ugrad men join)	12 (11)
# of sororities (% ugrad women join)	7 (15)
% African American	1
% Asian	1
% Caucasian	88
% Hispanic	2
% Native American	<1
% Pacific Islander	<1
% Two or more races	3
% Race and/or ethnicity unknown	2
% international	3
# of countries represented	35

ACADEMICS

Academic Rating	84
% students returning for sophomore year	83
% students graduating within 4 years	28
% students graduating within 6 years	67
Calendar	Semester
Student/faculty ratio	12:1
Profs interesting rating	78
Profs accessible rating	77

Most classes have 10–19 students. Most lab/discussion sessions have fewer than 10 students.

MOST POPULAR MAJORS
Chemical Engineering; Civil Engineering; Mechanical Engineering

ABOUT THE SCHOOL

Michigan Technological University gives students a "big city education in a small town setting." Some students say this public research university in Michigan's "often snowy" Upper Peninsula boils down to "Engineering, Nerds, and the Great Outdoors" while others stress that "Michigan Tech was a school created for engineering but [its] other departments are just as strong and the education you receive is great." For students looking to pursue an engineering focus, though, Michigan Tech excels at "preparing [tomorrow's] engineers to create the future today." With its small, rural campus, "Michigan Tech is the type of school where you're not just a student, you're a family." According to one Civil Engineering major, "The experience gets better with more time you put into your program, the professors become more interactive and the experience becomes more meaningful." Students say the professors are mostly "helpful and accommodating" while "a few have been dull, but those are the minority;" the fact that the majority "have high expectations…helps in learning." Small class sizes (usually between two and nine students) for non-general education classes and a 13:1 student-to-faculty ratio "allows for a great professor-student relationships."

BANG FOR YOUR BUCK

Though some students say that "Financial Aid usually does a good job at keeping us covered," other students wish that Michigan Tech would "allocate financial resources more effectively" and "consider [its] students more when making financial decisions." The average Michigan Tech freshman receives a total of $8,040 in need-based gift aid (the average for a Michigan Tech undergrad is $7,481) and the average amount received in need-based loans is $3,331. Scholarships are available to qualifying Michigan residents, including the Presidential Scholars program, the Wade McCree scholarship, and the School of Business Impact Scholarship. Since Michigan Tech is located so close to Canada, there are special scholarship opportunities, such as through the McAllister Foundation, available to qualified incoming Canadian students.

STUDENT LIFE

"They are smart, studious, but know how to have fun," Michigan Tech students say of their classmates. They are "great at balancing school and hanging out." Some say it's hard to define the "typical" student and that "it all depends on the department. There is a great deal of diversity apart from the large white male majority." According to one Biology major, "There's little diversity ethnically, but everyone feels welcome. There's many more men than women, so girls get doors opened for them across campus. If you have any problems, anyone will help you. It's easy to fit in." Around campus, "students play a lot of intramural sports and are in a lot of student organizations." There are a total of 226 registered student organizations on campus. Some students say "embrace the Greek system" because "it is a big thing here"—11 percent of men at Michigan Tech join a fraternity, while 15 percent of women join a sorority. Winter sports are especially popular, "[skiing], snowboarding, snowshoeing, ice fishing and [snowmobiling] are all very popular" during Michigan's long, snowy winter months.

CAREER

"Career services are unbelievable here. If you work for your degree and earn it, participate in co-ops or internships (and the opportunities to do so are ample), you are almost guaranteed a job out of college." Not all students have quite such high praise, saying that they wished there were "more internships etc. for majors that are not engineering." But overall, Michigan Tech gets high marks, with students saying "the [school's] biggest strength is the Career Services…There is a fall and

Michigan Technological University

FINANCIAL AID: 906-487-2622 • E-MAIL: MTU4U@MTU.EDU • WEBSITE: WWW.MTU.EDU

spring career fair so getting internships and co-ops is slightly better than other universities." The Career Services department is "really helpful in working with you to find a job/internship/co-op." During the month of the career fair, Michigan Tech also offers lots of informal events that make up CareerFEST, which helps prepare students for interviews, résumé-writing, and more. From the school's website, students can access Handshake, which helps connect students and potential employers and internship leaders.

GENERAL INFO

Activities: Choral groups, concert band, dance, drama/theater, jazz band, literary magazine, music ensembles, musical theater, pep band, radio station, student government, student newspaper, student-run film society, symphony orchestra, campus Ministries. **Organizations:** 226 registered organizations, 16 honor societies, 9 religious organizations. 12 fraternities, 7 sororities. **Athletics (Intercollegiate):** *Men:* basketball, cross-country, football, ice hockey, skiing (nordic/cross-country), tennis, track/field (outdoor). *Women:* basketball, cross-country, skiing (nordic/cross-country), soccer, tennis, track/field (outdoor), volleyball. **On-Campus Highlights:** Student Development Complex, Rozsa Center for the Performing Arts, Mont Ripley Ski Hill, Portage Lake Golf Course, Memorial Union Building, Gates Tennis Center, Great Lakes Research Center, and Sustainable Futures Institute.

FINANCIAL AID

Students should submit: FAFSA. Priority filing deadline is 3/1. The Princeton Review suggests that all financial aid forms be submitted as soon as possible after October 1. *Need-based scholarships/grants offered:* College/university scholarship or grant aid from institutional funds, Federal Pell, private scholarships, SEOG, state scholarships/grants. *Loan aid offered:* Direct PLUS Loans, Direct Subsidized Loans, Direct Unsubsidized Loans. Applicants will be notified of awards on a rolling basis beginning late December. Federal Work-Study program, institutional employment, and paid undergraduate research opportunities are available.

BOTTOM LINE

Tuition for in-state students is roughly $15,346, with an additional $300 in fees and approximately $1,200 in books and supplies. Tuition for out-of-state students is roughly $33,426. In terms of scholarships and grants, the average freshman receives roughly $10,959 and the average loan debt per Michigan Tech graduate is $35,834. Financial aid is available to international students.

CAREER INFORMATION FROM PAYSCALE.COM	
ROI Rating	89
Bachelors and No Higher	
Median starting salary	$64,600
Median mid-career salary	$110,200
At Least Bachelors	
Median starting salary	$65,400
Median mid-career salary	$113,200
Alumni with high job meaning	48%
Degrees awarded in STEM subjects	80%

SELECTIVITY	
Admissions Rating	84
# of applicants	5,469
% of applicants accepted	74
% of acceptees attending	32

FRESHMAN PROFILE	
Range SAT EBRW	570–660
Range SAT Math	590–680
Range ACT Composite	25–30
Minimum paper TOEFL	550
Minimum internet-based TOEFL	79
Average HS GPA	3.7
% graduated top 10% of class	32
% graduated top 25% of class	65
% graduated top 50% of class	91

DEADLINES	
Regular	
Priority	1/15
Nonfall registration?	Yes

FINANCIAL FACTS	
Financial Aid Rating	83
Annual in-state tuition	$15,346
Annual out-of-state tuition	$33,426
Room and board	$10,756
Required fees	$300
Room and board	NR
Average frosh need-based scholarship	$8,040
Average UG need-based scholarship	$7,481
% needy frosh rec. need-based scholarship or grant aid	85
% needy UG rec. need-based scholarship or grant aid	78
% needy frosh rec. non-need-based scholarship or grant aid	87
% needy UG rec. non-need-based scholarship or grant aid	82
% needy frosh rec. need-based self-help aid	80
% needy UG rec. need-based self-help aid	85
% frosh rec. any financial aid	98
% UG rec. any financial aid	92
% UG borrow to pay for school	69
Average cumulative indebtedness	$35,834
% frosh need fully met	18
% ugrads need fully met	15
Average % of frosh need met	79
Average % of ugrad need met	71

Middlebury College

THE EMMA WILLARD HOUSE, MIDDLEBURY, VT 05753-6002 • ADMISSIONS: 802-443-3000 • FAX: 802-443-2056

ABOUT THE SCHOOL

Home to "smart people who enjoy Aristotelian ethics and quantum physics, but aren't too stuck up to go sledding in front of Mead Chapel at midnight," Middlebury College is a small, exclusive liberal arts school with "excellent foreign language programs" as well as standout offerings in environmental studies, the sciences, theatre, and writing. The successful Middlebury candidate excels in a variety of areas, including academics, athletics, the arts, leadership, and service to others. These strengths and interests permit students to grow beyond their traditional comfort zones and conventional limits. The classrooms are as varied as the Green Mountains, the Metropolitan Museum of Art, or the great cities of Russia and Japan. Outside the classroom, students informally interact with professors in activities such as intramural basketball games and community service. At Middlebury, students develop critical-thinking skills, enduring bonds of friendship, and the ability to challenge themselves. Middlebury offers majors and programs in forty-five different fields, with particular strengths in languages, international studies, environmental studies, literature and creative writing, and the sciences. Opportunities for engaging in individual research with faculty abound at Middlebury.

BANG FOR YOUR BUCK

Distribution requirements and other general requirements ensure that a Middlebury education "is all about providing students with a complete college experience, including excellent teaching, exposure to many other cultures, endless opportunities for growth and success, and a challenging (yet relaxed) environment." Its "small class size and friendly yet competitive atmosphere make for the perfect college experience," as do "the best facilities of a small liberal arts college in the country." A new squash center and new field house recently opened. Students are grateful for the stellar advantages the school is able to provide them with. "I think that even if I didn't have classes or homework, I wouldn't be able to take advantage of all of the opportunities available on campus on a day-to-day basis." "The academics here are unbeatable. I'd come here over an Ivy League school any day."

STUDENT LIFE

Middlebury students are, in three words: "Busy, friendly, and busy." Everyone "will talk about how stressed they are, but it's not just from preparing for a Chinese exam while also trying to finish up a lab report for biology; it's doing both of those while also playing a club or a varsity sport and finding time to enjoy long meals in the cafeteria with friends." Weekends are for much-deserved relaxation: hiking or skiing (the school has its own ski mountain, the Snow Bowl, and cross-country ski area, Rikert Nordic Center), attending shows and concerts, film screenings, dance parties, and parties are put on by sports teams and other clubs on campus. The student activity board "does a pretty good job, but if you don't like it, you are always welcome to apply to be on the board." Many here are politically active in some way, and "the environment is big for most."

Middlebury College

E-MAIL: ADMISSIONS@MIDDLEBURY.EDU • WEBSITE: WWW.MIDDLEBURY.EDU

CAREER

Middlebury students "know how to take advantage of resources that aid their success." The Center for Careers & Internships helps students to find internships or even develop their own, and the online resources include a comprehensive series of Five-Minute Workshops. Funding is even available for unpaid internships, conferences, service projects, international volunteer programs, and local public service projects. Experiential learning is a heavy focus of the college, and there are numerous centers for students to enhance academic work, or explore possible career paths. Middlebury College graduates who visited PayScale.com had an average starting salary of $56,300; 52 percent said they felt their job had a meaningful impact on the world.

GENERAL INFO

Activities: Choral groups, dance, drama/theater, jazz band, literary magazine, music ensembles, musical theater, radio station, student government, student newspaper, student-run film society, symphony orchestra, yearbook. **Organizations:** 185 registered organizations. **Athletics (Intercollegiate):** *Men:* Baseball, basketball, cross-country, diving/swimming, football, golf, ice hockey, lacrosse, skiing (downhill/alpine), skiing (nordic/cross-country), soccer, squash. tennis, track/field (outdoor), track/field (indoor). *Women:* Basketball, cross-country, diving/swimming, field hockey, golf, ice hockey, lacrosse, skiing (downhill/alpine), skiing (nordic/cross-country), soccer, softball, squash, tennis, track/field (outdoor), track/field (indoor), volleyball.

FINANCIAL AID

Students should submit: CSS Profile, FAFSA; Institution's own financial aid form, Noncustodial PROFILE. Priority filing deadline is 4/1. The Princeton Review suggests that all financial aid forms be submitted as soon as possible after October 1. *Need-based scholarships/grants offered:* College/university scholarship or grant aid from institutional funds, Federal Pell, private scholarships, SEOG, state scholarships/grants. *Loan aid offered:* Direct PLUS Loans, Direct Subsidized Loans, Direct Unsubsidized Loans. Applicants will be notified of awards on or about 4/1. Federal Work-Study Program available. Institutional employment available.

BOTTOM LINE

Middlebury College is not the most expensive institution in the country, but it is a substantial investment. Fortunately, the opportunity for financial aid and other support is provided for needy students. Tuition is $52,080 per year, and Middlebury meets full demonstrated need for all admitted students. About 42 percent of enrollees receive some form of financial aid. Forty-five percent of students borrow to help offset the cost of their education and, upon graduating, are looking at a total loan debt of under $18,736; extremely reasonable for an education of the caliber provided by Middlebury.

CAREER INFORMATION FROM PAYSCALE.COM

ROI Rating	91
Bachelors and No Higher	
Median starting salary	$58,400
Median mid-career salary	$112,400
At Least Bachelors	
Median starting salary	$61,000
Median mid-career salary	$121,800
Alumni with high job meaning	52%
Degrees awarded in STEM subjects	16%

SELECTIVITY

Admissions Rating	97
# of applicants	8,909
% of applicants accepted	17
% of acceptees attending	42
# offered a place on the wait list	1,259
% accepting a place on wait list	43
% admitted from wait list	4
# of early decision applicants	834
% accepted early decision	48

FRESHMAN PROFILE

Range SAT EBRW	660–750
Range SAT Math	660–760
Range ACT Composite	30–34

DEADLINES

Early decision	
Deadline	11/1
Notification	mid-Dec
Other ED Deadline	1/1
Other ED Notification	early Feb
Regular	
Deadline	1/1
Notification	late March
Nonfall registration?	Yes

FINANCIAL FACTS

Financial Aid Rating	97
Annual tuition	$54,032
Room and board	$15,530
Required fees	$418
Books and supplies	$1,000
Average frosh need-based scholarship	$47,092
Average UG need-based scholarship	$47,439
% needy frosh rec. need-based scholarship or grant aid	100
% needy UG rec. need-based scholarship or grant aid	98
% needy frosh rec. non-need-based scholarship or grant aid	0
% needy UG rec. non-need-based scholarship or grant aid	0
% needy frosh rec. need-based self-help aid	91
% needy UG rec. need-based self-help aid	90
% frosh rec. any financial aid	48
% UG rec. any financial aid	42
% UG borrow to pay for school	46
Average cumulative indebtedness	$19,382
% frosh need fully met	100
% ugrads need fully met	100
Average % of frosh need met	100
Average % of ugrad need met	100

Mills College

5000 MacArthur Boulevard, Oakland, CA 94613 • Admissions: 510-430-2135 • Fax: 510-430-3298

CAMPUS LIFE

Quality of Life Rating	**89**
Fire Safety Rating	**78**
Green Rating	**87**
Type of school	Private
Environment	Metropolis

STUDENTS

Total undergrad enrollment	774
% male/female	0/100
% from out of state	20
% frosh from public high school	62
% frosh live on campus	76
% ugrads live on campus	60
# of fraternities (% ugrad men join)	0 (0)
# of sororities (% ugrad women join)	0 (0)
% African American	10
% Asian	10
% Caucasian	36
% Hispanic	29
% Native American	<1
% Pacific Islander	<1
% Two or more races	9
% Race and/or ethnicity unknown	4
% international	1
# of countries represented	8

ACADEMICS

Academic Rating	**87**
% students returning for sophomore year	74
% students graduating within 4 years	69
% students graduating within 6 years	71
Calendar	Semester
Student/faculty ratio	11:1
Profs interesting rating	95
Profs accessible rating	90
Most classes have 10–19 students.	

MOST POPULAR MAJORS

Psychology; English; Pre-Nursing; Sociology; Child Dev; Econ; Studio Art

ABOUT THE SCHOOL

Even though it's been around since 1852, the all-women's liberal arts Mills College continues to adapt and advance, introducing the MPOWER signature academic experience to all undergraduate programs in the fall of 2018. Under MPOWER, each student has a personalized academic support system (including a faculty advisor, an academic navigator), completes a faculty-mentored project, and takes part in community-engaged learning projects such as internships and study abroad. In this "cooperative learning environment," professors bring in their own experiences and "encourage you to work on projects that reflect your own interests as they relate to the class." Between the curriculum and the student body, Mills "really integrates individual fields of study and the concept of social justice and community advocacy." Classes are often non-traditional, especially in the Ethnic Studies, and Women's Studies departments, and teachers are always very supportive of the students: "If you need more time on an essay, you'll likely get the time." There is very little busy work, and professors often come up with "unusual and open-ended group and solo projects" that let students learn while at the same time letting them do valuable work that they are passionate about.

BANG FOR YOUR BUCK

Professors "always have research opportunities that are open for students" and "make learning in the classroom interesting and understandable" while still challenging. It's a very small school so "offices and people become very part of a community quickly," and there is "a lot of leeway for flexibility." A lot of the professors record their lectures and post their slides online, so "you can essentially redo the lecture and learn like that"; this is "an incredible resource for learners that work with repetition well." The diverse student body includes women from all backgrounds, and 98 percent of students that attend Mills receive some form of financial aid.

STUDENT LIFE

The 750 women that call Mills home during their undergraduate years are "socially aware activists who value education and community." There is a strong LGBTQ component here (more than half of the student body), and there are "plenty of cute little events going on" on campus, such as "movie night, craft making, a cultural food event, experimental music performances, dance performance, [and] traveling art exhibitions." The school itself is beautiful (and includes "a dorm on top of a hill that looks like a castle") and it is "easy to fall in love with the campus and the overall Mills vibe." Mills is located in the Bay Area, so trips to San Francisco and Oakland are frequent (for both classes and fun), and "almost every area of the campus is a good place to study."

Mills College

FINANCIAL AID: 510-430-2000 • E-MAIL: ADMISSION@MILLS.EDU • WEBSITE: WWW.MILLS.EDU

CAREER

MPOWER also provides a career-focused program in which the career services office looks for personalized opportunities such as internships, career treks, and skills development, while also connecting students with Mills alumnae. Many of the classes have required community outreach for extra units, like volunteering at a local elementary school, and professors are "able to connect you to mentors or other faculty that could help you on your journey to fellowships, internships, or even job opportunities." Here at Mills, the "first and only step to get in on a professor's personal research is to express interest." It may be that there's not a spot for you on the team, but "they are all almost always willing to find something for you to do." Not only does this look good on transcripts, but "directed research under these highly qualified professionals makes you qualified, too."

GENERAL INFO

Activities: Campus Ministries; Choral groups; Dance; Drama/theater; International Student Organization; Literary magazine; Model UN; Music ensembles; Student government; Student newspaper; Yearbook. 47 registered organizations, 2 honor societies, 4 religious organizations. **Athletics (Intercollegiate):** *Women:* crew/rowing, cross-country, soccer, swimming, tennis, volleyball. **On-Campus Highlights:** The Mills College Art Museum, Haas Pavilion & Trefethen Aquatic Center, Rothwell Student Center, Lorry I. Lokey School of Business and Public Policy,, Littlefield Concert Hall.

FINANCIAL AID

Students should submit: FAFSA; Noncustodial PROFILE. Priority filing deadline is 3/1. The Princeton Review suggests that all financial aid forms be submitted as soon as possible after October 1. *Need-based scholarships/grants offered:* College/university scholarship or grant aid from institutional funds, Federal Pell, private scholarships, SEOG, state scholarships/grants. *Loan aid offered:* Direct PLUS Loans, Direct Subsidized Loans, Direct Unsubsidized Loans. Applicants will be notified of awards on a rolling basis beginning 2/15. Federal Work-Study Program available. Institutional employment available.

CAREER INFORMATION FROM PAYSCALE.COM	
ROI Rating	88
Bachelors and No Higher	
Median starting salary	$50,500
Median mid-career salary	$85,600
At Least Bachelors	
Median starting salary	$52,100
Median mid-career salary	$89,300
Alumni with high job meaning	51%
Degrees awarded in STEM subjects	7%

SELECTIVITY

Admissions Rating	**77**
# of applicants	1098
% of applicants accepted	78
% of acceptees attending	19

FRESHMAN PROFILE

Range SAT EBRW	530–670
Range ACT Composite	29–29
Minimum paper TOEFL	550
Minimum internet-based TOEFL	80
Average HS GPA	3.6
% graduated top 10% of class	11
% graduated top 25% of class	24
% graduated top 50% of class	96

DEADLINES

Early action	
Deadline	11/15
Notification	12/1
Regular	
Priority	1/15
Nonfall registration?	Yes

FINANCIAL FACTS

Financial Aid Rating	**82**
Annual tuition	$28,765
Room and board	$13,448
Required fees	$1,492
Books and supplies	$1,612
Average frosh need-based scholarship	$29,219
Average UG need-based scholarship	$27,995
% needy frosh rec. need-based scholarship or grant aid	95
% needy UG rec. need-based scholarship or grant aid	96
% needy frosh rec. non-need-based scholarship or grant aid	100
% needy UG rec. non-need-based scholarship or grant aid	92
% needy frosh rec. need-based self-help aid	70
% needy UG rec. need-based self-help aid	73
% frosh rec. any financial aid	100
% UG rec. any financial aid	95
% UG borrow to pay for school	60
Average cumulative indebtedness	$28,544
% frosh need fully met	7
% ugrads need fully met	7
Average % of frosh need met	70
Average % of ugrad need met	68

Missouri University of Science and Technology

300 West 13th Street; 106 Parker Hall, Rolla, MO 65409-1060 • Admissions: 573-341-4165 • Fax: 573-341-4082

CAMPUS LIFE

Quality of Life Rating	87
Fire Safety Rating	88
Green Rating	85
Type of school	Public
Environment	Village

STUDENTS

Total undergrad enrollment	6,920
% male/female	76/24
% from out of state	15
% frosh from public high school	85
% ugrads live on campus	30
# of fraternities	20
# of sororities	6
% African American	3
% Asian	4
% Caucasian	81
% Hispanic	4
% Native American	<1
% Pacific Islander	<1
% Two or more races	3
% Race and/or ethnicity unknown	2
% international	3
# of countries represented	60

ACADEMICS

Academic Rating	78
% students returning for sophomore year	81
% students graduating within 4 years	23
% students graduating within 6 years	64
Calendar	Semester
Student/faculty ratio	20:1
Profs interesting rating	79
Profs accessible rating	80

Most classes have 20–29 students. Most lab/discussion sessions have 10–19 students.

MOST POPULAR MAJORS

Civil Engineering; Electrical and Electronics Engineering; Mechanical Engineering

ABOUT THE SCHOOL

Missouri University of Science and Technology is one of the premier engineering and science-centered institutions in the Midwest. Though a "small school compared to other public universities," we've been assured that "the quality of education and availability of resources here is second to none." Of course, given the engineering focus, prospective students should anticipate a rigorous curriculum. Fortunately, students truly seem to value that their "classes really push you to learn and master the content." Undergrads also appreciate that they have the ability to participate in "lots of undergraduate research." Yes, these Miners love their time in the classroom. That's due in large part to some "incredibly capable and accessible" professors who really "want [to see] you succeed." Perhaps most impressively "they are always willing to spend time with you to understand the material [and they don't] hesitate to get to know you outside of the classroom at social events and such."

BANG FOR YOUR BUCK

If you're looking for a school that won't break the proverbial bank, Missouri S&T just might be the university for you. As one thrilled sophomore explains, "Missouri S&T offers a quality degree at a low price." And it's not just a bargain for Missouri residents. A relieved senior shares, "[Missouri S&T is even] affordable for an out-of-state student like myself; [it was actually cheaper] than some [of my] in-state institutions." Beyond just a state school price tag, undergrads often benefit from generous financial aid packages. A lot of that generosity can be attributed to the numerous merit scholarships available. For example, S&T offers the Excellence Scholarship, which provides a minimum of $5,500 for in-state students and $11,000 for out-of-state students. The Trustees Scholarship offers a minimum of $4,000 and $10,000 respectively. There are also many departmental awards to be had. Upon receiving an acceptance letter, students are encouraged to inquire with their intended degree program.

SCHOOL LIFE

Undergrads here don't mince words; "academics are everyone's top priority." As one knowledgeable senior admits, "People are usually very weighed down by classes." However, even the most diligent students need to take the occasional break. And when these undergrads do, there's plenty of fun to be had. Indeed, "for a school as small as S&T, our range of student organizations is mind-boggling. Who knew a small school in the middle of Missouri would have a thriving salsa club?" Students can also participate in activities such as "scavenger hunts, video game nights, cooking classes, viewing parties, dance lessons, and much more." Additionally, we're told that "Greek life is pretty big here [...] it feels like everyone is Greek." Thankfully, undergrads assure us that there's a friendly vibe and everyone is welcome at parties no matter their affiliation.

Missouri University of Science and Technology

FINANCIAL AID: 573-341-4282 • E-MAIL: ADMISSIONS@MST.EDU • WEBSITE: WWW.MST.EDU

CAREER

Success is often synonymous with Missouri S&T graduates. And this does not go unnoticed by current students. As one senior boasts, "Many employers place Missouri S&T candidates at the top of their list." A fellow senior concurs adding, "Missouri S&T provides a first class education and employers know the quality of student that graduates from this institution so finding a job is no problem at all!" Certainly, some of this professional achievement can be chalked up to a "fantastic" career services office. After all, the industrious individuals who work here put up some remarkable statistics. For starters, the office facilitates roughly 4,700 on-campus interviews a year. It also arranges approximately 3,330 job postings for Missouri S&T students and provides access to an additional 16 million job postings worldwide. And, as if that all weren't enough, according to PayScale.com, the median starting salary of S&T graduates is $65,200.

GENERAL INFO

Activities: Choral groups, concert band, dance, drama/theater, jazz band, literary magazine, marching band, music ensembles, musical theater, pep band, radio station, student government, student newspaper, symphony orchestra, yearbook, campus ministries, International Student Organization. **Organizations:** 202 registered organizations, 29 honor societies, 13 religious organizations. 23 fraternities, 5 sororities. **Athletics (Intercollegiate):** *Men:* baseball, basketball, cross-country, football, soccer, swimming, track/field (outdoor), track/field (indoor). *Women:* basketball, cross-country, soccer, softball, track/field (outdoor), track/field (indoor), volleyball. **On-Campus Highlights:** Havener Student Center, Residential College, Student Design Team Center, Castleman Performing Arts Center, Student Recreation Center.

FINANCIAL AID

Students should submit: FAFSA. Priority filing deadline is 2/1. The Princeton Review suggests that all financial aid forms be submitted as soon as possible after October 1. *Need-based scholarships/grants offered:* College/university scholarship or grant aid from institutional funds, Federal Pell, private scholarships, SEOG, state scholarships/grants. *Loan aid offered:* Applicants will be notified of awards on a rolling basis beginning 4/1. Federal Work-Study Program available. Institutional employment available.

BOTTOM LINE

Missouri residents attending Missouri S&T will receive a tuition bill of $8,286. Undergrads hailing from out-of-state face a higher bill, one priced at $25,554. Additionally, all students must pay another $1,351 in required fees. And undergrads should anticipate spending around $836 for books and supplies. Finally, students can expect to pay $9,145 for on-campus room and board.

CAREER INFORMATION FROM PAYSCALE.COM	
ROI Rating	90
Bachelors and No Higher	
Median starting salary	$66,700
Median mid-career salary	$116,400
At Least Bachelors	
Median starting salary	$67,400
Median mid-career salary	$121,100
Alumni with high job meaning	51%
Degrees awarded in STEM subjects	80%

SELECTIVITY	
Admissions Rating	85
# of applicants	3,876
% of applicants accepted	84
% of acceptees attending	37

FRESHMAN PROFILE	
Range SAT EBRW	520–640
Range SAT Math	580–700
Range ACT Composite	25–31
Minimum internet-based TOEFL	79
Average HS GPA	3.6
% graduated top 10% of class	39
% graduated top 25% of class	72
% graduated top 50% of class	94

DEADLINES	
Regular	
Priority	12/1; 2/1 for final scholarship
Deadline	7/1

FINANCIAL FACTS	
Financial Aid Rating	81
Annual in-state tuition	$7,974
Annual out-of-state tuition	$25,082
Room and board	$10,274
Required fees	$1,626
Average frosh need-based scholarship	$10,079
Average UG need-based scholarship	$7,978
% needy frosh rec. need-based scholarship or grant aid	95
% needy UG rec. need-based scholarship or grant aid	88
% needy frosh rec. non-need-based scholarship or grant aid	30
% needy UG rec. non-need-based scholarship or grant aid	40
% needy frosh rec. need-based self-help aid	100
% needy UG rec. need-based self-help aid	100
% frosh rec. any financial aid	94
% UG rec. any financial aid	91
% UG borrow to pay for school	66
Average cumulative indebtedness	$27,500
% frosh need fully met	14
% ugrads need fully met	30
Average % of frosh need met	40
Average % of ugrad need met	48

Montana Tech of the University of Montana

1300 West Park Street, Butte, MT 59701 • Admissions: 406-496-4256 • Fax: 406-496-4710

CAMPUS LIFE

Quality of Life Rating	**84**
Fire Safety Rating	**98**
Green Rating	**60***
Type of school	Public
Environment	Town

STUDENTS

Total undergrad enrollment	2,096
% male/female	64/36
% from out of state	14
% frosh live on campus	54
% ugrads live on campus	12
# of fraternities (% ugrad men join)	0 (0)
# of sororities (% ugrad women join)	0 (0)
% African American	1
% Asian	1
% Caucasian	78
% Hispanic	2
% Native American	2
% Two or more races	<1
% Race and/or ethnicity unknown	6
% international	10
# of countries represented	10

ACADEMICS

Academic Rating	**74**
% students returning for sophomore year	77
% students graduating within 6 years	44
Calendar	Semester
Student/faculty ratio	13:1
Profs interesting rating	75
Profs accessible rating	74

Most classes have 20–29 students. Most lab/discussion sessions have 10–19 students.

MOST POPULAR MAJORS
Engineering; Petroleum Engineering; Management Information Systems and Services

ABOUT THE SCHOOL

If you're on the hunt for school with top-notch programs in the sciences or engineering, you'll want to consider Montana Tech. While the courses here can be "difficult," students really appreciate that they graduate with a "true understanding of [their] major." And they readily assert that the academic rigor helps to foster a "feeling of community" amongst students. Montana Tech undergrads also love that their courses are quick to "evolve with changing technology." Moreover, students here benefit from "small" class sizes which allows them to form "strong bonds" with their professors. Speaking of professors, we're told that Montana Tech attracts instructors who are "extremely knowledgeable and easy to approach." Many professors at the university worked in "their respective fields for a long time before going into teaching," so "they teach real life scenarios rather than out of a book." Best of all, they are "genuinely interested in their students learning" and "do everything in their power to help students become successful without giving answers directly."

BANG FOR YOUR BUCK

Montana Tech is a school that's truly committed to providing its undergraduates with an affordable education. This isn't mere lip service; approximately 72 percent of the school's first-time students receive some form of financial aid. And several students themselves praise the university's "incredible scholarships. Montana Tech distributes over $1.4 million in scholarship money to each incoming class. To be considered, students must submit a general scholarship application by January 15th. These are competitive and undergrads are encouraged to apply as early as possible. The university also sets aside an addition $2 to 3 million in funding for continuing students.

STUDENT LIFE

We won't mince words; many undergrads at Montana Tech spend a fair amount of time in the library tackling homework. But even these diligent workers need to kick back every now and then. We're told that "sporting events are very popular and well attended." And many people participate in "co-ed intramural sports [such as] flag football, volleyball, basketball and softball." The school also attracts a lot of outdoor enthusiasts and you'll frequently find students "hiking, camping, hunting and fishing." Montana Tech's hometown Butte "is central to many great ski resorts and many hills offer discounts to students." And finally, the surrounding area has a decent number of "local breweries and distilleries" and many (of-age) students enjoy sampling.

Montana Tech of the University of Montana

FINANCIAL AID: 406-496-4213 • E-MAIL: ENROLLMENT@MTECH.EDU • WEBSITE: WWW.MTECH.EDU

CAREER

Undergrads at Montana Tech proudly boast of the school's "high job placement." Of course, this is not too surprising given that from "the first week of freshman year they are preparing us to get a job in our field." Specifically, students are constantly encouraged to "[craft] a resume, [attend] career fair[s], talk...to job recruiters, figure out what [their] ideal job would be [and read] up interview strategies." "Montana Tech's career fair [helps] many students [land both] paid internships and permanent positions." All of this groundwork helps to guarantee that students earn a great return on their (educational) investment. You'll find alums working at top companies such as Chevron Corporation, Enterprise Rent-A-Car, Devon Energy, and Sherwin Williams.

GENERAL INFO

Activities: concert band, pep band, radio station, student government, student newspaper, yearbook, campus ministries. **Organizations:** 58 registered organizations, 2 honor societies, 3 religious organizations. **Athletics (Intercollegiate):** *Men:* basketball, football, golf. *Women:* basketball, golf, volleyball. **On-Campus Highlights:** Mineral Museum, Mil Building (which houses Starbucks and, HPER (athletic facility), Student Union, Mall area.

FINANCIAL AID

Students should submit: FAFSA. Priority filing deadline is 12/1. The Princeton Review suggests that all financial aid forms be submitted as soon as possible after October 1. *Need-based scholarships/grants offered:* College/university scholarship or grant aid from institutional funds, Federal Pell, private scholarships, SEOG, state scholarships/grants. *Loan aid offered:* Direct PLUS Loans, Direct Subsidized Loans, Direct Unsubsidized Loans. Applicants will be notified of awards on a rolling basis beginning 2/15. Federal Work-Study Program available. Institutional employment available.

THE BOTTOM LINE

As a state school, Montana Tech charges Montana residents a modest tuition fee of $7,139. Undergraduates coming from out-of-state face a somewhat heftier bill of $21,969. Moreover, room and board costs students $8,932. They will also need another $1,100 for books and supplies. Transportation typically runs between $1,700 and $1,900 (depending on whether an individual is from the state).

CAREER INFORMATION FROM PAYSCALE.COM	
ROI Rating	88
Bachelors and No Higher	
Median starting salary	$61,900
Median mid-career salary	$107,200
At Least Bachelors	
Median starting salary	$63,300
Median mid-career salary	$111,600
Alumni with high job meaning	61%
Degrees awarded in STEM subjects	61%

SELECTIVITY	
Admissions Rating	78
# of applicants	981
% of applicants accepted	92
% of acceptees attending	43

FRESHMAN PROFILE	
Range SAT EBRW	540–630
Range SAT Math	575–670
Range ACT Composite	22–27
Minimum paper TOEFL	525
Minimum internet-based TOEFL	71
Average HS GPA	3.6
% graduated top 10% of class	25
% graduated top 25% of class	56
% graduated top 50% of class	87

DEADLINES	
Nonfall registration?	Yes

FINANCIAL FACTS	
Financial Aid Rating	81
Annual in-state tuition	$7,411
Annual out-of-state tuition	$22,575
Room and board	$9,828
Books and supplies	$1,100
Average frosh need-based scholarship	$5,777
Average UG need-based scholarship	$5,768
% needy frosh rec. need-based scholarship or grant aid	87
% needy UG rec. need-based scholarship or grant aid	83
% needy frosh rec. non-need-based scholarship or grant aid	15
% needy UG rec. non-need-based scholarship or grant aid	7
% needy frosh rec. need-based self-help aid	58
% needy UG rec. need-based self-help aid	73
% frosh rec. any financial aid	72
% UG rec. any financial aid	67
% UG borrow to pay for school	54
Average cumulative indebtedness	$27,926
% frosh need fully met	22
% ugrads need fully met	13
Average % of frosh need met	64
Average % of ugrad need met	59

Mount Holyoke College

NEWHALL CENTER, SOUTH HADLEY, MA 01075 • ADMISSIONS: 413-538-2023 • FAX: 413-538-2409

CAMPUS LIFE

Quality of Life Rating	**92**
Fire Safety Rating	**91**
Green Rating	**91**
Type of school	Private
Environment	Town

STUDENTS

Total undergrad enrollment	2,186
% male/female	0/100
% from out of state	53
% frosh from public high school	65
% frosh live on campus	99
% ugrads live on campus	95
# of fraternities (% ugrad men join)	0 (0)
# of sororities (% ugrad women join)	0 (0)
% African American	5
% Asian	10
% Caucasian	45
% Hispanic	7
% Native American	<1
% Pacific Islander	<1
% Two or more races	4
% Race and/or ethnicity unknown	1
% international	27
# of countries represented	69

ACADEMICS

Academic Rating	**98**
% students returning for sophomore year	91
% students graduating within 4 years	81
% students graduating within 6 years	86
Calendar	Semester
Student/faculty ratio	9:1
Profs interesting rating	98
Profs accessible rating	97
Most classes have 10–19 students.	

MOST POPULAR MAJORS

Biology/Biological Sciences; Psychology;
Social Sciences

ABOUT THE SCHOOL

At this original member of the Seven Sisters schools, founded in 1837, young women find "an ideal environment for curious and engaged students of different backgrounds." Mount Holyoke College reinforces the idea of a global, twenty-first century education for its students, giving them the broad education of a true liberal arts curriculum while providing the practical tools needed to adapt to different career paths and jobs. More than 200 faculty members guide over 2,100 students (about 25 percent of whom are international citizens) through the halls of academia, providing "a vastly engaging classroom experience" that "excels in empowering students to lead on-campus organizations and programs." There are fifty majors to choose from (as well as an option to design your own), and professors "not only help you with your homework, but often give you words of wisdom about life in general."

BANG FOR YOUR BUCK

Despite the high sticker price, Mount Holyoke does everything in its power to make sure that "significant financial aid" is given to students who require it. The school is highly focused on the employability of its students down the road, so the return on whatever level of investment students do end up making is solid. Numerous merit-based scholarships are available on top of grants. The Trustee Scholarship offers full tuition to a select group of high-achieving first-year students; around twenty-five freshman Twenty-First Century Scholars also receive $25,000 annually based upon scholarship, extracurricular achievement, and leadership potential. Scholarships ranging from $10,000 to $20,000 are also available via the Mount Holyoke Leadership Awards.

STUDENT LIFE

From the bond of sisterhood to the numerous college traditions, this "truly unique" campus community is very close knit. The "racially and ethnically diverse, internationally representative" student body is also "inclusive of many sexual orientations and gender identities," embraces variety in terms of student organizations and social life, and is "pretty active socially on campus." "If you want to be considered a MoHo, you have to be intelligent and love to raise dialogue." There is "always plenty going on here" and at the other colleges in the Five College Consortium, from lectures to theatre to concerts to exhibits to parties. Students can "take a walk around the lake, see an a cappella performance, go to a celebration of the scientific measurement...or a lecture on ancient manuscripts," or attend one of the "big five-college parties in Chapin Auditorium."

CAREER

Many who attend Mount Holyoke choose to go on to a secondary degree (nearly 80 percent enroll in grad school within ten years of graduation), and 84 percent of the class of 2014 reported being employed or in school six months after graduation. The college has adapted to the needs of students facing a volatile job market with curriculum-to-career classes and other job training endeavors (The Lynk), and students are able to call on an alumnae network of more than 35,000 to supplement the already "excellent internship and career resources" provided. The active Career Development Center helps connect students with internships, advisers, preparatory workshops, and funding for unpaid internships and research opportunities, and an employer partnership with Smith and Amherst Colleges helps bolster job opportunities. For those Mount Holyoke graduates who visited PayScale.com, 52 percent reported that they had a career with high job meaning.

Mount Holyoke College

FINANCIAL AID: 413-538-2291 • E-MAIL: ADMISSION@MTHOLYOKE.EDU • WEBSITE: WWW.MTHOLYOKE.EDU

GENERAL INFO

Activities: Choral groups, dance, drama/theater, jazz band, literary magazine, music ensembles, musical theater, radio station, student government, student newspaper, student-run film society, symphony orchestra, yearbook, campus ministries, International Student Organization, Model UN. **Organizations:** 130 registered organizations, 5 honor societies, 9 religious organizations. **Athletics (Intercollegiate):** *Women:* basketball, crew/rowing, cross-country, diving, equestrian sports, field hockey, golf, horseback riding, lacrosse, soccer, squash, swimming, tennis, track/field (outdoor), track/field (indoor), volleyball. **On-Campus Highlights:** Unified Science Center, Kendall Sports and Dance Complex, The Equestrian Center, Blanchard Campus Center, Williston Memorial Library. The entire campus is an exquisitely maintained botanic garden which includes an arboretum, numerous gardens, and the Talcott Greenhouse.

FINANCIAL AID

Students should submit: CSS Profile; FAFSA; Noncustodial PROFILE. Priority filing deadline is 3/15. The Princeton Review suggests that all financial aid forms be submitted as soon as possible after October 1. *Need-based scholarships/grants offered:* College/university scholarship or grant aid from institutional funds, Federal Pell, private scholarships, SEOG, state scholarships/grants. *Loan aid offered:* Direct PLUS Loans, Direct Subsidized Loans, Direct Unsubsidized Loans. Applicants will be notified of awards on or about 4/1. Federal Work-Study Program available. Institutional employment available.

BOTTOM LINE

Tuition at this private school runs $49,780, with room and board adding an additional $14,660 to the bill; however, financial aid, scholarships (both need- and merit-based), and financing opportunities are plentiful. Most students receive some sort of financial assistance, with the average undergraduate total need-based gift running $35,067.

CAREER INFORMATION FROM PAYSCALE.COM	
ROI Rating	91
Bachelors and No Higher	
Median starting salary	$50,500
Median mid-career salary	$94,400
At Least Bachelors	
Median starting salary	$52,800
Median mid-career salary	$100,200
Alumni with high job meaning	52%
Degrees awarded in STEM subjects	28%

SELECTIVITY	
Admissions Rating	93
# of applicants	3,446
% of applicants accepted	51
% of acceptees attending	30
# offered a place on the wait list	437
% accepting a place on wait list	44
% admitted from wait list	1
# of early decision applicants	311
% accepted early decision	55

FRESHMAN PROFILE	
Range SAT EBRW	640–713
Range SAT Math	630–750
Range ACT Composite	29–33
Minimum internet-based TOEFL	100
Average HS GPA	3.8
% graduated top 10% of class	54
% graduated top 25% of class	91
% graduated top 50% of class	98

DEADLINES	
Early decision	
Deadline	11/15
Notification	1/1
Other ED Deadline	1/1
Other ED Notification	2/1
Regular	
Deadline	1/15
Notification	4/1
Nonfall registration?	Yes

FINANCIAL FACTS	
Financial Aid Rating	97
Annual tuition	$49,780
Room and board	$14,660
Required fees	$218
Books and supplies	$950
Average frosh need-based scholarship	$37,011
Average UG need-based scholarship	$35,067
% needy frosh rec. need-based scholarship or grant aid	100
% needy UG rec. need-based scholarship or grant aid	100
% needy frosh rec. non-need-based scholarship or grant aid	18
% needy UG rec. non-need-based scholarship or grant aid	16
% needy frosh rec. need-based self-help aid	86
% needy UG rec. need-based self-help aid	88
% frosh rec. any financial aid	81
% UG rec. any financial aid	80
% UG borrow to pay for school	66
Average cumulative indebtedness	$23,827
% frosh need fully met	100
% ugrads need fully met	100

Muhlenberg College

2400 West Chew Street, Allentown, PA 18104-5596 • Admissions: 484-664-3200 • Fax: 484-664-3032

ABOUT THE SCHOOL

At this private Lutheran college in Allentown, Pennsylvania, "the education is wonderful, and there isn't a day that goes by without learning something." This small school—enrollment is roughly 2,400—is "an excellent place to go if you're serious about academics, and you want to try a lot of different things throughout your undergraduate career. There are tons of options for extra-curriculars, and there are many majors and minors to explore." The liberal arts mentality appeals to students who praise "strong academics" and the ability to sample lots of different classes by professors who "are willing to help and listen, which significantly [increases] the learning experience." The "highly accepting and friendly" environment and the ease of access to professors "is extremely encouraging" and students find that "[they] work harder" because of it.

BANG FOR YOUR BUCK

In addition to offering an online catalogue of current internship opportunities, the school's website also provides students with the Muhlenberg College Internship Manual, which includes "tips on how to make the most of your internship, various guidelines, as well as important forms." One Environmental Science and Sociology major praised the "strong science program and honors program," where students "could conduct research and take part in an internship" instead of having to sacrifice internship opportunities for academic ones. Muhlenberg meets roughly 91 percent of students' need for aid, with students praising "generous" and "incredible" financial aid packages. Muhlenberg students are also encouraged to participate in the Student Research and Scholarship program, where they take part in "a variety of extracurricular experiences in which students conduct an independent scholarly investigation of a field under the guidance of a faculty member," according to the school's website.

STUDENT LIFE

Students describe Muhlenberg campus life as "a bubble" with little venturing out to downtown Allentown. Even for a small school, "there is such a wide variety of talented students here at Muhlenberg." Greek life does play a role on campus, where there are five sororities and four fraternities; approximately 25 percent of women join a sorority, while roughly 17 percent of men join a fraternity. "When the weather is nice," says one Neuroscience and Spanish major, "everyone is outside, whether playing pickup Frisbee, lacrosse, football or just relaxing on a blanket in the sun." Most students don't have classes on Friday, so the weekend begins on Thursday evening. One Political Science major described the school as "very accepting and open" and if "students want to try something new (clubs, etc.), they're welcome to. At Muhlenberg, the sky is the limit." There are roughly 100 registered student organizations and around 98 percent of all undergraduates living on campus, making for a college that "works hard to make sure that there are always fun events going on."

CAREER

PayScale.com reports that 43 percent of Muhlenberg graduates would describe their careers as helping to improve society and earn a median starting salary of $50,000. Popular careers for graduates include web project manager, high school teacher, and software developer. The Muhlenberg website offers two helpful services to students looking to gain traction in the work world: Collegefeed.com, where students upload a profile and the site "connect[s] [students] directly to hiring managers and founders at 500+ great companies;" and Interviewstream.com, a "virtual interviewing system" where students

Muhlenberg College

FINANCIAL AID: 484-664-3175 • E-MAIL: ADMISSIONS@MUHLENBERG.EDU • WEBSITE: WWW.MUHLENBERG.EDU

can "record an unlimited amount of practice interviews before seeking employment" and view "video clips on interviewing with tips from experts." A French and Business double major says that "Muhlenberg is very strong in academics and I feel that I will be well prepared for whatever career I [choose]."

GENERAL INFO

Activities: concert band, dance, drama/theater, jazz band, literary magazine, music ensembles, musical theater, pep band, radio station, student government, student newspaper, student-run film society, symphony orchestra, yearbook. **Organizations:** 100 registered organizations, 12 honor societies, 7 religious organizations. 4 fraternities, 4 sororities. **Athletics (Intercollegiate):** *Men:* baseball, basketball, cheerleading, cross-country, football, golf, lacrosse, soccer, tennis, track/field (outdoor), track/field (indoor), wrestling. *Women:* basketball, cheerleading, cross-country, field hockey, golf, lacrosse, soccer, softball, tennis, track/field (outdoor), track/field (indoor), volleyball. **On-Campus Highlights:** Seegers Union by fireplace & Java Joe's, The Life Sports Center-Athletic Facility, Parents Plaza-Outdoor Courtyard, GQ, Seegers Union, Trexler Pavilion for Threatre & Dance.

FINANCIAL AID

Students should submit: CSS Profile, FAFSA; Institution's own financial aid form, Noncustodial PROFILE. Priority filing deadline is 2/1. The Princeton Review suggests that all financial aid forms be submitted as soon as possible after October 1. *Need-based scholarships/grants offered:* College/university scholarship or grant aid from institutional funds, Federal Pell, private scholarships, SEOG, state scholarships/grants. *Loan aid offered:* Direct PLUS Loans, Subsidized Direct Loans, and Unsubsidized Direct Loans. Applicants will be notified of awards on or about 3/15. Federal Work-Study Program available. Institutional employment available.

BOTTOM LINE

Tuition is roughly $51,860 annually, with an additional $11,765 for room and board, and around $2,130 for books and fees, making a year at Muhlenberg cost $65,755. Ninety-two percent of freshmen receive some sort of financial aid, with 88 percent of other undergraduates receiving aid. The average need-based gift aid awarded is $32,257. The typical Muhlenberg student graduates with approximately $32,241 in debt.

CAREER INFORMATION FROM PAYSCALE.COM

ROI Rating	88
Bachelors and No Higher	
Median starting salary	$51,700
Median mid-career salary	$101,700
At Least Bachelors	
Median starting salary	$53,300
Median mid-career salary	$106,800
Alumni with high job meaning	43%
Degrees awarded in STEM subjects	20%

SELECTIVITY

Admissions Rating	89
# of applicants	4,636
% of applicants accepted	48
% of acceptees attending	25
# offered a place on the wait list	1,530
% accepting a place on wait list	16
% admitted from wait list	5
# of early decision applicants	341
% accepted early decision	85

FRESHMAN PROFILE

Range ACT Composite	25–30
Range SAT	1140–1340
Minimum internet-based TOEFL	80
Average HS GPA	3.3
% graduated top 10% of class	31
% graduated top 25% of class	61
% graduated top 50% of class	90

DEADLINES

Early decision 1	
Deadline	11/15
Notification	12/15
Early decision 2	
Deadline	2/1
Notification	3/1
Regular decision	
Deadline	2/1
Notification	3/15
Nonfall registration?	Yes

FINANCIAL FACTS

Financial Aid Rating	89
Annual tuition	$51,860
Room and board	$11,765
Required fees	$735
Books and supplies	$1,395
Average frosh need-based scholarship	$33,460
Average UG need-based scholarship	$32,257
% needy frosh rec. need-based scholarship or grant aid	100
% needy UG rec. need-based scholarship or grant aid	98
% needy frosh rec. non-need-based scholarship or grant aid	19
% needy UG rec. non-need-based scholarship or grant aid	15
% needy frosh rec. need-based self-help aid	75
% needy UG rec. need-based self-help aid	75
% frosh rec. any financial aid	92
% UG rec. any financial aid	88
% UG borrow to pay for school	59
Average cumulative indebtedness	$32,241
% frosh need fully met	27
% ugrads need fully met	25

New College of Florida

5800 Bay Shore Road, Sarasota, FL 34243-2109 • Admissions: 941-487-5000 • Fax: 941-487-5001

ABOUT THE SCHOOL

New College of Florida distinguishes itself from other elite colleges and universities through its unique collaborative curriculum, emphasis on independent learning, and "deep and stimulating academics." With a total enrollment of 861 students, New College offers a "small, intimate atmosphere" in which faculty and students engage collaboratively in in-depth exploration of ideas and subject matter, all at a public college price. "It [feels] like a family," says a student. With no graduate students on campus, undergraduates receive the full attention of their professors and work one-on-one with them to map their own intellectual journey, which culminates in a senior thesis. There is no rigid core curriculum required of all students ("Our school has been tailored to us"). The cornerstone of the New College experience is that, in addition to traditional course offerings, the student has the ability to work with "dedicated and wise professors" to design their own independent study and research projects during the month of January, which is set aside for independent projects. Course work at NCF is intense and can be stressful. However, with fewer than 1,000 students on campus, all students are guaranteed to receive plenty of personal attention from passionate and accessible professors. The student body takes "active participation in the running of the school," and The Center for Engagement and Opportunity helps students coordinate internships, make career decisions, conduct job searches, apply to graduate and professional schools, and network with New College alumni. This leads to impressive outcomes, as evidenced by the seventy Fulbright Scholarships that have been awarded to NCF students since 2001 (there were eight in 2011 alone).

BANG FOR YOUR BUCK

The combination of NCF's incredibly low tuition and rigorous, individualized academic program make it a tremendous value for both in-state and out-of-state students. Students and their families can take advantage of many funding opportunities, including grants, loans, book advances, and work-study. Scholarships are guaranteed to all admitted applicants meeting the February 15 application deadline. Additional scholarship opportunities may be available to students based upon their specialized high school curriculum. In addition to an academic scholarship, gift assistance is available for qualifying students who submit the FAFSA by the February 15 priority deadline.

STUDENT LIFE

New College students share "a few things in common: Most…are friendly, passionate about the things they believe in, very hard workers, liberal, and most of all, try to be open to new experiences." Put another way: "New College is a bunch of incredibly intelligent hippies exploring every facet of existence." On campus, students enjoy everything "from club meetings to public speakers to 'hip' bands playing shows. There's usually something to do and usually free food to be found!" Weekends usually mean going to see "the Wall," which are the "school-wide parties every Friday and Saturday night in a courtyard outside of the dorms" or a visit to nearby Lido and Siesta Beaches, "where [students] enjoy unlimited swimming, sunning and Frisbee playing." Undergrads praise the overall emphasis on "freedom, intelligence, creativity, and challenging yourself" that permeates student culture in class and out.

CAREER

The Center for Engagement and Opportunity (CEO), a new office in 2014–2015, houses everything related to career services, internships, and

New College of Florida

FINANCIAL AID: 941-487-5000 • E-MAIL: ADMISSIONS@NCF.EDU • WEBSITE: WWW.NCF.EDU

fellowships for students thinking strategically about their future. Beyond CEO, faculty advisors also act as career mentors and help their students locate experiential learning opportunities like study abroad or off-campus research—students have recently interned at the Jane Goodall Institute in Washington, D.C., and the Early Intervention Program in Massachusetts. The Alumnae/i Association boasts professional connections at University of Florida, University of South Florida, UC Berkeley, and Apple and serves as another resource for students seeking opportunities or advice about life after graduation.

GENERAL INFO

Activities: Choral groups, dance, drama/theater, literary magazine, music ensembles, musical theater, radio station, student government, student newspaper, student-run film society, campus ministries. **Organizations:** 90 registered organizations, 5 religious organizations. **Athletics (Intercollegiate):** *Men:* Sailing. *Women:* Sailing. **On-Campus Highlights:** The R.V. Heiser Natural Sciences Complex, Pritzker Marine Biology Research Center, The Caples Fine Arts Complex, Four Winds Cafe (Student owned and operated), Jane Bancroft Cook Library, Historic bay-front mansions. **Environmental Initiatives:** Waste management efforts—recycling of all paper, newsprint, cardboard, phone books, magazines, junk mail, soft-cover books, cotton goods, cans (all types), glass and plastic, jars and bottles, auto batteries, used oil and filters, used antifreeze, toner cartridges, chemicals and solvents, white goods, scrap metal, precious metals, wastewater solids, used pallets, yard debris, masonry and concrete, fluorescent tubes, used lumber, etc. Purchasing efforts—all new appliances are EnergyStar.

FINANCIAL AID

Students should submit: FAFSA. Priority filing deadline is November 1. The Princeton Review suggests that all financial aid forms be submitted as soon as possible after October 1. *Need-based scholarships/grants offered:* College/university scholarship or grant aid from institutional funds, Federal Pell, private scholarships, SEOG, state scholarships/grants. *Loan aid offered:* Direct PLUS Loans, Direct Subsidized Loans, Direct Unsubsidized Loans. Applicants will be notified of awards on a rolling basis beginning 3/1. Federal Work-Study Program available. Institutional employment available.

THE BOTTOM LINE

Even in the era of rising higher education costs, tuition at New College of Florida is still incredibly low, as evidenced by the comparatively low average debt for graduating students: $16,577. The sticker price is further offset by loans, grants, and scholarships. The average scholarship for students with demonstrated need is $8,832. The school estimates that books and supplies may run another $1,200 per year. Independent study projects and senior theses may involve additional costs for travel, research expenses, and equipment.

CAREER INFORMATION FROM PAYSCALE.COM	
ROI Rating	90
Bachelors and No Higher	
Median starting salary	$45,800
Median mid-career salary	$91,500
At Least Bachelors	
Median starting salary	$49,200
Median mid-career salary	$96,200
Alumni with high job meaning	38%
Degrees awarded in STEM subjects	4%

SELECTIVITY	
Admissions Rating	87
# of applicants	1,353
% of applicants accepted	69
% of acceptees attending	21
# offered a place on the wait list	92
% accepting a place on wait list	41
% admitted from wait list	53
# of early decision applicants	0

FRESHMAN PROFILE	
Range SAT EBRW	620–710
Range SAT Math	570–670
Range ACT Composite	25–30
Minimum paper TOEFL	560
Minimum internet-based TOEFL	83
Average HS GPA	3.99
% graduated top 10% of class	37
% graduated top 25% of class	71
% graduated top 50% of class	95

DEADLINES	
Early decision	
Deadline	11/1
Notification	1/4
Other ED Deadline	N/A
Other ED Notification	N/A
Regular	
Priority	11/1
Deadline	4/15
Nonfall registration?	No

FINANCIAL FACTS	
Financial Aid Rating	88
Annual in-state tuition	$6,916
Annual out-of-state tuition	$29,944
Room and board	$9,370
Books and supplies	$1,200
Average frosh need-based scholarship	$11,802
Average UG need-based scholarship	$9,932
% needy frosh rec. need-based scholarship or grant aid	90
% needy UG rec. need-based scholarship or grant aid	91
% needy frosh rec. non-need-based scholarship or grant aid	13
% needy UG rec. non-need-based scholarship or grant aid	13
% needy frosh rec. need-based self-help aid	79
% needy UG rec. need-based self-help aid	80
% frosh rec. any financial aid	100
% UG rec. any financial aid	97
% UG borrow to pay for school	34
Average cumulative indebtedness	$16,297
% frosh need fully met	26
% ugrads need fully met	31

New Jersey Institute of Technology

OFFICE OF UNIVERSITY ADMISSIONS, NEWARK, NJ 07102 • ADMISSIONS: 973-596-3300 • FAX: 973-596-3461

CAMPUS LIFE

Quality of Life Rating	83
Fire Safety Rating	99
Green Rating	60*
Type of school	Public
Environment	Metropolis

STUDENTS

Total undergrad enrollment	7,489
% male/female	78/22
% from out of state	3
% frosh from public high school	85
% frosh live on campus	53
% ugrads live on campus	22
# of fraternities (% ugrad men join)	18 (6)
# of sororities (% ugrad women join)	6 (6)
% African American	8
% Asian	22
% Caucasian	35
% Hispanic	21
% Native American	<1
% Pacific Islander	<1
% Two or more races	3
% Race and/or ethnicity unknown	6
% international	5
# of countries represented	65

ACADEMICS

Academic Rating	72
% students returning for sophomore year	88
% students graduating within 4 years	28
% students graduating within 6 years	64
Calendar	Semester
Student/faculty ratio	17:1
Profs interesting rating	70
Profs accessible rating	68

Most classes have 10–19 students. Most lab/discussion sessions have 20–29 students.

MOST POPULAR MAJORS

Computer Science; Information Technology; Mechanical Engineering

ABOUT THE SCHOOL

Newark-based New Jersey Institute of Technology (NJIT) has doubled the size of its campus within the past decade, in a direct answer to the call for more STEM-oriented skill sets in the workplace. This mid-sized public research university offers more than 50 undergraduate degrees in six specialized schools and colleges, and is constantly developing new curriculums to adapt to the marketplace. It spent $140 million on research expenditures in 2017. The industrious types who go to NJIT all recognize that their four years are all about "putting your best work forward so that you can achieve what you want in life after graduation" and find that classes here mean that they are "constantly supplied with knowledge applicable to my field" and "constantly challenged." Professors "bring practical knowledge to even the [driest] lectures." One of NJIT's greatest strengths is the help and support on offer, including "a math tutoring center, physics tutoring center, and a writing center where you can have your papers looked at and looked over," in order to receive feedback on the paper.

BANG FOR YOUR BUCK

A return on an NJIT investment is a beautiful thing, and the school is among the top 1 percent in the United States for occupational earnings power. "Great job placement and high starting salaries" are a huge draw for most who attend. "Financial aid is very helpful" for many at NJIT—it is "unmatched" for honors students—and allows good students to focus on the academic tasks at hand. Students can apply for a variety of need- and merit-based scholarships, including the $1,000 Governor's Urban Scholarship for high-achieving New Jersey residents, the $7,260 Engineering Technology Scholarship for academically talented transfer and out-of-state students, and the $2,500 William S Guttenberg '44 Endowed Scholarship to be used toward tuition, books, fees and/or residency for each qualified student.

STUDENT LIFE

NJIT has "a very diverse campus" and more than half of all first years and around a quarter of all undergraduates live there with commuters constantly streaming throughout. Students admit they are "more work than play," but the school "has a very active and fun resident community." One of the central social hubs on campus is the game room, where students "can come and relax, play some billiards, or even go bowling on their six-lane bowling alley." Soccer and basketball are popular, and these busy, "highly independent" students have "a plethora of different activities for student to take part in." The closeness to New York City is "a major plus" and "can provide the socialization needed when you have some free time."

CAREER

A big selling point of NJIT is "the prestige of it and how many companies love NJIT students: it is "a magical place to learn engineering." Many of the faculty have worked at Bell Labs and other nearby research think tanks and "have supreme hands-on engineering experience" and connections. The Career Development Services Office makes sure students are prepared via workshops, practice interviews, and two career fairs (and preparatory sessions), and are very good at providing students with job experience. "There are a lot of connections with companies that will give students internships and full-time positions," says one. Essentially, "if you make it through the academic program you will get a job." Of all of the New Jersey Institute of Technology alumni visiting PayScale.com, 52 percent report that their jobs make the world a better place.

New Jersey Institute of Technology

FINANCIAL AID: 973-596-3479 • E-MAIL: ADMISSIONS@NJIT.EDU • WEBSITE: WWW.NJIT.EDU

GENERAL INFO

Activities: concert band, dance, drama/theater, literary magazine, marching band, musical theater, radio station, student government, student newspaper, yearbook, Student Organization. 70 registered organizations, 10 honor societies, 5 religious organizations. 15 fraternities, 7 sororities. **Athletics (Intercollegiate):** *Men:* baseball, basketball, cheerleading, cross-country, fencing, soccer, swimming, tennis, track/field (outdoor), track/field (indoor), volleyball. *Women:* basketball, cheerleading, cross-country, fencing, soccer, swimming, tennis, track/field (outdoor), track/field (indoor), volleyball. **On-Campus Highlights:** Campus Center, Van Houten Library, Zoom Fleisher Athletic Center, East Building—Admissions, Student Mall.

FINANCIAL AID

Students should submit: FAFSA. Priority filing deadline is 3/1. The Princeton Review suggests that all financial aid forms be submitted as soon as possible after October 1. *Need-based scholarships/grants offered:* College/university scholarship or grant aid from institutional funds; Federal Pell; Private scholarships; SEOG; State scholarships/grants; United Negro College Fund. *Loan aid offered:* Direct PLUS Loans, Direct Subsidized Loans, Direct Unsubsidized Loans. Applicants will be notified of awards on a rolling basis beginning 12/15. Federal Work-Study Program available. Institutional employment available.

BOTTOM LINE

Tuition for in-state students is $14,174 for a full course load, and $29,586 for out-of-state residents. Full-time students can expect an additional $3,162 in fees. Ninety-six percent of incoming undergraduates receive financial aid with the average undergraduate need-based scholarship totaling $12,484.

CAREER INFORMATION FROM PAYSCALE.COM	
ROI Rating	89
Bachelors and No Higher	
Median starting salary	$62,800
Median mid-career salary	$121,100
At Least Bachelors	
Median starting salary	$64,100
Median mid-career salary	$125,900
Alumni with high job meaning	52%
Degrees awarded in STEM subjects	75%

SELECTIVITY	
Admissions Rating	**87**
# of applicants	7,254
% of applicants accepted	61
% of acceptees attending	25

FRESHMAN PROFILE	
Range SAT EBRW	580–670
Range SAT Math	610–700
Range ACT Composite	24–30
Minimum paper TOEFL	550
Minimum internet-based TOEFL	79
Average HS GPA	3.6
% graduated top 10% of class	37
% graduated top 25% of class	66
% graduated top 50% of class	89

DEADLINES	
Regular	
Deadline	3/1
Nonfall registration?	Yes

FINANCIAL FACTS	
Financial Aid Rating	**78**
Annual in-state tuition	$14,174
Annual out-of-state tuition	$29,586
Room and board	$13,560
Required fees	$3,162
Books and supplies	$2,600
Average frosh need-based scholarship	$12,671
Average UG need-based scholarship	$12,484
% needy frosh rec. need-based scholarship or grant aid	97
% needy UG rec. need-based scholarship or grant aid	96
% needy frosh rec. non-need-based scholarship or grant aid	67
% needy UG rec. non-need-based scholarship or grant aid	39
% needy frosh rec. need-based self-help aid	62
% needy UG rec. need-based self-help aid	71
% frosh rec. any financial aid	87
% UG rec. any financial aid	72
% UG borrow to pay for school	62
Average cumulative indebtedness	$40,979
% frosh need fully met	17
% ugrads need fully met	9
Average % of frosh need met	51
Average % of ugrad need met	41

North Carolina State University

Box 7103, Raleigh, NC 27695 • Admissions: 919-515-2434 • Fax: 919-515-5039

CAMPUS LIFE

Quality of Life Rating	**90**
Fire Safety Rating	**97**
Green Rating	**97**
Type of school	Public
Environment	Metropolis

STUDENTS

Total undergrad enrollment	22,755
% male/female	55/45
% from out of state	10
% frosh from public high school	87
% frosh live on campus	93
% ugrads live on campus	39
# of fraternities (% ugrad men join)	28 (12)
# of sororities (% ugrad women join)	20 (17)
% African American	6
% Asian	6
% Caucasian	69
% Hispanic	5
% Native American	<1
% Pacific Islander	<1
% Two or more races	4
% Race and/or ethnicity unknown	5
% international	5
# of countries represented	102

ACADEMICS

Academic Rating	**80**
% students returning for sophomore year	94
% students graduating within 4 years	50
% students graduating within 6 years	79
Calendar	Semester
Student/faculty ratio	13:1
Profs interesting rating	75
Profs accessible rating	80

Most classes have 10–19 students. Most lab/discussion sessions have 20–29 students.

MOST POPULAR MAJORS
Engineering; Biology/Biological Sciences; Business Administration and Management

ABOUT THE SCHOOL

Science and technology are big at North Carolina State University, a major research university and the largest four-year institution in its state. While the College of Engineering and the College of Sciences form the backbone of the academic program, the school also boasts nationally reputable majors in architecture, design, textiles, management, agriculture, humanities and social sciences, education, physical and mathematical sciences, natural resources, and veterinary medicine, providing "big-school opportunity with a small-school feel." The "vicinity to top-of-the-line research" is palpable, as more than 70 percent of NC State's faculty is involved in sponsored research, and the school is "an incubator for outstanding engineering and scientific research." For undergraduates, many of whom grew up wanting to attend the school, this opportunity to participate in important research is a major advantage. It makes sense, given that NC State "is all about developing skills in school that will help you throughout your professional career." In addition, an education at NC State includes many opportunities for students to get a head start on a real-world job, and the school also has "a great [Exploratory Studies] for students . . . who aren't sure what major they want to go into." The university's co-op program is one of the largest in the nation, with more than 1,000 work rotations a year, all due to the school's excellent reputation. "I want my degree to pack a punch when people see it, without having to be ridiculously rich or a prodigy of some sort," says a student of his decision to go to NC State.

BANG FOR YOUR BUCK

NC State continues to be a best value for North Carolina residents. Offering financial assistance to qualified students is an integral part of NC State's history. In 2017, NC State awarded $3,520,520 in institutional scholarships.

STUDENT LIFE

North Carolina State offers a lot for students to do both on and off campus. Though students report that they spend a great deal of time studying, social life is very big as well: "Everyone manages to have some fun doing what they want to do while maintaining their GPA. And there is something for everyone here at State." "The school offers various activities throughout each semester that are usually lots of fun, and the best part is they're free," says a student. "There are also a lot of club events. Outdoor Adventures usually does something about every weekend, involving a trip to the mountains or something. There's always a lot of support for the sports teams and tons of school spirit." In addition to attending sporting events, "it's easy to get out and play yourself" through a variety of intramural teams and clubs. For those looking to venture out at night, "students love to go to downtown Raleigh to have fun in clubs or wander Hillsborough Street. There is opportunity to do just about anything in the area."

CAREER

Students at NC State work hard and are concerned about their future careers, and most feel that the school prepares them very well for life after college. The Career Development Center offers one-on-one academic advising and career planning; job and internship search resources; career fairs and on-campus recruiting in many different fields; and help with resume building, job interviews, and other professional skills. The school also offers a Cooperative Education program that allows students to pursue paid work in their field while studying for their degree. "I have had several good academic advisors that have helped me decide what courses I should take based on the different career paths I have been considering," says a student. "Also,

North Carolina State University

FINANCIAL AID: 919-515-2421 • E-MAIL: UNDERGRAD_ADMISSIONS@NCSU.EDU • WEBSITE: WWW.NCSU.EDU

all of my professors always wish to do whatever they can in order to help out the students." Out of NC State alumni visiting PayScale.com, 53 percent report that they derive a high level of meaning from their jobs.

GENERAL INFO

Activities: Choral groups, concert band, dance, drama/theater, jazz band, literary magazine, marching band, music ensembles, musical theater, pep band, radio station, student government, student newspaper, symphony orchestra, yearbook, campus ministries, international student organization. **Organizations:** 637 registered organizations, 26 honor societies, 50 religious organizations. 30 fraternities, 20 sororities. **Athletics (Intercollegiate):** *Men:* Baseball, basketball, cheerleading, cross-country, diving, football, golf, riflery, soccer, swimming, tennis, track/field (outdoor), track/field (indoor), wrestling. *Women:* Basketball, cheerleading, cross-country, diving, golf, gymnastics, riflery, soccer, softball, swimming, tennis, track/field (outdoor), track/field (indoor), volleyball.

FINANCIAL AID

Students should submit: FAFSA. Priority filing deadline is 3/1. The Princeton Review suggests that all financial aid forms be submitted as soon as possible after October 1. *Need-based scholarships/grants offered:* College/university scholarship or grant aid from institutional funds; Federal Pell; Private scholarships; SEOG; State scholarships/grants; United Negro College Fund. *Loan aid offered:* Direct PLUS Loans, Direct Subsidized Loans, Direct Unsubsidized Loans. Applicants will be notified of awards on a rolling basis beginning 4/1. Federal Work-Study Program available. Institutional employment available.

BOTTOM LINE

Annual tuition and fees for North Carolina residents are $9,100. For nonresidents, tuition and fees reach $28,444. For both residents and nonresidents, room and board runs about $11,078 per year, while books and supplies average just over $1,000 annually. Around 54 percent of all NC State students take out loans—students who borrow money graduate with an average loan debt of roughly $24,053.

CAREER INFORMATION FROM PAYSCALE.COM	
ROI Rating	91
Bachelors and No Higher	
Median starting salary	$55,800
Median mid-career salary	$104,700
At Least Bachelors	
Median starting salary	$56,900
Median mid-career salary	$109,200
Alumni with high job meaning	52%
Degrees awarded in STEM subjects	47%

SELECTIVITY	
Admissions Rating	90
# of applicants	26,859
% of applicants accepted	51
% of acceptees attending	34
# offered a place on the wait list	2,479
% accepting a place on wait list	42
% admitted from wait list	1

FRESHMAN PROFILE	
Range SAT EBRW	610–680
Range SAT Math	620–710
Range ACT Composite	27–31
Average HS GPA	3.7
% graduated top 10% of class	46
% graduated top 25% of class	88
% graduated top 50% of class	99

DEADLINES	
Early action	
Deadline	10/15
Notification	1/30
Regular	
Priority	10/15
Deadline	1/15
Nonfall registration?	Yes

FINANCIAL FACTS	
Financial Aid Rating	85
Annual in-state tuition	$6,535
Annual out-of-state tuition	$25,878
Room and board	$11,078
Required fees	$2,566
Books and supplies	$1,082
Average frosh need-based scholarship	$10,144
Average UG need-based scholarship	$9,974
% needy frosh rec. need-based scholarship or grant aid	93
% needy UG rec. need-based scholarship or grant aid	91
% needy frosh rec. non-need-based scholarship or grant aid	18
% needy UG rec. non-need-based scholarship or grant aid	13
% needy frosh rec. need-based self-help aid	72
% needy UG rec. need-based self-help aid	71
% frosh rec. any financial aid	76
% UG rec. any financial aid	68
% UG borrow to pay for school	52
Average cumulative indebtedness	$24,053
% frosh need fully met	23
% ugrads need fully met	22
Average % of frosh need met	77
Average % of ugrad need met	75

Northeastern University

360 Huntington Avenue, Boston, MA 02115 • Admissions: 617-373-2200 • Fax: 617-373-8780

CAMPUS LIFE

Quality of Life Rating	92
Fire Safety Rating	94
Green Rating	93
Type of school	Private
Environment	Metropolis

STUDENTS

Total undergrad enrollment	18,463
% male/female	49/51
% from out of state	75
% frosh live on campus	99
% ugrads live on campus	49
# of fraternities (% ugrad men join)	NR (10)
# of sororities (% ugrad women join)	NR (16)
% African American	6
% Asian	16
% Caucasian	31
% Hispanic	8
% Native American	<1
% Pacific Islander	<1
% Two or more races	5
% Race and/or ethnicity unknown	17
% international	20
# of countries represented	122

ACADEMICS

Academic Rating	85
% students returning for sophomore year	97
% students graduating within 6 years	87
Calendar	Semester
Student/faculty ratio	14:1
Profs interesting rating	79
Profs accessible rating	75
Most classes have 10–19 students.	

MOST POPULAR MAJORS
Engineering; Health Services/Allied Health/
Health Sciences

ABOUT THE SCHOOL

Experiential learning is the name of the game at Boston's Northeastern University, which integrates a "stellar" global cooperative learning program within its classroom education. Over 11,000 students were placed in co-ops last year which is up by nearly 75 percent from a decade prior). Northeastern regularly sends more than 3,000 students abroad to more than 133 locations to study, work, and research each year. Service-learning is also a huge part of the Northeastern education, and students complete thousands of hours of service learning courses, workshops, and trips. Northeastern's learning model "actively pushes students to gain real world experience" and students can take part in multiple co-ops (even around the world), which feeds into strong job placement rates and a "pretty grueling but completely worth it" academic experience. "The co-op specifically puts the school well beyond anywhere else I would have wanted to go," says one student.

BANG FOR YOUR BUCK

All eligible applicants are considered for merit awards during the Admissions review process, where real life work experience through the co-op program combines with top-level academics in order to "provide the best preparation possible for students post-college." The school's commitment to education is reflected in the Northeastern Promise, which guarantees that need will be met and need-based grants will be raised in accordance with tuition each year. Additionally, plenty of other institutional aid is available for research and creative projects; study abroad and co-op scholarships are for students who might not be able to participate otherwise, and more than one hundred students receive undergraduate research awards each year. Students who are in the top 15 percent of the applicant pool are also considered for competitive merit awards, including the Dean's Scholarship, with awards valued at $15,000 and $30,000 annually.

STUDENT LIFE

Northeastern students are "pretty diverse, from their backgrounds to their majors" and no one is cookie-cutter in any way: "everyone has their quirks and qualities that shine through." It is "not unusual to hear ten languages in ten minutes walking across campus." On the whole, this bunch is "globally-minded and career-focused," and many students are "actively liberal" and have entrepreneurial interests. People are mainly focused on school and work, so "there aren't many parties or great sports," but Northeastern "has worked hard to support many clubs so that people can stay busy and involved." There are over 400 student organizations to choose from. Additionally, "Boston is an amazing city in which to go to school."

CAREER

Northeastern's great strength is "creating co-op opportunities that enhance what we learn in the classroom to best prepare us for the future." This incredible amount of work experience automatically gives graduates an edge when it comes time to enter the workforce. Typically, students get up to a year-and-a-half of real experience in their fields, which "is a huge advantage when it comes to looking for jobs post-graduation." Having a "strong academic pipeline to university cultivated co-ops and jobs," all in the center of Boston, is half the battle, and the Career Development Office further aids students on their professional paths by hosting career fairs, panels, and workshops. According to PaysScale.com, alumni with bachelor's degrees from Northeastern report an average starting salary of $58,300.

Northeastern University

FINANCIAL AID: 617-373-3190 • E-MAIL: ADMISSIONS@NORTHEASTERN.EDU • WEBSITE: WWW.NORTHEASTERN.EDU/ADMISSIONS

GENERAL INFO

Activities: Choral groups, dance, drama/theater, jazz band, literary magazine, music ensembles, musical theater, radio station, student government, student newspaper, symphony orchestra, television station, yearbook, International Student Organization, Model UN. **Organizations:** 400+ registered organizations, 14 honor societies, 20 religious organizations. 12 fraternities, 11 sororities. **Athletics (Intercollegiate):** *Men:* baseball, basketball, crew/rowing, cross-country, ice hockey, soccer, track/field (outdoor), track/field (indoor). *Women:* basketball, crew/rowing, cross-country, diving, field hockey, ice hockey, soccer, swimming, track/field (outdoor), track/field (indoor), volleyball. **On-Campus Highlights:** International Village, Curry Student Center, Marino Health and Fitness Center, Levine Marketplace & Stetson West Dining, Cyber Cafe.

FINANCIAL AID

Students should submit: CSS Profile; FAFSA; Noncustodial PROFILE. Priority filing deadline is 3/1. The Princeton Review suggests that all financial aid forms be submitted as soon as possible after October 1. *Need-based scholarships/grants offered:* College/university scholarship or grant aid from institutional funds, Federal Pell, private scholarships, SEOG, state scholarships/grants. *Loan aid offered:* Direct PLUS Loans, Direct Subsidized Loans, Direct Unsubsidized Loans. Applicants will be notified of awards alongside of their admissions decision if all application materials have been received. Federal Work-Study Program available. Institutional employment available.

BOTTOM LINE

Tuition costs $50,450 a year with an additional $1,072 in fees and around $16,270 in room and board. Luckily, the Northeastern Promise is more than just lip service: over 75 percent of students receive some form of financial aid.

CAREER INFORMATION FROM PAYSCALE.COM	
ROI Rating	88
Bachelors and No Higher	
Median starting salary	$61,200
Median mid-career salary	$105,900
At Least Bachelors	
Median starting salary	$62,200
Median mid-career salary	$108,900
Alumni with high job meaning	47%
Degrees awarded in STEM subjects	40%

SELECTIVITY	
Admissions Rating	96
# of applicants	54,209
% of applicants accepted	27
% of acceptees attending	21
# of early decision applicants	953
% accepted early decision	38

FRESHMAN PROFILE	
Range SAT EBRW	680–750
Range SAT Math	690–770
Range ACT Composite	32–34
Minimum internet-based TOEFL	92
% graduated top 10% of class	75
% graduated top 25% of class	93
% graduated top 50% of class	99

DEADLINES	
Early decision	
Deadline	11/1
Notification	12/15
Early action	
Deadline	11/1
Notification	2/1
Regular	
Deadline	1/1
Notification	4/1
Nonfall registration?	Yes

FINANCIAL FACTS	
Financial Aid Rating	87
Annual tuition	$50,450
Room and board	$16,270
Required fees	$1,072
Books and supplies	$1,000
% needy frosh rec. need-based scholarship or grant aid	98
% needy UG rec. need-based scholarship or grant aid	91
% needy frosh rec. non-need-based scholarship or grant aid	45
% needy UG rec. non-need-based scholarship or grant aid	36
% needy frosh rec. need-based self-help aid	89
% needy UG rec. need-based self-help aid	86
% frosh need fully met	100
% ugrads need fully met	37
Average % of frosh need met	100
Average % of ugrad need met	86

Northwestern University

PO Box 3060, 1801 Hinman Avenue, Evanston, IL 60204-3060 • Admissions: 847-491-7271

CAMPUS LIFE
Quality of Life Rating	**69**
Fire Safety Rating	**83**
Green Rating	**96**
Type of school	Private
Environment	City

STUDENTS
Total undergrad enrollment	8,278
% male/female	50/50
% from out of state	68
% frosh from public high school	65
% frosh live on campus	100
% ugrads live on campus	52
# of fraternities (% ugrad men join)	17 (32)
# of sororities (% ugrad women join)	12 (40)
% African American	6
% Asian	17
% Caucasian	46
% Hispanic	13
% Native American	<1
% Pacific Islander	0
% Two or more races	5
% Race and/or ethnicity unknown	3
% international	9
# of countries represented	77

ACADEMICS
Academic Rating	**87**
% students returning for sophomore year	98
% students graduating within 4 years	84
% students graduating within 6 years	94
Calendar	Quarter
Student/faculty ratio	6:1
Profs interesting rating	75
Profs accessible rating	73

Most classes have 10–19 students. Most lab/discussion sessions have 20–29 students.

MOST POPULAR MAJORS
Journalism; Engineering; Economics

ABOUT THE SCHOOL
One student relates that Northwestern University "is all about balance—academically it excels across the academic spectrum, its location is just the right balance between urban and suburban, and its student body, while not incredibly ethnically diverse, still has a range of people." The total undergraduate enrollment is more than 8,000 students; adding to the school's diversity, nearly three-quarters of kids come from out-of-state. Northwestern University is a school built on communities, be they social, political, or academic. It's a rigorous, "very challenging" multidisciplinary school that is preprofessional and stimulating, and students are pleased by the fact that "Northwestern is not an easy school. It takes hard work to be average here." Northwestern not only has a varied curriculum, but "everything is given fairly equal weight." Northwestern students and faculty "do not show a considerable bias" toward specific fields. Excellence in competencies that transcend any particular field of study is highly valued.

BANG FOR YOUR BUCK
Northwestern University works hard to empower students to become leaders in their professions and communities. People are goal-oriented and care about their academic success, and they're pleased that Northwestern helps provide "so many connections and opportunities during and after graduation." Numerous resources established by administrators and professors, including tutoring programs such as Northwestern's Gateway Science Workshop, provide needy students with all of the support they desire.

STUDENT LIFE
The typical Northwestern student "was high school class president with a 4.0, swim team captain, and on the chess team." So it makes sense everyone here "is an excellent student who works hard" and "has a leadership position in at least two clubs, plus an on-campus job." Students also tell us "there's [a] great separation between North Campus (think: fraternities, engineering, state-school mentality) and South Campus (think: closer to Chicago and its culture, arts and letters, liberal arts school mentality). Students segregate themselves depending on background and interests, and it's rare for these two groups to interact beyond a superficial level." The student body here includes sizeable Jewish, Indian, and East-Asian populations.

CAREER
The University Career Services at Northwestern aims to empower students to "assess, explore, decide and act" on their future professional goals, according to its website. The office offers resources on finding a major, an internship, or a job, applying to graduate school, and on honing employment skills like writing resumes and cover letters or being a fantastic interviewee. CareerCat is the online internship and job database through which students and alumni also get updates on programming, special events, and other services. If students are unsure about which career path is for them, they can participate in a Career Trek to cities like New York City or Washington D.C. where they meet with professionals and are given some perspective on industries like Finance, Media & Marketing or Law, Government & Policy. Northwestern graduates who visited PayScale.com report a median starting salary of $59,500.

Northwestern University

FINANCIAL AID: 847-491-7400 • E-MAIL: UG-ADMISSION@NORTHWESTERN.EDU • WEBSITE: WWW.NORTHWESTERN.EDU

GENERAL INFO

Activities: Choral groups, concert band, dance, drama/theater, jazz band, literary magazine, marching band, music ensembles, musical theater, opera, pep band, radio station, student government, student newspaper, student-run film society, symphony orchestra, television station, yearbook, campus ministries, international student organization. **Organizations:** 415 registered organizations, 23 honor societies, 29 religious organizations. 17 fraternities, 12 sororities. **Athletics (Intercollegiate):** *Men:* Baseball, basketball, cheerleading, diving, football, golf, soccer, swimming, tennis, wrestling. *Women:* Basketball, cheerleading, cross-country, diving, fencing, field hockey, golf, lacrosse, soccer, softball, swimming, tennis, volleyball. **On-Campus Highlights:** Shakespeare Garden, Dearborn Observatory, Norris Student Center, Henry Crown Sports Pavilion and Aquatic Center, the lakefill on Lake Michigan. **Environmental Initiatives:** Commitment to purchase of renewable energy credits for 20 percent of the University's usage. Commitment to LEED certifications awarded (LEED NC Silver and LEED CI Gold).

FINANCIAL AID

Students should submit: CSS Profile; FAFSA; Noncustodial PROFILE. Priority filing deadline is 3/1. The Princeton Review suggests that all financial aid forms be submitted as soon as possible after October 1. *Need-based scholarships/grants offered:* College/university scholarship or grant aid from institutional funds; Federal Pell; SEOG; State scholarships/grants. *Loan aid offered:* Direct PLUS Loans, Direct Subsidized Loans, Direct Unsubsidized Loans. Applicants will be notified of awards on or about 4/15. Federal Work-Study Program available. Institutional employment available.

BOTTOM LINE

Northwestern is among the nation's most expensive undergraduate institutions, a fact that sometimes discourages some qualified students from applying. The school is increasing its efforts to attract more low-income applicants by increasing the number of full scholarships available for students whose family income is less than $45,000. Low-income students who score well on the ACT may receive a letter from the school encouraging them to apply. With tuition more than $50,000 a year, any and all support is greatly appreciated by undergrads and their parents.

CAREER INFORMATION FROM PAYSCALE.COM

ROI Rating	91
Bachelors and No Higher	
Median starting salary	$61,500
Median mid-career salary	$115,800
At Least Bachelors	
Median starting salary	$63,500
Median mid-career salary	$122,200
Alumni with high job meaning	47%
Degrees awarded in STEM subjects	20%

SELECTIVITY

Admissions Rating	98
# of applicants	37,259
% of applicants accepted	9
% of acceptees attending	55
# offered a place on the wait list	2,905
% accepting a place on wait list	65
% admitted from wait list	3
# of early decision applicants	3830
% accepted early decision	27

FRESHMAN PROFILE

Range SAT EBRW	700–770
Range SAT Math	720–790
Range ACT Composite	32–34
% graduated top 10% of class	91
% graduated top 25% of class	100
% graduated top 50% of class	100

DEADLINES

Early decision	
Deadline	11/1
Notification	12/15
Regular	
Deadline	1/1
Notification	4/1
Nonfall registration?	Yes

FINANCIAL FACTS

Financial Aid Rating	92
Annual tuition	$50,424
Room and board	$15,489
Required fees	$431
Books and supplies	$1,620
Average frosh need-based scholarship	$49,645
Average UG need-based scholarship	$46,720
% needy frosh rec. need-based scholarship or grant aid	97
% needy UG rec. need-based scholarship or grant aid	98
% needy frosh rec. non-need-based scholarship or grant aid	0
% needy UG rec. non-need-based scholarship or grant aid	0
% needy frosh rec. need-based self-help aid	69
% needy UG rec. need-based self-help aid	72
% UG borrow to pay for school	37
Average cumulative indebtedness	$19,718
% frosh need fully met	100
% ugrads need fully met	100
Average % of frosh need met	100
Average % of ugrad need met	100

Oberlin College

101 NORTH PROFESSOR STREET, OBERLIN, OH 44074 • ADMISSIONS: 440-775-8411 • FAX: 440-775-6905

CAMPUS LIFE

Quality of Life Rating	79
Fire Safety Rating	89
Green Rating	99
Type of school	Private
Environment	Village

STUDENTS

Total undergrad enrollment	2,827
% male/female	42/58
% from out of state	94
% frosh from public high school	66
% frosh live on campus	100
% ugrads live on campus	93
# of fraternities (% ugrad men join)	0 (0)
# of sororities (% ugrad women join)	0 (0)
% African American	5
% Asian	4
% Caucasian	64
% Hispanic	8
% Native American	<1
% Pacific Islander	<1
% Two or more races	8
% Race and/or ethnicity unknown	1
% international	10

ACADEMICS

Academic Rating	88
% students returning for sophomore year	91
% students graduating within 4 years	75
% students graduating within 6 years	86
Calendar	4/1/4
Student/faculty ratio	10:1
Profs interesting rating	86
Profs accessible rating	83

Most classes have 10–19 students. Most lab/discussion sessions have fewer than 10 students.

MOST POPULAR MAJORS

Environmental Studies; Economics; Political Science and Government

ABOUT THE SCHOOL

Oberlin is known as a school that emphasizes the "liberal" in liberal arts. Oberlin's forward thinking and progressive values can be seen in its history. It was the first school to institute a policy of admitting students without regard to race and was the first coeducational school to grant bachelor's degrees to women. Academics are excellent here. An Oberlin education "focus[es] on learning for learning's sake rather than making money in a career." Oberlin can boast having more graduates earn PhDs than any other liberal arts college. Oberlin's academics are strong all around, but "the sciences, English, politics, religion, music, environmental studies, and East Asian studies are particularly noteworthy." The campus is also home to the Oberlin Conservatory of Music, which is the oldest continually active conservatory in America. Consequentially, music is a huge part of campus, and there are "400-plus musical performances every year, due to the conservatory." "I am lucky to be involved in the music scene at Oberlin," one student says, "so most of my social life revolves around the numerous house parties that host live bands." Oberlin alumni have gone on to perform in such bands as Deerhoof, Tortoise, Liz Phair, and Yeah Yeah Yeahs. The professors are the "heart and soul of the school" and "an absolute dream." The dedicated faculty "treat you more like collaborators." "Academically, my classes are stimulating and my professors are engaging," one student says.

BANG FOR YOUR BUCK

With an undergrad population of about 2,800 students, Oberlin is a small and selective school. The "excellent instructors" are easily accessible to students, as Oberlin boasts an impressive nine to one student-to-faculty-ratio. "Because of the small-town atmosphere, you can get to know professors quite personally," one student explains. Oberlin students tend to love their experience: a full 94 percent of freshmen return for sophomore year. Sixty-nine percent of students graduate in four years. "The beautiful campus" has, in addition to the worldclass music conservatory, a great art museum with a peculiar art rental program. For a mere five dollars, students are able to rent out original works of art by such renowned artists as Pablo Picasso, Salvador Dali, and Andy Warhol to hang in their dorm rooms. This is just one example of the kind of unique and forward-thinking ideas that you will find while receiving Oberlin's one-of-a-kind education.

STUDENT LIFE

"If you're a liberal, artsy, indie loner," then Oberlin might be the place for you. "We're all different and unusual, which creates a common bond between students." "Musicians, jocks, science geeks, creative writing majors, straight, bi, questioning, queer, and trans [students]," all have their place here, alongside "straight-edge, international, local, and joker students." Oberlin has a reputation for a left-leaning and active student body. One undergrad observes, "They are less active politically than they would like to think, but still more active than most people elsewhere." Another adds, "Most students are very liberal, but the moderates and (few) Republicans have a fine time of it. Every student has different interests and isn't afraid to talk about them."

CAREER

Oberlin offers abundant opportunities for students to gain experience that may be valuable to future employers. The Career Center, for example, coordinates Winter Term internships in various fields (past sites have included the Smithsonian Institution, Global Green, and Discovery Communications), usually sponsored by Oberlin alumni. Oberlin's recruiting database, ObieOpps, makes the sometimes daunting search for internships and jobs a simple process. The Office of Undergraduate Research provides support for students interested in faculty-mentored research, and OSU has special scholars programs

Oberlin College

FINANCIAL AID: 440-775-8142 • E-MAIL: COLLEGE.ADMISSIONS@OBERLIN.EDU • WEBSITE: WWW.OBERLIN.EDU

in areas like law, business, and entrepreneurship for undergraduates who wish to hone their skills. To draw upon the experience of Oberlin graduates, students can visit TAPPAN, an online directory with thousands of alumni career profiles. Finally, there are frequent information sessions about anything you might be interested in pursuing after graduation from Google to grad school. Oberlin graduates who visited PayScale.com reported an average starting salary of about $49,400.

GENERAL INFO

Activities: Choral groups, concert band, dance, drama/theater, jazz band, literary magazine, marching band, music ensembles, musical theater, opera, radio station, student government, student newspaper, student-run film society, symphony orchestra, yearbook, campus ministries, International Student Organization. **Organizations:** 125 registered organizations, 3 honor societies, 10 religious organizations. **Athletics (Intercollegiate):** *Men:* baseball, basketball, cross-country, diving, football, golf, lacrosse, soccer, swimming, tennis, track/field (outdoor), track/field (indoor). *Women:* basketball, cross-country, diving, field hockey, golf, lacrosse, soccer, softball, swimming, tennis, track/field (outdoor), track/field (indoor), volleyball. **On-Campus Highlights:** Allen Art Museum, Oberlin College Science Center, Adam Joseph Lewis Center for Environmental Studies, Mudd Library, Jesse Philips Recreational Center.

FINANCIAL AID

Students should submit: Business/Farm Supplement; CSS Profile, FAFSA; Institution's own financial aid form, Noncustodial PROFILE. Priority filing deadline is 2/1. The Princeton Review suggests that all financial aid forms be submitted as soon as possible after October 1. *Need-based scholarships/grants offered:* College/university scholarship or grant aid from institutional funds, Federal Pell, private scholarships, SEOG, state scholarships/grants. *Loan aid offered:* Direct PLUS Loans, Direct Subsidized Loans, Direct Unsubsidized Loans. Applicants will be notified of awards on or about 4/1. Federal Work-Study Program available. Institutional employment available.

BOTTOM LINE

Oberlin's top-notch education does not come free. The annual tuition is $51,324 and students will spend another $14,688 a year on room, board, and required fees. That said, Oberlin is very committed to helping students financially. Eighty-seven percent of needy freshmen receive need-based financial aid here, and 61 percent of first-years as a whole receive some form of financial aid. The average need-based scholarship is $37,059. Oberlin is also one of the few American universities that offer a substantial amount of aid to international students. Those who get into Oberlin will get a truly unique education. As one student exclaims, "Oberlin has let me expand my horizons in ways I never would have imagined before I got to college!"

CAREER INFORMATION FROM PAYSCALE.COM	
ROI Rating	88
Bachelors and No Higher	
Median starting salary	$51,400
Median mid-career salary	$100,600
At Least Bachelors	
Median starting salary	$53,300
Median mid-career salary	$106,600
Alumni with high job meaning	50%
Degrees awarded in STEM subjects	21%

SELECTIVITY	
Admissions Rating	94
# of applicants	7,762
% of applicants accepted	34
% of acceptees attending	29
# offered a place on the wait list	1,125
% accepting a place on wait list	67
% admitted from wait list	16
# of early decision applicants	505
% accepted early decision	49

FRESHMAN PROFILE	
Range SAT EBRW	650–720
Range SAT Math	630–730
Range ACT Composite	28–33
Minimum paper TOEFL	600
Minimum internet-based TOEFL	100
Average HS GPA	3.6
% graduated top 10% of class	58
% graduated top 25% of class	79
% graduated top 50% of class	97

DEADLINES	
Early decision	
Deadline	11/15
Notification	12/15
Other ED Deadline	1/2
Other ED Notification	1/15
Regular	
Priority	1/15
Deadline	1/15
Notification	4/1
Nonfall registration?	No

FINANCIAL FACTS	
Financial Aid Rating	94
Annual tuition	$52,762
Room and board	$15,212
Required fees	$698
Books and supplies	$1,958
Average frosh need-based scholarship	$37,998
Average UG need-based scholarship	$38,289
% needy frosh rec. need-based scholarship or grant aid	95
% needy UG rec. need-based scholarship or grant aid	85
% needy frosh rec. non-need-based scholarship or grant aid	82
% needy UG rec. non-need-based scholarship or grant aid	80
% needy frosh rec. need-based self-help aid	88
% needy UG rec. need-based self-help aid	89
% UG borrow to pay for school	42
Average cumulative indebtedness	$29,781
% frosh need fully met	100
% ugrads need fully met	100

Occidental College

1600 CAMPUS ROAD, OFFICE OF ADMISSION, LOS ANGELES, CA 90041-3314 • ADMISSIONS: 323-259-2700 • FAX: 323-341-4875

CAMPUS LIFE

Quality of Life Rating	90
Fire Safety Rating	81
Green Rating	87
Type of school	Private
Environment	Metropolis

STUDENTS

Total undergrad enrollment	2,055
% male/female	42/58
% from out of state	51
% frosh from public high school	58
% frosh live on campus	100
% ugrads live on campus	81
# of fraternities (% ugrad men join)	4 (13)
# of sororities (% ugrad women join)	4 (19)
% African American	5
% Asian	14
% Caucasian	51
% Hispanic	14
% Native American	<1
% Pacific Islander	<1
% Two or more races	8
% Race and/or ethnicity unknown	2
% international	7
# of countries represented	56

ACADEMICS

Academic Rating	91
% students returning for sophomore year	91
% students graduating within 4 years	80
% students graduating within 6 years	84
Calendar	Semester
Student/faculty ratio	9:1
Profs interesting rating	91
Profs accessible rating	92

Most classes have 10–19 students. Most lab/discussion sessions have 10–19 students.

MOST POPULAR MAJORS
Economics; Biology; Psychology; International Relations

ABOUT THE SCHOOL

Although the curriculum is reportedly difficult, students actually appreciate it. Occidental College is a "very prestigious school," and "tough academically," but "the benefits of getting an education here are worth all the work." Professors really care about their students and desperately want them to be successful. Undergrads are pleased that profs here don't exist to "publish or perish"; "they actually are at Oxy to teach—and not to teach so they can research." Students say it is "really easy" to get "independent study, internships, and grants" that would "not be offered anywhere else to undergraduates." "I've been working with postdoctoral researchers as an undergraduate. It's very rewarding." There is also the highly respected Center for Academic Excellence, which provides free tutoring. With a total student body of only 2,100 or so students—women being more highly represented—individual attention is a wonderful advantage for all undergrads.

Occidental offers a semester-long, residential United Nations program, one of the few programs of its kind; the country's only Campaign Semester program, which every two years offers students the opportunity to earn academic credit while working on House, Senate, and presidential campaigns; one of the few opportunities to pursue fully funded undergraduate research overseas (almost 50 percent of Occidental students study overseas); and one of the country's best undergraduate research programs, which has sent more than 170 students to the National Conference on Undergraduate Research over the past six years.

BANG FOR YOUR BUCK

Occidental emphasizes experiential learning. Internships for academic credit are available for sophomores, juniors, and seniors through the Hameetman Career Center; the Center also offers a limited number of paid summer internships through its Intern LA and Intern PDX programs. The Center also offers a career-shadowing program with alumni professionals (the Walk in My Shoes program). "I've gotten a broader sense of self and have been able to fulfill my learning goals," said one student appreciatively. The admission team at Occidental is adamant about not adhering to formulas. They rely heavily on essays and recommendations in their mission to create a talented and diverse incoming class. The college attracts some excellent students, so a demanding course load in high school is essential for the most competitive candidates. Successful applicants tend to be creative and academically motivated. A stellar total of 80 percent of students graduate within four years.

STUDENT LIFE

There's no doubt that Occidental students lead full and fulfilling lives. After all, there's so much of which to take advantage. For starters, "the school brings amazing speakers and musicians to campus...and every weekend [features] a movie screening." There are also "regular campus-wide dances...that everyone attends." Even better, the "Office of Student Life...[frequently] organizes outdoor pool parties, theme parties like Toga...[and events such as] Septemberween." For those undergrads wishing to remain substance free, the residence "halls usually provide alternative event/activities for people who do not partake in drinking/partying." And, naturally, students "love to [simply] explore Los Angeles [whether it involves] going to the beach, farmers market, museums, or hiking." Oxy undergrads truly have it all!

Occidental College

FINANCIAL AID: 323-259-2548 • E-MAIL: ADMISSION@OXY.EDU • WEBSITE: WWW.OXY.EDU

CAREER

Overall, "Occidental does a great job of providing its students with excellent resources and opportunities." And this certainly extends to career services. Indeed, as one happy junior succinctly states, the "career development support is fantastic." Undergrads really appreciate the fact that Oxy runs a robust internship program, one in which they can earn course credit. Students also have the unique opportunity to participate in job shadowing. More specifically, the "Walk in My Shoes (WIMS)" program matches undergrads with alumni and professionals from the surrounding area. They can experience a day-in-the-life of all types of jobs—from marine biology and green business to jobs within the fine arts. Ultimately, WIMS provides students with invaluable insight into potential career tracks. Lastly, according to PayScale.com, the median starting salary for recent Oxy graduates is $51,800.

GENERAL INFO

Activities: Choral groups, concert band, dance, drama/theater, jazz band, literary magazine, music ensembles, musical theater, radio station, student government, student newspaper, student-run film society, symphony orchestra, yearbook, international student organization. **Organizations:** 8 honor societies, 5 religious organizations. 4 fraternities, 4 sororities. **Athletics (Intercollegiate):** *Men:* Baseball, basketball, cross-country, diving, football, golf, soccer, swimming, tennis, track/field (outdoor), water polo. *Women:* Basketball, cross-country, diving, golf, lacrosse, soccer, softball, swimming, tennis, track/field (outdoor), volleyball, water polo.

FINANCIAL AID

Students should submit: CSS Profile; FAFSA; Noncustodial PROFILE; State aid form. Priority filing deadline is 1/15. The Princeton Review suggests that all financial aid forms be submitted as soon as possible after October 1. *Need-based scholarships/ grants offered:* College/university scholarship or grant aid from institutional funds, Federal Pell, private scholarships, SEOG, state scholarships/grants. *Loan aid offered:* Direct PLUS Loans, Direct Subsidized Loans, Direct Unsubsidized Loans. Applicants will be notified of awards on or about 3/25. Federal Work-Study Program available. Institutional employment available.

BOTTOM LINE

About three out of four Occidental students receive some form of financial aid, including need-based aid and merit scholarships. The average need-based financial scholarship is $40,172. Oxy actively seeks out talented students from all backgrounds. There are more than 300 student scholarships available. "They gave me gave me extraordinary financial aid," says one undergrad.

CAREER INFORMATION FROM PAYSCALE.COM	
ROI Rating	89
Bachelors and No Higher	
Median starting salary	$54,100
Median mid-career salary	$111,100
At Least Bachelors	
Median starting salary	$55,400
Median mid-career salary	$113,900
Alumni with high job meaning	47%
Degrees awarded in STEM subjects	25%

SELECTIVITY	
Admissions Rating	93
# of applicants	6,775
% of applicants accepted	42
% of acceptees attending	20
# offered a place on the wait list	1,088
% accepting a place on wait list	44
% admitted from wait list	0
# of early decision applicants	307
% accepted early decision	49

FRESHMAN PROFILE	
Range SAT EBRW	650–720
Range SAT Math	630–720
Range ACT Composite	27–32
Minimum paper TOEFL	600
Average HS GPA	3.6
% graduated top 10% of class	62
% graduated top 25% of class	86
% graduated top 50% of class	99

DEADLINES	
Early decision	
Deadline	11/15
Notification	12/15
Other ED Deadline	1/1
Other ED Notification	2/1
Regular	
Deadline	1/15
Notification	3/25
Nonfall registration?	No

FINANCIAL FACTS	
Financial Aid Rating	96
Annual tuition	$54,090
Room and board	$15,496
Required fees	$596
Books and supplies	$1,220
Average frosh need-based scholarship	$41,801
Average UG need-based scholarship	$40,172
% needy frosh rec. need-based scholarship or grant aid	99
% needy UG rec. need-based scholarship or grant aid	99
% needy frosh rec. non-need-based scholarship or grant aid	54
% needy UG rec. non-need-based scholarship or grant aid	51
% needy frosh rec. need-based self-help aid	84
% needy UG rec. need-based self-help aid	86
% frosh rec. any financial aid	71
% UG rec. any financial aid	71
% UG borrow to pay for school	57
Average cumulative indebtedness	$32,008
% frosh need fully met	100
% ugrads need fully met	100

The Ohio State University—Columbus

STUDENT ACADEMIC SVCS. BLDG. 281 WEST LANE AVE., COLUMBUS, OH 43210 • ADMISSIONS: 614-292-3980 • FAX: 614-292-4818

CAMPUS LIFE

Quality of Life Rating	84
Fire Safety Rating	87
Green Rating	94
Type of school	Public
Environment	Metropolis

STUDENTS

Total undergrad enrollment	44,853
% male/female	52/48
% from out of state	19
% frosh from public high school	84
% frosh live on campus	94
% ugrads live on campus	32
# of fraternities (% ugrad men join)	45 (13)
# of sororities (% ugrad women join)	25 (14)
% African American	6
% Asian	7
% Caucasian	69
% Hispanic	4
% Native American	<1
% Pacific Islander	<1
% Two or more races	3
% Race and/or ethnicity unknown	3
% international	8
# of countries represented	66

ACADEMICS

Academic Rating	71
% students returning for sophomore year	94
% students graduating within 4 years	59
% students graduating within 6 years	83
Calendar	Semester
Student/faculty ratio	19:1
Profs interesting rating	71
Profs accessible rating	73

Most classes have 20–29 students. Most lab/discussion sessions have 20–29 students.

MOST POPULAR MAJORS
Psychology; Communication; Finance

ABOUT THE SCHOOL

Twelve thousand courses, more than 200 majors and a student-to-faculty ratio of 19:1 help convey just how solid an institution The Ohio State University—Columbus is. This first tier research university "hires the best and the brightest" faculty from around the world, and provides its students with many opportunities to become involved. The facilities are "state of the art," the administration is "extremely approachable," and "Ohio State is always trying to stay ahead of the game." "Ohio State combines the love of tradition with the excellence of modern facilities and technology," says an undergrad. Students praise the work ethic instilled in them by a blue-chip education, and "the spirit instilled by citizenship in the living experience that is Buckeye Nation." "No two students leave Ohio State with the same experience, proving you are not just a number," says a student.

BANG FOR YOUR BUCK

Seventy-nine percent of undergraduate students receive some form of financial aid, with the average freshman need-based award being $11,497. There are numerous merit-based scholarships available to qualified students, including those associated with the Eminence Fellows Scholarship, the Morrill Scholarship Program, and the Maximus, Provost, and Trustees scholarships, which consider those students who graduate high school within various rankings of their class. Non-Ohio residents attending the Columbus campus may be eligible for the National Buckeye Scholarship, worth $12,500 per year. Two students from each of Ohio's eighty-eight counties receive the equivalent of the full cost of attendance thanks to the Land Grant Opportunity Scholarship. Departmental scholarships are also available.

STUDENT LIFE

People here like to have a good time. In the fall "campus is in a frenzy for Buckeye Football," and in the spring "the Oval turns into a beach." Columbus is a major metro area, so "there is never a shortage of stuff to do." Athletics play a big role here, and this is "a sport fan's paradise. Campus is bursting with Buckeye spirit and it's infectious." Not only do students love attending games, but "we also have so many intramural sports that students get involved in for fun." Though the size of OSU can be daunting, students say not to worry, as there are more than 1,000 student organizations, which really facilitate students in finding people with similar interests. Students have free transportation provided to downtown Columbus, and the Ohio Union Activities Board also does a great job of bringing in speakers and comedians, and hosting free movie events on campus. "OSU has a great way of breaking down the large school into much smaller communities," says a student.

CAREER

The sheer size of the school results in an overflow of resources and opportunities, and "the alumni base is outstanding." The university is committed to helping students advance themselves academically and personally through club/organization involvement and career/internship services, and maintains the Buckeye Careers Network online database for helping to foster such connections. There are also plenty of "top-notch research opportunities for undergraduates in every academic area on campus." The "international recognition" automatically attracts employers, and there are plenty of Career Days throughout the year for this to happen. OSU alumni who visited PayScale.com report a median starting salary of $51,900.

The Ohio State University—Columbus

FINANCIAL AID: 614-292-0300 • E-MAIL: ASKABUCKEYE@OSU.EDU • WEBSITE: WWW.OSU.EDU

GENERAL INFO

Activities: Choral groups, dance, drama/theater, jazz band, literary magazine, marching band, music ensembles, musical theater, opera, pep band, student government, student newspaper, student-run film society, symphony orchestra, television station, yearbook, international student organizations. **Organizations:** 1,000+ registered organizations, 60 honor societies, 85 religious organizations. 45 fraternities, 25 sororities. **Athletics (Intercollegiate):** *Men:* baseball, basketball, cheerleading, cross-country, diving, fencing, football, golf, gymnastics, ice hockey, lacrosse, pistol, riflery, soccer, swimming, tennis, track/field (outdoor), track/field (indoor), volleyball, wrestling. *Women:* baseball, basketball, cheerleading, crew/rowing, cross-country, diving, fencing, field hockey, golf, gymnastics, ice hockey, lacrosse, pistol, riflery, soccer, softball, swimming, synchronized swimming, tennis, track/field (outdoor), track/field (indoor), volleyball. **On-Campus Highlights:** Hale Cultural Center, Chadwick Arboretum, Jack Nicklaus Golf Museum, Schottenstein Center and Value City Arena, Wexner Center for the Arts, Wexner Medical Center.

FINANCIAL AID

Students should submit: FAFSA. Priority filing deadline is 2/1. The Princeton Review suggests that all financial aid forms be submitted as soon as possible after October 1. *Need-based scholarships/grants offered:* College/university scholarship or grant aid from institutional funds, Federal Pell, private scholarships, SEOG, state scholarships/grants. *Loan aid offered:* Direct PLUS Loans, Direct Subsidized Loans, Direct Unsubsidized Loans. Federal Work-Study Program available. Institutional employment available.

BOTTOM LINE

Ohio residents pay $10,591 in tuition each year (or $10,726 for first-year students). Non-Ohio residents pay an annual tuition of $30,608 (or $30,742 for first-year students), including an out-of-state surcharge. The most popular room and board plan runs $12,434, though cheaper options are available. Over 80 percent of OSU students are Ohio residents, and 53 percent borrow to pay for school.

CAREER INFORMATION FROM PAYSCALE.COM	
ROI Rating	88
Bachelors and No Higher	
Median starting salary	$54,000
Median mid-career salary	$95,100
At Least Bachelors	
Median starting salary	$55,100
Median mid-career salary	$98,800
Alumni with high job meaning	49%
Degrees awarded in STEM subjects	27%

SELECTIVITY	
Admissions Rating	91
# of applicants	47,782
% of applicants accepted	48
% of acceptees attending	31
# offered a place on the wait list	5,051
% accepting a place on wait list	25
% admitted from wait list	66

FRESHMAN PROFILE	
Range SAT EBRW	610–700
Range SAT Math	650–750
Range ACT Composite	27–31
Minimum paper TOEFL	550
Minimum internet-based TOEFL	79
% graduated top 10% of class	64
% graduated top 25% of class	95
% graduated top 50% of class	99

DEADLINES	
Early action	
Deadline	11/1
Notification	1/15
Regular	
Deadline	2/1
Notification	3/31
Nonfall registration?	Yes

FINANCIAL FACTS	
Financial Aid Rating	81
Annual in-state tuition	$10,726
Annual out-of-state tuition	$30,742
Room and board	$12,434
Books and supplies	$1,168
Average frosh need-based scholarship	$11,497
Average UG need-based scholarship	$10,325
% needy frosh rec. need-based scholarship or grant aid	93
% needy UG rec. need-based scholarship or grant aid	87
% needy frosh rec. non-need-based scholarship or grant aid	8
% needy UG rec. non-need-based scholarship or grant aid	4
% needy frosh rec. need-based self-help aid	74
% needy UG rec. need-based self-help aid	83
% frosh rec. any financial aid	86
% UG rec. any financial aid	78
% UG borrow to pay for school	53
Average cumulative indebtedness	$28,158
% frosh need fully met	24
% ugrads need fully met	19
Average % of frosh need met	73
Average % of ugrad need met	70

Ohio Wesleyan University

61 South Sandusky Street, Delaware, OH 43015 • Admissions: 740-368-3020 • Fax: 740-368-3314

CAMPUS LIFE

Quality of Life Rating	87
Fire Safety Rating	86
Green Rating	60*
Type of school	Private
Affiliation	Methodist
Environment	Town

STUDENTS

Total undergrad enrollment	1,554
% male/female	47/53
% from out of state	54
% frosh from public high school	77
% frosh live on campus	94
% ugrads live on campus	86
# of fraternities (% ugrad men join)	6 (36)
# of sororities (% ugrad women join)	7 (33)
% African American	10
% Asian	3
% Caucasian	69
% Hispanic	6
% Native American	<1
% Pacific Islander	<1
% Two or more races	5
% Race and/or ethnicity unknown	2
% international	5
# of countries represented	41

ACADEMICS

Academic Rating	90
% students returning for sophomore year	78
% students graduating within 4 years	62
% students graduating within 6 years	60
Calendar	Semester
Student/faculty ratio	9:1
Profs interesting rating	94
Profs accessible rating	93

Most classes have 10–19 students. Most lab/discussion sessions have 10–19 students.

MOST POPULAR MAJORS
Zoology/Animal Biology; Psychology; Economics

ABOUT THE SCHOOL

Ohio Wesleyan University makes no secret that it wants students who want to learn. Small class sizes and distribution requirements are structured so that "everyone experiences many of the different academic departments on campus" and "are well-versed in many different disciplines." This small liberal arts school offers over 90 majors, and more than a quarter of students choose two. Ohio Wesleyan is constantly adding to its disciplines; the business administration major added in 2016 is now one of its most popular, and in the past year, it launched new programs in growing areas such as data analytics, nutrition, and social justice. It's "quite easy to become close to professors, as well as combine their interests with your own." The undergraduate research program allows students to work with a professor over the summer, and "involves everything from biology to chemistry and even psychology," ensuring Ohio Wesleyan students "get a rare opportunity to get paid to do research—almost always one-on-one with a PhD."

BANG FOR YOUR BUCK

Ohio Wesleyan seeks to "provide students with unique experiences while also allowing them to make their own unique experiences." No graduate students means that "all research opportunities [and] TA jobs go to undergrad students," and there is "a huge focus on international awareness, exploration, and education" that students of any discipline can take into the global workplace. In addition to its stellar reputation with employers, "Ohio Wesleyan University is more generous with financial aid than almost any other college that I've heard of," says a student. "Many students...benefit from the large amount of scholarships available," and admitted students are automatically considered for institutional scholarships such as the Schubert Scholarship for students in the Honors program, the Branch Rickey Scholarship for outstanding first-year students, and the Bishop Scholarship for first-year students with true potential for success.

STUDENT LIFE

Ohio Wesleyan's Small Living Units (SLUs) are communities of students who share an interest, ranging from spiritual athletes to sustainability, and students often find their niche in the SLUs, in addition to Greek life and sports. The Delaware community is a great place for students to explore and they can often be found downtown at night or in nearby Columbus; students "have a great relationship with our community." There is "a strong social aspect in terms of events and clubs" and "starting new clubs is fully supported by the university." There's always something going on on-campus, "whether it be a cultural immersion experience, study abroad opportunity, or a campus event." Students and faculty alike "push for acceptance of everyone," and "it is very easy to make friends in this type of environment."

CAREER

Ohio Wesleyan "strives to prepare [its] students with the necessary experience to be employed after college" and to that end, the Office of Career Services provides individual counseling, creative programming, and technological services, and invites students and faculty to request workshops on topics they feel would benefit the student career path, such as salary negotiation or graduate school preparation. "A good percentage of students [get] jobs right out of college" and the administration excels at "getting alumni support on projects or on when helping students network outside of class." Of the Ohio Wesleyan University alumni who visited PayScale.com, 46 percent report that their jobs make the world a better place..

Ohio Wesleyan University

FINANCIAL AID: 740-368-3050 • E-MAIL: OWUADMIT@OWU.EDU • WEBSITE: WWW.OWU.EDU

GENERAL INFO

Activities: Choral groups, dance, drama/theater, jazz band, literary magazine, marching band, music ensembles, musical theater, opera, pep band, student government, student newspaper, symphony orchestra, yearbook, campus ministries, Model UN. 86 registered organizations, 26 honor societies, 10 religious organizations. 6 fraternities, 7 sororities. **Athletics (Intercollegiate):** *Men:* baseball, basketball, cross-country, diving, football, golf, lacrosse, soccer, swimming, tennis, track/field (outdoor), track/field (indoor), and wrestling. *Women:* basketball, cross-country, diving, field hockey, lacrosse, rowing, soccer, softball, swimming, tennis, track/field (outdoor), track/field (indoor), volleyball. **On-Campus Highlights:** Science Center, Hamilton-Williams Campus Center, Selby Stadium, Delaware Entrepreneurial Center, Sanborn Hall (music), Simpson Querrey Fitness Center, Meek Aquatics and Recreation Center, Beeghly Library and Ross Museum are additional popular places on campus.

FINANCIAL AID

Students should submit: FAFSA. Priority filing deadline is January 15. The Princeton Review suggests that all financial aid forms be submitted as soon as possible after October 1. *Need-based scholarships/grants offered:* University scholarship or grant aid from institutional funds, Federal Pell, private scholarships, SEOG, state scholarships/grants. *Loan aid offered:* Direct PLUS Loans, Direct Subsidized Loans, Direct Unsubsidized Loans. Federal Work-Study Program available. Institutional employment available.

BOTTOM LINE

Tuition at Ohio Wesleyan runs $45,000 a year for students and on-campus residents pay an additional $12,430 in room and board. All students must also pay a $260 student activities fee. All admitted students are automatically considered for merit-scholarships, and 100 percent of needy Ohio Wesleyan students receive need-based scholarship or grant aid with the average scholarship coming in at $29,200.

CAREER INFORMATION FROM PAYSCALE.COM	
ROI Rating	87
Bachelors and No Higher	
Median starting salary	$48,800
Median mid-career salary	$103,900
At Least Bachelors	
Median starting salary	$49,800
Median mid-career salary	$106,200
Alumni with high job meaning	48%
Degrees awarded in STEM subjects	21%

SELECTIVITY	
Admissions Rating	80
# of applicants	4,160
% of applicants accepted	71
% of acceptees attending	15
# of early decision applicants	38
% accepted early decision	84

FRESHMAN PROFILE	
Range SAT EBRW	530–640
Range SAT Math	510–630
Range ACT Composite	22–28
Minimum paper TOEFL	550
Average HS GPA	3.4
% graduated top 10% of class	22
% graduated top 25% of class	47
% graduated top 50% of class	78

DEADLINES	
Early decision	
Deadline	11/15
Notification	11/30
Other ED Deadline	1/15
Other ED Notification	1/30
Early action	
Deadline	12/15
Notification	1/15
Regular	
Priority	1/15
Deadline	3/1
Notification	4/1
Nonfall registration?	Yes

FINANCIAL FACTS	
Financial Aid Rating	86
Annual tuition	$45,000
Room and board	$12,430
Required fees	$240
Average frosh need-based scholarship	$32,215
Average UG need-based scholarship	$30,716
% needy frosh rec. need-based scholarship or grant aid	100
% needy UG rec. need-based scholarship or grant aid	100
% needy frosh rec. non-need-based scholarship or grant aid	15
% needy UG rec. non-need-based scholarship or grant aid	17
% needy frosh rec. need-based self-help aid	88
% needy UG rec. need-based self-help aid	86
% UG borrow to pay for school	70
Average cumulative indebtedness	$35,221
% frosh need fully met	16
% ugrads need fully met	20
Average % of frosh need met	80
Average % of ugrad need met	80

Pennsylvania State University

201 SHIELDS BUILDING, BOX 3000, UNIVERSITY PARK, PA 16802-3000 • ADMISSIONS: 814-865-5471 • FAX: 814-863-7590

CAMPUS LIFE

Quality of Life Rating	93
Fire Safety Rating	97
Green Rating	92
Type of school	Public
Environment	Town

STUDENTS

Total undergrad enrollment	40,552
% male/female	53/47
% from out of state	34
% ugrads live on campus	35
# of fraternities (% ugrad men join)	47 (17)
# of sororities (% ugrad women join)	30 (20)
% African American	4
% Asian	6
% Caucasian	66
% Hispanic	7
% Native American	<1
% Pacific Islander	<1
% Two or more races	3
% Race and/or ethnicity unknown	2
% international	12
# of countries represented	105

ACADEMICS

Academic Rating	81
% students returning for sophomore year	93
% students graduating within 4 years	67
% students graduating within 6 years	85
Calendar	Semester
Student/faculty ratio	16:1
Profs interesting rating	80
Profs accessible rating	83

Most classes have 20–29 students. Most lab/discussion sessions have 20–29 students.

MOST POPULAR MAJORS

Communication, Journalism, and Related Programs; Engineering; Business, Management, Marketing, and Related Support Services

ABOUT THE SCHOOL

At 8,556 acres, the campus at Pennsylvania State University is enormous. Penn State offers a whopping 160 majors, with students having special commendations for the well-regarded Smeal College of Business and the Schreyer Honors College. What is big on Penn State besides the campus itself? Football. Football and School Spirit. Cries of "We Are Penn State!" echo across the campus, and the nation itself. Students note that the initial core classes "had such a huge amount of students in the classes that it was hard to get much professor interaction," but that as you progress through the school classes get "down to about fifteen to forty people and there are a lot more discussions." Students find the faculty and administration to be available, but advise that, given the size of the school, students should take the initiative to reach out.

BANG FOR YOUR BUCK

Penn State students feel that the "fantastic alumni association" provides them with "financial funds for scholarships and programs," ("the Penn State networking web is incredible!") though some note that due to the enormous size of the campus, "scholarships, grants, and student recognition is extremely competitive." The school offers solid value for in-state students—66 percent of the student body hail from the great Keystone State.

STUDENT LIFE

Students at Penn State attend many football games, and after football season comes THON, the "forty-six-hour dance marathon for children with pediatric cancer" at Hershey's Children's Hospital, one of the largest student run philanthropies in the country with "almost 15,000 students involved each year." State College contains multitudes of restaurants and stores, and malls and movie theaters that can all be reached on the CATA bus. The CATA bus-system is "high tech" with an iPhone/Android application that "shows real time tracking of every bus on every loop, which is very convenient." As for social life, students feel that "Greek Life dominates the social scene. There are forty-plus fraternities and twenty-plus sororities on and off campus." And again, for students not that wild about the large size of the school, "you really do need to get involved to meet people and really find your place at PSU. Coming from smaller high schools it can be a little overwhelming and hard to transition at first, but once you find your niche it makes all the difference."

CAREER

The typical Penn State graduate has a starting salary of around $55,200, and 47 percent report that their job has a great deal of meaning. Past that, students choose Penn State for its vast alumni network. How vast, you ask? Students boast of "access to an alumni network of over half a million, and...of its job-recruiting power out of major metropolitan areas such as Philadelphia, New York, Pittsburgh, Baltimore, Washington D.C., and across the country." A student notes that the "giant alumni base and brand name make getting internships so much easier. I loved our career fair when just about every company was here. I was offered four summer internships...as a freshman!" and this theme is reiterated by a member of the Smeal College of Business, who notes, "One of the best things about Penn State overall is the fact that the alumni network is one of the largest in the United States. Because of this, PSU alums seek out Penn State grads for jobs at their companies."

Pennsylvania State University

FINANCIAL AID: 814-865-6301 • E-MAIL: ADMISSIONS@PSU.EDU • WEBSITE: WWW.PSU.EDU

GENERAL INFO

Activities: Choral groups, concert band, dance, drama/theater, jazz band, literary magazine, marching band, music ensembles, musical theater, opera, pep band, radio station, student government, student newspaper, student-run film society, symphony orchestra, television station, yearbook, campus ministries, International Student Organization, Model UN. **Organizations:** 1,062 registered organizations, 40 honor societies, 58 religious organizations. 43 fraternities, 27 sororities. **Athletics (Intercollegiate):** *Men:* baseball, basketball, cheerleading, cross-country, diving, fencing, football, golf, gymnastics, lacrosse, soccer, swimming, tennis, track/field (outdoor), track/field (indoor), volleyball, wrestling. *Women:* basketball, cheerleading, cross-country, diving, fencing, field hockey, golf, gymnastics, lacrosse, soccer, softball, swimming, tennis, track/field (outdoor), track/field (indoor), volleyball. **On-Campus Highlights:** HUB-Robeson Union Building, Pattee Paterno Library, The Creamery, Old Main, The Lion Shrine.

FINANCIAL AID

Students should submit: FAFSA. Priority filing deadline is 2/15. The Princeton Review suggests that all financial aid forms be submitted as soon as possible after October 1. *Need-based scholarships/grants offered:* College/university scholarship or grant aid from institutional funds, Federal Pell, private scholarships, SEOG, state scholarships/grants, and United Negro College Fund. *Loan aid offered:* Direct PLUS Loans, Direct Subsidized Loans, Direct Unsubsidized Loans. Federal Work-Study Program available. Institutional employment available.

BOTTOM LINE

The tuition at Pennsylvania State University comes to about $17,416 for in-state students and $33,820 for out-of-state students. Seventy-three percent of Penn State undergraduates receive some form of financial aid. And with its intense, dedicated, and enormous alumni network at your back, a Penn State grad will have a good shot out there in the employment market.

CAREER INFORMATION FROM PAYSCALE.COM

ROI Rating	88
Bachelors and No Higher	
Median starting salary	$57,300
Median mid-career salary	$103,100
At Least Bachelors	
Median starting salary	$58,400
Median mid-career salary	$107,600
Alumni with high job meaning	47%
Degrees awarded in STEM subjects	37%

SELECTIVITY

Admissions Rating	88
# of applicants	56,114
% of applicants accepted	50
% of acceptees attending	28
# offered a place on the wait list	2,168
% accepting a place on wait list	63
% admitted from wait list	0

FRESHMAN PROFILE

Range SAT EBRW	580–660
Range SAT Math	580–680
Range ACT Composite	25–30
Minimum paper TOEFL	550
Minimum internet-based TOEFL	80
Average HS GPA	3.6
% graduated top 10% of class	35
% graduated top 25% of class	73
% graduated top 50% of class	96

DEADLINES

Regular	
Priority	11/30
Deadline	Rolling
Nonfall registration?	Yes

FINANCIAL FACTS

Financial Aid Rating	81
Annual in-state tuition	$17,416
Annual out-of-state tuition	$33,820
Room and board	$11,570
Required fees	$1,038
Books and supplies	$1,840
Average frosh need-based scholarship	$6,536
Average UG need-based scholarship	$6,629
% needy frosh rec. need-based scholarship or grant aid	33
% needy UG rec. need-based scholarship or grant aid	40
% needy frosh rec. non-need-based scholarship or grant aid	58
% needy UG rec. non-need-based scholarship or grant aid	57
% needy frosh rec. need-based self-help aid	74
% needy UG rec. need-based self-help aid	80
% frosh rec. any financial aid	60
% UG rec. any financial aid	73
% UG borrow to pay for school	54
Average cumulative indebtedness	$37,307
% frosh need fully met	34
% ugrads need fully met	30
Average % of frosh need met	64
Average % of ugrad need met	63

Pitzer College

1050 NORTH MILLS AVENUE, CLAREMONT, CA 91711-6101 • ADMISSIONS: 909-621-8129 • FAX: 909-621-8770

CAMPUS LIFE

Quality of Life Rating	93
Fire Safety Rating	60*
Green Rating	96
Type of school	Private
Environment	Town

STUDENTS

Total undergrad enrollment	1,074
% male/female	46/54
% from out of state	55
% frosh live on campus	100
% ugrads live on campus	72
# of fraternities (% ugrad men join)	0 (0)
# of sororities (% ugrad women join)	0 (0)
% African American	6
% Asian	10
% Caucasian	47
% Hispanic	15
% Native American	<1
% Pacific Islander	<1
% Two or more races	7
% Race and/or ethnicity unknown	5
% international	9
# of countries represented	33

ACADEMICS

Academic Rating	92
% students returning for sophomore year	95
% students graduating within 4 years	83
% students graduating within 6 years	88
Calendar	Semester
Student/faculty ratio	11:1
Profs interesting rating	91
Profs accessible rating	91
Most classes have 10–19 students.	

MOST POPULAR MAJORS
Biological and Physical Sciences;
Psychology; Political Science and
Government

ABOUT THE SCHOOL

Pitzer College, one of five undergraduate institutions comprising the Claremont Consortium, located 35 miles from downtown Los Angeles, is an intimate liberal arts school with a student body overwhelmingly committed to social justice. Classes are small (with a 11:1 student-faculty ratio), academics have a "strong interdisciplinary focus," and "power is placed in students' hands" through "shared governance, student-run eateries, and strong student organizations." It is worth highlighting the college's "super progressive environment" and the strength of the psychology and media studies departments, but students also crow over access to the four other Claremont Colleges (Harvey Mudd, Pomona, Scripps, and Claremont McKenna) that offer "extensive cross-enrollment" and allow undergraduates "to enjoy both the tight-knit passionate Pitzer atmosphere and the larger intellectual community of the...nearby campuses." The "brilliant and creative" faculty are praised for their "discussion-based classes" and for being "supportive and accommodating." Community engagement is a core element of a Pitzer education. All students participate in service-learning courses before graduation, and its students, faculty, and staff "commit approximately 100,000 hours to community-based projects each year."

BANG FOR YOUR BUCK

The Claremont University Consortium offers great value to students, offering more than 2,000 classes across colleges. And with just over 1,000 students, about 70 full-time faculty members, and an average class size of 16, students can still reap the benefits of the personalized attention associated with small, liberal-arts colleges. Pitzer offers under 50 percent of its students financial aid, which many students say could be boosted. For incoming first-year students, the average need-based financial aid package comes to $42,956.

STUDENT LIFE

A Pitzer student can expect to be engaged in a "constant, evolving dialogue...regarding a...myriad of environmentally- and socially-centered topics." Though "liberal" and "progressive" attitudes are common at liberal arts colleges, students emphasize that they and their peers are more than likely identify as "activists" and far left of center. So many students spend their time volunteering and developing various advocacy initiatives. It is not "abnormal by any means" to be "president of Pitzer advocates for survivors of sexual assault, a writing center fellow, and intern at a local nonprofit law firm, and a Planned Parenthood volunteer." But students aren't all work: they "love to spend time on the Mounds, the small, grassy hills in the center of campus" and the Grove House, "an old log cabin-turned social space that features its own student-run kitchen." An art collective "gets school funding" for extracurricular art projects. There are mountains nearby for hiking, and the proximity to Los Angeles offers opportunities for weekend outings and beach parties.

CAREER

Pitzer is a top producer of Fulbright Scholars. Career Services offers programs such as the Pitzer Internship Fund (to fund students with unpaid or low-pay internships), the Pitzer Shadowing Program (in partnership with alumni and parents), the Field Trip Friday program (to visit potential employer sites), and a yearly non-profit and public service career fair. Students seeking preparation for careers in computer science, law, and economics will benefit from taking classes at Harvey Mudd, Claremont McKenna, and Pomona, respectively. Nearly 60 percent of alumni report to Payscale.com that they derive a high level of meaning from their careers. The average "early career" (alumni with 0-5 years of experience) yearly salary is $49,000.

Pitzer College

FINANCIAL AID: 909-621-8208 • E-MAIL: ADMISSION@PITZER.EDU • WEBSITE: WWW.PITZER.EDU

GENERAL INFO

Activities: Choral groups, dance, drama/theater, literary magazine, music ensembles, radio station, student government, student newspaper, symphony orchestra, campus ministries, International Student Organization, Model UN 120 registered organizations, 1 honor societies. **Athletics (Intercollegiate):** *Men:* baseball, basketball, cross-country, diving, football, golf, soccer, swimming, tennis, track/field (outdoor), water polo. *Women:* basketball, cross-country, diving, soccer, softball, swimming, tennis, track/field (outdoor), volleyball, water polo. **On-Campus Highlights:** Grove House, McConnell Center, Gloria and Peter Gold Student Center, Marquis Library, The Mounds, The Claremont Colleges Consortium. Pitzer students may cross-register at any of The Claremont Colleges, and may utilize all Claremont facilities, including Honnold Library, the third-largest academic library in the state, with more than 2 million volumes; Huntley Bookstore; Baxter Medical Center; McAlister Center for Religious Activities and Monsour Counseling Center. Pitzer sponsors the Joint Science Program with Claremont McKenna and Scripps colleges, and the five undergraduate colleges offer a wide range of recreational facilities, student gathering places and dining areas. Pitzer combines with Pomona College for NCAA Division III sports.

FINANCIAL AID

Students should submit: Business/Farm Supplement; CSS Profile, FAFSA; Institution's own financial aid form, Noncustodial PROFILE; State aid form. Priority filing deadline is 1/1. The Princeton Review suggests that all financial aid forms be submitted as soon as possible after October 1. *Need-based scholarships/grants offered:* College/university scholarship or grant aid from institutional funds, Federal Pell, private scholarships, SEOG, state scholarships/grants. *Loan aid offered:* Direct PLUS Loans, Direct Subsidized Loans, Direct Unsubsidized Loans. Applicants will be notified of awards on or about 3/15. Federal Work-Study Program available. Institutional employment available.

BOTTOM LINE

Pitzer College "produces engaged socially responsible citizens of the world through an academically rigorous, interdisciplinary liberal arts program emphasizing social justice, intercultural understanding, and environmental sensitivity." At an annual cost of around $69,200, which includes tuition at $51,964 fees of $272, and room and board of $16,264, students are making a serious financial investment in their education; yet students also gain access to four other liberal arts colleges (The Claremont Colleges) with their own networks and strong academic reputations.

CAREER INFORMATION FROM PAYSCALE.COM	
ROI Rating	88
Bachelors and No Higher	
Median starting salary	$51,000
Median mid-career salary	$96,200
At Least Bachelors	
Median starting salary	$52,100
Median mid-career salary	$103,100
Alumni with high job meaning	52%
Degrees awarded in STEM subjects	18%

SELECTIVITY	
Admissions Rating	97
# of applicants	3,753
% of applicants accepted	16
% of acceptees attending	43
# offered a place on the wait list	675
% accepting a place on wait list	43
% admitted from wait list	8
# of early decision applicants	381
% accepted early decision	32

FRESHMAN PROFILE	
Range SAT EBRW	640–740
Range SAT Math	670–750
Range ACT Composite	29–32
Minimum paper TOEFL	190
Minimum internet-based TOEFL	70
Average HS GPA	3.9
% graduated top 10% of class	63
% graduated top 25% of class	88
% graduated top 50% of class	100

DEADLINES	
Early decision	
Deadline	11/15
Notification	12/18
Other ED Deadline	1/1
Other ED Notification	2/12
Regular	
Deadline	1/1
Notification	4/1
Nonfall registration?	No

FINANCIAL FACTS	
Financial Aid Rating	95
Annual tuition	$53,776
Room and board	$16,844
Required fees	$280
Average frosh need-based scholarship	$43,050
Average UG need-based scholarship	$44,048
% needy frosh rec. need-based scholarship or grant aid	99
% needy UG rec. need-based scholarship or grant aid	97
% needy frosh rec. non-need-based scholarship or grant aid	2
% needy UG rec. non-need-based scholarship or grant aid	4
% needy frosh rec. need-based self-help aid	92
% needy UG rec. need-based self-help aid	86
% frosh rec. any financial aid	39
% UG rec. any financial aid	37
% UG borrow to pay for school	32
Average cumulative indebtedness	$20,947
% frosh need fully met	100
% ugrads need fully met	100

Pomona College

333 North College Way, Claremont, CA 91711-6312 • Admissions: 909-621-8134 • Fax: 909-621-8952

#24 BEST VALUE COLLEGE

CAMPUS LIFE

Quality of Life Rating	92
Fire Safety Rating	97
Green Rating	98
Type of school	Private
Environment	Town

STUDENTS

Total undergrad enrollment	1,704
% male/female	50/50
% from out of state	74
% frosh from public high school	55
% frosh live on campus	100
% ugrads live on campus	98
# of fraternities (% ugrad men join)	3 (5)
# of sororities (% ugrad women join)	0 (0)
% African American	9
% Asian	14
% Caucasian	35
% Hispanic	16
% Native American	<1
% Pacific Islander	<1
% Two or more races	7
% Race and/or ethnicity unknown	6
% international	12
# of countries represented	63

ACADEMICS

Academic Rating	89
% students returning for sophomore year	98
% students graduating within 4 years	92
% students graduating within 6 years	97
Calendar	Semester
Student/faculty ratio	8:1
Profs interesting rating	93
Profs accessible rating	93

Most classes have 10–19 students. Most lab/discussion sessions have 10–19 students.

MOST POPULAR MAJORS

Economics; Computer Science; Mathematics; Neuroscience

ABOUT THE SCHOOL

Students here are among the most happy and comfortable in the nation. To help ease the transition to college life, first-year students are assigned to sponsor groups of ten to twenty fellow first-years who live in adjacent rooms, with two sophomore sponsors who help them learn the ropes of college life. Students rave that the sponsor program is "the single best living situation for freshmen." It "makes you feel welcome the second you step on campus as a new student" and is "amazing at integrating the freshmen into the community smoothly." Greek life is almost nonexistent, but you'll never hear a complaint about a lack of (usually free and awesome) things to do. There's virtually always an event or a party happening either on campus or just a short walk away on one of the other Claremont campuses (Scripps, Pitzer, Claremont McKenna, and Harvey Mudd). Students say that the Claremont Consortium offers "an abundance of nightlife that you wouldn't expect at a small elite liberal arts school." There are also quite a few quirky traditions here throughout the academic year. If you find yourself craving some big-city life, Los Angeles is just a short train ride away.

BANG FOR YOUR BUCK

The financial aid program here is exceedingly generous and goes beyond just covering tuition, room and board, and fees, for which Pomona can and does meet 100 percent of students' demonstrated financial need. The financial aid packages consist wholly of grants and scholarships, probably along with a campus job that you work maybe ten hours a week. For students on financial aid who wish to participate in study abroad, Pomona ensures that cost is not a barrier. All programs carry academic credit and no extra cost for tuition or room and board. To ensure that all Pomona students are able to participate in the college's internship program, funding is provided in the form of an hourly wage for semester-long internships, making it possible for students to take unpaid positions. The Career Development Office (CDO) also subsidizes transportation to and from internships. In addition, the college offers funding, based on need, to students with job interviews on the East Coast during the Winter Break Recruiting Days program.

STUDENT LIFE

Due to its location in Southern California, "life [at Pomona] consists of a lot of school work but always done out in the beautiful sun. I think most people love it here." "People usually are athletic or at least interested in outdoor activities like hiking, camping, and rock climbing." For those with access to cars "the beach, the mountains, and Joshua Tree National Park are other popular locations for a day or weekend," and many students will venture into nearby Los Angeles for fun. However it's not necessary to get away to have a good time, as "at Pomona, there's usually so much happening on campus that you don't need to venture out." "While partying is a big deal—as it is at almost any college—it certainly isn't the only deal. There are movie nights all over campus, music festivals, plays, impromptu games of Frisbee going on at all times of the year." Many students also say that talking the night away with their friends is one of the things they love about Pomona. "Deep conversations" are a frequent occurrence and "people engage in AMAZING conversations

Pomona College

FINANCIAL AID: 909-621-8205 • E-MAIL: ADMISSIONS@POMONA.EDU • WEBSITE: WWW.POMONA.EDU

about EVERYTHING." "Whatever you like to do for fun," students say, "there's a good chance that you'll find others who like to do the same."

CAREER

Pomona's Career Development Office offers advising and counseling to help students explore their interests and discover careers to which they might be suited; hosts career fairs and recruiting events; and provides resources for networking job searches. It also hosts a Prestigious Scholarships and Fellowships Expo that brings representatives from foundations and universities to discuss postgraduate opportunities. However despite the number of offerings, many students list the Career Office as an area that "could definitely be better" and say that the school needs "more resources for internships and career development." On the other hand, several students cite their professors as a helpful resource to "get the internships and jobs that we want or need for our desired careers," and more than 200 students conduct mentored research, with a stipend, each summer. Overall, students say that Pomona provides "a diverse education that will prepare students for whatever they choose to do afterward" and out of alumni visiting PayScale.com, 46 percent report that they derive meaning from their career.

GENERAL INFO

Activities: Choral groups, concert band, dance, drama/theater, jazz band, literary magazine, music ensembles, musical theater, pep band, radio station, student government, student newspaper, student-run film society, symphony orchestra, television station, yearbook, campus ministries, international student organization.

FINANCIAL AID

Students should submit: Business/Farm Supplement; CSS Profile; FAFSA; Noncustodial PROFILE; State aid form. Priority filing deadline is 2/15. The Princeton Review suggests that all financial aid forms be submitted as soon as possible after October 1. *Need-based scholarships/grants offered:* College/university scholarship or grant aid from institutional funds, Federal Pell, private scholarships, SEOG, state scholarships/grants. *Loan aid offered:* Direct PLUS Loans, Direct Subsidized Loans, Direct Unsubsidized Loans. Applicants will be notified of awards on or about 4/1. Federal Work-Study Program available. Institutional employment available.

THE BOTTOM LINE

Tuition, fees, and room and board at Pomona run about $50,720 for a year. At the same time, the mantra here is that no one should hesitate to apply because of the cost. Pomona College has need-blind admissions and meets the full, demonstrated financial aid need of every accepted student with scholarships and work-study. Students say that Pomona "has a reputation of providing great financial aid packages."

CAREER INFORMATION FROM PAYSCALE.COM	
ROI Rating	94
Bachelors and No Higher	
Median starting salary	$60,500
Median mid-career salary	$119,900
At Least Bachelors	
Median starting salary	$64,100
Median mid-career salary	$132,100
Alumni with high job meaning	47%
Degrees awarded in STEM subjects	37%

SELECTIVITY	
Admissions Rating	98
# of applicants	9,045
% of applicants accepted	8
% of acceptees attending	54
# offered a place on the wait list	934
% accepting a place on wait list	58
% admitted from wait list	3
# of early decision applicants	1080
% accepted early decision	19

FRESHMAN PROFILE	
Range SAT EBRW	690–760
Range SAT Math	680–770
Range ACT Composite	30–34
Minimum paper TOEFL	600
Minimum internet-based TOEFL	100
% graduated top 10% of class	94
% graduated top 25% of class	100
% graduated top 50% of class	100

DEADLINES	
Early decision	
Deadline	11/1
Notification	12/15
Other ED Deadline	1/1
Other ED Notification	2/15
Regular	
Deadline	1/1
Notification	4/1
Nonfall registration?	No

FINANCIAL FACTS	
Financial Aid Rating	99
Annual tuition	$50,720
Room and board	$16,150
Required fees	$355
Books and supplies	$900
Average frosh need-based scholarship	$50,686
Average UG need-based scholarship	$50,069
% needy frosh rec. non-need-based scholarship or grant aid	0
% needy UG rec. non-need-based scholarship or grant aid	0
% needy frosh rec. need-based self-help aid	100
% needy UG rec. need-based self-help aid	100
% frosh rec. any financial aid	57
% UG rec. any financial aid	56
% UG borrow to pay for school	31
Average cumulative indebtedness	$17,408
% frosh need fully met	100
% ugrads need fully met	100
Average % of frosh need met	100
Average % of ugrad need met	100

Princeton University

PO Box 430, Admission Office, Princeton, NJ 08542-0430 • Admissions: 609-258-3060 • Fax: 609-258-6743

CAMPUS LIFE

Quality of Life Rating	**87**
Fire Safety Rating	**94**
Green Rating	**86**
Type of school	Private
Environment	Town

STUDENTS

Total undergrad enrollment	5,246
% male/female	51/49
% from out of state	82
% frosh from public high school	60
% frosh live on campus	100
% ugrads live on campus	96
# of fraternities (% ugrad men join)	0 (0)
# of sororities (% ugrad women join)	0 (0)
% African American	8
% Asian	21
% Caucasian	43
% Hispanic	10
% Native American	<1
% Pacific Islander	<1
% Two or more races	4
% Race and/or ethnicity unknown	1
% international	12
# of countries represented	99

ACADEMICS

Academic Rating	**89**
% students returning for sophomore year	98
% students graduating within 4 years	89
% students graduating within 6 years	97
Calendar	Semester
Student/faculty ratio	5:1
Profs interesting rating	80
Profs accessible rating	72

Most classes have 10–19 students. Most lab/discussion sessions have 10–19 students.

MOST POPULAR MAJORS
Computer Engineering; Public Administration; Economics

#3 BEST VALUE COLLEGE

ABOUT THE SCHOOL

Princeton offers its 5,000 undergraduate students a top-notch liberal arts education, taught by some of the best minds in the world. The university is committed to undergraduate teaching, and all faculty, including the president, teach undergraduates. "You get the attention you deserve—if you seek it," says a student. Supporting these efforts are exceptional academic and research resources, including the world-class Firestone Library, the new Frick Chemistry Laboratory that emphasizes hands-on learning in teaching labs, a genomics institute, the Woodrow Wilson School of Public and International Affairs that trains leaders in public service, and an engineering school that enrolls more than 900 undergraduates. Freshman seminars take students into a variety of settings, such as to theaters on Broadway, geological sites in the West, art museums, and more. Princeton students can choose between more than seventy-five fields of concentration (majors) and interdisciplinary certificate programs, of which history, political science, economics, and international affairs are among the most popular. The school's excellent faculty-student ratio of five to one means that many classes are discussion-based, giving students a direct line to their brilliant professors, and "once you take upper-level courses, you'll have a lot of chances to work closely with professors and study what you are most interested in." All "unfailingly brilliant, open, and inspirational" faculty members also work closely with undergraduates in the supervision of junior-year independent work and senior theses. "Professors love teaching, and there are many fantastic lecturers," giving students a chance "to meet and take classes from some of the most brilliant academic minds in the world." Even before they start taking Princeton classes, select students each year are chosen for the Bridge Year Program, which provides funding for students to engage in public-service opportunities in one of four countries: India, Peru, Ghana, or Serbia. There are "pools of resources available for students for all sorts of nonacademic or extracurricular pursuits."

BANG FOR YOUR BUCK

Princeton operates need-blind admissions, as well as one of the strongest need-based financial aid programs in the country. Once a student is admitted, Princeton meets 100 percent of each student's demonstrated financial need. One of the first schools in the country to do so, Princeton has eliminated all loans for students who qualify for aid—it is possible to graduate from this Ivy League school without debt. Financial awards come in the form of grants, which do not need to be repaid. About 60 percent of Princeton students receive financial aid, with an average grant of about $44,890. No need to pinch yourself, you're not dreaming. In recent years, the amount of grant aid available at Princeton has outpaced the annual increase in school fees. Good news for international students: Financial aid packages extend to international admits as well.

STUDENT LIFE

"Academics come first" at this hallowed Ivy, but an "infinite number of clubs" on campus means that "almost everyone at Princeton is involved with something other than school about which they are extremely passionate." Students "tend to participate in a lot of different activities from varsity sports (recruits), intramural sports (high school athletes)...[to] Engineers Without Borders, and the

Princeton University

FINANCIAL AID: 609-258-3330 • E-MAIL: UAOFFICE@PRINCETON.EDU • WEBSITE: WWW.PRINCETON.EDU

literary magazine." If you need to relax, "sporting events, concerts, recreational facilities," "a movie theater that frequently screens current films for free," and "arts and crafts at the student center" will help you de-stress. Others enjoy Princeton's eating clubs—private houses that service as social clubs and cafeterias for upperclassmen. Campus is located in a quaint little bubble of a New Jersey town and is full of traditions (some dating back hundreds of years), but if you crave some city-life "there's NJ transit if you want to go to New York, Philly, or even just the local mall."

CAREER

As one student tells us, "Princeton is a place that prepares you for anything and everything, providing you with a strong network every step of the way." Career Services lends a hand the moment students arrive on campus by guiding undergrads through self-assessments, educating about majors and careers, updating HireTigers—which holds hundreds of listings for jobs, fellowships, and internships—and, of course, strategize regarding resumes, cover letters, and online profiles. "Princeternships" allow students to experience "a day in the life" by shadowing an alumnus at their workplace for a few days. According to PayScale.com, the average starting salary for recent grads is $69,800.

GENERAL INFO

Activities: Choral groups, concert band, dance, drama/theater, jazz band, literary magazine, marching band, music ensembles, musical theater, opera, pep band, radio station, student government, student newspaper, student-run film society, symphony orchestra, yearbook, campus ministries, international student organization. **Organizations:** 300+ registered organizations, 30 honor societies, 28 religious organizations.

FINANCIAL AID

Students should submit: FAFSA; Institution's own financial aid form. Priority filing deadline is 2/1. The Princeton Review suggests that all financial aid forms be submitted as soon as possible after October 1. *Need-based scholarships/grants offered:* College/university scholarship or grant aid from institutional funds, Federal Pell, private scholarships, SEOG, state scholarships/grants. *Loan aid offered:* Direct PLUS Loans, Direct Subsidized Loans, Direct Unsubsidized Loans. Applicants will be notified of awards on or about 4/1. Federal Work-Study Program available. Institutional employment available.

THE BOTTOM LINE

If you can afford it, Princeton is far from cheap. A year's tuition is $45,320, plus about $14,770 in room and board. These figures are nothing to scoff at. However, if you qualify for aid, you'll be granted the amount you need, without loans.

CAREER INFORMATION FROM PAYSCALE.COM	
ROI Rating	99
Bachelors and No Higher	
Median starting salary	$72,700
Median mid-career salary	$141,300
At Least Bachelors	
Median starting salary	$74,500
Median mid-career salary	$147,800
Alumni with high job meaning	47%
Degrees awarded in STEM subjects	45%

SELECTIVITY	
Admissions Rating	99
# of applicants	31,056
% of applicants accepted	6
% of acceptees attending	66
# offered a place on the wait list	1,168
% accepting a place on wait list	71
% admitted from wait list	12

FRESHMAN PROFILE	
Range SAT EBRW	710–780
Range SAT Math	720–790
Range ACT Composite	32–35
Minimum paper TOEFL	600
Average HS GPA	3.9
% graduated top 10% of class	94
% graduated top 25% of class	99
% graduated top 50% of class	100

DEADLINES	
Early action	
Deadline	11/1
Notification	12/15
Regular	
Deadline	1/1
Notification	4/1
Nonfall registration?	No

FINANCIAL FACTS	
Financial Aid Rating	99
Annual tuition	$47,140
Room and board	$15,610
Books and supplies	$1,050
Average frosh need-based scholarship	$52,800
Average UG need-based scholarship	$51,365
% needy frosh rec. need-based scholarship or grant aid	100
% needy UG rec. need-based scholarship or grant aid	100
% needy frosh rec. non-need-based scholarship or grant aid	0
% needy UG rec. non-need-based scholarship or grant aid	0
% needy frosh rec. need-based self-help aid	100
% needy UG rec. need-based self-help aid	100
% frosh rec. any financial aid	60
% UG rec. any financial aid	60
% UG borrow to pay for school	18
Average cumulative indebtedness	$9,005
% frosh need fully met	100
% ugrads need fully met	100
Average % of frosh need met	100
Average % of ugrad need met	100

Purdue University—West Lafayette

1080 Schleman Hall, West Lafayette, IN 47907-2050 • Admissions: 765-494-1776 • Fax: 765-494-0544

CAMPUS LIFE

Quality of Life Rating	**91**
Fire Safety Rating	**96**
Green Rating	**96**
Type of school	Public
Environment	Town

STUDENTS

Total undergrad enrollment	30,831
% male/female	57/43
% from out of state	36
% frosh live on campus	94
% ugrads live on campus	41
# of fraternities (% ugrad men join)	30 (18)
# of sororities (% ugrad women join)	25 (22)
% African American	3
% Asian	8
% Caucasian	63
% Hispanic	5
% Native American	<1
% Pacific Islander	<1
% Two or more races	3
% Race and/or ethnicity unknown	2
% international	16
# of countries represented	123

ACADEMICS

Academic Rating	**83**
% students returning for sophomore year	92
% students graduating within 4 years	51
% students graduating within 6 years	79
Calendar	Semester
Student/faculty ratio	13:1
Profs interesting rating	73
Profs accessible rating	86

Most classes have 10–19 students. Most lab/discussion sessions have 20–29 students.

MOST POPULAR MAJORS

Computer Science; Mechanical Engineering; Mechanical Engineering/Mechanical Technology/Technician

ABOUT THE SCHOOL

Located in rural Indiana, Purdue University, with close to 30,000 students, is one of the most educationally and ethnically diverse universities in the United States. Purdue has rich tradition and has one of the oldest colleges of agriculture in the nation. "An institution filled with brain power and immense achievement, yet at the same time exceedingly humble and saturated with the warm-hearted hospitality of the Midwest," a contented undergrad tells us. Academics are taken seriously here. Purdue is research-intensive but retains great faculty-student interaction inside and outside of the classroom. "It allows undergraduates to enter laboratory research very early in their college career," says one student excitedly. Purdue has excellent research opportunities that are open to almost anyone who shows interest and dedication, and prides itself on being strong in STEM (science, technology, engineering, and math) education, with heavy emphasis on real-world practical research and knowledge. When combined with an emphasis on innovation and creative thinking, Purdue becomes a great choice for anyone looking to have a successful future. A well-networked university, that is incorporated into the surrounding town through collaborative learning, field experiences, and service opportunities, allows students to learn in and out of the classroom.

BANG FOR YOUR BUCK

One student describes the value of a Purdue education by saying, "I considered the problem mathematically. Math + science + social skills = engineering. Engineering + Midwest = Purdue." Others add, "I knew that I would be receiving an excellent education and that I would be prepared for my chosen career field," and explain that Purdue offers "a great education that will prepare you for a career, and it won't break the bank," and "tries its hardest to ensure everyone comes out of college with a job lined up." Purdue also draws a lot of employers for internships and full-time positions at many of their career fairs; the school produces marketable graduates who are in high demand by a number of top employers. Students are not hesitant with their praise. "I love Purdue and all of the doors it has opened for me in terms of engineering jobs and opportunities." The school's "emphasis on real-world practical research and knowledge, combined with an emphasis on innovation and creative thinking, make Purdue a great choice for anyone looking to have a successful future." High expectations ensure that the students at Purdue are well prepared for the future. "Nurturing a strong work ethic and high moral accountability" is important at Purdue, one student tells us. "It's been extremely tough, and a lot of work, but I feel like a much better engineer than I would have been had I gone anywhere else," says another appreciative enrollee.

STUDENT LIFE

"Students do work hard in the classroom throughout the week because we know that we are getting an outstanding education here. Come weekend time though, we definitely like to cut loose." Football and basketball games are major draws at the school, and "a lot of people on our campus think about when the next sporting event is. Big Ten Sports are huge here on campus. But not so huge that those who are uninterested in sports feel left out." When students are looking for ways to unwind that don't involve either sporting events or parties, they can choose from "so many different organizations" that are designed to "meet whatever your interests are whether it be sports, music, art, or may be even medieval jousting." A student raves that "Lafayette has plenty of restaurants, movie theatres, bowling, shopping, etc....Chicago and Indianapolis are also near enough for day trips! I am so busy on campus because there are so many great organizations to join! I could be busy every night, if I wanted!" General consensus about life at Purdue seems to be that "there's always something going on on-campus, no one can TRULY say they have NOTHING to do."

Purdue University—West Lafayette

FINANCIAL AID: 765-494-0998 • E-MAIL: ADMISSIONS@PURDUE.EDU • WEBSITE: WWW.PURDUE.EDU

CAREER

"The programs to help people out with career development are countless. That's definitely a strength at Purdue," raves one student, and students definitely seem to feel that the school leaves them well prepared to navigate life after graduation. The Center for Career Opportunities offers counseling on academic majors and career paths, networking and recruiting opportunities, resources for job and internship searches, and coaching on résumés, cover letters, and interviews. Overall, "Purdue has an outstanding reputation for developing difference makers, role models, and individuals who can think outside the box." Out of Purdue alumni visiting PayScale.com, 49 percent report feeling as though they derive a high level of meaning from their careers.

GENERAL INFO

Activities: Choral groups, concert band, dance, drama/theater, jazz band, literary magazine, marching band, music ensembles, musical theater, opera, pep band, radio station, student government, student newspaper, student-run film society, symphony orchestra, television station, yearbook, campus ministries, international student organization. **Organizations:** 970 registered organizations, 51 honor societies, 30 religious organizations, 31 fraternities, 31 sororities. **Athletics (Intercollegiate):** *Men:* Baseball, basketball, cross-country, diving, football, golf, swimming, tennis, track/field (outdoor), track/field (indoor), wrestling. *Women:* Basketball, cross-country, diving, golf, soccer, softball, swimming, tennis, track/field (outdoor), track/field (indoor), volleyball.

FINANCIAL AID

Students should submit: FAFSA. Priority filing deadline is 3/1. The Princeton Review suggests that all financial aid forms be submitted as soon as possible after October 1. *Need-based scholarships/grants offered:* College/university scholarship or grant aid from institutional funds, Federal Pell, private scholarships, SEOG, state scholarships/grants. *Loan aid offered:* Direct PLUS Loans, Direct Subsidized Loans, Direct Unsubsidized Loans. Applicants will be notified of awards on or about 4/15. Federal Work-Study Program available. Institutional employment available.

BOTTOM LINE

Tuition is about $9,200 for in-state students, with those from other states looking at a substantial increase to over $28,000. Room, board, books, and fees will increase this amount by another $12,000. "The financial aid package was the best offered to me, along with a very good scholarship." Purdue is "cheaper than a private school but it is a world-renowned engineering school at the same time." One student reports, "[Purdue] gave me a very generous scholarship package."

CAREER INFORMATION FROM PAYSCALE.COM

ROI Rating	91
Bachelors and No Higher	
Median starting salary	$60,200
Median mid-career salary	$105,800
At Least Bachelors	
Median starting salary	$61,500
Median mid-career salary	$110,800
Alumni with high job meaning	48%
Degrees awarded in STEM subjects	38%

SELECTIVITY

Admissions Rating	89
# of applicants	48,912
% of applicants accepted	57
% of acceptees attending	27
# offered a place on the wait list	2,235
% accepting a place on wait list	164
% admitted from wait list	3

FRESHMAN PROFILE

Range SAT EBRW	570–670
Range SAT Math	580–710
Range ACT Composite	25–31
Minimum internet-based TOEFL	80-88
Average HS GPA	3.8
% graduated top 10% of class	44
% graduated top 25% of class	78
% graduated top 50% of class	97

DEADLINES

Early action	
Deadline	11/1
Notification	12/12
Regular	
Priority	2/1
Notification	12/12
Nonfall registration?	Yes

FINANCIAL FACTS

Financial Aid Rating	87
Annual in-state tuition	$9,208
Annual out-of-state tuition	$28,010
Room and board	$10,030
Required fees	$784
Books and supplies	$1,160
Average frosh need-based scholarship	$12,990
Average UG need-based scholarship	$12,782
% needy frosh rec. need-based scholarship or grant aid	68
% needy UG rec. need-based scholarship or grant aid	73
% needy frosh rec. non-need-based scholarship or grant aid	37
% needy UG rec. non-need-based scholarship or grant aid	30
% needy frosh rec. need-based self-help aid	53
% needy UG rec. need-based self-help aid	60
% frosh rec. any financial aid	74
% UG rec. any financial aid	77
% UG borrow to pay for school	42
Average cumulative indebtedness	$27,617
% frosh need fully met	40
% ugrads need fully met	33
Average % of frosh need met	76
Average % of ugrad need met	77

Reed College

3203 SE WOODSTOCK BOULEVARD, PORTLAND, OR 97202-8199 • ADMISSIONS: 503-777-7511 • FAX: 503-777-7553

CAMPUS LIFE

Quality of Life Rating	91
Fire Safety Rating	96
Green Rating	60*
Type of school	Private
Environment	Metropolis

STUDENTS

Total undergrad enrollment	1,447
% male/female	46/54
% frosh from public high school	93
% frosh live on campus	99
% ugrads live on campus	65
# of fraternities (% ugrad men join)	0 (0)
# of sororities (% ugrad women join)	0 (0)
% African American	2
% Asian	6
% Caucasian	59
% Hispanic	10
% Native American	<1
% Pacific Islander	<1
% Two or more races	8
% Race and/or ethnicity unknown	3
% international	11
# of countries represented	46

ACADEMICS

Academic Rating	99
% students returning for sophomore year	88
% students graduating within 4 years	65
% students graduating within 6 years	80
Calendar	Semester
Student/faculty ratio	10:1
Profs interesting rating	99
Profs accessible rating	97
Most classes have 20–29 students.	

MOST POPULAR MAJORS
Biology; English; Psychology

ABOUT THE SCHOOL

The "academic emphasis and open-minded, quirky student body," is right at home in Portland, Oregon, where the "absolutely beautiful" Reed College campus is located. Reed's "intellectually rigorous" liberal arts curriculum "teaches you to think highly critically and to present your thoughts so that a variety of people will be able to understand you." A "mandatorily broad cluster" of courses provides students with "an understanding of how different fields of study interact with each other." One student tells us "the sciences are incomparable to any other college," and STEM distinctions at Reed include with the school's "nuclear reactor where undergrads can do research," the only such reactor in the country run primarily by undergraduate students. Reed maintains a distinctive grading philosophy where most students don't see their grades before graduation. But you can opt into seeing them. According to students this places the "emphasis on learning, as opposed to getting good grades," while creating an environment "conducive to growing as a person." "We get pages of comments that are so much more helpful than a letter grade," another student explains. Reed has "small, conference-based classes" that emphasize the Socratic method and create "a very engaging and effective style of teaching." "The relationships with faculty that I've developed are invaluable; you meet these experts in their field, then become their academic and social peers. Professors not only get to know you in small classes, but are available and approachable." Reed exalts the individual and the independent thinker. Even if a student doesn't start off with these qualities, they will likely develop them.

BANG FOR YOUR BUCK

Of fundamental importance at Reed is how you contribute to the intellectual life inside and outside the college. "Reed is an academically rigorous institution that not only prepares students for graduate school but also provides students with opportunities to advance in life beyond academia." High-level research and scholarship at the cutting edge of each academic discipline are important to the school. With outstanding professors, and a healthy social environment, "for students who are interested both in exploring great ideas and in developing personal autonomy, it makes very good sense." Aptly put by another undergrad, "The institution nurtures learning for the sake of learning and ensures students have opportunities to succeed at and outside of Reed."

STUDENT LIFE

"Remember that one, quirky kid in class that had a huge intellect and a passion for (insert passion here)? Well, they all went to Reed." While this "quirky Reedy" is a common description, students also emphasize that Reed's social and cultural life are built around the schools ability to "[foster] intellectual relationships between peers that will last a lifetime." With no Greek system or varsity sports, and student groups that change year to year based on students' interest, freedom and flexibility abound on campus. "Students at Reed are able to pursue their own intellectual curiosities very easily," on and off campus through "on-campus jobs, clubs, student organizations, or volunteer work." Politics tilt strongly to the left, and "in recent years, Reed has also had a real upsurge in activist organizations especially concerning people of color on our campus."

Reed College

FINANCIAL AID: 503-777-7223 • E-MAIL: ADMISSION@REED.EDU • WEBSITE: WWW.REED.EDU

CAREER

The aptly named Center for Life After Reed is dedicated to connecting students with experiential learning during their time in college and with professional contacts for their future careers. Paid summer internships abound through the Internship Advantage Initiative, and winter Externships let Reedies learn even more about interesting career paths. SEEDS links students to service learning gigs throughout the year, and the weekly e-mail digest Beyond Campus Opportunities reminds them about upcoming fellowship deadlines, interesting employment opportunities, and more. According to PayScale.com, Reed graduates report average starting salaries of $53,400, and 51 percent derive a high level of meaning from their work.

GENERAL INFO

Activities: A capella groups, theatre productions, literary magazine, radio station, foreign language clubs, student government, student newspaper, symphony orchestra, feminist student union, social activist groups, international student organization. **Organizations:** 105 registered organizations, 1 honor society, 5 religious organizations. **On-Campus Highlights:** Thesis Tower, Nuclear Research Reactor, Crystal Springs Canyon, Cerf Amphitheatre, Paradox and Paradox Lost Cafes. **Environmental Initiatives:** LEED construction, recycling, installation for energy efficiency across campus (i.e., lighting, windows, heating).

FINANCIAL AID

Students should submit: CSS Profile; FAFSA; Noncustodial PROFILE. Priority filing deadline is 1/15. The Princeton Review suggests that all financial aid forms be submitted as soon as possible after October 1. *Need-based scholarships/grants offered:* College/university scholarship or grant aid from institutional funds, Federal Pell, private scholarships, SEOG, state scholarships/grants. *Loan aid offered:* Direct PLUS Loans, Direct Subsidized Loans, Direct Unsubsidized Loans. Applicants will be notified of awards on or about 4/1. Federal Work-Study Program available. Institutional employment available.

BOTTOM LINE

Annual tuition at is $53,900; with books, room, board, and fees, you can tack another $13,670. Reed meets 100 percent of demonstrated need through need-based scholarships or grant assistance; it is commonly heard from students, "Financial aid is terrific at Reed." "Reed was really generous with my financial aid package and made it possible for me to go out of state to college."

CAREER INFORMATION FROM PAYSCALE.COM

ROI Rating	90
Bachelors and No Higher	
Median starting salary	$53,900
Median mid-career salary	$109,800
At Least Bachelors	
Median starting salary	$56,200
Median mid-career salary	$117,100
Alumni with high job meaning	47%
Degrees awarded in STEM subjects	26%

SELECTIVITY

Admissions Rating	95
# of applicants	5,652
% of applicants accepted	36
% of acceptees attending	21
# offered a place on the wait list	1,659
% accepting a place on wait list	31
% admitted from wait list	0
# of early decision applicants	310
% accepted early decision	57

FRESHMAN PROFILE

Range SAT EBRW	670–740
Range SAT Math	640–760
Range ACT Composite	30–33
Minimum paper TOEFL	600
Minimum internet-based TOEFL	100
Average HS GPA	3.9
% graduated top 10% of class	59
% graduated top 25% of class	85
% graduated top 50% of class	98

DEADLINES

Early decision	
Deadline	11/15
Notification	12/15
Other ED Deadline	12/20
Other ED Notification	2/1
Early action	
Deadline	11/15
Notification	1/31
Regular	
Deadline	1/15
Notification	4/1
Nonfall registration?	No

FINANCIAL FACTS

Financial Aid Rating	94
Annual tuition	$56,030
Room and board	$14,210
Required fees	$310
Books and supplies	$1,050
Average frosh need-based scholarship	$39,129
Average UG need-based scholarship	$38,994
% needy frosh rec. need-based scholarship or grant aid	100
% needy UG rec. need-based scholarship or grant aid	100
% needy frosh rec. non-need-based scholarship or grant aid	0
% needy UG rec. non-need-based scholarship or grant aid	0
% needy frosh rec. need-based self-help aid	100
% needy UG rec. need-based self-help aid	100
% frosh rec. any financial aid	55
% UG rec. any financial aid	58

Rensselaer Polytechnic Institute

110 EIGHTH STREET, TROY, NY 12180-3590 • ADMISSIONS: 518-276-6216 • FAX: 518-276-4072

CAMPUS LIFE

Quality of Life Rating	**83**
Fire Safety Rating	**94**
Green Rating	**60***
Type of school	Private
Environment	City

STUDENTS

Total undergrad enrollment	6,314
% male/female	68/32
% from out of state	67
% frosh from public high school	70
% frosh live on campus	100
% ugrads live on campus	57
# of fraternities (% ugrad men join)	29 (30)
# of sororities (% ugrad women join)	5 (16)
% African American	4
% Asian	12
% Caucasian	53
% Hispanic	9
% Native American	<1
% Pacific Islander	<1
% Two or more races	7
% Race and/or ethnicity unknown	1
% international	14
# of countries represented	44

ACADEMICS

Academic Rating	**80**
% students returning for sophomore year	93
% students graduating within 4 years	61
% students graduating within 6 years	83
Calendar	Semester
Student/faculty ratio	13:1
Profs interesting rating	68
Profs accessible rating	80
Most classes have fewer than 10 students.	

MOST POPULAR MAJORS

Engineering; Computer & Information Science; Mathematics/Statistics; Business/Marketing

ABOUT THE SCHOOL

As the first technological research university in the country, Rensselaer Polytechnic Institute has some legs to stand on in the higher education world. Though primarily an engineering institution, RPI offers degrees through five schools and encourages its students to take part in interdisciplinary programs that combine work from different areas of study. A focus on bringing the skills and technology from the lab to the real world has kept the school current and provided many a career showpiece for students. For instance, according to the school, in the last thirty years RPI has helped launch almost 300 start-up companies, many of which grew out of class projects. Classes are sized so that students can get to know their professors, who "make it a point to be accessible to students, either personally or through other venues like phone or email."

BANG FOR YOUR BUCK

Ninety-three percent of Rensselaer students receive need-based financial aid, and the school meets an average of 77 percent of need. The school offers numerous merit-based scholarships and grants, most prominently the Rensselaer Leadership Award for academic and personal achievements, and the Rensselaer Medal, which offers a $25,000 per year to students who have distinguished themselves in mathematics and science. A relatively large number of RPI students receive the Rensselaer Medal (13 percent of the most recently admitted class). International students are not eligible to receive financial aid outside of the Medal.

STUDENT LIFE

RPI draws a significant portion (nearly one-third) of its "very diverse" students from outside of the northeast. The typical student "may be considered 'nerdy' by the liberal arts world, but being a nerd is totally cool here," says a student. "Everyone has quirks that are appreciated here, and people with similar quirks tend to flock together." There "is always something going on, especially with all the student clubs," of which there are over 180, and the intramural sports (hockey is especially big at Rensselaer), and most people stay on campus over the weekends (even those who are local) since it is "packed full of concerts, sporting events, plays, and club events." Students often split up the weekend with some homework and pick and choose which events to attend; they "are really focused and goal-oriented, but know when and how to have a good time."

CAREER

RPI is all about ensuring every student gets legitimate experience in his or her field of study as soon as possible, and looks to "equip each student with the skills needed to be a valuable member of any research team or company." The focus on problem-solving and "opportunities to be involved in hands-on research" are just two of the ways the school accomplishes this, and "the research buildings are amazing." The RPI name has a great reputation with science and tech employers, and many take part in co-ops throughout the academic year. The Center for Career & Professional Development maintains JobLink, an online job recruiting and posting system, offers career programming tailored to your class year, and hosts a Spring Career Fair. Forty-eight percent of the RPI graduates who visited PayScale.com reported feeling that their jobs had a high level of meaningful impact on the world, and brought in an average starting salary of $71,000.

Rensselaer Polytechnic Institute

FINANCIAL AID: 518-276-6813 • E-MAIL: ADMISSIONS@RPI.EDU • WEBSITE: WWW.RPI.EDU

GENERAL INFO

Activities: Choral groups, concert band, dance, drama/theater, jazz band, literary magazine, music ensembles, musical theater, pep band, radio station, student government, student newspaper, student-run film society, symphony orchestra, television station, yearbook, campus ministries, International Student Organization. **Organizations:** 177 registered organizations, 40 honor societies, 11 religious organizations. 29 fraternities, 5 sororities. **Athletics (Intercollegiate):** *Men:* baseball, basketball, cross-country, diving, football, golf, ice hockey, lacrosse, soccer, swimming, tennis, track/field (outdoor), track/field (indoor). *Women:* basketball, cross-country, diving, field hockey, ice hockey, lacrosse, soccer, softball, swimming, tennis, track/field (outdoor), track/field (indoor). **On-Campus Highlights:** Rensselaer Union, Mueller Fitness Center, Experimental Media & Performing Arts Ctr, Houston Field House (hockey arena), ECAV.

FINANCIAL AID

Students should submit: CSS Profile; FAFSA. Priority filing deadline is 2/1. The Princeton Review suggests that all financial aid forms be submitted as soon as possible after October 1. *Need-based scholarships/grants offered:* College/university scholarship or grant aid from institutional funds, Federal Pell, private scholarships, SEOG, state scholarships/grants. *Loan aid offered:* Direct PLUS Loans, Direct Subsidized Loans, Direct Unsubsidized Loans. Applicants will be notified of awards on or about 3/15. Federal Work-Study Program available. Institutional employment available.

BOTTOM LINE

Tuition runs a hefty $52,550, with an additional $15,260 needed for room and board. With fees and supplies added in the estimated cost of attendance is $71,997, but the vast majority of students receive aid so as not to pay the sticker price. The average need-based scholarship award is $34,894.

CAREER INFORMATION FROM PAYSCALE.COM

ROI Rating	90
Bachelors and No Higher	
Median starting salary	$69,600
Median mid-career salary	$131,600
At Least Bachelors	
Median starting salary	$71,200
Median mid-career salary	$136,100
Alumni with high job meaning	48%
Degrees awarded in STEM subjects	78%

SELECTIVITY

Admissions Rating	94
# of applicants	19,505
% of applicants accepted	43
% of acceptees attending	20
# offered a place on the wait list	4,803
% accepting a place on wait list	55
% admitted from wait list	1
# of early decision applicants	903
% accepted early decision	57

FRESHMAN PROFILE

Range SAT EBRW	640–730
Range SAT Math	680–770
Range ACT Composite	28–32
Minimum paper TOEFL	570
Minimum internet-based TOEFL	88
Average HS GPA	3.8
% graduated top 10% of class	63
% graduated top 25% of class	91
% graduated top 50% of class	98

DEADLINES

Early decision	
Deadline	11/1
Notification	12/15
Other ED Deadline	12/15
Other ED Notification	1/12
Regular	
Deadline	1/15
Nonfall registration?	Yes

FINANCIAL FACTS

Financial Aid Rating	83
Annual tuition	$52,550
Room and board	$15,260
Required fees	$1,330
Books and supplies	$2,858
Average frosh need-based scholarship	$36,478
Average UG need-based scholarship	$34,894
% needy frosh rec. need-based scholarship or grant aid	100
% needy UG rec. need-based scholarship or grant aid	100
% needy frosh rec. non-need-based scholarship or grant aid	18
% needy UG rec. non-need-based scholarship or grant aid	12
% needy frosh rec. need-based self-help aid	99
% needy UG rec. need-based self-help aid	98
% frosh rec. any financial aid	89
% UG rec. any financial aid	89
% UG borrow to pay for school	65
% frosh need fully met	22
% ugrads need fully met	17
Average % of frosh need met	84

Rhodes College

2000 North Parkway, Memphis, TN 38112 • Admissions: 901-843-3700 • Fax: 901-843-3631

CAMPUS LIFE

Quality of Life Rating	93
Fire Safety Rating	87
Green Rating	75
Type of school	Private
Affiliation	Presbyterian
Environment	Metropolis

STUDENTS

Total undergrad enrollment	1,975
% male/female	44/56
% from out of state	72
% frosh from public high school	46
% frosh live on campus	97
% ugrads live on campus	70
# of fraternities (% ugrad men join)	8 (32)
# of sororities (% ugrad women join)	7 (42)
% African American	8
% Asian	6
% Caucasian	70
% Hispanic	6
% Native American	<1
% Pacific Islander	<1
% Two or more races	4
% Race and/or ethnicity unknown	2
% international	4
# of countries represented	18

ACADEMICS

Academic Rating	95
% students returning for sophomore year	91
% students graduating within 4 years	76
% students graduating within 6 years	80
Calendar	Semester
Student/faculty ratio	10:1
Profs interesting rating	98
Profs accessible rating	98

Most classes have 20–29 students. Most lab/discussion sessions have 20–29 students.

MOST POPULAR MAJORS

English Language and Literature; Biology/Biological Sciences; Business Administration and Management

ABOUT THE SCHOOL

Located in the heart of Memphis, Tennessee, Rhodes College was founded in 1848 by Freemasons, but came to be affiliated with the Presbyterian Church. This private liberal arts college encourages students to study "as many different disciplines as possible in order to gain a broader understanding of the world." Rhodes students can expect small classes—averaging ten to nineteen students—and "rigorous" academics. Students who put in the work can expect to succeed: "Most people here work hard and see it academically pay off." The school's "very dedicated professors" "really care about their students and make an effort to get to know us and help us succeed." One student proudly explains that "Rhodes offers a close, personalized environment where teachers and faculty are not just willing, but enthusiastic to help you find your unique path to achievement." The school's 110-acre campus, situated right in the middle of historic Memphis, is known for its "beautiful" grounds and architecture. Over a dozen of Rhodes's buildings are listed in the National Register of Historic Places. The campus is located near Overton Park and the Memphis Zoo, and a short walk to many entertainment, internship, and research opportunities, including institutions such as St. Jude Children's Research Hospital and the National Civil Rights Museum.

BANG FOR YOUR BUCK

"Memphis is a city with character, and Rhodes is an institution [that] helps foster it," one student explains. The city of Memphis offers it all to students, from internships to "great restaurants" and weekend activities. Despite being located in a city, the college provides a secluded college atmosphere for those who want it. The professors are "great and helpful," and with a faculty-to-student ratio of 10:1, they are easily accessible. The student body is "actually really diverse and tends to have some great opportunities for students to learn about other cultures and countries."

STUDENT LIFE

"Stereotypically, Rhodes is a white, private college full of men in sweater-vests and women in pearls. But, there is an incredible diversity at Rhodes between upper socioeconomic backgrounds to lower socioeconomic backgrounds, between different races, between different ethnic backgrounds, between political backgrounds, and between genders. There are 'preppy' students, 'hippies,' 'punks,' and 'nerds.' The one thing that unites us all is that, on the inside, we're all just a bunch of geeks who love to learn and want to broaden our horizons." The school is full of hard workers ("academic but not full of nerds") and its honor code is taken very seriously. One thing is for certain—students here are "busy" in all areas of their life: studying, taking advantage of the "countless service opportunities," arts, athletics, and Greek life. At Rhodes, "there is an emphasis on academics, a friendly atmosphere, and plenty of extra-curriculars to get involved in."

CAREER

The typical Rhodes College graduate has a starting salary of around $47,900, and 46 percent report that their job has a great deal of meaning. Students feel that Rhodes "is the epitome of opportunity: from service to sports to academics to internships and jobs to career services and professors. Rhodes has it all." A Biochemistry major notes that "I get to do cutting edge biomedical Cancer research at St. Jude Children's Research hospital. This is an invaluable internship I got through Rhodes." Many students feel that the internship opportunities at Rhodes are not only "invaluable," but the sort of things that "helped pull us here."

Rhodes College

FINANCIAL AID: 901-843-3810 • E-MAIL: ADMINFO@RHODES.EDU • WEBSITE: WWW.RHODES.EDU

GENERAL INFO

Activities: Choral groups, dance, drama/theater, jazz band, literary magazine, music ensembles, musical theater, pep band, radio station, student government, student newspaper, student-run film society, symphony orchestra, television station, yearbook. **Organizations:** campus ministries, International Student Organization, Model UN, 115 registered organizations, 14 honor societies, 8 religious organizations. 8 fraternities, 7 sororities. **Athletics (Intercollegiate):** *Men:* baseball, basketball, cross-country, football, golf, lacrosse, soccer, swimming, tennis, track/field (outdoor). *Women:* basketball, cross-country, field hockey, golf, lacrosse, soccer, softball, swimming, tennis, track/field (outdoor), volleyball. **On-Campus Highlights:** Barret Library (includes a Starbucks coffee shop), Burrow Center for Student Opportunity, Bryan Campus Life Center (home to the Lynx Lair pub, East Village (apartment-style dorms), McCoy Theater, The Burrow Center for Student Opportunity opened in Spring, 2008. It consolidates most student services under one roof, including a one-stop transaction center, enrolling and financing, student development and academic support, and out of class experiences. It also includes space for student organizations and is open to students 24x7. **Environmental Initiatives:** $500,000 Andrew W. Mellon Foundation grant to expand environmental studies initiatives through community partnerships; comprehensive campuswide recycling program; centralized energy management system; Green Power Switch.

FINANCIAL AID

Students should submit: FAFSA; Noncustodial PROFILE. Priority filing deadline is 2/1. The Princeton Review suggests that all financial aid forms be submitted as soon as possible after October 1. *Need-based scholarships/grants offered:* College/university scholarship or grant aid from institutional funds, Federal Pell, private scholarships, SEOG, state scholarships/grants. *Loan aid offered:* Direct PLUS Loans, Direct Subsidized Loans, Direct Unsubsidized Loans. Federal Work-Study Program available. Institutional employment available.

BOTTOM LINE

Annual tuition at Rhodes is $44,632 to which a student should expect to add another $11,068 for living and other school expenses. However, in addition to working hard to meet students with financial needs—a full 94 percent of undergraduates receive aid—the school offers many merit-based scholarships. The Rhodes Student Associate Program is a unique work program that matches students with "meaningful employment that requires advanced skills and dedication." The program currently offers more than 100 positions in a variety of both academic and administrative departments. Rhodes also facilitates many off-campus student employment opportunities with local non-profits.

CAREER INFORMATION FROM PAYSCALE.COM	
ROI Rating	91
Bachelors and No Higher	
Median starting salary	$49,400
Median mid-career salary	$107,400
At Least Bachelors	
Median starting salary	$52,900
Median mid-career salary	$111,100
Alumni with high job meaning	47%
Degrees awarded in STEM subjects	25%

SELECTIVITY	
Admissions Rating	**90**
# of applicants	4,733
% of applicants accepted	51
% of acceptees attending	21
# offered a place on the wait list	1,008
% accepting a place on wait list	21
% admitted from wait list	24
# of early decision applicants	155
% accepted early decision	63

FRESHMAN PROFILE	
Range SAT EBRW	620–720
Range SAT Math	600–690
Range ACT Composite	27–32
Minimum paper TOEFL	600
Average HS GPA	3.9
% graduated top 10% of class	51
% graduated top 25% of class	90
% graduated top 50% of class	98

DEADLINES	
Early decision	
Deadline	11/1
Notification	12/1
Other ED Deadline	1/1
Other ED Notification	2/1
Early action	
Deadline	11/15
Notification	1/15
Regular	
Priority	1/15
Notification	4/1
Nonfall registration?	Yes

FINANCIAL FACTS	
Financial Aid Rating	**91**
Annual tuition	$46,194
Room and board	$11,358
Required fees	$310
Books and supplies	$1,125
Average frosh need-based scholarship	$31,593
Average UG need-based scholarship	$31,751
% needy frosh rec. need-based scholarship or grant aid	98
% needy UG rec. need-based scholarship or grant aid	99
% needy frosh rec. non-need-based scholarship or grant aid	48
% needy UG rec. non-need-based scholarship or grant aid	34
% needy frosh rec. need-based self-help aid	51
% needy UG rec. need-based self-help aid	64
% frosh rec. any financial aid	95
% UG rec. any financial aid	94
% UG borrow to pay for school	48

Rice University

MS 17, PO Box 1892, Houston, TX 77251-1892 • Admissions: 713-348-7423 • Fax: 713-348-5952

CAMPUS LIFE

Quality of Life Rating	99
Fire Safety Rating	95
Green Rating	92
Type of school	Private
Environment	Metropolis

STUDENTS

Total undergrad enrollment	3,970
% male/female	53/47
% from out of state	52
% frosh from public high school	71
% frosh live on campus	99
% ugrads live on campus	72
# of fraternities (% ugrad men join)	0 (0)
# of sororities (% ugrad women join)	0 (0)
% African American	7
% Asian	26
% Caucasian	35
% Hispanic	15
% Native American	<1
% Pacific Islander	<1
% Two or more races	4
% Race and/or ethnicity unknown	2
% international	12
# of countries represented	42

ACADEMICS

Academic Rating	92
% students returning for sophomore year	97
% students graduating within 4 years	83
% students graduating within 6 years	91
Calendar	Semester
Student/faculty ratio	6:1
Profs interesting rating	84
Profs accessible rating	86

Most classes have 10–19 students.

MOST POPULAR MAJORS

Chemical Engineering; Biology/Biological Sciences;Computer Science

ABOUT THE SCHOOL

Texas' Rice University is a leading research institution that marries an academic environment with dozens of unique traditions, creating an intellectual and fun framework in which its nearly 4,000 students can thrive. An undergraduate student-to-faculty ratio of just under 6 to 1 and vast opportunities for undergraduate research are just the tip of the iceberg. Rice is full of "extremely smart people who also have many other dimensions outside of one subject or the classroom"; for instance, each new student is required to take a First Year Writing Intensive Seminar, each of which covers a niche topic/subject (such as Time Travel Narratives, Science Fiction and Shakespeare, Fake Art and Forgeries). Professors are "easily accessible outside the classroom" and are "experts in their specific fields"; this is a "world class faculty teaching small classes surrounded by like-minded individuals that really want to be there." There is "a strong desire for expanding intellectual horizons and engaging in meaningful dialogue about any number of issues" both inside and outside of the classroom, and there is "a good support system to make everyone feel welcomed and safe."

BANG FOR YOUR BUCK

As a premier research university, there are "many job/research/fellowship opportunities," and the community "is one of such cultural and intellectual diversity that is at the same time unified and supportive." The opportunities afforded for research and collaboration "cannot be understated," and the "funding for students in the humanities tends to be particularly good." Grants are readily available for research in all areas, as is financial aid. Rice Merit Aid is a scholarship fund that is awarded to academically outstanding students, who are automatically considered for each award via their admissions application, while there is separate funding that ensures that a student's unmet financial need is entirely covered through various financial aid types.

STUDENT LIFE

Located in the heart of the museum district in the "unique and vibrant city of Houston," students here prioritize academics and "spend a ton of time studying," but all welcome distractions from the daily routine of class and work. On any given night of the week, there "is likely some kind of event happening," and "crawls and parties tend to be quite frequent starting Thursday night through the weekend." There is a "good mix between races, ethnicities, [and] socioeconomic classes" here, and nearly three-quarters of students (including 99% of all first-years) live on campus via the school's residential college system, which "provides an inclusive community/culture of care"; between this system and the school's small size, it is "easy to feel like you belong and that you have a second family." This "quirky, uniquely interesting" group is composed of "intellectual, happy human beings who are passionate about the topics they're pursuing." They are "motivated," and "constantly thinking about ways to improve our campus systems as well as those in our city and world," and there is "never any competition."

CAREER

The academic flexibility at Rice lets students change majors easily as their career paths develop, and the school offers "lots of academic planning and job preparation." The "autonomy and ability of...students to test ideas and create change" is one of the greatest tools that Rice provides,

Rice University

FINANCIAL AID: 713-348-4958 • E-MAIL: ADMI@RICE.EDU • WEBSITE: WWW.RICE.EDU

and the plethora of research opportunities and "ease of entering research programs regardless of experience level" helps students build their resume right out of the gate. The university is also located close to the Texas Medical Center, which offers many opportunities for pre-med students. The Center for Career Development helps students with their internship and job searches, holds job fairs, and has weekly drop-in hours. Additionally, the office helps set up Owl Edge Externships, which are one to five-day job shadowing experiences with Rice alumni in different fields.

GENERAL INFO

Activities: Campus Ministries; Choral groups; Concert band; Dance; Drama/theater; International Student Organization; Jazz band; Literary magazine; Marching band; Music ensembles; Musical theater; Opera; Pep band; Radio station; Student government; Student newspaper; Student-run film society; Symphony orchestra; Television station; Yearbook 215 registered organizations, 11 honor societies, 14 religious organizations. **Athletics (Intercollegiate):** *Men:* baseball, basketball, cross-country, football, golf, tennis, track/field (outdoor), track/field (indoor). *Women:* basketball, cross-country, soccer, swimming, tennis, track/field (outdoor), track/field (indoor), volleyball. **On-Campus Highlights:** Rice Memorial Center, Baker Institute for Public Policy, Brochstein Pavilion (cafe), Shepherd School of Music, Reckling Park—baseball stadium.

FINANCIAL AID

Students should submit: Business/Farm Supplement; CSS Profile; FAFSA; Noncustodial PROFILE. Priority filing deadline is 3/1. The Princeton Review suggests that all financial aid forms be submitted as soon as possible after October 1. *Need-based scholarships/grants offered:* College/university scholarship or grant aid from institutional funds, Federal Pell, private scholarships, SEOG, state scholarships/grants. *Loan aid offered:* Direct PLUS Loans, Direct Subsidized Loans, Direct Unsubsidized Loans. Applicants will be notified of awards on or about 4/1. Federal Work-Study Program available. Institutional employment available.

THE BOTTOM LINE

Tuition comes in at $46,600; the total cost, including $14,000 for room and board and $750 in mandatory fees, is $61,350. Rice meets the full need of admitted students, and 72% of students graduate without debt. Beginning in fall 2019 under the school's new initiative, The Rice Investment, middle-income families with demonstrated need and typical assets will receive grant aid to cover full tuition if they earn up to $130,000 per year, and half tuition for families earning between $130,001-$200,000. Students with family incomes below $65,000 and typical assets will receive grant aid covering not only their full tuition, but also mandatory fees and room and board. Students receiving aid under The Rice Investment will have all demonstrated need met without any loans.

CAREER INFORMATION FROM PAYSCALE.COM	
ROI Rating	95
Bachelors and No Higher	
Median starting salary	$69,200
Median mid-career salary	$133,600
At Least Bachelors	
Median starting salary	$70,500
Median mid-career salary	$134,700
Alumni with high job meaning	49%
Degrees awarded in STEM subjects	43%

SELECTIVITY	
Admissions Rating	97
# of applicants	18,063
% of applicants accepted	16
% of acceptees attending	37
# offered a place on the wait list	2,080
% accepting a place on wait list	64
% admitted from wait list	1
# of early decision applicants	1603
% accepted early decision	21

FRESHMAN PROFILE	
Range SAT EBRW	730–780
Range SAT Math	760–800
Range ACT Composite	33–35
Minimum internet-based TOEFL	100
% graduated top 10% of class	89
% graduated top 25% of class	97
% graduated top 50% of class	99

DEADLINES	
Early decision	
Deadline	11/1
Notification	12/15
Regular	
Deadline	1/1
Notification	4/1
Nonfall registration?	No

FINANCIAL FACTS	
Financial Aid Rating	97
Annual tuition	$46,600
Room and board	$14,000
Required fees	$750
Books and supplies	$1,200
Average frosh need-based scholarship	$41,572
Average UG need-based scholarship	$40,285
% needy frosh rec. need-based scholarship or grant aid	99
% needy UG rec. need-based scholarship or grant aid	98
% needy frosh rec. non-need-based scholarship or grant aid	4
% needy UG rec. non-need-based scholarship or grant aid	3
% needy frosh rec. need-based self-help aid	66
% needy UG rec. need-based self-help aid	72
% frosh rec. any financial aid	57
% UG rec. any financial aid	55
% UG borrow to pay for school	25
Average cumulative indebtedness	$26,555
% frosh need fully met	100
% ugrads need fully met	100
Average % of frosh need met	100
Average % of ugrad need met	100

Rochester Institute of Technology

60 LOMB MEMORIAL DRIVE, ROCHESTER, NY 14623-5604 • ADMISSIONS: 585-475-5502 • FAX: 585-475-7424

CAMPUS LIFE

Quality of Life Rating	**88**
Fire Safety Rating	**89**
Green Rating	**96**
Type of school	Private
Environment	City

STUDENTS

Total undergrad enrollment	12,858
% male/female	67/33
% from out of state	48
% frosh from public high school	85
% frosh live on campus	96
% ugrads live on campus	52
# of fraternities (% ugrad men join)	19 (4)
# of sororities (% ugrad women join)	10 (2)
% African American	5
% Asian	9
% Caucasian	66
% Hispanic	7
% Native American	<1
% Pacific Islander	<1
% Two or more races	4
% Race and/or ethnicity unknown	2
% international	7
# of countries represented	71

ACADEMICS

Academic Rating	**82**
% students returning for sophomore year	90
% students graduating within 4 years	28
% students graduating within 6 years	70
Calendar	Semester
Student/faculty ratio	13:1
Profs interesting rating	79
Profs accessible rating	79
Most classes have 20–29 students.	

MOST POPULAR MAJORS
Computer Science; Game Design and Development; Mechanical Engineering

ABOUT THE SCHOOL

Rochester Institute of Technology is a school that prioritizes "innovation and creativity." It's also an institution that's deeply "committed to helping its students achieve their goals." Hence, it's none too surprising to learn that RIT places a tremendous "focus on undergraduate research" and experiential learning, especially cooperative education. Students also happily report that their school frequently attracts "talented nerds," and they wouldn't have it any other way. Academically, RIT is especially strong when it comes to "science, technology, engineering, and the arts." And a handful of undergrads rush to highlight the fact that the school has "one of the best video game design/development programs in the country." Fortunately, regardless of the course of study, undergrads here will find "knowledgeable" professors who are "very dedicated to their subjects." Just as critical, the vast majority "are willing to stay after hours, meet with [individuals] and hold group study/review sessions to help their students understand the material."

BANG FOR YOUR BUCK

We're all painfully aware that attending college can be a pricey endeavor. Thankfully, RIT's Office of Financial Aid and Scholarships works diligently to help bring down the cost. In fact, over 13,500 students (undergraduate and graduate combined) receive more than $320 million in aid from state, federal, and institutional resources. Importantly, all applicants will be considered for merit-based scholarships. These include the RIT Presidential Scholarship which awards $14,000–$20,000, the RIT Founders Scholarship which awards $8,000–$12,000, the RIT National Hispanic Scholar Award which provides $2,000 and the RIT Recognition Scholarship which awards a minimum of $1,000. We should note that all of these scholarships are renewable.

STUDENT LIFE

Undergrads at RIT are never at a loss for something to do. Students can enjoy "free on-campus movies, see guest speakers, listen to comedians, and attend events hosted by the College Activities Board." Of course, we'd remiss if we neglected to mention that "hockey is a huge part of RIT and it is very common to see a large number of students at the games." The school also has plenty of resources undergrads love to take advantage of including "free ice skating at the rink," the "rock climbing barn," and a "game room with pool and ping pong." Additionally, a number of individuals participate in a "campus wide game" of Humans vs. Zombies. And you can always find "multiple parties every weekend if that's what interests you."

Rochester Institute of Technology

FINANCIAL AID: 585-475-5502 • E-MAIL: ADMISSIONS@RIT.EDU • WEBSITE: WWW.RIT.EDU

CAREER

RIT students are incredibly successful on the job market. After all, the university's "mandatory co-op/internship program almost guarantees graduates a job in an area they love." Students are also able to easily capitalize on RIT's "amazing connections with companies throughout the world." And they can no doubt turn to the school's stellar Office of Career Services can Cooperative Education as well. Beyond helping undergrads land their co-ops, the office holds networking events with companies like Apple, Nike, and Bristol Meyers Squibb. They also host career fairs every semester. Best of all, the office maintains drop-in hours Monday–Friday allowing students to get all of their questions answered and their resumes tweaked.

GENERAL INFO

Activities: Campus Ministries; Choral groups; Concert band; Dance; Drama/theater; International Student Organization; Jazz band; Literary magazine; Music ensembles; Musical theater; Pep band; Radio station; Student government; Student newspaper; Student-run film society; Symphony orchestra; Yearbook 300+ registered organizations, 9 honor societies, 5 religious organizations. 19 fraternities, 10 sororities. **Athletics (Intercollegiate):** *Men:* baseball, basketball, crew/rowing, cross-country, diving, ice hockey, lacrosse, soccer, swimming, tennis, track/field (outdoor), track/field (indoor), wrestling. *Women:* basketball, cheerleading, crew/rowing, cross-country, diving, ice hockey, lacrosse, soccer, softball, swimming, tennis, track/field (outdoor), track/field (indoor), volleyball. **On-Campus Highlights:** Java Wally's (Wallace Library coffee sho, Student Life Center/Field House/Ice Aren, ESPN Zone @ RIT Student Alumni Union, Ben and Jerry's (RIT Student Alumni Uni, The Cafe and Market at Crossroads.

FINANCIAL AID

Students should submit: FAFSA, state aid form. Priority filing deadline is November 1 for Early Decision I; January 1 for Early Decision II; and January 15 for Regular Decision. *Need-based scholarships/grants offered:* College/university scholarship or grant aid from institutional funds, Federal Pell, private scholarships, SEOG, state scholarships/grants. *Loan aid offered:* Direct PLUS Loans, Direct Subsidized Loans, Direct Unsubsidized Loans. Applicants will be notified of awards on a rolling basis beginning 3/1. Federal Work-Study Program available. Institutional employment available.

CAREER INFORMATION FROM PAYSCALE.COM	
ROI Rating	87
Bachelors and No Higher	
Median starting salary	$60,400
Median mid-career salary	$102,600
At Least Bachelors	
Median starting salary	$61,500
Median mid-career salary	$105,700
Alumni with high job meaning	43%
Degrees awarded in STEM subjects	50%

SELECTIVITY	
Admissions Rating	88
# of applicants	20,451
% of applicants accepted	57
% of acceptees attending	24
# offered a place on the wait list	376
% accepting a place on wait list	98
% admitted from wait list	22
# of early decision applicants	1349
% accepted early decision	66

FRESHMAN PROFILE	
Range SAT EBRW	590–680
Range SAT Math	600–700
Range ACT Composite	26–32
Minimum paper TOEFL	550
Minimum internet-based TOEFL	79
Average HS GPA	3.6
% graduated top 10% of class	40
% graduated top 25% of class	74
% graduated top 50% of class	95

DEADLINES	
Early decision I	
Deadline	11/1
Early decision II	
Deadline	1/1
Regular	
Deadline	1/15
Nonfall registration?	Yes

FINANCIAL FACTS	
Financial Aid Rating	92
Annual tuition	$41,046
Room and board	$13,046
Required fees	$584
Books and supplies	$1,066
Average frosh need-based scholarship	$23,968
Average UG need-based scholarship	$22,200
% needy frosh rec. need-based scholarship or grant aid	95
% needy UG rec. need-based scholarship or grant aid	95
% needy frosh rec. non-need-based scholarship or grant aid	23
% needy UG rec. non-need-based scholarship or grant aid	33
% needy frosh rec. need-based self-help aid	90
% needy UG rec. need-based self-help aid	90
% frosh rec. any financial aid	87
% UG rec. any financial aid	77
% UG borrow to pay for school	76
Average cumulative indebtedness	$38,927
% frosh need fully met	77
% ugrads need fully met	81
Average % of frosh need met	87

Rose-Hulman Institute of Technology

5500 Wabash Ave., Terra Haute, IN 47803 • Admissions: 812-877-8213 • Fax: 812-877-8941

CAMPUS LIFE

Quality of Life Rating	91
Fire Safety Rating	96
Green Rating	79
Type of school	Private
Environment	Town

STUDENTS

Total undergrad enrollment	2,146
% male/female	75/25
% from out of state	64
% frosh from public high school	63
% frosh live on campus	99
% ugrads live on campus	58
# of fraternities (% ugrad men join)	8 (36)
# of sororities (% ugrad women join)	3 (34)
% African American	3
% Asian	5
% Caucasian	68
% Hispanic	5
% Native American	<1
% Pacific Islander	<1
% Two or more races	5
% Race and/or ethnicity unknown	1
% international	15
# of countries represented	11

ACADEMICS

Academic Rating	85
% students returning for sophomore year	91
% students graduating within 4 years	67
% students graduating within 6 years	81
Calendar	Quarter
Student/faculty ratio	11:1
Profs interesting rating	92
Profs accessible rating	95

Most classes have 20–29 students. Most lab/discussion sessions have 10–19 students.

MOST POPULAR MAJORS

Computer Science; Chemical Engineering; Mechanical Engineering

ABOUT THE SCHOOL

Though ostensibly dedicated to the study of engineering, science and mathematics, the Rose-Hulman Institute of Technology seeks to create a "collaborative rather than competitive" environment that sends its graduates into the real world with the tools needed to secure employment. "Everyone from the housekeepers and residence life to professors and staff truly wants you to succeed, academically and at life in general," says a student. The professors in the small classes "genuinely care about your learning and advancing you in your career path," the "accommodating" administration creates an "intimate family atmosphere," and there is an open door policy that extends "from your fellow students all the way up to the president." Additionally, there are many resources for students who are struggling, and the school makes it a point to encourage students to take advantage of the artwork and cultural opportunities available at the school (including the Rose-Hulman art collection, drama club productions, and the Performing Arts Series).

BANG FOR YOUR BUCK

Almost every single student attending Rose-Hulman receives aid of some sort, and the college makes the application process as ingrained with the admissions process as possible. In addition to federal grants and scholarships, there are several institutional scholarships available. Rose-Hulman Merit Scholarships are based on both academic and non-academic measures (such as extracurricular activities, leadership and community service), and all admitted students are automatically considered. Rose-Hulman Named Scholarships are more limited in number and have specific restrictions placed on them by the donor; all students are also considered upon admission.

STUDENT LIFE

Students at this 2,100 strong school "are time- and efficiency-oriented" and while they may put a lot of hours into school, they all "choose a few extracurriculars with which to get very involved." Rose-Hulman "is a sort of social oasis for the kids that knew everything in high school" and "we are all proud to be nerds together," beams a student. "Students are pretty goofy and creative" so "random games like 'owling' and fruit golf pop up," says one. The excellent residential life program means that "floor residents become extremely close and participate in many events together" and people call it the "Rose bubble" because "life on campus is amazing (although unrealistic to the outside world because of how nice everyone is)." Indeed, there's so much to do on campus that people leave very rarely: "If we aren't busy studying or getting homework done, we are out participating in intramurals, varsity athletics, community service, religious groups, gaming groups, campus jobs, greek life...the list goes on and on," says a student.

Rose-Hulman Institute of Technology

FINANCIAL AID: 812-877-8259 • E-MAIL: ADMISSIONS@ROSE-HULMAN.EDU • WEBSITE: WWW.ROSE-HULMAN.EDU

CAREER

This is one of the top undergraduate engineering schools in the country, and "the job placement rate and average starting salary are amazing." The importance is set strictly on academics and employers recognize that, and "the opportunities for gaining experience in your field of study are endless." Career Services brings in numerous companies to help provide jobs, co-ops, and internships to students, and sets up mock interviews, résumé reviews, and numerous career and graduate school fairs to help the job hunt process run smoothly. Fifty-one percent of Rose-Hulman graduates who visited PayScale. com felt their job had a meaningful impact on the world; an average starting salary of $71,600 was reported.

GENERAL INFO

Activities: Choral groups, concert band, dance, drama/theater, jazz band, literary magazine, music ensembles, musical theater, pep band, radio station, student government, student newspaper, International Student Organization. **Organizations:** 105 registered organizations, 7 honor societies, 2 religious organizations. 8 fraternities, 3 sororities. **Athletics (Intercollegiate):** *Men:* baseball, basketball, cross-country, diving, football, golf, soccer, swimming, tennis, track/field (outdoor), track/field (indoor). *Women:* basketball, cross-country, diving, golf, soccer, softball, swimming, tennis, track/field (outdoor), track/field (indoor), volleyball. **On-Campus Highlights:** Sports and Recreation Center, Hatfield Hall, White Chapel, Moench Hall, Mussallem Union, and Branam Innovation Center.

FINANCIAL AID

Students should submit: FAFSA. Priority filing deadline is 3/10. The Princeton Review suggests that all financial aid forms be submitted as soon as possible after October 1. *Need-based scholarships/grants offered:* College/university scholarship or grant aid from institutional funds; Federal Pell; SEOG; State scholarships/grants. *Loan aid offered:* Direct PLUS Loans, Direct Subsidized Loans, Direct Unsubsidized Loans. Applicants will be notified of awards on or about 3/10. Federal Work-Study Program available. Institutional employment available.

BOTTOM LINE

Tuition rings in at $46,641, with another $14,766 going towards room and board. Fortunately, 98 percent of students receive financial aid. Of the 60 percent of students who borrow through a loan program, the average debt upon graduation is $45,345. About 60 percent of Rose-Hulman students also participate in Federal Work-Study or Work Opportunity to help offset costs while they are at school.

CAREER INFORMATION FROM PAYSCALE.COM	
ROI Rating	91
Bachelors and No Higher	
Median starting salary	$73,400
Median mid-career salary	$129,900
At Least Bachelors	
Median starting salary	$74,600
Median mid-career salary	$134,400
Alumni with high job meaning	52%
Degrees awarded in STEM subjects	96%

SELECTIVITY	
Admissions Rating	92
# of applicants	4,473
% of applicants accepted	61
% of acceptees attending	20
# offered a place on the wait list	379
% accepting a place on wait list	40
% admitted from wait list	25

FRESHMAN PROFILE	
Range SAT EBRW	610–690
Range SAT Math	650–760
Range ACT Composite	27–32
Minimum paper TOEFL	550
Minimum internet-based TOEFL	88
Average HS GPA	4.0
% graduated top 10% of class	64
% graduated top 25% of class	91
% graduated top 50% of class	100

DEADLINES	
Early action	
Deadline	11/1
Notification	12/15
Regular	
Priority	11/1
Deadline	2/1
Notification	3/15
Nonfall registration?	No

FINANCIAL FACTS	
Financial Aid Rating	83
Annual tuition	$46,641
Room and board	$14,766
Required fees	$930
Books and supplies	$1,500
Average frosh need-based scholarship	$29,035
Average UG need-based scholarship	$26,898
% needy frosh rec. need-based scholarship or grant aid	100
% needy UG rec. need-based scholarship or grant aid	100
% needy frosh rec. non-need-based scholarship or grant aid	78
% needy UG rec. non-need-based scholarship or grant aid	82
% needy frosh rec. need-based self-help aid	77
% needy UG rec. need-based self-help aid	79
% frosh rec. any financial aid	99
% UG rec. any financial aid	98
% UG borrow to pay for school	60
Average cumulative indebtedness	$45,345
% frosh need fully met	76
% ugrads need fully met	80
Average % of frosh need met	71
Average % of ugrad need met	69

Rutgers University—New Brunswick

100 Sutphen Road, Piscataway, NJ 08854-8097 • Admissions: 732-445-4636 • Fax: 732-445-8088

CAMPUS LIFE

Quality of Life Rating	82
Fire Safety Rating	89
Green Rating	60*
Type of school	Public
Affiliation	No Affiliation
Environment	Small Urban

STUDENTS

Total undergrad enrollment	35,296
% male/female	50/50
% from out of state	6
% frosh live on campus	85
% ugrads live on campus	43
# of fraternities	50
# of sororities	25
% African American	7
% Asian	27
% Caucasian	39
% Hispanic	13
% Native American	<1
% Pacific Islander	<1
% Two or more races	3
% Race and/or ethnicity unknown	2
% international	9
# of countries represented	113

ACADEMICS

Academic Rating	71
% students returning for sophomore year	94
% students graduating within 4 years	60
% students graduating within 6 years	80
Calendar	Semester
Student/faculty ratio	13:1
Profs interesting rating	65
Profs accessible rating	67
Most classes have 20–29 students.	

MOST POPULAR MAJORS
Business Administration and Management; Nursing; Engineering

ABOUT THE SCHOOL

As New Jersey's premiere state institution, Rutgers attracts "friendly and intelligent students" bursting with "school pride [and] spirit." And it's no surprise why. After all, undergrads here immediately tout Rutgers as "a diverse university in all aspects of the word—academically, culturally, politically, ethnically, linguistically, and socially." And they find that this "enriches" their collegiate experience tenfold. Aside from diversity, students happily report that opportunities abound for "undergraduates to conduct research and work with professors in any number of fields." However, they do caution that since the university "is so big, you have to learn to make your own way . . . no one is going to hold your hand for you." Despite the need for assertiveness, students do enjoy their academic experience. Many find their professors "engaging" and state that they know how to make "course material interesting." And, thankfully, they "are very accessible outside of classes in their office hours and by email."

BANG FOR YOUR BUCK

If forced to summarize Rutgers in one word, many undergraduates would likely say "affordable." Indeed, students here wholeheartedly agree that "the price is right" at their alma mater. In fact one very contented senior even brags, "I am getting an Ivy League education at an in-state tuition price!" Certainly, it's not just state school prices that leave these students grateful. The financial aid office also works hard to make higher education affordable for all undergraduates. In fact, 71 percent of Rutgers undergraduates receive some form of aid, either based on need or merit. Even more impressive, the average undergraduate need-based gift aid is a whopping $11,124. Not too shabby, eh?

STUDENT LIFE

Undergrads at Rutgers have to work extremely hard if they want to find themselves bored. That's because there's "ALWAYS something going on, whether it's a football game...arcade games at the RutgersZone, performing arts [shows]...[a] university-sponsored concert, free food events, community service days, Greek life...EVERYTHING!" An ecstatic math major rushes to add, "RUPA, our programming association, plans many different events...anything from movie nights to Rock, Paper, Scissor tournaments." Undergrads can also enjoy "free ice cream on Thursdays, free seminars...and the attractions of downtown New Brunswick." In addition, students readily admit that "Rutgers has a great party scene. Every night is an adventure in one of the many fraternities or house parties going on." Fortunately, there's a place for drinkers and non-drinkers alike. Lastly, students love that Rutgers is close to the Jersey Shore and "half-way between NYC and Philly, so getting away for the weekend is easy."

CAREER

Employment opportunities are plentiful for both Rutgers students and alums. Of course, this should probably be expected. After all, a Middle Eastern studies major emphatically tells us that, "Career Services is awesome." And many undergrads are able to land "amazing internships." One thrilled journalism major confirms this stating, "I work at NBC in 30 Rockefeller Plaza, and will continue my internship for my last semester." Numerous students attribute this success to Career Service's robust internship and co-op program. Beyond internships, the office also hosts a massive fall career fair featuring over 250 companies from a variety of industries as well as government

Rutgers University—New Brunswick

FINANCIAL AID: 848-932-7057 • E-MAIL: ADMISSIONS@UGADM.RUTGERS.EDU • WEBSITE: WWW.RUTGERS.EDU

and nonprofit organizations. And undergrads are also privy to a bevy of career events—including everything from drop-in resume clinics to sixty-minute job search boot camps. Finally, prospective (and current!) students should be pleased to discover that, according to PayScale.com, the average starting salary for a Rutgers alum is $58,900.

GENERAL INFO

Activities: Choral groups, concert band, dance, drama/theater, jazz band, literary magazine, marching band, music ensembles, musical theater, opera, pep band, radio station, student government, student newspaper, student-run film society, symphony orchestra, television station, yearbook, campus ministries, International Student Organization. **Organizations:** 750 registered organizations, 30 honor societies. 50 fraternities and 25 sororities. **Athletics (Intercollegiate):** *Men:* baseball, basketball, cheerleading, cross-country, football, golf, lacrosse, soccer, track/field (outdoor), track/field (indoor), wrestling. *Women:* basketball, cheerleading, crew/rowing, cross-country, diving, field hockey, golf, gymnastics, lacrosse, soccer, softball, swimming, tennis, track/field (outdoor), track/field (indoor), volleyball. **On-Campus Highlights:** Geology Museum, Jane Voorhees Zimmerli Art Museum, Rutgers Display Gardens and Heylar Woods, Hutcheson Memorial Forest.

FINANCIAL AID

Students should submit: FAFSA. Priority filing deadline is 12/1. The Princeton Review suggests that all financial aid forms be submitted as soon as possible after October 1. *Need-based scholarships/grants offered:* Federal Pell, FSEOG, State scholarships/grants, College/university scholarship or grant aid from institutional funds, Federal Nursing Scholarships. *Loan aid offered:* Direct Subsidized Loans, Direct Unsubsidized Loans, Direct PLUS loans, Federal Perkins Loans, Federal Nursing Loans, State Loans, College/university loans from institutional funds. Applicants are notified of awards on a rolling basis beginning 3/1. Federal Work-Study Program available. Institutional employment available.

THE BOTTOM LINE

New Jersey residents joining Rutgers ranks face a tuition bill of $11,886. Students hailing from out-of-state have a tuition bill that comes in at $28,194. Further, undergraduates who decide to live on-campus pay another $12,706 in room and board. Students (and their families) must also pay $3,088 in required fees. And they'll need an additional $1,350 for books and supplies. Finally, those undergraduates commuting from off-campus should expect roughly $3,082 in transportation fees.

CAREER INFORMATION FROM PAYSCALE.COM	
ROI Rating	87
Bachelors and No Higher	
Median starting salary	$57,800
Median mid-career salary	$111,600
At Least Bachelors	
Median starting salary	$58,900
Median mid-career salary	$115,900
Alumni with high job meaning	42%
Degrees awarded in STEM subjects	28%

SELECTIVITY	
Admissions Rating	87
# of applicants	38,384
% of applicants accepted	58
# of acceptees attending	28

FRESHMAN PROFILE	
Range SAT EBRW	590–680
Range SAT Math	600–720
Minimum paper TOEFL	550
Minimum internet-based TOEFL	79
% graduated top 10% of class	40
% graduated top 25% of class	75
% graduated top 50% of class	96

DEADLINES	
Early action	
Deadline	11/1
Notification	1/31
Regular	
Priority	12/1
Notification	2/28
Nonfall registration?	Yes

FINANCIAL FACTS	
Financial Aid Rating	77
Annual in-state tuition	$11,886
Annual out-of-state tuition	$28,194
Room and board	$12,706
Required fees	$3,088
Books and supplies	$1,350
Average frosh need-based scholarship	$12,943
Average UG need-based scholarship	$11,124
% needy frosh rec. need-based scholarship or grant aid	65
% needy UG rec. need-based scholarship or grant aid	70
% needy frosh rec. non-need-based scholarship or grant aid	29
% needy UG rec. non-need-based scholarship or grant aid	17
% needy frosh rec. need-based self-help aid	84
% needy UG rec. need-based self-help aid	82
% frosh rec. any financial aid	71
% UG rec. any financial aid	71
% ugrads need fully met	48
Average % of frosh need met	52

Saint Anselm College

100 SAINT ANSELM DRIVE, MANCHESTER, NH 03102-1310 • ADMISSIONS: 603-641-7500 • FAX: 603-641-7550

CAMPUS LIFE

Quality of Life Rating	93
Fire Safety Rating	85
Green Rating	60*
Type of school	Private
Affiliation	Roman Catholic
Environment	City

STUDENTS

Total undergrad enrollment	1,956
% male/female	39/61
% from out of state	78
% frosh from public high school	65
% frosh live on campus	97
% ugrads live on campus	92
# of fraternities (% ugrad men join)	0 (0)
# of sororities (% ugrad women join)	0 (0)
% African American	2
% Asian	1
% Caucasian	88
% Hispanic	4
% Native American	<1
% Pacific Islander	<1
% Two or more races	2
% Race and/or ethnicity unknown	3
% international	1
# of countries represented	6

ACADEMICS

Academic Rating	89
% students returning for sophomore year	89
% students graduating within 4 years	78
% students graduating within 6 years	80
Calendar	Semester
Student/faculty ratio	11:1
Profs interesting rating	87
Profs accessible rating	90

Most classes have 10–19 students. Most lab/discussion sessions have 10–19 students.

MOST POPULAR MAJORS
Nursing, Business, Biology

ABOUT THE SCHOOL

This picturesque, quaint, Catholic college is located on a New Hampshire hilltop, offering its almost 2,000 students a traditional liberal arts education while emphasizing preparation for real-world careers. The school has forty-six majors and fifty-one minors, as well as several pre-professional programs for advanced studies. All freshmen begin in the humanities program (Conversatio) and follow a core curriculum throughout their four years (including required philosophy and theology courses), with average class sizes of eighteen students and a focus on "improving the academic skills of the student to the maximum." Students get out what they put in, but "there is a strong sense of encouragement to do well," and students agree that one of the best parts about the college is the personal interaction between students and both administrators and faculty members. "They are ready and willing to meet with you at a time convenient for you."

BANG FOR YOUR BUCK

Plenty of need- and merit-based scholarships are available to students to offset the cost of the private school: Chancellor Honors Scholarships provide academically strong students with Honors Program admission and up to $25,000 annually; the Presidential Scholarship offers up to $21,000 a year; and the Dean's Scholarship is up to $15,000 a year. Furthermore, the school has multiple scholarships set aside for talent-based achievements, and for families who have two or more children attending the college.

STUDENT LIFE

The campus is separate from the city of Manchester so students tend to stay local for their fun, and most are "very involved in activities here, especially sports (a lot of people do intramurals) and service activities" (indeed, "volunteering is HUGE here at Saint Anselm College"). During the week, there are usually club-run events students can go to, as well as "a lot of speakers and political candidates who come to the New Hampshire Institute of Politics." Students are typically from a religious private high school, and the environment at the college is "very intellectual," with "debates and discussions on politics, philosophy and society in general [being] typical."

CAREER

The college is heavily vested in its students' future careers, and employment readiness is incorporated into the curriculum from day one. Credit-bearing internships, study abroad, and faculty-student research opportunities abound, and the Career Development Center also offers personal guidance, professional development workshops, and HawkCareers, a Saint-Anselm specific job and internship database. Additionally, the Meelia Center for Community Engagement helps connect students with agencies throughout the Greater Manchester area, in order to gain service experience. For the Class of 2017, 99 percent were employed, in graduate school, or engaged in service within six months of graduation. Saint Anselm graduates who visited Payscale.com reported an early career salary of $54,900 annually.

Saint Anselm College

FINANCIAL AID: 603-641-7110 • E-MAIL: ADMISSION@ANSELM.EDU • WEBSITE: WWW.ANSELM.EDU

GENERAL INFO

Activities: Choral groups, dance, drama/theater, jazz band, literary magazine, musical theater, radio station, student government, student newspaper, television station, yearbook, campus ministries, International Student Organization, Model UN 120 registered organizations, 11 honor societies, 7 religious organizations. **Athletics (Intercollegiate):** *Men:* baseball, basketball, cross-country, football, golf, ice hockey, lacrosse, soccer, tennis. *Women:* basketball, cross-country, field hockey, golf, ice hockey, lacrosse, soccer, softball, tennis, volleyball. **On-Campus Highlights:** Joseph Hall Academic Building, Chapel Arts Center, Davidson Hall Dining Hall, Sullivan Ice Arena & Fitness Center, Abbey Church, Coffee Shop and Pub Roger & Francine Jean Student Center Complex.

FINANCIAL AID

Students should submit: CSS Profile; FAFSA. Priority filing deadline is 12/1. The Princeton Review suggests that all financial aid forms be submitted as soon as possible after October 1. *Need-based scholarships/grants offered:* College/university scholarship or grant aid from institutional funds, Federal Pell, private scholarships, SEOG, state scholarships/grants. *Loan aid offered:* Direct PLUS Loans, Direct Subsidized Loans, Direct Unsubsidized Loans. Applicants will be notified of awards on a rolling basis beginning 2/1. Federal Work-Study Program available. Institutional employment available.

BOTTOM LINE

It costs $39,900 in tuition and $14,500 in room and board (as well as an additional $1,300 in fees) to attend Saint Anselm, but a whopping 98 percent of first-year students are awarded some form of financial aid, with the average need-based grant/scholarship coming in at $24,300. All averages considered, a first-year student receiving need-based aid can expect a total price of around $25,350.

CAREER INFORMATION FROM PAYSCALE.COM	
ROI Rating	88
Bachelors and No Higher	
Median starting salary	$54,900
Median mid-career salary	$98,800
At Least Bachelors	
Median starting salary	$56,600
Median mid-career salary	$103,500
Alumni with high job meaning	58%
Degrees awarded in STEM subjects	10%

SELECTIVITY

Admissions Rating	**81**
# of applicants	3,892
% of applicants accepted	76
% of acceptees attending	18
# offered a place on the wait list	410
% accepting a place on wait list	33
% admitted from wait list	3
# of early decision applicants	37
% accepted early decision	86

FRESHMAN PROFILE

Range SAT EBRW	580–650
Range SAT Math	560–650
Range ACT Composite	24–28
Minimum paper TOEFL	550
Minimum internet-based TOEFL	80
Average HS GPA	3.3
% graduated top 10% of class	24
% graduated top 25% of class	55
% graduated top 50% of class	88

DEADLINES

Early decision	
Deadline	12/1
Notification	1/1
Early action	
Deadline	11/15
Regular	
Deadline	2/1
Notification	3/15
Nonfall registration?	Yes

FINANCIAL FACTS

Financial Aid Rating	**86**
Annual tuition	$39,900
Room and board	$14,500
Required fees	$1,300
Books and supplies	$1,000
Average frosh need-based scholarship	$24,780
Average UG need-based scholarship	$23,682
% needy frosh rec. need-based scholarship or grant aid	100
% needy UG rec. need-based scholarship or grant aid	100
% needy frosh rec. non-need-based scholarship or grant aid	22
% needy UG rec. non-need-based scholarship or grant aid	17
% needy frosh rec. need-based self-help aid	76
% needy UG rec. need-based self-help aid	81
% frosh rec. any financial aid	98
% UG rec. any financial aid	98
% UG borrow to pay for school	84
Average cumulative indebtedness	$36,567
% frosh need fully met	27

Saint Louis University

ONE NORTH GRAND BOULEVARD, SAINT LOUIS, MO 63103 • ADMISSIONS: 314-977-2500 • FAX: 314-977-7136

CAMPUS LIFE

Quality of Life Rating	**91**
Fire Safety Rating	**93**
Green Rating	**82**
Type of school	Private
Affiliation	Roman Catholic-Jesuit
Environment	Metropolis

STUDENTS

Total undergrad enrollment	7,209
% male/female	40/60
% from out of state	59
% frosh live on campus	92
% ugrads live on campus	51
# of fraternities (% ugrad men join)	7 (4)
# of sororities (% ugrad women join)	7 (7)
% African American	6
% Asian	10
% Caucasian	69
% Hispanic	6
% Native American	<1
% Pacific Islander	<1
% Two or more races	3
% Race and/or ethnicity unknown	1
% international	5
# of countries represented	69

ACADEMICS

Academic Rating	**88**
% students returning for sophomore year	90
% students graduating within 4 years	70
% students graduating within 6 years	78
Calendar	Semester
Student/faculty ratio	9:1
Profs interesting rating	85
Profs accessible rating	84
Most classes have 20–29 students.	

MOST POPULAR MAJORS

Biology/Biological Sciences; Registered Nursing; Liberal Arts and Sciences, General Studies

ABOUT THE SCHOOL

One of the oldest Catholic universities in the nation, St. Louis University in Missouri follows the Jesuit mission of educating the whole person. More than 80 courses at SLU directly integrate service into the curriculum, giving these 7,209 undergraduates "a well-rounded education to mold the best possible adults for an ever changing world." The institution spends an incredible $52.5 million in research each year. SLU offers 90 academic majors and 100 minors to complement the overall academic experience. In fact, students find that the SLU curriculum is "flexible based on the student's needs" and that the university does "a good job in trying to make sure that everyone feels included." "Professors here are very passionate about their field of study" and "incredible at relating class material to real world events." "You get professors like that from day one."

BANG FOR YOUR BUCK

SLU "does a great job of catering to the needs of all people from all backgrounds," and is incredibly generous with need-based financial aid. Both need- and merit-based scholarships are available, including the Billiken, Ignatian, University, Deans', and Vice Presidents' scholarships for high-achieving incoming freshman, ranging from $3,000 to $18,000 per year. Additionally the Presidential Scholarship is a four-year, full-tuition award for exemplary student leaders, and the esteemed Martin Luther King Jr. Scholarship is an academic award (averaging $24,000 per year) for students who have demonstrated leadership as agents of change or influence.

STUDENT LIFE

Most SLU students are "incredibly busy" throughout the day, and the campus "is always buzzing with life because people are coming and going all day long between their various activities." Two activities seem to be the bare minimum for extracurriculars. Intramural sports are popular, as is Greek life, and students take advantage of the beautiful campus simply by lounging in hammocks out on the quad or playing Frisbee in the green space. There are a bowling alley and movie theatre adjacent to campus, and many also "go downtown or other bustling areas of the city to get off campus." Optional mass is held daily, and there are plenty of religious retreats for those who are interested.

CAREER

SLU students are looking for "careers that strive to improve our society and our own wellbeing." The faculty are more than willing to help students outside of established hours and parameters, and many offer "valuable career advice, support, and connections." In addition, the Career Services office offers career counseling, two career fairs, and a 16-week, hour-long class each semester called Career Decision Making, designed for first- and second- years who are unsure about their major or career direction.

Saint Louis University

FINANCIAL AID: 314-977-2350 • E-MAIL: ADMISSION@SLU.EDU • WEBSITE: WWW.SLU.EDU

GENERAL INFO

Activities: Choral groups, dance, drama/theater, jazz band, literary magazine, music ensembles, musical theater, pep band, radio station, student government, student newspaper, television station, campus ministries, International Student Organization, Model UN. 150 registered organizations, 23 honor societies, 17 religious organizations. 7 fraternities, 7 sororities. **Athletics (Intercollegiate):** *Men:* baseball, basketball, cross-country, diving, soccer, swimming, tennis, track/field (outdoor), track/field (indoor). *Women:* basketball, cross-country, diving, field hockey, soccer, softball, swimming, tennis, track/field (outdoor), track/field (idoor), volleyball. **On-Campus Highlights:** St. Francis Xavier Church, Busch Student Center, Saint Louis University Museum of Art, Simon Recreation Center, Robert R. Hermann Soccer Stadium, Chaifetz Arena.

FINANCIAL AID

Students should submit: FAFSA. Priority filing deadline is 2/1. The Princeton Review suggests that all financial aid forms be submitted as soon as possible after October 1. *Need-based scholarships/grants offered:* College/university scholarship or grant aid from institutional funds, Federal Nursing Scholarships, Federal Pell, Private scholarships, SEOG, State scholarships/grants. *Loan aid offered:* Direct PLUS Loans, Direct Subsidized Loans, Direct Unsubsidized Loans, Federal Nursing Loans, State Loans, and College/university loans from institutional funds. Applicants will be notified of awards on a rolling basis beginning 2/1. Federal Work-Study Program available. Institutional employment available.

THE BOTTOM LINE

It costs $43,160 in tuition to attend SLU, and students should budget for an additional $724 going to student fees, as well as for room and board, which comes to about $12,290. There is plenty of assistance to go around. Ninety-seven percent of first-time frosh receive aid—and 45 percent of SLU students complete their degree without taking on loans.

CAREER INFORMATION FROM PAYSCALE.COM	
ROI Rating	89
Bachelors and No Higher	
Median starting salary	$53,100
Median mid-career salary	$92,400
At Least Bachelors	
Median starting salary	$54,400
Median mid-career salary	$97,300
Alumni with high job meaning	56%
Degrees awarded in STEM subjects	12%

SELECTIVITY	
Admissions Rating	89
# of applicants	13,431
% of applicants accepted	64
% of acceptees attending	19
# offered a place on the wait list	195

FRESHMAN PROFILE	
Range SAT EBRW	590–690
Range SAT Math	580–700
Range ACT Composite	25–31
Minimum paper TOEFL	550
Minimum internet-based TOEFL	80
Average HS GPA	3.9
% graduated top 10% of class	50
% graduated top 25% of class	76
% graduated top 50% of class	94

DEADLINES	
Regular	
Priority	12/1
Deadline	8/15
Nonfall registration?	Yes

FINANCIAL FACTS	
Financial Aid Rating	88
Annual tuition	$43,160
Room and board	$12,290
Required fees	$724
Average frosh need-based scholarship	$34,048
Average UG need-based scholarship	$27,300
% needy frosh rec. need-based scholarship or grant aid	97
% needy UG rec. need-based scholarship or grant aid	95
% needy frosh rec. non-need-based scholarship or grant aid	17
% needy UG rec. non-need-based scholarship or grant aid	14
% needy frosh rec. need-based self-help aid	65
% needy UG rec. need-based self-help aid	67
% frosh rec. any financial aid	96
% UG rec. any financial aid	90
% UG borrow to pay for school	55
Average cumulative indebtedness	$21,292
% frosh need fully met	51
% ugrads need fully met	34
Average % of frosh need met	86
Average % of ugrad need met	78

San Diego State University

5500 Campanile Drive, San Diego, CA 92182-7455 • Admissions: 619-594-6336 •

CAMPUS LIFE

Quality of Life Rating	**90**
Fire Safety Rating	**95**
Green Rating	**83**
Type of school	Public
Environment	Metropolis

STUDENTS

Total undergrad enrollment	30,165
% male/female	46/54
% from out of state	10
% frosh from public high school	91
% frosh live on campus	62
% ugrads live on campus	14
# of fraternities (% ugrad men join)	23 (11)
# of sororities (% ugrad women join)	22 (13)
% African American	4
% Asian	13
% Caucasian	33
% Hispanic	31
% Native American	<1
% Pacific Islander	<1
% Two or more races	7
% Race and/or ethnicity unknown	4
% international	7
# of countries represented	114

ACADEMICS

Academic Rating	**75**
% students returning for sophomore year	89
% students graduating within 4 years	36
% students graduating within 6 years	75
Calendar	Semester
Student/faculty ratio	27:1
Profs interesting rating	76
Profs accessible rating	75

Most classes have 20–29 students. Most lab/discussion sessions have 20-29 students.

MOST POPULAR MAJORS
Health and Physical Education/Fitness; Psychology; Criminal Justice/Safety Studies

ABOUT THE SCHOOL

San Diego State University, a public research university juggernaut, boasts more than 30,000 undergraduates, nearly 100 undergraduate majors (including the renowned business school and pre-professional programs), and $135 million in grant funding in 2017-2018. Excellent study abroad options, a diverse student body, and a military-friendly setup (for students who are veterans or in ROTC) make for "a laid-back atmosphere with perfect weather and driven students." Classrooms are "conducted with enthusiasm and passion for both educating and the subjects themselves" and "there are some lectures, but overall most classes are dynamic." Overall, professors are "easy to contact, easy to understand, and very patient. " In addition to the research opportunities available for hands-on learning, there are various extracurricular programs that are both for pleasure and education, so students "can learn in the process of having fun."

BANG FOR YOUR BUCK

SDSU students are "very focused on applying their education into real world application" and the university "[encourages] its students to participate in the high impact research that SDSU is involved in." Resources and potential for recognition are everywhere, and an ambitious student can leave the school with a fully stocked resume. On top of need-based aid, there are tons of scholarships available for just about every qualification under the sun, including the Middle Class Scholarship for California residents who attend a California State University and have a family income up to $150,000 (structured like a grant) and the Benjamin A. Gilman International Scholarship Program, which grants up to $5,000 to students wishing to study abroad and may not have been able to without financial assistance.

STUDENT LIFE

SDSU has "a very active and healthy student body," which pairs nicely with the "perfect location, determined students, and strong athletics." People often go to football and basketball games and the campus is "never empty"; there are "always familiar faces when walking to class." "It is a fun campus to be on and hard to get bored," says a student. Greek life is "very active in philanthropy" and provides a "great community on campus." The SDSU student population is "diverse, kind, and interactive," and it's not uncommon to be surrounded by people who aren't originally from San Diego "which makes exploring the city fun." Most students have a full or part-time job in addition to classes, and are also actively involved in a wide variety of activities ranging from "attending club meetings, going to the library, or going to the beach."

CAREER

San Diego State does a wonderful job of "ensuring students have local and abroad opportunities during college, as well as job offers waiting at graduation." One in seven adults in San Diego with a college degree attended SDSU, which, needless to say, makes for excellent alumni networking and internship opportunities. The popular Aztec Mentor Program connects alumni and professional mentors with juniors, seniors and graduate students to help them prepare for a career, and even alumni can use the online Aztec Career Connection (also available as an app) to find jobs and internships. The school partners with thousands of alumni and organizations to provide as many opportunities as possible, and the school hosts a two-day career and internship fair to accommodate them. Of all of the San Diego State alumni visiting PayScale.com, 53 percent report that they derive a high level of meaning from their jobs.

San Diego State University

FINANCIAL AID: 619-594-6323 • E-MAIL: • WEBSITE: WWW.SDSU.EDU

GENERAL INFO

Activities: Choral groups, concert band, dance, drama/theater, jazz band, literary magazine, marching band, music ensembles, musical theater, opera, pep band, radio station, student government, student newspaper, student-run film society, symphony orchestra, television station, campus ministries. 264 registered organizations, 6 honor societies, 14 religious organizations. 22 fraternities, 22 sororities. **Athletics (Intercollegiate):** *Men:* baseball, basketball, football, golf, soccer, tennis. *Women:* basketball, crew/rowing, cross-country, diving, golf, soccer, softball, swimming, tennis, track/field (outdoor), track/field (indoor), volleyball, water polo.

FINANCIAL AID

Students should submit: FAFSA, state aid form. Regular filing deadline is 3/1. The Princeton Review suggests that all financial aid forms be submitted as soon as possible after October 1. *Need-based scholarships/grants offered:* College/university scholarship or grant aid from institutional funds, Federal Pell, private scholarships, SEOG, state scholarships/grants. *Loan aid offered:* Direct PLUS Loans, Direct Subsidized Loans, Direct Unsubsidized Loans. Applicants will be notified of awards on a rolling basis beginning 3/15. Federal Work-Study Program available. Institutional employment available.

BOTTOM LINE

In-state residents get a steal of a sticker price with $7,488 in tuition and fees, while non-residents pay $11,880. Room and board is another $16,735. The school anticipates books, supplies, transportation, and other expenses will add another $4,900 or so onto the price.

CAREER INFORMATION FROM PAYSCALE.COM

ROI Rating	89
Bachelors and No Higher	
Median starting salary	$53,400
Median mid-career salary	$102,900
At Least Bachelors	
Median starting salary	$54,200
Median mid-career salary	$104,900
Alumni with high job meaning	52%
Degrees awarded in STEM subjects	16%

SELECTIVITY

Admissions Rating	**90**
# of applicants	60,697
% of applicants accepted	35
% of acceptees attending	25
# offered a place on the wait list	3,279
% accepting a place on wait list	50
% admitted from wait list	1

FRESHMAN PROFILE

Range SAT EBRW	550–640
Range SAT Math	540–650
Range ACT Composite	23–28
Minimum paper TOEFL	550
Minimum internet-based TOEFL	80
Average HS GPA	3.7
% graduated top 10% of class	31
% graduated top 25% of class	70
% graduated top 50% of class	95

DEADLINES

Regular	
Deadline	11/30
Notification	March
Nonfall registration?	No

FINANCIAL FACTS

Financial Aid Rating	**82**
Annual in-state tuition	$5,742
Annual out-of-state tuition	$17,622
Room and board	$16,735
Required fees	$1,746
Books and supplies	$1,915
Average frosh need-based scholarship	$9,500
Average UG need-based scholarship	$9,500
% needy frosh rec. need-based scholarship or grant aid	60
% needy UG rec. need-based scholarship or grant aid	72
% needy frosh rec. non-need-based scholarship or grant aid	48
% needy UG rec. non-need-based scholarship or grant aid	34
% needy frosh rec. need-based self-help aid	92
% needy UG rec. need-based self-help aid	94
% frosh rec. any financial aid	55
% UG rec. any financial aid	63
% UG borrow to pay for school	47
Average cumulative indebtedness	$19,633
% frosh need fully met	8
% ugrads need fully met	19
Average % of frosh need met	65
Average % of ugrad need met	67

Santa Clara University

500 El Camino Real, Santa Clara, CA 95053 • Admissions: 408-554-4700 • Fax: 408-554-5255

CAMPUS LIFE

Quality of Life Rating	**91**
Fire Safety Rating	**95**
Green Rating	**98**
Type of school	Private
Affiliation	Roman Catholic
Environment	City

STUDENTS

Total undergrad enrollment	5,481
% male/female	50/50
% from out of state	29
% frosh from public high school	46
% frosh live on campus	96
% ugrads live on campus	56
# of fraternities (% ugrad men join)	0 (0)
# of sororities (% ugrad women join)	0 (0)
% African American	3
% Asian	16
% Caucasian	50
% Hispanic	18
% Native American	<1
% Pacific Islander	<1
% Two or more races	7
% Race and/or ethnicity unknown	2
% international	4
# of countries represented	37

ACADEMICS

Academic Rating	**90**
% students returning for sophomore year	94
% students graduating within 4 years	85
% students graduating within 6 years	90
Calendar	Differs By Program
Student/faculty ratio	11:1
Profs interesting rating	86
Profs accessible rating	92

Most classes have 10–19 students. Most lab/discussion sessions have 10–19 students.

MOST POPULAR MAJORS
Speech and Communication; Finance; Psychology

ABOUT THE SCHOOL

Santa Clara University is a mid-sized Jesuit University that offers undergraduate and graduate degrees through six different colleges on a beautiful campus in Silicon Valley. Though Jesuit philosophy and spirituality are central to the school's identity, students hail from many different backgrounds and "other than occasionally seeing a Jesuit walking around campus, you can make it four years without any contact with religion" if that is your preference. Rather, the emphasis is firmly on academic excellence, and Santa Clara has received many accolades in undergraduate education. Fifty-two undergraduate majors are offered through the schools of Arts and Sciences, Engineering, and Business. The University offers abundant opportunities for undergraduate research, and a third of students take advantage of study abroad programs in more than fifty countries. 74 percent of classes contain under thirty students, and though some professors "don't connect to students" the majority "invest their out of class time to help students achieve their academic and personal development goals." "I have been able to form personal relationships with all of my professors if I make the effort," so if "you are willing to put in work, your professor is likely to be willing to work as hard as you towards your success."

BANG FOR YOUR BUCK

Santa Clara offers many opportunities for Federal or State aid via well-known programs like the Pell Grant as well as many grants and scholarships from the University. Its prestigious Johnson Scholars Program offers full tuition, room, and board, along with a number of specialized academic opportunities, to a small selection of top-tier applicants for four years. The University's other top award is the Presidential at Entry Scholarship, which also offers full tuition to outstanding applicants and is likewise renewable for four years. Several smaller awards, both need and merit based, are offered through the University or through specific departments such as Music, Theater and Dance, or Military Science. In addition to scholarships students can qualify for loans and Federal Work Study, and opportunities for student employment are available through the Career Center. About seventy-three percent of students at Santa Clara receive some manner of financial aid.

STUDENT LIFE

Due to its location in sunny California and an appealing outdoor campus, "the social scene really takes life when the weather is nice." "It's not uncommon to see kids sitting outside the cafeteria or the library doing homework on any given day," and during less studious moments "going to school in California means lots of day-parties, lots of time spent tanning on the lawn." Santa Clara has a fairly robust party scene on and off campus, "but no more or less than I think you'd find at a school of comparable size." The school has a top-tier athletic program and many activities are available through the University: "the typical student is very active on campus in all sorts of clubs and groups, and usually works out at least once a week." A special feature of life at the school is the beautiful regional geography, and students with access to a car can enjoy "so many incredible things, just distant from school: hiking in the Santa Cruz mountains, the Santa Cruz beach, travelling to Lick Observatory, exploring Marin County, and of course, skiing at Tahoe!" Trips to nearby San Francisco on the weekends are also common. So while Santa Clara offers a great deal on campus, one of the best features of student life may be the fun of getting away.

Santa Clara University

FINANCIAL AID: 408-554-4505 • E-MAIL: ADMISSION@SCU.EDU • WEBSITE: WWW.SCU.EDU

CAREER

Santa Clara University has an "exceptionally helpful" Career Center which offers counseling, networking opportunities, and professional development services from traditional resume building to how to craft a great LinkedIn profile. Praise for career services is widespread, with many students citing it as one of the school's strengths. "The University has a phenomenal career center that was able to find me a top notch internship" and "they have so many connections [that] there is no reason why anyone should not have a job or internship because of all the resources they provide." Outside of the Career Center, students praise an environment where "my professors all have access to the type of resources that will help us further our careers" and the Business and Engineering schools are particularly known for "placing graduates at top firms throughout the valley."

GENERAL INFO

Activities: Choral groups, dance, drama/theater, jazz band, literary magazine, music ensembles, musical theater, opera, pep band, radio station, student government, student newspaper, symphony orchestra, yearbook, campus ministries, International Student Organization, Model UN. **Organizations:** 134 registered organizations, 27 honor societies, 15 religious organizations. **Athletics (Intercollegiate):** *Men:* baseball, basketball, crew/rowing, cross-country, golf, soccer, tennis, track/field (outdoor), water polo. *Women:* basketball, crew/rowing, cross-country, golf, soccer, softball, tennis, track/field (outdoor), volleyball, water polo.

FINANCIAL AID

Students should submit: CSS Profile; FAFSA. Priority filing deadline is 2/1. The Princeton Review suggests that all financial aid forms be submitted as soon as possible after October 1. *Need-based scholarships/grants offered:* College/university scholarship or grant aid from institutional funds, Federal Pell, private scholarships, SEOG, state scholarships/grants. *Loan aid offered:* Direct PLUS Loans, Direct Subsidized Loans, Direct Unsubsidized Loans, Private credit-based loans. Applicants will be notified of awards on or about 4/1. Federal Work-Study Program available. Institutional employment available.

BOTTOM LINE

Tuition and fees for a year at Santa Clara University are listed at $51,081, with room and board totaling $14,910. Combined with books, supplies, and expenses, students can expect to spend approximately $68,000 per year to attend Santa Clara. That's not cheap, and while some students describe their peers as largely "upper middle class," others refer to students "who are on almost complete full scholarship and financial aid." The average need-based award package for all undergraduates is around $28,976 in scholarships or grants and $4,563 in loans, and for students who land one of the school's substantial merit scholarships the deal is even sweeter.

CAREER INFORMATION FROM PAYSCALE.COM	
ROI Rating	91
Bachelors and No Higher	
Median starting salary	$66,800
Median mid-career salary	$139,100
At Least Bachelors	
Median starting salary	$68,300
Median mid-career salary	$143,100
Alumni with high job meaning	44%
Degrees awarded in STEM subjects	29%

SELECTIVITY	
Admissions Rating	91
# of applicants	15,061
% of applicants accepted	54
% of acceptees attending	17
# offered a place on the wait list	2,397
% accepting a place on wait list	62
% admitted from wait list	3
# of early decision applicants	305
% accepted early decision	74

FRESHMAN PROFILE	
Range SAT EBRW	630–710
Range SAT Math	640–730
Range ACT Composite	28–32
Minimum paper TOEFL	575
Minimum internet-based TOEFL	90
Average HS GPA	3.7
% graduated top 10% of class	57
% graduated top 25% of class	87
% graduated top 50% of class	99

DEADLINES	
Early decision	
Deadline	11/1
Notification	Late December
Early action	
Deadline	11/1
Regular	
Deadline	1/7
Notification	Late March
Nonfall registration?	No

FINANCIAL FACTS	
Financial Aid Rating	84
Annual tuition	$51,081
Room and board	$14,910
Required fees	$630
Books and supplies	$1,917
Average frosh need-based scholarship	$30,051
Average UG need-based scholarship	$28,976
% needy frosh rec. need-based scholarship or grant aid	86
% needy UG rec. need-based scholarship or grant aid	73
% needy frosh rec. non-need-based scholarship or grant aid	48
% needy UG rec. non-need-based scholarship or grant aid	35
% needy frosh rec. need-based self-help aid	51
% needy UG rec. need-based self-help aid	43
% frosh rec. any financial aid	75
% UG rec. any financial aid	71
% UG borrow to pay for school	42
Average cumulative indebtedness	$28,808
% frosh need fully met	42

Scripps College

1030 COLUMBIA AVENUE, CLAREMONT, CA 91711 • ADMISSIONS: 909-621-8149 • FAX: 909-607-7508

CAMPUS LIFE

Quality of Life Rating	96
Fire Safety Rating	79
Green Rating	79
Type of school	Private
Environment	Town

STUDENTS

Total undergrad enrollment	1,059
% male/female	0/100
% from out of state	51
% frosh live on campus	100
% ugrads live on campus	100
# of fraternities (% ugrad men join)	0 (0)
# of sororities (% ugrad women join)	0 (0)
% African American	4
% Asian	16
% Caucasian	53
% Hispanic	13
% Native American	0
% Pacific Islander	<1
% Two or more races	4
% Race and/or ethnicity unknown	4
% international	5

ACADEMICS

Academic Rating	97
% students returning for sophomore year	92
% students graduating within 4 years	83
% students graduating within 6 years	88
Calendar	Semester
Student/faculty ratio	10:1
Profs interesting rating	95
Profs accessible rating	97

Most classes have 10–19 students. Most lab/discussion sessions have fewer than 10 students.

MOST POPULAR MAJORS

Biology/Biological Sciences; Psychology; Economics

ABOUT THE SCHOOL

Scripps College in California is a women's college where interdisciplinary thinking is a priority and classes are purposefully small. As a member of The Claremont Colleges, which includes seven institutions, five undergraduate and two graduate, Scripps offers its 1,059 students a diverse co-ed community and students may cross-register for courses and use facilities at the other schools. Students find this system "very beneficial because it offers opportunities and resources that a small school would not otherwise have access to, and makes for interesting class discussions with people from very diverse academic backgrounds." A Scripps education begins with the Core Curriculum, a three-semester, interdisciplinary track where students gain new perspectives on complex issues facing the world today. Students say they appreciate how the core program "strengthens your understanding of Western thought in ways you'd never imagined." Students say their professors, who are accomplished scholars and researchers, are always accessible and consistently excellent. Every student also completes a thesis or senior project prior to graduation.

BANG FOR YOUR BUCK

Scripps College meets 100 percent of an eligible student's demonstrated financial need for all four years with the combination of grants, scholarships, part-time employment, and loans. Additionally, all applicants are considered for merit-based scholarships ranging from $15,000 to $27,000 annually. No separate application is required in order to be considered for these merit awards. A biology major says that she chose Scripps College "because of the fantastic merit scholarships. Not only did they defray the expense of attending a private college, but they convinced me I could be a big fish in a small pond here."

STUDENT LIFE

Prospective students interested in Scripps will be delighted to discover that there's rarely a dull moment on this campus in the picturesque town of Claremont, just 35 miles from Los Angeles. As one knowing senior shares, "There are so many activities to become involved in. Whether you're interested in feminist issues, journalism, baking, sports or music, Scripps has a place for you to belong." When it comes to simply kicking back, "Scripps women love sunning on the lawn or at the pool...[and] they also love grabbing a cup of coffee at our amazing student run and eco-friendly coffee shop, the Motley!" Students also attend events at the "surrounding schools in the [Claremont Colleges ...including] 'art after hours' and 'Thursday Night Club' on Thursdays." And, as another senior boasts, "there are many off campus activities like trips to LA, rock climbing, and skiing...You can be on the slopes and at the beach on the same day! How do you beat that?"

CAREER

Scripps alumnae find success in a variety of paths post-graduation. Eighty-six percent of graduates have held at least one internship, with nearly 40 percent holding three or more. In fact, over 50 percent of seniors who intend to work full-time after graduation had secured at least one job offer prior to graduation. Recent graduates have landed positions with companies such as the Congressional Budget Office, National Museum of African American History and Culture, 21st Century Fox, Facebook, Ernst & Young, Los Angeles County

Scripps College

FINANCIAL AID: : 909-621-8275 • E-MAIL: ADMISSION@SCRIPPSCOLLEGE.EDU • WEBSITE: WWW.SCRIPPSCOLLEGE.EDU

Museum of Art, Nextdoor, National Institute of Health and Morgan Stanley. Between 12–15 percent of alumnae go straight to graduate school, with 67 percent having enrolled or completed a graduate degree within five years. Scripps alums have enrolled in institutions such as Brown University, the Courtauld Institute of Art, George Washington University School of Medicine, University of California, Berkeley, UCLA, University of Chicago, Cornell University, and Yale. Other resources unique to Scripps include a personalized freshman orientation to the Career Planning & Resources office and an online Resume Book for seniors embarking on their job hunts. Scripps graduates regularly receive prestigious fellowships and grants like the Fulbright and Watson Fellowship to continue their studies/research.

GENERAL INFO

Activities: Choral groups, dance, drama/theater, literary magazine, music ensembles, radio station, student government, student newspaper, symphony orchestra, yearbook, campus ministries, international student organization. **Organizations:** 200 registered organizations, 7 honor societies, 7 religious organizations. **Athletics (Intercollegiate):** *Women:* Basketball, cross-country, diving, golf, lacrosse, soccer, softball, swimming, tennis, track/field, volleyball, water polo. **On-Campus Highlights:** Williamson Gallery, Motley Coffee House, Denison Library, Margaret Fowler Garden, Malott Commons, Graffiti Wall, Sallie Tiernan Field House.

FINANCIAL AID

Students should submit: FAFSA, CSS Profile. Business/Farm Supplement, if applicable; CAL Dream Act Application, if applicable. Priority filing deadline is 11/15 for Early Decision I, and 2/1 for Early Decision II and Regular Decision. The Princeton Review suggests that all financial aid forms be submitted as soon as possible after October 1. *Need-based scholarships/grants offered:* College/university scholarship or grant aid from institutional funds, Federal Pell, private scholarships, SEOG, state scholarships/grants. *Loan aid offered:* Direct PLUS Loans, Direct Subsidized Loans, Direct Unsubsidized Loans. Applicants who meet filing deadlines will be notified with their admission decision. Federal Work-Study Program available.

BOTTOM LINE

The retail price for tuition, room and board, and fees at Scripps is around $69,260 a year. Financial aid is superabundant here; please don't let the cost keep you from applying. Also worth noting: the average total need-based indebtedness for Scripps graduates is $20,205—well below the national average at private colleges and universities.

CAREER INFORMATION FROM PAYSCALE.COM	
ROI Rating	89
Bachelors and No Higher	
Median starting salary	$53,700
Median mid-career salary	$95,600
At Least Bachelors	
Median starting salary	$55,000
Median mid-career salary	$98,000
Alumni with high job meaning	49%
Degrees awarded in STEM subjects	28%

SELECTIVITY	
Admissions Rating	96
# of applicants	2,841
% of applicants accepted	33
% of acceptees attending	34
# offered a place on the wait list	495
% accepting a place on wait list	48
% admitted from wait list	<1
# of early decision applicants	292
% accepted early decision	39

FRESHMAN PROFILE	
Range SAT EBRW	660–730
Range SAT Math	630–730
Range ACT Composite	29–33
Minimum paper TOEFL	600
Minimum internet-based TOEFL	100
Average HS GPA	4.1
% graduated top 10% of class	73
% graduated top 25% of class	94
% graduated top 50% of class	98

DEADLINES	
Early decision	
Deadline	11/15
Notification	Mid Dec
Other ED Deadline	1/4
Other ED Notification	Mid Feb
Regular	
Deadline	1/4
Notification	4/1
Nonfall registration?	No

FINANCIAL FACTS	
Financial Aid Rating	95
Annual tuition	$54,806
Room and board	$16,932
Required fees	$218
Books and supplies	$800
Average frosh need-based scholarship	$38,332
Average UG need-based scholarship	$37,532
% needy frosh rec. need-based scholarship or grant aid	100
% needy UG rec. need-based scholarship or grant aid	100
% needy frosh rec. non-need-based scholarship or grant aid	0
% needy UG rec. non-need-based scholarship or grant aid	0
% needy frosh rec. need-based self-help aid	30
% needy UG rec. need-based self-help aid	33
% UG borrow to pay for school	41
Average cumulative indebtedness	$19,639
% frosh need fully met	100
% ugrads need fully met	100
Average % of frosh need met	100

Skidmore College

815 NORTH BROADWAY, SARATOGA SPRINGS, NY 12866-1632 • ADMISSIONS: 518-580-5570 • FAX: 518-580-5584

CAMPUS LIFE

Quality of Life Rating	**96**
Fire Safety Rating	**98**
Green Rating	**94**
Type of school	Private
Environment	Town

STUDENTS

Total undergrad enrollment	2,659
% male/female	40/60
% from out of state	66
% frosh from public high school	57
% frosh live on campus	100
% ugrads live on campus	89
# of fraternities (% ugrad men join)	0 (0)
# of sororities (% ugrad women join)	0 (0)
% African American	5
% Asian	5
% Caucasian	63
% Hispanic	9
% Native American	0
% Pacific Islander	0
% Two or more races	4
% Race and/or ethnicity unknown	3
% international	11
# of countries represented	61

ACADEMICS

Academic Rating	**94**
% students returning for sophomore year	93
% students graduating within 4 years	84
% students graduating within 6 years	87
Calendar	Semester
Student/faculty ratio	8:1
Profs interesting rating	92
Profs accessible rating	94

Most classes have 10–19 students. Most lab/discussion sessions have 10–19 students.

MOST POPULAR MAJORS
Psychology; Social Sciences; Fine Arts

ABOUT THE SCHOOL

Set on a pristine 890-acre campus in Saratoga Springs, New York, this prestigious liberal arts hamlet is celebrated for its creative arts, student-centered learning, low student/faculty ratio, and multidisciplinary academic approach. Skidmore's strong majors in the liberal arts and sciences are complemented by an "excellent and intimate" theater program, as well as strong programs in art, music, and dance. Faculty here are "accessible, interested and most importantly—student-centered." Students at Skidmore are well aware that they are attending a "first-rate academic institution," and tell us that the learning atmosphere on campus fosters a "relaxed intensity." The library "is packed on weeknights" and "many people would be surprised to find how often a Skidmore student is cramming his or her weekend with serious studying." The low student-to-teacher ratio offers "smaller class sizes for more personalized and individual attention." Beyond the caliber of its academics, Skidmore is "the perfect size in the perfect town." The surrounding city of Saratoga Springs is "beautiful and vibrant."

BANG FOR YOUR BUCK

From the moment students step onto campus freshman year, they are embraced by the school's commitment to student-centered learning and community involvement. The journey begins with Skidmore's First-Year Experience, which places students from each seminar in close proximity to one another in the residence halls, where they can cohabitate intellectually and creatively with their peers while establishing lasting relationships with close faculty mentors. Skidmore is one of few liberal arts colleges to offer majors in preprofessional disciplines, including business, education, exercise science, and social work. In fact, business consistently ranks as a popular major alongside English and psychology. Always ready to extend learning beyond the classroom, more than 60 percent of students study abroad at some point. Many Skidmore students complete a culminating project in their major—68 percent complete senior capstones, 52 percent complete independent studies, and 27 percent complete theses or advanced research projects. In addition, the Career Development Center provides one-on-one career counseling for life, including pre-health, pre-law, and graduate school preparation advising. Twenty-nine percent of students do an internship for academic credit, and the school's network boasts approximately 80 funded internships and more than 2,200 alumni mentors, which extends Skidmore's community well beyond graduation.

STUDENT LIFE

"I love life at Skidmore," says one sociology major. "There is no excuse to be bored because something is [always] going on. If you're not into the [party] scene, student clubs always have events going on during the weekend." The fairly small student body—roughly 2,500 students—makes for a close community feeling, particularly with 89 percent of undergraduates living on campus. There are 110 registered student organizations on campus and no Greek life presence at the school. Performances, particularly by visiting musicians and DJs, are a "big thing" at Skidmore, especially near the "end of the semester [when] a typical weekend night would be a performance and then the after party." One History and Theater major notes that "Skidmore students are very involved in the Saratoga community through everything from sustainability efforts to mentoring local children." The town of Saratoga Springs can be "a great town" with "amazing food options."

CAREER

According to PayScale.com, the average starting salary for a Skidmore graduate is roughly $51,200. Popular jobs and majors include research associate, financial analyst, graphic designer, software engineer, and marketing manager, and business, English and psychology, respectively.

Skidmore College

FINANCIAL AID: 518-580-5750 • E-MAIL: ADMISSIONS@SKIDMORE.EDU • WEBSITE: WWW.SKIDMORE.EDU

Thirty-five percent of Skidmore graduates consider their careers to be instrumental in helping improve the world. According to the school's website, Skidmore's "Career Development Center helps students develop a holistic view of their career development plan, offering programs and services for students in each year to foster enhanced self-awareness, exposure to a variety of career fields, participation in off-campus experiential activities, [and] effective career decision-making." A Summer Funded Internship program provides grants to students interning locally, nationally, or abroad. Another unique feature on the school's website is the "What Can I Do With This Major?" section, where students can "learn about the typical career areas and the types of employers that hire people with each major, as well as strategies to make [them] more marketable candidate[s]."

GENERAL INFO

Activities: Admissions ambassador, campus committees, chorus, collaborative faculty-student research, community garden, community service, dance, drama/theater, student-run EMS program, jazz ensemble, literary and art magazines, music ensembles (guitar, vocal, concert band, small jazz, chamber), peer mentor, peer tutor, radio station, residential life, student government, student newspaper, orchestra, television station, yoga. **Athletics (Intercollegiate):** *Men:* baseball, basketball, rowing, golf, ice hockey, lacrosse, soccer, swimming and diving, tennis. *Women:* basketball, rowing, riding, field hockey, lacrosse, soccer, softball, swimming and diving, tennis, volleyball.

FINANCIAL AID

Students should submit: CSS Profile. Regular filing deadline is 2/1. The Princeton Review suggests that all financial aid forms be submitted as soon as possible after October 1. *Need-based scholarships/grants offered:* College/university scholarship or grant aid from institutional funds, Federal Pell, private scholarships, SEOG, state scholarships/grants. *Loan aid offered:* Direct PLUS Loans, Direct Subsidized Loans, Direct Unsubsidized Loans. Applicants will be notified of awards on or about 4/1. Federal Work-Study Program available. Institutional employment available.

BOTTOM LINE

With a price tag in line with other prestigious liberal arts colleges, Skidmore culls an annual tuition of $53,258, and students can expect to spend an additional $14,494 on room and board. However, with 100 percent of needy incoming freshmen receiving either need-based scholarship or grant aid, the school recognizes the significance of a hefty academic price tag for many and works hard to make sure all eligible students find their needs met. Thirty-nine percent of undergraduates borrow to finance their education. Upon graduation, the average Skidmore student can expect to shoulder about $23,916 of debt.

CAREER INFORMATION FROM PAYSCALE.COM

ROI Rating	89
Bachelors and No Higher	
Median starting salary	$52,700
Median mid-career salary	$99,400
At Least Bachelors	
Median starting salary	$53,500
Median mid-career salary	$103,700
Alumni with high job meaning	39%
Degrees awarded in STEM subjects	22%

SELECTIVITY

Admissions Rating	94
# of applicants	10,053
% of applicants accepted	25
% of acceptees attending	27
# offered a place on the wait list	2,300
% accepting a place on wait list	20
% admitted from wait list	13
# of early decision applicants	629
% accepted early decision	55

FRESHMAN PROFILE

Range SAT EBRW	610–700
Range SAT Math	595–700
Range ACT Composite	27–31
Minimum paper TOEFL	590
Minimum internet-based TOEFL	96-97
% graduated top 10% of class	29
% graduated top 25% of class	73
% graduated top 50% of class	92

DEADLINES

Early decision	
Deadline	11/15
Notification	12/15
Other ED Deadline	1/15
Other ED Notification	2/15
Regular	
Deadline	1/15
Notification	4/1
Nonfall registration?	No

FINANCIAL FACTS

Financial Aid Rating	96
Annual tuition	$53,258
Room and board	$14,494
Required fees	$1,012
Average frosh need-based scholarship	$45,900
Average UG need-based scholarship	$44,600
% needy frosh rec. need-based scholarship or grant aid	100
% needy UG rec. need-based scholarship or grant aid	100
% needy frosh rec. non-need-based scholarship or grant aid	4
% needy UG rec. non-need-based scholarship or grant aid	4
% needy frosh rec. need-based self-help aid	78
% needy UG rec. need-based self-help aid	79
% frosh rec. any financial aid	56
% UG rec. any financial aid	50
% UG borrow to pay for school	39
Average cumulative indebtedness	$23,916
% frosh need fully met	100
% ugrads need fully met	94
Average % of frosh need met	100

Smith College

Seven College Lane, Northampton, MA 01063 • Admissions: 413-585-2500 • Fax: 413-585-2527

CAMPUS LIFE

Quality of Life Rating	**92**
Fire Safety Rating	**84**
Green Rating	**97**
Type of school	Private
Environment	Town

STUDENTS

Total undergrad enrollment	2,521
% male/female	0/100
% from out of state	79
% frosh from public high school	62
% frosh live on campus	100
% ugrads live on campus	95
# of fraternities (% ugrad men join)	0 (0)
# of sororities (% ugrad women join)	0 (0)
% African American	7
% Asian	11
% Caucasian	48
% Hispanic	10
% Native American	<1
% Pacific Islander	<1
% Two or more races	4
% Race and/or ethnicity unknown	6
% international	14
# of countries represented	68

ACADEMICS

Academic Rating	**89**
% students returning for sophomore year	93
% students graduating within 4 years	82
% students graduating within 6 years	88
Calendar	Semester
Student/faculty ratio	9:1
Profs interesting rating	89
Profs accessible rating	86

MOST POPULAR MAJORS
Psychology; Economics; Government

ABOUT THE SCHOOL

Located in western Massachusetts in the idyllic college town of Northampton, Smith College boasts "extremely challenging academics" in a setting where "women come first." Along with the school's "global and interdisciplinary focus," women at Smith enjoy an "excellent academic atmosphere, close-knit community, small class size, top-notch professors, [and] fantastic resources" in a "beautiful New England" setting. Smith's "open curriculum" "doesn't have course requirements," and the school boasts "lots of unique traditions that make it enjoyable." Smith professors are "strikingly committed to their students." Students routinely attend "class dinners with professors," where mentors "volunteer to read drafts, and help with research." As one student attests, "not only that, but [professors] always get excited when you visit office hours—the one-on-one is not only available here, but encouraged." Another incoming freshman recalls, "Walking onto Smith College campus was like a breath of fresh air. The old brick buildings (mixed in with the newer ones), the gorgeous campus (designed by Fredrick Law Olmsted), and atmosphere pulled me in. The academics were superb and the people welcoming." In a nutshell, this highly prestigious women's college is "all about being socially aware and making a positive impact in the environment, economy, politics, and everyday life."

BANG FOR YOUR BUCK

One of the cornerstones of a Smith education is the ability to design your own academic experience within a plethora of curricular opportunities. Students here are routinely engaged in one-on-one research as undergraduates, with professors in the arts, humanities, sciences, and social sciences. There are no required courses outside of the freshman year writing-intensive seminar. In addition, students have the added benefit of the larger academic community of the Five Colleges Consortium, which includes Amherst, Hampshire, Mount Holyoke, and the University of Massachusetts Amherst. Smith has the largest and oldest women-only ABET-accredited Engineering program in the country, and more than 43 percent of Smithies major in the hardcore sciences. Praxis, Smith's unique internship program, guarantees all students access to at least one college-funded internship during their four years at the college.

STUDENT LIFE

Undergrads at Smith certainly cultivate full and varied lives. Of course, it helps that "a range of social activities" abound. The student government continually sponsors a number of events "like movie showings, outdoor activities [and] bowling nights." As you might expect, these ladies are also incredibly politically savvy. Hence, there's also "a lot of involvement in community service and activism for global issues, women's rights, LGBTQ rights, the environment, and pretty much anything that fights oppression." Further, during the weekend "there are always house parties on campus and students can go to other college parties at surrounding campuses." Additionally, "downtown Northampton [is] always bustling with events. Indeed, "there are...concerts, restaurants, and cute shops...to provide us with distractions."

CAREER

Hands down, "Smith provides so many opportunities for [undergrads]!" Indeed, from "on-campus resources to internship and job opportunities—Smith gives students the means to thrive in the world." To begin with, it's definitely not uncommon for professors to "[go] out of their way to help [students] find contacts and resources for jobs." What's more, according to a grateful American

Smith College

FINANCIAL AID: 413-585-2530 • E-MAIL: ADMISSION@SMITH.EDU • WEBSITE: WWW.SMITH.EDU

studies major, "The Career Development Office will do everything in its power to help you get a job/internship." With its myriad of workshops, Preparing for Finance Interviews or Marketing Your Study Abroad Experience for example, Smith students can confidently enter the job market. They can visit the office to get assistance in tweaking their resumes and cover letters or to gain insight in the grad school admissions process. And they may definitely take advantage of the career fairs the college hosts. Organizations in attendance have included the Peace Corps, Bloomingdale's, Verizon Wireless and Teach for America.

GENERAL INFO

Activities: Choral groups, concert band, dance, drama/theater, jazz band, literary magazine, music ensembles, musical theater, radio station, student government, student newspaper, television station, yearbook, International Student Organization, Model UN. **Organizations:** 141 registered organizations, 3 honor societies, 17 religious organizations. **Athletics (Intercollegiate):** *Women:* basketball, crew/rowing, cross-country, diving, field hockey, lacrosse, soccer, softball, swimming, tennis, track/field (outdoor), track/field (indoor), volleyball. **On-Campus Highlights:** Smith Art Museum, The Botanic Garden, Campus Center, Mendenhall Center for Performing Arts, Lyman Plant House.

FINANCIAL AID

Students should submit: CSS Profile, FAFSA; Institution's own financial aid form. Regular filing deadline is 1/15. The Princeton Review suggests that all financial aid forms be submitted as soon as possible after October 1. *Need-based scholarships/grants offered:* College/university scholarship or grant aid from institutional funds, Federal Pell, private scholarships, SEOG, state scholarships/grants. *Loan aid offered:* Direct PLUS Loans, Direct Subsidized Loans, Direct Unsubsidized Loans. Applicants will be notified of awards on or about 4/1. Federal Work-Study Program available. Institutional employment available.

BOTTOM LINE

Smith makes no bones about its commitment to finding inroads to making a serious private education available to women of all stripes, no matter their financial background. Though the cost of education here doesn't come at a discount—annual tuition is currently $52,120, with room and board tallying an additional $17,520—according to our recent statistics, over the past several years Smith has boasted a 100 percent success rate when it comes to meeting not just freshman financial need but financial need across all four years. The average student indebtedness after four years totals $24,501, with 62 percent of undergraduates receiving some form of need-based financial aid.

CAREER INFORMATION FROM PAYSCALE.COM	
ROI Rating	90
Bachelors and No Higher	
Median starting salary	$51,100
Median mid-career salary	$100,900
At Least Bachelors	
Median starting salary	$52,600
Median mid-career salary	$108,900
Alumni with high job meaning	49%
Degrees awarded in STEM subjects	26%

SELECTIVITY	
Admissions Rating	97
# of applicants	5,432
% of applicants accepted	32
% of acceptees attending	37
# offered a place on the wait list	931
% accepting a place on wait list	51
% admitted from wait list	4
# of early decision applicants	538
% accepted early decision	54

FRESHMAN PROFILE	
Range SAT EBRW	650–740
Range SAT Math	640–750
Range ACT Composite	30–33
Minimum paper TOEFL	600
Minimum internet-based TOEFL	90
Average HS GPA	3.8
% graduated top 10% of class	72
% graduated top 25% of class	96
% graduated top 50% of class	100

DEADLINES	
Early decision	
Deadline	11/15
Notification	12/15
Other ED Deadline	1/1
Other ED Notification	late Jan.
Regular	
Deadline	1/15
Notification	late March
Nonfall registration?	No

FINANCIAL FACTS	
Financial Aid Rating	95
Annual tuition	$52,120
Room and board	$17,520
Required fees	$284
Books and supplies	$800
Average frosh need-based scholarship	$48,185
Average UG need-based scholarship	$45,819
% needy frosh rec. need-based scholarship or grant aid	99
% needy UG rec. need-based scholarship or grant aid	98
% needy frosh rec. non-need-based scholarship or grant aid	5
% needy UG rec. non-need-based scholarship or grant aid	2
% needy frosh rec. need-based self-help aid	93
% needy UG rec. need-based self-help aid	94
% frosh rec. any financial aid	73
% UG rec. any financial aid	72
% UG borrow to pay for school	58
Average cumulative indebtedness	$24,501
% frosh need fully met	100

Southwestern University

OFFICE OF ADMISSION, GEORGETOWN, TX 78627-0770 • OFFICE OF ADMISSION: 512-863-1200 • FAX: 512-863-9601

CAMPUS LIFE

Quality of Life Rating	**91**
Fire Safety Rating	**96**
Green Rating	**88**
Type of school	Private
Affiliation	Methodist
Environment	Town

STUDENTS

Total undergrad enrollment	1,387
% male/female	43/57
% from out of state	10
% frosh from public high school	79
% frosh live on campus	99
% ugrads live on campus	77
# of fraternities (% ugrad men join)	4 (28)
# of sororities (% ugrad women join)	4 (23)
% African American	5
% Asian	3
% Caucasian	60
% Hispanic	24
% Native American	<1
% Pacific Islander	<1
% Two or more races	5
% Race and/or ethnicity unknown	1
% international	1
# of countries represented	12

ACADEMICS

Academic Rating	**90**
% students returning for sophomore year	86
% students graduating within 4 years	67
% students graduating within 6 years	74
Calendar	Semester
Student/faculty ratio	11:1
Profs interesting rating	94
Profs accessible rating	94

Most classes have 10–19 students. Most lab/discussion sessions have 10–19 students.

MOST POPULAR MAJORS
Speech Communication and Rhetoric; Psychology; Business/Commerce

ABOUT THE SCHOOL

Located in Georgetown, Texas, just thirty miles from Austin, Southwestern University is a liberal arts college for people who "like to be challenged and have fun at the same time." Students here say they receive a "well-rounded education" that allows them to "build… connections between different disciplines." And they are taught how to "think [both] creatively and critically." Many students said they were attracted to Southwestern due to its "low professor-to-student ratio"—currently 11:1—which fosters "relationship[s] with faculty" and leads to "many research opportunities." Undergrads report that their "professors are extremely invested in student success," and "they really emphasize student learning and [encourage them to] ask…questions." While SU professors certainly make their classes "challenging," they are also exceedingly "approachable." Additionally, the clear majority "share the course material with passion and [offer] interesting perspectives…that allow for better retention." Finally, as this grateful undergrad concludes, "The professors have absolutely made the difference in my time here."

BANG FOR YOUR BUCK

Undergrads are quick to note that "Southwestern gives excellent financial aid." As one student shares, "I know a lot of people who thought they wouldn't be able to attend because of the cost, but [the administration] worked with [them] to ensure their attendance." The university strives to offer comprehensive aid packages replete with both need-based and merit-based aid. And all admitted students are automatically considered for scholarships. These include the Cody Scholarship, which provides $27,000 annually; the Mood Scholarship. which provides $25,000 annually; and the Ruter Scholarship, which provides $23,500/annually. Southwestern's most competitive scholarship is perhaps the Brown Scholar Award. This award amount starts at $33,000 per year. Recipients must rank in the top 5 percent of their graduating class, have a 3.8 GPA and SAT/ACT minimum score of 1400 and 31 respectively. An interview will also be required.

SCHOOL LIFE

There's plenty of fun to be had at Southwestern. To begin with, undergrads highlight the school's robust Greek life noting that it's "very prevalent…and is sort of the social heart of the campus." Southwestern "offers lots of other activities for students who are not involved with Greek Life," as "there are a multitude of clubs and organizations to join." We're told that "people like to participate in recreational activities around campus like sand volleyball, ping pong, and pool." Every weekend there are numerous entertainment options like "Friday Night Live and Cinematic Saturday," which include events with music acts, comedians, or magicians. It's common for students to spend time in Austin "due to the [city's close] proximity" to campus.

Southwestern University

FINANCIAL AID: 512-863-1259 • E-MAIL: ADMISSION@SOUTHWESTERN.EDU • WEBSITE: WWW.SOUTHWESTERN.EDU

CAREER

Many students say that Southwestern's "stellar career services program" helps to distinguish the school. They can turn to the Office of Career Services for help "creat[ing] resumes, apply[ing] to grad school and find[ing] the perfect career." SU students frequently attend the myriad of events career services sponsors throughout the year. These offerings consist of everything from GRE strategy sessions and pre-med previews to cover letter writing workshops and industry-specific panels. The office even holds photo shoots for undergrads to get the perfect professional picture for their LinkedIn account. Best of all, SU hosts multiple career fairs which enables students to network with a wide variety of employers.

GENERAL INFO

Activities: Choral groups, concert band, dance, drama/theatre, jazz band, literary magazine, music ensembles, musical theater, student government, student newspaper, radio. **Organizations:** 99 registered organizations, 17 honor societies, 9 religious organizations. 4 fraternities, 4 sororities. **Athletics (Intercollegiate):** *Men:* baseball, basketball, cross-country, diving, football, golf, lacrosse, soccer, swimming, tennis, track/field (outdoor). *Women:* basketball, cross-country, diving, golf, lacrosse, soccer, softball, swimming, tennis, track/field (outdoor), volleyball. **On-Campus Highlights:** Robertson Center—indoor Olympic size pool, McCombs Center—Student Center, Fountainwood Observatory, Korouva Milkbar—student run coffee house, Academic Mall.

FINANCIAL AID

Students should submit: FAFSA. Priority filing deadline is 2/1. The Princeton Review suggests that all financial aid forms be submitted as soon as possible after October 1. *Need-based scholarships/grants offered:* College/university scholarship or grant aid from institutional funds, Federal Pell, private scholarships, SEOG, state scholarships/grants. *Loan aid offered:* Direct PLUS Loans, Direct Subsidized Loans, Direct Unsubsidized Loans. Applicants will be notified of awards on a rolling basis beginning 12/15. Federal Work-Study Program available. Institutional employment available.

THE BOTTOM LINE

At Southwestern University, tuition and fees for the academic year total $42,00. Undergrads living on campus can expect to pay $5,820 for room and another $5,520 for board. Books and various supplies often end up costing an additional $1,300. Southwestern also recommends having another $1,300 on hand for travel and personal expenses. These figures come to a total of $55,940.

CAREER INFORMATION FROM PAYSCALE.COM	
ROI Rating	89
Bachelors and No Higher	
Median starting salary	$51,600
Median mid-career salary	$89,700
At Least Bachelors	
Median starting salary	$53,500
Median mid-career salary	$91,400
Alumni with high job meaning	52%
Degrees awarded in STEM subjects	19%

SELECTIVITY	
Admissions Rating	89
# of applicants	4,133
% of applicants accepted	43
% of acceptees attending	20
# offered a place on the wait list	117
% accepting a place on wait list	26
% admitted from wait list	30
# of early decision applicants	81
% accepted early decision	25

FRESHMAN PROFILE	
Range SAT EBRW	570–670
Range SAT Math	540–650
Range ACT Composite	23–29
Minimum paper TOEFL	570
Minimum internet-based TOEFL	88
% graduated top 10% of class	37
% graduated top 25% of class	73
% graduated top 50% of class	96

DEADLINES	
Early decision	
Deadline	11/1
Notification	12/1
Early action	
Deadline	12/1
Notification	3/1
Regular	
Deadline	2/1
Notification	4/1
Nonfall registration?	No

FINANCIAL FACTS	
Financial Aid Rating	87
Annual tuition	$42,000
Room and board	$11,340
Books and supplies	$1,300
Average frosh need-based scholarship	$31,462
Average UG need-based scholarship	$30,483
% needy frosh rec. need-based scholarship or grant aid	98
% needy UG rec. need-based scholarship or grant aid	99
% needy frosh rec. non-need-based scholarship or grant aid	97
% needy UG rec. non-need-based scholarship or grant aid	98
% needy frosh rec. need-based self-help aid	87
% needy UG rec. need-based self-help aid	84
% frosh rec. any financial aid	98
% UG rec. any financial aid	98
% UG borrow to pay for school	58
Average cumulative indebtedness	$34,788
% frosh need fully met	23
% ugrads need fully met	23

St. John's College (MD)

60 COLLEGE AVE., ANNAPOLIS, MD 21401 • ADMISSIONS: 410-626-2522 • FAX: 410-269-7916

CAMPUS LIFE

Quality of Life Rating	93
Fire Safety Rating	97
Green Rating	60*
Type of school	Private
Environment	Town

STUDENTS

Total undergrad enrollment	458
% male/female	53/47
% from out of state	62
% frosh from public high school	47
% frosh live on campus	96
% ugrads live on campus	70
# of fraternities (% ugrad men join)	0 (0)
# of sororities (% ugrad women join)	0 (0)
% African American	2
% Asian	4
% Caucasian	64
% Hispanic	6
% Native American	0
% Pacific Islander	0
% Two or more races	3
% Race and/or ethnicity unknown	0
% international	22
# of countries represented	35

ACADEMICS

Academic Rating	98
% students returning for sophomore year	87
% students graduating within 4 years	63
% students graduating within 6 years	67
Calendar	Semester
Student/faculty ratio	7:1
Profs interesting rating	99
Profs accessible rating	99

Most classes have 10–19 students.

MOST POPULAR MAJORS

Liberal Arts and Sciences.

ABOUT THE SCHOOL

Great books are the bedrock of a St. John's College education. At this Annapolis institution (which also has a campus in Santa Fe, New Mexico), the interdisciplinary curriculum is based around important books and ideas of Western civilization "fostering the best educational experience any lover of learning could ask for." All students share the same course of study—"the Program"—fully conducted in seminar-style courses in the humanities, literature, and philosophy with three years of laboratory science, four years of math, three years of language, and two years of music. Students "don't memorize formulas, we learn the logic and reason through the steps." Professors are called tutors here, and they are "always thoughtful and well-spoken, incredibly intelligent, and interested in being a part of the community." St. John's is "unique in its approach but is so oddly accessible," and its educational model really gives the student control. It "allows the student to solve problems and answer their own personal questions… in such a way that one truly feels empowered in one's education."

BANG FOR YOUR BUCK

St. John's was founded in 1696 and received its charter in 1784 and has a longstanding tradition of churning out incredibly bright, capable critical thinkers who have no aversion to hard work. In fact, 70 percent of students continue their studies after graduation in graduate or professional school programs. St. John's recently announced the college is lowering tuition to $35,000. The college's financial aid program both rewards academic merit and recognizes financial need. To that end, St. John's awarded over $3.7 million in merit scholarships to students in the most recent incoming class. All students who apply are considered for merit-based scholarships.

STUDENT LIFE

The St. John's student body is unique because "our social and our academic [lives] are completely blurred." Due to the unusual nature of the curriculum, everyone has read the same books so socially, "most things revolve around the Program," and a popular student in this "curious bunch" is one who does their work. Campus boasts a smorgasbord of activities for eager students, including those put on by the Waltz committee, which organizes a ton of swing dances each semester. "The entire college (almost) knows how to swing dance." The school also has a "robust intramural program," as well as an intercollegiate croquet team for which the school is famous, and the community formed within "leads to many friendships that would not have happened otherwise." There is also a very active theater program, which usually holds four shows a year, and four publications on campus.

CAREER

Simply by getting everyone to talk to one another in their seminars, the Program "allows the community the freedom and opportunity to shape St. John's into what they want and need it to be," and even if career paths aren't as apparent, students leave happy. The Career Services Office is ready to help any student with finding an internship, application strategies for graduate programs, or securing research positions. Information sessions, workshops, and career and "experience fairs" showcasing student projects are held throughout the year, and a newsletter is published twice a month with information about career development opportunities, internships, graduate school, and life planning.

St. John's College (MD)

FINANCIAL AID: 410-626-2502 • E-MAIL: ADMISSIONS@SJC.EDU • WEBSITE: WWW.SJC.EDU

GENERAL INFO

Activities: Choral groups, dance, drama/theater, literary magazine, music ensembles, student government, student newspaper, student-run film society, yearbook. **Organizations:** 55 registered organizations, 3 religious organizations. **On-Campus Highlights:** Mitchell Art Gallery, Greenfiled Library, McDowell Hall, Caroll Barrister House, French Monument, The entire campus is a registered national landmark.

FINANCIAL AID

Students should submit: FAFSA, state aid form. Priority filing deadline is 2/15. The Princeton Review suggests that all financial aid forms be submitted as soon as possible after October 1. *Need-based scholarships/ grants offered:* College/university scholarship or grant aid from institutional funds, Federal Pell, private scholarships, SEOG, state scholarships/grants. *Loan aid offered:* Direct PLUS Loans, Direct Subsidized Loans, Direct Unsubsidized Loans. Applicants will be notified of awards on a rolling basis beginning 12/15. Federal Work-Study Program available. Institutional employment available.

BOTTOM LINE

St. John's has lowered tuition starting in the 2019-20 academic year to $35,000 with about $14,000 in room and board and a $510 activity fee. Currently, around 99 percent of St. John's student receive assistance and The Princeton Review expects this history of financial aid excellence to continue. Additionally, the Maryland Higher Education Commission offers a variety of state scholarships for residents of Maryland.

CAREER INFORMATION FROM PAYSCALE.COM	
ROI Rating	91
Bachelors and No Higher	
Median starting salary	$54,900
Median mid-career salary	$108,600
At Least Bachelors	
Median starting salary	$56,600
Median mid-career salary	$110,100
Alumni with high job meaning	
Degrees awarded in STEM subjects	0%

SELECTIVITY	
Admissions Rating	90
# of applicants	753
% of applicants accepted	55
% of acceptees attending	30
# offered a place on the wait list	32
% accepting a place on wait list	100
% admitted from wait list	25

FRESHMAN PROFILE	
Range SAT EBRW	630–710
Range SAT Math	650–740
Range ACT Composite	26–32
Minimum paper TOEFL	600
Minimum internet-based TOEFL	100
Average HS GPA	3.5
% graduated top 10% of class	36
% graduated top 25% of class	59
% graduated top 50% of class	87

DEADLINES	
Early action	
Deadline	11/15
Notification	12/15
Regular	
Priority	1/15
Nonfall registration?	No

FINANCIAL FACTS	
Financial Aid Rating	89
Annual tuition	$52,734
Room and board	$12,602
Required fees	$484
Books and supplies	$630
Average frosh need-based scholarship	$38,747
Average UG need-based scholarship	$36,575
% needy frosh rec. need-based scholarship or grant aid	98
% needy UG rec. need-based scholarship or grant aid	99
% needy frosh rec. non-need-based scholarship or grant aid	16
% needy UG rec. non-need-based scholarship or grant aid	19
% needy frosh rec. need-based self-help aid	89
% needy UG rec. need-based self-help aid	87
% frosh rec. any financial aid	99
% UG rec. any financial aid	99
% UG borrow to pay for school	74
Average cumulative indebtedness	$16,705
% frosh need fully met	23
% ugrads need fully met	25
Average % of frosh need met	88
Average % of ugrad need met	87

St. John's College (NM)

1160 Camino Cruz Blanca, Santa Fe, NM 87505 • Admissions: 505-984-6060 • Fax: 505-984-6162

CAMPUS LIFE

Quality of Life Rating	91
Fire Safety Rating	73
Green Rating	73
Type of school	Private
Environment	Town

STUDENTS

Total undergrad enrollment	322
% male/female	56/44
% from out of state	89
% frosh from public high school	50
% frosh live on campus	96
% ugrads live on campus	83
# of fraternities (% ugrad men join)	0 (0)
# of sororities (% ugrad women join)	0 (0)
% African American	1
% Asian	2
% Caucasian	55
% Hispanic	9
% Native American	0
% Pacific Islander	0
% Two or more races	6
% Race and/or ethnicity unknown	1
% international	26
# of countries represented	28

ACADEMICS

Academic Rating	97
% students returning for sophomore year	68
% students graduating within 4 years	53
% students graduating within 6 years	65
Calendar	Semester
Student/faculty ratio	8:1
Profs interesting rating	99
Profs accessible rating	98

Most classes have 10–19 students.

ABOUT THE SCHOOL

There's no denying that St. John's is a budding intellectual's paradise. The university's curriculum is predicated upon the "Great Books" of western civilization. Essentially, students study the "history of human ideas." Through that, undergrads really learn how to "think critically and analytically." It's important to note that all classes are "discussion based"; there are "no lectures or tests" here. What's more, each course has no more than "twelve to fifteen students" per class. This helps to foster a certain level of "intimacy" and often "leads to a better understanding of the topic at hand." Despite the fact that "there are no departments or specialties," St. John's students seem to love their "insanely smart and fascinating" professors. They're also "friendly, funny, bring in donuts from time to time and seem to genuinely care about the students." And perhaps most impressively, "they are open to criticism—even on how the specific class is being taught." Students believe that all of this makes for an extremely "rewarding" experience.

BANG FOR YOUR BUCK

St. John's strives to provide an affordable education for all students and has announced tuition to the college will be reduced to $35,000 in the 2019-2020 academic year. Impressively, the average aid package often covers more than half the total current cost of attendance. And the university does a stellar job of tailoring packages to each undergrad's specific circumstances. Of course, most aid is distributed as a combination of scholarships, grants, work-study, and loans. Fortunately, all students are eligible for a number of merit-based scholarships. These can range anywhere from $2,000 to the full cost of tuition. St. John's also proudly participates in the Yellow Ribbon Program, providing funding for both veterans and their dependents. Finally, New Mexico residents are eligible for state incentive grants. These awards vary from $200 to $2,500 per year. The amount distributed is based upon need.

STUDENT LIFE

The academics at St. John's are rather demanding and most students spend their days "reading" and "doing homework together." Nevertheless, when they need a break there's plenty to enjoy. For starters, though the university doesn't maintain any varsity sports teams, students do love participating in intramurals. And we're told that "pick up basketball and soccer are probably the two most popular sports." The school also hosts numerous "outdoors trips, like rock climbing, river rafting, hiking, etc." Additionally, undergrads can join lots of organizations including the "student-run coffee shop, a sustainability club, painting club and woodworking club." Perhaps not surprisingly, "there isn't too big a party culture" at St. John's. Indeed, the school has "no frats or sororities." However, "people do drink...but [it's] usually [relegated to] small gatherings 10-15 people."

St. John's College (NM)

FINANCIAL AID: 505-984-6058 • E-MAIL: ADMISSIONS@SJC.EDU • WEBSITE: WWW.SJC.EDU

CAREER

St. John's Office of Personal and Professional Development truly helps prepare undergrads for life beyond the university. Starting from the first year, the office meets with students to strategize career paths. Undergrads have access to all sorts of opportunities such as job shadowing (for organizations as diverse as the Department of Justice, United Airlines and NPR), fellowship programs to assist with the transition to graduate study and the Ariel Internship Program which provides stipends to students wishing to intern during the summer months. Past internships have included apprenticing with a custom guitar maker, training in legal mediation and teaching aspiring first-generation students. Undergrads also come to the office for help writing resumes and cover letters and to kickstart their job search.

GENERAL INFO

Activities: Choral groups; Dance; Drama/theater; International Student Organization; Literary magazine; Music ensembles; Student government; Student newspaper. **Organizations:** 27 registered organizations. **On-Campus Highlights:** Student Activities Center, The Cave, Coffee Shop, Placita/Fish Pnd, Common rooms.

FINANCIAL AID

Students should submit: FAFSA. The Princeton Review suggests that all financial aid forms be submitted as soon as possible after October 1. *Need-based scholarships/grants offered:* College/university scholarship or grant aid from institutional funds, Federal Pell, private scholarships, SEOG, state scholarships/grants. *Loan aid offered:* Direct PLUS Loans, Direct Subsidized Loans, Direct Unsubsidized Loans. Applicants will be notified of awards on a rolling basis beginning 12/15. Federal Work-Study Program available. Institutional employment available.

THE BOTTOM LINE

St. John's has lowered tuition starting in the 2019-20 academic year to $35,000 with about $13,000 in room and board and a $510 activity fee. Take note: Around 97 percent of St. John's student receive assistance, with the average cost of attendance after financial aid coming in at $24,800.

CAREER INFORMATION FROM PAYSCALE.COM	
ROI Rating	88
Bachelors and No Higher	
Median starting salary	$49,700
Median mid-career salary	$88,700
At Least Bachelors	
Median starting salary	$53,300
Median mid-career salary	$101,000
Alumni with high job meaning	
Degrees awarded in STEM subjects	0%

SELECTIVITY	
Admissions Rating	86
# of applicants	342
% of applicants accepted	63
% of acceptees attending	32
# offered a place on the wait list	14
% accepting a place on wait list	100
% admitted from wait list	100
# of early decision applicants	0

FRESHMAN PROFILE	
Range SAT EBRW	630–670
Range SAT Math	560–680
Range ACT Composite	23–32
Minimum paper TOEFL	550
Minimum internet-based TOEFL	79
Average HS GPA	3.5
% graduated top 10% of class	37
% graduated top 25% of class	48
% graduated top 50% of class	74

DEADLINES	
Early action	
Deadline	11/15
Notification	12/15
Regular	
Priority	11/15
Nonfall registration?	Yes

FINANCIAL FACTS	
Financial Aid Rating	87
Annual tuition	$52,734
Room and board	$12,148
Required fees	$484
Books and supplies	$400
Average frosh need-based scholarship	$42,153
Average UG need-based scholarship	$39,930
% needy frosh rec. need-based scholarship or grant aid	100
% needy UG rec. need-based scholarship or grant aid	100
% needy frosh rec. non-need-based scholarship or grant aid	28
% needy UG rec. non-need-based scholarship or grant aid	17
% needy UG rec. need-based self-help aid	89
% frosh rec. any financial aid	97
% UG rec. any financial aid	84
% UG borrow to pay for school	71
Average cumulative indebtedness	$18,434
% frosh need fully met	41
% ugrads need fully met	21
Average % of frosh need met	86
Average % of ugrad need met	88

St. Lawrence University

Payson Hall, Canton, NY 13617 • Admissions: 315-229-5261 • Fax: 315-229-5818

CAMPUS LIFE

Quality of Life Rating	**90**
Fire Safety Rating	**81**
Green Rating	**87**
Type of school	Private
Environment	Village

STUDENTS

Total undergrad enrollment	2,373
% male/female	44/56
% from out of state	64
% frosh from public high school	71
% frosh live on campus	100
% ugrads live on campus	98
# of fraternities (% ugrad men join)	2 (12)
# of sororities (% ugrad women join)	4 (16)
% African American	3
% Asian	1
% Caucasian	78
% Hispanic	5
% Native American	<1
% Pacific Islander	0
% Two or more races	2
% Race and/or ethnicity unknown	1
% international	9
# of countries represented	53

ACADEMICS

Academic Rating	**90**
% students returning for sophomore year	92
% students graduating within 4 years	82
% students graduating within 6 years	85
Calendar	Semester
Student/faculty ratio	11:1
Profs interesting rating	90
Profs accessible rating	89

Most classes have 10–19 students. Most lab/discussion sessions have 10–19 students.

MOST POPULAR MAJORS
Economics; Business in the Liberal Arts; Psychology

ABOUT THE SCHOOL

Founded 1856, St. Lawrence University truly "allows students to broaden their horizons." Campus is spread across 1,000 acres in far upstate New York, known as "the North Country," where 2,400 undergrads receive a top-notch "liberal arts education" and join a "tight-knit community" that deftly "balanc[es] a fun and social environment with a serious workload." Students love that both "study abroad [programs]" and "research opportunities" abound. And they benefit from classes that often place an "emphasis on reading and writing skills." Many call attention to the university's "strong science program" as well. With an average class size of sixteen students, the "small class sizes allow you to get to know your professors and ask them questions." Speaking of professors, undergrads here say that they are "amazing" and "extremely accessible." As one student shares, "I know most on a first name basis and can ask any of them for help with class material or academic advising at any time." And another undergrad concludes, "They are more than just professors, they are mentors."

BANG FOR YOUR BUCK

St. Lawrence does its utmost to ensure all students, no matter their economic background, can further their education. As many undergrads note, "SLU gives a lot of financial aid and makes it possible for even low income students to attend." In fact, 96 percent of undergraduates receive some type of assistance. Of course, it's easy to help your students when you're able to distribute over $64.2 million each year. A substantial portion of this money comes in the form of merit-based scholarships. And fortunately for incoming SLU students, most scholarship decisions are based upon their admissions application. Importantly, merit awards can range anywhere from $5,000 to full tuition coverage.

STUDENT LIFE

SLU may be remotely located, but with over 100 student organizations, there's plenty to take advantage of beyond the classroom. "There are music concerts, comedians, movies and sporting events on campus almost every weekend: and the popular Outing Club frequently organizes "camping trips, hikes, ski trips and more." Most everyone here is involved in varsity or intramural sports—the men and women's hockey teams compete at the Division I level—and the athletic facilities are of such good quality that "even if you don't play sports or work out often, you want to go there to try it out." Like at most colleges, you can find "plenty [of parties] each weekend, as well as an 18 and over club off campus." And for those students anxious to get off campus for a bit, downtown Canton offers "farmers markets… plenty of small shops, restaurants…a sculpture garden and nature walks."

CAREER

St. Lawrence students are rather fortunate in that they can both tap into a "great alumni network" and take advantage of a fabulous career services office. In fact, undergrads here make a point of mentioning that the office does "a good job with providing resources for students." Indeed, it's one of the school's "greatest strengths." As one impressed undergrad explains, "Sophomore year at St. Lawrence offers a career boot-camp [in which] a very large [number] of students participate. This career boot-camp made sure my resume, LinkedIn [profile] and networking skills were on point." And best of all, "the career services advisers go out of their way to make sure as many students as possible are taking advantage of the panels, networking events and internships available." Ninety-seven percent of the Class of 2017 were employed or enrolled in graduate school within a year after commencement.

St. Lawrence University

FINANCIAL AID: 315-229-5265 • E-MAIL: ADMISSIONS@STLAWU.EDU • WEBSITE: WWW.STLAWU.EDU

GENERAL INFO

Activities: Choral groups, concert band, dance, drama/theater, jazz band, literary magazine, music ensembles, radio station, student government, student newspaper, student-run film society, yearbook, campus ministries, International Student Organization, Model UN, Outdoor Club. **Organizations:** Over 100 registered organizations, 22 honor societies, 4 religious organizations. 2 fraternities, 4 sororities. **Athletics (Intercollegiate):** *Men:* baseball, basketball, crew/rowing, cross-country, equestrian sports, football, golf, ice hockey, lacrosse, skiing (downhill/alpine), skiing (nordic/cross-country), soccer, squash, swimming, tennis, track/field (outdoor), track/field (indoor). *Women:* basketball, crew/rowing, cross-country, equestrian sports, field hockey, golf, ice hockey, lacrosse, skiing (downhill/alpine), skiingnordiccross-country, soccer, softball, squash, swimming, tennis, track/field (outdoor), track/field (indoor), volleyball. **On-Campus Highlights:** Newell Field House, Brewer Bookstore, Johnson Hall of Science, Owen D. Young Library, Student Center, Newell Center for Arts Technology.

FINANCIAL AID

Students should submit: FAFSA. Filing deadline is 2/1 for regular decision. The Princeton Review suggests that all financial aid forms be submitted as soon as possible after October 1. *Need-based scholarships/grants offered:* College/university scholarship or grant aid from institutional funds, Federal Pell, private scholarships, SEOG, state scholarships/grants. *Loan aid offered:* Direct PLUS Loans, Direct Subsidized Loans, Direct Unsubsidized Loans. Federal Work-Study Program available. Institutional employment available.

THE BOTTOM LINE

At present, St. Lawrence University charges $54,454 for tuition. On-campus housing typically costs $7,614 (for non-single rooms; singles cost $4,669 per semester). Meal plans tend to run students another $6,300 for the academic year. Undergrads are also charged $382 for an activities fee and $10 for class dues. St. Lawrence suggests that students have an additional $1,650 in which to cover books, transportation and personal expenses. Lastly, undergrads who enroll in the school's health insurance plan will be charged $1,780.

CAREER INFORMATION FROM PAYSCALE.COM	
ROI Rating	90
Bachelors and No Higher	
Median starting salary	$53,800
Median mid-career salary	$104,300
At Least Bachelors	
Median starting salary	$55,500
Median mid-career salary	$112,800
Alumni with high job meaning	50%
Degrees awarded in STEM subjects	24%

SELECTIVITY	
Admissions Rating	90
# of applicants	5,866
% of applicants accepted	48
% of acceptees attending	25
# offered a place on the wait list	85
# of early decision applicants	299
% accepted early decision	90

FRESHMAN PROFILE	
Range SAT EBRW	590–680
Range SAT Math	580–675
Range ACT Composite	25–30
Minimum paper TOEFL	600
Minimum internet-based TOEFL	82
Average HS GPA	3.6
% graduated top 10% of class	46
% graduated top 25% of class	79
% graduated top 50% of class	95

DEADLINES	
Early decision	
Deadline	11/1
Notification	continual
Other ED Deadline	2/1
Other ED Notification	continual
Regular	
Deadline	2/1
Notification	late March
Nonfall registration?	Yes

FINANCIAL FACTS	
Financial Aid Rating	82
Annual tuition	$54,454
Room and board	$14,134
Required fees	$382
Books and supplies	$750
Average frosh need-based scholarship	$39,769
Average UG need-based scholarship	$37,572
% needy frosh rec. need-based scholarship or grant aid	100
% needy UG rec. need-based scholarship or grant aid	100
% needy frosh rec. non-need-based scholarship or grant aid	79
% needy UG rec. non-need-based scholarship or grant aid	73
% needy frosh rec. need-based self-help aid	76
% needy UG rec. need-based self-help aid	77
% frosh rec. any financial aid	100
% UG rec. any financial aid	99
% UG borrow to pay for school	60
Average cumulative indebtedness	$32,627
% frosh need fully met	22
% ugrads need fully met	27
Average % of frosh need met	88

St. Mary's College of Maryland

ADMISSIONS, 47645 COLLEGE DRIVE, ST. MARY'S CITY, MD 20686-3001 • ADMISSIONS: 240-895-5000 • FAX: 240-895-5001

CAMPUS LIFE

Quality of Life Rating	88
Fire Safety Rating	88
Green Rating	98
Type of school	Public
Environment	Rural

STUDENTS

Total undergrad enrollment	1,544
% male/female	42/58
% from out of state	7
% frosh from public high school	80
% frosh live on campus	94
% ugrads live on campus	82
# of fraternities (% ugrad men join)	0 (0)
# of sororities (% ugrad women join)	0 (0)
% African American	9
% Asian	4
% Caucasian	71
% Hispanic	8
% Native American	<1
% Pacific Islander	<1
% Two or more races	5
% Race and/or ethnicity unknown	2
% international	<1
# of countries represented	11

ACADEMICS

Academic Rating	87
% students returning for sophomore year	87
% students graduating within 4 years	70
% students graduating within 6 years	78
Calendar	Semester
Student/faculty ratio	10:1
Profs interesting rating	92
Profs accessible rating	92

Most classes have 10–19 students. Most lab/discussion sessions have 10–19 students.

MOST POPULAR MAJORS

Biology/Biological Sciences; Psychology; Economics

ABOUT THE SCHOOL

Tucked away in rural Maryland, St. Mary's is a "prestigious" public honors college that's "all about connecting the liberal arts experience to the real world." The school also does a tremendous job of fostering a "sense of community" and a "welcoming atmosphere." And there is a strong culture of "accepting everyone for who they are." While the academics here are no doubt "rigorous," St. Mary's undergrads benefit from "small," "intimate" classes as well as "hands on learning experiences." They're also privy to "passionate" professors who "actively want to get to know their students and make teaching their first priority." Indeed, "despite doing important research and work in their fields, many St. Mary's professors also go above and beyond in ensuring that their students succeed academically." As this thrilled undergrad concludes, "I consider many of them friends and feel that I can come to them with any problem, no matter how abstract, out-of-the-blue, or insolvable it might seem."

BANG FOR YOUR BUCK

St. Mary's firmly believes that a great education should be within reach no matter the size of your bank account. To that end, the university works tirelessly with families to carve out a financial plan that works well for them. Impressively, 52 percent of incoming first-years are granted some type of merit-based scholarship. That's because the school likes to reward both hard work and academic excellence. For example, there's the St. Mary's Academic Achievement Scholarship which provides $1,000–$5,000 to Maryland residents and $5,000–$15,000 to out-of-state students. Beyond scholarships and grants, the university runs a robust work-study program with nearly a quarter of students participating.

STUDENT LIFE

St. Mary's students definitely prioritize their academics. Nevertheless, they still love to indulge in study breaks and there's plenty of fun to be had when they do. For starters, "there are about 200 clubs and organizations to join." Additionally, the student government association (SGA) hosts events "every weekend" bringing performers like "comedians and magicians" to campus. Undergrads also love to take advantage of the fact that St. Mary's is located near the banks of a river. Therefore, it's pretty common to find students "[on] the water kayaking, paddle boarding, swimming, and sailing." While there is a "drinking" culture, we're told that it doesn't dominate the social scene. And students who choose to abstain will discover "many non-alcoholic weekend parties includ[ing] a murder mystery party, karaoke night, poker, and mafia the game."

St. Mary's College of Maryland

FINANCIAL AID: 240-895-3000 • E-MAIL: ADMISSIONS@SMCM.EDU • WEBSITE: WWW.SMCM.EDU

CAREER

There's no denying that St. Mary's students flourish when it's time to hit the job market. To begin with, undergrads can easily reach out to their "department chairs [who] are great about sending out internship opportunities and creating events where students can learn from and network with alumni in their field." Indeed, "everyone in the faculty has contacts they're willing to leverage for students' benefit, and this is really the best thing about coming here." Of course, undergrads can also turn to the Career Development Center for guidance and support. The office sponsors a number of terrific events including the Professional Network Program which connects students with informational interviews and MicroInternships which provide students with short job shadowing experiences.

GENERAL INFO

Activities: Campus Ministries; Choral groups; Dance; Drama/theater; Jazz band; Literary magazine; Model UN; Music ensembles; Radio station; Student government; Student newspaper; Symphony orchestra; Yearbook 117 registered organizations, 8 honor societies, 4 religious organizations. **Athletics (Intercollegiate):** *Men:* baseball, basketball, cross-country, lacrosse, rowing, sailing, soccer, swimming, tennis. *Women:* basketball, cross-country, field hockey, lacrosse, rowing, sailing, soccer, swimming, tennis, volleyball. On-Campus Highlights: Campus Center, Waterfront, Library, Athletics and Recreation Center, The Pub.

FINANCIAL AID

Students should submit: FAFSA. Priority filing deadline is 2/28. The Princeton Review suggests that all financial aid forms be submitted as soon as possible after October 1. *Need-based scholarships/grants offered:* College/university scholarship or grant aid from institutional funds, Federal Pell, private scholarships, SEOG, state scholarships/grants. *Loan aid offered:* Direct PLUS Loans, Direct Subsidized Loans, Direct Unsubsidized Loans. Applicants will be notified of awards on a rolling basis beginning 12/15. Federal Work-Study Program available. Institutional employment available.

CAREER INFORMATION FROM PAYSCALE.COM	
ROI Rating	88
Bachelors and No Higher	
Median starting salary	$52,300
Median mid-career salary	$93,400
At Least Bachelors	
Median starting salary	$53,200
Median mid-career salary	$98,900
Alumni with high job meaning	36%
Degrees awarded in STEM subjects	27%

SELECTIVITY	
Admissions Rating	78
# of applicants	1,655
% of applicants accepted	82
% of acceptees attending	25

FRESHMAN PROFILE	
Range SAT EBRW	540–650
Range SAT Math	530–630
Range ACT Composite	22–28
Minimum paper TOEFL	550
Minimum internet-based TOEFL	90
Average HS GPA	3.3

DEADLINES	
Early Decision	
Deadline	11/1
Notification	12/1
Early action	
Deadline	11/1
Notification	1/1
Regular	
Priority	11/1
Deadline	1/15
Notification	4/1
Nonfall registration?	Yes

FINANCIAL FACTS	
Financial Aid Rating	80
Annual in-state tuition	$11,878
Annual out-of-state tuition	$27,640
Room and board	$13,202
Required fees	$2,928
Books and supplies	$800
Average frosh need-based scholarship	$11,527
Average UG need-based scholarship	$10,240
% needy frosh rec. need-based scholarship or grant aid	91
% needy UG rec. need-based scholarship or grant aid	92
% needy frosh rec. non-need-based scholarship or grant aid	0
% needy UG rec. non-need-based scholarship or grant aid	0
% needy frosh rec. need-based self-help aid	78
% needy UG rec. need-based self-help aid	79
% frosh rec. any financial aid	92
% UG rec. any financial aid	86
% UG borrow to pay for school	53
Average cumulative indebtedness	$21,911
% frosh need fully met	5
% ugrads need fully met	4
Average % of frosh need met	72
Average % of ugrad need met	68

St. Olaf College

1520 St. Olaf Avenue, Northfield, MN 55057 • Admissions: 507-786-3025 • Fax: 507-786-3832

CAMPUS LIFE

Quality of Life Rating	93
Fire Safety Rating	82
Green Rating	60*
Type of school	Private
Affiliation	Lutheran
Environment	Village

STUDENTS

Total undergrad enrollment	3,004
% male/female	42/58
% from out of state	53
% frosh from public high school	73
% frosh live on campus	100
% ugrads live on campus	94
# of fraternities (% ugrad men join)	0 (0)
# of sororities (% ugrad women join)	0 (0)
% African American	3
% Asian	7
% Caucasian	71
% Hispanic	6
% Native American	<1
% Pacific Islander	<1
% Two or more races	3
% Race and/or ethnicity unknown	1
% international	10
# of countries represented	80

ACADEMICS

Academic Rating	92
% students returning for sophomore year	92
% students graduating within 4 years	85
% students graduating within 6 years	88
Calendar	4/1/4
Student/faculty ratio	12:1
Profs interesting rating	91
Profs accessible rating	93

Most classes have 10–19 students. Most lab/discussion sessions have 10–19 students.

MOST POPULAR MAJORS

Biology/Biological Sciences; Mathematics; Economics

ABOUT THE SCHOOL

Located in Northfield, Minnesota, less than an hour drive from the Twin Cities, St. Olaf College boasts a combination of top-rated programs and academic rigor with an uncommon emphasis on community-building. Historically connected to the Evangelical Lutheran Church, the college offers a secular educational experience rooted in Norwegian traditions. The small class size allows for "strong relationships" between faculty and students, and professors are "passionate," "incredibly accessible," and "challenging." Along with the top-ranked, "incredible" study abroad program, its music program is highly prized and "nationally recognized." The mathematics/statistics and religion/theology programs are also highly ranked, and professors across disciplines receive "tens across the board." The clear majority of its approximately 3,000 students (nicknamed "Oles") live on the "beautiful" 300-acre campus, building a tight-knit community students call "inclusive" and true to the school's unofficial motto of "Never leave an Ole behind." "St. Olaf has this inherent spirit of possibility and collaboration that drew me in…" says one student. "There is a feeling that…everyone is there to work hard and achieve."

BANG FOR YOUR BUCK

St. Olaf's mission sets out "to be a globally engaged community" and "to explore meaningful vocation," a philosophy institutionalized in the Piper Center, which "works tirelessly to make sure Oles have the resources to land their dream internship, job, or service opportunity." Paired with the ample study abroad opportunities, students can expect to be prepared for life after St. Olaf, whether that means gaining full-time employment, entering competitive graduate programs, or joining the large cohort of graduating seniors who become Fulbright Scholars. Over ninety percent of students receive institutional gift aid, averaging about $37,000 per student. Notably, students point out that the centrality of the school's music program to the campus means that they can "give scholarships in music to non-music majors."

STUDENT LIFE

The "highly residential" and dry campus help shape the culture on campus for students, which is described as a "busy…but fulfilled life." Most Oles engage in at least one extracurricular activity every day—and the offerings are vast. With "over 200 clubs," frequent dances at "The Pause," a campus hangout and concert venue, [and] student government-sponsored activities…" most students balance "a full course load, in addition to a music ensemble, club sport, or some other type of group—sometimes all of the above." The Tostrud Recreation Center—with its varied offerings that include a rock climbing wall—is a popular place to blow off steam, along with intramural sports teams and the "surrounding natural lands for…walks and de-stressing." The music program (including its celebrated St. Olaf Christmas Festival) is world renowned and deeply integrated into campus culture.

CAREER

Students say that one of St. Olaf's greatest strengths is its Piper Center for Vocation and Career. By maintaining "strategic relationships with employers, faculty, staff, alumni, parents, and donors," the center can "maximize opportunities for students and alumni." Furthermore, students say that the "vocational retreats, alumni luncheons, [and] one-on-one coaching…makes sure that all the hard work put into classes pays off." According to PayScale.com, over 50 percent of St. Olaf alumni report that they derive a high level of meaning from their careers. The average "early career" (alumni with 0-5 years of experience) yearly salary is $49,000.

St. Olaf College

FINANCIAL AID: 507-786-3019 • E-MAIL: ADMISSIONS@STOLAF.EDU • WEBSITE: WWW.STOLAF.EDU

GENERAL INFO

Activities: Choral groups, concert band, dance, drama/theater, jazz band, literary magazine, music ensembles, musical theater, opera, pep band, radio station, student government, student newspaper, student-run film society, symphony orchestra. **Organizations:** campus ministries, International Student Organization, Model UN, 257 registered organizations, 20 honor societies, 19 religious organizations. **Athletics (Intercollegiate):** *Men:* baseball, basketball, cross-country, diving, football, golf, ice hockey, skiing (downhill/alpine), skiing (nordic/cross-country), soccer, swimming, tennis, track/field (outdoor), track/field (indoor), wrestling. *Women:* basketball, cross-country, diving, golf, ice hockey, skiing (downhill/alpine), skiing (nordic/cross-country), soccer, softball, swimming, tennis, track/field (outdoor), track/field (indoor), volleyball.

FINANCIAL AID

Students should submit: CSS Profile; FAFSA. Priority filing deadline is 2/1. The Princeton Review suggests that all financial aid forms be submitted as soon as possible after October 1. *Need-based scholarships/grants offered:* College/university scholarship or grant aid from institutional funds, Federal Pell, private scholarships, SEOG, state scholarships/grants. *Loan aid offered:* Direct PLUS Loans, Direct Subsidized Loans, Direct Unsubsidized Loans. Applicants will be notified of awards on or about 4/1. Federal Work-Study Program available. Institutional employment available.

BOTTOM LINE

If you are seeking a small, community-oriented, academically rigorous environment with an emphasis on social values and cooperation, St. Olaf fits the bill. The $47,840 tuition and $10,850 room and board costs are offset by St. Olaf's commitment to providing a financially manageable education: its financial aid packages meet 97 percent of undergraduate need across all four years.

CAREER INFORMATION FROM PAYSCALE.COM	
ROI Rating	91
Bachelors and No Higher	
Median starting salary	$51,900
Median mid-career salary	$102,100
At Least Bachelors	
Median starting salary	$53,700
Median mid-career salary	$106,000
Alumni with high job meaning	48%
Degrees awarded in STEM subjects	30%

SELECTIVITY

Admissions Rating	91
# of applicants	5,949
% of applicants accepted	43
% of acceptees attending	31
# offered a place on the wait list	784
% accepting a place on wait list	22
% admitted from wait list	12
# of early decision applicants	278
% accepted early decision	80

FRESHMAN PROFILE

Range SAT EBRW	580–690
Range SAT Math	570–710
Range ACT Composite	25–31
Minimum internet-based TOEFL	90
Average HS GPA	3.6
% graduated top 10% of class	44
% graduated top 25% of class	77
% graduated top 50% of class	94

DEADLINES

Early decision	
Deadline	11/15
Notification	12/15
Other ED Deadline	1/8
Other ED Notification	2/1
Regular	
Deadline	1/15
Notification	3/20
Nonfall registration?	No

FINANCIAL FACTS

Financial Aid Rating	95
Annual tuition	$47,840
Room and board	$10,850
Books and supplies	$1,000
Average frosh need-based scholarship	$35,083
Average UG need-based scholarship	$33,553
% needy frosh rec. need-based scholarship or grant aid	100
% needy UG rec. need-based scholarship or grant aid	100
% needy frosh rec. non-need-based scholarship or grant aid	36
% needy UG rec. non-need-based scholarship or grant aid	28
% needy frosh rec. need-based self-help aid	95
% needy UG rec. need-based self-help aid	98
% frosh rec. any financial aid	92
% UG rec. any financial aid	93
% UG borrow to pay for school	57
Average cumulative indebtedness	$27,002
% frosh need fully met	93
% ugrads need fully met	74

Stanford University

Undergraduate Admission, Montag Hall, 355 Galvez Street, Stanford, CA 94305-6106 • Admission: 650-723-2091

#2 BEST VALUE COLLEGE

CAMPUS LIFE

Quality of Life Rating	93
Fire Safety Rating	89
Green Rating	99
Type of school	Private
Environment	Suburban

STUDENTS

Total undergrad enrollment	7,056
% male/female	50/50
% from out of state	59
% frosh from public high school	59
% frosh live on campus	100
% ugrads live on campus	97
# of fraternities (% ugrad men join)	15 (19)
# of sororities (% ugrad women join)	14 (27)
% African American	7
% Asian	22
% Caucasian	36
% Hispanic	15
% Native American	1
% Pacific Islander	<1
% Two or more races	9
% Race and/or ethnicity unknown	<1
% international	9
# of countries represented	93

ACADEMICS

Academic Rating	95
% students returning for sophomore year	98
% students graduating within 4 years	73
% students graduating within 6 years	94
Calendar	Quarter
Student/faculty ratio	4:1
Profs interesting rating	84
Profs accessible rating	86

Most classes have fewer than 10 students. Most lab/discussion sessions have fewer than 10 students.

MOST POPULAR MAJORS

Computer Science; Engineering; Human Biology

ABOUT THE SCHOOL

Stanford University is widely recognized as one of the nation's most outstanding universities, considered by many to be the West Coast's answer to the Ivy League. Stanford alumni, who can be found in 143 countries, eighteen territories, and all fifty states, have distinguished themselves in many fields, from government service to innovation to business to arts and entertainment. -0Academics are simply top-notch, and despite the fact that this is a research-driven university, professors are seriously interested in getting to know their undergrads. Students say that teachers at Stanford are "wonderful resources for guidance and tutoring," and there is "an opportunity to engage with them on a regular basis." The classroom experience is discussion-oriented and otherwise awesome. There are tons of majors, and, if you don't like any of the ones on offer, it's a breeze to design your own. The dorms are like palaces. The administration runs the school like a finely tuned machine. There's very little not to like about this place. "The classes, campus, and faculty are amazing," reports one contented undergrad; another is happy to find that Stanford "has incredible resources, incredible people...and an unrivaled atmosphere of openness and collaboration."

BANG FOR YOUR BUCK

Like a handful of other spectacularly wealthy schools in the United States, Stanford maintains a wholly need-blind admission policy, and it demonstrates a serious commitment to making its world-class education available to talented and well-prepared students regardless of economic circumstances. All of Stanford's scholarship funds are need-based. For parents with total annual income and typical assets below $65,000, Stanford will not expect a parent contribution toward educational costs. For parents with total annual income and typical assets below $125,000, the expected parent contribution will be low enough to ensure that all tuition charges are covered with need-based scholarship, federal and state grants, and/or outside scholarship funds. Families with incomes at higher levels (typically up to $200,000 or higher) may also qualify for assistance, especially if more than one family member is enrolled in college. The hard part is getting admitted. If you can do that, the school will make sure you have a way to pay. The vast majority of successful applicants will be among the strongest students (academically) in their secondary schools.

STUDENT LIFE

"People often use the duck metaphor to describe Stanford," says a student, "on the surface they are calm and serene, under the surface they are paddling really hard." But it's not all hard work and studying for the student body, as "life at Stanford has the potential to be both extremely stressful (due to the strenuous academics) and very carefree (due to the wide variety of 'releases' available to students)." "We aren't a typical party school, but about a third of the student body tries to party enough for everyone else." For the other two-thirds, "there are tons of ways to be involved" and "clubs for every type of person." "Some dance, some sing, some play instruments, some plan events" and "students constantly 'roll out' to whatever performance, sports event, or talk they can in order to support their fellow classmates and the hard work that is put in to it." And of course, students can turn to the beautiful natural surroundings when in need of a little relaxation. "Life at Stanford is like a vacation. The campus with its palm trees and

Stanford University

Financial Aid: 650-723-3058 • E-mail: admission@stanford.edu • Fax: 650-725-2846 • Website: www.stanford.edu

surrounding foothills is the most beautiful in the world." But while "anything you could possibly need is pretty much on campus" getting away can be great too: "Only at Stanford can you go from snowy mountains, to sunny beaches, to bustling city life [in San Francisco] all in one day."

CAREER

As a top-notch school, Stanford can lead to "great job opportunities" for motivated students looking to enter a wide variety of careers. Stanford students tend to be very focused on the future, with "about a 50/50 divide of people who are planning for careers to make money and people who are planning for careers to 'make a difference.'" Stanford's Career Development Center provides standard services such as job fairs and recruiting events, resume critique, and one-on-one counseling. The Center also offers "career communities" in specific fields, and a special community devoted solely to the needs of underclassmen still a few years from their job search. Most agree that Stanford "provides a great opportunity to pursue greater careers with a wide array of resources and support." Out of Stanford alumni visiting PayScale.com, 56 percent report that they derive meaning from their jobs.

GENERAL INFO

Activities: Choral groups, concert band, dance, drama/theater, jazz band, literary magazine, marching band, music ensembles, musical theater, opera, pep band, radio station, student government, student newspaper, student-run film society, symphony orchestra, television station, yearbook, campus ministries, international student organization. **Organizations:** 600 registered organizations, 30 religious organizations. 15 fraternities, 14 sororities.

FINANCIAL AID

Students should submit: CSS Profile; FAFSA; Noncustodial PROFILE. Priority filing deadline is 2/16. The Princeton Review suggests that all financial aid forms be submitted as soon as possible after October 1. *Need-based scholarships/grants offered:* College/university scholarship or grant aid from institutional funds, Federal Pell, private scholarships, SEOG, state scholarships/grants. *Loan aid offered:* Direct PLUS Loans, Direct Subsidized Loans, Direct Unsubsidized Loans. Applicants will be notified of awards on a rolling basis beginning 4/1. Federal Work-Study Program available. Institutional employment available.

BOTTOM LINE

A year of tuition, fees, room and board, and basic expenses at Stanford costs about $64,729. While that figure is staggering, you have to keep in mind that few students pay anywhere near that amount. Financial packages here are very generous. Most aid comes with no strings attached. Only 18 percent of undergrads borrow to pay for school, and those who do walk away with an average of $20,205 in loan debt.

CAREER INFORMATION FROM PAYSCALE.COM	
ROI Rating	99
Bachelors and No Higher	
Median starting salary	$76,500
Median mid-career salary	$143,100
At Least Bachelors	
Median starting salary	$80,900
Median mid-career salary	$156,700
Alumni with high job meaning	57%
Degrees awarded in STEM subjects	51%

SELECTIVITY	
Admissions Rating	99
# of applicants	44,073
% of applicants accepted	5
% of acceptees attending	82
# offered a place on the wait list	842
% accepting a place on wait list	78
% admitted from wait list	5

FRESHMAN PROFILE	
Range SAT EBRW	690–760
Range SAT Math	700–780
Range ACT Composite	32–35
Average HS GPA	4.0
% graduated top 10% of class	94
% graduated top 25% of class	99
% graduated top 50% of class	100

DEADLINES	
Early action	
Deadline	11/1
Notification	12/15
Regular	
Deadline	1/2
Notification	4/1
Nonfall registration?	No

FINANCIAL FACTS	
Financial Aid Rating	98
Annual tuition	$48,987
Room and board	$15,112
Required fees	$630
Books and supplies	$1,455
Average frosh need-based scholarship	$53,337
Average UG need-based scholarship	$50,234
% needy frosh rec. need-based scholarship or grant aid	96
% needy UG rec. need-based scholarship or grant aid	97
% needy frosh rec. non-need-based scholarship or grant aid	2
% needy UG rec. non-need-based scholarship or grant aid	4
% needy frosh rec. need-based self-help aid	64
% needy UG rec. need-based self-help aid	74
% frosh rec. any financial aid	86
% UG rec. any financial aid	84
% UG borrow to pay for school	18
Average cumulative indebtedness	$20,205
% frosh need fully met	98
% ugrads need fully met	99
Average % of frosh need met	100
Average % of ugrad need met	100

State University of New York—Binghamton University

PO Box 6001, Binghamton, NY 13902-6001 • Admissions: 607-777-2171 • Fax: 607-777-4445

CAMPUS LIFE

Quality of Life Rating	86
Fire Safety Rating	95
Green Rating	96
Type of school	Public
Environment	City

STUDENTS

Total undergrad enrollment	13,693
% male/female	51/49
% from out of state	7
% frosh from public high school	90
% frosh live on campus	98
% ugrads live on campus	52
# of fraternities (% ugrad men join)	36 (14)
# of sororities (% ugrad women join)	17 (11)
% African American	5
% Asian	14
% Caucasian	57
% Hispanic	11
% Native American	<1
% Pacific Islander	<1
% Two or more races	2
% Race and/or ethnicity unknown	2
% international	8
# of countries represented	97

ACADEMICS

Academic Rating	79
% students returning for sophomore year	91
% students graduating within 4 years	73
% students graduating within 6 years	82
Calendar	Semester
Student/faculty ratio	19:1
Profs interesting rating	74
Profs accessible rating	74

Most classes have 10–19 students. Most lab/discussion sessions have 10–19 students.

MOST POPULAR MAJORS
Engineering; Psychology; Business Administration and Management

ABOUT THE SCHOOL

Boasting "affordability, reputation, care and attention towards students," Binghamton University is a central institution in one of the nation's strongest public university systems. According to students, whether you're interested in nursing, engineering, science research, or you want to design your own major, this research university has a place for you. As one student says, "The greatest strengths of my school are having a lot of activities to do on campus, friendly students, intelligent students, living communities giving the large school a smaller feeling and the overall helpfulness of the staff. Most of the professors and other staff that I have spoken to are very willing to help you and want to see you succeed as a student. Even for my large lecture classes, the teachers are willing to get to know students when you go to their office hours, creating a more personal connection." Students also highlight Binghamton University's beautiful natural setting on 930 acres in upstate New York. One student notes that "the living communities really help break it up and make it feel smaller. Also, the nature preserve on campus is amazing, and I love hiking there with friends. I didn't see anything like it at any of the other schools I visited before making my final decision to become a Bearcat."

BANG FOR YOUR BUCK

Binghamton University offers "a fantastic amount of academic and extracurricular opportunities for your money." One student sums up: "The price is the number one strength of Binghamton University, followed by the rigor of its academic programs, [and] the availability of job placement and training." All students who apply and submit a Free Application for Federal Student Aid (FAFSA) are considered for scholarships at Binghamton. The school also offers competitive merit based scholarships, and students are encouraged to apply for state scholarships and grants also. Due to "high quality research endeavors, in the sciences especially, with programs such as the Freshman Research Immersion program," (through which students in science and engineering programs earn course credit as they work directly with faculty on cutting-edge research projects), "one of [Binghamton University's] greatest strengths is its ability to attract high achieving, motivated students."

STUDENT LIFE

There's something for everyone at Binghamton University with "the multiple programs and organizations we have on campus. Students always have a place that they can fit into and feel a sense of belonging." With lots of students, everyone finds their niche on campus, whether it's through research, school groups, or social events. Current undergraduates find that "[their] peers are supportive and outgoing" so that they often find themselves working together on projects. Another student says, "The location is great, our community and our city is constantly improving, change happens all of the time and the students are getting ready for it. We strive to be the best public university in New York and it shows." Binghamton University hosts a diverse student body, which students praise as an important asset at the school. One student says, "My peers are motivated and dedicated to their schoolwork as well as to helping others. There is a very friendly and homey atmosphere at the school."

CAREER

Binghamton University has many opportunities for students to combine their education with career prep, and "the most important would be integration with the industries within the area." The university works very closely with the industries in the city and surrounding areas of Binghamton, New York. The Fleishman Center for Career and Professional Development is "one of the greatest strengths of Binghamton University through its innovative programming and dedicated professional staff." Students in

State University of New York—Binghamton University

FINANCIAL AID: 607-777-2428 • E-MAIL: ADMIT@BINGHAMTON.EDU • WEBSITE: WWW.BINGHAMTON.EDU

all disciplines have opportunities for research, thanks to Binghamton University's emphasis on faculty research, and many graduate students stay and continue to work at the school. One student says that they "love how there are so many different opportunities that Binghamton provides for the students—whether [it's through] internships, jobs, or volunteering opportunities, the students are given the tools they need to gain as much experience as possible in order to prepare them for life after graduation." Of the Binghamton University alumni who visited PayScale.com, average early-career salaries for Binghamton graduates is $56,400.

GENERAL INFO

Activities: Choral groups, concert band, dance, drama/theater, jazz band, literary magazine, music ensembles, musical theater, opera, pep band, radio station, student government, student newspaper, student-run film society, symphony orchestra, television station, yearbook, campus ministries, international student organization.

FINANCIAL AID

Students should submit: FAFSA, state aid form. Priority filing deadline is 3/1. The Princeton Review suggests that all financial aid forms be submitted as soon as possible after October 1. *Need-based scholarships/grants offered:* College/university scholarship or grant aid from institutional funds, Federal Pell, private scholarships, SEOG, state scholarships/grants. *Loan aid offered:* Direct PLUS Loans, Direct Subsidized Loans, Direct Unsubsidized Loans. Applicants will be notified of awards on a rolling basis beginning 1/31. Federal Work-Study Program available. Institutional employment available.

BOTTOM LINE

Students appreciate Binghamton University for being a "great school at a great price." And with tuition and housing costs adding up to just $24,866 for in-state students, they aren't exaggerating. Out-of-state students can expect $39,546 for the same treatment, but both types of students are eligible for federal and state aid and grants.

CAREER INFORMATION FROM PAYSCALE.COM	
ROI Rating	91
Bachelors and No Higher	
Median starting salary	$58,900
Median mid-career salary	$111,200
At Least Bachelors	
Median starting salary	$60,500
Median mid-career salary	$115,300
Alumni with high job meaning	44%
Degrees awarded in STEM subjects	34%

SELECTIVITY	
Admissions Rating	92
# of applicants	33,467
% of applicants accepted	40
% of acceptees attending	20
# offered a place on the wait list	1,543
% accepting a place on wait list	0

FRESHMAN PROFILE	
Range SAT EBRW	640–711
Range SAT Math	650–720
Range ACT Composite	28–31
Minimum paper TOEFL	560
Minimum internet-based TOEFL	83
Average HS GPA	3.7

DEADLINES	
Early action	
Deadline	11/1
Notification	1/15
Regular	
Priority	1/15
Nonfall registration?	Yes

FINANCIAL FACTS	
Financial Aid Rating	81
Annual in-state tuition	$6,870
Annual out-of-state tuition	$21,550
Room and board	$15,058
Required fees	$2,938
Books and supplies	$1,000
Average frosh need-based scholarship	$10,101
Average UG need-based scholarship	$9,356
% needy frosh rec. need-based scholarship or grant aid	80
% needy UG rec. need-based scholarship or grant aid	81
% needy frosh rec. non-need-based scholarship or grant aid	15
% needy UG rec. non-need-based scholarship or grant aid	7
% needy frosh rec. need-based self-help aid	97
% needy UG rec. need-based self-help aid	97
% frosh rec. any financial aid	81
% UG rec. any financial aid	70
% UG borrow to pay for school	51
Average cumulative indebtedness	$27,022
% frosh need fully met	15
% ugrads need fully met	14
Average % of frosh need met	70
Average % of ugrad need met	69

State University of New York—College of Environmental Science and Forestry

OFFICE OF UNDERGRADUATE ADMISSIONS, SUNY-ESF, SYRACUSE, NY 13210 • ADMISSIONS: 315-470-6600

CAMPUS LIFE

Quality of Life Rating	86
Fire Safety Rating	98
Green Rating	99
Type of school	Public
Environment	City

STUDENTS

Total undergrad enrollment	1,793
% male/female	53/47
% from out of state	15
% frosh from public high school	90
% frosh live on campus	96
% ugrads live on campus	35
# of fraternities (% ugrad men join)	26 (2)
# of sororities (% ugrad women join)	21 (2)
% African American	2
% Asian	4
% Caucasian	80
% Hispanic	6
% Native American	<1
% Two or more races	3
% Race and/or ethnicity unknown	4
% international	2
# of countries represented	8

ACADEMICS

Academic Rating	76
% students returning for sophomore year	83
% students graduating within 6 years	78
Calendar	Semester
Student/faculty ratio	13:1
Profs interesting rating	82
Profs accessible rating	72

Most classes have 20–29 students. Most lab/discussion sessions have 20–29 students.

MOST POPULAR MAJORS

Environmental Science; Landscape Architecture; Environmental Biology

ABOUT THE SCHOOL

The State University of New York—College of Environmental Science and Forestry (SUNY-ESF) is a small institution dedicated entirely to the environment and sustainability studies. Based in Syracuse, New York, SUNY-ESF students can expect to spend a lot of time outdoors. Campus occupies 12 acres in Syracuse in addition to 25,000 acres of "regional campuses" and "field stations" throughout Central New York and the Adirondacks, which are used for hands-on research projects. With 24 official courses of study from chemistry to landscape architecture on on their own campus these lucky undergraduates also have access to classes and facilities at nearby Syracuse University. On SUNY-ESF's "beautiful historic campus," expect to find "unique and fun clubs, lots of student involvement, rigorous classes, eco-consciousness, great dorms, and kind, knowledgeable staff." Described by current students as being a "small, well-funded school with a faculty that is very interested in helping the student body," the SUNY-ESF "has the potential to be one of the few institutions that can greatly contribute to the future by affecting environmental aspects of the planet."

BANG FOR YOUR BUCK

SUNY ESF Students say that the "small campus size" has its perks and "allows plentiful opportunities for students to gain close relationships with professors, eventually leading to research, projects, or teaching assistant positions." In fact, one student says "the job placement rates straight out of college" were a deciding factor on their enrollment at the university. In addition to offering financial aid in the form of federal and state packages, loans, scholarships, and grants, SUNY-ESF offers their own Presidential Scholarships which provide up to $3,000 per year for New York State residents or up to $8,000 per year for out-of-state residents.

STUDENT LIFE

SUNY-ESF has a small campus with an enrollment of 1,750, but "students also have access to Syracuse University's clubs, activities, and classes, [which] helps to round out the specificity of SUNY-ESF. There is also countless opportunities to get involved and pursue a particular passion." The College offers internships, research opportunities, and 30 student organizations, sponsored by the ESF student government, for this environmentally-conscious student body. As a current undergrad divulges, SUNY ESF students are "generally very smart, informed young people who have a passion for the environment and tend to very knowledgeable and eager to learn more in their field. Most students are fairly outdoorsy and well rounded, as well as motivated to make a difference in the world. [They] care about our planet and our community and one another. [They] make a point to make connections, and are generally very friendly, welcoming, and inclusive." Many students mentioned "integrity, environmentalism, and equality" as key components of their life at SUNY-ESF.

CAREER

SUNY-ESF students take "specific courses with specialized programs that allow for very high job placement after graduation." Many believe they are also getting a career boost in terms of the "opportunities for interaction with professors and administrators. First year students are doing research and we have the ability to become close to high level administrators including the president." One unique offering, the Job Location and Development Program, matches students with careers right after school, and has made connections in the paper industry, conservation, wildlife management, and environmental research. SUNY-ESF alumni who visited PayScale.com reported an average starting salary of $49,700 with an average mid-career salary of $87,500.

State University of New York—College of Environmental Science and Forestry

FINANCIAL AID: 315-470-6706 • E-MAIL: ESFINFO@ESF.EDU • FAX: 315-470-6933 • WEBSITE: WWW.ESF.EDU

GENERAL INFO

Activities: Choral groups, concert band, dance, drama/theater, jazz band, literary magazine, marching band, music ensembles, musical theater, pep band, radio station, student government, student newspaper, student-run film society, symphony orchestra, television station, yearbook, campus ministries, International Student Organization, 300 registered organizations. **Athletics (Intercollegiate):** *Men:* basketball, cross-country, golf, soccer, track. *Women:* cross-country, golf, soccer, track. **On-Campus Highlights:** Library, Green houses, Wildlife collection, Laboratories & Studios, Gateway Center, snack bar, student store. SUNY-ESF is on the campus of Syracuse University. Popular sites include: Carrier Dome, Crouse College (a historic building), Schine Student Center, Hendricks Chapel. **Environmental Initiatives:** (1) ESF's new student center is a LEED platinum rated building with a wood pellet fueled heating system. (2) Photovoltaic arrays/green roof. (3) College owns and manages 25,000 acres of forest (providing carbon offsets). Faculty are conducting government supported research in the development of ethanol and other renewable products from wood biomass. ESF has partnered with the NY State government and private industry to develop the state's first "biorefinery" aimed at producing ethanol and other chemical products from wood sugars. ESF has also developed a genetically engineered species of fast growth willow that is being grown as an alternative to corn use in ethanol production. Forty percent of all College vehicles (cars, maintenance vehicles, buses, GEM, etc.) are powered with renewable fuels, electric or hybrid technologies.

FINANCIAL AID

Students should submit: FAFSA, state aid form. Priority filing deadline is 2/1. The Princeton Review suggests that all financial aid forms be submitted as soon as possible after October 1. *Need-based scholarships/grants offered:* College/university scholarship or grant aid from institutional funds, Federal Pell, private scholarships, SEOG, state scholarships/grants. *Loan aid offered:* Direct PLUS Loans, Direct Subsidized Loans, Direct Unsubsidized Loans. Applicants will be notified of awards on a rolling basis beginning 2/1. Federal Work-Study Program available. Institutional employment available.

BOTTOM LINE

Tuition for in-state students totals $6,670, but incoming students should also budget $8,300 for room and $7,100 for board. Additional costs like textbooks are estimated at $1,200. Living off campus or changing housing affects costs, as does hailing from out of state. All students are eligible for federal loans, aid, scholarships, and grants. Determination of the specific scholarship amount will be based upon the student's academic record, recommendations, activities, and requirements for their intended major.

CAREER INFORMATION FROM PAYSCALE.COM	
ROI Rating	88
Bachelors and No Higher	
Median starting salary	$51,800
Median mid-career salary	$94,800
At Least Bachelors	
Median starting salary	$52,700
Median mid-career salary	$97,400
Alumni with high job meaning	61%
Degrees awarded in STEM subjects	49%

SELECTIVITY

Admissions Rating	88
# of applicants	1,815
% of applicants accepted	52
% of acceptees attending	35
# offered a place on the wait list	452
% accepting a place on wait list	45
% admitted from wait list	16
# of early decision applicants	175
% accepted early decision	73

FRESHMAN PROFILE

Range SAT EBRW	580–650
Range SAT Math	570–650
Range ACT Composite	24–28
Minimum paper TOEFL	550
Minimum internet-based TOEFL	79
Average HS GPA	3.8
% graduated top 10% of class	32
% graduated top 25% of class	62
% graduated top 50% of class	95

DEADLINES

Early decision	
Deadline	12/1
Notification	1/15
Regular	
Priority	2/1
Nonfall registration?	Yes

FINANCIAL FACTS

Financial Aid Rating	87
Annual in-state tuition	$6,670
Annual out-of-state tuition	$16,320
Room and board	$15,160
Required fees	$1,898
Books and supplies	$1,200
Average frosh need-based scholarship	$7,510
Average UG need-based scholarship	$6,648
% needy frosh rec. need-based scholarship or grant aid	98
% needy UG rec. need-based scholarship or grant aid	92
% needy frosh rec. non-need-based scholarship or grant aid	72
% needy UG rec. non-need-based scholarship or grant aid	65
% needy frosh rec. need-based self-help aid	69
% needy UG rec. need-based self-help aid	66
% frosh rec. any financial aid	91
% UG rec. any financial aid	93
% UG borrow to pay for school	68
Average cumulative indebtedness	$26,679
% frosh need fully met	35
% ugrads need fully met	48
Average % of frosh need met	70
Average % of ugrad need met	66

State University of New York—Purchase College

735 Anderson Hill Road, Purchase, NY 10577 • Admissions: 914-251-6300 • Fax: 914-251-6314

CAMPUS LIFE

Quality of Life Rating	**84**
Fire Safety Rating	**60***
Green Rating	**60***
Type of school	Public
Environment	Town

STUDENTS

Total undergrad enrollment	4,102
% male/female	43/57
% from out of state	15
% frosh live on campus	87
% ugrads live on campus	67
% African American	12
% Asian	4
% Caucasian	53
% Hispanic	22
% Native American	<1
% Pacific Islander	<1
% Two or more races	5
% Race and/or ethnicity unknown	1
% international	3
# of countries represented	39

ACADEMICS

Academic Rating	**78**
% students returning for sophomore year	83
Calendar	Semester
Student/faculty ratio	14:1
Profs interesting rating	84
Profs accessible rating	71
Most classes have 20–29 students.	

MOST POPULAR MAJORS

Liberal Arts and Sciences; Psychology; Arts, Entertainment, and Media Management

ABOUT THE SCHOOL

Imbued with a "strong sense of school spirit," SUNY Purchase is an institution that actively celebrates "diversity," "creativity," and "the weird." Many undergrads are drawn to Purchase due to the "excellent" performing and fine arts programs. And while it can often feel like these "phenomenal" conservatories dominate the academic scene, we've been assured that "there is something for everyone at this school." As one undergrad interjects, "Yes, we are an arts school, but we also have majors in sciences, math, and even an awesome Arts Management program that bridges the gap between business and the arts." Students also love the fact that many courses are "discussion" based. And they are quick to note that professors here make a point of "get[ting] to know [students] on a personal level" and continually demonstrate that "they really want to share what they know with you." Finally, this pleased undergrad concludes, "I absolutely love my professors. I couldn't have asked for or received better people who are more qualified for their positions."

BANG FOR YOUR BUCK

Students in search of a good school with a reasonable price tag will definitely want to consider SUNY Purchase. After all, during the last academic year, the university doled out roughly $2.2 million in aid. And every student is considered for scholarships when his or her admissions application is reviewed. Recipients are generally chosen based upon standardized test scores and academic achievement. Awards range anywhere from $200 to the full cost of tuition. Moreover, it's also important to note that when distributing aid packages, Purchase always endeavors to first award grants and then work-study options. Loans are often the last resort.

STUDENT LIFE

Purchase students love that their campus is constantly abuzz with activity. There's always something fun to attend be it "special lectures...movie screenings [or various] games." Of course, many undergrads flock to the "huge dance parties in the Stood" that are held "every Friday night." Additionally, there are "concerts [most] weekend[s]." And given the university's emphasis on the arts, you can frequently find a "play, dance, music or opera" performance being staged somewhere. We're also told that there are "usually parties in the campus apartments." But if drinking "isn't your thing" don't fret. After all, "there's an on-campus museum, [tons] of places to sit and relax, lots of free yoga classes, zumba, the gym, etc." And don't forget that New York City is only a quick train ride away!

State University of New York—Purchase College

FINANCIAL AID: 914-251-6350 • E-MAIL: ADMISSIONS@PURCHASE.EDU • WEBSITE: WWW.PURCHASE.EDU

CAREER

SUNY Purchase's Career Development Center truly excels at helping students turn their passions into tangible careers. The office hosts a myriad of events pertaining to specific fields and industries including Museum Career Day, Opportunities in Book Publishing, Opportunities in Healthcare, etc. Undergrads may also visit the Center to develop the skills they need to be successful on the job market. They can receive assistance with resume writing, practice interviewing and get some hot tips on networking. Additionally, Purchase hosts an annual job fair. Undergrads here have the opportunity to meet with a number of illustrious companies and organizations and maybe even walk away with a job or internship offer in hand!

GENERAL INFO

Activities: Choral groups; Dance; Drama/theater; International Student Organization; Jazz band; Literary magazine; Music ensembles; Musical theater; Radio station; Student government; Student newspaper; Student-run film society; Television station 30 registered organizations. **Athletics (Intercollegiate):** *Men:* baseball, basketball, cross-country, golf, soccer, tennis, volleyball. *Women:* basketball, cross-country, soccer, softball, tennis, volleyball. **On-Campus Highlights:** The Performing Arts Center, The Neuberger Museum, State-of-the-Art Athletic Complex, Starbucks, Fort Awesome .

FINANCIAL AID

Students should submit: FAFSA, state aid form. Priority filing deadline is 2/15. The Princeton Review suggests that all financial aid forms be submitted as soon as possible after October 1. *Need-based scholarships/grants offered:* College/university scholarship or grant aid from institutional funds, Federal Pell, private scholarships, SEOG, state scholarships/grants. *Loan aid offered:* Direct PLUS Loans, Direct Subsidized Loans, Direct Unsubsidized Loans. Applicants will be notified of awards on a rolling basis beginning 3/1. Federal Work-Study Program available. Institutional employment available.

CAREER INFORMATION FROM PAYSCALE.COM

ROI Rating	87
Bachelors and No Higher	
Median starting salary	$48,100
Median mid-career salary	$88,800
At Least Bachelors	
Median starting salary	$49,000
Median mid-career salary	$90,300
Alumni with high job meaning	42%
Degrees awarded in STEM subjects	5%

SELECTIVITY

Admissions Rating	**87**
# of applicants	4,056
% of applicants accepted	74
% of acceptees attending	25

FRESHMAN PROFILE

Range SAT EBRW	530–630
Range SAT Math	490–570
Range ACT Composite	20–26
Minimum paper TOEFL	550
Average HS GPA	3.2

DEADLINES

Early action	
Deadline	11/15
Notification	12/15
Regular	
Priority	3/1
Deadline	7/15
Nonfall registration?	Yes

FINANCIAL FACTS

Financial Aid Rating	**78**
Annual in-state tuition	$6,870
Annual out-of-state tuition	$16,650
Room and board	$13,764
Required fees	$1,828
Books and supplies	$1,250
Average frosh need-based scholarship	$9,119
Average UG need-based scholarship	$9,926
% needy frosh rec. need-based scholarship or grant aid	98
% needy UG rec. need-based scholarship or grant aid	98
% needy frosh rec. non-need-based scholarship or grant aid	11
% needy UG rec. non-need-based scholarship or grant aid	16
% needy frosh rec. need-based self-help aid	91
% needy UG rec. need-based self-help aid	90
% frosh need fully met	1
% ugrads need fully met	2
Average % of frosh need met	44
Average % of ugrad need met	48

State University of New York— Stony Brook University

OFFICE OF ADMISSIONS, STONY BROOK, NY 11794-1901 • ADMISSIONS: 631-632-6868 • FINANCIAL AID: 631-632-6840

CAMPUS LIFE

Quality of Life Rating	85
Fire Safety Rating	91
Green Rating	96
Type of school	Public
Environment	Town

STUDENTS

Total undergrad enrollment	17,215
% male/female	53/47
% from out of state	6
% frosh from public high school	90
% frosh live on campus	83
% ugrads live on campus	53
# of fraternities (% ugrad men join)	14 (2)
# of sororities (% ugrad women join)	16 (2)
% African American	7
% Asian	24
% Caucasian	33
% Hispanic	12
% Native American	<1
% Pacific Islander	<1
% Two or more races	3
% Race and/or ethnicity unknown	6
% international	14
# of countries represented	130

ACADEMICS

Academic Rating	79
% students returning for sophomore year	90
% students graduating within 4 years	53
% students graduating within 6 years	72
Calendar	Semester
Student/faculty ratio	18:1
Profs interesting rating	71
Profs accessible rating	72

Most classes have 20–29 students. Most lab/discussion sessions have 20–29 students.

MOST POPULAR MAJORS

Biology/Biological Sciences; Psychology; Health Services/Allied Health/Health Sciences; Computer Science; Business

ABOUT THE SCHOOL

SUNY's Stony Brook University in Long Island is a "research-oriented university" that provides both "excellent academics and atmosphere." The institution, located just 60 miles from New York City, also does a stellar job of cultivating a "diverse community" which helps students expand their world views. Additionally, Stony Brook smartly capitalizes on its "connection to the hospital" and thus offers some "renowned" programs within STEM subjects and the health sciences. Undergrads further note that the university is "very student focused," with faculty and staff "willing to help in every which way possible to ensure the success of every student." And in general, professors here are all "very enthusiastic about the courses they teach." They're also great about peppering their lectures with their "personal research experiences." And they truly excel at "bringing the material to life and offering creative problems that show the real-world applications of our studies." Best of all, professors are "readily available to answer questions you may have during and outside of class."

BANG FOR YOUR BUCK

Stony Brook University maintains a strong commitment to providing an affordable education to all students. Every admitted undergraduate is automatically considered for merit scholarships. The university emails all selected students starting in late March to inform them of their awards. Importantly, scholarships are available within a range of categories. These include diversity, disability, leadership and general academic excellence. There are also scholarships offered for specific courses of study including music, business and international relations. Many students also participate in the federal work study program. Priority is given to students who complete their FAFSA by their respective deadline designations.

STUDENT LIFE

Students who attend Stony Brook can participate in "hundreds of student organizations and clubs ranging from intramural basketball to a cappella to college Republicans." Of course, many undergrads here flock to the "spectacular recreational center where students can play sports with their friends, work out, or take fitness classes such as kick boxing, self defense and yoga." However, some people do bemoan the fact that "many students do go home on the weekends." Therefore, the campus can sometimes feel a little dead at times. Conversely, others insist that "there's plenty to do" and note that "the university sends out twice weekly emails to the student body publicizing events on campus." And many undergrads love participating in "great Stony Brook traditions such as Roth Regatta (a boat race of boats made from only cardboard and duct tape), Earthstock, and [annual] concerts."

CAREER

To ensure that they're ready for their post-collegiate life, Stony Brook undergrads frequently turn to the university's Career Center. The office offers numerous resources starting with Handshake, a database for both on- and off-campus jobs, internships and volunteer opportunities. Students can also take advantage of Career Communities which connects undergrads with employers, faculty and staff who have common career interests. The Career Center provides both individual and group coaching and it sponsors numerous career fairs tailored to specific fields or academic disciplines, such as engineering, business, or health care. Finally, students can also attend information sessions with top companies such as Wells Fargo, Credit Suisse, KPMG, and Bloomberg (among others).

State University of New York—Stony Brook University

E-MAIL: ENROLL@STONYBROOK.EDU • FAX: 631-632-9898 • WEBSITE: WWW.STONYBROOK.EDU

GENERAL INFO

Activities: Choral groups, concert band, dance, drama/theater, jazz band, literary magazine, marching band, music ensembles, musical theater, pep band, radio station, student government, student newspaper, student-run film society, yearbook, campus ministries. **Organizations:** 425 registered clubs and organizations. 18 fraternities, 14 sororities. **Athletics (Intercollegiate):** *Men:* Baseball, basketball, cross-country, football, lacrosse, soccer, track/field (outdoor), track/field (indoor). *Women:* Basketball, cross-country, diving, lacrosse, soccer, softball, swimming, tennis, track/field (outdoor), track/field (indoor), volleyball. **On-Campus Highlights:** Staller Center for the Arts, Sports Complex (including a new 4,000-seat arena) and Stadium, Student Activities Center, University Hospital, The Charles B. Wang Center.

FINANCIAL AID

Students should submit: FAFSA; State aid form. Priority filing deadline is 2/15. The Princeton Review suggests that all financial aid forms be submitted as soon as possible after October 1. *Need-based scholarships/grants offered:* College/university scholarship or grant aid from institutional funds, Federal Pell, private scholarships, SEOG, state scholarships/grants. *Loan aid offered:* Direct PLUS Loans, Direct Subsidized Loans, Direct Unsubsidized Loans. Applicants will be notified of awards on a rolling basis beginning 3/1. Federal Work-Study Program available. Institutional employment available.

THE BOTTOM LINE

Tuition for New York State residents who opt to attend Stony Brook is $6,870 for the 2018–2019 academic year. On the other hand, out-of-state and international students pay $24,540. Stony Brook charges an additional $2,755 in fees. On-campus housing will cost another $8,654 and the meal plan runs students $5,044. Undergrads should need another $900 for books and supplies. Stony Brook ballparks personal expenses (including transportation needs) at around $1,868.

CAREER INFORMATION FROM PAYSCALE.COM	
ROI Rating	90
Bachelors and No Higher	
Median starting salary	$57,000
Median mid-career salary	$110,000
At Least Bachelors	
Median starting salary	$58,300
Median mid-career salary	$114,500
Alumni with high job meaning	49%
Degrees awarded in STEM subjects	35%

SELECTIVITY	
Admissions Rating	91
# of applicants	35,313
% of applicants accepted	42
% of acceptees attending	21
# offered a place on the wait list	3,778
% accepting a place on wait list	45
% admitted from wait list	4

FRESHMAN PROFILE	
Range SAT EBRW	590–680
Range SAT Math	620–730
Range ACT Composite	26–31
Minimum paper TOEFL	550
Minimum internet-based TOEFL	80
Average HS GPA	3.8
% graduated top 10% of class	48
% graduated top 25% of class	81
% graduated top 50% of class	95

DEADLINES	
Regular	
Priority	1/15
Notification	4/1
Nonfall registration?	Yes

FINANCIAL FACTS	
Financial Aid Rating	82
Annual in-state tuition	$6,870
Annual out-of-state tuition	$24,540
Room and board	$13,698
Required fees	$2,755
Books and supplies	$900
Average frosh need-based scholarship	$10,601
Average UG need-based scholarship	$8,641
% needy frosh rec. need-based scholarship or grant aid	93
% needy UG rec. need-based scholarship or grant aid	85
% needy frosh rec. non-need-based scholarship or grant aid	12
% needy UG rec. non-need-based scholarship or grant aid	6
% needy frosh rec. need-based self-help aid	89
% needy UG rec. need-based self-help aid	90
% frosh rec. any financial aid	77
% UG rec. any financial aid	67
% UG borrow to pay for school	54
Average cumulative indebtedness	$26,219
% frosh need fully met	16
% ugrads need fully met	18
Average % of frosh need met	70
Average % of ugrad need met	67

Stevens Institute of Technology

1 Castle Point Terrace, Hoboken, NJ 07030 • Admissions: 201-216-5194 • Fax: 201-216-8348

CAMPUS LIFE

Quality of Life Rating	**90**
Fire Safety Rating	**99**
Green Rating	**77**
Type of school	Private
Environment	Town

STUDENTS

Total undergrad enrollment	3,114
% male/female	70/30
% from out of state	39
% frosh live on campus	91
% ugrads live on campus	64
# of fraternities (% ugrad men join)	12 (31)
# of sororities (% ugrad women join)	6 (49)
% African American	2
% Asian	12
% Caucasian	67
% Hispanic	10
% Native American	<1
% Race and/or ethnicity unknown	4
% international	4
# of countries represented	39

ACADEMICS

Academic Rating	**74**
% students returning for sophomore year	94
% students graduating within 4 years	42
% students graduating within 6 years	83
Calendar	Semester
Student/faculty ratio	10:1
Profs interesting rating	71
Profs accessible rating	69
Most classes have 20–29 students.	

MOST POPULAR MAJORS

Computer Science; Mechanical Engineering; Chemical Engineering

ABOUT THE SCHOOL

Technological innovation leads the way at Stevens Institute of Technology in Hoboken, where 3,114 undergraduates, spread across three schools and one college (as well as two national research centers), gain interdisciplinary knowledge through a curriculum that incorporates classroom lectures, innovative technologies, team projects, and actual work in the field. Most who come here participate in the strong engineering programs, which "challenge students but is also flexible, allowing students time to make up their minds about which field they would like to pursue." All students participate in some form of experiential learning, with most completing at least two activities (internships, co-ops, or faculty-mentored research) prior to graduation; students say that the co-op program is "the best part about Stevens," as "it offsets the cost of the college and gives the students real life experience." In fact, "all academics are applied to upcoming technology and students learn to adapt to the changing world."

BANG FOR YOUR BUCK

The Stevens job placement rate is "incredibly high and at renowned companies," and more than three quarters of students have finalized their career or post-graduate study plans prior graduation. Ninety-six percent of Class of 2017 grads had secured their career outcomes within six months of graduation, The cooperative education and internship programs play a big role in students' job placement success as students have opportunities to gain experience in both corporate and laboratory settings with employers such as Google, Microsoft, JPMorgan Chase, Exxon Mobil, L'Oreal, Goldman Sachs, Citigroup, and Panasonic. The school has plenty of scholarships available, including the prestigious Neupauer Scholarship, which is a four-year, full tuition award, and the Martha Bayard Stevens Scholarship, which is a four-year award to a woman pursuing any field of study at Stevens.

STUDENT LIFE

Stevens offers a "small-knit environment where you see familiar faces everywhere," which makes the experience all the more enriching. Everyone here is a friendly high-achiever that "understands teamwork and cooperation lead to success rather than competition and divisiveness." People are "really involved in clubs, sports, organizations, and Greek Life," which "does a ton of community service for the local area." With plenty to do in the surrounding area—New York City is a mere ten minutes away—"fun is practically endless." There are also "lots of gamers at the school, given its technical background," and "LAN parties are weekly and fill up an entire lecture hall and go on all night long." Many students "have very technical interests" and hobbies relating to their majors.

CAREER

With several career fairs held through the year and more than 300 employers recruiting and otherwise involved on campus, The Stevens Career Center does an excellent job of facilitating connections between companies and organizations that want to hire their grads: "You're free to get as much help from the Career Center as you want." Stevens also uses Handshake, a mobile job-posting and recruitment resource utilized by hundreds of schools and organizations. Additionally, the Career Center hosts workshops and seminars, arranges co-ops and internships, and sets up one-day job shadowing externships during the winter recess. All seniors at Stevens, regardless of their major, are required to complete a capstone Senior Design Project. Seniors are encouraged to develop their Senior Design Projects with the collaboration of an industrial sponsor, providing another route for students to secure post-college employment. It also "really helps to be located so close to the city, as there are tons of opportunities

Stevens Institute of Technology

FINANCIAL AID: 201-216-5555 • E-MAIL: ADMISSIONS@STEVENS.EDU • WEBSITE: WWW.STEVENS.EDU

available to you as a Stevens student." Of the Stevens Institute of Technology alumni visiting PayScale.com, 50 percent report that they derive a high level of meaning from their jobs.

GENERAL INFO

Activities: Choral groups, concert band, dance, drama/theater, jazz band, literary magazine, music ensembles, musical theater, radio station, student government, student newspaper, symphony orchestra, television station, yearbook, campus ministries, Ethnic Student Council, StevensTHON, Entertainment Committee, Alpha Phi Omega Service Fraternity. **Organizations:** 120 registered organizations, 13 honor societies. 12 fraternities, 6 sororities. **Athletics (Intercollegiate):** *Men:* baseball, basketball, cross-country, fencing, golf, lacrosse, soccer, swimming, tennis, track/field (outdoor), track/field (indoor), volleyball, wrestling. *Women:* basketball, cross-country, equestrian sports, fencing, field hockey, lacrosse, soccer, softball, swimming, tennis, track/field (outdoor), track/field (indoor), volleyball. **On-Campus Highlights:** Schaefer Athletic Center, DeBaun Auditorium, Castle Point Lookout, NYC skyline views, Babbio Center, Wesley J. Howe Center.

FINANCIAL AID

Students should submit: CSS Profile; FAFSA. Priority filing deadline is 3/1. The Princeton Review suggests that all financial aid forms be submitted as soon as possible after October 1. *Need-based scholarships/grants offered:* College/university scholarship or grant aid from institutional funds; Federal Pell; Private scholarships; SEOG; State scholarships/grants. *Loan aid offered:* Direct PLUS Loans, Direct Subsidized Loans, Direct Unsubsidized Loans. Federal Work-Study Program available. Institutional employment available.

BOTTOM LINE

Though the sticker price is steep—$50,370 in tuition and $15,244 for room and board—the Stevens Office of Financial Aid partners with any student that wishes to develop a plan for paying for their education. About 92 percent of students receive some form of financial assistance, to the annual tune of more than $67 million.

CAREER INFORMATION FROM PAYSCALE.COM	
ROI Rating	87
Bachelors and No Higher	
Median starting salary	$73,600
Median mid-career salary	$138,900
At Least Bachelors	
Median starting salary	$74,900
Median mid-career salary	$142,400
Alumni with high job meaning	50%
Degrees awarded in STEM subjects	79%

SELECTIVITY	
Admissions Rating	95
# of applicants	8,335
% of applicants accepted	44
% of acceptees attending	21
# offered a place on the wait list	1,672
% accepting a place on wait list	35
% admitted from wait list	15
# of early decision applicants	689
% accepted early decision	56

FRESHMAN PROFILE	
Range SAT EBRW	640–710
Range SAT Math	680–760
Range ACT Composite	29–33
Minimum internet-based TOEFL	80
Average HS GPA	3.8
% graduated top 10% of class	72
% graduated top 25% of class	91
% graduated top 50% of class	99

DEADLINES	
Early decision	
Deadline	11/15
Notification	12/15
Other ED Deadline	1/15
Other ED Notification	2/15
Regular	
Deadline	1/15
Notification	4/1
Nonfall registration?	No

FINANCIAL FACTS	
Financial Aid Rating	82
Annual tuition	$50,370
Room and board	$15,244
Required fees	$1,832
Books and supplies	$1,200
Average frosh need-based scholarship	$13,787
Average UG need-based scholarship	$12,741
% needy frosh rec. need-based scholarship or grant aid	68
% needy UG rec. need-based scholarship or grant aid	59
% needy frosh rec. non-need-based scholarship or grant aid	98
% needy UG rec. non-need-based scholarship or grant aid	92
% needy frosh rec. need-based self-help aid	71
% needy UG rec. need-based self-help aid	74
% frosh rec. any financial aid	97
% UG rec. any financial aid	92
% frosh need fully met	17
% ugrads need fully met	18
Average % of frosh need met	71
Average % of ugrad need met	69

Stonehill College

320 Washington Street, Easton, MA 02357-5610 • Admission: 508-565-1373 • Fax: 508-565-1545

CAMPUS LIFE

Quality of Life Rating	91
Fire Safety Rating	98
Green Rating	87
Type of school	Private
Affiliation	Roman Catholic
Environment	Village

STUDENTS

Total undergrad enrollment	2,494
% male/female	41/59
% from out of state	38
% frosh from public high school	67
% frosh live on campus	93
% ugrads live on campus	89
# of fraternities (% ugrad men join)	0 (0)
# of sororities (% ugrad women join)	0 (0)
% African American	4
% Asian	2
% Caucasian	85
% Hispanic	4
% Native American	<1
% Pacific Islander	0
% Two or more races	2
% Race and/or ethnicity unknown	2
% international	1
# of countries represented	11

ACADEMICS

Academic Rating	88
% students returning for sophomore year	85
% students graduating within 4 years	77
% students graduating within 6 years	80
Calendar	Semester
Student/faculty ratio	12:1
Profs interesting rating	88
Profs accessible rating	85
Most classes have 10–19 students.	

MOST POPULAR MAJORS
Biology/Biological Sciences; Psychology; Accounting

ABOUT THE SCHOOL

Stonehill College is a "Catholic institution" that places an emphasis on building a "tight knit community." Moreover, the school really pushes students to go "beyond the classroom" and gain experience by taking advantage of "volunteer[ing]...internships and...research opportunities." Thankfully, there's plenty to be gained inside the classroom as well. And since courses tend to be "small," there's a "more intimate [learning] environment." In turn, this really allows students and faculty to "build strong...relationships." Of course, it is rather easy to connect with professors since they "genuinely want to be here." Not only do they have a "passion" for their chosen discipline, they strive to see their students "do well." Indeed, they are always "willing to meet with you to go over a test or paper." What's more, Stonehill professors "make an effort to get to know" each student as individuals. As one amazed undergrad illustrates, "I had a professor first semester freshman year who still says hi to me when he [sees] me in the hallways (and I haven't had him as a professor in three years)."

BANG FOR YOUR BUCK

Stonehill is a college that is deeply committed to both affordability and helping families with the financial aid process. To that end, the school offers a number of both need-based and merit-based scholarships. Certain awards, such as the Fr. Basil Moreau Scholarship, are renewable for four years and may cover more than half the cost of tuition. Stonehill undergrads can also receive grants to cover specific needs such as room and board. Finally, undergrads who have a parent working at a participating institution may be eligible for a Tuition Exchange Scholarship. This is also renewable assuming the recipient demonstrates satisfactory academic progress.

STUDENT LIFE

It's rather easy to have an active social life at Stonehill College. After all, "during the weekends we have so many events going on that it is hard to choose from." For example, there are "Bingo Nights every Friday that are actually really fun." Additionally, the "campus bar" frequently hosts "concerts" and we're also told that "sports games" are well attended. Of course, undergrads here are equally adept at making their own fun. And when the weather's nice, you can always find "people playing frisbee or spikeball on the quad." A number of students can also be found "hiking at local parks." Finally, if students are anxious for some big city excitement, they're just a shuttle ride away from Boston!

Stonehill College

FINANCIAL AID: 508-565-1088 • E-MAIL: ADMISSION@STONEHILL.EDU • WEBSITE: WWW.STONEHILL.EDU

CAREER

Undergrads at Stonehill love to brag about the college's "high job placement rate." They often tout the strong "connections" they're able to form with both "alumni and...professors" as these relationships frequently lead to "internships, jobs, etc." Students can obviously also turn to the college's Career Development Center, which takes an individualized approach to the job hunt and really helps empower each undergraduate. The Center also hosts numerous events that place students on the path to career success. Perhaps the ultimate event is the annual Job and Internship Expo which brings top companies to campus including Massachusetts General Hospital, PricewaterhouseCoopers, W.B. Mason Company, Inc., Talbots, Northwestern Mutual and the Department of Homeland Security.

GENERAL INFO

Activities: Campus Ministries; Choral groups; Concert band; Dance; Drama/theater; International Student Organization; Jazz band; Literary magazine; Model UN; Music ensembles; Musical theater; Pep band; Radio station; Student government; Student newspaper; Student-run film society; Symphony orchestra; Yearbook. **Organizations:** 76 registered organizations, 19 honor societies, 3 religious organizations. **Athletics (Intercollegiate):** *Men:* baseball, basketball, cross-country, football, ice hockey, soccer, tennis, track/field (outdoor), track/field (indoor). *Women:* basketball, cross-country, equestrian sports, field hockey, lacrosse, soccer, softball, tennis, track/field (outdoor), track/field (indoor), volleyball. **On-Campus Highlights:** The Hill (entertainment/dining social space), The MacPhaidin Library, The Roche Dining Commons, The Shields Science Center, The Sally Blair Ames Sports Complex. The Leo J. Meehan School of Business building opening fall 2019.

FINANCIAL AID

Students should submit: CSS Profile; FAFSA; Noncustodial PROFILE. Regular filing deadline is 3/1. The Princeton Review suggests that all financial aid forms be submitted as soon as possible after October 1. *Need-based scholarships/grants offered:* College/university scholarship or grant aid from institutional funds, Federal Pell, private scholarships, SEOG, state scholarships/grants. *Loan aid offered:* Direct PLUS Loans, Direct Subsidized Loans, Direct Unsubsidized Loans. Applicants will be notified of awards two to four weeks after receiving their decision. Federal Work-Study Program available. Institutional employment available.

CAREER INFORMATION FROM PAYSCALE.COM

ROI Rating	87
Bachelors and No Higher	
Median starting salary	$54,000
Median mid-career salary	$104,900
At Least Bachelors	
Median starting salary	$55,500
Median mid-career salary	$107,400
Alumni with high job meaning	43%
Degrees awarded in STEM subjects	18%

SELECTIVITY

Admissions Rating	81
# of applicants	6,260
% of applicants accepted	72
% of acceptees attending	15
# offered a place on the wait list	936
% accepting a place on wait list	34
% admitted from wait list	15
# of early decision applicants	84
% accepted early decision	92

FRESHMAN PROFILE

Range SAT EBRW	550–640
Range SAT Math	530–630
Range ACT Composite	23–28
Minimum paper TOEFL	550
Minimum internet-based TOEFL	80
Average HS GPA	3.3
% graduated top 10% of class	22
% graduated top 25% of class	51
% graduated top 50% of class	88

DEADLINES

Early decision	
Deadline	12/1
Notification	12/31
Early action	
Deadline	11/1
Notification	12/31
Regular	
Deadline	1/15
Notification	3/15
Nonfall registration?	Yes

FINANCIAL FACTS

Financial Aid Rating	90
Annual tuition	$42,746
Room and board	$16,000
Average frosh need-based scholarship	$23,901
Average UG need-based scholarship	$25,209
% needy frosh rec. need-based scholarship or grant aid	99
% needy UG rec. need-based scholarship or grant aid	98
% needy frosh rec. non-need-based scholarship or grant aid	27
% needy UG rec. non-need-based scholarship or grant aid	25
% needy frosh rec. need-based self-help aid	69
% needy UG rec. need-based self-help aid	74
% frosh rec. any financial aid	99
% UG rec. any financial aid	95
% UG borrow to pay for school	77
Average cumulative indebtedness	$36,502
% frosh need fully met	46

Swarthmore College

500 College Avenue, Swarthmore, PA 19081 • Admissions: 610-328-8300 • Fax: 610-328-8580

CAMPUS LIFE

Quality of Life Rating	78
Fire Safety Rating	92
Green Rating	85
Type of school	Private
Environment	Village

STUDENTS

Total undergrad enrollment	1,641
% male/female	49/51
% from out of state	87
% frosh from public high school	56
% frosh live on campus	100
% ugrads live on campus	96
# of fraternities (% ugrad men join)	2 (9)
# of sororities (% ugrad women join)	1 (4)
% African American	7
% Asian	17
% Caucasian	41
% Hispanic	12
% Native American	<1
% Pacific Islander	<1
% Two or more races	7
% Race and/or ethnicity unknown	3
% international	13
# of countries represented	79

ACADEMICS

Academic Rating	91
% students returning for sophomore year	98
% students graduating within 4 years	89
% students graduating within 6 years	94
Calendar	Semester
Student/faculty ratio	8:1
Profs interesting rating	91
Profs accessible rating	92

Most classes have between 2–9 students.
Most lab/discussion sessions have 10–19 students.

MOST POPULAR MAJORS
Economics; Computer Science; Biology

ABOUT THE SCHOOL

Swarthmore College is among the most renowned liberal arts schools in the country. The locus of Swarthmore's greatness lies in the quality and passion of its faculty ("Some of my professors have knocked me to the floor with their brilliance"). A student/faculty ratio of eight to one ensures that students have close, meaningful engagement with their professors. "It's where to go for a real education—for learning for the sake of truly learning, rather than just for grades," says a student. The college's Honors Program features small groups of dedicated and accomplished students working closely with faculty, with an emphasis on independent learning, and helps further the school's reputation as "a community where everyone pushes each other toward success." External examiners who are experts in their fields, such as theater professionals from the Tisch School at NYU and Google software engineers, evaluate seniors in the Honors Program through written and oral examinations. Swatties are a bright and creative lot "who don't get enough sleep because they're too busy doing all they want to do in their time here." Professors and administrators are extremely supportive and "view the students as responsible adults, and thus leave them to their own devices when they are out of class." Students also enjoy an expansive curriculum—about 600 course offerings each year. Swarthmore is part of the Tri-College Consortium (along with Bryn Mawr and Haverford), which means that students can take courses at those schools and use their facilities.

BANG FOR YOUR BUCK

Swarthmore College maintains a need-blind admission policy. Admission here is not contingent on your economic situation, and financial aid awards meet 100 percent of admitted students' demonstrated need. Financial aid is also available for some international students. Best of all, all Swarthmore financial aid awards are loan-free (though some students choose to borrow to cover their portion). In most cases, Swarthmore students may apply their financial aid toward the cost of participation in a study abroad program. Finally, the annual activity fee covers everything from digital printing to sports matches, campus movie screenings to lectures and dance performances, making for a cash-free campus.

STUDENT LIFE

Students are "not sure if there is a typical Swattie," but suspect that "the defining feature among us is that each person is brilliant at something: maybe dance, maybe quantum physics, maybe philosophy." One undergrad sums up, "While it is tough to generalize…one word definitely applies to us all: busy." Swarthmore's small size combined with its vast number of clubs and organizations provide opportunities to participate in pretty much whatever you want, and if not "you can start your own club." "There are student musical performances, drama performances, movies, speakers, and comedy shows," along with all kinds of school-sponsored events, so "there is almost always something to do on the weekend." When they can spare a couple of hours, many Swatties like to blow off steam in nearby Philadelphia, which is easily accessible by public transportation, including the train station located right on campus.

Swarthmore College

FINANCIAL AID: 610-328-8358 • E-MAIL: ADMISSIONS@SWARTHMORE.EDU • WEBSITE: WWW.SWARTHMORE.EDU

CAREER

Swarthmore's Career Services does its part to help students reach their fullest potential by offering a variety of useful resources. Personalized career counseling advises undergrads on their options for major selection, internships, externships, and graduate school applications. The Career Cafés engage the community on broad topics, like women in leadership or sustainable farming, that may have career implications. And, of course, a packed events calendar lets students network with alumni, attend panel discussions, and impress potential employers at recruiting consortiums. Take note of Swarthmore's extensive externship program. It matches students with alumni volunteers for week-long job-shadowing experiences in laboratories, museums, publishing companies, labor unions, leading think-tanks, and other places where you might like to work someday. Alumni who visited PayScale.com reported an average starting salary of $60,000, and 44 percent think their work makes the world a better place.

GENERAL INFO

Activities: Choral groups, dance, drama/theater, jazz band, literary magazine, music ensembles, opera, student government, student newspaper, student-run film society, symphony orchestra, yearbook, campus ministries, international student organization. **Organizations:** 150 registered organizations, 3 honor societies, 12 religious organizations. 2 fraternities, 1 sorority. **Athletics (Intercollegiate):** *Men:* Baseball, basketball, cross-country, golf, lacrosse, soccer, swimming, tennis, track/field (outdoor), track/field (indoor). *Women:* Badminton, basketball, cross-country, field hockey, lacrosse, soccer, softball, swimming, tennis, track/field (outdoor), track/field (indoor), volleyball.

FINANCIAL AID

Students should submit: CSS Profile; FAFSA; State aid form. Priority filing deadline is 1/1. The Princeton Review suggests that all financial aid forms be submitted as soon as possible after October 1. *Need-based scholarships/grants offered:* College/university scholarship or grant aid from institutional funds, Federal Pell, private scholarships, SEOG, state scholarships/grants. *Loan aid offered:* Direct PLUS Loans, Direct Subsidized Loans, Direct Unsubsidized Loans. Applicants will be notified of awards on or about 4/1. Federal Work-Study Program available. Institutional employment available.

THE BOTTOM LINE

Swarthmore has staggeringly generous financial aid resources, and it will meet 100 percent of your demonstrated need without loans. The average need-based financial aid award here is more than $45,000. Don't assume you won't receive aid because your family is too wealthy and definitely—please!—don't assume you can't afford Swarthmore because your family isn't wealthy enough.

CAREER INFORMATION FROM PAYSCALE.COM	
ROI Rating	94
Bachelors and No Higher	
Median starting salary	$63,800
Median mid-career salary	$129,200
At Least Bachelors	
Median starting salary	$65,400
Median mid-career salary	$131,700
Alumni with high job meaning	46%
Degrees awarded in STEM subjects	45%

SELECTIVITY	
Admissions Rating	98
# of applicants	9,382
% of applicants accepted	11
% of acceptees attending	39
# of early decision applicants	712
% accepted early decision	28

FRESHMAN PROFILE	
Range SAT EBRW	690–760
Range SAT Math	690–780
Range ACT Composite	31–34
% graduated top 10% of class	91
% graduated top 25% of class	99
% graduated top 50% of class	100

DEADLINES	
Early decision	
Deadline	11/15
Notification	12/15
Other ED Deadline	1/1
Other ED Notification	2/15
Regular	
Deadline	1/1
Notification	4/1
Nonfall registration?	No

FINANCIAL FACTS	
Financial Aid Rating	94
Annual tuition	$50,424
Room and board	$14,952
Required fees	$398
Books and supplies	$1,336
Average frosh need-based scholarship	$50,505
Average UG need-based scholarship	$48,661
% needy frosh rec. need-based scholarship or grant aid	100
% needy UG rec. need-based scholarship or grant aid	100
% needy frosh rec. non-need-based scholarship or grant aid	0
% needy UG rec. non-need-based scholarship or grant aid	0
% needy frosh rec. need-based self-help aid	98
% needy UG rec. need-based self-help aid	98
% frosh rec. any financial aid	57
% UG rec. any financial aid	57
% UG borrow to pay for school	27
Average cumulative indebtedness	$20,209
% frosh need fully met	100
% ugrads need fully met	100
Average % of frosh need met	100
Average % of ugrad need met	100

Texas A&M University—College Station

PO Box 30014, College Station, TX 77842-3014 • Admissions: 979-845-3741 • Fax: 979-847-8737

CAMPUS LIFE

Quality of Life Rating	**89**
Fire Safety Rating	**95**
Green Rating	**91**
Type of school	Public
Environment	City

STUDENTS

Total undergrad enrollment	53,065
% male/female	52/48
% from out of state	4
# of fraternities	30
# of sororities	28
% African American	3
% Asian	7
% Caucasian	62
% Hispanic	23
% Native American	<1
% Pacific Islander	<1
% Two or more races	3
% Race and/or ethnicity unknown	<1
% international	1
# of countries represented	92

ACADEMICS

Academic Rating	**68**
% students returning for sophomore year	92
% students graduating within 4 years	54
% students graduating within 6 years	82
Calendar	Semester
Student/faculty ratio	20:1
Profs interesting rating	72
Profs accessible rating	70

Most classes have 20–29 students. Most lab/discussion sessions have 20–29 students.

MOST POPULAR MAJORS

Engineering; Biomedical Sciences; Business Administration and Management

ABOUT THE SCHOOL

As one of the ten largest universities in the country—the school is home to over 50,000 students, about 40,000 of whom are undergraduates—Texas A&M may embody the idea that everything is bigger in Texas. However, that doesn't mean that students don't feel at home here. The community of Texas A&M bonds over its traditions and pervasive school spirit. Students at Texas A&M have a great "sense of pride that...motivates them to do well because they're part of something bigger than themselves." Students tend to feel that they are "part of a huge family" at Texas A&M. As one student says, "From the outside looking in, you can't understand it. From the inside looking out, you can't explain it." Perhaps part of that mysterious spirit lies in the school's devotion to their "Aggies" athletic teams. From women's volleyball to baseball, Texas A&M fields top-quality athletic teams, and of course, "Saturdays in the fall are owned by football." Founded back in the 1890s, the Aggies Football team has appeared in thirty bowls, winning thirteen of them as well as three national championships. The professors "all have life experiences working with the topics that they teach, making them the perfect resource for information," one student says. Another sums up the Texas A&M experience thusly: "Texas A&M University is not only one of the best universities in terms of higher education. At Texas A&M you learn to be a well-rounded, moral, and ethical person."

BANG FOR YOUR BUCK

If you love college sports, and especially football, it is hard to do better than Texas A&M. About 650 student athletes compete in twenty varsity sports. In 2012, Texas A&M officially joined the storied Southeastern Conference (SEC). Kyle Field is always "packed for home games." This is all part of the Aggie school spirit which extends to the vast Aggie alumni network. "Aggie alumni are loyal to their school forever" and can be a great source of support for students looking to enter postcollege life. The school has a wealth of resources for students and over 950 student organizations for students to participate in. Those who attend Texas A&M tend to enjoy the experience. A full 91 percent of freshmen return for sophomore year.

STUDENT LIFE

These Aggies proudly declare that "there is rarely a dull moment" at Texas A&M. First off, sports fans should rejoice since we're told that "football is central to [student's] live[s] in the fall, with [the] stadium routinely seeing 80,000 in attendance." And, in general, Texas A&M students are pretty active. Many undergrads "spend their free time in the state-of-the-art rec center equipped with a climbing wall, a boulder wall, numerous [pieces of] exercise equipment, an indoor track, and countless exercise classes such as Zumba, Pilates, yoga, and many more." Additionally, "two-stepping and dancing is popular on the weekends." There are also plenty of "frat parties or house parties" to attend. And just off-campus students will find "four dollar movies, many dance halls, endless restaurants to eat at...a large mall...an ice skating rink, bowling alley, and miniature golf place." What more could a college student desire?

CAREERS

The Career Center at Texas A&M does a tremendous job of assisting undergraduates in their career search. Students can connect with over 3,000 potential employers, including more than eighty percent of the Fortune 500 companies. Clearly, these undergrads are in demand. Many students happily share that "the Aggie Network is [another] good [avenue] for getting jobs after graduation." Of course, prior to seeking

Texas A&M University—College Station

FINANCIAL AID: 979-845-3236 • E-MAIL: ADMISSIONS@TAMU.EDU • WEBSITE: WWW.TAMU.EDU

out interviews, undergrads can arrange one-on-one meetings to review resumes, cover letters, etc. Lastly, prospective (and current) students will be delighted to discover that the average starting salary, according to PayScale.com, for recent A&M grads is $57,200.

GENERAL INFO

Activities: Choral groups, concert band, dance, drama/theater, jazz band, literary magazine, marching band, music ensembles, musical theater, radio station, student government, student newspaper, student-run film society, symphony orchestra, television station, yearbook. **Organizations:** campus ministries, International Student Organization 1,000 registered organizations, 34 honor societies, 77 religious organizations. 20 fraternities, 36 sororities. **Athletics (Intercollegiate):** *Men:* baseball, basketball, cross-country, diving, football, golf, riflery, swimming, tennis, track/field (outdoor), track/field (indoor). *Women:* basketball, cross-country, diving, equestrian sports, golf, riflery, soccer, softball, swimming, tennis, track/field (outdoor), track/field (indoor), volleyball. **On-Campus Highlights:** Student Recreation Center, Kyle Field, Corps of Cadets, George Bush Presidential Library/Museum, Memorial Student Center. **Environmental Initiatives:** Aggie Green Fund, sustainable land use, green building practices, smart energy, optimization of energy clusters, waste management through recycling and composting.

FINANCIAL AID

Students should submit: FAFSA. Priority filing deadline is 12/15. The Princeton Review suggests that all financial aid forms be submitted as soon as possible after October 1. *Need-based scholarships/grants offered:* College/university scholarship or grant aid from institutional funds, Federal Pell, private scholarships, SEOG, state scholarships/grants. *Loan aid offered:* Direct PLUS Loans, Direct Subsidized Loans, Direct Unsubsidized Loans. Applicants will be notified of awards on a rolling basis beginning 2/25. Federal Work-Study Program available. Institutional employment available.

BOTTOM LINE

Texas A&M's price tag depends on whether you are from the great state of Texas or not. In-state students pay only $7,052 in tuition, while out-of-state students will pay $33,083. In addition, student should expect to spend another $13,719 in room, board, and fees. Three-quarters of the freshmen student body receive some aid, while almost half will take out loans. The average student will accrue $24,072 in debt during their Texas A&M career. The bottom line is that Texas A&M is a big school with big resources and big pride.

CAREER INFORMATION FROM PAYSCALE.COM	
ROI Rating	89
Bachelors and No Higher	
Median starting salary	$59,000
Median mid-career salary	$115,900
At Least Bachelors	
Median starting salary	$60,200
Median mid-career salary	$119,300
Alumni with high job meaning	53%
Degrees awarded in STEM subjects	36%

SELECTIVITY	
Admissions Rating	88
# of applicants	37,191
% of applicants accepted	70
% of acceptees attending	45

FRESHMAN PROFILE	
Range SAT EBRW	570–670
Range SAT Math	570–690
Range ACT Composite	25–30
Minimum paper TOEFL	550
Minimum internet-based TOEFL	80
% graduated top 10% of class	60
% graduated top 25% of class	88
% graduated top 50% of class	98

DEADLINES	
Regular	
Deadline	12/1
Nonfall registration?	Yes

FINANCIAL FACTS	
Financial Aid Rating	80
Annual in-state tuition	$7,052
Annual out-of-state tuition	$33,803
Room and board	$12,250
Required fees	$3,351
Books and supplies	$1,054
Average frosh need-based scholarship	$12,201
Average UG need-based scholarship	$10,569
% needy frosh rec. need-based scholarship or grant aid	90
% needy UG rec. need-based scholarship or grant aid	82
% needy frosh rec. non-need-based scholarship or grant aid	10
% needy UG rec. non-need-based scholarship or grant aid	7
% needy frosh rec. need-based self-help aid	48
% needy UG rec. need-based self-help aid	56
% frosh rec. any financial aid	76
% UG rec. any financial aid	70
% UG borrow to pay for school	43
Average cumulative indebtedness	$23,505
% frosh need fully met	25
% ugrads need fully met	22
Average % of frosh need met	76
Average % of ugrad need met	72

Texas Christian University

OFFICE OF ADMISSIONS, TCU BOX 297013, FORT WORTH, TX 76129 • ADMISSIONS: 817-257-7490 • FAX: 817-257-7268

CAMPUS LIFE

Quality of Life Rating	**97**
Fire Safety Rating	**98**
Green Rating	**78**
Type of school	Private
Affiliation	Disciples of Christ
Environment	Metropolis

STUDENTS

Total undergrad enrollment	8,983
% male/female	41/59
% from out of state	46
% frosh from public high school	57
% frosh live on campus	97
% ugrads live on campus	48
# of fraternities (% ugrad men join)	17 (41)
# of sororities (% ugrad women join)	21 (58)
% African American	5
% Asian	3
% Caucasian	71
% Hispanic	13
% Native American	1
% Pacific Islander	<1
% Two or more races	<1
% Race and/or ethnicity unknown	1
% international	5
# of countries represented	69

ACADEMICS

Academic Rating	**90**
% students returning for sophomore year	91
% students graduating within 4 years	69
% students graduating within 6 years	83
Calendar	Semester
Student/faculty ratio	13:1
Profs interesting rating	92
Profs accessible rating	94

Most classes have 20–29 students. Most lab/discussion sessions have 20–29 students.

MOST POPULAR MAJORS

Speech Communication and Rhetoric; Public Relations, Advertising, and Applied Communication; Registered Nursing

ABOUT THE SCHOOL

Texas Christian University is a bit like the "Disney World of American universities." After all, it boasts a "beautiful campus" just three miles from downtown Fort Worth, "amazing traditions," and "a great sense of community." More importantly, it offers "strong academics" and attracts a "driven student body." As if that wasn't enough, "small class sizes" help to foster an "intimate learning environment." And while there are a myriad of majors from which to choose, students highlight the fabulous business school as well as the "great honors program" as particular TCU strengths. Undergrads do caution that courses are "rigorous." You'll certainly be "pushed by the professors and faculty," who are "commit[ed] to serving and helping students." And they make sure they "are readily available through office hours and emails." Ultimately, "they're very supportive and want you to succeed."

BANG FOR YOUR BUCK

TCU recognizes that paying for higher education can be a huge burden for families. The university strives to alleviate that stress by providing solid aid packages to undergraduates who demonstrate need. And it offers "large amounts of merit-based financial aid" to candidates who demonstrate outstanding academic achievement. These recipients are selected regardless of family income. The financial aid office uses the application for undergraduate admission to identify contenders. No additional application materials are needed. Most of these scholarships, such as the Chancellor's Scholarship and the Dean's Scholarship, are renewable. Of course, renewal is contingent upon the student maintaining a minimum GPA (3.0 their first year and 3.25 in subsequent years) and taking a full course schedule.

STUDENT LIFE

Life at TCU is certainly action packed with a "a plethora of on campus organizations for students to participate in." One club in particular, "theCREW" organizes weekly activities for the campus. Put on by the programming arm of the Student Government, these programs can "range from petting zoos to bouncy houses to circus performers." The university also hosts various "concerts and comedians" throughout the year. Students admit, "Saturdays in the Fall are strictly dedicated to football." Lastly, TCU undergrads love "exploring the DFW (Downtown Fort Worth) area," which has lots of shopping and dining options.

CAREER

When it comes to the job hunt, TCU students are destined for success. Many undergrads benefit from having professors who "use their contacts with employers to help students land internships and job interviews." They may also tap into a very "involved alumni network." Further, a number of "job opportunities" come through TCU's fantastic Center for Career & Professional Development. Indeed, the office sponsors multiple career fairs throughout the year, each focused on a different discipline (ex. nursing, social work, engineering and technology, etc.) And it hosts a number of networking events wherein students can meet employers from various industries like criminal justice, media and interior design.

Texas Christian University

FINANCIAL AID: 817-257-7858 • E-MAIL: FROGMAIL@TCU.EDU • WEBSITE: WWW.TCU.EDU

GENERAL INFO

Activities: Choral groups, concert band, dance, drama/theater, jazz band, literary magazine, marching band, music ensembles, musical theater, opera, pep band, radio station, student government, student newspaper, television station, yearbook, campus ministries, Student Organization, Model UN. 200 registered organizations, 29 honor societies, 17 religious organizations. 19 fraternities, 20 sororities. **Athletics (Intercollegiate):** *Men:* baseball, basketball, cross-country, diving, football, golf, swimming, tennis, track/field (outdoor), track/field (indoor). *Women:* basketball, cross-country, diving, equestrian sports, golf, riflery, soccer, swimming, tennis, track/field (outdoor), track/field (indoor), volleyball(beach), volleyball(indoor). **On-Campus Highlights:** Amon Carter Stadium, University Recreation Center, Monnig Meteorite Collection, Brown-Lupton University Union, Campus Commons/Frog Fountain. **Environmental Initiatives:** American Colleges and Universities President's Climate Commitment; Energy MBA; minor in Sustainability.

FINANCIAL AID

Students should submit: CSS Profile; FAFSA. Priority filing deadline is 2/1 for first year; 4/1 for transfer. The Princeton Review suggests that all financial aid forms be submitted as soon as possible after October 1. *Need-based scholarships/grants offered:* College/university scholarship or grant aid from institutional funds, Federal Pell, private scholarships, SEOG, state scholarships/grants. *Loan aid offered:* Direct PLUS Loans, Direct Subsidized Loans, Direct Unsubsidized Loans. Applicants will be notified of awards on a rolling basis beginning 12/15. Federal Work-Study Program available. Institutional employment available.

THE BOTTOM LINE

Texas Christian University charges $44,860 for tuition. Undergrads are also charged a $90 Student Government Association fee. And they're likely to spend approximately $970 on books and supplies. Transportation is estimated to cost $1,280 for the year. Finally, TCU recommends budgeting another $3,600 for personal expenses.

CAREER INFORMATION FROM PAYSCALE.COM	
ROI Rating	87
Bachelors and No Higher	
Median starting salary	$54,700
Median mid-career salary	$97,000
At Least Bachelors	
Median starting salary	$56,000
Median mid-career salary	$101,000
Alumni with high job meaning	51%
Degrees awarded in STEM subjects	9%

SELECTIVITY	
Admissions Rating	90
# of applicants	19,740
% of applicants accepted	41
% of acceptees attending	24

FRESHMAN PROFILE	
Range SAT EBRW	570–660
Range SAT Math	560–670
Range ACT Composite	25–30
Minimum paper TOEFL	550
Minimum internet-based TOEFL	80

DEADLINES	
Early decision	
Deadline	11/1
Notification	12/5
Early action	
Deadline	11/1
Notification	12/15
Regular	
Deadline	2/1
Notification	4/1
Nonfall registration?	Yes

FINANCIAL FACTS	
Financial Aid Rating	84
Annual tuition	$46,860
Room and board	$12,804
Required fees	$90
Books and supplies	$970
Average frosh need-based scholarship	$28,394
Average UG need-based scholarship	$27,790
% needy frosh rec. need-based scholarship or grant aid	93
% needy UG rec. need-based scholarship or grant aid	93
% needy frosh rec. non-need-based scholarship or grant aid	73
% needy UG rec. non-need-based scholarship or grant aid	66
% needy frosh rec. need-based self-help aid	71
% needy UG rec. need-based self-help aid	76
% frosh rec. any financial aid	77
% UG rec. any financial aid	76
% UG borrow to pay for school	36
Average cumulative indebtedness	$42,212
% frosh need fully met	36
% ugrads need fully met	27
Average % of frosh need met	71
Average % of ugrad need met	64

Trinity College (CT)

300 SUMMIT STREET, HARTFORD, CT 06106 • ADMISSIONS: 860-297-2180 • FAX: 860-297-2287

CAMPUS LIFE

Quality of Life Rating	77
Fire Safety Rating	95
Green Rating	78
Type of school	Private
Environment	Metropolis

STUDENTS

Total undergrad enrollment	2,174
% male/female	49/51
% from out of state	81
% frosh from public high school	45
% frosh live on campus	100
% ugrads live on campus	90
# of fraternities (% ugrad men join)	7 (29)
# of sororities (% ugrad women join)	3 (17)
% African American	6
% Asian	4
% Caucasian	65
% Hispanic	8
% Native American	<1
% Pacific Islander	0
% Two or more races	3
% Race and/or ethnicity unknown	3
% international	12
# of countries represented	70

ACADEMICS

Academic Rating	89
% students returning for sophomore year	89
Calendar	Semester
Student/faculty ratio	9:1
Profs interesting rating	83
Profs accessible rating	78

Most classes have 10–19 students. Most lab/discussion sessions have 10–19 students.

MOST POPULAR MAJORS
Economics; Political Science; Psychology

ABOUT THE SCHOOL

Trinity College is an "elite liberal arts school with a reputation matched by few other schools." Serious students flock here for the "gorgeous campus, outstanding teacher accessibility, good athletics, and an overall great academic environment." Replete with traditional New England architecture and set on a green campus which encompasses over 100 acres in downtown Hartford, Connecticut, students' number one reason for attending Trinity is "the strong sense of community and its unique identity as a college located on a beautiful green campus that is also in the heart of a city." From its "strong Division III athletics," to its "close faculty-student interaction," to "amazing study abroad opportunities," and a "great political science department" that benefits from being "two blocks away from the state capitol, which is great for internships," at Trinity "you get a chance to figure out what you are truly passionate about." Trinity's unique Guided Studies program, in which students undertake a fixed curriculum of interdisciplinary study to survey the entirety of Western civilization from the classical age to the present, forms the backbone of the school's academics for some and "really gives the student body an opportunity to try new fields of study." Says one happy Trinity undergraduate, "Even the president of the school...is accessible. They go on the quest orientation hiking trip for first-year students and regularly attends various student events on campus."

BANG FOR YOUR BUCK

Trinity offers the prestige and individual attention of a small liberal arts school with the benefits its urban backdrop provides. Though the school's price tag is in line with other serious private colleges of its rank, students at Trinity are offered two main advantages: real personalized attention and truly distinct curricular options, which allow students to craft an individualized academic course of study. From its "interdisciplinary neuroscience major and a professionally accredited engineering degree program," to its "unique Human Rights Program, a Health Fellows Program, and interdisciplinary programs such as the Cities Program, Interdisciplinary Science Program, and InterArts," active learning with a host of flexibility forms the backbone of academic experience at Trinity.

STUDENT LIFE

Many students here hail from the tri-state area and the word "preppy" gets tossed about a lot in this "great community" where "you can walk across campus at any point in the day and run into ten of your friends." "Trinity's campus is beautiful and students here like to stick pretty close to home," says one of this "definitely not a suitcase school." Off campus, there are "concerts, plays, and all kinds of ways to entertain yourself"; Hartford has "amazing restaurants," movie theaters, and bowling alleys, and the campus movie theater (the Cinestudio) is a big haunt. Events thrown by the arts and cultural houses are popular weekend pastimes, and Greek life and school sponsored concerts/events are very well-attended. Mostly because of Trinity's small size, "the social scene is so unique and is one of the aspects that students past and present value the most."

CAREER

Trinity students are "very engaged and involved outside of class, often expanding their maturity and job experiences in internships [and] leadership opportunities." Career Services helps students out a lot with these jobs and internship searches through Handshake (the online job listing service) with more than 200 internships for credit, and "alums are eager to help out the student body as well." Each student can take part in the two-day intensive Bantam Sophomore Success program, and alumni mentoring is available to everyone. Networking opportunities are especially fruitful if you want to go into finance or investment banking.

Trinity College

FINANCIAL AID: 860-297-2047 • E-MAIL: ADMISSIONS.OFFICE@TRINCOLL.EDU • WEBSITE: WWW.TRINCOLL.EDU

The starting salary for Trinity College graduates who visited PayScale.com was $55,600, and 49 percent said they felt their job had a meaningful impact on the world.

GENERAL INFO

Activities: Choral groups, dance, drama/theater, jazz band, literary magazine, music ensembles, musical theater, radio station, student government, student newspaper, student-run film society, yearbook. **Organizations:** campus ministries, International Student Organization, Model UN 105 registered organizations, 5 honor societies, 5 religious organizations. 7 fraternities, 3 sororities. **Athletics (Intercollegiate):** *Men:* baseball, basketball, crew/rowing, cross-country, diving, football, golf, ice hockey, lacrosse, soccer, squash, swimming, tennis, track/field (outdoor), track/field (indoor), wrestling. *Women:* basketball, crew/rowing, cross-country, diving, field hockey, ice hockey, lacrosse, soccer, softball, squash, swimming, tennis, track/field (outdoor), track/field (indoor), volleyball.

FINANCIAL AID

Students should submit: CSS Profile; FAFSA. Priority filing deadline is 1/15. The Princeton Review suggests that all financial aid forms be submitted as soon as possible after October 1. *Need-based scholarships/grants offered:* College/university scholarship or grant aid from institutional funds, Federal Pell, private scholarships, SEOG, state scholarships/grants. *Loan aid offered:* Direct PLUS Loans, Direct Subsidized Loans, Direct Unsubsidized Loans. Applicants will be notified of awards on or about 4/1. Federal Work-Study Program available. Institutional employment available.

BOTTOM LINE

Whether they're drawn to this liberal arts hamlet for its "school spirit, amazing alumni, and career placement," or the feeling that they are attending a truly competitive college with "a city at your fingertips," undergraduates at Trinity have access to all the luxuries and opportunities that Trinity's reputation as a "little Ivy" affords. However, what sets the college apart is its small student-to-faculty ratio and commitment to individualized attention, which promises the added assurance that talented students won't fall between the cracks. The school earns high marks when it comes to financial aid despite its significant tuition of $54,340, with another $14,750 in room and board.

CAREER INFORMATION FROM PAYSCALE.COM	
ROI Rating	89
Bachelors and No Higher	
Median starting salary	$57,600
Median mid-career salary	$111,600
At Least Bachelors	
Median starting salary	$60,500
Median mid-career salary	$116,600
Alumni with high job meaning	50%
Degrees awarded in STEM subjects	22%

SELECTIVITY	
Admissions Rating	92
# of applicants	6,085
% of applicants accepted	34
% of acceptees attending	28
# of early decision applicants	552
% accepted early decision	57

FRESHMAN PROFILE	
Range ACT Composite	28–32
% graduated top 10% of class	49
% graduated top 25% of class	81
% graduated top 50% of class	95

DEADLINES	
Early decision	
Deadline	11/15
Notification	12/15
Other ED Deadline	1/1
Other ED Notification	2/15
Regular	
Deadline	1/1
Notification	4/1
Nonfall registration?	Yes

FINANCIAL FACTS	
Financial Aid Rating	95
Annual tuition	$54,340
Room and board	$14,750
Required fees	$2,570
Books and supplies	$1,000
Average frosh need-based scholarship	$47,478
Average UG need-based scholarship	$47,156
% needy frosh rec. need-based scholarship or grant aid	97
% needy UG rec. need-based scholarship or grant aid	98
% needy frosh rec. non-need-based scholarship or grant aid	4
% needy UG rec. non-need-based scholarship or grant aid	4
% needy frosh rec. need-based self-help aid	62
% needy UG rec. need-based self-help aid	66
% frosh rec. any financial aid	51
% UG rec. any financial aid	48
% UG borrow to pay for school	45
Average cumulative indebtedness	$25,958
% frosh need fully met	100
% ugrads need fully met	100
Average % of frosh need met	100
Average % of ugrad need met	100

Trinity University

One Trinity Place, San Antonio, TX 78212-7200 • Admissions: 210-999-7207 • Fax: 210-999-8164

CAMPUS LIFE

Quality of Life Rating	93
Fire Safety Rating	94
Green Rating	74
Type of school	Private
Affiliation	Presbyterian
Environment	Metropolis

STUDENTS

Total undergrad enrollment	2,428
% male/female	45/55
% from out of state	22
% frosh from public high school	66
% frosh live on campus	100
% ugrads live on campus	80
# of fraternities (% ugrad men join)	6 (17)
# of sororities (% ugrad women join)	7 (32)
% African American	4
% Asian	8
% Caucasian	58
% Hispanic	19
% Native American	<1
% Pacific Islander	0
% Two or more races	4
% Race and/or ethnicity unknown	2
% international	5
# of countries represented	60

ACADEMICS

Academic Rating	95
% students returning for sophomore year	89
% students graduating within 4 years	72
% students graduating within 6 years	80
Calendar	Semester
Student/faculty ratio	9:1
Profs interesting rating	94
Profs accessible rating	96

Most classes have 10–19 students. Most lab/discussion sessions have 10–19 students.

MOST POPULAR MAJORS
Communication; Engineering Science; Business Administration and Management

ABOUT THE SCHOOL

This private school in San Antonio, Texas, gives students a "great environment, great people, [and a] great education." The small student body—roughly 2,428—and the requirement that undergraduates must live on campus for three years gives the school a small-town feel in a big state. Trinity is a "small, liberal arts college...that has the comfort of a small secluded area [with the added] wonders of a big city." One Communication major says, Trinity is "a close-knit university with high standards of excellence and competency that challenge students, while creating a comfortable environment." The student to teacher ratio of roughly 9:1 helps foster this sense of community and the professors "know all of their students by name and are extremely accessible outside of class." With 47 majors offered, Trinity has something for everyone: "Some of the best aspects of Trinity are its emphasis on academic goals, assistance in preparing students for life after college, and, most importantly, the sense of community it provides between students, faculty, and alumni."

BANG FOR YOUR BUCK

Trinity meets an average of 94 percent of its students' financial needs and scholarship options draw in many prospective students, including international ones, who are eligible for financial assistance. One French and art history double major notes that Trinity is "warm and supportive but challenging—kind of like San Antonio's weather. The plentiful scholarship money didn't hurt either." Ninety-eight percent of freshmen get some form of financial aid, and 92 percent of other undergraduates receive financial assistance. A Political Science major says that Trinity's "financial aid packages are great so there are many middle-class students and with such a smorgasbord of ethnicities, economic statuses, and cultures," the students "all learn from one another." According to the school's website, "All Trinity scholarships are renewable on an annual basis for up to eight semesters of undergraduate study, as long as the recipient meets each award's specified criteria." Most of these scholarships are merit-based but there are some that combine merit with financial need.

STUDENT LIFE

While "it's not uncommon to hear students worrying about tests," they are also "often looking forward to some big event over the weekend" such as themed parties or fundraisers for local charities. The school's location in San Antonio—"we are about five minutes from downtown"—also affords students access to clubs and restaurants. On campus, Greek life plays a significant role: the school has seven sororities and six fraternities, with roughly 32 percent of women joining a sorority and 19 percent of men joining a fraternity. Though "Greek life is a popular way of getting involved," students can find "almost any type of...group on campus," where there are more than 115 registered student organizations. Even though students like to kick back and have fun, "when it's time to study, people study hard" and it's "not considered anti-social to not hang out with your friends a couple of nights before a big test. Overall, Trinity's students are an accepting fun-loving lot."

CAREER

According to PayScale.com, 51 percent of Trinity graduates consider their careers to be instrumental in making the world a better place. The average starting salary for a Trinity graduate is roughly $51,100, and popular jobs include marketing manager, financial analyst, and executive director. Popular majors at Trinity include Communication, Business Administration, and Engineering Science. One Communication major singled out a grant the school received from AT&T that allowed Trinity to "renovate the...communications lab [so] that is has [state-of-the-art] equipment," which helps to

Trinity University

FINANCIAL AID: 210-999-8315 • E-MAIL: ADMISSIONS@TRINITY.EDU • WEBSITE: WWW.TRINITY.EDU

"further [the] interests and careers of students going into a media field." According to the school's website, Career Services "fosters career advancement and contributes to the growth and success of Trinity graduates." The office's website offers students access to Hire a Tiger, the school's online recruitment system. The school's website emphasizes that "Career Services at Trinity is a comprehensive and centralized service that works with both students (from first-years to seniors) and alumni." Trinity's small size makes it so "everyone really knows everyone, even alumni, which is really great because it makes networking so much easier."

GENERAL INFO

Activities: Choral groups, concert band, dance, drama/theater, jazz band, literary magazine, music ensembles, musical theater, opera, pep band, radio station, student government, student newspaper, student-run film society, symphony orchestra, television station, yearbook, campus ministries, International Student Organization, Model UN. **Organizations:** 115 registered organizations, 24 honor societies, 7 religious organizations. 6 fraternities, 7 sororities. **Athletics (Intercollegiate):** *Men:* baseball, basketball, cross-country, diving, football, golf, soccer, swimming, tennis, track/field (outdoor). *Women:* basketball, cross-country, diving, golf, soccer, softball, swimming, tennis, track/field (outdoor), volleyball. **On-Campus Highlights:** Stieren Theater, Laurie Auditorium, Coates Library, Bell Athletic Center, Coates University Center, Northrup Hall, and the Center for the Sciences and Innovation.

FINANCIAL AID

Students should submit: CSS Profile; FAFSA. Priority filing deadline is 2/15. The Princeton Review suggests that all financial aid forms be submitted as soon as possible after October 1. *Need-based scholarships/grants offered:* College/university scholarship or grant aid from institutional funds, Federal Pell, private scholarships, SEOG, state scholarships/grants. *Loan aid offered:* Direct PLUS Loans, Direct Subsidized Loans, Direct Unsubsidized Loans. Applicants will be notified of awards on or about 3/15. Federal Work-Study Program available. Institutional employment available.

BOTTOM LINE

A year at Trinity costs roughly $55,824, including tuition, room and board. With the average need-based gift aid for undergraduates being approximately $32,078, 44 percent of the previous graduating class borrowed to finance their education with an average cumulative debt of $40,800.

CAREER INFORMATION FROM PAYSCALE.COM	
ROI Rating	91
Bachelors and No Higher	
Median starting salary	$53,400
Median mid-career salary	$104,100
At Least Bachelors	
Median starting salary	$55,500
Median mid-career salary	$109,500
Alumni with high job meaning	46%
Degrees awarded in STEM subjects	27%

SELECTIVITY	
Admissions Rating	92
# of applicants	7,663
% of applicants accepted	38
% of acceptees attending	22
# offered a place on the wait list	592
% accepting a place on wait list	51
% admitted from wait list	14
# of early decision applicants	97
% accepted early decision	66

FRESHMAN PROFILE	
Range SAT EBRW	610–710
Range SAT Math	610–700
Range ACT Composite	27–32
Average HS GPA	3.6
% graduated top 10% of class	44
% graduated top 25% of class	76
% graduated top 50% of class	97

DEADLINES	
Early decision	
Deadline	11/1
Notification	12/15
Other ED Deadline	1/1
Other ED Notification	2/15
Early action	
Deadline	11/1
Notification	12/15
Regular	
Deadline	2/1
Notification	4/1
Nonfall registration?	Yes

FINANCIAL FACTS	
Financial Aid Rating	91
Annual tuition	$42,360
Room and board	$13,464
Required fees	$616
Books and supplies	$1,000
Average frosh need-based scholarship	$32,078
Average UG need-based scholarship	$31,374
% needy frosh rec. need-based scholarship or grant aid	99
% needy UG rec. need-based scholarship or grant aid	99
% needy frosh rec. non-need-based scholarship or grant aid	37
% needy UG rec. non-need-based scholarship or grant aid	20
% needy frosh rec. need-based self-help aid	62
% needy UG rec. need-based self-help aid	68
% frosh rec. any financial aid	99
% UG rec. any financial aid	96
% UG borrow to pay for school	44
Average cumulative indebtedness	$40,800

Truman State University

100 East Normal Avenue, Kirksville, MO 63501 • Admissions: 660-785-4114 • Fax: 660-785-7456

CAMPUS LIFE

Quality of Life Rating	**86**
Fire Safety Rating	**98**
Green Rating	**60***
Type of school	Public
Environment	Village

STUDENTS

Total undergrad enrollment	5,241
% male/female	42/58
% from out of state	29
% frosh from public high school	82
% frosh live on campus	98
% ugrads live on campus	42
# of fraternities (% ugrad men join)	22 (9)
# of sororities (% ugrad women join)	7 (9)
% African American	4
% Asian	3
% Caucasian	79
% Hispanic	3
% Native American	<1
% Pacific Islander	<1
% Two or more races	3
% Race and/or ethnicity unknown	1
% international	7
# of countries represented	45

ACADEMICS

Academic Rating	**83**
% students returning for sophomore year	86
% students graduating within 4 years	59
% students graduating within 6 years	75
Calendar	Semester
Student/faculty ratio	16:1
Profs interesting rating	79
Profs accessible rating	83

Most classes have 10–19 students. Most lab/discussion sessions have 10–19 students.

MOST POPULAR MAJORS

Biology/Biological Sciences; Psychology; Business Administration, Management and Operations

ABOUT THE SCHOOL

Truman students aren't shy about discussing their school's "extremely well-deserved academic reputation," nor should they be: the school is Missouri's only highly selective public university, and students are here due to hard work, in order to work hard. The "grade-conscious" students here at the "Harvard of the Midwest" receive an education grounded in the liberal arts and sciences, and the school keeps a constant eye on its applicability to their futures, incorporating critical thinking, writing, and leadership-skill-building opportunities along the way to a degree. Many experiential-learning opportunities exist all across campus, in which students can gain practical knowledge that will be relevant to future schooling and careers; the Career Center sets up a yearly Career Expo and Non-Profit Fair in order to expose students to employers and give them the chance to hone their interviewing, résumé, and professional skills. The classes are difficult, but "serve to develop the students into well-prepared graduates ready to face postcollege life"; many include a service learning component. Students are also able to diversify their studies across multiple subjects and throughout multiple countries by taking advantage of the numerous study abroad options, many of which can be covered by financial aid.

BANG FOR YOUR BUCK

Truman offers a private school education at a public price; students and their families can even set up a flexible payment plan through the Business Office. The school offers four separate types of loans for students, covering everything from tuition to a new computer to study abroad, and there are numerous federal and state aid options also available. Automatic scholarships are offered to incoming freshmen based on academic merit, and additional opportunities to apply for endowed foundation scholarships occur each spring. The school understands that everything costs money (except the application—it's free!), and their comprehensive financial aid programs can be used to make sure that students are able to focus on their studies. One out-of-stater says, "Between Truman scholarships and private scholarships, I'm basically being paid to go here." Basically, if a student wants to attend Truman, then numbers can be crunched.

While the deal Truman offers may seem too good to be true, the quality of the education on offer here remains high. Students report their professors "really push you to work hard," and "are available beyond their scheduled office hours and do their best to make sure we understand the material." Classes are "small and engaging," enabling a "fantastic one-on-one experience between professors and students."

STUDENT LIFE

Students coined the "term T.T.S. (Typical Truman Student) [...] to describe academically focused, very studious students." Here, "college life is hectic and amazing all at the same time." Truman brings "tons of really great activities, shows, bands, etc., to campus to keep us entertained," and though homework consumes much of a student's day, "there is always time to [... see] a comedian or performance." Kirksville, Missouri may not be a buzzing metropolis, but "part of the fun of Truman is to find unorthodox things to do"—"you can be a huge political advocate, involved in protests on the quad; you can become involved in community service locally and nationwide; or you can work in a lab to make discoveries." Students are pleased with the facilities, including "newly renovated" dorms, and the "excellent" library and say the campus is "beautiful, and the atmosphere is very welcoming."

Truman State University

FINANCIAL AID: 660-785-4130 • E-MAIL: ADMISSIONS@TRUMAN.EDU • WEBSITE: WWW.TRUMAN.EDU

CAREER

The fall semester gets a jumpstart at Truman with Career Week, hosted by the Career Center, complete with speakers, employer information sessions, and a career expo that has included Boeing, the Federal Bureau of Investigation, IBM, and Target. Other career calendar highlights are a spring Non-Profit conference, Alumni Mock Interview Day, and a host of grad school prep events like "How to Attend Graduate School for Free." Alumni who visited PayScale.com report an average starting salary of $45,000, and 53 percent believe their works hold a high level of meaning.

GENERAL INFO

Activities: Choral groups, concert band, dance, drama/theater, jazz band, literary magazine, marching band, music ensembles, musical theater, opera, pep band, radio station, student government, student newspaper, student-run film society, symphony orchestra, television station, campus ministries, international student organization. **Organizations:** 227 registered organizations, 18 honor societies, 16 religious organizations. 12 fraternities, 6 sororities. **Athletics (Intercollegiate):** *Men:* Baseball,basketball, cross-country, football, golf, soccer, swimming, tennis, track/field (outdoor), track/field (indoor), wrestling. *Women:* Basketball, cross-country, golf, soccer, softball, swimming, tennis, track/field (outdoor), track/field (indoor), volleyball.

FINANCIAL AID

Students should submit: FAFSA. Priority filing deadline is 2/15. The Princeton Review suggests that all financial aid forms be submitted as soon as possible after October 1. *Need-based scholarships/grants offered:* College/university scholarship or grant aid from institutional funds, Federal Pell, private scholarships, SEOG, state scholarships/grants. *Loan aid offered:* Direct PLUS Loans, Direct Subsidized Loans, Direct Unsubsidized Loans. Applicants will be notified of awards on a rolling basis beginning 1/1. Federal Work-Study Program available. Institutional employment available.

BOTTOM LINE

Residents of Missouri pay $7,352 in tuition; nonresidents pay just $14,136, which is still a bargain. There is one full-ride award offered to incoming freshmen: the General John J. Pershing Scholarship, which includes an additional stipend for a future study abroad experience. The Harry S. Truman Leadership scholarship (for Missouri residents only) offers a limited number of $10,000 awards and a four-year leadership development program. Financial aid programs to help fund undergraduate research and study abroad experiences are also available.

CAREER INFORMATION FROM PAYSCALE.COM	
ROI Rating	90
Bachelors and No Higher	
Median starting salary	$46,500
Median mid-career salary	$85,400
At Least Bachelors	
Median starting salary	$49,000
Median mid-career salary	$90,600
Alumni with high job meaning	50%
Degrees awarded in STEM subjects	16%

SELECTIVITY	
Admissions Rating	89
# of applicants	5,263
% of applicants accepted	67
% of acceptees attending	37

FRESHMAN PROFILE	
Range SAT EBRW	605–705
Range SAT Math	580–715
Range ACT Composite	24–30
Minimum paper TOEFL	550
Minimum internet-based TOEFL	79
Average HS GPA	3.8
% graduated top 10% of class	51
% graduated top 25% of class	83
% graduated top 50% of class	98

DEADLINES	
Regular	
Priority	12/1
Nonfall registration?	Yes

FINANCIAL FACTS	
Financial Aid Rating	89
Annual in-state tuition	$7,426
Annual out-of-state tuition	$14,277
Room and board	$8,630
Required fees	$304
Books and supplies	$1,000
Average frosh need-based scholarship	$8,717
Average UG need-based scholarship	$7,824
% needy frosh rec. need-based scholarship or grant aid	99
% needy UG rec. need-based scholarship or grant aid	94
% needy frosh rec. non-need-based scholarship or grant aid	98
% needy UG rec. non-need-based scholarship or grant aid	80
% needy frosh rec. need-based self-help aid	69
% needy UG rec. need-based self-help aid	77
% frosh rec. any financial aid	99
% UG rec. any financial aid	83
% UG borrow to pay for school	57
Average cumulative indebtedness	$24,938
% frosh need fully met	41
% ugrads need fully met	36
Average % of frosh need met	88
Average % of ugrad need met	84

Tufts University

BENDETSON HALL, MEDFORD, MA 02155 • ADMISSIONS: 617-627-3170 • FAX: 617-627-3860

CAMPUS LIFE

Quality of Life Rating	92
Fire Safety Rating	99
Green Rating	92
Type of school	Private
Environment	Metropolis

STUDENTS

Total undergrad enrollment	5,492
% male/female	49/51
% from out of state	75
% frosh from public high school	59
% frosh live on campus	100
% ugrads live on campus	63
# of fraternities (% ugrad men join)	9 (10)
# of sororities (% ugrad women join)	4 (9)
% African American	4
% Asian	12
% Caucasian	57
% Hispanic	7
% Native American	0
% Pacific Islander	0
% Two or more races	5
% Race and/or ethnicity unknown	6
% international	10
# of countries represented	74

ACADEMICS

Academic Rating	92
% students returning for sophomore year	97
% students graduating within 4 years	87
% students graduating within 6 years	93
Calendar	Semester
Student/faculty ratio	9:1
Profs interesting rating	89
Profs accessible rating	87

Most classes have 10–19 students. Most lab/discussion sessions have 10–19 students.

MOST POPULAR MAJORS

Computer Science; Economics; International Relations and Affairs

ABOUT THE SCHOOL

Some of the reasons Tufts students love their school are the "beautiful campus," "international focus," "diverse community," "proximity to Boston," and the "really chill vibe." This is a university that wants students to be "exploring passions and relating them to the world today." The size of the school is "not too big, not too small," but just right for many students. "Tufts is well known for being very liberal, focused on internationalism and global citizenship," a Religion major states. This is a place where "people aren't afraid to study and be intellectual." Often regarded as a "Little Ivy," Tufts offers a world-class academic education. Tufts professors are "highly accessible," "engaging and knowledgeable." "Professors have the students best interest at heart, so they do all they can to make sure we succeed," one student reports. A Political Science major says that "at Tufts, you're surrounded by so many intelligent, engaged, and interesting people in a supportive, collaborative learning environment."

BANG FOR YOUR BUCK

Although Tufts tuition is not insignificant, there are many opportunities for aid, loans, and scholarships. "There are a lot of work study programs offered at Tufts and a lot of people on complete financial aid," an International Relations student confirms. The Student Employment Office helps students get jobs on-campus or off and regularly posts jobs to the JobX and TuftsLife websites. The school has forty-four Tufts-specific scholarships and awards for everything from Fine Arts and Social Justice to various STEM majors. Prospective applicants can view the entire list online. Prospective applicants can also use the school's online Net Price Calculator to get an idea what kind of aid they can expect if accepted.

STUDENT LIFE

"The campus culture is thriving and alive," one student says, "and as such it really encourages students to merge their academic and social interests and pursue both in a passionate way." Your average student at Tufts is "fun, passionate," "geeky" and likely an "activist." "The variety of clubs and activities available is amazing" and most students get "involved in many clubs and activities, campaigns, grassroots organizing, athletic teams, volunteer organizations, jobs, etc." "The Tufts Dance Collective and Quidditch clubs are some of the most popular and fun," one student helpfully suggests. Unlike many universities, there are "not too many 'cliques'" here and students tend to get along with each other. "The best way to fit in at Tufts is to be yourself, even if that sounds cheesy." If there is a Tufts uniform, it's "skinny jeans, a vintage sweater, worn-in shoes, and framed glasses" along with a "MacBook Pro" softly playing indie music. On campus, there are "extensive" student-run events and many students show up "for theater, dance and musical performances." When students need to get off campus, Boston is "less than an hour" away.

Tufts University

Financial Aid: 617-627-2000 • E-mail: admissions.inquiry@ase.tufts.edu • Website: www.tufts.edu

CAREER

"The school's strong reputation has helped me get summer jobs and internships," one student reports. This is a common sentiment among Tufts students. The university's reputation and proximity to Boston provide students with many opportunities to get a head start on their post-college careers. The "great alumni network" also helps students find "jobs or internships after college." The school frequently holds events like the Career Carnival and Tufts Career Fair along with consulting sessions. Fully 91 percent of the Class of 2013 had found full-time employment or were in graduate school by 2014. The website PayScale.com reports an average starting salary of $60,400 for Tufts grads and an average mid-career salary of $120,200.

GENERAL INFO

Activities: Choral groups, concert band, dance, drama/theater, jazz band, literary magazine, marching band, music ensembles, musical theater, opera, pep band, radio station, student government, student newspaper, student-run film society, symphony orchestra, television station, yearbook, campus ministries, International Student Organization, Model UN. **Organizations:** 160 registered organizations, 4 honor societies, 6 religious organizations. 9 fraternities, 4 sororities. **Athletics (Intercollegiate):** *Men:* baseball, basketball, crew/rowing, cross-country, diving, football, golf, ice hockey, lacrosse, sailing, soccer, squash, swimming, tennis, track/field (outdoor), track/field (indoor). *Women:* basketball, cheerleading, crew/rowing, cross-country, diving, fencing, field hockey, golf, lacrosse, sailing, soccer, softball, squash, swimming, tennis, track/field (outdoor), track/field (indoor), volleyball. **On-Campus Highlights:** The Aidekman Arts Center, Tisch Library, Edwin Ginn Library, Tisch Sports and Fitness Center, Ellis Oval, Meyer Campus Center.

FINANCIAL AID

Students should submit: CSS Profile; FAFSA. Regular filing deadline is 3/1. The Princeton Review suggests that all financial aid forms be submitted as soon as possible after October 1. *Need-based scholarships/grants offered:* College/university scholarship or grant aid from institutional funds, Federal Pell, private scholarships, SEOG, state scholarships/grants. *Loan aid offered:* Direct PLUS Loans, Direct Subsidized Loans, Direct Unsubsidized Loans. Applicants will be notified of awards on or about 4/1. Federal Work-Study Program available. Institutional employment available.

BOTTOM LINE

The baseline tuition at Tufts is $55,172. Room and board are an additional $14,560. Adding the various fees, a student can expect a bill of $73,500 before any aid or scholarships.

CAREER INFORMATION FROM PAYSCALE.COM	
ROI Rating	91
Bachelors and No Higher	
Median starting salary	$63,200
Median mid-career salary	$120,500
At Least Bachelors	
Median starting salary	$64,900
Median mid-career salary	$129,700
Alumni with high job meaning	50%
Degrees awarded in STEM subjects	25%

SELECTIVITY	
Admissions Rating	97
# of applicants	21,101
% of applicants accepted	15
% of acceptees attending	45
# offered a place on the wait list	1,504
% accepting a place on wait list	42
% admitted from wait list	0

FRESHMAN PROFILE	
Range SAT EBRW	700–760
Range SAT Math	710–780
Range ACT Composite	31–34
Minimum paper TOEFL	600
Minimum internet-based TOEFL	100

DEADLINES	
Early decision	
Deadline	11/1
Notification	12/15
Other ED Deadline	1/1
Other ED Notification	2/15
Regular	
Deadline	1/1
Notification	4/1
Nonfall registration?	No

FINANCIAL FACTS	
Financial Aid Rating	95
Annual tuition	$55,172
Room and board	$14,560
Required fees	$1,210
Average frosh need-based scholarship	$44,967
Average UG need-based scholarship	$42,763
% needy frosh rec. need-based scholarship or grant aid	93
% needy UG rec. need-based scholarship or grant aid	94
% needy frosh rec. non-need-based scholarship or grant aid	3
% needy UG rec. non-need-based scholarship or grant aid	8
% needy frosh rec. need-based self-help aid	86
% needy UG rec. need-based self-help aid	89
% frosh rec. any financial aid	38
% UG rec. any financial aid	36
% UG borrow to pay for school	34
Average cumulative indebtedness	$27,367
% frosh need fully met	100
% ugrads need fully met	94
Average % of frosh need met	100
Average % of ugrad need met	100

Tulane University

6823 St. Charles Avenue, New Orleans, LA 70118 • Admissions: 504-865-5731 • Fax: 504-862-8715

CAMPUS LIFE

Quality of Life Rating	98
Fire Safety Rating	95
Green Rating	83
Type of school	Private
Environment	Metropolis

STUDENTS

Total undergrad enrollment	6,571
% male/female	41/59
% from out of state	77
% frosh from public high school	57
% frosh live on campus	98
% ugrads live on campus	48
# of fraternities (% ugrad men join)	12 (29)
# of sororities (% ugrad women join)	12 (50)
% African American	4
% Asian	5
% Caucasian	75
% Hispanic	7
% Native American	<1
% Pacific Islander	<1
% Two or more races	4
% Race and/or ethnicity unknown	1
% international	4
# of countries represented	48

ACADEMICS

Academic Rating	90
% students returning for sophomore year	93
% students graduating within 4 years	73
% students graduating within 6 years	83
Calendar	Semester
Student/faculty ratio	8:1
Profs interesting rating	86
Profs accessible rating	90

Most classes have 10–19 students. Most lab/discussion sessions have 10–19 students.

ABOUT THE SCHOOL

Tulane "is a place where learning is put center-stage." "The academic opportunities are unending" and are all about "preparing students for the 'real-world.'" "The campus is beautiful, the atmosphere is vibrant and professors are very friendly and helpful," one student says. Perhaps the biggest draw is the "location, location, location!" Students cannot stop raving about "the culturally diverse classroom of the city of New Orleans." "The people, the food, the vibe, the city, the weather, the festivals, the irreplaceable and second to none culture!" gushes one student. Perhaps this is why "the smart 'cool' kids go to Tulane." Tulane instituted a core curriculum as part of their post-Katrina Renewal Plan. This includes seminars for freshmen, public services classes, and a capstone program that gives students experience in their field. Tulane has "small classes taught by real professors." The "extremely personable and engaging" professors are "easy to talk to" and "very interested in their subject." As one student explains, "just like New Orleans, Tulane is quirky, classy (with underlying chaos), optimistic, and not without a sense of humor."

BANG FOR YOUR BUCK

Tulane is an especially attractive school to Louisiana residents. The school awards millions in both need-based aid and merit-based scholarships to applicants living in Louisiana. Tulane even offers guaranteed admission to Louisiana students who meet their academic requirements through the Focus Louisiana program. Students from other states have plenty of opportunity for aid and scholarships too. Tulane offers "no-loan assistance" to students whose families gross income is less than $75,000 a year. Everyone who applies is considered for Tulane's partial tuition merit scholarships, which range from $10,000 to $32,000. In addition, the school awards full-tuition scholarships that students can apply for as well as alternative financing options like a monthly payment plan to help families spread out expenses. Students who stay on as 5th Year masters students get discounted tuition during their additional year of graduate study.

STUDENT LIFE

The student body at Tulane reflects "the vivacious and colorful culture of New Orleans." The "super diverse student body" is hard to generalize, but most students are "smart, quirky, and unique." "The typical student is very friendly, academically motivated, and usually has some hidden talent," one student explains. "We're mainly Ivy-league rejects who all wanted to get out of our hometowns and have a new experience," a Philosophy student says. Greek life is big and "MARDI GRAS IS HUGE." "There's frequently live music," and students are always busy. "If you ask a Tulane student what they do in their free time be prepared for a laundry list of clubs and activities," one student warns. "Campus is a wonderful setting with just enough trees, quads, and bikes around to let you forget that you're in a major city." However, most students "love to explore the city" of New Orleans, which "is absolutely the best city to go to college in."

Tulane University

FINANCIAL AID: 504-865-5723 • E-MAIL: UNDERGRAD.ADMISSION@TULANE.EDU • WEBSITE: WWW.TULANE.EDU

CAREER

One of the biggest benefits of Tulane is the dedicated professors, many of whom make the extra effort to help students on their career paths. "I've had professors email me links to internships," one student reports. Another tells us, "My neuroscience advisor, Dr. Wee, is always working to network us with professionals so we can have a leg up after we graduate." As a core requirement of the undergrad curriculum, public service allows students to apply knowledge and skills from classroom study to real-world projects. Students also have good things to say about the jobs and opportunities that Tulane's Career Center provides. The Hire Tulane Grads website makes it easy for employers to post jobs and find qualified students, and Career Wave, an all day event, brings speakers from companies like Saks, Gil Group, and the NBA to campus. Payscale reports an average starting salary of $52,300.

GENERAL INFO

Activities: Choral groups, concert band, dance, drama/theater, jazz band, literary magazine, marching band, music ensembles, musical theater, pep band, radio station, student government, student newspaper, student-run film society, television station, yearbook. **Organizations:** 250+ registered organizations, 43 honor societies, 11 religious organizations. 12 fraternities, 12 sororities. **Athletics (Intercollegiate):** *Men:* baseball, basketball, cross-country, football, tennis, track/field (outdoor). *Women:* basketball, cross-country, diving, golf, swimming, tennis, track/field (outdoor), track/field (indoor), volleyball. **On-Campus Highlights:** Amistad Research Center, Newcomb Art Gallery, Reily Recreation Center, Howard Tilton Memorial Library, PJ's Coffee Shop.

FINANCIAL AID

Students should submit: Business/Farm Supplement; CSS Profile; FAFSA. Priority filing deadline is 2/15. The Princeton Review suggests that all financial aid forms be submitted as soon as possible after October 1. *Need-based scholarships/grants offered:* College/university scholarship or grant aid from institutional funds, Federal Pell, private scholarships, SEOG, state scholarships/grants. *Loan aid offered:* Direct PLUS Loans, Direct Subsidized Loans, Direct Unsubsidized Loans. Applicants will be notified of awards on a rolling basis beginning 3/15. Federal Work-Study Program available. Institutional employment available.

BOTTOM LINE

The cost of tuition and fees at Tulane is $54,820. Room and board add another $15,190. Adding that together with the estimated costs of books and other miscellaneous fees, Tulane expects a total of $71,210 for resident students. As noted above, Tulane has several programs aimed at providing aid to in-state applicants.

CAREER INFORMATION FROM PAYSCALE.COM	
ROI Rating	89
Bachelors and No Higher	
Median starting salary	$54,600
Median mid-career salary	$108,800
At Least Bachelors	
Median starting salary	$57,100
Median mid-career salary	$115,400
Alumni with high job meaning	44%
Degrees awarded in STEM subjects	22%

SELECTIVITY	
Admissions Rating	96
# of applicants	35,622
% of applicants accepted	21
% of acceptees attending	25
# offered a place on the wait list	5,596
% accepting a place on wait list	30
% admitted from wait list	1
# of early decision applicants	1394
% accepted early decision	36

FRESHMAN PROFILE	
Range SAT EBRW	670–740
Range SAT Math	660–750
Range ACT Composite	30–33
Minimum paper TOEFL	550
Average HS GPA	3.6
% graduated top 10% of class	62
% graduated top 25% of class	88
% graduated top 50% of class	96

DEADLINES	
Early decision	
Deadline	11/1
Notification	12/15
Other ED Deadline	1/5
Other ED Notification	1/19
Early action	
Deadline	11/15
Notification	1/15
Regular	
Deadline	1/15
Notification	4/1
Nonfall registration?	Yes

FINANCIAL FACTS	
Financial Aid Rating	93
Annual tuition	$50,780
Room and board	$15,190
Required fees	$4,040
Books and supplies	$1,200
Average frosh need-based scholarship	$32,464
Average UG need-based scholarship	$34,996
% needy frosh rec. need-based scholarship or grant aid	98
% needy UG rec. need-based scholarship or grant aid	97
% needy frosh rec. non-need-based scholarship or grant aid	37
% needy UG rec. non-need-based scholarship or grant aid	28
% needy frosh rec. need-based self-help aid	72
% needy UG rec. need-based self-help aid	78
% UG borrow to pay for school	37
Average cumulative indebtedness	$33,717
% frosh need fully met	67

Union College (NY)

Grant Hall, Schenectady, NY 12308 • Admissions: 518-388-6112 • Fax: 518-388-6986

CAMPUS LIFE

Quality of Life Rating	87
Fire Safety Rating	92
Green Rating	93
Type of school	Private
Environment	Town

STUDENTS

Total undergrad enrollment	2,163
% male/female	53/47
% from out of state	62
% frosh from public high school	66
% frosh live on campus	99
% ugrads live on campus	90
# of fraternities (% ugrad men join)	11 (32)
# of sororities (% ugrad women join)	7 (41)
% African American	4
% Asian	6
% Caucasian	72
% Hispanic	7
% Native American	<1
% Pacific Islander	0
% Two or more races	3
% Race and/or ethnicity unknown	<1
% international	7
# of countries represented	37

ACADEMICS

Academic Rating	95
% students returning for sophomore year	92
% students graduating within 4 years	79
% students graduating within 6 years	85
Calendar	Trimester
Student/faculty ratio	10:1
Profs interesting rating	97
Profs accessible rating	97
Most classes have 10–19 students.	

MOST POPULAR MAJORS
Mechanical Engineering; Biology; Economics

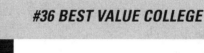

#36 BEST VALUE COLLEGE

ABOUT THE SCHOOL
Union College is a small, private institution located in upstate New York that operates on the trimester schedule. It offers more than forty majors, the most prominent of which are Biology, Economics, and Psychology, and a thriving study abroad program in which roughly 60 percent of students take part. Additionally, Union boasts a ten to one student-to-faculty ratio, with the most frequent class size coming in at between ten and nineteen students. Fifty-four percent of the student body is male, 46 percent is female, and 72 percent is white. A neuroscience major reports that "they give amazing scholarships, they have a great program for what I want to pursue, the atmosphere suited me extremely well, and I've never met friendlier people." Most students feel that "Union College is the perfect balance of the interdisciplinary liberal arts and engineering, where your extracurricular activities are just as important as academics," and also that there are "strong faculty-student interaction both in and out of the classroom," with one student noting "it is nice that the President of the school is willing to stop and talk with you, and knows your name." All students and faculty are assigned to one of seven Minerva Houses, community spaces which offer further opportunities for leadership, service, and faculty interaction. Overall, "Union is a work hard, play hard school with an active student body and accessible professors who are always willing to help."

BANG FOR YOUR BUCK
Tuition at Union College comes to $53,019, with the average aid package coming to around $44,649. Union meets the full demonstrated need of admitted students, and roughly 82 percent of students receive some form of aid. Students feel that "Union College is very generous with its financial aid and scholarship money," which is the sort of thing that practically anyone would want to hear. Multiple students report receiving full rides, and many others report receiving at least a partial merit scholarship. Union College also participates in academic opportunity programs like POSSE Scholars and Yellow Ribbon.

STUDENT LIFE
Every student on campus belongs to a Minerva House, and 39 percent of students of either gender are involved in Greek Life. The average Union student "comes from a upper middle class background in the northeast," and many find it remarkable that "students are able to have so much fun and do so well in their classes." It is noted that though there are students who are not from upper middle-class northeastern backgrounds, these students tend to fit in rather well. However, "while the rich New Englander is the 'typical' student, it is not saying that he isn't playing Dungeons and Dragons with the gaming kids." Drinking is a popular weekend activity, and yet there are atypical students in this aspect as well. Students feel that Union is making an effort to diversify the "typical" student body.

CAREER
Union College graduates report their average starting salary at around $58,500, and 51 percent report that their job has a great deal of meaning. Past that, students feel that "Union has an awesome career center that is always reaching out to students to help them with life after college with jobs, internships, resumes, etc. . . ."

Union College (NY)

FINANCIAL AID: 518-388-6123 • E-MAIL: ADMISSIONS@UNION.EDU • WEBSITE: WWW.UNION.EDU

Others add that "there are so many resources available in terms of funding, internships, and leadership opportunities." Students report being thrilled about the "undergraduate research opportunities" like the Sophomore Research Seminar or those through National Science Foundation awards, and the annual Steinmetz Symposium allows them to present their work to the entire campus community. A distinctive Union institution, the Minerva House program has produced sixty-two fellows selected to spend a year after graduation working on a global service project.

GENERAL INFO

Activities: Choral groups, concert band, dance, drama/theater, jazz band, literary magazine, music ensembles, radio station, student government, student newspaper, student-run film society, symphony orchestra, television station, yearbook, campus ministries, International Student Organization, Model UN. **Organizations:** 120 registered organizations, 12 honor societies, 7 religious organizations. 13 fraternities, 5 sororities. **Athletics (Intercollegiate):** *Men:* baseball, basketball, crew/rowing, cross-country, diving, football, ice hockey, lacrosse, soccer, swimming, tennis, track/field (outdoor), track/field (indoor). *Women:* basketball, crew/rowing, cross-country, diving, field hockey, ice hockey, lacrosse, soccer, softball, swimming, tennis, track/field (outdoor), track/field (indoor), volleyball. **On-Campus Highlights:** The Nott Memorial, Schaffer Library, Reamer Campus Center, Jackson's Garden, Memorial Chapel.

FINANCIAL AID

Students should submit: CSS Profile; FAFSA.; State aid form. Priority filing deadline is 1/15. The Princeton Review suggests that all financial aid forms be submitted as soon as possible after October 1. *Need-based scholarships/grants offered:* College/university scholarship or grant aid from institutional funds, Federal Pell, private scholarships, SEOG, state scholarships/grants. *Loan aid offered:* Direct PLUS Loans, Direct Subsidized Loans, Direct Unsubsidized Loans. Applicants will be notified of awards on or about 3/25. Federal Work-Study Program available. Institutional employment available.

BOTTOM LINE

The tuition at Union College comes to about $53,019. The average aid package comes to $44,649, with 82 percent of students receiving some aid. On average 100 percent of student demonstrated need is met. Union isn't cheap, but offers a great deal of financial aid to those who need it.

CAREER INFORMATION FROM PAYSCALE.COM	
ROI Rating	92
Bachelors and No Higher	
Median starting salary	$60,900
Median mid-career salary	$122,400
At Least Bachelors	
Median starting salary	$63,500
Median mid-career salary	$129,900
Alumni with high job meaning	51%
Degrees awarded in STEM subjects	47%

SELECTIVITY	
Admissions Rating	93
# of applicants	6,676
% of applicants accepted	37
% of acceptees attending	23
# offered a place on the wait list	1,066
% accepting a place on wait list	49
% admitted from wait list	7
# of early decision applicants	408
% accepted early decision	63

FRESHMAN PROFILE	
Range SAT EBRW	630–700
Range SAT Math	640–730
Range ACT Composite	29–32
Minimum paper TOEFL	600
Minimum internet-based TOEFL	90
Average HS GPA	3.4
% graduated top 10% of class	63
% graduated top 25% of class	88
% graduated top 50% of class	99

DEADLINES	
Early decision	
Deadline	11/15
Notification	12/15
Other ED Deadline	1/15
Other ED Notification	2/8
Regular	
Deadline	1/15
Notification	4/1
Nonfall registration?	Yes

FINANCIAL FACTS	
Financial Aid Rating	96
Annual tuition	$53,019
Room and board	$13,119
Required fees	$471
Books and supplies	$1,500
Average frosh need-based scholarship	$37,841
Average UG need-based scholarship	$37,748
% needy frosh rec. need-based scholarship or grant aid	97
% needy UG rec. need-based scholarship or grant aid	100
% needy frosh rec. non-need-based scholarship or grant aid	8
% needy UG rec. non-need-based scholarship or grant aid	9
% needy frosh rec. need-based self-help aid	97
% needy UG rec. need-based self-help aid	97
% frosh rec. any financial aid	79
% UG rec. any financial aid	79
% UG borrow to pay for school	56
Average cumulative indebtedness	$34,221
% frosh need fully met	100

University of Alabama—Tuscaloosa

Box 870132, Tuscaloosa, AL 35487-0132 • Admissions: 205-348-5666 • Fax: 205-348-9046

CAMPUS LIFE

Quality of Life Rating	**90**
Fire Safety Rating	**81**
Green Rating	**60***
Type of school	Public
Environment	City

STUDENTS

Total undergrad enrollment	32,387
% male/female	44/56
% from out of state	60
% frosh live on campus	95
% ugrads live on campus	24
# of fraternities (% ugrad men join)	37 (28)
# of sororities (% ugrad women join)	23 (44)
% African American	10
% Asian	1
% Caucasian	78
% Hispanic	5
% Native American	<1
% Pacific Islander	<1
% Two or more races	3
% Race and/or ethnicity unknown	<1
% international	2
# of countries represented	60

ACADEMICS

Academic Rating	**77**
% students returning for sophomore year	87
% students graduating within 4 years	44
% students graduating within 6 years	68
Calendar	Semester
Student/faculty ratio	23:1
Profs interesting rating	79
Profs accessible rating	81

Most classes have 20–29 students. Most lab/discussion sessions have 20–29 students.

MOST POPULAR MAJORS

Nursing; Mechanical Engineering, Marketing

ABOUT THE SCHOOL

Undergrads at this public research university proudly assert that "the University of Alabama is all about academics, athletics, and having a good time." Therefore, it's not too surprising to learn that there's also "amazing campus spirit." The Tuscaloosa campus is the flagship of the state of Alabama, where students rush to highlight the "great" honors college as well as the nursing, business and engineering programs. And they steadfastly assert that the "academics are plenty challenging" for virtually all disciplines. Even better, "opportunities [abound to conduct] undergraduate research." UA also works diligently to ensure that its students "foster critical thinking skills" and aim "to create a more thoughtful society." Just as essential, Alabama manages to attract "passionate" professors who excel at "bring[ing their] material to life." They're also "kind and caring...and highly intelligent." And they "genuinely want their students to grasp and retain the information." To that end, professors here are "very personable and willing to help each and every one of their students individually."

BANG FOR YOUR BUCK

Many students are drawn to the University of Alabama thanks to the "large amount of financial aid" they offer undergraduates. Indeed, the school's generous packages "make it easy [for students] to attend." And undergrads can easily apply for merit-based scholarships. These typically demand that students meet certain GPA and standardized test minimums. Top applicants will be in the running for scholarships such as the Academic Elite which covers the cost of tuition, one year of housing at a regular room rate, provides an $8,500 stipend (per year) and a book scholarship totaling $2,000 ($500/year). That certainly makes it worth your while to hit the books!

STUDENT LIFE

The University of Alabama is overflowing with extracurricular options. To begin with, "there are hundreds of student organizations [with which] to get involved." Additionally, "the university also holds many functions and events every week for people to attend." Several undergrads can also be found at "Riverwalk, a walking trail close to campus that goes along the Black Warrior River." Of course, during the fall semester, most students flock "to football games and tailgate." And no matter what time of year, once the weekend rolls around "a lot of people go to parties at fraternities and sororities [or they head] to the local bars and hang out."

CAREER

One of the University of Alabama's "greatest strengths is the career center." Indeed, the office has "a staff of the best people" who work closely with students and help them plan far before (and beyond) graduation. Students can seek advice on everything from selecting a major to job search strategies. And they may easily log onto Handshake, an online portal that connects them with the latest job and internship postings. The Career Center also does a stellar job of bringing recruiters to campus. In fact, it hosts multiple career fairs throughout the year and manages to attract companies like Abercrombie & Fitch, Apple, Deloitte, Geico, Mercedes Benz, Southwest Airlines, and Target.

GENERAL INFO

Activities: Choral groups, concert band, dance, drama/theater, jazz band, literary magazine, marching band, music ensembles, musical theater, opera, pep band, radio station, student government,

University of Alabama—Tuscaloosa

FINANCIAL AID: 205-348-6756 • E-MAIL: ADMISSIONS@UA.EDU • WEBSITE: WWW.UA.EDU

student newspaper, student-run film society, symphony orchestra, television station, campus ministries, Student Organization, Model UN. 567 registered organizations, 45 honor societies, 44 religious organizations. 37 fraternities, 23 sororities. **Athletics (Intercollegiate):** *Men:* baseball, basketball, cross-country, diving, football, golf, swimming, tennis, track/field (outdoor), track/field (indoor). *Women:* basketball, crew/rowing, cross-country, diving, golf, gymnastics, soccer, softball, swimming, tennis, track/field (outdoor), track/field (indoor), volleyball. **On-Campus Highlights:** University of Alabama Museum of Natural History, Amelia Gayle Gorgas Library, Bryant-Denny Stadium, The Gorgas House Museum (built in 1829), Paul W. Bryant Museum, Located right on campus is a wonderful blend of cultures and ethnic foods. Interesting shops, a new shopping center, great coffee shops, and local and visiting musical talent—all located on University Blvd.

FINANCIAL AID

Students should submit: FAFSA and Application for Academic Scholarships. Priority filing deadline is 3/1. The Princeton Review suggests that all financial aid forms be submitted as soon as possible after October 1. *Need-based scholarships/grants offered:* College/university scholarship or grant aid from institutional funds, Federal Nursing Scholarships, Federal Pell, Private scholarships, SEOG, State scholarships/grants. *Loan aid offered:* Direct PLUS Loans, Direct Subsidized Loans, Direct Unsubsidized Loans. Applicants will be notified of awards on a rolling basis beginning 4/1. Federal Work-Study Program available. Institutional employment available.

BOTTOM LINE

The price of tuition at University of Alabama depends upon whether a student is an Alabama resident. Undergrads who hail from the state pay $10,780 versus $29,230 for out-of-state students. Further, individuals who live on campus can expect to pay $8,900 for housing and $3,802 for board. Books and supplies often cost students $1,200. There's also a loan fee estimate of $70. Lastly, Alabama recommends setting aside $2,390 for miscellaneous expenses.

CAREER INFORMATION FROM PAYSCALE.COM	
ROI Rating	87
Bachelors and No Higher	
Median starting salary	$51,200
Median mid-career salary	$93,900
At Least Bachelors	
Median starting salary	$52,600
Median mid-career salary	$96,900
Alumni with high job meaning	50%
Degrees awarded in STEM subjects	15%

SELECTIVITY	
Admissions Rating	89
# of applicants	38,129
% of applicants accepted	53
% of acceptees attending	36

FRESHMAN PROFILE	
Range SAT EBRW	530–640
Range SAT Math	520–640
Range ACT Composite	23–32
Minimum paper TOEFL	550
Minimum internet-based TOEFL	79
Average HS GPA	3.7
% graduated top 10% of class	39
% graduated top 25% of class	60
% graduated top 50% of class	83

DEADLINES	
Regular	
Priority	2/1
Nonfall registration?	Yes

FINANCIAL FACTS	
Financial Aid Rating	82
Annual in-state tuition	$10,780
Annual out-of-state tuition	$29,230
Room and board	$10,102
Required fees	$0
Room and board	$9,974
Books and supplies	$1,200
Average frosh need-based scholarship	$15,053
Average UG need-based scholarship	$12,730
% needy frosh rec. need-based scholarship or grant aid	77
% needy UG rec. need-based scholarship or grant aid	73
% needy frosh rec. non-need-based scholarship or grant aid	62
% needy UG rec. non-need-based scholarship or grant aid	51
% needy frosh rec. need-based self-help aid	64
% needy UG rec. need-based self-help aid	74
% frosh rec. any financial aid	81
% UG rec. any financial aid	73
% UG borrow to pay for school	46
Average cumulative indebtedness	$34,305
% frosh need fully met	28
% ugrads need fully met	21
Average % of frosh need met	58
Average % of ugrad need met	54

University of Arizona

PO Box 210073, Tucson, AZ 85721-0073 • Admissions: 520-621-3237 • Fax: 520-621-9799

CAMPUS LIFE

Quality of Life Rating	88
Fire Safety Rating	91
Green Rating	94
Type of school	Public
Environment	Metropolis

STUDENTS

Total undergrad enrollment	34,049
% male/female	48/52
% from out of state	31
% frosh from public high school	86
% frosh live on campus	72
% ugrads live on campus	19
# of fraternities	24
# of sororities	24
% African American	4
% Asian	5
% Caucasian	50
% Hispanic	27
% Native American	1
% Pacific Islander	<1
% Two or more races	5
% Race and/or ethnicity unknown	1
% international	7
# of countries represented	129

ACADEMICS

Academic Rating	78
% students returning for sophomore year	83
% students graduating within 4 years	45
% students graduating within 6 years	64
Calendar	Semester
Student/faculty ratio	15:1
Profs interesting rating	76
Profs accessible rating	77

Most classes have 10–19 students. Most lab/discussion sessions have 10–19 students.

MOST POPULAR MAJORS

Cell/Cellular and Molecular Biology; Psychology; Political Science and Government

ABOUT THE SCHOOL

Undergrads at the University of Arizona have "a lot of pride" in their school and it's easy to understand why. Though the overall university is "large," students report that most academic departments feel "small" and manage to provide "individual attention" as well as "foster student growth." Arizona also offers "many opportunities for research, study abroad, and experiential learning through internships and/or campus jobs." Another advantage is the sheer breadth of "programs and majors" available to undergrads. While virtually all of these programs are "strong," students especially highlight the "engineering" and "nursing" schools along with the "Eller College of Management." Thankfully, no matter the course of study, the majority of professors here are "passionate" and "teach in a way that engages the students and makes them think [about] the topic outside of class." Even better, they are truly "invested" in their students and endeavor to make themselves "accessible outside of the classroom."

BANG FOR YOUR BUCK

There is little doubt that the University of Arizona prioritizes affordability. After all, over 85 percent of their undergraduates receive some form of financial assistance. And all students are eligible to apply for a number of merit-based scholarships. These awards can range anywhere from $3,000-$12,000 (for in-state applicants) and $2,000-$35,000 (for out-of-state applicants). Recipients are chosen based upon GPA and standardized test scores. Importantly, many of these awards are renewable for up to four years. Undergrads here may also capitalize on Arizona's nationally recognized Scholarship Universe. This database, compiled by the university, allows students to easily search for legitimate scholarship opportunities at the school and beyond.

STUDENT LIFE

It's virtually impossible to be bored at the University of Arizona. After all, the school offers "a lot of extracurricular activities" ranging from "honoraries and student government to Greek life and professional societies." UA also sponsors numerous events including "cultural festivals," music "recitals," "poetry reading[s]," comedy shows and much more." Additionally, Arizona students are a sporty lot and they love to support their fellow Wildcats. Hence, athletic games are really well attended "especially [when it comes to] football and basketball." Of course, students also love to take advantage of Tucson's "fantastic" weather. It's quite common to find undergrads "playing frisbee or simply reading on a bench." And opportunities also abound for "hiking" as well as "mountain bik[ing]," "slacklining," "hammocking," and "rock climbing on Mount Lemmon."

CAREER

Undergrads at Arizona are quick to boast that their university does an "amazing [job] with getting people career ready." Indeed, the school provides a myriad of opportunities for "network[ing]" and helps students "learn...important job and interview skills." This is all largely thanks to a stellar Office of Student Engagement and Career Development that shows undergrads how to meld their passions with their job search. Through numerous employer information sessions and

University of Arizona

FINANCIAL AID: 520-621-1858 • E-MAIL: ADMISSIONS@ARIZONA.EDU • WEBSITE: WWW.ARIZONA.EDU

job fairs, students are able to meet and interview with representatives from hundreds of industries. In fact, the university often draws big name corporations such as Vanguard, Allstate Insurance Company, AmeriCorps, Macy's, the U.S. State Department, Honeywell, American Express, Deloitte and DISH Network. Students can easily prepare for these meetings (as well as their job hunts in general) via workshops offered by Career Development. Topics cover everything from resume writing to crafting the perfect LinkedIn profile.

GENERAL INFO

Activities: Campus Ministries; Choral groups; Concert band; Dance; Drama/theater; International Student Organization; Jazz band; Literary magazine; Marching band; Model UN; Music ensembles; Musical theater; Opera; Pep band; Radio station; Student government; Student newspaper; Symphony orchestra; Television station; Yearbook, Intramurals, Campus Recreation Center. 504 registered organizations, 13 honor societies, 13 religious organizations. 25 fraternities, 20 sororities. **Athletics (Intercollegiate):** *Men:* baseball, basketball, cross-country, diving, football, golf, swimming, tennis, track/field (outdoor). *Women:* basketball, cross-country, diving, golf, gymnastics, soccer, softball, swimming, tennis, track/field (outdoor), track/field (indoor), volleyball. **On-Campus Highlights:** Flandrau Science Center, Center for Creative Photography, UA Museum of Art, Athletics Events, Arizona State Museum.

FINANCIAL AID

Students should submit: FAFSA. The Princeton Review suggests that all financial aid forms be submitted as soon as possible after October 1. *Need-based scholarships/grants offered:* College/university scholarship or grant aid from institutional funds, Federal Pell, private scholarships, SEOG, state scholarships/grants. *Loan aid offered:* Direct PLUS Loans, Direct Subsidized Loans, Direct Unsubsidized Loans. Applicants will be notified of awards on a rolling basis beginning 2/1. Federal Work-Study Program available. Institutional employment available.

THE BOTTOM LINE

Total cost of attendance for Arizona residents is about $22,944. A deal by any measure but over 70 percent of undergraduates receive some form of financial assistance making this gem even more of a bargain.

CAREER INFORMATION FROM PAYSCALE.COM	
ROI Rating	87
Bachelors and No Higher	
Median starting salary	$55,000
Median mid-career salary	$99,000
At Least Bachelors	
Median starting salary	$56,200
Median mid-career salary	$102,900
Alumni with high job meaning	50%
Degrees awarded in STEM subjects	23%

SELECTIVITY	
Admissions Rating	81
# of applicants	33,608
% of applicants accepted	84
% of acceptees attending	26

FRESHMAN PROFILE	
Range SAT EBRW	540–650
Range SAT Math	560–690
Range ACT Composite	21–28
Minimum internet-based TOEFL	70
Average HS GPA	3.3
% graduated top 10% of class	34
% graduated top 25% of class	61
% graduated top 50% of class	85

DEADLINES	
Regular	
Priority	5/1
Deadline	5/1
Nonfall registration?	Yes

FINANCIAL FACTS	
Financial Aid Rating	80
Annual in-state tuition	$10,262
Annual out-of-state tuition	$31,067
Room and board	$11,300
Required fees	$1,382
Room and board	$11,300
Required fees	$1,382
Books and supplies	$800
Average frosh need-based scholarship	$13,402
Average UG need-based scholarship	$10,555
% needy frosh rec. need-based scholarship or grant aid	99
% needy UG rec. need-based scholarship or grant aid	90
% needy frosh rec. non-need-based scholarship or grant aid	16
% needy UG rec. non-need-based scholarship or grant aid	9
% needy frosh rec. need-based self-help aid	50
% needy UG rec. need-based self-help aid	63
% frosh rec. any financial aid	70
% UG rec. any financial aid	71
% UG borrow to pay for school	54
Average cumulative indebtedness	$23,956
% frosh need fully met	18
% ugrads need fully met	11
Average % of frosh need met	68
Average % of ugrad need met	58

University of California—Berkeley

110 Sproul Hall, #5800, Berkeley, CA 94720-5800 • Admissions: 510-642-3175 • Fax: 510-642-7333

CAMPUS LIFE

Quality of Life Rating	**84**
Fire Safety Rating	**91**
Green Rating	**97**
Type of school	Public
Environment	City

STUDENTS

Total undergrad enrollment	30,574
% male/female	47/53
% from out of state	14
% frosh live on campus	96
% ugrads live on campus	15
# of fraternities (% ugrad men join)	38 (10)
# of sororities (% ugrad women join)	19 (10)
% African American	2
% Asian	35
% Caucasian	26
% Hispanic	15
% Native American	<1
% Pacific Islander	<1
% Two or more races	6
% Race and/or ethnicity unknown	4
% international	12

ACADEMICS

Academic Rating	**85**
% students returning for sophomore year	97
% students graduating within 4 years	76
% students graduating within 6 years	91
Calendar	Semester
Student/faculty ratio	18:1
Profs interesting rating	76
Profs accessible rating	69

Most classes have 10–19 students. Most lab/discussion sessions have 20–29 students.

MOST POPULAR MAJORS

Computer Engineering; Political Science and Government; Economics

#11 BEST VALUE COLLEGE

ABOUT THE SCHOOL

University of California—Berkeley enjoys a reputation for quality and value that few other colleges can match. Large, diverse, and highly regarded, Berkeley is often ranked among the top public institutions in the world. Berkeley offers around 350 undergraduate and graduate degree programs in a wide range of disciplines. Best known for research, the school counts Nobel laureates, MacArthur Fellowship recipients, and Pulitzer Prize and Academy Award winners among its faculty. With an "all-star faculty and resources," professors here are "intelligent [and] accessible," with many departments boasting "the best [academics] in their field." Needless to say, undergraduate education is first-rate. The school maintains a low student-to-teacher ratio, and opportunities to get in on cutting-edge research at Berkeley abound. In fact, approximately half of the school's undergraduates assist faculty in creative or research projects during their time here. As some students note, "you don't get the coddling that the private universities show. You don't have a billion counselors catering to your every need." Though students note that survey classes here can sometimes be "enormous," professors "make themselves very accessible via e-mail and office hours." Berkeley maintains an incredibly high number of nationally ranked programs; however, engineering, computer science, molecular and cell biology, and political science are the most popular majors for undergraduates.

BANG FOR YOUR BUCK

Berkeley's Undergraduate Scholarships, Prizes and Honors unit of the Financial Aid Office administers three different scholarship programs. Twenty-five Berkeley Undergraduate Scholarships are awarded each year. The Regent's and Chancellor's Scholarship is Berkeley's most prestigious scholarship, and is awarded annually to approximately 200 incoming undergraduates. The by-invitation-only Cal Opportunity Scholarship is designed to attract high-achieving students who have overcome challenging socioeconomic circumstances. Award amounts vary for each of these scholarship programs, and are often based on financial need. All applicants to Berkeley are automatically considered for these scholarship programs. As a public institution, UC Berkeley's low in-state tuition makes this school very affordable. With a low cost and an active financial aid program, Berkeley is an ideal choice for high-achieving students from low-income families. According to its website, Berkeley serves more economically disadvantaged students than all the Ivy League universities combined. More than 30 percent of Berkeley undergraduates are eligible for Pell Grants. The Middle Class Access Plan helps middle-class families keep debt down by capping the parents' contribution.

STUDENT LIFE

At Berkeley "you are free to express yourself." "Conversations vary from the wicked party last night" to "debates about the roles of women in Hindu mythology." To simply label this school as "diverse" seems like an oversimplification. Here, people "think about everything." Students regard fellow students as "passionate" and "intelligent." Full of their signature optimism, they believe that "life at Berkeley has no limits"; they "study and hear obscure languages, meet famous scientists, engage with brilliant students, eat delicious food, and just relax with friends daily." Student life includes taking advantage of everything San Francisco has to offer across the bay, but

University of California—Berkeley

even when remaining on campus, "there are clubs and classes that cater to everybody's needs and such a diverse group of people that it would be hard to not fit in."

CAREER

"Berkeley's greatest strengths are the amount of resources and opportunities it provides to students not only to allow them to explore numerous academic fields but to engage them in the community, in the country, and in the world." "There are internship opportunities for students from all disciplines, both on campus and in the surrounding cities of Berkeley, Oakland, and San Francisco." "Research opportunities are abundant" and "the career center is amazing." There are "endless options for student involvement" and employers like the school's "prestigious" reputation. According to the website PayScale.com, the average starting salary for graduates is $65,400 and 49 percent of alumni find their jobs to be highly meaningful.

GENERAL INFO

Activities: Choral groups, concert band, dance, drama/theater, jazz band, literary magazine, marching band, music ensembles, musical theater, pep band, radio station, student government, student newspaper, student-run film society, symphony orchestra, television station, yearbook, international student organization. **Organizations:** 300 registered organizations, 6 honor societies, 28 religious organizations. 38 fraternities, 19 sororities. **Athletics (Intercollegiate):** *Men:* Baseball, basketball, crew/rowing, cross-country, diving, football, golf, gymnastics, rugby, sailing, soccer, swimming, tennis, track/field (outdoor), water polo. *Women:* Basketball, crew/rowing, cross-country, diving, field hockey, golf, gymnastics, lacrosse, sailing, soccer, softball, swimming, tennis, track/field (outdoor), volleyball, water polo.

FINANCIAL AID

Students should submit: FAFSA, state aid form. Priority filing deadline is 3/1. The Princeton Review suggests that all financial aid forms be submitted as soon as possible after October 1. *Need-based scholarships/grants offered:* College/university scholarship or grant aid from institutional funds, Federal Pell, private scholarships, SEOG, state scholarships/grants. *Loan aid offered:* Direct PLUS Loans, Direct Subsidized Loans, Direct Unsubsidized Loans. Applicants will be notified of awards on or about 3/31. Federal Work-Study Program available. Institutional employment available.

BOTTOM LINE

For California residents, Berkeley is a great deal, ringing in at $11,220 annually for tuition and fees. In addition to tuition, the school estimates expenditures of $1,240 for books and supplies, though these costs vary by major. Nonresident tuition alone is $37,902 annually.

CAREER INFORMATION FROM PAYSCALE.COM	
ROI Rating	95
Bachelors and No Higher	
Median starting salary	$68,300
Median mid-career salary	$132,300
At Least Bachelors	
Median starting salary	$69,900
Median mid-career salary	$140,100
Alumni with high job meaning	49%
Degrees awarded in STEM subjects	36%

SELECTIVITY	
Admissions Rating	98
# of applicants	85,057
% of applicants accepted	17
% of acceptees attending	44
# offered a place on the wait list	3,454
% accepting a place on wait list	50
% admitted from wait list	55

FRESHMAN PROFILE	
Range SAT EBRW	650–760
Range SAT Math	650–780
Range ACT Composite	29–34
Minimum paper TOEFL	550
Minimum internet-based TOEFL	80
Average HS GPA	3.9
% graduated top 10% of class	98
% graduated top 25% of class	100
% graduated top 50% of class	100

DEADLINES	
Regular	
Deadline	11/30
Nonfall registration?	Yes

FINANCIAL FACTS	
Financial Aid Rating	84
Annual in-state tuition	$11,442
Annual out-of-state tuition	$40,434
Room and board	$16,160
Required fees	$2,742
Books and supplies	$894
Average frosh need-based scholarship	$21,384
Average UG need-based scholarship	$20,900
% needy frosh rec. need-based scholarship or grant aid	89
% needy UG rec. need-based scholarship or grant aid	93
% needy frosh rec. non-need-based scholarship or grant aid	4
% needy UG rec. non-need-based scholarship or grant aid	2
% needy frosh rec. need-based self-help aid	45
% needy UG rec. need-based self-help aid	40
% UG borrow to pay for school	35
Average cumulative indebtedness	$18,197
% frosh need fully met	22
% ugrads need fully met	24
Average % of frosh need met	78
Average % of ugrad need met	81

University of California—Davis

550 ALUMNI LANE, ONE SHIELDS AVE, DAVIS, CA 95616 • ADMISSIONS: 530-752-2971 • FAX: 530-752-1280

CAMPUS LIFE

Quality of Life Rating	**92**
Fire Safety Rating	**95**
Green Rating	**98**
Type of school	Public
Environment	Town

STUDENTS

Total undergrad enrollment	29,982
% male/female	41/59
% from out of state	5
% frosh from public high school	84
% frosh live on campus	92
% ugrads live on campus	25
# of fraternities	28
# of sororities	21
% African American	2
% Asian	28
% Caucasian	25
% Hispanic	21
% Native American	<1
% Pacific Islander	<1
% Two or more races	5
% Race and/or ethnicity unknown	2
% international	16
# of countries represented	121

ACADEMICS

Academic Rating	**75**
% students returning for sophomore year	92
Calendar	Differs By Program
Student/faculty ratio	19:1
Profs interesting rating	76
Profs accessible rating	74

Most classes have 20–29 students. Most lab/discussion sessions have 20–29 students.

MOST POPULAR MAJORS

Biology/Biological Sciences; Psychology; Economics

ABOUT THE SCHOOL

"A top-tier research institution," University of California—Davis is a school that "provides…tremendous opportunities." Undergrads are enamored with the "beautiful" campus and value the UC Davis focus on "green energy." Students can study virtually any academic discipline here, many call out the university's "top ranked" animal science and agriculture programs. Just as critical, students appreciate that they can make their "voices…heard." As one undergrad explains, "When we want change or we are upset about the way the school is being run, the Dean or Chancellor addresses it." This praise also extends to the "awesome" professors who are typically "world-renowned in their field." Not only do they want their students "learn the material," they work diligently to ensure said students understand how to "apply" that knowledge. Further, their "passion" for their subject matter is often infectious. And while the "course load is heavy," the professors here make sure that they're "very accessible and helpful outside of the classroom."

BANG FOR YOUR BUCK

UC Davis really does an admirable job in providing an affordable education. Impressively, 44 percent of their students graduate debt free. Even better, approximately 75 percent of the aid offered comes in the form of grants, scholarships and work-study. California residents can take advantage of a handful of plans meant to ease the financial burden for low and middle income families. For example, the Blue and Gold opportunity plan covers UC tuition as well as the student services fee for undergrads whose parents earn $80,000 or less. And the Aggie Grant Plan awards $3,000 annually to students whose annual family income ranges from $80,000 to 120,000. Thankfully, there are also plenty of merit scholarships for which all students can be considered. In fact, Davis doles out over $6 million in scholarships every year. Awards can be anywhere from $100 to $13,000.

STUDENT LIFE

There's no shortage of extracurricular options at Davis. After all, the university offers "700+ clubs…including 71 Greek organizations." It's also quite common to find people simply "playing Frisbee or throwing a football on the quad, with students reading and eating lunch on the grass beside them." Many undergrads also enjoy participating in "intramural sports [as a] fun way to [take a break] from studying." As one student shares, "Volleyball, and inter-tube water polo are some of my favorites." There is also a party scene but we're told that mostly takes place at "people's houses" and these events are relatively "discreet." When students need a little break from campus life, they can easily head "to neighboring cities [like] Sacramento, San Francisco [and] Tahoe."

CAREER

Without a doubt, UC Davis provides students with "numerous career and internship resources." Undergrads have easy access to an outstanding Career Center that assists with all aspects of career planning. Students can use the office to explore career paths associated with various major, find opportunities for job shadowing, connect with various professional associations. Students can receive individual counseling on everything from how to conduct a job search to interview techniques and salary negotiation. UC Davis also does a tremendous of attracting top companies to recruit on campus. The university hosts multiple career fairs throughout the year allowing undergrads to network with hundreds of employers.

University of California—Davis

Financial Aid: 530-752-2396 • E-mail: undergraduateadmissions@ucdavis.edu • Website: www.ucdavis.edu

GENERAL INFO

Activities: Choral groups, concert band, dance, drama/theater, jazz band, literary magazine, marching band, music ensembles, musical theater, radio station, student government, student newspaper, student-run film society, symphony orchestra, video production studio, campus ministries, international student organizations. **Organizations:** 700+ registered student organizations, 1 honor society, 67 religious/philosophical organizations. 28 fraternities, 21 sororities. **Athletics (Intercollegiate):** *Men:* Baseball, basketball, cross-country, football, golf, soccer, swimming, track/field, track/field, water polo. *Women:* Basketball, cross-country, field hockey, golf, gymnastics, lacrosse, soccer, softball, swimming & diving, tennis, track/field, volleyball, water polo.

FINANCIAL AID

Students should submit: FAFSA, state aid form. Priority filing deadline is 3/2. The Princeton Review suggests that all financial aid forms be submitted as soon as possible after October 1. *Need-based scholarships/grants offered:* College/university scholarship or grant aid from institutional funds, Federal Pell, private scholarships, SEOG, state scholarships/grants. *Loan aid offered:* Direct PLUS Loans, Direct Subsidized Loans, Direct Unsubsidized Loans. Applicants will be notified of awards on or about 3/14.

THE BOTTOM LINE

UC Davis charges California residents $14,046 for its annual tuition (and fees). Undergraduates hailing from out of state can expect a tuition bill of $37,902. All students will likely spend around $1,253 for books and supplies. Undergrads living on campus will pay another $14,838 for room and board. UC Davis suggests that students budget $1,281 for personal expenses and $381 for transportation. Students who opt to get health insurance through the university will spend $2,298.

CAREER INFORMATION FROM PAYSCALE.COM	
ROI Rating	91
Bachelors and No Higher	
Median starting salary	$59,400
Median mid-career salary	$113,800
At Least Bachelors	
Median starting salary	$60,600
Median mid-career salary	$119,800
Alumni with high job meaning	53%
Degrees awarded in STEM subjects	35%

SELECTIVITY	
Admissions Rating	**89**
# of applicants	70,214
% of applicants accepted	44
% of acceptees attending	19
# offered a place on the wait list	8,263
% accepting a place on wait list	35
% admitted from wait list	15

FRESHMAN PROFILE	
Range SAT EBRW	550–650
Range SAT Math	570–710
Range ACT Composite	25–31
Minimum paper TOEFL	550
Minimum internet-based TOEFL	60
Average HS GPA	4.0

DEADLINES	
Regular	
Deadline	11/30
Notification	3/31
Nonfall registration?	No

FINANCIAL FACTS	
Financial Aid Rating	**81**
Annual in-state tuition	$11,502
Annual out-of-state tuition	$40,497
Room and board	$15,765
Required fees	$2,961
Books and supplies	$1,601
Average frosh need-based scholarship	$20,111
Average UG need-based scholarship	$17,591
% needy frosh rec. need-based scholarship or grant aid	96
% needy UG rec. need-based scholarship or grant aid	96
% needy frosh rec. non-need-based scholarship or grant aid	2
% needy UG rec. non-need-based scholarship or grant aid	1
% needy frosh rec. need-based self-help aid	60
% needy UG rec. need-based self-help aid	56
% UG rec. any financial aid	55
% UG borrow to pay for school	56
Average cumulative indebtedness	$19,588
% frosh need fully met	16
% ugrads need fully met	15
Average % of frosh need met	80
Average % of ugrad need met	78

University of California—Los Angeles

1147 MURPHY HALL, LOS ANGELES, CA 90095-1436 • ADMISSIONS: 310-825-3101 • FAX: 310-206-1206

#35 BEST VALUE COLLEGE

CAMPUS LIFE
Quality of Life Rating	86
Fire Safety Rating	92
Green Rating	90
Type of school	Public
Environment	Metropolis

STUDENTS
Total undergrad enrollment	30,990
% male/female	43/57
% from out of state	12
% frosh from public high school	75
% frosh live on campus	98
% ugrads live on campus	48
# of fraternities (% ugrad men join)	35 (11)
# of sororities (% ugrad women join)	35 (13)
% African American	3
% Asian	28
% Caucasian	27
% Hispanic	22
% Native American	<1
% Pacific Islander	<1
% Two or more races	5
% Race and/or ethnicity unknown	2
% international	12
# of countries represented	120

ACADEMICS
Academic Rating	77
% students returning for sophomore year	97
% students graduating within 4 years	75
% students graduating within 6 years	91
Calendar	Quarter
Student/faculty ratio	18:1
Profs interesting rating	66
Profs accessible rating	62
Most classes have 10–19 students.	

MOST POPULAR MAJORS
Biology/Biological Sciences; Psychology;
Business/Managerial Economics

ABOUT THE SCHOOL

In a word, the University of California, Los Angeles is about diversity—in what you can study, in what you can do with your free time, in ethnicity, in gender and sexuality, in everything. With more than 200 undergraduate and graduate degree programs on offer for its 40,000 students, there truly is something for everyone. The technology and research resources here are dreamy. There is comprehensive quality across the broad range of disciplines. There are almost 9,000 undergraduate and graduate courses. You can take classes here in pretty much any academic endeavor, and you will likely run across some of the best and brightest professors in the world. Brushes with fame are common here—with a location near Hollywood and a world-famous film and television school, the UCLA campus has attracted film productions for decades. That being said, you should be aware that bigness and breadth have their limitations (lots of teaching assistants, big classes, anonymity). But if you don't mind being a small fish in a big pond, chances are you'll have a great experience here. And with just a little bit of initiative, you might even make a splash. Perhaps more notable, "UCLA is the kind of school that pushes you to work hard academically but reminds you that interaction with people outside of the classroom is just as important."

BANG FOR YOUR BUCK

Even in a time of rising fees, UCLA remains far below most of the other top research universities in total costs for undergraduate study. A little more than half of the student population here receives need-based financial aid. This school prizes its diversity, and that definitely includes economic diversity. UCLA ranks at the top among major research universities in the percentage of its students that receive Pell Grants (which is free government money for low-income students). The university also offers the prestigious Regents Scholarship, intended to reward extraordinary academic excellence and exemplary leadership and community service accomplishments. Also, the career-planning operation here is first-rate, and there are extensive opportunities for internships with local employers. UCLA Financial Aid and Scholarships has both advisors and counselors available to help students complete financial aid applications, and to provide guidance throughout the process. In-person appointments can be scheduled, but the office also has walk-in hours. The UCLA website also provides access to certain scholarship opportunities, but the school also has a resource center on campus. The Scholarship Resource Center opened in 1996 to provide scholarship information, resources, and support services to all UCLA students, regardless of financial aid eligibility.

STUDENT LIFE

"UCLA is the mold that fits to you," says a happy student. "There is no 'typical student,' and everyone can easily find a group of students to fit in with. The benefits of 30,000 students and over 1,000 student groups!" The school has an extremely large campus and a very diverse student body, but it fosters an environment where everyone can find a place in the community: "Whether it be in Greek life, a club or organization, everybody has somewhere they can go to relax and have some fun. The apartments are close to campus, so nearly everybody lives in a small area with close proximity." And the benefits of going to school in a big, busy city are manifold: "LA is a vibrant and multicultural city. You have the beach to the west and the deserts/mountains to the east. EVERYTHING is accessible here in this city. If you want to go

University of California—Los Angeles

FINANCIAL AID: 310-206-0400 • E-MAIL: UGADM@SAONET.UCLA.EDU • WEBSITE: WWW.UCLA.EDU

surf during the week it's ten minutes away. The food here is amazing and brings out the inner foodie in everyone!" One student puts the student experience at UCLA very succinctly: "I, like most people here, love [my] life."

CAREER

"UCLA is about getting a top notch education at a (currently) affordable price that will start your career off on an excellent path," is a popular sentiment regarding how the school equips students for their future. The Career Center offers standard services like advising and counseling; job fairs; on-campus recruiting; job and internship search tools; resources for those applying to grad school or looking for international opportunities; and "JumpStart" workshops covering professional development topics in a wide variety of fields. Students seem very satisfied with what the school affords them: "Networking and marketing, you're always told of a ton of activities, internships, resource opportunities—there are constant career fairs and activities. Also, location-wise, L.A. is a huge cosmopolitan city, you've got the opportunity to work in anything." Out of UCLA alumni visiting PayScale.com, 47 percent report that they derive a high level of meaning from their job.

GENERAL INFO

Activities: Choral groups, concert band, dance, drama/theater, jazz band, literary magazine, marching band, music ensembles, musical theater, opera, pep band, radio station, student government, student newspaper, student-run film society, symphony orchestra, television station, yearbook, campus ministries, international student organization.

FINANCIAL AID

Students should submit: FAFSA. Priority filing deadline is 3/15. The Princeton Review suggests that all financial aid forms be submitted as soon as possible after October 1. *Need-based scholarships/grants offered:* College/university scholarship or grant aid from institutional funds; Federal Nursing Scholarships; Federal Pell; Private scholarships; SEOG; State scholarships/grants; United Negro College Fund. *Loan aid offered:* Direct PLUS loans; Direct Subsidized Loans. Applicants will be notified of awards on a rolling basis beginning 3/15. Federal Work-Study Program available. Institutional employment available.

BOTTOM LINE

For Californians, the cumulative price tag to attend UCLA for a year—when you add up fees, room and board, and basic expenses—is somewhere around $30,721. Your living arrangements can make a noticeable difference. If you can't claim residency in the Golden State, the cost totals $58,735. Almost all students who demonstrate need receive some form of aid, and the average cumulative indebtedness, at just $22,013, is relatively reasonable.

CAREER INFORMATION FROM PAYSCALE.COM

ROI Rating	92
Bachelors and No Higher	
Median starting salary	$60,000
Median mid-career salary	$118,500
At Least Bachelors	
Median starting salary	$62,200
Median mid-career salary	$124,100
Alumni with high job meaning	47%
Degrees awarded in STEM subjects	31%

SELECTIVITY

Admissions Rating	98
# of applicants	102,242
% of applicants accepted	16
% of acceptees attending	37

FRESHMAN PROFILE

Range SAT EBRW	630–730
Range SAT Math	610–760
Range ACT Composite	27–33
Minimum paper TOEFL	550
Minimum internet-based TOEFL	83
Average HS GPA	4.4
% graduated top 10% of class	97
% graduated top 25% of class	100
% graduated top 50% of class	100

DEADLINES

Regular	
Deadline	11/30
Notification	3/31
Nonfall registration?	No

FINANCIAL FACTS

Financial Aid Rating	84
Annual in-state tuition	$11,502
Annual out-of-state tuition	$39,516
Room and board	$15,991
Required fees	$1,778
Books and supplies	$1,450
Average frosh need-based scholarship	$20,953
Average UG need-based scholarship	$20,489
% needy frosh rec. need-based scholarship or grant aid	96
% needy UG rec. need-based scholarship or grant aid	96
% needy frosh rec. non-need-based scholarship or grant aid	3
% needy UG rec. non-need-based scholarship or grant aid	2
% needy frosh rec. need-based self-help aid	56
% needy UG rec. need-based self-help aid	59
% frosh rec. any financial aid	53
% UG rec. any financial aid	54
% UG borrow to pay for school	43
Average cumulative indebtedness	$22,013
% frosh need fully met	28
% ugrads need fully met	26
Average % of frosh need met	83
Average % of ugrad need met	83

University of California—Riverside

3106 STUDENT SERVICES BUILDING, RIVERSIDE, CA 92521 • ADMISSIONS: 951-827-3411 • FAX: 951-827-6344

CAMPUS LIFE

Quality of Life Rating	**87**
Fire Safety Rating	**94**
Green Rating	**98**
Type of school	Public
Environment	City

STUDENTS

Total undergrad enrollment	20,044
% male/female	46/54
% from out of state	1
% frosh from public high school	90
% frosh live on campus	71
% ugrads live on campus	31
# of fraternities (% ugrad men join)	19 (4)
# of sororities (% ugrad women join)	19 (7)
% African American	3
% Asian	34
% Caucasian	11
% Hispanic	41
% Native American	<1
% Pacific Islander	<1
% Two or more races	6
% Race and/or ethnicity unknown	1
% international	3
# of countries represented	100

ACADEMICS

Academic Rating	**79**
% students returning for sophomore year	89
% students graduating within 4 years	53
% students graduating within 6 years	75
Calendar	Quarter
Student/faculty ratio	22:1
Profs interesting rating	75
Profs accessible rating	73

Most classes have 20–29 students. Most lab/discussion sessions have 20–29 students.

MOST POPULAR MAJORS

Biological and Biomedical Sciences; Psychology; Business Administration and Management

ABOUT THE SCHOOL

Committed to promoting a top-notch research and academic environment, the University of California—Riverside (UCR), part of the esteemed University of California system, is on the rise. With plans in place to expand faculty and facilities, this school is looking to further build on its established record as an accessible and vibrant campus. Alongside one of the country's best undergraduate business administration programs, UCR's engineering and sciences programs are highly regarded by students. The university's inland, southern California location makes it ideal for the study of "air, water, energy, biodiversity, sustainability, land use, [and] the habitat/agriculture interface." The campus is very diverse, and, as one student puts it, it is truly "a place where everyone will feel at home and welcomed." Despite a sizable undergraduate body of about 20,000, professors here are more than willing to provide individualized attention and mentorship. While about 70 percent of students commute, several on-campus clubs and events help foster a distinct sense of community.

BANG FOR YOUR BUCK

A state school with a demonstrated commitment to making higher education accessible and attainable, UCR offers eligible students a wide range of scholarship and grant opportunities. California students from families making less than $80,000 are eligible for The Blue and Gold Opportunity Plan, which, by combining applicable scholarships and grants, ensures they do not pay out of pocket for tuition and fees. In addition, merit-based scholarships, such as the Regent's and Chancellor's Scholarship, are always an option. Eighty-six percent of students receive some sort of aid. UCR also has a robust internship program and regularly works with major companies to help students to gain real, on-the-job experience prior to graduation. Not only that, the school regularly organizes career fairs and professional coaching sessions to help students enter the workforce smoothly and successfully.

STUDENT LIFE

Asked about the atmosphere at UCR, most students report "studying" being a focus, but according to one, "if you are looking to get involved, meet like-minded individuals, and learn outside of the classroom, it is very easy to do so at UCR." Even though most students live off-campus, there's a distinct culture; as one student notes, "there are over 400 clubs...many of which organize their own activities." The Student Recreation Center is well-liked and features "a rock wall, assorted sport courts, [and] Olympic-style pool." Popular as well are concerts and parties organized by the school. "Every week there is a mini-concert in the middle of campus," one student says. Not only that, many students join fraternities and sororities, and there are plenty of opportunities to "attend a party" or "hang out at the restaurants or bars near campus." More outdoorsy types are also in the right place because of UCR's "1,200-acre, park-like campus" featuring the stunning Botanic Gardens.

CAREER

UCR students are known for being driven and focused, so it's no wonder that most graduate feeling well-prepared for their careers. The university offers numerous resources for those looking to enter the job market with their feet on the ground, and one student notes the school "takes pride in preparing students for jobs by encouraging them to dive into research and internships." For engineers and those going into sciences, UCR's centers and institutes such as the Center for Environmental Research and Technology and the Agricultural Experimentation Station provide ample opportunities

University of California—Riverside

FINANCIAL AID: 951-827-3878 • E-MAIL: ADMIN@UCR.EDU • WEBSITE: WWW.UCR.EDU

for students to gain research experience. The Career Center further helps by organizing fairs and offering training in professional skills, and their SCOTjobs online database lists numerous internships and job opportunities. It certainly pays off: graduates enter their careers making an average of $51,600 per year, with 44 percent reporting that their work as "high meaning."

GENERAL INFO

Activities: Choral groups, concert band, dance, drama/theater, jazz band, literary magazine, music ensembles, musical theater, pep band, radio station, student government, student newspaper, student-run film society, international student organization. **Organizations:** 439 registered organizations, 9 honor societies, 27 religious organizations. 19 fraternities, 20 sororities. **Athletics (Intercollegiate):** *Men:* Baseball, basketball, cross-country, golf, soccer, tennis, track/field (outdoor), track/field (indoor). *Women:* Basketball, cross-country, golf, soccer, softball, tennis, track/field (outdoor), track/field (indoor), volleyball. **On-Campus Highlights:** Music festival-style concerts, new Lattitude 55, basketball games, Student Recreation Center and intramural sports, The Barn (music and comedy acts), Coffee Bean and Tea Leaf. The Highlander Union Building (HUB).

FINANCIAL AID

Students should submit: FAFSA, state aid form. Priority filing deadline is 3/2. The Princeton Review suggests that all financial aid forms be submitted as soon as possible after October 1. *Need-based scholarships/grants offered:* College/university scholarship or grant aid from institutional funds, Federal Pell, private scholarships, SEOG, state scholarships/grants. *Loan aid offered:* Direct PLUS Loans, Direct Subsidized Loans, Direct Unsubsidized Loans. Applicants will be notified of awards on a rolling basis beginning 3/1. Federal Work-Study Program available. Institutional employment available.

BOTTOM LINE

In-state tuition and fees for UCR is only $15,633 per year, making it a very affordable institution of higher learning. Out-of-state students, however, pay considerably more: $44,625. For those opting to live in dorms, room and board is $17,475 a year. Books and supplies typically add $1,400 in annual cost for both in-state and out-of-state students.

CAREER INFORMATION FROM PAYSCALE.COM	
ROI Rating	91
Bachelors and No Higher	
Median starting salary	$54,000
Median mid-career salary	$109,300
At Least Bachelors	
Median starting salary	$55,400
Median mid-career salary	$113,500
Alumni with high job meaning	47%
Degrees awarded in STEM subjects	31%

SELECTIVITY	
Admissions Rating	92
# of applicants	43,682
% of applicants accepted	57
% of acceptees attending	18
# offered a place on the wait list	5,499
% accepting a place on wait list	57
% admitted from wait list	10

FRESHMAN PROFILE	
Range SAT EBRW	550–640
Range SAT Math	540–660
Range ACT Composite	23–29
Minimum paper TOEFL	550
Minimum internet-based TOEFL	80
Average HS GPA	3.7
% graduated top 10% of class	94
% graduated top 25% of class	100
% graduated top 50% of class	100

DEADLINES	
Regular	
Deadline	11/30
Notification	3/31
Nonfall registration?	No

FINANCIAL FACTS	
Financial Aid Rating	87
Annual in-state tuition	$11,442
Annual out-of-state tuition	$40,434
Room and board	$17,000
Required fees	$4,191
Books and supplies	$1,300
Average frosh need-based scholarship	$20,892
Average UG need-based scholarship	$18,125
% needy frosh rec. need-based scholarship or grant aid	98
% needy UG rec. need-based scholarship or grant aid	98
% needy frosh rec. non-need-based scholarship or grant aid	2
% needy UG rec. non-need-based scholarship or grant aid	2
% needy frosh rec. need-based self-help aid	81
% needy UG rec. need-based self-help aid	68
% frosh rec. any financial aid	89
% UG rec. any financial aid	86
% UG borrow to pay for school	66
Average cumulative indebtedness	$21,104
% frosh need fully met	22
% ugrads need fully met	25
Average % of frosh need met	91
Average % of ugrad need met	89

University of California—San Diego

9500 GILMAN DRIVE, 0021, LA JOLLA, CA 92093-0021 • ADMISSIONS: 858-534-4831 • FAX: 858-534-5723

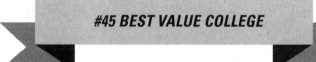

#45 BEST VALUE COLLEGE

ABOUT THE SCHOOL

Mathematics and the sciences reign supreme at the University of California—San Diego, and the school has an excellent reputation, huge research budgets, and an idyllic climate that have helped it attract eight Nobel laureates to its faculty. While research and graduate study garner most of the attention, undergraduates still receive a solid education that results in an impressive degree. The division of the undergraduate program into six smaller colleges helps take some of the edge off UC San Diego's big-school vibe (roughly 23,000 undergraduates) and allows students easier access to administrators. A quarterly academic calendar also keeps things moving. Campus life is generally pretty quiet. Students are divided on whether this school in scenic but sleepy La Jolla has a boring social scene or whether one simply has to look hard to find recreation. "There is always something to do on campus, and it is always changing! I never get bored!" But one thing is certain: some students work way too hard to afford the luxury of a social life. Students are often too busy with schoolwork to spend a lot of time partying, and when they have free time, they find hometown La Jolla a little too tiny for most college students. The town won't sanction a frat row, so Greek life doesn't include raucous parties, but the new 1,000-bed Village at Torrey Pines, built especially for transfer students, is one of the most environmentally sustainable student housing structures in the nation. Students also spend a lot of time at the beach or enjoying the school's intramural sports programs. One student summed up the dichotomy perfectly: "My school is all about science and the beach." Trying to study the hard sciences despite the distraction of the Pacific only a few blocks away is a mammoth task. And a fine public transit system makes downtown San Diego very accessible.

BANG FOR YOUR BUCK

More than half of UC San Diego's undergraduate students receive need-based support. The University of California's Blue and Gold Opportunity Plan (B&G) will cover students' UC fees if they are California residents and their families earn $80,000 or less and the student also qualifies for UC financial aid. For needy middle-class families earning up to $120,000, UC offers additional grant money that offsets half of any UC fee increase. In response to California's current economic climate, UC San Diego launched the $50 million Invent the Future student-support fundraising campaign, which will help fund scholarships and fellowships for all who need them.

STUDENT LIFE

A handful of undergrads seem to continually gripe that UC San Diego is "socially dead." However, plenty of students counter that there are definitely good times to be had, you simply have to "take control of your own college experience" and not just "go to class and [then retreat] to your room." For starters, San Diego offers "beautiful scenery and the perfect weather to go outside and play sports, chill at the beach or just hang out." Indeed, many undergrads tell us that there's a "huge surfing community." Additionally, students can typically find "small concerts or raves going on every week." The residence counsels also host lots of "fun programs such as Jell-o Fight, drive-in movies, casino nights, and much more." And there are a number of "spectacular" dance and play performances "that happen on campus."

University of California—San Diego

FINANCIAL AID: 858-534-4480 • E-MAIL: ADMISSIONSINFO@UCSD.EDU • WEBSITE: WWW.UCSD.EDU

CAREER

Professional success is practically synonymous with UCSD. Indeed, according to PayScale.com, the average starting salary for San Diego grads is $58,600. Students looking to jumpstart their search can easily turn to the Career Services Center. Here undergrads have the opportunity to meet with advisors to explore the breadth of career options, conduct assessments and research various industries. Most importantly, the Center hosts job fairs and networking events every quarter. These present great opportunities for undergrads to learn about internships, part-time gigs and full-time positions. Companies that have recently attended include Amazon, Boeing, Apple, Chevron Corporation, California State Auditor, Hulu, Groupon, Intel Corporation, and the Peace Corps.

GENERAL INFO

Activities: Choral groups, concert band, dance, drama/theater, jazz band, literary magazine, marching band, music ensembles, musical theater, opera, pep band, radio station, student government, student newspaper, student-run film society, symphony orchestra, television station, yearbook, campus ministries, international student organization. **Organizations:** 406 registered organizations, 5 honor societies, 46 religious organizations. 26 fraternities, 22 sororities. **Athletics (Intercollegiate):** *Men:* Baseball, basketball, crew/rowing, cross-country, diving, fencing, golf, soccer, swimming, tennis, track/field (outdoor), volleyball, water polo. *Women:* Basketball, crew/rowing, cross-country, diving, fencing, soccer, softball, swimming, tennis, track/field (outdoor), volleyball, water polo.

FINANCIAL AID

Students should submit: FAFSA, state aid form. Priority filing deadline is 3/2. The Princeton Review suggests that all financial aid forms be submitted as soon as possible after October 1. *Need-based scholarships/grants offered:* College/university scholarship or grant aid from institutional funds, Federal Pell, private scholarships, SEOG, state scholarships/grants. *Loan aid offered:* Direct PLUS Loans, Direct Subsidized Loans, Direct Unsubsidized Loans. Applicants will be notified of awards on a rolling basis beginning 3/15. Federal Work-Study Program available. Institutional employment available.

BOTTOM LINE

California residents attending UC San Diego full-time pay roughly $15,983 in tuition and fees. Room and board costs come to about $13,254, not to mention additional costs for transportation, books, and personal expenses. Nonresidents pay more than $40,600 in tuition alone.

CAREER INFORMATION FROM PAYSCALE.COM

ROI Rating	92
Bachelors and No Higher	
Median starting salary	$61,300
Median mid-career salary	$126,800
At Least Bachelors	
Median starting salary	$63,100
Median mid-career salary	$133,300
Alumni with high job meaning	52%
Degrees awarded in STEM subjects	58%

SELECTIVITY

Admissions Rating	97
# of applicants	88,428
% of applicants accepted	34
% of acceptees attending	19

FRESHMAN PROFILE

Range SAT EBRW	550–660
Range SAT Math	590–720
Range ACT Composite	26–32
Minimum paper TOEFL	550
Average HS GPA	4.1
% graduated top 10% of class	100
% graduated top 25% of class	100
% graduated top 50% of class	100

DEADLINES

Regular	
Deadline	11/30
Notification	3/31

FINANCIAL FACTS

Financial Aid Rating	84
Annual in-state tuition	$12,630
Annual out-of-state tuition	$40,644
Room and board	$13,733
Required fees	$1,643
Books and supplies	$1,198
Average frosh need-based scholarship	$19,028
Average UG need-based scholarship	$18,412
% needy frosh rec. need-based scholarship or grant aid	90
% needy UG rec. need-based scholarship or grant aid	95
% needy frosh rec. non-need-based scholarship or grant aid	3
% needy UG rec. non-need-based scholarship or grant aid	2
% needy frosh rec. need-based self-help aid	72
% needy UG rec. need-based self-help aid	71
% frosh rec. any financial aid	77
% UG rec. any financial aid	63
% UG borrow to pay for school	53
Average cumulative indebtedness	$21,830
% frosh need fully met	37
% ugrads need fully met	34
Average % of frosh need met	87
Average % of ugrad need met	86

University of California—Santa Barbara

Office of Admissions, 1210 Cheadle Hall, Santa Barbara, CA 93106-2014 • Admissions: 805-893-2881 • Fax: 805-893-2676

CAMPUS LIFE

Quality of Life Rating	92
Fire Safety Rating	95
Green Rating	97
Type of school	Public
Environment	City

STUDENTS

Total undergrad enrollment	22,186
% male/female	46/54
% from out of state	4
% frosh from public high school	80
% frosh live on campus	95
% ugrads live on campus	38
# of fraternities (% ugrad men join)	12 (4)
# of sororities (% ugrad women join)	20 (8)
% African American	2
% Asian	21
% Caucasian	34
% Hispanic	26
% Native American	<1
% Pacific Islander	<1
% Two or more races	6
% Race and/or ethnicity unknown	1
% international	8
# of countries represented	82

ACADEMICS

Academic Rating	86
% students returning for sophomore year	92
% students graduating within 4 years	70
% students graduating within 6 years	87
Calendar	Quarter
Student/faculty ratio	17:1
Profs interesting rating	83
Profs accessible rating	84
Most classes have fewer than 10 students.	

MOST POPULAR MAJORS
Biology/Biological Sciences; Psychology; Economics

#21 BEST VALUE COLLEGE

ABOUT THE SCHOOL

UCSB's beautiful campus is located 100 miles north of Los Angeles, with views of the ocean and the mountains, and typically benevolent Southern California weather. Perched above the Pacific coast, the University of California—Santa Barbara is a top-ranked public university with a multitude of world-class academic, extracurricular, and social opportunities. University of California–Santa Barbara is "a beautiful, laid-back learning institute on the beach," yet students say it's much more than a great place to get a tan. This prestigious public school is "one of the best research universities in the country," which "attracts many excellent professors" as well as a cadre of dedicated students. Maybe it's the sunny weather, but "professors here are more accessible than [at] other universities," and they are "genuinely interested in helping the students learn." This large university offers more than 200 major programs, of which business, economics, biology, communications, psychology, and engineering are among the most popular. Students agree that the competent and enthusiastic faculty is one of the school's greatest assets. Teaching assistants are also noted for being dedicated and helpful, especially in leading small discussion sessions to accompany large lecture courses. There are six Nobel laureates on the UCSB faculty, and the school offers many opportunities for undergraduates to participate in research.

BANG FOR YOUR BUCK

As a part of the prestigious University of California system, UCSB fuses good value and strong academics. It is a state school with over 20,000 students enrolled, so many classes are large. But with all the resources of a major research school at your fingertips, it's a definite bargain. The University of California operates the Blue and Gold Opportunity Plan. For in-state students with household incomes of less than the state median of $80,000, the Blue and Gold Opportunity plan will fully cover the mandatory UC fees for four years. California residents are also eligible for Cal Grants, a grant program administered by the state and open to college students that meet certain minimum GPA requirements. In addition to state and federal aid, there are a number of scholarships available to UCSB undergraduates. New freshmen with outstanding academic and personal achievement may be awarded the prestigious Regents Scholarship. There are additional merit awards offered through each of the university's four colleges, as well as through the alumni association.

STUDENT LIFE

University of California—Santa Barbara is "a place for strong academics, excellent research opportunities, all with a laid-back and vibrant student life." With its large student body—there are over 20,000 undergraduates—there's something for everyone. Students note that outdoor activities are popular, from surfing to hiking, and underscore that UCSB has "a beach on campus." There are about 500 registered student organizations on campus and students participate in activities as varied as "a Shakespeare flash mob group" and "aerial dancing class." The Greek system is also a mainstay of campus life, with the school housing eighteen sororities and seventeen fraternities. Roughly 12 percent of women join a sorority, with 8 percent of men joining a fraternity. The school strikes a balance, though, according to one Literature major, who describes the population at UCSB as "lots of Greeks [and] lots of geeks." For another student, the number of "clubs, internships, research opportunities, and avenues to create... your own extracurricular activities is almost intimidating."

University of California—Santa Barbara

FINANCIAL AID: 805-893-2118 • E-MAIL: ADMISSIONS@SA.UCSB.EDU • WEBSITE: WWW.UCSB.EDU

CAREER

According to PayScale.com, the average starting salary for a UCSB graduate is roughly $55,000 and popular careers include software engineer, mechanical engineer, and marketing manager. The most popular majors for UCSB students are Communication, Economics, and Sociology. While one Biochemistry major laments there are "basically too many students, and not enough open positions," other students praise the range of internship and post-graduation career opportunities, with one describing UCSB as "a springboard for the greatest young minds to launch into highly successful research and careers." The Career Services department at UCSB encourages students to take advantage of "GauchoLink," a frequently updated database of job and internship opportunities that also lists upcoming career-oriented events hosted by the school or by potential employers. Students are also able to store letters of recommendation with the Career Services department so as to streamline the process of applying for internships or jobs during their school tenure or after graduation.

GENERAL INFO

Activities: Choral groups, concert band, dance, drama/theater, jazz band, literary magazine, music ensembles, musical theater, opera, pep band, radio station, student government, student newspaper, student run film society, symphony orchestra, television station, yearbook, campus ministries, international student organization. **Organizations:** 508 registered organizations, 5 honor societies, 19 religious organizations. 12 fraternities, 18 sororities. **Athletics (Intercollegiate):** *Men:* Baseball, basketball, cross-country, diving, golf, gymnastics, soccer, swimming, tennis, track/field (outdoor), volleyball, water polo. *Women:* Basketball, cross-country, diving, gymnastics, soccer, softball, swimming, tennis, track/field (outdoor), volleyball, water polo.

FINANCIAL AID

Students should submit: FAFSA. Priority filing deadline is 3/2. The Princeton Review suggests that all financial aid forms be submitted as soon as possible after October 1. *Need-based scholarships/grants offered:* College/university scholarship or grant aid from institutional funds; Federal Pell; SEOG; State scholarships/grants. *Loan aid offered:* Direct PLUS Loans, Direct Subsidized Loans, Direct Unsubsidized Loans. Federal Work-Study Program available. Institutional employment available.

BOTTOM LINE

Depending on where you live and what you study, the cost of attending UC Santa Barbara fluctuates. For California residents, the school estimates that total expenses come to about $35,289 annually. For out-of-state residents, the estimated annual cost comes to $61,917.

CAREER INFORMATION FROM PAYSCALE.COM

ROI Rating	94
Bachelors and No Higher	
Median starting salary	$57,300
Median mid-career salary	$121,500
At Least Bachelors	
Median starting salary	$59,000
Median mid-career salary	$125,900
Alumni with high job meaning	47%
Degrees awarded in STEM subjects	29%

SELECTIVITY

Admissions Rating	97
# of applicants	80,319
% of applicants accepted	33
% of acceptees attending	17
# offered a place on the wait list	6,650
% accepting a place on wait list	60
% admitted from wait list	24

FRESHMAN PROFILE

Range SAT EBRW	620–710
Range SAT Math	620–760
Range ACT Composite	26–32
Minimum paper TOEFL	550
Minimum internet-based TOEFL	80
Average HS GPA	4.1
% graduated top 10% of class	100
% graduated top 25% of class	100
% graduated top 50% of class	100

DEADLINES

Regular	
Deadline	11/30
Notification	March 1-31
Nonfall registration?	No

FINANCIAL FACTS

Financial Aid Rating	83
Annual in-state tuition	$12,630
Annual out-of-state tuition	$40,644
Room and board	$14,778
Required fees	$1,779
Books and supplies	$1,143
Average frosh need-based scholarship	$21,491
Average UG need-based scholarship	$18,698
% needy frosh rec. need-based scholarship or grant aid	94
% needy UG rec. need-based scholarship or grant aid	93
% needy frosh rec. non-need-based scholarship or grant aid	1
% needy UG rec. non-need-based scholarship or grant aid	1
% needy frosh rec. need-based self-help aid	62
% needy UG rec. need-based self-help aid	60
% UG rec. any financial aid	61
% UG borrow to pay for school	59
Average cumulative indebtedness	$20,978
% frosh need fully met	15
% ugrads need fully met	16
Average % of frosh need met	80
Average % of ugrad need met	79

University of California—Santa Cruz

OFFICE OF ADMISSIONS, COOK HOUSE, 1156 HIGH STREET, SANTA CRUZ, CA 95064 • ADMISSIONS: 831-459-4008

CAMPUS LIFE

Quality of Life Rating	**69**
Fire Safety Rating	**80**
Green Rating	**98**
Type of school	Public
Environment	City

STUDENTS

Total undergrad enrollment	17,577
% male/female	50/50
% from out of state	4
% frosh from public high school	85
% frosh live on campus	98
% ugrads live on campus	52
# of fraternities (% ugrad men join)	6 (6)
# of sororities (% ugrad women join)	11 (8)
% African American	2
% Asian	22
% Caucasian	31
% Hispanic	28
% Native American	<1
% Pacific Islander	<1
% Two or more races	8
% Race and/or ethnicity unknown	2
% international	6
# of countries represented	56

ACADEMICS

Academic Rating	**70**
% students returning for sophomore year	90
% students graduating within 4 years	53
% students graduating within 6 years	77
Calendar	Quarter
Student/faculty ratio	19:1
Profs interesting rating	64
Profs accessible rating	61

Most classes have 10–29 students. Most lab/discussion sessions have 20–29 students.

MOST POPULAR MAJORS
Computer Science; Psychology; Business/Managerial Economics

ABOUT THE SCHOOL

UC Santa Cruz is a world-class research and teaching university, featuring interdisciplinary learning and a distinctive residential college system that provides a small-college environment within the larger research institution. Tucked within "a friendly and diverse community full of lovely scenery," a student observes how easy it is to "focus on scholastic endeavors in a beautiful forest setting." The university combines a multicultural, open community with a high-quality education, and the campus is very politically aware. Students enjoy the "medium-size school, where it is possible to get a university experience but the professors also want to learn your name." Undergraduates are provided with significant access to faculty and have a valuable opportunity to incorporate creative activities into their studies; they conduct and publish research and work closely with faculty on leading-edge projects. What sets instructors apart from those at a typical research-driven university is that "they are very passionate about their subject even when teaching undergrads," according to a surprised student.

BANG FOR YOUR BUCK

Along with quality instruction, internships and public service are common elements of the educational experience at UC Santa Cruz, which seeks to extend the classroom into the real world. Alternative Spring Break, for example, is an opportunity for students to immerse themselves in a service project such as building homes in Mexico and assisting with the rebuilding efforts in New Orleans. A unique human biology major requires an internship in the health field in a Spanish-speaking community, where students can volunteer in a hospital, spend time shadowing a physician, or assist in providing health services to underserved populations. Student Organization Advising and Resources (SOAR) sponsors internships which help students gain skills in leadership, networking, program planning, and outreach. To support students financially, UC's Blue and Gold Opportunity Plan covers UC tuition for students who qualify. In addition, a range of grants and scholarships can help cover student costs, including a scholarship sponsored by the UCSC Alumni Association, honoring high-achieving students who have compelling financial need.

STUDENT LIFE

"The 'stereotypical' Santa Cruz student is a hippie," and the school certainly has its fair share of those: "The typical student is very hardworking until about 9:00 P.M., when hikes to the forest are common practice and returning to your room smelling like reefer is acceptable," one undergrad explains—but "there are many different types who attend UCSC." "It seems that almost every student here has a personal passion, whether it be an activism or cause of some sort, etc.," one student writes. "Everyone is so...alive." "Most are liberal," and there's a definite propensity for earnestness; it's the sort of place where students declare without irony that they "not only possess a great respect for one another but the world and life in general. The world to an average UCSC student is a sacred and beautiful place to be shared and enjoyed by all its inhabitants."

University of California—Santa Cruz

Financial Aid: 831-459-2963 • E-mail: admissions@ucsc.edu • Fax: 831-459-4452 • Website: www.ucsc.edu

CAREER

UC Santa Cruz's Career Services creates hundreds of opportunities each semester for students looking to hone their skills and explore their options. On-campus internships through the Chancellor's Undergraduate Internship Program come with mentorship, a leadership seminar for credit, and a scholarship of $8,200 toward school registration fees. Students may also apply to spend a quarter in Sacramento, interning with students from other University of California campuses. It's easy to find federal, regional, and on-campus research gigs through an online database where students can search by major. Plus, Career Fairs, informational sessions, and Meet & Greets throughout the year ensure that students have plenty of chances to network and research potential fields.

GENERAL INFO

Activities: Choral groups, dance, drama/theater, jazz band, literary magazine, music ensembles, musical theater, opera, radio station, student government, student newspaper, student-run film society, symphony orchestra, television station, campus ministries, international student organization. **Organizations:** 138 registered organizations, 3 honor societies, 19 religious organizations. 6 fraternities, 11 sororities. **Athletics (Intercollegiate):** *Men:* Basketball, diving, soccer, swimming, tennis, volleyball. *Women:* Basketball, cross-country, diving, golf, soccer, swimming, tennis, volleyball. **On-Campus Highlights:** Arboretum, Farm and Garden, East Field House, Bay Tree Bookstore/Grad Student Commons, Pogonip Open Area Reserve.

FINANCIAL AID

Students should submit: FAFSA; State aid form. Regular filing deadline is 3/1. The Princeton Review suggests that all financial aid forms be submitted as soon as possible after October 1. *Need-based scholarships/grants offered:* College/university scholarship or grant aid from institutional funds, Federal Pell, private scholarships, SEOG, state scholarships/grants. *Loan aid offered:* Direct PLUS Loans, Direct Subsidized Loans, Direct Unsubsidized Loans. Applicants will be notified of awards on a rolling basis beginning 4/1. Federal Work-Study Program available. Institutional employment available.

BOTTOM LINE

Over 17,000 students are enrolled at the university, Almost everyone is originally from California, and the student population is split evenly between residents and commuters. Total cost of attendance for in-state students is $30,416 and $58,430 for out-of-state residents.

CAREER INFORMATION FROM PAYSCALE.COM	
ROI Rating	88
Bachelors and No Higher	
Median starting salary	$56,100
Median mid-career salary	$104,700
At Least Bachelors	
Median starting salary	$57,200
Median mid-career salary	$108,200
Alumni with high job meaning	45%
Degrees awarded in STEM subjects	38%

SELECTIVITY	
Admissions Rating	93
# of applicants	52,975
% of applicants accepted	51
% of acceptees attending	15
# offered a place on the wait list	10,378
% accepting a place on wait list	58
% admitted from wait list	37

FRESHMAN PROFILE	
Range SAT EBRW	580–680
Range SAT Math	580–690
Range ACT Composite	24–30
Minimum paper TOEFL	550
Minimum internet-based TOEFL	80
Average HS GPA	3.5
% graduated top 10% of class	96
% graduated top 25% of class	100
% graduated top 50% of class	100

DEADLINES	
Regular	
Deadline	11/30
Notification	3/31
Nonfall registration?	No

FINANCIAL FACTS	
Financial Aid Rating	80
Annual in-state tuition	$11,502
Annual out-of-state tuition	$39,516
Room and board	$16,407
Required fees	$2,507
Books and supplies	$1,152
Average frosh need-based scholarship	$20,079
Average UG need-based scholarship	$20,041
% needy frosh rec. need-based scholarship or grant aid	92
% needy UG rec. need-based scholarship or grant aid	93
% needy frosh rec. non-need-based scholarship or grant aid	2
% needy UG rec. non-need-based scholarship or grant aid	1
% needy frosh rec. need-based self-help aid	77
% needy UG rec. need-based self-help aid	75
% frosh rec. any financial aid	66
% UG rec. any financial aid	70
% UG borrow to pay for school	70
Average cumulative indebtedness	$22,582
% frosh need fully met	21
% ugrads need fully met	26
Average % of frosh need met	83
Average % of ugrad need met	84

University of Central Florida

PO Box 160111, Orlando, FL 32816-0111 • Admissions: 407-823-3000 • Fax: 407-823-5625

CAMPUS LIFE

Quality of Life Rating	**88**
Fire Safety Rating	**96**
Green Rating	**92**
Type of school	Public
Environment	City

STUDENTS

Total undergrad enrollment	56,458
% male/female	46/54
% from out of state	6
% frosh live on campus	68
% ugrads live on campus	18
# of fraternities (% ugrad men join)	27 (6)
# of sororities (% ugrad women join)	22 (7)
% African American	11
% Asian	6
% Caucasian	49
% Hispanic	26
% Native American	<1
% Pacific Islander	<1
% Two or more races	4
% Race and/or ethnicity unknown	1
% international	2
# of countries represented	147

ACADEMICS

Academic Rating	**72**
% students returning for sophomore year	90
% students graduating within 4 years	40
% students graduating within 6 years	70
Calendar	Semester
Student/faculty ratio	30:1
Profs interesting rating	73
Profs accessible rating	69
Most classes have 20–29 students.	

MOST POPULAR MAJORS
Biomedical Sciences; Psychology; Health Services/Allied Health/Health Sciences

ABOUT THE SCHOOL

Orlando's University of Central Florida is the largest research university in the state—the "Pride of Central Florida"—educating more than 56,000 undergraduates across more than two hundred majors and 1,400 acres of a main campus. The faculty are all "helpful, interactive teachers who strive to deliver meaningful content" and many professors (including online classes, which are abundant) "create a great academic environment with their varied methods of teaching and outside resources." They "all care about student success," hold regular office hours, and "know their stuff, and try to engage students as much as they can." Anything a student needs can be found at UCF, where "financial aid packages are generous, tuition is low, classes are convenient, [and] school spirit is amazing." Basically, "UCF lays the perfect framework necessary in order to find a successful career in the field of your choosing."

BANG FOR YOUR BUCK

UCF's size provides the momentum any student needs to get where they want to go, and the school excels at giving them an "excellent, well-rounded education and offering them a massive amount of resources and opportunities." People of all levels of aspiration and talent "interact and coexist in the same environment," and the university provides "a nice emphasis on STEM fields." Cream can rise to the top easily here if they put in the work; the Burnett Honors College enrolls nearly 1,700 students ("a very nice facet that I couldn't imagine attending UCF without," according to one), and the College of Undergraduate Studies lets students tailor their course of study to suit their individual career goals.

STUDENT LIFE

A school this big is "not a cookie cutter place," and the UCF student population is "a mix of races, a balance of genders, all with a variety of interests and ambitions." Everything you need is on campus, "from advice to food," but students will still go to local malls or restaurants when not studying, and if they're willing to make a small trip, "they will go downtown or to one of the many amusement parks in the area." UCF students are "fun loving and always willing to help someone out," and there is a "wide variety of clubs and recreational sports so it is easy to make friends."

University of Central Florida

Financial Aid: 407-823-2827 • E-mail: admission@ucf.edu • Website: www.ucf.edu

CAREER

"The opportunities in this school are amazing," and Career Services offers the whole panoply of job assistance tools for undergraduates, from practice interviews to alumni mentoring to on-campus recruitment. The university receives nearly $150 million in research funding each year, and "professors at UCF are always willing to put a student in a research position if they are interested." Though people come to UCF with all career designs and at all ages, the school is "all about...putting [you] in good positions to succeed." There is "a multitude of majors, people, clubs, and opportunities," so "you never have to struggle to find what you need to be successful." Out of UCF alumni visiting PayScale.com, fifty percent report that they derive a high level of meaning from their jobs.

GENERAL INFO

Activities: Campus Ministries; Choral groups; Concert band; Drama/theater; International Student Organization; Jazz band; Literary magazine; Marching band; Model UN; Music ensembles; Musical theater; Pep band; Radio station; Student government; Student-run film society; Symphony orchestra; Television station. **Organizations:** 565 registered organizations, 28 honor societies, 37 religious organizations. 27 fraternities, 22 sororities. **Athletics (Intercollegiate):** *Men:* baseball, basketball, cheerleading, football, golf, soccer, tennis. *Women:* basketball, cheerleading, crew/rowing, cross-country, golf, soccer, softball, tennis, track/field (outdoor), track/field (indoor), volleyball. **On-Campus Highlights:** Student Union, Recreation and Wellness Center, Bookstore (Starbucks cafe), Reflecting Pond, Spectrum Stadium & CFE Arena.

FINANCIAL AID

Students should submit: FAFSA. Priority filing deadline is 12/1. The Princeton Review suggests that all financial aid forms be submitted as soon as possible after October 1. *Need-based scholarships/grants offered:* College/university scholarship or grant aid from institutional funds, Federal Pell, private scholarships, SEOG, state scholarships/grants. *Loan aid offered:* Direct PLUS Loans, Direct Subsidized Loans, Direct Unsubsidized Loans. Applicants will be notified of awards on a rolling basis beginning 3/1. Federal Work-Study Program available. Institutional employment available.

CAREER INFORMATION FROM PAYSCALE.COM

ROI Rating	87
Bachelors and No Higher	
Median starting salary	$48,200
Median mid-career salary	$88,000
At Least Bachelors	
Median starting salary	$49,400
Median mid-career salary	$90,400
Alumni with high job meaning	50%
Degrees awarded in STEM subjects	16%

SELECTIVITY

Admissions Rating	89
# of applicants	37,693
% of applicants accepted	50
% of acceptees attending	36
# offered a place on the wait list	4,801
% accepting a place on wait list	60
% admitted from wait list	2

FRESHMAN PROFILE

Range SAT EBRW	580–660
Range SAT Math	570–660
Range ACT Composite	24–29
Minimum paper TOEFL	550
Minimum internet-based TOEFL	80
Average HS GPA	3.9
% graduated top 10% of class	31
% graduated top 25% of class	70
% graduated top 50% of class	96

DEADLINES

Regular	
Priority	1/1
Deadline	5/1
Nonfall registration?	Yes

FINANCIAL FACTS

Financial Aid Rating	80
Annual in-state tuition	$6,368
Annual out-of-state tuition	$22,467
Room and board	$9,617
Required fees	$0
Books and supplies	$1,200
Average frosh need-based scholarship	$6,002
Average UG need-based scholarship	$5,796
% needy frosh rec. need-based scholarship or grant aid	60
% needy UG rec. need-based scholarship or grant aid	69
% needy frosh rec. non-need-based scholarship or grant aid	63
% needy UG rec. non-need-based scholarship or grant aid	40
% needy frosh rec. need-based self-help aid	50
% needy UG rec. need-based self-help aid	59
% frosh rec. any financial aid	80
% UG rec. any financial aid	74
% UG borrow to pay for school	50
Average cumulative indebtedness	$21,818
% frosh need fully met	9
% ugrads need fully met	7
Average % of frosh need met	55
Average % of ugrad need met	55

The University of Chicago

1101 E 58TH STREET, ROSENWALD HALL SUITE 105, CHICAGO, IL 60637 • ADMISSIONS: 773-702-8650 • FAX: 773-702-4199

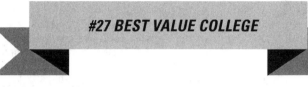

#27 BEST VALUE COLLEGE

CAMPUS LIFE

Quality of Life Rating	90
Fire Safety Rating	97
Green Rating	95
Type of school	Private
Environment	Metropolis

STUDENTS

Total undergrad enrollment	6,264
% male/female	51/49
% from out of state	82
% frosh live on campus	100
% ugrads live on campus	54
# of fraternities (% ugrad men join)	NR (8)
# of sororities (% ugrad women join)	NR (12)
% African American	5
% Asian	18
% Caucasian	42
% Hispanic	13
% Native American	<1
% Pacific Islander	0
% Two or more races	6
% Race and/or ethnicity unknown	2
% international	13
# of countries represented	77

ACADEMICS

Academic Rating	97
% students returning for sophomore year	99
% students graduating within 4 years	88
% students graduating within 6 years	93
Calendar	Quarter
Student/faculty ratio	5:1
Profs interesting rating	85
Profs accessible rating	84

Most classes have fewer than 10 students.
Most lab/discussion sessions have fewer than 10 students.

MOST POPULAR MAJORS

Biology/Biological Sciences; Mathematics; Economics

ABOUT THE SCHOOL

The University of Chicago has a reputation as a favorite destination of the true intellectual: students here are interested in learning for learning's sake, and they aren't afraid to express their opinions. A rigorous, intellectually challenging, and world-renowned research university, the University of Chicago continues to offer a community where students thrive and ideas matter. Here, an attitude of sharp questioning seems to be the focus, rather than the more relaxed inquiry and rumination approach at some schools of equal intellectual repute. Many find welcome challenges in the debates and discussions that define the campus atmosphere; the typical Chicago student is task-oriented, intellectually driven, sharp, vocal, and curious. As one student surveyed said, "There is nothing more exciting, challenging, and rewarding than the pursuit of knowledge in all of its forms." The undergraduate program at Chicago emphasizes critical thinking through a broad-based liberal arts curriculum. At the heart of the experience is the Common Core, the foundation for any major and all future endeavors. No lecture courses here—Core courses are discussion-based, and enrollment is limited to twenty. Chicago's numerous major programs range from religious studies to linguistics, history, economics, and molecular engineering.

BANG FOR YOUR BUCK

The University of Chicago operates a need-blind admissions process, admitting qualified students regardless of their financial situation. Once admitted, the school guarantees to meet 100 percent of a student's demonstrated financial need. Under a program called "No Barriers," grants replace student loans for every student's need-based financial aid package. Highly qualified freshman candidates may also be considered for competitive merit scholarships. Scholarships are awarded to applicants on the basis of outstanding academic and extracurricular achievement, demonstrated leadership, and commitment to their communities. Notable merit scholarships include: the Odyssey Scholarship, a renewable scholarship and guaranteed summer internship for students from low- and moderate-income families; and University Scholarships, which are guaranteed for four years of study.There are also scholarship programs for first-generation students, children of police officers and firefighters, and a partnershp with the Posse Foundation's Veterans Program.

STUDENT LIFE

Students rejoice! The "social scene at UChicago is truly vibrant and encompasses a very wide spectrum." Indeed, it "allows you to dabble in a variety of groups; one weekend you can hang out at a frat playing flip cup or pong, while another weekend you can go out in downtown Chicago, drink wine with your sorority sisters, discuss Marx and Smith at an apartment party, or just simply watch a movie with your roommates." There are also "tons of [clubs to join], from numerous different martial arts to gymnastics to multiple magazines to event planning for the school to tutoring kids and community service to cultural groups to a vegan society." And, of course, the city of Chicago also helps to guarantee boredom will be kept at bay. There is "always something to do like going to festivals, trying new restaurants, shopping, seeing a performance, listening to a concert, visiting museums, or experiencing a different culture."

The University of Chicago

FINANCIAL AID: 773-702-8655 • E-MAIL: COLLEGEADMISSIONS@UCHICAGO.EDU • WEBSITE: WWW.UCHICAGO.EDU

CAREER

Without a doubt, a University of Chicago education means that students will "enter a competitive job market prepared." This sentiment is supported by the fact that 94 percent of students have jobs or post-grad plans soon after leaving school. In fact, the average starting salary (according to PayScale.com) for recent UChicago grads is $58,100. The school's Career Advancement office maintains some unique programs to help ensure this success. For example, students can participate in the Jeff Metcalf Internship Program, which provides more than 2,500 paid internships each year throughout the country and abroad, or the Alumni Board Job Shadowing Program where they can shadow an accomplished professional.

GENERAL INFO

Activities: Choral groups, concert band, dance, drama/theater, jazz band, literary magazine, music ensembles, musical theater, pep band, radio station, student government, student newspaper, student-run film society, symphony orchestra, yearbook, campus ministries, international student organization. **Organizations:** More than 400 registered organizations, 5 honor societies, 36 religious organizations. 10 fraternities, 8 sororities.

FINANCIAL AID

Students should submit: FAFSA; Institution's own financial aid form, Parents' last-year income tax return. Priority filing deadline is 2/15. The Princeton Review suggests that all financial aid forms be submitted as soon as possible after October 1. *Need-based scholarships/grants offered:* College/university scholarship or grant aid from institutional funds, Federal Pell, private scholarships, SEOG, state scholarships/grants. *Loan aid offered:* Direct PLUS Loans, Direct Subsidized Loans, Direct Unsubsidized Loans. Applicants will be notified of awards on or about 3/15. Federal Work-Study Program available. Institutional employment available.

BOTTOM LINE

Yearly tuition to University of Chicago is a little more than $55,425, plus an additional $1,581 in mandatory fees. For campus residents, room and board is about $16,350 per year. Once you factor in personal expenses, transportation, books, and supplies, an education at University of Chicago costs about $77,331 per year. At University of Chicago, all demonstrated financial need is met through financial aid packages.

CAREER INFORMATION FROM PAYSCALE.COM

ROI Rating	93
Bachelors and No Higher	
Median starting salary	$61,600
Median mid-career salary	$117,500
At Least Bachelors	
Median starting salary	$63,700
Median mid-career salary	$123,200
Alumni with high job meaning	43%
Degrees awarded in STEM subjects	22%

SELECTIVITY

Admissions Rating	99
# of applicants	27,694
% of applicants accepted	9
% of acceptees attending	72

FRESHMAN PROFILE

Range SAT EBRW	730–780
Range SAT Math	750–800
Range ACT Composite	32–35
Minimum paper TOEFL	600
Minimum internet-based TOEFL	100
Average HS GPA	4.5
% graduated top 10% of class	99
% graduated top 25% of class	100
% graduated top 50% of class	100

DEADLINES

Early decision	
Deadline	11/1
Notification	12/18
Other ED Deadline	1/2
Other ED Notification	2/15
Early action	
Deadline	11/1
Notification	12/18
Regular	
Deadline	1/2
Nonfall registration?	No

FINANCIAL FACTS

Financial Aid Rating	97
Annual tuition	$55,425
Room and board	$16,350
Required fees	$1,581
Books and supplies	$1,800
Average frosh need-based scholarship	$48,203
Average UG need-based scholarship	$46,460
% needy frosh rec. need-based scholarship or grant aid	99
% needy UG rec. need-based scholarship or grant aid	99
% needy frosh rec. non-need-based scholarship or grant aid	0
% needy UG rec. non-need-based scholarship or grant aid	0
% needy frosh rec. need-based self-help aid	82
% needy UG rec. need-based self-help aid	69
% frosh rec. any financial aid	54
% UG rec. any financial aid	57
% UG borrow to pay for school	29
Average cumulative indebtedness	$23,401
% frosh need fully met	100
% ugrads need fully met	100
Average % of frosh need met	100
Average % of ugrad need met	100

University of Colorado Boulder

552 UCB, Boulder, CO 80309-0552 • Admissions: 303-492-6301 • Fax: 303-492-7115

ABOUT THE SCHOOL

A large research institution of more than 29,000 undergraduates, the University of Colorado Boulder offers more than 150 fields of study. The school operates particularly strong programs in engineering and the sciences; students also hold the architecture, journalism, mass communications, and aerospace programs in high esteem. (The university is consistently among the top universities to receive NASA funding.) Since the school is large, there are many available academic choices and the diverse faculty reflects that, among them five Nobel Prize winners, nineteen Rhodes Scholars, and eight MacArthur Genius Grant Fellowships. "Being in a class taught by a Nobel laureate is not something everyone gets to experience." It is not uncommon for students to be on a five- or six-year plan as a result of the extensive amount of academic choices. When they do finish, CU graduates are likely to find themselves well prepared for the real world. The career services office offers counseling, job and internship listings, and on-campus recruiting to the general student population; in addition, the university has numerous online tools to help students prepare for the job market.

BANG FOR YOUR BUCK

For Colorado residents, scholarship opportunities include the Esteemed Scholars Program for freshmen, the CU Promise Program for freshmen and transfers, and the First Generation Scholarship, for students whose parents do not have college degrees. For both in-state and out-of-state students, CU offers this enticing guarantee: there will be no tuition increases during your four years of study. In addition, the top 25 percent of out-of-state admissions are eligible to receive the Chancellor's Achievement Scholarship. With well over 5,000 new freshman "Buffaloes" on campus each year, the school nonetheless provides an incredible array of resources. "CU is an amazing place because you can find an array of challenges and opportunities whether your drive is research, the arts, sports, a job, or tough classwork." "I am able to research in one of my professor's labs while receiving a great education." In select programs, students may earn a bachelors and a masters degree concurrently in five years.

STUDENT LIFE

University of Colorado Boulder tends to attract "very social" students. Therefore, that pretty much guarantees that undergrads can almost "always [find] something going on." For example, "during the weekends, there is always a party or two to attend, and once you are twenty-one the bar scene is quite popular." Moreover, CU Boulder is "a very politically aware campus and the students tend to have an opinion about different issues going on in the world." They also love simply chilling in their dorm. As one civil engineering major shares, "We have a ping pong table constantly in use, and it seems like there's always somebody playing music or playing a game or just hanging out and talking." Additionally, "most people usually watch the Broncos games together in the common room." Finally, seeing as though "Boulder is a beautiful place" many undergrads love participating in outdoor activities. Yes, this student population counts a number of "rock climbers, skiers, and backpackers" among their ranks.

CAREER

Students at University of Colorado Boulder are flush with career opportunities. Clearly, the fantastic Career Services office ensures that these undergrads know how to compete in competitive job markets. Freshman start with the StrengthsQuest program, to learn how to better maximize their skillsets on campus and beyond. Then the Buffs Professional Program leads them through professional development activities to help them stand out to future employers. Throughout the academic year, the office sets up a number of information sessions. This allows students to both network and explore a variety of career

University of Colorado Boulder

FINANCIAL AID: 303-492-5091 • WEBSITE: WWW.COLORADO.EDU

paths. Aside from the usual internship and job searches, the office helps undergrads find research opportunities that align with their interests and passions. In fact, many students are involved with cutting edge research. Of course, undergrads who have their sights set on finding a job will be happy to discover that CU hosts numerous career fairs. Even better—they are organized by industry. Therefore, students can attend events based around creative jobs, green jobs, finance jobs, and more.

GENERAL INFO
Activities: Choral groups, concert band, dance, drama/theater, jazz band, literary magazine, marching band, music ensembles, musical theater, opera, pep band, radio station, student government, student newspaper, student-run film society, symphony orchestra, campus ministries, international student organization. **Organizations:** 400 registered organizations, 28 honor societies, 30 religious organizations. 25 fraternities, 31 sororities. **Athletics (Intercollegiate):** *Men:* Basketball, cross-country, football, golf, skiing (downhill/alpine), skiing (nordic/cross-country), track/field (outdoor), track/field (indoor). *Women:* Basketball, cross-country, golf, lacrosse, skiing (downhill/alpine), skiing (nordic/cross-country), soccer, tennis, track/field (outdoor), track/field (indoor), volleyball. **On-Campus Highlights:** University Memorial Center (UMC), Student Recreation Center, Norlin Library, ATLAS Building, Farrand Field, CU Boulder's Outdoor Program at the Recreation Center.

FINANCIAL AID
Students should submit: FAFSA. Priority filing deadline is 2/15. The Princeton Review suggests that all financial aid forms be submitted as soon as possible after October 1. *Need-based scholarships/grants offered:* College/university scholarship or grant aid from institutional funds, Federal Pell, private scholarships, SEOG, state scholarships/grants. *Loan aid offered:* Direct PLUS Loans, Direct Subsidized Loans, Direct Unsubsidized Loans. Applicants will be notified of awards on a rolling basis beginning 3/15. Federal Work-Study Program available. Institutional employment available.

THE BOTTOM LINE
CU Boulder's reasonable tuition is one of the school's major selling points. Tuition (including mandatory fees) for Colorado residents averages just about $11,500 annually. For nonresidents, tuition and fees average about $37,000. Room and board is an additional $14,418 annually. Books average $1,800 per year. Each year, more than 60 percent of CU Boulder's undergraduates apply for and receive financial aid through a combination of loans, work-study programs, and scholarships. The average total need-based aid package amounts to over $16,000. The need-based gift aid to freshmen is approximately $11,000.

CAREER INFORMATION FROM PAYSCALE.COM	
ROI Rating	88
Bachelors and No Higher	
Median starting salary	$55,600
Median mid-career salary	$111,500
At Least Bachelors	
Median starting salary	$56,800
Median mid-career salary	$115,300
Alumni with high job meaning	48%
Degrees awarded in STEM subjects	36%

SELECTIVITY	
Admissions Rating	83
# of applicants	36,149
% of applicants accepted	80
% of acceptees attending	23
# offered a place on the wait list	1,159
% accepting a place on wait list	15
% admitted from wait list	100

FRESHMAN PROFILE	
Range SAT EBRW	580–665
Range SAT Math	570–680
Range ACT Composite	25–30
Minimum paper TOEFL	537
Minimum internet-based TOEFL	75
Average HS GPA	3.7
% graduated top 10% of class	29
% graduated top 25% of class	59
% graduated top 50% of class	90

DEADLINES	
Early action	
Deadline	11/15
Notification	2/1
Regular	
Priority	11/15
Deadline	1/15
Notification	4/1
Nonfall registration?	Yes

FINANCIAL FACTS	
Financial Aid Rating	88
Annual in-state tuition	$10,728
Annual out-of-state tuition	$35,482
Room and board	$14,418
Required fees	$1,804
Books and supplies	$1,800
Average frosh need-based scholarship	$11,013
Average UG need-based scholarship	$11,091
% needy frosh rec. need-based scholarship or grant aid	74
% needy UG rec. need-based scholarship or grant aid	76
% needy frosh rec. non-need-based scholarship or grant aid	5
% needy UG rec. non-need-based scholarship or grant aid	4
% needy frosh rec. need-based self-help aid	83
% needy UG rec. need-based self-help aid	84
% frosh rec. any financial aid	72
% UG rec. any financial aid	63
% UG borrow to pay for school	42
Average cumulative indebtedness	$27,680
% frosh need fully met	46
% ugrads need fully met	40
Average % of frosh need met	82

University of Dallas

1845 East Northgate Drive, Irving, TX 75062 • Admissions: 972-721-5266 • Fax: 972-721-5017

CAMPUS LIFE

Quality of Life Rating	89
Fire Safety Rating	88
Green Rating	60*
Type of school	Private
Affiliation	Roman Catholic
Environment	City

STUDENTS

Total undergrad enrollment	1,450
% male/female	46/54
% from out of state	48
% frosh from public high school	45
% frosh live on campus	85
% ugrads live on campus	43
# of fraternities (% ugrad men join)	0 (0)
# of sororities (% ugrad women join)	0 (0)
% African American	2
% Asian	6
% Caucasian	61
% Hispanic	23
% Native American	1
% Pacific Islander	<1
% Two or more races	3
% Race and/or ethnicity unknown	1
% international	4
# of countries represented	19

ACADEMICS

Academic Rating	84
% students returning for sophomore year	85
% students graduating within 4 years	65
% students graduating within 6 years	68
Calendar	Semester
Student/faculty ratio	11:1
Profs interesting rating	93
Profs accessible rating	95

Most classes have 20–29 students. Most lab/discussion sessions have 30–39 students.

MOST POPULAR MAJORS
Business; English Language and Literature; Biology/Biological Sciences; History

ABOUT THE SCHOOL

The University of Dallas "rigorously and liberally educates students" both intellectually and morally in order "to prepare them to fulfill their lives to the best of their abilities." This tiny Texas Catholic school boasts small class sizes, a 10:1 student-to-faculty ratio, and an academically renowned two-year core curriculum, which is sixty credits of classes focused on the Great Books of Western literature and culture. The curriculum is connected from one course to the next, and the professors are "faithful to the goal of creating a Catholic university for independent thinkers," teaching students to know the greats of Western culture, and giving them "the skills and context in which to evaluate modernity and continue searching for the truth, wherever it may be found." Every class incorporates "a religious and ethical sense so that we learn to be responsible in our future careers." Additionally, faculty members are all "incredible both in their depth of knowledge which inevitably extends far beyond their field, and in their accessibility to students."

BANG FOR YOUR BUCK

The core curriculum typically culminates with a semester abroad at the school's sister campus in Rome, which is "a great incentive for students to work hard", as "being able to travel Europe with one hundred of your classmates is an amazing experience." The core curriculum enriches the academic experience of the school greatly, adding to what a student gets out of class and "enabling serious academic discussions to take place anywhere on campus with any UD student regardless of their major." The small nature of the school and the shared curriculum means "a lot of personal attention is given to the students," and the faculty "take a personal interest in you as a person, physically, mentally, and spiritually."

STUDENT LIFE

UD students are "very lively, reverent, and smart"; with just 1,400 undergraduates, this is a close-knit community, and "one would have to work very hard to be a complete outsider." There are almost always school events planned on weekends, particularly "music events such as Groundhog Day and Oktoberfest," and the university works to provide opportunities to go into Dallas with their Dallas-year program, which includes trips to the symphony, the Galleria mall, and museums.

The characteristics of the typical UD student are "primarily intellectual," and "very few students who are not enthusiastic about this intellectual pursuit come to the school." Students love to keep the chat going beyond the classroom: "We argue about everything from Plato's 'Republic' to what is the best food in the cafeteria," says one. Many of the students have a strong life of faith, but there is also "careful attention payed to respect the beliefs or lack of belief of all students."

University of Dallas

Financial Aid: 972-721-5266 • E-mail: crusader@udallas.edu • Website: www.udallas.edu

CAREER

The core really strengthens the students as educated people, and students are taught "how to think rather than what to think," and graduate with the ability to discuss all aspects of Western thought intelligently. The Office of Personal Career Development has relationships with a number of employers and organizations, and the campus' location of Irving (just fifteen minutes from downtown Dallas) is home to the headquarters of six Fortune 500 companies. More than 97 percent of students find employment or continuing education within six months of graduation. Out of UD alumni visiting PayScale.com, 51 percent report that they derive a high level of meaning from their jobs.

GENERAL INFO

Activities: Campus Ministries; Choral groups; Dance; Drama/theater; International Student Organization; Literary magazine; Music ensembles; Musical theater; Student government; Student newspaper; Student-run film society; Yearbook. **Organizations:** 35 registered organizations, 4 honor societies, 5 religious organizations. **Athletics (Intercollegiate):** *Men:* baseball, basketball, cross-country, golf, lacrosse, soccer, track/field (outdoor). *Women:* basketball, cross-country, lacrosse, soccer, softball, track/field (outdoor), volleyball. **On-Campus Highlights:** Church of the Incarnation, Cappuccino Bar, The Mall, The Rathskeller, Art Village.

FINANCIAL AID

Students should submit: FAFSA. Priority filing deadline is 1/15. The Princeton Review suggests that all financial aid forms be submitted as soon as possible after October 1. *Need-based scholarships/grants offered:* College/university scholarship or grant aid from institutional funds, Federal Pell, private scholarships, SEOG, state scholarships/grants. *Loan aid offered:* Direct PLUS Loans, Direct Subsidized Loans, Direct Unsubsidized Loans. Applicants will be notified of awards on a rolling basis beginning 12/1. Federal Work-Study Program available. Institutional employment available.

CAREER INFORMATION FROM PAYSCALE.COM	
ROI Rating	88
Bachelors and No Higher	
Median starting salary	$51,300
Median mid-career salary	$99,600
At Least Bachelors	
Median starting salary	$53,900
Median mid-career salary	$100,800
Alumni with high job meaning	48%
Degrees awarded in STEM subjects	16%

SELECTIVITY	
Admissions Rating	89
# of applicants	3,857
% of applicants accepted	47
% of acceptees attending	23

FRESHMAN PROFILE	
Range SAT EBRW	590–700
Range SAT Math	550–670
Range ACT Composite	24–31
Minimum internet-based TOEFL	79
Average HS GPA	3.9
% graduated top 10% of class	37
% graduated top 25% of class	71
% graduated top 50% of class	95

DEADLINES	
Early action	
Deadline	12/1
Notification	1/15
Regular	
Priority	1/15
Deadline	9/15
Nonfall registration?	Yes

FINANCIAL FACTS	
Financial Aid Rating	86
Annual tuition	$37,652
Room and board	$12,400
Required fees	$3,000
Books and supplies	$1,000
Average frosh need-based scholarship	$30,746
Average UG need-based scholarship	$28,420
% needy frosh rec. need-based scholarship or grant aid	100
% needy UG rec. need-based scholarship or grant aid	99
% needy frosh rec. non-need-based scholarship or grant aid	60
% needy UG rec. non-need-based scholarship or grant aid	66
% needy frosh rec. need-based self-help aid	67
% needy UG rec. need-based self-help aid	65
% frosh rec. any financial aid	96
% UG rec. any financial aid	94
% UG borrow to pay for school	57
Average cumulative indebtedness	$35,161
% frosh need fully met	28
% ugrads need fully met	20
Average % of frosh need met	85
Average % of ugrad need met	79

University of Dayton

300 COLLEGE PARK, DAYTON, OH 45469-1669 • ADMISSIONS: 800-837-7433 • FAX: 937-229-4729

CAMPUS LIFE

Quality of Life Rating	93
Fire Safety Rating	81
Green Rating	90
Type of school	Private
Affiliation	Roman Catholic
Environment	City

STUDENTS

Total undergrad enrollment	8,617
% male/female	53/47
% from out of state	52
% frosh from public high school	43
% frosh live on campus	94
% ugrads live on campus	75
# of fraternities (% ugrad men join)	11 (12)
# of sororities (% ugrad women join)	9 (21)
% African American	3
% Asian	1
% Caucasian	78
% Hispanic	6
% Native American	<1
% Pacific Islander	<1
% Two or more races	5
% Race and/or ethnicity unknown	1
% international	6
# of countries represented	39

ACADEMICS

Academic Rating	80
% students returning for sophomore year	91
% students graduating within 4 years	63
% students graduating within 6 years	79
Calendar	Semester
Student/faculty ratio	15:1
Profs interesting rating	82
Profs accessible rating	83

Most classes have 20–29 students. Most lab/discussion sessions have 20–29 students.

MOST POPULAR MAJORS

Speech Communication and Rhetoric; Mechanical Engineering; Marketing/ Marketing Management

ABOUT THE SCHOOL

A Catholic research institution in the Marianist tradition, the University of Dayton (UD) in Ohio offers undergraduates more than just a top-notch education; it's a place where students truly engage with one another. "The sense of community that is shared among everyone," as one student puts it, is one of the most commonly admired traits of this campus. Class sizes are small, and "the staff and faculty really care." Another student notes, "The administration [is] very inclusive and always looking to diversify and make the campus safe." But the mission of UD moves beyond fostering interactions on campus and emphasizes building bridges to the world at large. According to one student, "Students at UD also are very likely...to spend their time volunteering," and the school's mission emphasizes service and leadership in the community. A mid-sized, private university on a gorgeous campus, UD is a welcoming school that allows students to learn and grow into model citizens and driven professionals.

BANG FOR YOUR BUCK

The University of Dayton prides itself in being "one of the most affordable private, Catholic universities in the country." Not only that, between the numerous athletic, academic, and legacy scholarships, as well as need-based grants, the school's Office of Financial Aid does a lot to help families with the cost of education. In fact, 94 percent of students receive some form of financial aid. Notably, annual budgets are established for every student, reflecting the actual and complete cost of attendance. Students aren't left in the dark when it comes to how much they and their families will need to pay.

STUDENT LIFE

At this "aggressively inclusive" campus, students can be described as "laid-back, fun, loving, yet hardworking people." While smaller class sizes ensure a thriving academic community, students feel supported in other ways. "Each individual is there to help no matter what," reports one student. Much social activity is centered in the "student neighborhood," made up of university-run houses with porches that play host to barbecues and parties. Students also hit the Recreation Complex, or "RecPlex," to take part in intramural sports. Extracurricular activities are big here, and "almost every student is involved in some sort of club." For many, though, campus life is all about the university's Division I basketball team. It's no wonder the largest student organization on campus is the Red Scare, "dedicated to doing whatever it takes to give the Flyers a home advantage at games." "There's something here about the people and the campus that's just magical," says one student.

CAREER

On average, the starting salary of the typical University of Dayton graduate is $53,700 per year, with 44 percent of alums reporting that their work has "high meaning" to them. Students credit this to UD's mission to integrate class time with real working experience. As one student puts it, among the "greatest strengths as a university are our internship opportunities." For budding engineers and scientists, the University of Dayton Research Institute offers a chance to partner with companies to conduct research and aid in innovation. Not only that, the university offers inroads to a variety of other co-op and professional development opportunities, and its Career Services center offers interview coaching, resume development sessions, and career fairs. It's no wonder that 96 percent of graduates are either employed, accepted into graduate schools, or working in meaningful volunteer programs within six months of graduation.

University of Dayton

FINANCIAL AID: 800-837-7433 • E-MAIL: ADMISSION@UDAYTON.EDU • WEBSITE: WWW.UDAYTON.EDU

GENERAL INFO

Activities: Choral groups, concert band, dance, drama/theater, jazz band, literary magazine, marching band, music ensembles, musical theater, opera, pep band, radio station, student government, student newspaper, sustainability club, symphony orchestra, television station, yearbook, Campus Ministry, Model UN. **Organizations:** 240 registered organizations, 15 honor societies, 35 service groups. 11 fraternities, 9 sororities. **Athletics (Intercollegiate):** *Men:* baseball, basketball, cheerleading, cross-country, football, golf, soccer, tennis. *Women:* basketball, cheerleading, crew/rowing, cross-country, golf, soccer, softball, tennis, track/field (outdoor), track/field (indoor), volleyball. **On-Campus Highlights:** John F. Kennedy Memorial Union, Ryan C. Harris Learning-Teaching Center, University of Dayton Arena, Science Center, Kettering Laboratories, University of Dayton Research Institute, ArtStreet, Marianist Hall, Chapel of the Immaculate Conception, RecPlex.

FINANCIAL AID

Students should submit: FAFSA. Priority filing deadline is 2/1. The Princeton Review suggests that all financial aid forms be submitted as soon as possible after October 1. *Need-based scholarships/grants offered:* College/university scholarship or grant aid from institutional funds, Federal Pell, private scholarships, SEOG, state scholarships/grants. *Loan aid offered:* Direct PLUS Loans, Direct Subsidized Loans, Direct Unsubsidized Loans. Applicants will be notified of awards on a rolling basis beginning 2/17. Federal Work-Study Program available. Institutional employment available.

THE BOTTOM LINE

Annual tuition at University Dayton is $42,900, and there are no additional fees or surcharges. In fact, what a student pays their first year is guaranteed to stay the same for all four years. Students' UD scholarships and grants increase each year to offset any tuition increases. On-campus room and board total $13,580. Ninety-four percent of UD students receive financial aid; merit scholarships can get up to $88,000 over four years, and need-based grants can amount up to $21,000 per year.

CAREER INFORMATION FROM PAYSCALE.COM	
ROI Rating	87
Bachelors and No Higher	
Median starting salary	$56,100
Median mid-career salary	$104,500
At Least Bachelors	
Median starting salary	$57,000
Median mid-career salary	$108,300
Alumni with high job meaning	44%
Degrees awarded in STEM subjects	33%

SELECTIVITY	
Admissions Rating	85
# of applicants	16,824
% of applicants accepted	72
% of acceptees attending	19

FRESHMAN PROFILE	
Range SAT EBRW	550–650
Range SAT Math	550–660
Range ACT Composite	24–29
Minimum internet-based TOEFL	54
Average HS GPA	3.7

DEADLINES	
Early decision	
Deadline	11/1
Notification	12/15
Regular	
Priority	12/15
Deadline	3/1
Notification	2/15
Nonfall registration?	Yes

FINANCIAL FACTS	
Financial Aid Rating	95
Annual tuition	$42,900
Room and board	$13,580
Required fees	$0
Books and supplies	$1,000
Average frosh need-based scholarship	$28,208
Average UG need-based scholarship	$27,594
% needy frosh rec. need-based scholarship or grant aid	100
% needy UG rec. need-based scholarship or grant aid	96
% needy frosh rec. non-need-based scholarship or grant aid	9
% needy UG rec. non-need-based scholarship or grant aid	9
% needy frosh rec. need-based self-help aid	76
% needy UG rec. need-based self-help aid	79
% frosh rec. any financial aid	98
% UG rec. any financial aid	94
% UG borrow to pay for school	55
Average cumulative indebtedness	$35,689
% frosh need fully met	82
% ugrads need fully met	81
Average % of frosh need met	82
Average % of ugrad need met	81

University of Denver

Undergraduate Admission, Denver, CO 80208 • Admissions: 303-871-2036 • Fax: 303-871-3301

CAMPUS LIFE
Quality of Life Rating	91
Fire Safety Rating	82
Green Rating	86
Type of school	Private
Environment	Metropolis

STUDENTS
Total undergrad enrollment	5,753
% male/female	47/53
% from out of state	62
% frosh live on campus	93
% ugrads live on campus	50
# of fraternities (% ugrad men join)	9 (25)
# of sororities (% ugrad women join)	13 (30)
% African American	2
% Asian	4
% Caucasian	69
% Hispanic	11
% Native American	<1
% Pacific Islander	<1
% Two or more races	4
% Race and/or ethnicity unknown	2
% international	8
# of countries represented	51

ACADEMICS
Academic Rating	89
% students returning for sophomore year	87
% students graduating within 4 years	65
% students graduating within 6 years	75
Calendar	Quarter
Student/faculty ratio	11:1
Profs interesting rating	89
Profs accessible rating	88

Most classes have fewer than 20 students.
Most lab/discussion sessions have 10–19 students.

MOST POPULAR MAJORS
Psychology; Finance; Biological Sciences

ABOUT THE SCHOOL
There's no denying that University of Denver's profile is on the rise. And with its "small classroom settings," "focus on innovation [and] sustainability" and "excellent study abroad program[s]" it's easy to understand why. Of course, "being able to see the sun set over the mountains out [your] dorm window" doesn't hurt either. Academically, students have the opportunity to pursue a wide variety of disciplines. For starters, the university is "well-known for its hospitality and business programs." We'd also be remiss if we didn't highlight Denver's Josef Korbel School of International Studies, "regarded as one of the best schools for international relations in the world." Fortunately, no matter what they study, undergrads typically encounter "passionate" professors who are "experts in their field." And while their "expectations are high," they are also "actively engaged" and "willing to do [whatever it takes] to help students be successful."

BANG FOR YOUR BUCK
A number of undergrads are drawn to the University of Denver for the "great financial aid." And it's easy to understand why. The school truly strives to make sure its programs are affordable for all students, no matter their background. For example, Denver offers a variety of generous scholarships including the Chancellor award which provides $24,000 annually and the Provost award which offers $22,000 annually. Thankfully, DU's scholarships aren't limited to a select few. Indeed, roughly 70 percent of Denver's first-year students receive some type of merit-based aid. And these rewards are typically renewable assuming the student remains in good academic standing.

STUDENT LIFE
Overall, DU's student body tends to skew "preppy," though we've been assured that everyone, "no matter their race, ethnicity, religion [or] sexual preference [is] accepted and fit[s] in." Perhaps some of this openness can be attributed to the fact that the university is overflowing with extracurricular and social opportunities. To begin with, "Greek life is big." Additionally, "students love to cheer on their own sports teams as well as the professional teams in Denver." Of course, there's no need to fret if fraternities or athletics aren't your scene. A sophomore tells us that DU "has different activities like parades and fairs that students and their friends can enjoy, so it is really easy to be entertained." Lastly, given the school's proximity to the Rockies, it's no surprise that undergrads are "constantly driving up to the mountains to go skiing, snowboarding, hiking, etc."

CAREER
By and large, undergrads at University of Denver are confident in their post-graduation job prospects (The school reports that 97 percent of alumni have jobs and/or are enrolled in graduate school six months following graduation.) And many students happily report that there are "countless opportunities for internships." This sunny outlook can certainly be attributed to the tireless efforts of DU's career services office. For starters, the office hosts multiple fairs throughout the academic year, including an innovative reverse career fair where students set up tables and employers circulate the room to share their job opportunities. Moreover, the office recently launched AlumniFire, which helps current students connect with Denver alums. And many students love to take advantage of the Career Center's drop-in program which allows them to swing by the office and quickly meet with a career advisor.

University of Denver

FINANCIAL AID: 303-871-4020 • E-MAIL: ADMISSION@DU.EDU • WEBSITE: WWW.DU.EDU

GENERAL INFO

Activities: Choral groups, concert band, dance, drama/theater, jazz band, literary magazine, music ensembles, musical theater, opera, pep band, radio station, student government, student newspaper, student-run film society, symphony orchestra, campus ministries, International Student Organization, Model UN. **Organizations:** 160 registered organizations, 19 honor societies, 14 religious organizations. 9 fraternities, 7 sororities. **Athletics (Intercollegiate):** *Men:* basketball, diving, golf, ice hockey, lacrosse, skiing (downhill/alpine), skiing (nordic/cross-country), soccer, swimming, tennis. *Women:* basketball, diving, golf, gymnastics, lacrosse, skiing (downhill/alpine), skiing (nordic/cross-country), soccer, swimming, tennis, volleyball. **On-Campus Highlights:** Daniel Felix Ritchie School of Engineering and Computer Science, Ritchie Center (athletic facility), Newman Center (performing arts), Daniels College of Business building, Anderson Academic Commons (library).

FINANCIAL AID

Students should submit: CSS Profile; FAFSA. Priority filing deadline is 11/15 for Early Action and 2/1 for Regular Decision. The Princeton Review suggests that all financial aid forms be submitted as soon as possible after October 1. *Need-based scholarships/grants offered:* College/university scholarship or grant aid from institutional funds, Federal Pell, private scholarships, SEOG, state scholarships/grants. *Loan aid offered:* Direct PLUS Loans, Direct Subsidized Loans, Direct Unsubsidized Loans. Applicants will be notified of awards once their financial aid application is complete. Federal Work-Study Program available. Institutional employment available.

BOTTOM LINE

Traditional, full-time undergraduates at University of Denver will face a tuition bill of $47,520 for the 2017-2018 academic year. Additionally, there are miscellaneous fees totaling $1,149. Students can also expect room and board to cost roughly $12,612. And they'll need to set aside another $1,200 for books (and various school supplies) as well as $1,536 for transportation. Lastly, it's estimated that undergrads will need $1,359 for personal expenses.

CAREER INFORMATION FROM PAYSCALE.COM	
ROI Rating	88
Bachelors and No Higher	
Median starting salary	$54,000
Median mid-career salary	$101,600
At Least Bachelors	
Median starting salary	$55,600
Median mid-career salary	$106,700
Alumni with high job meaning	49%
Degrees awarded in STEM subjects	12%

SELECTIVITY	
Admissions Rating	89
# of applicants	19,904
% of applicants accepted	58
% of acceptees attending	13
# offered a place on the wait list	500
% accepting a place on wait list	47
% admitted from wait list	0
# of early decision applicants	363
% accepted early decision	46

FRESHMAN PROFILE	
Range SAT EBRW	590–680
Range SAT Math	570–670
Range ACT Composite	25–30
Minimum paper TOEFL	550
Minimum internet-based TOEFL	80
Average HS GPA	3.7
% graduated top 10% of class	38
% graduated top 25% of class	73
% graduated top 50% of class	95

DEADLINES	
Early decision	
Deadline	11/1
Notification	12/15
Other ED Deadline	1/15
Other ED Notification	2/20
Early action	
Deadline	11/1
Notification	1/15
Regular	
Deadline	1/15
Notification	3/15
Nonfall registration?	Yes

FINANCIAL FACTS	
Financial Aid Rating	89
Annual tuition	$49,392
Room and board	$13,005
Required fees	$1,164
Books and supplies	$1,200
Average frosh need-based scholarship	$34,932
Average UG need-based scholarship	$34,077
% needy frosh rec. need-based scholarship or grant aid	99
% needy UG rec. need-based scholarship or grant aid	99
% needy frosh rec. non-need-based scholarship or grant aid	23
% needy UG rec. non-need-based scholarship or grant aid	24
% needy frosh rec. need-based self-help aid	68
% needy UG rec. need-based self-help aid	69
% frosh rec. any financial aid	85

University of Florida

201 CRISER HALL, GAINESVILLE, FL 32611-4000 • ADMISSIONS: 352-392-1365 • FAX: 352-392-3987

CAMPUS LIFE

Quality of Life Rating	86
Fire Safety Rating	88
Green Rating	94
Type of school	Public
Environment	City

STUDENTS

Total undergrad enrollment	35,247
% male/female	44/56
% from out of state	6
% frosh from public high school	70
% frosh live on campus	73
% ugrads live on campus	22
# of fraternities (% ugrad men join)	36 (18)
# of sororities (% ugrad women join)	28 (23)
% African American	6
% Asian	8
% Caucasian	54
% Hispanic	22
% Native American	<1
% Pacific Islander	1
% Two or more races	3
% Race and/or ethnicity unknown	3
% international	3
# of countries represented	152

ACADEMICS

Academic Rating	78
% students graduating within 4 years	68
% students graduating within 6 years	88
Calendar	Semester
Student/faculty ratio	19:1
Profs interesting rating	72
Profs accessible rating	75

Most classes have 10–19 students. Most lab/discussion sessions have 20–29 students.

MOST POPULAR MAJORS

Biology/Biological Sciences; Psychology; Finance

#47 BEST VALUE COLLEGE

ABOUT THE SCHOOL

The University of Florida is the prototypical large, state school that "provides its students with a well-rounded experience: an excellent education coated in incomparable school camaraderie." With a total enrollment of just over 55,000, this school is among the five largest universities in the nation, proffering "first class amenities, athletics, academics, campus, and students." Those students hail from all fifty states and more than 150 countries, all of whom are looking for more than your standard academic fare. UF certainly doesn't disappoint, as the school has "a great reputation and…great academic programs for the tuition price." The campus is home to more than 100 undergraduate degree programs, and undergraduates interested in conducting research with faculty can participate in UF's University Scholars Program. One unique learning community, Innovation Academy, pulls together students from thirty majors who share a common minor in innovation. The Career Connection Center (CCC) is a major centralized service that helps students prepare for their post-graduation experiences—UF "seeks to graduate academically ahead and 'real-world-prepared' alumni"—and organized career fairs are conducted regularly and the university is very successful in attracting top employers nationally to recruit on campus.

BANG FOR YOUR BUCK

The cost of attending University of Florida is well below the national average for four-year public universities. Annual tuition and fees hover are $6,381 (based on a typical schedule of thirty credit hours per year), while campus room and board will run you another $9,000-plus. Overall, Florida residents are the main benefactors of this great value. Out-of-state undergraduates pay a little over $22,000 more in tuition and fees and must also factor in higher transportation costs. The school prides itself on providing prospective students with financial aid packages that will help lower educational costs through a variety of "Gator Aid" options. Their website offers a net price calculator to help students and their families get a better idea of exactly how much it would cost to attend the school. In-state students should be sure to check out the Florida Bright Futures Scholarship Program, which offers scholarships based on high school academic achievement. The program has different award levels, each with its own eligibility criteria and award amounts.

STUDENT LIFE

Though students at UF study hard and things can get very serious during finals and midterms, fun abounds at school. "A lot of UF culture is based around sports. We are always going to or watching something," is a sentiment expressed by many students. "The sporting events are top notch and everyone [can] find a sport to cheer for because we are great at them all! Our intramural program and gym are also amazing." With sports tend to come parties, but while "many activities revolve around drinking and partying (especially during football season)," there are lots of other ways to enjoy yourself at school. "GatorNights are always fun," says a student. "Every Friday, there are different events from wax hands to comedians to sand candy and a lot more. Also, the clubs are great here. They have so many clubs, from Software Development to Aerial Dance and everything in

University of Florida

between." There are opportunities to get away as well: "Occasionally when looking for a change of scenery we embrace the nature around us and float down...Ginnie Springs or go to the school's lake." So no matter how you like to spend your time, UF should have something to offer.

CAREER

Students widely feel that UF does a great job at preparing them for life after school, from the first-rate academics to the "excellent" career services. The Career Resource Center offers an abundance of services, including academic advising and career planning, job fairs and recruiting events, resume critique and mock interviews, and resources for job and internship searches. Gator Shadow Day allows student to learn about careers by shadowing a professional at work. The Center also offers a program called Gator Launch to provide "underrepresented" students in the science and technology fields with special mentoring opportunities. All in all, students seem to leave happy. Of University of Florida alumni visiting PayScale.com, 52 percent report that they derive a high level of meaning from their jobs.

GENERAL INFO

Organizations: 1,052 registered organizations. **Athletics (Intercollegiate):** *Men:* Baseball, basketball, cross-country, diving, football, golf, swimming, tennis, track/field (outdoor), track/field (indoor). *Women:* Basketball, cross-country, diving, golf, gymnastics, lacrosse, soccer, softball, swimming, tennis, track/field (outdoor), track/field (indoor), volleyball.

FINANCIAL AID

Students should submit: FAFSA. Priority filing deadline is 4/1. The Princeton Review suggests that all financial aid forms be submitted as soon as possible after October 1. *Need-based scholarships/grants offered:* College/university scholarship or grant aid from institutional funds; Federal Pell; Private scholarships; SEOG; State scholarships/grants; United Negro College Fund. *Loan aid offered:* Direct PLUS Loans, Direct Subsidized Loans, Direct Unsubsidized Loans. Applicants will be notified of awards on a rolling basis beginning 4/2. Federal Work-Study Program available. Institutional employment available.

THE BOTTOM LINE

With relatively low tuition and a strong scholarship program for in-state students, UF is an especially good value for Florida residents. The Machen Florida Opportunity Scholars (MFOS) is a scholarship program for first-generation college freshmen from economically disadvantaged backgrounds. The scholarship provides a full grant scholarship aid package for up to four years of undergraduate education.

SELECTIVITY	
Admissions Rating	**93**
# of applicants	32,747
% of applicants accepted	42
% of acceptees attending	47

FRESHMAN PROFILE	
Range SAT EBRW	620–710
Range SAT Math	620–690
Range ACT Composite	28–32

DEADLINES	
Regular	
Deadline	11/1

FINANCIAL FACTS	
Financial Aid Rating	**88**
Annual in-state tuition	$6,381
Annual out-of-state tuition	$28,658
Room and board	$10,120
Books and supplies	$1,030
Average frosh need-based scholarship	$8,328
Average UG need-based scholarship	$7,612
% needy frosh rec. need-based scholarship or grant aid	59
% needy UG rec. need-based scholarship or grant aid	65
% needy frosh rec. non-need-based scholarship or grant aid	88
% needy UG rec. non-need-based scholarship or grant aid	70
% needy frosh rec. need-based self-help aid	37
% needy UG rec. need-based self-help aid	49
% frosh rec. any financial aid	98
% UG rec. any financial aid	91
% UG borrow to pay for school	38
Average cumulative indebtedness	$22,192
% frosh need fully met	28
% ugrads need fully met	23
Average % of frosh need met	99
Average % of ugrad need met	97

CAREER INFORMATION FROM PAYSCALE.COM	
ROI Rating	92
Bachelors and No Higher	
Median starting salary	$54,200
Median mid-career salary	$101,400
At Least Bachelors	
Median starting salary	$56,300
Median mid-career salary	$106,300
Alumni with high job meaning	52%
Degrees awarded in STEM subjects	29%

University of Georgia

TERRELL HALL, ATHENS, GA 30602 • ADMISSIONS: 706-542-8776 • FAX: 706-542-1466

CAMPUS LIFE

Quality of Life Rating	**90**
Fire Safety Rating	**88**
Green Rating	**95**
Type of school	Public
Environment	City

STUDENTS

Total undergrad enrollment	28,723
% male/female	44/56
% from out of state	11
% frosh from public high school	69
% frosh live on campus	98
% ugrads live on campus	33
# of fraternities (% ugrad men join)	36 (20)
# of sororities (% ugrad women join)	28 (31)
% African American	8
% Asian	10
% Caucasian	69
% Hispanic	6
% Native American	<1
% Pacific Islander	<1
% Two or more races	4
% Race and/or ethnicity unknown	1
% international	2
# of countries represented	97

ACADEMICS

Academic Rating	**73**
% students returning for sophomore year	96
% students graduating within 4 years	63
% students graduating within 6 years	85
Calendar	Semester
Student/faculty ratio	17:1
Profs interesting rating	75
Profs accessible rating	68
Most classes have 10–19 students.	

MOST POPULAR MAJORS
Biology/Biological Sciences; Psychology; Finance

ABOUT THE SCHOOL

Programs in journalism, science, agriculture, and literature, among others, are the backbone of UGA's increasingly attractive profile as a world-class research institution that draws top faculty and students. "Everyone in Georgia strives to go to UGA," says a student. Students make note of the stellar, "experienced professors and research participation" opportunities, pointing out many of the classes—especially in the first two years—are large, and that it is to a student's advantage to go beyond just showing up. Smaller student-faculty ratios are available in honors program classes. UGA students are educated on a beautiful, 759-acre main campus located in Athens, Georgia, a quintessential college town known for its vibrant music and arts scene. "When classes are over and your studying is done, there is fun to be had all around Athens," including a full slate of on-campus and out-of-class activities on offer. Students can choose from more than 600 extracurricular organizations ranging from sororities and fraternities to pre- professional ("a great way to meet people"), environmental, and civic groups. There's an "incomparable" music scene, a hippie scene, and a jock scene—to name just a few—and all 34,000 students on campus have an easy time finding a group where they feel welcome. "I never tire of meeting new people, and UGA has so many people to offer. It's incredible," says a student. Students often gather around that other constant of UGA, the Georgia Bulldogs. "There are so many choices here, it's difficult to manage your time between studying and getting involved in all UGA has to offer," says a student. The University of Georgia Career Center provides centralized career services for students and is among the first in the nation to develop iPhone apps that connect students with potential employers. The university also offers an innovative Career Boot Camp, a day-long, intensive program that brings representatives of Fortune 100 companies to the campus to conduct exercises such as mock interviews.

BANG FOR YOUR BUCK

Georgia's merit-based HOPE Scholarship provides high school graduates who have a minimum 3.0 grade point average with a scholarship to cover the cost of tuition and a percentage of student fees and books. Ninety-seven percent of Georgia-resident freshmen at UGA receive the scholarship. UGA also offers the prestigious Foundation Fellowship, which provides an annual stipend of approximately $9,000 for in-state students (in addition to the HOPE Scholarship) and $15,700 for out-of-state students (plus an out-of-state tuition waiver). The fellowship provides numerous opportunities for national and international travel-study, faculty-directed academic research, and participation in academic conferences.

STUDENT LIFE

"Students are generally white, upper-middle-class, smart, [and] involved, and [they] have a good time," "seem to be predominantly conservative," and "are usually involved in at least one organization, whether it be Greek, a club, or sports." "The typical student at UGA is one who knows how and when to study but allows himself or herself to have a very active social life." The majority are Southerners, with many students from within Georgia. "The stereotype is Southern, Republican, football-loving, and beer-drinking. While many, many of UGA's students do not fit this description, there is no lack of the above," and "there is a social scene for everyone in Athens." "There are a great number of atypical students in the liberal arts," which "creates a unique and exciting student body with greatly contrasting opinions."

University of Georgia

FINANCIAL AID: 706-542-6147 • E-MAIL: ADMPROC@UGA.EDU • WEBSITE: WWW.UGA.EDU

CAREER

The UGA Career Center is a one-stop resource for major and career exploration, graduate school information, interviewing and resume prep, and, of course, the job search. On that front, DAWGLink has postings for full-time, part-time work, or internships, and the Intern For A Day program lets students get a taste of a particular field or career while shadowing a professional. The Center for Leadership and Service can connect students who want to volunteer (the Volunteer UGA Calendar is loaded with relevant panels and service opportunities) and even offers grants for student groups on campus to engage with the Athens community at large. Graduates generally earn average starting salaries of $50,200 (according to PayScale.com), and 44 percent derive a high level of meaning from their work.

GENERAL INFO

Activities: Choral groups, concert band, dance, drama/theater, jazz band, literary magazine, marching band, music ensembles, musical theater, opera, pep band, radio station, student government, student newspaper, student-run film society, symphony orchestra, television station, yearbook, campus ministries, international student organization. **Organizations:** 597 registered organizations, 22 honor societies, 35 religious organizations. 35 fraternities, 27 sororities. **Athletics (Intercollegiate):** *Men:* Baseball, basketball, cross-country, diving, football, golf, swimming, tennis, track/field (outdoor), track/field (indoor). *Women:* Basketball, cross-country, diving, equestrian sports, golf, gymnastics, soccer, softball, swimming, tennis, track/field (outdoor), track/field (indoor), volleyball. **On-Campus Highlights:** Zell B. Miller Learning Center, Sanford Stadium, Ramsey Student Center for Physical Activity, Performing and Visual Arts Complex, Tate Student Center.

FINANCIAL AID

Students should submit: FAFSA. Priority filing deadline is 3/1. The Princeton Review suggests that all financial aid forms be submitted as soon as possible after October 1. *Need-based scholarships/grants offered:* College/university scholarship or grant aid from institutional funds, Federal Pell, private scholarships, SEOG, state scholarships/grants. *Loan aid offered:* Direct PLUS Loans, Direct Subsidized Loans, Direct Unsubsidized Loans. Applicants will be notified of awards on a rolling basis beginning 5/1. Federal Work-Study Program available. Institutional employment available.

THE BOTTOM LINE

The average in-state Georgia freshman pays $9,552 in tuition, while those from out of state cough up more than $28,126 a year. On-campus room and board costs just over $10,038. Recent graduates left UGA with approximately $23,403 in cumulative debt, on average.

CAREER INFORMATION FROM PAYSCALE.COM	
ROI Rating	90
Bachelors and No Higher	
Median starting salary	$52,600
Median mid-career salary	$100,000
At Least Bachelors	
Median starting salary	$53,700
Median mid-career salary	$102,500
Alumni with high job meaning	44%
Degrees awarded in STEM subjects	13%

SELECTIVITY	
Admissions Rating	92
# of applicants	24,165
% of applicants accepted	54
% of acceptees attending	45
# offered a place on the wait list	889
% accepting a place on wait list	60
% admitted from wait list	6

FRESHMAN PROFILE	
Range SAT EBRW	610–690
Range SAT Math	590–680
Range ACT Composite	26–31
Minimum paper TOEFL	550
Minimum internet-based TOEFL	80
Average HS GPA	4.0
% graduated top 10% of class	54
% graduated top 25% of class	90
% graduated top 50% of class	99

DEADLINES	
Early action	
Deadline	10/15
Notification	12/1
Regular	
Priority	10/15
Deadline	1/1
Nonfall registration?	Yes

FINANCIAL FACTS	
Financial Aid Rating	83
Annual in-state tuition	$9,552
Annual out-of-state tuition	$28,126
Room and board	$10,038
Required fees	$2,278
Room and board	NR
Average frosh need-based scholarship	$10,769
Average UG need-based scholarship	$9,317
% needy frosh rec. need-based scholarship or grant aid	97
% needy UG rec. need-based scholarship or grant aid	92
% needy frosh rec. non-need-based scholarship or grant aid	24
% needy UG rec. non-need-based scholarship or grant aid	17
% needy frosh rec. need-based self-help aid	47
% needy UG rec. need-based self-help aid	53
% frosh rec. any financial aid	47
% UG rec. any financial aid	48
% UG borrow to pay for school	47
Average cumulative indebtedness	$23,403
% frosh need fully met	28
% ugrads need fully met	23
Average % of frosh need met	77
Average % of ugrad need met	72

University of Houston

4400 University, Houston, TX 77204-2023 • Admissions: 713-743-1010 • Financial Aid: 713-743-9051

CAMPUS LIFE

Quality of Life Rating	**85**
Fire Safety Rating	**98**
Green Rating	**87**
Type of school	Public
Environment	Metropolis

STUDENTS

Total undergrad enrollment	36,088
% male/female	51/49
% from out of state	1
% frosh from public high school	93
% frosh live on campus	46
% ugrads live on campus	17
# of fraternities (% ugrad men join)	25 (4)
# of sororities (% ugrad women join)	23 (5)
% African American	10
% Asian	22
% Caucasian	24
% Hispanic	35
% Native American	<1
% Pacific Islander	<1
% Two or more races	3
% Race and/or ethnicity unknown	2
% international	4
# of countries represented	107

ACADEMICS

Academic Rating	**77**
% students returning for sophomore year	85
% students graduating within 4 years	25
% students graduating within 6 years	54
Calendar	Semester
Student/faculty ratio	22:1
Profs interesting rating	75
Profs accessible rating	76

Most classes have 20–29 students. Most lab/discussion sessions have 20–29 students.

MOST POPULAR MAJORS
Biology/Biological Sciences; Psychology; Business Administration and Management

ABOUT THE SCHOOL

Situated in the heart of the fourth largest city in the United States, the University of Houston is a tier one public research university located in an urban setting. UH is one of the most ethnically diverse universities in the country, having "a thriving multicultural mix" within one of the nation's most international cities, also known as "the energy capital of the world." One undergraduate here loves the fact that "you meet people from different social/economic backgrounds every day and it's humbling and amazing!" Students communicate, share ideas, and build relationships with people from all over the world, enabling "political discussion and religious awareness to flow freely throughout the university." Despite the metropolitan environment, there is still a close-knit feel to the campus. With a great balance of residents and commuters, UH is also nontraditional, "so you'll meet lots of people who are coming back to school after serving our country, having kids, or trying a few classes at a community college first." The location also makes it convenient for students who wish to work while attending, and the University of Houston tries hard to accommodate them by providing evening, distance-learning, online, and Saturday classes. Enthused one satisfied beneficiary of these services, "commuters can still have school spirit!"

BANG FOR YOUR BUCK

Students tell us that the school's financial aid packages are "considerably higher than other institutions" and are instrumental in "helping bright kids from low-middle-income households build an optimistic future." Also, "tuition rates are quite low compared to its competitors." These and other accolades from students (and parents!) are quite common. "Such a great value." "Amazingly affordable." "A quality education that will be long-lasting and nationally recognized." Described as "amazing," "generous," and "substantial" by students, there are an abundance of scholarships available at UH. "I got an all-expenses paid scholarship for being a National Merit Scholar!" The Tier One Scholarship program offers a distinguished, high-profile award intended to attract highly qualified students. Awarded to first-time-in-college freshmen, it covers tuition and mandatory fees for up to five years of undergraduate study. Selection is based on merit and consideration of a student's need for financial assistance. Tier One Scholars also receive stipends for undergraduate research and for study abroad programs.

STUDENT LIFE

Students at UH are outgoing, friendly, and ambitious." "You will see every ethnicity and nationality you can think of" because "minorities are the majorities here!" Even though most students are commuters, many with full-time jobs and families, those who do live on campus seem quite happy to do so. "The spirit on campus is intoxicating!" remarks one resident. Others cite "the famous cougar paw hand signal" as a familiar gesture. Since students here are "like snowflakes," UH "has a club for everyone, for whatever you're into." There is also a bowling alley on campus, "rock climbing at the rec," and "a hangout spot, always bursting with life." Another UH tradition is "humans vs. zombies, where we wear bandanas and chase each other with nerf guns in between classes!"

University of Houston

E-MAIL: VC@UH.EDU • FAX: 713-743-7542 • WEBSITE: HTTP://WWW.UH.EDU/

CAREER

"Opportunities are bountiful at UH." In the "nationally recognized" Bauer College of Business, students feel ready for the job market. They believe that UH prepares them "for a long-term successful life in the career of their choosing." Professors at UH have an "amazing" amount of experience and "push their students to do their absolute best." "Not ONLY do they teach you about your subject, they show you how it applies to your career and how to make yourself a better person." "There are a number of student organizations that people participate in to show their enthusiasm for their chosen profession, which also helps them find gainful employment doing what they love." Students take advantage of internships in Houston as well as opportunities with the major corporations that have "close ties to the University." According to the website PayScale.com, the average salary for recent graduates is $53,100.

GENERAL INFO

Activities: Choral groups, concert band, dance, drama/theatre, jazz band, literary magazine, marching band, music ensembles, musical theatre, opera, pep band, radio station, student government, student newspaper, student-run film society, symphony orchestra, television station, yearbook, campus ministries, international student organization. **Organizations:** 448 registered organizations, 29 honor societies, 53 religious organizations. 25 social fraternities, 23 social sororities. **Athletics (Intercollegiate):** *Men:* Baseball, basketball, cross-country, football, golf, track/field (outdoor), track/field (indoor). *Women:* Basketball, cross-country, diving, soccer, softball, swimming, tennis, track/field (outdoor), track/field (indoor), volleyball. **On Campus Highlights:** Student Center, Campus Recreation and Wellness Center, Student Center Satellite, Blaffer Art Museum, TDECU Stadium.

FINANCIAL AID

Students should submit: FAFSA. Priority filing deadline is 3/15. The Princeton Review suggests that all financial aid forms be submitted as soon as possible after October 1. *Need-based scholarships/grants offered:* College/university scholarship or grant aid from institutional funds, Federal Pell, private scholarships, SEOG, state scholarships/grants. *Loan aid offered:* Direct PLUS Loans, Direct Subsidized Stafford Loans, Direct Unsubsidized Stafford Loans. Applicants will be notified of awards on a rolling basis beginning 3/1. Federal Work-Study Program available. Institutional employment available.

BOTTOM LINE

In-state tuition is around $9,888 per year; for out-of-state students, the cost is $25,338. Room and board will come to $9,104; required fees, $1,002; books and supplies, $1,300. Nearly 50 percent of students borrow in some way to pay for school, and those that do can envision a cumulative indebtedness of $23,746.

CAREER INFORMATION FROM PAYSCALE.COM	
ROI Rating	88
Bachelors and No Higher	
Median starting salary	$55,000
Median mid-career salary	$100,900
At Least Bachelors	
Median starting salary	$55,800
Median mid-career salary	$103,800
Alumni with high job meaning	50%
Degrees awarded in STEM subjects	24%

SELECTIVITY	
Admissions Rating	87
# of applicants	20,768
% of applicants accepted	61
% of acceptees attending	39

FRESHMAN PROFILE	
Range SAT EBRW	560–640
Range SAT Math	550–640
Range ACT Composite	23–27
Minimum paper TOEFL	550
Minimum internet-based TOEFL	79
% graduated top 10% of class	32
% graduated top 25% of class	65
% graduated top 50% of class	88

DEADLINES	
Regular	
Priority	11/15
Deadline	6/15
Nonfall registration?	Yes

FINANCIAL FACTS	
Financial Aid Rating	80
Annual in-state tuition	$9,888
Annual out-of-state tuition	$25,338
Room and board	$9,104
Required fees	$1,002
Books and supplies	$1,300
Average frosh need-based scholarship	$9,811
Average UG need-based scholarship	$8,306
% needy frosh rec. need-based scholarship or grant aid	89
% needy UG rec. need-based scholarship or grant aid	81
% needy frosh rec. non-need-based scholarship or grant aid	5
% needy UG rec. non-need-based scholarship or grant aid	3
% needy frosh rec. need-based self-help aid	48
% needy UG rec. need-based self-help aid	59
% frosh rec. any financial aid	85
% UG rec. any financial aid	76
% UG borrow to pay for school	50
Average cumulative indebtedness	$23,746
% frosh need fully met	16
% ugrads need fully met	14
Average % of frosh need met	63
Average % of ugrad need met	60

University of Idaho

UI ADMISSIONS OFFICE, MOSCOW, ID 83844-4264 • ADMISSIONS: 208-885-6326 • FAX: 208-885-9119

CAMPUS LIFE

Quality of Life Rating	**89**
Fire Safety Rating	**89**
Green Rating	**76**
Type of school	Public
Environment	Town

STUDENTS

Total undergrad enrollment	7,685
% male/female	52/48
% from out of state	21
% frosh from public high school	90
% frosh live on campus	85
% ugrads live on campus	36
# of fraternities (% ugrad men join)	20 (22)
# of sororities (% ugrad women join)	14 (17)
% African American	1
% Asian	1
% Caucasian	74
% Hispanic	11
% Native American	1
% Pacific Islander	<1
% Two or more races	4
% Race and/or ethnicity unknown	2
% international	5
# of countries represented	57

ACADEMICS

Academic Rating	**78**
% students returning for sophomore year	82
% students graduating within 4 years	30
% students graduating within 6 years	55
Calendar	Semester
Student/faculty ratio	14:1
Profs interesting rating	76
Profs accessible rating	75

Most classes have 10–19 students. Most lab/discussion sessions have 10–19 students.

MOST POPULAR MAJORS
Mechanical Engineering; General Studies; Psychology

ABOUT THE SCHOOL

The University of Idaho is a "community oriented" institution that's wholly "dedicated to students' success." Though it's a "large" state school, Idaho is still "very personable" and able to provide "small class sizes." Academically, the university is a powerhouse when it comes to "engineering, agriculture, business, and law." And students certainly appreciate the "diverse range of degrees and programs" offered overall. They also value attending "a great research institution." Praise extends to their "knowledgeable and experienced" professors as well. By and large, undergrads here find their instructors to be "very open and welcoming." And it's clearly evident that they "really care about their students." Just as critical, "they don't want students who can suck up information and then vomit it back on a test[. T]hey want well educated students with the ability to think, not [just] memorize." Perhaps best of all, Idaho professors "are very interesting and really bring their lectures to life."

BANG FOR YOUR BUCK

Rest assured that a degree from the University of Idaho comes with an "affordable" price tag. After all, students here report that the school provides "fantastic" financial aid. Even better, Idaho makes the process fairly painless. That's because all candidates are automatically considered for scholarships; there's no separate application to fill out. What's more, the university distributes over $25 million in scholarship awards each year. These are doled out based upon merit, financial need and/or achievement in specialized fields. For example, in-state applicants are eligible for the Go! Idaho Scholarship Program which offers anywhere from $1,000-$4,000 a year. Recipients are selected based upon GPA. The university also participates in the Western Undergraduate Exchange, providing a price break to out-of-state students who hail from western states, Guam and the Commonwealth of Northern Mariana Islands. Finally, east coast and midwestern students will be considered for the Discover Idaho program, which provides students with $2,000–$8,000 each year. These scholarship amounts are also determined by GPA.

STUDENT LIFE

There's plenty of fun to be had at the University of Idaho. For starters, athletics are pretty popular and "many people participate…in intramural sports." Students also love to take advantage of the school's "wonderful state-of-the-art recreation center which includes several gymnasiums, an indoor running track, exercise equipment, and the tallest indoor rock climbing wall in the Northwest." Moreover, the university is a paradise for outdoor enthusiasts. We're told that "there are [a handful of] places…to go hiking, rock climbing, kayaking, etc." and "many nearby waterways which are nice for fishing and swimming." A large number of students participate in fraternities and sororities as well. And most weekends "the Greek community [hosts] a philanthropic event…that anyone is welcome to attend." And, of course, "there are many student organizations people can join that focus on their preferred activities (chess, video games, Harry Potter, ballroom dancing, etc)." In other words, Idaho offers something for everyone.

University of Idaho

FINANCIAL AID: 208-885-6312 • E-MAIL: ADMISSIONS@UIDAHO.EDU • WEBSITE: WWW.UIDAHO.EDU

CAREER

Simply put, the University of Idaho has "great job placement rates." Of course, this should probably be expected given that the school provides students with numerous "networking opportunities." For example, Career Services hosts multiple job fairs every year. These events bring hundreds of employers to campus. As one thrilled undergrad explains, "Being here at UI, I've had the chance to meet many people in [my prospective] industry, which helped me land an internship at NASA JPL this past summer." Beyond networking, students can turn to Career Services for interview tips and tricks, salary and benefit negotiations, help crafting cover letters and even career assessment tests.

GENERAL INFO

Activities: Campus Ministries; Choral groups; Concert band; Dance; Drama/theater; International Student Organization; Jazz band; Literary magazine; Marching band; Model UN; Music ensembles; Musical theater; Opera; Pep band; Radio station; Student government; Student newspaper; Student-run film society; Symphony orchestra; Television station 190 registered organizations, 13 honor societies, 20 religious organizations. 18 fraternities, 9 sororities. **Athletics (Intercollegiate):** *Men:* basketball, cross-country, football, golf, track/field (outdoor), track/field (indoor). *Women:* basketball, cross-country, golf, soccer, swimming, track/field (outdoor), track/field (indoor), volleyball. **On-Campus Highlights:** Idaho Commons -common areas, food and meeting rooms, Student Recreation Center, Bruce M. Pitman Center, Kibbie Dome—athletics, Integrated Research and Innovation Center.

FINANCIAL AID

Students should submit: FAFSA. Priority filing deadline is 12/1. The Princeton Review suggests that all financial aid forms be submitted as soon as possible after October 1. *Need-based scholarships/grants offered:* College/university scholarship or grant aid from institutional funds, Federal Pell, private scholarships, SEOG, state scholarships/grants. *Loan aid offered:* Direct PLUS Loans, Direct Subsidized Loans, Direct Unsubsidized Loans. Applicants will be notified of awards on a rolling basis beginning 12/20. Federal Work-Study Program available. Institutional employment available.

THE BOTTOM LINE

The University of Idaho is an incredible deal for both residents of Idaho and those who would like to spend their formative years in the Gem state.

CAREER INFORMATION FROM PAYSCALE.COM	
ROI Rating	87
Bachelors and No Higher	
Median starting salary	$51,300
Median mid-career salary	$95,200
At Least Bachelors	
Median starting salary	$52,400
Median mid-career salary	$97,900
Alumni with high job meaning	54%
Degrees awarded in STEM subjects	22%

SELECTIVITY	
Admissions Rating	81
# of applicants	7,087
% of applicants accepted	73
% of acceptees attending	30

FRESHMAN PROFILE	
Range SAT EBRW	510–620
Range SAT Math	500–610
Range ACT Composite	20–26
Minimum paper TOEFL	525
Minimum internet-based TOEFL	70
Average HS GPA	3.4
% graduated top 10% of class	20
% graduated top 25% of class	42
% graduated top 50% of class	74

DEADLINES	
Regular	
Priority	2/15
Deadline	8/1
Nonfall registration?	Yes

FINANCIAL FACTS	
Financial Aid Rating	86
Annual in-state tuition	$5,778
Annual out-of-state tuition	$23,414
Room and board	$8,880
Required fees	$2,086
Books and supplies	$1,292
Average frosh need-based scholarship	$4,537
Average UG need-based scholarship	$4,596
% needy frosh rec. need-based scholarship or grant aid	61
% needy UG rec. need-based scholarship or grant aid	69
% needy frosh rec. non-need-based scholarship or grant aid	84
% needy UG rec. non-need-based scholarship or grant aid	63
% needy frosh rec. need-based self-help aid	75
% needy UG rec. need-based self-help aid	74
% frosh rec. any financial aid	90
% UG rec. any financial aid	80
% UG borrow to pay for school	59
Average cumulative indebtedness	$25,145
% frosh need fully met	34
% ugrads need fully met	32
Average % of frosh need met	80
Average % of ugrad need met	78

University of Illinois at Urbana-Champaign

901 WEST ILLINOIS STREET, URBANA, IL 61801 • ADMISSIONS: 217-333-0302 • FAX: 217-244-0903

CAMPUS LIFE

Quality of Life Rating	84
Fire Safety Rating	60*
Green Rating	98
Type of school	Public
Environment	City

STUDENTS

Total undergrad enrollment	32,752
% male/female	55/45
% from out of state	14
% frosh live on campus	99
% ugrads live on campus	50
# of fraternities (% ugrad men join)	NR (21)
# of sororities (% ugrad women join)	NR (27)
% African American	6
% Asian	18
% Caucasian	47
% Hispanic	10
% Native American	<1
% Pacific Islander	<1
% Two or more races	3
% Race and/or ethnicity unknown	<1
% international	16
# of countries represented	90

ACADEMICS

Academic Rating	74
% students returning for sophomore year	94
Calendar	Semester
Profs interesting rating	69
Profs accessible rating	72

Most classes have 10–19 students. Most lab/discussion sessions have 20–29 students.

ABOUT THE SCHOOL

In many ways, the flagship campus of the University of Illinois at Urbana-Champaign is the prototypical large, state-funded research university. It's hard to get admitted, but not too hard; however, it does stand apart. The admissions office reviews every candidate individually, which is rare. The library is stellar, and the amazing research resources are practically endless. With seventeen colleges and about 150 undergraduate programs to offer, students have a wide range of options, but even the best professors aren't going to hold your hand, and lower-level class sizes are mostly lectures filled with students. Despite this, many students agree that the professors are incredibly passionate and intelligent. Incredibly, nearly all faculty have PhDs. The engineering and business schools are the most prestigious and, therefore, offer the most competition. Agriculture, architecture, and psychology are also quite well respected.

University of Illinois is a magnet for engineering and sciences research. "The research resources are amazing," one pleased undergrad enthuses. Another student relates that "the library has almost any resource an undergraduate or even an advanced researcher would ever need." The university has been a leader in computer-based education and hosted the PLATO project, which was a precursor to the Internet and resulted in the development of the plasma display. That legacy of leading computer-based education and research continues today—Microsoft hires more graduates from the University of Illinois than from any other university in the world. The University of Illinois media organization (the Illini Media Co.) is also quite extensive, featuring a student newspaper that isn't censored by the administration since it receives no direct funding from it.

BANG FOR YOUR BUCK

The University of Illinois provides an incredibly wide array of undergraduate programs at a great price. A large percentage of the student population receives some form of financial assistance. The usual set of work-study, loans, and need-based grants is available, of course, along with a bounty of private and institutional scholarships. The school confers more than 1,500 individual merit-based scholarships each year. These awards vary considerably in value, and they are available to students who excel in academics, art, athletics, drama, leadership, music, and pretty much anything else. Alumni scholarships are available, too, if someone in your family is a graduate of U of I. There's an online scholarship database at Illinois's website that is definitely worth perusing. Application procedures vary, and so do the deadline dates.

STUDENT LIFE

The University of Illinois at Urbana-Champaign has a decidedly Midwestern feel. "Kids from out-of-state and small-town farm students" definitely have a presence, but, sometimes, it seems like "practically everyone is from the northwest suburbs of Chicago." There's a lot of ethnic diversity "visible on campus." On the whole, the majority of students are "very smart kids who like to party." "They really study fairly hard, and when you ask, it turns out that they're majoring in something like rocket science." One student notes that "students fit in through about 1,000 different ways. They find work friends, classmates, group members in an organization, you name it." A media studies student notes that "the townie culture here is what gets me. The bars in downtown Champaign are great and super relaxed, plus there is an awesome music scene that most people don't expect from a college town."

University of Illinois at Urbana-Champaign

FINANCIAL AID: 217-333-0100 • E-MAIL: UGRADADMISSIONS@UIUC.EDU • WEBSITE: WWW.ILLINOIS.EDU

CAREER

The typical University of Illinois at Urbana-Champaign graduate has a starting salary of around $58,600, and 46 percent report that their job has a great deal of meaning. Students feel that "you can't get any better alumni networking and leadership opportunities than you do at UIUC." Many students feel that "there are a lot of UIUC alumni in agencies" that they want to work for. Students applaud "the availability of highly regarded finance internships and full-time opportunities." The Career Center at Illinois offers multiple job fairs for several different sorts of careers and majors as well as other excellent resources like the job board I-Link and drop-in career counseling.

GENERAL INFO

Activities: Choral groups, concert band, dance, drama/theater, jazz band, literary magazine, marching band, music ensembles, musical theater, opera, pep band, radio station, student government, student newspaper, student-run film society, symphony orchestra, television station, yearbook, campus ministries, international student organization. **Organizations:** 1,000 registered organizations, 30 honor societies, 95 religious organizations. 60 fraternities, 36 sororities. **Athletics (Intercollegiate):** *Men:* Baseball, basketball, cheerleading, cross-country, football, golf, gymnastics, tennis, track/field (outdoor), wrestling. *Women:* Basketball, cheerleading, cross-country, diving, golf, gymnastics, soccer, softball, swimming, tennis, track/field (outdoor), volleyball. **On-Campus Highlights:** Campus Town restaurants and shops, Krannert Center for Performing Arts, Assembly Hall, Multiple Campus Recreation Centers, Illini Student Union, on-campus Arboretum; The Japan House; extensive athletic facilities; historic round barns; Siebel Computer Science Center; spacious green space at the Central and Bardeen Quads; Papa Dels Pizza and Za's Italian Cafe.

FINANCIAL AID

Students should submit: FAFSA. Priority filing deadline is 3/15. The Princeton Review suggests that all financial aid forms be submitted as soon as possible after October 1. *Need-based scholarships/grants offered:* College/university scholarship or grant aid from institutional funds; Federal Pell; Private scholarships; SEOG; State scholarships/grants; United Negro College Fund. *Loan aid offered:* Direct PLUS Loans, Direct Subsidized Loans, Direct Unsubsidized Loans. Applicants will be notified of awards on a rolling basis beginning 3/10. Federal Work-Study Program available. Institutional employment available.

THE BOTTOM LINE

The University of Illinois requires all first-year undergraduate students (who do not commute) to live on campus. The cost for a year of tuition, fees, room and board, and basic expenses averages $26,708 for Illinois residents. For nonresidents, the average is about $41,868. The average student indebtedness upon graduation is $25,448. Around three-quarters of students are recipients of financial aid; the average need-based gift aid comes to nearly $13,700.

CAREER INFORMATION FROM PAYSCALE.COM	
ROI Rating	89
Bachelors and No Higher	
Median starting salary	$61,000
Median mid-career salary	$113,800
At Least Bachelors	
Median starting salary	$62,400
Median mid-career salary	$119,700
Alumni with high job meaning	45%
Degrees awarded in STEM subjects	36%

SELECTIVITY	
Admissions Rating	89
# of applicants	38,093
% of applicants accepted	60
% of acceptees attending	33
# offered a place on the wait list	2,846
% accepting a place on wait list	74
% admitted from wait list	17

FRESHMAN PROFILE	
Range ACT Composite	26–32
% graduated top 10% of class	49
% graduated top 25% of class	82
% graduated top 50% of class	99

DEADLINES	
Early action	
Deadline	11/1
Notification	12/16
Regular	
Priority	11/1
Deadline	12/1
Nonfall registration?	No

FINANCIAL FACTS	
Financial Aid Rating	77
Annual in-state tuition	$12,036
Annual out-of-state tuition	$27,658
Room and board	$11,308
Required fees	$3,832
Books and supplies	$1,200
Average frosh need-based scholarship	$14,652
Average UG need-based scholarship	$14,244
% needy frosh rec. need-based scholarship or grant aid	81
% needy UG rec. need-based scholarship or grant aid	64
% needy frosh rec. non-need-based scholarship or grant aid	17
% needy UG rec. non-need-based scholarship or grant aid	8
% needy frosh rec. need-based self-help aid	74
% needy UG rec. need-based self-help aid	60
% UG borrow to pay for school	47
Average cumulative indebtedness	$25,222
% frosh need fully met	14
% ugrads need fully met	12
Average % of frosh need met	67
Average % of ugrad need met	65

University of Maryland—College Park

MITCHELL BUILDING, COLLEGE PARK, MD 20742-5235 • ADMISSIONS: 301-314-8385 • FAX: 301-314-9693

CAMPUS LIFE

Quality of Life Rating	**69**
Fire Safety Rating	**90**
Green Rating	**93**
Type of school	Public
Environment	Metropolis

STUDENTS

Total undergrad enrollment	29,273
% male/female	53/47
% from out of state	22
% frosh live on campus	92
% ugrads live on campus	41
# of fraternities (% ugrad men join)	32 (15)
# of sororities (% ugrad women join)	24 (20)
% African American	12
% Asian	17
% Caucasian	50
% Hispanic	10
% Native American	<1
% Pacific Islander	<1
% Two or more races	4
% Race and/or ethnicity unknown	1
% international	5
# of countries represented	63

ACADEMICS

Academic Rating	**68**
% students returning for sophomore year	96
% students graduating within 4 years	67
% students graduating within 6 years	85
Calendar	Semester
Student/faculty ratio	18:1
Profs interesting rating	64
Profs accessible rating	61

Most classes have 10–19 students. Most lab/discussion sessions have 20–29 students.

MOST POPULAR MAJORS

Biology/Biological Sciences; Criminology; Economics

ABOUT THE SCHOOL

The University of Maryland—College Park is a big school. There are many different people from various backgrounds, as well as numerous student organizations on campus. Some incoming freshmen might find this intimidating, but thanks to the university's system of living-and-learning communities, which allows students with similar academic interests to live in the same residential community, take specialized courses, and perform research; this campus of almost 27,000 can feel a lot smaller and more intimate than it actually is. UMD offers a "top-notch honors program" for academically talented students, which offers special access and opportunities with a community of intellectually gifted peers. More than 100 undergraduate degrees are on offer here, and the university's location near Washington, D.C. means that top-notch research and internship opportunities are literally in your backyard. The university recently received funding from the Department of Homeland Security to create a new research center to study the behavioral and social foundations of terrorism. It's no surprise then that UMD's political science program is strong. A well-respected business program, top-ranked criminology program, and solid engineering school are also available. The school is also extremely invested in promoting sustainability across the university curriculum, and developing a sustainability ethic in campus culture.

BANG FOR YOUR BUCK

University of Maryland—College Park offers a comprehensive aid program for students who demonstrate financial need. But it's the university's full suite of merit-based scholarships that make a UMD degree an exceptional value. Highlights include the Banneker/Key Scholarship, the university's most prestigious merit scholarship, which may cover up to the full the cost of tuition, mandatory fees, room and board, and a book allowance each year for four years. The President's Scholarship provides four-year awards of up to $12,000 per year to exceptional entering freshmen. Maryland Pathways is a new financial assistance program set up by the university to assist low-income families by reducing the debt component and increasing grants to those who receive it. National Merit, creative and performing arts, and departmental scholarships are also available. To be considered for most merit scholarships, entering freshmen applying for the fall semester must submit their complete application for undergraduate admission by the priority deadline of November 1. The eligibility requirements for each scholarship vary. Award notifications begin in early March.

STUDENT LIFE

"The University of Maryland is a very large school," so "there is no 'typical' student here. Everyone will find that they can fit in somewhere." UMD is "an especially diverse school," and this makes people "more tolerant and accepting of people from different backgrounds and cultures." A student from New Jersey explains it this way: "Coming from a very diverse area, I thought it was going to be hard to find a school that had that same representation of minority and atypical students until I found Maryland. I don't think I have ever learned so much about different religions, cultures, orientations, or lifestyles. All of them are accepted and even celebrated" at UMD.

University of Maryland—College Park

FINANCIAL AID: 301-314-9000 • E-MAIL: UM-ADMIT@UGA.UMD.EDU • WEBSITE: WWW.MARYLAND.EDU

CAREER

The President's Promise initiative is the cornerstone of UMD's career philosophy, which focuses on helping students to articulate classroom learning in real-world settings. In cooperation with the comprehensive University Career Center, President's Promise connects students with career exposure and experiential learning opportunities (internships, job shadowing, service learning, study abroad, and research) in ways that complement the academic curriculum. One program, the Bright Futures Fund, supports unpaid interns with awards that range from $250 to $1,250. Opportunities to work with nearby federal agencies and labs, such as NASA's Goddard Space Flight Center and the National Institute of Standards and Technology, abound. More than 1,200 employers participate in UMD's career fairs annually or visit for on-campus interviews and networking events. Alumni who visited PayScale.com report a median starting salary of $57,600, and 50 percent derive a high level of meaning from their work.

GENERAL INFO

Activities: Choral groups, concert band, dance, drama/theater, jazz band, literary magazine, marching band, music ensembles, musical theater, opera, pep band, radio station, student government. **Organizations:** 724 registered organizations, 49 honor societies, 55 religious organizations. 32 fraternities, 24 sororities. **Athletics (Intercollegiate):** *Men:* Baseball, basketball, football, golf, lacrosse, soccer, track/field (outdoor), track/field (indoor), wrestling. *Women:* Basketball, cross-country, field hockey, golf, gymnastics, lacrosse, soccer, softball, swimming, tennis, track/field (outdoor), track/field (indoor), volleyball.

FINANCIAL AID

Students should submit: FAFSA. Priority filing deadline is 2/15. The Princeton Review suggests that all financial aid forms be submitted as soon as possible after October 1. *Need-based scholarships/grants offered:* College/university scholarship or grant aid from institutional funds, Federal Pell, private scholarships, SEOG, state scholarships/grants. *Loan aid offered:* Direct PLUS Loans, Direct Subsidized Loans, Direct Unsubsidized Loans. Applicants will be notified of awards on a rolling basis beginning 4/1. Federal Work-Study Program available. Institutional employment available.

THE BOTTOM LINE

College costs may be on the upswing, but the cost of an education at the University of Maryland—College Park is still a very good deal. Tuition and fees for Maryland residents comes to just $10,595 drawing in many from around the area; though nonresidents can expect to pay three times as much. All students who decide to live on campus can expect to pay an additional $12,429 in room and board. When you factor in the cost of books and supplies, the total cost of a UMD degree is $23,024 for all those who hail from the state, and $47,645 for those who don't.

CAREER INFORMATION FROM PAYSCALE.COM	
ROI Rating	89
Bachelors and No Higher	
Median starting salary	$60,000
Median mid-career salary	$109,700
At Least Bachelors	
Median starting salary	$61,300
Median mid-career salary	$113,800
Alumni with high job meaning	51%
Degrees awarded in STEM subjects	33%

SELECTIVITY	
Admissions Rating	94
# of applicants	33,907
% of applicants accepted	44
% of acceptees attending	27

FRESHMAN PROFILE	
Range SAT EBRW	640–720
Range SAT Math	650–750
Range ACT Composite	29–33
Minimum internet-based TOEFL	100
Average HS GPA	4.3
% graduated top 10% of class	72
% graduated top 25% of class	90
% graduated top 50% of class	99

DEADLINES	
Early action	
Deadline	11/1
Notification	1/31
Regular	
Priority	11/1
Deadline	1/20
Notification	4/1
Nonfall registration?	Yes

FINANCIAL FACTS	
Financial Aid Rating	80
Annual in-state tuition	$8,651
Annual out-of-state tuition	$33,272
Room and board	$12,429
Required fees	$1,944
Books and supplies	$1,250
Average frosh need-based scholarship	$10,122
Average UG need-based scholarship	$9,978
% needy frosh rec. need-based scholarship or grant aid	76
% needy UG rec. need-based scholarship or grant aid	76
% needy frosh rec. non-need-based scholarship or grant aid	10
% needy UG rec. non-need-based scholarship or grant aid	5
% needy frosh rec. need-based self-help aid	86
% needy UG rec. need-based self-help aid	92
% frosh rec. any financial aid	86
% UG rec. any financial aid	72
% UG borrow to pay for school	42
Average cumulative indebtedness	$28,122
% frosh need fully met	19
% ugrads need fully met	16
Average % of frosh need met	64
Average % of ugrad need met	66

University of Massachusetts Amherst

UNIVERSITY ADMISSIONS CENTER, AMHERST, MA 01003-9291 • ADMISSIONS: 413-545-0222 • FAX: 413-545-4312

CAMPUS LIFE

Quality of Life Rating	**89**
Fire Safety Rating	**93**
Green Rating	**98**
Type of school	Public
Environment	Town

STUDENTS

Total undergrad enrollment	23,010
% male/female	50/50
% from out of state	18
% frosh live on campus	99
% ugrads live on campus	61
# of fraternities (% ugrad men join)	23 (9)
# of sororities (% ugrad women join)	14 (9)
% African American	4
% Asian	10
% Caucasian	64
% Hispanic	6
% Native American	<1
% Pacific Islander	<1
% Two or more races	3
% Race and/or ethnicity unknown	6
% international	6
# of countries represented	78

ACADEMICS

Academic Rating	**79**
% students returning for sophomore year	91
% students graduating within 4 years	67
% students graduating within 6 years	77
Calendar	Semester
Student/faculty ratio	17:1
Profs interesting rating	74
Profs accessible rating	68

Most classes have 10–19 students. Most lab/discussion sessions have 20–29 students.

MOST POPULAR MAJORS
Biology/Biological Sciences; Psychology; Finance

ABOUT THE SCHOOL

University of Massachusetts Amherst is one of the East Coast's most highly-regarded public research universities, with students enjoying the resources of a major university while living in a quintessential college town. With more than 100 academic majors, including the opportunity to create a customized major, students have "a lot of opportunity and wiggle room for students who don't know what they want to be when they are older." rofessors are "very approachable and take a sincere interest in the students, and they "understand the stresses" inherent in undergraduate life. A surge of construction in recent years provides students with state-of-the-art facilities for living and learning. As part of the undergraduate admissions process, the highest academically achieving students are invited to join the Commonwealth Honors College, which includes a nationally recognized residential complex. The university is also part of the Five College Interchange, which allows students to broaden their course offerings by taking classes at nearby Amherst College, Hampshire, Mount Holyoke, and Smith Colleges. All in all, this is a driven university with "a great amount of resources looking for their diverse and unique student body to excel in the world."

BANG FOR YOUR BUCK

UMass Amherst "has so many resources and reasons for so many of us to be here," according to students. This is an "affordable education in a caring, inclusive environment," and the school does everything it can to fill the gap between a family's ability to pay for school and actual costs. Most students here receive some form of financial aid, and both need- and merit-based scholarships are available. Chancellor's, Director's and Dean's Scholarships and Awards are for students with high academic and personal achievement, and the Flagship and the Community Scholarships and Awards are for applicants who are low income and/or who are first generation college students.

STUDENT LIFE

With around 23,000 undergraduates, diversity is baked into UMass life in terms of both background and interests, and campus is full of "accepting students" who "embrace individuality." People are very active here. Undergads fill their days with "studying, intramural [sports], and hanging out with friends," and in the winter months you'll find students "outside sledding." Most are members of one or more of the 400+ clubs and organizations present on campus and represent UMass Amherst with pride: "Lots of students wear our colors and are proud of where we come from." Defined Residential Communities (DRCs) are open to students who want to live with friends and hall mates who share similar interests, backgrounds, and identities. Sustainability is big here, and "everyone is very passionate about their causes."

CAREER

The Career Services department provides all the standard guidance and tools (including job and career fairs, advising, and workshops), as well as several online tools to help make the search easier. The UMass Amherst Alumni Advisor Network is a platform that allows undergraduates access to mentorship and advice from alumni in their fields of choice, and the CareerConnect 3.0 Jobs and Internships Database helps connect student with open opportunities. Most alumni are "very helpful to UMass graduates," and a majority are in the New England and New York area so "finding and getting a job is immediately easier than a smaller university." Of the University of Massachusetts Amherst alumni visiting PayScale.com, 46 percent report that they derive a high level of meaning from their jobs.

University of Massachusetts Amherst

FINANCIAL AID: 413-545-0801 • E-MAIL: MAIL@ADMISSIONS.UMASS.EDU • WEBSITE: WWW.UMASS.EDU

GENERAL INFO

Activities: Choral groups, concert band, dance, drama/theater, jazz band, literary magazine, marching band, music ensembles, musical theater, opera, pep band, radio station, student government, student newspaper, student-run film society, symphony orchestra, television station. **Organizations:** campus ministries, International Student Organization, Model UN. **Organizations:** 488 registered organizations, 37 honor societies, 25 religious organizations. 23 fraternities, 14 sororities. **Athletics (Intercollegiate):** *Men:* baseball, basketball, cross-country, diving, football, ice hockey, lacrosse, soccer, swimming, track/field (outdoor), track/field (indoor). *Women:* basketball, crew/rowing, cross-country, diving, field hockey, lacrosse, soccer, softball, swimming, tennis, track/field (outdoor), track/field (indoor). **On-Campus Highlights:** The Campus Center / Student Union, The Learning Commons, Recreation Center, The Mullins Center, The Fine Arts Center. **Environmental Initiatives:** Student-led effort resulted in first major public university to divest from direct fossil fuel holdings; new School of Earth and Sustainability; nationally recognized leader for using local food sources, recycling efforts, and clean and efficient energy infrastructure.

FINANCIAL AID

Students should submit: FAFSA. Priority filing deadline is 3/1. The Princeton Review suggests that all financial aid forms be submitted as soon as possible after October 1. *Need-based scholarships/grants offered:* College/university scholarship or grant aid from institutional funds, Federal Pell, private scholarships, SEOG, state scholarships/grants. *Loan aid offered:* Direct PLUS Loans, Direct Subsidized Loans, Direct Unsubsidized Loans. Applicants will be notified of awards on a rolling basis beginning 12/15. Federal Work-Study Program available. Institutional employment available.

BOTTOM LINE

In-state residents pay a tuition of $15,406, while out-of-staters pay $34,089; the annual average room and board cost is $13,202. Several schools within UMass Amherst have additional fees. Legal residents of other New England states (including Connecticut, New Hampshire, Maine, Rhode Island, and Vermont) may also qualify for a reduced tuition rate for specific majors. Aid is also available to students who wish to take courses over the summer or study abroad.

CAREER INFORMATION FROM PAYSCALE.COM

ROI Rating	88
Bachelors and No Higher	
Median starting salary	$55,800
Median mid-career salary	$102,000
At Least Bachelors	
Median starting salary	$57,000
Median mid-career salary	$105,400
Alumni with high job meaning	46%
Degrees awarded in STEM subjects	23%

SELECTIVITY

Admissions Rating	87
# of applicants	41,922
% of applicants accepted	57
% of acceptees attending	20
# offered a place on the wait list	6,736
% accepting a place on wait list	23
% admitted from wait list	3

FRESHMAN PROFILE

Range SAT EBRW	590–670
Range SAT Math	590–690
Range ACT Composite	26–31
Minimum internet-based TOEFL	80
Average HS GPA	3.9
% graduated top 10% of class	34
% graduated top 25% of class	73
% graduated top 50% of class	97

DEADLINES

Early action	
Deadline	11/1
Regular	
Deadline	1/15
Nonfall registration?	Yes

FINANCIAL FACTS

Financial Aid Rating	83
Annual in-state tuition	$15,406
Annual out-of-state tuition	$34,089
Room and board	$13,202
Required fees	$481
Average frosh need-based scholarship	$10,965
Average UG need-based scholarship	$10,708
% needy frosh rec. need-based scholarship or grant aid	93
% needy UG rec. need-based scholarship or grant aid	88
% needy frosh rec. non-need-based scholarship or grant aid	9
% needy UG rec. non-need-based scholarship or grant aid	7
% needy frosh rec. need-based self-help aid	88
% needy UG rec. need-based self-help aid	90
% frosh rec. any financial aid	88
% UG rec. any financial aid	90
% UG borrow to pay for school	68
Average cumulative indebtedness	$31,860
% frosh need fully met	14
% ugrads need fully met	14
Average % of frosh need met	83
Average % of ugrad need met	86

University of Michigan—Ann Arbor

1220 STUDENT ACTIVITIES BUILDING, ANN ARBOR, MI 48109-1316 • ADMISSIONS: 734-764-7433 • FAX: 734-936-0740

CAMPUS LIFE

Quality of Life Rating	90
Fire Safety Rating	88
Green Rating	90
Type of school	Public
Environment	City

STUDENTS

Total undergrad enrollment	29,550
% male/female	50/50
% from out of state	41
% frosh live on campus	98
% ugrads live on campus	32
# of fraternities (% ugrad men join)	41 (17)
# of sororities (% ugrad women join)	26 (25)
% African American	4
% Asian	14
% Caucasian	61
% Hispanic	6
% Native American	<1
% Pacific Islander	<1
% Two or more races	4
% Race and/or ethnicity unknown	4
% international	7
# of countries represented	92

ACADEMICS

Academic Rating	85
% students returning for sophomore year	97
% students graduating within 4 years	77
% students graduating within 6 years	92
Calendar	Trimester
Student/faculty ratio	15:1
Profs interesting rating	70
Profs accessible rating	72

Most classes have 10–19 students. Most lab/discussion sessions have 20–29 students.

MOST POPULAR MAJORS

Computer Science; Business Administration and Management; Psychology

ABOUT THE SCHOOL

The University of Michigan—Ann Arbor is a big school with big opportunities, and we do mean big. The university has a multibillion-dollar endowment and one of the largest research expenditures of any American university, also in the billions. Its physical campus includes more than 34 million square feet of building space, and its football stadium is the largest college football stadium in the country. With more than 28,000 undergraduates, the scale of the University of Michigan's stellar offerings truly is overwhelming. But for those students who can handle the "first-class education in a friendly, competitive atmosphere," there are a lot of advantages to attending a university of this size and stature, and they will find "a great environment both academically and socially." You get an amazing breadth of classes, excellent professors, a "wide range of travel abroad opportunities," unparalleled research opportunities, and inroads into an alumni network that can offer you entry into any number of postgraduate opportunities. The school "provides every kind of opportunity at all times to all people," and students here get "the opportunity to go far within their respective concentrations."

BANG FOR YOUR BUCK

UM spent $351 million in 2015–16 on total undergraduate need-based and merit-aid. That is truly staggering and reflects an amount more than the total endowment of many schools. Students who are Pell-grant eligible may benefit from UM's debt-elimination programs. All in-state students can expect to have 100 percent of their demonstrated need met. The Go Blue Guarantee will cover full tuition for students whose family income is less than $65,000. The university's schools, colleges, and departments administer their own scholarship programs, so you should feel free to check with them directly. UM's Office of Financial Aid also administers a variety of scholarship programs that recognize superior academic achievement, leadership qualities, and potential contribution to the scholarly community. The majority of these scholarships are awarded automatically to eligible students. A full list of UM scholarships is available on the university's website. In addition to the scholarship programs offered by the school, there are also private scholarships available to prospective students. These are offered by a variety of corporate, professional, trade, governmental, civic, religious, social and fraternal organizations. While these applications can be time consuming, they can be worth it. Some are worth thousands of dollars. The University of Michigan has a full list of these scholarships—and their deadlines—on their website. The school is dedicated to helping prospective students gain a better understanding of how to pay for their education by providing access to financial aid counselors. Their website also features an application called M-Calc, a net price calculator, which allows students and their families to access an early estimate of the full-time cost of attendance the University of Michigan.

STUDENT LIFE

The Michigan student body is "hugely diverse," which "is one of the things Michigan prides itself on." There is a place for everyone here, because "there are hundreds of mini-communities within the campus, made of everything from service fraternities to political organizations to dance groups." As one undergrad puts it, "That's part of the benefit of 40,000-plus students!" Students also rave about "great programs like UMix...phenomenal cultural opportunities in Ann Arbor especially music and movies," and "the hugely popular football Saturdays. The sense of school spirit here is impressive." With over 1,200 registered student organizations on campus, "if you have an interest, you can find a group of people who enjoy the same thing."

University of Michigan—Ann Arbor

FINANCIAL AID: 734-763-6600 • WEBSITE: WWW.UMICH.EDU

CAREER

The Career Center offers a wealth of resources to students learning to be advocates for themselves post-graduation. The massive fall Career Fair jumpstarts the process for job-seekers (the Career Center even offers a smartphone App for navigating the floor plan), and the semester schedule is packed with programs and workshops like Career Crawls, which focus on themes such as choosing a major, or Immersions, a program which hosts half-day visits to an organization's workplace. Career Center Connector lists tons of job and internship opportunities while Alumni Profiles provide glimpses into grad's career choices and job search strategies. Other structured programs, like the Public Service Intern Program, link students with internship openings in the U.S. and abroad. Graduates who visited PayScale. com report an average starting salary of $59,300, and 46 percent believe that their jobs make the world a better place.

GENERAL INFO

Activities: Choral groups, concert band, dance, drama/theater, ethnic/environmental/gender groups, intramural sports, jazz band, literary magazine, marching band, music ensembles, musical theater, opera, pep band, radio station, social activism, student government. **Organizations:** >1,200 registered organizations, 31 honor societies, 98 religious organizations. 41 fraternities, 26 sororities. **Athletics (Intercollegiate):** *Men:* Baseball, basketball, cross-country, diving, football, golf, gymnastics, ice hockey, lacrosse, soccer, swimming, tennis, track/field (outdoor), track/field (indoor), wrestling. *Women:* Basketball, crew/rowing, cross-country, diving, field hockey, golf, gymnastics, lacrosse, soccer, softball, swimming, tennis, track/field (outdoor), track/field (indoor), volleyball, water polo.

FINANCIAL AID

Students should submit: CSS Profile; FAFSA. Priority filing deadline is 3/1. The Princeton Review suggests that all financial aid forms be submitted as soon as possible after October 1. *Need-based scholarships/grants offered:* College/university scholarship or grant aid from institutional funds, Federal Pell, private scholarships, SEOG, state scholarships/grants. *Loan aid offered:* Direct PLUS Loans, Direct Subsidized Loans, Direct Unsubsidized Loans. Applicants will be notified of awards on a rolling basis beginning 3/15. Federal Work-Study Program available. Institutional employment available.

BOTTOM LINE

UM's top-of-the-line education and comparatively low tuition make this school the definition of a best value. For Michigan residents, the estimated total cost of attendance for one year is about $28,807, including tuition, fees, room and board, books and supplies. For nonresidents, the price is roughly double the in-state rate at $63,664.

CAREER INFORMATION FROM PAYSCALE.COM	
ROI Rating	91
Bachelors and No Higher	
Median starting salary	$62,000
Median mid-career salary	$107,900
At Least Bachelors	
Median starting salary	$63,800
Median mid-career salary	$115,200
Alumni with high job meaning	45%
Degrees awarded in STEM subjects	38%

SELECTIVITY	
Admissions Rating	96
# of applicants	59,886
% of applicants accepted	27
% of acceptees attending	43
# offered a place on the wait list	11,127
% accepting a place on wait list	37
% admitted from wait list	11

FRESHMAN PROFILE	
Range SAT EBRW	660–730
Range SAT Math	670–770
Range ACT Composite	30–33
Minimum paper TOEFL	600
Minimum internet-based TOEFL	100
Average HS GPA	3.9

DEADLINES	
Early action	
Deadline	11/1
Notification	12/24
Regular	
Priority	11/1
Deadline	2/1
Nonfall registration?	Yes

FINANCIAL FACTS	
Financial Aid Rating	88
Annual in-state tuition	$15,897
Annual out-of-state tuition	$50,754
Room and board	$11,534
Required fees	$328
Books and supplies	$1,048
Average frosh need-based scholarship	$19,099
Average UG need-based scholarship	$19,648
% needy frosh rec. need-based scholarship or grant aid	78
% needy UG rec. need-based scholarship or grant aid	80
% needy frosh rec. non-need-based scholarship or grant aid	72
% needy UG rec. non-need-based scholarship or grant aid	64
% needy frosh rec. need-based self-help aid	69
% needy UG rec. need-based self-help aid	77
% frosh rec. any financial aid	71
% UG rec. any financial aid	62
% UG borrow to pay for school	41
Average cumulative indebtedness	$25,712
% frosh need fully met	72
% ugrads need fully met	78
Average % of frosh need met	92
Average % of ugrad need met	93

University of Minnesota, Twin Cities

240 Williamson Hall, 231 Pillsbury Drive SE, Minneapolis, MN 55455-0213 • Admissions: 612-625-2008

CAMPUS LIFE
Quality of Life Rating	89
Fire Safety Rating	88
Green Rating	94
Type of school	Public
Environment	Metropolis

STUDENTS
Total undergrad enrollment	31,535
% male/female	48/52
% from out of state	27
% frosh live on campus	88
% ugrads live on campus	23
# of fraternities	31
# of sororities	12
% African American	5
% Asian	10
% Caucasian	68
% Hispanic	4
% Native American	<1
% Pacific Islander	<1
% Two or more races	4
% Race and/or ethnicity unknown	1
% international	9
# of countries represented	139

ACADEMICS
Academic Rating	81
% students returning for sophomore year	93
% students graduating within 4 years	64
% students graduating within 6 years	80
Calendar	Semester
Student/faculty ratio	17:1
Profs interesting rating	75
Profs accessible rating	72

Most classes have 20–29 students. Most lab/discussion sessions have between 10–19 students.

MOST POPULAR MAJORS
Journalism; Rhetoric and Composition; Psychology

ABOUT THE COLLEGE

The University of Minnesota, Twin Cities, offers more than 150 majors to its undergraduate student body of over 30,000. That equals a whole lot of opportunity. The university's top-ranked College of Pharmacy is complemented by exceptional programs in business and engineering. Off-the-beaten track majors are also available, as U of M has enough academic offerings to cover almost every esoteric interest you can imagine. This is a big research university, which means "there are incredible opportunities [for undergraduates] to work in ANY field of research." Instructors "enjoy teaching the material and getting to know the students personally." Qualified undergraduates may take graduate-level classes, too. It's a large school, so lower-level courses can get crowded—though freshman seminars, freshman composition, and foreign language classes are usually capped at twenty-five students or less. Study abroad opportunities here are expansive, and a good proportion of students take advantage.

BANG FOR YOUR BUCK

University of Minnesota offers a comprehensive program of need-based and merit-based aid. Each year, the incoming freshmen class receives over $25 million in academic scholarships to be used over the course of their college careers. Awards last four years, and range from $1,000–$15,000 each year. U of M offers a national scholarship program for nonresident freshmen that covers the difference between in-state and nonresident tuition. There are nine conventional residence halls, plus three new apartment-style facilities.

STUDENT LIFE

As is often the case at large schools, U of M offers a diversity of options depending on where your interests lie. "There is a lot of partying, but it can be avoided if you are not interested in it," is a sentiment echoed by many students, and both the University itself and the surrounding urban area offer many ways for students to have fun outside of class. "There are endless intramural sports, and sporting events, concerts, and different student groups and clubs that plan activities and have regular meetings," says one student, and another affirms that "there are so many events and activities on campus, it's hard to be bored." For those looking to explore, "uptown [Minneapolis] features some fantastic ethnic restaurants and kitschy shops as well as frequent art fairs and comedy clubs. Downtown features several theaters where student rates give us access to the best local performances." Students of all varieties seem to find the environment welcoming, and one raves that "we are also the most gay friendly, hipster, and bike friendly city in the nation (not to mention we're really proud of these three things)." So whatever it is you're into, at U of M you should be able to find exactly what you're looking for.

CAREER

U of M Career Services is somewhat unique in that each college has its own career center catering to the specific needs of its students. While these centers are linked through a main Career Services office, the majority of the services available at U of M, such as advising, career fairs, and job search tools, are offered through the individual colleges. As such, "academic advising and career services differ from college to college," but most students seem to be pleased with the quality of what is offered. One student reports that "my advisor and the career center are excellent guides," and another states that, "I'm always getting emails [from] the career center, all on-campus jobs offer training for finding jobs after graduation, and the information on post grad options are extremely easy to find." There are also resources available specifically for women, LGBT students, international students, and other demographic groups. According to the school, U

University of Minnesota, Twin Cities

Fax: 612-626-1693 • Financial Aid: 612-624-1111 • Website: www.umn.edu

of M alumni have founded over 19,000 companies. Out of graduates visiting PayScale.com, 52 percent report feeling as though they derive a high level of meaning from their careers.

GENERAL INFO

Activities: Choral groups, concert band, dance, drama/theater, jazz band, literary magazine, marching band, music ensembles, musical theater, opera, pep band, radio station, student government, student newspaper, student-run film society, symphony orchestra, television station, international student organization. **Organizations:** 900 registered organizations, 76 religious organizations. 22 fraternities, 12 sororities, 7 multicultural fraternities, 5 multicultural sororities. **Athletics (Intercollegiate):** *Men:* Baseball, basketball, cross-country, diving, football, golf, gymnastics, ice hockey, swimming, tennis, track/field (outdoor), track/field (indoor), wrestling. *Women:* Basketball, cheerleading, cross-country, diving, golf, gymnastics, ice hockey, soccer, softball, swimming, tennis, track/field (outdoor), track/field (indoor), volleyball. **On-Campus Highlights:** Weisman Art Museum, McNamara Alumni Center, TCF Bank Stadium, Goldstein Gallery, Northrup Memorial Auditorium, Coffman Memorial Union, Mariucci Arena, University Theater, Rarig Center, Bell Museum of Natural History.

FINANCIAL AID

Students should submit: FAFSA; Institution's own financial aid form. Priority filing deadline is 3/1. The Princeton Review suggests that all financial aid forms be submitted as soon as possible after October 1. *Need-based scholarships/grants offered:* College/university scholarship or grant aid from institutional funds, Federal Nursing Scholarships, Federal Pell, Private scholarships, SEOG, State scholarships/grants. *Loan aid offered:* Direct PLUS Loans, Direct Subsidized Loans, Direct Unsubsidized Loans. Applicants will be notified of awards on a rolling basis beginning 2/15. Federal Work-Study Program available. Institutional employment available.

THE BOTTOM LINE

Tuition and fees at the University of Minnesota—Twin Cities runs about $14,693 per year for Minnesota, North Dakota, South Dakota, and Manitoba, Wisconsin residents. Nonresidents get a pretty good deal also: they can expect to pay in the range of $26,603 a year. Room and board is an additional $10,312, bringing the total cost of attendance to $25,005 for residents and $40,683 for nonresidents. University of Minnesota also fosters both learning and frugality with its unique thirteenth-credit tuition incentive in which every credit after thirteen is free of charge, keeping costs down for families and helping students achieve graduation in four years. Students typically take fifteen to sixteen credits each semester or 120 credits over four years.

CAREER INFORMATION FROM PAYSCALE.COM	
ROI Rating	89
Bachelors and No Higher	
Median starting salary	$55,800
Median mid-career salary	$101,600
At Least Bachelors	
Median starting salary	$56,400
Median mid-career salary	$105,200
Alumni with high job meaning	52%
Degrees awarded in STEM subjects	30%

SELECTIVITY	
Admissions Rating	90
# of applicants	43,720
% of applicants accepted	50
% of acceptees attending	29

FRESHMAN PROFILE	
Range SAT EBRW	620–720
Range SAT Math	650–760
Range ACT Composite	26–31
Minimum internet-based TOEFL	79
% graduated top 10% of class	50
% graduated top 25% of class	84
% graduated top 50% of class	99

DEADLINES	
Regular	
Priority	11/1
Notification	3/31
Nonfall registration?	Yes

FINANCIAL FACTS	
Financial Aid Rating	82
Annual in-state tuition	$13,058
Annual out-of-state tuition	$28,736
Room and board	$10,312
Required fees	$1,635
Room and board	NR
Average frosh need-based scholarship	$11,119
Average UG need-based scholarship	$10,444
% needy frosh rec. need-based scholarship or grant aid	86
% needy UG rec. need-based scholarship or grant aid	85
% needy frosh rec. non-need-based scholarship or grant aid	9
% needy UG rec. non-need-based scholarship or grant aid	7
% needy frosh rec. need-based self-help aid	79
% needy UG rec. need-based self-help aid	77
% UG borrow to pay for school	58
Average cumulative indebtedness	$26,568
% frosh need fully met	26
% ugrads need fully met	22
Average % of frosh need met	76
Average % of ugrad need met	72

University of Nebraska—Lincoln

1410 Q STREET, LINCOLN, NE 68588-0417 • ADMISSIONS: 402-472-2023

CAMPUS LIFE

Quality of Life Rating	91
Fire Safety Rating	85
Green Rating	90
Type of school	Public
Environment	City

STUDENTS

Total undergrad enrollment	20,954
% male/female	52/48
% from out of state	22
% frosh live on campus	87
% ugrads live on campus	37
# of fraternities (% ugrad men join)	26 (17)
# of sororities (% ugrad women join)	21 (24)
% African American	3
% Asian	3
% Caucasian	75
% Hispanic	6
% Native American	<1
% Pacific Islander	<1
% Two or more races	3
% Race and/or ethnicity unknown	1
% international	9
# of countries represented	107

ACADEMICS

Academic Rating	77
% students returning for sophomore year	83
% students graduating within 4 years	39
% students graduating within 6 years	68
Calendar	Semester
Student/faculty ratio	21:1
Profs interesting rating	73
Profs accessible rating	77

Most classes have 20–29 students. Most lab/discussion sessions 20–29 students.

MOST POPULAR MAJORS
Public Relations, Advertising, and Applied Communication; Psychology; Business Administration and Management

ABOUT THE SCHOOL

The University of Nebraska is a public research university in Lincoln that "challenges students and gives them the best opportunity to succeed." This large state school treats its undergrads "like [people], not…number[s]." Moreover, the institution heavily "supports research and innovation, promotes diversity in education, and fosters a sense of community." And it maintains some fantastic departments and schools including journalism and public relations, engineering, agriculture, and actuarial science. When it comes to professors, most work hard to be "engaging" and try to ensure their lessons are both "interesting and applicable." Even better, they make every effort to "know and support their students both inside and outside of the classroom." And because they are so invested in what they are teaching…learning from them [is] easy and exciting." Certainly, it also helps that they are "very willing to answer questions and [want students] succeed academically."

BANG FOR YOUR BUCK

The administration recognizes that financing an undergraduate degree can be burdensome. To that end, the school strives to create "many opportunities for financial aid." In fact, more than two thirds of students receive some form of assistance. Moreover, many of these individuals report that their aid packages are quite "generous." And there are a wide variety of scholarships to which students can apply. For example, the Regents Scholarship offers full tuition for up to 135 credit hours or completion of degree (whichever comes first). There's also the Chancellor's Scholarship which provides recipients with full tuition plus a $2,000 annual stipend. And, to help off-set tuition costs for out-of-state students who score between a 23 and 36 on the ACT may qualify for scholarships worth $5,000-$22,000.

STUDENT LIFE

If you simply wander around Nebraska's campus, you're bound to run into something fun. That's because there are "always events going on." "Students here are heavily invested in the football team" and "tailgating" is quite popular. And many undergrads are "involved in intramurals" as well. Students also love simply kicking back in their "residence halls, [playing] ping pong [or] pool, [or watching] television. Several Huskers reveal that "there are a lot of parties," mostly sponsored by the active Greek community. Fortunately, these same students assure us that there are plenty of "people who aren't into parties too." Therefore, no one ever feels pressured to participate. Lastly, Nebraska's "campus is a five-minute walk away from downtown, where there are a variety of restaurants, bars, shops, and anything else you could want."

CAREER

At the University of Nebraska, "opportunities for internships and other career connections" abound at Nebraska, due in large part to one of the school's "greatest strengths"—career services. Students can use the Career Services office to explore careers, majors, and graduate schools as well as search for jobs and internships and connect with employers. More specifically, Nebraska hosts numerous career fairs throughout the year. These are often focused on different areas and industries, such as education, business, agriculture, and STEM-related jobs. Undergrads can also capitalize on free advising sessions, getting individual advice on everything from cover letters to navigating Nebraska's job search tools. Finally, you can often find Nebraska alums working at such illustrious companies as KPMG, Target, TD Ameritrade, Union Pacific Railroad, Hudl, and Union Bank and Trust.

University of Nebraska—Lincoln

Fax: 402-472-0670 • Financial Aid: 402-472-2030 • E-mail: admissions@unl.edu • Website: www.unl.edu

GENERAL INFO

Activities: Choral groups, concert band, dance, drama/theater, jazz band, literary magazine, marching band, music ensembles, musical theater, opera, pep band, radio station, student government, student newspaper, student-run film society, symphony orchestra, television station, campus ministries, Model UN. **Organizations:** 580 registered organizations, 30 honor societies, 31 religious organizations. 26 fraternities, 21 sororities. **Athletics (Intercollegiate):** *Men:* baseball, basketball, cross-country, football, golf, gymnastics, tennis, track/field (outdoor), track/field (indoor), wrestling. *Women:* basketball, bowling, cross-country, diving, golf, gymnastics, riflery, soccer, softball, swimming, tennis, track/field (outdoor), track/field (indoor), volleyball. **On-Campus Highlights:** Student Union, Campus Recreation Center, Memorial Stadium and Hewitt Center, Residence Halls. **Environmental Initiatives:** Recycling of paper, plastic, aluminum and many other materials A student government initiative has resulted in Nebraska eliminating the use of polystyrene, also known as Styrofoam, for food packaging in 2016.

FINANCIAL AID

Students should submit: FAFSA. Priority filing deadline is 4/1. The Princeton Review suggests that all financial aid forms be submitted as soon as possible after October 1. *Need-based scholarships/grants offered:* College/university scholarship or grant aid from institutional funds, Federal Pell, private scholarships, SEOG, state scholarships/grants. *Loan aid offered:* Direct PLUS Loans, Direct Subsidized Loans, Direct Unsubsidized Loans. Applicants will be notified of awards on a rolling basis beginning 4/1. Federal Work-Study Program available. Institutional employment available.

BOTTOM LINE

For the 2018-2019 academic year, Nebraska residents attending UNL will be expected to pay $7,350 in tuition. Undergrads attending from outside of Nebraska face a tuition bill that totals $23,145. All students pay an additional $1,896 in fees. Housing and meal plans will run a combined $11,430. These costs are all based upon 15 credit hours, a standard double room, and a 7-day unlimited meal plan. Estimates do not include differential tuition for some programs, books, transportation, or personal expenses.

CAREER INFORMATION FROM PAYSCALE.COM

ROI Rating	88
Bachelors and No Higher	
Median starting salary	$50,600
Median mid-career salary	$94,800
At Least Bachelors	
Median starting salary	$52,000
Median mid-career salary	$98,300
Alumni with high job meaning	54%
Degrees awarded in STEM subjects	20%

SELECTIVITY

Admissions Rating	87
# of applicants	14,947
% of applicants accepted	64
% of acceptees attending	51

FRESHMAN PROFILE

Range SAT EBRW	550–680
Range SAT Math	550–700
Range ACT Composite	22–29
Minimum paper TOEFL	523
Minimum internet-based TOEFL	70
Average HS GPA	3.6
% graduated top 10% of class	26
% graduated top 25% of class	53
% graduated top 50% of class	85

DEADLINES

Regular	
Priority	3/1
Deadline	5/1
Nonfall registration?	Yes

FINANCIAL FACTS

Financial Aid Rating	83
Annual in-state tuition	$7,350
Annual out-of-state tuition	$23,145
Room and board	$11,430
Required fees	$1,896
Books and supplies	$1,016
Average frosh need-based scholarship	$8,007
Average UG need-based scholarship	$7,482
% needy frosh rec. need-based scholarship or grant aid	82
% needy UG rec. need-based scholarship or grant aid	78
% needy frosh rec. non-need-based scholarship or grant aid	8
% needy UG rec. non-need-based scholarship or grant aid	6
% needy frosh rec. need-based self-help aid	70
% needy UG rec. need-based self-help aid	68
% frosh rec. any financial aid	87
% UG rec. any financial aid	75
% UG borrow to pay for school	52
Average cumulative indebtedness	$22,918
% frosh need fully met	20
% ugrads need fully met	17
Average % of frosh need met	79
Average % of ugrad need met	74

The University of North Carolina at Chapel Hill

CAMPUS BOX #2200, CHAPEL HILL, NC 27599-2200 • ADMISSIONS: 919-966-3621 • FAX: 919-962-3045

#16 BEST VALUE COLLEGE

CAMPUS LIFE
Quality of Life Rating	91
Fire Safety Rating	97
Green Rating	95
Type of school	Public
Environment	Town

STUDENTS
Total undergrad enrollment	18,682
% male/female	41/59
% from out of state	16
% frosh from public high school	82
% frosh live on campus	100
% ugrads live on campus	51
# of fraternities (% ugrad men join)	34 (18)
# of sororities (% ugrad women join)	24 (18)
% African American	8
% Asian	11
% Caucasian	62
% Hispanic	8
% Native American	<1
% Pacific Islander	<1
% Two or more races	4
% Race and/or ethnicity unknown	4
% international	3
# of countries represented	93

ACADEMICS
Academic Rating	88
% students returning for sophomore year	97
% students graduating within 4 years	84
% students graduating within 6 years	91
Calendar	Semester
Student/faculty ratio	13:1
Profs interesting rating	83
Profs accessible rating	80

Most classes have 10–19 students. Most lab/discussion sessions have 20–29 students.

MOST POPULAR MAJORS
Biology/Biological Sciences; Psychology; Economics

ABOUT THE SCHOOL
The University of North Carolina at Chapel Hill has a reputation for top academics, top athletics, and great overall value. Chartered in 1789 as the first public university in America, UNC Chapel Hill has a long legacy of excellence. Although its relative low cost makes Carolina a great value in higher education, and the school is all about "top-notch academics while having the ultimate college experience." Professors are at the top of their fields and "will work with you above and beyond the normal scope of their position to help you with any concerns or interests you could possibly have." The chancellor even "holds meetings for students to meet with her to discuss school issues." The journalism, business, and nursing programs are ranked among the best in the country, and students of any major may minor in entrepreneurship and compete for start-up funding in the Carolina Challenge. Study abroad programs are available in more than seventy countries. The student body is composed of students from every state and nearly 100 countries, and the university has produced more Rhodes Scholars during the past twenty-five years than any other public research university. There are "many opportunities to gain experience for a future career," and just by applying to Carolina, students are considered for opportunities such as the school's Honors Program, Carolina Research Scholars Program, Global Gap Year Fellowship, and assured enrollment in the university's business and journalism programs. The university's extensive career center counsels students throughout every stage of their education, and students are "at ease knowing that their hard work pays off."

BANG FOR YOUR BUCK
Carolina meets 100 percent of students' demonstrated need, regardless of whether they are North Carolinians or out-of-state residents (entering students with need even receive laptop computers). Aid packages generally contain at least 65 percent in grant and scholarship assistance, with the remainder in work-study and loans. Low-income students whose family income is below 200 percent of the federal poverty standard have the opportunity to graduate debt-free—Carolina Covenant Scholars receive packages of grants, scholarships, and student employment. The university awards about 250 merit scholarships each year to students in the first-year class. These scholarships range in value from $2,500 to a full ride. Best of all, there is no separate application for merit scholarships; students are awarded scholarships based on information provided in the regular admissions application — and all admissions are need-blind.

STUDENT LIFE
A feeling of generosity pervades UNC—"the epitome of Southern hospitality"—and extends beyond mere school spirit and the wearing of Tar Heels colors on game days. "Carolina is family," one student says. "Many of us here are crazy about sports," (even the fire trucks here are Carolina blue), "but most will do anything at all to help a fellow UNC student." Still, "there are few experiences that can top being in the risers at a UNC basketball game or rushing Franklin Street when UNC beats Duke," says a student. No matter what you're into, "life at UNC is full throttle," and "there are hundreds of active clubs and student organizations in which you can meet people with the same interests, or different interests." Students can participate in anything "from ballroom dancing" to "sports clubs to service organizations" plus downtown Chapel Hill is just out the door.

The University of North Carolina at Chapel Hill

FINANCIAL AID: 919-962-8396 • E-MAIL: UNCHELP@ADMISSIONS.UNC.EDU • WEBSITE: WWW.UNC.EDU

CAREER

UNC-Chapel Hill's comprehensive Career Services assists students throughout their entire undergraduate education. First, volunteer Career Peers can help prep undergrads for the job hunt by facilitating anything from mock interviews to marathon résumé-writing sessions. Handshake is a one-stop shop for job and internship postings but also for information about on-campus recruiting, career fairs (recent guests include IBM, The Hershey Company, and NBC/Universal), and an assortment of workshops on topics like LinkedIn profiles or graduate school applications. Recent grads report average starting salaries of $53,500, and 50 percent believe their job holds a great deal of meaning.

GENERAL INFO

Activities: Choral groups, concert band, dance, drama/theater, jazz band, literary magazine, marching band, music ensembles, musical theater, opera, pep band, radio station, student government, student newspaper, student-run film society, symphony orchestra, television station, yearbook, campus ministries, international student organization. **Organizations:** 796 registered organizations, 30 honor societies, 55 religious organizations. 34 fraternities, 24 sororities. **Athletics (Intercollegiate):** *Men:* Baseball, basketball, cross-country, diving, fencing, football, golf, lacrosse, soccer, swimming, tennis, track/field (outdoor), track/field (indoor), wrestling. *Women:* Basketball, crew/rowing, cross-country, diving, fencing, field hockey, golf, gymnastics, lacrosse, soccer, softball, swimming, tennis, track/field (outdoor), track/field (indoor), volleyball. **On-Campus Highlights:** The Pit, McCorkle Place, Polk Place, Dean Smith Center, Student Union, Old Well, Coker Arboretum, Morehead Planetarium, Ackland Art Museum, Kenan Stadium.

FINANCIAL AID

Students should submit: CSS Profile; FAFSA. Priority filing deadline is 3/1. The Princeton Review suggests that all financial aid forms be submitted as soon as possible after October 1. *Need-based scholarships/grants offered:* College/university scholarship or grant aid from institutional funds, Federal Pell, private scholarships, SEOG, state scholarships/grants. *Loan aid offered:* Direct PLUS Loans, Direct Subsidized Loans, Direct Unsubsidized Loans, institutional loans. Applicants will be notified of awards on a rolling basis beginning 2/1. Federal Work-Study Program available. Institutional employment available.

THE BOTTOM LINE

The cost of attending Carolina is a real bargain—especially if your home state is North Carolina. In-state students can expect to pay about $8,987 in tuition and fees. Out-of-state students have it pretty good too; they can expect to cough up about $35,170 for the cost of tuition and fees for one year. Cost of living in Chapel Hill is pretty cheap too—you can expect room and board to run you just $11,190 per year.

CAREER INFORMATION FROM PAYSCALE.COM	
ROI Rating	95
Bachelors and No Higher	
Median starting salary	$53,500
Median mid-career salary	$97,800
At Least Bachelors	
Median starting salary	$55,300
Median mid-career salary	$102,000
Alumni with high job meaning	50%
Degrees awarded in STEM subjects	19%

SELECTIVITY	
Admissions Rating	97
# of applicants	40,918
% of applicants accepted	24
% of acceptees attending	45
# offered a place on the wait list	5,097
% accepting a place on wait list	46
% admitted from wait list	1

FRESHMAN PROFILE	
Range SAT EBRW	640–720
Range SAT Math	620–720
Range ACT Composite	27–32
Minimum paper TOEFL	600
Minimum internet-based TOEFL	100
Average HS GPA	4.7
% graduated top 10% of class	78
% graduated top 25% of class	96
% graduated top 50% of class	100

DEADLINES	
Early action	
Deadline	10/15
Notification	1/31
Regular	
Deadline	1/15
Notification	3/31
Nonfall registration?	No

FINANCIAL FACTS	
Financial Aid Rating	94
Annual in-state tuition	$7,019
Annual out-of-state tuition	$32,202
Room and board	$11,190
Required fees	$1,967
Books and supplies	$948
Average frosh need-based scholarship	$15,882
Average UG need-based scholarship	$17,607
% needy frosh rec. need-based scholarship or grant aid	92
% needy UG rec. need-based scholarship or grant aid	89
% needy frosh rec. non-need-based scholarship or grant aid	11
% needy UG rec. non-need-based scholarship or grant aid	5
% needy frosh rec. need-based self-help aid	58
% needy UG rec. need-based self-help aid	70
% frosh rec. any financial aid	67
% UG rec. any financial aid	63
% UG borrow to pay for school	40
Average cumulative indebtedness	$22,214
% frosh need fully met	83
% ugrads need fully met	80
Average % of frosh need met	100
Average % of ugrad need met	100

University of Notre Dame

220 Main Building, Notre Dame, IN 46556 • Admissions: 574-631-7505 • Fax: 574-631-8865

CAMPUS LIFE

Quality of Life Rating	70
Fire Safety Rating	98
Green Rating	92
Type of school	Private
Affiliation	Roman Catholic
Environment	City

STUDENTS

Total undergrad enrollment	8,527
% male/female	53/47
% from out of state	92
% frosh from public high school	42
% frosh live on campus	100
% ugrads live on campus	79
# of fraternities (% ugrad men join)	0 (0)
# of sororities (% ugrad women join)	0 (0)
% African American	4
% Asian	5
% Caucasian	69
% Hispanic	11
% Native American	<1
% Pacific Islander	<1
% Two or more races	5
% Race and/or ethnicity unknown	<1
% international	6
# of countries represented	68

ACADEMICS

Academic Rating	79
% students returning for sophomore year	98
% students graduating within 4 years	92
% students graduating within 6 years	95
Calendar	Semester
Student/faculty ratio	10:1
Profs interesting rating	68
Profs accessible rating	73
Most classes have 10–19 students.	

MOST POPULAR MAJORS
Psychology; Political Science and Government; Finance

ABOUT THE SCHOOL

As a private school with traditions of excellence in academics, athletics, and service, and with a vast, faithful alumni base that provides ample resources, the University of Notre Dame draws on its Catholic values to provide a well-rounded, world-class education. One student is thrilled to attend, noting that "as an Irish Catholic, Notre Dame is basically the equivalent of Harvard. I've always viewed the school as an institution with rigorous academics as well as rich tradition and history—and a symbol of pride for my heritage." Not all are Catholic here, although it seems that most undergrads "have some sort of spirituality present in their daily lives" and have a "vibrant social and religious life." Total undergraduate enrollment is just more than 8,000 students. ND is reportedly improving in diversity concerning economic backgrounds, according to members of the student body here. An incredible 90 percent are from out-of-state, and ninety countries are now represented throughout the campus. Undergrads say they enjoy "a college experience that is truly unique," "combining athletics and academics in an environment of faith." "It's necessary to study hard and often, [but] there's also time to do other things." Academics are widely praised, and one new student is excited that even "large lectures are broken down into smaller discussion groups once a week to help with class material and...give the class a personal touch."

BANG FOR YOUR BUCK

Notre Dame is one of the most selective colleges in the country. Almost everyone who enrolls is in the top 10 percent of their graduating class and possesses test scores in the highest percentiles. But, as the student respondents suggest, strong academic ability isn't enough to get you in here. The school looks for students with other talents and seems to have a predilection for athletic achievement. Each residence hall is home to students from all classes; most will live in the same hall for all their years on campus. An average of 93 percent of entering students will graduate within five years. Students report that "the administration tries its best to stay on top of the students' wants and needs." The school is also extremely community-oriented, and Notre Dame has some of the strongest alumni support nationwide.

STUDENT LIFE

Undergrads at Notre Dame report "the vast majority" of their peers are "very smart" "white kids from upper to middle-class backgrounds from all over the country, especially the Midwest and Northeast." The typical student "is a type-A personality that studies a lot, yet is athletic and involved in the community. They are usually the outstanding seniors in their high schools," the "sort of people who can talk about the BCS rankings and Derrida in the same breath." Additionally, something like "85 percent of Notre Dame students earned a varsity letter in high school." "ND is slowly improving in diversity concerning economic backgrounds, with the university's policy to meet all demonstrated financial need." As things stand now, those who "don't tend to fit in with everyone else hang out in their own groups made up by others like them (based on ethnicity, sexual orientation, etc.)."

CAREER

At Notre Dame, The Career Center's mantra to students is "YOU must take ownership of your future." But, of course, career counselors and staff are there to support and assist students every step of the way. To that end, experiential career opportunities abound for freshmen

University of Notre Dame

FINANCIAL AID: 574-631-6436 • E-MAIL: ADMISSIONS@ND.EDU • WEBSITE: WWW.ND.EDU

and seniors alike: students can complete a Wall Street externship, shadow an alum at work, or be matched to a mentor in the industry of their choice. The Career Center funding program will even support students who need financial assistance to participate in a full-time summer internship. The university hosts several career and internship fairs each semester, along with networking programs like a Civil Engineering Luncheon or Consulting Night. Finally, Students visit Go IRISH, the center's primary recruiting database, for information about interviewing opportunities, employer information sessions, or opportunities that specifically seek a ND student or alum.

GENERAL INFO

Activities: Choral groups, concert band, dance, drama/theater, jazz band, literary magazine, marching band, music ensembles, musical theater, opera, pep band, radio station, student government, student newspaper, student-run film society, symphony orchestra, yearbook, campus ministries, international student organization. **Organizations:** 299 registered organizations, 10 honor societies, 11 religious organizations. **Athletics (Intercollegiate):** *Men:* Baseball, basketball, cross-country, diving, fencing, football, golf, ice hockey, lacrosse, soccer, swimming, tennis, track/field (outdoor). *Women:* Basketball, crew/rowing, cross-country, diving, fencing, golf, lacrosse, soccer, softball, swimming, tennis, track/field (outdoor), volleyball.

FINANCIAL AID

Students should submit: Business/Farm Supplement; CSS Profile; FAFSA. The Princeton Review suggests that all financial aid forms be submitted as soon as possible after October 1. *Need-based scholarships/grants offered:* College/university scholarship or grant aid from institutional funds, Federal Pell, private scholarships, SEOG, state scholarships/grants. *Loan aid offered:* Direct PLUS Loans, Direct Subsidized Loans, Direct Unsubsidized Loans. Applicants will be notified of awards on a rolling basis beginning 2/15. Federal Work-Study Program available. Institutional employment available.

BOTTOM LINE

Notre Dame, while certainly providing a wonderful academic environment and superb education, does reflect this in the cost of attending the college. Annual tuition is $52,884. With room, board, and required fees, students are looking at close to $69,000 a year. Fortunately, over 75 percent of undergrads receive some form of financial aid.

CAREER INFORMATION FROM PAYSCALE.COM

ROI Rating	90
Bachelors and No Higher	
Median starting salary	$64,700
Median mid-career salary	$131,500
At Least Bachelors	
Median starting salary	$67,200
Median mid-career salary	$137,300
Alumni with high job meaning	46%
Degrees awarded in STEM subjects	28%

SELECTIVITY

Admissions Rating	98
# of applicants	19,564
% of applicants accepted	19
% of acceptees attending	55
# offered a place on the wait list	1,508
% accepting a place on wait list	60
% admitted from wait list	11

FRESHMAN PROFILE

Range SAT EBRW	680–750
Range SAT Math	690–770
Range ACT Composite	32–34
Minimum internet-based TOEFL	110.2
% graduated top 10% of class	91
% graduated top 25% of class	98
% graduated top 50% of class	100

DEADLINES

Early action	
Deadline	11/1
Notification	12/15
Regular	
Deadline	1/1
Notification	4/1
Nonfall registration?	Yes

FINANCIAL FACTS

Financial Aid Rating	92
Annual tuition	$52,884
Room and board	$15,410
Required fees	$507
Books and supplies	$1,050
Average frosh need-based scholarship	$38,673
Average UG need-based scholarship	$38,921
% needy frosh rec. need-based scholarship or grant aid	96
% needy UG rec. need-based scholarship or grant aid	97
% needy frosh rec. non-need-based scholarship or grant aid	16
% needy UG rec. non-need-based scholarship or grant aid	16
% needy frosh rec. need-based self-help aid	83
% needy UG rec. need-based self-help aid	83
% frosh rec. any financial aid	66
% UG rec. any financial aid	77
% UG borrow to pay for school	46
Average cumulative indebtedness	$29,254
% frosh need fully met	99
% ugrads need fully met	99
Average % of frosh need met	100
Average % of ugrad need met	100

University of Oklahoma

1000 Asp Avenue, Norman, OK 73019-4076 • Admissions: 405-325-2252 • Fax: 405-325-7124

CAMPUS LIFE

Quality of Life Rating	**97**
Fire Safety Rating	**97**
Green Rating	**90**
Type of school	Public
Environment	City

STUDENTS

Total undergrad enrollment	22,324
% male/female	49/51
% from out of state	33
% frosh live on campus	86
% ugrads live on campus	31
# of fraternities (% ugrad men join)	31 (25)
# of sororities (% ugrad women join)	26 (31)
% African American	5
% Asian	6
% Caucasian	61
% Hispanic	10
% Native American	4
% Pacific Islander	<1
% Two or more races	8
% Race and/or ethnicity unknown	2
% international	4
# of countries represented	120

ACADEMICS

Academic Rating	**82**
% students returning for sophomore year	92
% students graduating within 4 years	41
% students graduating within 6 years	67
Calendar	Semester
Student/faculty ratio	18:1
Profs interesting rating	82
Profs accessible rating	86

Most classes have 10–19 students. Most lab/discussion sessions have 20–29 students.

MOST POPULAR MAJORS
Registered Nursing; Accounting; Finance

ABOUT THE SCHOOL

The University of Oklahoma combines a unique mixture of academic excellence, varied social cultures, and a variety of campus activities to make your educational experience complete. At OU, comprehensive learning is the goal for your life. OU students receive a valuable classroom learning experience, but OU is considered by many students to be one of the finest research institutions in the United States. Students appreciate the opportunity to be a part of technology in progress. With 441 student organizations on campus, "there's no way you could possibly be bored." "From the Indonesian Student Association to the Bocce Ball League of Excellence, there's a group for" everyone. "The programming board here brings in a lot of great acts and keeps us very entertained in the middle of Oklahoma," adds one student. "School spirit is rampant," and intercollegiate athletics are extremely popular—particularly football. "Not everyone likes Sooner football," but it sure seems that way. Students at OU "live and breathe football" in the fall when "the campus goes into a frenzy." Fraternities and sororities are also "a large part of social life." Some students insist that the Greek system isn't a dominant feature of the OU landscape. "You hardly notice their presence" if you're not involved, they say, and "the majority of students aren't involved." The "friendly and cute little town" of Norman is reportedly an ideal place to spend a day when not in class. Right next to campus is an area "full of" boutique shops and "a fine selection of bars and restaurants." "Norman is such a great town," gushes one student. "It's not too little to be boring but not too big to be impersonal."

BANG FOR YOUR BUCK

The University of Oklahoma's tuition and fees remain perennially low when compared to its peer institutions in the Big Twelve athletic conference, and OU is mighty proud of its dedication to providing financial assistance to students who want to attend. Alumni are loyal, and the fundraising machine is epic. In fact, OU's Campaign for Scholarships has raised over $247 million since its launch in 2005. As far as scholarships go, OU offers several merit- and need-based aid programs to students including those based on such criteria as academics, leadership, and extracurricular interests. Funds cover up to the full cost of tuition, and are available to Oklahoma residents and nonresidents.

STUDENT LIFE

"Greek life tends to dominate the social scene" at OU with sororities and fraternities making up a significant portion of the population. "Almost all students are in one or more student organizations." Most are "from Oklahoma or Texas, white, Christian, self-motivated, family oriented." Still OU is home to "a wide variety of students with different political, religious, and economic backgrounds." "Everybody is able to find other kindred spirits among the school community." And, more importantly, "there's a niche (and bar)" for everyone. It seems most students are involved in athletics in some capacity, even if it's just as a fan. "During football season, the campus is electric." The school also offers "amazing opportunities to see incredible art through theatre, dance, orchestra, and art exhibits." OU students attend free movies at the Union on the weekends, and Norman itself is "friendly and cute," a true "college town to the core."

University of Oklahoma

FINANCIAL AID: 405-325-5505 • E-MAIL: ADMREC@OU.EDU • WEBSITE: WWW.OU.EDU

CAREER

At OU, the "career services are impeccable," so naturally students feel "ready for the future." There are "creative programs that provide real-world experience" and "opportunities to really develop oneself outside the classroom." A student-run advertising and public relations agency or the National Weather Center are just a few places where students may hone their skills on campus. OU emphasizes community service through "million dollar help programs like the Writing Center, Free Action Tutoring, Project Threshold, etc." Students also receive career advice and counseling from professors who "leave their office doors open" and are happy to discuss "not only class but life after OU." Students feel a sense of global awareness at OU and a desire to better the world. Nearly sixty percent of alumni who visited the website PayScale.com regard their jobs as meaningful. And, according to the same site, the average salary for recent grads is $51,900.

GENERAL INFO

Environment: City. **Activities:** Choral groups, concert band, dance, drama/theater, literary magazine, marching band, music ensembles, musical theater, opera, pep band, model UN, radio station, student government, student newspaper, student-run film society, symphony orchestra, television station, yearbook, campus ministries, international student organization. **Organizations:** 441 registered organizations, 18 honor societies, 44 religious organizations. 35 fraternities, 24 sororities. **Athletics (Intercollegiate):** *Men:* Baseball, basketball, cheerleading, cross-country, football, golf, gymnastics, tennis, track/field (outdoor), track/field (indoor), wrestling. *Women:* Basketball, cheerleading, crew/rowing, cross-country, golf, gymnastics, soccer, softball, tennis, track/field (outdoor), track/field (in door), volleyball.

FINANCIAL AID

Students should submit: FAFSA. Priority filing deadline is 3/1. The Princeton Review suggests that all financial aid forms be submitted as soon as possible after October 1. *Need-based scholarships/grants offered:* College/university scholarship or grant aid from institutional funds; Federal Pell; Private scholarships; SEOG; State scholarships/grants; United Negro College Fund. *Loan aid offered:* Direct PLUS Loans, Direct Subsidized Loans, Direct Unsubsidized Loans. Applicants will be notified of awards on a rolling basis beginning 1/15. Federal Work-Study Program available. Institutional employment available.

BOTTOM LINE

Total cost of attendance at OU runs about $19,651 per year for Oklahoma residents. Nonresidents can expect to pay about $35,032 a year. About 85 percent of undergrads here receive some type of financial assistance in the form of scholarships, grants, loans, work-study, and tuition waivers.

CAREER INFORMATION FROM PAYSCALE.COM	
ROI Rating	89
Bachelors and No Higher	
Median starting salary	$53,500
Median mid-career salary	$99,200
At Least Bachelors	
Median starting salary	$54,900
Median mid-career salary	$102,300
Alumni with high job meaning	52%
Degrees awarded in STEM subjects	23%

SELECTIVITY	
Admissions Rating	86
# of applicants	16,777
% of applicants accepted	69
% of acceptees attending	39
# offered a place on the wait list	1,929
% accepting a place on wait list	100
% admitted from wait list	8

FRESHMAN PROFILE	
Range SAT EBRW	580–690
Range SAT Math	570–690
Range ACT Composite	23–29
Minimum paper TOEFL	550
Minimum internet-based TOEFL	79
Average HS GPA	3.6
% graduated top 10% of class	36
% graduated top 25% of class	65
% graduated top 50% of class	92

DEADLINES	
Regular	
Priority	12/15
Deadline	2/1
Nonfall registration?	Yes

FINANCIAL FACTS	
Financial Aid Rating	92
Annual in-state tuition	$4,788
Annual out-of-state tuition	$20,169
Room and board	$10,994
Required fees	$4,275
Room and board	NR
Average frosh need-based scholarship	$6,946
Average UG need-based scholarship	$6,077
% needy frosh rec. need-based scholarship or grant aid	45
% needy UG rec. need-based scholarship or grant aid	56
% needy frosh rec. non-need-based scholarship or grant aid	63
% needy UG rec. non-need-based scholarship or grant aid	53
% needy frosh rec. need-based self-help aid	64
% needy UG rec. need-based self-help aid	69
% frosh rec. any financial aid	86
% UG rec. any financial aid	77
% UG borrow to pay for school	45
Average cumulative indebtedness	$29,283
% frosh need fully met	76
% ugrads need fully met	76
Average % of frosh need met	77
Average % of ugrad need met	80

University of Pennsylvania

1 COLLEGE HALL, PHILADELPHIA, PA 19104 • ADMISSIONS: 215-898-7507 • FAX: 215-898-9670

CAMPUS LIFE

Quality of Life Rating	87
Fire Safety Rating	84
Green Rating	94
Type of school	Private
Environment	Metropolis

STUDENTS

Total undergrad enrollment	10,033
% male/female	49/51
% from out of state	81
% frosh from public high school	60
% frosh live on campus	99
% ugrads live on campus	52
# of fraternities (% ugrad men join)	36 (30)
# of sororities (% ugrad women join)	13 (29)
% African American	7
% Asian	21
% Caucasian	43
% Hispanic	10
% Native American	<1
% Pacific Islander	<1
% Two or more races	5
% Race and/or ethnicity unknown	2
% international	13
# of countries represented	126

ACADEMICS

Academic Rating	89
% students returning for sophomore year	98
% students graduating within 4 years	86
% students graduating within 6 years	96
Calendar	Semester
Student/faculty ratio	6:1
Profs interesting rating	70
Profs accessible rating	71
Most classes have 10–19 students.	

MOST POPULAR MAJORS
Economics; Registered Nursing; Finance

#25 BEST VALUE COLLEGE

ABOUT THE SCHOOL

The University of Pennsylvania (commonly referred to as Penn), as one of the eight members of the Ivy League, gives you all of the advantages of an internationally recognized degree with none of the attitude. Founded by Benjamin Franklin, Penn is the fourth-oldest institution of higher learning in the United States. The university is composed of four undergraduate schools, including The Wharton School, home to Penn's well-known and intense undergraduate business program. This, along with other career-focused offerings, contributes to a preprofessional atmosphere on campus. That comes with an element of competition, especially when grades are on the line. Penn students love the opportunity to take classes with professors who are setting the bar for research in his or her field. Professors are praised for being "enthusiastic and incredibly well-versed in their subject," a group who is "passionate about teaching" and who will "go out of their way to help you understand the material." Penn students don't mind getting into intellectual conversations during dinner, but "partying is a much higher priority here than it is at other Ivy League schools." Students here can have intellectual conversations during dinner, and hit the frat houses later that night. Trips to New York City and Center City Philadelphia are common, and students have plenty of access to restaurants, shopping, concerts, and sports games around campus.

BANG FOR YOUR BUCK

Transparency is embedded in Penn's financial aid process. The Student Financial Services website provides a chart of the percent of applicants offered aid and median award amounts for family income levels ranging from $0–$220,000 and higher. For 2015–2016, Penn committed more than $206 million of its resources for grant aid to undergraduate students. Over 78 percent of freshman who applied for aid received an award, and Penn's financial aid packages meet 100 percent of students' demonstrated need through an all grant, all grant aid program. According to the school, the average financial aid package for incoming awarded furst years in 2015 was $48,605. University Named Scholarships are provided through direct gifts to the university and privately endowed funds and enable Penn to continue to admit students solely on the basis of academic merit. The scholarship amount varies according to determined financial need. Staff at Penn provide strong support for applicants, with one student noting, "It was the only school to call me during the admissions process instead of just e-mailing me extra information."

STUDENT LIFE

This "determined" bunch "is either focused on one specific interest, or very well-rounded." Pretty much everyone "was an overachiever ('that kid') in high school," and some students "are off-the-charts brilliant," making everyone here "sort of fascinated by everyone else." Everyone has "a strong sense of personal style and his or her own credo," but no group deviates too far from the more mainstream stereotypes. There's a definite lack of "emos" and hippies. There's "the career-driven Wharton kid who will stab you in the back to get your interview slot" and "the nursing kid who's practically nonexistent," but on the whole, there's tremendous school diversity, with "people from all over the world of all kinds of experiences of all perspectives."

University of Pennsylvania

FINANCIAL AID: 215-898-1988 • E-MAIL: INFO@ADMISSIONS.UPENN.EDU • WEBSITE: WWW.UPENN.EDU

CAREER

Penn's Career Services is an amazing resource for students who wish to discover opportunities on- and off-campus. A bursting job board (with over 13,000 individual position postings), trips to New York City and Washington D.C. to learn about organizations and industries, as well as hundreds of employer information sessions give students tons of chances to network and research fields. One neat perk: along with other offices like Civic House, Kelly Writers House, and Penn Global, Career Services provides funding to finance research and unpaid (or lowly paid) summer internships. Career days a year bring over 600 employers to campus (Amazon, IBM, and Bloomberg, to name a few), and PennApps, a weekend-long "hackathon" for student developers, draws prospective employers like Intel and Microsoft for sponsorship and presentations. Alumni mentoring is also available to help students find their path. Penn grads who visited PayScale.com report median starting salaries of $68,100.

GENERAL INFO

Activities: Choral groups, concert band, dance, drama/theater, jazz band, literary magazine, marching band, music ensembles, student government, student newspaper, symphony orchestra. **Organizations:** 500+ registered organizations, 9 honor societies, 29 religious organizations. 36 fraternities, 13 sororities.

FINANCIAL AID

Students should submit: Business/Farm Supplement; CSS Profile, FAFSA; Institution's own financial aid form. Priority filing deadline is 2/15. The Princeton Review suggests that all financial aid forms be submitted as soon as possible after October 1. *Need-based scholarships/grants offered:* College/university scholarship or grant aid from institutional funds, Federal Pell, private scholarships, SEOG, state scholarships/grants. *Loan aid offered:* Direct PLUS Loans, Direct Subsidized Loans, Direct Unsubsidized Loans. Applicants will be notified of awards on or about 4/1. Federal Work-Study Program available. Institutional employment available.

BOTTOM LINE

A year's tuition is $47,416. You'll pay another $15,066 in room and board. Don't be alarmed: Penn offers loan-free packages to all dependent students who are eligible for financial aid, regardless of the family's income level. The average student debt, for the students who choose to borrow, is approximately $26,157. Students have noted the school's "generous aid program" as being "phenomenal."

CAREER INFORMATION FROM PAYSCALE.COM

ROI Rating	93
Bachelors and No Higher	
Median starting salary	$70,100
Median mid-career salary	$135,800
At Least Bachelors	
Median starting salary	$72,900
Median mid-career salary	$145,200
Alumni with high job meaning	42%
Degrees awarded in STEM subjects	21%

SELECTIVITY

Admissions Rating	99
# of applicants	40,413
% of applicants accepted	9
% of acceptees attending	65
# of early decision applicants	6147
% accepted early decision	22

FRESHMAN PROFILE

Range SAT EBRW	700–770
Range SAT Math	720–790
Range ACT Composite	32–35
Average HS GPA	3.9
% graduated top 10% of class	96
% graduated top 25% of class	100
% graduated top 50% of class	100

DEADLINES

Early decision	
Deadline	11/1
Notification	12/15
Regular	
Deadline	1/5
Nonfall registration?	No

FINANCIAL FACTS

Financial Aid Rating	93
Annual tuition	$49,220
Room and board	$15,616
Required fees	$6,364
Average frosh need-based scholarship	$47,114
Average UG need-based scholarship	$46,177
% needy frosh rec. need-based scholarship or grant aid	98
% needy UG rec. need-based scholarship or grant aid	99
% needy frosh rec. non-need-based scholarship or grant aid	0
% needy UG rec. non-need-based scholarship or grant aid	0
% needy frosh rec. need-based self-help aid	100
% needy UG rec. need-based self-help aid	100
% frosh rec. any financial aid	47
% UG rec. any financial aid	45
% UG borrow to pay for school	27
Average cumulative indebtedness	$23,224
% frosh need fully met	100
% ugrads need fully met	100
Average % of frosh need met	100
Average % of ugrad need met	100

University of Pittsburgh

4227 Fifth Avenue, First Floor Alumni Hall, Pittsburgh, PA 15260 • Admissions: 412-624-7488 • Fax: 412-648-8815

CAMPUS LIFE

Quality of Life Rating	**90**
Fire Safety Rating	**91**
Green Rating	**92**
Type of school	Public
Environment	City

STUDENTS

Total undergrad enrollment	19,326
% male/female	49/51
% from out of state	28
% frosh live on campus	97
% ugrads live on campus	43
# of fraternities (% ugrad men join)	24 (10)
# of sororities (% ugrad women join)	18 (12)
% African American	5
% Asian	10
% Caucasian	72
% Hispanic	4
% Native American	<1
% Pacific Islander	<1
% Two or more races	4
% Race and/or ethnicity unknown	1
% international	4
# of countries represented	55

ACADEMICS

Academic Rating	**81**
% students returning for sophomore year	93
% students graduating within 4 years	64
% students graduating within 6 years	81
Calendar	Semester
Student/faculty ratio	14:1
Profs interesting rating	76
Profs accessible rating	77

Most classes have 10–19 students. Most lab/discussion sessions have 20–29 students.

MOST POPULAR MAJORS

Psychology; Biology/Biological Services; Finance

ABOUT THE SCHOOL

An academic powerhouse, University of Pittsburgh is one of Pennsylvania's premier institutions. With 110 degree programs spread throughout eight undergraduate schools, students can study virtually any topic they desire. Impressively, strong prospective freshmen can be considered for guaranteed admission to fourteen graduate/professional schools, including dentistry, medicine and law. Additionally, Pitt has established a number of fantastic programs that enhance (and encourage) learning beyond the classroom. For example, the Outside the Classroom Curriculum (OCC) assists undergrads in finding internship, research, and volunteer opportunities where students gain practical experience (and a résumé boost). The Engineering Co-Op Program also helps students pair their education with a professional setting. And the stellar Honors College (offering a unique BPhil degree) maintains several prestigious programs, including the Brackenridge Summer Research Fellowships and the Yellowstone Field Program. Finally, hometown Pittsburgh provides students with a number of educational and cultural opportunities. Recently voted one of the most livable cities in the country, students frequently take advantage of the city's myriad bars, restaurants, museums and theaters (even getting a discount through PITTARTS).

BANG FOR YOUR BUCK

Pitt endeavors to help all students with financial need and limited resources. To begin with, all prospective freshmen who present an outstanding academic record (and complete an application by December 15) will automatically be considered for merit scholarships. These awards range from $2,000 to full coverage for tuition and room and board. Importantly, these scholarships are renewable up to three years, provided recipients meet predetermined GPA and progress requirements.

STUDENT LIFE

"The best part about Pitt is that there is no cookie cutter student." Although most do come from the northeast, "there are many atypical students when considering backgrounds, ethnicity, and beliefs." Students are "motivated," "studious," "hard working and friendly," "career minded, but not obsessive." They "balance school work and free time," and there are a "variety of ways to have fun" at Pitt "from museums, concerts, theatre, ballet, lectures, movie theaters, shopping, dining, and of course parties." Pitt is "a big school with all the perks of a small school" and most students "are involved in at least one activity." Students use their "free bus passes" to explore the city, dine at restaurants in Squirrel Hill and Southside, and attend Steelers and Pirates' games.

CAREER

"Pitt is excellent at helping students find jobs, internships, job shadowing opportunities, and other activities to help solidify a career path." There is an internship "guarantee" for all students after their first semester and "an entire department devoted to internships and job placement." "Pitt is one of the best schools to help students with experiential learning, whether it be through an internship, research experience, or even service learning experience." Students describe the career office as "very helpful and...always willing to point you in the right direction." There are career consultants available to help students along the way as well. Many also extol Pittsburgh itself as a hotbed of "career opportunities." According to alumni who've visited the website PayScale.com, the average starting salary for recent graduates is $52,100.

University of Pittsburgh

FINANCIAL AID: 412-624-7488 • E-MAIL: OAFA@PITT.EDU • WEBSITE: WWW.PITT.EDU

GENERAL INFO

Activities: Choral groups, concert band, dance, drama/theater, jazz band, literary magazine, marching band, music ensembles, pep band, radio station, student government, student newspaper, student-run film society, television station, campus ministries, international student organization. **Organizations:** 570 registered organizations, 23 honor societies, 24 fraternities, 18 sororities. **Athletics (Intercollegiate):** *Men:* Baseball, basketball, cross-country, diving, football, soccer, swimming, track/field (outdoor), wrestling. *Women:* Basketball, cross-country, diving, gymnastics, soccer, softball, swimming, tennis, track/field (outdoor), volleyball. **On-Campus Highlights:** Cathedral of Learning, William Pitt Union, Heinz Chapel, Petersen Event Center, Sennott Square. **Environmental Initiatives:** Steam plant which houses six 100,000 pound per hour national gas fired boilers; the Carillo Street Steam Plant provides partial steam service for both the University and the University of Pittsburgh Medical Center. Comprehensive building automation/energy management system that provides automatic control of building temperatures, lighting upgrades, occupancy sensors, and the expansion of the university's central steam and chilled water infrastructure to eliminate stand-alone chillers and boilers. The University pursues LEED certification for many large projects.

FINANCIAL AID

Students should submit: FAFSA, state aid form. Priority filing deadline is 3/1. The Princeton Review suggests that all financial aid forms be submitted as soon as possible after October 1. *Need-based scholarships/grants offered:* College/university scholarship or grant aid from institutional funds, Federal Nursing Scholarships, Federal Pell, Private scholarships, SEOG, State scholarships/grants. *Loan aid offered:* Direct PLUS Loans, Direct Subsidized Loans, Direct Unsubsidized Loans. Applicants will be notified of awards on a rolling basis beginning 2/1. Federal Work-Study Program available. Institutional employment available.

BOTTOM LINE

Pennsylvania residents should expect to pay $18,130 per academic year. Out-of-state undergraduates will need to shell out $31,102 annually. There are also additional, required fees totaling $950. Of course, the university offers a variety of grants, loans, and work-study opportunities.

CAREER INFORMATION FROM PAYSCALE.COM	
ROI Rating	87
Bachelors and No Higher	
Median starting salary	$54,600
Median mid-career salary	$97,600
At Least Bachelors	
Median starting salary	$55,900
Median mid-career salary	$101,000
Alumni with high job meaning	50%
Degrees awarded in STEM subjects	27%

SELECTIVITY	
Admissions Rating	90
# of applicants	27,679
% of applicants accepted	60
% of acceptees attending	24
# offered a place on the wait list	2,098
% accepting a place on wait list	37
% admitted from wait list	14

FRESHMAN PROFILE	
Range SAT EBRW	620–700
Range SAT Math	620–720
Range ACT Composite	27–32
Minimum paper TOEFL	600
Minimum internet-based TOEFL	100
Average HS GPA	4.0
% graduated top 10% of class	53
% graduated top 25% of class	87
% graduated top 50% of class	99

DEADLINES	
Nonfall registration?	Yes

FINANCIAL FACTS	
Financial Aid Rating	79
Annual in-state tuition	$18,130
Annual out-of-state tuition	$31,102
Room and board	$11,050
Required fees	$950
Books and supplies	$752
Average frosh need-based scholarship	$10,945
Average UG need-based scholarship	$9,771
% needy frosh rec. need-based scholarship or grant aid	78
% needy UG rec. need-based scholarship or grant aid	73
% needy frosh rec. non-need-based scholarship or grant aid	13
% needy UG rec. non-need-based scholarship or grant aid	8
% needy frosh rec. need-based self-help aid	73
% needy UG rec. need-based self-help aid	80
% frosh rec. any financial aid	61
% UG rec. any financial aid	54
% UG borrow to pay for school	62
Average cumulative indebtedness	$38,322
% frosh need fully met	17
% ugrads need fully met	12
Average % of frosh need met	55
Average % of ugrad need met	53

University of Richmond

CAMPUS LIFE	
Quality of Life Rating	97
Fire Safety Rating	94
Green Rating	93
Type of school	Private
Environment	City

STUDENTS	
Total undergrad enrollment	2,907
% male/female	48/52
% from out of state	80
% frosh from public high school	61
% frosh live on campus	100
% ugrads live on campus	92
# of fraternities (% ugrad men join)	8 (21)
# of sororities (% ugrad women join)	8 (28)
% African American	7
% Asian	9
% Caucasian	57
% Hispanic	9
% Native American	<1
% Pacific Islander	0
% Two or more races	4
% Race and/or ethnicity unknown	4
% international	9
# of countries represented	60

ACADEMICS	
Academic Rating	96
% students returning for sophomore year	93
% students graduating within 4 years	83
% students graduating within 6 years	88
Calendar	Semester
Student/faculty ratio	8:1
Profs interesting rating	96
Profs accessible rating	97
Most classes have 10–19 students.	

MOST POPULAR MAJORS
Biology/Biological Sciences; Business Administration; Leadership Studies

#43 BEST VALUE COLLEGE

ABOUT THE SCHOOL

At the University of Richmond, situated right in the West End of Virginia's capital, academic opportunities abound. No matter if they want to study abroad or conduct research, these 2,950 students have access to "unparalleled resources" and can easily broaden their horizons. Under The Richmond Guarantee, for example, every undergraduate student is eligible to receive a fellowship of $4,000 for a summer internship or a faculty-mentored research project. Of course, University of Richmond is quite strong in the sciences, as evidenced by their "good...admission rate to med school." And the university is also home to the "highly respected" Robins School of Business. Even better, all students benefit from "small" courses which allows for an "AMAZING" classroom experience. All courses are taught by members of the faculty (no teaching assistants), and most instructors endeavor to "make their classes difficult because they know we can rise to the challenge." They also make it quite evident that "they all really want their students to understand the material and succeed." Best of all, they are always "willing to meet outside of class to help."

BANG FOR YOUR BUCK

Undergrads proudly proclaim that "the financial aid programs [at Richmond] are amazing." Indeed, the university "gives great...aid to those who need it." The University of Richmond has a need-blind admission process and a guarantee to meet 100 percent of demonstrated need. For Virginia residents, whose parents earn $60,000 or less a year, University of Richmond will cover full tuition, room, and meal plan—with no loans. And all students, no matter their financial circumstances, are automatically considered for merit-based aid. This includes the Presidential Scholarship which covers one third of the cost of tuition, the Richmond Scholars Program which covers full tuition, room and board, and the Davis United World College Scholars which provides up to $10,000.

STUDENT LIFE

It's easy to have a good time at University of Richmond. After all, "there are endless clubs and activities that you can get involved in." Indeed, students can participate in everything from "service organizations [and] religious groups [to] a cappella and dance troupes [to] academic [and] social fraternities." Additionally, "club sports teams and IM Sports (intramural) are pretty popular." Many undergrads assert that "Greek Life definitely dominates the social scene." We're told that a "high percentage of students are [involved]" and that "[frat] parties are the main attractions on weekend nights." Fortunately, these tend to be "open to all members of the student body" no matter your affiliation. And if fraternities and sororities aren't your scene, "there are always events being put on by the Center for Student Involvement and various student groups."

CAREER

Students at the University of Richmond triumphantly declare that the school's Career Services office is "incredibly helpful and thorough." It's "constantly reaching out to students" and manages to "foster great relationships" with several companies. Undergrads flock there to explore various majors and careers (the Career Advisors are even certified in analyzing the Myers-Brigg Type Indicator assessment)

University of Richmond

E-MAIL: ADMISSION@RICHMOND.EDU • FAX: 804-287-6003 • WEBSITE: WWW.RICHMOND.EDU

and to take advantage of fantastic programs like Spider Shadowing, which provides individuals with the opportunity to spend time with an alum or employer to learn more about a particular career. As if that wasn't enough, students can turn to the office for résumé reviews and interview prep. Industry-specific preparedness programs like Q-camp, A&S NEXT, and the Jepson EDGE Institute ensure undergrads are able to translate their skills when it's time to job hunt.

GENERAL INFO

Activities: Choral groups, concert band, dance, drama/theater, jazz band, literary magazine, music ensembles, musical theater, pep band, radio station, student government, student newspaper, student-run film society, symphony orchestra, campus ministries, international student organization, Model UN. **Organizations:** 190 registered organizations, 6 honor societies, 14 religious organizations. 8 fraternities, 8 sororities. **Athletics (Intercollegiate):** *Men:* Baseball, basketball, cross-country, football, golf, lacrosse, tennis. *Women:* Basketball, cross country, diving, field hockey, golf, lacrosse, soccer, swimming, tennis, track/field (outdoor), track/field (indoor). **On-Campus Highlights:** Tyler Haynes Commons, Weinstein Center for Recreation and Wellness (Fitness Center), Robins Center (Athletic Center), Boatwright Memorial Library and Coffee Shop, Carole Weinstein International Center, Westhampton Green (Modlin Center for the Arts). **Environmental Initiatives:** Signing the ACUPCC and subsequent creation of the Climate Action Plan; waste diversion initiatives; energy conservation and efficiency projects.

FINANCIAL AID

Students should submit: CSS Profile; FAFSA. Regular filing deadline is 2/1. The Princeton Review suggests that all financial aid forms be submitted as soon as possible after October 1. *Need-based scholarships/grants offered:* College/university scholarship or grant aid from institutional funds, Federal Pell, private scholarships, SEOG, state scholarships/grants. *Loan aid offered:* Direct PLUS Loans, Direct Subsidized Loans, Direct Unsubsidized Loans. Applicants will be notified of awards on or about 4/1. Federal Work-Study Program available. Institutional employment available.

THE BOTTOM LINE

The University of Richmond charges $50,910 for tuition. Beyond that, students and their families pay $5,440 for room and another $6,380 for board. UR estimates that books and supplies will cost undergrads an additional $1,100. And it's recommended that individuals set aside $1,000 to cover personal expenses. There are also $60 worth of direct loan fees. These figures add up to $64,890.

CAREER INFORMATION FROM PAYSCALE.COM	
ROI Rating	92
Bachelors and No Higher	
Median starting salary	$57,900
Median mid-career salary	$109,000
At Least Bachelors	
Median starting salary	$59,300
Median mid-career salary	$115,300
Alumni with high job meaning	46%
Degrees awarded in STEM subjects	13%

SELECTIVITY	
Admissions Rating	94
# of applicants	10,013
% of applicants accepted	33
% of acceptees attending	24
# offered a place on the wait list	3,383
% accepting a place on wait list	38
% admitted from wait list	4
# of early decision applicants	674
% accepted early decision	49

FRESHMAN PROFILE	
Range SAT EBRW	630–710
Range SAT Math	640–750
Range ACT Composite	29–32
Minimum paper TOEFL	550
Minimum internet-based TOEFL	80
% graduated top 10% of class	62
% graduated top 25% of class	92
% graduated top 50% of class	98

DEADLINES	
Early decision	
Deadline	11/1
Notification	12/15
Other ED Deadline	1/15
Other ED Notification	2/15
Early action	
Deadline	11/1
Notification	1/20
Regular	
Deadline	1/15
Notification	4/1
Nonfall registration?	No

FINANCIAL FACTS	
Financial Aid Rating	95
Annual tuition	$52,610
Room and board	$12,250
Required fees	$0
Books and supplies	$1,100
Average frosh need-based scholarship	$42,218
Average UG need-based scholarship	$41,831
% needy frosh rec. need-based scholarship or grant aid	98
% needy UG rec. need-based scholarship or grant aid	98
% needy frosh rec. non-need-based scholarship or grant aid	22
% needy UG rec. non-need-based scholarship or grant aid	18
% needy frosh rec. need-based self-help aid	74
% needy UG rec. need-based self-help aid	79
% frosh rec. any financial aid	61
% UG rec. any financial aid	67
% UG borrow to pay for school	40

University of Rochester

300 Wilson Boulevard, Rochester, NY 14627 • Admissions: 585-275-3221 • Fax: 585-461-4595

CAMPUS LIFE

Quality of Life Rating	87
Fire Safety Rating	95
Green Rating	79
Type of school	Private
Environment	City

STUDENTS

Total undergrad enrollment	5,570
% male/female	52/48
% frosh from public high school	74
% frosh live on campus	100
% ugrads live on campus	90
# of fraternities (% ugrad men join)	18 (20)
# of sororities (% ugrad women join)	15 (26)
% African American	5
% Asian	11
% Caucasian	42
% Hispanic	7
% Native American	<1
% Pacific Islander	<1
% Two or more races	3
% Race and/or ethnicity unknown	6
% international	26
# of countries represented	114

ACADEMICS

Academic Rating	85
% students returning for sophomore year	97
Calendar	Semester
Student/faculty ratio	10:1
Profs interesting rating	77
Profs accessible rating	76

Most classes have 10–19 students. Most lab/discussion sessions have 10–19 students.

MOST POPULAR MAJORS

Biology/Biological Sciences; Psychology; Economics

ABOUT THE SCHOOL

Tucked away in lovely upstate New York, the University of Rochester offers students a "unique" collegiate experience. Undergrads rave about UR's "innovative curriculum," which "essentially [dictates that there are] no required classes." Alternatively, "students...chart out their own academic paths." In turn, this "encourages personal exploration rather than conventional general education." And with so many renowned disciplines, from its outstanding music conservatory to phenomenal programs in the applied sciences, it's understandable why students relish the opportunity to explore. Inside the classroom, undergrads delight in their "amazing" professors who "are at the top of their [respective] fields." Just as essential, they are "very approachable [in] a one-on-one situation." Finally, Rochester students cheerfully report that their peers "seem genuinely engaged and happy, and possess a quirky sense of humor." And they greatly appreciate that "while everyone here strives to do better it is in no way a cut-throat environment."

BANG FOR YOUR BUCK

Though a private university, Rochester strives to ensure that it's still affordable for qualified and capable students. These efforts are definitely appreciated and many an undergrad remarked that they chose UR because they received a "great financial aid [package]." In fact, 82 percent of the students here are receiving some form of need-based aid. And the average package is roughly $38,021. That includes a combination of loans, grants, scholarships and work-study. For undergrads wary about going into debt, be assured that Rochester does provide a variety of merit-based scholarships ranging anywhere from $2,000 per year to covering the full cost of tuition.

STUDENT LIFE

If you attend Rochester, you can virtually guarantee that you'll never be at a loss for something to do. As one senior explains, "Almost every weekend there are movies shown, dance performances, athletic events and other special programs held by one of our 250+ students organizations." A fellow senior rushes to add, "The a cappella shows here are immensely popular and easily sell out our biggest auditorium (we have four different a cappella groups)." Certainly, numerous undergrads can also be found at one of the many "parties hosted by the various frats." Fortunately, students assure us that everyone is welcome and no one is pressured to drink. Further, the "school has its own bus lines" which makes venturing into Rochester pretty easy. And we're told these undergrads love to head "off campus to bowl, ice skate, or go to the mall."

CAREER

University of Rochester students do pretty well for themselves. Indeed, according to PayScale.com, the average starting salary for these grads is $57,500. And how do these undergrads land such lucrative jobs? Why, through an excellent career services office! Rochester's Career & Internship Center sponsors weekly seminars that cover everything from finding internships to discussions of networking techniques and tips. The office also offers specialized boot camps for targeted career areas. For example, students may attend boot camps based around non-profit jobs or ones centered upon engineering and applied sciences. And, of course, we'd be remiss if we neglected to mention that the center also hosts several career fairs throughout the year. Students can connect with companies such as Apple, the Rochester Museum and Science Center, the Federal Bureau of Investigations (FBI), Wegmans Food Markets and Teach for America.

University of Rochester

FINANCIAL AID: 585-275-3226 • E-MAIL: ADMIT@ADMISSIONS.ROCHESTER.EDU • WEBSITE: WWW.ROCHESTER.EDU

GENERAL INFO

Activities: Choral groups, concert band, dance, drama/theater, jazz band, literary magazine, music ensembles, musical theater, opera, pep band, radio station, student government, student newspaper, student-run film society, symphony orchestra, television station, International Student Organization, Model UN. **Organizations:** 275 registered organizations, 4 honor societies, 14 religious organizations. 18 fraternities, 15 sororities. **Athletics (Intercollegiate):** *Men:* baseball, basketball, cross-country, diving, football, golf, soccer, squash, swimming, tennis, track/field (outdoor), track/field (indoor). *Women:* basketball, crew/rowing, cross-country, diving, field hockey, golf, lacrosse, soccer, softball, swimming, tennis, track/field (outdoor), track/field (indoor), volleyball. **On-Campus Highlights:** Eastman Theater, Memorial Art Gallery, Rush Rhees Library, Interfaith Chapel, Robert B. Goergen Athletic Center, Robert B. Goergen Hall for Biomedical Engineering, The Gleason Library.

FINANCIAL AID

Students should submit: CSS Profile; FAFSA; State aid form. Priority filing deadline is 3/1. The Princeton Review suggests that all financial aid forms be submitted as soon as possible after October 1. *Need-based scholarships/grants offered:* College/university scholarship or grant aid from institutional funds, Federal Pell, private scholarships, SEOG, state scholarships/grants. *Loan aid offered:* Direct PLUS Loans, Direct Subsidized Loans, Direct Unsubsidized Loans. Applicants will be notified of awards on or about 4/1. Federal Work-Study Program available. Institutional employment available.

THE BOTTOM LINE

Tuition at this private university will cost undergraduates $52,867. On top of that, on-campus room and board runs approximately $15,860. Students will face an additional $930 in required fees. And the university advises setting aside another $1,310 for books and miscellaneous supplies. Finally, undergrads commuting from off-campus should expect to spend roughly $300 for transportation.

CAREER INFORMATION FROM PAYSCALE.COM	
ROI Rating	90
Bachelors and No Higher	
Median starting salary	$58,900
Median mid-career salary	$110,300
At Least Bachelors	
Median starting salary	$61,500
Median mid-career salary	$121,400
Alumni with high job meaning	52%
Degrees awarded in STEM subjects	32%

SELECTIVITY

Admissions Rating	93
# of applicants	18,069
% of applicants accepted	35
% of acceptees attending	24
# offered a place on the wait list	3,203
% accepting a place on wait list	55
% admitted from wait list	<1
# of early decision applicants	797
% accepted early decision	51

FRESHMAN PROFILE

Range SAT EBRW	600–720
Range SAT Math	650–770
Range ACT Composite	29–33
Minimum paper TOEFL	600
Minimum internet-based TOEFL	100
Average HS GPA	3.8

DEADLINES

Early decision	
Deadline	11/1
Notification	12/15
Regular	
Deadline	1/5
Notification	4/1
Nonfall registration?	Yes

FINANCIAL FACTS

Financial Aid Rating	95
Annual tuition	$52,867
Room and board	$15,860
Required fees	$958
Books and supplies	$1,310
Average frosh need-based scholarship	$47,440
Average UG need-based scholarship	$43,502
% needy frosh rec. need-based scholarship or grant aid	100
% needy UG rec. need-based scholarship or grant aid	99
% needy frosh rec. non-need-based scholarship or grant aid	11
% needy UG rec. non-need-based scholarship or grant aid	11
% needy frosh rec. need-based self-help aid	84
% needy UG rec. need-based self-help aid	84
% frosh rec. any financial aid	85
% UG borrow to pay for school	51
Average cumulative indebtedness	$29,393
% frosh need fully met	100
% ugrads need fully met	99
Average % of frosh need met	100
Average % of ugrad need met	99

University of Southern California

OFFICE OF ADMISSION/JOHN HUBBARD HALL, LOS ANGELES, CA 90089-0911 • ADMISSIONS: 213-740-1111 • FAX: 213-821-0200

CAMPUS LIFE

Quality of Life Rating	**81**
Fire Safety Rating	**97**
Green Rating	**84**
Type of school	Private
Environment	Metropolis

STUDENTS

Total undergrad enrollment	19,059
% male/female	49/51
% from out of state	35
% frosh from public high school	54
% frosh live on campus	98
% ugrads live on campus	30
# of fraternities (% ugrad men join)	32 (26)
# of sororities (% ugrad women join)	26 (27)
% African American	5
% Asian	21
% Caucasian	40
% Hispanic	14
% Native American	<1
% Pacific Islander	<1
% Two or more races	6
% Race and/or ethnicity unknown	1
% international	13
# of countries represented	114

ACADEMICS

Academic Rating	**76**
% students returning for sophomore year	96
% students graduating within 4 years	77
% students graduating within 6 years	92
Calendar	Semester
Student/faculty ratio	8:1
Profs interesting rating	67
Profs accessible rating	63

Most classes have 10–19 students. Most lab/discussion sessions have 20–29 students.

MOST POPULAR MAJORS

Social Sciences; Visual and Performing Arts; Business Administration and Management

ABOUT THE SCHOOL

Based in Los Angeles and known world round, the University of Southern California is a premier research institution and academic/athletic haven. USC "wants its students to do what they love without any restraint"; the school "is all about tailoring an education to the individual, and not vice-versa." Despite the size of the school, most classes are "very intimate and comfortable in setting" and students say that "even though it's a big school, it definitely has a small school feel." Professors are very passionate about their field of study and "always incorporate their personal experiences," but remain friendly and accessible. "Most of my professors insist that we call them by their first names," says a student. Make no mistake about the breezy SoCal life: the academics at USC are taken very seriously, and happily so. "It's clear that people do actually enjoy their classes," says one student.

BANG FOR YOUR BUCK

Though the sticker price may be high, USC administers one of the largest financial aid programs in the country and the majority of USC students receive financial aid to offset the cost. In addition to need-based aid, USC has more than a dozen robust scholarship programs, including departmental awards. USC Merit Scholarships (ranging in value from a few thousand dollars up to full tuition) include ten Mork Family Scholarships for full tuition plus a stipend; Stamps Leadership Scholarships for exceptional students whose test scores are in the top 1 to 2 percent nationwide; one hundred Trustee Scholarships for full tuition; and two hundred Presidential Scholarships offering half tuition.

STUDENT LIFE

The USC campus is "extremely diverse": the school enrolls more international students than any other U.S. university. The "great weather" of southern California goes without saying (the majority of students here are from in-state), and the sports scene here is huge. USC "is all about school spirit, great academics, Greek life, and football." There is plenty to keep students occupied outside of the classroom, including clubs, organizations, theatre, and music groups, and "the school does a really good job of bringing speakers and other events to campus." "There really is always something to do... Even walking to class everyday is awesome because you can definitely feel the vibe of an active campus." Many academic aspects and social aspects "combine for an ideal college experience" at USC, and "everyone can find their niche."

CAREER

The USC Career Center runs continuous workshops, counseling, information sessions, and events to help students discover and progress on their careers. An Internship Week and CareerFest (including career panels, networking mixers, and Employer Resume Review) are held every fall and spring, as are Explore@4 Career Panels where students can interact with alumni and industry professionals. The school also offers extensive internship and study abroad opportunities. USC graduates who visited PayScale.com reported an average starting salary of $59,400, and 47 percent felt they had a job with a meaningful impact on the world.

University of Southern California

FINANCIAL AID: 213-740-1111 • E-MAIL: ADMITUSC@USC.EDU • WEBSITE: WWW.USC.EDU

GENERAL INFO

Activities: Choral groups, concert band, dance, drama/theater, jazz band, literary magazine, marching band, music ensembles, musical theater, opera, pep band, radio station, student government, student newspaper, student-run film society, symphony orchestra, television station, yearbook, campus ministries, International Student Organization, Model UN. **Organizations:** 676 registered organizations, 49 honor societies, 74 religious organizations. 32 fraternities, 26 sororities. **Athletics (Intercollegiate):** *Men:* baseball, basketball, diving, football, golf, swimming, tennis, track/field (outdoor), volleyball, water polo. *Women:* basketball, crew/rowing, cross-country, diving, golf, soccer, swimming, tennis, track/field (outdoor), volleyball, water polo. **On-Campus Highlights:** USC Fisher Museum of Art, Galen Center (event & training pavilion), Leavey Library (open twenty-four hours), Heritage Hall, Tutor Campus Center.

FINANCIAL AID

Students should submit: Business/Farm Supplement; CSS Profile; FAFSA. Priority filing deadline is 2/17. The Princeton Review suggests that all financial aid forms be submitted as soon as possible after October 1. *Need-based scholarships/grants offered:* College/university scholarship or grant aid from institutional funds, Federal Pell, private scholarships, SEOG, state scholarships/grants. *Loan aid offered:* Direct PLUS Loans, Direct Subsidized Loans, Direct Unsubsidized Loans. Applicants will be notified of awards on or about 4/1. Federal Work-Study Program available. Institutional employment available.

BOTTOM LINE

Though tuition runs around $51,442, 65 percent of USC undergrads (including international students) receive financial aid, with an average need-based scholarship of $35,011. A whopping one hundred percent of average need is met. Of the 41 percent of students who took out a loan of some kind, the average debt upon graduation was $27,882.

CAREER INFORMATION FROM PAYSCALE.COM	
ROI Rating	87
Bachelors and No Higher	
Median starting salary	$62,000
Median mid-career salary	$122,600
At Least Bachelors	
Median starting salary	$63,700
Median mid-career salary	$126,300
Alumni with high job meaning	47%
Degrees awarded in STEM subjects	23%

SELECTIVITY	
Admissions Rating	98
# of applicants	55,676
% of applicants accepted	16
% of acceptees attending	37

FRESHMAN PROFILE	
Range SAT EBRW	650–730
Range SAT Math	650–770
Range ACT Composite	30–34
Average HS GPA	3.8
% graduated top 10% of class	88
% graduated top 25% of class	96
% graduated top 50% of class	100

DEADLINES	
Regular	
Priority	12/1
Deadline	1/15
Notification	4/1
Nonfall registration?	Yes

FINANCIAL FACTS	
Financial Aid Rating	91
Annual tuition	$55,320
Room and board	$15,395
Required fees	$905
Books and supplies	$1,200
Average frosh need-based scholarship	$38,196
Average UG need-based scholarship	$36,496
% needy frosh rec. need-based scholarship or grant aid	87
% needy UG rec. need-based scholarship or grant aid	90
% needy frosh rec. non-need-based scholarship or grant aid	66
% needy UG rec. non-need-based scholarship or grant aid	48
% needy frosh rec. need-based self-help aid	88
% needy UG rec. need-based self-help aid	93
% frosh rec. any financial aid	68
% UG rec. any financial aid	65
% UG borrow to pay for school	36
Average cumulative indebtedness	$29,080
% frosh need fully met	88
% ugrads need fully met	84
Average % of frosh need met	100
Average % of ugrad need met	100

The University of Texas at Austin

PO Box 8058, Austin, TX 78713-8058 • Admissions: 512-475-7399 • Fax: 512-475-7478

CAMPUS LIFE

Quality of Life Rating	**88**
Fire Safety Rating	**84**
Green Rating	**90**
Type of school	Public
Environment	Metropolis

STUDENTS

Total undergrad enrollment	39,965
% male/female	47/53
% from out of state	6
% frosh live on campus	65
% ugrads live on campus	18
# of fraternities (% ugrad men join)	43 (15)
# of sororities (% ugrad women join)	30 (18)
% African American	4
% Asian	21
% Caucasian	41
% Hispanic	23
% Native American	<1
% Pacific Islander	<1
% Two or more races	4
% Race and/or ethnicity unknown	1
% international	5
# of countries represented	96

ACADEMICS

Academic Rating	**74**
% students returning for sophomore year	95
% students graduating within 4 years	58
% students graduating within 6 years	83
Calendar	Semester
Student/faculty ratio	18:1
Profs interesting rating	74
Profs accessible rating	64

Most classes have 10–19 students. Most lab/discussion sessions have 10–19 students.

MOST POPULAR MAJORS
Computer and Information Sciences; Biology/Biological Sciences; Economics

ABOUT THE SCHOOL

Some students at the University of Texas at Austin (UT Austin) boldly make the claim that their school is considered the "Harvard of the South," and they would probably be able to make a strong case for it. Considered one of the best public schools in Texas, the massive UT Austin campus offers a world-class education through its wide array of programs in the sciences and humanities as well as state-of-the-art laboratories. Despite the large size of some of the classes, the students find their professors to be supportive. According to one student, "They are always willing to meet you outside of class, and they try their best to encourage students to speak up during class." Students flock to this research university not only for its robust academics but also for its famed athletic offerings. One student raves, "I think the greatest strengths are the level of education we receive and the athletics program. The classes here are very difficult and will prepare students very well for graduate schools or careers. The athletics program here is awesome." The football team (Go Longhorns!) certainly helps inspire the school's contagious school spirit. The school's 431-acre campus serves as home to a student body of over 51,000 (including graduate students) and offers boundless opportunities for students to get a rich and diverse social education. With over 1,100 student organizations, the campus is bustling with activities such as sports games, festivals, movie screenings, concerts, and cultural events. For those who need the rush of city life, the campus is just a few blocks away from downtown Austin, where students often frequent the numerous restaurants, bars, clubs, and live music venues, especially those on 6th Street, a major hot spot. Competitive academic programs, legendary athletics, a huge sprawling campus, the eclectic allure of Austin, a strong sense of Texas pride, and an unabashed love of a good party are the hallmarks of an education at the University of Texas at Austin.

BANG FOR YOUR BUCK

UT Austin works hard to make college affordable for the families of students who wish to attend. One effort, Texas Advance, provides scholarships to students with a family adjusted gross income up to $100,000. Many of these top-performing students will also be invited to participate in one of the university's selective academic-enrichment communities. 360 Connections set the tone once new students arrive on campus—these small groups help first-years make the most of all the opportunities for mentorship, research, internships and experiential learning that UT Austin has to offer. Meanwhile, the Office of Financial Aid offers money management information and programming needed to help all students and their families reduce the burden of unnecessary debt.

STUDENT LIFE

"Because of the huge Greek life at UT, a 'typical student' would be a sorority girl or fraternity boy," but—and it's a big but—such students "are hardly the majority, since UT is actually made of more 'atypical' people than most other schools. Everyone here has his own niche, and I could not think of any type of individual who would not be able to find one of his own." Indeed, "everyone at Texas is different! When you walk across campus, you see every type of ethnicity. There are a lot of minorities at Texas. Also, I see many disabled people, whom the school accommodates well. Everyone seems to get along. The different types of students just blend in together." Especially by Texas standards, "Austin is known for being 'weird.' If you see someone dressed in a way you've never seen before, you just shrug it off and say 'That's Austin!'"

The University of Texas at Austin

FINANCIAL AID: 512-475-6203 • WEBSITE: WWW.UTEXAS.EDU

CAREER

There is a huge career services presence at UT Austin, where each college has its own dedicated office. This way while all students have access to HireUTexas, the university's campus-wide job board, they also have resources tailored to their particular schools and interests. For instance, students in the College of Liberal Arts may take courses (for credit!) that complement and make the most of their internship experiences. And ScienceWorks is the online hub for College of Natural Sciences students looking for jobs, internships, mentors and professional development events. Job and Internship Fairs are usually organized by school as well with multiple chances to network and meet potential employers each year. UT Austin graduates who visited PayScale.com report a median starting salary of $59,100, and 48 percent derive a high level of meaning from their work.

GENERAL INFO

Environment: Metropolis. **Activities:** Choral groups, concert band, dance, drama/theater, jazz band, literary magazine, marching band, music ensembles, musical theater, opera, pep band, radio station, student government, student newspaper, student-run film society, symphony orchestra, television station, yearbook, campus ministries, international student organization. **Organizations:** 1,000 registered organizations, 12 honor societies, 110 religious organizations. 40 fraternities, 32 sororities. **Athletics (Intercollegiate):** *Men:* Baseball, basketball, cross-country, diving, football, golf, swimming, tennis, track/field (outdoor). *Women:* Basketball, crew/rowing, cross-country, diving, golf, soccer, softball, swimming, tennis, track/field (outdoor), volleyball. **On-Campus Highlights:** Student Activities Center, Frank Erwin Special Events Center, Performing Arts Center, Harry Ransom Humanities Research Center, Blanton Museum of Art.

FINANCIAL AID

Students should submit: FAFSA; Institution's own financial aid form. Priority filing deadline is 3/15. The Princeton Review suggests that all financial aid forms be submitted as soon as possible after October 1. *Need-based scholarships/grants offered:* College/university scholarship or grant aid from institutional funds, Federal Pell, private scholarships, SEOG, state scholarships/grants. *Loan aid offered:* Direct PLUS Loans, Direct Subsidized Loans, Direct Unsubsidized Loans. Applicants will be notified of awards on a rolling basis beginning 3/15. Federal Work-Study Program available. Institutional employment available.

THE BOTTOM LINE

For students who are Texas residents, the cost of tuition is $10,610, which makes the school very affordable for many. For any out-of-state students, the price tag jumps to $37,580 plus another $10,804 for room and board. Whether you're an in-state or out-of-state student, do not forget to factor in the additional cost of books and supplies, which add up to $700.

CAREER INFORMATION FROM PAYSCALE.COM	
ROI Rating	90
Bachelors and No Higher	
Median starting salary	$59,100
Median mid-career salary	$111,400
At Least Bachelors	
Median starting salary	$60,300
Median mid-career salary	$115,400
Alumni with high job meaning	48%
Degrees awarded in STEM subjects	27%

SELECTIVITY	
Admissions Rating	93
# of applicants	51,033
% of applicants accepted	36
% of acceptees attending	45

FRESHMAN PROFILE	
Range SAT EBRW	620–720
Range SAT Math	610–740
Range ACT Composite	26–33
Minimum paper TOEFL	550
Minimum internet-based TOEFL	79
% graduated top 10% of class	74
% graduated top 25% of class	17
% graduated top 50% of class	99

DEADLINES	
Regular	
Priority	None
Deadline	12/1
Nonfall registration?	Yes

FINANCIAL FACTS	
Financial Aid Rating	79
Annual in-state tuition	$10,610
Annual out-of-state tuition	$37,580
Room and board	$10,804
Required fees	$0
Books and supplies	$700
Average frosh need-based scholarship	$9,596
Average UG need-based scholarship	$9,457
% needy frosh rec. need-based scholarship or grant aid	78
% needy UG rec. need-based scholarship or grant aid	81
% needy frosh rec. non-need-based scholarship or grant aid	42
% needy UG rec. non-need-based scholarship or grant aid	24
% needy frosh rec. need-based self-help aid	65
% needy UG rec. need-based self-help aid	66
% UG rec. any financial aid	40
% UG borrow to pay for school	43
Average cumulative indebtedness	$24,883
% frosh need fully met	21
% ugrads need fully met	23
Average % of frosh need met	70
Average % of ugrad need met	71

The University of Texas at Dallas

800 West Campbell Road, Richardson, TX 75080 • Admissions: 972-883-2270 • Fax: 972-883-2599

CAMPUS LIFE

Quality of Life Rating	87
Fire Safety Rating	94
Green Rating	77
Type of school	Public
Environment	Metropolis

STUDENTS

Total undergrad enrollment	18,091
% male/female	57/43
% from out of state	4
% frosh from public high school	92
% frosh live on campus	59
% ugrads live on campus	26
# of fraternities (% ugrad men join)	12 (5)
# of sororities (% ugrad women join)	11 (7)
% African American	6
% Asian	31
% Caucasian	34
% Hispanic	18
% Native American	<1
% Pacific Islander	<1
% Two or more races	4
% Race and/or ethnicity unknown	2
% international	4
# of countries represented	78

ACADEMICS

Academic Rating	73
% students returning for sophomore year	87
% students graduating within 4 years	52
% students graduating within 6 years	69
Calendar	Semester
Student/faculty ratio	23:1
Profs interesting rating	73
Profs accessible rating	73
Most classes have 10–19 students.	

MOST POPULAR MAJORS
Computer and Information Sciences;
Mechanical Engineering; Biology/Biological
Sciences

ABOUT THE SCHOOL

A member of the UT system—it was founded as a graduate-level research center in 1969—the University of Texas at Dallas is working toward attaining the national prestige associated with its sister school, UT Austin. It is now home to more than forty centers, labs, and institutes. UTD administrators call its Academic Excellence Scholarship Program "the flagship program" of the university, and admitted students are automatically reviewed on the basis of grades in all course work, success in AP, IB, or dual credit courses, SAT or ACT scores, and class rank. AES is highly competitive and no specific acheivement will guarantee a scholarship. UTD is also competitive in its admissions process: its 61 percent acceptance rate is much lower than many state universities.

UTD focuses on producing employable graduates. The university offers a growing number of courses of study in science, engineering, arts, technology, and the social sciences, and boasts one of the top business schools in the state. In addition, the school's location just north of Dallas, in the heart of the Telecom Corridor, poises graduates for employment at one of the Dallas-Fort Worth area's over 3,000 tech companies. UTD students enjoy the free Handshake online job-recruiting system, which administrators call its "signature program."

BANG FOR YOUR BUCK

For high-performing students, UTD can provide the ultimate value: a free education. As a result of the Academic Excellence Scholarship Program and others, UTD attracts many of Texas's best and brightest with competitive scholarship offers: a striking number of students name scholarship funds as one of their top reasons for attending UTD, and the Eugene McDermott Scholars Program, which covers all expenses of a UTD education, stands out as a hallmark value opportunity. Academic Excellence scholarships are awarded each year to first-year students. Like the university itself, its ability to offer financial subsidies to its students is growing rapidly: "An ever-expanding breadth of degree programs and capital improvements," one administrator explains, "promise to push the university to the fore of education excellence" in the future. And on the employability point, UTD's Career Center "sponsors on-campus career expos, externships/job-shadowing programs, internships, and co-ops and industrial-practice programs in conjunction with the Jonsson School of Engineering and Computer Science and the Naveen Jindal School of Managements in-house career services."

STUDENT LIFE

Life on campus at UT Dallas is very focused on academics, with the consensus being that "people are here to work" and, as one student succinctly put it, "Study, study, study. Homework, homework, homework." "UT Dallas is not a party school," says a student, and others echo that sentiment, so "if you are into the party scene, you might have to look for it a little." A fair number of students report that "life at UTD consists of making your own fun, [so] don't rely on too many actual activities." However some students report a different experience: "There are a lot of clubs, even if some people may not know about them, meaning that there's something for everyone. Recently there's been a lot of campus improvement and it went from being ok looking to really nice, with a lot more areas for people to congregate. As a result campus has become a lot more lively." Additionally, students love to take advantage of the school's urban location in order to find things to do: "A lot of people go downtown for concerts/shows, museum visits, and general entertainment. There's plenty of delicious restaurants all over the place and people go out for bowling, laser tag, or the movies a lot because there's a lot of choices."

The University of Texas at Dallas

FINANCIAL AID: 972-883-2941• E-MAIL: INTEREST@UTDALLAS.EDU • WEBSITE: WWW.UTDALLAS.EDU

CAREER

The UT Dallas Career Center offers many services for students looking ahead towards their futures. Advising is available to help students focus on their interests and develop professional goals; jobs and internship listings can be accessed via Handshake; and seminars are offered on résumé and cover letter writing and interview strategies. In addition to career fairs and on-campus recruiting, UTD offers an externship and job-shadowing program that pairs students with professionals from a variety of fields. Overall, students at UT Dallas report finding the Career Center "very helpful." Out of UT Dallas alumni visiting PayScale.com, 42 percent say that they derive a high level of meaning from their careers.

GENERAL INFO

Activities: Choral groups, concert band, dance, drama/theater, jazz band, literary magazine, music ensembles, musical theater, pep band, radio station, student government, student newspaper, student-run film society, symphony orchestra, television station. **Organizations:** 300+ registered organizations, 11 honor societies, 25 fraternities and sororities. **Athletics (Intercollegiate):** *Men:* baseball, basketball, cross-country, golf, soccer, tennis. *Women:* basketball, cross-country, golf, soccer, softball, tennis, volleyball. **On-Campus Highlights:** The Pub (coffeehouse), Comet Cafe, Student Union, Activity Center, University Village clubhouses, University Commons, Dining Hall, Food Court.

FINANCIAL AID

Students should submit: FAFSA. Priority filing deadline is 4/15. The Princeton Review suggests that all financial aid forms be submitted as soon as possible after October 1. *Need-based scholarships/grants offered:* College/university scholarship or grant aid from institutional funds, Federal Pell, private scholarships, SEOG, state scholarships/grants. *Loan aid offered:* Direct PLUS Loans, Direct Subsidized Loans, Direct Unsubsidized Loans. Applicants will be notified of awards on a rolling basis. Federal Work-Study Program available. Institutional employment available.

BOTTOM LINE

UTD undergraduates give their alma mater high marks on its dedication to rewarding academic performance with financial support. There are two options for tuition for incoming students: Variable and Guaranteed. Students see overall value in their UTD experience even beyond scholarships; one notes that he enjoyed "excellent and extremely affordable/convenient," living facilities, "especially in comparison to other college housing options offering the same services or lower-quality ones for double the price."

CAREER INFORMATION FROM PAYSCALE.COM

ROI Rating	88
Bachelors and No Higher	
Median starting salary	$55,500
Median mid-career salary	$98,800
At Least Bachelors	
Median starting salary	$56,600
Median mid-career salary	$102,400
Alumni with high job meaning	41%
Degrees awarded in STEM subjects	44%

SELECTIVITY

Admissions Rating	85
# of applicants	11,791
% of applicants accepted	76
% of acceptees attending	35

FRESHMAN PROFILE

Range SAT EBRW	600–700
Range SAT Math	620–730
Range ACT Composite	26–32
Minimum paper TOEFL	550
Minimum internet-based TOEFL	80
% graduated top 10% of class	36
% graduated top 25% of class	64
% graduated top 50% of class	89

DEADLINES

Regular	
Deadline	7/1
Nonfall registration?	Yes

FINANCIAL FACTS

Financial Aid Rating	83
Annual in-state tuition	$13,034 (Variable)
Annual out-of-state tuition	$36,876 (Variable)
Room and board	$11,532
Books and supplies	$1,200
Average frosh need-based scholarship	$10,751
Average UG need-based scholarship	$9,183
% needy frosh rec. need-based scholarship or grant aid	87
% needy UG rec. need-based scholarship or grant aid	88
% needy frosh rec. non-need-based scholarship or grant aid	12
% needy UG rec. non-need-based scholarship or grant aid	6
% needy frosh rec. need-based self-help aid	84
% needy UG rec. need-based self-help aid	88
% frosh rec. any financial aid	78
% UG rec. any financial aid	71
% UG borrow to pay for school	33
Average cumulative indebtedness	$23,565
% frosh need fully met	25
% ugrads need fully met	17
Average % of frosh need met	71
Average % of ugrad need met	65

The University of Tulsa

800 SOUTH TUCKER DRIVE, TULSA, OK 74104 • ADMISSIONS: 918-631-2307 • FAX: 918-631-5003

CAMPUS LIFE

Quality of Life Rating	**90**
Fire Safety Rating	**97**
Green Rating	**83**
Type of school	Private
Affiliation	none
Environment	Metropolis

STUDENTS

Total undergrad enrollment	3,316
% male/female	56/44
% from out of state	41
% frosh from public high school	72
% frosh live on campus	80
% ugrads live on campus	65
# of fraternities (% ugrad men join)	8 (20)
# of sororities (% ugrad women join)	6 (23)
% African American	5
% Asian	5
% Caucasian	57
% Hispanic	6
% Native American	3
% Pacific Islander	<1
% Two or more races	3
% Race and/or ethnicity unknown	2
% international	19
# of countries represented	53

ACADEMICS

Academic Rating	**85**
% students returning for sophomore year	88
% students graduating within 4 years	50
% students graduating within 6 years	69
Calendar	Semester
Student/faculty ratio	11:1
Profs interesting rating	79
Profs accessible rating	82

Most classes have 10–19 students. Most lab/discussion sessions have 20–29 students.

MOST POPULAR MAJORS

Computer Science; Psychology; Finance

ABOUT THE SCHOOL

Integrity, diversity, and curiosity are a few of the values that underlie an education at The University of Tulsa, a nondenominational global research university that attracts the best and the brightest students not just from Oklahoma, but around the world. More than three quarters of students come here from the top 10 percent of their high school classes, and over a quarter have international backgrounds, attracted by the "small size…[and] the resources of a big school." More than sixty degree programs are offered to TU's 3,400 undergraduates, many of whom can take advantage of the Tulsa Undergraduate Research Challenge, which lets students collaborate with faculty on advanced research projects. The city of Tulsa also provides "plenty of opportunities for students to be active in the community," and TU students rack up more than 70,000 hours of volunteer service each year.

BANG FOR YOUR BUCK

The University of Tulsa churns out scholarship and fellowship winners regularly, and the school's "reputation as a challenging and rewarding university" is a confidence boost for employers. The "wonderful" professors are also "great resources for internships and real world advice": "They have helped me gain internships and eventually a job offer, while consistently being available to talk about everything from career advice to the football game last weekend," says a student. Almost every person comes to TU with the help of financial aid, and there are several scholarships available to students, including the $24,000 Capstone Scholarship, the $22,000 TU Excellence Scholarship, and the $20,000 Royal Blue Scholarship. The average package (aid and scholarships) was $29, 598 for the most recent incoming class.

STUDENT LIFE

The University of Tulsa student body is made up of "a diverse range of cultures and origins that help create a unique experience." One thing students appreciate most about TU is the "very inclusive environment": "We are all here to do well, but we are here to do well together." Most students are "incredibly involved," whether in Greek life, athletics, music, or research, and the school has seventeen Division 1 athletic teams. Student organization meetings, philanthropic events, intramural sports, and "so much more" take place every night of the week, and there's "always an event to attend or free food to eat;" people also often go downtown for the First Friday Art Crawl. Everyone is "friendly and happy to be here," and "most students live in on-campus housing, which makes for a close community."

CAREER

TU students can find all the resources they need for interview preparation, academic planning, and internship seeking at the Career Services' website. The department also hosts multiple industry-specific job fairs and internship workshops in both the fall and spring semesters. There are a "vast amount of research opportunities" to stock résumés, and career prep programs take place (often with free lunches) almost daily throughout the week. Of The University of Tulsa alumni visiting PayScale.com, 51 percent report that they derive a high level of meaning from their jobs.

University of Tulsa

FINANCIAL AID: 918-631-2526 • E-MAIL: ADMISSION@UTULSA.EDU • WEBSITE: WWW.UTULSA.EDU

GENERAL INFO

Activities: Choral groups, concert band, dance, drama/theater, jazz band, literary magazine, marching/pep band, music ensembles, musical theater, opera, preprofessional groups, radio station, student government, student newspaper, orchestra, television station, campus ministries, multicultural organizations, recreational clubs. **Organizations:** 178 chartered organizations, 37 honor societies, 19 religious organizations, 8 fraternities, 6 sororities. **Athletics (Intercollegiate):** *Men:* basketball, cross-country, football, soccer, tennis, track/field (outdoor), track/field (indoor). *Women:* basketball, cross-country, golf, rowing, soccer, softball, tennis, track/field (outdoor), track/field (indoor), volleyball.

FINANCIAL AID

Students should submit: FAFSA. *Need-based scholarships/grants offered:* College/university scholarship or grant aid from institutional funds, Federal Pell, private scholarships, SEOG, state scholarships/grants. *Loan aid offered:* Direct PLUS Loans, Direct Subsidized Loans, Direct Unsubsidized Loans. Applicants will be notified of awards on a rolling basis in January. Federal Work-Study Program available. Institutional employment available.

BOTTOM LINE

Tuition is $40,484 with another $11,116 for room and board, but the school has no intention of letting cost keep qualified students from attending. A whopping 94 percent of students receive some form of financial assistance, including more than $20 million given to the most recent incoming class alone.

CAREER INFORMATION FROM PAYSCALE.COM	
ROI Rating	89
Bachelors and No Higher	
Median starting salary	$58,500
Median mid-career salary	$103,200
At Least Bachelors	
Median starting salary	$62,400
Median mid-career salary	$108,900
Alumni with high job meaning	52%
Degrees awarded in STEM subjects	36%

SELECTIVITY

Admissions Rating	94
# of applicants	7,869
% of applicants accepted	39
% of acceptees attending	24

FRESHMAN PROFILE

Range SAT EBRW	590–720
Range SAT Math	560–720
Range ACT Composite	25–32
Minimum paper TOEFL	525
Minimum internet-based TOEFL	70
Average HS GPA	3.9
% graduated top 10% of class	70
% graduated top 25% of class	85
% graduated top 50% of class	97

DEADLINES

Early action	
Deadline	11/1
Notification	12/15
Regular	
Priority	1/15
Nonfall registration?	Yes

FINANCIAL FACTS

Financial Aid Rating	89
Annual tuition	$40,484
Room and board	$11,116
Required fees	$540
Books and supplies	$1,200
Average frosh need-based scholarship	$8,034
Average UG need-based scholarship	$7,945
% needy frosh rec. need-based scholarship or grant aid	92
% needy UG rec. need-based scholarship or grant aid	89
% needy frosh rec. non-need-based scholarship or grant aid	99
% needy UG rec. non-need-based scholarship or grant aid	94
% needy frosh rec. need-based self-help aid	58
% needy UG rec. need-based self-help aid	62
% frosh rec. any financial aid	91
% UG rec. any financial aid	86
% UG borrow to pay for school	50
Average cumulative indebtedness	$34,869
% frosh need fully met	38
% ugrads need fully met	35
Average % of frosh need met	88
Average % of ugrad need met	82

University of Utah

201 South 1460 East, Room 250 S, Salt Lake City, UT 84112 • Admissions: 801-581-7281 • Fax: 801-585-7864

CAMPUS LIFE

Quality of Life Rating	90
Fire Safety Rating	89
Green Rating	94
Type of school	Public
Environment	Metropolis

STUDENTS

Total undergrad enrollment	23,402
% male/female	54/46
% from out of state	19
% frosh from public high school	91
% frosh live on campus	50
% ugrads live on campus	14
# of fraternities (% ugrad men join)	10 (6)
# of sororities (% ugrad women join)	7 (7)
% African American	1
% Asian	6
% Caucasian	69
% Hispanic	13
% Native American	<1
% Pacific Islander	<1
% Two or more races	5
% Race and/or ethnicity unknown	1
% international	5
# of countries represented	87

ACADEMICS

Academic Rating	78
% students returning for sophomore year	91
% students graduating within 4 years	31
% students graduating within 6 years	67
Calendar	Semester
Student/faculty ratio	16:1
Profs interesting rating	79
Profs accessible rating	73

Most classes have 10–19 students. Most lab/discussion sessions have 10–19 students.

MOST POPULAR MAJORS

Commnication; Psychology; Economics

ABOUT THE SCHOOL

Salt Lake City's University of Utah, affectionately called "the U," is a large public school that offers extensive "academics and research [in] a student-oriented institution" with a "fun atmosphere." Over 100 majors and minors are offered in nineteen colleges and schools, including a university studies major that allows students to create an "individualized major in an area not otherwise available" at the university. The university awards BA, BS, BFA and BMus degrees, and its well-respected Hinckley Institute of Politics hosts "one of the best internship programs in the country." Additionally, the U boasts "one of the best music programs in the state" and "the Middle East department is second-to-none." Student can also customize their degree by adding an emphasis to their major or by pursuing one of the school's two-dozen undergraduate certificates. The U has "incredible" professors who bring "a challenging curriculum and a wide variety of perspectives" to their classrooms, and many have "won awards and recognition in the academic world."

BANG FOR YOUR BUCK

The U has a wide array of scholarships for incoming, first-year students, including academic scholarships, diversity scholarships, and need-based awards. There are also grants to help students with financial need, which the university describes as the cornerstone of its aid program for students with demonstrated need. The University of Utah says that it places a high-priority on providing need-based aid "to ensure that an economically diverse student population can enroll at the university." Many students cite "good scholarship" opportunities as a major factor when deciding to attend the University of Utah.

STUDENT LIFE

According to one student, anyone who is willing to put in the effort will find plenty of opportunities to take advantage of at the U: "The opportunities are not limited to the brightest students; rather, they are available to any proactive student." Campus events through "student government, clubs, and other extracurricular activities" abound at the U, where involved students become "very close-knit." Students praise the ample research opportunities available on campus and say that many students get "involved in the local community." Students say that the free "lecturers and discussion panels hosted by the school are intriguing and insightful." Campus activities include seasonal sports and "some of the best outdoors in the nation. Killer snow, amazing hills, mountains, lakes and streams." While "the typical student is probably married and working on completing a degree to support themselves, their spouses, and possibly their children," everyone can "fit in great because there are hundreds of different student groups and opportunities to get involved. It's easy to find a niche."

CAREER

The University of Utah's Career Services office offers students a number of ways to prepare themselves for the job market. Career coaches help students understand how to leverage their talents and interests into fulfilling careers by planning research opportunities and experiential learning. Career services also hosts three on-campus volunteer, internship and job fairs throughout the year, including a

University of Utah

FINANCIAL AID: 801-581-6211 • E-MAIL: ADMISSIONS@SA.UTAH.EDU • WEBSITE: WWW.UTAH.EDU

science and engineering focused career fair. The renowned Hinckley Institute for Politics places student from all disciples into internships every year. Students say they are able participate "in several meaningful extracurricular activities," and have access to top-notch "lab equipment, job opportunities, internships, or study abroad programs." University of Utah graduates who visited PayScale.com report an average early career salary of $51,100 and mid-career salaries average at $97,500. Sixty percent of graduates say their job helps to make the world a better place.

GENERAL INFO

Activities: Choral groups, concert band, dance, drama/theater, jazz band, literary magazine, marching band, music ensembles, musical theater, opera, pep band, radio station, student government, student newspaper, student-run film society, symphony orchestra, television station, campus ministries, International Student Organization, Model UN 238 registered organizations, 41 honor societies, 9 religious organizations. 10 fraternities, 7 sororities. **Athletics (Intercollegiate):** *Men:* baseball, basketball, cheerleading, diving, football, golf, skiing (downhill/alpine), skiing (nordic/cross-country), swimming, tennis. *Women:* basketball, cheerleading, cross-country, diving, gymnastics, skiing (downhill/alpine), skiing (nordic/cross-country), soccer, softball, swimming, tennis, track/field (outdoor), track/field (indoor), volleyball. **On-Campus Highlights:** Rice Eccles Stadium, Jon M. Huntsman Center, Huntsman Cancer Institute, Utah Museum of Fine Arts, Utah Museum of Natural History, Marriott Library Red Butte Gardens Olympic Cauldron Park Fort Douglas Museum and Cemetery Kingsbury Hall/Gardner Hall.

FINANCIAL AID

Students should submit: FAFSA. Priority filing deadline is 2/15. The Princeton Review suggests that all financial aid forms be submitted as soon as possible after October 1. *Need-based scholarships/grants offered:* College/university scholarship or grant aid from institutional funds, Federal Nursing Scholarships, Federal Pell, Private scholarships, SEOG, State scholarships/grants. *Loan aid offered:* Direct PLUS Loans, Direct Subsidized Loans, Direct Unsubsidized Loans. Applicants will be notified of awards on a rolling basis beginning 3/1. Federal Work-Study Program available. Institutional employment available.

BOTTOM LINE

In-state tuition at the University of Utah is $7,408 and out-of-state tuition runs $25,929 per academic year. On campus room and board is $9,425 and students pay $1,110 in fees. The average undergraduate need-based scholarship is $7,029, and on average students leave with $21,081 in student loan debt. Only 39 percent of students take out some form of loan during their U of U undergraduate education.

CAREER INFORMATION FROM PAYSCALE.COM	
ROI Rating	88
Bachelors and No Higher	
Median starting salary	$53,400
Median mid-career salary	$101,600
At Least Bachelors	
Median starting salary	$55,700
Median mid-career salary	$107,700
Alumni with high job meaning	57%
Degrees awarded in STEM subjects	22%

SELECTIVITY	
Admissions Rating	84
# of applicants	22,400
% of applicants accepted	66
% of acceptees attending	28

FRESHMAN PROFILE	
Range SAT EBRW	560–670
Range SAT Math	550–680
Range ACT Composite	22–29
Minimum paper TOEFL	550
Minimum internet-based TOEFL	80
Average HS GPA	3.6

DEADLINES	
Early action	
Deadline	12/1
Notification	1/15
Regular	
Priority	12/1
Deadline	4/1
Nonfall registration?	Yes

FINANCIAL FACTS	
Financial Aid Rating	81
Annual in-state tuition	$7,997
Annual out-of-state tuition	$27,990
Room and board	$10,262
Required fees	$1,225
Room and board	NR
Average frosh need-based scholarship	$7,754
Average UG need-based scholarship	$7,178
% needy frosh rec. need-based scholarship or grant aid	87
% needy UG rec. need-based scholarship or grant aid	81
% needy frosh rec. non-need-based scholarship or grant aid	13
% needy UG rec. non-need-based scholarship or grant aid	6
% needy frosh rec. need-based self-help aid	90
% needy UG rec. need-based self-help aid	85
% frosh rec. any financial aid	75
% UG rec. any financial aid	64
% UG borrow to pay for school	39
Average cumulative indebtedness	$21,188
% frosh need fully met	20
% ugrads need fully met	15
Average % of frosh need met	66
Average % of ugrad need met	65

University of Virginia

OFFICE OF ADMISSION, CHARLOTTESVILLE, VA 22906 • ADMISSIONS: 434-982-3200 • FAX: 434-924-3587

CAMPUS LIFE

Quality of Life Rating	88
Fire Safety Rating	90
Green Rating	96
Type of school	Public
Environment	City

STUDENTS

Total undergrad enrollment	16,089
% male/female	46/54
% from out of state	27
% frosh from public high school	72
% frosh live on campus	100
% ugrads live on campus	39
# of fraternities (% ugrad men join)	31 (24)
# of sororities (% ugrad women join)	16 (28)
% African American	7
% Asian	14
% Caucasian	58
% Hispanic	7
% Native American	<1
% Pacific Islander	<1
% Two or more races	4
% Race and/or ethnicity unknown	6
% international	4
# of countries represented	122

ACADEMICS

Academic Rating	89
% students returning for sophomore year	97
% students graduating within 4 years	88
% students graduating within 6 years	95
Calendar	Semester
Student/faculty ratio	15:1
Profs interesting rating	80
Profs accessible rating	82

Most classes have 10–19 students. Most lab/discussion sessions have 20–29 students.

MOST POPULAR MAJORS
Biology/Biological Sciences; Economics; Business/Commerce

#10 BEST VALUE COLLEGE

ABOUT THE SCHOOL
The University of Virginia's offerings live up to Thomas Jefferson's presidential legacy. UVA seamlessly blends the academic advantages of the Ivy League with the social life and the price tag of a large state school. The wealth of academic and extracurricular activities available here is paralleled at just a handful of schools around the country, and the school "values academia while fostering an enjoyable atmosphere for students." While class sizes can be large, and getting into the courses you want can be difficult, students rave about their engaging and inspiring professors, "who care and keep students from being 'numbers.'" Graduation rates are among the highest in the country, and the university has one of the highest graduation rates for African-American students. UVA also takes its history and traditions very seriously. The student-administered honor code is a case in point; sanctions can be harsh, but only for those who disrespect it. "Students claim full responsibility for their grades and actions, while being engaged and challenged in all aspects of life," says a student.

BANG FOR YOUR BUCK
UVA has one of the largest per-capita endowments of any public school in the country and exerts a tremendous effort to ensure that its undergraduates have access to an affordable education regardless of economic circumstances. Around half of undergraduates receive some form of financial aid, and the university aims to meet 100 percent of every student's demonstrated need. There are loan-free financial aid packages for low-income students and new Blue Ridge Scholarships for high achieving students with high financial need. There are caps on need-based loans for middle-income families. By limiting debt—or eliminating it altogether, in the case of students with the most need—UVA ensures that you can afford to attend the university as long as you can get admitted and maintain decent grades. Scholarships abound for Virginia residents, including the Virginia Commonwealth Award, which gives recipients up to $3,000 per academic year. There are plenty of other scholarships, too, available based upon need, academic achievement, and specific donor criteria. UVA's signature program, Jefferson Scholars, covers the tuition, fees, room and board of extraordinary students.

STUDENT LIFE
Students here "often get typecast as homogeneous and preppy." Overall "life at UVA is pretty chill, but when exams roll around life can be very hectic." Due to the top-notch academics, one student says, "during the week I typically spend most of my time studying." It's not all work and no play, however, as "people are committed to academics but play hard on the weekends. Parties off-grounds, going to bars, hanging out with friends, seeing shows and performances, going to dinner, etc." are all popular. "While the UVA party scene is definitely predominant, both the University and the city of Charlottesville provide plenty of alternative opportunities for entertainment." "It seems that almost every day of the week there is something university-sponsored to attend," says a student, and physical activity is big too: "[Students] like playing sports, going running, going hiking in the areas around Charlottesville, playing Frisbee on the lawn, etc. Everyone always seems to be outdoors during nice weather." The

University of Virginia

FINANCIAL AID: 434-982-6000 • E-MAIL: UNDERGRADADMISSION@VIRGINIA.EDU • WEBSITE: WWW.VIRGINIA.EDU

wealth of things to keep busy pays off for students. "Life at school is usually buzzing," says a student, and another raves that "I can't imagine being happier anywhere else."

CAREER

University Career Services offers all of the standard resources for undergrads, including advising and one-on-one career planning; job fairs and on-campus recruitment; internship and job search services; and professional development services like résumé building and interview coaching. It also offers specialized career events in a variety of fields, such as commerce, engineering, nursing, education, and government and non-profits. The new Internship Center is a hub for all things internship related, like the University Internship Program that provides field placement based on what students are learning in the classroom. One student raves that "UVA really excels in career training and placement." Career Exploration Workshops and other self-assessments ensure that undergrads are attuned to their personal styles and interests. "The students [at UVA] are very ambitious and career-focused," and out of alumni visiting PayScale.com, 48 percent report that they derive a high level of meaning from their jobs.

GENERAL INFO

Activities: Choral groups, concert band, dance, drama/theater, jazz band, literary magazine, marching band, music ensembles, musical theater, opera, pep band, radio station, student government, student newspaper, student-run film society, symphony orchestra, television station, campus ministries, international student organization.

FINANCIAL AID

Students should submit: CSS Profile; FAFSA. Priority filing deadline is 3/1. The Princeton Review suggests that all financial aid forms be submitted as soon as possible after October 1. *Need-based scholarships/grants offered:* College/university scholarship or grant aid from institutional funds, Federal Nursing Scholarships, Federal Pell, Private scholarships, SEOG, State scholarships/grants. *Loan aid offered:* Direct PLUS Loans, Direct Subsidized Loans, Direct Unsubsidized Loans. Applicants will be notified of awards on or about 4/5. Federal Work-Study Program available. Institutional employment available.

BOTTOM LINE

There is a large disparity here between tuition and fees for in-state versus out-of-state students. That's not unusual, just something to note. It's also important to keep in mind that 100 percent of applicants with financial need have their needs met. The sticker price for tuition, fees, room and board, and personal expenses for Virginia residents is somewhere in the neighborhood of $26,500 per year. For residents of other states, it's more than twice as much at $56,700. The average undergraduate need-based scholarship totals $30,980.

CAREER INFORMATION FROM PAYSCALE.COM	
ROI Rating	95
Bachelors and No Higher	
Median starting salary	$62,300
Median mid-career salary	$119,900
At Least Bachelors	
Median starting salary	$64,100
Median mid-career salary	$125,100
Alumni with high job meaning	46%
Degrees awarded in STEM subjects	23%

SELECTIVITY	
Admissions Rating	97
# of applicants	36,779
% of applicants accepted	27
% of acceptees attending	38
# offered a place on the wait list	5,961
% accepting a place on wait list	61
% admitted from wait list	3

FRESHMAN PROFILE	
Range SAT EBRW	650–730
Range SAT Math	640–740
Range ACT Composite	29–33
Average HS GPA	4.3
% graduated top 10% of class	88
% graduated top 25% of class	98
% graduated top 50% of class	100

DEADLINES	
Early action	
Deadline	11/1
Notification	1/31
Regular	
Deadline	1/1
Notification	4/1
Nonfall registration?	No

FINANCIAL FACTS	
Financial Aid Rating	94
Annual in-state tuition	$14,505
Annual out-of-state tuition	$46,046
Room and board	$11,220
Required fees	$2,845
Books and supplies	$1,320
Average frosh need-based scholarship	$21,517
Average UG need-based scholarship	$20,980
% needy frosh rec. need-based scholarship or grant aid	85
% needy UG rec. need-based scholarship or grant aid	84
% needy frosh rec. non-need-based scholarship or grant aid	8
% needy UG rec. non-need-based scholarship or grant aid	7
% needy frosh rec. need-based self-help aid	63
% needy UG rec. need-based self-help aid	65
% frosh rec. any financial aid	59
% UG rec. any financial aid	52
% UG borrow to pay for school	33
Average cumulative indebtedness	$24,598
% frosh need fully met	100
% ugrads need fully met	100
Average % of frosh need met	100
Average % of ugrad need met	100

University of Washington

1410 NORTHEAST CAMPUS PARKWAY, SEATTLE, WA 98195-5852 • ADMISSIONS: 206-543-9686 • FAX: 206-685-3655

CAMPUS LIFE

Quality of Life Rating	78
Fire Safety Rating	95
Green Rating	99
Type of school	Public
Environment	Metropolis

STUDENTS

Total undergrad enrollment	30,475
% male/female	47/53
% from out of state	18
% frosh live on campus	70
% ugrads live on campus	27
# of fraternities (% ugrad men join)	32 (16)
# of sororities (% ugrad women join)	16 (15)
% African American	3
% Asian	24
% Caucasian	40
% Hispanic	8
% Native American	<1
% Pacific Islander	<1
% Two or more races	7
% Race and/or ethnicity unknown	1
% international	15
# of countries represented	84

ACADEMICS

Academic Rating	76
% students returning for sophomore year	94
% students graduating within 4 years	65
% students graduating within 6 years	84
Calendar	Quarter
Student/faculty ratio	19:1
Profs interesting rating	71
Profs accessible rating	68

Most classes have 20–29 students. Most discussion/lab session have 20–29 students.

MOST POPULAR MAJORS

Computer Science; Engineering; Business Administration and Management

ABOUT THE SCHOOL

Known as "U-Dub," the University of Washington's flagship campus in Seattle is the largest university on the West Coast, providing excellent "course options, location, and a good price range." Its resources are truly astonishing, creating a "diverse student body with an aim to learn about diverse subjects." The school's "great libraries and huge online databases... make researching for papers (almost) a snap!" The Career Center at UW ensures that students have access to a myriad of internship and other experiential-learning opportunities. UW International Programs and Exchanges (IPE) provides hundreds of study abroad and internship options to UW students, and the school "boasts a great level of awareness of international issues." UW offers more than seventy student exchanges with universities around the world that are available to undergraduates from most fields. Husky athletics always draw huge crowds, and the school "has an electric campus" even on nongame days. More than 850+ student clubs and organizations are on offer. The Greek community is big without being overwhelming.

BANG FOR YOUR BUCK

The University of Washington is committed to making students' education affordable by providing financial assistance in a number of areas—from grants and loans to scholarships and work-study opportunities. The University of Washington offers a full range of grant opportunities for students who qualify. More than $152 million in grants were received by UW undergraduates in 2010–11. The average freshman grant was $11,800. Both merit- and need-based scholarship awards are also available, and the university provided $28.5 million in scholarships. UW's Husky Promise program guarantees full tuition and standard fees will be covered via grant or scholarship support for eligible Washington residents. The cutoff income level that UW has set for eligibility is the highest in the nation for comparable programs.

STUDENT LIFE

"At such a large university, there is no 'typical' student," undergrads tell us, observing that "one can find just about any demographic here and there is a huge variety in personalities." There "are quite a lot of yuppies, but then again, it's Seattle," and by and large "the campus is ultraliberal. Most students care about the environment, are not religious, and are generally accepting of other diverse individuals." Otherwise, "you've got your stereotypes: the Greeks, the street fashion pioneers, the various ethnic communities, the Oxford-looking grad students, etc." In terms of demographics, "the typical student at UW is middle-class and is from the Seattle area," and "there are a lot of African American students and a very large number of Asian students." All groups "seem to socialize with each other."

CAREER

Internship, leadership, and service learning experiences are all on the menu at the University of Washington, where offices like The Career Center and the Center for Experiential Learning and Diversity are dedicated to connecting students with opportunity. For example, students and faculty work side-by-side on projects through the Undergraduate Research Program, or undergrads may join in the Community for Social Progress, which links academics with service learning in the community. HuskyJobs consolidates job postings, internships, and volunteer opportunities, as well as information about employers who are interviewing on campus, all

University of Washington

FINANCIAL AID: 206-543-6101 • WEBSITE: WWW.WASHINGTON.EDU

in one handy place. Even better, career workshops aren't just for enrolled students—the two-day Dependable Strengths Seminars are geared toward alumni or community members "in any stage of career transition."

GENERAL INFO

Activities: Choral groups, concert band, dance, drama/theater, jazz band, literary magazine, marching band, music ensembles, musical theater, opera, pep band, radio station, student government, student newspaper, student-run film society, symphony orchestra, television station, campus ministries, international student organization. **Organizations:** 850 registered organizations, 13 honor societies, 52 religious organizations. 32 fraternities, 16 sororities. **Athletics (Intercollegiate):** *Men:* Baseball, basketball, crew/rowing, cross-country, football, golf, soccer, tennis, track/field (outdoor). *Women:* Basketball, crew/rowing, cross-country, golf, gymnastics, soccer, softball, tennis, track/field (outdoor), volleyball. **On-Campus Highlights:** Henry Art Gallery, Burke Museum, Meany Hall for Performing Arts, football games at Husky Stadium, Waterfront Activities Center (WAC). **Environmental Initiatives:** College of the Environment. Environmental Stewardship and Sustainability Office; Strategy Management Finance and Facilities. This office supports the Environmental Stewardship Advisory Committee (ESAC). Charter signatory of the American College & University Presidents Climate Commitment (ACUPCC); development and submission of a Climate Action Plan.

FINANCIAL AID

Students should submit: FAFSA;. Priority filing deadline is 1/15. The Princeton Review suggests that all financial aid forms be submitted as soon as possible after October 1. *Need-based scholarships/grants offered:* College/university scholarship or grant aid from institutional funds, Federal Pell, private scholarships, SEOG, state scholarships/grants. *Loan aid offered:* Direct PLUS Loans, Direct Subsidized Loans, Direct Unsubsidized Loans. Applicants will be notified of awards on or about 4/1. Federal Work-Study Program available. Institutional employment available.

BOTTOM LINE

In-state tuition at the University of Washington is about $9,694 annually, and out-of-state tuition is in the ballpark of $33,732. Room and board can be as much as an additional $11,691. Students graduate with about $21,900 in debt on average.

CAREER INFORMATION FROM PAYSCALE.COM	
ROI Rating	90
Bachelors and No Higher	
Median starting salary	$59,900
Median mid-career salary	$111,800
At Least Bachelors	
Median starting salary	$61,100
Median mid-career salary	$116,000
Alumni with high job meaning	52%
Degrees awarded in STEM subjects	34%

SELECTIVITY	
Admissions Rating	91
# of applicants	44,877
% of applicants accepted	46
% of acceptees attending	33

FRESHMAN PROFILE	
Range SAT EBRW	590–690
Range SAT Math	600–730
Range ACT Composite	27–32
Minimum paper TOEFL	540
Minimum internet-based TOEFL	76
Average HS GPA	3.8

DEADLINES	
Regular	
Deadline	11/15
Nonfall registration?	No

FINANCIAL FACTS	
Financial Aid Rating	80
Annual in-state tuition	$9,909
Annual out-of-state tuition	$34,473
Room and board	$12,117
Required fees	$1,375
Books and supplies	$825
Average frosh need-based scholarship	$15,650
Average UG need-based scholarship	$15,550
% needy frosh rec. need-based scholarship or grant aid	88
% needy UG rec. need-based scholarship or grant aid	85
% needy frosh rec. non-need-based scholarship or grant aid	24
% needy UG rec. non-need-based scholarship or grant aid	15
% needy frosh rec. need-based self-help aid	49
% needy UG rec. need-based self-help aid	56
% frosh rec. any financial aid	42
% UG rec. any financial aid	40
% UG borrow to pay for school	35
Average cumulative indebtedness	$19,880
% frosh need fully met	34
% ugrads need fully met	26
Average % of frosh need met	79
Average % of ugrad need met	77

University of Wisconsin—Madison

702 West Johnson Street, Suite 101, Madison, WI 53715-1007 • Admissions: 608-262-3961 • Fax: 608-262-7706

CAMPUS LIFE

Quality of Life Rating	**93**
Fire Safety Rating	**83**
Green Rating	**60***
Type of school	Public
Environment	City

STUDENTS

Total undergrad enrollment	29,931
% male/female	49/51
% from out of state	34
% frosh live on campus	92
% ugrads live on campus	25
# of fraternities (% ugrad men join)	26 (9)
# of sororities (% ugrad women join)	11 (8)
% African American	2
% Asian	6
% Caucasian	73
% Hispanic	5
% Native American	<1
% Pacific Islander	<1
% Two or more races	3
% Race and/or ethnicity unknown	1
% international	9
# of countries represented	102

ACADEMICS

Academic Rating	**86**
% students returning for sophomore year	95
% students graduating within 4 years	61
% students graduating within 6 years	87
Calendar	Semester
Student/faculty ratio	18:1
Profs interesting rating	82
Profs accessible rating	80

Most classes have 10–19 students. Most lab/discussion sessions have 10–19 students.

MOST POPULAR MAJORS

Biology/Biological Sciences; Economics; Political Science and Government; Computer Sciences

ABOUT THE SCHOOL

A prolific public research institution, the University of Wisconsin-Madison is home to almost 30,000 undergraduates, who avail themselves of more than 200 majors, 4,700 classes, and the independent opportunities provided by a university that spends a whopping one billion dollars in research expenditures annually. Education at UW-Madison is guided by the mission of "The Wisconsin Idea," which holds that research and teaching at the school should also be done for the good of the state. There are "endless opportunities": "working in research labs, a huge variety of classes, clubs," free tutoring and learning support units throughout campus, and a "good athletic program and engineering program." Professors are "up-to-date on research, allowing them to bring the most recent information into the classroom," and are "not only top-ranked in research, but the majority care about the student experience."

BANG FOR YOUR BUCK

UW-Madison is chockablock with strong academic programs that "offer so many avenues for future careers." Students find there are "wonderful opportunities to get involved in research," which allows them "to contribute to scientific discovery, meet and bond with professors, and add things to your résumé." The Wisconsin Idea as a school mission helps students "acquire the theoretical background to succeed and do well at their jobs." Each school has its own individual merit scholarships to award to deserving students, and the University's Scholarships @ UW-Madison is a handy site that matches student data with possible open scholarship opportunities.

STUDENT LIFE

At UW-Madison, there are "many students from the Midwest, particularly Wisconsin, Illinois, and Minnesota," but plenty come here from the East and West coasts, and the diversity of such a large school is as high as one would expect. Besides participation in the hundreds of student organizations on-campus, people also "enjoy spending time at the beautiful Memorial Union Terrace, running on the Lakeshore path, and getting involved with the many recreational opportunities." During the week, students are mostly putting their time towards class and work, but on the weekends "everyone goes out and has fun at bars and house parties but then buckles down on Sunday." State Street offers lots of options for "shopping and really amazing restaurants," and "the students here are definitely the life of the party." Everyone "loves the Badgers," and athletic games are popular anchors to social life.

CAREER

Individual colleges and schools at UW-Madison have their own dedicated career and advising centers with "good job placement and recruiting," and the Career Exploration Center (CEC) hosts a series of workshops on a variety of topics throughout the year designed to help students winnow down or channel their passions and strengths into concrete paths. The alumni network is gigantic, and there are "great networking connections with important businesses and institutions through the East and Midwest." Says one student: "Often times when you meet a Wisconsin graduate, and exchange of words is unnecessary. You both understand that your experience in college surpasses what anyone else has experienced." Of the University of Wisconsin-Madison alumni visiting PayScale.com, 50 percent report that they derive a high level of meaning from their jobs.

University of Wisconsin—Madison

FINANCIAL AID: 608-262-3060 • E-MAIL: ONWISCONSIN@ADMISSIONS.WISC.EDU • WEBSITE: WWW.WISC.EDU

GENERAL INFO

Activities: Choral groups, concert band, dance, drama/theater, jazz band, literary magazine, marching band, music ensembles, musical theater, opera, pep band, radio station, student government, student newspaper, student-run film society, symphony orchestra, television station, yearbook, international student organization. **Organizations:** 985 registered organizations, 27 honor societies, 26 fraternities, 11 sororities. **Athletics (Intercollegiate):** *Men:* Basketball, cheerleading, crew/rowing, cross-country, football, golf, ice hockey, soccer, swimming, tennis, track/field (outdoor), wrestling. *Women:* Basketball, cheerleading, crew/rowing, cross-country, golf, ice hockey, soccer, softball, swimming, tennis, track/field (outdoor), volleyball. **On-Campus Highlights:** Allen Centennial Gardens, Kohl Center, Memorial Union Terrace, Chazen Museum of Art, Babcock Hall Dairy Plant and Store.

FINANCIAL AID

Students should submit: FAFSA. Priority filing deadline is 12/1. The Princeton Review suggests that all financial aid forms be submitted as soon as possible after October 1. *Need-based scholarships/grants offered:* College/university scholarship or grant aid from institutional funds, Federal Pell, private scholarships, SEOG, state scholarships/grants. *Loan aid offered:* Direct PLUS Loans, Direct Subsidized Loans, Direct Unsubsidized Loans. Applicants will be notified of awards on a rolling basis beginning 3/1. Federal Work-Study Program available. Institutional employment available.

BOTTOM LINE

Wisconsin residents pay a steal of $10,556 for tuition and fees while out-of-state residents must cough up $36,805.28. Minnesota residents get a break at $14,340.08. Room and board runs another $11,114 and new first-year students must pay an additional fee of $275. Aid is available to all students; the UW-Madison website offers a clean step-by-step process for obtaining financial assistance.

CAREER INFORMATION FROM PAYSCALE.COM	
ROI Rating	91
Bachelors and No Higher	
Median starting salary	$55,700
Median mid-career salary	$101,800
At Least Bachelors	
Median starting salary	$57,000
Median mid-career salary	$105,600
Alumni with high job meaning	49%
Degrees awarded in STEM subjects	33%

SELECTIVITY	
Admissions Rating	92
# of applicants	35,615
% of applicants accepted	54
% of acceptees attending	35

FRESHMAN PROFILE	
Range SAT EBRW	620–690
Range SAT Math	660–760
Range ACT Composite	27–31
Average HS GPA	3.8
% graduated top 10% of class	52
% graduated top 25% of class	89
% graduated top 50% of class	99

DEADLINES	
Early action	
Deadline	11/1
Notification	1/31
Regular	
Deadline	2/1
Notification	3/31
Nonfall registration?	Yes

FINANCIAL FACTS	
Financial Aid Rating	89
Annual in-state tuition	$9,273
Annual out-of-state tuition	$33,523
Room and board	$11,114
Required fees	$1,260
Books and supplies	$1,200
Average frosh need-based scholarship	$12,746
Average UG need-based scholarship	$11,806
% needy frosh rec. need-based scholarship or grant aid	78
% needy UG rec. need-based scholarship or grant aid	79
% needy frosh rec. non-need-based scholarship or grant aid	10
% needy UG rec. non-need-based scholarship or grant aid	11
% needy frosh rec. need-based self-help aid	72
% needy UG rec. need-based self-help aid	76
% UG borrow to pay for school	45
Average cumulative indebtedness	$27,979
% frosh need fully met	45
% ugrads need fully met	42
Average % of frosh need met	79
Average % of ugrad need met	80

Vanderbilt University

2305 West End Avenue, Nashville, TN 37203 • Admissions: 615-322-2561 • Fax: 615-343-7765

CAMPUS LIFE

Quality of Life Rating	99
Fire Safety Rating	91
Green Rating	98
Type of school	Private
Environment	Metropolis

STUDENTS

Total undergrad enrollment	6,885
% male/female	49/51
% from out of state	90
% frosh from public high school	66
% frosh live on campus	100
% ugrads live on campus	90
# of fraternities (% ugrad men join)	17 (34)
# of sororities (% ugrad women join)	15 (50)
% African American	10
% Asian	13
% Caucasian	48
% Hispanic	10
% Native American	1
% Pacific Islander	<1
% Two or more races	5
% Race and/or ethnicity unknown	5
% international	8
# of countries represented	49

ACADEMICS

Academic Rating	95
% students returning for sophomore year	97
% students graduating within 4 years	86
% students graduating within 6 years	92
Calendar	Semester
Student/faculty ratio	7:1
Profs interesting rating	97
Profs accessible rating	96

Most classes have 10–19 students. Most lab/discussion sessions have 10–19 students.

MOST POPULAR MAJORS

Economics; Human and Organizational Development; Medicine, Health, and Society

ABOUT THE SCHOOL

Undergraduates are attracted to Nashville's Vanderbilt University, a mid-sized private research university, by its "diverse student body," "strong research" opportunities, and a "collaborative classroom culture." And while the education is "top-notch," Vanderbilt's 6,800 undergrads here appreciate that there's a healthy "balance between academics, extracurriculars and social life." Student apply directly to one of Vandy's four undergraduate schools (College of Arts and Science, School of Engineering, Peabody College of Education and Human Development, or Blair School of Music). Across all four schools are opportunities for research, internships, and involvement in honors programs. Many students, especially individuals who are undeclared, really value the school's "good pre-major advising program." They're also quick to mention that they have access to "great tutoring services" as well. Even better, the clear majority of professors at Vanderbilt are "really invested in their students and go out of their way to see them succeed." Further, they know how to create a classroom environment that's "engaging." And they work hard to ensure that the course-work is both "challenging [and] rewarding." Best of all, professors here are "very accessible" and quite "willing [to offer both] their time and [their] resources."

BANG FOR YOUR BUCK

At first glance, it's easy to experience sticker shock when looking at the cost of a Vanderbilt education. In fact, every year the university distributes more than $42 million in aid. Vanderbilt has pledged to meet 100 percent of a family's demonstrated need solely with grants so students don't have to worry about paying back loans. Vanderbilt also sponsors several merit-based scholarships. Rather competitive, these scholarships are awarded to incoming students who demonstrate exceptional intellectual prowess. The three signature scholarships–The Ingram Scholarship Program, The Cornelius Vanderbilt Scholarship, and The Chancellor's Scholarship–all cover full-tuition and offer a summer stipend for research, study abroad, a creative endeavor, community service, or the required immersion Vanderbilt experience.

STUDENT LIFE

At Vanderbilt, life beyond the classroom is full of opportunity. As one student explains, "There are so many student-run and university-run events going on every single day. It's hard to choose which interesting and fun [ones] to go to!" For starters, there are numerous "cultural events [such as] Diwali, Cafe Con Leche, and the Asian New Year Festival." Many undergrads can also be found heading to the "student recreational center to either work out, play basketball, rock climb, play racquetball, or attend yoga, spinning, and other classes." Certainly, there are "tons of clubs and volunteer opportunities" with which to get involved as well. And, like many schools, students admit that "Thursday nights, Friday nights, and Saturday days are usually parties at frats, bars, or tailgates." Of course, when undergrads want a break from campus, they can "explore the food, music and culture" scene that Nashville has to offer.

Vanderbilt University

FINANCIAL AID: 800-288-0204 • E-MAIL: ADMISSIONS@VANDERBILT.EDU • WEBSITE: WWW.VANDERBILT.EDU

CAREER

Vanderbilt's stellar Career Center does its utmost to help students meet their professional goals and dreams. Right from the beginning, undergrads can meet with a Career Coach assigned to work with their specific major. What's more, the Center makes meeting with said coach incredibly easy; you can get together in person, via Skype, or speak over the phone. Students can also tap into numerous online resources, taking career assessments, searching for internship listings, etc. Additionally, the Career Center sponsors a myriad of events throughout the academic year. For example, the office hosts industry specific "slams." These operate as fun, casual networking events wherein companies pitch themselves to students in rapid-fire rounds and then set up tables so interested individuals can further the conversation. Of course, students can rest assured that there are more traditional career fairs as well.

GENERAL INFO

Activities: Choral groups, concert band, dance, drama/theater, jazz band, literary magazine, marching band, music ensembles, musical theater, opera, pep band, radio station, student government. **Organizations:** 430 registered organizations, 20 honor societies, 24 religious organizations. 17 fraternities, 15 sororities. **Athletics (Intercollegiate):** *Men:* Baseball, basketball, cross-country, football, golf, tennis. *Women:* Basketball, bowling, cross-country, golf, lacrosse, soccer, swimming, tennis, track and field.

FINANCIAL AID

Students should submit: CSS Profile; FAFSA. Priority filing deadline is 2/1. The Princeton Review suggests that all financial aid forms be submitted as soon as possible after October 1. *Need-based scholarships/grants offered:* College/university scholarship or grant aid from institutional funds; Federal Pell; Private scholarships; SEOG; State scholarships/grants; United Negro College Fund. *Loan aid offered:* Direct PLUS Loans, Direct Subsidized Loans, Direct Unsubsidized Loans. Applicants will be notified of awards on or about 4/1. Federal Work-Study Program available. Institutional employment available.

THE BOTTOM LINE

Vanderbilt students are currently charged $48,600 for tuition. Undergrads who opt to live on campus pay $10,620 for housing and $5,614 for meals. All students also pay another $1,216 to cover student activity and recreation fees. Books and supplies typically cost students an additional $1,294. And Vanderbilt ballparks personal expenses at around $2,802. These figures come to a total of $70,146.

CAREER INFORMATION FROM PAYSCALE.COM	
ROI Rating	95
Bachelors and No Higher	
Median starting salary	$63,800
Median mid-career salary	$118,400
At Least Bachelors	
Median starting salary	$65,900
Median mid-career salary	$124,800
Alumni with high job meaning	49%
Degrees awarded in STEM subjects	23%

SELECTIVITY	
Admissions Rating	**99**
# of applicants	31,462
% of applicants accepted	11
% of acceptees attending	47
# of early decision applicants	3592
% accepted early decision	24

FRESHMAN PROFILE	
Range SAT EBRW	700–760
Range SAT Math	700–790
Range ACT Composite	32–35
Minimum internet-based TOEFL	100
Average HS GPA	3.8
% graduated top 10% of class	90
% graduated top 25% of class	96
% graduated top 50% of class	98

DEADLINES	
Early decision	
Deadline	11/1
Notification	12/15
Other ED Deadline	1/1
Other ED Notification	2/15
Regular	
Priority	1/1
Deadline	1/1
Notification	4/1
Nonfall registration?	No

FINANCIAL FACTS	
Financial Aid Rating	**99**
Annual tuition	$48,600
Room and board	$16,234
Required fees	$1,216
Books and supplies	$1,294
Average frosh need-based scholarship	$48,559
Average UG need-based scholarship	$47,294
% needy frosh rec. need-based scholarship or grant aid	97
% needy UG rec. need-based scholarship or grant aid	98
% needy frosh rec. non-need-based scholarship or grant aid	9
% needy UG rec. non-need-based scholarship or grant aid	6
% needy frosh rec. need-based self-help aid	43
% needy UG rec. need-based self-help aid	50
% frosh rec. any financial aid	70
% UG rec. any financial aid	66
% UG borrow to pay for school	21
Average cumulative indebtedness	$23,973
% frosh need fully met	100
% ugrads need fully met	100
Average % of frosh need met	100
Average % of ugrad need met	100

Vassar College

124 RAYMOND AVENUE, POUGHKEEPSIE, NY 12604 • ADMISSIONS: 845-437-7300 • FAX: 845-437-7063

CAMPUS LIFE
Quality of Life Rating	89
Fire Safety Rating	87
Green Rating	88
Type of school	Private
Environment	Town

STUDENTS
Total undergrad enrollment	2,323
% male/female	41/59
% from out of state	75
% frosh from public high school	66
% frosh live on campus	100
% ugrads live on campus	95
# of fraternities (% ugrad men join)	0 (0)
# of sororities (% ugrad women join)	0 (0)
% African American	4
% Asian	13
% Caucasian	57
% Hispanic	11
% Native American	<1
% Pacific Islander	0
% Two or more races	7
% Race and/or ethnicity unknown	<1
% international	7
# of countries represented	54

ACADEMICS
Academic Rating	95
% students returning for sophomore year	96
% students graduating within 4 years	85
% students graduating within 6 years	90
Calendar	Semester
Student/faculty ratio	8:1
Profs interesting rating	96
Profs accessible rating	90

Most classes have 10–19 students. Most lab/discussion sessions have 20–29 students.

MOST POPULAR MAJORS
Psychology; Economics; Political Science and Government

#41 BEST VALUE COLLEGE

ABOUT THE SCHOOL
A coed institution since 1969, Vassar was founded in 1861 as the first of the Seven Sister colleges. Located in Poughkeepsie, New York, this private liberal arts school where there is very little in the way of a core curriculum allows students the freedom to design their own courses of study. This approach, students agree, "really encourages students to think creatively and pursue whatever they're passionate about, whether medieval tapestries, neuroscience, or unicycles. Not having a core curriculum is great because it gives students the opportunity to delve into many different interests."

Student life is campus-centered, in large part because hometown Poughkeepsie does not offer much in the way of entertainment. It's a very self-contained social scene; virtually everyone lives on Vassar's beautiful campus. A vibrant oasis, it's easy for students here to get caught in the "Vassar Bubble." There are clubs and organizations aplenty, and the school provides interesting lectures, theatre productions, and a wide array of activities pretty much every weeknight. Weekends, on the other hand, are more about small parties and gatherings. More adventurous students make the relatively easy trek to New York to shake up the routine.

The lack of core requirements is valued by students as "a great opportunity… to explore anything they want before settling into a major." The faculty is "super accessible" and "fully engaged in the total Vassar community." "My professors are…spectacular at illuminating difficult material," says a junior psychology major. Classes are small and "most are very discussion-based"; while academics are rigorous and challenging here, students describe themselves as self-motivated rather than competitive, contributing to a relaxed and collaborative atmosphere.

BANG FOR YOUR BUCK
Vassar has a need-blind admissions policy and is able to meet 100 percent of the demonstrated need of everyone who is admitted for all four years. Vassar awards more than $69 million dollars in scholarships. Funds come from Vassar's endowment, money raised by Vassar clubs, and gifts from friends of the college and all are need-based. In addition to a close-knit community, beautiful campus, engaged professors, and rigorous academics, study abroad opportunities abound.

STUDENT LIFE
The students at Vassar are an eclectic group who "will do things in any way but the traditional way" and who revel in their individuality. Think "smart and passionate hipsters" out to prove they have something to offer the world. Students say "the vibe of the whole school is so chill," but does not hamper a "vibrant extracurricular scene." In fact, Vassar is "bursting at the seams" with over 170 student organizations. There are "a ton of intramural sports teams," several very popular a cappella groups, plenty of political organizations, a large performing arts contingent, and "basically anything else you can think of." New York City isn't far, but there are always a decent amount of weekend activities right on this close-knit campus such as "concerts, comedy shows, plays, dances, etc."

Vassar College

FINANCIAL AID: 845-437-5230 • E-MAIL: ADMISSIONS@VASSAR.EDU • WEBSITE: WWW.VASSAR.EDU

CAREER

The Career Development Office at Vassar "helps students and almumnae/i envision and realize a meaningful life" after graduation. To that end, the CDO provides career and major exploration, sets up information interviews, and will even help students put together a four-year plan to maximize their college experience. Both Handshake and The Vassar Alumnifire network provide job and internship listings for summer and post-college. Typically, more than 90% of Vassar graduates report having employment, graduate school, or fellowships within six months of graduation. PayScale.com reports that the starting salary for recent grads averages $52,100 and that 51 percent of grads visiting their website believe their work makes the world a better place.

GENERAL INFO

Activities: Choral groups, concert band, dance, drama/theater, jazz band, literary magazine, marching band, music ensembles. **Organizations:** 105 registered organizations, 11 religious organizations. **Athletics (Intercollegiate):** *Men:* Baseball, basketball, crew/rowing, cross-country, diving, fencing, lacrosse, rugby soccer, squash, swimming, tennis, track/field (outdoor), volleyball. *Women:* Basketball, crew/rowing, cross-country, diving, fencing, field hockey, golf, lacrosse, rugby, soccer, squash, swimming, tennis, track/field (outdoor), volleyball. **On-Campus Highlights:** Library, Shakespeare Garden, Class of 1951 Observatory, Frances Lehman Loeb Art Center, Center for Drama and Film, Bridge Building for Laboratory Sciences. **Environmental Initiatives:** climate action plan in place for campus to become carbon neutral by 2030, purchasing of local food; a half-acre organic student-run garden.

FINANCIAL AID

Students should submit: CSS Profile for all parents, including non-custodial parents; FAFSA. Regular filing deadline is 2/1. The Princeton Review suggests that all financial aid forms be submitted as soon as possible after October 1. *Need-based scholarships/grants offered:* College/university scholarship or grant aid from institutional funds, Federal Pell, private scholarships, SEOG, state scholarships/grants. *Loan aid offered:* Direct PLUS Loans, Direct Subsidized Loans, Direct Unsubsidized Loans. Applicants will be notified of awards on or about 3/30. Federal Work-Study Program available. Institutional employment available.

BOTTOM LINE

The sticker price at Vassar for tuition, fees, and room and board runs about $70,510 for a year. That said, Vassar has a need-blind admission policy, and financial aid is extremely generous. It's probably harder to get admitted here than it is to afford going here. Meeting financial standards is less important than exceedingly high academic standards and intellectual pursuits that venture far outside the classroom.

CAREER INFORMATION FROM PAYSCALE.COM	
ROI Rating	92
Bachelors and No Higher	
Median starting salary	$54,200
Median mid-career salary	$99,300
At Least Bachelors	
Median starting salary	$56,900
Median mid-career salary	$110,500
Alumni with high job meaning	53%
Degrees awarded in STEM subjects	24%

SELECTIVITY	
Admissions Rating	96
# of applicants	7,746
% of applicants accepted	24
% of acceptees attending	34
# offered a place on the wait list	985
% accepting a place on wait list	48
% admitted from wait list	17
# of early decision applicants	657
% accepted early decision	42

FRESHMAN PROFILE	
Range SAT EBRW	690–750
Range SAT Math	680–760
Range ACT Composite	31–33
Minimum paper TOEFL	600
Minimum internet-based TOEFL	100
% graduated top 10% of class	65
% graduated top 25% of class	93
% graduated top 50% of class	99

DEADLINES	
Early decision	
Deadline	11/15
Notification	12/15
Other ED Deadline	1/1
Other ED Notification	2/1
Regular	
Deadline	1/1
Notification	4/1
Nonfall registration?	No

FINANCIAL FACTS	
Financial Aid Rating	99
Annual tuition	$56,130
Room and board	$13,550
Required fees	$830
Books and supplies	$900
Average frosh need-based scholarship	$46,709
Average UG need-based scholarship	$48,194
% needy frosh rec. need-based scholarship or grant aid	100
% needy UG rec. need-based scholarship or grant aid	99
% needy frosh rec. non-need-based scholarship or grant aid	0
% needy UG rec. non-need-based scholarship or grant aid	0
% needy frosh rec. need-based self-help aid	100
% needy UG rec. need-based self-help aid	100
% frosh rec. any financial aid	61
% UG rec. any financial aid	58
% UG borrow to pay for school	45
Average cumulative indebtedness	$19,439
% frosh need fully met	100
% ugrads need fully met	100

Villanova University

AUSTIN HALL, 800 LANCASTER AVENUE, VILLANOVA, PA 19085 • ADMISSIONS: 610-519-4000 • FAX: 610-519-6450

CAMPUS LIFE

Quality of Life Rating	92
Fire Safety Rating	97
Green Rating	92
Type of school	Private
Affiliation	Roman Catholic
Environment	Village

STUDENTS

Total undergrad enrollment	6,966
% male/female	47/53
% from out of state	79
% frosh from public high school	54
% frosh live on campus	98
% ugrads live on campus	66
# of fraternities (% ugrad men join)	14 (17)
# of sororities (% ugrad women join)	14 (32)
% African American	5
% Asian	6
% Caucasian	74
% Hispanic	8
% Native American	<1
% Pacific Islander	0
% Two or more races	3
% Race and/or ethnicity unknown	2
% international	2
# of countries represented	44

ACADEMICS

Academic Rating	83
% students returning for sophomore year	95
% students graduating within 4 years	87
% students graduating within 6 years	90
Calendar	Semester
Student/faculty ratio	12:1
Profs interesting rating	88
Profs accessible rating	94

Most classes have 10–19 students. Most lab/discussion sessions have fewer than 10 students.

MOST POPULAR MAJORS

Business; Engineering; Registered Nursing

ABOUT THE SCHOOL

The rich Augustinian Catholic tradition creates a real sense of community at Villanova University, stemming from rigorous academics, service, spirit, and a perennially good basketball team. "Everyone actively [pursues] their own area of academic interest," and "if you want to succeed, the community will do everything in its power to make sure you can do so." There is a great support system set up to help students achieve academically (professors, advisors, tutors, writing/math/language learning centers) and there are "a lot of projects across majors that have real-world applications and are designed to help students in the long run." All degree programs—from science to engineering, business to nursing—are rooted in the liberal arts. The writing-intensive curriculum begins freshman year with the two-semester Augustine and Culture Seminar Program, in which students are divided into small discussion- and dialogue-driven classes; students are also housed near their classmates in "learning communities" to further foster relationships and create "a healthy, competitive environment that helps students grow together."

BANG FOR YOUR BUCK

Though the sticker price is high, the vast majority of Villanova students receive need- or merit-based scholarships and grants to offset the cost. Many scholarships are available. The merit-based Presidential Scholarship covers all tuition, room and board, books, and fees; twenty-eight are awarded each year, six of which go to historically underrepresented groups. Villanova Scholarships begin at $2,000 a year for academic achievers; students commuting from their families' homes can receive partial tuition Commuter Scholarships; and the Villanova/Coca-Cola First Generation Scholarship Program awards five partial scholarships per year to academically outstanding undergraduates who are the first in their families to attend college and have financial need.

STUDENT LIFE

Students here are active. Most of campus has a focused atmosphere during the week ("This isn't a school where people wear sweat pants or pajamas to class."), with extracurriculars (community service is big here) and intramurals taking up swaths of time. However, weekends are more relaxed. The school is "close enough to Philadelphia that you take advantage of all the city has to offer" and there are shuttles to the nearby King of Prussia mall. Performances (musicians, hypnotists, cultural shows) are well attended, and students "get creative when staying on campus." The orientation program means "each new student makes twenty new friends off the bat" and "it seems like everyone falls into a niche here very easily and everyone is happy." To top it off, nothing is quite like a basketball game at the Pavilion, the stands "packed with students proudly wearing their navy blue Nova Nation t-shirts."

Villanova University

FINANCIAL AID: 610-519-4010 • E-MAIL: GOTOVU@VILLANOVA.EDU • WEBSITE: WWW.VILLANOVA.EDU

CAREER

The Villanova Career Center hosts career fairs in the spring and fall to help hook students up with internships and jobs, and there are smaller, industry-based fairs held throughout the year for students interested in nursing and teaching. There is a "great presence of recruiters on campus," and potential employers collect student résumés and conduct on-campus interviews through the Career Center. Hundreds of alumni also take part in the Career Connections Advisor Program, and Villanova "does an impeccable job coordinating volunteer opportunities for students." Villanova reports that the average starting salary for recent graduates was $59,235 and the university had a 96 percent success placement rate (employed, continuing education or other planned activities).

GENERAL INFO

Activities: Choral groups, concert band, dance, drama/theater, jazz band, literary magazine, marching band, music ensembles, musical theater, pep band, radio station, student government, student newspaper, student-run film society, symphony orchestra, television station, yearbook, campus ministries, International Student Organization, Model UN. **Organizations:** 260 registered organizations, 34 honor societies, 15 religious organizations. 13 fraternities, 14 sororities. **Athletics (Intercollegiate):** *Men:* baseball, basketball, cheerleading, cross-country, diving, football, golf, lacrosse, soccer, swimming, tennis, track/field (outdoor), track/field (indoor). *Women:* basketball, cheerleading, crew/rowing, cross-country, diving, field hockey, lacrosse, soccer, softball, swimming, tennis, track/field (outdoor), track/field (indoor), volleyball, water polo. **On-Campus Highlights:** St. Thomas of Villanova Church, Finneran Pavilion, Davis Center for Athletics and Fitness, Villanova University Shop, Connelly Center and Cinema, Bartley Hall, Kevin M. Curley Family Exchange.

FINANCIAL AID

Students should submit: CSS Profile. Priority filing deadline is 2/15. The Princeton Review suggests that all financial aid forms be submitted as soon as possible after October 1. *Need-based scholarships/grants offered:* College/university scholarship or grant aid from institutional funds, Federal Pell, private scholarships, SEOG, state scholarships/grants. *Loan aid offered:* Direct PLUS Loans, Direct Subsidized Loans, Direct Unsubsidized Loans. Applicants will be notified of awards on or about 4/1. Federal Work-Study Program available. Institutional employment available.

BOTTOM LINE

It costs $50,554 in tuition to attend Villanova, and an additional $13,548 for room and board. Forty-seven percent of undergraduates receive some sort of financial aid, and the average need-based scholarship running $30,497.

CAREER INFORMATION FROM PAYSCALE.COM

ROI Rating	88
Bachelors and No Higher	
Median starting salary	$63,600
Median mid-career salary	$117,900
At Least Bachelors	
Median starting salary	$65,200
Median mid-career salary	$124,300
Alumni with high job meaning	41%
Degrees awarded in STEM subjects	23%

SELECTIVITY

Admissions Rating	96
# of applicants	21,112
% of applicants accepted	36
% of acceptees attending	23
# offered a place on the wait list	6,276
% accepting a place on wait list	41
% admitted from wait list	8

FRESHMAN PROFILE

Range SAT EBRW	620–710
Range SAT Math	630–730
Range ACT Composite	30–33
Minimum paper TOEFL	550
Minimum internet-based TOEFL	85 (IETLS 7)
Average HS GPA	4.1
% graduated top 10% of class	65
% graduated top 25% of class	95
% graduated top 50% of class	98

DEADLINES

Early decision	
Deadline	11/1
Notification	12/15
Early action	
Deadline	11/1
Notification	1/15
Regular	
Priority	12/15
Deadline	1/15
Notification	4/1

FINANCIAL FACTS

Financial Aid Rating	81
Annual tuition	$50,554
Room and board	$13,548
Required fees	$670
Books and supplies	$1,100
Average frosh need-based scholarship	$34,470
Average UG need-based scholarship	$32,405
% needy frosh rec. need-based scholarship or grant aid	92
% needy UG rec. need-based scholarship or grant aid	90
% needy frosh rec. non-need-based scholarship or grant aid	9
% needy UG rec. non-need-based scholarship or grant aid	5
% needy frosh rec. need-based self-help aid	92
% needy UG rec. need-based self-help aid	91
% frosh rec. any financial aid	67
% UG rec. any financial aid	68
% UG borrow to pay for school	60
Average cumulative indebtedness	$24,752
% frosh need fully met	12
% ugrads need fully met	10

Virginia Polytechnic Institute and State University

Undergraduate Admissions, 201 Burruss Hall, Blacksburg, VA 24061 • Admissions: 540-231-6267

CAMPUS LIFE

Quality of Life Rating	97
Fire Safety Rating	87
Green Rating	96
Type of school	Public
Environment	Town

STUDENTS

Total undergrad enrollment	27,120
% male/female	57/43
% from out of state	24
% frosh live on campus	99
% ugrads live on campus	35
# of fraternities (% ugrad men join)	29 (13)
# of sororities (% ugrad women join)	12 (19)
% African American	4
% Asian	10
% Caucasian	66
% Hispanic	6
% Native American	<1
% Pacific Islander	<1
% Two or more races	4
% Race and/or ethnicity unknown	3
% international	6
# of countries represented	116

ACADEMICS

Academic Rating	72
% students returning for sophomore year	93
% students graduating within 4 years	63
% students graduating within 6 years	84
Calendar	Semester
Student/faculty ratio	14:1
Profs interesting rating	75
Profs accessible rating	79

Most classes have fewer than 20 students.
Most lab/discussion sessions have 10–19 students.

MOST POPULAR MAJORS

Engineering; Family and Consumer Sciences; Business Administration and Management

ABOUT THE SCHOOL

Virginia Polytechnic University (Virginia Tech) is one of only two senior military colleges within a larger state university. (Texas A&M is the other.) This affords students a unique learning experience while benefiting from opportunities in a university with 174 undergraduate degree options. Unlike at your typical tech school, students at Virginia Tech happily discover that they don't have to forfeit a variety of exciting extracurricular activities in order to achieve an excellent education. VT's programs in engineering, architecture, agricultural science, and forestry are all national leaders, while the outstanding business program offers top-notch access to occupations in the field. Significant research is being conducted in each of the school's nine colleges. Nonetheless, undergrads are continually surprised by the genuine interest the school's first-rate faculty takes in students and their educations. At Virginia Tech, professors are dedicated to their students, a fact that is continually demonstrated by their open office doors, frequent email communication, and willingness to accept undergraduates as researchers.

BANG FOR YOUR BUCK

Sixty percent of Virginia Tech students receive some form of financial aid. Students can receive funds from federal, state, private, and university scholarships, as well as Stafford and Perkins loans, work-study, and federal Pell Grants. Some scholarships consider a student's financial need, while others are awarded independently, based on a student's academic or athletic achievement. Students can browse the numerous scholarship opportunities online through the school's scholarship database.

Membership in the Virginia Tech Corps of Cadets offers excellent opportunities for supplemental scholarships. About 650 cadets receive $1.5 million in Emerging Leaders Scholarships. In addition, 429 cadets garnered $7.8 million in Army, Navy, and Air Force ROTC scholarships. The cadets, of course, have access to other scholarships and financial aid. But the Emerging Leaders and ROTC scholarships provide more than $9 million in total aid to members of the 857-student corps.

STUDENT LIFE

Virginia Tech is "the perfect mix of studies and fun." People here are generally intellectual and "will have discussions on almost anything, including political issues and global issues." Off the clock, most students love Hokie Sports, and a typical student is "someone who has a love for all things Virginia Tech. You will find them at every…football game." "There is nothing like a home game during football season," agrees another student. Blacksburg is "in the middle of nowhere" but there is a nearby mall, grocery stores, and lots of local restaurants, and "school-related and Greek life functions are the main sources of weekend activities." There are hundreds of student organizations to get involved with, and "there are 30,000 people around you that are the same age as you. You find stuff to do."

CAREER

Virginia Tech "does excellent with job placement after graduation." There are many opportunities for internships and full-time positions through the "amazing Career Services" as well as career fairs for

Virginia Polytechnic Institute and State University

FINANCIAL AID: 540-231-5179 • E-MAIL: VTADMISS@VT.EDU FAX: 540-231-3242 • WEBSITE: WWW.VT.EDU

every major. Though Virginia Tech isn't necessarily known for liberal arts, the College of Liberal Arts and Human Science has been gaining serious momentum over the years, and "there are also a lot of connections to D.C. for jobs in these fields." The department maintains a host of online and in-person resources, such as Resumania! résumé review services, on-campus interviewing programs, and an online database of jobs and internships. Fifty percent of Virginia Tech graduates who visited PayScale.com said they thought their job had a meaningful impact on the world, and reported an average starting salary of $58,600.

GENERAL INFO

Environment: Town. **Activities:** Choral groups, concert band, dance, drama/theater, jazz band, literary magazine, marching band, music ensembles, musical theater, pep band, radio station, student government, student newspaper, year book. **Organizations:** 600 registered organizations, 32 honor societies, 53 religious organizations. 29 fraternities, 12 sororities. **Athletics (Intercollegiate):** *Men:* Baseball, basketball, cheerleading, cross-country, diving, football, golf, soccer, swimming, tennis, track/field (outdoor), track/field (indoor), ultimate Frisbee, water polo. *Women:* Basketball, cheerleading, cross-country, diving, lacrosse, soccer, softball, swimming, tennis, track/field (outdoor), track/field (indoor), ultimate Frisbee, volleyball, water polo. **Environmental Initiatives:** The Virginia Tech Climate Action Commitment Resolution and Sustainability Plan.

FINANCIAL AID

Students should submit: FAFSA. Regular filing deadline is 1/15. The Princeton Review suggests that all financial aid forms be submitted as soon as possible after October 1. *Need-based scholarships/grants offered:* College/university scholarship or grant aid from institutional funds; Federal Pell; Private scholarships; SEOG; State scholarships/grants; United Negro College Fund. *Loan aid offered:* Direct PLUS Loans, Direct Subsidized Loans, Direct Unsubsidized Loans. Applicants will be notified of awards on or about 4/1. Federal Work-Study Program available. Institutional employment available.

BOTTOM LINE

Virginia Tech's high-quality education and low tuition make this school an excellent investment. For Virginia residents, the estimated total cost of attendance for one year is $23,909, including tuition, fees, and room and board. For nonresidents, the price is around $41,693. In the popular school of engineering, the cost per credit hour is a bit higher than other major fields.

CAREER INFORMATION FROM PAYSCALE.COM	
ROI Rating	88
Bachelors and No Higher	
Median starting salary	$60,900
Median mid-career salary	$112,800
At Least Bachelors	
Median starting salary	$61,800
Median mid-career salary	$117,600
Alumni with high job meaning	48%
Degrees awarded in STEM subjects	42%

SELECTIVITY	
Admissions Rating	87
# of applicants	27,423
% of applicants accepted	70
% of acceptees attending	36
# offered a place on the wait list	3,485
% accepting a place on wait list	69
% admitted from wait list	0
# of early decision applicants	2596
% accepted early decision	63

FRESHMAN PROFILE	
Range SAT EBRW	590–670
Range SAT Math	590–690
Range ACT Composite	25–30
Minimum paper TOEFL	550
Average HS GPA	4.0
% graduated top 10% of class	38
% graduated top 25% of class	77
% graduated top 50% of class	98

DEADLINES	
Early decision	
Deadline	11/1
Notification	12/15
Early action	
Deadline	12/1
Notification	2/22
Regular	
Deadline	1/15
Notification	3/5
Nonfall registration?	Yes

FINANCIAL FACTS	
Financial Aid Rating	79
Annual in-state tuition	$11,420
Annual out-of-state tuition	$29,104
Room and board	$8,934
Required fees	$2,200
Books and supplies	$1,150
Average frosh need-based scholarship	$7,664
Average UG need-based scholarship	$7,097
% needy frosh rec. need-based scholarship or grant aid	67
% needy UG rec. need-based scholarship or grant aid	71
% needy frosh rec. non-need-based scholarship or grant aid	53
% needy UG rec. non-need-based scholarship or grant aid	53
% needy frosh rec. need-based self-help aid	65
% needy UG rec. need-based self-help aid	70
% UG rec. any financial aid	75
% UG borrow to pay for school	49
Average cumulative indebtedness	$30,221
% frosh need fully met	64

Wabash College

PO Box 352, 301 W. Wabash Av, Crawfordsville, IN 47933 • Admissions: 765-361-6225

CAMPUS LIFE

Quality of Life Rating	90
Fire Safety Rating	92
Green Rating	65
Type of school	Private
Environment	Village

STUDENTS

Total undergrad enrollment	864
% male/female	100/0
% from out of state	22
% frosh from public high school	83
% frosh live on campus	100
% ugrads live on campus	97
# of fraternities (% ugrad men join)	10 (63)
# of sororities (% ugrad women join)	0 (0)
% African American	6
% Asian	1
% Caucasian	73
% Hispanic	8
% Native American	<1
% Pacific Islander	0
% Two or more races	3
% Race and/or ethnicity unknown	2
% international	7
# of countries represented	16

ACADEMICS

Academic Rating	95
% students returning for sophomore year	87
% students graduating within 4 years	72
% students graduating within 6 years	77
Calendar	Semester
Student/faculty ratio	10:1
Profs interesting rating	99
Profs accessible rating	99

Most classes have 10–19 students. Most lab/discussion sessions have 10–19 students.

MOST POPULAR MAJORS
Economics; Political Science and Government; History

ABOUT THE SCHOOL

Wabash College in Indiana is one of only three all-male liberal arts schools in the country, filling its sixty-acre campus with twenty-five majors, and a full roster of professors, admissions, and career services staff "who will more than match a student's efforts if they see he is willing to apply himself." The student body conducts itself by the Gentleman's Rule and "holds itself responsible for ensuring no one falls through the cracks," so if a student is struggling, "classmates will reach out to them in an attempt to help."

Due to its small size, Wabash can acknowledge and interact with students on a one-on-one basis, and "students are recognized by faculty as individuals, and not some part of a collection." There "is always a person behind a process" so that "extenuating circumstances can always be addressed and accommodated." Every professor at Wabash challenges their students "to think critically about subject material, rather than learn it and regurgitate it for a test," and most also encourage group work, which "often turns into casual conversations over the subject material or mini instruction sessions." Unique experiences such as immersion and field trips abound—"We actually went rowing to learn more about Grecian war boats"—and professors also include students in research, even in their first year.

BANG FOR YOUR BUCK

Students say that the best part about Wabash is that once you're registered as a student, "everyone is treated on an equal basis," and for the most part, all students have equal opportunities "to enjoy programs such as immersion classes and career workshops…that at many other schools, students would have to pay extra for." A longstanding scholarship program (due in great part to generous alumni) ensures that all academically-qualified students have a shot at attending Wabash; the school maintains transparent guidelines for the level of merit-based scholarship that a student's GPA and test scores qualify them for. Indiana residents who receive Pell Grants will have all tuition and fees not covered under grants paid for, while students from families residing in Indiana with adjusted gross incomes up to $125,000 will receive grants to lower tuition and fees the equivalent to tuition and fees at the state's flagship university.

STUDENT LIFE

The school spirit and "tradition-oriented culture" at the college is second to none; everyone goes to games and "activities that started over 150 years ago still happen each year at Wabash." Extracurriculars are "easy to come by and active," fraternities are wildly popular (about half of the student population), and "it is never a question of if a student is involved in these activities, rather a question of how many." About 70 percent of students are from Indiana; the surrounding area is very rural, so life is centered around the campus, and students are required to live on campus all four years (there are a variety of housing options available). The school admittedly isn't very diverse, given its location and nature, but it is "quite open to progressive dialogue": this is truly a "brotherhood" where everyone is "very familiar with each other."

Wabash College

E-MAIL: ADMISSIONS@WABASH.EDU • FAX: 765-361-6437 • WEBSITE: WWW.WABASH.EDU

CAREER

Wabash has one of the most fervently loyal alumni networks in the nation (they "are willing to help out any way they can if you reach out"), and the resulting scholarships and internship opportunities are excellent benefits. The beloved Schroeder Center for Career Development—"if all else fails, Career Services will not fail"—helps students develop leadership and civic experience and provides a variety of tools and workshops for students to avail themselves of (such as cover letter, LinkedIn, and resume guides), as well as career counseling, internship and employment opportunities, and 86 percent of students in the Class of 2018 had jobs on their graduation day. A little more than a quarter of graduates enroll in professional or graduate school, and of those entering the work force, 31 percent begin careers in business. Out of Wabash alumni visiting PayScale.com, 46 percent report that they derive a high level of meaning from their jobs.

GENERAL INFO

Activities: Choral groups, concert band, drama/theater, jazz band, literary magazine, music ensembles, pep band, radio station, student government, student newspaper, student-run film society. **Organizations:** 65 registered organizations, 7 honor societies, 5 religious organizations. 10 fraternities. **Athletics (Intercollegiate):** *Men:* Baseball, basketball, cross-country, diving, football, golf, lacrosse, soccer, swimming, tennis, track/field (outdoor), track/field (indoor), wrestling. **On-Campus Highlights:** Allen Athletics and Recreation Center, Wabash Chapel, Hays Hall, Trippet Hall, Lilly Library, Malcolm X Institute of Black Studies. **Environmental Initiatives:** Campus-wide recycling. Environmental Concerns Committee driving LEED Certification. Green bikes.

FINANCIAL AID

Students should submit: FAFSA. Priority filing deadline is 2/1. The Princeton Review suggests that all financial aid forms be submitted as soon as possible after October 1. *Need-based scholarships/grants offered:* College/university scholarship or grant aid from institutional funds; Federal Pell; Private scholarships; SEOG; State scholarships/grants; United Negro College Fund. *Loan aid offered:* Direct PLUS Loans, Direct Subsidized Loans, Direct Unsubsidized Loans. Applicants will be notified of awards on a rolling basis beginning 12/15. Federal Work-Study Program available. Institutional employment available.

BOTTOM LINE

Tuition runs $42,800, with room and board tacking on another $9,800, plus an additional $850 in Student Activity and Student Health fees. It may be a small school (around nine hundred students), but Wabash has one of the country's highest per-student endowments, and 99 percent of all students receive some form of financial aid.

CAREER INFORMATION FROM PAYSCALE.COM	
ROI Rating	93
Bachelors and No Higher	
Median starting salary	$60,200
Median mid-career salary	$116,000
At Least Bachelors	
Median starting salary	$64,200
Median mid-career salary	$131,900
Alumni with high job meaning	40%
Degrees awarded in STEM subjects	34%

SELECTIVITY	
Admissions Rating	86
# of applicants	1,304
% of applicants accepted	63
% of acceptees attending	28
# offered a place on the wait list	173
% accepting a place on wait list	35
% admitted from wait list	75
# of early decision applicants	20
% accepted early decision	85

FRESHMAN PROFILE	
Range SAT EBRW	530–630
Range SAT Math	540–650
Range ACT Composite	23–28
Minimum paper TOEFL	550
Minimum internet-based TOEFL	80
Average HS GPA	3.7
% graduated top 10% of class	27
% graduated top 25% of class	57
% graduated top 50% of class	95

DEADLINES	
Early decision	
Deadline	10/15
Notification	11/16
Early action	
Deadline	11/1
Notification	12/11
Regular	
Priority	10/15
Deadline	1/15
Nonfall registration?	Yes

FINANCIAL FACTS	
Financial Aid Rating	93
Annual tuition	$42,800
Room and board	$9,800
Required fees	$850
Books and supplies	$1,200
Average frosh need-based scholarship	$34,044
Average UG need-based scholarship	$30,123
% needy frosh rec. need-based scholarship or grant aid	99
% needy UG rec. need-based scholarship or grant aid	99
% needy frosh rec. non-need-based scholarship or grant aid	16
% needy UG rec. non-need-based scholarship or grant aid	15
% needy frosh rec. need-based self-help aid	83
% needy UG rec. need-based self-help aid	84
% frosh rec. any financial aid	99
% UG rec. any financial aid	95
% UG borrow to pay for school	94
Average cumulative indebtedness	$35,726

Wake Forest University

P.O. Box 7305, Reynolda Station, Winston Salem, NC 27109 • Admissions: 336-758-5201 • Fax: 336-758-4324

CAMPUS LIFE

Quality of Life Rating	**89**
Fire Safety Rating	**96**
Green Rating	**85**
Type of school	Private
Environment	City

STUDENTS

Total undergrad enrollment	5,101
% male/female	46/54
% from out of state	78
% frosh from public high school	65
% frosh live on campus	98
% ugrads live on campus	75
# of fraternities (% ugrad men join)	14 (35)
# of sororities (% ugrad women join)	9 (60)
% African American	7
% Asian	4
% Caucasian	70
% Hispanic	7
% Native American	<1
% Pacific Islander	<1
% Two or more races	3
% Race and/or ethnicity unknown	<1
% international	10
# of countries represented	27

ACADEMICS

Academic Rating	**95**
% students returning for sophomore year	94
% students graduating within 4 years	84
% students graduating within 6 years	88
Calendar	Semester
Student/faculty ratio	11:1
Profs interesting rating	97
Profs accessible rating	98

Most classes have 10–19 students. Most lab/discussion sessions have 10–19 students.

MOST POPULAR MAJORS

Psychology; Political Science and Government; Business/Commerce

ABOUT THE SCHOOL

Wake Forest combines the best tradition of a small liberal arts college with the resources of a national research university. Founded in 1834, the university believes deeply in its responsibility to educate the whole person, mind, body, and spirit. One student says, "I was very impressed with the quality of the facilities and professors." Wake has a nurturing environment, with professors and faculty that care about the well-being and personal growth of their students. "Small classes with a lot of discussion are common." Small class sizes create opportunities for intense discussion, and though the workload may be heavy at times, professors are extremely accessible outside of class for additional help or questions. Professors, not graduate assistants, are the primary instructors. Students have access to top-flight scholars from the very first day of their college career. Wake Forest also offers extraordinary opportunities for undergraduate students to get involved in faculty research projects.

BANG FOR YOUR BUCK

"Wake Forest's generous financial aid program allows deserving students to enroll regardless of their financial circumstances." Wake Forest is one of a small group of private institutions that agrees to meet 100 percent of each regularly admitted student's demonstrated financial need. More than half of the students here receive some form of financial aid. In addition, each year Wake Forest awards merit-based scholarships to less than 3 percent of its first-year applicants. These scholarships are renewable through four years, subject to satisfactory academic, extracurricular, and civic performance. Though criteria differ slightly, the programs all recognize extraordinary achievement, leadership, and talent. Most scholarships do not require a separate merit-based scholarship application. The competition is steep, with recipients generally standing at least in the top 10 percent of the class. "Wake Forest's Reynolds and Carswell merit-based scholarships cover tuition, room, board, and summer grants for individually-designed study projects. Gordon Scholarships are awarded to up to seven students each year to students among constituencies historically underrepresented at Wake Forest."

STUDENT LIFE

There are a ton of traditions peppered throughout the school year, and a good percentage of students are involved in the Greek system. "Most people go out on Fridays and Saturdays, and some go out for 'Wake Wednesdays' as well," says a student. Movies and shopping are common ways to relax, and it is "very accessible to get to downtown Winston-Salem to spend the night in a more upscale part of town." A lot of students are strongly involved in community service, and also love going and supporting the Wake football and basketball teams "in southern attire." On warm days you will find students out on the quad "throwing [the] football...or just sitting around talking," or hiking and rock climbing at nearby Pilot Mountain. Shorty's (an on-campus restaurant) is "a great place to hang out with friends any night of the week," and there is also "an impressive variety of on-campus dining options."

Wake Forest University

FINANCIAL AID: 336-758-5154 • E-MAIL: ADMISSIONS@WFU.EDU • WEBSITE: WWW.WFU.EDU

CAREER
The Office of Career and Professional Development is known to be one of the best in the nation, and "for a school this size, that's incredible." The resources that are available there "almost guarantee you the best internships and jobs" and whether it's résumé reviews, career counseling, intern searches, or job application help, the OPCD provides all students with unprecedented career support. There are numerous career fairs during the academic year including a STEM Slam for students in any major interested in talking to STEM employers. There are also optional Career Treks to Washington, New York and San Francisco that students can apply to attend. Wake Forest graduates who visited PayScale.com reported an average starting salary of $56,000, and 48 percent said they felt their job had a meaningful impact on the world.

GENERAL INFO
Activities: Choral groups, concert band, dance, drama/theater, jazz band, literary magazine, marching band, music ensembles, pep band, radio station, student government, student newspaper, student-run film society, symphony orchestra, television station, yearbook, campus ministries, international student organization. **Organizations:** 168 registered organizations, 16 honor societies, 16 religious organizations. 14 fraternities, 9 sororities. **Athletics (Intercollegiate):** *Men:* Baseball, basketball, cheerleading, cross-country, football, golf, soccer, tennis, track/field (outdoor), track/field (indoor). *Women:* Basketball, cheerleading, cross-country, field hockey, golf, soccer, tennis, track/field (outdoor), track/field (indoor), volleyball. **On-Campus Highlights:** Charlotte and Philip Hanes Art Gallery, Museum of Anthropology, The Z. Smith Reynolds Library, Wait Chapel, Benson University Center.

FINANCIAL AID
Students should submit: CSS Profile; FAFSA; State aid form. Priority filing deadline is 2/1. The Princeton Review suggests that all financial aid forms be submitted as soon as possible after October 1. *Need-based scholarships/grants offered:* College/university scholarship or grant aid from institutional funds; Federal Pell; Private scholarships; SEOG; State scholarships/grants; United Negro College Fund. *Loan aid offered:* Direct PLUS Loans, Direct Subsidized Loans, Direct Unsubsidized Loans. Applicants will be notified of awards on a rolling basis beginning 4/1. Federal Work-Study Program available. Institutional employment available.

BOTTOM LINE
At Wake Forest University, the total cost for tuition and fees, room and board, books, and supplies comes to about $69,000. Fortunately, the average financial aid package for freshman includes a grant totaling $42,000. Additional aid is available in the form of scholarships, work-study, and loans.

CAREER INFORMATION FROM PAYSCALE.COM	
ROI Rating	90
Bachelors and No Higher	
Median starting salary	$58,200
Median mid-career salary	$118,600
At Least Bachelors	
Median starting salary	$61,100
Median mid-career salary	$122,300
Alumni with high job meaning	47%
Degrees awarded in STEM subjects	13%

SELECTIVITY
Admissions Rating	95
# of applicants	13,071
% of applicants accepted	28
% of acceptees attending	37
# of early decision applicants	1842
% accepted early decision	44

FRESHMAN PROFILE
Range SAT EBRW	630–710
Range SAT Math	630–730
Range ACT Composite	28–32
Minimum paper TOEFL	600
% graduated top 10% of class	77
% graduated top 25% of class	93
% graduated top 50% of class	98

DEADLINES
Early decision	
Deadline	11/15
Notification	Rolling
Other ED deadline	1/1
Regular	
Priority	12/1
Deadline	1/1
Notification	Most by 4/1
Nonfall registration?	No

FINANCIAL FACTS
Financial Aid Rating	96
Annual tuition	$52,348
Room and board	$16,032
Required fees	$974
Books and supplies	$1,500
Average frosh need-based scholarship	$49,145
Average UG need-based scholarship	$44,338
% needy frosh rec. need-based scholarship or grant aid	96
% needy UG rec. need-based scholarship or grant aid	96
% needy frosh rec. non-need-based scholarship or grant aid	95
% needy UG rec. non-need-based scholarship or grant aid	95
% needy frosh rec. need-based self-help aid	93
% needy UG rec. need-based self-help aid	94
% frosh rec. any financial aid	39
% UG rec. any financial aid	34
% UG borrow to pay for school	33
Average cumulative indebtedness	$35,434
% frosh need fully met	100
% ugrads need fully met	100
Average % of frosh need met	100
Average % of ugrad need met	100

Washington College

300 WASHINGTON AVENUE, CHESTERTOWN, MD 21620 • ADMISSIONS: 410-778-7700 • FAX: 410-778-7287

CAMPUS LIFE

Quality of Life Rating	**90**
Fire Safety Rating	**97**
Green Rating	**63**
Type of school	Private
Environment	Rural

STUDENTS

Total undergrad enrollment	1,449
% male/female	42/58
% from out of state	55
% frosh live on campus	98
% ugrads live on campus	85
# of fraternities (% ugrad men join)	4 (15)
# of sororities (% ugrad women join)	3 (17)
% African American	8
% Asian	3
% Caucasian	69
% Hispanic	6
% Native American	1
% Pacific Islander	<1
% Two or more races	1
% Race and/or ethnicity unknown	3
% international	9
# of countries represented	32

ACADEMICS

Academic Rating	**90**
% students returning for sophomore year	85
% students graduating within 4 years	73
% students graduating within 6 years	76
Calendar	Semester
Student/faculty ratio	11:1
Profs interesting rating	94
Profs accessible rating	92

Most classes have 20–29 students. Most lab/discussion sessions have 10–19 students.

MOST POPULAR MAJORS

Biology/Biological Sciences; Psychology; Business Administration and Management

ABOUT THE SCHOOL

A "small" school with "a rich history," Washington College provides students with "the opportunity to grow socially, personally, emotionally, and academically." Undergrads here receive a "great liberal arts education" that's steeped in "personal attention." And no matter what they study, students are encouraged to make "connections, however strange, between all academics, whether [it's] art and business [or] history and science." A number of undergrads also highlight Washington's "good study abroad program." Additionally, many love the fact that professors often encourage students to "work with them on research projects." Speaking of the faculty, undergrads report that they are "excellent" by and large. The vast majority are "witty, incredibly engaging, and wildly enthusiastic about the subject matter." And, as this thrilled student sums up, "they are willing to work with each student out of class, they push you to get the education you are paying for, and most importantly are great educators."

BANG FOR YOUR BUCK

Washington College works closely with families to ensure that attendance is within financial reach of all students. And undergrads happily report that they have access to some "very good financial aid and scholarship" opportunities. In fact, over 50 percent of accepted students receive merit-based tuition scholarship. These range anywhere from $18,000 to $23,000 annually and are awarded at the time of admission. There are also scholarships allocated for specific disciplines. For example, English majors who demonstrate outstanding potential are eligible for the Sophie Kerr Scholarship worth $1,500. And environmental studies students may be considered for the Environment and Society Fellowship. This scholarship also awards $1,500 annually to high-achieving students. Finally, the college operates a robust work-study program as well.

STUDENT LIFE

At Washington College there's always an activity to enjoy. For example, "there are movie nights practically every week" and "band[s] or comedian[s]" at the Student Center most weekends. Additionally, the college hosts Guitar Hero, Madden, and Wii Sports tournaments" and even "de-stress days with yoga lessons, snacks and tea, and a massage therapist." We must also note students report that "drinking is prevalent on campus." Fortunately, many undergrads assure us that "you don't have to drink to fit in here[;] people are cool with whatever you decide." And when students need a respite from campus life they simply head into Chestertown, a "rural" area that "offers quaint shops and restaurants as well as waterfront activities such as kayaking, canoeing, and sailing." Finally, if students want a little more excitement, "Annapolis, DC, Baltimore, and Philadelphia" are all fairly accessible.

CAREER

Students here feel very prepared to enter the job market. That can certainly be attributed to the fact that "Washington College isn't just about teaching you the specific skills you think you need for one job, it's about teaching you the analytical and critical thinking skills that

Washington College

FINANCIAL AID: 410-778-7214 • E-MAIL: ADM.OFF@WASHCOLL.EDU • WEBSITE: WWW.WASHCOLL.EDU

you KNOW you will need for any job." Of course, credit is also due to the school's Career Development Office which has some amazing resources. For example, students can participate in mock interviews as well as sit for GMAT/LSAT/MCAT test prep courses. The office also runs programs like Washington to Wall Street which helps undergrads prepare for a career in the financial services industry. Further, there's an extensive job shadowing program which pairs students with professionals in any number of fields from the arts and education to social justice and science and tech. All in all, Washington students graduate knowing they are prepared to conquer their next steps.

GENERAL INFO

Activities: Campus Ministries; Choral groups; Concert band; Dance; Drama/theater; International Student Organization; Jazz band; Literary magazine; Model UN; Music ensembles; Musical theater; Student government; Student newspaper; Yearbook. **Organizations:** 50 registered organizations, 13 honor societies, 4 religious organizations. 4 fraternities, 3 sororities. **Athletics (Intercollegiate):** *Men:* baseball, basketball, crew/rowing, lacrosse, sailing, soccer, swimming, tennis. *Women:* basketball, crew/rowing, field hockey, lacrosse, sailing, soccer, softball, swimming, tennis, volleyball. **On-Campus Highlights:** Miller Library, Johnson Lifetime Fitness Center, Gibson Center for the Arts, O'Neill Literary House, Hodson Commons Student Center.

FINANCIAL AID

Students should submit: FAFSA. Priority filing deadline is 3/1. The Princeton Review suggests that all financial aid forms be submitted as soon as possible after October 1. *Need-based scholarships/grants offered:* College/university scholarship or grant aid from institutional funds, Federal Pell, private scholarships, SEOG, state scholarships/grants. *Loan aid offered:* Direct PLUS Loans, Direct Subsidized Loans, Direct Unsubsidized Loans. Applicants will be notified of awards on a rolling basis beginning 2/1. Federal Work-Study Program available. Institutional employment available.

THE BOTTOM LINE

Washington College offers many avenues to defray the coast of attendence with 92 percent of students receiving some form of financial assistance.

CAREER INFORMATION FROM PAYSCALE.COM	
ROI Rating	87
Bachelors and No Higher	
Median starting salary	$52,700
Median mid-career salary	$88,100
At Least Bachelors	
Median starting salary	$53,300
Median mid-career salary	$90,700
Alumni with high job meaning	53%
Degrees awarded in STEM subjects	21%

SELECTIVITY	
Admissions Rating	88
# of applicants	5,515
% of applicants accepted	48
% of acceptees attending	14

FRESHMAN PROFILE	
Range SAT EBRW	550–670
Range SAT Math	540–630
Range ACT Composite	23–29
Minimum paper TOEFL	550
Minimum internet-based TOEFL	79
Average HS GPA	3.7
% graduated top 10% of class	38
% graduated top 25% of class	70
% graduated top 50% of class	91

DEADLINES	
Early decision	
Deadline	11/15
Notification	12/15
Other ED Deadline	12/15
Other ED Notification	1/15
Early action	
Deadline	12/1
Notification	1/15
Regular	
Deadline	2/15
Nonfall registration?	Yes

FINANCIAL FACTS	
Financial Aid Rating	84
Annual tuition	$45,888
Room and board	$12,190
Required fees	$1,118
Books and supplies	$1,400
Average frosh need-based scholarship	$33,601
Average UG need-based scholarship	$29,254
% needy frosh rec. need-based scholarship or grant aid	99
% needy UG rec. need-based scholarship or grant aid	99
% needy frosh rec. non-need-based scholarship or grant aid	15
% needy UG rec. non-need-based scholarship or grant aid	14
% needy frosh rec. need-based self-help aid	72
% needy UG rec. need-based self-help aid	76
% frosh rec. any financial aid	95
% UG rec. any financial aid	92
% UG borrow to pay for school	66
Average cumulative indebtedness	$30,462
% frosh need fully met	18
% ugrads need fully met	17
Average % of frosh need met	83
Average % of ugrad need met	76

Washington State University

PO Box 641067, Pullman, WA 99164-1067 • Admissions: 509-335-5586 • Fax: 509-335-4902

CAMPUS LIFE

Quality of Life Rating	**93**
Fire Safety Rating	**92**
Green Rating	**96**
Type of school	Public
Environment	Town

STUDENTS

Total undergrad enrollment	25,277
% male/female	48/52
% from out of state	13
% frosh live on campus	82
% ugrads live on campus	24
# of fraternities (% ugrad men join)	26 (23)
# of sororities (% ugrad women join)	14 (25)
% African American	3
% Asian	6
% Caucasian	61
% Hispanic	15
% Native American	1
% Pacific Islander	<1
% Two or more races	7
% Race and/or ethnicity unknown	2
% international	5
# of countries represented	78

ACADEMICS

Academic Rating	**77**
% students returning for sophomore year	81
% students graduating within 4 years	38
% students graduating within 6 years	62
Calendar	Semester
Student/faculty ratio	15:1
Profs interesting rating	74
Profs accessible rating	81

Most classes have 10–19 students. Most lab/discussion sessions have 20–29 students.

MOST POPULAR MAJORS

Engineering; Social Sciences; Business, Management, Marketing, and Related Support Services

ABOUT THE SCHOOL

A large public research institution in Pullman, Washington State University does an admirable job of making the campus feel like a "home away from home" for its 20,000 undergrads, where everyone has the opportunity to succeed." What's more, "a sense of community and unity" permeate the school. When it comes to academics, undergrads note that the "business program is well respected," and the engineering school maintains an "excellent reputation within the power and utility industry." And many students, regardless of their major, love that WSU offers "numerous study abroad opportunities." Undergrads are also united in their praise for their "challenging and rewarding" professors who encourage students to often "think outside the grain" and frequently "bring [their] practical experience [into] the classroom." Another hallmark of WSU's professors is their accessibility: They "want students to understand the material and urge us to ask questions." As one relieved student shares, "Whenever I struggle with an issue I know I can reach my professors and they will be willing to help me."

BANG FOR YOUR BUCK

The folks at Washington State do their utmost to ensure an undergraduate education is within financial reach. The university offers over 700 scholarship programs, and a single application allows students to be considered for everything available. Individuals who choose to apply will be in the running for scholarships such as the WUE/Cougar Award. This scholarship provides lucky recipients with $10,000 (renewable for up to four years). There's also the Glenn Terrell Presidential Award which grants $4,000/year for four years. Students are selected based upon the general strength of their scholarship application. Importantly, the university even has provisions for students who are undocumented. In other words, this financial aid office has your back!

STUDENT LIFE

Students at Washington State happily report that "the university does an excellent job [of] providing events, activities and performances to attend." Moreover, many undergrads here are athletic and active. They love "the awesome" student recreation center. As one individual brags, "We have a pool shaped like the state of Washington and a hot tub that can hold fifty people." There's also a robust Greek system which sponsors "plenty of activities…like going to the cliffs to swim, sisterhoods at the movie theater, and performing community service with friends to make a difference." What's more, outdoor enthusiasts will be delighted to learn that opportunities for skiing, hiking, camping, and boating" abound. Hometown Pullman has "many great restaurants" so students often "go out to eat for fun!"

CAREER

Washington State excels at "creating connections to job opportunities… and internships." For starters, numerous professors "strive to provide [students] with resources for internships and other ways to gain experience." Additionally, students can turn to the university's Career Center which offers individuals ample tools for professional development. For example, all undergrads have access to CougLink, a great resource for job and internship postings. It can also be used to schedule appointments with career counselors and peruse upcoming events. And speaking of events, every semester the Career Center hosts a campus-wide expo that attracts upwards of 100 recruiters from a variety of industries. It's a great way for undergrads to explore potential jobs and practice networking.

Washington State University

FINANCIAL AID: 509-335-9711 • E-MAIL: ADMISSIONS@WSU.EDU • WEBSITE: WWW.WSU.EDU

GENERAL INFO

Activities: Choral groups, concert band, dance, drama/theater, jazz band, literary magazine, marching band, music ensembles, musical theater, opera, pep band, radio station, student government, student newspaper, student-run film society, symphony orchestra, television station, yearbook, campus ministries, Student Organization, Model UN. **Organizations:** 300 registered organizations, 36 honor societies, 19 religious organizations. 26 fraternities, 14 sororities. **Athletics (Intercollegiate):** *Men:* baseball, basketball, cross-country, football, golf, track/field (outdoor). *Women:* basketball, crew/rowing, cross-country, golf, soccer, swimming, tennis, track/field (outdoor), volleyball. **On-Campus Highlights:** Compton Union Building (CUB), Terrell Friendship Mall, Student Recreation Center, Beasley Performing Arts Coliseum, Martin Stadium.

FINANCIAL AID

Students should submit: FAFSA; State aid form. Priority filing deadline is 1/31. The Princeton Review suggests that all financial aid forms be submitted as soon as possible after October 1. *Need-based scholarships/grants offered:* College/university scholarship or grant aid from institutional funds, Federal Pell, Private scholarships, SEOG, State scholarships/grants. *Loan aid offered:* Direct PLUS Loans, Direct Subsidized Loans, Direct Unsubsidized Loans. Applicants will be notified of awards on a rolling basis beginning mid-December. Federal and State Work-Study Programs available. Institutional employment available.

BOTTOM LINE

As you have no doubt realized, the cost of attendance at Washington State differs for residents and nonresidents. Undergrads who hail from Washington will face a tuition bill of $9,720. The tuition bill for non-residents is a tad steeper, coming in at $23,956. Additionally, all students must also pay a mandatory fee of $1,864. Room and board typically runs another $11,398. Finally, undergrads here can expect to pay another $960 for books.

CAREER INFORMATION FROM PAYSCALE.COM	
ROI Rating	88
Bachelors and No Higher	
Median starting salary	$54,600
Median mid-career salary	$102,200
At Least Bachelors	
Median starting salary	$55,200
Median mid-career salary	$104,800
Alumni with high job meaning	50%
Degrees awarded in STEM subjects	20%

SELECTIVITY	
Admissions Rating	81
# of applicants	22,565
% of applicants accepted	73
% of acceptees attending	28
# offered a place on the wait list	453
% accepting a place on wait list	0

FRESHMAN PROFILE	
Range SAT EBRW	510–610
Range SAT Math	510–610
Range ACT Composite	20–26
Minimum paper TOEFL	550
Minimum internet-based TOEFL	79
Average HS GPA	3.4

DEADLINES	
Regular	
Priority	1/31
Nonfall registration?	Yes

FINANCIAL FACTS	
Financial Aid Rating	81
Annual in-state tuition	$9,720
Annual out-of-state tuition	$23,956
Room and board	$11,398
Required fees	$1,864
Books and supplies	$960
Average frosh need-based scholarship	$10,895
Average UG need-based scholarship	$10,650
% needy frosh rec. need-based scholarship or grant aid	92
% needy UG rec. need-based scholarship or grant aid	85
% needy frosh rec. non-need-based scholarship or grant aid	76
% needy UG rec. non-need-based scholarship or grant aid	50
% needy frosh rec. need-based self-help aid	65
% needy UG rec. need-based self-help aid	69
% frosh rec. any financial aid	86
% UG rec. any financial aid	73
% UG borrow to pay for school	58
Average cumulative indebtedness	$26,807
% frosh need fully met	17
% ugrads need fully met	12
Average % of frosh need met	65
Average % of ugrad need met	63

Washington University in St. Louis

CAMPUS BOX 1089, ST. LOUIS, MO 63130-4899 • ADMISSIONS: 314-935-6000 • FAX: 314-935-4290

CAMPUS LIFE
Quality of Life Rating	98
Fire Safety Rating	97
Green Rating	95
Type of school	Private
Environment	City

STUDENTS
Total undergrad enrollment	7,253
% male/female	47/53
% from out of state	91
% frosh from public high school	56
% frosh live on campus	100
% ugrads live on campus	74
# of fraternities (% ugrad men join)	12 (25)
# of sororities (% ugrad women join)	9 (44)
% African American	8
% Asian	17
% Caucasian	52
% Hispanic	9
% Native American	<1
% Pacific Islander	<1
% Two or more races	5
% Race and/or ethnicity unknown	2
% international	7
# of countries represented	50

ACADEMICS
Academic Rating	93
% students returning for sophomore year	97
% students graduating within 4 years	88
% students graduating within 6 years	94
Calendar	Semester
Student/faculty ratio	8:1
Profs interesting rating	86
Profs accessible rating	84

Most classes have 10–19 students. Most lab/discussion sessions have 20–29 students.

MOST POPULAR MAJORS
Engineering; Social Sciences; Business Administration and Management

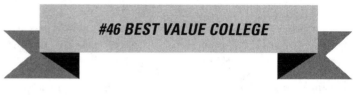

#46 BEST VALUE COLLEGE

ABOUT THE SCHOOL
Washington University in St. Louis is a nationally-renowned research university that encourages interdisciplinary study through its flexible curriculum, spread across five different schools and ninety majors; three out of four students pursue multiple majors or degrees, and 40 percent of students study abroad. First-year seminars sometimes include out-of-class components like research or travel, and academics are "rigorous": professors expect students to be able to handle a higher level of learning and material, but "there are homework help sessions and tutoring groups that you can access easily." Additionally, faculty invite student input and "often like to transfer skills to out-of-the-classroom contexts" within the framework of their classes. Students don't have to adhere to general education requirements, and can transfer within undergraduate schools and departments easily and without other applications, and there are an "array of academic courses available" (more than 1,500, to be exact). The support systems in place for first-year students "help ease the college transition immensely," and the administrators" deeply care about the well-being of the students."

BANG FOR YOUR BUCK
Washington University has resources in spades, and "there's always funding for student groups, student initiatives, university-run activities, research… and it shows." Even though the student body may skew wealthier and the tuition may appear high on paper, each family is assigned a designated financial assistance counselor to make sure that a Washington University education is accessible. As proof 100 percent of admitted students have financial aid fully covered. Merit scholarships are offered by each academic division and do not require a separate application beyond the school's admission process; each school has at least one merit-based full tuition scholarship (as well as other partial scholarships).

STUDENT LIFE
Campus life is "exciting and lively" among this "incredibly kind, inquisitive, and collaborative" bunch, and people here are "intelligent beyond belief." This is a community where everyone cares about their studies, but "really do it for the love of learning in great part, as well as for the grades." The infrastructure is unmatched: "Dorms are five-star hotels, food is delicious with tons of variety," and the buildings are "gorgeous." People are likely "to take breaks during lunch to just hang out or play Frisbee on the field," and on the weekends, students will go to the Loop (a stretch of restaurants near campus) for dinner out with friends. The social scene is "largely Greek life-based," though big clubs or student groups also have a very strong social aspect.

CAREER
Washington University is truly an individualized school, and encourages students to explore and combine their interests. The "supportive" Career Center has "a great relationship with alumni" and makes sure that academic and career advisers are available to all students to help them translate these interests into a career path, and faculty associates and fellows interact with

Washington University in St. Louis

FINANCIAL AID: 888-547-6670 • E-MAIL: ADMISSIONS@WUSTL.EDU • WEBSITE: WUSTL.EDU

students in the residence halls to provide additional on-the-ground guidance throughout the year. The Center for Experiential Learning allows students to consult for real companies; job placement is excellent, and the school is a "recruiting hub for top companies." Out of Washington University alumni visiting PayScale.com, 44 percent report that they derive a high level of meaning from their jobs.

GENERAL INFO

Activities: Choral groups, concert band, dance, drama/theater, jazz band, literary magazine, music ensembles, musical theater, opera, pep band, radio station, student government, student newspaper, student-run film society, symphony orchestra, television station, campus ministries, international student organization. **Organizations:** 380 registered organizations, 19 honor societies, 18 religious organizations. 10 fraternities, 8 sororities. **Athletics (Intercollegiate):** *Men:* Baseball, basketball, cross-country, diving, football, soccer, swimming, tennis, track/field (outdoor), track/field (indoor). *Women:* Basketball, cross-country, diving, golf, soccer, softball, swimming, tennis, track/field (outdoor), track/field (indoor), volleyball.

FINANCIAL AID

Students should submit: CSS Profile; FAFSA. Regular filing deadline is 2/1. The Princeton Review suggests that all financial aid forms be submitted as soon as possible after October 1. *Need-based scholarships/grants offered:* College/university scholarship or grant aid from institutional funds; Federal Pell; Private scholarships; SEOG; State scholarships/grants; United Negro College Fund. *Loan aid offered:* Direct PLUS Loans, Direct Subsidized Loans, Direct Unsubsidized Loans. Applicants will be notified of awards on or about 4/1. Federal Work-Study Program available. Institutional employment available.

THE BOTTOM LINE

Tuition is a hefty $52,400 and room and board is an equally hefty $16,440, but fear not: the sticker price is just for show. The school is committed to cost not being a barrier, and it has eliminated need-based loans to students from low- and middle-income families, and those coming from families with incomes below a certain threshold instead receive grants from the university that will not have to be repaid.

CAREER INFORMATION FROM PAYSCALE.COM	
ROI Rating	92
Bachelors and No Higher	
Median starting salary	$62,700
Median mid-career salary	$113,100
At Least Bachelors	
Median starting salary	$65,300
Median mid-career salary	$119,900
Alumni with high job meaning	42%
Degrees awarded in STEM subjects	30%

SELECTIVITY	
Admissions Rating	98
# of applicants	30,463
% of applicants accepted	16
% of acceptees attending	37
# of early decision applicants	1808
% accepted early decision	38

FRESHMAN PROFILE	
Range SAT EBRW	720–770
Range SAT Math	750–800
Range ACT Composite	32–34
% graduated top 10% of class	87
% graduated top 25% of class	98
% graduated top 50% of class	100

DEADLINES	
Early decision	
Deadline	11/1
Notification	12/15
Other ED Deadline	1/2
Other ED Notification	2/15
Regular decision	
Deadline	1/2
Notification	4/1
Nonfall registration?	No

FINANCIAL FACTS	
Financial Aid Rating	99
Annual tuition	$52,400
Room and board	$16,440
Required fees	$999
Books and supplies	$1,010
Average frosh need-based scholarship	$45,567
Average UG need-based scholarship	$43,745
% needy frosh rec. need-based scholarship or grant aid	95
% needy UG rec. need-based scholarship or grant aid	97
% needy frosh rec. non-need-based scholarship or grant aid	9
% needy UG rec. non-need-based scholarship or grant aid	6
% needy frosh rec. need-based self-help aid	73
% needy UG rec. need-based self-help aid	68
% frosh rec. any financial aid	50
% UG rec. any financial aid	49
% UG borrow to pay for school	29
Average cumulative indebtedness	$22,592
% frosh need fully met	100
% ugrads need fully met	100
Average % of frosh need met	100
Average % of ugrad need met	100

Wellesley College

BOARD OF ADMISSION, 106 CENTRAL STREET, WELLESLEY, MA 02481-8203 • PHONE: 781-283-2270

CAMPUS LIFE

Quality of Life Rating	**89**
Fire Safety Rating	**98**
Green Rating	**89**
Type of school	Private
Environment	Town

STUDENTS

Total undergrad enrollment	2,374
% male/female	0/100
% from out of state	87
% frosh from public high school	62
% frosh live on campus	100
% ugrads live on campus	98
# of fraternities (% ugrad men join)	0 (0)
# of sororities (% ugrad women join)	0 (0)
% African American	6
% Asian	23
% Caucasian	39
% Hispanic	12
% Native American	<1
% Pacific Islander	0
% Two or more races	6
% Race and/or ethnicity unknown	<1
% international	13
# of countries represented	88

ACADEMICS

Academic Rating	**93**
% students returning for sophomore year	95
% students graduating within 4 years	78
% students graduating within 6 years	90
Calendar	Semester
Student/faculty ratio	7:1
Profs interesting rating	97
Profs accessible rating	93

Most classes have 10–19 students. Most lab/discussion sessions have 10–19 students.

MOST POPULAR MAJORS
Computer Science; Psychology; Economics

ABOUT THE SCHOOL

Students spend a tremendous amount of time reading and writing papers at Wellesley. Spending part of junior year abroad is a staple of a Wellesley education. Wellesley Career Education offers grants and stipends, which allow students to pursue what would otherwise be unpaid research and internship opportunities. When they get their diplomas, Wellesley graduates are able to take advantage of a tenaciously loyal network of more than 35,000 alums who are ready to help students with everything from arranging an interview to finding a place to live. Wellesley's close-knit student population collectively spends large segments of its weekdays in stressed-out study mode. Students don't spend all of their weekdays this way, though, because there are a ton of extracurricular activities available on this beautiful, state-of-the-art campus. Wellesley is home to more than 160 student organizations. Lectures, performances, and cultural events are endless. Wellesley is twelve miles west of Boston, and access to cultural, academic, social, business, and medical institutions is a powerful draw. On the weekends, many students head to Boston to hit the bars or to parties on nearby campuses. While enrolling nearly 2,400 undergraduates, Wellesley offers a remarkable array of more than 1,000 courses and fifty-four major programs; plus, "you can cross-register at MIT (and to a limited extent at Brandeis, Babson, and Olin.)" From research to internships to overseas studies, Wellesley "provides great resources and opportunities to all its students."

BANG FOR YOUR BUCK

With an endowment worth more than $1.5 billion, Wellesley is rolling in the riches. Admission is completely need-blind for U.S. citizens and permanent residents. If you get admitted (no easy task), Wellesley will meet 100 percent of your calculated financial need. Most financial aid comes in the form of a grant; it's free money, and you'll never have to pay it back. Packaged student loan amounts are correlated to family income. No student will graduate with more than $15,200 in packaged student loans. Students from families with a calculated income between $60,000-$100,000 will graduate with no more than $10,100 in packaged student loans. And students from families with the greatest need, with a calculated income of $60,000 or less, will graduate with $0 in packaged student loans.

STUDENT LIFE

Because Wellesley is an academically rigorous school full of driven women, "most of the weekday is spent in class or studying." But when students want to take a break from the books, "there are always seminars and panel discussions and cultural events to attend. The diverse community and the multitudes of campus groups means there's always something to do." Once the weekend hits, "there's a large split. There are girls that don't party, or hardly party. And then there are girls who party every weekend." "On campus parties are hard to find and are normally broken up because of a noise complaint from a studying neighbor." As such, "the girls who are interested in men frequently spend their weekends venturing off campus to MIT or Harvard for parties," or head into Boston for "a girl's night out— go to a movie, maybe see a play, go karaoke, or just have dinner in the city." But no matter how you want to spend your free time, Wellesley has you covered: "It's nice to know that whatever you feel like doing on a Friday night, you'll always have company—whether you want to stay in and watch a movie or go into Boston to party."

Wellesley College

FINANCIAL AID PHONE: 781-283-2360 • E-MAIL: ADMISSION@WELLESLEY.EDU • FAX: 781-283-3678 • WEBSITE: WWW.WELLESLEY.EDU

CAREER

The typical Wellesley woman is often described as "career oriented" by her peers, and fortunately "Wellesley has an amazing alumni network and a career service center that helps students gain access to all sorts of job, internship, and community service opportunities." Wellesley Career Education offers ample resources, including career advising, help with finding jobs and internships, and tools for students seeking to continue their education in graduate school. True to its name, the center also offers guidance for women looking for service opportunities within existing organizations on and off-campus, and even offers funding for students looking to start their own initiatives. The support doesn't end after students graduate: "Wellesley's alumnae network is one of the strongest I found in my college research, and Wellesley's career placement services will assist alumnae no matter how much time has passed since they graduated."

GENERAL INFO

Activities: Choral groups, dance, debate society, drama/theater, jazz band, literary magazine, music ensembles, neuroscience club, quidditch team, radio station, Shakespeare society, student government, student newspaper, student-run film society, symphony orchestra, ultimate frisbee team, yearbook, campus ministries, international student organizations. **Organizations:** 160 registered organizations, 6 honor societies, 30 religious organizations. **Athletics (Intercollegiate):** *Women:* Basketball, crew/rowing, cross-country, diving, fencing, field hockey, golf, lacrosse, soccer, softball, swimming, tennis, track/field, volleyball.

FINANCIAL AID

Students should submit: CSS Profile; FAFSA. Priority filing deadline is 3/1. The Princeton Review suggests that all financial aid forms be submitted as soon as possible after October 1. *Need-based scholarships/grants offered:* College/university scholarship or grant aid from institutional funds; Federal Pell; Private scholarships; SEOG; State scholarships/grants; United Negro College Fund. *Loan aid offered:* Direct PLUS Loans, Direct Subsidized Loans, Direct Unsubsidized Loans. Applicants will be notified of awards on or about 4/1. Federal and institutional work-study programs are available.

BOTTOM LINE

The total cost for a year of tuition, fees, and room and board at Wellesley is over $70,000. However, this school has the financial resources to provide a tremendous amount of financial aid. Your aid package is likely to be quite extensive, and students leave with just $13,283 in loan debt on average. That's chump change for an education worth more than $250,000.

CAREER INFORMATION FROM PAYSCALE.COM

ROI Rating	91
Bachelors and No Higher	
Median starting salary	$56,600
Median mid-career salary	$103,900
At Least Bachelors	
Median starting salary	$58,300
Median mid-career salary	$108,100
Alumni with high job meaning	50%
Degrees awarded in STEM subjects	34%

SELECTIVITY

Admissions Rating	**97**
# of applicants	5,666
% of applicants accepted	22
% of acceptees attending	48
# offered a place on the wait list	1,153
% accepting a place on wait list	36
% admitted from wait list	3
# of early decision applicants	714
% accepted early decision	35

FRESHMAN PROFILE

Range SAT EBRW	690–760
Range SAT Math	670–770
Range ACT Composite	30–33
% graduated top 10% of class	81
% graduated top 25% of class	96
% graduated top 50% of class	99

DEADLINES

Early decision	
Deadline	11/1
Notification	Mid December
Other ED Deadline	1/1
Other ED Notification	Mid February
Regular	
Deadline	1/15
Notification	4/1
Nonfall registration?	No

FINANCIAL FACTS

Financial Aid Rating	**95**
Annual tuition	$53,408
Room and board	$16,468
Required fees	$324
Average frosh need-based scholarship	$48,433
Average UG need-based scholarship	$47,375
% needy frosh rec. need-based scholarship or grant aid	97
% needy UG rec. need-based scholarship or grant aid	97
% needy frosh rec. non-need-based scholarship or grant aid	0
% needy UG rec. non-need-based scholarship or grant aid	0
% needy frosh rec. need-based self-help aid	89
% needy UG rec. need-based self-help aid	91
% frosh rec. any financial aid	60
% UG rec. any financial aid	63
% UG borrow to pay for school	49
Average cumulative indebtedness	$13,283
% frosh need fully met	100
% ugrads need fully met	100
Average % of frosh need met	100
Average % of ugrad need met	100

Wesleyan University

70 Wyllys Avenue, Middletown, CT 06459-0265 • Admissions: 860-685-3000 • Fax: 860-685-3001

CAMPUS LIFE	
Quality of Life Rating	**88**
Fire Safety Rating	**93**
Green Rating	**96**
Type of school	Private
Environment	Town

STUDENTS	
Total undergrad enrollment	2,887
% male/female	46/54
% from out of state	92
% frosh from public high school	52
% frosh live on campus	100
% ugrads live on campus	100
# of fraternities (% ugrad men join)	4 (4)
# of sororities (% ugrad women join)	1 (1)
% African American	6
% Asian	8
% Caucasian	54
% Hispanic	11
% Native American	<1
% Pacific Islander	<1
% Two or more races	5
% Race and/or ethnicity unknown	3
% international	12
# of countries represented	53

ACADEMICS	
Academic Rating	**92**
% students returning for sophomore year	95
% students graduating within 4 years	85
% students graduating within 6 years	90
Calendar	Semester
Student/faculty ratio	8:1
Profs interesting rating	93
Profs accessible rating	88

Most classes have 10–19 students. Most lab/discussion sessions have 10–19 students.

MOST POPULAR MAJORS
Psychology; Economics

ABOUT THE COLLEGE

Connecticut's Wesleyan University emphasizes a "practical idealism" in its open curriculum, in which students propose an academic plan to their faculty advisors and readjust each semester as interests and strengths develop. The school offers forty-five majors, seventeen minors, and twelve certificates, with over one thousand classes available to just 3,000 students, not to mention countless study abroad opportunities and First-Year Seminars (all of which are writing-focused). The school is "very good about making sure you can study a range of things and still get the credits you need in your major(s)," and "the course offerings are diverse and great." Professors are "experts in their field and make learning challenging, yet rewarding," and class sizes are so small that "student-professor relationships are more easily facilitated." In addition, "student-student relationships are easier to maintain." In fact, students themselves are often core of the curriculum, as "everyone contributes wonderfully idiosyncratic thoughts built from past experiences within their own niches through the same mode of communication: education."

BANG FOR YOUR BUCK

Resources abound at Wesleyan, and there are more than 800 individual tutorials and private music lessons available to students, as well as numerous opportunities to get involved in graduate-level research. The school participates in the Twelve-College Exchange Program, where students can apply to study at one of eleven New England colleges for a semester or the full year, like a domestic study abroad. Most students also complete a senior thesis or capstone project (such as independent research) in an area that interests them most, which is an excellent showcase for results. There is no time lost to mindlessness here; the fluid general education requirements set up by Wesleyan University "really allows students to explore a broad spectrum of subjects while also figuring out what they like or dislike," so they can figure out if they like something else while still fulfilling their major requirements with a "lower risk factor."

STUDENT LIFE

Wesleyan students are "Hip, passionate, socially conscious," as well as "really dedicated and artsy," but there is a surprisingly strong athletic culture to be found, and games of all sport teams are in high attendance. Students take full advantage of the liberal arts experience and curiosity runs far and wide (a "very strange brilliance"), and "many are passionate about their niche interest." People "don't generally take themselves too seriously, even as they're doing incredible things academically," and overall, students are "hard-working and know how to relax with friends, too." The school is "big enough not to feel suffocating, small enough to feel comfortable," and even has its own movie theater that plays new releases. There is a highly diverse international student population (the school offers a full tuition scholarship to one student from each of eleven Asian countries each year), and all are "reflective snapshots of the various cultures around the world"; "everyone has something unique or weird (in a good way) about them."

CAREER

The Gordon Career Center has "many helpful resources for applying to summer internships and jobs after graduation," and works individually with students to design career paths based on the overlap of interests, rather than straight trajectories from a major. Due to the

Wesleyan University

FINANCIAL AID: 860-685-2800 • E-MAIL: ADMISSIONS@WESLEYAN.EDU • WEBSITE: WWW.WESLEYAN.EDU

interdisciplinary nature of the school, students have multiple and wildly varying interests (for instance, a double major in physics and theatre), and "no one can be placed in a traditional box." Students are truly free to make their own schedules and pursue the career they desire here, all with the support of the faculty. "Not once have I been discouraged from pursuing my interests, and the encouragement to follow these passions has caused a spark in me to bring them together," says a theater and science in society double major.

GENERAL INFO

Activities: Choral groups, concert band, dance, drama/theater, jazz band, literary magazine, music ensembles, musical theater, pep band, radio station, student government, student newspaper, student-run film society, symphony orchestra, yearbook, campus ministries. **Organizations:** 220 registered organizations, 2 honor societies, 10 religious organizations. 4 fraternities, 1 sorority. **Athletics (Intercollegiate):** *Men:* Baseball, basketball, crew/rowing, cross-country, diving, football, golf, ice hockey, lacrosse, soccer, squash, swimming, tennis, track/field (outdoor), track/field (indoor), wrestling. *Women:* Basketball, crew/rowing, cross-country, diving, field hockey, ice hockey, lacrosse, soccer, softball, squash, swimming, tennis, track/field (outdoor), track/field (indoor), volleyball.

FINANCIAL AID

Students should submit: CSS Profile; FAFSA. Priority filing deadline is 11/15. The Princeton Review suggests that all financial aid forms be submitted as soon as possible after October 1. *Need-based scholarships/grants offered:* College/university scholarship or grant aid from institutional funds, Federal Pell, private scholarships, SEOG, state scholarships/grants. *Loan aid offered:* Direct PLUS Loans, Direct Subsidized Loans, Direct Unsubsidized Loans. Applicants will be notified of awards on or about 4/1. Federal Work-Study Program available. Institutional employment available.

THE BOTTOM LINE

Tuition, room and board, books (estimated), and fees run $69,674 for first-year and sophomores, but the university is committed to price not being a barrier to those who want to attend and meets all financial need. Almost $59 million of solely need-based financial aid is distributed to 48 percent of Wesleyan students, with the average award coming in at $51,397.

CAREER INFORMATION FROM PAYSCALE.COM

ROI Rating	91
Bachelors and No Higher	
Median starting salary	$59,300
Median mid-career salary	$114,700
At Least Bachelors	
Median starting salary	$61,300
Median mid-career salary	$128,400
Alumni with high job meaning	56%
Degrees awarded in STEM subjects	21%

SELECTIVITY

Admissions Rating	97
# of applicants	12,360
% of applicants accepted	16
% of acceptees attending	38
# offered a place on the wait list	2,267
% accepting a place on wait list	54
% admitted from wait list	9
# of early decision applicants	1153
% accepted early decision	38

FRESHMAN PROFILE

Range SAT EBRW	660–740
Range SAT Math	640–760
Range ACT Composite	29–33
Minimum paper TOEFL	600
Minimum internet-based TOEFL	100
% graduated top 10% of class	60
% graduated top 25% of class	92
% graduated top 50% of class	98

DEADLINES

Early decision	
Deadline	11/15
Notification	12/15
Other ED Deadline	1/1
Other ED Notification	2/15
Regular	
Deadline	1/1
Notification	4/1
Nonfall registration?	No

FINANCIAL FACTS

Financial Aid Rating	96
Annual tuition	$54,314
Room and board	$15,060
Required fees	$300
Books and supplies	$1,200
Average frosh need-based scholarship	$47,653
Average UG need-based scholarship	$47,206
% needy frosh rec. need-based scholarship or grant aid	94
% needy UG rec. need-based scholarship or grant aid	93
% needy frosh rec. non-need-based scholarship or grant aid	3
% needy UG rec. non-need-based scholarship or grant aid	3
% needy frosh rec. need-based self-help aid	94
% needy UG rec. need-based self-help aid	93
% frosh rec. any financial aid	48
% UG rec. any financial aid	48
% UG borrow to pay for school	39
Average cumulative indebtedness	$22,930
% frosh need fully met	100
% ugrads need fully met	100

Wheaton College (IL)

501 COLLEGE AVENUE, WHEATON, IL 60187 • ADMISSIONS: 800-222-2419 • FAX: 630-752-5285

CAMPUS LIFE

Quality of Life Rating	96
Fire Safety Rating	94
Green Rating	70
Type of school	Private
Affiliation	Christian non-denominational
Environment	Town

STUDENTS

Total undergrad enrollment	2,356
% male/female	45/55
% from out of state	72
% frosh from public high school	48
% frosh live on campus	99
% ugrads live on campus	89
# of fraternities (% ugrad men join)	0 (0)
# of sororities (% ugrad women join)	0 (0)
% African American	3
% Asian	9
% Caucasian	75
% Hispanic	6
% Native American	<1
% Pacific Islander	0
% Two or more races	4
% Race and/or ethnicity unknown	<1
% international	3
# of countries represented	40

ACADEMICS

Academic Rating	90
% students returning for sophomore year	93
% students graduating within 4 years	80
% students graduating within 6 years	89
Calendar	Semester
Student/faculty ratio	11:1
Profs interesting rating	98
Profs accessible rating	95

Most classes have 20–29 students. Most lab/discussion sessions have fewer than 10 students.

MOST POPULAR MAJORS

English Language and Literature; Biology/Biological Sciences; Business/Managerial Economics; Applied Health Science

ABOUT THE SCHOOL

Tucked away in suburban Illinois, Wheaton is a small college that offers "academic excellence" within a "distinctly Christian environment." The school maintains a "welcoming community" that is certainly "commit[ted] to Christ." Many individuals also rush to highlight the school's "strong leadership development training program." Academically, students love that the "liberal arts" curriculum provides them with a "well-rounded" education. And they greatly appreciate that at Wheaton, "small" class sizes are a given. "Wheaton retains exceptional faculty members who are leading experts in their fields," and "building close relationships with professors is normal and highly encouraged." Students find that their instructors frequently prove themselves to be "very knowledgeable and interesting" and that they "generally love teaching and invest in their students both inside and outside of class." As one incredulous undergrad illustrates, "Their doors are literally always open. They work extremely hard, but their lives are transparent so you [even] know their families [and] what they are doing over the weekend!"

BANG FOR YOUR BUCK

Undergrads who attend Wheaton can rest assured that the college remains steadfast in its commitment to provide an affordable education. In fact, nearly 81 percent of the student body received some form of aid in the 2017 academic year. And the school awarded over $28 million through scholarships and grants. Wheaton offers several renewable merit scholarships. For example, the Blanchard Presidential Scholarship provides $16,000 per year and the Edman Presidential Scholarship provides $12,000 per year. Every applicant is given consideration for academic scholarships, based on standardized test scores, unweighted GPA, academic riigor of curriculum, and class rank (if available).

STUDENT LIFE

There's no denying that Wheaton students are a diligent lot and spend copious amounts of time studying. Yet somehow, they also manage to carve out space for fun and extracurricular activities. For example, "many students…participate in music programs" or "attend a weekly Bible study in addition to church and school chapel." Students also like to take advantage of the "numerous opportunities for community service." Both the "College Union and Residence Life organize dances, concerts, and other on-campus entertainment, while academic departments sponsor a variety of speakers." Undergrads do caution that "Wheaton is not a party school." For time away from campus, students love the college's proximity to Chicago and frequently head into the city for some sightseeing.

CAREER

Wheaton does a tremendous job of helping students "develop…a career path that is right [for them.]" For starters, the college fosters "great opportunities for research and internships." Of course, much of this success can be attributed to Wheaton's Center for Vocation and Career. Every year, the office runs a handful of programs that walk undergrads through every aspect of a job hunt. For example, there's Canvas which guides sophomores through the process of career exploration. There's also the Senior Series which helps seniors prepare for life after Wheaton. And we can't forget everyone's favorite program—Taco Tuesday. This scrumptious event pairs students with alumni and lets them chat about jobs industries over a casual taco dinner.

Wheaton College (IL)

FINANCIAL AID: 630-752-5021 • E-MAIL: ADMISSIONS@WHEATON.EDU • WEBSITE: WHEATON.EDU

GENERAL INFO

Activities: Choral groups, concert band, dance, drama/theater, jazz band, literary magazine, music ensembles, musical theater, opera, pep band, student government, student newspaper, student-run film society, symphony orchestra, campus ministries, International Student Organization, Model UN. **Organizations:** 85 registered organizations, 13 honor societies, 12 religious organizations. **Athletics (Intercollegiate):** *Men:* baseball, basketball, cross-country, football, golf, soccer, swimming, tennis, track/field (outdoor), track/field (indoor), wrestling. *Women:* basketball, cross-country, golf, soccer, softball, swimming, tennis, track/field (outdoor), track/field (indoor), volleyball. **On-Campus Highlights:** Billy Graham Center, archive, museum, Wade Center—English authors collections, Meyer Science Center, Todd M. Beamer Student Center, Wheaton College Center for Faith, Politics and Economics.

FINANCIAL AID

Students should submit: FAFSA. Priority filing deadline is 11/10. The Princeton Review suggests that all financial aid forms be submitted as soon as possible after October 1. *Need-based scholarships/grants offered:* College/university scholarship or grant aid from institutional funds, Federal Pell, private scholarships, SEOG, state scholarships/grants. *Loan aid offered:* Direct PLUS Loans, Direct Subsidized Loans, Direct Unsubsidized Loans. Applicants will be notified of awards on a rolling basis beginning 12/31. Federal Work-Study Program available. Institutional employment available.

THE BOTTOM LINE

Wheaton College charges $36,420 for one academic year. Beyond tuition, dining services cost students another $4,180. This figure can vary depending on the meal plan selected. Individuals living on campus will be charged $6,000 for their dormitory. That price covers both double and triple rooms. Students who wish to live in a single, apartment or housing designated for married couples will be charged more. Lastly, undergrads will also need to budget for books, personal expenses, and travel.

CAREER INFORMATION FROM PAYSCALE.COM

ROI Rating	89
Bachelors and No Higher	
Median starting salary	$51,500
Median mid-career salary	$101,300
At Least Bachelors	
Median starting salary	$52,900
Median mid-career salary	$105,600
Alumni with high job meaning	55%
Degrees awarded in STEM subjects	12%

SELECTIVITY

Admissions Rating	88
# of applicants	1,693
% of applicants accepted	85
% of acceptees attending	40
# offered a place on the wait list	184
% accepting a place on wait list	15
% admitted from wait list	54

FRESHMAN PROFILE

Range SAT EBRW	630–720
Range SAT Math	600–690
Range ACT Composite	27–32
Minimum paper TOEFL	587
Minimum internet-based TOEFL	95
Average HS GPA	3.7
% graduated top 10% of class	47
% graduated top 25% of class	73
% graduated top 50% of class	93

DEADLINES

Early action	
Deadline	11/1
Notification	12/31
Regular	
Deadline	1/10
Notification	4/1
Nonfall registration?	Yes

FINANCIAL FACTS

Financial Aid Rating	85
Annual tuition	$36,420
Room and board	$10,180
Average frosh need-based scholarship	$23,361
Average UG need-based scholarship	$21,171
% needy frosh rec. need-based scholarship or grant aid	100
% needy UG rec. need-based scholarship or grant aid	99
% needy frosh rec. non-need-based scholarship or grant aid	28
% needy UG rec. non-need-based scholarship or grant aid	27
% needy frosh rec. need-based self-help aid	76
% needy UG rec. need-based self-help aid	77
% frosh rec. any financial aid	86
% UG rec. any financial aid	79
% UG borrow to pay for school	57
Average cumulative indebtedness	$27,543
% frosh need fully met	18
% ugrads need fully met	22
Average % of frosh need met	84
Average % of ugrad need met	84

Wheaton College (MA)

Office of Admission, Norton, MA 02766 • Admissions: 508-286-8251 • Fax: 508-286-8271

CAMPUS LIFE

Quality of Life Rating	88
Fire Safety Rating	99
Green Rating	74
Type of school	Private
Environment	Village

STUDENTS

Total undergrad enrollment	1,678
% male/female	39/61
% from out of state	63
% frosh from public high school	69
% frosh live on campus	98
% ugrads live on campus	96
# of fraternities (% ugrad men join)	0 (0)
# of sororities (% ugrad women join)	0 (0)
% African American	6
% Asian	5
% Caucasian	65
% Hispanic	8
% Native American	<1
% Pacific Islander	<1
% Two or more races	3
% Race and/or ethnicity unknown	2
% international	10
# of countries represented	71

ACADEMICS

Academic Rating	92
% students returning for sophomore year	88
% students graduating within 4 years	72
% students graduating within 6 years	78
Calendar	Semester
Student/faculty ratio	10:1
Profs interesting rating	92
Profs accessible rating	91

Most classes have 10–19 students. Most lab/discussion sessions have 10–19 students.

MOST POPULAR MAJORS

Psychology; Economics; Business and Management

ABOUT THE SCHOOL

In Norton, Massachusetts, Wheaton College delivers the ultimate collegiate trifecta—a "beautiful campus," a "welcoming student body" and the promise of "academic rigor." Beyond that, the college truly aims to help each of its 1,750 undergrads reach their "full potential." To that end, Wheaton ensures that class sizes remain "small" and they offer students the ability to create an "individualized program" if they so desire. Current students praise the "diversity" of departments and disciplines available. And they value the "liberal arts program [that] allows for flexibility in education and makes dabbling in multiple subjects easier." Students are also quick to celebrate their peers, noting they are "very motivated and seek every opportunity to increase their academic knowledge." They partially attribute this to their "amazing" professors who "want their students to succeed." What's more, Wheaton instructors are "insightful" and "invested" and "work really hard to put the students' interests first." And their "genuine passion" continually shines through in the classroom.

BANG FOR YOUR BUCK

Prospective students will be delighted to learn that Wheaton tends to offer "generous financial aid" packages. What's more, the college can dole out that aid to "a great amount of the students." Wheaton administers over $40 million in funding annually. Additionally, all applicants are considered for academic scholarships. And Wheaton makes it so easy to apply; there's no separate application involved. Ultimately, roughly 35 percent of the incoming class will receive a merit scholarship. And these awards are often quite significant awards, covering up to a whopping $30,000 per year.

STUDENT LIFE

While Wheaton undergrads are undoubtedly dedicated to their studies, they also manage to carve out plenty of time for fun. Students here are "very committed to extracurricular activities." For example, we're told that "musical groups are big on campus as well as other performing arts groups." Additionally, many individuals are "involved in community service and there are numerous opportunities to get involved in the Norton community through classes and clubs." It's also quite common to find these undergrads hanging out at "the student run coffee shop (the Lyons Den) [which] is open late and hosts open mics on Wednesdays." Once the weekend rolls around, you'll discover "anything from a movie in one of the auditoriums to food trucks to dance and music performances." And of course, parties can be found on "Thursday, Friday and Saturday [nights]." These are "usually hosted by theme houses" which are Wheaton's "alternative to Greek life."

CAREER

Students at Wheaton proudly proclaim that the college provides "many great resources for...career building." As this undergrad boasts, "The greatest strength of our school is the career services department which has a high placement rate for both internships and full time positions." In fact, "about 99 percent of students complete an internship during their time at Wheaton." This is due to the Wheaton Edge program, which guarantees funding for an internship, research position, or other experiential learning opportunity for every student. Wheaton invests more than $1.2 million each year into this program. Importantly, the office works closely with undergrads to create a customized career development plan. Students can take advantage of one-on-one advising and receive fantastic guidance on resume writing and interview prep. Career services also sponsors several great programs and events. For example, students can attend "Career Conversations" which are

Wheaton College (MA)

FINANCIAL AID: 508-286-8232 • E-MAIL: ADMISSION@WHEATONCOLLEGE.EDU • WEBSITE: WWW.WHEATONCOLLEGE.EDU

informal round-table discussions with a variety of industry insiders. With events like this it's no wonder why Wheaton grads do so well!

GENERAL INFO

Activities: Choral groups, multiple a cappella groups, dance, drama/theater, jazz band, literary magazine, music ensembles, musical theater, radio station, student government, student newspaper, student-run film society, symphony orchestra, yearbook, Student Organization, Model UN. **Organizations:** 100+ registered organizations, 8 honor societies, 4 religious organizations. **Athletics (Intercollegiate):** *Men:* baseball, basketball, cross-country, diving, lacrosse, soccer, swimming, tennis, track/field (outdoor), track/field (indoor). *Women:* basketball, cross-country, diving, field hockey, lacrosse, soccer, softball, swimming, synchronized swimming, tennis, track/field (outdoor), track/field (indoor), volleyball. **On-Campus Highlights:** Mars Center for Science and Technology, Haas Athletic Center, Lyon's Den—coffee house, Mary Lyon Hall—college's oldest building, Balfour-Hood Student Center.

FINANCIAL AID

Students should submit: Business/Farm Supplement; CSS Profile; FAFSA. Regular filing deadline is 2/1. The Princeton Review suggests that all financial aid forms be submitted as soon as possible after October 1. *Need-based scholarships/grants offered:* College/university scholarship or grant aid from institutional funds, Federal Pell, private scholarships, SEOG, state scholarships/grants. *Loan aid offered:* Direct PLUS Loans, Direct Subsidized Loans, Direct Unsubsidized Loans. Applicants will be notified of awards on or about 3/15. Federal Work-Study Program available. Institutional employment available.

BOTTOM LINE

It's easy to experience sticker shock when you see that tuition at Wheaton costs $52,288 for the 2018–2019 academic year. Additionally, students will have to pay another $7,160 for room and another $6,261 for board. There's also a $338 student activity fee. Hence, the total amount is $66,050. Though that's a hefty sum, prospective students can breathe a sigh of relief. The average need-based aid package is $45,220. And the average academic merit scholarship is $23,400.

CAREER INFORMATION FROM PAYSCALE.COM	
ROI Rating	88
Bachelors and No Higher	
Median starting salary	$51,300
Median mid-career salary	$101,300
At Least Bachelors	
Median starting salary	$53,000
Median mid-career salary	$104,000
Alumni with high job meaning	45%
Degrees awarded in STEM subjects	28%

SELECTIVITY	
Admissions Rating	88
# of applicants	6,089
% of applicants accepted	48
% of acceptees attending	17
# offered a place on the wait list	96
% accepting a place on wait list	18
% admitted from wait list	29
# of early decision applicants	165
% accepted early decision	73

FRESHMAN PROFILE	
Range SAT EBRW	590–680
Range SAT Math	560–670
Range ACT Composite	26–30
Minimum paper TOEFL	580
Minimum internet-based TOEFL	90
Average HS GPA	3.4
% graduated top 10% of class	26
% graduated top 25% of class	55
% graduated top 50% of class	85

DEADLINES	
Early decision	
Deadline	11/1
Notification	12/15
Other ED Deadline	1/1
Other ED Notification	2/1
Early action	
Deadline	11/1
Notification	1/15
Regular	
Deadline	1/1
Notification	4/1
Nonfall registration?	Yes

FINANCIAL FACTS	
Financial Aid Rating	91
Annual tuition	$52,288
Room and board	$13,424
Required fees	$338
Books and supplies	$940
Average frosh need-based scholarship	$38,565
Average UG need-based scholarship	$34,058
% needy frosh rec. need-based scholarship or grant aid	100
% needy UG rec. need-based scholarship or grant aid	97
% needy frosh rec. non-need-based scholarship or grant aid	6
% needy UG rec. non-need-based scholarship or grant aid	2
% needy frosh rec. need-based self-help aid	75
% needy UG rec. need-based self-help aid	84
% frosh rec. any financial aid	98
% UG rec. any financial aid	98

Whitman College

345 Boyer Ave, Walla Walla, WA 99362 • Admissions: 509-527-5176 • Fax: 509-527-4967

CAMPUS LIFE

Quality of Life Rating	**95**
Fire Safety Rating	**90**
Green Rating	**89**
Type of school	Private
Environment	Town

STUDENTS

Total undergrad enrollment	1,468
% male/female	43/57
% from out of state	66
% frosh from public high school	62
% frosh live on campus	100
% ugrads live on campus	64
# of fraternities (% ugrad men join)	4 (33)
# of sororities (% ugrad women join)	4 (41)
% African American	2
% Asian	5
% Caucasian	69
% Hispanic	7
% Native American	1
% Pacific Islander	<1
% Two or more races	7
% Race and/or ethnicity unknown	2
% international	7
# of countries represented	26

ACADEMICS

Academic Rating	**96**
% students returning for sophomore year	94
% students graduating within 4 years	79
% students graduating within 6 years	88
Calendar	Semester
Student/faculty ratio	9:1
Profs interesting rating	96
Profs accessible rating	99

Most classes have 10–19 students. Most lab/discussion sessions have 10–19 students.

MOST POPULAR MAJORS
Biology; Psychology

ABOUT THE SCHOOL

Whitman College attracts students who represent the Whitman mosaic: down-to-earth high achievers with diverse interests. One student says, "I wanted to attend a college where I would be intellectually challenged and stimulated. Now that I'm a second-semester senior, I can say that what I've learned in my classes at Whitman will benefit me for the rest of my life." The college is known for combining academic excellence with a down-to-earth, collaborative culture, which includes "professors who take the time to chat with students, invite them to dinner in their homes, organize field trips, [and] enlist students to help them in their research projects." For a real-life example, look no further than Whitman's tradition of awarding summer, annual, and per-semester grants for student-faculty research collaboration, aimed at turning each student into a "whole, intelligent, [and] interesting person." "Internships, study abroad, work, research opportunities (in and out of the sciences) are abundant at Whitman. Grants are easily accessible for those who have valid reason to seek them." The recently established Whitman Internship Grant program provides a stipend of approximately $2,500 to students completing unpaid summer internships that are relevant to their educational goals and career interests. It allows them to get creative with internships and to take part in opportunities that best match their academic or career interests. "Whitman has so many strengths, but I think the most important is that the students and faculty at Whitman promote and maintain a great, collaborative, and intellectually active atmosphere for academics," says one student.

BANG FOR YOUR BUCK

A full suite of scholarships are on offer here, covering up to the full cost of tuition and fees for four years. Highlights include the Whitman awards, which are renewable, four-year merit-based scholarships, ranging from $9,000 to $14,000 to entering students who have excelled academically. Whitman's Paul Garrett and Claire Sherwood Memorial Scholarships range from $2,500 to $50,000 depending on demonstrated financial need. The scholarship includes a trip to NYC to visit corporate headquarters and graduate schools on the East Coast. The Eells Scholarship covers the full cost of tuition for four years and includes a research grant. Talent awards are available in art, music, and theater. Whitman's outside scholarship policy allows students to add scholarships they receive from non-Whitman sources on top of the college's awarded scholarship up to the total budget.

STUDENT LIFE

Whitman students widely report that the school is a "work hard, play hard" kind of place. While students "do not let partying or other non-academic endeavors get in the way of their studies," they find many ways to unwind and have fun. They cite games and sports, from organized intramural events to pick-up Frisbee on the lawn, as a constant activity, especially in nice weather. On the weekends there are plentiful parties thrown by fraternities, clubs, or informal groups of friends, but "there is also absolutely no pressure to drink or do drugs." There are also "many school-sponsored dances and events that are well-attended," and Whitman often brings in guest lecturers, "cool indie bands," and other acts to entertain students. The school also sponsors "numerous outdoor program trips and activities, like hiking, cliff jumping, kayaking, climbing, etc." And no matter where their interests lie students love to spend time with their peers, who provide "the perfect combination of silliness and actually being able to have an intelligent and enlightening conversation."

Whitman College

FINANCIAL AID: 509-527-5178 • E-MAIL: ADMISSION@WHITMAN.EDU • WEBSITE: WWW.WHITMAN.EDU

CAREER

Whitman's Student Engagement Center provides a number of services to help students prepare for life after college. It offers traditional resources like job and internship search tools, career counseling, help with resumes and cover letters, and career fairs. The school also organizes "Whitman Hubs" in several cities to provide students and alumni with professional networking opportunities. The SEC sponsors special events and programs geared towards students interested in entrepreneurship and community service. Many students praise the career resources that the school offers, and of Whitman alumni visiting PayScale.com, 48 percent report that they derive meaning from their jobs.

GENERAL INFO

Activities: Choral groups, concert band, dance, drama/theater, jazz band, literary magazines, music ensembles, musical theater, radio station, student government, student newspaper, student-run film series, symphony orchestra, campus ministries, international student organization. **Organizations:** 80 registered organizations, 3 honor societies, 7 religious organizations. 4 fraternities, 4 sororities. **Athletics (Intercollegiate):** *Men:* Baseball, basketball, cross-country, golf, soccer, swimming, tennis. *Women:* Basketball, cross-country, golf, lacrosse, soccer, swimming, tennis, volleyball. **On-Campus Highlights:** Reid Campus Center, Penrose Library.

FINANCIAL AID

Students should submit: CSS Profile; FAFSA. Priority filing deadline is 11/15. The Princeton Review suggests that all financial aid forms be submitted as soon as possible after October 1. *Need-based scholarships/grants offered:* College/university scholarship or grant aid from institutional funds, Federal Pell, private scholarships, SEOG, state scholarships/grants. *Loan aid offered:* Direct PLUS Loans, Direct Subsidized Loans, Direct Unsubsidized Loans. Applicants will be notified of awards on or about 4/1. Federal Work-Study Program available. Institutional employment available.

BOTTOM LINE

The total cost of tuition, room and board, and fees adds up to around $65,000 per year. Both need-based and merit aid is available to help offset costs. Every spring, Whitman offers a financial-planning night that addresses not only loans but also financial issues for graduating students. Whitman offers internships during the summer that allow the students to work in the same area as their degree and hopefully help with employment when they graduate.

CAREER INFORMATION FROM PAYSCALE.COM

ROI Rating	90
Bachelors and No Higher	
Median starting salary	$52,200
Median mid-career salary	$109,000
At Least Bachelors	
Median starting salary	$55,100
Median mid-career salary	$117,100
Alumni with high job meaning	52%
Degrees awarded in STEM subjects	28%

SELECTIVITY

Admissions Rating	92
# of applicants	4,081
% of applicants accepted	52
% of acceptees attending	18
# offered a place on the wait list	998
% accepting a place on wait list	19
% admitted from wait list	41
# of early decision applicants	179
% accepted early decision	71

FRESHMAN PROFILE

Range SAT EBRW	630–720
Range SAT Math	620–730
Range ACT Composite	26–31
Minimum paper TOEFL	560
Minimum internet-based TOEFL	85
Average HS GPA	3.8
% graduated top 10% of class	59
% graduated top 25% of class	88
% graduated top 50% of class	98

DEADLINES

Early decision	
Deadline	11/15
Notification	12/20
Other ED Deadline	1/1
Other ED Notification	2/1
Regular	
Priority	11/15
Deadline	1/15
Notification	4/1
Nonfall registration?	No

FINANCIAL FACTS

Financial Aid Rating	86
Annual tuition	$51,370
Room and board	$13,118
Required fees	$394
Books and supplies	$1,400
Average frosh need-based scholarship	$36,332
Average UG need-based scholarship	$36,371
% needy frosh rec. need-based scholarship or grant aid	99
% needy UG rec. need-based scholarship or grant aid	100
% needy frosh rec. non-need-based scholarship or grant aid	41
% needy UG rec. non-need-based scholarship or grant aid	33
% needy frosh rec. need-based self-help aid	81
% needy UG rec. need-based self-help aid	81
% frosh rec. any financial aid	83
% UG rec. any financial aid	76
% UG borrow to pay for school	46
Average cumulative indebtedness	$23,254

Willamette University

900 State Street, Salem, OR 97301 • Admissions: 844-232-7228 • Fax: 503-375-5363

CAMPUS LIFE

Quality of Life Rating	**90**
Fire Safety Rating	**98**
Green Rating	**87**
Type of school	Private
Affiliation	Methodist
Environment	City

STUDENTS

Total undergrad enrollment	1,772
% male/female	42/58
% from out of state	77
% frosh from public high school	75
% frosh live on campus	94
% ugrads live on campus	62
# of fraternities (% ugrad men join)	5 (24)
# of sororities (% ugrad women join)	4 (18)
% African American	2
% Asian	9
% Caucasian	61
% Hispanic	13
% Native American	1
% Pacific Islander	<1
% Two or more races	9
% Race and/or ethnicity unknown	3
% international	1
# of countries represented	30

ACADEMICS

Academic Rating	**93**
% students returning for sophomore year	86
% students graduating within 4 years	66
% students graduating within 6 years	73
Calendar	Semester
Student/faculty ratio	11:1
Profs interesting rating	94
Profs accessible rating	95

Most classes have 20–29 students, Most lab/discussion sessions have 10–19 students.

MOST POPULAR MAJORS
Biology/Biological Sciences; Psychology; Economics

ABOUT THE SCHOOL

As soon as you set foot on Willamette University's campus, you instantly feel the "great [sense of] community" that surrounds you. And with its "great reputation" and countless "study abroad and internship opportunities" enrolling here is a no-brainer for many students. Importantly, Willamette's "small size fosters a support system that allows students to branch out and be involved with a wide range of academic and extracurricular activities." Students also appreciate the school's liberal arts curriculum, quickly highlighting the "strong" biology and psychology programs along with an "amazing" politics department. Just as essential, undergrads generally feel "respected" by both professors and the administration and mention that all parties "are very receptive to new ideas." And, of course, accessibility is paramount. As one senior boasts, "It's not unusual to be asked to dinner at a professor's house...and there is no one—not even our president—who doesn't have open office hours, or isn't willing to make an appointment to meet with a student."

BANG FOR YOUR BUCK

Undergrads at Willamette really value the diversity found on their campus. And many chalk that up to a stellar financial aid office. An art history major explains, "The student body is more than just rich white kids. People come from everywhere and it's the financial aid packages that make it possible." Still skeptical? Well, the average scholarship doled out to undergrads is $29,689. Though, we should mention that the average need-based loan is $5,335. Fortunately, there are also plenty of merit scholarships to be had. And the beauty is that all applicants are automatically considered, so there's no additional paperwork.

STUDENT LIFE

Don't let their laid back demeanor fool you; Willamette undergrads are a busy and active lot. As one student shares, "There is a huge population that is involved in clubs on campus, anything from soccer club to juggling club or knitting club." These Bearcats are also full of school spirit. Hence they "love to support varsity sports teams, attend theatre productions [and] listen to our a cappella groups perform." We're also told that "parties happen" but "they're low-key compared to larger schools." Finally, there's plenty to take advantage of when students are itching to get off-campus. Undergrads frequently "take trips to Portland and the ocean, and also head out to the mountains for skiing as well as hiking along paths decorated with waterfalls."

Willamette University

FINANCIAL AID: 877-744-3736 • E-MAIL: BEARCAT@WILLAMETTE.EDU • WEBSITE: WWW.WILLAMETTE.EDU

CAREER

Willamette students are surrounded by professional opportunity. Though hometown Salem might not be a bustling metropolis, undergrads insist that plenty of job possibilities exist, especially given that "the capitol [building is] across the street to one side, and the [Salem] hospital to the other." Moreover, students don't have to go the search alone. Indeed, "professors are very willing to help students find internships, jobs and research opportunities." And undergrads can surely turn to Career Services as well. The office provides everything from job postings to résumé advice. Additionally, students who are unsure of the professional path they want to pursue can receive career counseling and testing. And all undergrads may use the office to connect with successful alumni. Lastly, PayScale.com reports that the average starting salary for Willamette alums is $47,700.

GENERAL INFO

Activities: Choral groups, concert band, dance, drama/theater, jazz band, literary magazine, music ensembles, musical theater, opera, student government, student newspaper, student-run film society, symphony orchestra, campus ministries, International Student Organization, Model UN. **Organizations:** 107 registered organizations, 7 honor societies, 4 religious organizations. 4 fraternities, 4 sororities. **Athletics (Intercollegiate):** *Men:* baseball, basketball, cross-country, football, golf, soccer, swimming, tennis, track/field (outdoor), track/field (indoor). *Women:* basketball, cross-country, golf, soccer, softball, swimming, tennis, track/field (outdoor), track/field (indoor), volleyball. **On-Campus Highlights:** Hallie Ford Museum of Art, Montag Student Center, Sparks Athletic Center, Willamette Bistro, Mill Stream and Star Trees on campus.

FINANCIAL AID

Students should submit: FAFSA. Priority filing deadline is 2/1. The Princeton Review suggests that all financial aid forms be submitted as soon as possible after October 1. *Need-based scholarships/grants offered:* College/university scholarship or grant aid from institutional funds, Federal Pell, private scholarships, SEOG, state scholarships/grants. *Loan aid offered:* Direct PLUS Loans, Direct Subsidized Loans, Direct Unsubsidized Loans. Applicants will be notified of awards on a rolling basis beginning 4/1. Federal Work-Study Program available. Institutional employment available.

THE BOTTOM LINE

Tuition at Willamette generally runs undergrads (and their families) $47,840. In addition, those students opting to live on-campus will likely pay another $11,880 for room and board. Beyond that, the university also charges $317 in required fees. Lastly, undergrads should anticipate spending approximately $950 on books and other academic supplies.

CAREER INFORMATION FROM PAYSCALE.COM	
ROI Rating	88
Bachelors and No Higher	
Median starting salary	$49,900
Median mid-career salary	$102,600
At Least Bachelors	
Median starting salary	$52,200
Median mid-career salary	$107,200
Alumni with high job meaning	48%
Degrees awarded in STEM subjects	14%

SELECTIVITY

Admissions Rating	86
# of applicants	4,484
% of applicants accepted	89
% of acceptees attending	11
# offered a place on the wait list	56
% accepting a place on wait list	48
% admitted from wait list	11
# of early decision applicants	20
% accepted early decision	85

FRESHMAN PROFILE

Range SAT EBRW	570–680
Range SAT Math	550–660
Range ACT Composite	26–31
Minimum paper TOEFL	560
Minimum internet-based TOEFL	85
Average HS GPA	3.8
% graduated top 10% of class	47
% graduated top 25% of class	75
% graduated top 50% of class	93

DEADLINES

Early decision	
Deadline	11/15
Notification	12/30
Early action	
Deadline	11/15
Notification	12/31
Regular	
Priority	1/15
Deadline	1/15
Nonfall registration?	Yes

FINANCIAL FACTS

Financial Aid Rating	86
Annual tuition	$49,750
Room and board	$12,440
Required fees	$324
Books and supplies	$950
Average frosh need-based scholarship	$30,353
Average UG need-based scholarship	$30,571
% needy frosh rec. need-based scholarship or grant aid	97
% needy UG rec. need-based scholarship or grant aid	98
% needy frosh rec. non-need-based scholarship or grant aid	26
% needy UG rec. non-need-based scholarship or grant aid	16
% needy frosh rec. need-based self-help aid	79
% needy UG rec. need-based self-help aid	84
% frosh rec. any financial aid	100
% UG rec. any financial aid	99
% UG borrow to pay for school	65
Average cumulative indebtedness	$32,117

William Jewell College

500 College Hill, Liberty, MO 64068 • Admissions: 816-781-7700 • Fax: 816-415-5040

CAMPUS LIFE

Quality of Life Rating	**89**
Fire Safety Rating	**88**
Green Rating	**60***
Type of school	Private
Environment	Town

STUDENTS

Total undergrad enrollment	928
% male/female	41/59
% from out of state	42
% frosh from public high school	90
% frosh live on campus	94
% ugrads live on campus	85
# of fraternities (% ugrad men join)	3 (38)
# of sororities (% ugrad women join)	4 (44)
% African American	5
% Asian	1
% Caucasian	79
% Hispanic	4
% Native American	<1
% Pacific Islander	<1
% Two or more races	5
% Race and/or ethnicity unknown	2
% international	4
# of countries represented	19

ACADEMICS

Academic Rating	**89**
% students returning for sophomore year	77
% students graduating within 4 years	54
% students graduating within 6 years	59
Calendar	Semester
Student/faculty ratio	9:1
Profs interesting rating	93
Profs accessible rating	95

Most classes have 20–29 students. Most lab/discussion sessions have 10–19 students.

MOST POPULAR MAJORS

Biology/Biological Sciences; Registered Nursing; Business Administration and Management

ABOUT THE SCHOOL

This small liberal arts college—enrollment is roughly 1,000 students—in rural Missouri "is all about being personal—both in classes and student life." One Political Science major sums up Jewell as "a serious school with serious students, wonderful professors, and a satisfying student life." Even though Liberty, Missouri, might not be on everyone's radar, Kansas City is within driving distance and students will frequent its restaurants and other attractions. "A typical student at Jewell," says a Business Administration major, "is...committed to academics but knows how to balance a social life as well. Students at Jewell fit in right away due to the [welcoming] upperclassmen." The small class sizes—the average student to professor ratio is 10:1—are important and students emphasize that they feel like individuals "not like a number." Students praise the "great" and "intelligent" professors and emphasize that "Jewell has strong academics and great athletics"—it's a Division II school—and "gives everyone the chance to feel...involved" due to the size of the student body.

BANG FOR YOUR BUCK

Though some students note the economic equality imbalance, others praise the school for its "substantial" financial aid and scholarships. The school meets an average of 67 percent of its students' demonstrated need and 100 percent of freshmen (and 99 percent of other undergraduates) receive some form of financial assistance; in 2014–2015, the school awarded $18.5 million in aid. Every student who applies to Jewell is automatically considered for academic, merit-based scholarships, says the school's website. Sports scholarships are common among the large number of student-athletes at Jewell and several students cite the generous sports-related financial aid offers as key motivators in choosing the school. The school's website also provides, in an easily searchable list separated by major, outside scholarships for current and prospective Jewell students.

STUDENT LIFE

"Jewell offers incredible opportunities to become involved," says one Political Science major. "My first year, I averaged sixteen meetings per week." It's "easy to become involved" on campus, where there are seventy registered student organizations. The school sponsors events like "free bowling, ice skating, [and] movies" and students often travel to Kansas City. Greek life plays a significant role on campus—there are four sororities and three fraternities. Roughly 40 percent of women join a sorority and 40 percent of men join a fraternity. A Nonprofit Leadership major notes that even as an "independent," it's easy to become "very close to numerous Greeks and also participate in many Greek events." Jewell is "like a big family" and you "cannot go anywhere on campus without running into a friendly face." As of fall of 2014, Jewell introduced "Jewellverse," a program that provides an iPad to all students and faculty—to be kept after graduation—to facilitate "mobile learning" and the move towards a "paperless campus."

William Jewell College

FINANCIAL AID: 816-415-5975 • E-MAIL: ADMISSION@WILLIAM.JEWELL.EDU • WEBSITE: WWW.JEWELL.EDU

CAREER

According to PayScale.com, the average starting salary for a Jewell graduate is roughly $48,200. Sixty percent of Jewell graduates state that their careers are beneficial to making the world a better place. According to the school's website, 99 percent of Jewell graduates are employed or in graduate school within six months of graduation. On the school's Outcomes and Career Services pages, students are able to search a database of alumni in order to facilitate networking connections for potential jobs and internships. The school's proximity to Kansas City allows students to gain career experience in a variety of internship settings. One Psychology major notes that "if you're not in class, you're at an internship." Jewell offers seven-week, one-credit sessions for career planning multiple times throughout the year, as well as giving students the opportunity to apply to the Career Mentor Program, which matches them up with a professional in their chosen field.

GENERAL INFO

Activities: Choral groups, concert band, dance, drama/theater, jazz band, literary magazine, music ensembles, pep band, student government, student newspaper, symphony orchestra, campus ministries. **Organizations:** 70 registered organizations, 13 honor societies, 7 religious organizations. 3 fraternities, 4 sororities. **Athletics (Intercollegiate):** *Men:* baseball, basketball, cheerleading, cross-country, football, golf, soccer, swimming, tennis, track/field (outdoor), track/field (indoor). *Women:* basketball, cheerleading, cross-country, golf, soccer, softball, swimming, tennis, track/field (outdoor), track/field (indoor), volleyball. **On-Campus Highlights:** The Perch—campus coffee shop, Mabee Center—athletic facility, The Quad—central campus quadrangle, Yates-Gill College Union—student union building, Ely Triangle—first-year residence hall, Fitness Center.

FINANCIAL AID

Students should submit: FAFSA. Priority filing deadline is 2/1. The Princeton Review suggests that all financial aid forms be submitted as soon as possible after October 1. *Need-based scholarships/grants offered:* College/university scholarship or grant aid from institutional funds; Federal Pell; Private scholarships; SEOG; State scholarships/grants; United Negro College Fund. *Loan aid offered:* Direct PLUS Loans, Direct Subsidized Loans, Direct Unsubsidized Loans. Applicants will be notified of awards on a rolling basis beginning 11/1. Federal Work-Study Program available. Institutional employment available.

BOTTOM LINE

A year at Jewell costs roughly $43,230: $32,850 for tuition, $9,640 for room and board, and $1,200 for books and supplies. The average need-based scholarship for undergraduates is $21,406. Sixty-nine percent of undergraduates have borrowed from one of the various loan programs; financial assistance is not available to international students. The typical Jewell student graduates with roughly $31,183 of debt.

SELECTIVITY

Admissions Rating	**87**
# of applicants	1,608
% of applicants accepted	49
% of acceptees attending	25

FRESHMAN PROFILE

Range SAT EBRW	440–630
Range SAT Math	550–610
Range ACT Composite	23–28
Minimum paper TOEFL	550
Minimum internet-based TOEFL	79
Average HS GPA	3.7
% graduated top 10% of class	26
% graduated top 25% of class	57
% graduated top 50% of class	88

DEADLINES

Regular	
Priority	10/15
Nonfall registration?	Yes

FINANCIAL FACTS

Financial Aid Rating	**85**
Annual tuition	$33,500
Room and board	$9,930
Required fees	$900
Books and supplies	$800
Average frosh need-based scholarship	$26,878
Average UG need-based scholarship	$24,739
% needy frosh rec. need-based scholarship or grant aid	100
% needy UG rec. need-based scholarship or grant aid	94
% needy UG rec. non-need-based scholarship or grant aid	86
% needy frosh rec. need-based self-help aid	96
% needy UG rec. need-based self-help aid	72
% frosh rec. any financial aid	100
% UG rec. any financial aid	99
% UG borrow to pay for school	70
Average cumulative indebtedness	$33,326
% frosh need fully met	60
% ugrads need fully met	27
Average % of frosh need met	74
Average % of ugrad need met	72

CAREER INFORMATION FROM PAYSCALE.COM

ROI Rating	88
Bachelors and No Higher	
Median starting salary	$50,100
Median mid-career salary	$92,700
At Least Bachelors	
Median starting salary	$51,300
Median mid-career salary	$96,400
Alumni with high job meaning	61%
Degrees awarded in STEM subjects	12%

Williams College

PO Box 487, Williamstown, MA 01267 • Admissions: 413-597-2211 • Fax: 413-597-4052

CAMPUS LIFE

Quality of Life Rating	91
Fire Safety Rating	60*
Green Rating	91
Type of school	Private
Environment	Village

STUDENTS

Total undergrad enrollment	2,030
% male/female	53/47
% from out of state	86
% frosh from public high school	49
% frosh live on campus	100
% ugrads live on campus	93
# of fraternities (% ugrad men join)	0 (0)
# of sororities (% ugrad women join)	0 (0)
% African American	8
% Asian	13
% Caucasian	51
% Hispanic	13
% Native American	<1
% Pacific Islander	0
% Two or more races	6
% Race and/or ethnicity unknown	1
% international	8
# of countries represented	57

ACADEMICS

Academic Rating	99
% students returning for sophomore year	98
% students graduating within 4 years	86
% students graduating within 6 years	94
Calendar	4/1/4
Student/faculty ratio	7:1
Profs interesting rating	98
Profs accessible rating	99

Most classes have 2–9 students. Most lab/discussion sessions have 10–19 students.

MOST POPULAR MAJORS
English Language and Literature; Mathematics; Economics

#5 BEST VALUE COLLEGE

ABOUT THE SCHOOL

Founded in 1793, Williams College emphasizes the learning that takes place in the creation of a functioning community: life in the residence halls, expression through the arts, debates on political issues, leadership in campus governance, exploration of personal identity, pursuit of spiritual and religious impulses, the challenge of athletics, and direct engagement with human needs. The school is an "amalgamation of the most thoughtful, quirky, and smart people that you will ever meet as an undergraduate." The rigorous academic experience "is truly excellent," and a typical student says, "I feel like I am learning thoroughly." Professors are accessible and dedicated. Distinctive academic programs include Oxford-style tutorials between two students and a faculty member that call for intense research and weekly debates. These tutorial programs offer students an opportunity to take a heightened form of responsibility for their own intellectual development. In January, a four-week Winter Study term allows students to take unique, hands-on pass/fail classes.

BANG FOR YOUR BUCK

The endowment at Williams totals over $2.5 billion. This colossal stash bountifully subsidizes costs for all students, including the cost of books and course materials for any student receiving financial aid and the costs to study all over the world. The fact that Williams is simply awash in money also enables the school to maintain a need-blind admission program for domestic students—including those who are undocumented or have DACA status—and meets 100 percent of the demonstrated need of all students. More than half of the college's international students—58 percent to be exact—receive financial aid and their average grant exceeds $60,000 annually. Merit-based scholarships are a historical artifact here. All financial aid is based purely on need. Convincing this school that you belong here is the difficult part. If you can just get admitted, Williams guarantees that it will meet 100 percent of your financial need for four years. You will walk away with a degree from one of the best schools in the country with little to no debt.

STUDENT LIFE

The typical Williams student is "quirky, passionate, zany, and fun." As one junior reports, "Williams is a place where normal social labels tend not to apply...So that football player in your theater class has amazing insight on Checkhov and that outspoken environmental activist also specializes in improv comedy." Nestled in the picturesque Berkshires of Massachusetts, campus is "stunning" and secluded, which means there is a real sense of community and caring here. Entertainment options include "lots of" performances, art exhibits, plays, and lectures. Some students have a healthy "obsession" with a cappella groups, and intramurals are popular, especially Ultimate Frisbee and broomball ("a sacred tradition involving a hockey rink, sneakers, a rubber ball, and paddles"). On Mountain Day, a unique fall tradition, bells ring announcing the cancellation of classes for the day, and students hike Stony Ledge to celebrate with donuts, cider, and, of course, a cappella performances. Opportunities for outdoor activities abound.

Williams College

FINANCIAL AID: 413-597-4181 • E-MAIL: ADMISSION@WILLIAMS.EDU • WEBSITE: WWW.WILLIAMS.EDU

CAREER

The Career Exploration Center at Williams empowers students to forge their own career path and gives them all the tools they need to get started. Each semester's calendar is packed with informational sessions, and cover letter writing or job fair success workshops. The aptly named "Who Am I & Where Am I Going" workshops helps students explore potential fields, and many students complete "real world" internships or work experience before graduation. The Williams Network connects students with opportunities and the "extensive alumni network" helps graduates get plum jobs all over the world. Graduates who visited PayScale.com report an average starting salary of $62,000 and 44 percent find a great deal of meaning in their work.

GENERAL INFO

Activities: Choral groups, dance, drama/theater, literary magazine, music ensembles, radio station, student government, student newspaper, student-run film society, symphony orchestra, yearbook, international student organization. **Organizations:** 150 registered organizations, 2 honor societies, 10 religious organizations. **Athletics (Intercollegiate):** *Men:* Baseball, basketball, crew/rowing, cross-country, diving, football, golf, ice hockey, lacrosse, skiing (downhill/alpine), skiing (nordic/cross-country), soccer, squash, swimming, tennis, track/field (outdoor), track/field (indoor), wrestling. *Women:* Basketball, crew/rowing, cross-country, diving, field hockey, golf, ice hockey, lacrosse, skiing (downhill/alpine), skiing (nordic/cross-country), soccer, softball, squash, swimming, tennis, track/field (outdoor), track/field (indoor), volleyball. **On-Campus Highlights:** Paresky Student Center, Schow Science Library, Williams College Museum of Art, '62 Center for Theatre and Dance, Chandler Gymnasium, Sawyer Library.

FINANCIAL AID

Students should submit: CSS Profile; FAFSA. Regular filing deadline is 1/15. The Princeton Review suggests that all financial aid forms be submitted as soon as possible after October 1. *Need-based scholarships/grants offered:* College/university scholarship or grant aid from institutional funds; Federal Pell; SEOG; State scholarships/grants. *Loan aid offered:* Federal Perkins Loans, Direct PLUS Loans, Direct Subsidized Loans, Direct Unsubsidized Loans, institutional loans for international students. Applicants will be notified of awards on or about 4/1. Federal Work-Study Program available. Institutional employment available.

THE BOTTOM LINE

Williams College is very similar to an Ivy League school. It has boundless, state-of-the-art resources in everything; a diploma with the Williams brand name on it will kick down doors for the rest of your life; and it's absurdly expensive. The total retail price here for tuition, room and board, and fees comes to about $70,750 per year. Financial aid here is beyond generous, though, and you'd be insane to choose a lesser school instead because of the sticker price.

CAREER INFORMATION FROM PAYSCALE.COM	
ROI Rating	98
Bachelors and No Higher	
Median starting salary	$64,000
Median mid-career salary	$135,500
At Least Bachelors	
Median starting salary	$66,700
Median mid-career salary	$140,900
Alumni with high job meaning	48%
Degrees awarded in STEM subjects	32%

SELECTIVITY	
Admissions Rating	98
# of applicants	8,593
% of applicants accepted	15
% of acceptees attending	44
# offered a place on the wait list	1,796
% accepting a place on wait list	37
% admitted from wait list	0
# of early decision applicants	727
% accepted early decision	35

FRESHMAN PROFILE	
Range SAT EBRW	710–780
Range SAT Math	690–790
Range ACT Composite	31–35
% graduated top 10% of class	88
% graduated top 25% of class	98
% graduated top 50% of class	99

DEADLINES	
Early decision	
Deadline	11/15
Notification	12/15
Regular	
Deadline	1/1
Notification	first week of April
Nonfall registration?	No

FINANCIAL FACTS	
Financial Aid Rating	99
Annual tuition	$55,140
Room and board	$14,500
Required fees	$310
Books and supplies	$800
Average frosh need-based scholarship	$53,866
Average UG need-based scholarship	$51,773
% needy frosh rec. need-based scholarship or grant aid	100
% needy UG rec. need-based scholarship or grant aid	100
% needy frosh rec. non-need-based scholarship or grant aid	0
% needy UG rec. non-need-based scholarship or grant aid	0
% needy frosh rec. need-based self-help aid	83
% needy UG rec. need-based self-help aid	86
% frosh rec. any financial aid	52
% UG rec. any financial aid	51
% UG borrow to pay for school	35
Average cumulative indebtedness	$16,230
% frosh need fully met	100
% ugrads need fully met	100
Average % of frosh need met	100
Average % of ugrad need met	100

Wofford College

429 North Church Street, Spartanburg, SC 29303-3663 • Admissions: 864-597-4130 • Fax: 864-597-4147

CAMPUS LIFE

Quality of Life Rating	89
Fire Safety Rating	94
Green Rating	60*
Type of school	Private
Affiliation	Methodist
Environment	City

STUDENTS

Total undergrad enrollment	1,582
% male/female	47/53
% from out of state	46
% frosh from public high school	63
% frosh live on campus	99
% ugrads live on campus	93
# of fraternities (% ugrad men join)	6 (50)
# of sororities (% ugrad women join)	4 (55)
% African American	8
% Asian	2
% Caucasian	79
% Hispanic	4
% Native American	<1
% Pacific Islander	<1
% Two or more races	4
% Race and/or ethnicity unknown	<1
% international	2
# of countries represented	24

ACADEMICS

Academic Rating	90
% students returning for sophomore year	90
% students graduating within 4 years	77
% students graduating within 6 years	81
Calendar	4/1/4
Student/faculty ratio	10:1
Profs interesting rating	92
Profs accessible rating	92
Most classes have 10–19 students.	

MOST POPULAR MAJORS
Biology/Biological Sciences; Business/
Managerial Economics; Finance

ABOUT THE SCHOOL

As soon as students set foot on campus in downtown Spartanburg, South Carolina, they immediately sense that the Wofford College community is one "big family." At this "liberal arts college," undergrads are also free to explore a variety of 67 majors and programs, forge "relationships," and create "opportunities" for themselves. While the coursework is challenging, students say the effort is well worth it, due to Wofford's "high acceptance rate to graduate schools." They also love the "small" class sizes, which foster an "intimate" learning experience and "allow for engaged discussions." Of course, students also insist that their courses tend to be "interactive because many of the professors like to keep it fun." Plus, it helps that instructors here "are excited about their subjects" and "enthusiastic" about teaching. Moreover, Wofford professors "are accessible and willing to answer questions and help where they can." And "their enthusiasm and encouragement helps students...maintain a positive attitude throughout the entire semester."

BANG FOR YOUR BUCK

At Wofford College, over 90 percent of the student body receives some form of financial assistance. And that's likely why undergrads praise the school's "incredible financial aid." Wofford awards over $55 million in scholarships and grants, and they make the process easy for incoming students as all applicants are automatically considered for merit scholarships. Recipients may find themselves awarded the Richardson Family Scholarship, with full tuition and other amenities, or the Launch Program scholarship to support, develop or direct their entrepreneurial talents. Wofford also offers scholarships for study-abroad opportunities. Several students also receive funding by participating in Wofford's robust work-study program.

SCHOOL LIFE

Wofford students admit that since "classes are rigorous" a large portion of the week is spent "studying and [completing] homework." Fortunately, these dedicated academics still find time to relax. We're told that "there are always student organizations putting on activities like Campus Outreach will have bonfires with s'mores, and WAC (the Wofford Activities Council) will host trivia night." Undergrads here also love to support their fellow Wofford Terriers, and you'll quickly discover that "basketball and baseball games are very popular in the Spring Semester." And, of course, you can spot plenty of students hanging out on the "main street of Spartanburg [which] has several good restaurants and bars," that undergrads love to patronize.

CAREER

Undergrads at Wofford feel that the college provides them with "many opportunities to pursue [their] career goals." For starters, it does a great job "keep[ing] students extremely connected to alumni." Ultimately, this provides tremendous "help [when it comes to] job searches and internships." At Wofford's amazing The Space Mungo Center, a full-service office for both professional development and entrepreneurship, undergrads can jump-start on their interview prep, networking, and resume writing skills. The career counselors here provide students with actionable job search strategies that make landing that first gig surprisingly easy. The average starting salary for recent Wofford graduates is $48,800, according to PayScale.com.

Wofford College

FINANCIAL AID: 864-597-4160 • E-MAIL: ADMISSION@WOFFORD.EDU • WEBSITE: WWW.WOFFORD.EDU

GENERAL INFO

Activities: Choral groups, concert band, dance, drama/theater, literary magazine, music ensembles, pep band, student government, student newspaper, yearbook, campus ministries. **Organizations:** 105 registered organizations, 10 honor societies, 8 religious organizations. 7 fraternities, 4 sororities. **Athletics (Intercollegiate):** *Men:* baseball, basketball, cross-country, football, golf, riflery, soccer, tennis, track/field (outdoor), track/field (indoor). *Women:* basketball, cross-country, golf, lacrosse, riflery, soccer, tennis, track/field (outdoor), track/field (indoor), volleyball. **On-Campus Highlights:** The Roger Milliken Arboretum, Roger Milliken Science Center/Great Oaks Hall, Main Building/Leonard Auditorium, Franklin W. Olin Building, The Village (student housing), Gibbs Stadium, Richardson Physical Activities Building, Russell C. King Field and Switzer Stadium, Stewart H. Johnson Greek Village, Joe E. Taylor Athletic Center, Rosalind Sallenger Richardson Center for the Arts and the Jerry Richardson Indoor Stadium..

FINANCIAL AID

Students should submit: FAFSA. Priority filing deadline is 3/1. The Princeton Review suggests that all financial aid forms be submitted as soon as possible after October 1. *Need-based scholarships/grants offered:* College/university scholarship or grant aid from institutional funds, Federal Pell, private scholarships, SEOG, state scholarships/grants. *Loan aid offered:* Direct PLUS Loans, Direct Subsidized Loans, Direct Unsubsidized Loans. Applicants will be notified of awards on or about 3/1. Federal Work-Study Program available. Institutional employment available.

THE BOTTOM LINE

Tuition at Wofford College currently costs undergrads (and their families) $40,510. Additionally, room and board for the academic year comes to $12,140. Though that figure can vary a bit depending on the chosen meal plan. All students must also pay a reservation deposit every year—$300 for commuters and $500 for residents. And there are miscellaneous fees such as the $250 damage deposit. Finally, undergrads will need to set aside additional funds for books, supplies, and personal expenses.

CAREER INFORMATION FROM PAYSCALE.COM	
ROI Rating	89
Bachelors and No Higher	
Median starting salary	$49,300
Median mid-career salary	$100,600
At Least Bachelors	
Median starting salary	$50,700
Median mid-career salary	$105,000
Alumni with high job meaning	50%
Degrees awarded in STEM subjects	28%

SELECTIVITY	
Admissions Rating	86
# of applicants	3,092
% of applicants accepted	69
% of acceptees attending	21
# offered a place on the wait list	232
% accepting a place on wait list	42
% admitted from wait list	8
# of early decision applicants	102
% accepted early decision	96

FRESHMAN PROFILE	
Range SAT EBRW	570–660
Range SAT Math	550–650
Range ACT Composite	24–30
Minimum paper TOEFL	550
Minimum internet-based TOEFL	80
Average HS GPA	3.7
% graduated top 10% of class	43
% graduated top 25% of class	76
% graduated top 50% of class	95

DEADLINES	
Early decision	
Deadline	11/1
Notification	12/1
Early action	
Deadline	11/15
Notification	2/1
Regular	
Deadline	1/15
Notification	3/1

FINANCIAL FACTS	
Financial Aid Rating	89
Annual tuition	$42,335
Room and board	$12,685
Required fees	$1,510
Books and supplies	$1,200
Average frosh need-based scholarship	$32,581
Average UG need-based scholarship	$32,355
% needy frosh rec. need-based scholarship or grant aid	100
% needy UG rec. need-based scholarship or grant aid	100
% needy frosh rec. non-need-based scholarship or grant aid	40
% needy UG rec. non-need-based scholarship or grant aid	31
% needy frosh rec. need-based self-help aid	49
% needy UG rec. need-based self-help aid	56
% frosh rec. any financial aid	96
% UG rec. any financial aid	94
% UG borrow to pay for school	50
Average cumulative indebtedness	$32,043
% frosh need fully met	47

SCHOOL PROFILES ■ 457

Worcester Polytechnic Institute

ADMISSIONS OFFICE, BARTLETT CENTER, WORCESTER, MA 01609 • ADMISSIONS: 508-831-5286 • FAX: 508-831-5875

CAMPUS LIFE

Quality of Life Rating	92
Fire Safety Rating	91
Green Rating	91
Type of school	Private
Environment	City

STUDENTS

Total undergrad enrollment	4,337
% male/female	64/36
% from out of state	57
% frosh live on campus	99
% ugrads live on campus	59
# of fraternities (% ugrad men join)	13 (27)
# of sororities (% ugrad women join)	6 (45)
% African American	3
% Asian	3
% Caucasian	64
% Hispanic	9
% Native American	<1
% Pacific Islander	0
% Two or more races	2
% Race and/or ethnicity unknown	8
% international	11
# of countries represented	69

ACADEMICS

Academic Rating	94
% students returning for sophomore year	95
% students graduating within 4 years	82
% students graduating within 6 years	89
Calendar	Semester
Student/faculty ratio	13:1
Profs interesting rating	87
Profs accessible rating	91

MOST POPULAR MAJORS
Computer Science; Electrical and Electronics Engineering; Mechanical Engineering

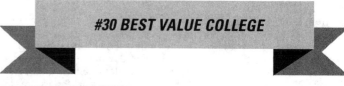

#30 BEST VALUE COLLEGE

ABOUT THE SCHOOL

Worcester Polytechnic Institute is a small university in Massachusetts with a primary focus on technology and the applied sciences. Undergraduates can choose from more than fifty majors and minors across fourteen academic departments, and though the school is world-renowned for engineering WPI prides itself on offering an extremely flexible curriculum that emphasizes the importance of a well-rounded education. In addition to abundant research opportunities the school offers several to complete projects in the sciences and humanities. These include an Interactive Qualifying Project that challenges students to apply technology to solve a societal problem, often by working and studying abroad. Students say that these programs "give [them] a chance to learn real world skills and work together rather than against each other." "I love the fact that WPI develops technical professionals' soft skills and doesn't only focus on the numbers," students say, and while there are some unpopular professors most "genuinely want all of their students to not just succeed academically but to understand the material." Furthermore, the majority are "interested in helping students, and don't prioritize their own research above being a good professor."

BANG FOR YOUR BUCK

WPI offers several financial aid options in the form of scholarships and grants, loans, and work-study. Need-based aid comes from a variety of State and Federal programs, such as the Pell Grant, as well as institutional scholarships. The school also offers an extremely high number of merit-based scholarships for which students are automatically considered upon application, with several awards that average $12,500 to $25,000. There are special merit scholarships available to students of color, and to students studying in specific disciplines such as chemistry or pre-med. Ninety-seven percent of students are receiving merit- and/or need-based aid, and many students cite financial assistance as a determining factor in their decision to attend WPI.

STUDENT LIFE

Though "the work in classes requires you to spend significant time studying," WPI is "a place for more than just rigorous academics." Thirty to 40 percent of students are involved in Greek life and there are abundant clubs and activities on campus. "Students are very involved in campus organizations" and in addition to structured groups there are dances, a winter carnival, Saturday gaming nights, a comedy festival, a play festival, and weekend movie nights, among many other offerings. Off campus in Worcester, "there are constantly shows and concerts, there is an ice rink, a climbing gym, and movie theaters." Many students also travel to Boston on weekends. "At WPI you are always on the go with work, academics, and extra curricular activities, but we are the best time managers I know."

CAREER

Due to WPI's emphasis on real-world experience and applied science and technology, it's not surprising that the students are a career-focused bunch. All students participate in three projects, some with external sponsors, before graduation. The Career Development Center is generally well regarded, offering career fairs and company presentations, services like résumé building and interview prep, and

Worcester Polytechnic Institute

FINANCIAL AID: 508-831-5469 • E-MAIL: ADMISSIONS@WPI.EDU • WEBSITE: WWW.WPI.EDU

advice for students on how to use networking and social media to their advantage. A WPI education is "about preparing students for successful careers in their respective fields upon graduation through practical applications of the knowledge and skills that are taught," and "a large percentage of the student body will leave WPI with a fairly good job when they graduate." Evidence seems to bear out that observation, as WPI has been frequently cited for graduating their students into high-paying careers. Beyond the finances, 48 percent WPI alumni visiting PayScale.com report feeling as though their job has a high level of meaning.

GENERAL INFO

Activities: Choral groups, concert band, dance, drama/theater, jazz band, literary magazine, marching band, music ensembles, musical theater, pep band, radio station, student government, student newspaper, student-run film society, symphony orchestra, yearbook, International Student Organization. **Organizations:** 200+ registered organizations, 14 honor societies, 7 religious organizations. 13 fraternities, 6 sororities. **Athletics (Intercollegiate):** *Men:* baseball, basketball, crew/rowing, cross-country, diving, football, soccer, swimming, track/field (outdoor), track/field (indoor), wrestling. *Women:* basketball, crew/rowing, cross-country, diving, field hockey, soccer, softball, swimming, track/field (outdoor), track/field (indoor), volleyball. **On-Campus Highlights:** makerspace, Student invented fountain, Campus Center, Robotics Lab, Fire Protection Engineering Lab, biomedical and life sciences research center at Gateway Park, Sports & Recreation Center.

FINANCIAL AID

Students should submit: CSS Profile; FAFSA. Priority filing deadline is 2/15. The Princeton Review suggests that all financial aid forms be submitted as soon as possible after October 1. *Need-based scholarships/grants offered:* College/university scholarship or grant aid from institutional funds, Federal Pell, private scholarships, SEOG, state scholarships/grants. *Loan aid offered:* Direct PLUS Loans, Direct Subsidized Loans, Direct Unsubsidized Loans. Applicants will be notified of awards on a rolling basis. Federal Work-Study Program available. Institutional employment available.

THE BOTTOM LINE

Tuition and fees for a year at WPI are listed as just over $48,800, with room and board totaling an additional $14,218. In addition to many merit-based scholarships WPI offers a numerous need-based programs, with 98 percent of first year students receiving some form of financial aid. Between robust aid packages and lucrative career prospects for graduating students, Worcester Polytechnic Institute could be a great investment for those interested in the science, technology, and engineering fields.

CAREER INFORMATION FROM PAYSCALE.COM	
ROI Rating	93
Bachelors and No Higher	
Median starting salary	$71,700
Median mid-career salary	$132,500
At Least Bachelors	
Median starting salary	$73,200
Median mid-career salary	$138,000
Alumni with high job meaning	48%
Degrees awarded in STEM subjects	86%

SELECTIVITY	
Admissions Rating	94
# of applicants	10,331
% of applicants accepted	48
% of acceptees attending	22
# offered a place on the wait list	2,187
% accepting a place on wait list	50
% admitted from wait list	9

FIRST YEAR PROFILE	
Range SAT EBRW	620–710
Range SAT Math	660–730
Range ACT Composite	28–32
Minimum paper TOEFL	550
Minimum internet-based TOEFL	80
Average HS GPA	3.9
% graduated top 10% of class	68
% graduated top 25% of class	92
% graduated top 50% of class	100

DEADLINES	
Early action	
Deadline	11/1
Notification	12/20
Regular	
Deadline	2/1
Notification	4/1
Nonfall registration?	No

FINANCIAL FACTS	
Financial Aid Rating	89
Annual tuition	$49,860
Room and board	$14,774
Required fees	$670
Books and supplies	$1,000
Average frosh need-based scholarship	$22,795
Average UG need-based scholarship	$22,942
% needy frosh rec. need-based scholarship or grant aid	99
% needy UG rec. need-based scholarship or grant aid	97
% needy frosh rec. non-need-based scholarship or grant aid	27
% needy UG rec. non-need-based scholarship or grant aid	29
% needy frosh rec. need-based self-help aid	49
% needy UG rec. need-based self-help aid	49
% frosh rec. any financial aid	98
% UG rec. any financial aid	95
% frosh need fully met	58
% ugrads need fully met	47
Average % of frosh need met	80
Average % of ugrad need met	81

Yale University

PO Box 208234, New Haven, CT 06520-8234 • Admissions: 203-432-9300 • Fax: 203-432-9392

#7 BEST VALUE COLLEGE

CAMPUS LIFE

Quality of Life Rating	91
Fire Safety Rating	62
Green Rating	92
Type of school	Private
Environment	City

STUDENTS

Total undergrad enrollment	5,746
% male/female	50/50
% from out of state	93
% frosh from public high school	57
% frosh live on campus	100
% ugrads live on campus	84
% African American	7
% Asian	18
% Caucasian	45
% Hispanic	13
% Native American	1
% Pacific Islander	<1
% Two or more races	6
% Race and/or ethnicity unknown	<1
% international	11
# of countries represented	118

ACADEMICS

Academic Rating	91
% students returning for sophomore year	99
% students graduating within 4 years	87
% students graduating within 6 years	97
Calendar	Semester
Student/faculty ratio	6:1
Profs interesting rating	85
Profs accessible rating	82
Most classes have 10–19 students.	

MOST POPULAR MAJORS

Economics; Political Science and
Government; History

ABOUT THE SCHOOL

As one of the triple towers of the Ivy League, when you say you attend "Yale, you don't really have to say much else—those four letters say it all." Beyond the gothic spires ("It reminds me of Hogwarts," says a student) and ivy-clad residence halls, Yale University truly lives up to its reputation as one of the preeminent undergraduate schools in the nation. At this world-class research institution, 5,000-plus undergraduates (who are "are passionate about everything") benefit not only from "amazing academics and extensive resources" that provide "phenomenal in- and out-of-class education," but also from participation in "a student body that is committed to learning and to each other." Cutting-edge research is commonplace and great teaching the norm, and three quarters of courses enroll fewer than twenty students. A popular test-the-waters registration system allows students to sample classes for up to two weeks before they commit to their schedule, and the school "encourages its students to take a range of courses." "The wealth of opportunities in and out of the classroom made the choice very clear to me," says a student. The education they're getting prepares them for leadership on a massive scale. Case in point: Yale alumni were represented on the Democratic or Republican ticket in every U.S. presidential election between 1972 and 2004. Still, no matter the end result, it's clear that "the people at Yale are genuinely interested in learning for learning's sake, not so that they can get a job on Wall Street."

BANG FOR YOUR BUCK

Here's a shocker: you don't have to be wealthy to have access to a Yale education. Thanks to a multibillion-dollar endowment, Yale operates a need-blind admissions policy and guarantees to meet 100 percent of each applicant's demonstrated need. In fact, Yale's annual expected financial aid budget is larger than many schools' endowments. Yale spends more than $140 million dollars on student financial aid annually. The average scholarship award is around $50,000, and it's entirely need-based—no athletic or merit scholarships are available. Seven hundred and fifty Yale undergraduates will have a $0 expected parent contribution next year—that's more than 10 percent of its student body. Yale even provides undergraduates on financial aid with grant support for summer study and unpaid internships abroad.

STUDENT LIFE

A typical Yalie is "tough to define because so much of what makes Yale special is the unique convergence of different students to form one cohesive entity. Nonetheless, the one common characteristic of Yale students is passion—each Yalie is driven and dedicated to what he or she loves most" which "creates a palpable atmosphere of enthusiasm on campus." Yale is, of course, extremely challenging academically, but work doesn't keep undergrads from participating in a "a huge variety of activities for fun." "Instead of figuring out what to do with my free time, I have to figure out what not do during my free time," says a student. There are more than 300 student groups on campus including the Yale Daily News, the oldest collegiate daily newspaper still in existence, as well as "singing, dancing, juggling fire, theater . . . the list goes on." Many students are politically active and "either volunteer or try to get involved in some sort of organization to make a difference in the world."

Yale University

FINANCIAL AID: 203-432-2700 • E-MAIL: STUDENT.QUESTIONS@YALE.EDU • WEBSITE: WWW.YALE.EDU

CAREER

As its name would suggest, the Yale Office of Career Strategy (OCS) offers a host of resources to students before they even embark on the job hunt. A comprehensive collection of online career profiles helps students gain an overview of potential fields, and walk-in appointments with career advisers ensure that all of their questions get answered. OCS sponsors numerous internship programs, often drawing upon Yale's extensive alumni network for leads on opportunities. The Yale Career Network is another great way to network with keen alumni. Yalies report average starting salaries of about $66,800, and 53 percent of those grads who visited PayScale.com say they find a high level of meaning in their work.

GENERAL INFO

Activities: Choral groups, concert band, dance, drama/theater, jazz band, literary magazine, marching band, music ensembles, musical theater, opera, pep band, radio station, student government, student newspaper, student-run film society, symphony orchestra, television station, yearbook, campus ministries, international student organization. **Organizations:** 350 registered organizations.

FINANCIAL AID

Students should submit: CSS Profile; FAFSA; Institution's own financial aid form. Priority filing deadline is 3/1. The Princeton Review suggests that all financial aid forms be submitted as soon as possible after October 1. *Need-based scholarships/grants offered:* College/university scholarship or grant aid from institutional funds; Federal Pell; Private scholarships; SEOG; State scholarships/grants; United Negro College Fund. *Loan aid offered:* Direct PLUS Loans, Direct Subsidized Loans, Direct Unsubsidized Loans. Applicants will be notified of awards on or about 4/1.

THE BOTTOM LINE

Annual tuition to Yale is $49,480. Room and board in one of Yale's residential colleges is $15,170 per year, bringing the total cost to about $64,650 annually, not to mention costs of books, supplies, health insurance, and personal expenses. Yale guarantees to meet 100 percent of all students' demonstrated financial need; as a result, the cost of Yale education is often considerably lower than the sticker price.

CAREER INFORMATION FROM PAYSCALE.COM	
ROI Rating	97
Bachelors and No Higher	
Median starting salary	$68,300
Median mid-career salary	$135,400
At Least Bachelors	
Median starting salary	$72,300
Median mid-career salary	$146,300
Alumni with high job meaning	54%
Degrees awarded in STEM subjects	20%

SELECTIVITY	
Admissions Rating	99
# of applicants	32,879
% of applicants accepted	7
% of acceptees attending	69

FRESHMAN PROFILE	
Range SAT ERBW	710–790
Range SAT Math	710–790
Range ACT Composite	32–35
Minimum paper TOEFL	600
Minimum internet-based TOEFL	100
% graduated top 10% of class	82
% graduated top 25% of class	93
% graduated top 50% of class	99

DEADLINES	
Early action	
Deadline	11/1
Notification	12/15
Regular	
Deadline	1/1
Notification	4/1
Nonfall registration?	No

FINANCIAL FACTS	
Financial Aid Rating	99
Annual tuition	$49,480
Room and board	$15,170
Required fees	$0
Books and supplies	$3,670
Average frosh need-based scholarship	$55,568
Average UG need-based scholarship	$53,412
% needy frosh rec. need-based scholarship or grant aid	100
% needy UG rec. need-based scholarship or grant aid	100
% needy frosh rec. non-need-based scholarship or grant aid	0
% needy UG rec. non-need-based scholarship or grant aid	0
% needy frosh rec. need-based self-help aid	76
% needy UG rec. need-based self-help aid	84
% frosh rec. any financial aid	51
% UG rec. any financial aid	52
% UG borrow to pay for school	16
Average cumulative indebtedness	$13,050
% frosh need fully met	100
% ugrads need fully met	100
Average % of frosh need met	100
Average % of ugrad need met	100

INDEX OF SCHOOLS BY NAME

NOTES

NOTES

NOTES

NOTES

NOTES

NOTES

NOTES

NOTES

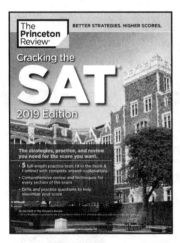
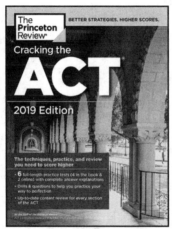

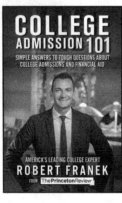

31901064091442